encyclopedia of religion and war

ROUTLEDGE ENCYCLOPEDIAS OF RELIGION AND SOCIETY

David Levinson, *Series Editor*

The Encyclopedia of Millennialism and Millennial Movements

Richard A. Landes, *Editor*

The Encyclopedia of African and African-American Religions

Stephen D. Glazier, *Editor*

The Encyclopedia of Fundamentalism

Brenda E. Brasher, *Editor*

The Encyclopedia of Religious Freedom

Catharine Cookson, *Editor*

The Encyclopedia of Religion and War

Gabriel Palmer-Fernandez, *Editor*

encyclopedia of
religion and war

Gabriel Palmer-Fernandez
Editor

Religion & Society
A Berkshire Reference Work

ROUTLEDGE
New York London

Published in 2004 by

Routledge
29 West 35th Street
New York, NY 10001
www.routledge-ny.com

Published in Great Britain by Routledge
11 New Fetter Lane
London EC4P 4EE
www.routledge.uk.com

A Berkshire Reference Work
Routledge is an imprint of Taylor & Francis Group.

Printed in the United States of America on acid-free paper.

10 9 8 7 6 5 4 3 2 1

Library of Congress Cataloging-in-Publication Data

The encyclopedia of religion and war / Gabriel Palmer-Fernandez, editor.
p. cm. — (Routledge encyclopedias of religion and society)
Includes bibliographical references and index.
ISBN 0-415-94246-2 (alk. paper)
1. Religions—Encyclopedias. 2. War—Religious aspects—Encyclopedias. I. Palmer-Fernandez, Gabriel, 1953- II. Series.
BL80.3.E53 2003
291.1′7873—dc21

2003012412

Contents

Editorial Advisory Board

List of Entries

Introduction

"I acted alone and on orders from God," Yigal Amir, the young Jewish extremist who assassinated Israeli prime minister Yitzhak Rabin in 1995, said to police (quoted in Kifner 1995, 12). Those words could have come easily from members of any of a number of religiously motivated groups that in the past twenty-five years have engaged in acts of political violence around the globe—in Japan, Algeria, Kashmir, Egypt, and the United States, among other places. War and violence motivated in whole or in part by religious beliefs have become increasingly prominent features of the contemporary religious and political landscape. Yet few scholars or clergy would have imagined fifty years ago that in the dawn of the twenty-first century religion would emerge as a vital political force or that theocracies would compete to compete with authoritarian systems and liberal democracies.

The Rise in Religiously Motivated Violence

On the contrary, in the 1960s and 1970s scholars of religion, theologians, and social scientists had predicted that the importance of religion in public life would gradually decrease as societies modernized, until ultimately religion became a private matter without power in the public domain. That prediction was sometimes expressed as a historical thesis, the truth of which was confirmed by the secularization of European nations. "From the religious point of view," the Italian sociologist and professor of religion Sabino Acquaviva wrote, "humanity has entered a long night that will become darker and darker with the passing of the generations, and of which no end can be seen" (1979, 201). In all modern industrial societies, "a normative order based on religious beliefs and values," Richard Fenn, also a scholar of religion, wrote, "is no longer possible" (1972, 19). But by the early 1980s the prediction was already proving false. In some important ways, politics were becoming an instrument of religion. The impact of Christian fundamentalists in the presidential politics of the United States, the establishment of the Islamic Republic of Iran, and the emergence of the powerful religiously inspired Bharatiya Janata Party in India were just some of the evidence that convincingly disproved theories of secularization.

As religion has asserted itself in public life, it has appeared also as an important contributing factor in defining the belligerents in, and the nature of, armed hostilities. From the late twentieth century onward, wars between nation-states have seemed less prominent than conflicts between groups representing different religious, ethnic, and linguistic communities, whether Hindus and Muslims in India, Protestants and Catholics in Northern Ireland, or Turkic Muslims and Slavic Orthodox Russians in Central Asia. The number of groups involved in conflicts with significant religious dimensions has increased dramatically in the more than half-century since the end of World War II: from 26 between 1945 and 1949 to 70 in the 1990s, with the greatest increase in the 1960s and 1970s. By the 1980s militant religious sects accounted for one-quarter of all armed rebellions. "[T]here appears every prospect," the Israeli military historian Martin van Creveld wrote, "that religious attitudes, beliefs, and fanaticism will play a larger role in the motivation of armed conflict than it has, in the West at any rate, for the last 300 years" (1991, 214).

The Peace of Westphalia (1648) saw the start of an era in which only nation-states, acting through the agency of armies, made war. Now that era may be coming to a close, and new kinds of war-making organizations and warriors are emerging. The new controlling images are profoundly religious. The hymns, narratives, and images tell of divine warfare and struggles of cosmic proportions. The great wars of the Hindu *Mahabarata* and *Ramayana* epics, the triumphant battles of Buddhist kings recounted in the *Dipavamsa* and *Mahavamsa* Pali chronicles, and Christological understandings of Jesus as liberator from structures of oppression all invest present-day conflicts with spiritual meaning—and similar examples could be given for almost any world religion.

Religious Terrorism

The salience of religion in armed conflicts is most evident in the advent of religious terrorism. Religion and terrorism share a long history; among the ancient religious groups whose actions might be labeled terrorism are the Hindu Thuggees (whence the English word *thug*), the Jewish Zealots, and the Muslim Assassins. The medieval Christian doctrine of tyrannicide might also be considered a form of religiously sanctioned terrorism. "Sacred terror," as the U.S. political scientist David Rapoport calls it, "never disappeared altogether, and there are signs that it is reviving in new and unusual forms" (1984, 659). While none of the internationalist terrorist groups active in the 1960s could be classified as religious, by 1980 the modern religious terrorist group had begun to emerge, and by 1992 the number of these groups had increased from two to twelve. In 1994 sixteen of the forty-five identifiable international terrorist groups had a significantly if not predominantly religious character, and in 1995 the number grew to twenty-six. Unlike the ideologically or politically driven terrorism of the late nineteenth and early twentieth centuries (such as European anarchists or the Irish Sinn Fein employed, for example), religious terrorism does not appear to be motivated solely by a political objective or publicity for its cause. Instead, its distinguishing feature seems to be the desire to please a deity or to fulfill some spiritual purpose, as with ancient sacred terror. Future historians may well look upon this new century as a period in which religion returned as one of the prime motives for violence and war, and assumed what some writers refer to as a premodern form.

Millenarian Violence

Alongside the renewed political vitality of religions, the increase in armed conflicts partly motivated by religious differences, and the emergence of contemporary religious terrorism, we must note also in a growing number of oppositional groups an ascendant religious enthusiasm of a millenarian, apocalyptic, or messianic nature. Members of these groups await either a radical societal transformation, a cosmic war, or a celestial figure whose appearance on earth will mark the beginning of a new age. Although millenarian, apocalyptic, and messianic ideas belong to the biblical tradition, such enthusiasm can also be found in Islam, Buddhism, Daoism, Confucianism, Baha'i, and Zoroastrianism, as well as in the religions of indigenous peoples of North America, Malaysia, and sub-Saharan Africa. Two important examples are the Brüder Schweigen (Silent Brotherhood) and other U.S. white-supremacist, anti-Semitic, paramilitary groups associated with Christian Identity that prepare for a war believed to be imminent, and Aum Shinrikyo, a Japanese new religion that achieved notoriety as the only nonstate group to have carried out a nerve gas attack.

But the close relationship between religion and war (as well as other forms of political violence) is neither unique to this period of history nor limited to any particular religion or geographical region. The history of religion provides abundant examples of this relationship, even among those religious traditions considered otherworldly or nonpolitical. The medieval Christian Crusades are perhaps the most noteworthy instance of that relationship, but other notable examples are the violent conflicts between competing Buddhist sects in Japan during the Heian period (794–1185), the violent overthrow of China's Yuan dynasty in 1368, influenced by the messianic ideas of the Buddhist millenarian sect known as the Red Turbans, and the Ghost Dance among the Sioux in the Messiah War against the U.S. government in 1890–1891.

Scope of the Encyclopedia

The *Encyclopedia of Religion and War* has a narrow focus. It looks to one part of religion, not to the whole. And the part of religion that this volume examines might rightly be called, in the words of the sociologist Mark Juergensmeyer (2000, xi), "the dark alliance between religion and violence." An encyclopedia that examined religious teachings on love, compassion, and benevolent service to others, or that focused on spiritual enlightenment and salvation or on devotional practices, would paint an entirely different portrait of religion. But even with such a focus, religious iconography would still involve images of violence, warfare, and martial exploits, as these are among the most prevalent and enduring images in the world's religions. At or very near the core of many religions we find a universal battle between order, equated with all that is righteous and good, and confusion, equated with all that is evil and bad, and we find heroes, martyrs, and holy warriors arrayed against the legendary foes of the cherished divinities and ultimately receiving vast and eternal rewards. Such is the case with proto-Indo-European religions, such as the ancient Vedic traditions and the complex of Hittite, Aryan, Celtic, and Greek religions, as well as the later religions of Zoroastrianism, Judaism, Christianity, and Islam.

This volume provides authoritative historical and cross-cultural information that will help readers understand war and other forms of political violence in the major religions of the world. It also covers violent religious conflict in different regions, particular religious movements, and religious wars. The terms *religion* and *war* are left unanalyzed and undefined here. To do otherwise would involve us in a number of unsettled and contested issues far beyond the scope of this volume. There is no generally agreed-upon or unequivocal definition either of religion or war. During the past century, European and North American scholars introduced categories for understanding other peoples' religion—for example, primitive, pagan, premonotheistic—that frequently belittled the religions and justified colonial expansion and racist viewpoints. Many contemporary scholars of religion therefore argue that any attempt to define religion will be tainted by the values and biases of a particular point of view, secular or religious. Others argue that the concept of religion itself is neither intelligible nor valid. Similarly, war is hardly a value-neutral concept. It can be taken as a legal or a moral category applicable only to certain entities—nation-states—under particular conditions. All else is criminality on a mass scale.

This volume aims to be inclusive, but it is not exhaustive of all the world religions. The traditions covered include the Western religions of Judaism, Christianity, and Islam, and the Eastern religions of Jainism, Hinduism, Buddhism, Confucianism, and Daoism. Attention is given also to indigenous religions of the Americas and sub-Saharan Africa, but the religions of the indigenous people of Australia are not covered. Certain less popular religions, such as Zoroastrianism, and nonliving religions, such as Manichaeanism, are also covered. I have sought to take into account two important facts about religions: They change over time, and at any given time they exhibit significant internal diversity. Each is therefore divided by historical periods (more easily defined for some than for others) and denominations or branches. For example, there is an article on Hinduism in the Vedic period and another on Judaism in the rabbinic period, and there are also articles on Sunni Islam, Zen Buddhism, Reformed Judaism, Orthodox Christianity, and the like.

Salient Themes

Three salient themes are worth noting here. First, most religions have explicitly scriptural and doctrinal views on war. Second, many religions have supported states when those states have waged wars. Finally, the values of nonviolence and, more generally, pacifism are widely represented in the religions of the world.

Scriptural and Doctrinal Views on War

Articulated scriptural views on war are most clearly evident in the biblical traditions. Judaism in its biblical period, like many religions of the ancient Near East, looked upon the deity as itself a warrior, fighting with or without human armies, commanding and often deciding the outcome of battles, sometimes employing defeat as a punishment, and glorifying the courage and skill of warriors. In the Hebrew Bible, there is evidence of concern with the conduct of war, legitimate targets of destruction, the treatment of enemies and prisoners, and conditions of surrender. While Christianity may initially have had a strong pacifist impulse, it shows significant evolution over its first few centuries, particularly after the conversion of Constantine in the fourth century of the common era. By the fifth century and the writings of Augustine, bishop of the ancient city of Hippo in North Africa, the view of war found in the Hebrew Bible served as the basic framework for the development of Christian doctrine on war. Christian theologians of the Middle Ages developed a doctrine of holy war, and in the early modern period a secularized just-war tradition that continues to the present day. There is a striking similarity between the Jewish, Christian, and Qur'anic views of war: All three traditions see war as a way of establishing the divine will on earth, and they believe that warfare is constrained by divine pronouncements concerning the conduct of war, particularly the treatment of prisoners.

In South Asia, the array of religious beliefs and practices that now come under the appellation of Hinduism classify in a hierarchy those functions essential to a martial society and enshrine the Kshatriya (warrior caste) in its sacred writings. The Rig Veda, a sacred text dating as far back as the fifteenth century BCE, gives war a largely uncontested place within the economy of salvation. The most frequently appearing deity in that text is Indra, the god of thunder and ruler of the space between the heavens and earth, who, much like the Hebrew Yahweh, is a warrior god and patron of the Kshatriya. The religio-juridical teachings of Manu (the Vedic mythological analogue to the biblical Adam) proclaimed war an eternal duty, and in the *Mahabarata* a warrior's death guarantees entry into heaven. The section of the *Mahabarata* known as the Bhagavad-Gita ("Song of the Lord"), arguably the most important single text in Hinduism, upholds the Rig Veda's teaching on war. Krishna, an incarnation of the god Vishnu, instructs the ambivalent warrior Arjuna, saying, "[If] you will not engage in this lawful war: then you give up your Law and honor, and incur guilt. Creatures will tell of your undying shame, and for one who has been honored dishonor is worse than death . . . and what is more miserable than that?" (Buitenen 1981, 77).

In East Asia, Mahayana Buddhism elaborated doctrines that served as a basis for war. In China, for example, the belief in a future Buddha led to various rebellions to secure the survival of peasant communities, and Buddhist millenarian cults periodically rebelled against the ruling dynasty. In Japan, Mahayana Buddhism accepted the samurai warrior and set the stage for political insurrection and a number of violent confrontations among competing sects.

Religions in Alliance with States, in Support of War

Most people will assert that religion is a system of beliefs concerning the cause, nature, and purpose of the universe organized in response to some perceived spiritual reality. But even a cursory glance at the history of religions discloses that religion also serves important social needs, including the military needs of the state. In the *Zen and Japanese Culture*, D. T. Suzuki, one of the most compelling modern apologists for Zen Buddhism, wrote: "A good fighter is generally an ascetic, or stoic, which means he has an iron will. This, when needed, Zen can supply" (Suzuki 1959, 62). Suzuki had long held the view that religion in general and Zen in particular preserves the state and its various interests, including commerce, and when needed may be called upon to defend those interests by arms. In 1942, Yamada Mumon, a Zen master of the Rinzai school, edited a pro-war book titled *The Promotion of the Way of the Warrior*. In 1976 he referred to World War II as a holy war. Japan's oldest religion, Shinto, similarly linked religious devotion with service to the emperor and the state's imperial campaigns.

Christianity has similarly served various states' interests in conquest or recovery of lands. In the late fifteenth century, Pope Alexander VI (1431–1503) divided the lands discovered by Columbus between Portugal and Spain. Non-Christian kingdoms, whether in Europe, as in the case of the pagan peoples of the Baltic coast, or in the New World, could be designated to secular rulers whose armies would oppose by force and violence those who hindered preachers of the Gospel. Several centuries earlier, threatened by Muslim converts, the Byzantine Emperor Alexius I sought the assistance of the pope and Church. Pope Urban II (c. 1035–1099) responded by exhorting Christians to recover the Holy Lands, launching the first of the Crusades. Led mainly by French feudal lords, the crusaders captured Constantinople in 1096, Nicaea in 1097, Antioch in 1098, and finally in 1099 Jerusalem, where crusaders murdered thousands of Muslims and Jews. Encouraged by these military successes, Urban II sought to recover Spain from Muslin rule. Later Crusades were led by King Conrad III of Germany, King Louis VII of France, Holy Roman Emperor Frederick I Barbarossa, Richard I Lionheart of England, and Phillip II of France, all responding to papal calls.

In the history of Islam, particularly in that period known as the Age of Conquest, war played an important role in spreading the new faith, quickly establishing Muslim rule throughout the Mediterranean and beyond. By 637, five years after the death of the Prophet Muhammad, Muslim armies had conquered the Sasanid empire, which was centered in what is now Iran. Muslim forces conquered Jerusalem in 638 and Egypt in 641. Within a few decades, Muslims took control of Syria, North and parts of sub-Saharan Africa, and Spain in the west (reaching as far north in Europe as Tours, France), Central Asia in the east, and parts of the Indian subcontinent in the southeast. In 1453, nomadic Islamic Turkish tribes from Central Asia seized control of Constantinople and the Muslim Ottoman empire that soon followed came to control much of eastern Europe. Though its power began to wane in the late seventeenth century, it did not die until 1918.

Religion can also help secure a state's internal order and stability. In China, several rival schools of thought emerged in response to a breakdown of feudal order and the subsequent social chaos of the Warring States period in the fifth century BCE. One of the most lasting of these is Confucianism. Its founder, Master Kong (Confucius) delineated orderly hierarchical social relations based on moral cultivation and educational enrichment of the people under an imperial head of state fulfilling a heavenly mandate. War, though always regrettable, was seen as sometimes necessary to return to or to protect the essential orderliness of the state. Around the beginning of the common era, Buddhism gained some prominence in China. It adopted the values of social order articulated by the Confucian tradition and spread into Korea, Vietnam, and other parts of East Asia. Centuries later armies of Buddhist monks would fight to protect the imperial orders of China and Japan.

Pacifism and Nonviolence in World Religions

Of the philosophies that emerged from the Warring States period in China, Daoism is unique in the importance it assigns to pacifism and in its opposition to ambition, worldly authority, and political power. "He who would assist a lord of men in harmony with the Tao will not assert his mastery in the kingdom by force of arms" (Legge 1891, 72). While religions have legitimized the coercive powers of the state, its military campaigns, and imperial, colonial aspirations, enveloping them in an aura of spiritual ultimacy, they have also developed pacifistic doctrines that oppose those same powers and aspirations. Religious pacifism is found in virtually every religion. During the Reformation, for example, a number of Protestant sects revived the pacifism of the early Christian Church. Those groups that collectively are called the Anabaptists forbid violence and war, a prohibition that has frequently brought them in conflict with the state. Pacifism is found also in Roman Catholicism, Eastern Orthodoxy, and Judaism, though as a minority position. Some Qur'anic pronouncements also tend in this direction, though a thoroughgoing rejection of war is hardly an option for Muslims.

The doctrine of *ahimsa*, or nonviolence, gives Hinduism and other religious traditions in South Asia a strong pacifist streak. This is clearly the case with two religions that began as reform movements within Hinduism: Jainism and Buddhism. Both were established by individuals born in the Kshatriya caste, Mahavira (Jainism) and Siddhartha Gautama (Buddhism), who rejected the caste system and reworked the martial virtues of their caste into a spiritual struggle requiring the courage of a warrior to free oneself from the cycle of death and rebirth. Although the Jains hold that some violence is unavoidable (for example, even a vegetarian must harm plant life to eat), on the whole they have developed a way of life relatively removed from social functions that might involve them in direct violence. Jains are most frequently found among the merchant classes in India and rarely in the political or military classes. Similarly, Buddhism, prior to its division into the Theravada and Mahayana traditions in the first century CE, explicitly prohibited killing, including ceremonial sacrifice of animals, and rejected the use of violence as a necessary instrument of politics.

In the twentieth century, Mahatma Gandhi successfully led a nonviolent revolution that ended British colonial rule in India. And in the United States a Christianized version of the Hindu *ahimsa*, adopted by Martin Luther King, Jr., was a cornerstone of the civil-rights movement in the 1960s.

Acknowledgments

David Levinson came up with the idea for this volume—and indeed, for the *Religion and Society* series as a whole. I am very grateful to him for giving me full freedom with it. His staff at Berkshire Publishing, especially Elizabeth Eno, the project coordinator, made pleasurable the work of author contact, manuscript submission, and review. My associate editor, Iain Maclean, and the editorial board, comprising Jonathan Herman, Zayn Kassam, and Timothy Lubin, together did the bulk of the work. Their advice on topics and contributors and their efforts on manuscript review have made this volume the strong, interesting, and accurate work that it is.

My department chairperson, Thomas A. Shipka, worked another of his many small miracles in granting me release time from my teaching duties to complete this project. Students in my seminars on war and peace, and particularly those in my course Contemporary Philosophical and Religious Approaches to War and Terrorism, challenged me to get things right. I consulted and benefited from the expertise of several colleagues: John Cort, Denison University; Mustansir Mir, Youngstown State University; Louis Newman, Carleton College; Kimberley Patton, Harvard University; Ralph B. Potter, Harvard University; and John P. Reeder, Brown University. Finally, my spouse, Sarah Verrill Lown, frequently expressed her delight with this project and, as always, gave me her friendship and love.

Gabriel Palmer-Fernandez

Further Reading

Acquaviva, S. (1979). *Decline of the sacred in industrial society*. New York: Harper & Row.

Anscombe, G. E. M. (1981). War and murder. In G.E.M. Anscombe (Ed.), *Collected philosophical papers, Vol. III: Ethics, religion and politics* (pp. 51–61). Minneapolis: University of Minnesota Press.

Buitenen, J. A. B. van. (Ed. and Trans.). (1981). *The Bhagavadgita*. Chicago: University of Chicago Press.

Creveld, M. van. (1991). *The transformation of war*. New York: Free Press.

Fenn, R. (1972). A new sociology of religion. *Journal for the Scientific Study of Religion, 2*(1), 16–32.

Gurr, T. R. (1993). *Minorities at risk: A global view of ethnopolitical conflicts*. Washington, DC: United States Institute of Peace Press.

Hoffman, B. (1998). *Inside terrorism*. New York: Columbia University Press.

Jenkins, P. (2002, October). The next Christianity. *The Atlantic Monthly, 290*(3), 53–68.

Juergensmeyer, M. (2000). *Terror in the mind of God: The global rise of religious violence*. Berkeley and Los Angeles: University of California Press.

Kaplan, R. D. (1994, February). The coming anarchy. *The Atlantic Monthly, 273*(2), 44–76.

Kifner, J. (1995, November 8). Israelis investigate far right; may crack down on speech. *New York Times*, p. A12.

Landes, R. A., & Levinson, D. (2000). Introduction. In R. Landes (Ed.), *Encyclopedia of millennialism* (pp. xi–xxi). New York: Routledge.

Legge, J. (1891). *The sacred books of China: The texts of Taoism* (The Sacred Books of the East, No. 39). London: Oxford University Press.

Potter, R. B. (1996). The moral logic of war. In G. Palmer-Fernandez (Ed.), *Moral issues: Philosophical and religious perspectives* (pp. 291–304). Upper Saddle River, NJ: Prentice-Hall.

Rapoport, D. C. (1984). Fear and trembling: Terrorism in three religious traditions. *The American Political Science Review, 78*(3), 658–677.

Smith, W. C. (1978). *The meaning and end of religion*. New York: Harper & Row.

A

Afghanistan

Since the 1979 Soviet invasion, Afghanistan has seen successive rounds of war, with its accompanying death and destruction. However, the greatest source of trouble for the Afghan nation, its neighborhood, and the world has been the rise of Islamic extremism and its global implications, particularly after the September 11 terrorist attacks against the United States.

Decades of warfare have resulted in abysmally low levels of human and economic development in Afghanistan, which can improve only if diverse sectors of the international community commit themselves to the country's long-term social rehabilitation and economic reconstruction. Afghanistan also needs to develop viable forms of political governance and a working security structure. Afghanistan is strategically located at the crossroads of Central Asia, and, therefore, has been the hub of foreign military invasions and great power rivalries for centuries. In the nineteenth century it occupied a central place in what was known as the Great Game, a power struggle between imperial Russia and the British Empire in which Afghanistan was a pawn. Analysts such as the journalist Ahmed Rashid see present-day Afghanistan as caught up in a new Great Game, as the United States, China, and Russia vie for influence in oil-rich Central Asia.

Ethnic and Religious Diversity

Afghanistan has a population of over 25 million, excluding around 4 million Afghan refugees who started to return home from Pakistan, Iran, and other countries after the fall of the Taliban by the end of 2001. Afghanistan has a multiethnic and multi-religious society, settled across the country in geographically distinct zones. Ethnically, Pashtuns are the dominant group, constituting about 38 percent of the population. Tajiks comprise 25 percent, Hazaras 19 percent, Uzbeks 6 percent, and the remaining 12 percent include Turkmen, Balochis, Aimaqs, Nuristanis, and Kizilbash. Pashtuns are concentrated mostly in southern, southeastern, and southwestern Afghanistan, with the other ethnic groups inhabiting mostly the northern, northeastern, and northwestern regions of the country.

Religiously, around 84 percent of the Afghans belong to Sunni Hanafi sect of Islam, but Shiʿites constitute 15 percent, and others 1 percent. Although the religious identity mostly cuts across varied ethnic identities, members of major ethnic groups tend to have the same religious identity. For instance, Pashtuns are predominantly Sunnis and Hazaras are generally Shiʿites.

Roots of Radical Islam

Islam had been a unifying factor in Afghanistan since its introduction by the Arabs in the eighth century. The enormous popularity of Sufism, a mystical and undogmatic branch of Islam, contributed to Afghans' general religious tolerance. Sectarianism was never an issue, with Sunnis and Shiʿites and even Muslims and non-Muslims coexisting peacefully. The Loya Jirgah, an assembly of tribal notables and elders, resolved ethnic or tribal feuds by consensus.

Despite Soviet attempts to secularize Afghan society during the period of Soviet control (1979–1989),

Selection from the Bonn Agreement on an International Security Force for Afghanistan

ANNEX I
INTERNATIONAL SECURITY FORCE

1. **The participants in the UN Talks on Afghanistan recognize that the responsibility for providing security and law and order throughout the country resides with the Afghans themselves. To this end, they pledge their commitment to do all within their means and influence to ensure such security, including for all United Nations and other personnel of international governmental and non-governmental organizations deployed in Afghanistan.**
2. **With this objective in mind, the participants request the assistance of the international community in helping the new Afghan authorities in the establishment and training of new Afghan security and armed forces.**
3. **Conscious that some time may be required for the new Afghan security and armed forces to be fully constituted and functioning, the participants in the UN Talks on Afghanistan request the United Nations Security Council to consider authorizing the early deployment to Afghanistan of a United Nations mandated force. This force will assist in the maintenance of security for Kabul and its surrounding areas. Such a force could, as appropriate, be progressively expanded to other urban centres and other areas.**
4. **The participants in the UN Talks on Afghanistan pledge to withdraw all military units from Kabul and other urban centers or other areas in which the UN mandated force is deployed. It would also be desirable if such a force were to assist in the rehabilitation of Afghanistan's infrastructure.**

Source: **Agreement on Provisional Arrangements in Afghanistan Pending the Re-Establishment of Permanent Government Institutions. (2001, December 5). Retrieved 1 May, 2003, from www.uno.de/frieden/afghanistan/talks/agreement.htm**

Islam survived as a principal means of controlling personal conduct and settling legal disputes in the country. Islam also emerged as a key force opposing the occupation. In the process, however, it got radicalized.

There were three main reasons for its radicalization. First, there was the involvement of Arab mujahideen (Islamist guerrillas) in the U.S.-sponsored anti-Soviet jihad. Second, there was the struggle for power among the eight Iran-based mujahideen groups and the seven Pakistan-based mujahideen groups by the end of this jihad, and the aftermath of that struggle. Finally, there was the anarchy that enveloped the nation as a consequence of the factional warfare.

The Arab Mujahideen

While the eight mujahideen groups operating from Iran were mostly Hazara Shiʿites, the seven based in Pakistan were mostly Sunnis of Pashtun and Tajik origins. The Arab mujahideen included tens of thousands of radicalized Sunni Hanafi Muslims of North African and Middle Eastern origin. The radicalization of the seven Pakistan-based Afghan mujahideen groups was an outcome of their common sectarian link with Arab mujahideen, whose leaders hailed from radical Islamic organizations in the Middle East and North Africa, such as Ikhwan-ul-Muslamin and Gama'alIslamiya in Egypt, and the Islamic Salvation Front of Algeria.

It was the former Arab mujahideen leaders who constituted the leadership of al-Qaeda, the transnational Islamic terrorist movement created in 1989 by Osama bin Laden (b. 1957), Saudi millionaire and one of the Arab mujahideen leaders. Until their ouster from Kabul, Afghanistan's capital, the Taliban harbored al-Qaeda and bin Laden. Afghanistan under their rule became the chief exporter of Islamic extremism in the region and key sponsor of international terrorism in the world.

Factional Fighting

In addition to the radical Arab dimension of its emergence, radical Islam in Afghanistan in the post-Soviet era grew as a result of the struggle for power among various Afghan mujahideen groups. Some of them were Shiite of Hazara and Tajik ethnic origins, such as Hizb-i-Wahadat of Ali Mazari (later Karim Khalili). Others were Sunni of predominantly Pashtun origin, such as Burhanuddin Rabbani's Jamiat-e-Islami. These mujahideen groups were led by leaders exploiting Islam for political ends. Even the leadership of the same group, such as Hizb-i-Islami, was claimed by rival leaders like Gulbadin Hikmatyar and Younus Khalis. None of these groups participated in or negotiated the 1988 U.N.-supervised Geneva accords, under which the Soviet withdrawal from Afghanistan took place. Consequently, as soon as the Communist government of Mohammed Najibullah (c. 1941–1996) collapsed in March 1992, the mujahideen, acting independently of the United Nations, established an interim Islamic Jihad Council in Kabul under the leadership of Sibghatullah Mojaddedi, the moderate chief of the Afghanistan National Liberation Front. It did not survive long; in June Mojaddedi had to surrender power to Burhanuddin Rabbani (b. 1940), a more radical Islamist. Later that year, Rabbani's forces clashed with the forces of another radical mujahideen leader, Gulbadin Hikmatyar (b. 1940).

Until its fall at the hands of the Taliban, the Rabbani regime in Kabul continued to fight on two military fronts: against the forces of Gulbadin Hikmatyar's Hizb-i-Islami and its Shiʿite ally, the Hizb-i-Wahdat, east and southwest of the Afghan capital; and the Jumbish-i-Milli Islami forces of a former Communist commander, General Abdul Rashid Dostum (b. 1954), an Uzbek, in the north.

Anarchy and the Taliban Takeover

The struggle for power among various Afghan factions and the ensuing anarchy and warlordism across the country created a political and ideological vacuum that was filled by the Taliban, a new extremist Islamic movement. Under the spiritual leadership of Mullah Mohammed Omar (b. 1961), the Taliban established a reign of terror in Afghanistan, persecuting religious minorities, political opponents, and women, and exporting Islamic extremism and terrorism abroad.

The Taliban's conception of Islamic *shariʿa* was based on an idiosyncratic interpretation of Deobandism, an Islamic reformist movement in British India whose intention was to regenerate Muslim society through reinterpreting Islam according to new realities. After Pakistan's creation, Deobandis established the Jamiat-ul-Ulema-i-Islam (JUI), a religiously based political party. Students were taught Deobandisim at *madrasah*s run by JUI's "barely literate mullahs who knew nothing about the original reformist Deobandi agenda" (Rashid 1999, 26). Saudi Arabia's funding of the *madrasah*s resulted in teachings that leaned toward Wahhabism, the ultraconservative form of Islam practiced in that country. The students at those *madrasah*s became the Taliban.

The end result was horrific, not just for the Afghan nation but also for the outside world, particularly the neighboring states. The Taliban's practice of *shariʿa* in Afghanistan tarnished the image of Islam in the eyes of the world. Through a series of fatwas (Islamic edicts), Mullah Omar barred women from work, required women to cover up from head to foot in public places, and forbade the education of girls. *Shariʿa* punishments such as the amputation of limbs, stoning, beheading, and shootings at public gatherings, mostly at football stadiums, became the norm of the day.

Lessons from Afghanistan

While radical Islam had horrendous effects on the Afghan people, the outside world also paid a huge price. U.S. indifference and the U.N.'s failure to achieve a political settlement in post-Soviet Afghanistan not only resulted in the growth of radicalized Islam but also nurtured an anti-American rage among the former Afghan and Arab mujahideen that expressed itself in a series of acts of international terrorism culminating in the September 11 attacks on New York City's World Trade Center and the Pentagon. The journalist John Cooley, considering the fact that the United States had at one time sponsored the very groups that sponsored acts of terror against it, observed that "When you decide to go to war . . . take a good, long look at the people behind you whom you chose as your friends, allies or mercenary fighters. Look well to see whether these allies already have unleashed their knives—and are pointing them at your own back." (Cooley 1999, 141).

In the post–September 11 period, expansion of Islamic extremism has been met with the war against terrorism. The war has not yet ended. Western engagement in the postwar peacekeeping and rebuilding of Afghanistan indicates that Islam and the West can march together for a common cause that the world of

FBI TEN MOST WANTED FUGITIVE

MURDER OF U.S. NATIONALS OUTSIDE THE UNITED STATES; CONSPIRACY TO MURDER U.S. NATIONALS OUTSIDE THE UNITED STATES; ATTACK ON A FEDERAL FACILITY RESULTING IN DEATH

USAMA BIN LADEN

Date of Photograph Unknown

Aliases: Usama Bin Muhammad Bin Ladin, Shaykh Usama Bin Ladin, the Prince, the Emir, Abu Abdallah, Mujahid Shaykh, Hajj, the Director

DESCRIPTION

Date of Birth:	1957	**Hair:**	Brown
Place of Birth:	Saudi Arabia	**Eyes:**	Brown
Height:	6' 4" to 6' 6"	**Complexion:**	Olive
Weight:	Approximately 160 pounds	**Sex:**	Male
Build:	Thin	**Nationality:**	Saudi Arabian
Occupation:	Unknown		
Remarks:	Bin Laden is the leader of a terrorist organization known as Al-Qaeda, "The Base". He is left-handed and walks with a cane.		
Scars and Marks:	None		

The Federal Bureau of Investigation's Ten Most Wanted poster, depicting Osama bin Laden. Bin Laden founded the transnational terrorist organization, al-Qaeda, which was harbored by the Taliban in Afghanistan.

tomorrow may be based on a partnership of civilizations rather than a clash of civilizations. Instead of sharpening the divide between Islam and the West, the demise of the Taliban and al-Qaeda may liberate Muslim nations and people across the world from the religious attitudes upon which transnational militant movements such as al-Qaeda have thrived in the past.

Future Challenges

After decades of death and destruction, Afghanistan needs a stable peace in which the millions of suffering Afghan people inside and outside the country can recover and the nation's thoroughly decimated infrastructure can be reconstructed. The key challenge facing Afghanistan today is economic and social. It will require billions of dollars in international financial and developmental assistance, part of which has been committed by international and national donors, even though not delivered in full. It also requires the establishment of credible political and security foundations across Afghanistan.

Since December 2001, Afghanistan has been under the rule of a transitional administration established under the U.N.-supervised Bonn Agreement on Afghanistan. The Pashtun leader Hamid Karzai (b. 1957) was elected president of the Afghan Interim Authority in June 2002 under the symbolic leadership of the former Afghan king Mohammed Zahir Shah (b. 1914). Under the Bonn Agreement of 3 December 2001, the transitional administration will hold free and fair national elections in December 2003 in order to establish a broad-based political setup in the country, which should be representative of all of the nation's ethnic and religious groups.

It took decades for radical Islam to establish its roots inside Afghanistan and endanger regional and global peace. Since the fall of the Taliban, U.S.-led coalition forces have been busy eliminating the remnants of the Taliban and al-Qaeda from Afghanistan and preventing their regrouping, especially from their hideouts across the Afghan border in Pakistan's tribal Pashtun areas. The international war against Islamic extremism and terrorism in Afghanistan and its neighborhood may be a long haul.

For that reason, the International Security Assistance Force (ISAF), established under U.N. Security Council Resolution 1386, needs to expand its operational scope and mandate so that it can help create a stable and secure environment for the socioeconomic rebuilding of Afghanistan and for the establishment of democratic institutions and processes.

Ishtiaq Ahmad

See also Deobandism; Taliban; Wahhabism

Further Reading

Ahmad, I. (2000–2001). Containing the Taliban: The path to peace in Afghanistan. *Perceptions, 5*(4), 67–87.

Ahmad, I. (2002). Post-war Afghanistan: Rebuilding a ravaged nation. *Perceptions, 7*(2), 25–39.

Cooley, J. K. (2002). *Unholy wars: Afghanistan, America and international terrorism*. London: Pluto Press.

Evans, M. (2001). *Afghanistan: A brief history*. Richmond, UK: Curzon Press.

Gohari, M. J. (2000). *The Taliban: Ascent to power*. New York: Oxford University Press.

Goodson, L. P. (2001). *Afghanistan's endless war: State failure, regional politics, and the rise of the Taliban*. Seattle: University of Washington Press.

Griffin, M. (2001). *Reaping the whirlwind: The Taliban movement in Afghanistan*. London: Pluto Press.

Khalilzad, Z., & Byman, D. (2000). Afghanistan: the consolidation of a rogue state. *The Washington Quarterly, 23*(1), 65–78.

Maley, W. (1998). *Fundamentalism reborn? Afghanistan and the Taliban*. London: C. Hurst.

Marsden, P. (1999). *The Taliban: War, religion and the new order in Afghanistan*. London: Zed Books.

Marsden, P., & Minority Rights Group. (2001). *Afghanistan: Minorities, conflict and the search for peace*. London: Minority Rights Group International.

Nojumi, N. (2002). *The rise of the Taliban in Afghanistan: Mass mobilization, civil war, and the future of the region*. New York: Palgrave.

Rashid, A. (2002). *Jihad: The rise of militant Islam in Central Asia*. New Haven, CT: Yale University Press.

Rashid, A. (1999). The Taliban: Exporting extremism. *Foreign Affairs, 78*(6), 22–35.

Rashid, A. (2000). *Taliban: Islam, oil and the new Great Game in Central Asia*. London: I. B. Tauris.

Rubin, M. (2002). Who is responsible for the Taliban? *Middle East Review of International Affairs, 6*(1), 1–16.

Africa *See* Africa, West; African Religion: Warrior Cult; Apartheid; Fundamentalism in Egypt and Sudan; Genocide in Rwanda; Islam: Age of Conquest; Nigeria; Yoruba; Zimbabwe; Zulu

Africa, West

The history of West Africa over the last several centuries is one of recurrent struggle between Christianity and Islam. Often entangled in that conflict is ethnic strife and intra- and interregional conflict.

Establishment and Spread of Islam

Much of the spread of Islam throughout West Africa was tied initially to commerce; later it was on occasion imposed through conquest. Several kingdoms in the region had an Islamic presence dating back to the eighth century; these include Songhai (an empire in present-day Mali on the central portion of the Niger River), the Mali empire (centered on the upper portion of the Niger River), and the ancient kingdom of Ghana. By the eleventh century there was a movement to impose a more rigorous Islamic structure throughout the region by banishing certain customs and practices that were viewed as contrary to the belief. Even though stricter religious practices were carried out with great vehemence, the unique character of Islam in West Africa was its variation on standard customs. By the sixteenth century Islam was well established in large sections of West Africa.

A new dimension was present in the religious dynamic from the mid-1600s until the end of the eighteenth century: the slave trade. The capture, enslavement, and deportation of Africans by European powers gave impetus to various jihads, or holy wars, in the region because the conquered groups could be sold for a profit, or traded for goods. This was the experience among the Hausa states and elsewhere in West Africa. While much scholarly attention has gone to the exportation of enslaved Africans, there was also internal enslavement throughout the region prior to any contact with Europeans.

The Spread of Christianity and Styles of Colonial Rule

Roman Catholicism was introduced to coastal areas of West Africa by the fifteenth century by the Portuguese in the form of clergy who served Portuguese traders in the area. The Portuguese sought to break the Muslim control of the maritime trade in the region. By the 1460s, the Cape Verde islands had been colonized, and the Portuguese began building forts on the Island of Goree and in other coastal areas such as Elmina, in what later became known as the Gold Coast (modern-day Ghana). This trading in gold provided a lucrative incentive for the Portuguese and later other European powers to establish contact with Africans who were in a position to mine gold and other precious commodities. The Portuguese also acted as middlemen to facilitate internal enslavement for laborers in the mines. By the end of the eighteenth century, however, much of this activity waned as more emphasis was placed on the export-oriented African slave trade.

Although there was a Christian (Catholic) presence in the region as early as the fifteenth century, the real effort at converting Africans to Christianity did not begin until the 1840s, when missionary work was undertaken by the British, the French, and the Portuguese in much of the western part of the continent. So, in addition to the commerce, trade, and slavery dynamic, the colonization and missionization of Africans became a part of the complex equation which set the tone throughout the nineteenth century.

The general strategy of the French was to weaken if not minimize the Islamic presence in its colonies so as to gain greater cooperation. The French and Portuguese adopted a policy of assimilation whereby the Africans in their colonies were equipped with the language, culture, and customs of the colonial power and afterward could be considered French or Portuguese citizens. They thus divided their colonial populations into those who were assimilated and those who remained indigenous. The indigenous were frequently Muslims, who had well-honed trading skills but did not have a Western-style education and were therefore looked down upon by the colonial powers.

The British took a less integrative approach. They employed a strategy of indirect rule, which was based on the British belief that African culture was fundamentally incompatible with its own. The British therefore utilized local leaders, customs, languages, and laws, to a degree, to maintain order. They then placed British colonial representatives in the various localities for the indigenous leaders to account to. This system worked well among peoples such as the Yoruba, whose style of governance was hierarchical, but less well among peoples such as the Igbo, whose culture was more egalitarian and who resented the imposition of what were called "warrant chiefs." In the southern part of British-controlled Nigeria, Christian missionaries were free to proselytize, build churches, and convert Africans. One of the major missionary organizations, the British-based Church Missionary Society (CMS),

Islam, Colonialism and Christianity in Northern Nigeria

The following text describes the suspicion and separation that has long existed and continues to define relations between Muslims and Christians in much of West Africa. The text describes attitudes in a town of the Kanuri people of northern Nigeria.

One busy place almost any day or time of the year is Nola Primary School, built by order of the education authority in Maiduguri about twenty years ago. It opened with a single room and grew until in 1967 it became a complete seven-class institution. Because education in the colonial period was so closely associated with Christian initiative, even locally sponsored, nonmission schools were suspect as Christian places. Western education was, and often still is, perceived as a threat to Islamic beliefs. Consequently, Nola, primarily a Muslim village, did not welcome its new school. Many parents hid their children in the bush or fled the village, fearing not only the school's "godlessness" but also that their young ones would be shipped abroad and eaten by Europeans. Even today such fears have not been totally dispelled.

Source: Peshkin, Alan. (1972). *Kanuri Schoolchildren: Education and Social Mobilization in Nigeria.* New York: Holt, Rinehart and Winston, Inc., p. 12.

was firmly established by the mid-nineteenth century, but it was soon joined by missionary groups from Catholic and other Protestant denominations.

Nineteenth-Century Regional Conflicts

In what is now northern Nigeria, the British indirect-rule strategy meant giving local Muslim emirs power over both Muslims and non-Muslims; the British also kept Christian missionary activity to a minimum throughout the region as an appeasement to the northern Islamic leaders. The indirect-rule strategy seems to have facilitated greater ethnic polarization and greater regional conflict than did the French and Portuguese strategy of assimilation. Developing a firm grip in the northern portion of West Africa (modern-day Burkina Faso, Chad, Niger, and Mali, among others), activist Muslims led by Usman dan Fodio (d. 1817) waged war on nearby states beginning in 1804. Usman dan Fodio established the Sokoto caliphate in 1809; it had a strong presence in northern Nigeria for the remainder of the nineteenth century.

Among the Yoruba people of present-day Nigeria, the nineteenth century saw conflict between those Yoruba who embraced Islam or Christianity and those who retained their traditional religion. With roughly proportionate numbers of Yoruba being either Christian or Muslim, competing identities which were based around one's town of origin, often resulted in religious, economic, and political struggles. Certain Yoruba—the Ijebu for example—tended to embrace both Christianity and Western education and frequently used these skills for profit as interpreters or letter writers for less-skilled Yoruba (including traditional chiefs) from the interior. This produced yet greater animus among various Yoruba groups.

After the Yoruba Oyo empire fell to Muslim Fulani tribesmen from the north sometime between 1800 and 1820, there was full-scale civil war throughout much of Yorubaland within a decade. While there was a religious component, these wars were fought over access to lucrative routes for trade purposes. One outcome of these wars was that large numbers of enslaved Africans were sold to Western powers. Although in 1833 Britain and its colonies officially abandoned the practice of importing slaves and stationed ships off of the West African coast to enforce such a band, many slave ships continued to slip through its blockade.

The Europeans Formalize Colonial Power

By the mid-1880s, fearing territorial claims on the African continent might lead to war, the major European powers arranged a conference in Berlin between 1884 and 1885 to establish formal boundaries. Of course, many of these powers had staked their claims in the region long before the Berlin conference. Britain had, for example, claimed Sierra Leone in 1808, along with the areas of the Gambia, Lagos (annexed in 1861), and the Gold Coast, which was declared a colony in the mid-1870s after the British defeated the Ashanti nation in 1874 in the last of several wars the British and Ashanti fought. France laid its colonial claimed to Senegal in the eighteenth century, but also pulled in Algeria in 1830, Gabon in 1849, and Tunisia in 1881. The Portuguese had a complete monopoly on the Cape Verde islands, but also brought Guinea-Bissau and other areas into its colonial sphere. The conference also included colonial powers such as Germany, Belgium, and the Netherlands (among others) that were active in other parts of Africa.

Among the guidelines participants at the Berlin Conference agreed upon for the proper establishment of an African colony were that a colonial power had to establish control of a territory, either through armed occupation or through some form of indirect rule, that it had to ensure access to trade routes to allow for free trade, that it had to be committed to the abolition of slavery in the claimed territory, and it had to recognize all Christian denominations. The last requirement met with resistance in areas such as in northern Nigeria, where the British tacitly agreed to keep Christian missionary activity to a bare minimum. The only area in West Africa left untouched by these events was Liberia, which was a pseudoprotectorate of the United States.

The African response to these events was pacifistic in some instances and violent in others. In Dahomey (modern day Benin), Chad, and the Gold Coast, Africans fought the French and British imposition of colonialism. Similar resistance was seen in other parts of the continent, too, as when the Ethiopians defeated the Italians at Adowa in 1896.

Religion and Conflict in the Twentieth Century: Nigeria as a Case Study

Once the colonial system was firmly in place in the twentieth century and railways made long-distance travel relatively easy, both Christianity and Islam spread more rapidly than ever. Without question, the history of Nigeria presents the most vivid regional example of how these major world religions' different sacred views and the different ethnic identities of their adherents have placed local interests above national ones. These often conflicting interests have repeatedly led to violence in the decades since Nigeria's independence in 1960.

The Nigerian Civil War, also known as the Biafran War (1967–1970), demonstrated the severity of ethnic and religious tensions in the independent country. Even before independence was declared, the country had been divided into three regions (northern, western, and eastern) along relatively clear ethnic and regional lines. In terms of religion, the northern region had a Muslim majority and the eastern region had a Christian majority. Intra-ethnic violence among the Yoruba in the western region of the country led to the jailing of certain politicians and the support of others who appeared to have aligned themselves with the northern Muslims, ethnically Hausas/Fulani. Rigged elections in 1964 and 1965 as well as general violence and mayhem throughout the country led several mid-level officers to stage the country's first coup d'état, in which major politicians and military leaders were killed. The fact that most of the coup plotters were Igbo (a people originally from the eastern part of the country) and that eastern political leaders were spared being assassinated led to northern Nigerians to suspect an eastern plot to take over the country. A subsequent countercoup led to the removal of the original plotters, but easterners (mostly Christians) who resided in the north of the country had their businesses burned and many were killed. In the turmoil the eastern region declared its independence as the state of Biafra, and a three-year-long struggle ensued to bring the eastern region back into the federal fold.

In the last decades of the twentieth century, while the country made efforts to reunite the Christian and Muslim communities, politicians continued to use religion as a tool in politics. The case of the military president of the 1980s, General Ibrahim Babangida, is often cited. Widely perceived to have become a Muslim after joining the military to advance his political ambitions, Babangida secretly added Nigeria to the ranks of the Organization of Islamic Conference in 1986. When this became known among the country's Christians, there was widespread protest and anger from that population, with accusations that he intended to transform Nigeria into an Islamic country.

In fall 2002, the Miss World contest (a beauty contest based in London) announced its intentions to hold that year's contest in Lagos, formerly Nigeria's capital. The move was supported by the federal government, which hoped to attract international attention to the country's development and boost tourism. Instead, the decision angered Nigeria's Muslim population, who thought young ladies displaying themselves in bathing suits was immodest and inappropriate. When a reporter suggested in a journal article that the prophet Muhammad would have approved of such young ladies, it sparked rioting in several northern cities that left close to two hundred people dead.

Other Parts of Contemporary West Africa

In other parts of West Africa there continue to be religious tensions, but they are not nearly so severe as in Nigeria. The Mano River Basin, comprising Guinea, Sierra Leone, and Liberia, has been economically devastated by civil conflict that has raged throughout much of the 1980s and 1990s. Religious institutions have played a significant role in helping to resettle refugees displaced by the fighting and have functioned as a conflict resolution vehicle. The World Conference on Religion and Peace (WCRP; founded 1970), a coalition of representatives of the world's great religions, has encouraged Christian and Muslim leaders in the region to work together through the formation of organizations such as the Inter-religious Council of Sierra Leone (IRCSL; 1997), which in 1999 helped bring about the signing of the Lome Peace Accord in that nation.

There are many African organizations that seek to address the delicate issue of religious intolerance on the continent. The Project for Christian-Muslim Relations in Africa (PROCMURA) has, among its primary aims, the facilitation of constructive engagement between Christians and Muslims and reduction of worrying and negative relations. As part of the effort to improve relations, participants have shared gifts and sent greetings and goodwill messages on the occasion of major religious festivals. They have also formed joint committees of Christians and Muslims to address such issues as the implementation of Islamic law *(shariʿa)* in northern Nigeria and to encourage governments to stop making aid and political appointments dependent on one's religious affiliation. They have spoken out against the polarization of society into Christian and Muslim; their efforts represent an African solution to an ongoing challenge in the region.

Christopher Brooks

See also Nigeria; Yoruba

Further Reading

Clarke, P. B. (1982). *West Africa and Islam*. London: Edward Arnold.

Fage, J. D. (1969). *A history of West Africa: An introductory survey*. Cambridge, UK: Cambridge University Press.

Hastings, A. (1976). *African Christianity*. New York: The Seabury Press.

Hastings, A. (1994). *The church in Africa, 1450–1950*. Oxford, UK: Clarendon Press.

Hiskett, M. (1984). *The development of Islam in West Africa*. London and New York: Longman.

Ramussen, L. (1993). *Christian-Muslim relations in Africa: The case of northern Nigeria and Tanzania compared*. London: British Academic Press.

African Religion: Warrior Cult

This article examines the place of the warrior cult in West Africa in the late eighteenth century and throughout the nineteenth century. The Warrior Cult also existed in other parts of Africa among the Zulus and the Masai. During that period, preparations for war, war itself, and the conduct of war were all organized around the central figure of the sacred warrior. The Nso' of Cameroon and the Ashanti of Ghana illustrate the effectiveness of the concept of the sacred warrior in traditional African society and illustrate how societies thus organized resisted colonialism, albeit with limited success.

Warfare in precolonial West Africa was never solely the isolated function of state; it also involved religious specialists, since West African peoples believed that the spiritual world had transformative power in the material world. Rules for the conduct of war reflected these beliefs and made accommodation for ritual specialists. In general, the conduct of warfare in precolonial West African societies was similar to the conduct of warfare in other ancient or traditional societies.

Preparations for War

Rules of war are generally agreed upon by neighboring nation-states or ethnic groups and expressed in customary mutual laws that specify how war is to be declared and how warring parties will treat outsiders and neighbors who share a common border. These laws attempt to minimize the element of surprise attacks and to encourage ways of resolving differences peaceably. Attempts to resolve conflicts may include direct talks or consultation, but most of the time initiatives are indirect and involve third parties or traditionally recognized diplomatic channels.

Two of the critical decisions facing leaders of traditional African societies were how to treat war prisoners or captives and how to formulate peace treaties governing the relationship between the victors and the vanquished. In this regard, it is important to remember that the objective of most West African wars was not

Masai Warrior Cult

The following ethnographic account describes the formation and structure of the warrior cult of the Masai, a herding people of Kenya.

After some years the boys are circumcised, and become *moran* warriors. As soon as most of them are circumcised the *ingopiri* plan to form into separate companies in readiness for residence in warrior villages called *imanyab*. Messages are sent and the warriors of all clans are called together by means of an *ol-amal* just as the boys did before the *endungore* ceremony. The number of companies, called *i'sirit*, to be formed, also the names to be given to them are decided on beforehand by the *ingopiri* warriors. After discussion a division is decided upon. One warrior representing each company to be formed leaves the assembly, goes a little way and striking the haft of his spear with his club to attract attention, he calls: "En alo Il Mirisho" or "En alo Il Tetiauri"—"This way the Mirisho, this way the Tetiuri." The warriors then rise and join the man calling the name of the company they wish to join.

Groups of five will go together, to join the same company. A company may include warriors of more than one clan though as a rule the majority are of the same clan.

If the warriors of one clan are too few to form a separate unit they join the unit of another clan. If the clan is a very big one, the warriors may form two or even more *sirits*. Having joined a *sirit* a warrior may retract at any time before that *sirit* forms the first warrior village. Once the warrior villages are formed, any warrior who leaves *nis sirit* to join another, incurs the bitter resentment of the others. In some cases a fine of cattle is inflicted.

The *sirits* once formed, the warriors now approach the *il-piron* elders with a view to holding the ceremony of drilling—without which the first warrior village or *manyata* of new age-group may not be erected.

Source: Whitehouse, L. E. (n.d.) "Masai Social Customs." *Journal of the East Africa and Uganda Natural History Society*, 47–48, 150.

so much the long-term occupation or annexation of foreign territory, but peaceful coexistence. Warfare was declared to settle longstanding grudges and disputes or in response to a perceived threat by neighboring ethnic groups.

The environment dictated terms of combat insofar as it affected means of combat and mobility of combatants. In the northern Sahel and Sahara savannahs of West Africa, the shrub and grass vegetation presented few physical obstacles to travel and communication or to establishing trade links between ethnic groups. The lack of difficult terrain meant that the conduct of war was more fast paced than it was in the southern rain forests. Because forest dwellers were more isolated from their neighbors, social intercourse and warfare were definitely slower, and the likelihood of developing suspicions toward and a sense of distance from outsiders was high.

Conceptual Framework of War

The conceptual framework of the warrior tradition in Africa can best be understood in terms of what the historian and anthropologist Anthony Wallace calls the forces of "severe disorganization of a socio-cultural system" (Wallace 1961, 144). His observations regarding the Seneca Indians of New York at the close of the eighteenth century apply both to precolonial African societies and to African societies during the Western colonial incursion. There are differences between the Seneca and West African cases, however. The Seneca seem to have attached high value to the concept of individualism, which in times of crisis was subordinated and transcended for the sake of the common good. In contrast, West African cultures are rooted in the communitarian ethic, although they do recognize and encourage individual talent and acts of heroism during hunting expeditions and times of war. In the Seneca case study, Wallace argues that the incursion of outsiders from 1754 to 1797 and the loss of Indian hunting grounds diminished the role of the good hunter and destroyed that of the forest statesman. Similar consequences followed in Africa when the African warrior tradition came under attack by the Europeans. The warrior personality may have been reduced to irrelevance by modern warfare and Western governance, but the heroic virtues of the African warrior tradition have been preserved in oral tradition.

The Conduct of War and the Warrior

In West African societies, a warrior could assume a leadership position among his peers during a hunting expedition, but more often he gained it during war. The defining moments for a would-be warrior were those that called for courage and fearlessness. To be recognized as a warrior, the individual should understand the use of deadly force and the necessity of loss of life—including, possibly, one's own—in order to secure peace and the greater good of the community. The scholar Clyde Ford provides a good summary of the ideals of a warrior: "Warriors march along the razor's edge. They thread a treacherous path between the considered use of deadly force and the indiscriminate slaughter of lives; between destroying obstacles to the well-being of self and society, and raging berserk in the midst of battle; between fearlessness in the face of death and recklessness for life itself. The noble warrior also answers the bugle of the battlefield but is the trumpet of the soul, sounding a higher note of loyalty to the ideal, a cause, a god, or a nation" (Ford 1999, 68).

Sacred Warriors

A sacred warrior, as distinguished from an ordinary warrior, was "a uniquely talented individual whose bravery and harnessing of spiritual forces moves in the inescapable dance of death yielding to life yielding to death again. The sacred warrior moves in step with this eternal rhythm of life" (Ford 1999, 69). He was unquestionably an extraordinary citizen. His life and deeds would be celebrated and recounted in epic narratives. The Mwindo Epic of the Nyanga, a people living in what is now the Democratic Republic of Congo, depicts the sacred warrior as one who is gifted and precocious from birth. He is associated with strange happenings and signs that often accompany religious figures. Mwindo for example, was born laughing, speaking, walking, and holding a conga-scepter in his right hand and an ax in his left. More importantly, he was born wearing a little bag of the spirit of Kihindo, the goddess of good fortune. In all Mwindo's struggles, whether against physical or spiritual forces, he was never hurt. The warrior's place in traditional society was earned and tested in warfare. The claim to fame for a warrior was rewarded by an honorary title or disctinction. Among the Nso', the Amfome are honored and greeted with respect and deference.

Waging War

In discussing how West African precolonial societies waged war, it is essential to recall that the modern concept of the nation-state was alien to West African peoples. Precolonial West Africa knew tribes and kingdoms, but not nation-states.

Precolonial wars ranged from skirmishes and raids to full-blown warfare among neighboring groups and tribes. Armed insurgents used spears, bows and arrows, and slings. Although war could be waged not for the primary reason of establishing peace, there are circumstances when wars are fought for the sake of expanded territory or to dominate and usurp hostile or weaker states (examples include the wars of the great empires of medieval West Sudan, Ghana, and Kanem (in present-day Chad). Second, they went to war to acquire wealth in the form of tribute or by opening up new trade routes. This was the dominant reason for the rivalry between the Fante (on the southern coast of what is now Ghana) and the Ashanti (present-day southern Ghana and nearby portions of Togo and Ivory Coast) in their wars of the eighteenth and nineteenth centuries. Third, the need for a reliable work force in certain African societies led them to carry out raids to obtain slaves.

Divine Kingship

In societies that were ruled by chiefs or kings, the divine king embodied the unity of the people and religion. In his role as the chief ritual specialist and intercessor of his people, the king was treated with deference and great respect. He had at his service other religious specialists with whom he could consult on matters that determined the survival of the kingdom. As a general principle, priestly diviners were consulted prior to a formal declaration of war on an enemy country or ethnic group. In the Dahomey kingdom (present-day central Benin), after the priestly diviners had determined that the chances of winning a battle were good, spies would be sent into enemy territory to bury magical substances that were calculated to assure the Dahomey kingdom victory. Then, before the army made its move into enemy territory, sacrifices were made to the war god or the war standard, weapons were smeared with sacrificial blood, and warriors' bodies were rubbed with ointment to make them invisible.

Among the Nso' of Cameroon, religious ideology played an important role in the execution of war. The paramount ruler, the Fon, is considered sacred, and he is served by ritual specialists who work in close collaboration with military leaders, called the Amfome (plural) of the military organization of which the Fon was the formal head. Before the Nso' went to war, the Fon would consult his council, which was made up mostly of the Amfome, who represented different villages. As with the Dahomeans, spies would be sent out to enemy country. Generally, the divination precedes the sending of the spies. The spies are involved in reconnaissance work which involves intelligence gatherings, strategy, and eavesdropping on enemy plans for war. Among these spies would be special warriors believed to possess magical or supernatural powers, including the power to become invisible and the power to transform into big cats or birds. The last phase in the preparation for war was divination: A goat or cock would be sacrificed and its entrails examined. In the case of an offensive war, if the omen was bad the war effort would be aborted or suspended indefinitely; in the case of a defensive war, a bad omen prompted the removal of women and children to some hidden location where they would be safe.

Challenges and Adaptation to Colonial Rule

The colonial era tested the African ability to wage war. African resistance to colonial rule was remarkable, and the numerous struggles that were made in West Africa have not been fully recounted. If we judge African resistance to colonial occupation solely in terms of its success in Western military terms, we fail to appreciate a crucial element contained in the African conception of the warrior. The historian Michael Crowder suggests that battles that Africans fought against outside enemies should be measured by the prowess of defeated leaders who became heroes in the oral tradition.

In the history of African resistance to European rule, the Ashanti presented a formidable challenge. In the eighteenth century, the large Ashanti empire was the envy of both the British and the Ashantis' local rivals, the Fante. The British, who had already established trade relations with the Fanti, resented the idea of the Ashanti king extending his rule over the European settlements in the coastal region. The British made an alliance with the Fante to fight the Ashanti, but the Ashanti defeated their enemies in the war of 1807. The Ashanti had acquired additional guns and gunpowder from other European traders on the coast, and the Ashanti military was highly disciplined and motivated. Their guiding principle at war was summed up in the saying, "if it is a matter of choosing between disgrace and death then I should choose death" (Crowder 1971, 27). The Ashanti, like other West African peoples, conducted sacrifices to the gods and ancestors to guarantee success. In the latter part of the eighteenth century and in the nineteenth century, Ashanti warriors sought prayers from the Muslim community written in Ashanti. Ashanti warriors also believed that wearing amulets and talismans containing Qur'anic texts would help bring victory in battle.

The Idea of the Sacred Warrior in Postcolonial Africa

Traditional African religions continue to be practiced in present-day Africa, but a large percentage of Africans today are Christian or Muslim. African-initiated forms of Christianity retain attenuated roles for ritual specialists and sacred kings, but there is not much of a role for warriors. African Islam accommodates and reinforces the sacred warrior title to the extent that traditional Muslim mullahs prepare charms and prophylactics which warriors consider useful for self-defense, immunity, or to render themselves invisible to their enemies. Tales of heroic warriors of the past continue to be recounted, and continue to inspire young men—although now the field on which they must prove themselves has changed.

Victor F. Wan-Tatah

See also Africa, West; Zulu

Further Reading

Campbell, J. (1968). *The hero with a thousand faces*. Princeton, NJ: Princeton University Press.

Crowder, M. (Ed.). (1971). *West African resistance: The military response to colonial occupation*. New York: Africana Publishing Corporation.

Ford, C. W. (1999). *The hero with an African face: Mythic wisdom of traditional Africa*. New York: Bantam Books.

Fowler, I., & Zeitlyn, D. (1996). *African crossroads: Intersections between history and anthropology in Cameroon*. Oxford, UK: Berghahn.

Mbiti, J. (1969, 1999). *African religions and philosophy*. Oxford, UK: Heinemann.

Rotberg, R. (Ed.). (1971). *Rebellion in black Africa*. London: Oxford University Press.

Saul, M., & Royer, P. (2001). *West African challenge to empire: Culture and history in the Volta-Bani anticolonial war*. Athens: Ohio University Press.

Smith, R. S. (1976). *Warfare and diplomacy in pre-colonial West Africa*. London: Methuen.

Wallace, A. F. C. (1961). *Culture and personality*. New York: Random House.

Werbner, R. P. (Ed.). (1977). *Regional cults*. London: Academic Press.

Anabaptist Pacifism

Sixteenth-century Europe gave rise to a number of movements within Christianity more radical than the Reformation, indeed sometimes called, collectively, the "Radical Reformation." The Anabaptists were those who believed with the reformers that a break with Rome was necessary, but that the Reformation of Martin Luther (1483–1546), Huldrych Zwingli (1484–1531), John Calvin (1509–1564), and others did not go far enough. The Anabaptist intent was to restore the church to its New Testament roots rather than to merely reform it somewhat closer to that ideal.

Anabaptism began in 1522 when students of Zwingli who were meeting in Zurich, led by a humanist named Konrad Grebel (c. 1498–1526), took several actions to demonstrate what they believed were New Testament Christian communal commitments and at the same time vocally opposed local Catholic monks. Whereas Zwingli wanted a popular or "people's church," the radicals wanted a "free church": free from all authority other than that established explicitly by the New Testament, and free in the sense that only those who freely joined of their own volition would be members. On 21 January 1525, these believers baptized a number of adults who had previously been baptized as infants. They were reinstituting the New Testament conception of baptism as they understood it—believer's baptism—and this event signifies their complete break with the Zurich Reformation, which was, even aside from the movement led by Grebel and others, the most radical of all Reformation movements at the time. It wasn't long before these radicals were called Anabaptists or "rebaptizers" by their enemies.

This communal Christianity spread rapidly, and in February 1527 a meeting was called near the Swiss community of Schleitheim, principally under the direction of Michael Sattler (c. 1490–1527), a former Catholic monk and one of the first Anabaptist martyrs. The meeting produced the Schleitheim Confession, a statement of identity and order of discipline among the Anabaptists. Briefly, some Anabaptist distinctives can by summarized as follows. Baptism was an ordinance received by those who made a personal confession of faith in Jesus Christ, pledging themselves to "repentance and amendment of life" and living in the "resurrection of Jesus Christ." The Lord's Supper was to be shared by all baptized believers. Authority within the church was not hierarchically but communally conceived; it was not a matter of office, but a matter of practice. The Bible (especially the New Testament with primacy given to the Gospels), the direction of the Holy Spirit, and "the rule of love" were to direct believers' lives, rather than religious superiors. The church was to practice "separation" from the evil of the world: "To us, the, the commandment of the Lord is obvious, whereby he orders us to be and to become separated from the evil one" (Klaassen 1981, 304). Further, the Anabaptists confessed that "The sword is ordained of God outside the perfection of Christ" (Klaassen 1981, 268). In short, the Anabaptists believed that they were to live as the New Testament directed in all matters, that discipleship or Christ-likeness was the hallmark of true Christian faith, and that living as Christ's disciples meant, among other things, that baptism was for believers only and that pacifism was a part of Christian life by definition.

Anabaptist Pacifism

Thus we can see that pacifism for Anabaptists is not an element of piety added on to the essential character of their faith, but rather part of the essence of faith, which is discipleship, living as Jesus commanded his disciples to live. This view of pacifism continues to hold true for Anabaptists today, for example, among Mennonites and members of the Church of the Brethren and Brethren in Christ churches. But why do Anabaptists understand pacifism as essential to living the Christian life? How is this pacifism different from other kinds of pacifism? And how do Anabaptists conceive of their relationship to the state?

In respect to the first of these questions, Anabaptists believe discipleship means living as Jesus told his disciples to live. This is to say that the ethics enjoined in the New Testament are not ideals that (tragically) cannot be made manifest, as for example in the theological ethics of Reinhold Niebuhr. Rather, the New Testament's ethics, especially the primacy of love, are to be made real through communal as well as personal practices regardless of how impractical such ethical mandates may look to nonbelievers. The Anabaptist

Matthew 5:38–48

38. Ye have heard that it hath been said, An eye for an eye, and a tooth for a tooth:

39. But I say unto you, That ye resist not evil: but whosoever shall smite thee on thy right cheek, turn to him the other also.

40. And if any man will sue thee at the law, and take away thy coat, let him have thy cloke also.

41. And whosoever shall compel thee to go a mile, go with him twain.

42. Give to him that asketh thee, and from him that would borrow of thee turn not thou away.

43. Ye have heard that it hath been said, Thou shalt love thy neighbour, and hate thine enemy.

44. But I say unto you, Love your enemies, bless them that curse you, do good to them that hate you, and pray for them which despitefully use you, and persecute you;

45. That ye may be the children of your Father which is in heaven: for he maketh his sun to rise on the evil and on the good, and sendeth rain on the just and on the unjust.

46. For if ye love them which love you, what reward have ye? do not even the publicans the same?

47. And if ye salute your brethren only, what do ye more than others? do not even the publicans so?

48. Be ye therefore perfect, even as your Father which is in heaven is perfect.

method of interpretation, then, is to understand Scripture's ethical injunctions literally. Further, Jesus himself is the model of faithful life (Matthew 20:25–28; Ephesians 5:1–2; Philippians 2:5–8). Anabaptists, taking Jesus as the model for Christian living, are, among other things, then, forbidden to use violence. Anabaptists believe Jesus, whose cause was perfectly just, and who lived a perfectly innocent life, rejected violence and even submitted himself to it. He taught his disciples,

> You have heard it said, "An eye for an eye and a tooth for a tooth." But I say to you, Do not resist an evildoer. But if anyone strikes you on the right cheek, turn the other also. . . . You have heard that it was said, "You shall love your neighbor and hate your enemy." But I say to you, Love your enemies and pray for those who persecute you, so that you may be children of your Father in heaven. . . . Be perfect, therefore, as your heavenly Father is perfect." (Matthew 5:38–48 NRSV)

If Jesus is a model to be followed with complete seriousness, then pacifism is required.

Anabaptists see in the cross event the perfect unfolding of God's will and love for humanity, a model of the love that believers are to embody. The cross is the paradigmatic event for understanding God. God, in Christ, suffered and died innocently in order to make salvation available to all. And this act of supreme sacrificial love is a pattern to be followed. This unconditional sacrifice is held up by Paul as an example when he writes, "Let the same mind be in you that was in Christ Jesus, who, though he was in the form of God . . . humbled himself and became obedient to the point of death—even death on a cross" (Philippians 2:5–8 NRSV).

The ecclesiology of Anabaptists, then, is inextricably tied to nonviolence. Anabaptists understand the true Christian community, that is, the church, normatively, as those disciples who, living after the model of Jesus, practice pacifism as a part of the practice of forgiveness and of servanthood. Again, nonviolence is not an add-on to Anabaptist theology or ethics, but intricately tied to all aspects of the Anabaptist understanding of the Christian faith. As Christians are called to sacrificially forgive, love, and serve all others, pacifism is not only explicitly commanded, but implicit in all of the Christian life. Normatively, an Anabaptist believer is incapable of seeing the coherence of the gospel and of Christianity apart from the call to nonviolence.

In sum, while there are many varieties of pacifism, religious and secular, Anabaptist pacifism is rooted in a theological understanding of God and God's purposes for humankind in general and Christ's disciples in particular. God so understood is ontological, Trinitarian love, a love that gave up life on a cross not only as a redemptive act, but also as an ethical act. Jesus' life and the cross event, then, provide an example for his disciples.

Goshen College students at the October 2002 School of Americas Protest in Georgia. Goshen College is affiliated with the Mennonites and traces its roots to Anabaptism.
Photo courtesy Marten Beels.

The Anabaptists and the State

Such a commitment to nonresistance clearly brings Anabaptist Christians in conflict with the state over the matter of state-sanctioned violence. Indeed, many Anabaptist communities throughout history have understood the Christian's relationship to the state to be difficult in a number of ways. Since Christ's disciples call him "Lord," they cannot give ultimate allegiance to the state. Since Jesus forbade the taking of oaths (Matthew 5:33–37), the Anabapists refused to serve on juries and in other capacities that required the swearing of oaths. Because in early Anabaptist history, and in other times throughout history, Anabaptists have been persecuted by the state, Anabaptist Christians have viewed the state with caution. Yet, Anabaptists also have maintained that the state exists purposefully in God's economy, that is, it has its rightful, God-ordained functions, and concomitantly Anabaptists have consistently sought to be good citizens whenever doing so was not seen to violate the gospel. Thus, in the Anabaptist understanding, Christian nonviolence is not meant as defiance, protest, or subversion to the state. Anabaptists have often, for example, served as medical personnel in time of war, even on the battlefield. After registering as Contentious Objectors, Anabaptists have usually served their countries, where permitted, by doing alternative service such as the Peace Corps or in hospitals instead of going to war. Such service in the United States has usually lasted for two years or more and was common during World Wars I and II and the Korean and Vietnam conflicts. Biblical nonresistance, for the Anabaptist, is not directed against the state, but rather is a response of obedience to God. Furthermore, Anabaptists believe that they are called to witness to the gospel to all, so that their witness must include witness to the state. The Anabaptist wants to be a good citizen in whatever state he or she resides, and believes that the way to be the best citizen one can be is to be faithful to the gospel, a disciple of Christ.

In one respect, it can be said that Anabaptists have understood the kingdom of God as an alternative *polis*, the church as its own political community. Certainly the concept of kingdom and reign (*basileia* in New Testament Greek) is a political conception. But Anabaptists, as do other Christians, seek to live lives of dual citizenship, as they must be citizens of God's *polis* first, but also citizens of their respective states, or even "of the world." Pacifism does not, for the Anabaptist, keep one from serving or giving witness to the state; rather, it is a necessary part of doing so as a disciple of Christ, and thus doing so in the best way possible.

It should be mentioned that whereas scholars generally understand Anabaptism and pacifism to be inherent correlates, a few take a broader view of Anabaptism such that all sixteenth-century groups which rejected both the Catholic church and the Reformers, and baptized believers only, were, on this understanding, Anabaptist. These scholars, notably Michael G. Baylor and George H. Williams, tend to conflate groups constituting the "Radical Reformation" and Anabaptists; most scholars, however, understand the category of "radicals" to be broader than the category "Anabaptist." The broader interpretation, which usually conflates the two categories, can be seen to fail in two respects. First, Anabaptist groups, in nearly overwhelming consensus, produced documents which make it clear that they understood nonresistance to be constitutive of their self-understanding and identity. Second, Anabaptists were persecuted for their pacifism (among other reasons); thus their enemies understood them as defined in part by their commitment to nonresistance, which was seen as subversive to the state. Thomas Müntzer (1468 or 1489/90–1525) and later, Melchior Hoffmann (c. 1495–1543 or 1544) are the two figures, sometimes identified as Anabaptist, who taught that violence could be legitimately used by Christians. In any event, Anabaptists are generally understood for both historical and theological reasons to be, by definition, those who rejected and still reject violent resistence.

More important still are the reasons why Anabaptist pacifists saw and continue to see nonresistance as an essential part of the Christian faith. In short, Anabaptists believe that the Christian life is by definition a life lived in imitation of Jesus Christ. Such imitation includes the renouncing of violent resistence to all forms of injustice or violence. 1 John 2:5–6 records this injunction simply, "This is how we can be sure that we are in union with God: if we say that we remain in union with God, we should live just as Jesus Christ did." In his "Armaments and Eschatology," the important twentieth-century Anabaptist theologian John Howard Yoder put it this way:

> The point . . . is not only that people who wear crowns and who claim to foster justice by the sword are not as strong as they think—true as that is: we still sing "O where are Kings and Empires now of old that went and came?" It is that people who bear crosses are working with the grain of the universe. One does not come to that belief by reducing social processes to mechanical and statistical models, nor by winning some of one's battles for the control of the fallen world. One comes to it by sharing the life of those who sing about the Resurrection of the slain Lamb.

Michael L. Minch

Further Reading

Baylor, M. G. (2000). *The radical Reformation*. New York: Cambridge University Press.

Estep, W. R. (1996). *The Anabaptist story: An introduction to sixteenth-century Anabaptism*. Grand Rapids, MI: Wm. B. Eerdmans Publishing Co.

Goertz, H. (1996). *The Anabaptists* (Trevor Johnson, Trans.). New York: Routledge.

Hershberger, G. F. (Ed.). (1962). *The recovery of the Anabaptist vision*. Scottdale, PA: Herald Press.

Klaassen, W. (Ed.). (1981) *Anabaptism in outline: Selected primary sources*. Scottdale, PA: Herald Press.

Sider, R. J. (1979). *Christ and violence*. Scottdale, PA: Herald Press.

Stayer, J. M. (1976). *Anabaptists and the sword*. Lawrence, KS: Coronado Press.

Williams, G. H. (1992). *The radical Reformation*. Kirksville, MO: Sixteenth Century Publishers.

Yoder, J. H. (1979). *The politics of Jesus*. Grand Rapids, MI: Wm. B. Eerdmans Publishing Co.

Yoder, J. H. (2001). Armaments and eschatology. In S. Hauerwas (Ed.), *With the grain of the universe: The church's witness and natural theology*. Grand Rapids, MI: Brazos Press.

Apartheid

Apartheid is a system of racial discrimination that was implemented by the National Party (NP) during its reign in South Africa from 1948 to 1994. It is a system of thought that was premised on the superiority of whites over blacks. Nigel Worden has pointed out that apartheid was not static or monolithic as "each decade was marked by differences in both content and the implementation of the policy as well as in the ways of resistance" (Worden 2000, 107). Moreover, according to David Chidester there was no one understanding of apartheid among the Afrikaner groups. First, there was "pure" apartheid—the idea that the purity of the white Afrikaner nation needed to be protected. This group advocated for the total separation from blacks; even contact with black workers was supposed to be eliminated. A second understanding of apartheid was that of the National Party, which believed in preserving and safeguarding the white race. They believed that they had a Christian religious duty to exercise trusteeship over blacks in South Africa. In their application of apartheid, the NP believed that it was protecting all the different racial groups. The separation did not end with blacks and whites; blacks were further divided into separate ethnic groups that were confined to certain areas determined by the NP. Such areas were called homelands. The third type was practical apartheid, which recognized that white economy is dependent on cheap labor. In this understanding, apartheid was more about power than about purity.

The Development of the Ideology

Saul Dubow is of the view that the development of the ideology of apartheid is linked to the development of Afrikaner nationalism. There were a number of factors that created favorable conditions for the development of the ideology. The first was the defeat of the Afrikaner during the South African War (Anglo-Boer war; 1899–1902) and the birth of the Union of South Africa in 1910 as a member of the British Empire. Giliomee described the union as a compromise that favored the English. The South African Party and later the United Party, which ruled the union between 1910 and 1948, perpetuated the compromise and promoted links with Britain. They even promoted the idea of amalgamation between the English and the Afrikaners. During the aftermath of the war and the alienating political and economic climate, Afrikaners were a defeated and powerless people. Afrikaner thinkers wanted to find ways of getting power. Resources like history, culture, language, and religion were mobilized in constructing an Afrikaner identity

A second factor in the development of the ideology of apartheid was that, due to rapid industrialization, more Afrikaners moved to the cities and towns to seek employment. They "often entered the job market on the lowest rungs, hardly any higher than the equally unskilled black labor force and far beneath the skilled English worker. Viewed from a Nationalist perspective, the dominant feature of the South African economy was the vast gap between Afrikaner and English wealth" (Giliomee 1979, 107). World War II saw secondary industry undergoing rapid expansion as a result of the need for more materials. During this period there was a massive influx of African work seekers, which threatened the privileged position of Afrikaans-speaking workers. Unskilled Afrikaner workers could not compete with their African counterparts, as they were willing to work for less pay.

The term "apartheid" first appeared on the scene in 1936. According to Dubow, it was first used by the *Suid-Afrikaanse Bond vir Rassestudie* (South African Bond for Racial Studies) as its political slogan distinguishing the radical Afrikaner form of segregation from that propagated by the state. It only rose to prominence in 1943 when Dr. D. F. Malan started using it in his speeches. It was on the basis of this radical segregation that the Nationalist Party won the 1948 election.

According to Johann Kinghorn, the Dutch Reformed Church was involved in debates on the desirability of segregation prior to 1948. They even sent a delegation to Prime Minister Jan Smuts in 1942 for him to implement some of the measures to ensure segregation. Biblical justification of apartheid was only sought in 1948 in a report submitted to the Transvaal Synod of the Dutch Reformed Church entitled *Racial and National Apartheid in the Bible*. More sophisticated attempts were made after 1948.

Apartheid in Practice

There are three main phases that apartheid underwent between 1948 and 1994: construction (1950s), consolidation (1960s), and crisis (1970s to the early 1990s).

Phase 1: Construction (1950s)

During this period various apartheid legislations were passed extending racial discrimination. Colored people were also disenfranchised during this period. The central pillar of apartheid was the separation of all South Africans according to race. The Prohibition of Mixed Marriages Act was enacted in 1949. It was followed by the Immorality Act in 1950, which prohibited sex between people from different racial groups. These two acts made it illegal for people from different racial groups to have any intimate contact. Nineteen fifty was a very busy year for the legislature as it passed three other acts. First, the Population Registration Act en-

In New York on 15 June 2000, retired Archbishop of Cape Town Desmond Tutu lights a peace candle during ceremonies launching a Peace Center honoring his struggle against apartheid in South Africa. Courtesy the Episcopal News Service; photo by James Solheim.

forced the classification of people into four racial categories, i.e., white, Asiatic, colored, and native (Bantu and later African). Second, the Group Areas Act segregated residential areas for different racial groups. This act was followed by forced removal of people who were deemed to be living in inappropriate areas. Third, the Suppression of Communism Act gave the state power to outlaw any person or organization understood to be promoting Communist ideas. The 1953 Separate Amenities Act ensured the segregation of public amenities like sports facilities, public toilets, cinemas, transport, and schools.

During the 1950s the government gradually introduced its policies in the educational sector. In fact, "educational apartheid was enforced in schools (1953), technical colleges (1955) and universities (1959)" (Worden 2000, 108). The Bantu Education Act was introduced in 1953. This act "brought all African schools under the control of the Department of Native Affairs, thus phasing out independent missionary institutions which had previously led the field in African education" (Worden 2000, 108).

The measures that the Nationalist Party had taken were not without any resistance. The 1940s saw the emergence of the Congress Youth League, which transformed and radicalized the African National Congress (ANC). "In 1952 the ANC and the Communist Party jointly launched the Defiance campaign to protest against the government's new discriminatory legislation, with the aim of mobilizing widespread defiance of unjust laws such as curfews, pass laws and segregation of amenities" (Worden 2000, 112). A mass demonstration of over 20,000 women from different parts of the country under the banner of the Federation of South African Women marched to the union buildings in Pretoria in 1956. The highlight of the 1950s was the drafting and adoption of the Freedom Charter in 1955 by the National Congress of the People (ANC, Congress of Democrats, Indian Congress Movement, and South African Coloured People's Organization) as well as the South African Communist Party. The Freedom Charter was adopted by the ANC as its policy document. The state responded to the Congress of the People by arresting 156 of its leaders for treason and conspiracy to overthrow the state in 1956. The Supreme Court overturned the case in 1961.

Phase 2: Consolidation (1960s)

The period of consolidation is when the Nationalist Party consolidated its position of power and implemented more measures to complete the apartheid project. A number of historians have identified the main feature of this period as the economic boom accompanied by state repression of any form of resistance. On 21 March 1960, sixty-nine Pan Africanist Congress (PAC) supporters who were protesting against pass laws were killed by the police at Sharpville, south of Johannesburg. The government responded by banning the ANC, PAC, and the SACP. The leadership of the liberation movement was forced to turn to armed resistance. The ANC formed its military wing, Umkhonto we Sizwe (Spear of the Nation). The majority of the leadership of the liberation movement ended up either in exile or in jail.

The government consolidated its policy of separate development, creating homelands for all Africans. The aim of this strategy was to leave South Africa without any African citizens. Dubow pointed out that "[i]n the 1960s Verwoerd defended Apartheid on the grounds that it was giving blacks similar opportunities to those in the newly independent states to the north" (Dubow 1995, 276). The African population was divided into ethnic groups, each with a designated area. The idea was that Africans should be allowed to develop in their own areas without white interference. As this policy was implemented more and more Africans lost their South African citizenship.

The government implemented its Bantustan policy by giving nominal independence to Transkei (1976), Bophuthatswana (1977), Venda (1979), and Ciskei (1981). These "independent" states were not recognized outside the South African borders. They promoted narrow ethnic nationalisms but they were not completely cut off from South Africa as large numbers of their populations still worked in South Africa. The other ethnic homelands were called self-governing territories.

Phase 3: Crisis (1970s to the early 1990s)

During this period signs of discord within the Nationalist Party became visible. There was also an increase in the levels of resistance among the oppressed population. Toward the end of the 1960s the seeds of the Black Consciousness Movement (BCM) were sown. The South African Students Organization (SASO) was formed after black students left the white-dominated National Union of South African Students (NUSAS).

Worden further states that when the BCM started, the state thought that it would serve its purposes of separate development. However, the state was surprised when the Black Consciousness Movement rejected the Bantustan policy, Bantustan leaders, and ethnically based movements like Inkatha (founded in 1975 by Mangosuthu Buthelezi in Natal).

The defining moment in the 1970s was the 1976 Soweto student uprising, which has since become an important symbol of black resistance. After learning that their curriculum was to be taught in Afrikaans, students organized and marched through Soweto. The police confronted them and several students were killed. The Soweto uprisings were followed by a period of state repression, which culminated with the banning of all Black Consciousness–aligned organizations and the death of Steve Biko in detention in 1977.

The winds of change were sweeping Southern Africa, as both Angola and Mozambique got their independence from Portugal. The governments that took over these countries were hostile to South Africa. The P. W. Botha government felt that it was in its interest to curtail the threat of military incursion by the armed wings of the ANC and the PAC through direct military incursion into neighboring countries as well as through supporting organizations that were friends of South Africa like UNITA (National Union for the Total Independence of Angola) and RENAMO (National Resistance Movement of Mozambique).

During the 1980s the crisis deepened as the leaders of the Nationalist Party introduced various reforms to counter international and local pressure. There was disagreement within the Nationalist Party about how to implement and defend apartheid. A split occurred in 1982 and a right-wing Conservative Party was born. In 1983 a new constitution came into being, which extended parliamentary representation to Coloreds and Indians. Parliament had three chambers, one for each of the represented groups. Elections for the Colored House of Representatives and the Indian House of Delegates were marred by low voter turnouts and widely rejected by the opposition.

The NP was increasingly under pressure from the right wing, which was eroding their support base among white voters. In the 1987 whites-only election the Conservative Party gained enough support to become the official opposition. The international community put both economic and political pressure on South

Africa. International bodies like the United Nations and the British Commonwealth criticized the violation of human rights in South Africa. Some international companies heeded the international sanctions call and disinvested from South Africa. Local business that had supported Botha's political reformism in 1979 became more critical of the government. Extraparliamentary opposition gained more momentum in 1983 with the formation of the United Democratic Front (UDF), whose first task was to organize the boycott of tricameral parliamentary elections. Black labor was becoming more organized; different sectors of the labor market became unionized. In 1985 a federation of South African trade unions, COSATU (Congress of South African Trade Unions), was formed.

In 1985 violence broke out between the supporters of the ANC-aligned UDF and Inkatha and went on until 1994. Hundreds of lives were lost during this conflict, which Buthelezi called a low-intensity civil war. There were allegations that the government was sponsoring this conflict through its support of Inkatha. Between 1985 and 1990 the government imposed three states of emergencies, giving police power to detain individuals for up to ninety days without trial; as a response to unrests in other parts of the country. A number of activists were arrested and others disappeared without trace.

The failure of the P. W. Botha government to lead South Africa out of international isolation led to disillusionment among local business; as a result a delegation met with the ANC in Dakar, Senegal. The then NP Transvaal leader F. W. de Klerk organized a trip to Lusaka, Zambia, to meet with the ANC without Botha's approval. In 1989 Botha resigned the presidency and was replaced by de Klerk. During the opening of Parliament on 2 February 1990, the government announced the unbanning of all banned extraparliamentary organizations and the release of Nelson Mandela, who had been a political prisoner for 27 years in Robben Island, Pollsmoor, and Victor Verster prisons in South Africa.

Implications

When studying the history of apartheid, it is important to realize that it was not a monolithic and static system. There were disagreements among the Afrikaner about the meaning and substance of apartheid. Throughout the various phases it was evident that the minor differences turned into ideological differences, especially as the NP responded to pressure from the international community and local business. The Truth and Reconciliation Commission, established by the government following the first free elections on 27 April 1994, uncovered some of the atrocities that were committed by state operatives, which led to human suffering. Resistance changed with each phase. During the last phase extraparliamentary opposition was better organized than in the previous decades and it was able to mobilize both local and international support against apartheid.

Sibusiso Masondo

Further Reading

Boonzaier, E. (1988). "Race" and the race paradigm. In E. Boonzaier & J. Sharp (Eds.), *South African keywords: The uses and abuses of political concepts* (pp. 58–67). Cape Town, South Africa: David Philip.

Chidester, D. (1992). *Religions of South Africa*. London and New York: Routledge.

De Gruchy, J. W. (1979). *The church struggle in South Africa*. London: William Eerdmans; Cape Town, South Africa: David Philip.

De Gruchy, J. W. (1997). Grappling with a colonial heritage: English-speaking churches under imperialism and apartheid. In R. Elphick & R. Davenport (Eds.), *Christianity in South Africa: A political, social, and cultural history* (pp. 155–172). Oxford, U.K.: James Currey; Cape Town, South Africa: David Philip.

Dubow, S. (1995). *Scientific racism in modern South Africa*. Cambridge, UK: Cambridge University Press.

Giliomee, H. (1979). The growth of Afrikaner identity. In H. Adam & H. Giliomee (Eds.), *The rise and crisis of Afrikaner power* (pp. 83–127). Cape Town, South Africa: David Philip.

Hofmeyr, I. (1987). Building a nation from words: Afrikaans language, literature, and ethnic identity, 1902–1924. In S. Marks & S. Tropido (Eds.), *The politics of race, class, and nationalism in twentieth century South Africa* (pp. 95–123). London: Longmans.

Kinghorn, J. (1990). The theology of separate equality: A critical outline of the DRC position on Apartheid. In M. Prozensky (Ed.), *Christianity in South Africa* (pp. 57–80). Bergvlei, South Africa: South Book Publishers.

Kinghorn, J. (1997). Modernization and apartheid: The Afrikaner churches. In R. Elphick & R. Davenport (Eds.), *Christianity in South Africa: A political, social, and cultural history* (pp. 135–154). Oxford, U.K.: James Currey; Cape Town, South Africa: David Philip.

Reader's Digest. (1994). *Illustrated history of South Africa: The real story* (3rd ed). New York: Author.

Rhoodie, N. J., & Venter, H. J. (1960). *Apartheid: A socio-historical exposition of the origin and development of the Apartheid idea*. Cape Town, South Africa: HAUM.

Sharp, J. (1988). Ethnic group and nation: The apartheid vision in South Africa. In E. Boonzaier & J. Sharp (Eds.), *South African keywords: The uses and abuses of political concepts* (pp. 79–99). Cape Town, South Africa: David Philip.

Villa-Vicencio. (1988). *Trapped in apartheid: A socio-theological history of the English-speaking churches*. Cape Town, South Africa: David Philip; Maryknoll, NY: Orbis Books.

West, M. (1988). Confusing categories: Population groups, national states, and citizenship. In E. Boonzaier & J. Sharp (Eds.), *South African keywords: The uses and abuses of political concepts* (pp. 100–110). Cape Town, South Africa: David Philip.

Worden, N. (2000). *The making of modern South Africa: Conquest, segregation, and apartheid*. Oxford, U.K.: Blackwell Publishers.

Art

While the artistic representation of human conflict is as old as war itself, the juxtaposition of religious themes and motifs with realistic battlefield settings in art is a relatively recent phenomenon. It was only in the late nineteenth century that the first such images began to appear. However, in the famous picture *Death of General Wolfe* painted in 1771 by Benjamin West (1738–1820), the dying figure bears strong similarities to images of Jesus taken down from the cross, and it has been argued that the artist intentionally composed this apotheosis in order to create a spiritual countenance around the personality. Other "death tableaux" paintings from the period had similar religious connotations. So, too, did several paintings of Napoleon, particularly *Napoleon on the Battlefield of Eylau*, by Baron Gros (1771–1835), in which the artist imbued the emperor with Christlike qualities.

Although prints of visions, dreams, and solace appeared in popular prints during the U.S. Civil War, the artwork avoided any overt religious themes, and it was only later that such themes were incorporated directly into paintings of war. In *Faithful unto Death*, the German historical painter Ferdinand Pauwels (1830–1904) chose a battlefield setting from the Franco-Prussian War of 1870–1871. A German soldier with bandaged head stares up at Christ, whose hand is on the warrior's shoulder. A few decades later, in 1901, the British artist George Joy (1844–1925) painted *Dreams on the Veldt*, in which three casualties of the Boer War (1899–1902) are visited by angels. In contrast was the realism of Richard Caton Woodville (1856–1927), as seen in *Lindlay: Whitsunday 1900*, which shows a church service on the veldt. It was during the Great War however, that the full flowering of war art in concert with religious themes emerged.

World War I

No modern war has invoked more religious and spiritual sentiment than the Great War, and the art of the period certainly reflected this. Artists used popular religious motifs to link death on the battlefield with spiritual intervention. The war catalyzed a growing preoccupation with spiritualism and inspired the production of numerous such images.

Christian symbols were employed in various forms on postcards and memorials, as well as in prints, posters, and paintings. Portrayals of visions were a popular method for instilling nationalism, a sense of inspiration, and patriotic fervor. Artists sought to inspire patriotic feelings by depicting Saint George of England and Saint Michael of France. And when depicting the inspired recruits who had met their death on the battlefield, artists replaced images of saints with the crucified or risen Christ. The use of such motifs was designed to comfort those who grieved, a steady stream of religious iconography providing a visual assurance of loved ones' eternal salvation. There were also more naturalistic scenes of soldiers praying on the battlefield or attending makeshift church services.

Death, Sacrifice, and Resurrection

Sacrifice emerged as a popular motif throughout the war. One of the earliest pictures in this vein was the inspirational painting *The Great Sacrifice* (1914), by James Clark (1858–1943), showing a young soldier "sacrificed" at the foot of a cross, reflecting universal attitudes of approval and respect for a soldier's sacrifice for his country, to war and death. Images of sacrifice and resurrection frequently employed the figure of Jesus; one example is *The Hero*, by Hal Hurst (1865–1938), in which Christ holds the dead body of a soldier in his hands. Similarly, a postcard printed by the Bamforth Company in aid of the Red Cross depicts a

Conservet Corpus Tuum et Animam Tuam (1915) by W. H. Y. Titcomb, depicting British soldiers taking communion at the front. Courtesy Anne S. K. Brown Military Collection, Brown University Library.

The Great Sacrifice (1914) by James Clark. Anne S. K. Brown Military Collection, Brown University Library.

wounded or dying soldier looking up to a vision of Jesus, a scene repeated frequently throughout the war in the art of all the belligerents.

Understandably, the idea of resurrection and life everlasting found expression in several paintings and prints. James Clark's sequel to *The Great Sacrifice*, entitled *The Greater Reward*, showed his young soldier, having ascended from the battlefield on his journey to eternal life, holding the hand of an angel while he looks heavenward. Another picture that employed the angel motif was *Happy Warrior*, painted in 1918 by Henry Lintott (1877–1965). That work shows four angels rising through the clouds carrying on their shoulders a stretcher bearing a dead soldier covered by a blanket atop which is a sword.

The Cross

Wayside crucifixes were a common sight throughout northern France and Belgium during the war, and a number of artists chose deliberately to incorporate crosses in realistic settings. A profound expression of grief employing the cross motif was the 1916 piece *Youth Mourning*, by George Clausen (1852–1944), depicting a group of over fifty crude wooden crosses set in a plain level grassy landscape in the middle distance. The main subject was a crouching naked women with her head down in her hands grieving. Three crosses suggestive of swords stuck into the earth and symbolizing Calvary are spaced equidistant behind her. Later the artist painted out all but a single cross planted on the edge of a pockmarked battlefield covered with water-filled shell holes. *Anno Domini 1917*, by James Dollman, employs small, crude crosses arranged haphazardly, protruding here and there across a wasteland. Looking out across the wilderness is Christ, wearing a loose tunic which touches the ground and casts a long shadow. The theme of harvesting souls was popular at the time, and an example was the late-war canvas *Harvest 1918*, by William Orpen (1878–1931), in which farmers are shown cultivating in a field of crosses.

Visions

Rumors of battlefield visions abounded at the beginning of the war. One example, the angels of Mons, an angelic host that was widely reported to have intervened in battle on the side of the British, was portrayed by several artists. *The White Comrade*, painted by George Hillyard Swinstead (1860–1926), showed a medical officer sustaining a badly wounded soldier, while with an expression of hope and courage he gazes at a white vision of Christ. The White Comrade was inspired by accounts from soldiers of seeing a white figure on the battlefield.

Postwar

Some artists used religious and spiritual metaphors after the war to symbolize the human and physical destruction. While such postwar memorial imagery was criticized by returning soldiers, the bereaved could relate to it and found it to be therapeutic, and many religious symbols were incorporated into war memorials. In general, such themes were out of favor with the official war artists, although Stanley Spencer (1891–1959) invoked sacrifice and resurrection in one of his murals at the Sandham Memorial Chapel at Burghclere in Hampshire, England.

In contrast to World War I, World War II and subsequent wars were virtually secularized and devoid of religious iconography and pathos when it came to war art, although images of soldiers at church services or praying occasionally appeared.

Peter Harrington

See also Martyrdom

Further Reading

Mosse, G. (1990). *Fallen soldiers: Reshaping the memory of the world wars*. Oxford, UK: Oxford University Press.

Harrington, P. (1992). Early paintings of the Great War. *Imperial War Museum Review, 7*: 46–54.

Harrington, P. (1993). *British artists and war: The face of battle in paintings and prints 1700–1914*. London: Greenhill Books.

Harrington, P. (1994). *The great sacrifice:* The First World War's most graphic painting. *This England, 27*(3), 14–15.

Wilkinson, A. B. (1978). *The Church of England and the First World War*. London: SPCK.

Winter, J. (1995). *Sites of memory, sites of mourning: The Great War in European cultural history*. Cambridge, UK: Cambridge University Press.

Assassins

The common contemporary meaning of the word *assassin* is one who murders another; specifically, it is one who murders a politically important person, either for hire or for fanatical reasons. But the word developed out of a derogatory term applied by Sunni Muslims (Sunni Islam being the branch of Islam encompassing the majority of the world's Muslims) to the Nizaris, breakaway members of the Ismaili sect of Shiʿa Islam who were active between the eleventh and the thirteenth centuries. The original Arabic term is *hashshahshin*, meaning "one who smokes the narcotic hashish."

For more than two centuries, from 909 CE to 1171 CE, the Fatimid dynasty, an Ismaili dynasty, ruled Egypt and North Africa. Ismailis everywhere looked to the Fatimid ruler, the imam, for spiritual leadership. In 1094 CE, a dispute arose when the Fatimid imam al-Mustansir died and was succeeded by his younger son, al-Mustaʿli, rather than his eldest son, Nizar. The choice caused a schism among the Ismailis, and a new branch emerged known as the Nizaris, whose members argued that Nizar rather than al-Mustaʿli was the rightful imam.

Spiritually, the Nizaris did not differ greatly from other Ismailis. They did, however, emphasize the imam's unique role as one who conveys authoritative teaching *(talim)* to the people, and the bond that exists between him and his followers. The Nizaris continued to observe orthodox religious practices as defined by Islamic law *(shariʿa)*, but believed these practices should be carried out not just for the sake of obedience to the law, but also as a means to individual spiritual transformation.

The Nizaris are notable for the revolutionary political ideology they embraced during this period. From bases in Iran and Syria, where the movement had its strongest support, they took part in sporadic conflict with the Seljuks, their ethnically Turkish Sunni rulers, aiming to bring about the downfall of the Sunni caliphate and its orthodox institutions. The Nizaris also engaged in the killing of prominent Sunnis, mainly government officials and religious leaders, in pursuit of this goal. These acts of violence had the dual effect of eliminating enemies of the movement as well as generally intimidating the opposition. The Nizaris glorified as heroic martyrs the devotees, known as fidaʿis, who carried out these usually suicidal missions. The tactic of assassination was not, however, pioneered by the Nizaris. The Ismailis and members of other Islamic sects had carried out similar killings in the past.

During this period, a number of fortresses in Iran and Syria were occupied and converted into Nizari strongholds. The first and most prominent of these was a fortress at Alamut in the Elburz Mountains of northern Iran, which was captured in 1090 under the leadership of Hasan bin Sabbah (1034–1124). Hasan became a key figure in the Nizari movement, helping to turn the network of fortresses into a fledgling Ismaili state that was eventually ruled by imams descended from Nizar. Repeated Seljuk attempts to reclaim the fortresses and suppress the Nizari revolt were unsuccessful and, against the odds, the state survived for more than 150 years.

As the Nizaris became increasingly radicalized and alienated from mainstream society, legends about the sect spread. Among these was a belief popular among Sunnis that, prior to carrying out the assassinations, Nizari *fidaʿis* used hashish to induce visions of paradise and inspire them to martyrdom, hence the disparaging use of the term *hashshahshin* in reference to the Nizaris collectively. Although there is no evidence that hashish was used in this way, the legend persisted, and during the Crusades the term was introduced to Western Europe, where it was translated as "assassins" and eventually acquired its current meaning.

The Nizari state collapsed with the Mongol invasion of 1256 CE. Alamut and the other Iranian fortresses were captured, and a massacre of the Ismailis followed. Shortly after, forces of the Mamluk sultan Baybars I (1223–1277; reigned 1260–1277) occupied the Syrian fortresses, ending any hope of ongoing Nizari political power in the region. The Nizaris nevertheless survived as a minor Ismaili sect, and branches of the movement spread throughout the world. Today its strongest presence is in India and Pakistan, where its followers are known as Khojas.

Diane Rixon

Further Reading

Lewis, B. (1987). *The assassins: A radical sect in Islam*. New York: Oxford University Press.

Daftary, F. (1990). *The Ismailis: Their history and doctrines*. Cambridge, UK: Cambridge University Press.

Hodgson, M. G. S. (1968–1991). *The Cambridge history of Iran, Vol. 5*. Cambridge, UK: Cambridge University Press.

Aum Shinrikyo

The Japanese religious sect Aum Shinrikyo ("religion of supreme truth") represents the clearest contemporary case of an apocalyptic movement that mobilized for a violent encounter with the host society. Although the group was founded in the mid-1980s, Japanese authorities paid relatively little attention to Aum until 1994–1995, when police investigators began to suspect its involvement in terrorism and other criminal activity. On 20 March 1995, at the direction of Aum's spiritual leader, members of the group deployed a chemical nerve gas (sarin) in the Tokyo subway system. While the attack killed twelve commuters and injured several thousand more, the results would have been far worse had the group engineered a more sophisticated means of dispersing the gas. The Aum case stands as the most successful terrorist operation involving the use of a weapon of mass destruction.

Early History of Aum Shinrikyo

Until the time of its nerve gas attack in the Tokyo subway, Aum had existed as a controversial sect within the broad milieu of the new religious movements that had blossomed by the thousands in Japan throughout the 1970s and 1980s. Propelled by the work of the charismatic mystic Matsumoto Chizuo (b. 1955), the nearly blind son of a poor weaver, Aum began as a tiny spiritual movement established in a one-room Tokyo yoga school. While in his early thirties, Matsumoto changed his name to Asahara Shoko. "Shoko," meaning "bright light," suggested his gift of divine enlightenment. Even at this early stage in his life, it is apparent that Asahara believed that he had achieved great spiritual power and was destined to be a revered guru. Although Aum began with only a handful of devoted followers, Asahara's efforts at self-promotion and his bombastic claims of spiritual authority quickly resulted in the organization's development as one of the fastest-growing new religious movements in Japan.

Throughout the late 1980s, Asahara Shoko committed himself to the group's further growth. In order to put himself, and Aum, in the public eye, he wrote widely in Japanese New Age and alternative-spirituality magazines about his approach to harnessing the "secret extraordinary powers" that human beings possess. He also traveled to Nepal and India where it is claimed he took the final step in the journey to enlightenment. Asahara's self-proclaimed divine mission was to establish a utopian Buddhist kingdom in Japan by constructing Aum-operated communal villages throughout the country. These communities were to serve primarily as separatist, monastic enclaves where Aum members could rid themselves of bad karma through spiritual exercise, fasting, and by receiving Asahara's instruction in the ways of mystical self-realization. After the organization received recognition as a tax-exempt religious body in 1989, the Aum communes became home to some 1,200 to 1,400 of the group's most devoted followers. A large majority of these adherents were young (mainly in their twenties or thirties) and well educated, which was consistent with the overall membership makeup of the organization. For Aum's core following in the villages, all connections with the outside world were severed and an ascetic lifestyle was adopted to allow believers to gain the level of detachment deemed necessary to achieve the exalted state of enlightenment attributed to their leader.

Religious Beliefs and Apocalypse

Aum's doctrine included a highly syncretic mix of esoteric Tibetan Buddhism, aspects of Hinduism, and

Shinto, as well as Christian millennialism, New Age beliefs, and occult themes. The eclectic blend had its basis in Asahara's interests and experiences. Like most of the other late-twentieth-century new religions that emerged in Japan, Aum attracted many young upper-middle-class adherents who were dissatisfied with their condition of spiritual desolation in highly materialistic and stress-producing modern society. For these converts, Aum's emphasis on meditation, asceticism, and, most importantly, renunciation of contemporary Japanese materialism, offered both a way out of a corrupted, spiritually vacuous world and a pathway to enlightenment. Aum drew heavily from elements of Buddhist and Hindu cosmology and in particular tapped into their ideas on attaining higher consciousness, emphasizing the role of the guru and rejecting the ways of the outside world. However, Asahara also included Christian apocalyptic thinking in Aum's religious belief structure. The most prominent of these apocalyptic images was shaped by the discussion of the Apocalypse in the Revelation of St. John, which informed Asahara's view on an imminent, final war between the forces of good and evil.

Asahara's fondness for science fiction also found its way into Aum's worldview. Belief in UFOs, X-ray vision, trips to the fourth dimension, and other fantastic notions percolated through the sect's membership and became part of the secret knowledge reserved for Aum's members. The science fiction writings of Issac Asimov (1920–1992), particularly his classic multivolume *Foundation* series, formed an important part of Aum's mythology. The *Foundation* series tells of a heroic scientist's efforts to save humanity from catastrophic wars by forming an elite secret society dedicated to rebuilding civilization. The story made a major impact on Asahara and certainly influenced his thinking on Aum's ultimate goals. The more disaster-oriented predictions of Nostradamus also gained the attention of the guru, who increasingly ratcheted up the level of apocalyptic panic within his movement and began by 1990 to predict that end of the world would occur sometime around the beginning of the twenty-first century. In preparation for Armageddon, Aum launched an aggressive recruiting campaign aimed at winning new converts and urged its adherents to seek safety in its communes.

Aum's turn toward the apocalyptic marked the beginning of violence within the organization. As Asahara became more and more committed to the idea of an imminent worldwide war, he grew more paranoid about people and institutions that he felt were plotting against Aum. Around 1990, he began to proclaim to his followers that those who threatened the movement should be killed. The guru justified this directive by explaining that such persons had accumulated excessive bad karma and that killing them was actually an act of love that transformed the failed life of the nonbeliever. It was approximately at this time that Asahara's own Action Squad, a select enforcement unit within the sect, began to carry out the abductions and killings of Aum defectors and critics. Though these actions did not become public knowledge until 1995, rumors of the organization's authoritarian style and bizarre behavior began to circulate in the media and among opposition groups comprising parents whose children had joined the sect.

Failed Political Goals and Conspiracies

In early 1990, encouraged by his followers, Asahara made a bid to attain parliamentary office in Japan. Having organized his own party, Shinri To (the Party of Truth), Asahara and twenty-four other members of the sect planned to lead a grassroots campaign that they believed would place Aum in a position of political authority. The Party of Truth lacked any coherent program, and the media regarded Aum's election campaign as a strange stage play. When all the candidates, including Asahara, lost heavily in the elections, the guru responded by claiming that Aum's enemies had joined together to engineer the political defeat. Shortly after the embarrassing experience, Asahara turned more directly to conspiratorialism and began to deliver talks before Aum devotees that singled out those who were said to be responsible for the group's persecution, including Jews, the Japanese and U.S. governments, Freemasons, and others. In Asahara's view, the election made clear that evil forces in the world opposed his efforts to save from global disaster those enlightened enough to accept Aum's truth. Furthermore, the public, which had been invited to follow the guru and find salvation, had instead turned its back on Aum's teachings. From this point onward, Asahara preached that the outside world had rejected his message and that unbelievers should be punished.

Asahara's failed dream of political power filled him with rage and, it appears, put the guru on a path of further detachment from reality. Shortly after the elections he declared himself to be "Jesus the Christ" and, in a book written for Aum's membership, maintained that he had been sent to take away the sins of the world. His concern by now, however, was no longer to rescue all of humanity from Armageddon through conversion; rather, he focused on quickly mobilizing his movement to survive a forthcoming disaster of sweeping proportions. To prepare for what Asahara prophesied would be a U.S. nuclear attack as early as the mid-1990s, Aum purchased a large tract of ranch property in Australia that was to function as a retreat site for the group when global war began. At the conclusion of the nuclear conflict, which followers believed would destroy all existing governments and most of human civilization, Aum would be left to repopulate the globe and establish the perfect society.

Weapons of Mass Destruction

From the time of its founding, Aum had been successful in attracting scientists, physicians, and engineers into its ranks. The technical knowledge of these recruits proved especially important to Asahara in his efforts to create weapons of mass destruction, a secret program that came into operation in some of the closed Aum communes in 1990. Asahara believed that his movement needed to develop such devices because the U.S. government would use them against Japan and, therefore, Aum would require the same types of exotic weapons to survive the apocalyptic war. In order to gain information on how to develop biological and chemical weapons, Asahara's scientists traveled to Russia, where they attempted both to recruit the country's unemployed defense technicians and to gain knowledge about the military use of toxins. Evidence indicates that Asahara ordered the use of a weapon of mass destruction (botulinum toxin) against the Japanese public as early as April 1990 in an attempt to demonstrate to nonbelievers the validity of his disaster prophecies. This crude operation, as well as several others that took place in April 1990, involved outfitting a convoy of trucks with sprayers to spread the poison at various sites in Tokyo, including the imperial palace and near the U.S. naval base at Yokosuka. Then at several points in 1993, elite members of Aum's Action Squad tried to disseminate another biological agent (anthrax) in Tokyo. These failures with biological agents were followed by the more successful use of sarin, a chemical poison gas developed by Nazi scientists. Aum released sarin on at least four occasions in 1993 and 1994. The most deadly of these episodes occurred on 2 June 1994, when members of the sect used a fan-driven vaporizer to spread the gas in the city of Matsumoto in a plan to kill three judges living in the area who were about to rule on a civil case brought against Aum. Although Aum succeeded in only sickening the targeted judges, the gas attack killed 7 people and injured 144. Police did not initially suspect terrorism, although traces of the nerve gas were detected in the area.

With assets that exceeded $1 billion, Aum was able to fund its own private military program by buying the resources and information it needed. Aside from its experimentations with botulinum toxin, anthrax, and sarin, the sect's scientists also acquired (primarily from the international black market and Russia) the knowledge to develop other nerve gases, such as VX, tabun, and soman, and dispatched its experts to Zaire (now Democratic Republic of the Congo) to cultivate the Ebola virus for use as a weapon. Evidence also exists that the group sought to build its own nuclear device for deployment as a doomsday bomb.

The 20 March 1995 Attack

In the time immediately leading up to Aum's chemical attack on the Tokyo subway system, the sect had some forty thousand members worldwide. Approximately ten thousand of these adherents were in Japan, with the most devoted members residing in the twenty separatist communes where the weapons projects were undertaken. The great majority of the organization's membership (approximately thirty thousand) was located in Russia, where Aum had aggressively recruited since the late 1980s. It bears attention that only a tiny fraction of the organization's overall membership, specifically Asahara's hand-picked circle of advisers, clergy, and scientists, were active participants in Aum's crimes. The rest of the membership remained completely unaware of the group's illegal activities.

By the beginning of 1995, police inquiries into alleged incidents of abduction and murder by Aum led Asahara to conclude that the beginning of Armageddon had begun. With law enforcement pressure building on the organization, it is believed that Asahara thought it necessary to direct a forceful attack against the Japanese government. Aum's strike took place at the busy Kasumigaseki transfer station in the Tokyo subway, the stop for many government offices. There five Aum members equipped with plastic bags filled with sarin released the contents. The perpetrators of the attack escaped, but the incident resulted in the deaths of twelve commuters and the injury of almost four thousand others. Immediately following the episode, authorities raided Aum communes throughout the country and seized massive quantities of chemical and biological weapons, along with a stockpile of hallucinatory drugs.

Japanese authorities had been getting information on Aum since the Matsumoto gas raid and suspected that the group would again attempt to deploy sarin. In the weeks after the Tokyo subway incident, police arrested Asahara and forty of the sect's followers on charges of murder and attempted murder.

Aum Shinrikyo and Apocalyptic Violence

Asahara's interest in acquiring weapons of mass destruction was based on a defensive warfare strategy. He believed that these devices were necessary in order for his movement to gain protection from the events of Armageddon and to later reemerge to usher in its vision of utopia. However, Aum actually deployed these weapons offensively for a variety of more tactical and functional reasons. These included attempting to frighten authorities into halting their investigations, building Aum's membership base by demonstrating the accuracy of Asahara's predictions, and simply killing the group's opponents. Still, undergirding the sect's calculated acts of religiously inspired violence was its leader's conviction that the world was about to end, which fed the paranoia that came to engulf Aum and transformed it into an extremist millennial movement prepared to do battle with the outside world.

For Asahara, the lines of distinction blurred between weathering the ravages of an apocalyptic war he viewed as inevitable and provoking the world-ending conflict. This interplay between what might otherwise be seen as the antithetical actions of survival preparation and embracing disaster became more and more indistinguishable in Asahara's worldview as Aum evolved. When authorities began to close in on Aum, it is apparent that the sect's leader moved to trigger the arrival of the new millennium. The release of the nerve agent in the Tokyo subway system provided evidence for Aum's followers that Asahara's prophecies were correct and that the promised postapocalyptic world was not far off.

Extremist millennial movements such as Aum harbor hopes for the arrival of a new era that are invariably tied to the idea that the old order of things must be destroyed. Groups adhering to these convictions are not necessarily prone to violence, but those that have combined a separatist style and virulent conspiracism (as had Aum) are a source of concern, and their philosophies carry serious implications for public order.

Brad Whitsel

See also Buddhism: Tibet; Millenarian Violence: Latin America; Millenarian Violence: Thai Buddhism; Millenarian Violence: United States; Shinto, Modern

Further Reading

Benjamin, D., & Simon, S. (2002). *The age of sacred terror*. New York: Random House.

Disch, T. (1998). *The dreams our stuff is made of*. New York: The Free Press.

Hall, J., Schuyler, P., & Trinh, S. (2000). *Apocalypse observed: Religious movements and violence in North America, Europe, and Japan*. New York: Routledge.

Hoffman, B. (1998). *Inside terrorism*. New York: Columbia University Press.

Juergensmeyer, M. (2000). *Terror in the mind of God: The global rise of religious violence*. Berkeley and Los Angeles: University of California Press.

Kaplan, D. (2000). Aum Shinrikyo. In J. Tucker (Ed.), *Toxic terror* (pp. 207–227). Cambridge, MA: MIT Press.

Kaplan, D., & Marshall, A. (1996). *The cult at the end of the world*. New York: Crown Publishers.

Laqueur, W. (1996, September-October). Postmodern terrorism. *Foreign Affairs, 75*(5), 24–36.

Laqueur, W. (1999). *The new terrorism: Fanaticism and the arms of mass destruction*. New York: Oxford University Press.

Lifton, R. (1999). *Destroying the world to save it: Aum Shinrikyo, apocalyptic violence, and the new global terrorism*. New York: Metropolitan Books.

Reader, I. (1996). *A poisonous cocktail? Aum Shinrikyo's path to violence*. Copenhagen: Nordic Institute of Asian Studies.

Reader, I. (2002). Dramatic confrontations: Aum Shinrikyo against the world. In D. Bromley & J. Melton (Eds.), *Cults, religion, and violence* (pp. 189–209). Cambridge, UK: Cambridge University Press.

Robins, R. (1997). *Political paranoia: The psychopolitics of hatred*. New Haven, CT: Yale University Press.

Stern, J. (1999). *The ultimate terrorists*. Cambridge, MA: Harvard University Press.

Watanabe, M. (1998). Religion and violence in Japan today: A chronological and doctrinal analysis of Aum Shinrikyo. *Terrorism and Political Violence, 10*(4), 80–100.

Weber, E. (1999). *Apocalypses: Prophesies, cults, and millennial beliefs through the ages*. Cambridge, MA: Harvard University Press.

Whitsel, B. (1998). The Turner diaries and cosmotheism: William Pierce's theology of revolution. *Nova Religio:*

The Journal of Alternative and Emergent Religions, 1(2), 183–197.

Aztecs

The Aztecs of Mexico, whose empire flourished from 1427 to 1521, are perhaps best known for their human sacrifices, and their wars are widely interpreted as having been religiously motivated, driven by an insatiable demand for captives to be sacrificed in religious ceremonies. Human sacrifice in many forms and in various degrees was indeed common, from such self-sacrifice as drawing blood from ears, tongue, legs, and other parts of the body as offerings or penance, to the famous ritual involving the extraction of the beating heart of the still-living victim. The necessity for human sacrifice is explained in the Aztec creation myth. In that myth, after the world had been created and destroyed four times, the gods all gathered, built a bonfire, and one, Nanahuatzin, threw himself in, was consumed, and emerged as the new sun. But he would not come forth as he does today until the other gods offered their own blood; only then did he rise in the east, cross the arc of the sky, and set in the west, as he has done ever since. The Aztecs believed that he, the world, and the rest of the gods all depended on offerings of human blood, a necessity until that time in the uncertain future when this world too would be destroyed. Thus, while the Aztecs depended on the gods for their existence, the gods likewise depended on the Aztecs for the human sacrifices that sustained them. And this, it is argued, was the main imperative behind Aztec warfare, the relentless quest for human sacrifices.

While the interdependence of humans and gods did characterize Aztec views of the gods, and while sacrifice in various forms was important, the extent of warfare and the way the Aztecs practiced it far exceeded any religious imperative. Aztec religion undoubtedly had an impact on warfare, but the relationship is far more complex than the creation myth implies.

Aztec Religion

Most of the information on Aztec religion comes from their capital, Tenochtitlan, but practices there were not typical of Mexico generally; the city was many times larger than any other in Mexico, and was an imperial capital with more and larger cults and temples, and correspondingly larger, more frequent, and more elaborate ceremonies than seen elsewhere. Moreover, theirs was not a missionary religion, and despite the enormous expansion of their empire, the Aztecs spread neither their gods nor their religious beliefs and rituals. As a polytheistic religion the Aztec religion was tolerant of other gods and practices and placed no emphasis on conversion or exclusivity. Consequently, warfare was not used to spread religion. The lack of a missionary goal does not mean, however, that religion had no role in warfare. On the contrary, it was deeply involved, offering personal meaning and serving state goals, but the focus was on domestic benefits, not dissemination and conversion.

The Aztecs interpreted their world in fundamentally religious ways: Each natural phenomenon, such as wind, rain, hail, snow, clouds, fire, lightning, earthquakes, planets, sun, moon, and earth, had its own deity or set of deities that embodied it or controlled it; for each moment in time and so too for each major life event, a different cluster of gods prevailed; for every malady and cure a god was involved; for every location and every occupation there was a god. Each person, as a unique individual, had a slightly different relationship to the supernatural, viewing the gods and their rituals differently according to his or her own social and intellectual circumstances. While the gods controlled much about the world, the relationship of people to the supernatural was less one of moral imperatives, of supplicants learning how to live from divine teachers, than one of clients seeking the favors of supernatural patrons through offerings and the repetition of rituals. Overall, Aztec religion was not suited to providing ideological support for imperialism.

Aztec Religion in War

Aztec religion was not bereft of martial significance, however. Omens and portents were important; kings consulted priests for propitious days to begin campaigns, and prayers for magical or divine aid augmented more mundane armaments. Moreover, priests accompanied Aztec armies to war, marching one day ahead (a logistical rather than a ritual necessity), bearing statues of the gods on their backs. In battle, they carried out the sacrifice of the first captive.

Seizing and burning an enemy town's main temple was the quintessential symbol of conquest, but this act was not a demonstration of the superiority of Aztec gods, as the god whose temple was burned was generally also worshiped in Tenochtitlan. Rather, the town arsenal was generally associated with main temple, and the temple's size was the single most salient demonstration of that town's wealth and importance. Therefore, to burn the temple was not to destroy the enemy's god, but to destroy the visible sign of the enemy's wealth and importance, the enemy's arms, and it also meant they controlled the political center. Actual destruction of a temple or city was probably relatively infrequent, though always recorded, and most battles ended by surrender in advance, or on the battlefield before the city was actually ransacked. Destroying their adversaries offered few benefits, the Aztecs wanted viable tributaries out there, not smoldering ruins

Occasionally, vanquished gods were sometimes taken from their temples in conquered towns and deposited in Tenochtitlan in a temple constructed especially to house such foreign gods. But this happened rarely, to only a few foreign gods, and for purposes that are unclear. Scholars surmise that, as all recorded instances occurred with gods from nearby cities, and as their priests were allowed to accompany and care for their gods, the main purpose was probably to reorient the cult's tribute flow from their home towns to Tenochtitlan where feasible.

And at the end of the battles, priests oversaw the religious rituals accompanying the cremation of the dead. During military campaigns, as at other times, Aztec priests spent more time tending the gods and conducting their rituals than worshiping them.

Religious, Political, and Personal Motivations for War

Although a religious motivation cannot be ascribed to Aztec warfare directly, religion nevertheless affected individual attitudes toward war. Individual soldiers were not interested in forcing their religious beliefs on others, yet those beliefs nevertheless gave them some motivations for war. The need for captives to be sacrificed in religious ceremonies was one motivation that may have moved the individual soldier. Another was the belief that the best afterlife was guaranteed to those who died in battle—they would spend four years in heaven before returning to earth as birds and butterflies. But there was little else in Aztec religion that might prompt an individual to war. Dreams of glory and of rising socially and economically within Aztec society, which was possible for those who excelled in battle, were probably the primary personal motivations for going to war. Regardless of whether they were motivated or not, however, Aztec men were compelled to go to war on a rotating basis as part of a state-mandated obligation.

Although the state used religious reasons for going to war, its religious claims were more pretext for war than actual cause. For example, the Aztecs might request independent cities to provide materials to expand a temple in Tenochtitlan. If those cities acquiesced, it was tacit acknowledgment of vassalage, so they frequently refused, and the Aztecs could then declare war over the insult to the gods, a strategy that was probably aimed at mobilizing the support of the Aztecs' own people.

The Role of Human Sacrifice

Although captives were needed for sacrifice in all Mexican city-states, the scale on which the Aztecs waged war and took captives dwarfed that of other states. Sacrifices on the scale the Aztecs performed them were not essential to the fundamental religious exercise and were not widely seen outside Tenochtitlan.

Human sacrifice itself was not necessarily associated with war, nor were all of the victims captives. During the major ceremonies, human sacrifice was more common and the victims more numerous for nonmilitary gods than for military ones. Most monthly ceremonies involved sacrifice, and a majority of these honored nonmilitary gods. Even for the four annual festivals that all subordinate cities were required to attend and to which they brought their tribute, the gods celebrated were the rain god (Tlaloc), an agricultural god (Xipe), the goddess of medicine (Teteo Innan), and only one war god (Huitzilopochtli). The largest sacrifices of the year occurred during the month of Tlacaxipehualiztli, at the end of the war season, during the celebration of the rain god. So while war did supply most of the captives, sacrificing them did not especially glorify war. And on the infrequent occasions when truly large numbers of captives were sacrificed, the purpose was political control.

In perhaps the most famous instance of mass sacrifice, the rededication of the Great Temple in Tenochtitlan in 1487, an unprecedented 80,400 captives were sacrificed. Temple rededications occurred both before and after this, with no such massive sacrifices. But after the lethargic reign of King Tizoc, the Aztecs, and especially their newly chosen king, Ahuitzotl, desperately needed to demonstrate their power and resolve unambiguously, which they did by conducting the huge sacrifice before their wavering tributaries. So the ostensible goal of the 1487 rededication was religious, but the underlying purpose was political, and similar political motivations underlie most of the ostensibly religious public rationales for Aztec conquests. Aztec religion was first and foremost in the service of politics.

Priests and War

While it is easy to understand why political leaders would seek to use religion to justify their actions and generate popular support, why would the priests themselves collaborate in these exercises? Many, if not all, probably embraced the religious explanations for the need for war, and many were doubtless sincere in their convictions. But there were also sociopolitical considerations. Becoming a priest was a significant avenue of social advancement for commoners and lower nobles, and the priesthood offered significant incentives for joining. The many cults, with their priests and temples, required considerable financial resources for their support. Economic support came from donations and from the recompense the temples received for the services they provided to the citizenry; the greater number of temples in Tenochtitlan, and their greater elaboration, demanded more funds, some of which came simply from the city's greater size and prosperity, but much of which came directly from war. The temples were among the main beneficiaries of the allocation of tributary lands and goods the Aztecs took in warfare. It was natural, then, that the priests supported the wars. Indeed, church and state were inextricably interwoven, with the highest priests also acting as political advisers and blessing the investiture of new rulers, and political officials in turn supporting and participating in the cults and their activities. This interdependence of clergy and nobles was fostered by their education together in the city's elite, parochial schools.

Implications

So what, then, was the relationship between religion and warfare in Aztec society? Priests did provide advice and ritual services in war, but while their religion required sacrificial victims for a wide array of gods, it did not contain a religious imperative to conquer that would reflect supernatural favor. The scale on which the Aztec engaged in human sacrifice was an index of political success rather than religious favor. For the individual, there was merit in being a good warrior, and dying in battle entitled one to a better afterlife, but there was no religious or societal emphasis on seeking such a death. And aside from any religious purpose, taking captives was far more important to the individual warrior for the social and economic benefits it conveyed. Religion aided the prosecution of war and served as a justification in some instances, but was far from its primary cause.

Ross Hassig

Further Reading

Acuña, R. (1982–1987). *Relaciones geográficas del siglo XVI* [Geographic relations of the 16th century] (Vols 1–9). Mexico City, Mexico: Universidad Nacional Autónoma de México.

Alva Ixtlilxóchitl, F. (1975–1977). *Obras completas* [Complete works] (Vols. 1–2). Mexico City, Mexico: Universidad Nacional Autónoma de México.

Bierhorst, J. (Trans.). (1992). *History and mythology of the Aztecs: The Codex Chimalpopoca*. Tucson: University of Arizona Press.

Codex Borbonicus. (1974). Graz, Austria: Akademische Drück- und Verlagsanstalt.

Durán, D. (1971). *Book of the gods and rites and the ancient calendar*. Norman: University of Oklahoma Press.

Mendieta, G. (1971). *Historia eclesiastica Indiana* [Indian ecclesiastic history]. Mexico City, Mexico: Editorial Porrúa.

Motolinía [Toribio de Benavente]. (1971). *Memoriales o libro de las cosas de la Nueva España y de los Naturales de ella* [Memorials: or, a book of nature and the things of New Spain]. Mexico City, Mexico: Universidad Nacional Autónoma de México.

Primeros Memoriales [First Memorials] (Facsimile). (1993). Norman: University of Oklahoma Press.

Quiñones Keber, E. (Ed.). (1995). *Codex Telleriano-Remensis: Ritual, divination, and history in a pictorial Aztec manuscript*. Austin: University of Texas Press.

Ruiz de Alarcón, H. (1984). *Treatise on the heathen superstitions and customs that today live among the Indians native to this New Spain, 1629* (J. R. Andrews & R. Hassig, Eds.). Norman: University of Oklahoma Press

Sahagún, B. (1951–1982). *General history of the things of New Spain: Florentine Codex* (Vols 1–12). (J. O. A. Arthur & C. E. Dibble, Trans.). Salt Lake City: University of Utah Press.

Nicholson, H. B. (Ed.). (1997). *Primeros Memoriales* [First Memorials]. (Trans. T. Sullivan). Norman: University of Oklahoma Press.

Serna, J. (1953). *Tratado de las idolatrias, supersticiones, dioses, ritos, hechicerías y otras costumbres gentílicas de las razas aborigenes de México* [Treatise of idolatries, superstitions, gods, rites, witchcraft and other general customs of the races and aborigines of Mexico]. Mexico City, Mexico: Ediciones Fuente Cultural.

Torquemada, J. (1973–1983). *Monarquía Indiana* (Vols. 1–7). Mexico City, Mexico: Universidad Nacional Autónoma de México.

Zorita, A. (1971). *Life and labor in ancient Mexico* (B. Keen, Trans.). New Brunswick, NJ: Rutgers University Press.

B

Babí and Baha'i Religions

The Baha'í religion was founded in the Middle East toward the middle of the nineteenth century in what were then the Ottoman dominions of Iraq (in the city of Baghdad, c. 1863), Turkey (in Edirne, c. 1866–1868), and Palestine (1868–1892). The founder was the Persian-born messianic claimant Mirza Husayn ʿAli Nuri (1817–1892) who adopted the title Bahaʾuʾllah ("the Splendor of God"). During the mid- to late nineteenth century his followers came to be known as "people of Baha' " or Baha'is. Today they number 5–6 million and live in varying numbers in more than 160 countries worldwide. The Baha'i religion was developed and gradually globalized under ʿAbd al-Baha' (1844–1921), the son of Bahaʾuʾllah, and under Shoghi Effendi (c. 1896–1957), Bahaʾu'llah's great-grandson, who was called the Guardian of the Baha'i religion. Throughout the nineteenth and twentieth centuries Baha'is worked for international peace in light of the directives and teachings of Bahaʾuʾllah.

The Baha'i religion grew out of the religion initiated by the youthful ʿAli Muhammad Shirazi (1819–1850), who was known as the Bab (the Gate). That religion is often referred to as Babism or the Babi religion; it has its roots in Islam, but (like the Baha'i faith after it) was regarded as heretical by orthodox Islamic clerics. The Babi movement was in some respects a kind of proto-Baha'i religion, though there are many legalistic and other differences.

The architects of the Baha'i religion wrote a great deal about the folly of destructive warfare and the need for global peace underpinned and maintained by international agencies of justice and a spiritually rooted consciousness of the unity in diversity of humankind. Religion should, they frequently articulated, inspire genuine love and unity; otherwise it would be better to forego it. In Baha'i sacred texts, divisive and destructive religiosity that inclines to hatred and warfare is considered to be the antithesis of genuine spirituality and civilization. All human beings are considered by Bahaʾuʾllah to be the citizens of this one world, as the "fruits of one tree and the leaves of one branch" (Baha'u'llah 1988, 14). The founder of the Baha'i religion explicitly banned Islamic and other forms of jihad (holy war) and religious fanaticism. He exhorted all to freely socialize without prejudices of any kind and in an attitude of humble and loving fellowship.

The Bab, Jihad, and Divine Victory

Bahaʾuʾllah began as a follower of the Bab, who is considered by Baha'is today to be the revolutionary forerunner of Bahaʾuʾllah who fulfilled Islamic messianic and other last-days expectations relating to global war and peace. In commencing his religious mission on 22 May 1844, the Bab announced the onset of a new era. He claimed to be the inspired intermediary to the Mahdi, the messianic figure in Shiʿa Islam whose return is awaited, and from around 1848 the Bab claimed to be the Mahdi himself. This claim to be the Shiʿite messiah presupposed that he would be something of a warrior *Qa'im bi'l-sayf* (the Ariser armed with the sword). It presupposed his fulfilling numerous predictions surrounding the onset of the tumultuous "Day of Judgment," the "Day of Resurrection," and the ensuing era of victory and peace. As the Qa'im, or messianic ariser, the Bab was expected to wage universal, last-days jihad and, following his divine victory, to establish global justice.

From the first and several later chapters of his early and neo-qurʿanic *Qayyum al-asma'* (Self-Subsisting of the Divine Names; 1844) until his very late, last substantial work, the *Haykal al-din* (Temple of Religion; 1850), he anticipated or predicted future holy war scenarios in which converted monarchs would engage in jihad, so that earthly dominions, the kingdoms of this world, would become the kingdom of God, their Creator. It is in this light that the Baha'i leader ʿAbd al-Baha at one time stated that the religion of the Bab included teachings involving human slaughter *(qitl-iʿamm)* abrogated in the later Baha'i scripture.

Even though visions of a future jihad and divine victory are fairly common in the extensive writings of the Bab, it seems likely that this militaristic aspect of his religion found little concrete realization during the Babi-state struggles between 1848 and 1852 in Persia. Though at times the religious zeal of the Bab's followers appears to have been inspired by militaristic motifs rooted in Islamic last-days theology, for the most part they appear to have acted defensively. There are important pacifistic elements in the Bab's Persian and Arabic *Bayans* (Expositions; 1847–1848) and other writings, including a prohibition against carrying arms. It is not irrelevant to note in this connection that an early 1845 divine *bada'* ("cancellation"), communicated by divine revelation to the Bab, canceled a jihad-oriented congregation in Karbala in Iraq. Bahaʾu'llah's retelling of the story of Noah and explanation of sovereignty in his *Kitab-i iqan* (The Book of Certitude) appears in part to be a defense of the Bab's canceling this once anticipated holy war. It is also an explanation of the reality of the universal spiritual victory and sovereignty of the messianic Qa'im (the Bab).

Whether the largely unsuccessful late Babi uprisings in the Persian provinces of Mazandaran, Khurasan, and elsewhere should be considered episodes of jihad is unclear and continues to be debated. The Bab seems never to have specifically called for a concrete, full-scale holy war during the six years of his mission (1844–1850), even though several of his important writings envisage this and at least five thousand of his followers were martyred in Iran and Iraq during nineteenth-century episodes of religious persecution.

The Bab gave nonliteral, spiritual interpretations to many Islamic, end-time apocalyptic scenarios involving war, catastrophe, resurrection, and divine judgment. He made the full realization of end-time peace dependent upon another subsequent messiah figure: "Him whom God will make manifest" (a phrase that appears hundreds of times in the later writings of the Bab). The Bab predicted the advent of this future universal "Manifestation of God" (Persian: *mazhar-i ilahi*) in his numerous Persian and Arabic revelations. Though he was executed in Tabriz (Iran) in July 1850, the Bab was expected to usher in the imminent millennial age of peace and justice. For Baha'is, however, these expectations came to be fulfilled through the Bab's successor, Bahaʾu'llah.

Bahaʾu'llah, the Abrogation of Jihad, and the Promise of World Peace

Bahaʾu'llah's very early inclination to pacifism is illustrated by his youthful abhorance on reading the episode of the Muslim slaughter of the Jews of the Banu Qurayda, recounted in the encyclopedic *Bihar al-anwar* (Oceans of Lights) of Muhammad Baqir Majlisi (d. 1699). Bahaʾu'llah first intimated that he was a divine manifestation to a few followers of the Bab in a garden near Baghdad in late April–early May 1863, and his first declarative utterance in that capacity was the explicit abrogation of the permissibility of jihad. He repeated that abrogation most notably ten years later in his centrally important *al-Kitab al-aqdas* (Most Holy Book; c. 1873), but also in many other important writings, such as his late *Bisharat* ("Glad-Tidings"):

> O peoples of the world!
> The first Glad-Tiding which the Mother Book hath . . . imparted unto the peoples of the world is that the law of holy war *(jihad)* hath been blotted out from the Book"
> (Tablets of Bahaʾu'llah: 21–22)

From Edirne in Turkey in 1867–1868 and Acre in Ottoman Palestine between 1868 and 1873, Bahaʾu'llah addressed scriptural "tablets" to various heads of state and ecclesiastics. He exhorted them to rule with justice, cease oppression, and promote peace. In his message to Great Britain's Queen Victoria he spoke of a secular "lesser peace" (*sulh al-akbar;* literally, "greatest peace") which had been bypassed and a future (religious) "most great peace" *(sulh al-aʿzam)* that should be worked for and embraced wholeheartedly. According to Shoghi Effendi, this "most great peace" would come with the establishment of a Baha'i world commonwealth.

Bahaʾu'llah prophesied both apocalyptic catastrophe and millennial peace. He predicted, for example, the fall of the Ottoman officials ʿAli and Fuʿad Pasha and Sultan ʿAbd al-Aziz (reigned 1861–1876) as well as the French emperor Louis Napoleon Bonaparte III in the 1870 Battle of Sedan. He made cryptic reference to the banks of the Rhine being drenched in blood and to the lamentations of Berlin, which were understood later as alluding to World Wars I and II. Toward the end of his life, Bahaʾuʾllah predicted the eventual cessation of "ruinous wars" and the inevitability of the millennial most great peace.

Later Baha'i Developments

Though a prisoner and an exile for most of his life ʿAbd al-Baha' spent much of his life in exemplary servitude to humanity. He did much for the promotion of peace in expounding his father's teachings about the essential oneness of revealed religion and the need for all humankind to regard themselves as variegated citizens of a single planet, before the One, the incomprehensible father and creator of all.

ʿAbd al-Baha' toured the West from 1911 to 1913, giving hundreds of public addresses at which he tried to awaken in his diverse hearers a consciousness of the oneness of humankind. At Stanford University in October 1912 he is reported to have voiced a strong warning regarding a forthcoming "Battle of Armageddon" that would come in two years' time. In 1919 ʿAbd al-Baha' sent a lengthy letter of advice to the (unofficial) European Central Organization for a Durable Peace; that document was subsequently known as the Tablet to the Hague. Therein he remarked, "the recent war has proved to the world . . . that war is destruction while Universal Peace is construction." In a second, shorter letter, sent in 1920 to the same body, he wrote "Today the most important problem in the affairs of the world of humanity is that of Universal Peace" (ʿAbd al-Baha' n.d.).

ʿAbd al-Baha' supported equality of the sexes, predicting that world peace would never truly be realized until women played their rightful part in world affairs. The balanced universal moral, intellectual, and spiritual education of all humanity regardless of gender would foster world peace and a consciousness of world citizenship. Expounding explicit directives and predictions of Bahaʾuʾllah, ʿAbd al-Baha' was very much in favor of a future world parliament, a supreme tribunal, and a globally agreed-upon international auxiliary language to be taught in all the schools of the world alongside the various national languages.

On the theological level, Shoghi Effendi viewed World Wars I and II, along with other socioeconomic injustices and imbalances of the nineteenth and twentieth centuries, as apocalyptic upheavals suggestive of God's judgment upon a humanity that was failing to heed the Baha'i message of world unity and peace. This is clear from his two extended letters addressed to the Baha'is of the world, "The Advent of Divine Justice" (1939) and "The Promised Day is Come" (1941). He exhorted individual Baha'is to obey just governments and to avoid divisive partisan politics. He lauded sane patriotism, though he strongly condemned racism and excessive nationalism, capitalism, and atheistic Communism. When it comes to military service, Baha'is are advised to assent but to avoid when possible combatant service in favor of noncombatant duties, such as medical service. Baha'is are not, therefore, strict pacifists: They see themselves as citizens of a global community with active responsibilities for justice and peacemaking.

The Baha'i governing body, known since 1963 as the Universal House of Justice, is located at the Baha'i World Centre in Haifa, Israel. According to its constitution, it has the duty of promoting international peace and global justice. In 1985 it issued its widely distributed *The Promise of World Peace* and in April 2002 it made available a six-page *Message to World's Religious Leaders*, calling for the abandonment of religious fanaticism and exclusivity, which stand in the way of universal brotherhood.

Baha'is have published a considerable number of books and leaflets setting out their vision of global security, gender equality, world government, and pathways to true peace. They consider the rebirth of a new religiosity promoting world citizenship and a new world order to be fundamental to swords becoming ploughshares, and to the global achievement of that greater, peaceful, inner jihad that generates a lasting peace for all humanity.

Stephen N. Lambden

Further Reading

ʿAbd al-Baha'. (n.d.). *Tablet to the Hague*. London: NSA of the Baha'is of the British Isles.

ʿAbd al-Baha'. (1912). *Makatib-i hadrat-i ʿAbd al-Baha'* [Writings of ʿAbd al-Baha'] (Vol. 2). Cairo, Egypt: Matba'at Kurdistan al-ʿIlmiyya. (Original work published 1330)

ʿAbd al-Baha'. (1972). *Paris Talks: Addresses given by ʿAbdu'l-Baha in Paris in 1911–1912*. London: Baha'i Publishing Trust.

ʿAbd al-Baha'. (1982). *The promulgation of universal peace* (Rev. ed.). Wilmette, IL: Baha'i Publishing Trust.

ʿAbd al-Baha'. (2001). Lawh-i-Hague: The tablet to the Hague. Retrieved 10 April 2003, from http://bahai-library.org/provisionals/lawh.hague.html

Bahaʾuʾllah. (1961). *The book of certitude* (Shoghi Effendi, Trans.). London: Baha'i Publishing Trust.

Bahaʾuʾllah. (1978). *Tablets of Bahaʾuʾllah*. Haifa, Israel: Baha'i World Centre.

Bahaʾuʾllah. (1988). Epistle to the son of the wolf. In *Tablets of Bahaʾuʾllah* (164). Wilmette, IL: Baha'i Publishing Trust.

Bahaʾuʾllah. (1992). *The Kitab-i-Aqdas* [The most holy book]. Haifa, Israel: Baha'i World Centre.

Lambden, S. (1988). Eschatology, Part. IV. In E. Yarshater (Ed.), *Encyclopedia Iranica* (Vol. 8, p. 581). New York: Bibliotheca Persica Press.

Lambden, S. (1999–2000). Catastrophe, armageddon and millennium: Some aspects of the Babi-Baha'i exegesis of apocalyptic symbolism. *Baha'i Studies Review, 9*, 81–99.

MacEoin, D. (1982). The Babi concept of Holy War. *Religion, 12*, 93–129.

Sachedina, A. (1981). *Islamic messianism*. NewYork: SUNY Press.

Shoghi Effendi. (1980). *The promised day is come*. Wilmette, IL: Baha'i Publishing Trust.

Shoghi Effendi. (1990). *The advent of divine justice*. New Delhi, India: Baha'i Publishing Trust.

Shoghi Effendi. (1991). *The world order of Bahaʾuʾllah*. (Reprint).Wilmette, IL: Baha'i Publishing Trust. (Original work published 1938)

Shoghi Effendi. (1995). *God passes by* (Reprint). Wilmette, IL: Baha'i Publishing Trust. (Original work published 1944)

Universal House of Justice. (1995). *The promise of world peace*. Haifa, Israel: Baha'i World Centre.

Universal House of Justice. (2002). *To the world's religious leaders*. Haifa, Israel: Baha'i World Center.

Walbridge, J. (1996). The Babi uprising in Zanjan: Causes and issues. *Iranian Studies, 29*(3–4), 339–362.

Bishops' Wars

The Bishops' Wars were conflicts between England and Scotland in 1639 and 1640 that were a direct result of the religious uniformity policies imposed upon Scotland by Charles I and his Archbishop of Canterbury, William Laud; the pursuit of these policies presaged the larger civil conflict that would engulf England in the 1640s and, ultimately, lead to the deposition and execution of the king.

In 1638, Charles I was in the ninth year of his "Personal Rule"—a period in which he had consistently refused to call Parliament, relying instead on his prerogatives and an inherent belief in divine right monarchy. His isolation from Parliament during these years gave Charles an inflated sense of his abilities and power, and it was this misperception that was at the heart of the conflict with Scotland that led to the Bishops' Wars.

Over the years of Personal Rule, Charles and Laud had increasingly come to favor the anti-Calvinist precepts adumbrated by the Dutch priest Arminius (Arminianism), who emphasized free will as opposed to predestination, but still within a Protestant synthesis. Arminianism also incorporated ceremonial aspects of religious practice that seemed to emulate those in the Roman Catholic Church. Charles and Laud reformed the Anglican liturgy to reflect these tenets, and began to insist, vigorously, on uniformity of practice within the Church of England. Calvinists saw this move as an assault on their beliefs and resistance to the uniformity required by Charles and Laud in this regard was to be one of the issues that inflamed the Long Parliament.

Charles, never popular in Scotland, had alienated the Scottish nobles over the course of the 1630s; staunch Presbyterians, the Scots were particularly offended by his "high church" Anglicanism. Charles began to meddle with the Church of Scotland in 1636, when he insisted on a new Book of Canons for the Scottish Kirk without them having first approved it. The Scottish nobles began to fear further impositions, and they did not have to wait very long for them: in July 1637, Charles directed that the Kirk adopt a new prayer book that would bring the Scottish church into alignment with the English church in terms of its liturgy. The outraged Scots rejected the use of the prayer book and petitioned the king to withdraw it; his failure to do so resulted in the Prayer Book Rebellion of July 1637—occasioned by a riot by the opponents of the Anglican prayer book, later known as Covenanters, in St. Giles Cathedral in Edinburgh—that was solidified by the passage of the National Covenant in February 1638. The Covenanters sought Scottish autonomy both in politics and religion, and wished to impose a Presbyterian form of religious organization upon the Scottish church, a form that excluded the Anglican hierarchical system headed by bishops.

The First Bishops' War

With the words of his father, James I, echoing in his ears—"no bishop, no king"—Charles felt compelled to force the Scots to accept his plans for their church, particularly as he came to believe that the Scots were being encouraged in their rebellion by the French, which added an element of treason to the mix. Charles determined that the best course was to take Edinburgh and force the Covenanters to come to terms, but wished to do it with a flourish that would enhance his standing as king. Such a plan was expensive, and Charles would not turn to Parliament for funds as had historically been the case for his predecessors. He hoped that the Covenanters would be easily cowed, thus obviating the need to seek additional sources of revenue; further, he did not believe that the Scots would carry the war to England for fear of arousing the English against them. The king was supported in his beliefs by a very small circle of advisers who had as little knowledge of the reality of the situation as Charles himself.

Charles planned to organize troops and base them at York for an assault in the spring of 1639; similarly, the Covenanters anticipated this attack and began to arm themselves in preparation. Neither side possessed effective intelligence about the other's plans, and, as a result, speculation about the impending war ran rampant. At the beginning of 1639, Charles showed his hand by calling the English nobles to arms at York for April 1, and hoped to put together a force of 30,000 men. He was resolved not to call Parliament to help create and support this force, and his intransigence on this issue seemed to characterize a monarchy and government that was increasingly authoritarian and out of touch with its citizens. Charles did exploit all of his prerogatives and compelled local officials to cooperate in fielding his army, a largely unskilled force that eventually numbered some 20,000 men.

Charles assumed that, because England had been generally quiescent and cooperative during the years of the Personal Rule, they would continue to be so as the country went to war. However, the king's failure to pursue the war through normal channels—i.e., the calling of Parliament—and his dogmatic insistence on both his religious and political policies shattered this consensus. Charles seemed incapable of understanding that a vast majority of his English subjects were in sympathy with the Covenanters on religious issues and this shared vision doomed the king's plans before they were even put into action.

Charles placed Sir Jacob Astley in charge of the overall campaign, and Astley set about making sure that forces were being mustered, fortifications were being set up and maintained, and arms were purchased. A garrison on Holy Island south of Berwick was to be refurbished, again under Astley's aegis. Sir Thomas Morton was given responsibility for the northern counties, and organized the militias there, while the earl of Arundel was to prepare the garrison at Carlisle. It was believed that Carlisle and Berwick were strategic targets for the Scots, but despite all the preliminary preparations, neither garrison was properly staffed by the end of 1638. It seemed that the king and his advisers were reluctant to take the final steps that would lead to war, and hoped that negotiation might save the day; in any event, military preparations proved to be problematic at best and Charles feared exposing England to a Scottish assault if he concentrated his resources at Carlisle and Berwick.

By March 1639, it appeared that the delay had earned the king nothing and, indeed, had opened up northern England to attack by the Scots. Thomas Wentworth (later earl of Strafford) was ordered to take troops to Carlisle in late March 1639, while Astley hastened to Berwick in anticipation that the garrison might fall into Scottish hands and was able to secure it for the English by the beginning of April. These were small victories, considering that the Covenanters had taken, among other places, Edinburgh Castle. However, Charles was able to establish control on the borders; he then had to decide whether to attack the Scots or go on the defensive. A number of the king's advisers counseled the latter, but the king was reluctant to let the Covenanters continue to stand in rebellion to him. Charles decided to have his troops move slowly toward the borders starting in May 1639 and hoped that this display of force might convince the Covenanters to come to terms. Communication with the Scots made it clear that they had no intention of going back on their Covenant and they refused to disband without concessions on the king's part. Charles refused to consider their demands and stepped up his plans to bring the war to them.

At this point, Charles found himself in communications difficulties with his Privy Council, and the situation was further complicated by a number of lords who began to criticize the king publicly. While the king was in residence at York, Lords Saye and Sele and Lord Brooke refused to take the military oath, and used the occasion not just to state their opposition to the war, but to air grievances that dated back through the years of Personal Rule. Charles had asked the nobles to pledge their "life and fortune" in defending the kingdom against religious rebels—a sort of English Covenant—and the lords balked at fighting for such an issue. Charles's dealings with Saye and Sele and Brooke—he had them arrested and questioned—made him appear more arbitrary than ever and calls for Parliament to be convened grew louder.

Despite objections, Charles marched his troops to Newcastle in May 1639, and had them outside Berwick by the end of the month, despite fears for his safety. Toward the middle of the month, skirmishing between the opponents broke out, resulting in the wounding of one man on each side, but the engagement was extremely short-lived. On the fourth of June, English troops came up against a much larger and well-organized army of Scots at Kelso; some 4,000 English found they were being confronted by nearly 10,000 Scots (though their massive appearance may have been the result of trickery). The commander of the English, the earl of Holland, though initially willing to wade into the fray, was persuaded of the futility of the plan and decided to retreat. Though Holland suffered no losses either in men or matériel, the retreat seemed to symbolize the weakness of the king's cause. The Scots hoped to get the king to sign a treaty, and exploited the retreat in order to get the English to believe that an invasion of their country was in the offing. The truth was that the armies were roughly equal in size, and the English had simply let propaganda and poor intelligence convince them otherwise. The reluctance of Charles's nobles to continue the fight convinced him that negotiations were his only alternative.

The parties met in mid-June, agreed to disband the troops on both sides, and restored the conditions that existed before the war; further, a Parliament session was promised for a later date to resolve specific differences, and the king agreed to respect Scottish laws and their religion. The majority of combatants on both sides were relieved that hostilities would develop no further; however, many believed that the king was simply playing for time in signing the treaty and that he would not be content until he had forced the Scots to accept his terms and acknowledge his authority over them.

The Second Bishops' War

Indeed, this seemed to be the case. Anticipating another war with Scotland, Charles, on the advice of Wentworth and Laud, decided to summon Parliament and make the case for their support. This so-called "Short Parliament"—which met on 7 April and was prorogued on 5 May 1640—was a failure for both crown and Parliament. This Parliament marked the end of the king's Personal Rule and signaled a shift from cooperation to combativeness in the relationship between Charles and his Parliament. Stung by years of being ignored, the members of the Short Parliament refused to provide the funds for the upcoming Second Bishops' War, which was scheduled to begin in June. When the members started to discuss the motives for the war, Charles dismissed Parliament and made preparations for his second offensive against Scotland.

Mismanagement of the mobilization of the troops and incipient mutinies among the men because of pay issues allowed the Covenanters to take the early advantage; this time, the Scots determined to bring the war to England rather than wait for it to be brought to them. Marching on Northumberland, the Scots crossed the Tweed River on 20 August 1640, with the objective being the capture of Newcastle. The royal commanders failed to grasp the Scottish strategy and, in the event, when the Scots faced the English on 28 August at Newburn, the Covenanters enjoyed a significant advantage over the royal troops in size and in geographic position. As the Scots came across the river Tyne, the English defended their embankment gallantly, but were at last forced to retreat, leaving the field to the Scots.

In the end, the Second Bishops' War failed not just because of military blunders, but because the king and his advisers failed to understand that they could not make war without the necessary funds. Ultimately, the king was forced to come to terms in the Treaty of Ripon, in October 1640; he was required to pay a daily subsidy to the Scots and convene a new Parliament that would address their grievances. This "Long Parliament," meeting for the first time on 3 November 1640, would remain in session, in one form or another, for the next twenty years and would oversee the king's deposition and execution in 1649. The Bishops' Wars, therefore, while not very significant in a military sense, certainly set the stage for the profound upheaval that laid the foundations for the eventual primacy of Parliament.

Connie Evans

Further Reading

Fissel, M. C. (1994). *The Bishops' Wars: Charles I's campaigns against Scotland, 1638–1640*. Cambridge, UK: Cambridge University Press.

Fritze, R. H., & Robison, W. B. (Eds.). (1996). *Historical dictionary of Stuart England, 1603–1689*. Westport, CT: Greenwood Press.

Buddhism: China

The relationship between Buddhism and war in China is complex and multifaceted. It cannot be understood adequately or appreciated appropriately from the standpoint of Buddhist doctrine and philosophy alone. In the vast collection of Buddhist literature translated into Chinese, sutras and monastic codes for the most part suggest that killing and warfare are unwholesome actions that cause bad karma and are to be avoided. A few scattered passages in Mahayana Buddhist writings condone killing by a bodhisattva, but only if done out of compassion *(cibei)* to keep a murderer from harming others and from incurring further bad karma to him- or herself. Furthermore, a number of Buddhist scriptures emphasize the role of Buddhist monks and ritual in preserving and upholding the state, a concept known as "state-protection Buddhism" *(huguo fojiao)*. However, since Buddhism began as a foreign religion in China, the perception of Buddhism as subversive, or as supporting armed rebellion or millenarianism, has accompanied the religion's self-proclaimed role as a protector of the country.

Buddhism Enters China

Buddhist monks, ideas, doctrines, scriptures, and communities were introduced into China over a long period of time probably beginning in the first century BCE. In the early years, most of the Buddhists were foreign monks and merchants who established residences in China to participate in the lucrative Silk Road trade. In 65 CE, Prince Ying of the Eastern Han dynasty (25–220), a lay believer in Buddhism and Daoist gods, established the first Buddhist community at Pengcheng, located east of the capital at Luoyang. In 73 CE, Prince Ying committed suicide after a failed coup. After that, all Buddhist practitioners and monks and some associated Daoist miracle workers were brought back to Luoyang so that the government could observe the social and political activities of these religions not officially sanctioned by the Chinese government. From that time forward, the Buddhist church in Luoyang influenced the growth of the Buddhism in China.

Although Luoyang Buddhists were influential, there was no centralized organ for the governing of Buddhists in China. The Chinese state fell into rebellion and chaos during the second half of the second century, and over the next century Indian and Central Asian monks and merchants, many of Indo-European extraction, entered China and attempted to establish lay and monastic followings and communities. These communities received a measure of recognition and protection from local political leaders and served the needs of those rulers. Chinese rule of northern China came to an end in the early fourth century. As northern China was overridden and carved up into short-lived regional kingdoms by the nomadic peoples, the Chinese leadership and bureaucracy fled south of the Chang (Yangtze) River.

The Role of Buddhist Monks and Monasteries

Buddhism had remained a curious religion of foreigners, for the most part, prior to the disintegration of Chinese rule in the north. However, due to the influence of a new breed of Buddhist monks, Buddhism became an increasingly important factor in the non-Chinese tribal states. Beyond being vigorous proselytizers, these monks were renowned for their ability to demonstrate the magical efficacy of the religion and were willing to serve as advisers to kings and to recognize the royalty and aristocratic elite as important patrons and protectors of the Buddhist church. Initially perceived as a barbarian religion by the Chinese elite, Buddhism served to legitimate the non-Chinese dynasties in the north because of its connections to India, the only other great cultural power in Asia, because of its widespread following in Central Asia and along the Silk Road, and because it provided rituals for state protection that rivaled those of ancient China and by which it lauded powerful rulers who promoted Buddhism. Foreign and Chinese monks utilized warfare and associated interstate relations to propagate the Buddhist message. The Buddhist message did not promote peace and nonviolence so much as provide solace and hope for a better rebirth in this world or salvation in a nonviolent world ruled by a compassionate buddha.

The efficacy of Buddhism was also seen in the magical power of adept Buddhist monks. For example, the Central Asian monk Fotudeng (d. 348), who arrived in China in 310, converted the Xiongnu hegemons Shi Le (d. 333) and Shi Hu (d. 348) through the performance of miracles and served as their spiritual adviser. Fotudeng did not participate directly in the warfare waged by these hegemons, but he also did not oppose their wars. He was famous for his ability to foretell the outcome of battles.

Due to the efforts of many eminent monks, the Buddhist religion began to receive Chinese imperial patronage. Buddhist monasteries received official

Requirements of the Shaolin Warrior

1. **Be as graceful as a cat.**
2. **Be as aggressive as a tiger.**
3. **Step like a dragon**
4. **Be as quick as a lightning bolt.**
5. **Shout like thunder.**
6. **Move like a gust of wind.**
7. **Be as soft as cotton.**
8. **Be as hard as iron.**

Source: **Adapted from Shaolin Kung Fu OnLine Library. Retrieved 14 May 2003, from http://www.kungfulibrary.com**

sanction and support and began to play an important role in the development of the Chinese economy. Monasteries commonly served as storehouses, banks, and pawnshops, and played a vital role in the development of commerce and usury. Monasteries were a key factor in driving local economies and, for better or for worse, were either directly or indirectly associated with the political aspirations of nearby aristocrats. They were also used occasionally as facilities for the storage of weapons. In the winter of 445, a certain Ge Wu raised a rebellion in Chang'an. Emperor Taiwu (reigned 423–452) of the Northern Wei dynasty arrived in the second month of 446 to quell the uprising. While pasturing the emperor's horses on a monastery's grounds in Chang'an, attendants found a hoard of bows, arrows, spears, and shields stashed in a side building. Since he had not sanctioned the stockpiling of these weapons, Emperor Taiwu concluded that the monks in the monastery must be supporters of Ge Wu and ordered their immediate execution. This incident led to the first great persecution of Buddhism, which occurred between 446 and 452. The monks may not have been connected directly with the rebellion, but the connection between some Buddhist monasteries and the waging of war cannot be denied.

Later, during the Sui (581–618) and Tang (618–907) dynasties, the Buddhist church reached the pinnacle of imperial support. The founders of these dynasties established several Buddhist temples in which monks prayed and made offerings on behalf of the soldiers who died in the many wars fought during the reunification of the Chinese empire in 589, the decline of the Sui and the founding of the Tang, and in numerous wars with the various tribes that threatened Chinese interests on the Silk Road.

Imperial Buddhas and *Cakravartin* Kings

The legend of the Indian Buddhist King Asoka (reigned 274–232 BCE) had a profound effect on rulers in both north and south China during the period of disunion prior to the founding of the Sui dynasty. Although the traditional narrative suggests that Asoka turned to Buddhism and promoted nonviolence after waging a bloody war of conquest, the application of Asoka's example varied in China. A ruler who supported and patronized Buddhism is called a *cakravartin* king, "a king who turns the wheel [of the Buddhist teaching]" *(zhuanlun wang)*. Buddhist kings such as Fu Jian (reigned 357–384) of the Former Qin and Emperor Wu (reigned 502–549) of the Liang, conceived of themselves as *cakravartins* and distinguished themselves as patrons of the Buddhist church, commissioning elaborate icons and monasteries and holding large vegetarian feasts in order to obtain merit for their pious actions. However, although in medieval China to behave in a nonviolent manner often meant refraining from wanton killing of people and animals, belief in Buddhism did not keep rulers from waging wars to expand their domains. Although some devout Buddhist rulers of China were quite knowledgeable of Buddhist teachings, they never attempted to justify such wars using Buddhist doctrine.

The relationship between the Buddhist church and the Chinese state was always precarious. The Chinese Buddhist church never developed into a powerful religious bureaucracy that could wield political might the way the Catholic church did in medieval Europe. Although Buddhism provided legitimacy for rulers, it had to compete in this arena with the Confucian tradition as well as with Daoist movements. It was always dependent on imperial patronage, and rulers were suspicious of monks as seditionists because monks, as renouncers of the secular world, for the most part refused to bow to secular rulers.

In 396, at the beginning of the Northern Wei period (386–534), the Chinese monk Faguo (d. 419) attempted to solve the problem of bowing to the emperor by declaring that the emperor was himself the Tathagata (Buddha). The Northern Wei rulers identified themselves specifically with the buddha of the future, Maitreya (Chinese: Milofo). In Buddhist literature, Maitreya will descend from the Tsuita Heaven in the distant future to establish a messianic reign of peace during which the Buddhist teaching will be spread. In this way, warfare and bloodshed brought about by the Northern Wei kings in their conquest of the whole of northern China by 439 could be justified as necessary acts to bring about the transformation of the world.

Buddhist Rebellion and Messianic Movements in Medieval China

Although the first use of messianic Maitreya imagery was not intended to be revolutionary, it was used soon thereafter to legitimate uprisings. No canonical texts supported these messianic expectations, but once the idea of Maitreya's descent to the world was made current, opponents to the existing power could and did use it. There were at least ten different popular uprisings led by monks between the years 402 and 517. Many of the movements began as religious associations that were bound tightly by their performance of pious acts, although the official records emphasize their desire to deceive the people and to commit acts of banditry. Hope in the coming of Maitreya was disseminated through popular Chinese literature. In the mid-sixth century, for example, an apocryphal sutra called Prince Moonlight circulated that combined Buddhist and Daoist ideas of eschatology and promoted warfare to bring about the foundation of Maitreya's peaceful reign. In 613, a miracle worker from Hebei named Song Zixian claimed to be an incarnation of Maitreya. He recruited Buddhist laymen to make an attack upon the emperor of the Sui dynasty. Also that year, a monk from Shanxi named Xiang Haiming claimed to be an earthly manifestation of Maitreya and the new emperor. Both revolts failed. The popular cult of Maitreya continued throughout the Tang period, but Maitreyan imagery was always seen as a threat to legitimate dynastic rule. None of these groups tried to establish utopian societies as defined in the West. The more perfect world sought by the members of these groups was described in some detail in apocryphal sutras that combined canonical Buddhist and Daoist millenarian elements and would come of its own accord during the reign of a universal monarch, a *cakravartin* king. They did not raise questions of class or position in society directly but rather focused on the idea being one of the elect or faithful followers of Maitreya and that he would establish a more equitable society on earth and that the faithful would be rewarded with a blissful rebirth in a paradisiacal Buddha-land.

The White Lotus Society and Messianic Movements in Late Imperial China

The White Lotus Society emerged as a popular movement containing both monks and laymen in east and south China during the middle of the Song dynasty (960–1279), probably after the beginning of the Southern Song period in 1127. It was one of numerous folk Buddhist traditions influenced by the cult of the Buddha Amitabha (Chinese: Omito) and pious hope for rebirth in his Pure Land in the West. The lotus is one of the most powerful symbols in Buddhism. Just as a lotus is able to blossom on top of a murky pond, it is symbolic of one's leaving behind the mundane world and becoming enlightened. Furthermore, the scriptures describing rebirth in Amitabha's Pure Land say that aspirants are reborn in the calyx of a lotus flower and that they stay sealed in that state until their sins and wrong views are removed sufficiently for them to accept the Buddhist message. By the mid-fourteenth century the White Lotus Society incorporated Maitreyan and, later, Manichaean eschatology and began to appear throughout China. These groups attempted to establish millennial states by means of armed uprisings. During the Mongol Yuan dynasty (1279–1368), official memorials mention rebellion by a White Lotus group in southern China in 1281. Uprisings led by groups holding White Lotus symbols and beliefs played a significant role in overthrowing the Mongol dynasty. Zhu Yuanzhang, the founder of the Ming dynasty (1368–1644), abandoned his connections to White Lotus groups and Maitreyan eschatology and attempted to obliterate them, but rebellions led by sectarians with loose associations to the White Lotus movements continued and increased substantially by the end of the Ming dynasty. Between the years 1621 and 1627, for instance, there were twenty uprisings associated with the White Lotus movement. Many of the eschatological views associated with these groups appeared in a new genre of religious literature called "precious volumes" *(baojuan).* White Lotus rebellions occurred throughout the Manchu Qing dynasty (1644–1912). Liu Song and Liu Zhixie led one of the longest-lasting sect-driven uprisings, which began in Hubei province in 1796, spread to five provinces, and was finally quelled nine years later. In 1813, just a few years after the end of the previous uprising, Lin Qing and Li Wenchang led a White Lotus rebellion with a direct attack on the imperial palace. The folk Buddhist sects responsible for these uprisings all had different names but were united by core beliefs and shared religious literature.

The ideal society sought by the members of these Buddhist and Buddhist-inspired groups may be loosely described as utopian, but, as the Chinese were again threatened by wave after wave of invasions by nomadic and semi-nomadic peoples from Mongolia and Manchuria, the society they sought to establish was one ruled by someone ethnically and culturally Chinese. Poverty was always a motivating factor in these rebellions, but issues of class and position in society were not the defining factors since many rebellions were led by persons with some measure of wealth and social status. The popular religious literature of the time, the precious scrolls genre, combined many elements: ethnic, social, political, moral, religious, and millenarian; and constituted a potent message to people dissatisfied with many elements in society.

Shaolin Monastery, Chan, and Martial Arts

The Chan (Japanese: Zen) tradition emerged as the dominant Buddhist tradition in the aftermath of the An Lushan rebellion (755–763) during the Tang and received political patronage in the Song period. Although some Chan monks distinguished themselves as servants of the state by raising money for the war effort, there is no conclusive evidence of a Chan martial-arts tradition during the Tang period. During the Song period, the Chan tradition succeeded in codifying its myth of a patriarchal lineage tracing back through several Chinese Chan masters to the Indian Bodhidharma (c. 461–534), and thence back to the Buddha in India. The myth of Bodhidharma was then linked to a real martial-arts tradition at Shaolin Monastery—where Bodhidharma was said to have practiced his famous "wall contemplation"—that probably developed later during the Yuan or Ming period. Thus, according to the received popular tradition, the original Shaolin martial-arts techniques are either attributed to Bodhidharma or to Chinese who are associated with his protection. However, analysis of the philosophical principles associated with these kung-fu techniques suggests a synthesis of Daoist and Buddhist philosophy.

Shaolin martial arts techniques are divided into two main strands: internal *(neijia quanfa)*, or soft *(rou)*, and external *(waijia quanfa)*, or hard *(gang)*. The development of the will *(yi)* and vital energy *(qi)* lead to the perfection of inner strength. Internal techniques include *taiji* (or t'ai-chi), *bagua*, and *xingyi* and are similar to Daoist *qigong*, focusing on the cultivation of the cinnabar fields (*dantian*). The cinnabar fields refer to where the vital essences of life are produced and psychophysical power is cultivated in the pubic region of one's body. Shaolin boxing is an external technique.

Buddhist Resistance Against the Japanese in World War II

In September of 1931, Japan began its occupation of Manchuria. Armed conflict between Japan and China, already brimming over with internal strife between Chiang Kai-shek's Nationalist government and the Chinese Communists under the leadership of Mao Zedong, escalated gradually. The two sides eventually agreed to set aside their dispute to provide a unified front against the Japanese onslaught. As part of the general mobilization of the Chinese people, in July of 1936, the Nationalist government ordered that all young Buddhist monks should be trained to defend the nation. Later, in October of 1936, the government ordered that all monks and nuns must mobilize for war along with all other Chinese citizens. In December of 1936, the *Fohai deng* (The Illuminator of the Sea of Buddhism), a periodical produced by Mingnan Buddhist College, which is located at Nanputuo Monastery in Xiamen, sent out a call to monks and nuns to contribute papers to a special edition of the journal on the topic of the role of Buddhism in protecting the state *(huguo).*

In a very short period, three volumes were produced that circulated widely among the Buddhist monastic communities in China. In the articles, Chinese monks struggled to reconcile the prohibition against killing with the necessity of protecting the state. Some contributors voiced the opinion that monks would have to cease to be monks in order to fight, but that they would earn great merit for protecting the nation. Others felt that, despite the monastic precept against killing, there must be flexibility with regard to the monk's rules. Others argued that the precept against killing should not be an obstacle to a Buddhist's serving his country. Since Buddhists cannot look on without compassion while murderers (in this case, the Japanese) kill thousands of people, monks should protect the state by "killing with compassion." There is no doctrinal basis for this view, although the pithy expression "compassion as the basis and expediency as the way" has been used to describe Mahayana Buddhism in China. Thereafter, other monks wrote important treatises in which they culled passages from sutras and historical materials for evidence of monks' having protected their countries throughout Buddhist history. Chinese monks eventually were able to demonstrate not only that the necessity of killing a few to save many is justified in the Buddhist scriptures and monastic codes dealing with compassion, but that it was a wholesome, meritorious practice that led to good karmic results. Despite the overwhelming scriptural evidence against killing and violence, Chinese monks were able to craft their writings selectively, drawing on strong nationalistic sentiment, to form powerful propaganda against the Japanese invasion.

Richard D. McBride, II

See also Buddhism: India; Buddhism, Mahayana; Buddhism: Taiwan; Confucianism, Classical; Daoism, Classical; Daoism, Medieval; Zen: Samurai Tradition

Further Reading

Ch'en, K. (1964). *Buddhism in China: A historical survey*. Princeton, NJ: Princeton University Press.

Gernet, J. (1995). *Buddhism in Chinese society: An economic history from the fifth to the tenth centuries* (F. Verellen, Trans.). New York: Columbia University Press.

Overmyer, D. L. (1976). *Folk Buddhist religion: Dissenting sects in late traditional China* (Harvard East Asian Series No. 83). Cambridge, MA: Harvard University Press.

Overmyer, D. L. (1999). *Precious volumes: An introduction to Chinese sectarian scriptures from the sixteenth and seventeenth centuries*. Cambridge, MA: Harvard University Asia Center.

ter Haar, B. J. (1999). *The white lotus teachings in religious history*. Leiden, Netherlands: E. J. Brill.

Wong, J. I. (Ed.). (1978–1981). *A source book in the Chinese martial arts*. Stockton, CA: Koinonia Publications.

Wright, A. F. (1948). Fo-t'u-teng: A biography. *Harvard Journal of Asiatic Studies, 11*(3–4), 321–371.

Wright, A. F. (1978). *The Sui dynasty: The unification of China, A.D. 581–617*. New York: Alfred A. Knopf.

Zürcher, E. (1982) Prince Moonlight: Messianism and eschatology in early medieval Chinese Buddhism. *T'oung Pao, 98*(1–3), 1–71.

Buddhism: India

The history of Buddhism's decline and near disappearance in the land of its origin (by 1192 CE) still perplexes historians. Is one factor that might have influenced this destiny the tradition's ambivalence to warfare, even in self-defense? An exploration of this topic is illuminating for understanding the practical implications of a tradition that prescribed a solitary path to enlightenment for individuals, yet for over 2,500 years survived the vicissitudes of history across Asia.

To consider the Indian Buddhist understandings of war, we must note that the tradition is multivocalic, like all world religions. Since religious authority in Buddhism was never singular across Asia even in individual societies, constructing a composite "Buddhist view of war" entails broad generalizations.

Born a prince and trained in youth as a warrior, Siddhartha Gautama (c. 563–c. 483 BCE) renounced his throne to become the Buddha, a sage who conquered humanity's entrapment by redeath and rebirth. Feeling compassion for suffering beings, he founded the first missionary religion, created a community of monks and nuns (the *sangha*) who adopted his ascetic norms and meditative practices, and shared his teachings (dharma) with all interested in them. The seekers who joined the early *sangha* were taught to cultivate detachment and so avoid entanglements in politics or warfare. But as householders and kings were drawn to this faith, applications of Buddhist thought to worldly matters developed.

Karma Doctrine: War as Moral Failure and Cause for Retribution

As did other spiritual teachers in ancient India, the Buddha taught a doctrine of moral retribution, arguing that all deeds will "ripen" via natural law in this life and future lifetimes: good actions will result in reward, evil deeds will result in punishment. Although there were many views about how the calculus of this karma retribution actually work, it was widely held by Buddhists that only intended actions lead to karma creation and fruition.

According to Buddhist doctrine, retribution is shaped by beings acting under the influence of the "three great poisons" *(kleshas)*—greed, hatred, delusion—creating karma that binds them to certain rebirth, mortal suffering, and death. Since killing is the most serious immoral act, humans engaging in warfare are in most instances seen as acting out of wrong motives, creating bad karma by injuring and killing their victims, and undermining their own future in the moral universe by strengthening these *kleshas*. Thus, in early Buddhist thought, war is a disaster both for the victims and the perpetrators, "poisoning" the future of the world.

The Buddhist aversion to warfare is based upon this central philosophy and its view that compassion should guide action in the world. Just as it is a universal truth that all beings suffer, compassion is the central principle in Buddhist ethics and is intended to alleviate the world's pain. The existence of warfare is accordingly regarded as the failure of humans to resist the *kleshas* and live by compassion.

Buddhist Kingship: Ashoka's Rule by Dharma as Antidote for Warfare

Indian Buddhists clearly thought that kingship was needed in the violent, war-prone world of ancient India. A canonical creation myth describes kingship created to abet society's resistance to violent anarchy: "Then they instituted boundary lines [on the land] and one steals another's share. After . . . the third time . . . they beat the offender with fists, earth clods, with sticks, etc. When thus stealing, lying, and violence had sprung up among them, they came together and said, 'What if we elect some one of us, who shall get angry with him who merits anger, and banish him who merits banishment?' . . . He was called the 'King' " (Warren 1995, 326).

Though there were no treatises on statecraft known in Indian Buddhism, the tradition did evolve a model for kingship based on its greatest royal patron, King Ashoka (c. 265–236 or c. 273–232 BCE). Grandson to the unifier of India's first great empire, Ashoka followed Hindu norms of rulership by consolidating with brute force the coastal region of Kalinga. The resulting destruction and bloodshed greatly dismayed Ashoka, however:

> He [the king] has felt profound sorrow and regret because the conquest of a people previously unconquered involves slaughter, death, and deportation. Even those who escaped calamity themselves are deeply afflicted by the misfortunes suffered by those friends, acquaintances, companions, and relatives for whom they feel an undiminished affection. Thus all men share in the misfortune [of war], and this weighs on the King's mind. (Nikam and McKeon 1978, 28)

At just this time and in reaction to the horrors of war, Ashoka became a Buddhist devotee, and sent scribes throughout the Indian subcontinent to explain "the Dharma" that he embraced. In Pillar Edict I he writes, "Dharma is good. But what does Dharma consist of? It consists of few sins and many good deeds, of kindness, liberality, truthfulness, and purity" (Nikam and McKeon 1978, 41). Through later texts about Ashoka that elaborated on his acts and piety, Indian Buddhists adopted Ashoka's example for their norms of a "good Buddhist ruler."

Buddhist "Just War" vs. "Never War" Views

That some Buddhist kings ignored the ideal of total nonviolence should not be surprising. Even Ashoka did not disband his army and in one inscription warns, "The King seeks to induce even the forest peoples . . . to adopt this way of life. He reminds them, however, that he can exercise the power to punish, despite his repentance, in order to induce them to desist from their crimes and escape execution" (Nikam and McKeon 1978, 28–29.)

One famous example of a Buddhist king resorting to war comes from Sri Lanka, where Buddhism had but recently entered this island from India. King Dutthagamani (d. 77 BCE), a convert to Buddhism, waged an armed crusade to repel non-Buddhist invaders. In the national chronicle, the *Mahavamsa*, he is said to have attached a Buddha relic to his spear and marched into battle with five hundred monks in attendance, with "defense of the Dharma" as the justification. When afterwards arhats (enlightened monks) try to assuage his guilt for the killings he had caused, their words of comfort come in striking contrast to the norms of the early canon and the popular narratives: "From this deed arises no hindrance . . . Only one and a half human beings have been slain here by thee, O Lord of men, . . . unbelievers and men of evil life were the rest, not more to be esteemed than beasts. . . . [T]herefore cast away care from thy heart" (Smith 1972, 43).

Similar in its "just war" approach—though not result—is the widely popular tale, the *Simhalasarthabahu Avadana*. It tells the story of a caravan trader who is shipwrecked and sees his companions trapped and eaten by cannibalistic demonesses; when he later becomes king, he leads an army to attack these murderous spirits, but ultimately accepts their surrender:

> "O Demonesses! After seeing all of your crimes, you deserve to be killed immediately." But after hearing their entreaties for mercy, he continued, "And in this land, you should live no more. . . . If you ever return to this town, I will certainly kill you all." (Lewis 2000, 79)

Thus, one strain in Buddhist thought about war was to justify it for self-defense or in defense of the faith, and to portray an enemy as less than fully human.

Other Indian Buddhists clearly understood the possibility that violent intervention can be just when used to limit the violent from perpetuating widespread suffering. The Mahayana scholar Shantideva (active eighth century CE) illustrates this view when he argues for self-sacrifice and implicitly for violent intervention in his popular work, the *Bodhicaryavatara*: "If the suffering of one ends the suffering of many, then one who has compassion for others and himself must cause that [individual] suffering to arise" (Crosby and Skilton 1996, 97). This assertion may in part be related to the practice of monks in medieval Indian monasteries being appointed as guards who took up weapons in self-defense.

But there is also another view expressed in popular Buddhist literature, where kings do not even resist violent invaders. In one instance from the Pali Canon, a king throws open the city gates and admits a marauding army. After he is captured and thrown into a dungeon, the king's only defense is to extend thoughts of *maitri* (loving-kindness) to his chief tormenter. This causes his captor to feel "great torment in his body" and "be smitten with great pain" (Jataka 282 in Cowell 1957, 3:274). A similar story plot is found in Pali Jataka 351 and the result is the same: both kings regain their thrones without war or bloodshed.

This same spiritual method of nonviolent defense is evident in Mahayana narratives. In a story that is part of the *Pancaraksha*, one of the most popular Indian Buddhist ritual texts, the king responds to invasion by telling the citizens not to fight, as he resorts to ritual:

> He proclaimed, "My dear subjects! It is my duty to safeguard the country and countrymen. . . . I will do all that is needed." After saying this, King Brahmadatta bathed and . . . purified in body, speech, and mind, the king appended the amulets of the *Pratisara dharani* [chant] to his crown and armor, then went alone to meet the enemy. The men in the army of the enemy kings retreated in panic. (Lewis 2000, 135)

Thus, an observant Buddhist king need not perpetuate the endless cycle of war violence, even on those mindlessly assaulting them; he can rely instead on the power made available from tradition: the force of loving-kindness, the causality of karmic retribution, the power of rituals and chants bestowed by the Buddha.

War as Spiritual Metaphor

One final point can be made about Indian Buddhism regarding war. There are passages from the early texts that convey the Buddha's martial origins. *The Sutra of 42 Sections*, for example, compares war to the struggle for spiritual transformation: "A man practicing the Way is like a lone man in combat against ten thousand. Bearing armor and brandishing weapons, he charges through the gate eager to do battle, but if he is weak-hearted and cowardly he will withdraw and flee. Some get halfway . . . and retreat; some reach the battle and die; some are victorious and return to their kingdoms triumphantly" (Sharf 1996, 370). We find this same connection in an Ashokan inscription: "King Ashoka desires security, self-control, impartiality, and cheerfulness for all living beings. He considers moral conquest *[dharma-vijaya]* the most important conquest" (Nikam and McKeon 1978, 29).

Implications

Witness Tibetan exiles unable to expel the Chinese since 1959, the Buddhists in Burma incapable of overcoming military authoritarianism since 1960, and the inability of Buddhists to muster effective resistance to Communist regimes in Southeast Asia (Vietnam, Laos, and Cambodia): does the lack of a strong foundational doctrine of self-defense underlie Buddhist failures to resist persecution in the twentieth century?

Todd T. Lewis

See also Hinduism: Vedic Period; Jainism

Further Reading

Buddhaghosa, B. (1976). *The path of purification (Visuddhimagga)* (B. Nyanamoli, Trans.). Berkeley, CA: Shambhala.

Cowell, E. B. (Trans.). (1957). *The Jataka* (Vol. 6). London: Routledge and Kegan Paul.
Crosby, K., & Skilton, A. (1996). *The Bodhicaryavatara by Shantideva*. New York: Oxford University Press.
Gard, R. A. (1962). Buddhism and political authority. In H. W. Lasswell & H. F. Cleveland (Eds.), *The ethic of power: The interplay of religion, philosophy, and politics* (pp. 39–70). New York: Harper.
Geiger, W. (Ed. & Trans.). (1958). *The Mahavamsa*. London: Luzak and Company.
Lewis, T. T. (2000). *Popular Buddhist texts from Nepal: Narratives and rituals of Newar Buddhism*. Albany, NY: State University of New York Press.
Nikam, N. A., & McKeon, R. (Eds. and Trans.). (1978). *The edicts of Ashoka*. Chicago: University of Chicago Press.
Rahula, W. (1956). *History of Buddhism in Ceylon*. Colombo, Sri Lanka: Gunasena.
Reynolds, F. (1972). The two wheels of dhamma: A study of early Buddhism. In B. Smith (Ed.), *The two wheels of Dhamma* (pp. 6–30). Chambersburg, PA: American Academy of Religion.
Sharf, R. (Ed.). (1996). The scripture in forty-two sections. In D. S. Lopez, Jr. (Ed.), *Religions in China in practice* (pp. 360–371). Princeton, NJ: Princeton University Press.
Smith, B. L. (1972). The ideal social order as portrayed in the Chronicles of Ceylon. In B. Smith (Ed.), *The two wheels of Dhamma* (pp. 31–57). Chambersburg, PA: American Academy of Religion.
Strong, J. S. (1983). *The legend of King Asoka*. Princeton, NJ: Princeton University Press.
Warren, H. C. (1995). *Buddhism in translations*. Delhi, India: Motilal Banarsidass Reprint.

Buddhism, Mahayana

Mahayana Buddhism is one of the two major schools of Buddhist religious philosophy that emerged from the teachings of Siddhartha Gautama (c. 563–c. 483 BCE), known as the Buddha ("Enlightened One"). The term Mahayana ("Greater Vehicle") was adopted by the followers of this school to distinguish it from the earlier orthodox interpretation of the Buddha's teachings referred to as Hinayana ("Lesser Vehicle"), or Theravada ("Way of the Elders"). Mahayana Buddhism first appeared as a distinct school of thought during the centuries immediately following the death of the Buddha as differences arose among Buddhist scholars over the authority and authenticity of various sutras (scriptures) composing the early Buddhist canon. The Theravada school of Buddhism formulated an interpretation of the Buddha's teachings based upon the earliest Pali language discourses and commentaries compiled by the First Buddhist Council shortly after the Buddha's death. In subsequent Buddhist councils, Mahayanists rejected what they saw as the narrow orthodoxy of Hinayana and advocated a more liberal acceptance of apocryphal scriptures and traditions. In the early centuries of the first millennium CE, the Mahayana tradition expanded into East Asia, where it eventually became the predominant form of Buddhism practiced in China, Japan, Korea, and Vietnam. Theravada Buddhism, on the other hand, spread southward where it became the predominant form of Buddhism in Sri Lanka and the countries of Southeast Asia, such as Burma, Thailand, and Cambodia.

Essential Principles of Mahayana Buddhism

Mahayana Buddhism adopts a less analytical and more intuitive interpretation of the Buddha's teachings than the earlier Theravada tradition. It also accepts a much broader canon of sacred writings as authoritative sources of Buddhist doctrine. It nevertheless maintains the essential precepts that constitute the foundation of all schools of Buddhism. These include the "Four Noble Truths" that express the fundamental Buddhist creed that life in this world is one of inescapable suffering, in which all creatures are subjected to the inevitable ordeals of frustration, sickness, and death. The cause of this suffering, according to this creed, is craving and ignorance. Therefore, release from the suffering of existence, and the attainment of nirvana (extinction of ego), may only be achieved by dispelling craving and ignorance. This may be accomplished through devoted adherence to the "Eightfold Path" of right views, right aspirations, right speech, right conduct, right livelihood, right effort, right mindfulness, and right meditation. Inasmuch as Buddhism emerged in the context of the earlier Brahmanical traditions of ancient India, many of its key concepts have parallels in other schools of Indian philosophy and religion such as Hinduism and Jainism. These concepts include reincarnation (rebirth), karma (the positive or negative force of one's thoughts and deeds), and the notion that one's supreme spiritual destiny consists in release from samsara, the cycle of birth, death, and rebirth to which all creatures are bound. Buddhism departed from earlier Indian traditions by renouncing the Brahmanical emphasis on religious ritual and the extreme asceticism of Indian mystics, advocating instead the "Middle Way" between a life of indulgence and severe austerity as the most effective pathway to spiritual enlightenment.

Mahayana Buddhism diverged from the earlier Theravada orthodoxy by formulating new interpretations of the Buddha's teachings regarding spiritual enlightenment and the attainment of nirvana. Mahayanists renounced the Theravada contention that entrance into nirvana was the exclusive privilege of the arhat, who attains enlightenment only after a life immersed in meditation and adherence to the strict Vinaya code taught by the Buddha for the moral edification of Buddhist monks (the *sangha*). According to the Mahayanist, one who had truly attained spiritual enlightenment would not selfishly abandon the creatures of this world, but would be moved by infinite compassion to postpone entrance into nirvana for the sake of guiding all other beings to salvation. Such a perfected being was called a bodhisattva, or "one who has the essence of Buddhahood." The spiritual object of the Mahayanist therefore differed significantly from that of the Theravada arhat. The Mahayana tradition placed much greater emphasis on the devotee's intuitive capacity for love and compassion and adopted a conception of the Buddha that elevated him from the confines of history and nature to a station of absolute spiritual transcendence. The Mahayana tradition therefore opened the pathway of spiritual attainment to the devout layperson, lessening the distinction between the monkhood and the rest of society. Mahayanists believed that they had a more altruistic view of salvation than the analytical and individualistic approach of the Theravada school. And the more liberal acceptance by Mahayanists of sutras outside of the orthodox canon of the Theravada school opened the door for great variation in doctrinal interpretation and the assimilation of a broad array of new conceptions and deities.

Mahayana Teachings on War and Violence

Mahayana Buddhist ethics regarding war and violence must first be understood in the larger context of India's complex religious and political history. Buddhism arose during a period of incessant warfare and political fragmentation in northern India as the various Aryan tribes competed against one another for regional hegemony. The Buddha's emphasis on ahimsa, or nonviolence, may therefore be regarded in part as a response to the violence of the age in which Siddhartha Gautama lived. Buddhist teachings explicitly prohibited killing; and the Buddha renounced the caste system, which served to justify warfare in Aryan society by associating it with the caste dharma, or moral imperative, of the Kshatriya warrior caste. Buddhism even opposed those Brahmanic rituals that required the ceremonial sacrifice of animals. The renunciation of the use of violence for political purposes became an even more integral part of the Buddhist tradition during the reign of the Mauryan emperor Ashoka (reigned c. 273–232 BCE), who would become the foremost exemplar of the Buddhist ideal of benevolent kingship by rejecting the use of violence as an instrument of political coercion and upholding instead Buddhist righteousness as the chief principle of his imperial administration.

From another perspective, the Buddhist emphasis on nonviolence was closely related to its introspective and psychological approach to spiritual growth and purification. The quest for spiritual maturity and enlightenment that constituted the primary aspiration of the ideal Buddhist life necessitated the internalization of new sentiments and values, and the moral discipline that this required was given direction by the principles and injunctions associated with the Eightfold Path and the Vinaya code of monastic discipline. Among these was the need to cultivate a sincere love and compassion toward all living creatures and to refrain from killing. According to the *Metta Sutra*, the four cardinal virtues that constituted the essence of "right mindfulness" called on the faithful to "develop the state of mind of love *(metta)*, . . . for as you do hostility will grow less; and of compassion *(karuna)*, for anxiety will grow less; and of joy *(mudita)*, for aversion will grow less" (Pardue 1971, 13). And the first of the "Five Precepts" that defined the primary moral obligations of the Buddhist monkhood was the explicit injunction not to kill any living being. Indeed, adhering to the principle of nonviolence was regarded as a necessary prerequisite for spiritual development and one of the primary means for improving one's karma. As with most of the world's major religions, however, Mahayana Buddhism could also serve as the basis for political rebellion or, in some schools of thought, even develop elaborate justifications of warfare for the sake of securing its institutional interests.

Buddhist Millenarian Rebellion in China

One of the more notable examples of Mahayana Buddhism serving as the basis for warfare and rebellion is the occurrence of Buddhist millenarian rebellions in Chinese history. During periods of dynastic decline and social disorder, Buddhist lay societies have occasionally arisen in China to help secure the survival and welfare of their hungry and oppressed peasant constituents. The "Pure Land" tradition of folk Buddhism provided an appealing religious ideology for such periods of upheaval by promoting the belief in the imminent advent of the Buddha Maitreya (the future Buddha), a messianic boddhisattva who would rescue the faithful and reestablish an era of peace, justice, and prosperity. Seeing themselves as instruments of this redemptive process, followers of these cults have occasionally taken up arms against the established political authorities and fought with great passion and dedication. One of the best known examples of this was at the end of the Yuan dynasty (1279–1368), at which time the Chinese suffered under the oppressive rule of the Mongols. Following a period of disastrous floods and severe famines, the region around the lower reaches of the Huang (Yellow) River fell under the control of a Buddhist millenarian sect known as the Red Turbans. The leader of this insurrection, Han Shantong (d. 1351), was considered a reincarnation of Maitreya and was thus able to rally the peasant masses to his religious cause. Chu Yüan-chang (1328–1398), a Chinese peasant who would eventually overthrow the Yuan and take the throne as the first emperor of the Chinese Ming dynasty (1368–1644), was once a monk who had been deeply influenced by the messianic ideology of the Red Turbans. The rise of similarly inspired Buddhist millenarian cults during the reign of the Manchu Qing dynasty (1644–1912) would also serve as the basis of violent insurrections during a period of social and economic decline in the late eighteenth century.

Warrior Monks in Japan

Another notable example of organized violence by Mahayana Buddhist organizations is the phenomena of warrior monks in Japanese history. During the Heian period (794–1192 CE), state sponsorship of selected Buddhist establishments and the close relationship between the aristocracy and the *sangha* would set the stage for violent confrontations between competing sects. One of the most famous examples occurred in the years following the death of the emperor Kammu (736–806) in 806 CE. Kammu had lavishly supported the Tendai sect of Buddhism and its immense establishment on Mount Hiei located near the imperial capital, Heian-kyo (now Kyoto). His successor, however, shifted his support to a monk of aristocratic lineage named Kukai (774–835), founder of the influential Shingon sect, which erected a large monastery in direct competition with the Tendai establishment. Following Kukai's demand that the Tendai sect submit to a lesser status in his Ten Stages hierarchy and accept the appointment of one of his blood relatives as its leader, the Tendai community split into contending factions. The conflict between these factions became increasingly violent as the contending sects allied themselves with warring feudal clans. This sort of sectarian warfare became characteristic of Buddhism in Japan throughout the medieval period as the centralized imperial government gave way to centrifugal provincial loyalties that used their sectarian alliances as an integral part of their military strategy.

The transmission of Zen (Chan) Buddhism to Japan from China in the twelfth century and its adoption by the country's samurai elite marks another example of how Mahayana Buddhism could serve as a basis for violent action. Zen Buddhism represented an iconoclastic reaction against the scholasticism and emphasis on scriptural authority associated with some of Japan's classical schools of Buddhism, upholding instead the principle that the authentic transmission of the truths of Buddhism was best conveyed directly from master to pupil. Advocating a more immediate and intuitive approach to enlightenment, Zen practitioners sought to purify their consciousness through an austere lifestyle and rigorous monastic discipline. The discipline, grace, and spontaneity fostered by Zen produced a great influence on the arts in Japan, from the tea ceremony and flower arranging to swordsmanship and archery. Zen was therefore integrated easily with the warrior code (Bushido), becoming an essential component of military training for the Japanese samurai. Zen's mystical affirmation of the world also allowed for a relatively uncritical acceptance of the given social and political order; the samurai warrior trained in Zen could therefore be counted on to endure pain and hardship, and to accept with an unquestioned obedience the dictates of his feudal lord.

Significance

While Mahayana Buddhism has placed far greater emphasis on the ethic of nonviolence than many of the world's major religious traditions, historical forces and events have occasionally conspired to transform it into a basis for warfare and rebellion. Its liberal acceptance of variant schools of thought and interpretation has also served to weaken, in some cases, the authority of traditional Buddhist principles of morality and ethics. In short, while Mahayana Buddhism has throughout its history emphasized the values of love, compassion, and nonviolence, like many of the world's major religious traditions it has also served as the focus for sectarian violence and political insurrection.

Michael C. Lazich

See also Zen, Premodern; Zen: Samurai Tradition

Further Reading

Beasley, W. G. (1999). *The Japanese experience*. Berkeley, CA: University of California Press.

Conze, E. (1980). *A short history of Buddhism*. Boston: Allen and Unwin.

Gernet, J. (1995). *Buddhism in Chinese society: An economic history from the fifth to the tenth centuries*. New York: Columbia University Press.

Kalupahana, D. J. (1992). *A history of Buddhist philosophy: Continuities and discontinuities*. Honolulu, HI: University of Hawaii Press.

King, W. L. (1993). *Zen and the way of the sword: Arming the samurai psyche*. New York: Oxford University Press.

Lopez, D. S., Jr. (2001). *The story of Buddhism: A concise guide to its history and teachings*. San Francisco: Harper.

Pardue, P. A. (1971). *Buddhism: An historical introduction to Buddhist values and the social and political forms they have assumed in Asia*. New York: The Macmillan Company.

Reat, N. R. (1994). *Buddhism: A history*. Berkeley, CA: Asian Humanities Press.

Runzo, J., & Martin, N. M. (2001). *Ethics in the world religions*. New York: Oneworld Press.

Suzuki, B. L. (1969). *Mahayana Buddhism: A brief outline*. New York: The Macmillan Company.

Tamura, Y. (2000). *Japanese Buddhism: A cultural history* (J. Hunter, Trans.). Tokyo: Kosei Publishing Company.

Williams, P. (1989). *Mahayana Buddhism: The doctrinal foundations*. New York: Routledge.

Wright, A. F. (1990). *Studies in Chinese Buddhism* (R. M. Somers, Ed.). New Haven, CT: Yale University Press.

Buddhism: Myanmar (Burma) and Thailand

Buddhism is the religion that has dominated Myanmar (Burma) and Thailand for hundreds of years. It is the official religion of each country, with over 75 percent of the population in Myanmar being Buddhist and over 95 percent in Thailand. Buddhism has provided the basis for social organization and has sought to remain a factor in politics of each country.

Buddhist Beginnings

Traditions differ as to how Buddhism came to Myanmar, from which it then traveled to Thailand. One tradition states that in the third century BCE, after King Ashoka converted to Buddhism and conquered much of India, in addition to doing works of merit in India, he sent what today would be called missionaries, including either a son or a daughter, to Sri Lanka and Myanmar to spread Buddhism. Another tradition states that two merchants named Tapussa and Bhallika of the Mon ethnic group brought the faith to the region.

A schism in the first century BCE between Buddhism's two main schools, Mahayana and Theravada, found Mahayana spreading north to Tibet, Nepal, China, and then to Korea and Japan. Later, Theravada would move to Sri Lanka. Mahayana Buddhism then spread throughout mainland Southeast Asia beginning in the seventh century CE and was replaced later by Theravada Buddhism.

Ethnic groups that migrated from Tibet and southern China into the regions that came to be known as Burma and Thailand came into contact with Buddhism. The first group known to be impacted by Buddhism was the Mon. The Mon migrated south from the interior of Burma, occupying what is today Myanmar as well as part of Thailand and adopted Mahayana Buddhism from the Indian settlers who lived in the region. From the Mon, Buddhism spread to other ethnic groups in the region, including the Pyu, the Burmans, and the Thai.

The Pyu were one of the earliest of the Tibeto-Burman migrants who originated in eastern Tibet. Described by Chinese texts as tattooed cannibals, they moved into the Irrawaddy River valley and came into contact with the Mon, from whom they adopted Buddhism.

The Thai people's first kingdom is traced to the kingdom of Nanchao in Yunnan Province in southern China in the seventh century CE. From there the Thai migrated into Upper Burma and Thailand. The migration continued from the late eighth century on because of the threat of Chinese domination. The move into modern Thailand came several centuries later. By the

Buddhists praying at Shwedegon Pagoda, Rangoon, Burma, August 1996. Courtesy Steve Donaldson

eleventh century Thais lived in Mon territory. In this way they came under the influence of Theravada Buddhism from the Mon as well as the Hindu-Buddhist culture of the Khmers of neighboring Cambodia.

The Burmese appeared shortly after the kingdom of Nanchao defeated the Pyu. The remaining Pyu were absorbed into the Burmese as they settled in the region where the Irrawaddy and Chindwin Rivers meet. There the Burmese came into contact with the Mon and eventually conquered them. The victors, as is often the case, borrowed from the culture of the vanquished. In this way the Burmese became Buddhists. The person credited with the conversion of the Burmans to Theravada Buddhism was the eleventh-century king Anawrahta.

Expansion

During the thirteenth and fourteenth centuries Theravada Buddhism spread to Thailand, Cambodia, and Laos. As news of a revival of Theravada Buddhism in Sri Lanka in the twelfth century reached Southeast Asia, monks began to travel, with the support of local rulers, to the Theravada Buddhist centers in Sri Lanka, such as the Mahavihara monastery in Anuradhapura. They returned and began to proselytize, and Theravada Buddhism gained dominance in Thai society, pushing aside the influences of Hindu and Buddhist Mahayana cults. At the end of the thirteenth century Buddhism was still growing in importance in Myanmar.

Theravada Buddhism and Statecraft

Theravada Buddhism (the way of the elders) differs from Mahayana Buddhism in several significant areas. Pali is the sacred language of the Theravada school rather than Sanskrit, which is used in the Mahayana school. Thus, one finds the Pali words *dhamma, kamma,* and *nibbana* in place of the Sanskrit words *dharma* (divine law), *karma* (the force generated by a person's actions and held to perpetuate transmigration and to determine the nature of a person's next existence), and *nirvana* (the final beatitude that transcends suffering and is sought through the extinction of desire and consciousness). Theravada Buddhism emphasizes reproducing "the teachings that embody the way of salvation taught by the Buddha in precisely the same form from generation to generation ever since the original elders recited them" (Keyes 1987, 33). In addition, whereas the Mahayana school believes in numerous bodhisattvas (deities), the Theravada school believes that there was one bodhisattva—that is, the Buddha—and that one—Matreiya—is yet to come. It should be noted that the central concept among Theravada Buddhists is *kamma*, not *nibbana*.

Early Southeast Asian statecraft (the art of conducting state affairs) was marked by personal achievement. The ruler was a mediator, one who was accessible and able to maintain order and stability. Such rulers did not seek to develop political institutions as much as to initiate religious cults in which their subjects would be able to benefit from the rulers' relationship with local and universal sources of power. Yet, religion was never the exclusive concern of rulers.

Unlike Hindu kings, who had authority based on their divine status, Buddhist rulers in Southeast Asia were not divine, and their authority was based on personal achievement *and* their adherence to a system of morality—that is, they had to combine morality with power. Although it would seem that Mahayana Buddhism would be better suited to such rulers, particularly with the concept of the bodhisattva, Theravada

Buddhism was embraced for what Professor of Comparative Religions Trevor Ling calls "its socially and culturally cohesive qualities" (Ling 1979, 29). The other major institution in Theravadin societies is the *sangha*—the community of monks. Kings supported such communities and sought to be seen as not only the protectors of the *sangha* but also as propagators of Theravada. A symbiosis existed between the political aspect of the state and the religious aspect. (Such a distinction is artificial and reflective more of modern Western thinking.)

Sangha

The *sangha* is composed of boys and men; women cannot become members. Theravadin Buddhists believe that every male should spend some time as a member of the *sangha*, first by becoming a novice as a boy. Novices learn to read Buddhist texts, to write (in order to copy such texts), and to memorize chants used in rituals. Being a monk for a short time is believed to instill a high moral sense that will remain with the person after leaving the *sangha*. As a result, generally speaking, in both countries the *sangha* did not become an elite institution. Rather than acquire members from the nobility, the *sangha* acquired most of its members from rural villages.

Some persons remain in the *sangha* as monks, either to become better instructed about the *dhamma* or to engage in activities leading to enlightenment, including meditation. Far more monks have devoted themselves to the study of texts than have become expert in meditation.

The word "*sangha*" refers to the monastic institution and not to the physical location of Buddhist rituals and practice. Shrines, temples, and monasteries serve as the center of religious activities.

Local Elements and Theravada Buddhism

As in other societies that have embraced Theravada Buddhism, local beliefs and practices have been retained in Myanmar and Thailand. Buddhism provides the transcendent focus, and local religious beliefs give protection in day-to-day matters. In Myanmar the belief in the *nat* (spirit) and the use of magical amulets are examples of this distinction. Likewise, the Thais did not give up their beliefs in spirits *(phi)* and the essence *(khuan)* that animates each person. In addition, they retained the notion of a cosmic order. These beliefs were retained but subordinated to the orthodox Theravada doctrine of *kamma* and the teaching regarding enlightenment.

Texts

The Tripitaka (three baskets) of the *dhamma*, the Buddhist scriptures, does not perform the same role as the Qur'an (the book of sacred writings accepted as revelations made to Muhammad by Allah) for Muslims or the Bible for Protestant Christians. Most Thai Buddhists, either elite or peasants, gain their understanding of Buddhist teachings more from ritual presentations than from scriptural texts.

In Thailand three texts provide the basis for understanding the Theravadin view of the world: *Trai Phum Phra Ruang* (The Three Worlds According to Phra Ruang), *Phra Malai* (the story of a monk named Phra Malai), and *Maha Chat* (The Great Life). The first two works seek to make the doctrine of *kamma* understandable, whereas the third, in telling "birth stories" *(jataka)* of the Buddha, provides moral models for social relationships.

Although Myanmar and Thailand began the nineteenth century with new dynasties (Konbaung in Myanmar and Chakri in Thailand), their experiences in that century were different. Myanmar was taken in sections after a war with Britain that ended in 1885. Thailand, on the other hand, was never subject to European colonial rule. With the monarchy as a symbol of national unity and supporter of Buddhism, Thailand was involved in no major war or conflict during this period. These factors and others contributed to the different directions that Buddhism followed in each country.

The beginning of the Chakri dynasty was marked by a coup against Taksin, a general claiming to be a bodhisattva. His removal, aided by Buddhist leadership, placed another military leader on the throne, thus beginning what is known as the "Ratanakosin era," the era of the Emerald Buddha, which had been installed as the talisman of the kingdom. The fourth king of this dynasty, Mongkut (Rama IV), believing that the true message of Buddhism had become obscured, sought a purified *sangha*, which brought about a revival of Buddhism in Thailand. The efforts of Protestant missionaries and the spread of colonial power came to be seen as serious threats to Buddhism in each country. In response, people called for a new purification, which included a new interpretation of the Tripitaka and a more rigorous discipline among monks. Such reformation was successful in nineteenth-century Thailand. A fundamentalist form of Buddhism became an important component of emerging nationalism in Myanmar in the twentieth century.

With British rule in place, Myanmar experienced pressures that pulled at the threads of society. Buddhism was the common factor that held society together, "providing it with a worldview, a cosmology . . . and even a sense of identity as a people and a nation" (Matthews 1999, 27–28). Thus, Buddhism defined what it meant to be Burmese. Buddhist ideals came to be the foundations of emerging Burmese nationalism, perhaps the only unifying factor available. However, it was not able to accommodate to changes.

In Thailand nationalism was not tied to resisting a colonial power but rather to constructing the nation along Western models. In 1902 the *sangha* was made a national institution, recognized as one of the elements of the Thai state, along with the king, the officials, and the people. But the *sangha* is not wholly an instrument of the state because most of its members (monks) are recruited from local communities and rely on those communities for their support. The *sangha* has continued to be more concerned with and responsive to local than national interests. This has resulted in conflicts between the *sangha* and the government.

Differences between Burmese and Thai Buddhism

Although the people of Myanmar and Thailand share basic beliefs about the nature of the world, the ethical interpretations of those beliefs are different. Some of the differences are based in premodern practice, but most are based on the reforms in Thai Buddhism beginning in the middle of the nineteenth century. These reforms had different social implications.

In premodern practice both the Thais and the Burmans held to the Three Gems—the Buddha, the *dhamma*, and the *sangha*—and the practice of those actions that would accrue merit for future lives. Although each group "worshiped" the Buddha in the form of "reminders," Thais focused on images and the Burmans on stupas (shrines). Both groups believed in the temporary service of males as monks and offered alms to the members of the *sangha*. Thai Buddhism emphasizes the moral responsibility for one's present actions, in contrast to the emphasis of Burmese Buddhism on the limitations imposed on one's life based on actions in previous lives.

When Myanmar came under control of the British, the changes in Buddhist practice were strongly tied to opposition to the British presence. In Thailand the rethinking of Buddhism during the same time became the foundation for reform of the *sangha* supported by the state.

Post–World War II

After Myanmar gained independence in 1948, Prime Minister U Nu sought to restore Buddhism and the *sangha* to precolonial status, later seeking to make Buddhism the state religion, which did not take place until 1961. The *sangha* was becoming increasingly politically involved and gained in political stature. But the military takeover in 1962, led by General Ne Win, resulted in the *sangha* being totally cut off from political power and marginalized. Later, Ne Win sought to control the *sangha* through councils aimed at "reform." Due to governmental authority and interference, the *sangha* was forced to distance itself from the political arena. Upon Ne Win's resignation in 1988, monks participated in large numbers in demonstrations, when the military refused to relinquish control, but not in the violence accompanying the protests. Aung San Suu Kyi gave her famous speech at the Shwe Dagon, the central Buddhist shrine in Rangoon. The government has sought to control or crush all opposition, which came to include large numbers of monks.

In Thailand, by contrast, Buddhism remained a part of the national ideology dating back to King Chulalongkorn (1853–1910) and eventually became the national religion. However, after World War II, specifically after the coup in September 1957 and the authoritarian regime that lasted until 1973, the *sangha* was perceived to be a threat to the political order. The *sangha* was brought under closer state control and used by the various regimes since 1957 to promote governmental ideals, although not all members of the *sangha* have done so. Buddhism continues to inform the national consciousness in Thailand, and yet there is tolerance for different value systems.

Buddhism and War

Although Buddhism may be seen as a religion of peace, "Buddhist nations [including Myanmar and Thailand] in practice . . . are no strangers to the battlefield. They have frequently been found there, sometimes engaged in war with would-be conquerors and sometimes in aggressive imperial exploits of their own. In both cases Buddhist nation has been found warring against Buddhist nation" (Ling, 1979, xi).

This contradiction, if not confusion, is illustrated in positions taken by post–World War II Burmese leaders.

U Nu, on the one hand, stated, "Unlike the theistic creeds [Buddhism] cannot sanction (even) such acts of violence that are necessary for the preservation of public order and society" (Ling 1979, 135). On the other hand, another post–World War II Burmese leader, U Ba Swe expressed the view that Marxism and Buddhism are compatible and that a revolution program based on the two systems of thought was "very appropriate for Burma" (Ling 1979, 135). The history of Myanmar and Thailand clearly shows that U Ba Swe more accurately described the Buddhist position.

A number of explanations may be given to account for this apparent contradiction. The first explanation is that justification has been given for *national* participation in war. In a sermon at the coronation of King Rama VI of Thailand in 1910, the Buddhist patriarch reasoned that disputes will inevitably arise between people who live in countries that are near one another. These disputes may be over territory, the rights of their subjects, commerce, and other issues. In light of this reality, each country will find it necessary, even in times of peace, to be prepared to fight its enemies. The patriarch quoted some words of the Buddha to support his position: "As a town situated on the frontier must be prepared internally and externally, so too should you be prepared" (Ling 1979, 136–137). Recalling the past when all Thais were warriors, he lamented that with the separation of the military and the rest of society, civilians had "become totally inexperienced in warfare. . . ." (Ling 1979, 136–137) He praised the king for reversing this trend. The printed edition of this sermon stated that it is "an erroneous idea to suppose that the Buddha condemned all wars and people whose business it was to wage war" (Ling 1979, 136–137). Instead, the Buddha was seen as denouncing "intolerant and unreasoning hatred, vengeance and savagery which causes men to kill from sheer blood-lust" (Ling 1979, 136–137).

The second explanation is that the practice of peace and nonaggression has been limited to the arena of interpersonal relationships. The result has been that people in Myanmar and Thailand seek to live in such a way as to avoid incurring the displeasure of others. This means that overt expressions of aggression are often absent, with a variety of devices employed to avoid any direct, face-to-face conflict. On the surface personal encounters are marked by pleasantness but may also include "a high degree of brittleness" (Ling 1979, 141–142).

In terms of millenarian movements found in both countries, one finds another possible explanation to justify the use of violence to achieve one's ends. Anthropologist Charles Keyes has noted that *kamma* rather than *nibbana* is the governing principle of many Buddhists in Myanmar and Thailand. As such, violent struggle as seen in millenarian revolts in both countries need not affect negatively one's *kamma*. One is permitted to struggle, even employing violence, to improve one's life.

The Future

The current regime in Myanmar continues to restrict the activities of Buddhist monks. The government reportedly has imprisoned, tortured, and even killed monks who have campaigned for the freedoms of speech and association. Still, Buddhism continues to play an important role for the people of Myanmar with its strong tradition of social activism. Its potential to challenge political authority remains strong.

Buddhism and the monarchy remain central pillars of Thai society, with the king deriving certain political legitimacy and authority from his status as a Buddhist monarch. However, an increasingly secularized Thai public is unlikely to give unquestioning loyalty to the throne based on Buddhist precepts.

Damon L. Woods

Further Reading

Harris, I. (1999). Buddhism and politics in Asia: The textual and historical roots. In I. Harris (Ed.), *Buddhism and politics in twentieth-century Asia* (pp. 1–25). New York: Pinter.

Jackson, P. A. (1989). *Buddhism, legitimation, and conflict: The political functions of urban Thai Buddhism*. Singapore: Institute of Southeast Asian Studies.

Keyes, C. F. (1987). *Thailand, Buddhist kingdom as modern nation-state*. Boulder, CO: Westview Press.

Keyes, C. F. (1991). Buddhist economics and Buddhist fundamentalism in Burma and Thailand. In M. E. Marty & R. S. Appleby (Eds.), *Fundamentalisms and the state: Remaking politics, economies, and militance*. Chicago: University of Chicago Press.

King, W. L. (1989). *A thousand lives away: Buddhism in contemporary Burma*. Berkeley, CA: Asian Humanities Press.

Lester, R. C. (1973). *Theravada Buddhism in Southeast Asia*. Ann Arbor: University of Michigan Press.

Ling, T. (1979). *Buddhism, imperialism and war: Burma and Thailand in modern history*. London: George Allen & Unwin.

Matthews, B. (1999). The legacy of tradition and authority: Buddhism and the nation in Myanmar. In I. Harris (Ed.), *Buddhism and politics in twentieth-century Asia* (pp. 26–53). New York: Pinter.

Suksamran, S. (1976). *Political Buddhism in Southeast Asia: The role of the sangha in the modernization of Thailand.* New York: St. Martin's Press.

Swearer, D. K. (1999). Centre and periphery: Buddhism and politics in modern Thailand. In I. Harris (Ed.), *Buddhism and politics in twentieth-century Asia* (pp. 194–228). New York: Pinter.

Tambiah, S. J. (1976). *World conqueror and world renouncer: A study of Buddhism and polity in Thailand against a historical background.* Cambridge, UK: Cambridge University Press.

Buddhism: Taiwan

The spread of Buddhism from India to China occurred gradually as merchants, missionaries, and settlers made their way to the Middle Kingdom. Buddhism eventually made its way across the Formosa Strait to Formosa (now Taiwan) in the mid-seventeenth century as Chinese settlers from Fujian and Guangdong provinces in southeastern China began immigrating to Formosa to escape the chaos and confusion surrounding the collapse of the Ming dynasty (1368–1644).

The establishment of Buddhism on the island came slowly, as the Dutch governor-general (Formosa was then under Dutch control) discouraged the practice of Buddhism. It wasn't until 1662, when the Chinese military hero Zheng Chenggong (also known as Koxinga; 1624–1662) drove the Dutch out that Buddhism began to flourish. Zheng Chenggong's son established the first Buddhist temple on Taiwan. The Manchu Qing dynasty (1644–1912), which took control of China after the fall of the Ming, conquered the island in 1683; Buddhism flourished on Taiwan for much of the Qing dynasty.

In 1895, the Japanese occupied Taiwan and in doing so, brought Buddhism under Japanese oversight by requiring temples to register with local authorities. Most temples simply complied with the legislation hoping to retain control of their temples. Monasteries were closed and land confiscated as monks, nuns, and novices soon became corrupt. Soon thereafter, the Japanese authorities closed monasteries as well as confiscated adjacent landholdings when they exposed the rampant corruption of monks, nuns, and novices who had foresworn their vows of celibacy, choosing to marry. New organizations for Taiwanese Buddhist temples and lay groups were established by the Japanese to maintain control over the Buddhist religious community and the local population. These local religious organizations were meant to stabilize the political situation on Taiwan. The Japanese were defeated in 1945, and the governance of Taiwan went to the Nationalists (Kuomintang), who were at that point engaged in a civil war with the Communists. When the Communists proved victorious in 1949, the Kuomintang fled to Taiwan and declared their Taiwan-based Republic of China to be China's legitimate government. The Kuomintang integrated Buddhist temples and their affiliated organizations into the Kuomintang's local political organizations.

During the 1950s Buddhism in Taiwan underwent a renaissance of sorts, invigorated by the influx of refugee Buddhist monks and nuns from mainland China. Taiwanese monks and nuns, who had little Buddhist education, learned much from the Chinese Buddhist monks. Support for Buddhism grew steadily from 1950 to 1980 as Buddhism made inroads in Taiwanese society. Activities promoted or arranged by Buddhist groups, such as arranging health care for the poor, became increasingly visible. By the early 1980s, Buddhism was enjoying unparalleled growth. Buddhist lay organizations founded new schools, and Buddhist student groups became more active on college campuses across Taiwan. Buddhist monks and nuns became influential figures through engaging in social activism, such as the establishment of hospitals, schools, and orphanages. The Buddhist community remained neutral toward the authoritarian government.

Most modern Taiwanese Buddhists practice either Chan (Japanese: Zen) Buddhism or Pure Land Buddhism. The popularity of these schools is due largely to the influence of the monks and nuns who came to Taiwan following the Communist victory on the mainland.

Keith A. Leitich

See also Buddhism: China

Further Reading

Davidson, G. M., & Reed, B. E. (1998). *Culture and customs of Taiwan.* Westport, CT: Greenwood Press.

Davidson, J. (1988). *The island of Formosa: Past and present.* Oxford, UK: Oxford University Press.

Della Santini, P. (1988). *The tree of enlightenment: An introduction to the major traditions of Buddhism*. Taipei, Taiwan: Corporate Body of the Buddha Educational Foundation.

Hsing, L. F. (1983). *Taiwanese Buddhism and Buddhist temples*. Taipei, Taiwan: Pacific Cultural Foundation.

Jones, C. B. (1947). *Buddhism in Taiwan*. Taichung, Taiwan: Bodhedrum Publications.

Jones, C. B. (1999). *Buddhism in Taiwan: Religion and the state, 1660–1990*. Honolulu, HI: University of Hawaii Press.

Buddhism: Tibet

The physical and cultural contrasts between the bleak landscape of Central Asia and the distinctive Tibetan religious architecture, and between Tibetan Buddhism's meditative philosophy and its terrifying paintings have fascinated Americans and Europeans for a long time. Many clichés have blurred Westerners' understanding of Tibetan Buddhism. Lhasa used to be called the Forbidden City; from this capital city of the Land of Snow, the Dalai Lama was supposed to rule a mountain kingdom that geography and religious fanaticism had always isolated. In reality, Tibet has served for centuries as a cultural and commercial crossroad with connections to Kathmandu and Calcutta in the south, Chengdu in the east, Lanzhou and Beijing further north, and the oasis cities of the Silk Road. Caravans needed two months to cover the distance from Lhasa to the Silk Road and two weeks to reach the Indian border. The isolation of Tibet is therefore quite relative, even if the environment of Tibet is dramatically uncompromising.

The Geography and Demography of Tibet

As a physical entity, Tibet is defined by its size, elevation, aridity, and desolation. The collision of the Indian and Asian plates that began 50 million years ago has yielded extremely high and complex mountain ranges that prevent the monsoon rains from entering Tibet and Central Asia. The largest, harshest, and highest plateau in the world, with a mean elevation of 4,900 meters, occupies the center of Tibet. Its surface remains frozen eight months a year. The Tibetan valleys may be as low as 3,600 meters, which allows some agriculture, but the mountains that surround them are as high as 7,300 meters. The Himalaya and Karakoram mountains, the highest ranges in the world, are not to be found on the central plateau, but on its southern and western margins. The Indus, Zangbo/Bramaputra, Salween, Mekong, Jinsha (Chang, or Yangtze) and Huang (Yellow) rivers are among the major rivers of Asia that flow from the Tibetan plateau to the Indian and Pacific oceans.

Outside the international borders of China, Tibetan-speaking areas cover most of Bhutan and Sikkim as well as districts in Nepal, India, and Pakistan. Within China, Tibetan populations live in Xizang, Qinghai, southern Xinjiang, Gansu, western Sichuan, and northern Yunnan. The provinces of Tsang, Amdo, and Kham form historical Tibet, a vast area of 2.5 million square kilometers. The Chinese government has divided historical Tibet into different prefectures and provinces since 1950. Six prefectures administer the Tibetan Autonomous Region (TAR) of Xizang, which was created in 1965. The TAR corresponds to former Tsang and western Kham. Chinese statistics on Tibet do not merge together data on Xizang and the Tibetan-speaking areas of the other provinces of the People's Republic of China.

Population in historical Tibet is estimated to now be 6 million Tibetans and 7.5 million Han Chinese, most of whom inhabit Kham (Sichuan and Qinghai provinces) and Amdo (Gansu and Qinghai provinces). Most Tibetans live in small and scattered communities, all located in the sheltered valleys south and east of the central plateau. Lhasa, the capital of the TAR, is a large city whose inhabitants are largely Han Chinese immigrants, although government figures say the opposite. Lhasa has held a special significance for Tibetan pilgrims because the Dalai Lama, who is believed by Tibetan Buddhists to be the reincarnation of Chenserig (Sanskrit: Avalokitesvara), the Bodhisattva of Compassion, traditionally resided there. The fourteenth Dalai Lama (b. 1935) fled Lhasa in 1959 and has since established a government-in-exile in Dharamsala, India. Some 120,000 Tibetans are political refugees abroad, mostly in India.

Tibet in History and the Role of Religion in the Government

Most Tibetans view themselves as *Bod-pa* (Bhotia) people, or peaceful farmers who do not miss an opportunity for trade. Until 1909, when the explorer Sven Hedin published a sympathetic travel account, foreigners had a poor opinion of Tibetans. They frequently

Tibetan Buddhists and Chinese Rulers

The following description by two Christian missionaries of the killing of a Buddhist lama by Chinese officials illustrates the conflict and violence that have characterized Tibetan Buddhist-Chinese relations for centuries.

The Emperor Khang-Hi, during the great military expedition which he made in the west against the Oelets [Ölet], one day, in traversing the Blue Town, expressed a wish to pay a visit to the Guison-Tamba, at that time the Grand Lama of the Five Towers. The latter received the Emperor without rising from the throne, or manifesting any kind of respect. Just as Khang-Hi drew near to speak to him, a *Kiang-Kian*, or high military Mandarin, indignant at this unceremonious treatment of his master, drew his saber, fell upon the Guison-Tamba, and laid him dead on the steps of his throne. This terrible event roused the whole Lamasery, and indignation quickly communicated itself to all the Lamas of the Blue Town.

They ran to arms in every quarter, and the life of the Emperor, who had but a small retinue, was exposed to the greatest danger. In order to calm the irritation of the Lamas, he publicly reproached the *Kiang-Kian* with his violence. "If the Guison-Tamba," answered the *Kiang-Kian*, "was not a living Buddha, why did he not rise in the presence of the master of the universe? If he was a living Buddha, how was it he did not know I was going to kill him?" Meanwhile the danger to the life of the Emperor became every moment more imminent; he had no other means of escape than that of taking off his imperial robes, and attiring himself in the dress of a private solider. Under favour of this disguise, and the general confusion, he was enabled to rejoin his army, which was near at hand. The greater part of the men who had accompanied the Emperor into the Blue Town were massacred, and among the rest, the murderer of the Guison-Tamba.

***Source:* Huc, Evariste-Régis, & Gabet, Joseph. (1987). *Travels in Tartary, Thibet and China, 1844–1846.* New York: Dover, pp. 150–151.**

complained about the Tibetan wild brigands who were given to raiding and stealing. In 1720, China swiftly conquered Tibet, which in effect became a protectorate placed under the supervision of *ambans*, representatives who Beijing appointed in Lhasa. The Qing dynasty (1644–1912) implemented a policy of surveillance and control in 1788: Foreigners from the neighboring countries were tolerated in Lhasa as long as they were either Buddhist or Hindu pilgrims or Muslim traders. Russian and European scientific missions were routinely expelled from Tibet. This isolationist policy ended brutally in 1904 when Francis Younghusband (1863–1942), at the head of the British military expedition, entered Lhasa to impose a commercial treaty and more respect for international law. Sent from Beijing, a second military expedition entered Lhasa in 1950, reestablishing China's control of Tibet in a more direct fashion than that imposed by the Qing emperors. In that sense Tibet only ceased being a secluded country in the past half-century, but from another viewpoint the country stopped being a remote entity many centuries ago, with the diffusion of Buddhism. Its kings and later its Dalai Lamas played at times a major role in Central Asian affairs as they were engaged in alliances with the Chinese, Mongol, and Manchu empires.

Western scholars have all been impressed by the absolute domination of religion in Tibetan political life. Tibet is solidly Buddhist, although its brand of Buddhism includes several traditional elements that introduce some diversity in practices and rituals. Anthropologists have commented on the lack of social cohesion and the emphasis on individual salvation evident in Tibet, which contrasts with Buddhism elsewhere in Asia. Sociologists of religion have argued that the Buddhist religion of Tibet has features that differentiate the Tibetan society both from other Buddhist and from Hindu societies. The combination of two characteristics is considered unique: Monasteries provide the structures of secular power in Tibet, and their spiritual leaders are the only source of legitimacy because they have magical powers denied to others. The influence yielded by the dignitaries of the Tibetan church to the Dalai Lama has not resulted in the coalescence of an effective central authority. The Panchen Lama is not subject to the Dalai Lama, although the two dignitaries belong to the same church and are geographically neighbors. Far away from Lhasa, the Kumbum monastery in Amdo similarly recognizes the Dalai Lama's religious supremacy but remains autonomous in all affairs. The Dalai Lama's administration supervised and taxed only a minority of Tibetans in south-central Tibet until 1950. Tibet should therefore be regarded as a stateless society instead of a theocracy.

Historians provide explanations for why the powerful Tibetan church failed to engender an efficient state that would have unified all Tibetans within the same political framework. In the seventh century, the Tibetan King Srong-btsan sGam-po, or Songtsen Gampo (c. 608–650, reigned 629–650), unified Tibet and married two princesses, one Chinese and one Nepalese, who were both Buddhists. These state marriages may have accelerated the introduction of Buddhism and the use of an Indian alphabet. The Potala Temple of Lhasa and the oldest monasteries of Tibet date from the seventh century, which was a time of great expansion of Buddhism throughout Central and East Asia. The Indian school of Buddhism had become the official religion of Tibet by the end of the eighth century. Famous monasteries developed considerable influence as Tibetan Buddhism flourished with the establishment of the shamanistic Nyingmapa order. During the eleventh century the Kagyupa and Sakyapa orders monopolized all functions in society. The power held by the hereditary families in the Sakyapa or Red Hat Church aroused resentment over time. Attempts at reform during the fourteenth and fifteenth centuries resulted in the emergence of the dGe-lugs-pa, or Gelugpa, order also called "Yellow Hat Church," founded by Tsong-kha-pa, or Tsongkhapa (1357–1419). The third leader of the Gelugpa church received from the Mongols the title of Dalai Lama, which means "Ocean of Wisdom." Many monasteries were built or rebuilt during the reign of the fifth Dalai Lama (1617–1682), including the Potala and Labrang. The Gelugpa priests are committed to celibacy and poverty. The first pledge has reinforced the reincarnation doctrine since the new heads of the church must be found among toddlers away from Lhasa and not within the same dynastic families as was the case previously. The second pledge has added to the influence the monasteries had in Tibet's political and economic life since donations were encouraged to support their large resident populations. These institutions provided venues for education, justice, health care, and trade fairs. Together, these features have prevented the birth of the independent civil society since no center of administration existed outside the prestigious monasteries. In that respect, Tibet is different from other Buddhist countries.

Tibetan Buddhism's Tenets and Warfare

During its phase of expansion throughout Central, East, and Southeast Asia, Buddhism came in contact with local religions whose values and rituals eventually found themselves encompassed by the new native Buddhist churches. The ancient Bön religion, a Tibetan form of shamanism, had little impact on Buddhism when it entered the country, and instead was transformed by the newer religion. Buddhist institutions were usually not confrontational and accepted uncritically society as it was, "even serving as a spiritual tranquilizer for the oppressed peasantry by promising happiness in the world to come" (Kitagawa 1962, 4). In Buddhist countries, the king acted as head of state and protector of the monastic orders. In Tibet however, Buddhism turned the country into a theocracy that granted the Dalai Lama both spiritual and temporal power. As head of the Tibetan church, the Dalai Lama is subordinate to no one. This principle was not so absolute after Tibet became a dependency of the Qing empire, and it never was admitted by the Republican and Communist governments of China.

Passion for spiritual satisfaction does not preclude more violent forms of passion for power. Internal warfare has filled the history of Tibet since at least the country submitted to the Mongol empire in 1207. Wars imposed by foreign powers were less common. The brief 1240 Mongol expedition against Tibet, just like the British expedition of 1904, was a reconnaissance maneuver carefully planned to serve long-range objectives. Despite their limited scale, since only two monasteries were plundered in 1240, both expeditions wanted to ascertain the identity of Tibetan leaders and deny neighboring empires (Song China or Tsarist Russia) the control of the Tibet. The Mongol raid eventually resulted in the fusion of the religious hierarchy and political power even if Tibet remained fragmented. The British excursion created a division between the reformist Thirteenth Dalai Lama who had traveled abroad and the conservative clergy of Lhasa. The Dalai Lama tried to create the modern army Tibet needed to back claims for independence. Although successful, the Tibetan campaigns in Kham in 1918 and 1931 revealed how obstructive and provincial the hierarchy remained.

Violence in Domestic Laws

One of the outside world's most enduring images of Tibetan Buddhism, maybe the most popular one, is that it is a peace-loving religion that preaches nonviolence. Tibetan Buddhism's views on warfare are discussed above, but even with regard to internal affairs, the historical record tells a different story. Several Dalai Lamas died mysteriously when they turned eighteen years old and reached majority. Regents who did not kill conspirers fast enough languished in jail. The Fifth Dalai Lama and his son were vicious despots who murdered the powerful abbots of rival sects. Violence was not limited to the factions surrounding the Dalai and Panchen Lamas. Harsh Tibetan laws sought to deter and punish criminality through the flogging, amputating, branding, exiling, or executing of the offenders. An eighteenth-century traveler noted that the gallows is always standing in Tibet. Thieves were flogged, branded, and had their hands cut off; those who helped them had their mouths slit open on either side (de Filippi 1932, 174).

Tibetan Buddhism in the Twenty-First Century

Like other religions, Tibetan Buddhism provides systematic information on the nature of the world, on spiritual practice, and on the ways in which the individual should behave in society. We live in an infinite universe and are sentenced to an endless cycle of births and deaths if we do not take the path to liberation. Historically speaking, Tibetan Buddhism does not appear as a particularly peace-loving religion. The current Dalai Lama, who incarnates Avalokitesvara or the Bodhisattva of Compassion, has frequently spoken on nonviolence and published popular books on wisdom, happiness, and the meaning of life. The future Dalai Lama will probably amplify this trend in Tibetan Buddhism, which has helped in making Tibet a popular cause in the West.

Philippe Forêt

See also Buddhism: China; Buddhism: India

Further Reading

Batchelor, S. (1998). *The Tibet guide: Central and western Tibet*. Somerville, MA: Wisdom Publications.

de Filippi, F. (Ed.). (1932). *An account of Tibet: The travels of Ippolito Desideri of Pistoia, S. J., 1712–1727*. London: Routledge.

Dodin, T., & Raether, H. (Eds.). (2001). *Imagining Tibet: Perceptions, projections and fantasies*. Somerville, MA: Wisdom Publications.

Fletcher, J. (1979). A brief history of the Chinese northwestern frontier. China Proper's northwest frontier: Meeting place of four cultures. In M.E. Alonso (Ed.), *China's inner Asian frontiers: Photographs of the Wulsin expedition to northwest China in 1923*. Cambridge, MA: Peabody Museum of Archaeology and Ethnology, Harvard University Press.

Harrer, H. (1996). *Seven years in Tibet*. New York: Tarcher/Putman. (Original German work, *Sieben Jahre in Tibet*, published 1953)

Hedin, S. (1909). *Trans-Himalaya: Discoveries and adventures in Tibet*. London: Macmillan and Company.

Kitagawa, J. M. (1962). Buddhism and Asian Politics. *Asian Affairs*, 2(5), 1–11.

Lattimore, O. (1962). *Inner Asian frontiers of China*. Boston: Beacon Press.

Lopez, D. S. Jr. (1998). *Prisoner of Shangri-La. Tibetan Buddhism and the West*. Chicago: University of Chicago Press.

Rhie, M. M., & Thurman, R. A. F. (1991). *Wisdom and compassion: The sacred art of Tibet*. New York: Harry N. Abrams.

Rockhill, W. W. (1891). *The land of the lamas: Notes of a journey through China, Mongolia and Tibet*. New York: The Century Co.

Samuel, G. (1982). Tibet as stateless society and some Islamic parallels. *Journal of Asian Studies, 42*(2), 215–229.

Smith, W. W. Jr. (1996). *Tibetan nation: A history of Tibetan nationalism and Sino-Tibetan relations*. Boulder, CO: Westview Press.

Stein, R.A. (1996). *La civilisation tibétaine*. [Tibetan Civilization]. Paris: L'Asiathèque, 1996.

Tournadre, N., & Dorje, S. (1998). *Manuel de tibétain standard: Langue et civilisation*. [Handbook of standard Tibetan: Language and Civilization]. Paris: l'Asiathèque.

Tucci, G. (1987). *To Lhasa and beyond*. Ithaca, NY: Snow Lion Publications. (Original French work, *A Lhasa e oltre*, published 1956)

Waddell, L. A. (1988). *Lhasa and its mysteries, with a record of the British Tibetan expedition of 1903–1904*. New York: Dover Publications. (Original work published 1905)

Byzantine-Muslim War of 645

In 645 CE a struggle broke out between forces of the Byzantine Empire and the emerging Islamic empire. At stake was the control of Egypt. Formerly a Byzantine province, Egypt was invaded in 639 by Muslim forces who expelled the Byzantines and established a capital at Al-Fustat near present-day Cairo. The conflict of 645 took place in and around the coastal city of Alexandria, the former Byzantine capital in Egypt, which had come under Muslim control in 642. The war of 645 remains one of the lesser-known conflicts associated with the early Islamic expansion, yet it was an episode of the utmost importance, helping to set in motion the cultural transformation of the region.

The Byzantine Reoccupation of Alexandria and the Muslim Counterattack

The war began with the Byzantine reoccupation of Alexandria in late 645. Constans II (630–668 CE) the Byzantine emperor, apparently ordered the campaign after receiving letters from city leaders in Alexandria imploring him to reclaim the area and release its largely Christian population from Muslim rule. The letter-writers noted that Alexandria was weakly guarded and therefore unlikely to hold out in the face of a surprise Byzantine attack. In response, Constans sent a fleet consisting of perhaps as many as three hundred vessels to Alexandria under the leadership of a commander named Manuel the Eunuch. As predicted, the Byzantine soldiers encountered only slight resistance. Alexandria's defense had been left in the hands of just one garrison of around a thousand soldiers, most of whom were slaughtered when the Byzantines entered the city.

The Muslim military response to the reoccupation was led by ʿAmr ibn al-ʿAs (d. 663 CE), who had commanded the initial Muslim incursion into Egypt in 639 and governed the province for a time after the conquest. Rather than launch an immediate counterattack on Alexandria, ʿAmr challenged Manuel to lead his forces against the army he had assembled near the town of Nikiou. Manuel accepted and the two armies met soon after, engaging in battle under the walls of a fortress and near the canal that ran by the town. The fighting was intense. At one point ʿAmr had to dismount and fight on foot when his horse was wounded by an arrow, yet he nevertheless survived the battle. The Muslim army eventually proved to be the stronger of the two, and the Byzantines were forced to retreat to Alexandria. The pursuing Muslims besieged the city, setting up camp outside its eastern walls.

The siege was broken in the summer of 646 CE when the Muslims finally managed to enter the city, possibly due to the treason of a guard who is believed to have unlocked the city's gates in exchange for his own safety. The Muslim soldiers charged through the streets, killing and plundering as they went. Fires were lit during the chaos and among the landmarks destroyed by a blaze that ruined the city's eastern quarter was the historic Church of St. Mark. A mosque named the Mosque of Mercy was later built near the center of Alexandria to mark the spot where ʿAmr is said to have finally halted the rampage. Although some of the Byzantine soldiers managed to escape to their ships and set sail, most, including their leader Manuel, died in the battle for Alexandria.

The Role of Religion

On the surface, the Byzantine campaign against the Muslims might have seemed an attempt to liberate fellow Christians from Islamic rule, and this was certainly a rationale the Byzantines used. In reality, the war was more political than religious in nature, being essentially a struggle by two foreign powers for control of this productive and strategically important region. Relations between the Byzantines and the inhabitants of their former province were poor. The local people, mostly Coptic Christians, had endured persecution in the past because they adhered to a doctrine of belief other than the official Byzantine doctrine. Also, following the reoccupation of Alexandria the Byzantine soldiers acted more like conquerors than liberators, plundering the city and surrounding villages. Despite lingering loyalty from some quarters, there was therefore no widespread enthusiasm for a return to Byzantine rule.

As the Byzantines became less popular, a groundswell of support for the new Islamic regime began to appear. During this early period few attempts were made to impose the Islamic faith on the people. As a result, religious freedom was actually greater than it had been under the Christian Byzantines. After the war had ended, the Muslims also showed leniency toward those guilty of rebellion coupled with generosity toward the people as a whole. A case in point was ʿAmr's response to the discovery that, contrary to expectations, many locals had resisted the Byzantines and aided the Muslims during the conflict. Filled with remorse at not having prevented the destruction caused by the Byzantine army, he ordered that full compensation be paid to those whose property had been lost or damaged. Gestures such as this helped to ensure the increasing acceptance of Muslim rule.

Consequences of the War

The conflict alerted Muslim leaders to the need for a larger fighting force in Egypt. As a result, thousands more troops were sent to the region. Alexandria became especially heavily fortified, with perhaps 27,000 men stationed in the city during the 661–680 caliphate of Muʿawiyah I (c. 602–680 CE). Work also began immediately in Egypt and in Syria on the first Muslim naval vessels. The ease with which the Byzantine forces had been able to reoccupy Alexandria made clear to the Muslims the vulnerability of their coastal territories. Naval warfare, previously viewed as a foreign concept, quickly became integral to the empire's defense. Nine years after the war, when Constans sent another fleet to Alexandria in a last attempt to retake the city, the Muslims were able to confront their enemy at sea and prevent the Byzantine fleet from reaching land. Although the Byzantines continued to raid other coastal towns in the region, Alexandria became so well defended that further attacks were deterred.

Another consequence of the war was an increase in immigration to Egypt by Arab Muslim civilians. Space limitations in Al-Fustat led to the creation of new settlements, beginning with a new fortified quarter named Al-Jizah (Giza), located on the west bank of the Nile. Soon, encouraging Muslim immigration to the region became official policy, being an effective method of hastening Egypt's incorporation into the Islamic empire. Indeed, within the Islamic community Muslim immigrants were referred to as *amdad* or *madadiyyun*, literally meaning "reinforcements." Immigration also accelerated the spread of the Islamic faith and the emerging Islamic culture, which led in turn to the gradual decline of Coptic Christianity and the Greco-Roman civilization associated with the Byzantines.

Following its initial conquest Alexandria acquired a special symbolic significance for Muslims as a *ribat*, or fortified military and religious outpost. This significance became much stronger after the city was almost lost in 645. Muslims perceived the defense of the city as critical to the future of the Islamic empire. Jihad (holy war) and *fadaʿil* (praise) literature from that time refers frequently to Alexandria, along with other coastal towns also at risk from attack, extolling the willingness of Muslim soldiers and settlers to die in its defense.

In a sense, the Byzantine-Muslim War of 645 CE was merely a temporary setback in the sweeping early Islamic expansion. The conflict was of critical importance, however, determining once and for all which of the two foreign powers would control Egypt. When the Byzantine forces lost the battle for Alexandria in 646, they effectively lost the battle for the entire region—a significant loss to the Byzantine Empire. The conflict also brought about additional far-reaching consequences. For the Muslim conquerors, the shock of near-defeat brought about more vigorous efforts to defend Egypt and fully incorporate the region into the Islamic empire. For these reasons, the war of 645 was every bit as significant as the initial Muslim conquest, marking the ascension of Islam as a political and religious force in Egypt.

Diane Rixon

Further Reading

Athamina, K. (1997). Some administrative, military, and socio-political aspects of early Muslim Egypt. In Y. Lev (Ed.), *War and society in the eastern Mediterranean, 7th–15th centuries* (pp 101–113). Leiden, Netherlands: E. J. Brill.

Butler, A. J. (1978). *The Arab conquest of Egypt and the last thirty years of the Roman dominion* (2nd ed.; P. M. Fraser, Ed.). Oxford, UK: Clarendon Press.

Donner, F. M. (1981). *The early Islamic conquests*. Princeton, NJ: Princeton University Press.

Gabrieli, F. (1968). *Muhammad and the conquests of Islam* (V. Luling & R. Linell, Trans.). New York: McGraw-Hill.

Jenkins, R. J. H. (1967). *Byzantium: The imperial centuries, A.D. 610–1071*. New York: Random House.

Kaegi, W. E. (1992). *Byzantium and the early Islamic conquests*. New York: Cambridge University Press.

C

China *See* Buddhism: China; Buddhism: Taiwan; Buddhism: Tibet; Confucianism, Classical; Confucianism: Han Dynasty; Confucianism, Modern; Confucianism, Neo-Confucianism; Daoism, Classical; Daoism, Huang-Lao; Daoism, Medieval; Daoism, Modern

Christian Identity

Christian Identity is an influential religious faith among white supremacists. However, it is not organized as a denomination and has no central institutions. This makes Identity a community with unclear boundaries, knit together by beliefs that have a family resemblance to one another. Its significance lies in its emphasis on a history-ending, apocalyptic race war. This commitment to struggle exists within a racial theology.

The beliefs most commonly associated with Christian Identity are the following: (1) persons of northwestern European ancestry are considered the direct, biological descendants of the biblical tribes of Israel; (2) Jews are regarded as the offspring, through Cain, of a sexual liaison between Eve and Satan; and (3) the present is believed to be at or near the end-times, which will feature a final battle between "Israelites" (i.e., "Aryans", or white northern Europeans) on the one hand, and Jews and non-whites on the other. These doctrines have been used as a justification for attacks on non-Aryans and, in the most sweeping Identity scenarios, as a divine imperative for race war.

History

The immediate origins of Christian Identity lie in the British-Israel (or Anglo-Israel) movement, which developed in Great Britain during the second half of the nineteenth century and subsequently spread to other parts of the English-speaking world, including the United States. British-Israelism asserted that the inhabitants of the British Isles as well as descendants of northwestern Europeans in general were direct offspring of the "ten lost tribes of Israel." The tribes, they believed, had wandered north and west to eventually populate Great Britain and adjacent areas. British-Israelism was initially well disposed toward the Jewish people, whom they saw as literal relatives. Nonetheless, twentieth-century British-Israelism became increasingly anti-Semitic, particularly in the United States and Western Canada.

Christian Identity began to emerge as a distinct religious tendency in America after World War II. Its separation from British-Israelism, however, was never complete. Some American groups continued to advance a highly anti-Semitic Anglo-Israelism, adding only a belief in the satanic ancestry of Jews. Christian Identity's initial nucleus was made up of three preachers in Southern California: Bertrand Comparet, William Potter Gale, and Wesley Swift. All were closely associated with the anti-Semitic political organizer Gerald L. K. Smith.

Identity gradually spread from its West Coast beginnings, but, like British-Israelism, it never developed a denominational structure. Consequently, it appeared in many variants, including not only varying religious styles but also different styles of right-wing extremism.

These have included neo-Nazi groups, such as Aryan Nations; some Ku Klux Klan organizations; and local paramilitary groups, such as elements of the Posse Comitatus and militias. Hence Identity now overlaps upon many other styles of extremist organization. Right-wing extremists who do not consider themselves Identity believers may consequently work with Identity followers and absorb some Identity beliefs.

While Identity may be found throughout the country, it has been weakest in the Northeast and historically strongest in the Ozarks, southern Appalachians, Southwest, and Pacific Northwest. More recently, clusters have emerged in southern Ohio and central Pennsylvania. Because of its fragmented character, all estimates of total size have been guesses based upon such factors as the known size of some groups, the number of groups, and periodicals and websites. These estimates generally cover a substantial range—from about 10,000 to 100,000—but even the upper limits suggest a movement that remains extremely small. Its influence, however, has been greater than its size might suggest.

Political Activities

The political orientations of Christian Identity adherents have ranged from complete withdrawal from American society to violent engagement with it. Withdrawal has taken the form of *survivalism*, i.e., the cultivation of a lifestyle marked by both physical withdrawal and self-sufficiency. Those who adopt such a lifestyle have sometimes done so both as individual families and as small communities.

Communal separation has had varied political consequences. In some cases, such as that of Pastor Dan Gayman's Church of Israel in Schell, Missouri, it has been accomplished with minimum friction with the authorities. In other cases, however, the separation has been accompanied by conflict. A case in point was that of the Freemen of Montana, who were predominantly Identity followers and whose compound near Jordan, Montana, was the scene of a standoff with the FBI in 1996. The most militarized such community was Zarephath-Horeb in the Arkansas Ozarks, organized by a group called the Covenant, Sword and Arm of the Lord, led by James Ellison. Ellison's communal settlement included sophisticated military training, automatic weapons, electrically controlled minefields, and preparations for chemical warfare—all in anticipation of apocalyptic chaos. Although the organization as such never attacked outsiders, individual members committed or attempted murders, sabotage, and arson. Large-scale violence was averted when the community surrendered to a federal taskforce in 1985.

While most Identity believers appear to live in ways that do not bring them into conflict with the authorities, the exceptions have occurred among those who believe in the inevitability of a war between "Aryan Israelites" on one side and Jews and non-whites on the other. While some survivalists believe such a war will eventually take place, others in Identity have felt compelled to try to set the struggle off through deliberate violent acts. The most dramatic case was that of "The Order" (also called "The Silent Brotherhood" or "Bruders Schweigen") which, in the mid-1980s, engaged in a brief insurgency against the federal government consisting largely of a series of bank robberies and one murder. While only about half the organization's members were Identity believers, those who were saw such an undertaking as consistent with their religious commitments.

Since the late 1980s, more vigorous government intelligence gathering and prosecutions have reduced the propensity of Identity followers to engage in violence. However, since an unknown number of Identity believers are members of paramilitary groups, it is extremely difficult to determine the degree of Identity influence in these organizations.

The 1990s presented particularly acute challenges to Christian Identity. By this decade, the leadership generation that had assumed its roles in the 1950s and 1960s had died or was on the verge of retirement. The 1995 bombing of the Oklahoma City Federal Building greatly increased public concern about right-wing terrorism. Although it was never clear whether Timothy McVeigh had significant Christian Identity associations, the bombing made the anti-government subculture a major public concern for the first time. Partly in response to these stresses, the label *Christian Identity* itself has fallen out of favor within the movement (indeed, there were always Identity figures who used other terms, such as *Kingdom Message*).

Beliefs

Because of their conviction that they are the biological descendants of the biblical Israelites, Identity believers think of themselves as God's elect, the instruments for the fulfillment of His will on earth. British-Israelism held a similar view, but tended to identify nations, especially Great Britain and the United States, as the divine agents. Identity has been much more overtly racial, imputing to whites a special status in the divine scheme and implicitly or explicitly devaluing non-whites.

A theology of anti-Semitism lies at the heart of Christian Identity, for whom Jews are essentially non-white. More significantly, they see Jews as impostors, masquerading as Israelite descendants. The most fully developed version of this theology—found in such Identity writers as Wesley Swift, William Potter Gale, and Dan Gayman—is its so-called two-seed theology. According to the two-seed theory, Adam and Eve were the parents of Abel and Seth, but not of Cain. Cain's parents were supposedly Eve and Satan, Satan having seduced Eve in the Garden of Eden. Identity regards the Jews as the literal, biological descendants of Satan, through Cain. Hence they posit a continuing state of war between the white seed line of Adam and the diabolical seed line of Cain. Identity theology assumes blacks and other non-whites have resulted from separate creations in which Adam and Eve were not involved.

Identity Millennialism

Christian Identity followers believe the war between the seed lines is reaching its climax. This leads to an end-time scenario conceived in terms of race war (again, based upon Identity's view of Jews as racially non-white). Again, this view of history has been used to support both radical withdrawal and violent engagement. It can be used to justify survivalism, in which Identity believers seek separation in order to avoid the dangers of conflict in the last days; and it can be used to justify violent attacks on Jews, non-whites, and governmental authority, on the grounds that Satanic forces are poised to destroy God's people.

These differing orientations toward the end-times can be better understood in terms of Identity's relationship to broader millenarian currents in American society. While Identity is sometimes considered part of Christian fundamentalism, it in fact is quite different. The relationship between Christian Identity and Protestant Fundamentalism has generally been one of mutual hostility. That is because they differ radically about two important theological issues: the role of the Jewish people and the doctrine of the Rapture.

The great majority of Protestant Fundamentalists accept the millenarian system devised in the late nineteenth century by John Nelson Darby called *dispensational premillennialism*. It was Darby's contention that Christ's Second Coming would precede the millennium, but that the Second Coming could not take place until biblical prophecies concerning the Jewish people were fulfilled. There was no sign of this in Darby's time, and he and other dispensationalists believed the "prophetic clock" had stopped for an indefinite period. However, the creation of the State of Israel in 1948 and the reunification of Jerusalem in 1967 persuaded many fundamentalists that the prophetic clock was now ticking, and that consequently the world was moving rapidly toward the final events of history.

Darby believed these events would include a seven-year period of conflict and persecution, known as the *Tribulation*, the final half of which would be dominated by the figure of the Antichrist. However, dispensationalists have held that the saved would not have to endure the rigors of the Tribulation, because they would be *raptured*. That is, they would be taken up into heaven at the beginning of the Tribulation, be with Christ for the seven years, and then return with him at the time of the battle of Armageddon.

Christian Identity totally rejects this scenario. Since it believes Jews to be satanic impostors, it does not believe that biblical prophecies concerning Israel refer to them. Indeed, it believes such prophecies refer to Aryans. Thus, Identity adherents believe the support shown by Christian fundamentalists for the state of Israel signifies that the Christian community has been duped or co-opted by Jews. Identity also rejects the doctrine of the Rapture as a major theological error. It does not believe the faithful will be lifted off the earth. Instead, the saved (again, themselves) will have to live through the harrowing events of the Tribulation. This belief has significantly reinforced separatist tendencies, since a survivalist lifestyle is deemed to be not merely a way of escaping a society regarded as sinful, but also a way of protecting themselves against what they see as the dangers to come. It also fuels paramilitary tendencies, for they believe that during the Tribulation, public order will break down or the government will become the enemy of believers. Consequently, they see guns as an essential means of defense against encircling enemies.

Identity on the Wane

Throughout the roughly fifty years of its history, Christian Identity has shown itself capable of rapid and unpredictable changes. Because its constituent groups operate independently of one another, individual pastors and political organizers have been free to develop their own interpretations and programs. By closely interweaving anti-Semitism and racism with millennial expectation, Christian Identity has provided a theological rationalization for racial and religious conflict and inequality. Its assertion that these positions have a divine mandate has given Identity an influence in extremist circles far beyond its relatively small number of adherents.

That influence began to wane in the late 1990s and early 2000s, along with a more general decline of the extreme right. Perhaps the best-known Identity group, Aryan Nations, was torn by a leadership struggle. Dan Gayman faced a breach in his congregation. The militia groups that had multiplied in the early 1990s began to fragment and contract. Symbolic of the right's crisis was the sudden death in 2002 of William Pierce, leader of the neo-Nazi National Alliance. Although Pierce made no secret of his disdain for Christian Identity, his novel, *The Turner Diaries*, which described a successful racist uprising, was widely admired in Identity circles.

Michael Barkun

See also Ku Klux Klan; Millenarian Violence; Millennialism

Further Reading

Aho, J. (1990). *The politics of righteousness: Idaho Christian patriotism*. Seattle: University of Washington Press.

Barkun, M. (1997). Millenarians and violence: The case of the Christian identity movement. In T. Robbins & S. J. Palmer (Eds.), *Millennium, messiahs, and mayhem: Contemporary apocalyptic movements* (pp. 247–260). New York: Routledge.

Barkun, M. (1997). *Religion and the racist right: The origins of the Christian identity movement* (Rev. ed.). Chapel Hill: University of North Carolina Press.

Jeansonne, G. (1988). *Gerald L. K. Smith: Minister of hate*. New Haven, CT: Yale University Press.

Kaplan, J. (1997). *Radical religion in America: Millenarian movements from the far right to the children of Noah*. Syracuse, NY: Syracuse University Press.

MacDonald, A. (1980). *The Turner diaries* (2nd ed.). Washington, DC: National Alliance.

Robins, R. A., & Post, J. M. (1997). *Political paranoia: The psychopolitics of hatred*. New Haven, CT: Yale University Press.

Christianity: African-American Traditions

Throughout the African experience in the United States, Christianity has played a pivotal role in defining a unique identity. This is especially evident when one examines the place of African-Americans during periods of armed conflict.

With the statutory recognition of African enslavement during the 1660s, colonies were almost immediately confronted with the issue of how the enslaved population's religious status was to affect their status as slaves. Virginia encouraged the conversion of Africans to Christianity, but quickly resolved the vexing question of the enslaved African's status after embracing Christianity by enacting a law in 1667 that endorsed the religious conversion of Africans while stating that conversion did not affect their status as slaves. Other colonies quickly adopted variations on such laws.

The Eighteenth Century

Eighteenth-century American colonies witnessed a religious movement that swept through the population spreading its particular style of Christianity with great speed. Commonly called the Great Awakening, the movement ushered in a highly emotional and rhetorically powerful style of sermonizing in which the attainment of salvation was contrasted with hellfire and damnation. Some of these religious sentiments manifested themselves in 1739 in one of the first significant slave insurrections. Called the Stono Rebellion, it involved several enslaved Africans, who assembled outside Charleston, South Carolina, and marched toward the city with the intent of taking it over. Often disguising their meetings as religious assemblies, the leading participants planned the uprising. The small army was halted by colonial militia outside the city, but the assembled group held out for several days before being captured.

During the Revolutionary War George Washington initially barred the recruitment of enslaved or free Africans, but he quickly reversed his position after the deposed governor of Virginia, John Murray, Earl of Dunmore, promised freedom to any enslaved African who fought for the British in the conflict. Responding to the call, many Africans escaped from plantations to join the Loyalists. Indeed, the British shifted the focus of the battles to southern colonies to take advantage of the large presence of enslaved blacks.

Many colonies formally abolished the institution of slavery during or after the Revolutionary War, with Vermont being the first in 1777. By 1783 slavery was prohibited in Massachusetts, New Hampshire, and

Selection from David Walker's *Appeal to the Coloured Citizens of the World* (1829)

The Pagans, Jews and Mahometans try to make proselytes to their religions, and whatever human beings adopt their religions they extend to them their protection. But Christian Americans, not only hinder their fellow creatures, the Africans, but thousands of them *will absolutely beat a coloured person nearly to death, if they catch him on his knees, supplicating the throne of grace.* This barbarous cruelty was by all the heathen nations of antiquity, and is by the Pagans, Jews and Mahometans of the present day, left entirely to Christian Americans to inflict on the Africans and their descendants, that their cup which is nearly full may be completed. I have known tyrants or usurpers of human liberty in different parts of this country to take their fellow creatures, the coloured people, and beat them until they would scarcely leave life in them; what for? Why they say "The black devils had the audacity to be found *making prayers and supplications to the God who made them!!!!*" Yes, I have known small collections of coloured people to have convened together, for no other purpose than to worship God Almighty, in spirit and in truth, to the best of their knowledge; when tyrants, calling themselves *patrols*, would also convene and wait almost in breathless silence for the poor coloured people to commence singing and praying to the Lord our God, as soon as they had commenced, the wretches would burst in upon them and drag them out and commence beating them as they would rattle-snakes—many of whom, they would beat so unmercifully, that they would hardly be able to crawl for weeks and sometimes for months. Yet the American minister send out missionaries to convert the heathen, while they keep us and our children sunk at their feet in the most abject ignorance and wretchedness that ever a people was afflicted with since the world began. Will the Lord suffer this people to proceed much longer? Will he not stop them in their career? Does he regard the heathens abroad, more than the heathens among the Americans? Surely the Americans must believe that God is partial, notwithstanding his Apostle Peter, declared before Cornelius and others that he has no respect to persons, but in every nation he that feareth God and worketh righteousness is accepted with him. "The word," said he, which God sent unto the children of Israel, preaching peace, "by Jesus Christ, (he is Lord of all.").

Source: **Walker, David. (1930). *Walker's Appeal, in Four Articles; Together with a Preamble, to the Coloured Citizens of the World, but in Particular, and Very Expressly, to Those of the United States of America, Written in Boston, State of Massachusetts, September 28, 1829.* Boston: Revised and Published by David Walker, pp. 41–42.**

Pennsylvania, with Connecticut, Rhode Island, New York, and New Jersey to follow.

The post–Revolutionary War period saw the emergence of several benevolent societies and fraternal organizations to assist recently freed Africans in acquiring life skills. Organizations such as the African Union Society (Newport, Rhode Island), the Free African Society (Philadelphia, Pennsylvania), the Brown Fellowship (Charleston, South Carolina), the African Society of Boston, and the Society of Free Africans (Baltimore, Maryland), among others, became pillars within African-American communities. These self-help organizations tended to be quasi-religious societies, but in the case of the Free African Society in Philadelphia (which started as a burial society) under the leadership of Richard Allen (1760–1831) and Absalom Jones (1746–1818), an actual independent African church movement was launched.

By the late eighteenth century, Methodism had adopted an antislavery stance that caused a dramatic increase in its black membership. Allen and Jones were members in good standing at St. George Church in Philadelphia, which gained a substantial black membership after the two were elevated in position. Allen and Jones eventually staged a mass walkout of black congregants after they were required to worship in segregated seating in the building. While remaining in the folds of Methodism (Absalom Jones ultimately left to become the country's first black Anglican priest), Richard Allen subsequently established Bethel African Methodist Church. After some years of litigation, Allen established the African Methodist Episcopal Church and was consecrated as its first bishop in 1816. Even before Richard Allen's death in the 1830s, other all-black congregations had formed, including the African Methodist Episcopal Zion, the Ethiopian Church of Jesus, and the African Dutch Reformed Church.

Early Nineteenth-Century Insurrections

The tie between the African-American Christian experience and conflict continued to manifest itself throughout the early decades of the nineteenth century, when celebrated insurrections shook the nation. The first, Gabriel's Rebellion, took place outside Richmond, Virginia, in 1800. The slave of Thomas Prosser, Gabriel (1776–1800) was a influential figure throughout the area because of his knowledge and because he was a skilled blacksmith. Gabriel planned to take over the city of Richmond by commandeering the arsenal and other strategic entry and exit points. He also intended to hold the governor, James Monroe, hostage with follow-up plans to take over the cities of Petersburg and Norfolk. In this bold effort he recruited enslaved Africans from other plantations, Native Americans, several free blacks, and a few whites. The plan was to murder the whites of the city with the exception of the Quakers and the Mennonites because of their anti-enslavemnet positions and frequent involvement in abolitionist activities. Gabriel's plan was betrayed by two house servants, however, and torrential rains that slowed their progress gave Governor Monroe enough time to assemble a militia to scatter Gabriel's army and eventually capture and execute him and several of his followers.

A similar campaign was planned in Charleston, South Carolina, in 1821. At the center was Denmark Vesey (1767–1822), a former slave. As early as 1818 Vesey began planning the rebellion. He recruited as his captains other African-Americans of position and education. Vesey and his captains recruited followers throughout the state. Vesey cited the successful liberation of Santa Domingo, renamed Haiti by the leader Toussaint L'Ouverture (c. 1743–1803). He told his recruits that once the rebellion was underway, Haiti would join in to support their movement and help maintain their freedom. His campaign was scheduled to begin 14 July 1822, but like Gabriel, Vesey was betrayed by house servants. He and several followers were captured and secretly hanged in July and August of that year. Initially viewed as above suspicion as a conspirator, several of Vesey's lieutenants were held and charged with sedition before him. The delay in his inevitable arrest gave Vesey the opportunity to destroy records and conceal the names of the total number involved in this undertaking. Like Gabriel, Vesey used biblical quotes and interpretations to justify his cause and recruit followers, stating that it was not God's plan for one set to people to enslave another as had been done in the Americas.

The impact of the Gabriel and Denmark Vesey uprisings was to bring black churches in many parts of the South under much greater scrutiny because it was believed insurrectionary activity could be bred in such locations. These uprisings also inspired other blacks to engage in various forms of resistance to slavery.

Abolitionism and the Civil War

By the time of the Vesey episode, the abolitionist movement had gained considerable momentum and was actively carrying out its agenda. Several antislavery societies began emerging, mostly in northern states but with secret chapters in southern states.

The North-South divide deepened over the issue of African enslavement. Many white southern preachers advocated its continuation. Abolitionists were equally vehement in their opposition, arguing enslavement was an offense against man and God. Both sides supported their respective positions with scripture.

The later position was crystallized in an 1829 publication, *Appeal to the Coloured Citizens of the World* (1829) written by David Walker (1785–1830), a Boston-based journalist and a free black. The incendiary yet very Christian-oriented work referred to the United States' whites as the natural enemies of enslaved (and free) blacks. Walker also pointed out the hypocrisy of southern slaveholders who held the Bible in one hand and the bullwhip in the other. He argued in the *Appeal* that slavery degraded the individual who was subjected to it and it corrupted the perpetrators of it. The pamphlet was secretly circulated throughout the antebellum South, resulting in a price being put on Walker's head there. He was found dead at the age of thirty-five in Boston a year after its publication and is believed to have been poisoned.

Abolitionist sentiments only increased after Walker's murder, with the most violently executed rebellion carried out by Nat Turner (1800–1831), a slave, in August 1831 in Southampton, Virginia. Turner's religious zeal was apparent from when he was young. According to his account, he had prophetic visions that spurred him into action. Like Gabriel and Denmark Vesey, Turner used biblical and religious symbolism in his sermonizing against enslavement. Unlike them, his campaign was carried out with little apparent planning. For two days, he moved from plantation to plantation executing slaveholding men, women, and children and offered their enslaved blacks the choice of joining him or their slaughtered masters.

Although Turner was hastily captured, tried, and executed, the impact of the bloody campaign carried out in the name of God terrified whites in the South. It also emboldened other abolitionists to stage daring raids, like John Brown's 1859 failed attempt to capture a federal arsenal in Harpers Ferry, Virginia. There were also dramatic escapes made, such as those facilitated by the Underground Railroad, a network that offered systematic assistance to fugitives fleeing enslavement. "Conductors" such as the celebrated Harriet Tubman (c. 1820–1913) drew on a variety of techniques to lead people out of slavery to freedom. Among the practices were the use of alert songs, which were ostensibly religious but concealed encoded messages about a planned escape. Elaborate quilts, many employing ostensibly religious symbols, were also used to teach refugees safe routes to follow.

The southern states seceded from the United States in 1860 to form a Confederacy, leading to the U.S. Civil War (1861–1865). Both sides saw the war as a modern crusade with slavery as the primary issue. Both the Union and Confederacy claimed that God was on their side. Many African-Americans joined the war with similar convictions.

Initially rejecting African-Americans as combatants (based on an obscure 1792 Militia Act that banned black recruitment), President Abraham Lincoln ultimately succumbed to pressure from abolitionists such as Frederick Douglass (1817–1895), Sojourner Truth (c. 1797–1883), and William Lloyd Garrison (1805–1879) and encouraged blacks to join the ranks of the Union Army. More than fifty thousand African-American soldiers gave their lives for the Union during the war. The Confederacy also used blacks, but mostly for menial labor. While there were plans to use slaves as soldiers for combat on behalf of the South toward end of the war, nothing much came of them.

Black Missionary Work

Throughout much of the nineteenth century, an invisible African-American Protestant church tradition developed that crystallized at the end of the century. The more organized groups were the National Baptist Convention U.S.A, and the so-called "Holiness (Sanctified)," or Pentecostal, churches. Both promoted a less restrained style of religious behavior (for example, they encouraged speaking in tongues, holy dancing, and use of instruments like tambourines in the service). Several black churches, including the African Methodist Episcopal Church, began sending missionaries to Africa to evangelize continental Africans. The missionaries frequently met with colonial resistance.

In the background was the United States' involvement in the Spanish-American War, which was mostly fought in Cuba. Large numbers of African-American soldiers were involved in this conflict (including large numbers of black "Buffalo" soldiers shipped to Cuba from the United States' western territories) because of the belief that African-Americans were (because of their African ancestry) likely to be immune to tropical diseases such as malaria and yellow fever.

The Twentieth Century

Routinely subjected to second-class treatment and Jim Crow–style segregation in the military, African-American soldiers faced unfair court-martials (as in Brownsville, Texas, in 1906), harassment, and general lack of recognition for their military valor as the United States moved into the twentieth century. When the United States entered World War I in 1917, the battle over African-American soldiers' civil rights was also raging. Leaders such as W. E. B. Du Bois (1868–1963), who initially suggested African-Americans put aside their special grievances and join the war effort, later acknowledged the systemic indignities to which black soldiers were subjected. Following W. E. B. Du Bois' call to arms and rally around the American flag, African-American Protestant ministers also encouraged young Black men to sign up, thinking it would strengthen the race's chance for greater acceptance within American Society. Even the German forces in Europe used propaganda posters and messages in an effort to encourage African-American soldiers to defect because of their second-class status in the U.S. military and in the country as a whole. Kathryn Johnson, an African-American volunteer with the Young Men's Christian Association (YMCA) working in Europe during the war, was so discouraged by the blatant racism she saw African-American soldiers subjected to that she wrote a book (with Addie Hunton) chronicling her observations: *Two Colored Women with the American Expeditionary Forces* (1922).

Even as returning heroes, the black soldiers who had fought in support of European liberation faced serious violence once they returned to U.S. shores. The summer of 1919 saw no fewer than twenty race riots throughout the country. Several African-American soldiers were lynched or burned in their uniforms.

In 1935, Italy attacked the kingdom of Ethiopia, ruled by the emperor Haile Selassie (who had a following in the United States among African-Americans thanks to the work of Marcus Garvey, a black nationalist). African-American churches around the country but especially on the East Coast responded in the so-called Abyssinian Affair, mobilizing resources for the defense of Ethiopia and boycotting Italian-made goods.

The African-American press played a substantial role in the further erosion of segregation in the U.S. military as the country entered World War II by reporting on discriminatory practices against African-Americans as war correspondents. Often cited as one of the more significant advances toward the acceptance of Afircan-American soldiers as fighting equals was the creation of the all-black Tuskegee Airmen air squadron. Never before had the military entrusted such sophisticated weaponry in the hands of black soldiers. Trained as fighter pilots, many were kept from action for so long that Captain Benjamin Davis, Jr. (son of the first African-American general, Benjamin O. Davis, Sr.), had to fend off rumors started in other parts of the military that the black pilots were unwilling to fight.

After the conclusion of World War II, integrating the military became a pressing issue as a result of presidential Executive Order 9981, which permanently banned racial segregation in the military. Even with direct orders from President Truman, it was not until Douglas MacArthur (an ardent opponent of integration) was replaced by Matthew Ridgway that true integration was begun in any meaningful way.

The Vietnam War in the 1960s was the first conflict to which the United States sent an integrated fighting force. Many young African-Americans spoke out against fighting for the United States because of its history of racism. While Christianity was still the dominant religion among African-Americans within the military ranks, the institution had to accommodate its black soldiers' other religions, including Hinduism, Islam, and Judaism.

Since the 1960s, several African-Americans have been appointed generals, including Colin Powell, who became the Chairman of the Joint Chiefs of Staff, the highest military position in the United States. In the twenty-first century it appears that religious persuasion has diminished in influence among African-Americans in the military.

Christopher Brooks

Further Reading

Buckley, G. (2001). *American patriots: The story of blacks in the military from the Revolution to Desert Storm*. New York: Random House.

Huggins, N. (1986). *Dubois: Writings*. New York: Library of America.

Powell, C. (1995). *My American journey*. New York: Random House.

Quarles, B. (1996). *The Negro in the American Revolution*. Chapel Hill: University of North Carolina Press.

Walker, D. (1965). *Appeal: To the coloured citizens of the world (with introduction by Charles Wiltse)*. New York: Hill and Wang.

Walker, J. W. St. G. (1992). *The black loyalists: The search for a promised land in Nova Scotia and Sierra Leone, 1783–1870*. Toronto, Canada: University of Toronto Press.

Wright, K. (2002). *Soldiers of freedom: An illustrated history of African Americans in the armed forces*. New York: Black Dog & Leventhal Publishers.

Christianity and Revolution

The language of "revolution" has been invoked in contemporary discourse to refer to far-reaching and fundamental changes in the realms of agriculture, art, economics, industry, health care, political systems, religion, social structures, science, and technology. All such changes are watershed events; they are seen, often at the time they occur, but more definitively in retrospective reflection, as marking some of the great turning points in human history. Indeed, time itself is often measured with reference to a revolutionary event whose legacy has been inherited by a society or tradition.

This essay will focus specifically on the relationship between a religious tradition, Christianity, and revolution in its political and social forms, that is, those circumstances in which war and violence are characteristically part of the revolutionary process. Even in this more limited context, the relationship of Christianity and revolution is very complex. Christian political theologies rooted in biblical injunctions of submission to ruling powers have frequently expressed opposition to overthrow of oppressive governments or to revolutionary warfare. Christian ethical imperatives, such as love for the oppressed, vulnerable, and marginalized, may provide ideological support for a social revolutionary movement, as in the case of liberation theology. A major question is whether revolution is essentially "restorative," involving an attempt to return to an accepted social and political order, or whether revolution is "creative" and "innovative," seeking to bring into human existence a kind of person and society that is largely unprecedented (Gunneman). In either case, important questions remain about the justification and the limitation of revolutionary violence and warfare.

Portrait of John Calvin (1509–1564).

Revolution as Restoration

The political dimension of revolution is expressed in a definition from the *Oxford English Dictionary:* "a complete overthrow of the established government in any country or state by those who were previously subject to it; a forcible substitution of a new ruler or government." While this definition focuses on the event of political overthrow, and neglects the process by which a political system becomes discredited as well as the postoverthrow process of social change, both of which may be described as "revolutionary," it is fair to say that the question of insurrection, rebellion, or overthrow of an established government has historically loomed large in Christian political theologies and ethics.

The restorationist model of revolution makes three important presumptions that generate a cautious and exceptional-case approach to revolution:

- A coherent moral order that provides norms to assess the legitimacy of the political system.
- The legitimacy of political systems in normal circumstances.
- If a government fails repeatedly to measure up to these standards, then citizens may request or participate in political intervention to restore the system to its original ordering, but this is taken to be a very exceptional case.

Within these presumptions, the justification for political revolution does not challenge the moral structure and principles that legitimate political authority, but rather reaffirms the significance of this legitimating system by challenging particular political institutions and governments that have violated these standards.

The presumptions of moral order and political legitimacy have been influential in Christian political theologies since the letter of St. Paul to the Christian community at Rome. God is the source of normative moral order and God's ordering of the world legitimizes political systems. Thus, St. Paul prescribes a profoundly influential imperative of submission to Christians suffering under oppressive rule: "Let every person be subject to the governing authorities. For there is no authority except from God, and those that exist have been instituted by God. Therefore he who resists the authorities resists what God has appointed, and those who resist will incur judgment" (Romans 13:1–2, RSV).

The normativity of God's legitimizing power and the imperative of submission by the Christian is central to Augustine's (354–430 CE) project in the *City of God*, in which Augustine defends the Christian church from charges of political subversion and situates the breakup of the Roman Empire within the domain of divine providence. Nonetheless, the absolute nature of the apostolic claim of submission is challenged in the medieval era of Christianization of Europe. St. Thomas Aquinas (1225–1274) developed a theme embedded in Augustine, that an unjust law was not a binding law, and expanded this to an entire political order. Aquinas maintained that government as instituted by God was ordained to the promotion of the common good, and any insurrection against such a system constituted the mortal sin of sedition. Thus, the common good provides the norm against which laws and governments can be assessed, and this norm offered Aquinas some ground for what he described as "disturbance" of a tyrannical government. A tyrannical government, Aquinas claimed, was unjust because it was directed toward the private good of the tyrant, not the common good. Thus, "disturbance of tyranny," including communal removal of the tyrant, did not constitute sedition. The common good both justifies and restrains political disturbance, and such disturbance must be directed toward the restoration of a political regime that has the common good as its end.

The Protestant Reformation raised serious challenges to the idea of divine ordering of political legitimacy based on the common good. A "common" good between Catholic and Protestant could no longer be presupposed, and for Protestants living under Catholic rule, the question of freedom of worship became of paramount importance. Moreover, the ideology of the "divine right of kings" needed reconsideration when monarchs seemed to restrict or prevent rather than advance right worship. In this context, both magisterial and radical reformers give new content to concepts of justifiable political resistance and revolution.

The political theology of John Calvin (1509–1564) provided the most influential example of magisterial interpretations of revolution. Calvin's understanding of human sinfulness and depravity led him to prefer political order, even if tyrannical, to the potential for anarchy risked in a revolutionary uprising. Nonetheless, the Christian was not to be passive in the face of tyranny. The private Christian was encouraged to pray for providential deliverance from despotic princes. At the same time, Calvin admonished the "magistrates of the people" to resist misrule as part of their divine call to protect the freedoms, especially freedom to engage in right worship, of the people. Calvin's very cautious argumentation, which relied on a traditional distinction between public and private authority in the use of force, developed into a revolutionary legacy in the hands of John Knox in Scotland, the Puritans in England, and the French Huguenots.

The distinction between public and private authority was abandoned by the radical reformer Thomas Müntzer (1468 or 1489/90–1525), who appealed to "everyman" to purge the Christian church of evil, through use of the sword if necessary, in preparation for the imminent return of Christ and divine judgment. Müntzer's theologizing provided a warrant for the insurrections of peasants and commoners against European princes, especially in Central European locales in Germany and Switzerland, as well as Prague. He did not advocate the restoration of the old order, which had become corrupt beyond reparation, but provided an eschatological interpretation of scriptural history that anticipates the beginning of the "New Church." Müntzer introduces into Western thought and Christianity the idea of revolution as creative and innovative, which later becomes the defining characteristic of revolution in liberation thought and Marxism.

The Puritan and Scottish revolutions brought an end to the doctrine of the divine right of kings, and by the end of the seventeenth century, John Locke (1632–1704) drew on Christian (Calvinist and Puritan), philosophical (natural law), and political (Whig ideology) sources to develop his influential theory of legitimate political resistance and revolution against an unjust government. Locke argued that government was established, not by divine fiat, but by the people to ensure certain rights and protections, especially security of the person, liberty, and property. Systematic deprivation of these rights and protections by a government called the legitimacy of the political regime into question. Locke's case relied on an analogy between a foreign and a domestic invasion of fundamental rights, liberties, and protections; in both cases, the "invasion" violates the fiduciary trust between ruler and governed and places the parties in a "state of war." The same principles that motivated the formation of government in the first place, the duty of self-preservation and the right to punish in self-defense, now provide grounds for resistance and revolution. Locke's idea of revolution is thus ultimately restorative, as the goal of revolution is to reestablish the legitimate forms of contractual government. Aquinas's notion of the "common good" is rendered by Locke into the "will of the people" as both justification and limitation on resistance and political revolution. His interpretation of a justified political revolution relies heavily on concepts in Christian just-war tradition, including right authority, just cause, right intention, and last resort.

The moral and theological case for limits on the authority of the state, the violation of which permitted sedition, insurrection, rebellion, and revolution, found its practical expression in the political arguments made in the Declaration of Independence of the United States of America. The question was no longer whether or not Christian thought could justify or sanction revolution, but the methods by which such revolution could be conducted, and particularly the extent to which violence as a means was permissible. This informs contemporary discussions of the use of violence in debates over civil disobedience, irregular or revolutionary warfare, and assassination.

Creating Revolutionary Consciousness: Liberation Theology

According to a prominent exponent of liberation theology, Gustavo Gutiérrez, the process of liberation involves "a social revolution which will radically and qualitatively change the conditions in which [oppressed peoples] now live" (Gutiérrez 1973, 88). There are three important themes to emphasize in this understanding of revolution that stand in contrast to the restorationist model.

- The revolutionary change envisaged in liberation theology is not limited to the political context but encompasses social, economic, and religious structures, as well as the creation of revolutionary consciousness in the oppressed.
- The anticipated revolution brings radical and qualitative changes. It does not mean a "revolving" back and reaffirmation of accepted norms of political legitimization, as exemplified by Locke, but is an innovative process through which new norms for political and personal life are generated.
- The ordering norms of society, and not simply their application by specific political regimes, legitimize injustice and oppression. Indeed, on this analysis, the primary issue in revolutionary change is neither political order nor economic justice, but metaphysical. The question of theodicy—the issue of how convictions in an omnipotent and benevolent God can be reconciled with the presence of pain and evil in the world—and the cause of suffering and evil, is at the root of revolution.

The experience of oppression and social marginalization is coupled with a new Christological understanding. Christ is not portrayed as upholding unjust government, nor even primarily as savior, but as liberator. The 1968 Medellín Conference of Latin American Bishops understood salvation as *liberación* and declared that God's Son came to "liberate all men from the slavery to which sin has subjected them: hunger, misery, oppression, and ignorance, in a word, that injustice and hatred which have their origin in human selfishness" (Medellín 1977, 550). The liberating Christ embodies the teachings in the Christian Gospels, as well as the prophetic Hebrew tradition, that socially marginalized persons, such as widows and orphans, those living in poverty and deprivation, and those stigmatized by disease or cultural prejudice, are especially singled out for the expression of God's love and inclusion within the religious community. In some contemporary Christian traditions, this special distinction is designated by the phrase "preferential option for the poor."

Moreover, liberation theologians claim that the experience of oppression, and the effort to be faithful to a Christian witness, provides special or distinct insights into the nature of Christian discipleship within the religious community and within the larger society. This experientially based understanding is reflected in the language of the "epistemological privilege" of the oppressed. The world is seen differently, as constituted by a relationship of oppressed and oppressor; that is, the aberration in political and social relations for Aquinas, Calvin, and Locke is the customary norm within liberation thought. Because of this interpretation of the social context, Christians are called on to act differently, to struggle in solidarity and protest against oppression. This informs the liberation emphasis on right behavior, or "orthopraxis," rather than with traditional dogmatic debates over right belief or orthodoxy.

Because structures of oppression are embedded in the traditional social order, and legitimated by a moral worldview, the revolutionary strategy of innovative revolution is to challenge the coherence and validity of this moral order, and particularly its explanation (and legitimation) of evil. One theological analyst, Jon Gunneman, draws on the theory of scientific revolution developed by Thomas Kuhn to explicate this moral challenge. Gunneman contends that the revolutionary undergoes a paradigm shift in the perception of the moral universe. The prevailing structure of legitimation is shattered and an explanation of evil more congruent with experience is required: "A revolutionary is born . . . [when] he has undergone a transformation in consciousness that entails his seeing the world in a new way" (Gunneman 1979, 7).

This transformation in consciousness is so profound and fundamental to identity that Gunneman, drawing on liberationist language, contends it is analogous to religious conversion. It follows from this revolutionary posture that the dynamics of human interaction and relationships must also undergo dramatic alteration in order that they conform to the revolutionary paradigm of the world. The theologian Ignacio Ellacuria makes clear the connection between a conversion in consciousness and a conversion in conduct: "There must be complete conversion, a complete overthrow of our own ideas and the structures which objectify them. We must work for a complete change of structures (an objective revolution) and for a complete change of mind and heart (a subjective revolution). It is utopian to think that we can get one without the other" (Ellacuria 1976, 215).

This comprehensive change in both the person and the society have pointed liberation theologians to a different biblical narrative than that presented in the Christian Gospels. Instead, the primary interpretative narrative is that of the Exodus. The Hebrew peoples of the narrative must experience a transformed consciousness to make the transition from "slave" of pharaoh to "chosen" of God. Of necessity, however, this requires a transformed social structure, an escape from the oppression of Egypt, and the eventual establishment of the new society in Canaan, the land of promise.

Revolution and Violence

A persistent question for either the restorationist or the innovative meaning of revolution concerns the role of violence or warfare in bringing about revolutionary change. Both interpretations rely on a dual notion of violence. A first perspective understands violence to consist in the infliction of harm or injury through physical force. However, revolutionary literature does not consider this to be either a necessary or sufficient condition of violence. A supplementary account proposes that violence may also occur through the deprivation of basic rights and an assault on the dignity of the human person. John Locke's writing noted that the "state of war" between sovereign and citizen could be introduced not only through the sovereign's threat to the natural right to life (physical harm), but also through unwarranted and repeated invasions of the core rights to liberty and property.

Meanwhile, liberation theologians have articulated concepts of "structural" and "institutional" violence. That is, oppressive social situations and exploitative economic relationships are themselves violent, even if direct physical infliction of harm is absent. Revolutionary violence is thereby seen as "counterviolence," that is, a response to a degrading social structure that assaults human dignity. As Ellacuria puts it, "real violence" lies in the nature of the injustice committed, not the method. Indeed, the paradigm of exploitative relationships within liberation thought is the capitalistic economic system.

The perspective that revolutionary violence is *responsive*, employed against systematic oppression, provides a necessary ground for resort to modes of revolutionary warfare, including violent resistance, guerrilla war, and irregular war. There are three difficulties, however, with this justification of revolutionary warfare:

1. The revolutionary perception of systemic oppression is likely to be disputed, and certainly opposed, by those in power.
2. Other criteria, embedded in just war theory, including legitimate authority, right intention, and last resort, are required for revolutionary warfare to be justified on ethical grounds.
3. Even if revolutionary violence can be justified, the grounds for limitation of violence are not clear. Indeed, because of the customary disparities in military power, revolutionary war is often considered "dirty war" because it may employ tactics of terrorism to rectify the power imbalance.

Courtney S. Campbell

Further Reading

Aquinas, T. (1947). *Summa theologica*. New York: Benziger Bros.

Augustine. (1977). *The city of God*. Washington, DC: Catholic University of America Press.

Calvin, J. (1960). *Institutes of the Christian religion*. Philadelphia: Westminster Press.

Ellacuria, I. (1976). *Freedom made flesh*. Maryknoll, NY: Orbis Books.

Franklin, J. H. (1969). *Constitutionalism and resistance in the 16th century*. New York: Pegasus.

Gunneman, J. P. (1979). *The moral meaning of revolution*. New Haven, CT: Yale University Press.

Gunneman, J. P. (1986). Revolution. In J. Childress & J. Macquarrie (Eds.), *The Westminster dictionary of Christian ethics* (2d ed.; pp. 550–553). Philadelphia: Westminster Press.

Gutiérrez, G. (1973). *A theology of liberation*. Maryknoll, NY: Orbis Books.

Kuhn, T. (1970). *The structure of scientific revolutions*. Chicago: University of Chicago Press.

Little, D. (1984). *Religion, order, and law*. Chicago: University of Chicago Press.

Locke, J. (1960). The second treatise of civil government. In *Two treatises of government* (pp 307–477). New York: Cambridge University Press.

Medellín Conference. (1977). Justice. In D. O'Brien & T. A. Shannon (Eds.), *Renewing the earth*. Garden City, NY: Image Books.

Zuck, L. H. (1975) *Christianity and revolution: Radical Christian testimonies, 1520–1650*. Philadelphia: Free Church Press.

Christianity, Early: Constantinian Movement

The imperial reign of Constantine (273–337) at the beginning of the fourth century is a watershed in the history of Christianity. Within a few short decades, the Christian Church, which had just come off the heels of the most systematic and universal persecution it had endured in its first three centuries of existence, received imperial favor and became increasingly connected to the political, civic, and military activities of the Roman empire. The change from a persecuted church to a church of imperial patronage resulted in a rethinking of Christian attitudes towards war during the fourth and fifth centuries. Constantine's rule, beginning in the western half of the Roman Empire in 306 CE, marks a significant shift in the historical development of the Christian Church and tradition. The most dramatic change occurs in the relationship between the imperial government (the state) and the ecclesiastical organization (the Church). Christian involvement in the empire's public life meant that such state-sponsored activities as punishment of wrongdoers and defense of the state from external threats would necessarily receive the active support of Christians holding positions of civic responsibility. Growing membership in the Christian Church during the fourth century only increased Christian involvement in the public sphere. The distinction between what belonged to Caesar and what belongs to God became blurred (cf. Mark 12:17).

Emperor Constantine

The person and reign of Constantine are critical in any attempt to understand Christian attitudes and practices toward war and warfare in the fourth and fifth centuries. There are three main reasons for this. The first is the historical shift that occurred under his reign. Over night, Christianity was transformed from a persecuted faith to one receiving imperial benefaction. The historical landscape in which Christianity operated and functioned had been radically altered. Second, it is significant that Constantine himself underwent a conversion to Christianity. The sincerity and date of Constantine's conversion is debated; it is true, however, that he did not receive Christian baptism until ten days prior to his death in May 337. However, the story of his conversion as recorded by contemporary Christian historians becomes a permanent fixture within the historical consciousness of the Church. Although differing in details, the two accounts of Constantine's conversion, one by the Christian writer Lactantius (c. 240–325) and the other by the Church historian Eusebius of Caesarea (c. 260–339), both agree that Constantine had a dream (Eusebius reports that he first had a vision in the sky in the early afternoon) the evening before his victorious battle against the imperial usurper Maxentius (d. 312) at the Milvian Bridge. In that dream, Constantine is commanded (the military language in both accounts is undeniable) to place "the heavenly sign of God on the shields of his soldiers" and "to use it as a safeguard in all engagements with his enemies" (Eusebius, *Life of Constantine* n.d., I:31). This "sign of God" that Constantine used was a monogram consisting of a combination of the two Greek letters chi (X) and rho (R)—the first two letters in the Greek name for Christ—superimposed upon each other. This heavenly sign became known as the labarum, a word of unknown meaning but most likely Celtic in origin. The labarum became the insignia of the imperial reign of Constantine, appearing on several issues of coins during Constantine's reign. Eusebius, writing some twenty years later in his *Life of Constantine*, notes that the labarum became the Roman cavalry standard for the imperial armies.

The context of Constantine's conversion was significant. It came on the eve of his victory over the usurper Maxentius at Rome in 312—a victory that allowed Constantine to enter Rome as uncontested emperor of the Western Roman Empire. Whether or not at the time Constantine consciously connected his victory at the Milvian Bridge with the favor of the Christian God is debated. However, his Christian contemporaries made the connection, as most probably Constantine did at some later date. Twelve years after his victory at Rome, Constantine defeated Licinius (d. 325), the last rival to

The Council of Chalcedon (451 CE) on Military Service

CANON VII.

WE have decreed that those who have once been enrolled among the clergy, or have been made monks, shall accept neither a military charge nor any secular dignity; and if they shall presume to do so and not repent in such wise as to turn again to that which they had first chosen for the love of God, they shall be anathematized.

Source: **Schaff. P., & Wace, H. (Eds.). (1955).** ***The Seven Ecumenical Councils of the Undivided Church*** **(H. R. Percival, Trans.) Grand Rapids MI: Wm. B. Eerdmans, p. 272.**

universal imperial rule, and claimed the remarkable position as sole imperial ruler of the vast Roman empire. The association of Constantine's accession to universal imperial rule with the Christian faith is of fundamental historical importance for Western civilization.

The third reason Constantine's reign is important for understanding Christian attitudes toward war is that it was seized upon by Christian apologists, most notably Eusebius of Caesarea, as evidence of the victory of the Christian Gospel in the affairs of humanity. On the occasion of the celebration of Constantine's thirtieth anniversary as emperor, Eusebius delivered an oration in praise of the emperor, emphasizing the association of Constantine with Christ: Constantine's empire is a copy of the heavenly kingdom; Constantine rules as the ideal monarch of the earthly realm as Christ rules in heaven. For Eusebius, and certainly for many of his fellow Christians, Constantine's successful rule was a sign of the Church's worldly victory.

Christians in the Army

Since the mid-third century, Christians had been serving in the Roman army. During the Constantinian era, the issue of Christian service in the military becomes more acute. Two years after Constantine's victory at Rome, the Council of Arles (314), a gathering of western bishops, issued a canon (canon 3) legislating that "those who throw down their arms in time of peace are to be separated from the community." There is a lack of consensus regarding the meaning of this canon. The difficulty of interpretation comes from the phrase "in time of peace." It is most probable that this "time of peace" is in contrast to an earlier time when Christians were forcibly required to sacrifice in order to demonstrate their loyalty to the state and their renunciation of their Christian religion. With the threat of persecution gone, Christians are to remain in service of the empire. Should this interpretation be accurate, it marks a significant shift in Christian attitudes toward military service.

Evidence for Christians in the military multiplies during the fourth and fifth centuries. A few years after the meeting of bishops at Arles which Constantine himself had convened, Constantine acknowledged the presence of Christians in his army by granting them leave to attend liturgy on Sundays. Canon 15 of the so-called *Canons of Hippolytus* (c. 330) instructs Christians not to enlist voluntarily in the military. However, military service is acceptable if compulsory. Should a Christian serving in the military be required to shed blood, he is to abstain from the Eucharist "at least until he has been purified through tears and lamentation." Similarly, canon 13 of Basil of Caesarea (330–379) states that killing committed during times of war is not considered murder at all, "allowing men to fight in defense of sobriety and piety." Nonetheless, Basil suggests that those who have taken a life in their military service ought to refrain from the Eucharist for three years. Although not precluding Christians from military service, Basil's injunction and that found in the *Canons of Hippolytus* reflect early Christianity's moral abhorrence for war. In addition to utilization of repentance as a compromise for allowing Christians to spill blood in times of war, the Church proffered another means to mitigate the tension between Christian nonviolence and one's duty to the state, in the form of a distinction between clergy and laity. Canonical legislation of the fourth and fifth centuries prohibited clergy from enrollment in the military—most notably canon 7 of the Council of Chalcedon (451), which forbids both clergy and monks from entering military service but does not ban laity from military subscription.

Christian attitudes toward participation in the military were ambivalent, and Christian service in the military remained qualified. Clergy and monks, those who were in the service of religion, were to remain undefiled by refraining from participation in war. Ambrose (339–397), bishop of Milan in the last quarter of the fourth century, argued that clergy should not participate in war since their role is spiritual and to be expressed in peaceful activity. Although the taking of life during wartime was not considered murder, Christians who killed on the battlefield were in need of repentance. The Church did not issue indulgences for military service. Nonetheless, Christians could and did wear the military uniform, and therefore by the mid-fifth century Christian chaplains could be found in the Roman military.

A Necessary Evil

During the course of the fourth century Christian attitudes toward war and military service gradually shifted from the pre-Constantinian pacifist or nonviolence position to a sense that it was acceptable, if not a moral obligation, to defend one's country and fellow citizens. The change in opinion is explained in part by the fact that Christians were increasingly active in the public sphere, holding positions of increasing responsibility. As Christians became more engaged with the affairs of empire, their principles of peace and nonviolence came into conflict with the necessity of using force to defend the empire. Although Eusebius would have us believe that Constantine's rule ushered in a period of peace for the Roman Empire, the fourth century was as violent militarily as any in imperial Roman history. The survival of the state meant that Christians, now running the state, had to find a way to remain faithful to the Gospels' message of nonviolence while still maintaining the safety and prosperity of a violent empire.

Post-Constantinian Christians in the eastern half of the Roman Empire generally viewed war as a necessary evil. The emphasis in writers such as Basil of Caesarea and John Chrysostom (c. 340–407), bishop of Constantinople, is on peace rather than pacifism: "God is not a God of war and fighting. Make war and fighting cease, both that which is against Him, and that which is against your neighbor." In the sixth century, an anonymous military manual of strategy, written during the reign of Emperor Justinian I (reigned 483–565), acknowledged war as the greatest of evils. At the end of the sixth century, the *Strategikon of Maurice*, another Byzantine military manual, emphasized how the military leader should attempt to avoid open conflict between opposing armies. The emphasis here is on minimizing participation in a military conflict, which is by definition evil.

In the early Byzantine liturgical tradition, prayers for peace as well as for victory during war are quite common. Peace is generally understood in this context as having two meanings: the absence of war or strife and the biblical notion of peace, denoting well-being. The latter meaning further connotes a desirous condition of the human soul that leads to harmony among people and is the result of the salvific work of God among his people. Parallel to the liturgical use of the word *peace* are numerous prayers and references to military victory, the empire, and the armies in their roles as protectors of the citizens and defenders of the state. In addition to these prayers and liturgical petitions, other contexts in the fourth through seventh centuries combine religious sensibilities toward peace with the necessity of war: the cult of the warrior saints; sermons delivered on the occasion of battles, victories, and defeats; military religious services held for soldiers prior to engaging in battle; Christian bishops praying for the military success of troops defending their cities from external threats; and the use of religious objects (such as icons or relics) in processions to ward off attack and entreat God to grant victory. Christians in Nisibis (Syria) prayed for the success of the Roman troops defending their city in sieges (338, 342, and 349) by the Persians. One of the most celebrated defenses of a city by a Christian religious leader took place during the siege of the city of Constantinople in 626. Patriarch Sergios, being left in charge of the city in the absence of the emperor, led a procession of clergy and faithful along the city's walls with a miraculous icon of the Virgin Mary. The procession rallied the troops defending the city, and the city was spared.

Just War, Holy War

From the fourth through the sixth centuries, Christians populating the eastern half of the Mediterranean world continued to view war primarily as a necessary evil. Athanasius (c. 293–c. 373), bishop of Alexandria, treated killing during the time of war as an involuntary sin. Attitudes toward war remained fairly consistent during the Middle and Late Middle Ages in the Eastern Roman empire (commonly referred to as the Byzantine empire, 610–1453). There are only a handful of instances when Byzantine military campaigns took on the cloak, flimsy as it was, of a holy war. The campaign that the emperor Heraclius (c. 575–641) launched against the Persians to retrieve the cross of Christ, which the latter had taken as a trophy when they sacked Jerusalem (614), and some campaigns against Turkish forces in the eleventh and following centuries, utilized the rhetoric of holy war. The Eastern Church never developed a notion of holy war comparable with that of the Western Church, most fully expressed in the Crusades, because the theory of a just war, developed in its early stages by Ambrose of Milan and definitively articulated by Augustine of Hippo (354–430), is not found in the theological or political writings of Christian leaders in the eastern Mediterranean. For Christians in the east, war remained a necessary evil.

Constantine's personal and political acceptance of Christianity fundamentally altered the relationship between Christians and the state. Christians found themselves in the position of having to commit men to the horrors of war as well as having themselves to participate in them. In the new historical reality created by Constantine's religious conversion, the Eastern Church took a somewhat ambiguous road by viewing war as a necessary evil while simultaneously blessing, praying for, and supporting the men, instruments, and outcomes of war.

James Skedros

See also Eastern Orthodoxy, Pacifism in; Holy War Idea in the Biblical Tradition; Roman Catholicism: Just-War Doctrine

Further Reading

Bainton, R. (1960). *Christian attitudes toward war and peace.* Nashville, TN: Abingdon Press.

Baldovin, J. (1987). *The urban character of Christian worship: The origins, development and meaning of stational liturgy* (Oriental Christiana Analecta No. 228). Rome: Pontifical Oriental Institute.

Delehaye, H. (1909). *Les légends grecques des saints militaries.* Bruxelles: Bureaux de la Société des Bollandistes

Dennis, G. (1993). Religious services in the Byzantine army. In E. Carr, S. Parenti, & A. A Thiermeyer (Eds.), *Eulogema: Studies in honor of Robert Taft, S.J.* (Studia Anselmiana No. 110, pp. 1–11). Rome: Pontificio Ateneo di S. Anselmo.

Harakas, S. (1999). *Wholeness of faith and life: Orthodox Christian ethics: Vol. 1. Patristic Ethics.* Brookline, MA: Holy Cross Orthodox Press.

Helgeland, J. (1974). Christians and the Roman army: A.D. 173–337. *Church History*, 43, 149–163.

Helgeland, J., Daly, R., & Burns, S. (1985). *Christians and the military: The early experience.* Philadelphia: Fortress Press.

Hornus, J. M. (1980). *It is not lawful for me to fight: Early Christian attitudes toward war, violence and the state.* Scottsdale, PA: Herald Press.

Laiou, A. (1993). On just war in Byzantium. In S. Reinart, J. Langdon, & J. Allen (Eds.), *To Ellenikon: Studies in honor of Speros Vryonis, Jr.* (Vol. 1, pp. 153–174). New Rochelle, NY: Aristide D. Caratzas.

McCormick, M. (1987). *Eternal victory: Triumphal rulership in late antiquity, Byzantium and the early medieval west.* Cambridge, UK: Cambridge University Press.

Miller, T., & Nesbitt, J. (Eds.). (1995). *Peace and war in Byzantium: Essays in honor of George T. Dennis, S.J.* Washington, DC: The Catholic University of America Press.

Swift, L. J. (1983). *The early fathers on war and military service* (Message of the Fathers on the Church No. 19). Wilmington, DE: Michael Glazier.

Christianity, Early: Jesus Movement

Christian advocates of positions as different as pacifism, just-war theory, and justifiable revolution appeal to sources from the first centuries of Christianity for ethical warrants in formulating arguments on war and peace. Roland Bainton's classic *Christian Attitudes Toward War and Peace* (1960) emphasized the pacifist nature of Christianity for its first three centuries and implied that pacifism was ethically normative for Christianity since it characterized the period closest to Jesus. But early Christian perspectives on war were determined by sociological realities and theological commitments in addition to ethical principles arising from the teachings of Jesus. Hence it is important to understand the complex factors that shaped early Christian views on war and military service.

Evidence supports Bainton's assertion that the earliest followers of Jesus rejected war and military service. No extant Christian writings prior to Emperor Constantine's (d. 337 CE) legalization of Christianity (313) approved of Christian participation in military violence. Nor is there evidence of Christian participation in the military prior to 170 CE. Thus, Celsus, a second-century Roman critic of Christianity, wrote, "If all men were to do the same as you . . . the forces of the empire would fall into the hands of the wildest and most lawless barbarians" (Origen, *Against Celsus*, in Bainton 1960, 68). But references to participation in military service are increasingly common in the late second and third centuries, engendering negative responses in Christian writings. What factors influenced Christian views on war and military service?

The Life and Teachings of Jesus

Developing traditions about the life and teachings of Jesus were normative in early descriptions of discipleship. The ethic derived from Jesus' teachings was an ethic emphasizing love of God and love of neighbor. The canonical Gospels depict Jesus teaching and demonstrating a love expressed as spontaneous compassionate action that identifies with others and meets their needs. This love is unlimited in scope, based not on reciprocity but on the imitation of God's character (Matthew 5:46–48). So Jesus subverted the prevailing purity system in Palestine by accepting outcasts, eating with "sinners," and associating with those deemed unclean by the Levitical priests. This inclusive ethic broke down barriers and enlarged the community.

The Sermon on the Mount (Matthew 5–7) contains the central Christian teachings related to peace. In Matthew's formulation of Jesus' teachings, the meek, the merciful, and the peacemakers are blessed. Disciples are instructed not to resist those who are evil. Instead they should turn the other cheek, go the second mile, give to those who beg, pray for their persecutors, and talk to those with whom they have conflicts. Hence, the love ethic of the sermon seeks reconciliation by engaging in positive actions that break down the walls that divide people. The sermon's instruction to "love your enemies" (Matthew 5:44) was the "principle precept" of the ethic of Jesus, according to Tertullian (c. 155 or 160–after 220 CE), characteristic of children of God who participate in God's reign. Luke's version admonishes, "Love your enemies, do good to those who hate you, bless those who curse you, pray for those who abuse you" (Luke 6:27–28 NRSV).

That these teachings were central to the developing ethic of the Christian communities is evident in the numerous references in early Christian writings. Paul (whose writings predate the Gospels) exhorted the Roman Christians to

> Bless those who persecute you; bless and do not curse them. . . . Repay no one evil for evil . . . If possible, so far as it depends upon you, live peaceably with all. Beloved, never avenge yourselves, but leave it to the wrath of God; for it is written, "Vengeance is mine, I will repay, says the Lord." No, "if your enemy is hungry feed him; if he is thirsty, give him drink; for by so doing you will heap burning coals upon his head." Do not be overcome by evil, but overcome evil with good (Romans 12:14, 17–21 RSV).

No scripture was used in second century Christian writings more than the Sermon on the Mount. The ethical treatise called the *Didache* described the Christian "way" in terms closely parallel to the ethical prescriptions in Matthew 5 and Luke 6. Likewise, Justin (c. 100–c. 165) stated, "we who hated and destroyed one another . . . now since the coming of Christ, live familiarly with them, and pray for our enemies, and try to persuade those who unjustly hate us" (*First Apology* 14).

The teachings of the Sermon on the Mount must be understood in the context of Jesus' central theme of the kingdom of God (reign of God). Mark's Gospel begins with Jesus' programmatic declaration, "The time is fulfilled, and the kingdom of God is at hand; repent and believe in the gospel" (Mark 1:15 RSV; cf. Matthew 4:17). The sermon catalogues the most influential teachings about the way of life in this kingdom, understood as an alternative reality that calls the disciple to commitment. In the Gospels, Jewish eschatological expectation has become a present reality in the ministry of Jesus, although it will come to full realization at a future time. But disciples were to embody this present/future age of peace in the life of their communities in their current historical context.

Interpreters debate the meaning of "kingdom of God" and the relevance of early apocalyptic expectations for understanding the Sermon on the Mount, disagreeing on whether it was merely an "interim ethic" for first-century hearers awaiting an imminent end time, or a picture of the proper response to the proclamation of an already-present reign of God. But the kingdom ethic of the sermon was still a central feature of ethical exhortation after apocalyptic hopes had waned in the second and third centuries.

The Legacy of Judaism

Jewish traditions on war and peace inherited by Christianity are complex. Holy war traditions within the Hebrew scriptures were quoted in primitive Christianity, but were usually interpreted allegorically rather than employed in ethical arguments about war. Hebrew writings themselves reveal early debates within the covenant community that reflect discomfort with primitive ideologies justifying total annihilation. Even within the Scriptures, holy war ideology is supplemented with a competing "nonparticipation" tradition that "God will fight for us." A similar concept is present in the first-century apocalypticism that influenced the Jesus movement. This apocalyptic context for early Christianity reflected Jewish tensions between expectations of a messianic deliverer who would inaugurate the kingdom by conquering the forces of evil and one who would come as a "suffering servant" establishing a kingdom of peace. Both conceptions show up in early Christian writings, but developing Christian theology adopted the latter in interpretations of the meaning of Jesus, and projected the former into the future.

Also influential were prophetic critiques of warlike dependence on earthly might such as Hosea's warning of destruction because "you have trusted in your chariots and in the multitude of your warriors" (Hosea 10:13 RSV; cf. Isaiah 31:1). Perhaps more significant were prophetic visions of a future age when nations "shall beat their swords into plowshares, and their spears into pruning hooks" (Isaiah 2:4 NRSV), the "Prince of Peace" will establish a reign of justice (Isaiah 9:5–7), and the "wolf shall dwell with the lamb" (Isaiah 11:6–9 RSV).

Early Christian writers referred to Isaiah's visions of peace and interpreted them as images of the kingdom established in the ministry of Jesus. For example, Justin wrote, "We who were filled with war . . . have . . . changed our warlike weapons—our swords into ploughshares, and our spears into implements of tillage" (*Dialogue with Trypho*, CX, in Wogaman 1993, 33).

Finally, Jewish suspicion of monarchy colored early Christian views of the Roman state. Jewish history is full of negative experiences with imperial subjugation, but the disastrous results of nationalist insurrections and independent statehood left deep suspicion of political sovereigns even while hope for God's reign remained fervent.

The Sociopolitical Context

Early Christian teachings about war must also be understood within their sociopolitical context. The Jesus movement was a Jewish renewal movement that arose largely among the lower classes within an agrarian society in Palestine. In the second and third centuries the movement took root in urban commercialized contexts. The urban Christianity that eventually dominated was more conservative and likely to compromise with political authority than the more subversive rural expressions of the new religion.

The early Jesus movement embodied a communitarian ethic that was initially sectarian, politically powerless, and not responsible for affairs of state. Christians were subjects of the Roman Empire, living in minority communities with little influence, even in later urban settings under the patronage of householders. In fact, Christians experienced sporadic persecution by local or imperial authorities. A social ethic of intentional political transformation was not a practical possibility. So questions about the use of coercion in the service of political ends belong to a later time. These historical realities make it difficult to presume unanimous rejection of military violence *solely* on the basis of a theological ethic, especially considering the post-Constantinian shift in perspectives.

In fact, numerous Christian writers in the first three centuries already affirmed that God ordained the existing imperial powers, including their coercive functions, for maintaining order, restraining sin, and advancing the gospel. The injunction of Paul to "be subject to the governing authorities" whose authority has been "instituted by God" (Romans 13:1–7 NRSV; cf. 1 Peter 2:13–17) was echoed in the writings of Justin, Tertullian, and Origen (185?–254?). Each author acknowledged the benefits of Roman order as part of God's plan and assured the authorities of Christian support and prayers.

Such passages, in the context of insurrectionary ferment with which the vulnerable Christian movement did not want to be associated, repudiate revolutionary violence. In his classic work on Christian pacifism, *The Politics of Jesus*, John Howard Yoder understands this early Christian posture as a "revolutionary subordination" that might nonviolently undermine an evil system by revealing its inherent injustice through the suffering of the innocent. This interpretation is consistent with the sacrificial "ethic of the cross" that grounded Christian pacifism. But these early writers were also expressing appreciation for the value of a Pax Romana maintained by force.

The qualified legitimacy of state power was limited, however, by unwillingness to engage in bloodshed. For example, Origen wrote, "God did not deem it in keeping with such laws as His . . . to allow the killing of any individual whatever," and added, "We do not fight under [the emperor], although he require it, but we fight on his behalf, forming a special army—an army of piety—by offering our prayers to God" (*Contra Celsus*, in Holmes 1975, 48–49).

The legitimacy of state power was also qualified by refusal to worship the emperor or the deities of the empire. In this sense, Jesus' famous aphorism in response to a question about paying taxes, "Render to Caesar the things that are Caesar's, and to God the things that are God's" (Mark 12:17 RSV), was less an affirmation of the imperial system than a challenge to the hypocrisy of his Pharisaic questioners who were actually carrying coins that declared the divinity of Augustus.

In fact, the rejection of polytheism and emperor worship may be as important a reason for early Christian rejection of military service as any of the aforementioned factors. Roman legions were dedicated to deities, and service required oaths, prayers, and sacrifices considered idolatrous. Likewise, military adornment with insignia, laurels, and crowns dedicated to Roman gods was denounced by Christian writers. Refusal to serve in the military, then, was linked to rejection of the imperial cult and the deities of the empire. This refusal sometimes led to martyrdom.

The early Christian confession that "Jesus is Lord" implied an absolute loyalty that relativized earthly allegiances and challenged all pretensions to absolutism. So Tertullian wrote, "There is no agreement between . . . the standard of Christ and the standard of the devil. One soul cannot be due to two masters—God and Caesar . . . The Lord, in disarming Peter, unbelted every soldier" (*On Idolatry* 19, in Holmes 1975, 43). Here we have the combination of religious scruple and pacifist principle that characterized the complexity of Christian positions on military service.

The Problem for Christian Ethics

Christian writers prior to Constantine unanimously condemned killing in war. It was incompatible with the love ethic of Jesus and the injunction to love one's enemies. Yet a tension between ultimate allegiance to Christ and obedience to the love ideal on the one hand, and the legitimacy of state power on the other, was present in the earliest Christian communities. This tension became a crucial problem for Christian ethics after Constantine as Christians moved into the mainstream and gained influence in affairs of state in the fourth century. This development led to Christian appropriation of just-war theory alongside the continuing pacifist traditions.

Christian ethicists debate the degree to which biblical and theological arguments of the early church should be considered normative, especially in light of other religious and sociological reasons for rejecting military service. Does loyalty to Christ require pacifism? Might pacifism imply a lack of responsibility for justice? Is military force ever ethically justified? Answers require ethicists to resolve tough questions of balance on a dialectical continuum between Christ and culture, revelation and reason, sanctification and justification, love and justice, idealism and realism, deontology and teleology.

In addition, the proper way to interpret the Sermon on the Mount in relation to the question of the meaning of the kingdom of God as present and/or future reality remains a central question in contemporary debates. Recent interpretations written by Duane Friesen, John Langan, and Glen Stassen (which appear in Stassen [1998]), Pinchas Lapide (1986), and Walter Wink (2003) are moving this discussion fruitfully beyond the debate between pacifism and just war theory and into the realm of practical peacemaking.

Rick Axtell

Further Reading

Bainton, R. (1960). *Christian attitudes toward war and peace: A historical study and critical re-evaluation*. Nashville, TN: Abingdon Press.

Barnard, L. W. (Ed. & Trans.). (1997). *St. Justin Martyr: The First and Second Apologies*. New York: Paulist Press.

Cadoux, C. J. (1925). *The early church and the world*. Edinburgh, UK: T. & T. Clark.

Cadoux, C. J. (1982). *The early Christian attitude toward war*. London: New York: Seabury Press. (Original work published 1919).

Cahill, L. S. (1994). *Love your enemies: Discipleship, pacifism, and just war theory*. Minneapolis, MN: Fortress Press.

Crossan, J. D. (1998). *The birth of Christianity: Discovering what happened in the years immediately after the crucifixion of Jesus*. San Francisco: Harper.

Helgelund, J., Daly, R. H., & Burns, J. P. (1985). *Christians and the military: The early experience*. Philadelphia: Fortress.

Holmes, A. J. (Ed.). (1975). *War and Christian ethics*. Grand Rapids, MI: Baker.

Hunter, D. G. (1992). A decade of research on early Christians and military service. *Religious Studies Review, 18*(2), 87–94.

Jeremias, J. (1963). *The meaning of the Sermon on the Mount*. Philadelphia: Fortress.

Klassen, W. (1984). *Love of enemies: The way to peace*. Philadelphia: Fortress.

Kyrtatas, D. J. (1987). *The social structure of the early Christian communities*. New York: Verso.

Lapide, P. (1986). *The Sermon on the Mount: Utopia or program for action?* Maryknoll, NY: Orbis.

Niditch, S. (1993). *War in the Hebrew Bible: A study in the ethics of violence*. Oxford, UK: Oxford University Press.

Stassen, G. H. (1992). *Just peacemaking: Transforming initiatives for justice and peace*. Louisville, KY: Westminster/ John Knox Press.

Stassen, G. H. (Ed.). (1998). *Just Peacemaking: Ten Practices for Abolishing War*. Cleveland, OH: The Pilgrim Press.

Troeltsch, E. (1981). *The social teaching of the Christian churches*, vol. 1 (O. Wyon, Trans.). Chicago: University of Chicago Press. (Original work published 1931).

Wink, Walter. (2003). *Jesus and Nonviolence: The Third Way*. Philadelphia: Fortress Press.

Wogaman, J. P. (1993). *Christian ethics: A historical introduction*. Louisville, KY: Westminster/John Knox Press.

Yoder, J. H. (1994). *The politics of Jesus* (2nd ed.). Grand Rapids, MI: Eerdmans.

Confucianism, Classical

It is necessary to preface any discussion of the Confucian traditions with a cautionary note that the amalgam of Chinese phenomena we know as Confucianism is not a "religion" in the conventional sense of the term. Many of the characteristics that a Western audience may be accustomed to finding in the world's religious traditions—an institutional church structure, an ordained priesthood or clergy, a single God or standing pantheon of deities, a set of categorical moral injunctions, an established base of self-professed practitioners—are conspicuously absent in the Confucian context or present in such a manner that they are virtually unrecognizable. Moreover, there is considerable ambiguity as to what the label "Confucianism" describes. It can alternately refer to a body of anonymous classical texts, the philosophical writings of a subclass of scholar-officials, a state-administered bureaucratic and educational system, the cumulative legacy of Chinese literary and aesthetic disciplines, the ingrained family-based ethical substrate that has historically permeated Chinese (and other Asian) societies, the ritualized forms of social interaction, the various folk practices surrounding the popular cult of ancestors, or any combinations of the above. In short, the Confucian tradition cuts across several aspects of Chinese history and civilization, including philosophy, politics, education, aesthetics, ethics, and religious practice, and it is only an act of intellectual abstraction that renders it as a single consistent and intelligible entity. Rather, Confucianism is simply a convenient designation for a cluster of ideologies and resources that have contributed to China's syncretic philosophical and religious landscapes.

Obviously, the tradition is most closely identified with the historical figure of Confucius (551–479 BCE), the Latinized version of "Grand Master Kong" (Kong Fuzi). Nevertheless, it is not really accurate to characterize him as its "founder," since the *ru* lineage with which he identified himself had already been in existence for generations prior to his lifetime. The *ru* (a word that is ordinarily misleadingly translated as "Confucian" or "Confucianism") were a faction of "cultural experts" who viewed themselves as guardians of a range of ethical principles and social forms, while drawing on a fluid body of orally transmitted material that would later be canonized as the "Five Classics." In addition, they sought to inculcate their values in the hearts of the people at large by becoming public officials and applying moral suasion to the ruling class, with the understanding that such an ethical vanguard would set the tone for the entire community and beyond. But Confucius distinguished himself from the other intellectuals of his time, offering creative interpretations and syntheses of the established traditions, and attracting an extensive following of students and disciples who would eventually recite and transmit his teachings. Within a generation or so, the *ru* tradition was more or less equated with the teaching of Confucius. And although Confucianism would undergo considerable transformation over the next two-and-a-half millennia, the symbolic and conceptual primacy of Confucius would remain essentially unchallenged.

The "Hundred Schools" Period

The teachings of Confucius inaugurate in China a protracted epoch of intellectual ferment that has been traditionally remembered as the "Hundred Schools" period, unofficially stretching from the middle of the sixth century BCE until the end of the third century BCE. The era is marked by political and moral crisis—the collapse of the old feudal structure, the loss of land to the nomadic invaders from the north, a general sense of cultural and ethical decline—and it was in response to the exigencies of the era that intellectuals offered their various solutions. By the fourth century BCE or even earlier, the dynastic family had lost all but symbolic power and the hegemonic individual states were in open contention with one another. Local rulers, each hopeful of eventually unifying China under his or her own banner and seeking viable ideologies to facilitate that goal, took the initiative to sponsor academies for the purpose of luring scholars to engage in public debate. Over the course of time, several distinct strains of thinkers emerged, including those who would be later classified as Daoists, Mohists, Legalists, Cosmologists, and Dialecticians. Thus, the classical Confucians represented a single intellectual school engaged in a kind of public competition for the mantle of ideological orthodoxy. And though perhaps hundreds of *ru* exerted some influence at one time or another, only three of them—Confucius, Mencius (Meng-tzu: c. 371–c. 289 BCE), and Xunzi (c. 312–c. 238 BCE)—left behind complete texts, which make up our primary windows into classical Confucianism.

While the three seminal Confucian philosophers were addressing different audiences and operating in somewhat different historical contexts, they were in fundamental agreement on a number of issues that cumulatively make up the core of Confucian ideology. They all believed that humans are mandated by Heaven, the Chinese lexicon's ambiguous analogue to God, to fulfill their destinies as cultivated moral beings. However, the ethical framework is predicated on an assumption that humans are, most importantly, social beings, and that perfection of the individual entails the holistic education of a person who is inextricably woven into a complex, overlapping network of relationships, all of which are extensions of family ties and are innately hierarchical in nature. Thus, the traditional Confucian relationships are those of father to son, husband to wife, elder brother to younger brother, ruler to subject, and friend-as-mentor to friend-as-apprentice. These relationships are both learned and expressed through ritual propriety, explicitly prescribed formal actions that are thought to embody both the civilizing refinements of Chinese culture and the particular virtues—e.g., filiality, loyalty, reciprocity—that are appropriate to the particular social connection. This understanding of ritualistic harmonizing of human relationships extends beyond the overtly social sphere; or rather, it extends the understanding of "social" to include relationships with Heaven, various spirits, and, most importantly, deceased ancestors. Thus, even in the earliest formulations of the tradition, there are suggestions that human harmony is tantamount to cosmic harmony.

The main issue that separates the three primary Confucians of the Hundred Schools period from one another is the question of human nature, which has some theoretical bearing on attitudes toward war and military power. Confucius himself seemed reluctant to take a position on this matter; in fact, it is repeatedly noted in the *Analects*—the compendium of aphorisms, conversations, and vignettes which provides the most reliable historical record of Confucius's teachings—that human nature was one of the subjects which he specifically declined to address. Nevertheless, he did offer a single comment, subject to conflicting interpretations in subsequent generations, that human beings are fundamentally similar to one another by nature but differentiated through actual practice. For Mencius, this suggested that all people inherently possess the potential for goodness or even sageliness, which he articulated as four incipient virtuous qualities (human-heartedness, rightness, ritual propriety, and wisdom) that can be cultivated through the efforts of the human heart and mind within the appropriate traditional contexts. While this formulation still indicates the need for rigorous education and demands the ongoing efforts of each person, it also provides something of corroboration for the composite Chinese ethnic, ethical, and cultural identity. That is to say, the implicit ontological argument is that refined Chinese culture is the fitting historical extension of human beings' innate predilection toward goodness. In his rejection of this as a kind of veiled naturalism, Xunzi maintained that humans naturally incline toward evil—easily observable in children who have not learned manners or analogous to unfinished wood that needs to be shaped by a carpenter—and that the purpose of education is to redirect and ultimately transform the original nature. Thus, Xunzi valued Chinese culture, perhaps even more than did Mencius and Confucius, not because it reflects anything about human nature, but because it represents humankind's greatest achievement, the creative construction of an environment that is both *civilized* and *civilizing*. Xunzi's interpretations appeared to dominate the Confucian landscape for the next several generations, but it would ultimately be the Mencian line that would be universally recognized as the Confucian orthodoxy.

Classical Confucianism and War

Given the priorities articulated by Confucius and his subsequent defenders, it is not surprising that the earliest Confucians devoted little attention to discussing the justifications and methods of warfare, even with an acknowledged need for the government to take an active role in the unification of the fragmenting Chinese states. Still, the passing references from both Confucius and Mencius, in tandem with one complete chapter from Xunzi on military affairs, provide enough information to reconstruct an implicit ideology. The principal starting point, which follows from the primacy placed on ethical responsibility within hierarchical social relationships, is the belief that military undertakings are the exclusive province of the head of state and, furthermore, that such undertakings will succeed only when the sovereign has first secured the loyalty of his subjects through capable and compassionate rule. Interestingly, as the ancient Confucian philosophers became increasingly aware of the inevitability of military action, whether to resist invasion or to facilitate unification, they seldom directly addressed the conditions under which a war may be deemed legitimate. This is not to say that they found such a concern trivial or unimportant, or that they failed to differentiate between valid and invalid military campaigns, as they demonstrated no reluctance in criticizing the motivations of both current and historical figures in that capacity. Instead, they worked from the consistent Confucian assumption that a true ruler who lives up to the responsibilities of his office would take up arms only when it is appropriate to do so, and that the triumph or failure of his military operation would be contingent upon whether or not he has fulfilled the Heavenly mandate. Thus, the emphasis was not on what justifies war in general or any particular armed struggle—such a determination would be a matter for the ruler's moral judgment rather than a public policy debate—but on the more elemental question of what constitutes virtuous leadership. In this sense, attitudes toward war were ultimately subsidiary to broader ethical concerns, and specific conversations on the subject were often strategically redirected.

At this juncture, one could explore Confucian theories of rulership, rehearse the personal military histories of key Confucian figures, or elucidate Xunzi's guidelines for effective military administration, but each would digress substantially from the immediately relevant issue of religion and war. Of more significant concern is the matter of how classical Confucian thinkers understood war as a regrettable but sometimes necessary vehicle for achieving their ultimate aims, which remained focused on the moral cultivation, social harmony, and cultural enrichment of the Chinese people. Thus, the purpose of war was not to establish the centrality of a specific religious institution, to convert individuals to a particular religious persuasion, or even to assert an ideological orthodoxy, but to return stability to a civilization perceived to be under ethical siege or fraught with internal conflict. Ironically, this meant that war was discussed primarily as an in-house affair, as a struggle for control within a particular civilization, rather than as a clash between or among civilizations. This is, perhaps, an unusually fitting indicator and a provocative window into the overall classical Confucian worldview, which truly regarded China as the moral and cultural center of the universe, continually charged to justify its position as the predominant locus of Heaven's attentions.

Jonathan R. Herman

Further Reading

Ames, R. T., & Rosemont, H., Jr. (Trans.). (1998). *The analects of Confucius: A philosophical translation*. New York: Ballantine Books.

Knoblock, J. (1988). *Xunzi: A translation and study of the complete works, Books 1–6*. Stanford, CA: Stanford University Press.

Knoblock, J. (1990). *Xunzi: A translation and study of the complete works, Books 7–16*. Stanford, CA: Stanford University Press.

Knoblock, J., & Knoblock, O. (1994). *Xunzi: A translation and study of the complete works, Books 17–32*. Stanford, CA: Stanford University Press.

Lau, D. C. (Trans.). (2003). *Mencius*. Hong Kong, China: The Chinese University Press.

Shun, K. (2000). *Mencius and early Chinese thought*. Stanford, CA: Stanford University Press.

Tu Wei-ming. (1993). *Way, learning, and politics: Essays on the Confucian intellectual*. Albany: State University of New York Press.

Confucianism: Han Dynasty

Military exploits during China's Han dynasty (206 BCE–220 CE) would seem to owe much to the followers of Confucius. The first part of the dynasty saw the Chinese court dominated by officials who espoused Huang-Lao Daoism; under their influence, imperial foreign policy remained generally pacifistic. The status quo changedwith the accession in 141 BCE of Emperor Wu (Wudi, 140–87 BCE), who was much lauded by later

Chinese writers for having established Confucianism as the state's orthodox philosophy. He is reported to have dismissed all Huang-Lao and most other non-Confucian officials from court around 136 BCE, retaining only Confucians in high-ranking posts. Later, in 124 BCE, he established an imperial academy where only the Confucian classics could be taught and which was to funnel its students into the civil service.

The other major political change for which Wudi is famous reveals itself in his name, usually translated as "Martial Emperor." With an expedition against marauding tribes to the northwest in 133 BCE, Wudi began a series of far-flung conquests and campaigns that, for the first time, stretched China's borders to approximately those seen on modern maps. Since the transfer of power into Confucian hands had occurred three years previously, it might well seem as if the Confucians had repudiated the peace-oriented Huang-Lao policy, urging war instead. But matters were rather more complex than that.

Confucianism, Religion, and Politics

Many scholars would protest Confucianism's appearance in this encyclopedia, arguing that the Confucian tradition was solely philosophical and not religious at all. Confucius himself explicitly refused to discuss "spirits" when asked about them, and some later Confucians such as Xunxi (298–230 BCE) flatly denied an afterlife, coming very close to atheism. But other scholars observe that Confucius upheld the rituals of ancestor worship and, more importantly, claimed to have been sent by Heaven, which he seems to have conceptualized as an anthropomorphic force superior to humanity and earth but which, interacting with them, works to achieve cosmic harmony. And even if Confucianism in general should not be considered a religion, most scholars in the Han dynasty who identified themselves as followers of Confucius clearly held religious beliefs, vociferously expressed as they repeatedly petitioned their emperors to worship an abstract Heaven and Earth instead of the gods favored by the infamously oppressive Qin dynasty (221–206 BCE), whose religious practices Gaozu (256–195 BCE; reigned 202–195 BCE), the founder of the Han dynasty had largely accepted and continued. Somewhat paradoxically, Confucians also lobbied (successfully) for Confucius's deification. In addition, they adopted the highly metaphysical ideas of two other philosophical traditions, the yin-yang and five-elements schools, linking these to Heaven in a manner that more than one sinologist has dubbed theological. Dong Zhongshu (c. 179–c. 104 BCE) and his disciples, who synthesized the metaphysics popular with most Confucians after the first quarter of the dynasty, explained that Heaven set the patterns of yin, yang, and the five elements, or phases (wood, fire, earth, metal, water), to continuously constitute the earth in a harmonious manner. Wood feeds fire; fire results in earth (ashes); earth generates metal (ore in rocks); metal condenses, rarifying into water (perhaps an idea derived from observing condensation on cold metal); then water nourishes wood (as a tree) and the whole cycle of growth begins anew. The five elements governed all other components of Earth, which could usually be grouped into five-part units as well. Yin and yang, metaphysical principles of complementarity (as female to male, dark to light, and so forth), acted as Heaven's metaphysical aids to the five elements in the process of change.

These preternatural elements in Han Confucianism would be interesting but irrelevant to the topic of this encyclopedia if they had no impact on politics. In fact, however, Han Confucians regularly adduced this cosmic synthesis in support of proposals for political change. The minutes from a scholarly conference known as the *Comprehensive Discussions in the White Tiger Hall* (*Bo hu tong*, c. 79 CE) preserve the Han Confucian approach to the civil service. "According to what pattern does the Minister admonish his Ruler?" the scholars were asked. "He models himself on metal, which straightens wood," they unflinchingly replied (Pan 1952, 468). But they did not lack opponents. Despite the purported rejection of non-Confucian officials and the status of Confucianism as the orthodox imperial philosophy, Confucians at the court of Wudi (and at his son's court as well) often faced off with Legalists, who tended to hold more positions of genuine political power. Mocking the Confucian ideal of maintaining social order with proper education and benevolent leadership, Legalists followed the precedent set in the Qin dynasty and advocated aggressive government upheld by a harsh regime of law and punishment.

The Confucians refused to back down, though, and their numbers increased as time went on. Upon the occurrence of unsettling natural phenomena, the Confucians could be counted on to step forward and argue that Heaven had just expressed displeasure at the immorality engendered by non-Confucian behavior. They would support their contentions by fleshing out the details of Heaven's message with analyses based on which of the five elements had been involved, on the positions of the stars in Heaven, on the balance of yin and yang that day, or on some combination. A remarkably detailed example is preserved from the reign of Huandi (reigned 146–167 CE), who pardoned certain notorious criminals with ties to influential palace eunuchs in 166. Two officials disregarded the imperial proclamation and punished the miscreants anyhow, whereupon they themselves were arrested and scheduled for execution. One sympathizer, Xiang Kai, seized on a spring and summer of excessively cold temperatures and an unusual amount of precipitation to protest that Heaven was on the side of the officials. Xiang's divination soon progressed from earthly to heavenly portents; Huandi was told that "the stars and constellations are the adornments of heaven in the same way that the myriad kingdoms are in attendance on the true king. When those in lower positions are planning to rebel against the authority above them, it is then that the stars turn against heaven" (de Crespigny 1976, 22–27). Huan's insistence on these unrighteous executions, Xiang warned, had caused inauspicious movements by the " 'punishing' stars of Metal and Fire" (Venus and Mars, respectively identified with sharp weapons and warfare), which indicated "misfortune for the Son of Heaven." As Xiang warmed to his theme, he elaborated, "Either the emperor will die, or there will surely be a rebellion . . . This is a sign that there will be heavy fighting, that China is weak and the barbarians are strong" (de Crespigny 1976, 22–27). Xiang proved prescient on all three counts. Huandi soon died; major rebellions began to rip the empire apart only seventeen years later; and only a century after the dynasty's demise, steppe tribes from Central Asia conquered and occupied most of the traditional northern Chinese heartland.

Confucianism and War

The Confucian practice of interpreting omens was sometimes called upon to support the deployment of armed forces. In 112, when Chinese diplomats were killed in Nanyue (modern Vietnam), "on the last day of the month, there was an eclipse of the sun. In the autumn, toads and frogs fought together" (Pan 1938, 79–80). Finding in these phenomena a command (or at least a suggestion) from Heaven, Wudi dispatched six armies to conquer the recalcitrant kingdom. Nevertheless, Wudi's combination of Confucianism and conquest is a puzzling one, for Confucians were almost honor-bound to oppose war. A text that attained immense popularity during the Han period, the *Classic of Filial Piety* (*Xiao jing*, c. 350–222 BCE), decrees in the first paragraph, "Seeing that our body, with hair and skin, is derived from our parents, we should not allow it to be injured in any way" (Barnhart 1993). A conscientious Confucian, therefore, could not help but object to the practice of conscripting men into the army (Han forces were almost entirely comprised of draftees) and forcing them to risk bodily damage in combat.

A second bias against military endeavors grew from Confucius's promotion of rulers who held sway over their dominions not with violence but with persuasion, good example, and a kind of metaphysical charisma accrued by upright conduct. Resort to force was seen by Confucians as an admission of political incompetence. The only blanket exception to this general Confucian opposition to war concerned the famous mandate of Heaven, whereby Heaven withdrew its favor from an immoral ruler and produced another who was to assume leadership of the empire, usually by force of arms. However, Mencius (c. 371–c. 289 BCE), one of the most important pre-Han Confucians and probably the first to begin fleshing out the concept of a direct Heavenly mandate for earthly politics, went so far as to deny the veracity of the *Classic of History (Shu jing)* where it describes near-perfect King Wen—Heaven's new favorite—leading troops into battle. Because Wen was a sage, argued Mencius, his virtue was such that his opponents would all have given up without a fight.

Han Confucians were no less adamant. Despite the fact that Confucian ascendancy at Wudi's court coincided with militaristic policies, it is clear that the former did not lead to the latter; the incident during Huandi's time illustrates well the Confucians' view that armed conflict resulted from poor rulership. They also believed that war made bad conditions worse. Records of Wudi's reign are replete with Confucian memorials to the throne warning that yin and yang were being driven out of balance by the wars, protesting the hardship and disruption of peasant life caused by removing men from their farms or by raising taxes to fund campaigns. Some scholars attribute the incongruence of Wudi's regime, with its installation of Legalist-minded officials and its official support of Confucianism, to the emperor's early accession (he was only sixteen). Fresh from the teaching of his tutors, who happen to have been Confucians, he was led by youthful enthusiasm to make Confucianism the state orthodoxy. Soon thereafter he decided that the Legalists offered a better way to rule, but because of the outrage that would have arisen throughout the empire if he had openly espoused the methods of the despised

Qin tyrant, he continued to sponsor Confucianism as a smoke screen. Or perhaps the emperor was simply applying Dong Zhongshu's Confucian cosmology, balancing Confucianism's soft yin with Legalism's yang. Another theory holds that Wudi, notorious for being constantly duped by magicians who promised him the secret of immortality, liked Dong Zhongshu's metaphysics because they could easily be interpreted to support the possibility of living forever. This interest encouraged the emperor to retain Confucians at court, but mainly in capacities concerning state religious ceremonies and social protocol rather than direct political influence.

As the years passed, however, the Confucians gained ground. Under the eighth emperor, Yuandi (reigned 49–33 BCE), they achieved sufficient influence to greatly reduce the court's use of military force. The later *Comprehensive Discussions*, which seem to have introduced few new ideas or policies, can be assumed to reiterate earlier Confucian stipulations. For example, if conflict became inevitable, the emperor or his general were to don humble clothing to mirror the sorrow of Earth and the displeasure of Heaven at the impending exercise of force; thus did the Confucians cleverly play on Heaven and Earth's relationship to the emperor (as his metaphysical father and mother) in order to forbid the pomp and display often used to generate enthusiasm for war. Another ruling limited the draft to men over twenty-nine, so they could have sufficient time to procreate before being placed in harm's way. A particularly confining stricture reduced allowable time on campaign to a single season, for human affairs should follow the patterns Heaven had set in nature, and since the four seasons each accomplished their work in a span of roughly three months, the emperor should do the same.

The Confucians maintained their momentum through the reigns of three more emperors and into an interregnum during which a former official, Wang Mang (45 BCE–23 CE; reigned 8–23 CE), held sway. During the strife that overthrew the usurper and reinstated the legitimate dynasty, a wealthy member of the imperial family named Fan Hong was credited with an ideal Confucian response to the violence. When Fan's nephew, the imperial heir Guang Wu, offered to make Fan a general, the latter "made excuses, and said: 'A student of books does not practise the affairs of soldiers' " (Bielenstein 1953, 57). Later, when a different faction menaced his home, Fan sent them oxen, wine, rice, and grain as a present. Since Fan had always practiced Confucian principles of leadership, the rebels had already "heard of [his] . . . goodness and generosity, and they all praised him and said: 'The Lord Fan has always been kind. Besides, now that we have been treated like this, how could we have the heart to attack him?' They withdrew their soldiers and went away" (Bielenstein 1953, 57).

After this, during the second half of the dynasty (beginning in 26 CE), Confucians dominated the bureaucracy even more completely than before. Wang Mang's defeat, however, tainted the orthodox Confucianism taught at the state-sponsored academy. A staunch five-elements Confucian, Wang had been one of its products, yet he had been resoundingly rejected by Heaven. Despite Wang's debacle, Emperor Guang Wu continued to support the Confucianism established by his predecessors, but some scholars were less sanguine. Disillusioned or at least disturbed, they turned to a rival, minority school of Confucianism that advocated versions of the Classics significantly different from the texts embraced by state academicians. At the same time, orthodox careers in public scholarship and officialdom apparently became less rigorous, thus attracting the less talented. Fan Ye (398–446), a historian who had access to some of the scholarly works produced during the Han's last century, excoriated them as "trifling . . . [attempts at] outdoing each other in inaneness; the [old] tradition of the Confucians had fallen on evil days indeed" (Pan 1938, 149).

Records show that officials of the later Han indeed expressed less concern than their forerunners over the deleterious potential of military conflict. While later emperors never equaled Wudi's energetic campaigning, they launched expeditions against the steppe tribes often enough; the number of Confucian antiwar protests went down, however, as the number of ostensible Confucians went up. And apathy was a comparatively minor problem. The major one was increasing venality. Accusations of official corruption were voiced with mounting frequency, and historians have found evidence that yin-yang and five-element divinations and prognostications were indeed sometimes deliberately manipulated for political purposes. Well-known Confucians who were honest started refusing to serve in the government; immorality and greed, they insisted, ran so rampant in public life that they would either be unable to make positive changes or would be forced into corruption in order to accomplish anything. One highly respected statesman, Chen Fan (active from 158), strove to stem the tide, but even his spotless reputation was not enough to sway some of the conscientious recluses whom he invited to take office. Chen himself was killed in 168 trying to stop palace eunuchs from meddling with national politics.

The Confucian Eclipse

When the empire fell, Confucianism fell with it. Even a vigorous (and nearly rebellious) antiestablishment Confucian reform movement called the "Pure Stream" was itself reportedly corrupted toward the dynasty's end. Memories of the tradition's mid-dynasty vitality grew dim, and from a massive Daoist revolt in 184 CE to the formal abdication of the last puppet emperor in 220, scholars and gentlemen caught up in the chaos and conflict surrounding the Han dynasty's disintegration abandoned systematic Confucianism for Daoism. The latter dominated the thinking of the ensuing Six Dynasties period (220–618) and served as a vehicle for the introduction of Buddhism, which in turn became so popular that after the Tang emperors reunited China in 618, the foreign religion displaced native traditions as the preeminent intellectual influence on politics. When Confucianism reemerged triumphant in the Song dynasty (960–1279), most scholars dismissed Tong Zhongshu's Han synthesis as a superstitious betrayal of Confucius's teaching, and this attitude remained current for nearly a thousand years. It was only on the eve of the twentieth century that Kang Youwei (1858–1927) and other political reformers renewed the study of Han Confucianism. Notwithstanding their efforts, the imperial edifice toppled in 1912, this time never to rise again. But through those efforts the flavor of Confucianism first prominent in the empire was, perhaps fittingly, resurrected at the last, reappearing to bow out the political order that it had helped establish over two millennia before.

Michael L. Fitzhugh

See also Confucianism, Classical; Daoism, Huang-Lao

Further Reading

Barnhart, R.M. (Ed.). (1993). *Li Kung-lin's "Classic of filial piety."* New Haven, CT: Yale University Press.

Bielenstein, H. (1953). *The restoration of the Han dynasty.* Stockholm: Author.

Ching, J. (1993). *Chinese religions.* Maryknoll, NY: Orbis Books.

Confucius. (1979). *The analects (Lun yu)* (D. C. Lau, Trans.). Harmondsworth, UK: Penguin Books.

de Crespigny, R. (1976). *Portents of protest in the later Han dynasty: The memorials of Hsiang K'ai to Emperor Huan.* Canberra: Australian National University Press.

de Crespigny, R. (1984). *Northern frontier: The policies and strategy of the Later Han Empire.* Canberra: Australian National University Press.

Dreyer, E. L, Kierman, F. A., & Fairbank, J. K. (Eds.). (1974). *Chinese ways in warfare.* Cambridge, MA: Harvard University Press.

Fung, Y. (1952–1953). *A history of Chinese philosophy* (Vol. 1) (D. Bodde, Trans.). Princeton, NJ: Princeton University Press.

Graham, A. C. (1989). *Disputers of the Tao: Philosophical argument in ancient China.* La Salle, IL: Open Court.

Hulsewe, A. F. P. (1979). *China in Central Asia, the early stage: 125 BC–AD 23.* Leiden, Netherlands: E. J. Brill.

Lau, D. C. (Trans.). (1970). *Mencius.* Harmondsworth, UK: Penguin Books.

Loewe, M. (1961). *Military operations in the Han period.* London: China Society.

Loewe, M. (1968). *Everyday life in early Imperial China during the Han period, 202 B.C.–A.D. 220.* London: Putnam.

Loewe, M. (1974). *Crisis and conflict in Han China, 104 BC to AD 9.* London: Allen & Unwin.

Loewe, M. (1982). *Chinese ideas of life and death: Faith, myth, and reason in the Han period (202 BC–AD 220).* London: Allen & Unwin.

Loewe, M. (1994). *Divination, mythology and monarchy in Han China.* New York: Cambridge University Press.

Makra, M. L. (Trans.). (1961). *Hsiao Ching.* New York: St. John's University Press.

Needham, J. (1956). *Science and civilisation in China* (Vol. 2.). Cambridge, UK: Cambridge University Press.

Pan, K. (1938–1955). *The history of the former Han dynasty: A critical translation with annotations* (Vols. 1–3) (H. H. Dubs, T. Jen, & L. P'an, Trans.). Baltimore: Waverly Press.

Pan, K. (1949–1952). *Po hu t'ung: The comprehensive discussions in the White Tiger Hall* (Vols. 1–2) (T. S. Tjan, Trans.). Leiden, Netherlands: E. J. Brill.

Poo, M. (1998). *In search of personal welfare: A view of ancient Chinese religion.* Albany: State University of New York Press.

Queen, S. A. (1996). *From chronicle to canon: The hermeneutics of the* Spring and Autumn Annals *according to Tung Chung-shu.* New York: Cambridge University Press.

Taylor, R. L. (1990). *The religious dimensions of Confucianism.* Albany: State University of New York Press.

Thompson, L. G. (1996). *Chinese religion: An introduction* (5th ed.). Belmont, CA: Wadsworth Publishing Co.

Twitchett, D. C., Loewe, M., & Fairbank, J. K. (Eds.). (1986). *The Ch'in and Han empires, 221 B.C–A.D. 220.* Cambridge, UK: Cambridge University Press.

Xiao, G. (1978). *A history of Chinese political thought* (Vol. 1). Princeton, NJ: Princeton University Press.

Confucianism, Modern

In the middle of the nineteenth century, Confucianism was still the backbone of Chinese culture. However, strict thought censorship during the Qing dynasty (1644–1912) and other historical factors had reduced the tradition to a lifeless array of formalistic ritual norms and arid philological scholarship. After the two Opium Wars (1840–1842 and 1860) and as Western culture encroached, Confucianism gradually lost more ground as a spiritual tradition and as an inspiration for life. To make things worse, when Chinese intellectuals came to realize that China was technologically behind in comparison with the West, they identified the Confucian tradition as the culprit. Anger at the burden of Confucian tradition exploded with the May Fourth Movement (1919), an intellectual and political movement whose leaders rejected Confucianism in favor of Western science, political philosophy, and technology. The anti-Confucian trend reached its apex with the Cultural Revolution (1966–1976), which cast suspicion on all aspects of traditional culture.

Lone thinkers who went against the current, such as Liang Shuming (1893–1988), Zhang Junmai (also known as Carsun Chang, 1886–969), and Xiong Shili (1885–1968), had to face the challenging task of revitalizing Confucianism. Their main effort was directed toward rebuilding its metaphysics and cosmology as well as ethics. Their efforts were notable in rediscovering the true foundation of Confucian ethics hidden under accumulated centuries' worth of encrustations. It was a hard task, and they concentrated on basics. With regard to war, they had a set view inherited from Confucius (551–479 BCE) and Mencius (c. 371–c. 289 BCE), two foundational Confucian thinkers, who taught how to construct a lasting peace in the person, family, and society. Confucius did not deny the need at times for a just war, as one can discover by reading the *Chunqiu* (*Spring and Autumn Annals*), China's first chronological history, which Confucius revised. Living in a turbulent age, the Confucians of the twentieth century were often involved in wars and often had to take sides. The hardest and longest one was the second Sino-Japanese War (known in China as the War Against Japanese Aggression), which lasted from 1937 to 1945 and in which all the Confucian scholars of the time took part. During the Cold War, Mou Zongsan (1909–1995), another leading modern Confucian, criticized as excessive the pacifism of the British philosopher Bertrand Russell (1872–1970), who believed surrender of the West to the Soviet Union was preferable to nuclear war.

Liang Shuming

Modern Confucians believe that the supreme ideal of Confucianism for social life is harmony, as taught in various ancient classics. In 1921 Liang Shuming, forerunner of the contemporary Confucian movement, wrote in *Eastern and Western Cultures and Their Philosophies* that the essence of reality is change, according to the basic idea contained in the *Yijing (Book of Changes)*. He views the universe as not in a static state, but in a state of change and flow:

> The so-called change simply means [a process] from harmony to disharmony or from disharmony to harmony. (Liang 1989–1993, I, 445)

According to Liang, the cosmological view coming down from the *Book of Changes* has helped the Chinese people to live a life with harmony, yielding, and compromise. Liang felt that the Chinese are habitually inclined to regard themselves as being partners and friends of nature and as being compassionate members of their family and society. After receiving a Western-style education, Liang had a spiritual crisis and isolated himself at home for three years studying Buddhism. Later turning to Confucianism, he started teaching. His steadfast temper explains why even in Maoist China he would dare to speak out even facing Mao Zedong.

Fang Dongmei

Fang Dongmei (anglicized to Thomé Fang: 1899–1977) was a professor of Western philosophy in Nanjing (Nanking). He wrote books on Chinese philosophy in English during the last thirty years of his life while teaching in Taipei, Taiwan. Fang identified the two basic components of Confucianism by phrasing them as "creative creativity" (*sheng sheng bu yi)* and "comprehensive harmony" (by interpreting the Confucian traditional ideal of harmony [*he*] or Great Harmony [*taihe*]). Fang finds that Western thought is often permeated with what he calls "vicious bifurcation," which sets a number of things in implacable hostility—every-

Confucianism and Village Life

The following text describing life in a Taiwan village demonstrates the continuing central role played by Confucianism in Chinese life, despite the influences of Daoism, Buddhism, and Westernization.

While Confucianism is closely integrated within the religious system, there is no formal cult or official Confucian ritual in Hsin Hsing village. Although there is a Confucian temple in Lukang, usually only residents of that city worship there. However, the moral and ethical teachings of Confucianism are present in the rules of correct behavior which have been passed down from generation to generation of villagers. Filial piety, respect for age and authority, and worship of the ancestors are all considered both important and fundamental to correct behavior. Aptly expressing a rather general feeling, one villager said, "Everyone knows it's natural to act this way. What other way is there to act?"

***Source:* Gallin, Bernard. (1966). *Hsin Hsing, Taiwan: a Chinese Village in Change.* Berkeley and Los Angeles: University of California Press, p. 232–233.**

thing is separated into opposites, which, instead of being seen as complementary, are seen as in opposition. He perceives that in the Western scheme of things the universe seems to be a theater of war wherein all sorts of entities or phenomena are arrayed one against another:

> Among the great minds of mankind, there are those who, being versed in the method of bifurcation, tend, like a certain mythical giant, to see things doubled in image. Judged in the light of their imagined visions, the world is shot through with two irreconcilables. The Absolute Being is set in sheer contrast with the Not-Being. Existence is sharply divided into the authentic and the illusory. Life is disjoined from its natural conditions in the world—it is to be lived only after death, or in the phraseology of Socrates, after a long practice of dying. Values in the eternal forms of Truth, Goodness, Beauty, and Justice are severed from all the defiled disvalues, namely, the False, the Evil, the Ugly, and the Unjust. As William Blake is fond of saying, "Good is Heaven; Evil is Hell." Anything that cannot cling to Heaven must retreat into Hell. Similarly, man as an individual has the make-up of a soul and a body at odds with each other. The soul as the seat of reason is identified with the Good while the body as the source of energy is named as the Evil. And man will be tormented in eternity for following his bodily energies. We breathe the same air in the Platonic *Phaedo*, in the *Book of Revelation*, as well as in the *City of God*. (Fang 1981, 18)

Fang concludes his panoramic view of Western culture by saying that:

> As Nature is made incongruous with Man, so within man himself, the shrinking ego is out of keeping with the elevated transcendental Selfhood. The instances of antithesis of this kind might be infinitely multiplied. In a word, the extreme importance of harmony is either simply ignored or hopelessly misconstrued. (Fang 1980, 11)

As a response to this scenario, Fang offers Chinese metaphysics (which for Fang includes Confucianism, Daoism, and Buddhism) characterized by comprehensive harmony:

> For several thousands of years, we Chinese have been thinking of these vital problems in terms of comprehensive harmony, which permeates anything and everything. It sounds like an eternal symphony swaying and swinging all the sky, all the earth, all the air, all the water, merging all forms of existence in one supreme bliss of unity. (Fang, 1981, 18)

Fang saw his philosophical system as open to harmonizing and fitting together all kinds of doctrines and ideas, whether they originated from the West or the East, whether they were ancient, medieval, or modern, provided only that they offered profound insights into reality and human nature. Fang's views influenced the thousands of pupils who have studied him. No doubt, he has contributed a good deal toward the internationalization of Confucian philosophy.

On Confucianism

What I am speaking about are the soldiers of a benevolent man, the intentions of a true king. You speak of the value of plots and advantageous circumstances, of moving by sudden attack and stealth—but these are matters appropriate only to one of the feudal lords. Against the soldiers of a benevolent man, deceptions are of no use; they are effective only against a ruler who is rash and arrogant, whose people are worn out; they are effective only against a state in which the ruler and his subjects, superiors and inferiors, are torn apart and at odds.

Source: Xunzi. (1963). *Hsun Tzu, Basic Writings* (Burton Watson, Trans.). New York: Columbia University Press, p. 57.

In the Confucian tradition, human flourishing entails a series of concentric circles encompassing the self, family, community, society, nation, world, and cosmos. Since the self is conceived as a centre of relationships rather than an isolated individual, we can envision Confucian self-realization in terms of a gradual expansion of self-consciousness to embrace an ever-extending network of human-relatedness. The cultivation of the self provides a basis for cooperation in the family; the regulation of familial relationships enhances communal participation which, in turn, facilitates social solidarity. As national security is rooted in social well-being, peace in the world is built on the governance of states.

Source: Tu Wei-ming. (1999). "Humanity as Embodied Love: Exploring Filial Piety in a Global Ethical Perspective." In David Goicoechea & Marco Zlomislic (Eds.), *Jen Agape Tao with Tu Wei-Ming.* Binghamton, NY: Institute of Global Studies, pp. 28–29.

Tang Junyi

Tang Junyi (1909–1978) was a philosophy professor in Nanjing, who, after 1949, took refuge in Hong Kong. In the many books he wrote, Tang Junyi (Wade-Giles romanization: T'ang Chun-i) illustrates his discovery of the moral mind, "which is as divine as it is human" (Tang 1988, 329). One of his frequent themes is the religious import of Confucianism. Joining the debate over whether Confucianism is or is not a religion, Tang states that Confucianism is not totally on an equal footing with other religions. In outer structure, it is inferior to other religions: It lacks dogmas, a charismatic founder, and a well-defined organization. On the other hand, Tang finds that because Confucianism is based on the presence of the moral mind and on the innate impulse for transcendence, it is full of religious spirit, and from this point of view, it is not inferior to other religions. In Tang's view it is essential that all world faiths emphasize the presence of the moral mind and the impulse for transcendence. In other words, the foundation of Confucianism is exactly also the foundation of the other religions.

As Tang sees it, in Confucianism, the goal of human life is sagehood, which is, Tang argues, the goal of all religions. He views the various religions of the world as different ways to reach the same destination:

> All religions are only different expressions of the deepest human nature and at the same time the different channels where the mandates of Heaven flourish or are the different ways (Tao) by which different people attain their sagehood and likeness or conformity to Heaven. (Tang 1988, 330)

To summarize, Tang sees Confucianism as based on universal human nature, while the various religious denominations are based on belonging to a certain group or church, following a certain inspired founder, and keeping a certain set of beliefs. Since they are established on a different foundation from Confucianism, they are not in competition with it; thus Confucianism can easily combine with other religions in people's hearts. This explains the phenomenon, rather common in Chinese history and society, of multiple religious allegiances. Among the Chinese one can easily find Confucian Buddhists, Confucian Daoists, as well as Confucian Muslims and Confucian Christians, and even Confucian Daoist-Buddhists, and so on.

Moreover, in Tang's view there have never been religious wars in China:

> There have never been religious wars and only a few religious persecutions in Chinese history. The controversies among the Buddhists, the Taoists, and the Confucians in Chinese history usually culminated in

> a theory of reconciliation among the three teachings or of syncretism and mutual respect, each teaching performing a different function. The metaphor of the three rooms in a home, used by the Confucian Wang Lung-hsi (1498–1583) is apt and significant. (Tang 1988, p.330)

One view is that the persecution of the Buddhists under the Tang dynasty was basically an economic policy, not a religious issue as no one was killed, a huge amount of land was taken from the convents, hundreds of thousands of nuns were sent home, and countless indentured servants of the monasteries were set free.

Tang firmly believes that it has been thanks to the Confucian religious spirit that various religions could live together in China under the same roof for so many centuries. In his view, this tolerance only broke down after the entrance of Western religion on the Chinese scene. The only two religious wars he finds in Chinese history, both quite bloody, are the Taiping Rebellion (1850–1864) and the Boxer Uprising (1900). Both happened after the forced entrance of Western religion through the intervention of Great Britain (1840). Tang defines the Taiping Rebellion as a war between an indigenous Chinese version of Christianity and traditional Confucianism. The latter won the war. As for the Boxer Uprising, he defines it as a war of popular Chinese religion against foreign Christianity. Popular religion lost the war. Chinese intellectual historians for the most part agreed with Tang Junyi.

The Learning of Harmony

The renowned philosopher Feng Youlan (1895–1990) in his old age rejected his previous commitment to the Marxist notion of struggle and stressed the value of harmony not only in the human world, but also in the relationship between humans and nature. The renowned philosopher Feng Youlan (1895–1990) was the author of the first accurate *History of Chinese Philosophy*. Taking the lead and the vocabulary from the *Philosophy of Principle (lixue)* of Neo-Confucian China, Feng toiled at expounding his own *New Philosophy of Principle*, pouring Aristotelian content into Confucian vessels. During the last decades of the twentieth century other scholars have followed in the path of the contemporary Confucians discussed here. Scholars such as Tang Yijie (b. 1927), Meng Peiyuan (b. 1938), and Qian Xun (b. 1933), continued to develop the idea of harmony in Chinese thought, each from a special perspective. Tang Yijie, for instance, emphasizes the traditional concept of universal harmony, which he explains as inclusive of four dimensions: harmony in nature, between humans and nature, of humans among themselves, and harmony within a human person.

In China during the 1980s and 1990s, a whole current of thought defined as the learning of harmony has flourished. Its most active promoter has been Zhang Liwen (b. 1935). A well-known scholar and philosopher, Zhang writes from a Marxist background. He labors at reinterpreting the whole history and culture of China as centered on the key concept of harmony and cooperation. He also asserts that the learning of harmony is the best way to overcome all the challenges coming from the complex situation of conflict in the world today. At the same time, he endeavors to find a place inside the Confucian ideal of harmony for the Marxist concept of conflict. He suggests that reaching harmony is valuable because it ends a conflict (which implies that there needs first to be conflict).

Confucianism's Lessons for the Western World

On the whole, today's Confucians still have a mind-set shaped after Confucius, taking for granted that personal moral cultivation is always the root of a harmonious life among humans. As Tu Wei-ming, an outspoken U.S.-based expounder of Confucian values to Western audiences, says:

> If human relations are harmonized, it is because the people involved have cultivated themselves. To anticipate a harmonious state of affairs in one's social interaction as a favorable condition for self-cultivation is, in the Confucian sense, not only unrealistic but also illogical. Self-cultivation is like the root and trunk, and harmonious human relations are like the branches. Both temporally and in terms of importance, the priority is irreversible. (Tu 1985, 56)

When it comes to the topic of religion and war, the charges raised against Western culture by Fang Dongmei and Tang Junyi are especially serious. Fang pointed his finger at the drastic bifurcation (and implied conflict between the paired opposites) existing in Western minds, while Tang blamed China's few religious wars on Western culture. Scholars may be slow to accept these charges, due to the complex array of issues involved. They call for no less than a thorough analysis of China's long history and ancient culture. Many have argued that there were religious conflicts in China long before the coming of Westerners. Nevertheless, if the charges of the modern Confucians have even the slightest basis, they cannot but stimulate us and provoke deep reflection.

Umberto Bresciani

Further Reading

Berthrong, J. (1994). *All under heaven: Transforming paradigms in Confucian-Christian dialogue*, Albany: State University of New York Press.

Berthrong, J. (1998). *Transformations of the Confucian Way*. Boulder, CO: Westview Press.

Bresciani, U. (2001). *Reinventing Confucianism: The New Confucian Movement*. Taipei, Taiwan: Ricci Institute.

Chan, W. (1973). *A Source Book in Chinese Philosophy*. Princeton, NJ: Princeton University Press.

Cheng, C., & Bunnin, N. (Eds.). (2002). *Contemporary Chinese philosophy*. Malden, MA: Blackwell Publishers.

Ching, J. (1978). *Confucianism and Christianity: A Comparative Study*. Tokyo: Kodansha International.

de Bary, W. T., & Tu, W. (Eds.). (1998). *Confucianism and Human Rights*. New York: Columbia University Press.

Fang, T. H. (1980). *The Chinese view of life: A philosophy of comprehensive harmony*. Taipei, Taiwan: Linking Publishing.

Fang, T. H. (1981). *Chinese philosophy: Its spirit and its development*, Taipei, Taiwan: Linking Publishing.

Ivanhoe, P. J. (1993). *Confucian moral self-cultivation*. New York: Peter Lang.

Liang, S. (1989–1993). *Liang Shuming quanji* [The complete works of Liang Shuming] (Vols. 1–8). Jinan, China: Shandong Renmin Chubanshe.

Liu, S. (1998). *Understanding Confucian philosophy: Classical and Sung-Ming*. Westport, CT: Praeger Publishers.

T'ang, C. (1977). *Shengming cunzai yu xinling jingjie* [The existence of life and the world of the spirit] (Vols. 1–2). Taipei, Taiwan: Student Book Co.

T'ang, C. (1988). *Essays on Chinese philosophy and culture*. Taipei, Taiwan: Student Book Co.

Tu, W. (1976). *Centrality and commonality: An essay on Chung-yung*. Honolulu: The University Press of Hawaii.

Tu, W. (1976). *Neo-Confucian thought in action: The youth of Wang Yang-ming*. Berkeley & Los Angeles: University of California Press.

Tu, W. (1985). *Confucian thought: Selfhood as creative transformation*. Albany: State University of New York Press.

Zhang, L. (1997). *Hehexue gailun: 21 shiji wenhua zhanlue de gouxiang* [The learning of harmony and cooperation: An outline of the strategy for a culture for the 21st century] (Vols. 1–2). Beijing, China: Shifan daxue chubanshe.

Confucianism, Neo-Confucianism

Like Confucius (551–479 BCE), the founder of Confucianism, and Mencius (c. 372–c. 289 BCE), one of the earliest Confucian philosophers, the Neo-Confucians—those who revitalized Confucianism from the eleventh century—tended to speak little of military arts and war. Emphasizing ritual propriety, ethical rule, and equitable distribution, they viewed military conflict as Pyrrhic at best. Moreover, they thought military action for power and conquest often led to a state of incessant conflict difficult to pacify. Consequently, like Confucius, they sought to legitimate war only in the form of punitive action initiated by the highest level authority—the emperor.

Why the Neo-Confucians Pondered War and Military Arts

From early in the Han dynasty (206 BCE–220 CE) until the end of Imperial China in 1912, Confucians pondered warfare, particularly at times when the central plains lay in barbarian hands. Such was the situation when Neo-Confucian master Zhu Xi (1130–1200) contemplated those matters during the Southern Song dynasty (1127–1279) and when Wang Shouren (or Wang Yangming, 1472–1529) contemplated military arts to deal with marauding barbarians on the empire's frontier during the Ming dynasty (1368–1644). Generally, however, the court held absolute power in imperial China, and the Neo-Confucians' legitimization of punitive action initiated by the highest-level authority only served to strengthen the imperial hand. Even today, the Chinese government assumes this rationale in its harsh treatment of "separatist forces" in Tibet and especially in Xinjiang.

Roots in Classical Confucianism

Confucius embraced the ideal that only the emperor had the authority to conduct military campaigns because history had taught Confucius that states within the realm—even those claiming the best of intentions—generally resorted to war when they couldn't shore up their own state from within. Often blinded to the cost of war in lives and resources, they engaged in military assaults mainly to enlarge their share of land, thus triggering chain reactions of interstate aggression.

Living in a more warlike age, Mencius developed and expanded on Confucius's notion of justifiable military action. At the same time, while arguing that the

Selections from the Writings of Confucianists and Neo-Confucianists on War

In his punitive expedition, Tang began with Ge. With this, he gained the trust of the Empire, . . . so when he marched to the south, the northern barbarians complained, "Why does he not come to us first?" The people longed for his coming as they longed for a rainbow in time of severe drought. Those who were going to market did not stop; those who were plowing went on plowing. He only punished the evil rulers and brought security to the people, like the fall of timely rain, and the people rejoiced greatly in his coming. (*Mencius* 1B.11)

There are people who say, "I am expert at military formations; I am expert at waging war." This is a grave crime. If the ruler of a state is drawn to humanity, he will have no match in the Empire. Thus, "When he marched to the south, the northern barbarians complained; when he marched to the east, the western barbarians complained. They all said, 'Why does he not come to us first?' "

When King Wu marched on Yin, he had three hundred war chariots and three thousand brave warriors. He said, "Do not be afraid, I come to bring you peace, not to wage war on the people." Then, the sound of people knocking their heads on the ground—to show gratitude and respect—was like the collapse of a mountain. To wage a punitive war is to rectify. There is no one who does not wish himself to be rectified. What, then, is the need for war?' (*Mencius* 7B.4)

The humane man indeed loves others; because he loves others, he hates to see men bring harm to them. The righteous man acts on his sense of appropriateness, and so he hates to see men commit terrible wrongs. He takes up arms only in order to put an end to violence and harm, not in order to contend with others for spoils. Therefore, where the troops of a humane ruler are encamped, they too command respect, and where they pass, they transform the people. Their arrival is like the timely rains in which all men rejoice. . . . The [sagely] four emperors and two kings all marched through the Empire with their troops guided by humanity and appropriateness, The people close-by were won over by their goodness, and those afar were filled with longing for their excellence. They swords were not blood-stained, yet people near and far submitted willingly. Their excellence flourished in the center of the realm and spread out to the four quarters. This is what the *Odes* means when it says:

The good man, the noble gentleman,
In demeanor and conduct, he is without fault;
In demeanor and conduct, he is without fault;
He rectifies the states that fill the four quarters.

(*Xunxi*, ch.15)

authority to conduct war lies solely in the emperor's hands, he specified conditions under which a despotic ruler himself might be overthrown and replaced. The rationale for Mencius's view of war and military action was the primacy of the people: The people are the most important element of a state, and their welfare is the primary responsibility of the court. Since war and military action inevitably bring destruction and death to the common people, they are evil modes of conduct and should be contemplated solely as measures of last resort. Even then, armies should be raised only during seasons when the people are free—not, for example, when they are needed to harvest their crops.

Xunzi (c. 312–c. 238 BCE) lived in an even more chaotic age. He sharpened the teeth of Confucianism in arguing for the viability and indispensability of Confucianism, even in those anarchic times. Accordingly, he introduced penal regulations as a subcategory of ritual action and argued that the achievement of individual excellence and humaneness depended on rigorous training in ritual conduct and instruction in bona fide classics. He also encouraged a more activist government that would ensure public trust and order by taking such measures as standardizing weights and measures and even regulating word meanings and language use. While Confucius's *Analects* contain only occasional remarks on military affairs and the *Mencius* (the writings of Mencius) takes up warfare only in the course of discussing specific cases, the *Xunzi* (the writings of Xunzi) includes an essay on the topic of military affairs. Broadly, Xunzi insisted that it was the eminence of a just, ritually proper ruler and the vitality of his well-ordered state that attracted the favor and allegiance of people and rulers far and wide. While contextualizing the role of the military in state life and politics, Xunzi delineated the traits of the true king and went far beyond Confucius and Mencius by describing the effective general and offering practical advice on military training, command, intelligence, planning, and action.

Evolution of Confucianism

During the Han dynasty (206 BCE–220 CE) Confucian scholars, the conservators of ancient tradition and ministers of humane rule, confined themselves to the humanities and public affairs and did not pay particular heed to martial matters. Confucianism in this form persisted into the Tang dynasty (618–907), though it lost much of its broad public appeal to ascendant Chan Buddhism and religious Daoism. A new form of Confucianism—Neo-Confucianism—arose during the Northern Song dynasty (960–1126) that revived Confucius's original focus on self-cultivation. For the Neo-Confucians, war and military affairs remained secondary to pressing ethical and philosophical concerns. One of the founders of Neo-Confucianism, Zhang Zai (1020–1077), in youth loved to discuss military matters and sought to make a name for himself for his martial attainments. At age eighteen, however, when he posed a military question to the scholar-minister Fan Zhongyuan (989–1052), Fan asked him how a student of the Confucian Way could concern himself with military matters and told Zhang he should devote himself to the transmission contained in the *Doctrine of the Mean* (Zhongyong), a classic text of Confucianism. This exchange established a trend in Neo-Confucianism. Thereafter, Neo-Confucians tended to confine their study efforts to seminal texts of their own schools, the classics and the Four Books (the *Da xue* or *Great Learning*, *Mencius*, *Analects*, and *Doctrine of the Mean*) in particular.

Zhu Xi: Grand Synthesizer of Neo-Confucianism

The greatest Neo-Confucian, Zhu Xi, distinguished himself by mastering what he could of *all* the Chinese humanities, as well as some science and medicine. Zhu's studies thus included military strategy and tactics and military history, which he sought to master by contemplating ways that imperial forces might wrest the central plains of China back from barbarian Jurchen control. Unlike ordinary Confucian scholars, who believed that those conversant in humanity and appropriateness (cardinal Confucian virtues) couldn't master military and financial matters, Zhu asserted that it was precisely those conversant in humanity and appropriateness who *could* master military and financial matters. Following Confucius, Mencius, and Xunzi, Zhu believed that military affairs and finance were of secondary importance for a state's security and power (which depended primarily on upright, ritualized rule and fair distribution), but he insisted that military affairs and war must be managed by men of courage and integrity. Furthermore, military deployments and actions must be limited to those authorized by the emperor as punitive actions. An entire section of Zhu's *Dialogues* is devoted to military affairs, covering a range of issues, including leadership qualities, troop training and unit numbers, and tactics and strategy.

Strategy for Recovering the Central Plains from Barbarian Control

In considering possible military responses to the Jurchen presence on ancestral Chinese land, Zhu drew lessons from history. In 1162, the imperial court faced the dilemma of whether to prosecute a war (for which the cost of victory would be eventual defeat) or negotiate a treaty (that would yield internal dissent). Zhu's idea was to neither fight on nor sue for a peace treaty, but to maintain the status quo while the newly installed emperor took time to practice self-cultivation, improve his administration, and eventually increase the harmony, prosperity, and strength of the realm. Zhu believed that that course of action would make the regime stronger and nurture a state of readiness so that when the opportunity finally did arise to recover the central plains from the Jurchens, the emperor could initiate a successful military campaign. As it turned out, the court did negotiate with the Jurchens while not effectively improving the internal order of the empire, which led to a stalemate that lasted until the Mongol invasion in the mid-thirteenth century.

Wang Shouren: Great Neo-Confucian Scholar and Military Commander

Wang Shouren, a Neo-Confucian master of the Ming dynasty. championed the notion that "knowledge and action form a unity" (*zhixing heyi*) and that people possess an inborn capacity to know what is good and what course is most appropriate, and to act on this knowledge. He sought to revive Confucius's spirit of commitment and activism at a time when Confucian scholars often were pedantic and took excessive pride in their erudition. In response to imperial concerns about the problem of barbarian banditry on the frontier, Wang wrote a celebrated memorial outlining measures to be taken to meet the crisis. While premising his view on classical Confucian ideas, Wang drew freely from Sunzi's *Art of War* in making his case.

Advice to the Emperor: Steps for Strengthening Frontier Military Forces

Wang Shouren urged the imperial court to do eight things. First, build up military reserves (not professional soldiers but well-trained citizenry) to meet emergencies. This meant training potential officers well in administration and in military arts, then selecting those most qualified to lead. Second, overlook defects and utilize excellence. This meant reactivating daring commanders who had been retired for making mistakes. Often, Wang observed, those commanders were the most effective leaders in battle. Third, reduce the army (the full-time professional soldiers) to save expenditures: Do not dispatch a large army at an inopportune time, and keep smaller groups of elite forces in reserve to carry out well-focused assaults at opportune times. Fourth, rely on military farming to feed the troops, as long-distance food transport is costly and wasteful. Thus troops stationed along the frontier were to grow their own food. This would give them something to do and keep them strong. Fifth, enforce the laws and regulations. The court was to require district commanders to monitor their subordinates, rewarding successes and punishing blunders, and it was to enforce honesty and effectiveness in the field. Sixth, bestow imperial kindness to arouse indignation against the enemy: The court should show concern for the frontier guards, express sorrow for the fallen, and rouse the troops with a righteous cause. It should expose the evils of the enemy and post awards to promote valor. Seventh, sacrifice the small to preserve the large. This meant that when small units were baited and drawn into traps, the impulse to rescue them should be resisted, as giving in to the impulse could result in a larger defeat. Strength should be saved for the key matches. Eighth, keep a strong defensive position to exploit the enemy's weaknesses. Wang observed that the imperial forces were skillful at defense, whereas the enemy was superior in irregular, open fighting. Because China lacked the manpower for a complete border defense, Wang recommended concentrating troops around walled cities, dispatching scouts and spies, and staying vigilant.

Wang in Combat

Nearly twenty years later, Wang was appointed governor of a southern border area and charged with quelling a rebellion in the region. On arriving in Jiangxi in 1517, he recruited able-bodied fighters, reorganized the armies, instituted a ten-family joint-registration system under which families monitored and assisted each other for security, and restored social order. Wang succeeded in subduing the rebellion quickly. He secured the social order by rehabilitating the old bandits and by improving the local economy. Wang's greatest challenge came in 1519 when Prince Ning, a nephew of the emperor, assembled an army to take the capital at Nanjing and establish a new dynasty. Facing Ning's large, well-entrenched army, Wang maneuvered deftly—politically as well as militarily—to subdue the rebellion, and he captured the prince in just ten days. Unfortunately, court politics and jealousy tarnished Wang's achievement, and he didn't receive proper recognition for his exploits until the ascendance of the next emperor in 1521.

Wang Shouren was celebrated as a principled Confucian master with the wits and courage to fight for the integrity of the Way. His activist style of thought was taken up in the nineteenth century by the Japanese Meiji regime to spur their modernization efforts. In the twentieth century, the nationalist leader Chiang Kai-shek (1887–1975) attempted to apply this formula in modernizing China, while Mao Zedong (1893–1976), the leader of China's Communist revolution, adapted Wang's activist principle that "knowledge and action form a unity" into his revolutionary code.

Historical Fate of the Neo-Confucian View of War

During the nineteenth century, when the Western powers were striking at the imperial gates, the Qing court was ideologically stymied. The traditions and demands of imperial politics precluded the formation of effective institutions and policies for meeting the foreign threat. Court officials sought to fashion a compromise solution—termed "Chinese learning as the substance, Western learning as the function" (*zhongxue weiti, xixue weiyong*) by Zhang Zhidong (1837–1909)—by keeping to age-old traditions and policies while nurturing modern industry and military forces. The traditional considerations and criteria for making policy decisions were unsuited for developing and applying modern science and industry, and a series of misguided policy decisions resulted in mistakes and waste, climaxed by the Empress Dowager's using the budget allocated for building a modern navy to construct an idyllic park with a pond and a stone-crafted stationary boat. Yan Fu (1853–1921), who had translated the essential works of modern British science, thought, and values into Chinese, argued that effective use of Western science depends on absorption of modern culture and values, but his views went largely unheeded. Finally, radical changes in Chinese politics and economics in the early and mid-twentieth century ushered in radical changes in China's military thinking. For much of the twentieth century, Chinese armies were more instruments of contending political groups than guardians of the people or government. In Taiwan, after the termination of martial law and democratization in the late 1980s, the military forces at last became professionalized and are now clearly in the service of the people and the government. Mainland China's army became more professional and modern after 1990, but China remains a single-party state in which the military as well as the government are more instruments of party control over the people than they are guardians of the people. This situation cannot change until China becomes a democratic, multiparty state.

Root of True Power: Civilized, Noble Rule

As conservators of ritual culture and executors of order, Neo-Confucians tended to speak little of war or the military arts. They distrusted the use of force of arms except as a measure of last resort, ideally in the form of punitive action initiated at the highest level of the realm. Neo-Confucians believed that the realm would grow and flourish naturally under the auspices of wise and noble rulers, who attracted people outside the realm to join or pay tribute. Thus, they never held up force of arms as an instrument to wield and extend power or prestige. In principle, they would never seek to force their beliefs and traditions on others militarily.

Kirill Ole Thompson

Further Reading

Ames, R. (Trans.). (1993). *Sun-Tzu: The art of warfare*. New York: Ballantine Books.

Ames, R., & Hall, D. (Trans.). (2001). *Focusing the familiar: A translation and philosophical interpretation of the Zhongyong*. Honolulu: University of Hawaii Press.

Ames, R., & Lau, D. C. (Trans.). (1996). *Sun Pin: The art of warfare*. New York: Ballantine Books.

Ames, R., & Rosemont, H. (Trans.). (1998). *The Analects of Confucius: A philosophical translation*. New York: Ballantine Books.

Chan, W. (Trans.). (1963). *Instructions for practical living and other Neo-Confucian writings by Wang Yang-ming*. New York & London: Columbia University Press.

Chan, W. (Trans.). (1967). *Reflections on things at hand: The Neo-Confucian anthology compiled by Chu Hsi*. New York & London: Columbia University Press.

Dubs, H. (Trans.). (1928). *Hsun Tzu: Works from the Chinese*. London: Probsthain.

Hsu, C. (1965). *Ancient China in transition: An analysis of social mobility, 722–222 B.C.* Stanford, CA: Stanford University Press.

Lau, D. C. (Trans.). (1984). *Mencius* (Vols. 1–2). Hong Kong: Chinese University Press.

McKnight, B. (1986). Chu Hsi and his world. In W. Chan (Ed.), *Chu Hsi and Neo-Confucianism* (pp. 408–436). Honolulu: University of Hawaii Press.

Schirokauer, C. (1962). Chu Hsi's political career: A study in ambivalence. In A. F. Wright & D. Twitchett (Eds.), *Confucian personalities* (pp. 162–188). Stanford, CA: Stanford University Press.

Schirokauer, C. (1991). *A brief history of Chinese civilization*. San Diego, CA: Harcourt Brace Jovanovich.

Watson, B. (1964). *Hsun Tzu: Basic writings*. New York & London: Columbia University Press.

Crusades

The Crusades were a series of Christian military expeditions, prompted by papal declarations and aimed, at least initially, at the recovery of the Holy Land from Muslim control. Initiated by Pope Urban II (c. 1035–1099) at the Council of Clermont in 1095 CE, the Crusades promised participants the remission of their sins and the opportunity to fulfill the instructions of Jesus in Matthew 10:38: "No man is worthy of me who does not take up his cross and walk in my footsteps" (New English Bible [Oxford]). In fact, the word *crusade* derives from the Latin word for cross, *crux*. The Latin *Crucesignati*, often translated into English as "crusaders," literally means "those signed by the cross." Over the course of several centuries, crusading expeditions were launched periodically and with mixed results, their targets at times shifting from Muslims in the Holy Land to other alleged enemies of the church, including European Jews and Christian heretics. Contemporary historians disagree about when the Crusades came to a close, in part because the term designates a rather loose grouping of events rather than a unified movement. Some scholars place the end as early as 1270 and others argue that the Crusades continued into the sixteenth century. Contemporary Christian scholars also debate the ethical significance of the Crusades: Is there, within Christianity, a legitimate category of "holy war," or do the Crusades represent, from their very inception, an abuse of Christian ideals and the misdirection of religious fervor?

The Roots of the Crusades

The historical causes of the Crusades were varied.

The population of Western Europe was surging in the tenth and eleventh centuries, and the economy of the time struggled, and often failed, to keep pace with the demands of the growing population. Famine was common. Some historians, such as Kenneth Latourette, suggest that the Crusades, in part, stemmed from a desire for new land and a need for new economic markets. Others, however, question an explanation which holds that crusaders "took the cross merely as a pious pretext to enrich themselves with stolen booty and carve out a new home in a distant land" (Madden 1999, 11).

Another theory holds that the Crusades were politically motivated. Christianity faced a growing challenge from Islam. In the eighth century, Muslim armies conquered North Africa and crossed the straits of Gibraltar into Spain, setting up Moorish rule. In the eleventh century, Seljuk Turks, who were Muslim, conquered Armenia, Syria, and Palestine. They took over the city of Jerusalem (where they actually supplanted not Christian but Arab Muslim rule). By the last part of the twelfth century, Muslim Turks were challenging Christian Byzantium, including Greece, Asia Minor, and, most particularly, the city of Constantinople. The leaders of Byzantium and the Eastern Church turned to the West, and to the pope, for help. In March of 1095, at a council held at Piacenza, Byzantine Emperor Alexius I (1048–1118), through his ambassadors, made a formal plea to the Western Church for assistance in battling the Turks. Thus, according to this second theory, the motivation for the Crusades was the desire to reestablish the dominance of Christianity as an institution over Islam and, perhaps relatedly, "the desire of the Popes to heal the breach between the Western and Eastern wings of the Catholic Church and to restore Christian unity" (Latourette 1953, 499). In so doing, the popes might both mend their decades-old rift with the patriarchs of the Eastern Church and bolster papal prestige and power.

A third theory claims that the primary cause of the Crusades was theological, even spiritual, in nature. Christians had long been troubled by the fact that their holiest sites—including the place of Jesus' birth, Bethlehem, and the tomb of Christ, the Holy Sepulcher in Jerusalem—were under Islamic control. European Christians making pilgrimages to the Holy Land at times had been challenged, harassed, and even killed by Muslims—a situation which apparently worsened under Turkish rule. Did the control of Christian sacred spaces by Muslims not suggest the superiority of Islam over Christianity? And if so, was not it incumbent upon all able-bodied Christians to reverse this wrong? Such questions sparked a powerful religious fervor among Christian believers. As Roland Bainton writes, "The attempt [to raise crusading armies] would hardly have succeeded had not the Church been fired with a flaming zeal to Christianize the very fabric of society" (Bainton 1956, 285). Whatever the contributing factors, when the call to crusade came, the response was overwhelming.

The Call to Arms

In November 1095, several hundred archbishops, bishops, and abbots, mostly from southern France, gathered in the French town of Clermont. After ten days of meetings, Pope Urban II addressed the participants, as well as a group of gathered laity. While the accounts of what he said that day differ (many versions were not recorded until long after the event and display a somewhat mythical tenor), the basic components of his

Selection from Letter from Stephen, Count of Blois and Chartres, to his wife, Adele (1098)

Count Stephen to Adele, his sweetest and most amiable wife, to his dear children, and to all his vassals of all ranks—his greeting and blessing.

[. . .]

You have certainly heard that after the capture of the city of Nicaea we fought a great battle with the Turks and by God's aid conquered them. Next we conquered for the Lord all Romania. And we learned that there was a certain Turkish prince Assam, dwelling in Cappadocia; thither we directed our course. All his castles we conquered by force and compelled him to flee to a certain very strong castle situated on a high rock. We also gave the land of that Assam to one of our chiefs and in order that he might conquer the above-mentioned Assam, we left there with him many soldiers of Christ. Thence, continually following the wicked Turks, we drove them through the midst of Armenia, as far as the great river Euphrates. Having left all their baggage and beasts of burden on the bank, they fled across the river into Arabia.

[. . .]

We found the city of Antioch very extensive, fortified with incredible strength and almost impregnable. In addition, more than 5,000 bold Turkish soldiers had entered the city, not counting the Saracens, Publicans, Arabs, Tulitans, Syrians, Armenians and other different races of whom an infinite multitude had gathered together there. In fighting against these enemies of God and of our own we have, by God's grace, endured many sufferings and innumerable evils up to the present time. Many also have already exhausted all their resources in this very holy passion. Very many of our Franks, indeed, would have met a temporal death from starvation, if the clemency of God and our money had not saved them. Before the above-mentioned city of Antioch indeed, throughout the whole winter we suffered for our Lord Christ from excessive cold and enormous torrents of rain. What some say about the impossibility of bearing the heat of the sun throughout Syria is untrue, for the winter there is very similar to our winter in the west.

When truly Caspian [Bagi Seian], the emir of Antioch-that is, prince and lord-perceived that he was hard pressed by us, he sent his son Sensodolo [Chems Eddaulah] by name, to the prince who holds Jerusalem, and to the prince of Calep, Rodoam [Rodoanus], and to Docap [Deccacus Iba Toutousch], prince of Damascus. He also sent into Arabia to Bolianuth and to Carathania to Hamelnuth. These five emirs with 12,000 picked Turkish horsemen suddenly came to aid the inhabitants of Antioch. We, indeed, ignorant of all this, had sent many of our soldiers away to the cities and fortresses. For there are one hundred and sixty-five cities and fortresses throughout Syria which are in our power. But a little before they reached the city, we attacked them at three leagues' distance with 700 soldiers, on a certain plain near the "Iron Bridge." God, however, fought for us, His faithful, against them. For on that (lay, fighting in the strength that God gives, we conquered them and killed an innumerable multitude—God continually fighting for us-and we also carried back to the army more than two hundred of their heads, in order that the people might rejoice on that account. The emperor of Babylon also sent Saracen messengers to our army with letters and through these he established peace and concord with us.

Source: Translations and Reprints from the Original Sources of European History. (1894). Philadelphia: University of Pennsylvania. Retrieved 8 January 2003 from Hanover Historical Texts Project, http://history.hanover.edu/project.html.

THE CRUSADER STATES IN THE EARLY 12TH CENTURY

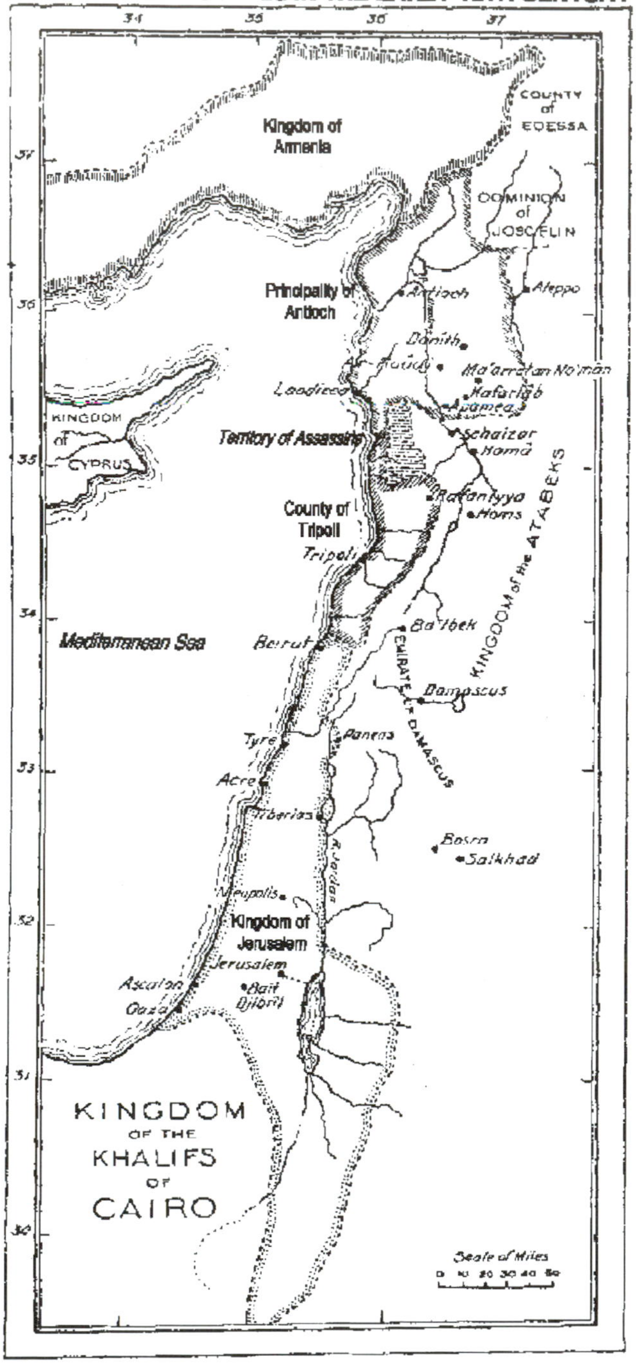

A map depicting the Crusader states in the early 12th century.
Source: George Richard Potter, *The Autobiography of Ousama*, (New York, 1929).

call to arms do not. As recounted by Fulcher of Chartres (c. 1059–c. 1127), Urban II first urged Christians to come to the aid of their brethren in Byzantium: "it is not I but God who beseeches and exhorts you as heralds of Christ, both poor and rich, to make haste to drive that vile breed [the Muslims] from the regions inhabited by our brethren" (Pernoud 1962, 23). Second, he pleaded for the restoration of the Holy Land: "You should be especially aroused by the fact that the Holy Sepulcher of the Lord our savior is in the hands of these unclean people, who shamefully mistreat and sacreligiously defile the Holy places with their filth . . . Remember the courage of your forefathers and do not dishonor them" (Brundage 1962, 19). Finally, Urban II promised to those Christians who perished in this undertaking the complete remission of their sins: "All who die on the way, whether by land or by sea, or in battle against the pagans, shall have immediate remission of sins. I grant them this through the power of God with which I am invested" (Van Voorst 1997, 121).

The response to the papal charge was sudden and strong. According to Thomas Madden:

> Approximately 150,000 people across Europe responded to Urban II's summons by donning the cross of the pilgrim. The vast majority of these were poor, and many were women or elderly (or both). During the course of the First Crusade, approximately 40,000 men marched to the East. Some left early, others late. Many did not make the entire journey. Only a small minority of that total were knights; nevertheless, it was the knights and barons who brought with them the armies, so their acceptance of the crusading vow was crucial to the success of the crusade. (Madden 1999, 12)

Urban II's plea would usher in one of the bloodiest periods of Christian history.

The Crusading Period

The most dramatic victories for Christians came in the early years of the Crusades. By the spring of 1093, thousands of crusaders—especially French, Flemish, and Norman knights but also French and German pilgrims who were inexperienced and poorly armed—assembled and embarked upon what became known as the First Crusade (1096–1102). On 15 July 1099, crusaders captured the city of Jerusalem. Two years later, another wave of crusaders defeated the Seljuk Turks in Asia Minor. Yet these successes came at great cost. The crusaders were often woefully equipped for the long journey ahead, and many, perhaps most, died before they ever reached their ultimate destination, the Holy Land. Thousands more perished in bloody battles. The cost to the noncrusaders was even higher. By some accounts, bands of crusaders during the First Crusade slaughtered Jews on their way through Germany. Muslims often were treated with unthinkable barbarism. In 1115, Guibert of Nogent (1053–c. 1124) recorded the following account of the actions of a crusading French lord named Thomas of Marle: "His thirst for blood was so unprecedented . . . that those who are themselves thought cruel seem milder when slaughtering animals than he did when killing people . . . [H]e had his prisoners strung up by their testicles—sometimes he did this with his own hands—and often the weight was too much to bear, so that their bodies ruptured and the viscera spilled out" (Riley-Smith 1995, 13). The brutal actions of Thomas of Marle and his like were not typical of the actions of every crusader, but they illustrate the pertinence of a question soon facing the triumphant Christians: Who has the ability, resources, and disposition to rule once a land has been conquered? The military successes of the First Crusade would prove impossible to sustain.

As news of victory came in from Jerusalem, Urban II attempted to extend the crusading movement to Spain, suggesting the liberation of Spain from Moorish rule was of an importance equal to the liberation of Jerusalem. The powerful French abbot Bernard of Clairvaux (1091–1153) preached passionately in favor of further expeditions against the Muslims in Asia Minor. In 1147, Pope Eugenius III (d. 1153) launched the Second Crusade (1147–1149) with the hope of waging a war concurrently on two fronts, in Spain and in the East. The efforts proved to be an unmitigated disaster, and the crusading forces were soundly defeated not only in Spain but in an attempted siege of Damascus.

In 1187, Muslim forces, under the powerful leadership of a Kurdish sultan, Saladin (1137 or 1138–1193), routed the Christians at Hattin in northern Palestine. Later that year, the Muslims under Saladin took back Jerusalem. The embarrassing loss of Jerusalem actually served to reenergize the crusading fervor in Europe. With great fanfare and confidence, the Third Crusade (1189–1192) was launched in 1189. It was led by three of the most powerful figures in Western Christendom: the Holy Roman Emperor Frederick Barbarossa (c. 1123–1190), King Philip Augustus (1165–1223) of France, and King Richard "the Lionhearted" (1157–1199) of England. The confidence faded quickly. The emperor accidentally drowned in Asia Minor before reaching the Holy Land, the French and English kings quarreled divisively, and the greatest achievement of the crusade was to take back some of the Palestinian coast, most particularly Acre. The Third Crusade closed when Richard negotiated a three-year truce with Saladin in 1192. Jerusalem remained firmly in Muslim hands.

A series of other crusades followed. The Fourth Crusade (1202–1204) was called by Pope Innocent III (1160 or 1161–1216) and initiated with the intent of attacking the Muslims in Egypt. Instead, the crusaders were diverted to Byzantium, eventually looting the Christian city of Constantinople and greatly weakening the Eastern Church in the process. By 1453, Constantinople would fall into the hands of the Muslim Ottoman Turks. The so-called Children's Crusade of 1212 was led by a boy, Nicholas (d. 1212), and consisted of young people swept up by the emotional appeals of the church to defend the faith. All trace of the group was lost as they crossed the Alps on their way to Mediterranean ports. Jerusalem returned to Christian control temporarily beginning in 1228, but this "victory" was a product not of military prowess but of a truce negotiated with the Muslims by Holy Roman Emperor Frederick II (1194–1250) of Hohenstaufen. By 1244, Muslims were back in control of the sacred city.

Increasingly during the thirteenth century and beyond, popes called for crusades against internal "threats" to the Western church. A savage crusade, perhaps better termed a massacre, was waged between 1209 and 1229 in southern France against the Albigensians—a group of allegedly heretical Christians who supported a radical dualism similar to that at the core of Manichaeism. Others crusades were undertaken against German peasants (1232–1234) and the Hussites (1441–1435). Crusades even were waged against other crusaders, including one declared by the pope against Frederick II and his followers (1240). Contemporary historians debate whether such actions, often pitting one faction of Christianity against another, truly can be considered part of the crusading movement.

By 1500, the impetus to crusade was clearly on the wane. Few of Pope Urban II's goals had been fulfilled, even temporarily. Muslims still controlled the Holy Land and threatened the eastern part of Christendom. Tens of thousands of Christians, Muslims, and Jews had died. By almost any standard, the Crusades were a failure. Their historical impact, on the other hand, was profound.

The Legacy of the Crusades

As with any major historical event, the Crusades brought changes that could not have been anticipated at their inception. The intellectual life of Christian Europe was profoundly impacted by exposure to the talented scholars and rich libraries of Islam. Many of the works of Aristotle, long suppressed by the church to the point of near-extinction in Europe, were discovered in Arabic translation among the booty brought back by the crusaders. In fact, the greatest Christian thinker of the thirteenth century, Thomas Aquinas (1225–1274), built his philosophical-Christian synthesis upon these rediscovered Aristotelian works, and was profoundly influenced by Muslim philosophers like Ibn Sina (Avicenna; 980–1037) and Ibn Rushd (Averroës; 1126–1198).

The Crusades, contrary to the initial intent of Urban II, also served to solidify and intensify the rift between the Western and Eastern Christian churches. Conceived in part as a means of aiding Byzantium and the church in the East, the Crusades by the thirteenth century often were being waged *against* Eastern Christians. The damage caused to East-West relations would prove irrevocable.

Perhaps most importantly, the Crusades changed what two religions, Islam and Christianity, had to say about war and violence.

For Islam, the impact of the Crusades was initially hidden. Syrian Muslims, among the first to be attacked by crusaders, thought they were being subjected to yet another incursion by Byzantines. Upon realizing their mistake, the Muslims referred to their attackers as "Franks," not "crusaders." By the early twelfth century, the significance of the Christian invasions was being reevaluated by Muslims. ʿAli ibn Tahir al-Sulami (1039–1106), a Sunni scholar from Damascus, was among the first Muslims to write a treatise on the attacks. In 1105, he labeled the incursion of the Franks a "Christian *jihad* [holy war]" and warned that the successes of the crusaders were a sign of the moral and political decline of Islam. Al-Sulami and others predicted an ultimate victory for Islam, though, citing a hadith (a statement attributed to the prophet Muhammad): "The Hour will not come until God gives my community victory over Constantinople" (Riley-Smith 1995, 217). Muslim clerics and poets produced a passionate (and still beloved) body of Arabic literature that sought to inspire Muslims to respond to the challenge posed by the infidels. Muslim scholars turned to the task of explaining and exploring the concept of jihad. Texts from the crusading period still constitute an integral part of contemporary Muslim discourse on such issues as the limits of warfare (including jihad), the nature of self-defense, the notion of noncombatants, and the concept of just authority during times of war. While Pope Urban II's original goal was to reverse the advances of Islam, the Crusades may well have had the opposite effect, raising militaristic interpretations of the concept of jihad to a more prominent place in Islam and forcing Muslims to reevaluate the threat posed to them by Christianity. As Karlfried Froehlich writes, "the Crusades led directly to the Turkish wars of later centuries, during which Ottoman expansion threatened even central Europe" (Froehlich 1995, 170).

The impact of the Crusades upon Christian views of war was equally profound. In effect, the Crusades represented the completion of a long process, initiated by Augustine in the fourth century, to reverse the attitude of the early church toward war. While the first centuries of Christianity were largely pacifistic, the Crusades took the Augustinian justification of Christian violence to its ultimate conclusion. The pacifistic monastic orders of previous centuries now were joined by monastic military orders like the Templars and the Teutonic Knights, charged with killing in the name of Christ. As such, the Crusades inspired an important period of intellectual introspection about the nature of war within Christianity and the West. Aquinas's seminal contributions to the formation of just war thought in the thirteenth century were written in the shadow of the Crusades and, almost surely, as a response to some of their excesses. The flowering of just war thought in the sixteenth century followed swiftly, and probably not coincidentally, upon the close of the crusading period.

To this day, the Crusades sit at the heart of the religious discourse on war, serving at times as an example of ultimate devotion and sacrifice in the name of God but more often as a cautionary tale about the potential excesses of religious fervor.

Timothy M. Renick

Further Reading

Bainton, R. (1956). The ministry in the middle ages. In H. R. Niebuhr & D. Williams (Eds.), *The ministry in historical perspectives* (pp. 82–109). New York: Harper Brothers.

Brundage, J. (1962). *The Crusades: A documentary survey*. Milwaukee, WI: Marquette University Press.

Eidelberg, S. (1977). *The Jews and the crusaders: The Hebrew chronicles of the First and Second Crusades*. Madison: University of Wisconsin Press.

Froehlich, K. (1995). Crusades: Christian perspective. In M. Eliade (Ed.), *The encyclopedia of religion* (pp. 167–171). New York: Macmillan Library Reference USA.

Fulcher of Chartres. (1969). *A history of the expedition to Jerusalem, 1095–1127* (H. Fink, Ed. & F. R. Ryan, Trans.). Knoxville, TN: University of Tennessee Press.

Gabrieli, F. (1969). *Arab historians and the Crusades*. New York: Routledge.

Green, V. (1996). *A new history of Christianity*. New York: Continuum.

Housley, N. (Ed.). (1996). *Documents on the later crusades, 1274–1580*. New York: St. Martin's Press.

Johnson, J. (1981). *Just war tradition and the restraint of war*. Princeton, NJ: Princeton University Press.

Latourette, K. (1953). *A history of Christianity*. New York: Harper and Brothers.

Madden, T. (1999). *A concise history of the Crusades*. New York: Rowman & Littlefield Publishers, Inc.

Pernoud, R. (Ed.). (1962). *The Crusades*. New York: G. P. Putnam's Sons.

Riley-Smith, J. (Ed.). (1995). *The Oxford illustrated history of the Crusades*. New York: Oxford University Press.

Riley-Smith, L., & Riley-Smith, J. (1981). *The Crusades: Idea and reality, 1095–1274*. London: Edward Arnold.

St. Bernard of Clairvaux. (1953). *The letters of St. Bernard of Clairvaux* (B. James, Trans.). London: Burns, Oates.

Van Voorst, R. (Ed.). (1997). *Readings in Christianity*. Belmont, CA: Wadsworth Publishing Company.

D

Daoism, Classical

Daoism is almost certainly the major religious tradition that is the least understood by Western audiences. This is in part due to the disproportionate attention given to a handful of ancient Chinese philosophical texts and a somewhat romantic fascination with practices loosely related to the historical tradition, such as feng shui (geomantic, or direction- and location-oriented, divination) and certain martial arts. But the bigger issue is that Daoism itself is an ambiguous term, and many modern Chinese are themselves reckless in its application or uninformed as to its nuances. It can alternately refer to a cluster of classical texts and later philosophical writings in the same vein, a two-thousand-year-old institutional "church," and, sometimes, the syncretic popular religion of the Chinese people that is subject to considerable regional variation. There has been Daoist mysticism, but also Daoist political theory; there has been Daoist monasticism, but also Daoist millenarian militarism. Moreover, there is much debate within scholarly circles as to how and whether the different faces of Daoism—including the various Western transmissions and transformations of it—are historically and conceptually related to one another. Thus, it is especially necessary that discussions of Daoism eschew overly broad generalizations and exhibit a marked precision in delimiting exactly which particular phenomena are being considered.

Daoism in the Hundred Schools Period

It should be made clear at the outset that classical Daoism is itself an anachronistic term, as the ancient period in China produced no intellectual tradition or social movement that was self-consciously Daoist. Rather, several authors who were active during what is known as the Hundred Schools period—a protracted epoch of intellectual ferment in China, unofficially stretching from the middle of the sixth century BCE through the end of the second or third century BCE—were subsequently identified as philosophically kindred and eventually linked to one another in hagiographic accounts. Their texts were grouped under the bibliographic heading *daojia*, which translates comfortably as "School of Dao" and is better known through dated Western scholarship as "philosophical Daoism." Early Chinese historiographers included a number of figures in this category, but only two documents, the cryptic *Daodejing* (traditionally attributed to the quasi-historical Laozi) and the eponymous *Zhuangzi*, have actually survived the centuries as relatively complete texts and been preserved by the later Daoist tradition. Other works do survive in fragmentary form, most notably the recently discovered *Neiye* (Inward Training) verses buried within an older heterogeneous philosophical compendium and portions of the largely forged later work *Liezi*, and the history of Daoist origins is continually being rewritten, but what has come to be known as the Laozhuang tradition (from the names Laozi and Zhuangzi) is at present more or less equated with Classical Daoism.

Although Laozi (traditionally sixth century BCE) and Zhuangzi (fourth century BCE) did not always speak with one voice, they did share similar perspectives on a number of important matters, particularly the belief that the goal of human life was to follow or

A Selection from Laozi

When people are born, they're supple and soft;
hen they die, they end up stretched out firm and rigid;
hen the ten thousand things and grasses and trees are alive, they're supple and pliant;
hen they're dead, they're withered and dried out.
Therefore we say that the firm and rigid are companions of death,
While the supple, the soft, the weak, and the delicate are companions of life.
If a solider is rigid, he won't win;
If a tree is rigid, it will come to its end.
Rigidity and power occupy the inferior position;
Suppleness, softness, weakness, and delicateness occupy the superior position.

Source: **Lao-Tzu, *Te-Tao Ching* (1989). Robert G. Henricks, Trans. New York: Ballantine Books, p. 47.**

realize the *Dao* (the Way), an ambiguous and ineffable principle that somehow underlies all existence. The creative impetus of this principle was consistently evoked through metaphorical images of nonbeing, nondifferentiation, and spontaneity, which translated ethically into a kind of intuitive naturalism. That is to say, the Classical Daoist response to the political and moral crises of the era—the collapse of the old feudal structure, the loss of land to the nomadic invaders from the north, a general sense of cultural and ethical decline—was not a moralistic solution, but both a challenge to how moral values are constructed and a suggestion for an alternative action guide. The new model, while not denying certain basic Chinese assumptions about the roles for organized government, family loyalties, and social cohesion, instead stressed the value of "nondoing," of acting in spontaneous harmony with the self-generating, self-perpetuating courses of the Way. Paradoxically, such nondoing is seen as efficacious and, ultimately, socially responsible, as the *Daodejing* contends, in chapter 48, that the sagely persons "do nothing, and yet there is nothing left undone" (Jonathan R. Herman, Trans.).

Classical Daoism and War

Modern readers of Daoism are quick to ascribe a blanket pacifism to the Classical Daoists, but it is on politics and military affairs that Laozi and Zhuangzi diverged most significantly. For the most part, Zhuangzi demonstrated no interest in such matters, often refusing even to be drawn into conversations about them and reportedly rejecting opportunities for civil service. His only comments on the role of government were to the effect that an enlightened ruler should somehow exert influence on the community and the world through his own emulation of the Way and perseverance in nondoing, thus allowing any transformations to seem as though they occurred spontaneously of their own accord. Zhuangzi's apparent indifference to political and community matters, in spite of his having lived during tumultuous times, led both his contemporaries and subsequent critics to charge that he espoused an amoral, asocial philosophy of retreat. Whether or not such a determination is defensible, one can reasonably extrapolate that Zhuangzi would have been unlikely to recognize a justification for war under any circumstance and that the Daoist tradition would find little textual basis for it if Zhuangzi were its sole canonical authority.

However, Laozi and the *Daodejing* presented a much more ambiguous understanding of war and military affairs. On the one hand, Laozi did on occasion sound very much the pacifist, as he suggested that violence is somehow unnatural and that trappings of war only flourish during times when the Way is not followed. On the other hand, much of the *Daodejing* appeared to be addressed to a ruler or aspiring ruler who seeks to exert control over the population or to expand the borders of his domain, or both. The *Daodejing* never specifically addresses the issue of what would justify military action, though the text is permeated by a vague intimation that war should only be undertaken by a discerning sovereign who has in mind the best interests of the state and the cosmos. Laozi devoted more attention to the questions of what constitutes a sagely ruler and which military strategies would prove most effective. As an answer to both these questions, Laozi essentially extends the idea of nondoing. A wise ruler is one who appears unconcerned about worldly matters, who makes no show of his power, and whose influences are so subtle that the common people scarcely know he exists. The recommended military tactics are those that emphasize concealment, stillness, and receptivity, with various metaphors of reflexive potential—water, femininity, uncarved wood—serving to illustrate how the soft can overcome the hard and a small state can annex a large one.

This sometimes incongruous juxtaposition of a stark utopianism with a cagy militarism foreshadows the kinds of developments in Daoist history that would begin to appear during the closing stages of the Classical period. The oldest extant commentary on the *Daodejing* was penned by Hanfeizi (d. 233 BCE), the architect of the much-reviled Legalist school, and several Hundred Schools scholars whose works survive only in reconstructed fragments are believed to have espoused some kind of amalgam of Daoism and Legalism. Moreover, many chapters of the *Zhuangzi* that were once considered simply spurious have since been demonstrated, through rigorous historical-critical inquiry, to have come from the hands of later proponents of such a synthesis, who were also the likely editors of the text. Other chapters of *Zhuangzi* likewise represent distinct philosophical voices—an apolitical anarchism, a doctrine of body-nurture—which offer twists on the bedrock Daoist principles of nondoing and spontaneity. The task of ascertaining how these various strains of early Daoism relate to one another historically and thematically is a high priority for the emerging generation of Sinologists.

Jonathan R. Herman

Further Reading

Allan, S., & Williams, K. (Eds.). (2000). *The Guodian Laozi: Proceedings of the international conference, Dartmouth College, May 1998* (Early China Special Series No. 5). Berkeley: Institute of East Asian Studies, University of California, Berkeley.

Ames, R. (Ed.). (1998). *Wandering at ease in the Zhuangzi.* Albany: State University of New York Press.

Graham, A. C. (Trans.). (1981). *Chuang-tzu: The seven inner chapters and other writings from the Chuang-tzu*. London: Allen & Unwin.

Henricks, R. G. (Trans.). (2000). *Lao Tzu's Tao Te Ching: A translation of the startling new documents found at Guodian*. New York: Columbia University Press.

Lao-tzu. (1989). *Te-Tao Ching* (R. G. Henricks, Trans.). New York: Ballantine Books.

Daoism, Huang-Lao

A movement of the Han dynasty (206 BCE–220 CE), Huang-Lao Daoism and its stance concerning war (or anything else) was an enigma until recently. Only with the 1973 discovery of new manuscripts at Mahuangdui (a small town in China's Hunan province) did any of writings by a representative of this tradition become available for modern study. This branch of Daoism may have originated during the Warring States period (475–221 BCE), but its early development is still obscure. By the beginning of Han times, however, it had matured into a coherent belief system complete with its own cosmology.

Prior to the newly discovered documents, scholars knew little more than that the tradition's name alluded to Huangdi (the Yellow Emperor, one of China's mythic founders) and Laozi (legendary founder of Daoism in the sixth century BCE). Parts of the *Huainanzi*, a treatise of political philosophy completed in 139 BCE, were supposed to reflect Huang-Lao ideas. This book, however, appeared to be an untrustworthy hodgepodge, containing too many philosophical perspectives lumped together for any one of them to be easily identified. The few other hints in scattered historical sources made Huang-Lao partisans seem schizophrenic, acting here like Daoists but there like Legalists (hardheaded advocates of realpolitik), Confucians, or yin-yang cosmologists.

We now know that the seeming confusion arose from Huang-Lao eclecticism: The movement amalgamated elements of various competing philosophies into its own synthesis. What made it a form of Daoism was its veneration of Laozi, whom Huang-Lao adherents held to be the semidivine teacher of Huangdi, and its core doctrine that the only valid laws stem directly from nature. Legalism's insistence on the strict enforcement of law was accepted, but unlike Legalism, Huang-Lao thought prohibited rulers from being above the law and from propounding their own arbitrary laws. Instead, nature—a direct manifestation of the cosmic order, or Dao—would reveal the laws. The ruler or his Huang-Lao officials were to divine these natural laws by meditation, readying themselves to perceive cosmic principles by emptying their minds of their own thought. The harsh potential of law-and-order regimes was also attenuated by another Huang-Lao doctrine, borrowed from Confucianism and embodied in legends about Huangdi, which specified that a ruler existed not so much to lead the state as to serve the people. He must always place their welfare before his own. In addition, rather than making decisions by himself, he should act only after consulting with his ministers and even representatives of the people.

The Huang-Lao attitude toward war looks Legalistic at first glance, embracing that school's penchant for a strong military. Legends portrayed Huangdi as the first to unify China under a single emperor, a position he had to achieve by force because—says the Huang-Lao writer—ungoverned humans will always selfishly contend with each other instead of being reasonable or virtuous. However, the writer continues, rulers often misuse their armies, so the laws of nature must determine military affairs. First, wars must be waged only against opponents who truly merit punishment, and second, armed expeditions should only be undertaken at the proper time. Nature gives life in spring and summer, waiting to take life until fall and winter, so the state should ideally prosecute a war only during the latter seasons.

Huang-Lao proponents, a major influence on four emperors and one regency, generally formed the dominant group of officials and political advisers during the entire first quarter of the four centuries of Han-dynasty rule. It is doubtful that seasonal prescriptions on warfare were followed very often, but the spirit of Huang-Lao law was largely observed throughout this early period. Internal rebellions were quickly suppressed, rebels obviously deserving punishment, but foreign policy remained remarkably pacifistic, emphasizing negotiation over force. Han Gaozu (256–195 BCE), the founder of the Han dynasty, after only a single attempt at retribution against barbarians marauding to the northwest, is said to have recognized, in good Huang-Lao fashion, that the time had not arrived for such expeditions and to have desisted from them henceforth. Gaozu's immediate successors followed this example. However, the situation changed abruptly with the accession of the fifth emperor, Wudi ("Martial Emperor," 156–87 BCE), who rejected Huang-Lao ideas and dismissed Huang-Lao officials along with those of other philosophical persuasions, patronizing Confucianism instead; Wudi's tutors had been Confucians. But the new emperor soon showed that he would not be ruled by Confucian precepts either. While never overtly rejecting Confucianism in favor of Legalism, he pursued a resolutely Legalistic method of rule. At home his reign was marked by harsh and arbitrary punishment (often death) even for minor offenses. Abroad, Wudi's reign was marked by a burst of military expansionism that remained unmatched for half a millennium afterward.

After its sudden fall under Wudi, Huang-Lao never regained its former influence. Reappearing only sporadically in the outlook of later officials, it had disappeared completely even before the dynasty that exalted and then abandoned it came to an end. Nevertheless, Huang-Lao Daoism may have had the last laugh. R. P. Peerenboom, to date the only Western scholar who has published a full-length study of the Mahuangdui Huang-Lao manuscripts (1993), argues that Huang-Lao ideas exercised a formative influence on the religious Daoism which, in the form of the massive Yellow Turban revolt (184 CE), sparked the Han dynasty's own descent into oblivion.

Michael L. Fitzhugh

See also Daoism, Classical; Confucianism: Han Dynasty

Further Reading

Bokenkamp, S. R. (1997). *Early Taoist scriptures*. Berkeley & Los Angeles: University of California Press.

Chan, W. (1963). *A source book in Chinese philosophy*. Princeton, NJ: Princeton University Press.

Dean, K. (1993). *Taoist ritual and popular cults of Southeast China*. Princeton, NJ: Princeton University Press.

Girardot, N. J. (1983). *Myth and meaning in early taoism: The theme of chaos (hun-tun)*. Berkeley & Los Angeles: University of California Press.

Huang, J., & Wurmbrand, M. (1987). *The primordial breath: An ancient Chinese Way of prolonging life through breath control*. Torrance, CA: Original Books.

Kohn, L. (1993). *The Taoist experience: An anthology*. Albany: State University of New York Press.

Robinet, I. (1997). *Taoism: Growth of a Religion*. Stanford, CA: Stanford University Press.

Saso, M. R. (1972). *Taoism and the rite of cosmic renewal*. Pullman: Washington State University Press.

Welch, H., & Seidel, A. (1979). *Facets of taoism*. New Haven, CT: Yale University Press.

Daoism, Medieval

During the Han dynasty (206 BCE–220 CE) and the era of the Northern and Southern dynasties (220–589) that followed, a number of sects of Daoism had their founding. Some movements were involved with rebellions; others were embraced by the ruling elites.

The Yellow Turbans

The Yellow Turbans were a Daoist movement that grew in influence in central and eastern China at the end of the Han dynasty. Toward the end of the Han, China experienced a number of natural disasters (floods, droughts, crop devastation by insects) that impoverished its peasant population. These conditions gave rise to a number of peasant rebellions, but the rebellion launched by the Yellow Turbans was the most successful. The Yellow Turbans worshiped the Yellow Emperor (China's mythical first man), and looked to a new era "under the reign of a 'Yellow Heaven' " (Robinet 1997, 54). Yellow, the color associated with the earth, would follow on red, the color associated with fire—and with the Han dynasty. The Yellow Turbans' leader, Zhang Jue (d. 184), got his start as a faith healer who worked his miracles by having the sick confess their sins. Soon the Yellow Turbans numbered in the tens of thousands. Zhang Yue, aided by his two brothers, organized them into paramilitary districts and was able to coordinate a simultaneous uprising in six provinces in 184. The Yellow Turbans took control of whole cities before being put down after the death (from natural causes) of Zhang Jue.

Tianshi Daoism

Tianshi ("Celestial Masters") Daoism grew out of a movement that was contemporaneous with the Yellow Turbans, known as Five Pecks of Rice. In 165 Zhang Daoling (c. 34–c. 156 CE) claimed to have received a commandment from Laozi (the semi-legendary founder of Daoism, who had come to be regarded as a deity) to establish a perfect society, which Zhang Daoling was to rule as the first in a line of celestial masters. Zhang Daoling's grandson, Zhang Lu (flourished 190–220), succeeded in establishing an independent state in Sichuan, in western China; the five pecks of rice that gave the sect its name were the taxes collected from the faithful in this state.

As the first of the Celestial Masters, Zhang Daoling stressed many of the notions associated with an organized religion, including clergy, canonical texts, and instructions on how to lead a moral life. On the spiritual front, the Celestial Masters opposed unregulated, popular religious practices, calling them "wrong paths" and blaming disease and other evils on the agents (shamans and mediums) of folk religion. On the political front, their well-organized state flourished as a successful polity, attracting refugees from the gradually disintegrating Han, until it was conquered in 215 by the forces of Cao Cao (155–220), who went on to found the Wei dynasty (200–265/6). With a policy of simultaneous fence mending and firm control Cao Cao both supported the defeated Zhang Lu, granting Zhang Lu's sons titles and arranging for the families to be joined by marriage ties, and managed him, requiring him, his family, and their followers to migrate north. Its organizational structure suffered from the move, but it nevertheless gained many converts in its new location.

The next two centuries were turbulent times in China, with no one dynasty uniting the entire country or lasting for very long. There were numerous uprisings; one in particular, the uprising (399–402) of Sun En (d. 402) against the tottering Eastern Jin dynasty (318–420) in southern China, has been taken as an example of a Celestial Masters uprising, though recent scholarship has disputed that assessment, arguing that the main points of contention were political (rebellious southerners were protesting what they saw as unfair treatment at the hands of the northern aristocrats who had fled from the north and established their dynasty in the south). During the Northern Wei dynasty (386–534) Celestial Masters Daoism received court favor. The celestial master Kou Qianzhi (365–448) emphasized hierarchy and state order and played down Daoism's egalitarian tendencies; he also promulgated a religious code that did away with such potentially antistate practices as religious taxation and forbade members of the sect to participate in rebellions. His success in establishing Celestial Masters Daoism as a state religion was so great that in 440 the Northern Wei emperor underwent a Daoist investiture ceremony. Folk religion and Buddhism were persecuted during this period, but after Kou's death Daoism's court influence rapidly declined and Buddhism became ascendant.

During the Tang dynasty (618–907) Celestial Masters Daoism was the lowest-ranking Daoist sect, but a new line of celestial masters was established that during the Song dynasty (960–1279) flourished as the Zhengyi (Orthodox Unity) sect. Zhengyi Daoism remains active in China today.

Shangqing Daoism

During the fourth century, the visionary Yang Xi (flourished c. 364) established the Shangqing (Supreme

Purity) sect of Daoism, based on revelations he reported receiving from various gods and spirits. Wei Huacun (251–334), a Daoist nun who appeared in Yang Xi's visions as his primary initiator, is also sometimes named as the sect's founder. During her lifetime she meditated on Mount Mao (in Chinese, Mao Shan), and the sect is also referred to as Mao Shan Daoism because of its headquarters on Mount Mao.

Yang Xi received patronage from a southern aristocratic family, and his visions, which came at a time when Celestial Masters Daoism was ascendant, were seized upon by southern aristocrats as a superior form of Daoism—hence the name Supreme Purity. Tao Hongjing (456–563), who had influence in the court of the Liang dynasty (502–556), compiled Shangqing texts. Persecution of Daoism in this era (this was the era when Buddhism was making inroads among the aristocracy) led some adherents to flee north and establish Shangqing Daoism there. By the Tang dynasty, Shangqing Daoism was the most influential Daoist sect. The first half of the Tang dynasty were characterized by religious tolerance; both native religions (Daoism and Confucianism) and foreign faiths (Buddhism, Zoroastrianism, Nestorian Christianity, and Islam) flourished, and ecumenical debates on China's "three faiths" (Confucianism, Daoism, and Buddhism) were held—a continuation of a tradition that had begun several hundred years earlier. In the waning years of the Tang, however, as China's borders were harried by tribal attacks, the court grew increasingly suspicious of nonnative faiths—and anxious over the power of the Buddhist temples—and in 845 a devastating persecution of Buddhism, during which many temples were destroyed, took place. Other foreign religions were outlawed altogether and their clergy laicized. Daoism, by contrast, continued to be patronized by the Tang imperial family.

Shangqing's most salient difference from earlier forms of Daoism was its emphasis on meditation. Salvation lay in internal transformation; through meditation the Daoist adept could ascend to the heavens and commune with the gods.

Lingbao Daoism

Lingbao (Numinous Treasure) Daoism emphasized scripture; it got its start around 397, when Ge Chaofu (flourished 397–402), inspired by Shangqing scriptures, compiled a number of texts, the foundational one being the *Wufujing* (Text of the Five Talismans). Lingbao Daoism was strongly influenced by popular Buddhism, as is evident from Lingbao Daoism's adoption of the notion of universal salvation. As in Buddhism, Lingbao Daoism dictated that salvation was attainable through the accumulation of merit over the course of a number of lives. The Lingbao sect also elaborated on apocalyptic elements it found in Shangqing texts, predicting End Times based on Yin-Yang theory (the theory of opposite and complementary forces in the universe) and Five Elements theory (the theory that the world is composed of five elements). To survive those end times and accumulate merit, Lingbao adherents made use of prayer, chanting, and ritual use of talismans. Ritual was a hallmark of Lingbao Daoism, and new rituals continued to be invented into the Song dynasty.

Francesca M. Forrest

See also Daoism, Classical; Daoism, Modern

Further Reading

Gernet, J. (1982). *A history of Chinese civilization* (J. R. Foster, Trans.). Cambridge, UK: Cambridge University Press.

Graff, D. A., & Higham, R. (2002). *A military history of China*. Boulder, CO: Westview.

Kohn, L. (n.d.) *Kou Qianzhi*. Retrieved 8 May 2003, from http://www.taoism.org.hk/taoist-world-today/taoism&us/pg7-5-3-5.htm

Lai, C. (1999). Daoism and political rebellion during the Eastern Jin dynasty. In F. H. Cheung & M. Lai (Eds.), *Politics and religion in ancient and medieval Europe and China* (pp. 77–100). Hong Kong: Chinese University Press.

Robinet, I. (1997). *Taoism: Growth of a religion* (P. Brooks, Trans.). Stanford, CA: Stanford University Press.

Yu, D. (Trans.) (2000). *History of Chinese Daoism: Vol 1*. Lanham, MD: University Press of America.

Daoism, Modern

Whether Daoism (Taoism) retains any vitality in the modern era is the subject of much debate. The question of how modern Daoists view war, on the other hand, has received comparatively little attention. Any discussion of modern Daoist attitudes toward war is intertwined with the controversies surrounding Daoism's modern fate. While Daoism as a living spiritual tradition has survived into the modern age, the nature of its primary concerns and practices tends to mute its voice on matters of war and peace, even as contemporary thinkers seek fresh insights into the nature of violence by rereading its oldest scriptures.

When Daoist institutions, along with other religious institutions in China, emerged from the long nightmare of repression known as the Cultural Revolution in the late 1970s, its membership was assessed by the Chinese government as numbering less than three thousand nationwide. This figure is based only on those claiming the status of "religious professional" (in other words, priests, monks, and nuns) and does not include the thousands, possibly millions, of laypeople who patronize Daoist institutions and clergy on a regular, if episodic, basis. Official Chinese government reports on Daoism continue to emphasize its low levels of membership and influence in modern Chinese society, however. It is fair to conclude that Daoism, as an institutional force in modern China, is relatively weak.

Nonetheless, Daoism persists today. Representatives of both the Northern (the *Quanzhen* or "Complete Perfection" sect, which maintains monastic communities and esoteric spiritual disciplines) and Southern (the *Tianshi* or "Celestial Master" sect, which offers public rituals performed by individual specialists at community functions) forms of institutional Daoism are active across mainland China, while Daoist practice in Taiwan and Hong Kong was never retarded by Communist persecution and thus remains strong today, albeit more so as a kind of ethos or spiritual legacy than as a powerful institutional presence. At the same time, a kind of Daoist readership has emerged, both in Asia and in the West, that is interested primarily in the classical literary products of the tradition.

Thus, in order to identify modern Daoist attitudes toward war, one must look for clues in modern Daoist institutional practices and the kinds of Daoist texts that interest modern readers.

Modern Daoism and War: Clues from Institutional Practices

Modern Daoism, as practiced in China and Chinese-speaking communities throughout the world, consists chiefly of ritual practices that fall into one of two categories: individual techniques of self-cultivation (meditation, calisthenics, and so forth) and communal celebrations of public importance (funerals, exorcisms, and the like). The former category is monopolized by the Complete Perfection sect, while the latter category is almost exclusively associated with the Celestial Masters sect.

Complete Perfection monasticism and meditation offer little in the way of clues to modern Daoist attitudes toward war, aside from the application of techniques such as *neidan* ("interior alchemy"—spiritual transformation through internal visualization) to popular, para-Daoist practices such as *qigong* ("energy work") and martial arts. The application of spiritual techniques to medicinal and martial ends often comes at the expense of the ethical framework, such as it is, that accompanies such techniques. Indeed, popular Chinese novels and films are thickly populated with stock characters who deploy Daoist tricks for immoral or amoral ends. Those affiliated with actual Daoist institutions, on the other hand, often present themselves as peaceful survivors of oppression and nonviolent resisters to further persecution. In the words of Min Zhiting, deputy secretary-general of the Chinese Daoist Association in Beijing during the late 1980s, "We believe in tranquillity, modesty, kindness—that weakness will defeat strength and that softness will defeat hardness" (quoted in MacInnis 1989, 205).

Apart from the rejection of blood sacrifice in most (although certainly not all) ritual performances of the Celestial Masters, there is not much to suggest the outlines, let alone the substance, of a modern Daoist view of violence in such ceremonies. In general, Celestial Masters clergy and their clients tend to focus on religious practice as an occasion of either personal concern (such as spirit possession requiring exorcism or deceased relatives requiring smooth passage to the underworld) or public welfare (as when a breach to the social fabric caused by untimely death or other sorts of catastrophe needs to be repaired), rather than as a vehicle for ethical reflection. To the extent that those who patronize modern Daoist institutions connect their Daoism with their moral lives, it is probably the case that they are responding to Buddhist influence (for example, the doctrine of karmic retribution) rather than to authentic Daoist notions, let alone specifically Daoist moral exhortation.

Modern Daoism and War: Clues from the Revival of Ancient Texts

While few clues to modern Daoist attitudes toward war can be gleaned from a survey of contemporary Daoist institutional practices, perhaps more may be said by examining the resurgent popularity of premodern Daoist scriptures among both Asian and Western audiences.

Since the late 1800s, approximately fifty translations of *Laozi* (also known as *Tao Te Ching* or *Daodejing*, c. third century BCE), an important early Daoist text, have appeared in English alone, and new editions appear every year. In fact, *Laozi* is second only to the Bible in the number of translations available worldwide. Perhaps more significantly, books sometimes only tangentially related to Daoism (examples include *The Tao of Leadership*, *Christ the Eternal Tao*, and *The Tao of Cleaning*) have proved to be extraordinarily popular in an increasingly unpredictable publishing market.

The questions of whether and how the interests of "nightstand Daoists," who engage the tradition largely or exclusively through reading and reflecting on texts, constitute evidence of a nascent Western Daoism are likely to be hotly debated in the decades to come. Nonetheless, it is clear that at least some Western Daoists espouse a pacifism which, if not directly drawn from Daoist sources, is seen by them as part and parcel of what it means to be a Daoist today.

Modern Asian interest in Daoist scriptures generally has tended in a more serious direction, drawing strength for contemporary philosophical and political projects from ancient texts. One example is the work of the Korean peace activist Sok Hon Ham (1901–1989), who claimed that the legendary Laozi (after whom the classical text is named) was the first pacifist and who located a basis for contemporary resistance to war in classical Daoist texts. It must be noted, however, that Sok borrowed as heavily from Christian traditions as from Daoist traditions, and that he refused to identify himself exclusively with any single religious tradition. Moreover, many scholars of early Daoist scriptures argue that, far from being blueprints for pacifist paradises, texts such as *Laozi* actually aim to provide tactical military advice to ancient Chinese rulers and generals.

Finally, other contemporary Asian thinkers who have appropriated ancient sources for their constructive ethical projects have tended to adopt Confucian, rather than Daoist, concepts. Perhaps this is because, as Henry Rosemont, Jr., has pointed out, "If Confucianism was the most socially and politically oriented of Chinese philosophies, Daoism was the least" (Rosemont 1997, 180).

Prospects for Modern Daoism as Ethical Resource

Modern Daoism, as a resource for thinking about war and violence, appears to be terribly impoverished. The aspects of the tradition that are most alive today are those that are least concerned with matters such as politics, social morality, and ethics in general. Conversely, the ethical legacy of the tradition is most forceful today through the popularity of ancient texts, with few if any links between an armchair readership and living communities of spiritual practice. Yet the voices of the classical texts, while subject to strenuous debate and interpretation, echo on, and the quiet sounds of contemporary Daoist practice, which owe much to a peaceful vision of life, have not been silenced.

Jeffrey L. Richey

See also Daoism, Classical; Daoism, Huang-Lao

Further Reading

Ames, R. T. (1997). Contemporary Chinese philosophy. In E. Deutsch & R. Bontekoe (Eds.), *A companion to world philosophies* (pp. 517–522). Oxford, UK: Blackwell Publishers.

Kim, S. S. (1994). *Sok Hon Ham and Taoism*. Retrieved 3 April 2003, from http://www2.gol.com/users/quakers/T&QhamTao.htm

Kohn, L. (Ed.). (2000). *Daoism Handbook*. Leiden, Netherlands: Brill.

MacInnis, D. E. (1989). *Religion in China today: Policy and practice*. Maryknoll, NY: Orbis Books.

Robinet, I. (1997). *Taoism: Growth of a religion* (P. Brooks, Trans.). Stanford, CA: Stanford University Press.

Rosemont, H., Jr. (1997). Chinese socio-political ideals. In E. Deutsch & R. Bontekoe (Eds.), *A companion to world philosophies* (pp. 174–184). Oxford, UK: Blackwell Publishers.

Schipper, K. (1993). *The Taoist body* (K. C. Duval, Trans.). Berkeley and Los Angeles: University of California Press.

Deobandism

Deobandism is an ideology of the orthodox Sunni branch of Islam (approximately 90 percent of the world's Muslims are Sunni Muslims). It emphasizes the enforcement of strict *shari*ʿ*a* rule (that is, rule according to Islamic law) in Muslim societies, promotes global jihad against non-Muslims, and is intolerant of other Islamic beliefs, especially Shiʿite beliefs. (Shiʿite beliefs are those held by adherents of Shiʿa Islam, approximately 10 percent of the world's Muslims.) Its followers include the Jamiyat Ulema-e-Islam (JUI) in Pakistan, the Taliban in Afghanistan and a number of extremist Islamic groups in South Asia, Southeast Asia, and Central Asia.

Based on the Hanafi legal school of thought (one of the four major Sunni juridical schools), Deobandism originated in British-ruled India during the mid-nineteenth century as a reformist ideology that aimed to regenerate Muslim society in the context of life in colonized state. Given its roots, its radicalization at the end of the twentieth century was quite ironic.

Roots

Deobandism takes its name from the Indian Himalayan town of Deoband, the location of an influential *madrasah* (religious school) called Darul uloom Deoband. The religious school was established in 1867 by Maulana Mohammad Qasim Nanauti, who was a student with Sir Sayyid Ahmad Khan (1817–1898), the founder of Aligarh Muslim University. Even though the two men were taught by the same teachers, they moved in different directions.

Darul uloom Deoband was established after the failed uprising of Indian Muslims against the British in 1857. Maulana Nanauti wanted to educate the demoralized Muslims in accordance with Islamic traditions, whereas Sir Sayyid wanted them to have a modern secular education. Consequently, while Aligarh University campaigned for Muslim accommodation to the British, Darul uloom Deoband preached confrontation with the British colonial rulers. In the 1920s, Maulana Ubaid Ullah Sindhi, a Deobandi scholar who founded the Jamiat al-Ulema-e-Hind (JUH), joined Mohandas (Mahatma) Gandhi and the Indian National Congress in the Khilafat movement in support of the Ottoman caliphate, an early indication of Deobandism's anticolonial and anti-Western stance.

Partition and After

Most conservative Deobandis opposed the creation of Pakistan. They instead envisioned life in a mixed Hindu and Muslim unified postcolonial state. Many saw Pakistan as an idea put forward by Westernized Muslims like Muhammed Ali Jinnah (1876–1948), the leader of the All-India Muslim League and the founder of Pakistan. The JUH, therefore, remained a major rival of the Muslim League. However, those Deobandis who had founded the Jamiyat Ulema-e-Islam in 1945 supported the formation of Pakistan.

In 1947, when India and Pakistan were separated from each other, the JUH stayed in India and the JUI shifted to Pakistan. In India, the followers of JUH and a faction of the Jamaʿat-e-Islami (JI), an Islamic party established by Maulana Mawdudi in 1941, have adhered to the reformist tradition of original Deobandism, despite Hindu nationalist violence against Indian Muslims, such as the December 1992 destruction of the Babri mosque, which fanned Muslim anger.

In Pakistan, the JI has dominated Islamic politics, though in the 1990s the JUI began to gain appeal when it adopted a neo-Deobandi ideology based on a rigid, militant, anti-American and anti-non-Muslim stance. The 1990s saw the emergence of two radical JUI offshoots, Sipah-e-Sahaba Pakistan and Lashkar-e-Jhangvi, which became notorious for their acts of violence against Shiʿites. Pakistan's conservative tribal Pashtun region bordering Afghanistan has constituted the traditional power base of the JUI. In October 2002, the JUI for the first time won seats in Pakistan's parliamentary elections.

The Taliban Connection

The Taliban grew out of a radical fringe of Deobandism. Their anomalous interpretation of Islam emerged from an extreme and perverse interpretation of Deobandism, preached by JUI mullahs at *madrasahs* in Afghan refugee camps in Pakistan's Pashtun region during and after the Afghan struggle against the Soviets during the 1980s. These *madrasahs* were run by barely literate mullahs untutored in the original reformist Deobandi agenda. They had little knowledge or appreciation of the classical Islamic tradition or for currents of Islamic thought in the broader Muslim world. "They espoused a myopic, self-contained, militant worldview in which Islam is used to legitimate their primitive Pushtun tribal customs and preferences. The classical Islamic belief in jihad as a defense of Islam and the Muslim community against aggression was transformed into a militant jihad culture and worldview that targets unbelievers, including Muslims and non-Muslims alike" (Esposito 2002, 16).

Many of these *madrasahs* were supported by Saudi funding that brought with it the influence of ultraconservative Wahhabi Islam (the denomination of Islam practiced in Saudi Arabia). Students received free education, and religious, ideological, and military training. Deoband teachings, like those of the Wahhabis, are puritanical in tone: They seek to purge Islam of Western and modernist influences and institutions and to establish the Qur'an and hadith (canonical Islamic traditions) as the sole guiding lights for Islamic thought. When the Taliban came to power in Afghanistan in 1996, they turned over many of their training camps to JUI militants, who in turn trained thousands of Pakistani and Arab militants as well as fighters from Southeast and Central Asia.

The Future

The Taliban fell in Afghanistan early in 2002, but the radicalized version of Deobandism continues to haunt South, Southeast, and Central Asia. For instance, inspired by Deobandism, Kashmiri militant groups such as Harkat-ul-Mujahideen, Jaish-e-Mohammed, Lashkar-e-Tayyiba—all included in the U.S. government's list of international terrorist organizations—continue to terrorize non-Muslims in the region in the name of jihad.

In Pakistan, Shiʿite-Sunni sectarianism has receded since the nation's military regime outlawed the two militant factions of JUI in August 2002. However, the Deobandi party's recent electoral success may not augur well for a politically stable Islamic Pakistan. Maulana Fazalur Rehman, the current leader of the JUI, issued a declaration of jihad against the United States in 1998, and JUI protested violently against the U.S. war in Afghanistan. Whether JUI will use its new clout in Pakistan's parliamentary politics to exercise its neo-Deobandi jihadist vision regionally and internationally in the violent manner of Deobandism's extremist fringe elements remains to be seen.

Ishtiaq Ahmad

See also Islam, Shiʿa; Islam, Sunni; Jihad; Kashmir; Taliban; Wahhabism

Further Reading

Ahmed, I. (1991). *The concept of an Islamic state in Pakistan.* Lahore, Pakistan: Vanguard Books.

Ali, T. (2002). *The clash of fundamentalisms: Crusades, jihads and modernity.* London: Verso.

Desker, B., & Ramakrishna, K. (2002). Forging an indirect strategy in South-East Asia. *The Washington Quarterly, 25*(2), 161–176.

Esposito, J. (2002). *Unholy war: Terror in the name of Islam.* New York: Oxford University Press.

Gohari, M. J. (2000). *The Taliban ascent to power.* New York: Oxford University Press.

Jones, O. (2002). *Pakistan: Eye of the storm.* New Haven, CT: Yale University Press.

Minault, G. (1999). *The Khilafat movement: Religious symbolism and political mobilization in India.* New York: Oxford University Press.

Nojumi, N. (2002). *The rise of the Taliban in Afghanistan: Mass mobilization, civil war, and the future of the region.* New York: Palgrave.

Rashid, A (1999). The Taliban: Exporting extremism. *Foreign Affairs, 78*(6), 22–35.

Rashid, A. (2000). *Taliban: Islam, oil and the new Great Game in Central Asia.* London: I. B. Tauris.

E

Eastern Orthodoxy, Pacifism in

The Eastern Orthodox Church understands itself as the church founded by Jesus Christ and living in unbroken apostolic succession of bishops and doctrine. It is preeminently the church of the Seven Ecumenical Councils (from I Nicea in 325 CE to II Nicea in 787 CE). Eastern Orthodoxy is the principal Christian church in the countries of Eastern Europe, with a worldwide membership of approximately 160 million. The church is organized in the four ancient patriarchates of Constantinople, Alexandria, Antioch, and Jerusalem; the autocephalous churches of Russia, Romania, Greece, Serbia, Bulgaria, Georgia, Poland, Cyprus, and Albania; and the autonomous churches of Finland, the Czech Republic and Slovakia, Japan, China, and the Sinai.

The Orthodox Moral Tradition

Eastern Orthodox moral theology differs significantly from its Western Christian counterparts. Stanley Harakas's taxonomy of Orthodox ethics in the last four centuries in *Toward Transfigured Life* illumines the significant continuities and discontinuities between East and West. The Athenian School associated with Chrestos Androutsos (1869–1935) is a rationalist approach grounded in philosophical idealism and influenced by Immanuel Kant. The Constantinopolitan School as seen in its major figure, Basil Antoniades (1851–1932), is distinguished by its reliance upon scriptural and early patristic texts, and even Western medieval writers such as Thomas Aquinas. The most distinctively Orthodox approach is that of the Thessalonian School associated with Christos Yannaras (b. 1935) and John Romanides (1927–2001). This approach draws from later Byzantine sources and stresses apophatic theology.

Orthodox moral theology, like its dogmatic theology, is grounded in the church's liturgy. Here the various sources of theological authority come together—tradition (including the Bible), the Seven Ecumenical Councils (especially the Symbol of Faith, i.e., the creed produced by the First and Second Councils, Nicea and Constantinople), the church fathers, the canons, and the holy icons. Evident throughout are the dogmatic and moral themes that characterize the Orthodox tradition and its moral theology—the Holy Trinity, the human being as created in the image of God and called to grow into God's likeness (*theosis* or deification), incarnation, and the kingdom of God. Moreover, these motifs are grounded in an eschatological understanding of the Eucharist and the church that situates the Christian's moral life in the context of one's journey of *theosis*. Such a journey is concerned with objectives different from those emphasized in Western ethics. Rather than a rational analysis of a normative notion of the moral good, prescriptive rules, and so forth, Orthodoxy insists that the goal of the moral life is nothing short of sainthood or *theosis*. The Christian will therefore be preoccupied not with moral theories and their prescriptions, but with living a life of continual repentance, confession, and thanksgiving.

No Just War

Unlike Western Christian traditions, Eastern Orthodoxy has never formulated a theory of just war. While

The Antiochian Orthodox Christian Archdiocese of North America Statement on Iraq

9 October 2002

STATEMENT ON IRAQ

While our country is on the brink of war with Iraq, it is the opinion of the Antiochian Orthodox Christian Archdiocese of North America that our esteemed President and governmental leaders rethink their position and the logic behind this impending conflict. Such an attack will destabilize the entire region, cause untold harm to countless children and other civilians as well as bring political and social unrest to an already troubled area of the world.

It is our conviction that all United Nations resolutions must be implemented in a consistent and meaningful way. We must add that we find it hypocritical that Iraq is threatened with war and destruction for failing to comply with UN resolutions while another state in the same region is in violation of about seventy UN resolutions which have never been implemented. This continues to be a reality even as this state occupies land that does not belong to it, illegally expands and builds settlements on occupied territories and implements collective punishment on masses of innocent people because of the distorted actions of a few. We are fully aware that Saddam Hussein and his government have committed atrocious acts which are in violation of international law.

We are gravely concerned, however, that a war against Iraq will create even more chaos in the region. The overthrowing of the Iraqi government could cause the breakup of the country into warring factions for many years to come. In addition, the geo-political imbalance this war would cause in the area will take generations to repair. It is said that our government will "rebuild Iraq and help the people of Iraq to form a democratic government." History has proven that this rarely comes to fruition. We need only look to the Balkans and Afghanistan as recent examples.

Therefore, we beseech our respected leaders and representatives and all those of good will to allow the United Nations inspectors to complete their mission. At the same time, we encourage our President and Congress to seek the difficult and tiresome road of peace rather than the bloody and dark road of war.

Issued by: Metropolitan Philip Saliba, Primate

Antiochian Orthodox Christian Archdiocese of North America

***Source:* Antiochian Orthodox Christian Archdiocese of North America. Retrieved 13 January 2003, from http://www.antiochian.org.**

Orthodox hierarchs and theologians have certainly invoked ideas typically associated with just war theory, e.g., that a war must be defensive in nature, such invocation is not an appeal to a moral theory that may be used to justify either the reasons for going to war *(jus ad bellum)* or the methods of conducting it *(jus in bello)*. While the Eastern Fathers do not articulate moral theories about wars such as those of Augustine and Aquinas, they do address the issue of Christian involvement in war. Their opinions represent a range from absolute pacifism to an acknowledgment that war is a necessary evil at best. Peace is the presumptive stance of Orthodox theology and one that cannot be abandoned without some degree of sin. The gospel standard is that of the Sermon on the Mount, wherein the eschatological ethics of the kingdom of God are the peaceful virtues of forgiveness, nonresistance to evil, and the love of enemies.

An important difference between East and West is their radically different appreciations of the soldier's moral standing. Under just war theory, a soldier who kills in a war justly entered and justly fought does not thereby sin. The theory serves to excuse the act of killing as long as it is a "just" killing. In the East, however, homicide is intrinsically sinful. Intention may mitigate the nature of a particular act's sinfulness, but killing in war, killing in self-defense, and even accidental manslaughter are all sinful acts. The Orthodox liturgy

This 13th-century icon of the Moscow School represents Saints Boris and Gleb, known as the Passion-Bearers who accepted death rather than fight in self-defense. Courtesy of Allyne Smith.

prays for the forgiveness of our sins, both "voluntary and involuntary." Thus St. Basil the Great (c. 329–379), while acknowledging that killing in war is sometimes justified, nonetheless counsels that someone who has killed in war is to be excommunicated for a period of three years.

Byzantium

The Byzantine Empire of the fourth through the fifteenth centuries is perhaps the best example of an Orthodox Christian nation, and aspects of its warmaking help to illustrate the Orthodox presumption in favor of peace, according to Harakas in *Wholeness of Faith and Life*. Various Byzantine military manuals demonstrate the Orthodox conviction that war is "the greatest of evils," and counsel the reader that paying tribute to an enemy is preferable to war and that open battle is to be avoided if at all possible. The slaughter of the enemy is excluded as a legitimate goal of warfare.

Russian Kenoticism

The theological concept of kenoticism is grounded in a particular New Testament text, Philippians 2:6–7, in which St. Paul writes that Christ, "who, though he was in the form of God, did not regard equality with God as something to be exploited, but emptied himself, taking the form of a slave, being born in human likeness" (NRSV). Christ's self-emptying, his *kenosis*, is understood as an expression of the humility of the incarnation. This theme flowered in Orthodoxy, especially in its Russian expression. Although Prince Vladimir's baptism of the Kievan Rus' (the medieval Russian state founded in the ninth century) took place in 988 CE, the paganism of the Kievan Rus' did not completely disappear until the fifteenth century. Shortly after the baptism, one of Prince Vladimir's (c. 956–1015) sons, Syvatopolk, decided to kill his brothers, Boris and Gleb, in order to take complete control of the Rus'. The two brothers refused to fight for power or even to defend themselves. After their martyrdom (1015 CE), the Russians created a new category of saint for them in reference to their voluntary acceptance of death in imitation of Christ, that of Passion-Bearers.

Inspired by Christ's voluntary death on the cross, and by the native example of St. Boris and St. Gleb, a theological movement characterized by kenoticism revitalized Russian Orthodox theology from 1725 to 1917. Important figures included St. Tikhon of Zadonsk (1722–1783), Metropolitan Philaret Drozdov of Moscow (1782–1867), Archimandrite Alexis M. Bukharev (1822–1871), Fyodor Dostoyevsky (1821–1881), and the theologian Mikhail M. Tareev (1866–1934). Traditional pacifist virtues of nonviolence and nonresistance to evil were joined to this kenotic notion of voluntary humiliation. These virtues, together with the emphasis upon universal forgiveness, reconciliation, and redemption that characterizes much of Russian theology, provide a solid theological grounding of Orthodox pacifism, according the A. F. C. Webster in *The Pacifist Option*.

Outlook for the Future

While it would not be accurate to identify the Orthodox Church as officially embracing the pacifist position, it would be fair to say that the presumption of its theology and practice is peace. And although Orthodox hierarchs and theologians have occasionally spoken of defensive wars as justified, it would also be wrong to say that the church embraces any theory of just war.

In recent years it has been increasingly common for Orthodox patriarchs, hierarchs, and theologians to criticize national decisions to wage war. In 2002, for example, numerous Orthodox churches communicated to the government of the United States their moral opposition to any American attack on Iraq. The likelihood of continued armed conflict throughout the world means that the Orthodox Church will continue to struggle to be faithful to its presumptive stance for peace amidst increasing pleas for armed response to aggression and terrorism.

Allyne L. Smith, Jr.

Further Reading

Berdyaev, N. (1954). *Christianity and anti-Semitism* (A. A. Spears & V. B. Kantner, Trans.). New York: Philosophical Library.

Bos, H., & Forest, J. (1999). *For the peace from above: An orthodox resource book on war, peace, and nationalism*. Bialystok, Poland: SYNDESMOS.

Dennis, G. T. (Trans.). (2001). *Maurice's* Strategikon: *Handbook of Byzantine military strategy*. Philadelphia: University of Pennsylvania Press.

Haldon, J. F. (1999). *Warfare, state and society in the Byzantine world 565–1204*. London: UCL Press.

Harakas, S. S. (1981). The morality of war: A synthesis of Christian views and individual response. In J. J. Allen (Ed.), *Orthodox synthesis: The unity of theological thought* (pp. 67–94). Crestwood, NY: St Vladimir's Seminary Press.

Harakas, S. S. (1983). *Toward transfigured life: The theoria of Eastern Orthodox ethics*. Minneapolis, MN: Light & Life Publishing.

Harakas, S. S. (1999). *Wholeness of faith and life: Orthodox Christian ethics*. Part 1: *Patristic ethics*. Brookline, MA: Holy Cross Orthodox Press.

Kartachov, A. (1996). The church and national identity (in Russian). In *Tserkov', Istoriya, Rossiya* (pp. 251–262). Moscow: Izd-vo "Probel."

Miller, T. S., & Nesbitt, J. (Eds.). (1995). *Peace and war in Byzantium: Essays in honor of George T. Dennis, S.J.* Washington, DC: Catholic University of America Press.

Treadgold, W. (1999). *Byzantium and its army 284–1081*. Stanford, CA: Stanford University Press.

Webster, A. F. C. (1995). *The price of prophecy: Orthodox churches on peace, freedom, and security*. Grand Rapids, MI: Eerdmans.

Webster, A. F. C. (1998). *The pacifist option: The moral argument against war in Eastern Orthodox theology*. San Francisco: International Scholars Publications.

English Civil Wars

The English Civil Wars (1642–1651) were armed conflicts that pitted King Charles I (1600–1649; reigned 1625–1649) and his Royalist forces against the Parliamentarians in a battle over constitutional and religious differences. The wars culminated in the king's execution and the establishment of a commonwealth under Oliver Cromwell (1599–1658), who took the title of lord protector (1653–1658).

Causes of the Civil Wars: The Authoritarianism of Charles I

Charles I was the second son of King James I (James VI of Scotland; 1566–1625) and his wife, Anne of Denmark. The reserved, slightly diffident Charles became king in 1625, married the devoutly Catholic Henrietta Maria, the sister of the French king Louis XII, and had nine children. Henrietta was disliked for her negative influence on Charles and her lack of concern for England.

Charles, like other monarchs before him, believed his actions were divinely endorsed. Accepting the belief that kings had a divine right to rule (the divine right of kings), Charles allowed no one to question his judgment. His strong-willed arrogance and frequently poor judgment led to severe mismanagement of state affairs. Charles inherited his father's unceasing financial problems and used various means to finance his government. Rather than deal with Parliament, which in the House of Commons was dominated by the middle class (gentry and merchants, many of whom were Calvinist Protestants—Puritans—who wished to rid the Church of England of its Catholic rituals and observances), Charles amassed finances by forced loans from nobles and knights, who were arrested if they refused to grant the loan. Charles also sold commercial monopolies at exorbitant rates and extracted ship money from towns that built naval warships, a policy he later applied to the whole country.

Parliament, for its part, claimed rights and privileges independent of the crown, and in response to Charles's abuses of power, forced the king to sign the Petition of Right in 1628. This petition ended the practice of forced loans, reasserted the principle (ignored by Charles) of due process of law, and reaffirmed that no one, including the commissioners Charles appointed to carry out his will, was above the law. Charles had summoned and dissolved Parliament three times between 1625 and 1629; thereafter, determined to rule without Parliament's interference, Charles commenced with arbitrary personal rule for the next eleven years.

Causes of the Civil Wars: Religious Differences

Conflict between the Church of England and dissenters played a secondary role in the Civil Wars. A precursor to the Civil Wars was the First Bishops' War (1638–1639), occasioned by the king's attempts to impose High Church Anglican reforms on the Scottish Presbyterian church. William Laud (1573–1645), whom Charles appointed archbishop of Canterbury in 1633, insisted on religious uniformity and supported the king's arbitrary religious reforms. The Scottish Assembly at Glasgow rejected the proposals in 1638. Charles was gravely affronted; he could not believe that the Scots would defy him. When the new Book of Common Prayer was read at St. Giles Cathedral in Edinburgh, however, overwhelming upheavals ensued. The Scots countered by establishing a National Covenant on 28 February 1638; the Covenanters swore to defend the Scottish Presbyterian Church and to do away with the office of bishop. Charles, despite being totally financially and militarily unprepared, invaded Scotland, but he never fought a battle. Instead he signed the Pacification of Berwick in 1639. That agreement gave the Scots the right to a free church assembly and a free parliament.

Despite this failure Charles promptly proceeded to invade Scotland again—without Parliament's support. In retaliation for Parliament's refusing to support him, Charles unknowingly made the greatest blunder of his monarchy when he dissolved the Short Parliament (so called because it lasted only three weeks) on 5 May 1640. He failed to anticipate the ramifications of dismissing Parliament and never realized the vehement discontent his personal rule was stirring up. The total unpreparedness of his mutinous and disorderly ragtag army also worked against Charles. The English soldiers were fighting for pay, while the Scots fought for their religion. The Second Bishops' War ended with Charles's humiliating defeat at Newburn; in the Treaty of Ripon (October 1640) he agreed to pay a temporary indemnity of £850 a day to the Scots until the war was over. The Scots occupied Northumberland and Durham and took control over the coal supplies in the region.

This English Civil War Society performs re-enactments of battles using authentic weapons, tactics, and clothing. Courtesy the English Civil War Society.

The Long Parliament

Charles summoned Parliament on November 1640, fully expecting them to quickly approve the indemnity payments. On the contrary, a bitter Parliament enacted a series of measures to severely curtail his power. The two-hundred-clause Grand Remonstrance, initiated by John Pym (1584–1643) and four other members of Parliament was promoted on 1 December 1641. It listed the transgressions of Charles's reign, noted what measures had already been taken to address his abuses of power, and suggested further measures that should be taken. Among the new laws enacted at this time were the Triennal Act, which ensured that only three years would elapse between sessions of Parliament, and the restriction of the right of taxation and financial affairs to Parliament. Episcopal (ecclesiastic) courts and other arbitrary prerogative courts were abolished. Charles complied with all of the demands issued by the Long Parliament (so called because members refused to disband when ordered to).

By this time a prominent religious split had emerged in Parliament between the Puritans, who considered the reforms that began when the Church of England split from the Roman Catholic Church (1534) to be only partly completed, and more moderate members who sided with Charles and were content with the Church of England as it was. Politically, many people outside of Parliament were satisfied with the degree of government reform already achieved and began to question Puritan members of Parliament who continued to speak of tyranny and conspiracy.

The landowners, gentry, and nobles were High Church Anglicans. For them, Charles represented social order and stability; they supported him and became known as Royalists or Cavaliers. The middle-class small landowners, tradesmen, city and town councilors, merchants, and manufacturers favored the less hierarchical Parliament. They were called Roundheads, so named because of their close-cropped hair (in contradistinction to the Cavaliers' long, curled locks). Geographically the areas of Royalist support tended to be the in the north, west, and in Wales, while Parliament was sustained by the richer south and east, including London. Parliament had access to more financial resources; Charles depended on donations. The common people, who made up the majority of the population were neutral in the Civil Wars.

In 1639 Charles made Thomas Wentworth (1593–1641), first earl of Strafford, his chief adviser. As lord deputy in Ireland Strafford had bolstered trade and industry, reorganized the Irish church, rid the sea of pirates, and reformed financial administration so effectively that income doubled; Strafford had also led the king's army in the Second Bishops' War. Parliament, suspecting that Strafford intended to use Irish troops against the king's opponents, charged him with treason, but, unable to prove the case against him, resorted to using a bill of attainder, which singles out an individual or group for punishment without trial. Strafford was executed on 12 May 1641. Fearing the same fate, many of the king's other ministers abandoned him and fled.

The First Civil War (1642–1646)

Emboldened by Royalist support, and still convinced that he ruled by divine right, Charles entered the House of Commons on 4 January 1642 supported by four hundred troops to arrest five members whom he viewed as traitors. This action caused public outrage, and Charles fled north to Oxford. Henrietta fled to Holland, taking the crown jewels as collateral to raise funds. Differences escalated and culminated in Charles raising his standard against Parliamentary forces at Nottingham on 22 August 1642.

Both sides aimed to take London. Parliamentarians had superior numbers, but the Royalists were militarily experienced and better trained. Robert Devereux, the third earl of Essex, became parliamentary commander and met Charles at the Battle of Edgehill on 23 October 1642; that battle proved indecisive. Charles then marched toward London, but on the way south lost the Battle of Turnham Green on 13 November 1642. He retreated to Oxford, which remained his headquarters throughout the war. The Royalist forces thereafter won the majority of battles in 1643: Grantham on 23 March, Stratton on 16 May, and Chalgrove Field on 18 June. At Adwalton Moor on 30 June 1643 the Royalists took control of Yorkshire; they won again at Lansdown on 5 July 1643 and at Roundway Down on 13 July 1643. They were also victorious at Newbury on 20 September 1643. Parliamentary forces, however, were victorious at Winceby on 11 October 1643, taking Lincoln.

Meanwhile Charles negotiated a cease-fire with the Irish, which was a blow to Parliament because it meant Charles could use the troops formerly occupied in Ireland to fight the Parliamentarians. Two attempts at peace negotiations conducted at Oxford in 1643 proved futile. John Pym arranged an alliance with Scotland in order to balance Charles's superior forces. On 25 September 1643 the Solemn League and Covenant promised the Scots religious reforms in return for their help. The Roundheads' military fortunes improved significantly in January 1644, when Scotland brought 18,000 troops.

In late 1644 Oliver Cromwell, a small landowner and member of Parliament who had achieved some influence as head of the Puritan Independent faction, set about to reorganize and improve the military. The various hitherto private armies were combined and restructured into the New Model Army, which came into being in April 1645. The *Soldier's Catechism* was drawn up, establishing rules, regulations, and correct drill and disciplinary procedures. Soldiers were offered standardized pay, food and clothing, and promotion based on merit. Conscription was used to fortify support. The 22,000-man force was headed by Sir Thomas Fairfax (1612–1671).

Many battles were fought from 1644 to 1646. The Parliamentarians won the decisive victory at Marston Moor on 2 July 1644, allowing them to take York. They also defeated the Royalist forces at Naseby on 14 June 1645. These battles effectively crushed Royalist hopes, although fighting went on for another year. In May 1646 Charles surrendered to the Scots, who ransomed him to Parliament for £400,000. In June 1646 the First Civil War ended when Oxford surrendered to the New Model Army.

The Second Civil War (1647–1648)

The Second Civil War began with Charles refusing the army's peace proposals. Charles surrendered to the Scots in 1636 who sold him to England for £400,000. He was in the custody of the army when he escaped and took refuge on the Isle of Wight in November 1647. He then foolishly proceeded to negotiate simultaneously with Cromwell and the Scots. On 28 December 1647 Charles concluded an agreement with the Scots known as the Engagement, in which he promised church reform in exchange for more favorable terms as king and the Scots' military support in an attack on the Parliamentarians. The Scots invaded England in July 1648. This war was more brutal than the first. Cromwell repeatedly defeated the Royalists. The Scots, who now allied with Charles, were soundly defeated at Preston on 17–19 August 1648. Cromwell also suppressed uprisings in Wales, Kent, and Essex, effectively ending the Second Civil War. Charles might have regained his throne had he negotiated in good faith with Cromwell, who by now fiercely hated his adversary. While Charles was held in protective custody at Holmby House, the discontent in the army over his returning as king gradually became more radical. The answer was to dispense with the king, who was condemned in Parliament in January 1648.

To accomplish this unprecedented task Parliament expelled by force all the Royalists and Presbyterian members who had opposed the king's condemnation in January1648. Some forty-five members were arrested and 146 were kept out. The 75 who remained were derisively named the Rump Parliament. Their objective was to try Charles I for treason and for making war on Parliament. Those members who had been ejected considered the Rump Parliament and its actions illegitimate.

There was no legal precedent for trying the king, so a court was set up based on a Roman statute that allowed the killing of a tyrant. Only 68 of 135 commissioners answered the call to the court at Whitehall on 1 January 1649. Charles refused to recognize the authority of the court, which found him guilty by one vote (68 to 67) on 26 January 1649. Charles was beheaded on 30 January 1649 in front of Whitehall in London. The public execution was witnessed by thousands of people, who groaned when his head was lifted for viewing. Regicide was not an accepted practice and the unpopular act turned the tragic, short-sighted Charles into a royal martyr. Most people had not wanted his death, they had merely wanted to control him.

The English Civil Wars did not end with the expurgation of the monarchy. The Rump Parliament abolished the monarchy and the House of Lords on 17 March. A Commonwealth was established that was governed by the Rump Parliament and by an executive council until 1653. Then the 140-member Barebones Parliament of 4 July to 11 December 1653 dissolved itself. What followed was known as the Interregnum.

The Irish rebelled from 1649 to 1650 after hearing of the king's execution. On 2 August, there was an uprising of Irish Royalists and even Irish Catholics supporting Charles II's claim to the English throne. The rebellion was harshly suppressed by Cromwell. The Irish forces were soundly defeated by Parliamentarian forces in battle near Dublin.

The Third Civil War (1650)

The Third Civil War occurred because the Scots accepted Charles I's son as king in Edinburgh upon the death of his father. Charles II (1630–1685; reigned 1660–1685) fought along with the Scots, but Cromwell defeated them at Dunbar on 2 September 1650, and Charles II fled to the continent. He invaded England in 1651 but was defeated at the Battle of Worcester, whereupon he went back into exile until after the death of Cromwell.

Cromwell had assumed the title of lord protector in February 1649. Upon his death on 3 September 1658 he was succeeded by his weak and ineffective son Richard (1626–1712; lord protector from September 1658 to May 1659). The Commonwealth ceased to exist in 1660 with the Restoration of the monarchy under Charles II.

Annette Richardson

Further Reading

Ashley, M. (1987). *Charles I and Oliver Cromwell: A study in contrasts and comparisons*. London: Methuen.

Ashley, M. (1996). *The English Civil War*. Stroud, UK: Sutton Publishing.

Hibbert, C. (1993). *Cavaliers and Roundheads*. New York: HarperCollins Publishers.

Kenyon, J. (1989). *The Civil Wars of England*. London: Weidenfield & Nicolson.

Ollard, R. (1976). *This war without an enemy: A history of the English Civil Wars*. New York: Atheneum.

Wedgwood, C. V. (1955). *The King's peace, 1637–1641: The great rebellion*. London: Collins.

Wedgwood, C. V. (1958). *The King's War, 1641–1647*. London: Collins.

Wedgwood C. V. (1964). *A coffin for King Charles: The trial and execution of Charles I*. New York: Macmillan.

European Wars of Religion

Religious differences divided early modern Europe, often leading to violence that undermined the state's social and political stability. Rulers needed to ensure that all subjects recognized their legitimate authority and, as all claimed some kind of divine right, preferred religious unity as an ideal platform upon which to base their power. Thus, even before Martin Luther challenged it, kings had been challenging papal authority over the church in their realms. Spanish monarchs controlled an Inquisition that from 1478 monitored religious issues with an eye toward enforcing Catholic orthodoxy, without reference to bishops or popes. (It did not disappear entirely until the nineteenth century.) Similarly, the Concordat of Bologna (1516) gave French monarchs the right of appointing all higher spiritual offices in France without reference to papal preferences. In many ways and under many guises, royal authority came to depend on political and religious unity and, hence, any threat to one sphere was a threat to both. The Protestant Reformation threatened both, and heresy became equated with treason. Religious schism led not only to a number of small clashes, but also to three major conflicts: the French Wars of Religion, the Revolt of the Netherlands, and the Thirty Years' War.

The French Wars of Religion (1559–1598)

The death in 1559 of Henry II left France in a politically and economically fragile state: Royal power fell to one weak-willed son after another and, while the church was still subordinate to the crown, the church was seen as little more than a steady source of income. As powerful quasi-royal families (the Guises, Bourbons, and Montmorencys) vied for political power, instability moved down the social scale as far as the peasantry in the countryside, the artisan and merchant classes in the towns, and poor and unappreciated parish priests everywhere. Into this volatile mix came the destabilizing influence of Calvinism, which disregarded the national hierarchy of priests, bishops, and cardinals and cemented the locals together under their own (self-elected) political and spiritual leaders. A combination of royal apathy, toleration, and inexperience allowed a rapid spread of Calvinism (particularly in the south and west). Small-scale riots against oppressive Catholic authorities, however, escalated out of control when the quasi-royal families, temporarily displaced from authority, noticed the potential of religious fanaticism (whether Catholic or Calvinist) of congregations who were, coincidentally, looking for powerful patrons able to aid their struggles and increase the social and political influence of their church. As the Calvinists (called Huguenots in France) were willing to die to defend their faith, the great magnates found ready-made soldiers who would fight for them. In order to secure and strengthen royal authority, Catherine de Médicis (1519–1589), acting on behalf of her three sons, kings Francis II (1544–1560; reigned 1559–1560), Charles IX (1550–1574; reigned 1560–1574), and Henry III (1551–1589; reigned 1574–1589), attempted accommodation with or acted ruthlessly against the Huguenots, achieving only mixed results while offending those on both sides of the religious divide. Political and religious tension led to eight civil wars in roughly three phases.

The first phase (c. 1562–1572), largely urban, saw the Huguenots trying to secure concessions from intolerant local Catholic hierarchies. In March 1562, the Massacre of Huguenots at Vassy led to similar events across France. To quell further rioting, the Pacification of Ambrose (1563) granted freedom of worship to the Huguenot nobles. Dissatisfaction, and fear that royal negotiations with Philip of Spain were aimed against them, led Huguenot radicals to try to kidnap the king (at Meaux) in September 1567. The peace of March 1568 forced restrictions on Huguenot worship and, by December, Catherine canceled all grants of toleration. The resultant rioting was ended in August 1570 with the Peace of St. Germain. The Huguenots gained limited religious freedom and the right to garrison four strongholds. By August 1572, fearing that Charles was falling too much under the influence of the leading Huguenot, Gaspard II de Coligny (1519–1572), Catherine arranged Coligny's assassination, but the attempt went spectacularly wrong and resulted in the infamous St. Bartholomew's Day Massacre (24 August 1572) in which thousands of Huguenots were murdered in Paris and, later, across France. The Edict of Boulogne (July 1573) restored Huguenot freedom of worship in La Rochelle, Nîmes, Mountauban, and some great noble homes, thus changing the nature of the conflict.

The second phase (c. 1572–1584) saw the surviving Huguenot communities form and pledge to defend a quasi-autonomous state within the state, creating serious political disjunction at court. For instance, February 1575 saw the duke of Alençon (the king's brother), join forces with Henry of Navarre (1553–1610), the leading Huguenot, in a revolt aimed ostensibly at the power of the Guise faction (the Catholic power around the king). The Peace of Monsieur (May 1576) and subsequent Edict of Beaulieu were trumpeted as a Huguenot triumph, as they signaled that the Huguenots had gained total religious freedom and judicial authority over their own people. The backlash came in 1577 with the formation of the "Catholic League" of magnates and quasi-independent towns over which Henry III was forced to assume leadership (or become a political nonentity); the resulting civil unrest was settled by the Peace of Bergerac (September 1577). Henry later issued the Edict of Poitiers, which restricted Huguenot worship, in an attempt to establish himself as the guarantor of religious peace. That action led to an indecisive, short-lived disturbance in 1580.

July 1585 ushered in the third phase. The king canceled all previous Huguenot liberties, just as circumstances made the Huguenot Henry of Navarre heir to his throne. This conflict is sometimes called the "war of three Henrys," as Henry, Duke of Guise (1550–1588) led the Catholic cause against a Protestant succession. The king tried to have Guise and his brother, a cardinal, assassinated, but ended up assassinated himself (1 August 1589). Henry IV (the former Henry of Navarre), facing the Catholic league and its Spanish supporters, realized his religious beliefs would always be a barrier to establishing uncontested authority. In July 1593 he converted to Catholicism, forging an alliance of sorts between politically minded Huguenots and moderate Catholics, ending the civil wars. He declared the Edict of Nantes (April 1598), which allowed a liberty of conscience and freedom of worship that lasted well into the seventeenth century.

Revolt of the Netherlands (1565–1598)

The underlying causes of the three revolts (1565–1567, 1567–1576, 1576–1581) in this geographically, linguistically, and culturally diverse region are similar to those underlying the French civil wars—religious tensions, governmental intolerance, and noble ambitions—with the added complication that it was part of the Habsburg empire (fashioned into a separate political entity in 1548) and very much dependent on the ruler for social, economic, and political stability. The region prospered under the first ruler, Holy Roman Emperor Charles V (Carlos I of Spain; 1500–1558) who, as a native Burgundian, was able to command the loyalty of his subjects in the Low Countries. His son, however, the staunchly Catholic and Spanish Philip II (1527–1598), was unable to retain that loyalty. He was determined to fight what he deemed heresy whatever the cost and to rule this commercially important region from Madrid. His attitude eventually led to the division of the Low Countries into the United Provinces of the north and the Spanish Netherlands of the south.

Here was a real clash of religious attitudes. Philip's uncompromising nature did not sit well with his Low Countries subjects, who were intentionally religiously tolerant as tolerance paid dividends in the world of international trade in which many were engaged. Provided monarchical demands did not infringe too seriously on their own powers and interests, the native nobles generally supported Habsburg rule, even joining Habsburg crusades against Anabaptists (radicals who rejected secular authority) in their midst. After

The Edict of Nantes (1598)

Henry, by the grace of God king of France and of Navarre, to all to whom these presents come, greeting:

Among the infinite benefits which it has pleased God to heap upon us, the most signal and precious is his granting us the strength and ability to withstand the fearful disorders and troubles which prevailed on our advent in this kingdom. The realm was so torn by innumerable factions and sects that the most legitimate of all the parties was fewest in numbers. God has given us strength to stand out against this storm; we have finally surmounted the waves and made our port of safety,—peace for our state. For which his be the glory all in all, and ours a free recognition of his grace in making use of our instrumentality in the good work. . . . We implore and await from the Divine Goodness the same protection and favor which he has ever granted to this kingdom from the beginning . . .

We have, by this perpetual and irrevocable edict, established and proclaimed and do establish and proclaim:

I. First, that the recollection of everything done be one party. or the other between March, 1585, and our accession to the crown, and during all the preceding period of troubles, remain obliterated and forgotten, as if no such things had ever happened.

[. . .]

III. We ordain that the Catholic Apostolic and Roman religion shall be restored and reestablished in all places and localities of this our kingdom and countries subject to our sway, where the exercise of the same has been interrupted, in order that it may be peaceably and freely exercised, without any trouble or hindrance: forbidding very expressly all persons, of whatsoever estate, quality, or condition, from troubling, molesting, or disturbing ecclesiastics in the celebration of divine service, in the enjoyment or collection of tithes, fruits, or revenues of their benefices, and all other rights and dues belonging to them: and that all those who during the troubles have taken possession of churches. houses, goods or revenues, belonging to the said ecclesiastics, shall surrender to them entire possession and peaceable enjoyment of such rights, liberties, and sureties as they had before they were deprived of them.

[. . .]

VI. And in order to leave no occasion for troubles or differences between our subjects, we have permitted, and herewith permit, those of the said religion called Reformed to live and abide in all the cities and places of this our kingdom and countries of our sway, without being annoyed, molested, or compelled to do anything in the matter of religion contrary to their consciences, . . . upon condition that they comport themselves in other respects according to that which is contained in this our present edict.

[. . .]

VII. It is permitted to all lords, gentlemen, and other persons making profession of the said religion called Reformed, holding the right of high justice [or a certain feudal tenure], to exercise the said religion in their houses.

[. . .]

IX. We also permit those of the said religion to make and continue the exercise of the same in all villages and places of our dominion where it was established by them and publicly enjoyed several and divers times in the year 1597, up to the end of the month of August, notwithstanding all decrees and judgments to the contrary.

Continues

Continued

[. . .]

XIII. We very expressly forbid to all those of the said religion its exercise, either in respect to ministry, regulation, discipline, or the public instruction of children, or otherwise, in this our kingdom and lands of our dominion, otherwise than in the places permitted and granted by the present edict.

[. . .]

XIV. It is forbidden as well to perform any function of the said religion in our court or retinue, or in our lands and territories beyond the mountains, or in our city of Paris or within five leagues of the said city . . .

[. . .]

XVIII. We also forbid all our subjects, of whatever quality and condition, from carrying off be force or persuasion, against the will of their parents, the children of the said religion, in order to cause them to be baptized or confirmed in the Catholic Apostolic and Roman Church; and the same is forbidden to those of the said religion called Reformed, upon penalty of being punished with especial severity.

[. . .]

XXI. Books concerning the said religion called Reformed may not be printed and publicly sold, except in cities and places where the public exercise of the said religion is permitted.

[. . .]

XXII. We ordain that there shall be no difference or distinction made in respect to the said religion, in receiving pupils to be instructed in universities, colleges, and schools; nor in receiving the sick and poor into hospitals, retreats and public charities.

[. . .]

XXIII. Those of the said religion called Reformed shall be obliged to respect the laws of the Catholic Apostolic and Roman Church, recognized in this our kingdom, for the consummation of marriages contracted, or to be contracted, as regards the degrees of consanguinity and kinship.

Source: **Robinson, James Harvey. (Ed.). (1906). *Readings in European History,* 2 vols. Boston: Ginn, 2, pp. 183–185.**

Calvinist influences from Geneva and Strasbourg came into the Low Countries on the back of Anabaptism and with Huguenots fleeing France, religious discontent infected the lower classes, the lesser nobles, and urban hierarchies, giving Calvinism a firm foothold.

The major divisive event occurred with a royal scheme to make over the local Catholic church on a clearer Spanish Catholic model (consequently increasing royal power). In 1559 three new archbishops and fourteen new bishops were installed (along with Inquisition associates). At a stroke Philip strengthened royal power at the expense of traditional and native noble authority (by removing their patronage over church appointments). Fear of the Inquisition resulted in civil unrest, with the threat that it might disrupt international trade agreements. Nor did the greater magnates (tolerant Catholics) welcome the further intrusion into their authorities by Cardinal Granvelle, Antoine Perrenot (1517–1586), the Spanish minister. (In 1564 they forced him into exile.) The lesser magnates (Calvinists)—with the support of their Huguenot counterparts—went further and established underground congregations and encouraged mob violence (in reaction to bad harvests in 1565) in an iconoclastic

Key Religious Differences

Early modern Western Christendom became divided into three distinguishable churches: Roman Catholics, Lutherans, and Calvinists (Protestants hereafter). Each provided a unique interpretation in four key areas of theology—justification (or salvation), the sacraments, authority (secular and spiritual), and on the use of scripture. The key to understanding the religious wars is having a firm grasp on the differences between the three sects on these issues. Protestants hold the Bible as the only source of religious truth while Catholics accept tradition and canon law (sacred and secular history) as well. Thus, as only Baptism and the Eucharist find undisputable scriptural support, Protestants agree that only these two are true sacraments (although the issue of the "real presence" divides them as Calvinists see only a spiritual presence), whereas Catholics discern five other sacraments. Thus, the Protestants disregard the office of priest (the sacrament of ordination) as nonscriptural, undermining the entire Catholic spiritual hierarchy as a result. Indeed, Protestants hold all believers as priests (regardless of any other qualifications), spiritual office being subject to community standard. Both sides hold that it is important, however, for the sake of social stability, that everyone within a specific locality belong to the same church.

Protestants view the spiritual and temporal spheres as complimentary, whereas Catholics hold them almost mutually exclusive. Regarding salvation, Catholics believe in a mixture of faith in God and the performance of faith affirming good works. Thus, acts of charity (and other good works) are blessed by God and increase personal grace, lessening the time a person must spend in purgatory atoning for their sins. After cleansing of sins (however long it takes), the soul moves on to heaven. Protestants hold the performance of good works as immaterial, holding purgatory as mere human invention (a means for Rome to raise funds through sharp practices). They are divided, however, over the larger issue of faith. Lutherans hold that genuine faith alone is sufficient—grace is a free gift from God—while Calvinists hold that as God determined at the point of creation who is damned and who is saved (in a way unexplainable to mortals) even genuine faith is not a guarantee of salvation.

***Source:* Andrew A. Chibi**

direction. If not for this, Philip might have been willing to relax the heresy laws. Instead, he signed the so-called Segovia Woods letter, rejecting concessions of any kind. This, the establishment of a Jesuit university at Douai, and his embracing of the decrees of the Council of Trent (1545–1563) led to greater anti-Spanish and anti-Catholic discontent. In April 1566 the regent, Margaret of Parma, received a petition (the First Request) against the threat of the inquisition; another (the Second Request) in July sought freedom of worship for the Calvinists. Philip's hard-line reaction encouraged further rioting, put down by the concerned magnates themselves (including William of Orange, at that time a Catholic). In August 1567, fearing further uprisings, Philip sent in an army of occupation under the Duke of Alva, Ferdinand Alvarez de Toledo (1508–1582), the most feared soldier on the continent.

Alva took over as governor-general and set up the Council of Troubles to enforce religious uniformity and Spanish power, initiating reign of terror. Having fled the country, William of Orange attempted invasions of his own (in 1568 and 1571) and the resultant second revolt (1567–1576) led to the deaths of thousands of so-called heretics but also to the founding of rebel strongholds in the towns of the north (supported by the so-called Sea Beggars, who were radical Calvinists). William converted to Calvinism in April 1573 to strengthen his authority as sovereign and supreme head of the Holland and Zealand provinces, promising freedom of worship in the north to all. Events outside of the Low Countries forced the withdrawal of Alva, and the reneging of payments to Spanish troops led to mutiny (lending a horrendously violent aspect to the third revolt). As a result, the States General (the native assembly) was summoned without Philip's permission by the Council of State in order to provide defense against the mutineers. The recruited forces (Calvinists and Catholics) were successful in the short term, leading to the so-called Pacification of Ghent (October-November 1576).

The States General then demanded that all divisive elements—the foreign troops, Spanish governors-general, and heresy measures—be removed from the region, thereby effecting a return of the traditional tolerant rule of the local magnates. In 1577, however, both William and Don Juan of Austria (Philip's new governor-general) entered Brussels expecting to assert political control. Philip supported Don Juan despite threats from the States General and exacerbated the situation by dispatching the Duke of Parma, Alexander Farnese (1546–1592) with another army. Farnese became governor-general in October 1578 on the death of Don Juan. The seeds of political division were sown when the states of the south refused to support northern uprisings against Parma. Instead, the southern states concluded the Union of Arras (6 January 1579), accepting Spanish rule in an attempt to reestablish traditional noble authorities. In light of Arras, the northern states had no option but to pursue a defensive military alliance via the Union of Utrecht (23 January 1579), laying the base for the independent United Provinces (a union of the northern provinces of Holland, Zeeland, Utrecht, Gelderland, Groningen, Friesland, and Overyssel). This division prolonged the third revolt, as William searched for foreign alliances based on shared religious beliefs and anti-Spanish political positions, in turn appealing to the main Huguenot leader (Francis, duke of Anjou) and Elizabeth I of England. Ultimately, however, William was assassinated (10 July 1584) and Parma racked up military successes (Brussels in 1585, Sluis in 1587), such that the sheer expense of continued warfare forced Philip into genuine truce talks (1598). Under Philip III (1578–1621), the Twelve-Year Truce was agreed in 1609, providing de facto recognition of the independent United Provinces.

The Thirty Years' War (1618–1648)

The Thirty Years' War was actually a series of five related conflicts that had grown out of religious and political instability. The first (1618–1620), the Bohemian war, was a war of Bohemian Protestants, supported by Czech nationalists, against their imperial Catholic overlords. The second (1625–1629), the Danish war, saw Denmark protecting Protestant German states against imperial Austrian troops and Catholic German forces. The third (1630–1648), the Swedish war, was a war of Swedish territorial expansion at the expense of Habsburg dynastic interests in northern Germany and in support of mercantile dominance of the Baltic region. The fourth (1635–1648), the Franco-Habsburg War, was largely a continuation of earlier Franco-Spanish conflicts, and the last (1543–1645), the Danish-Swedish conflict, was fought for dominance in the Baltic region and for control of trade.

The Catholic Habsburg dynasty (in Spain and in Austria) was targeted by discontented Protestant groups in the Holy Roman Empire, by military adventurers from Catholic France, and by the political and mercantile expansionist program of the Lutheran Swedes. Religious division was a backdrop for many of the important events and provided a cause for war, but politics was the greater issue outside of the Bohemian phase.

In 1547 many Czech nationalists made common cause with the Schmalkaldic League (the Protestant military wing of the German Lutheran princes) against Catholic power. While Emperor Ferdinand I (1503–1564; reigned 1558–1564) defeated the league, religious discontent and nascent nationalism later (c. 1610) combined and exploded into open revolt in Bohemia against Habsburg rule, German culture, and the Catholic Church. While the Czech-Bohemians were eventually crushed, their revolt had already fueled sympathy among German Protestant princes, and this blew up into a full-scale civil war. The main issue was the power struggle between Emperor Ferdinand II (elected in 1619) and Elector Frederick V of the Palatinate (a Calvinist), who had been offered the crown of Bohemia against Austrian Habsburg wishes. Frederick brought the Evangelical Union (a militant Protestant association) to the aid of the Czechs. When they were defeated, the Palatinate, Saxony, Baden, and Brunswick found themselves threatened by Catholic forces (a combination of Imperial, Spanish, and Bavarian troops). By 1629 Ferdinand II was in a position to proclaim the Edict of Restitution, declaring reclamation of all church lands secularized by the Lutherans. From this point, religious motivations took a backseat to political ones. Indeed, there are a number of cross-religious alliances (as in the 1630s, when Catholic France supported Protestant Sweden against the Habsburgs) and same-religion conflicts (as in the Danish-Swedish war).

In the final analysis, religion was a convenient justification for shady diplomatic practices and a smoke screen for predominantly political causes. The Treaty of Westphalia (1648), an amalgamation of treaty negotiations between the Imperial and Habsburg powers and French powers at Munster and the Imperial and

Habsburg powers and Swedish powers at Osnabruck, ostensibly ended the religious wars of Europe. In effect, Westphalia settled most of the outstanding religious questions of the previous century, and rulers on both sides were encouraged to toleration. Indeed, they gained greater power in the direction of state religions (while recognizing minority religions within their borders), which gave them the stability and political recognition they sought. Moreover, religious conflict as the basis of foreign policy died out as shared political aims clearly formed a more reliable basis for international associations.

Andrew Chibi

See also Reformed Christianity; Thirty Years' War; Tyrannicide, Medieval Catholic Doctrine of

Further Reading

Benicke, G. (1978). *Germany in the Thirty Years' War: Documents of modern history*. London: Edward Arnold.

Briggs, R. (1977). *Early modern France, 1560–1715*. Oxford, UK: Oxford University Press.

Cameron, E. (1991). *The European Reformation*. Oxford, UK: Oxford University Press.

Duke, A., Lewis, G., & Pettegree, A. (1992). *Calvinism in Europe, 1540–1610: A collection of documents*. Manchester, UK: Manchester University Press.

Greengrass, M. (1984). *The French Reformation*. London: Blackwell.

Greengrass, M. (1998). *The Longman companion to the European Reformation, c. 1500–1618*. London: Longman.

Höpfl, H. (Ed.). (1991). *Luther and Calvin on secular authority*. Cambridge, UK: Cambridge University Press.

Hughes, M. (1992). *Early modern Germany, 1477–1806*. London: Macmillan Education.

Kilsby, J. (1986). *Spain, rise and decline*. London: Hodder & Stoughton.

Lee, S. J. (1978). *Aspects of European history, 1494–1789*. London: Routledge.

Lotherington, J. (Ed.). (1988). *Years of renewal: European history, 1470–1600*. London: Hodder & Stoughton.

Mackenny, R. (1993). *Sixteenth century Europe: Expansion and conflict*. London: Macmillan.

McGrath, A. (1988). *Reformation thought*. Oxford, UK: Blackwell Publishers.

Parker, G. (Ed.). (1984). *The Thirty Years' War*. London: Routledge.

Rady, M. (1988). *France, 1494–1610: Renaissance, religion and recovery*. London: Hodder & Stoughton.

Sutherland, N. M. (1973). *The massacre of St. Bartholomew and the European conflict*. London: Macmillan.

Sutherland, N. M. (1980). *The Huguenot struggle for recognition*. New Haven, CT: Yale University Press.

F

Fundamentalism in Egypt and Sudan

Fundamentalism within the major religions of the world has generated tremendous scholarly interest in recent times. Historians, theologians, literary scholars, scholars of religion, and writers in international politics have all addressed the topic. With regard to Islamic fundamentalism, it is necessary to say from the outset that the application of the term *fundamentalism* to Islam is loaded with deep controversy. First, the term itself has a pejorative connotation. Many Muslims believe it connotes ignorance and narrow-mindedness, and therefore do not believe it is appropriate to apply the term to genuine Islamic revival movements. Second, many Muslims feel that there is no appropriate cognate term in Arabic for fundamentalism and therefore object to using the term in discussions of Islam. Last, scholars such as Frederick Denny, Bernard Lewis, Seyyed Hossein Nasr, and Riffat Hassan have objected to the application of the term to Muslims because of its Christian provenance. They contend that the application of the term to Islamic militant and revival groups is a misnomer because a group within a U.S. conservative Protestant setting coined the term. This group insisted on the literal divine origin and inerrancy of Christian scripture.

Be it as it may, there is a general consensus that revival movements, however they are characterized, are very important in Islam. Fundamentalism has become the most commonly used term for the various revivalist tendencies and impulses among Muslims all over the world; indeed, many scholars apply the term to the radical element in any religion that defines that religion in an absolutist and literalist way. Fundamentalism may also refer to the rejection by a certain religious group of the findings of historical-critical study of their sacred texts. The term has also been applied to a movement that is essentially characterized by firm authoritarianism that prevents individual deviation from the normative standard of faith. Fundamentalists generally reject secularism and its concomitant religious laxity. They bemoan the absence of divine rule in the public domain. In regions of the world that have suffered colonialism, such as Egypt and Sudan, fundamentalists see colonial rule as having disrupted the proper practice of their faiths and postcolonial rule as being given over to Westernization and therefore morally tainted. In the face of that reality, fundamentalists feel they must persist in their efforts to reform the current beliefs and practices. Fundamentalists have come to terms with the modern world, but they are vehemently opposed to it. Indeed, fundamentalism is defined by its reactions against modernity. The reactions can be an affirmation or outright rejection.

The debate about whether Islamic fundamentalism is a modern phenomenon or not continues to elicit passionate responses. Scholars like John O. Voll and Fazlur Rahman argue that throughout the long history of Islam, many movements have advocated a return to the essential fundamentals of the faith. From this perspective, it is possible to identify several premodern movements that advocate a fundamentalist agenda. They include the Hanbali tradition as articulated by Ibn Taymiyah (1263–1328) in the fourteenth century, the reform movements that were established by Ahmad Sirhindi (1564–1624) in many parts of South

Constitution of the Republic of Sudan, Article 48—Oath (entered into force 1 July 1998)

The Minister upon his appointment and before taking office shall take the following oath before the President of the Republic:

"In the name of Allah (God) the Almighty, I swear to perform my ministerial duties in worship and obedience to Allah; performing my duties diligently and honestly; working for the development and progress of the country and ignoring all personal or fanatical whims. I swear in the name of Allah, the Almighty, to respect the Constitution, law and consensus of public opinion and to accept shura and advice. Allah is the witness of what I say."

Source: **Constitution of the Republic of Iran. Retrieved 3 April 2003, from http://www.sudan.net/government/constitution/english.html**

Asia, and the Wahhabi movement in Arabia in the eighteenth century. These movements provide the foundation for Islamic fundamentalism in the modern period. Taking the opposite position, scholars like Martin Marty, Scott Appleby, and Martin Lawrence assert that fundamentalism is symptomatic of conditions in the modern period. They argue that fundamentalism is a concerted religious response to the religious challenges of modernity. From this perspective, the best examples of Islamic fundamentalism are not the sporadic religious revolts of the eighteenth or nineteenth centuries, but movements that were established in the twentieth century. The Muslim Brotherhood in many parts of the Muslim world will suffice as an apt example within this line of argument.

Egypt and Sudan provide important case studies for understanding the dynamic nature of Islamic radicalism. They are two core countries in the Arab world and they are very important to the future of the Middle East and the Muslim world.

Egypt

The movement to integrate tradition and a reforming impulse started with Jamal al-Din al-Afghani (1839–1997) and his protégé, Muhammad ʿAbduh (1849–1905). Al-Afghani was an Iranian who later became an Afghan in order to be well received within Sunni Islam (the stream of Islam of the majority of the world's Muslims). As a well-educated Shiʿite (adherent of Shiʿa Islam, the largest minority stream), he sought to educate Muslims about the virulent threat of European hegemonic domination. For him, the reform of Islam was crucial; he had a vision of restoring Islam to a pristine state. He became an important voice in Islamic revivalism in Iran, India, Turkey, and the entire Muslim world. He proclaimed the message of defensive reform and at the same time called for local and global Islamic uprisings. He used Egypt's prestigious al-Azhar University as the training ground for his resistance movement. Al-Afghani's ideals were taken further by Muhammad Rashid Rida (1865–1935). Rida aligned with the conservative Hanbali school of law and the early-eighteenth-century Arabian reform movement of Muhammad ibn ʿAbd al-Wahhab (1703–1791). He called for the absolute allegiance to the Qurʾan and the hadith as interpreted by orthodox religious teachers of each generation.

Hasan al-Banna' and the Muslim Brotherhood

Contemporary Islamic and political engagement in Egypt has been affected profoundly by the Jamiyat al-Ikhwan al-Muslimun (Society of Muslim Brothers; also known as the Muslim Brotherhood or the Ikhwan.), founded in 1928 by Hasan al-Banna' (1906–1949). Ikhwan has used activism, militancy, antiregime violence, charity, and alliances with opposition political parties to further its aims of purity in Islam and (eventually) rejection of Westernization.

Hasan al-Banna' was born in Buhayrah Province, northeast of Cairo. His father was an imam and teacher at the local mosque. Hasan al-Banna' received strict and rigid religious instruction from his father and from an early age was interested in the issues of piety and morality. At the young age of twelve al-Banna' became a member of the Hasafiyah Sufi order (an order of Islamic mysticism). At thirteen he became the secretary of Hasafiyah Society for Charity, whose objectives were to guarantee Islamic ethical standards and to resist Christian missionaries. In 1927 he graduated from

A Selection from Milestones by Sayyid Qutb

Sayyid Qutb (1906–1966) was one of the most influential thinkers in Islamic revivalism. In his *Milestones* he commented on women's roles in Western society.

If the family is the basis of the society, and the basis of the family is the division of labour between husband and wife, and the upbringing is the most important function of the family, then such a society is indeed civilised. In the Islamic system of life, this kind of a family provides the environment under which human values and morals develop and grow in the new generation; these values and morals cannot exist apart from the family unit. If, on the other hand, free sexual relationships and illegitimate children become the basis of a society, and if the relationship between man and woman is based on lust, passion and impulse, and the division of work is not based on family responsibility and natural gifts; if woman's role is merely to be attractive, sexy and flirtatious, and if woman is freed from her basic responsibility of bringing up children; and if, on her own or under social demand, she prefers to become a hostess or a stewardess in a hotel or ship or air company, thus using her ability for material productivity rather than the training of human beings, because material production is considered to be more important, more valuable and more honourable than the development of human character, then such a civilisation is "backward" from the human point of view, or "jahili" in Islamic terminology.

Source: Sayyid Qutb. (1980). *Milestones [Maʿalim fi] Tariq].* Beirut, Lebanon: The Holy Koran Publishing House, p. 182. Retrieved 17 April 2003, from http://www.nmhschool.org/tthornton/mehistorydatabase/sayyid_qutb_on_women.htm

Dar al-Ulum, a prestigious center for training teachers of Arabic. At the center, al-Banna' continued to be appalled by increasing moral laxity, decreasing respect for religious piety, and a pervasive gusto for Western secular culture. Highly influenced by the thought of Muhammad Rashid Rida, the Salafiyah movement (a dominant reform movement), and strict nationalism; al-Banna' called for a change in the religious landscape.

In Egypt, the Brotherhood joined with other Islamic youth movements to oppose the British and the moral slackness of the Egyptian regime. It campaigned for the establishment of an Islamic government based on the recommendations of the ulama (Islamic clerics) and the full application of *shariʿa* (Islamic law). For the Muslim Brotherhood and its allies, Islam presented the most authentic blueprint for a complete modern society and was the best ideological and political alternative to Communism.

Sayyid Qutb

Sayyid Qutb (1906–1966) provided the next critical voice within the Muslim Brotherhood. As a young man, Qutb was enamored of the West, but a visit to the United States from 1948 to 1950 changed his perspective. He was shocked by the anti-Arab prejudice he personally experienced, as well as by Americans' casual relations between the sexes. Qutb was distressed by the fact that Egypt's millions of Muslims were compelled to be governed by a system that he felt was basically un-Islamic. His calls for a violent change of political leadership in Egypt led to his eventual execution, and he has been described as the martyr of Islamic revivalism. Two years before his death he published *Maʿalim fiʿl Tariq (Milestones)*, a work that deeply influenced subsequent Islamic revivalists.

Egypt continues to produce radical Muslim groups that vehemently oppose the government and also have strong anti-Western sentiments. Nevertheless, the scholar Geveive Abdo has maintains that in Egypt today there are many moderate Muslim groups that believe that religious values are compatible with the demands of the modern world. These groups are vigorously working within and beyond the secular framework of the nation to gradually create a new society based on Islamic principles and values. These moderate groups are the religious movements popular in Egypt today, and they have allowed people from all walks of life to speak for themselves.

Sudan

Islam was introduced to the Sudan in the sixteenth century. At the present time, approximately 70 percent of Sudan's 22 million people are Muslims; they inhabit primarily the northern two-thirds of Africa's largest country. The non-Muslim minority population is located primarily in the Nuba Mountains and southern Sudan; these groups practice African indigenous religion and different denominations of Christianity.

The Madhist Revolution

By the nineteenth century, Islam was firmly established in Sudan after three centuries of continuous contact with Egypt, West Africa, and Arabia. The nineteenth century was also a period of intense imperial domination in the Sudan, beginning with the Ottoman Turkish-Egyptian invasion in 1821 and continuing with British occupation in 1898. Many observers have located the origin of Islamic revivalism in Sudan's Madhist movement, established by Muhammad Ahmad (al-Mahdi; 1844–1885) in the nineteenth century. Muhammad Ahmad received his Islamic education in northern Sudan and later joined the Sammaniyah Sufi order. He vigorously condemned the immorality and corruption of the political cabal of his day, and he called upon his people to fight the Turkish and Egyptian occupiers and to sanitize the society by introducing a government based on Islamic values and principles. In 1881 he revealed that he was al-Madhi al-Muntazar, a messianic figure in Islam. In 1885 he captured Khartoum, the capital of Sudan. His revolution is cited as the first modern success in establishing an Islamic state based on the notion of returning Islam to its pristine form.

Hasan al-Turabi

The next stage in Islamic revivalism in the Sudan was the establishment of a Sudanese branch of the Muslim Brotherhood. Sudanese students in Egypt in the 1940s came in contact with the Muslim Brotherhood, and in 1946 some of the organization's members came to Sudan to recruit more members. The Sudanese Muslim Brothers were officially established on 21 August 1954. In 1964 Hasan al-Turabi (b. 1932), a religious scholar and lawyer then teaching at the University of Khartoum, joined the organization. Turabi became one of the Muslim Brotherhood's most outspoken members, and when the organization established the Islamic Charter Front (ICF), they elected Turabi as its secretary general. Turabi used the ICF as a platform for his religious and political ideals. The ICF was able to formulate an Islamic constitution, but it was not implemented because of the Communist policies of Sudan's president at that time, Jaʿfar al-Nimeiri (b. 1930). The situation in the Sudan altered suddenly when the military regime of Nimeiri decided that Islamic law would be the only law of the land. His regime was repressive and intolerant of opposition. During his draconian rule many people were imprisoned without any trial and more than two hundred people had hands or other limbs amputated. Nimeiri fell from power in 1986. Another coup d'état in 1989 brought an Islamist government—that is, a government with radical Islamic views—to power. Turabi and his followers support this Islamist government. The constant issue in the Sudan, given its minority religious communities in the south, is how to resolve the relationship between religion and state and how to create new resources for national unity.

Looking Forward

Islam is a dynamic faith. It continues to vacillate between traditionalist and reformist ideals. In the nineteenth century and much of the twentieth century, most Muslim countries were aware of the dominance of the West and their own relative weakness. One of the dominant issues for countries like Sudan and Egypt in the twenty-first century is how to rejuvenate the Muslim world, and one of the approaches that will no doubt continue to be popular is fundamentalism.

Akintunde E. Akinade

Further Reading

Abdo, G. (2000). *No God but God: Egypt and the triumph of Islam*. New York: Oxford University Press.

Esposito, J. L. (1988). *Islam: The straight path*. New York: Oxford University Press.

Esposito, J. L. (1999). *The Islamic threat: Myth or reality?* New York: Oxford University Press.

Lawrence, B. B. (1995). *Defenders of God: The fundamentalist revolt against the modern age*. Columbia: University of South Carolina Press.

Lewis, B. (1988). *The political language of Islam*. Chicago: University of Chicago Press.

Fundamentalism in Iran

Iran's revolution of 1978–1979 brought in a fundamentalist theocratic government that replaced several thousand years of monarchy. The road to Iranian fundamentalism must be viewed in the context of the entirety of Iranian history, otherwise it easily misunderstood. Iran's historical development is characterized by three interweaving threads: national identity, autocracy, and Islam. Historically Iran is peaceful when all three function in equilibrium, but if an imbalance occurs political and social instability abound.

Iran's Dynastic History

In ancient times Iran was known as Persia. Strong charismatic leaders such as Cyrus the Great (c. 585–c. 529 BCE), Darius the Great (550–486 BCE; reigned 522–486 BCE), Xerxes (c. 519–465 BCE; reigned 486–465 BCE), and Alexander of Macedon (356–323 BCE) demanded complete obeisance from the meek Persians; this pattern has prevailed in Iran's history, being reinforced during the Seleucid dynasty (312–64 BCE), Parthian empire (flourished early first century BCE), and Sasanid dynasty (224/228–651 CE).

Persia was ruled by the Arab Umayyad caliphate (661–750) for a century until a revolt in 750 resulted in the establishment of the Abbasid caliphate (749/750–1258). The Abbasid caliphate witnessed the golden age of Islam, and Persia reached the peak of its cultural development. The Seljuk dynasty (1038–1157), a Turkmen dynasty that flourished in the eleventh and twelfth centuries, fell to the Mongols in 1243; successors to the Mongol Hulegu Khan established the independent Il-Khanid dynasty, which lasted until 1336. The Safavids (1502– 1722/1736) embraced Shiʿa Islam (the major minority branch of Islam), which at once made Persia distinct from the Ottoman Empire (which adhered to Sunni Islam, the majority branch of Islam) and helped establish national identity. The Zand dynasty (1747–1787) was replaced by the Qajar dynasty, which was overthrown in 1925 by the Pahlavi dynasty. Mohammad Reza Shah Pahlavi (1919–1980) was overthrown by the Islamic revolution in 1978–1979.

The Nineteenth and Early Twentieth Centuries

The first step on the road to fundamentalism was taken when Islam became a counterweight to the oppressive despotic secularism of kingship in the late eighteenth and early nineteenth centuries; religious power paralleled the authority of the king. Islam reached out to the oppressed, defined moral authority, and provided a vision of a just society.

Fundamentalism in Persia took on a modern hue during the inefficient and corrupt Qajar dynasty when the equalibrium changed toward greater adherence to the faith and away from allegiance to the monarchs. By the early nineteenth century Persia had lost much of its national identity: It lost Georgia, the districts of Azerbaijan, Baku, and Qarabag in 1813. In 1828 Iran lost Persian Armenia to Russia and was forced to grant extraterritorial rights. The Russian and British empires carved out spheres of influence in Persia in which they exercised economic control.

An attempt to reassert national identity was made with the 1905–1911 Constitutional Revolution, in which Persia established a parliament, the Majlis-e Shura, with authority deriving from the people. The parliament was meant to limit the power of the shah (Iran's king) and to curb overwhelming corruption and foreign manipulation. It proved to be the first step toward modernization.

By World War I, Iran was torn by internal divisions. The Qajar shah had become dependent on foreign financial subsidies that he squandered on personal enjoyment. Prior to the war, factions of pro-British and pro-German notables had gained control of the Majlis, causing political and economical disruption that resulted in famine and national bankruptcy. Persia was occupied by British, Russian, and Ottoman forces during the war. In 1919 the British offered Persia financial and military assistance, which the Majlis rejected, prompting British withdrawal, which allowed Iran to come into its own.

Persia was redeemed by an officer of the Persian Cossack Brigade, Reza Khan (1878–1944). This charismatic, strong personality with political acumen staged a coup d'état in 1921 and took control of all the military forces. Between 1921 and 1925 he served as war minister and then prime minister. He formed an army loyal to him and deposed Ahmad Mirza (1898–1930), the last Qajar shah. Reza Khan took the name Pahlavi and ruled Iran as Reza Shah Pahlavi from 1925. In 1935 the nation's name was officially changed to Iran.

Under his reign the pendulum swung away from religion, which he deemed an obstacle to modernization. Reza Shah looked to the glory of pre-Islamic Persia for inspiration as he undertook political restructuring and numerous economic development projects, including the construction of a new railway. Reza Shah also modernized the armed forces, created a police force and a national civil service, built schools, established the University of Tehran, and encouraged the elite to be educated in the West. Women received the right to vote and no longer were required to wear the

Selection from U.N. Resolution 598 (1987), Adopted by the Security Council on 20 July 1987

Acting under Articles 39 and 40 of the Charter of the United Nations,

1. Demands that, as a first step towards a negotiated settlement, Iran and Iraq observe an immediate cease-fire, discontinue all military actions on land, at sea and in the air, and withdraw all forces to the internationally recognized boundaries without delay;
2. Requests the Secretary-General to dispatch a team of United Nations Observers to verify, confirm and supervise the cease-fire and withdrawal and further requests the Secretary-General to make the necessary arrangements in consultation with the Parties and to submit a report thereon to the Security Council;
3. Urges that prisoners of war be released and repatriated without delay after the cessation of active hostilities in accordance with the Third Geneva Convention of 12 August 1949;
4. Calls upon Iran and Iraq to cooperate with the Secretary-General in implementing this resolution and in mediation efforts to achieve a comprehensive, just and honourable settlement, acceptable to both sides, of all outstanding issues in accordance with the principles contained in the Charter of the United Nations;
5. Calls upon all other States to exercise the utmost restraint and to refrain from any act which may lead to further escalation and widening of the conflict and thus to facilitate the implementation of the present resolution;
6. Requests the Secretary-General to explore, in consultation with Iran and Iraq, the question of entrusting an impartial body with inquiring into responsibility for the conflict and to report to the Security Council as soon as possible;
7. Recognizes the magnitude of the damage inflicted during the conflict and the need for reconstruction efforts, with appropriate international assistance, once the conflict is ended and, in this regard, requests the Secretary-General to assign a team of experts to study the question of reconstruction and to report to the Security Council;
8. Further requests the Secretary-General to examine in consultation with Iran and Iraq and with other states of the region measures to enhance the security and stability of the region;
9. Requests the Secretary-General to keep the Security Council informed on the implementation of this resolution;
10. Decides to meet again as necessary to consider further steps to insure compliance with this resolution.

Source: U.N. Security Council Resolution 1987. http://www.un.org/Docs

veil. Reza Shah abolished the special rights that had been granted to foreigners and pressured the Anglo-Persian Oil Company to increase the royalties it paid to Iran.

In time, however, as the pendulum swung increasingly far in Reza Shah's direction, autocracy overwhelmed the elements of religion and national identity. Reza Shah became regarded as a tyrant who modernized Iran too quickly, against the will of the masses. He was hated because he fought against the basic Shiʿite beliefs that made up the national identity. Many people were overjoyed when the British forced him to abdicate in 1941 because of his rapprochement with Nazi Germany—a political move on his point aimed at reducing Iran's dependence on the British. Reza Shah died in exile South Africa in 1944.

The Reign of Mohammad Reza Shah Pahlavi and the Islamic Revolution

Mohammed Reza Pahlavi, Reza Shah's eldest son, took the throne with Allied support on the understanding that he would rule as a constitutional monarch. He was a shy, weak, vacillating, initially well-meaning man; he made his father's reforms more efficient. The Shah struggled with Mohammad Mosaddeq (1880–1967), the prime minister the Majlis forced on him, from 1951 to 1953. Mosaddeq demanded that the Majlis nationalize the oil industry, which they did. He demanded the power to appoint the minister of war, which would give him control over the army. When the Shah refused this concession it led to a showdown, and the Shah left Iran temporarily. The CIA and Britain came to the Shah's aid, orchestrating riots and successfully removing Mosaddeq. However many Iranians had preferred Mosaddeq to the Shah and strongly resented U.S. interference in their domestic affairs. Iranians date their discontent with the monarchy to this incident.

On 20 May 1961, the shah used his royal authority to dissolve the Majlis. He continued his father's efforts to modernize Iran, carrying out land reform, increasing rights and opportunities for women, and undertaking numerous development projects. Per capita income rose from around $175 in 1960 to a high of $2,500 by 1978; this steadily rising standard of living improved the lifestyle of Iran's lower classes. It was the greatest economic leap in Iran's history. But the Shah was also given to extravagances. In 1967 he held his long-postponed coronation ceremony; it was elaborate and costly. In 1971 he held a $200 million extravaganza to celebrate 2,500 years of Persian monarchy. He purchased $9 billion in military weapons, far in excess of what the Iranian forces could use. By the late 1970s Iran faced economic stagnation, but dissent was repressed by the shah's secret police force, Savak.

The Shah's strong reliance on U.S. support alienated the Iranian people. The presence of U.S. military personnel and their dependents, who were highly insensitive to Iranian cultural norms, was resented by the clerics, and the sentiment echoed throughout Iran. Unequal distribution of oil wealth, government corruption, and the shah's severe autocratic rule were strong points of contention.

Ruhollah ibn Mustafa Musawi Khomeini Hindi (1902–1989), a popular Shiʿite religious leader, jurist, and teacher who had a huge following of students and other clerics, spoke up vigorously against the shah. He opposed the shah's reform program and denounced women's emancipation and the shah's land reforms. The shah forced Khomeini into exile in 1963; his arrest and deportation touched off rioting that was severely suppressed by Savak and the army. Popular dissent increased when some sixty thousand clergy were detained and theology students were conscripted. The shah granted liberal concessions and allowed protests in 1977, but by 1978, in the face of larger and more extreme protests, he instituted martial law in major cities. These controls led to religious activists' becoming more extreme.

From France the exiled Khomeini orchestrated a rebellion based on a revival of morality. It was time, he argued, for a return to fundamental Islamic principles, teachings, and norms. Twentieth-century Iranian kingship had clearly blundered by attempting to secularize the country along Western lines. The shah fled in January 1979, and Khomeini returned to Iran in February.

A national referendum on 1 April 1979 led to a landslide victory for Khomeini, who declared the Islamic Republic of Iran. A new constitution reflected his Shiʿite ideals of Islamic government. Strict Islamic dress and codes of behavior were enforced by revolutionary committees patrolling the streets. Summary trials, political purges, and executions made the populace fearful. All the impressive gains women had made under the last Pahlavi shah were rescinded. Western influence was suppressed and the Western-educated elite fled. Anti-American sentiment increased when the shah went to the United States to receive medical treatment for cancer; there were huge demonstrations demanding that he be extradited and stand trial for crimes against his people. On 4 November militant students seized sixty-nine U.S. citizens who worked in the foreign ministry and the U.S. embassy, demanding that the United States return the shah as a condition of the hostages' release. The hostages remained in captivity after the shah died on 27 July 1980; they were not released until 20 January 1981.

Iranian society remained in a state of disequilibrium, this time with the emphasis heavily on religion. In its early years, the revolutionary government replayed the shah's oppressive policies but cloaked them with Islamic doctrine. Unrelenting waves of executions, carried out with frenzied emotion in the name of Islam, sullied the Islamic Republic of Iran. Persecution of Baha'is (adherents of the Baha'i faith) increased.

In September 1980 a long-standing border dispute with Iraq erupted, with Iraq taking advantage of Iran's turmoil to launch an invasion of the southwestern oil-producing Iranian province of Khuzestan. An unbowed Iran achieved defensive successes by summer 1982, but the conflict quickly degenerated into a war of attrition, with huge civilian losses resulting from the bombing of populated areas. On 18 July 1988, Khomeini accepted UN Resolution 598, which brought a cease-fire into effect on 20 August 1988.

As the Revolution entered its second decade many Iranians were disillusioned with the government's ambiguous foreign policy (Khomeini, who had denounced the United States as the Great Satan, later accepted arms from the United States in exchange for Iranian help with a hostage crisis in Lebanonin 1985) and with the privation caused by the lengthy war.

On 3 June 1989 Khomeini died of a heart attack. The Iranian people genuinely grieved this loss. Ali Khamenei (b. 1939) was elected as the new supreme leader and promoted to the status of ayatollah although he was neither respected nor popular. A referendum on constitutional amendments and presidential elections was held on 28 July1989. Hojatolislam Ali Akbar Hashemi Rafsanjani (b. 1934), speaker of the Majlis since 1980, ran largely unopposed and was elected with 95 percent of the vote. The Majlis approved Rafsanjani's choices for ministers, and Rafsanjani commenced rebuilding Iran's economy. Considered a moderate or pragmatist and less closed-minded than his predecessors, Rafsanjani preferred economic liberalization, the privatization of industry, and reconciliation with the West, hoping to encourage foreign investment. Diplomatic ties with various countries were resumed. However his regime was blatantly corrupt. Iranian society had yet to achieve a stable equilibrium.

The Future

In subsequent years Iran has become deeply fragmented. The doubling of the population means that most of the population in Iran is under twenty-five. The children of the revolutionaries are not afraid of confronting the clerics; they not only demand more freedom, they demand equality. Pro-reform students staged riots in July 1999, clashing with hard-line vigilantes and police. The election of 2000 brought reform-minded Mohammad Khatami (b. 1943) to power when the Reformists won 170 seats in the 290-seat Majlis. His base was young people and women.

In the twenty-first century the equilibrium of Iranian society has been restored to some extent. The revolution was beneficial in that a despotic monarch was removed; Savak was debilitated; and Western ideas and economic methods were removed, allowing Islamic tenets to move to the forefront of life. However, the revolution was also detrimental in other ways, and it remains in flux. Fundamentalism is likely to remain a powerful force in Iran until the threads of national identity, autocracy, and Islam join and act congruently in a concerted effort to heal the wounds experienced over the last several hundred years.

Annette Richardson

Further Reading

Afshar, H. (1985). *Iran: A revolution in turmoil*. Albany: State University of New York Press.

Ansari, A. M. (2000). *Iran, Islam and democracy: The politics of managing change*. London: Royal Institute of International Affairs. (Distributed by the Brookings Institution, Washington DC).

Chehabi, H. E. (1990). *Iranian politics and religious modernism*. Ithaca, NY: Cornell University Press.

Ghani, S. (2000). *Iran and the rise of Reza Shah: From Qajar collapse to Pahlavi rule*. London: I. B. Tauris.

Irfani, S. (1983). *Iran's Islamic revolution: Popular liberation or religious dictatorship?* London: Zed Books.

Kamrava, M. (1992). *The political history of modern Iran: From tribalism to theocracy*. Westport, CT: Praeger.

Lenczowski, G. (Ed.). (1978). *Iran under the Pahlavis*. Stanford, CA: Hoover Institution Press.

Mackey, S. (1996). *The Iranians: Persia, Islam and the soul of a nation*. New York: Penguin Group.

Rizvi, A. A. (1980). *Iran royalty, religion and revolution*. Canberra, Australia: Maʿrifar Publishing House.

Wilber, D. N. (1981). *Iran, past and present: From monarchy to Islamic Republic* (9th ed.). Princeton, NJ: Princeton University Press.

Wright, M., & Danziger, N. (1989). *Iran: The Khomeini revolution*. Harlow, UK: Longman.

G

Genocide in Bosnia

The collapse of Yugoslavia in the early 1990s produced a human disaster in Europe of a kind that had not been seen since World War II. Interethnic warfare, inspired in part by religious nationalisms, destroyed tens of thousands of lives and dislocated even more. The epicenter of the conflict was the province of Bosnia-Herzegovina. Between 1992 and 1995, Bosnian Serbs, Croats, and Muslims engaged in fierce fighting there; Bosnia's Muslims ended up as the main victims. Genocide in Bosnia consisted of the calculated slaughter, forced removal, and cultural degradation of many Bosnian Muslims by militant Serbs and Croats who aspired to the division and control of the province. *Ethnic cleansing* was the euphemism for a brutal process that was shaped by the tangled political and religious history of a region where three major religions—Roman Catholicism, Orthodox Christianity, and Islam—have coexisted for centuries. Why did the twentieth-century state of Yugoslavia prove to be so fragile? How has religion influenced politics in this part of the world, and what role have religious ideas and authorities played in events in Bosnia?

Yugoslav State Politics

Socialist Yugoslavia after 1945 was the second twentieth-century effort to construct a state incorporating the groups of the "southern Slavs" in the Balkans. The first attempt was the post–World War I kingdom, dominated by Serbia; it was unable to contend with the demands of Croats for autonomy and dissolved in the face of the German invasion of 1941. The war years saw the establishment of a fascist Croatian state led by the Ustashe movement, the organization of Serb nationalist resistance, the Chetniks, to the Germans and the Ustashe, as well as the Communist partisan resistance movement under Josip Broz Tito. The civil war among these factions, especially Croat and Serb, was fierce, and memories of this wartime conflict would haunt Yugoslav politics into the 1990s.

Tito's Communist state, set up in 1945, was the second attempt at organizing a multiethnic Yugoslav politics; it did so by violently coercing both Serb and Croat nationalists, redrawing internal boundaries of the constituent ethnic republics, and relying on a police state to constrain ethno-national ambitions. Communism did not resolve the nationalist question of Yugoslav politics; it merely suppressed it. After Tito's death in 1980, Yugoslav politics faced ideological and political-economic decay. The general crisis and collapse of Communism in Eastern Europe in the 1980s gave rise to renewed forms of ethno-religious nationalism, and in Yugoslavia these drew on the still vivid memories of World War II and earlier ethno-religious ideas.

Religion and Ethno-Nationalisms in the Balkans

The national identities of Serbs and Croats are strongly influenced by historical forms of Christianity; historically, Croats are Roman Catholic and Serbs are Eastern Orthodox. These religious identities were powerfully shaped by the confrontation with Islam, given the Ottoman occupation of the Balkan peninsula from the fifteenth century. A particular by-product of this occu-

Muslim Identity in Bosnia

The following text based on research in a mixed Muslim-Catholic community in central Bosnia indicates how adherence to Islam defines the Bosnian community as separate from the Serbian and Croatian communities.

In Bosnia Islam attaches people to two symbolic communities, each different in content, function, and scale. On the one hand Islam (as cultural heritage, historical legacy, a set of practices and moral values) binds people together in a community of Bosnian Muslims (with the emphasis on Bosnian, as opposed to Serbian, Croatian, and the like, and on Muslim as opposed to Catholic or Orthodox Bosnian). On the other hand it unites them with a community of Muslims worldwide (the Islamic *umma*) as opposed to non-Muslims. During my research in Bosnia the former was the primary identification. The extent to which the latter was meaningful to Bosnian Muslims was dependent on devoutness, style of religiosity, and socioeconomic status. At the time it was an identification made by a small urban-oriented economic and religious elite, or what we might call the Islamic establishment. Typically one member of such a family would have been educated in the Islamic Middle East and the family would have a long tradition of religious instructors and learned men and women.

***Source:* Bringa, Tone. (1995). *Being Muslim the Bosnian Way: Identity and Community in a Central Bosnian Village.* Princeton, NJ: Princeton University Press, p. 197.**

pation was the conversion of part of the Slavic population to Islam, among them the so-called Bosniaks of Bosnia-Herzegovina. For Serbs, the Ottoman experience is also closely linked to the province of Kosovo, which today is populated largely by Albanian Muslims.

Both Serbs and Croats developed national mythologies that condemned Muslims in Bosnia as "Christ killers" and "race traitors," views that shaped a particular nineteenth-century religious ideology: *Christoslavism* (Sells 1996, 45). Christoslavism asserts that all Slavs are Christian, and that any Slav who converts from Christianity betrays the Slavic race; these ideas were popularized by later literary works that either glorified the extermination of Slavic Muslims or denigrated them as an alien and uncivilized race. Such ideas would rapidly become available to the political imagination when socialist Yugoslavia began to unravel by the mid-1980s

Yugoslavia's collapse was aggravated by the politics of renewed nationalisms that leaders like Franjo Tudjman in Croatia and Slobodan Milosevic in Serbia knew how to manipulate. Milosevic was particularly adept in exploiting the issue of Kosovo for his own nationalist leadership politics. Kosovo, linked to medieval stories of heroic Serb leadership, was in the mid–1980s the focal point of Serb fears of Muslim majorities threatening to undermine Serbia. Nationalist Serb intellectuals protested in 1986 that a genocide was already underway in Kosovo against remaining Serb culture there; the problem in Kosovo, however, was Serb suppression of Albanian aspirations for greater autonomy. Serb nationalists were most alarmed by the rapid growth of the Muslim population in Kosovo, and had never forgiven Tito's regime for recognizing the Bosnian Muslims as a constituent nation of the socialist republic in 1968. Muslim leaders such as Alija Izetbegovic, who wrote about the prospects for a kind of Islamic politics in Bosnia in the early 1970s, drew the ire of Serb nationalists in the next decade; when Izetbegovic became President of Bosnia in 1990, such Serbs immediately argued that he represented radical Islamist ideas and was in league with Islamic revolutionaries elsewhere in the region. The situation, inflamed by the specter of rising Islamic fundamentalism, fed the extremism of Serb nationalists, who saw Serbs throughout Yugoslavia threatened by dismaying demographic trends and hostile anti-Serb sentiments emanating from Tudjman's Croatia. This in turn produced the call for a "greater Serbia," a unified territorial state for Serbs who were spread out across three of Yugoslavia's republics: Croatia, Serbia, and Bosnia. Such a policy could only be realized by force, given the disintegration of the Yugoslav federation.

War and Genocide in Bosnia

The war in Bosnia began in spring 1992 when the Bosnian government declared its independence from Yugoslavia. Bosnian Serbs were intent on establishing their own republic, the Republika Srpska; they coordinated their efforts with Milosevic's government in Belgrade. The Bosnian government of Alija Izetbegovic was very weak militarily, and while recognized by the European Community and the United States, was subject to an arms embargo imposed by the United Nations on all parties in the region. Thus, Serb military attacks on Bosnian villages met with little resistance.

Serb actions in Bosnia were carried out by Bosnian Serb military forces and irregular militias, backed by Milosevic. As the Yugoslav Army had created a military infrastructure of supply depots and production facilities in Bosnia, it was a simple matter to arm these groups with overwhelming capabilities. Bosnian Serbs sought to create a contiguous Serb republic by seizing villages and towns in a large crescent from the northwest to the southeast in the province. After the villages were seized, the remaining Muslim civilian populations were expelled, terrorized, taken to detention centers and concentration camps, or selectively massacred. This process began in April 1992 and would continue until July 1995. Sarajevo came under a deadly artillery and sniper siege that destroyed the city's cultural institutions and Muslim neighborhoods.

Observers from the U.N. and Red Cross were vocal witnesses to such crimes, but Western countries were not willing to intervene in a meaningful way until 1995. U.N. efforts to deal with displaced refugees by establishing safe areas in selected Bosnian cities, beginning with Srebrenica in April 1993, proved ineffective; between fall 1994 and summer 1995, Serb military commanders brazenly entered these "safe" enclaves, intimidating U.N. commanders and carrying out further expulsions and massacres, most notoriously at Srebrenica. Such actions ultimately produced a series of decisions in the West that resulted in NATO military support of a Croat offensive against the Bosnian Serb army and compelled Milosevic to abandon his Bosnian allies and accept the peace accords negotiated at Dayton, Ohio.

While Serb responsibility for genocide against Mulsims in Bosnia is undeniable, that of Croatia is also significant. Croat President Franjo Tudjman, a religious nationalist whose drive for Croat independence contributed to the collapse of Yugoslavia and war with Serbia, sought to create his own "greater Croatia" at the expense of Bosnia. Tudjman backed the Croatian Defense Council (HVO), set up in Bosnia to defend Croats who lived in the western and southwestern areas of the province; the HVO originally cooperated with Izetbegovic against the Serbs, but by mid-1992 set out to establish a separate Croat ethnic republic in Bosnia: the Union of Herceg-Bosna. Subsequently, Croat military forces in Bosnia began to attack Muslim villages and towns, displaying the same genocidal zeal that characterized Serb actions elsewhere in the province. The Croat contribution to the destruction of multiethnic Bosnia went on until spring 1994, when the U.S. government brokered a deal between Bosnia and Croatia that created a "federation" between Bosnian Croats and the Bosnian government in Sarajevo. It would take another year, however, before events would conspire to produce decisive Western intervention and the Dayton Accords.

An ethnic Albanian man in April 2001, returning to Kosovo following Serb paramilitary attempts at "ethnic cleansing" in the former Yugoslav province. Courtesy Ssgt. Keith Brown, USAF.

Orthodox and Catholic Church Officials on Bosnia

How did Orthodox and Catholic church officials react to events in Bosnia? Attitudes and behaviors of many religious officials, especially Orthodox, reveal a general pattern of indifference or hostility toward Muslims and approval of the perpetrators of genocidal violence. The Serb Orthodox church was conspicuous for its support of "religious nationalist militancy" (Sells 1996, 79). Before the war, the church supported literary and academic figures who had rediscovered Christoslavic arguments against Muslims; during the war, notorious Serb militia leaders received public support from Orthodox clerics; the church leadership actively denied the atrocities of Bosnian Serb militias and criticized international peace plans for the division of Bosnia as unfair to Serbs. While not all Orthodox believers and clerics indulged in such behavior, evidence strongly suggests that much of the official institution was complicit with the rationalization and denial of genocidal actions in Bosnia.

The attitudes of Catholic church officials were divided. Croat Catholic church leaders in Zagreb, Sarajevo, and central Bosnia spoke out consistently against crimes committed by Croat religious nationalists; however, in Croat areas of Herzegovina, local Catholic priests and friars often shared anti-Muslim sentiments and did nothing to oppose the actions of the HVO against local Muslims. Croat President Tudjman paid no attention to the protests of Cardinal Kuharic in Zagreb; when Croat officials in Herzegovina were indicted in 1995 by the International Criminal Tribunal for massacres of local Muslims, he preferred to honor their efforts by promotion or awards. Whether supportive or divided, the attitudes and behaviors of official church leaders did little to restrain the ethnic political leadership or military operations that inflicted mayhem on the Bosnian population; at worst they provided a formal religious legitimacy for anti-Muslim atrocities.

Outlook

The outlook for recovery from the Bosnian war and genocide is somber. Bosnia, under NATO occupation and nominally pacified, remains deeply divided as a political entity. Contemporary Islamic fundamentalisms, whether inside of outside of Bosnia, will probably do little to reduce entrenched Serb and Croat views of the incompatibility of Muslim political ideas with their own. While internationally sponsored efforts have sought to cultivate projects that link up official religious communities in Bosnia, these have so far yielded only modest results. Religion remains a highly unpredictable force in Bosnia, in part because many religious leaders have reputations stained by what took place there in the last ten years, but also because religion at the popular level is connected to a set of historical and ethnic symbols that nationalistic leaders can manipulate, and that official Church leaders can constrain only with difficulty, even if they are so inclined.

Keith John Lepak

See also Genocide in Europe; Genocide in Rwanda; Religion, Violence and Genocide

Further Reading

Bennett, C. (1995). *Yugoslavia's bloody collapse: Causes, course and consequences*. New York: New York University Press.

Brown, J. F. (1994). *Hopes and shadows: Eastern Europe after communism*. Durham, NC: Duke University Press.

Cigar, N. (1995). *Genocide in Bosnia: The policy of "ethnic cleansing" in Eastern Europe*. College Station: Texas A & M University Press.

Faber, M. J. (Ed.). (1996). *The Balkans: A religious backyard of Europe*. Ravenna, Italy: Longo Editore.

Glenny, M. (1999). *The Balkans: Nationalism, war and the great powers*. New York: Viking.

Glenny, M. (1999). *The fall of Yugoslavia: The third Balkan war* (3d rev. ed.). New York: Penguin Books.

Gutman, R. (1993). *Witness to genocide*. New York: Macmillan.

Malcolm, N. (1994). *Bosnia: A short history*. New York: New York University Press.

Norris, H. T. (1993). *Islam in the Balkans: Religion and society between Europe and the Arab world*. Columbia: University of South Carolina Press.

Riskin, S. M. (Ed.). (1999). *Three dimensions of peacebuilding in Bosnia* (Peaceworks Rep. No. 32). Washington, D.C.: United States Institute of Peace.

Sells, M. A. (1996). *The bridge betrayed: Religion and genocide in Bosnia*. Berkeley: University of California Press.

Stokes, G. (1993). *The walls came tumbling down: The collapse of communism in Eastern Europe*. New York: Oxford University Press.

Udovicki, J., & Ridgeway, J. (1995). *Yugoslavia's ethnic nightmare: The inside story of Europe's unfolding ordeal*. New York: Lawrence Hill Books.

West, R. (1995). *Tito and the rise and fall of Yugoslavia*. New York: Carroll and Graf.

Genocide in Europe

Genocide is a twentieth-century neologism coined by Rafael Lemkin, a lawyer at the Nürnberg war crimes trials following World War II. It means the planned extermination of a religious, national, or racial group. The clearest example is a minority that has a history of persecution at the hands of a host nation. Should the dominant people become sufficiently frustrated (usually as a result of financial calamity or military setback), the minority is targeted as scapegoats. The continuum of rage proceeds from name-calling and propaganda to social and economic boycotts, then ultimately to physical assaults, pogroms, and mass murder.

Death but Not Destruction

Genocide is not predicated on numbers of victims. Since the dawn of Western civilization, Europe has endured migrating tribes and assorted world conquerors who left hundreds of thousands dead in their wake, yet these massacres were not genocide. The empire builders may have treated the conquered with disdain, but always wanted to keep some of their subjects alive as slaves.

Religious and ethnic clashes that have occurred in Europe since 1945 cannot be labeled genocide either. Deplorable as the interaction between Protestants and Catholics may be in Northern Ireland, no partisan has suggested eradicating the other side. Similarly, while the separation of Muslim men from their families and their subsequent murder in Bosnia in 1992 or Kosovo in 1999 evokes images of Nazi *Einsatzgruppen* ("shock troops") in Russia, expulsion, not annihilation, was the Serbian goal.

Genocide on the Periphery of Europe

Western ideology (anthropology, chauvinism, eugenics) and technology (development of the concentration camp, modern transportation, the gas chamber, weapons of mass destruction) have contributed to the eruption of several incidents of genocide on the periphery of Europe in the past century. The first (and, prior to World War II, the bloodiest) was the massacre of the Armenians in 1915–1916. Although the Turkish government continues to deny that there was any plan to exterminate the Armenians, the facts suggest otherwise. Following a botched invasion of Russia, Enver Pasa and Talat Bey, members of the Ottoman Empire's ruling triumvirate at that time, decided to blame Armenian traitors for the debacle. Historically, the Armenians had served as whipping boys for anything that went wrong in the Ottoman Empire. A successful, urban, mercantile class, Christians in an Islamic state, the Armenians were accused of following the lead of their catholicos, or patriarch, who lived beyond the Caucasus Mountains, at the expense of loyalty to the Ottoman Empire. Now they would pay by being deported by foot or boat or rail to death camps in the Syrian desert. The U.S. Ambassador Henry Morgenthau, Sr. and the German missionary Johannes Lepsius protested the massacres, to no avail. One million Armenians perished in towns along the Black Sea or in the steamy desert at Deir ez-Zor. The German-Jewish author Franz Werfel later wrote *The Forty Days of Musa Dagh* as a warning to civilization. Unfortunately, more Germans embraced the position of their ambassador, Hans von Wagenheim, who reported to Berlin that the inferior nation must make way for the superior one.

Some scholars might debate whether the Armenian tragedy was actually a genocide on technical grounds. It is doubtful the Turks would have killed all the Armenians in Russia had their invasion been successful. Even if they had, there still would have been 2 or 3 million others living in the West. For some inexplicable reason, non-Western states are held to a lower standard of accountability than Europeans. The rule insulates Africans and Asians from charges of wholesale genocide, although cases do exist. Economic oppression and tribal differences exploited by colonialists supposedly sparked "acts of genocide" in Nigeria in 1965 (1 million dead), Uganda three years later (100,000–300,000 dead), Cambodia during the 1970s (2 million dead), and Rwanda in 1994 (500,000 dead). The late Nora Levin, a leading authority on the Holocaust, argued that however we label these tragic chapters in human history, we cannot ignore their significance: They represent a failure on the part of humanity.

Killing the Contragenics

In World War II, the Nazis diverted great energy to the eradication of several groups of people dubbed contragenics (that is, impediments to the improvement

The Horror of Dachau: Irving Ross Remembers

At age 26, Irving Ross saw the horrors of the Nazi concentration camps, as a soldier in the U.S. military force that liberated Dachau. Ross, now a retired business owner in Punta Gorda, Florida, recounts what he witnessed.

At the end of April 1945, the most traumatic event of my life was about to begin—the liberation of the Dachau concentration camp. As usual, Colonel Doud was always the leader and the first to be in the midst of the action. We were with the infantry as they cut off the electricity from the barbed-wire fences and then proceeded to go after the guards that were still in the camp and in the towers. The infantrymen threw the guards to the ground and butted them to death. Later on we found out that they were mostly Russian and Polish inmates who had special duties and were given better treatment by the Germans in exchange for being guards.

Before entering the camp, I saw boxcars on the railroad tracks full of bodies. Along the track were bodies that had fallen out of the boxcars when they were opened. As I approached with amazement, I could see some of the bodies were still breathing—a sight that haunted me for years. The following morning our outfit took over the administration of the camp, and we were made into Military Police. We went back to the entrance of the camp and found a military hospital on the grounds. Before I could go back into the camp I had to get a tetanus shot.

I had confiscated a German camera a few weeks before, and I started to take photos of the camp. We were issued M. P. armbands and given duties to perform. On the road into the concentration camp stood a row of well-built houses that housed the commandant and the administrators of Dachau. Our outfit took over these buildings and from there we were given our daily orders.

I believe it was the day after the liberation that I was a driver for Colonel Doud and a few other officers. We entered the main administration building and went up a flight of stairs and into a large room where the 45th infantry were holding, I believe, six or seven top Nazis that ran the camp. (Most of the other camp officials had escaped.) Against the Geneva Convention rules relating to prisoners of war, we had them look at spots on the wall with their hands raised, and they were whipped by inmates that were strong enough to do the whipping. Colonel Doud also took a whip and beat them. When the Nazis fell to the floor, they were given water and made to stand again and the beating continued. I've never seen this fact written about in any publication.

The following day I was put on a detail to comb the buildings for papers that related to the inmates. We never found any documents; all the paperwork was probably destroyed by the Germans. Many inmates from other camps started coming to Dachau to try and find their parents or relations, not knowing that we had no records. They would often burst out crying, and I tried to console them—saying that I would try and get some information for them.

While on this detail many dignitaries from all over the world wanted to get a tour of the camp, and I was chosen to give tours and explain how the camp operated. I remember taking around Dorothy Thompson, a well-known reporter, and many other newspaper correspondents from different countries. My tour went as follows: I first took them along the railroad bedding where the boxcars were. (The first few days there were still piles of bodies on the railroad siding.) Then I took them toward the main gate, which had above the gates in large German letters, *Arbeit Macht Frei* ("Work Shall Make You Free"). Then I went to the barracks to show them how camp inmates were bunked, and continued to the field hospitals to show them the condition of the inmates. A terrible sight.

Continues

Continued

I moved on to show where they would line up prisoners (mostly Russian soldiers), make them kneel, and then shoot them in the back of their heads. The Russians would fall forward, and the heads would go into a trench so that the blood would run off into a pit. The Germans were very well organized and clean. From there I took them to show where they tied up some inmates and had vicious dogs rip off their testicles. We then continued to the crematorium.

I went down a flight of stairs under the ovens and showed them how all the ashes fell into a large metal pan. Above the pan on shelves were dozens of small bottles where the Germans would take some ashes and ship them back to the relatives of these people telling them that they died from some disease or from natural causes. This was probably done during the early years of the camp, because in the later years the inmates were probably Jews, and the Nazis didn't have to make excuses for them. The remaining ashes were used as fertilizer because outside of the camp there were small farms tended by the inmates and the soil was almost black from human ashes. I recall Colonel Doud getting a detail together to find residents of the city of Dachau and have them marched through the camp. Most of them claimed that they knew something was going on but they didn't know that they were burning bodies. They uttered the words *ich glaubish nicht* ("I don't believe it"). Some of them broke down, but I have my doubts if they were telling the truth. I could fill a book with what I saw at Dachau.

Source: Ross, I. (2003). *Fort Dix to Dachau: My War Experiences.* Punta Gorda, FL: author, pp. 19–21.

of the human species). These included Jehovah's Witnesses, homosexuals, Gypsies, Jews, and those euphemistically labeled "life unworthy of life." Because of their pacifist teachings, thousands of Jehovah's Witnesses were cast into concentration camps, where they were distinguished by a purple triangle. Perhaps eight thousand Jehovah's Witnesses died in places like Sachsenhausen and Buchenwald.

German machismo wrestled with the question of homosexuality for centuries, treating it as a capital offense. Bismarck modified the punishment, but homosexual activity remained a felony. Despite the behavior of several Brown Shirt leaders, the Nazis suppressed gay publications and arrested thousands of these alleged traitors. Fifteen thousand victims went to their deaths wearing the pink triangle, which indicated homosexuality.

Unfairly fettered with a tarnished history, Gypsies had been reviled in much of Europe. Although there were only forty thousand Gypsies in Germany, the Nazis tried to cluster them in state-supervised campgrounds before 1937. By 1942 they were being shipped off to extermination camps along with Jews. Estimates of the dead among Gypsies, who wore the brown triangle, range between 200,000 and 300,000.

"Life unworthy of life" included anyone suffering a physical or mental handicap. Intellectuals had debated the merits of sterilizing "useless eaters" during food shortages in World War I. Using U.S. sterilization laws as their models, Nazi eugenicists succeeded in passing a law against the procreation of defective offspring in 1933. Over the next six years more than 300,000 Germans were sterilized. It was only a matter of time before the question of *Gnadentod* (mercy killing) would be addressed. After Adolf Hitler (1889–1945) sanctioned the process in October 1939, more than seventy thousand Germans were killed in six facilities coordinated from an office at Tiergartenstrasse 4 in Berlin. When the T-4 program was officially terminated in the summer of 1941, many of its personnel were transferred to the east, where their expertise would be utilized in the extermination of the Jews.

Holocaust

Of all the groups targeted by the Nazis only one, the Jews, was regarded as irredeemable. SS guards tried to break the bonds among Jehovah's Witnesses, seeking a simple recantation from their prisoners. An oath of allegiance to Hitler and the sectarians could be released. Some Nazi physicians tried to "cure" homosexuals with drugs. (The gay inmate could also save himself by feigning "recovery.") Heinrich Himmler (1900–1945), head of the concentration camps and the extermination campaign against the Jews, intended to spare some of the Lalleri Gypsies who lived in Germany because they claimed descent from the ancient Aryans of India. And as bad as the sterilization and euthanasia programs were, they did not come close to eliminating all the alcoholics, Parkinsonians, or insane people in Germany.

Since the conquest of their homeland by the Romans between 63 BCE and 135 CE Jews were regarded as a pariah people. Cultural domination by Christians and Muslims with their anti-Jewish polemics made matters worse. Jews endured economic privation, imposition of badges and ghettos, accusations of ritual murder and host desecration, inquisitions, pogroms, and expulsions. In the worst of times, however, there was always a means of escape. Conversion might not secure equality, but this path, advocated by the Jewish philosopher Moses Maimonides (1135–1204), certainly was an alternative to martyrdom. That option was not available to Jews in World War II. According to the pseudoscience that constituted the foundation of Hitler's racism, Jews belonged to a different species that had to be exterminated.

The Intentionalist-Functionalist Debate

Holocaust historians are uncertain when Hitler decided to kill all the Jews in the world. Some academics (Intentionalists) maintain that genocide was central to his program from the start. Others (Functionalists) argue that there was a "twisted" or more pragmatic approach to mass murder in which other means of eliminating Jews such as pogroms, deportation, and reservations were considered before he settled on genocide. The historian Lucy Dawidowicz, for example, points to the many references of *Ausrottung* ("extermination") and a final solution that appear in *Mein Kampf*, even one prescient mention of poison gas in Hitler's political manifesto. Anti-Jewish rhetoric figures prominently in Hitler's table talk, his speeches, and the final testament he left in the Berlin bunker in 1945. Unquestionably, he hated Jews from his days as a struggling artist in Vienna. Given the opportunity, he probably would have killed many more when he came to power in January 1933. But there were always factors that tempered his actions—the influence of President Hindenburg, restoration of trade and the success of the 1936 Olympics, the waffling of his Wehrmacht generals. As bloody as Kristallnacht (9–10 November 1938) was, this statewide pogrom was orchestrated not so much to kill Jews as to terrorize them and prompt their flight from Germany.

It seems more reasonable to assume that Hitler was trying to encumber the democracies with 600,000 Jews from Germany, 250,000 from Austria, 100,000 from Bohemia and Moravia until the outbreak off war in September 1939. When the Nazis inherited 3 million Polish Jews, Hitler deferred to Himmler and to Hans Frank (1900–1946), Hitler's governor-general of Poland, who were plotting population shifts and the creation of a reservation near Lublin. When Germany celebrated its victory in Western Europe in 1940, members of Hitler's high command were giving thought to deporting Jews to Madagascar.

Only after his war plans went awry did Hitler sanction genocide. Even as his troops were entering Paris in the summer of 1940, Hitler instructed his generals to prepare for an invasion of the Soviet Union. By Christmas 1940, it was apparent that the Luftwaffe's aerial blitz was not bringing England to its knees. When 145 German divisions slashed into the Soviet Union in June 1941, they were accompanied by 3,000 specially trained shock troops whose mission it was to eliminate Bolshevik political officers, partisans, Jews, and other racial undesirables. With Hitler's spoken blessing (the Führer was especially cautious about penning his name to such orders) on 25 July 1941, Hermann Göring (1893–1946), Hitler's chancellor, instructed Reinhard Heydrich (1904–1942), Himmler's chief deputy, to take steps preparatory for the final solution of the Jewish Question in Europe.

Heydrich did attempt to hold a meeting in Prague that October, but several Nazi leaders were still conducting operations in the Baltic regions. On 20 January 1942, fifteen race specialists met to discuss the fate of the Jews at the offices of Interpol in the Berlin suburb of Grossen Wannsee. Heydrich chaired the ninety-minute conference, outlining the Jewish threat throughout the world (he counted 11 million Jews) and detailing German accomplishments to date. The goal was to establish a ghetto for prominent Jews at the fortress of Terezin outside Prague to delude humanitarian agencies. All other Jews would be sent to newly expanded concentration camps at Auschwitz and Chelmno in western Poland and Sobibor, Treblinka, Majdanek, and Belzec near the Bug River where they would "fall away" through forced labor. One million Jews in the former

Soviet territories had already been eliminated by the various shock troops—including nearly 100,000 in a great pit at Babi Yar outside Kiev and tens of thousands more murdered in vans that prowled the back woods of Serbia and Lithuania, gassing captives with carbon monoxide.

Heydrich was assassinated in Prague at the end of May 1942, but the roundups of Polish Jews that year were collectively dedicated to his memory as *Aktion Reinhard*. Three hundred fifty thousand Jews perished in Sobibor and 700,000 died in Treblinka before Jewish inmates rebelled and put an end to these death camps between August and October 1943. Majdanek flourished in full view of Lublin until the Soviets liberated the camp in 1945. At Auschwitz, 1.1 million Jews died.

A War against the Jews?

The question of when Hitler finally decided to kill all Jews seems moot. People knew of his hatred long before the war and did not do enough to stop him. Despite reports filtering out of Eastern Europe during the war years, statesmen and laymen in the democracies refused to believe that the Nazis were actually engaged in mass murder. In 1941 *Collier's* devoted eight pages to the deplorable conditions in the Warsaw Ghetto. On 23 February 1941, *Life* revealed the extent of Nazi brutality in a photographic essay on conditions in the Warsaw ghetto. Picture after picture showed stacks of bodies being dumped into common graves. The victims of starvation included children whose bodies were bloated with edema and one child held by a worker by its neck. In the next year the Polish military courier Jan Karski, Swedish businessmen, representatives of the World Jewish Congress and the Vatican, and escapees from Auschwitz confirmed the Nazi plan of genocide. Yet even after Allied troops began to overrun camps in December 1944, most Americans believed fewer than 100,000 Jews had been exterminated.

The Holocaust scholar Emil Fackenheim once said that since 1933 a war has been waged against every Jew in the world and it is difficult to dispute him. The Nazis intended to clear Warsaw of its Jews in 1943 and dedicate a victory stele in Hitler's honor. Today a monument to ghetto fighters stands there and the Polish government plans to create a museum to Jews who have vanished. Tourists visit Majdanek, a sprawling site of misery that was supposed to be six times larger when it was completed. They photograph gas chamber walls stained blue from hydrogen-cyanide gas to refute claims of revisionists who deny the Holocaust ever happened.

Saul S. Friedman

See also Genocide in Bosnia; Genocide in Rwanda; Nazism and Holocaust

Further Reading

Des Pres, T. (1976). *The survivor: An anatomy of life in the death camps*. New York: Oxford University Press.

Fackenheim, E. (1978). *The Jewish return into history*. New York: Schocken Press.

Fein, H. (1979). *Accounting for genocide*. New York: Free Press.

Friedlander, H. (1995). *The origins of Nazi genocide*. Chapel Hill: University of North Carolina Press.

Friedman, S. (1993). *Holocaust literature*. Westport, CT: Greenwood Press.

Glass, J. (1997). *Life unworthy of life*. New York: Basic Books

Hay, M. (1960). *Europe and the Jews*. Boston: Beacon.

Horowitz, I. (1976). *Genocide: State power and mass murder*. New Brunswick, NJ: Transaction Books.

Hovannisian, R. (1986). *The Armenian genocide in perspective*. New Brunswick, NJ: Transaction Books.

Kenrick, D., & Puxon, G. (1972). *The destiny of Europe's Gypsies*. New York: Basic Books.

Kogon, E. (1950). *The theory and practice of hell: The German concentration camps and the system behind them* (H. Norden, Trans.). New York: Berkeley Books.

Levin, N. (1968). *The Holocaust*. New York: Crowell.

Lifton, R. (1976). *The Nazi doctors*. New York: Basic Books.

Milgram, S. (1974). *Obedience to authority*. New York: Harper & Row.

Muller-Hill, B. (1988). *Murderous science*. New York: Oxford University Press.

Plant, R. (1986). *The pink triangle: The Nazi war against homosexuals*. New York: Henry Holt.

Viereck, P. (1951). *Metapolitics: The roots of the Nazi mind*. New York: Capricorn Books.

Genocide in Rwanda

The genocide that turned world attention to Rwanda in 1994 has been described in graphic terms. The May edition of *Time* magazine offered a damning headline: "There are no devils left in Hell. They are all in Rwanda."

Rwanda International Criminal Tribunal Pronounces Guilty Verdict in Historic Genocide Trial

Arusha, United Republic of Tanzania, 2 September (International Criminal Tribunal for Rwanda)—"Despite the indisputable atrociousness of the crimes and the emotions evoked in the international community, the judges have examined the facts adduced in a most dispassionate manner, bearing in mind that the accused is presumed innocent."

With these words, among others, the International Criminal Tribunal for Rwanda, in the first-ever judgement by an international court for the crime of genocide, today found Jean-Paul Akayesu guilty of genocide and crimes against humanity.

Mr. Akayesu, former bourgmestre (mayor) of Taba, was indicted on 15 counts of "genocide, crimes against humanity, and violations of Article 3 common to the Geneva Conventions and Additional Protocol II thereto". In its judgement, Trial Chamber I (Judges Laity Kama (Senegal), presiding, Lennart Aspegren (Sweden) and Navanethem Pillay (South Africa)) unanimously found Mr. Akayesu guilty of nine out of the 15 counts on which he was charged, and not guilty of six counts in his indictment. The former Rwandan official had pleaded not guilty to all 15 counts.

Specifically, he was found guilty of "genocide, direct and public incitement to commit genocide, and crimes against humanity (extermination, murder, torture, rape and other inhumane acts). But the Tribunal also held that he was not guilty of the crimes of complicity in genocide and violations of Article 3 common to the Geneva Conventions (murder and cruel treatment) and of Article 4(2)(e) of Additional Protocol II (outrage upon personal dignity, in particular, rape, degrading and humiliating treatment and indecent assault).

***Source:* Verdicts on the Crime of Genocide by the International Criminal Tribunal for Rwanda. Press release, 2 September 1998. Retrieved 6 April 2003 from http://www.un.org/law/rwanda.**

To understand the role of religion in the Rwanda genocide, a historical overview is necessary. Prior to 6 April 1994, Rwanda was an obscure and distant country in Africa except to people who had seen the film *Gorillas in the Mist*. Rwanda is the smallest country south of the Sahara Desert. It covers only 25,000 square kilometers, but 8 million people live in that area. They have been inaccurately identified in ethnic groups. The three major groupings share a culture and language (Kinyarwanda) but differ in physical appearance, social status, and occupation.

Myths of Origin

Myths of origin were fabricated to prove a separate origin for the Tutsi people of Rwanda. The Hamitic (relating to Noah's son Ham) "theory of origin" was introduced by John Hanning Speke in 1863 in his *Journal of the Discovery of the Source of the Nile*. According to his pseudoscientific theory, the Tutsis came from India. The main thesis of the Hamitic theory came from the first British administrator of the Ugandan protectorate, Sir Harry Johnston, who claimed that the Tutsis originated in Ethiopia. One variation of the Hamitic theory follows the biblical myth of the three sons of Noah. The variation emphasizes that although blacks are descendants of Ham, not all blacks, such as the Tutsi, are included.

The "superior race" concept and practices of the Germans in 1914 were limited but were formalized as colonial policy by the Belgian colonialists. Rwanda was colonized by the Germans in 1890 and by the Belgians from 1916 to 1946 under the League of Nations mandate along with Burubdi, and from 1946 to 1961 under the United Nations as a trust territory. During the 1930s the Belgians would ensure that most Hutu chiefs were deposed. They promoted Tutsis in every sphere of public life and expressed confidence in Tutsi leadership and their ability to succeed in education. Missionaries expressed the same bias in their evangelization methods. They first converted the Tutsi chiefs and sent them to Catholic schools and seminaries to prepare for leadership roles in the church. From 1931 to 1933 the Belgian colonialists introduced ethnic identity cards that would radically alter and solidify an otherwise fluid ethnic identity. After all, Tutsis and Hutus intermarried, and there was no untamable animosity between the two. The Roman Catholic Church was everything to the Tutsi in terms of ambition and substance. Its education system, including a school for children of kings, was the gateway to social position, based on its acceptance of the dangerous mythology.

Prelude to the Killings

The year 1959 was a major turning point because the anticolonial movement arose in European colonies, and the United Nations forced the Belgians to change their policies to accommodate the majority population's interests in representational government. This meant the replacement of the ruling Tutsi elite for the sake of democracy. Leading up to 1959, the first public expression of animosity against the Tutsis, which was shared by Catholic Church leaders, was the "Bahutu Manifesto" in 1957. The Parmehutu (the political party promoting Hutu emancipation) received strong support from Monsignor Perraudin, a Swiss bishop. By the time independence came in 1962, 20,000 Tutsis were massacred, and over 200,000 Tutsis would seek refuge in neighboring Burundi and Uganda. Since independence the country has been greatly favored for development by nongovernmental organizations and Western nations because it has been generally perceived to be stable under the power of the Hutus. In order to justify and maintain that image, the new leaders have employed two types of rhetoric: one for a domestic audience and the other for external aid donors. In order to maintain the urgent need for the Hutu power structure, "social revolution" was utilized to remind the majority Hutus that Hutus are the true and legitimate inhabitants of Rwanda and deserve to be freed from the oppressive rule of the outsider (the Tutsis). The second type of rhetoric focused on the need for "development," even though most of the money was diverted to bolster the president's power base.

After Gregoire Kayibanda took power as the first president, he established close ties with President Mobutu of Zaire with the hope that Mobutu would help demobilize the Tutsi rebel camps in eastern Zaire. President Kayibanda appeared to be an ineffective leader to his top military leaders. In 1973 General Juvenal Habyariman overthrew Kayibanda in a bloodless coup. Habyariman soon gained support from militant anti-Tutsi Hutu elements. The 1980s were difficult years for Rwanda. One reason was the growing strength of the Rwanda Patriotic Front (RPF), which was made up of mostly exiled Tutsi refugees in Uganda. They had been arming themselves in preparation for a return to their country. Their first attempt was made in 1990. The defeat of the group gave President Habyariman an excuse to make scapegoats of it and summon support for its elimination. Habyariman found ready support in President Francois Mitterand of France.

International pressure from Western donor countries, the International Monetary Fund, and the World Bank for greater democratization put the president in a tight spot. The Arusha Accords, to which he had been a signatory, required the inclusion of Tutsis in power sharing and the elimination of ethnic identifications on documents. For Habyariman and his northern Hutu clique (the Akazu), these accords spelled disaster because their implementation would mean the loss of power and privilege. In order to enforce the terms of the Arusha Accords, the United Nations peacekeeping force would supervise. Unfortunately, the Arusha Accords could not be carried out because of the growing suspicion and hatred of the Tutsis.

The Tragedy of Rwanda and the Role of Religion

Hell broke loose in Rwanda on 6 April 1994. Although the Hutus had identified moderate Hutus and Tutsis to be massacred, the immediate pretext came when the presidential plane carrying President Cyprien Ntaryamira of Burundi and Habyariman from a regional conference in Dar-es-Salaam, Tanzania, was struck by missiles. The purpose of the conference was to break the impasse over the accords. The killing and maiming of civilians by soldiers and Hutu extremists were methodical and brutal, using machetes, spiked tools, and weapons. Neighbors turned in neighbors, and some Tutsis paid killers to spare them the anguish of gruesome death as they pleaded to be shot. The two groups responsible for much of the carnage were the Interhamwe and the Impuzamugambi. All the while the state-run Hutu radio station, Radio Mille Collines (thousand hills) encouraged Hutu audiences with hate-filled messages to kill the Tutsis.

Church leaders stood by while the propaganda filled the airwaves. The Rwandan conversion to Christianity, when put to the test, turned out to be superficial and opportunistic. The example of Bishop Rwankeri illustrates the abandonment of Christianity among the Roman Catholic hierarchy. During the crisis he encouraged Christians to support the interim government and its policies. Also, in August 1994 twenty-nine Hutu priests wrote a letter to the Pope denying Hutu responsibility for the massacres. Protestant clergy and other Christians also gave in to evil. Pastor Elizaphan Ntakirutima of the Seventh-Day Adventist Church in Kibuye and his son, Dr. Gerard Ntakirutimana, a physician, gave public support to Hutu power and helped to assemble fleeing Tutsis in a church, where they were killed by Hutu militia. However, a few ordinary Christians and priests risked their lives for their fellow men and women.

The conspiracy of silence and the condoning of carnage have exposed the hypocrisy of Rwandan Christianity in the proceedings of the International Criminal Tribunal for Rwanda in Arusha, Tanzania. The tribunal was set up in November 1994 to try war criminals of the Rwanda massacre. Approximately 125,000 people have been jailed for war-related killings. Out of the twelve hundred tried in 1999, over one hundred were sentenced to death, and twenty-two have been executed. Convictions of prominent Church leaders followed, including those of Bishop Samuel Musabyimana, the Anglican bishop who, prior to the killings, declared that the situation for the Tutsis was dire and that their end had come; Father Athanase Seromba, who escaped to the diocese of Florence, Italy, in 1997; and two Rwandan nuns who were tried in Belgium and convicted. Upon the conviction of Sister Maria Kisito Mukabutera and Sister Gertrude Mukangango for handing over seven thousand Tutsis who were being sheltered in a southern Rwanda convent, the Vatican distanced itself from their actions. Perhaps the most notorious Church accomplice to be recently convicted is Pastor Ntakirutimana and his son, who fled to the United States.

The conviction of top Rwandan politicians, professionals, and religious authorities signals a new awareness about the gravity of crimes against humanity and the need for immediate action by the international community. The success of the Rwanda criminal tribunal brings hope and closure to those who long for justice and accountability in regions of the world that hardly make headlines in Western capitals. However, the success of the tribunal will be complete when the United Nations and Western nations, which had a stake in Rwanda but did nothing to stop the massacres, are made to own up to their complicity as well.

Victor Wan-Tatah

Further Reading

Ayittey, G. B. (1999). *Africa in chaos*. New York: St. Martin's Griffin.

Berry, J. A., & Berry, C. P. (Eds.). (1999). *Genocide in Rwanda: A collective memory*. Washington, DC: Howard University Press.

Destexhe, A. (1996). *Rwanda and genocide in the twentieth century*. New York: New York University Press.

Freeman, C. (1999). *Crisis in Rwanda*. Austin, TX: Steck-Vaughn.

Gouvevitch, P. (1998). *We wish to inform you that tomorrow we will be killed with our families: Stories from Rwanda*. New York: Farrar, Straus and Giroux.

Huband, M. (2001). *The skull beneath the skin: Africa after the Cold War*. Boulder, CO: Westview Press.

Jackson, R. H., & Rosberg, C. G. (1982). *Personal rule in black Africa: Prince, autocrat, prophet, tyrant*. Berkeley and Los Angeles: University of California Press.

Keane, F. (1995). *Season of blood: A Rwandan journey*. London: Penguin Books.

Klinghoffer, A. (1998). *The international dimension of genocide in Rwanda*. New York: New York University Press.

Madsen, W. (1994). *Genocide and covert operations in Africa 1993–1999*. New York: Edwin Press.

McCullum, H. (1995). *The angels have left us*. Geneva, Switzerland: WCC Publications.

Melvern, L. (2000). *A people betrayed: The role of the West in Rwanda's genocide*. New York: Zed Books.

Nyankanzi, E. L. (1998). *Genocide: Rwanda and Burundi*. Rochester, VT: Schenkman Books.

Prunier, G. (1995). *The Rwandan crisis: History of a genocide*. New York: Columbia University Press.

Sibomana, A. (1997). *Hope for Rwanda: Conversations with Laure Guiber and Herve Deguine*. London: Pluto Press.

Richburg, K. B. (1998). *Out of America: A black man confronts Africa*. New York: Harvest Books.

Taylor, C. (1994). *Sacrifice as terror: The Rwandan genocide of 1994*. Oxford, UK: Berg.

Uvin, P. (1998). *Aiding violence: The development enterprise in Rwanda*. West Hartford, CT: Kumarian Press.

Ghost Dance

The Ghost Dance was a major Native American revitalization movement of nineteenth century. It culminated in the Wounded Knee Massacre of 1890, the final battle in the war against the Native Americans of the Plains and an event of much symbolic meaning to Native Americans ever since. The Ghost Dance was a response to the catastrophic disruptions to Native American life that accompanied European conquest of North America. For Native Americans of the Plains these disruptions included a series of defeats by the American army, loss of land, confinement to reservations, and the near extinction of the bison. The Ghost Dance Movement was a spiritual mechanism that would enable them to transform the existing social order and improve their lives. Followers of the movement believed that participation in the ceremony would restore their traditional way of life, lead herds of bison to reappear, bring deceased ancestors back to earth, and cause white settlers and soldiers to leave Native American land.

There were actually two Ghost Dance movements. The first took place in 1870 and was limited to the western United States. It was led by Wodziwob (1844–1918?) a Northern Paiute from Nevada. He preached that to transform the world, Native Americans must dance the round dance at night to communicate their wishes to the other world and to call the ghosts of their ancestors. The movement lasted for several years in the West before disappearing.

The Impact of Wovoka

The prophet of the 1890 Ghost Dance was Wovoka (1856–1932), a Paiute in Nevada. Wovoka very likely knew of the 1870 dance, having either been told of it by his father or perhaps having even participated in it. In 1888 Wovoka received revelations from the supernatural world concerning the transformation of Indian society and a return to traditional ways. In January 1889, he had an out-of-body experience, which he described two years later: "When the sun dies, I went up to heaven and saw God and all the people who had died a long time ago. God told me to come back and tell my people that they must be good and love one another, and not fight, or steal, or lie. He gave me this dance to give to my people." He then began preaching the message of the dance:

> All Indians must dance, everywhere keep on dancing. Pretty soon in next spring Great Spirit Come. He bring back all game of every kind. The game be thick everywhere. All dead Indians come back and live again. They all be strong like young men, be young again. Old blind Indian see again and get young and have fine time. When Great Spirit comes this way, then all the Indians go the mountains, high up away from whites. Whites can't hurt Indians then. Then while Indians way high up, big flood comes like water and all white people die, get drowned. After that, water go away and then nobody but Indians everywhere and game all kinds thick. Then medicine man tell Indians to send word to all Indians to keep up dancing and the good time will come. Indians who don't dance, who don't believe in this word, will grow little, just about a foot high, and stay that way. Some of them will be turned into wood and be burned in fire. (Brown 1991, 416)

The first to join the movement were Native Americans in the Far West who were losing their land to Euroamerican ranchers, miners, and farmers. As Wovoka's message spread east, it caught the attention of Native American groups in the Plains including the Lakota, Caddo, Arapaho, Cheyenne, and Kiowa. These groups were suffering from nearly thirty years of skirmishes, battles, treaties, and relocations at the hands of the U.S. military and government agents. In addition, the bison which provided food, raw materials, and a focus of tribal organization were no nearly gone. Starving and disorganized, the Plains tribes had been herded onto reservations. Nonetheless, they were feared by settlers who sought their land.

Wovoka's message had special appeal for the Lakota (one of the major groups of the Sioux), whose situation was summed up by one of their leaders, Sitting Bull:

> If a man loses everything and goes back and looks carefully for it he will find it, and that is what the Indians are doing now when they ask you to give them the things that were promised them in the past; and I do not consider that they should be treated like beasts, and that is the reason I have grown up with the feelings I have. . . . I feel that my country has gotten a bad name, and I want it to have a good name; it used to have a good name; and I sit sometimes and wonder who it is that has given it a bad name. (Brown 1991, 415)

By 1880 some thirty-five Indian groups across the United States had joined the Ghost Dance Movement, with the most fervent believers among the Lakota and other groups in the northern Plains. They danced the round dance during the summer and fall of 1880. The dance was performed by hundreds of men and women over four or five nights. Although exhausting, participants were allowed to rest and they did not have visions or faint from exhaustion. The Lakota added new elements to the dance, including the wearing of white

Letter from General Nelson A. Miles to the Commissioner of Indian Affairs on 13 March 1917 concerning the Massacre at Wounded Knee in 1890

Washington, D. C. March 13, 1917

The Honorable Commissioner of Indian Afairs

Sir:

I am informed that there is a delegation in Washington now who came here from South Dakota and who are representatives of the remnant of what is known as the Big Foot Band of Northern Sioux Indians.

I was in command of that Department in 1889, 1890, and 1891, when what is known as the Messiah craze and threatened uprising of the Indians occurred. It was created by misrepresentations of white men then living in Nevada who sent secret messages to the different tribes in the great Northwest calling upon them to send representatives to meet Him near Walker Lake, Nevada.

[. . .]

This, together with the fact that the Indians had been in almost a starving condition in South Dakota, owing to the scarcity of rations and the nonfulfillment of treaties and sacred obligations under which the Government had been placed to the Indians, caused great dissatisfaction, dissension and almost hostility. Believing this superstition, they resolved to gather and go West to meet the Messiah, as they believed it was the fulfillment of their dreams and prayer and the prophecies as had been taught them by the missionaries.

[. . .]

While this was being done a detachment of soldiers was sent into the camp to search for any arms remaining there, and it was reported that their rudness frightened the women and children. It is also reported that a remark was made by some one of the soldiers that "when we get the arms away from them we can do as we please with them," indicating that they were to be destroyed. Some of the indians could understand English. this and other things alarmed the Indians and scuffle occured between one warrior who had rifle in his hand and two soldiers. The rifle was discharged and a massacre occurred, not only the warriors but the sick Chief Big Foot, and a large number of women and children who tried to escape by running and scattering over the prarie were hunted down and killed. The official reports make the number killed 90 warriors and approximately 200 women and children.

The action of the Commanding Officer, in my judgement at the time, and I so reported, was most reprehensible. The disposition of his troops was such that in firing upon the warriors they fired directly towards their own lines and also into the camp of the women and children and I have regarded the whole affair as most unjustifiable and worthy of the severest condemnation.

In my opinion, the least the Government can do is to make a suitable recompense to the survivors who are still living for the great unjustice that was done them and the serious loss of their relatives and property--and I earnestly recommend that this may be favorably considered by the Department and by Congress and a suitable appropriation be made.

I remain

Very truly yours,

(SGD.) NELSON A. MILES

Lt. General, U. S. Army

Source: Massacre at Wounded Knee. Retrieved May 23, 2003, from tp://woptura.com/milesltr1917.html

cotton "Ghost Shirts" to protect them from white bullets. Lakota leaders saw the movement as political as well as religious, and discussed the use of violence to escape from the reservation and to end white rule.

The gathering of thousands of people at some Ghost Dances, the donning of the ghost shirts for protection, and rumors of armed revolt alarmed white settlers and many abandoned their farms and ranches and sought protection in the towns. The U.S. government—seeking to end any all resistance—responded by charging that Sitting Bull, the most prominent Indian leader and symbol of Indian resistance, was the leader of the Ghost Dance movement. Fully half the troops in the entire U.S. army were assigned to the region to maintain order and protect settlers. Although the Indians did discuss violent resistance, they posed little threat. They were outnumbered ten to one by white settlers, outgunned by an even larger margin, and their food supply had recently been cut by 50 percent to force the Indians to cede more land through one-sided treaties.

The Wounded Knee Massacre

For some thirty years the Plains had been the scene of wars between the U.S. military and the indigenous Native Americans of the region. The final and tragic result of white fear and the huge military presence in the region was the Wounded Knee Massacre, which occurred on 29 December 1890. Before the massacre, Sitting Bull, had been arrested and then murdered by U.S. soldiers, at his home on 15 December. Other Lakota feared for their safety and fled north. Pursued by the cavalry, about 350 Indians were captured and forced to make camp along Wounded Knee Creek on 28 December. About 100 men were placed in one camp and about 250 women and children in another camp. The camps were guarded by a detachment of 500 heavily armed troops. Among their weapons were four Hotchkiss canons, each firing 50 two-pound shells a minute, aimed at the men's camp. After a night of drunken celebration, the troops entered the camps to search for and confiscate weapons. Women were mistreated and forced to expose themselves, men strip-searched, tipis ransacked, and property destroyed. A Lakota and a soldier fought over a rifle. When it discharged, both sides began to fire, although the Indians had only a few rifles. Over the next hour over 300 Indians were killed, including nearly all the men and most of the women and children, who were unarmed. Women and children were blown apart by the Hotchkiss shells and those who fled were shot in the back. Indian bodies were strewn across the plains for three miles around the camps. On New Year's Day the frozen bodies were gathered up, piled on wagons, and buried. Some 146 bodies were dumped in a mass grave, but only after the bodies were stripped of their ghost shirts as souvenirs for the soldiers.

The detachment commander Colonel Forsythe was later cleared of wrongdoing in the assault and three of his officers and fifteen of his enlisted men were awarded the Medal of Honor for their "valor" in combat. The Massacre at Wounded Knee was the last major engagement of the Indian wars in the West and also the last major massacre of Indians. It also marked the end of the Ghost Dance as a major movement, as the government quickly banned all new forms of Indian religious expression. The Ghost Dance was performed into the 1950s by some groups, but not as a revitalization movement.

Native Americans never forgot the massacre. The Lakota have asked for but have not received an apology from the U.S. government, and in 1973 the site was the locale of another uprising, know as Wounded Knee II or the Wounded Knee Takeover. It began on 27 February and ended on 8 May 1973. On 27 February, about two hundred Indians—mostly Lakota, led by several non-Lakota American Indian Movement (AIM) activists—took over Sacred Heart Catholic Church, a trading post, and museum near the mass grave at Wounded Knee on the Pound Ridge Sioux Reservation in South Dakota. As with the Ghost Dance that ended in the massacre eighty-three years earlier, the takeover was an act of resistance to white management of Indian affairs and more particularly to the mistreatment of Indians in South Dakota. Government response to the takeover was similar to the government response to the Ghost Dancers in 1890. Although no more than two hundred Indians ever occupied the site—some two thousand participated but only two hundred occupied the site at any given time—the U.S. government placed over two hundred FBI agents, Bureau of Indian Affairs police, and U.S. marshals at the scene. In a further parallel, the Indians had only a few dozen rifles while the U.S. force had machine guns, armed personnel carriers, and even helicopters. The standoff and negotiations were tense and disrupted by sniper fire, which claimed two Indians and two FBI agents. The takeover ended after seventy-one days when the parties agreed to a "peace pact" which was to bring a government review of Indian treaties and conditions on the reservation. Indians believe that the government never made good on these promises and a number of Indian leaders were prosecuted for the murder of the FBI agents.

On 29 Dec 1990 about four hundred people gathered at the mass grave to mark the centennial of the massacre. For Native Americans the massacre remains a vivid reminder of white oppression and Indian resistance.

David Levinson

Further Reading

Brown, D. (1991). *Bury my heart at Wounded Knee: An Indian history of the American West*. New York: Henry Holt.

Champagne, D. (Ed.). (1994). *Chronology of native North American history*. Detroit, MI: Gale Research.

Hittman, M. (1990). *Wovoka and the ghost dance: A sourcebook*. Carson City, NV: Grace Dabgberg.

Laubin, R., & Laubin, G. (1971). *Indian dances of North America*. Norman: University of Oklahoma Press.

Lazarus, E. (1991). *Black hills white justice: The Sioux nation versus the United States 1775 to the present*. New York: HarperCollins.

Lyman. S. D. (1991). *Wounded knee 1973*. Lincoln: University of Nebraska Press.

Matthiessen, P. (1983). *In the spirit of Crazy Horse*. New York: Viking.

Mooney, J. ([1896] 1965). *The ghost dance religion and Sioux outbreak of 1890*. Washington, DC: Government Printing Office; reprint, Chicago: University of Chicago Press.

Greek Religions

War was a certainty of life in the ancient world. Every free man at some point of his life should expect to be summoned to defend his homeland or invade another state as a citizen-soldier, and every woman had to accept the inevitable fact that her husband, father, or son would be called to arms. Moreover, every person could face captivity, slavery, and destruction of his or her homeland after defeat. In this uncertain world people turned to their gods before a battle, and presented them with presents, trophies, and thanksgiving prayers after victory. Many ancient civilizations held the belief that victory is a reward for piety, while defeat is fair punishment for human negligence of duty toward the gods, and the Greeks would not overtly object to this. They subscribed to the belief that a god or goddess might reward their favorite human with success, while they might punish an impious man with defeat and a cruel fate. Where they differed from all other civilizations is that they were deliberately rational and often tended to seek explanations for what was happening in their world not in supernatural causes but in the actions of humans. The modern student of ancient Greek society is confronted by some intriguing paradoxes: the Greeks were rational, and yet could be driven by irrational factors, and they were striving for logical explanations of events while, at the same time, their actions were often dictated by religious scruple and supernatural belief. They were the most humanist culture that has ever existed, and yet religion played a major role in people's lives, in peace or war. In order to understand these apparent contradictions, first we need to take a closer look at Greek mythology and theology, and try to explain how the Greeks understood the relationship between their gods and war.

Greek Mythology and War

Zeus, the supreme god of the Greek pantheon, came to power through a series of massive-scale battles among generations of gods and goddesses, giants, titans, and monsters, where mountains were shifted from their places and hurled at the combatant immortals. These epic wars among the gods, known as the Gigantomachy and Titanomachy, were popular themes of poetry and religious art, and have transcended through the centuries to inspire modern art (e.g., Leon Golub, *Gigantomachy*, 1967) and cinema (*Clash of the Titans*, 1980). Representations of these wars can be found on two of the most brilliant temples of the ancient Greek world, the Parthenon in Athens and the Altar of Pergamon. Hesiod's (c. 700 BCE) *Theogony*, arguably the earliest work of Greek theology, vividly describes this violent conflict, with no attempt to pass moral judgment on the rights or wrongs of war in the world of the gods. Later authors who revisited this old theme (e.g., Apollodoros, *Library*, Book 1; Hyginus, *Fabulae*, 1ff., 150ff.) also took it for granted that war and the struggle for supremacy were part of divine nature, and were neither inappropriate nor unsuitable activities for a god. In fact, the Greeks often imagined their gods fighting against each other, side by side with their favorite humans. In Greek drama war appears as one of the main characters in Aristophanes' (c. 450–c. 388 BCE) play *Peace*, while the gods fight and lose a war in the *Birds*. The gods of the Greeks thought humanly and acted human, and as such they hardly constituted perfect examples of good behavior. People did not look up to

Olympus to find out how they should act; this they would have to decide for themselves by using rational argument and debate. What they expected from their gods was their favor, protection, and goodwill. This is why their religious practices had much to do with ritual and little to do with theology or dogma. Through ritual the believer demonstrated his or her goodwill toward the god or goddess by offering a sacrifice, a prayer, or a gift, and hoped that this goodwill would be returned in the form of favorable attitude, protection, and help from the god. Thus the relationship between believer and god or goddess often resembles one of direct exchange and collaboration.

Religious Practices before and after a Battle

In a setting of war the goodwill of the gods ought to be secured with particular care. The Greeks would not engage the enemy without first obtaining divine approval. A sacrifice and study of the omens before the battle by prophets and oracles were standard procedures. Only when the omens were good did they proceed. Perhaps with the exception of marginal cults, like the Orphics or the Eleusinean Mysteries, Greek religion did not focus upon a deep metaphysical experience, but primarily consisted of an assemblage of rituals, sacred laws, ceremony, and communal celebration. These aspects were taken seriously, especially in critical situations, such as times of war. How seriously the Greeks could take religious scruple before going to war is very dramatically demonstrated by the infamous scandal of the Hermocopidai and the alleged divulgence of the Eleusinian Mysteries in 415 BCE. The Sicilian expedition was a daring undertaking by the city of Athens, which, if successful, would have substantially extended Athenian influence over the western Mediterranean, and might have led to the establishment of a naval empire that extended as far as the shores of Spain. This operation had the potential to make or break the city of Athens, as she invested heavily in it by dispatching more than two hundred warships. However, shortly before the departure of the fleet some of the statuettes of Hermes in the streets of Athens were vandalized. The Athenian assembly was alarmed. A witch-hunt followed, which implicated Alcibiades, the brains of the entire expedition project. Despite the importance of his position, he was suspended and recalled to face trial, but he fled to Sparta, where he helped ruin the expedition. This action of the Athenians had grave consequences: the Sicilian campaign failed catastrophically, and a few years later in 404 BCE a weakened Athens capitulated to the Spartan general Lysander (d. 395 BCE). Whether one interprets these events as superstitious paranoia, religious correctness, or simply a cynical ploy orchestrated by the opponents of Alcibiades, one thing is certain: even in the most critical moment of their history the Athenians, undoubtedly motivated by the belief that the favor of Olympus was essential precisely at this crucial moment before the big battle, were not prepared to tolerate an action that might have offended the gods.

After victory a share of the spoils would go to a temple, as a thanksgiving offering to the gods for their help. Defeat might also be attributed to the actions of a god. The historian Xenophon (c. 431–c. 352 BCE) is probably reflecting popular belief when he says in *Hellenica* that forces adverse to Sparta were in action during the catastrophic defeat by Thebes at Leuctra in 371 BCE, while the omens for the Thebans were excellent, and a whole range of supernatural phenomena and oracles predicted victory for the latter. However, the pro-Spartan Xenophon modifies this statement by adding that, according to some, the reported good omens for the Thebans were nothing more than a fabrication by the leaders of the city in order to boost morale before this critical battle.

The Delphic Oracle and the Sacred Wars of the Greeks

The Oracle of Apollo at Delphi played a particularly significant role in decisions over peace and war. In early times, during the second Greek colonization (eighth–seventh century BCE), the oracle functioned as a center directing colonists to their new homelands. The advice of the Oracle stretched well beyond religious matters; it made political and strategic decisions on the locations of new colonies. Thus the involvement of the Oracle with political matters had started well before the classical period, and by the sixth century its reputation stretched beyond the boundaries of the Greek world. In a famous episode narrated by Herodotus (c. 484–between 430 and 420 BCE), the king of Lydia Croesus asked the Oracle's advice whether he should go to war against the Persian king Cyrus II. The Greeks themselves consulted the Oracle before the Persian wars, but the Athenian general Themistocles (c. 524–c. 460 BCE) interpreted the response in a manner that condoned his policy of a naval engagement, rather than a land conflict with the enemy. The frequency and tenor of the Oracle's involvement in the wars of the Greeks suggests that its responses were often the result of intricate political consultations behind the scenes, not random words coming from the mouth of an elderly priestess (the Pythia) in a trance. This involvement was not impartial, either. Sparta had a particularly close relationship with Delphi, manipulated responses, and then used them to justify her war effort and domestic policy. The Athenians could recognize the pro-Spartan bias of the Delphic Oracle, and this is why in the late fifth and fourth centuries they maintained a respectful but cautious attitude toward it. Athens in more than one instance supported the claim of the neighboring Phocians upon the Sanctuary of Delphi, while Sparta opposed it, and enforced with military campaigns the rights of the Delphians. The Sanctuary of Apollo became the stage of major military conflicts on at least three different occasions.

The so-called "Sacred Wars" over the Delphic Oracle were events of political significance, even though the excuse for the conflicts was provided by incidents related to religious matters. In the first sacred war around 590 BCE, the combined forces of the Delphic Amphictyony and Cleisthenes (c. 600–c. 570 BCE), the tyrant of Sicyon, defeated the Crisaeans, who were trying to dominate the sanctuary, destroyed their city, and dedicated the field of Crisa to the temple. Solemn curses forbade the cultivation of the field of Crisa in later centuries. In the height of the Athenian Empire (448 BCE), an attempt by the Phocians to take over the sanctuary was supported by Athens, but Spartan military intervention restored the control of the sanctuary to the Delphians, and guaranteed its independence from Phocian control. About a century later, when Sparta had been substantially weakened, a rather unholy alliance of cities with anti-Spartan sentiments excluded the old defenders of Delphian independence from the god's temple, and sought to inflict more severe punishments for alleged religious infractions upon the neighbors of the sanctuary, the Phocians. Ironically this time the Spartans felt compelled to support the Phocian claims and the last and greatest sacred war broke out in 356, when the Phocians with secret Spartan support and Athenian connivance seized the temple and its treasures. The intervention of Philip II (382–336 BCE) of Macedon finally brought this war to an end after four years of bitter conflict, and forever changed the politics of southern Greece.

Religious Wars and Pagan Tolerance

The sacred wars of the Greeks were dictated by political expediency, not religious fanaticism. Religion provided the excuse for conflicts that had much deeper roots in historical resentments, financial benefits, territorial claims, or expansionist ambitions. Rarely do we hear about persecution on dogmatic grounds. Perhaps the most notorious case, the persecution of the Pythagoreans, is a historically disputable incident. In general the Greeks, along with most polytheistic religions of Europe and the Near East, were tolerant of other cults. Perhaps the reason for this lies in the fact that respect for one more alien deity or religious practice, in addition to the multitude of their own, would cost nothing, and might even bring some benefit to the individual believer. It is only from the moment that monotheistic religions emerge, with their firm devotion to the one true God, that there is no room for alien deities, and those who believe in them are now perceived as infidels and therefore dangerous, or simply raw material for proselytizing. But, on the other hand, complete denial of the existence of the gods would be perceived as threatening in pagan antiquity, as the ordinary person, who was convinced that the gods existed, feared their anger toward the entire community if it harbored the atheist. The philosopher Anaxagoras (c. 500–c. 428 BCE) barely escaped from Athens with his life, while Socrates (c. 380–c. 450 BCE) was put to death on the grounds that he denied the existence of the gods. The ordinary Greek might not look up to heaven to find the answers for all his questions, but he or she was not prepared to risk the wrath of the temperamental gods of Olympus. This is why ritual correctness, regular prayer, purification, sacrifices, offerings at the temples, and participation in the festivals in honor of a god or goddess were seen as indispensable activities for the individual and the community as a whole.

The Greeks were rational, and trusted their own judgment with regards to moral, political, social, and personal issues. However, at the same time they held strong religious beliefs, and expected every person to refrain from offending the gods, as well as to try to obtain their favor through ritual, prayer, and offerings at the temples. Anyone seen to be failing in his or her duties toward the gods was perceived as a threat to the entire community, as they could put everyone at risk by inviting divine anger. And when the Greek gods were in a bellicose mood, humans had to beware of their inexorable vengeance.

Konstantinos Kapparis

Further Readings

Buckler, J. (1989). *Philip II and the sacred war*. Leiden: E. J. Brill.

Burkert, W. (1983). *Homo Necans* (P. Bing, Trans.). Berkeley: University of California Press.

Burkert, W. (1985). *Greek religion* (J. Raffan, Trans.). Cambridge, MA: Harvard University Press.

Buxton, R. (Ed.). (2000). *Oxford readings in Greek religion*. Oxford, UK: Oxford University Press.

Guthrie, W. K. C. (1951). *The Greeks and their gods*. Boston: Beacon Press.

Hankinson, R. J. (1998). *Cause and explanation in ancient Greek thought*. Oxford, UK: Clarendon Press.

Lonis, R. (1979). *Guerre et religion en Grèce à l'époque classique: Recherches sur les rites, les dieux, l'idéologie de la victoire* [War and religion in Classical Greece: Studies on the rites, gods, and ideology of victory]. Paris: Belles Lettres.

Ruprecht, L. A., Jr. (2002). *Was Greek thought religious?* Milan: Palgrave.

van Wees, H. (Ed.). (2000). *War and violence in ancient Greece* (H. van Wees, Ed.). London: Duckworth.

H

Hamas

An acronym from the Arabic Harakat al-Muqawama al-Islamiyya or Islamic Resistance Movement, Hamas also means "zeal" or "fervor" in Arabic. This movement has two immediate goals: establishing a sovereign, independent state located in historic Palestine (present-day Israel, the West Bank, and the Gaza Strip); and providing religious, social, economic, and educational support to Palestinians, especially refugees. In furtherance of the first goal, Hamas activists have perpetrated large-scale suicide bombings against Israeli military and civilian targets, suspected Palestinian collaborators, and political rivals. The organization opposes the Oslo peace process, which was negotiated by the Palestine Liberation Organization (PLO), and its short-term aim is a complete Israeli withdrawal from the Palestinian territories, after which a sovereign, independent Palestine would be established. To achieve its second goal, Hamas has established an impressive social, religious, educational, and cultural infrastructure to serve Christian and Muslim Palestinians in the West Bank and Gaza.

Hamas's primary location of operation is the Gaza Strip, the West Bank, and Israel. Palestinian expatriates as well as Iran and Saudi Arabia largely fund Hamas activities in both its political/military and charitable wings. The group is also known as Students of Ayyash (Students of the Engineer) and Izz al-Din al-Qassim Brigades. Hamas's political arm has participated in a number of peaceful initiatives such as running candidates in West Bank Chamber of Commerce elections and involvement with political debate organizations at universities such as Al-Najah in Nablus and has established schools, charities, and health care facilities for poor Palestinians. Hamas's future as the voice for Palestinian nationalist aspirations is directly tied to the success of the Israeli-Palestinian peace process: as successful implementation of the PLO-negotiated Oslo Accords falters, Hamas gains credibility among Palestinians as a vehicle by which to establish a sovereign Palestinian state.

Historical Background and the Current Conflict

In its present form, Hamas emerged in the Gaza Strip in December 1987 as the organizational expression of the Muslim Brotherhood during the first *intifada* ("uprising"), when Palestinians took to the streets in often violent protests against the Israeli military occupation. Within one year, Hamas became a principal rival to Fatah, Yassir Arafat's faction and the largest of the groups represented in the coalition Palestine Liberation Organization (PLO). Hamas differs from Fatah and the PLO in at least one important way: while Fatah and the PLO uphold a gradual, phased approach to the creation of a Palestinian homeland, Hamas demands immediate Israeli withdrawal from all of historic Palestine and refuses to acknowledge its right to exist.

Islamic movements in Israel and Palestine were largely ineffectual until after the 1967 war, in which the Israeli military overwhelmingly defeated the surrounding Arab countries. After that, Hamas's social activities and economic support for the refugees of the Gaza Strip underscored the ineffectuality and corruption of the PLO. In 1978, Hamas legally registered with the Israeli government as al-Mujamma al-Islami (Islamic Association or Organization) and since then, largely servesas a political counterweight to Yasir Arafat's (b. 1929) PLO in providing social services to Palestinian refugees.

Structure and Current Funding

Much of Hamas's financial backing comes from wealthy Palestinian expatriates and private donors living in the West and from Saudi Arabia and other oil-rich Persian Gulf nations. There is some evidence that Iran provides funding to Hamas's military wing; the Israeli Ministry of Foreign Affairs estimates that $3 million flows between Iran and Hamas each year. The organization operates a complex network of fund-raising activities that focus on raising money for charitable activities. Some of the money is raised through Western-based Hamas aid agencies such as the Texas-based Holy Land Foundation, the Palestinian Development and Relief Fund based in Great Britain, Germany's Al-Aqsa Foundation, and France's Comité de Bienfaisance et Solidarité avec la Palestine. Funds donated through these organizations are ostensibly for charitable purposes, including funding sewing and weaving centers and cattle farms. But Western intelligence sources have determined that some of the aid earmarked for "orphans and the needy" is distributed to families of Hamas suicide bombers and those in Israeli prisons arrested for terrorist activities. In December 2001, President George W. Bush issued an executive order freezing the U.S. assets of individuals and groups with links to Hamas.

In addition to funding its military or terrorist operations, Hamas devotes much of its $70 million annual budget to an extensive network of social services, which includes schools, orphanages, mosques, health care clinics, soup kitchens, and sports leagues. According to Israeli scholar Reuven Paz, approximately nine-tenths of its funding is for social, welfare, and educational activities. Since the Palestinian Authority often fails to provide such services, Hamas's efforts in this area further explain much of its popularity.

Primary Leaders

A partially blind, wheelchair-bound cleric from Gaza Strip, Sheikh Ahmad Yassin (b. 1938) serves as the spiritual leader of Hamas. Yassin's fiery speeches have inspired numerous suicide bombings and an Israeli military court sentenced him to life imprisonment in 1991. Six years later, two Israeli intelligence operatives were arrested in Jordan for the attempted assassination of Hamas official Khalid Mishaal. In exchange for the return of their two agents, Israel released Sheikh Yassin to Jordanian authorities; he now lives in Gaza. Another founding member of Hamas, Khalid Mishaal (b. 1956), serves as the chair of the organization's political bureau.

Dr. Abdul Aziz Rantisi (b. 1947) acts as Hamas's official spokesman in Gaza. A physician and lecturer at the Islamic University in Gaza, Dr. Rantisi has been active in social and charitable causes such as the Palestinian Red Crescent Society and Arab Medical Society in Gaza and served on the administrative board of the Islamic Complex. He has been in and out of Israeli prisons since 1983, when he refused to pay taxes to the military government that administered the occupied territories.

Binyamin Netanyahu's and Ariel Sharon's Likud governments have implemented a policy of preemptive assassination against Hamas and Islamic Jihad officials. In April 1994, a leader of Hamas's military wing, Kamal Kuhail, was killed by a bomb planted in an apartment where he was visiting; three other Palestinian men died in that explosion. Nasir Sulouha, an active member of the Hamas movement, was killed in Gaza in June of the same year; six months later, the Israeli military killed Ibrahim Yaggi, another Hamas military official, outside his Jericho home. Dozens of Hamas's political and military figures have been assassinated in the past decade. During the first three months of 2003, the Israeli army killed over twenty Hamas operatives, including Riyad Abu Zaid, Nasser Asideh, and Ali Alan, in preemptive assassinations that also claimed the lives of more than thirty Palestinian civilians.

In what is probably the controversial assassination, the Israeli army killed a revered member of Hamas, Yahya Ayyash (1966–1996), with a small explosive planted in his mobile phone. Ayyash had become active in the Izz al-Din al-Qassim Brigades and specialized in developing explosives from ordinary materials readily available in the West Bank and Gaza. After the February 1994 al-Ibrahimi Mosque massacre, in which American-Israeli Baruch Goldstein killed twenty-nine Muslims during evening prayers, Ayyash assisted and encouraged suicide bombers in numerous attacks throughout Israel. Palestinian journalists estimate that a half million Palestinians attended his funeral.

Terrorist Activities

Since 1994, Hamas and Islamic Jihad (a militant Islamist group with ties to Iran) have conducted more than eighty suicide bombings, killing more than two hundred Israeli civilians. Its first suicide bombing occurred in April 1993. Polls taken since the outbreak of the second intifada (fall 2000) indicate that almost 70 percent of Palestinians in the West Bank and Gaza Strip favor suicide bombings as a way to force Israel to withdraw its troops and remove settlements from the occupied territories. The suicide bombings—and radical Hamas—were much less popular during the mid- to late 1990s. It was during this time that major gains were made after the peace accords signed in Oslo, Norway. Now that the peace accords have been all but scuttled, many Palestinians consider Hamas's terrorist activities as legitimate means by which to resist the occupation; they argue that the world pays less attention to Palestinian deaths than to suicide bombings. As of 30 April 2003, at least 2,013 Palestinians have died since the beginning of the second intifada; Israeli deaths numbered around 707.

Prior to 2000, Israeli–Palestinian Authority (PA) security cooperation was generally effective, but Israel's destruction of the PA's security infrastructure (2001–2002) has made it exceedingly difficult for the PA to undertake security operations against terrorists. Consequently, reduced Israeli-PA security cooperation and a lax security environment have allowed Hamas and other groups to rebuild terrorist infrastructure in the Palestinian territories. In June of 2001, a Hamas operative detonated explosives outside a nightclub frequented by young Russian Jews in Tel Aviv. The attacked left the bomber and twenty-one Israelis dead and injured more than sixty. Hamas claimed responsibility for the deaths of at least twenty-three people plus one hundred wounded in January 2003, when two suicide attackers set off charges in crowded and adjacent streets during rush hour in Tel Aviv, echoing an attack in July 2001.

The Foreign Policy of Hamas

Historically, Hamas has publicly stated that it is disinterested in and does not interfere with the domestic affairs of countries: "Hamas is keen on limiting the theatre of confrontation with the Zionist occupation to Palestine, and not to transfer it to any arena outside Palestine."(Retrieved 30 April 2003, from Hamas's official website, www.palestine-info.co.uk/hamas/about/index.htm). According to its publications, covenants and official statements, Hamas upholds the importance of dialogue with all governments and world parties without regard to religion, race, or political orientation and does not seek enmity with anyone on the basis of religious convictions or race. Hamas sees its struggle with Israel as one based on the latter's illegal occupation of historic Palestine; as Israel is not a bona fide government, military action is warranted and dialogue is not an alternative. Hamas does not recognize Israel, in its present form, as a nation-state and ostensibly rejects Israel's right to exist solely because of its role as an illegal occupier and not because of its Jewish character. "The main aim of the intifada is the liberation of the West Bank, Gaza and Jerusalem, and nothing more," said Abdul Aziz Rantisi in a November 2002 interview with the BBC. "It is forbidden in our religion to give up a part of our land, so we can't recognize Israel at all. But we can accept a truce with them, and we can live side by side and refer all the issues to the coming generations."

The attacks of 11 September 2002 brought quick condemnation by Sheikh Yassin. In an interview with a Spanish newspaper, the cleric said that he adamantly opposed the bombings but added, "The Palestinians die in bombardments by US-built helicopters and planes; they are victims of the Middle East policy of the United States which blindly supports Israel. How could they [Palestinians] not be glad?" (www.terrorismanswers.com/groups/hamas_print.html, retrieved 30 April 2003) Yassin has said that the attacks on the United States were un-Islamic. And, when U.S. and British forces invaded Iraq in March 2003, Yassin and other Hamas leaders sanctioned suicide bombers against American and British interests

Hamas in the Twenty-First Century

Conventional wisdom holds that the future of Hamas depends largely on the outcome of the Israeli-Palestinian peace accords. If the PLO is able to secure peace with Israel, Hamas and its radical call for the elimination of Israel will be less attractive options for Palestinians. If, however, the negotiations break down, Hamas is perfectly poised to challenge the PLO for leadership. During the Clinton era, as peace negotiations translated into real though extremely limited autonomy on the ground, Hamas did not post significant gains in membership. As George W. Bush's administration seems determined to withdraw U.S. support for peace negotiations, Hamas has attracted a wide following: more and more Palestinians consider it to be the only option for Palestinian national aspirations, despite its Islamic character.

Hamas and its military wing Izz al-Din al-Qassim continue to conduct suicide bombings and attacks against Israel and suspected Palestinian collaborators. Their primary targets are Israeli settlers (American and Israeli Jews who live in settlement compounds in the West Bank and Gaza Strip), whom Hamas considers legitimate military targets.

Kathryn M. Coughlin

Further Reading

Abu Shanab, I. H. (1999). An Islamic approach of the resistance against Israeli occupation in Palestine: The strategy of "Hamas" in the present and in the future. In W. Freund (Ed.), *Palestinian perspectives*. New York: Peter Lang.

Alexander, Y. (2002). *Palestinian religious terrorism: Hamas and Islamic Jihad*. New York: Transnational Publishers.

Esposito, J. L. (2002). *Unholy war: Terror in the name of Islam*. New York: Oxford University Press.

Hamas Covenant. (1988). Retrieved 30 April 2003 from http://www.yale.edu/lawweb/avalon/mideast/hamas.htm

Hamas, R. A. (1993). *Hamas: Palestinian politics with an Islamic hue*. Vienna, VA: United Association for Studies and Research.

Hroub, K. (2000). *Hamas: Political thought and practice*. Washington, DC: Institute for Palestine Studies.

Karsh, E. (1996). *Between war and peace: Dilemmas of Israeli security*. Portland, OR: F. Cass Publishers.

Legrain, J. F. (1999). Hamas: Legitimate Heir of Palestinian Nationalism? In J. L. Esposito (Ed.), *Political Islam: Revolution, radicalism, or reform?* Boulder, CO: Lynne Rienner Publishers.

Litvak, M. (1996). *The Islamization of Palestinian identity: The case of Hamas*. Tel Aviv, Israel: Moshe Dayan Center for Middle Eastern and African Studies.

Mishal, S., & Sela, A. (2000). *The Palestinian Hamas: Violence, vision, and co-existence*. New York: Columbia University Press.

Muslih, M. (1999). *The foreign policy of Hamas*. New York: Council on Foreign Relations.

Nüsse, A. (1998). *Muslim Palestine: An ideology of Hamas*. Amsterdam: Harwood Academic Publishers.

Rantisi, A. (1999). Hamas towards the west. In W. Freund (Ed.), *Palestinian perspectives*. New York: Peter Lang.

Rosaler, M. (2003). *Hamas: Palestinian terrorists*. New York: Rosen Publishing.

Hellenistic Religions

Hellenistic religions—that is, the religions of eastern Mediterranean peoples from the time of Alexander the Great (356–323 BCE) to the conquest of the region by the Romans in 30 BCE—were molded by conquest and its consequences. Alexander was, culturally, a transitional figure. Raised in a polytheistic culture that worshiped the Olympian gods, Alexander's personality was shaped by the traditional religious belief that the gods were violent and emotional beings who interacted with humans and involved themselves in the destinies of individual humans or whole peoples. Alexander's mother taught her son that he was sired by Zeus, that he had the strength of Achilles, and that the Homeric attributes of valor, glory, and irrepressible conquest were essential in the life of a warrior and king. Alexander's tutor Aristotle (384–322 BCE) brought a more metaphysical approach to Alexander's religious upbringing. When Alexander invaded the Persian Empire in 333 BCE, he was a complex character with diverse ideas, combining at once a belief in his own (possible) divinity, a willingness to listen to the messages of the gods through oracles, and an awareness of the infinite possibilities that he, Alexander, could bring to the world. Alexander's belief in the nearness and immediacy of the Homeric gods and heroes fed his continual hunger for war and conquest throughout his brief life.

Influence of Greek Religions

Traditional Greek polytheism, like polytheism in Asia and Africa, held that there was a supernatural basis to natural and human phenomena. The sea often appeared angry and vengeful, which were qualities personified by Poseidon. The terrifying thunderbolt that blazed from the sky must be the greatest power in nature, and therefore must belong to the greatest among the gods. The sun was not a mass of superheated gas; it was the shining presence of Helios. Goddesses of varying sorts controlled the fertility of crops, animals, and humans. In Homer's works, gods and goddesses served as the human conscience. Rumor and sleep, human phenomena and activities, were actual spiritual beings. Human jealousy, violence, and war had divine counterparts.

Stronger even than the gods was fate, an amorphous, anonymous force that had ultimate control over gods and humans. Not even Zeus himself could change something fated. The gods served as sources of information to help humans as they confronted the determined absoluteness of their future. One of the best ways to discover one's fate was to communicate directly with a god by means of a holy shrine or oracle.

The most famous oracle was at Delphi, where the god Apollo spoke through a priestess. Zeus was known to communicate at the shrine of Dodona in northwestern Greece and at the desert shrine at Siwa in northwestern Egypt. Fate guaranteed death for all humans. In Homer's world death was anticipated with dread as the afterlife was conceived as a dismal shadowy eternity. If only humans could join the eternal happiness of the gods. A few mortals, such as Heracles, did indeed become divine. This possibility of a more happy afterlife along with the strongly held belief of the Egyptians that an afterlife of bliss was possible served by the time of Alexander to stimulate the growth of various cults centered on gods and goddesses who, it was believed, could grant the faithful eternal life.

Hellenistic Multiculturalism

Alexander's conquest of the Persian empire brought Greek culture, art, literature, political institutions, and religious beliefs to the peoples of northern Africa and Asia. Macedonian and Greek soldiers stayed behind at varied garrisons (usually referred to as cities) in Egypt, Palestine, Iraq, Iran, Afghanistan, and Pakistan, where they married local women, adopted local customs, and traded with indigenous peoples even as they spoke and wrote in Greek, listened to itinerant Greek sophists, watched Greek plays in Greek amphitheatres, and worshiped Greek deities. Inevitably, there was a sharing of culture. Alexander intended for his empire to be Greco-Persian in language, custom, culture, and institutions. Following his death, the Hellenistic kingdoms of the Macedonians (who controlled Greece and the Balkan peninsula), the Egyptian Ptolemaic dynasty (c. 323–30 BCE), and the Seleucid god-kings (reigned 312–64 BCE) of western Asia all shared in that legacy.

The three hundred years that these Hellenistic kingdoms existed before eventually succumbing to the power of Rome witnessed a dynamic, violent mix of Asian, African, and Greek cultures. Such diversity resulted in new philosophies, new centers of culture, scientific discoveries, and varied religious expressions. Alexandria in Egypt, founded by Alexander in 331 BCE, was world cultural center for centuries. At Alexandria Euclid (flourished c. 300 BCE) wrote the *Elements*, Eratosthenes (c. 276 BCE–c. 194 BCE) estimated the circumference of the earth, Ptolemy (second century CE) wrote the *Almagest*, and Zeno of Citium (c. 335–c. 263 BCE) taught Stoicism.

Stoicism

Zeno, who was inspired by the achievements of Alexander and his legacy of multiculturalism, preached the brotherhood of mankind and human equality, and captured the attention of thoughtful men and women throughout the Mediterranean world. Zeno and his disciples, such as Cleanthes, believed that the universe was ordered by a divine fire, a central principle of thought and reason, the *logos* (Greek: "word"). The *logos* was the expressive idea of truth that united a universe of change, a world of diversity of thought and action, and the varying and contradictory emotions, thoughts, and actions of individual humans. The eternal *logos* was the source of all being, which was conceived of as material rather than spiritual in substance. The Stoics, then, were materialists who believed that the divine or holy spirit had a physical nature and was present, mysteriously, in all creation, including in every human. Stoicism, a philosophy of moderation, forbearance, and peace, ironically flourished at a time of constant war: Roman against Carthaginian, Greek against Greek, and the Hellenistic kingdoms competing for dominance.

At Alexandria believers in the Greek gods, Egyptian cults, Hebrew monotheism, Asian savior-gods, and the Anatolian mother goddess came together to think, discuss, and find new answers. As the Greek city-states declined in importance and the great, impersonal empires of Rome and the Hellenistic kingdoms came to prominence, the traditional civic religions of the city-states declined in importance. A confusing, uncertain world of manifold ideas and contradictory experiences inspired people increasingly to focus their spiritual attention on personal salvation. The mystery cults were one avenue.

Mystery Cults

Thanks to the wars of Alexander and his successors, Indian Brahmans and Zoroastrian priests were exposed to Hellenic philosophies and Greek thinkers were exposed to the notions of kings who were divine, of gods who died and were resurrected, of virgin births of saviors, and of ritual castrations. Devotees of gods from India, Egypt, and Iran welcomed Greek and European initiates into the mystery of salvation. The cult of Dionysus (Bacchus) had eastern origins, as indicated by the myth of his birth and upbringing in India, and his journey across Asia to Greece, where, assisted by maenads and satyrs, he introduced his mysteries. Initiates were scourged to purify them before enjoying orgiastic union with the god. The cult of Isis, an Egyptian fertility goddess, grew in importance as Greek seekers of salvation came in contact with her priests in Egypt and elsewhere in the eastern Mediterranean. Priests robed in white sacrificed to the goddess while worshippers looked on, their hands outstretched in praise and expectation. The cult of Cybele, the Anatolian mother goddess, was very old, but like many other such fertility cults, grew in popularity during the Hellenistic Age. Priests of Cybele were typically eunuchs; initiation rites often included bathing in the blood of a sacrificed bull. The cult of Mithras, a Persian savior god who represented the ongoing fight between good and evil and who was frequently identified with the sun, appealed to the military adventurers who journeyed to Asia in the wake of Alexander. The mystery cults of Demeter, the Hellenic earth goddess, preceded the Hellenistic Age by several centuries, but flourished in the Hellenistic kingdoms. The rites of Demeter were centered as Eleusis, near Athens. The Orphic mysteries were identified with Orpheus, the hero-singer who became a savior; his worshipers sought spiritual release from time and the body, an idea that was common among Greek philosophers before and during the Hellenistic Age. The rites of Asclepius, the healer, were indigenous to the Aegean, though their initiates during the Hellenistic Age spread throughout the Mediterranean. Asclepius's shrine was at Cos, which was also identified with Hippocrates. Initiates into the rites of Asclepius appealed to the god for help and spent nights in his temple to receive healing.

The most popular mysteries had rites of initiation, such as baptism, that led to a mystical cleansing to erase sin, or a ritual meal or drink that produced a divine intoxication and the mystical merging of man with god. Each of the mystery cults featured secret rites that resulted in communion with the divine, a transcending of body, time, and evil. Candidates for initiation usually went through ritual purifications; once cleansed and prepared to meet the divine, they were introduced to the god through an orgiastic union, or through the ritual of mourning the dying god then celebrating his resurrection. The mysteries were solemn, yet often highly emotional. The assumption of a mind-body duality, that the body must be suppressed so that the mind or soul can be released, united the mystery cults with philosophies such as Neoplatonism. When the Neoplatonist Plotinus (205–270 CE) "lifted himself to the primal and transcendent God by meditation" (Dodds 1965), he experienced what all cult members hoped to achieve. Where Neoplatonism was strongly intellectual and impersonal, mystery cults featured a personal savior, often a god who had once been a man, often born of a virgin and the son of the ultimate reality or God, who would live and die then experience resurrection—the ideal man resurrected to a divine status. Aelius Aristides, a mystic and a devotee of Asclepius, experienced communion, almost friendship, with the god in dreams. At one point Aristides says, "[I] thought I touched the god and felt him near, and I was then between waking and sleeping" (Dodds 1965). The goal of the mysteries was union, or identification, with the god—to be, or to be like, the god.

For some particularly introspective believers the mystical union brought them *gnosis* (Greek: knowledge), an awareness of the divine that is inherent in all humans. Gnostics believed in the essential equality of all humans, each of whom had the opportunity to arrive at this intuitive knowledge. *Gnosis* was a cosmic, natural force rather than a personal force of redemption. The essence of humanity was the mind and the spirit, not the body and feelings. Gnostics believed, for example, that Jesus' crucifixion and death was a metaphysical rather than physical experience. The appeal of Gnosticism for seekers of spiritual joy and contentment was that at any moment one might achieve *gnosis*: time was completely irrelevant; one's life in time, struggles and concerns, movement toward the end, pain and sickness, were unimportant, transcended by spiritual union with an altogether incomprehensible spiritual force—so incomprehensible, so beyond human understanding, that no word or concept could approach it.

Religion and Conflict

Some of the religious changes that occurred during the Hellenistic period were accompanied by violence. Notions of religious purity were central to some conflicts. For example, although the Jews of the eastern Mediterranean embraced the ideas and language of the Greeks, many resisted the polytheistic Hellenistic religions, particularly that of the Seleucids, who tried to convince their subjects of the divine nature of their kings. Jewish resistance led to bloodshed on many occasions, most notably during the Maccabean War of the second century BCE, which forms the basis for Maccabees I and II. Under the leadership of Judas Maccabaeus, the Jews successfully gained independence from the Seleucid kings in 164 BCE. Until the end of the Hellenistic Age, the Jews had an independent state in Palestine, ruled by two dynasties of priests-kings, the Hasmonaean and the Idumaean.

War during the Hellenistic Age was as varied as human experience. There were wars of expansion, such as those of Alexander and Hannibal (247–183 BCE); the ethnic and religious uprising of the Jews; the organized and ostensibly defensive imperialism of the Romans; the mercenary violence of leaders such as Pyrrhus of Epirus (319–272 BCE); the give-and-take conflicts of so-called "barbaric" and "civilized" peoples. Conflict and violence were so much a part of life that war was not even discussed in the context of theories of right and wrong or justice and injustice. War was a necessity. Each warrior, people, and state fought with the blessing and help of his god. Religion, however, generally had a secondary role in warfare.

The Hellenistic Age came to an end around 30 BCE, when the Hellenistic kingdoms fell to the power of Rome. The Roman Empire imposed an orderly if financially oppressive rule over the Greek-speaking peoples of the Balkans and the Near East. At the end of the Hellenistic Age, the Essenes, the Jewish ascetic sect who produced the Dead Sea Scrolls, withdrew from hectic contemporary life, its movement of peoples and ideas, and its political and religious conflicts. Withdrawal to seek righteousness became more common among thinkers and the discontented throughout the Hellenistic East. The Jewish wait for the coming of the Messiah and people's general expectation of a coming new age, were other characteristic responses to the experience of oppression. For many, seeking *gnosis* was the route to salvation.

Russell Lawson

See also Greek Religions; Indo-European Mythology; Jewish Revolt of 66–73; Roman Religions

Further Reading

Aurelius, M. (1964). *Meditations* (M. Staniforth, Ed. and Trans.). Harmondsworth, UK: Penguin.

Dodds, E. R. (1965). *Pagan and Christian in an age of anxiety: Some aspects of religious experience from Marcus Aurelius to Constantine*. Cambridge, UK: Cambridge University Press.

Grant, M. (1982). *From Alexander to Cleopatra: The Hellenistic world*. New York: Charles Scribner's Sons.

Grant, F. C. (1962). *Roman Hellenism and the New Testament*. Edinburgh, UK: Oliver & Boyd.

Nock, A. D. (1933). *Conversion*. Oxford, UK: Oxford University Press.

Noss, J. B. (1974). *Man's religions*. New York: Macmillan.

Pagels, E. (1979). *The Gnostic Gospels*. New York: Vintage Books.

Steiner, R. (1972). *Christianity as mystical fact* (C. Davy and A. Bittleston, Trans.). London: Rudolf Steiner Press. (Original work published 1902)

Hinduism, Classical

Hinduism flourished during India's early historical period (c. 500 BCE–600 CE). Brahmans (Hindus of the highest class traditionally assigned to the priesthood) incorporated tribal deities within their own pantheons and also were greatly influenced by the practices of regional devotional cults (bhakti) that worshipped one god, such as Shiva or Vishnu, as supreme. The establishment of extensive states connected by stable trade routes in northern India, as seen in the dynasties of the Maurya (c. 300–185 BCE), Kushana (c. 1–150 CE), and Gupta (c. 300–550 CE), allowed for increased trade and the movements of people such as missionaries from the Brahmanical tradition, settlers, agriculturalists, merchants, and mercenaries who stimulated social, economic, and religious changes.

This dynamic environment supported the freer dissemination of new religious practices that openly challenged Brahmanical orthodoxy (such as, Buddhism and Jainism: both traditions were founded by noble-born princes, who rejected Brahmanical animal sacrifice, and propagated nonviolence and self-reflection as means of salvation). It also supported the importation of orthodox practices into marginalized regions through a complex process of legitimation and authority seeking. Ethnic and religious ideologies subsequently clashed while adapting to the changing cultural milieu. Throughout this period numerous religious, political, legal, artistic, and dramatic sources were produced that are still highly significant for modern Indian religious and intellectual endeavors. For this reason the whole period is referred to as "classical." One should nevertheless be critical of such designations because they say more about modern identity politics in the West and in India than about historical events. The cultural and religious developments of this period continued to affect the identities of warrior groups well into early medieval times (c. 600–1000 CE). During the fifteen hundred years so outlined, sophisticated martial ideologies developed and connected intimately with religious and political realities.

The Maurya emperors for the first time brought much of northern and central India under a single political authority. The administrative and ritual knowledge of Brahmans placed them in a leading role in Maurya society, and under the Mauryas class hierarchy *(varna)* became rigid, with the priestly *(brahman)* and warrior classes *(kshatriya)* on top. The most significant Maurya ruler, Ashoka, who reigned about 274–232 BCE, instigated new social and economic reforms while also patronizing non-Brahmanical religious traditions. The evidence suggests that Ashoka publicly supported Buddhism in order to undermine the political and social dominance of orthodox Brahmanism (Buddhism records that Ashoka's conversion was motivated by remorse over the horrors of warfare and conquest). Buddhism was an influential countermovement that protested the social and spiritual practices of Brahmans. Ashoka's interests were furthered by the fact that many from the wealthy and powerful mercantile and warrior classes supported Buddhism. He erected massive stone pillars, known as "Ashokan edicts," throughout his empire. On them were carved inscriptions that promulgated Ashoka's own ethical and religious code (dharma), which upheld notions of nonviolence (ahimsa), social ethics, and civic responsibility (the concept of dharma reflects what was considered natural, ordered, and right in society and the cosmos). The ramifications were substantial because this new moral code transcended sectarian beliefs and instigated a new order of state control over daily life and religious practices.

The *Mahabharata*

Alf Hiltebeitel, the foremost scholar of Indian epic literature, argues that in post-Maurya times Brahman authors composed India's great epic, the *Mahabharata*, within several generations (c. 150 BCE onward). Although James Fitzgerald agrees that this represents the epic's formative period, he argues that the epic took its final form during the reign of the Gupta kings (300–550 CE). The *Mahabharata* is a cautionary tale about a class of martial experts *(kshatriya)* whose members must use physical force in order to preserve society and regain control of the throne. However, the king's duty to secure the social order distances him from that very institution because he is the superior individual in society yet represents a potential threat. He is viewed as radically different from his subjects and is worshiped as an incarnation of various deities. In fact, all the main characters in the *Mahabharata* are partial incarnations of gods and demons. Fitzgerald, a renowned interpreter of Indian epic literature, suggests that one of the *Mahabharata*'s lead characters, the eldest of the five Pandava brothers and rightful heir to the throne, Yudhishthira, represents a Brahmanical reaction to Ashoka's patronage of Buddhism and his promulgation of dharma, which the composers of the great epic implicitly viewed as arrogant and hypocritical. Yudhishthira is the pious and ideal king, an incarnation of the god Dharma, who upholds Brahmanical values while being conflicted between his duty as a warrior to kill, on the one hand, and the practice of nonviolence (ahimsa) on the other. A much shorter epic, the *Ramayana*, was composed around the same time as the *Mahabharata*—in fact, an abridged version of the former epic is contained in the latter. The *Ramayana* is also directly concerned with warrior ideologies and the duty of kings. However, unlike the *Mahabharata*'s complex characters, the *Ramayana*'s main actors are archetypal in nature and strictly adhere to good and duty, as seen in the human-god Rama and his divine wife Sita, on the one hand, and evil and chaos, as exemplified by the demon lord Ravana, on the other.

The concept of *kshatriya-dharma* (an ideal code of conduct and battle ethic for warriors) plays a pivotal yet problematic role in the *Mahabharata*. Central to *kshatriya-dharma* is the concept of honor. The most important expression of honor is to fight and be killed rather than flee battle or die at home. A warrior's death in battle reflected his quality as a Kshatriya and also guaranteed him heaven (the word for India's warrior class derives from *kshatra*, meaning "dominion"). The prescriptions of honorable combat also clearly state that one should fight only with another similarly armed, one should not kill a soldier who is already in combat with another or who has fled from the combat or who is unarmed or unprepared, and one should not harm noncombatants. The rules of mace fighting further prohibit a strike below the navel. On a more sobering note, Stephanie Jamison, a distinguished historian of ancient Indian culture, has shown that Kshatriyas were legally allowed to abduct brides for marriage, although the act of rapine had to be done in a highly ritualized manner and was considered demonic *(rakshasa)*. Hiltebeitel also highlights the fact that battle was considered a ritual sacrifice and that the gore and carnage were oblations (gifts offered in worship).

Central Tension

One of the central tensions in the epic lies in the conflict between fulfilling one's duty as a warrior *(kshatriya-*

dharma) and complying with the duty of being a king *(raja-dharma)*, which states that the security and protection of the kingdom must be achieved at all costs. Moreover, in times of chaos and warfare *(apad-dharma)* the use of stratagems, treachery, and assassination is legitimate. This is one of the major dilemmas for the heroes of the epic, the Pandavas, who are at once warriors and kings. The great battle begins with just intentions and a code of fair combat. However, as the fighting progresses in intensity many unfair and unjust episodes occur that clearly contravene the prescriptions of *kshatriya-dharma*. The battlefield is the scene of numerous questionable acts, which the *Mahabharata* itself does not hesitate to call "transgressions." Nearly all are committed by the heroic Pandavas, and the guiding hand seems almost always to be that of the god Krishna. In fact, the deity clearly and succinctly expresses the divinely sanctioned justification for warfare and violence through a martial theology contained in the famous Bhagavad Gita (a Hindu devotional work), which foreshadows the outbreak of war and outlines the central doctrine of duty above all else and action for action's sake *(karma-yoga)* without suffering any soteriological (relating to theology dealing with salvation) consequences of violent deeds. Moreover, Krishna is one of the few individuals who could have stopped the war in many instances. The deity is, however, driven by his role as an incarnation *(avatara)* of Vishnu, who descends to Earth to restore order (dharma) in times of chaos. Thus, Krishna constantly reminds the Pandavas of their duty as kings and also incites both sides so that the apocalyptic war is inevitable.

The *Mahabharata* skillfully portrays what must have been fundamental ethical concerns of the elites for whom it was created. Indian kings had to fulfill *raja-dharma* and were duty bound to protect their subjects and maintain the security of the kingdom at all costs. However, the epic contains one last moral: In violating their code of conduct as warriors in order to perform their duties as kings, the Pandavas ultimately cause their own individual deaths but preserve their legacy through the continuation of their lineage and the maintenance of the kingdom. Pandava Yudhishthira even states: "In all cases, war is evil. Who that strikes is not struck in return? Victory and defeat are the same to one who is killed. Defeat is not much better than death, I think; but he whose side gains victory also surely suffers some loss." (Narasimhan 1965, 101–02)

Within the epics one begins to see the worship of individual weapons and the appearance of divine weapons *(divya-astra)* that are associated with various deities and are deployed in mythologized battle scenes. Warriors also train in military schools and practice extreme forms of asceticism (*tapas*—strict self-denial as a measure of spiritual discipline) to condition their bodies. *Tapas* conveys the notion of heat, and the epics are replete with martial metaphors and allusions to fire. Warriors are thus further associated with the notion of fiery energy *(tejas)*, which they must acquire and maintain for efficacy in battle. The close relationship between fire, warriors, their weapons, and the raw power of the gods highlights the intimate religious nature of the martial lifestyle. In the first centuries of the common era, a practical manual on statecraft, the *Artha-Shastra*, was composed. It contains detailed information and advice for the king, ranging from mundane military organization and battle plans to the use of assassins, spies, and political intrigue, all of which are put within the framework of *raja-dharma*. During the same period the religious teachings of the orthodox Brahman Manu *(Manava-Dharmashastra)* proclaim honorable warfare the eternal duty of warriors *(sanatana yodhadharma)*. Manu further declares that booty won in single combat belongs to the victorious warrior, whereas all other spoils of war belong to the king.

Gupta Dynasty

During the Gupta (300–550 CE) dynasty traditional Brahmanical values centered on sacrifice, worship, and social hierarchy increased and were disseminated. The Guptas conquered most of northern and central India and demonstrated their political dominance through the performance of the "Horse-sacrifice" *(ashvamedha)*. In expertly crafted poems and plays *(kavya)* the renowned author Kalidasa praised the exploits of warriors and kings. The *Mahabharata* and *Ramayana* reached their final forms under Gupta rule. Likewise, many of the core *Puranas* (stories of the ancient past) were composed during this period and contain mythologized martial narratives and genealogies of kings while also documenting the rise of religious cults that worshiped a single deity above all others (either Vishnu, Shiva, or the Goddess). With the spread of Hinduism throughout southern and southeastern Asia, the eminent historian Hermann Kulke demonstrates that during the Gupta and post-Gupta periods human kings were aligned with a divine king, such as Vishnu or Shiva, in accordance with sectarian affiliations. In royal temples, images and statues of the god signified his cosmic and worldly authority. The human king was considered a counterpart, if not a portion, of the god-king. The royal divinity protected his human agent and legitimized his royal mandate. Richard Davis, a well-known South Asian art historian, argues that from the sixth century onward religious icons were important trophies of war and were direct symbols of the king and his empire; thus their capture and public display were highly significant indicators of conquest. Likewise, a defeated king could present sacred images as a gesture of submission, or else temple priests destroyed or hid them during times of danger. In opposition to the standard view that Muslims were rampant iconoclasts, Cynthia Talbot, a recognized historian of medieval India, asserts that only within periods of political turmoil were Hindu temples and icons desecrated and that such acts occurred only as part of the general chaos of warfare. The destruction was for political rather than religious reasons because destroyed royal temples symbolized the conquered power of the Hindu king.

Appearing throughout India from the second century CE onward, hero-stones commemorated the violent death of a warrior, either in battle or in cattle raids, and his subsequent ascension into heaven and worship of Shiva or Vishnu. The hero-stones also documented the assimilation of tribal religions with the spread and development of Brahmanical temple worship. The process of Hinduization typically occurred through an identification of an aboriginal god or goddess with a deity from the Brahmanical pantheon. The preponderance of Hinduized deities was female. Many pastoral tribes worshiped the goddess Devi as supreme, either in her warlike form of Durga or Kali, who was popular among warrior groups, or the fertility mother form of Uma or Parvati. The decisive step in this Hinduization process was the establishment of a temple for the tribal cult. Its success was contingent on donations by wealthy benefactors and royal patronage. The major reason for the patronization of a tribal deity was the kingdom's reliance on the loyalty and military support of local tribes. Potent local deities were incorporated into the courts of influential kings, and the cults were raised to fully developed temple cults with Hinduized rituals.

Jagannatha

This process was particularly intense in southern India from the sixth century onward due to the rise of bhakti devotionalism, which possessed an inclusive theology typically focused on the worship of one god (either Vishnu, Shiva, or the Goddess). Bhakti temples were important sites where regional traditions were assimilated into Hinduism. This was especially true in the case of the male deity Jagannatha, who underwent a gradual and multifaceted process of Hinduization in the northeastern state of Orissa (c. 400–1000 CE). Originally a martial tribal god, Jagannatha was readily aligned with Vishnu through this deity's more violent Varaha (boar) and Narasimha (man-lion) incarnations. In the final stages Jagannatha was associated with Shiva, which allowed the deity to be patronized by Shiva-worshipping kings. In the same vein Shiva in his destructive form as Nataraja, "Lord of the Cosmic Dance," functioned as an emblem of the Chola dynasty in tenth-century southern India. Shiva's dance was equated with warrior qualities such as heroism and victory, and the deity was utilized to form alliances with other kings and influential temple priests. A similar process was seen with the cult of Krishna. The cowherding Krishna was a minor northern Indian pastoral deity who had close affiliations with serpent *(naga)* and spirit *(yaksha)* cults, which date back to about 100 BCE. The pastoral god was fully incorporated into the Brahmanical and overtly martial Vishnu-Krishna cult of the *Mahabharata* and Bhagavad Gita toward the close of the Gupta period.

Jarrod L. Whitaker

Further Reading

Davis, R. H. (1997). *Lives of Indian images*. Princeton, NJ: Princeton University Press.

Eschmann, A., Kulke, H., & Tripathi, G. Ch., (Eds.). (1986). *The cult of Jagannath and the regional tradition of Orissa*. Delhi, India: Manohar.

Fitzgerald, J. L. (2003). Mahabharata. In G. Thursby & S. Mittal (Eds.), *The Hindu world*. New York: Routledge.

Fitzgerald, J. L. (in press). Introduction. In J. L. Fitzgerald (Ed.), *The Mahabharata:* Vol. 7. This volume translates Book Eleven (*The Book of the Women*) and the first half of Book Twelve (*The Book of Peace*). Chicago: University of Chicago Press.

Hiltebeitel, A. (1976). *The ritual of battle: Krishna in the Mahabharata*. Ithaca, NY: Cornell University Press.

Hiltebeitel, A. (1999). *Rethinking India's oral and classical epics: Draupadi among Rajputs, Muslims, and Dalits*. Chicago: University of Chicago Press.

Hiltebeitel, A. (2001). *Rethinking the Mahabharata: A reader's guide to the education of the dharma king*. Chicago: University of Chicago Press.

Jamison, S. W. (1996). *Sacrificed wife/sacrificer's wife: Women, ritual, and hospitality in ancient India*. New York: Oxford University Press.

Kaimal, P. (1999). Shiva Nataraja: Shifting meanings of an icon. *The Art Bulletin, 81*(3), 390–419.

Kulke, H. (1978). *The Devaraja cult* (I. W. Mabbet, Trans.) (Data Paper No. 108). Ithaca, NY: Cornell University Southeast Asia Program.

Kulke, H. (1993). *Kings and cults: State formation and legitimation in India and Southeast Asia*. New Delhi, India: Manohar.

Ludden, D. (1994). History outside civilization and the mobility of South Asia. *South Asia, 17*(2), 1–23.

Narasimhan, C. V. (1965). *The Mahabharata: An English Version based on Selected Verses*. New York: Columbia University Press.

Scharfe, H. (1993). *Investigations in Kautalya's manual of political science*. Wiesbaden, Germany: Otto Harrassowitz.

Settar, S., & Sontheimer, G. D. (Eds.). (1982). *Memorial stones: A study of their origins, significance, and variety*. Hubli-Dharwar, India: Institute for Indian Art History, Karnataka University.

Thapar, R. (1984). *From lineage to state: Social formations in the mid-first millennium* BC *in the Ganga Valley*. Bombay, India: Oxford University Press.

Whitaker, J. L. (2000). Divine weapons and *tejas* in the two Indian epics. *Indo-Iranian Journal, 43*(2), 87–113.

Whitaker, J. L. (2002). How the gods kill: The *Narayana Astra* episode, the death of Ravana, and the principles of *tejas* in the Indian epics. *Journal of Indian Philosophy, 30*(4), 403–430.

Hinduism: Early Medieval Period

The division of South Asian history into periods is highly controversial. For some scholars the early medieval period begins as far back as the end of the Gupta empire, some time around 500 CE. Other scholars would argue that the early medieval period begins roughly around the same time as the invasions by Turco-Afghan dynasties in about 1200 CE. The scholarly views about the end of the period embrace a narrower span of time but also lack any clear consensus. Most, however, associate the end of the period with the end of the Delhi sultanate and the rise to power of the Mughal dynasty in the sixteenth century. Virtually all these attempts to define what is meant by the early medieval period depend chiefly on major political events and economic changes and not on religious developments.

The Bhakti Ideal of Devotion

Whether we can identify a single thing that can be called early medieval Hinduism is an open question. Some scholars have even argued that Hinduism, as a unitary and self-conscious concept, did not exist until it was invented or constructed during the nineteenth century, chiefly under the impetus of studies by British scholars. Against this view, there is ample evidence, especially in vernacular religious literature, that Hindus had elaborated a conscious self-identity as Hindus long before 1800. Hindu tradition in fact has always claimed that its roots go back to the four Vedas, most probably composed sometime between 1500 and 1000 BCE. Tangible links to the Vedic period certainly do exist in modern Hinduism, but the essence of medieval and modern Hinduism undoubtedly lies in the development of a specific ideal of religious devotion, called bhakti, and its embodiment in a large corpus of mythological texts centered on the gods Vishnu and Shiva and a great goddess or Devi.

Although the basic features of this mythology can be dated back to at least the beginning of the common era, its most important early embodiments are the Sanskrit texts known as the *Ramayana* and the *Harivamsa* and a larger set of texts known collectively as Puranas. Although the *Ramayana* and the *Harivamsa* were probably composed before the early medieval period (however defined), the Puranas were composed over a long period from about 400 to about 1500 CE and are clearly the preeminent texts of early medieval Hinduism. Among the twenty or thirty extant Puranas (the traditional number is eighteen), the most important one is certainly the *Bhagavata-purana*, although others such as the *Skanda-purana*, the *Vishnu-purana*, and the *Markandeya-purana* have also been influential.

Many early medieval texts embodying this mythology and written in vernacular languages have also survived. Many are devotional songs dedicated to one or other form of the three principal Hindu gods, their avatars (mostly of Vishnu), or their principal associates (such as Hanuman). Other texts are retellings, in vernacular languages, of the mythological stories of the *Ramayana*, the *Harivamsha* and the Puranas. Particularly among the followers of Vishnu, the stories of the avatars Rama and Krishna became immensely popular.

Much of this medieval bhakti literature is associated with particular religious sects, often known as *sampradayas* or *panths*, which became a characteristic form of religious organization in the period. Each sect generally followed a genealogy of religious leaders going back to a famous founder, who was often also an important religious poet. Whether or not individual Hindus associated themselves with specific sects and lineages of gurus, most did maintain sentimental ties with one or more temples of their favorite deities. These temples, another characteristic institution of the period, served as centers for worship and pilgrimage open to virtually all Hindus.

Battles between Gods and Demons

Much of the mythology that lies at the heart of medieval and modern Hinduism consists of stories of battles between the gods and the demons. This tradition of celestial warfare can in fact be traced all the way back to the Vedas, where the gods, or *devas*, led by Indra battle against the demons, or *asuras*. In this Vedic context, the gods and demons symbolize good versus evil and order versus chaos, but they also transparently represent the human tribes of Vedic Aryas and non-Aryas. In the much later Puranic mythology, the gods and demons still symbolize good and evil, order and chaos, but their human referents become harder to identify. Nonetheless, the repeated migrations of conquering dynasties into South Asia via the region now known as Afghanistan throughout the ancient and medieval periods undoubtedly help explain the persistent popularity of stories of celestial warfare in Hindu mythology.

The most important god of the Hindu pantheon in the period after about 1200 CE is probably Rama, the royal avatar of Vishnu. Rama was a king of north India whose loyal wife Sita was abducted by a great demon king of the island of Lanka named Ravana. The abduction set in motion a great war, which finally ended in the defeat of Ravana and his demon armies by the armies of Rama. The popularity of this story in the medieval period is reflected in the composition of several important vernacular retellings of the epic *Ramayana*, most notably those of Kampan (c. 1050 CE) in the Tamil-speaking south and of Tulsidas (c. 1543–1623 CE) in the Hindi-speaking north. Particularly in the case of Tulsidas, the historical presence of royal dynasties of Turco-Afghans, who followed Islam, quite likely influenced the composition of his text as well as its subsequent popularity, although this presence provides only one of many aspects of the text's meanings and motivations.

The moral ambiguities of more human warfare occupy a central role in Hinduism's other great epic, the *Mahabharata*, the story of the great war between the Pandavas and the Kauravas. The famous episode of the Bhagavad Gita tells how the Pandava warrior Arjuna debates with his charioteer Krishna, the avatar of Vishnu, about whether it is just for him to fight against his Kaurava cousins. Krishna convinces him that to fight is the duty of a warrior and is moral as long as the action is taken without the motive of personal gain or glory and is dedicated to God. Although the Bhagavad Gita was composed sometime before the early medieval period, it retained its popularity throughout this period and was commented on by many important Hindu theologians including Sankara (or Sankaracarya; c. 700–c. 750 CE), Ramanuja (c. 1017–1137 CE), and Madhavacarya (c. 1296–c. 1386 CE).

David N. Lorenzen

Further Reading

Doniger, W. (Ed.). (1993). *Purana perennis: Reciprocity and transformation in Hindu and Jaina texts*. Albany: State University of New York Press.

Hawley, J. S., & Wulff, D. N. (Eds.). (1996). *Devi: Goddesses of India*. Berkeley: University of California Press.

Lorenzen, D. N. (Ed.). (2003). *Religious movements in South Asia, 600–1800*. Delhi, India: Oxford University Press.

Offredi, M. (Ed.). (2000). *The banyan tree: Essays on early literature in new Indo-Aryan languages* (Vols. 1–2). New Delhi, India: Manohar.

Richman, P. (Ed.). (2001). *Questioning Ramayanas: A South Asian tradition*. Berkeley: University of California Press.

Singer, M. (Ed.). (1968). *Krishna: Myths, rites, and attitudes*. Chicago: University of Chicago Press.

Hinduism: Late Medieval Period

The relationship between Hinduism and war in the late medieval period in India (c. 1200–1765 CE) can be considered in three contexts: war glorified as the religiously legitimate and ennobling exercise of royal power, war as a theme in religious literature, and war as a manifestation of conflicts between religious groups. Attacks on religious institutions during raids and conquests constitute a fourth context somewhat dependent upon the others. To a large extent, these contexts apply also to earlier centuries, but certain features of each are distinctive of the period in question. The most distinctive features of the period were the military conquests and founding of states by Muslims from Central Asia, mainly in the north (the Delhi sultanate, 1192–1394; the Mughal empire from 1526) but in some cases also in the south (from 1394 in the states of Bahmani, Bijapur, and Golconda), and the spread of Islam in India.

The Cult of Heroes

Ever since the classical period (c. 300 BCE–600 CE), Hindu kings had invoked *kshatriya-dharma* (the code of the warrior caste) as a sacred justification for waging war and for glorifying the warrior. Since antiquity heroes *(vira)* fallen in combat had sometimes been deified and venerated; this practice was evidently common in the late medieval period. Stone plaques *(kirtistambha, virakkal)* commemorating these deified heroes still stand today, and in some cases they remain sites of worship. Folk epics and ballads recorded the exploits of heroes small and great, including Prithviraja Chahamana, who fell opposing Muhammad of Ghur (1192), whose general, a former slave, Qutb-ud-din Aybak, occupied Delhi in India and became sultan in 1206.

Princely valor received not only popular recognition but also priestly warrant. Just as the classical epics and the early *dharmashastra* (the ethical code of the Brahman caste of priests) asserted the sacred duty of the *kshatriya* (Hindu upper caste traditionally assigned to governing and military occupations) to fight, late medieval contributions to the codes of *raja-niti* (royal policy), in the form of commentaries and digests, sometimes may reflect the special concerns and political circumstances of royal patrons of the time. For instance, Chandeshvara Thakkura, minister for peace and war and successful military leader in Nepal under the king of Mithila, a vassal of the sultan of Delhi, was ordered to add to his legal compendium, the *Smriti-Ratnakara* (Jewel-Mine of Tradition), a work on royal policy, the *Raja-Niti-Ratnakara* (around 1370). The increasing subjection of Hindu rulers to Muslim overlords in northern India is perhaps reflected in the fact that Mitramishra, in his *Vira-Mitrodaya* (compiled in the early seventeenth century by order of King Virasimha of Orchha, a vassal of the Mughals, treats manliness *(paurusha)* in the chapter on councils *(mantra)*, whereas Lakshmidhara, writing in the mid-twelfth century under the patronage of an independent king, had discussed it in the context of the military campaign *(yatra)*.

God as Conquering Hero

The late medieval period also brought the spread of vernacular devotionalism (bhakti) in the Deccan region and northern India. This movement began around the seventh century with the trend toward celebrating the deity according to the conventions of classical Tamil (an Indian language c. 100 BCE–300 CE) secular love-poetry *(akam)* and heroic poetry (*puram*). The *puram* genre thus transferred to the divine king the militant attributes and feats of the conquering hero.

The early works in old Kannada, Marathi, and regional varieties of Hindi addressed devotional themes. These early works included vernacular renderings of the Sanskrit epics, in which dharma is embodied in the military victories of divine king Rama or the Pandava brothers (under the guidance of the royal avatar [the incarnation of a Hindu deity] Krishna) over the forces of evil. It has been argued that the tremendous popularity of Tulasidasa's Hindi *Rama-Charita-Manasa* (sixteenth century) can be accounted for by the fact that northern Indian Vaishnavas (devotees of Vishnu) of the time, conscious of the ascendancy of state-sponsored Islam, embraced Rama as a traditional image of God victorious and the divine guide for the state.

Violent Conflict between Religious Groups

Building on a tradition of devotion to fierce divinities, some medieval northern Indian ascetic (practicing strict self-denial as a measure of spiritual discipline) groups began to emphasize wrestling and other martial exercises as part of their the training, which reinforced their popular reputation for superhuman powers derived from yoga. By the late medieval period Shaiva (belong to the tradition of devotion to the god Shiva) lineages such as the Naga Sannyasis (naked renouncers) were organized into named *akhadas* (corps, arenas), each with its patron deity. By the second half of the seventeenth century, the Vaishnava Ramanandis, or Bairagis (dispassionate ones), had become militant as well. The traditional explanation for this militancy has been the ostensible need to defend these Hindu groups from the depredations of Sufis (Islamic mystics) and other Muslims (a claim repeated by scholar Ghurye). However, most of the conflicts in which they were involved pitted Shaiva against Vaishnava, or one *akhada* against another. Besides small clashes, which appear to have been common, major battles occurred over the question of which group should have precedence and prime location in ceremonial bathing during the periodic Kumbha Mela festival. In 1760 such a battle at Hardwar established that the Shaiva Sannyasis could bathe before the Bairagis. On the other hand, not all fighting by ascetics was sectarian in motive; these groups also served the Rajputs and other rulers as mercenaries in political conflicts.

The competition between Shaivism, Jainism, and Brahmanical orthodoxy in southern India also sometimes turned bloody. One new movement in this period, the Virashaiva (heroic Shaivas) of Karnataka, presented the ascetic, the *jangama*, in rather militant terms. Many Virashaiva stories collected in the *Basava-Purana* approvingly depict Virashaiva ascetics killing "evil" Jains and other non-Shaivas, as well as Brahmans, and destroying their temples and images. This violence reflects the fierce competition between Shaivism and Jainism at the time as well as the initial hostility of the Virashaivas toward orthodox Brahmans. The hostility and militancy were gradually tempered as the Virashaiva tradition became Brahmanized.

Religion as a Factor in Interstate Conflict

Such religious disputes were largely driven by competition for patronage, especially royal patronage; in this context, conflicts between states were likely to be represented as conflicts between the religious establishments with which the respective rulers were aligned. The greatest southern kingdom in this period, Vijayanagara (City of Victory, 1336–1565), fostered a dramatic revival of Brahmanical piety and scholarship. The fourteenth-century scholar Sayana produced commentaries on many important Vedic (relating to the Hindu sacred writings) scriptures; his brother Madhava (who took the name "Vidyaranya") wrote an encyclopedic survey of philosophical schools and a major treatise defending the possibility of attaining spiritual liberation while still living. The foundation myth of the Vijayanagara empire asserts that Madhava reconverted the founding princes from Islam and chose the site for the capital.

In fact, it is widely taken for granted that the primary religious conflict of the late medieval period was between Hindus and Muslims. The Sangama kings of Vijayanagara were often at war with Islamic sultanates of the Deccan region. However, the conflict is more accurately described as political and ethnic: political insofar as Islam was identified as a feature of certain royal courts, and ethnic insofar as the dynasties and their courtiers were perceived to be foreign in origin. Hence, they are referred to most frequently not as "Muslims" (or some equivalent religious label) but as "Turks" *(turushka, turaka)* or "Tajiks" *(tajika)* (regardless of their actual ethnic origins). Moreover, *Hindu* was likewise an ethnic term used first by the "Turks" and Europeans. "Hindus" did not yet conceive of themselves as a religious unity in any sense except in opposition to "foreign" cultures (foreign religions included). Thus, the early seventeenth-century Telugu work the *Rayavachakamu*, one of the first southern Indian historiographical (relating to the writing of history) works to demonize the Muslims, condemns them for being foreign and barbarian *(mlechchha)* and only rarely for specifically religious traits (e.g., for not venerating *deva*s (Hindu deities) and Brahmans, for killing cows, for worshipping a distinct God and the *mulla-shastra*, "teachings of the mullahs" [Muslims trained in traditional religious law]). However, the military conflicts with the Islamic states were occasioned by political and territorial considerations, especially the threat they posed to Vijayanagara, which culminated in the capture and destruction of the capital in 1565.

The most frequently cited proof of the religious dimension of "the Hindu-Muslim conflict" was the desecration and destruction of Hindu temples by conquering Muslim kings, beginning with Mahmud of Ghazni (early eleventh century). It is true that the abhorrence of idolatry was sometimes offered as a justification. But even as early as the seventh century, Hindu kings looted the temples of their neighbors; desecration of a royal temple—and the capture of the shrine image—was a potent symbol of change of regime and the abolition of the divine warrant for the defeated king. In times of peace, by contrast, even Muslim kings not only tolerated and supported Hindu religious establishments, but also on occasion contributed to their refurbishment.

Nevertheless, a sense of Hindu identity regarding Muslims, religiously as well as ethnically, gradually became more widespread as the period wore on. In 1674 the Maharashtria leader Shivaji became the last of the Hindu rulers successfully to face down the Mughals prior to the establishment of British hegemony (influence) in the subcontinent, and for this he has become the symbol of Hindu resistance.

Timothy Lubin

Further Reading

Bakker, H. (1986). *Ayodhya*. Groningen, Netherlands: Egbert Forsten.

Davis, R. H. (1997). *Lives of Indian images*. Princeton, NJ: Princeton University Press.

Eaton, R. M. (2000). Temple desecration and Indo-Muslim states. In *Essays on Islam and Indian history* (pp. 94–132). New Delhi, India: Oxford University Press.

Ghurye, G. S. (1964). *Indian sadhus* (2nd ed.). Delhi, India: Popular Prakashan.

Kulke, H. (1993). *Kings and cults: State formation and legitimation in India and southeast Asia*. Delhi, India: Manohar.

Lutgendorf, P. (1991). *The life of a text*. Berkeley and Los Angeles: University of California Press.

Pinch, W. (1996). Soldier monks and militant *sadhus*. In D. Ludden (Ed.), *Contesting the nation: Religion, community, and the politics of democracy in India* (pp. 140–162). Philadelphia: University of Pennsylvania Press.

Rao, V. N. (1990). *Siva's warriors: The Basava Purana of Palkuriki Somanatha*. Princeton, NJ: Princeton University Press.

Settar, S., & Sontheimer, G. D. (Eds.). (1982). *Memorial stones: A study of their origins, significance, and variety*. Hubli-Dharwar: Institute for Indian Art History, Karnataka University.

Talbot, C. (1995). Inscribing the other, inscribing the self: Hindu-Muslim identities in pre-colonial India. *Comparative Studies in Society and History, 37*(4), 692–722.

Vaudeville, C. (1996). *Myths, saints and legends in medieval India*. Delhi, India: Oxford University Press.

Wagoner, P. B. (1993). *Tidings of the king: A translation and ethnohistorical analysis of the Rayavacakamu*. Honolulu: University of Hawaii Press.

Hinduism, Modern

Hinduism in modern times has undergone tremendous reformist changes and has tended to focus on peace rather than war. Though there has not been any scriptural development in Hinduism in relation to war, one stream of Hinduism espousing a theory similar to just war developed into the separate religion of Sikhism. Ancient doctrines of war and conflict continue to be important, but they are overshadowed by Hinduism's greater focus on peace.

In modern times, India was under British imperialism from 1757 to 1947. As part of this interaction, Hinduism was invoked on certain occasions of conflict. Hindu religious leaders focused on reform, and British imperialism hastened that process. Hindu theologians and leaders were concerned with combating Christian missionary propaganda, one element of imperialism, on theological grounds. This was done by engaging in debates with the missionaries and at the same time by bringing in reforms to the different institutions of Hinduism. These reforms started in Bengal province, where Ram Mohun Roy (1772–1833) initiated the Brahmo Samaj movement.

However, religious motivation was an important factor in the eruption of the civil rebellion of 1857 against the British. The rabid missionary criticism of Hindu religion was often extreme and people were sure that the British wanted to defile the religion and caste of the local population. The 1857 uprising started as a mutiny in Bengal province over the issue of the greased cartridges of the newly introduced Enfield rifles. The soldiers had to bite off the covering of the cartridge to use it. It was a widespread belief that this cartridge wrapper was made from materials that included the fat of cows and pigs. This was defiling for the Hindus in the army. This mutiny developed into a civil rebellion against British imperialism in which Hindus and Muslims fought side by side and also proclaimed the Mughal emperor as their leader. Modern historians see this event not as a religious war, but as the first war of independence.

Meanwhile, reform measures among Hindu believers addressed improving the status of women and bringing about equality in society by reforming the caste system. The two most influential reformers of the late nineteenth century were Dayananda Sarasvati (1824–1883) and Vivekananda (1863–1902). They were also influential as sources of inspiration to the freedom fighters opposing British colonialism.

At the political level religion came to be used as a rallying point as exemplified by B. G. Tilak's (1856–1920) use of the Ganapati festival, beginning in 1893, to propagate nationalist ideas. In such festivals, patriotic songs and speeches were incorporated that tended to radicalize the people. Another aspect was the use of religion by some of the revolutionary organizations, including swearing oaths by religion in pursuing revolutionary objectives against the imperial regime. By the 1920s, revolutionary organizations were influenced more by leftist ideology than by religion. But popular vernacular literature would use Hindu imagery to invoke patriotic sentiments against imperial rule; for example, India was depicted as a divine mother, Bharat Mata, that had been enslaved.

As imperialism developed, the imperial masters created a division between Hindus and Muslims. This on various occasions led to sectarian violence on religious grounds. The response of Hinduism to such developments was that of Gandhian nonviolence. Mohandas Karamchand Gandhi (1869–1948) was a political leader and social reformer with deep roots in the Hindu religious traditions. He brought to the fore the concept of ahimsa (nonviolence) as the theoretical and doctrinal dimension of his struggle against British imperialism and as a means of bringing about harmony between different sections of the population. The tradition of ahimsa has roots in the ancient scriptures of Hinduism. For Gandhi nonviolence was soul-force and was the positive kind of love. This meant that one should try to remove the evil, but not hate the evildoer. His concept of ahimsa was concomitant with his other formulations like that of satyagraha (meaning sticking to the truth or truth-force) even in situations of great adversity.

These concepts were useful in the struggle against imperialism as they helped to mobilize large numbers of unarmed people without any fear of the weapons of the state. Though Gandhi would draw inspiration from Hindu traditions, his nonviolence was not sectarian. In the latter part of his life, he also extended his nonviolence to the extent of being a pacifist who opposed all war. This also meant that he was for disarmament and against the atom bomb. As he said in his journal on 29 September 1946, the atom bomb symbolized "the most diabolical use of science." A related aspect of his thought was tolerance and equality between different religions; for him different religions were equally sacred. This doctrine of equality of religions was very useful in a culturally diverse and plural society like India in welding people to nationhood. Thus Gandhian ideas have great philosophical relevance for modern Hinduism.

Another aspect of Hinduism is a right-wing political movement, which has existed since British times. At the doctrinal level, this movement derives its roots from the writings of the revolutionary V. D. Savarkar (1883–1966). The movement sees India as a Hindu nation and aims to take it to glorious heights. In current times, it has developed into the Hindutva movement. This strand on different occasions has taken violent positions vis-à-vis other religions on issues like temple construction, killing of cows, and religious conversions. It is a form of cultural nationalism and considers that Hinduism should be assigned its prime position in its own land.

Two other aspects of modern Hinduism relate to social violence. These relate to the position of women in society and the ills of the caste system. Reformative Hinduism has led to considerable improvement in the position of women, and awareness and legal provisions have accomplished the eradication of the ills of the caste system.

The general tenor of modern Hinduism remains that of nonviolence combined with a pluralistic outlook and is influenced by liberal traditions of Vedanta (a branch of orthodox Hindu philosophy) and the Upanishads (Hindu philosophical writings). Outside India, the manifestation of Hinduism is generally not concerned with issues of war and violence, but is more concerned with bhakti (devotion) and its philosophical dimensions.

Anup Mukherjee

Further Reading

Andersen, W. K., & Damle, S. D. (1999). *The Brotherhood in Saffron*. New Delhi, India: Vistaar Publications.

Chandra, B. (1989). *India's struggle for independence*. New Delhi: Penguin India.

Desai, A. R. (1976). *Social background of Indian nationalism*. Bombay, India: Popular Prakashan.

Fischer, L. (1992). *The life of Mahatma Gandhi*. New Delhi, India: Indus. (Original work published 1951)

Gandhi, M. (1999). *Collected works* (CD-ROM). New Delhi: Publications Division, Government of India.

Savarkar, V. D. (1969). *Hindutva: Who is Hindu*? Bombay, India: Veer Savarkar Prakashan.

Trial of Tilak. (1986). New Delhi: Publications Division, Government of India.

Vivekananda. (1983). *Lectures from Colombo to Almora*. Calcutta, India: Advaita Ashram.

Hinduism: Vedic Period

A martial mind-set has played a fundamental role in the development of Vedic (relating to the Hindu sacred writings) religious beliefs and practices. Pastoralist tribes calling themselves "Arya" and speaking an archaic form of the Indo-European language Sanskrit arrived from central Asia and settled in the fertile Punjab of India around 1700–1500 BCE. The term *Arya* expresses a cultural (rather than racial) designation for groups of people who maintained distinct socio-religious beliefs and practices. The Arya referred in their earliest texts to other peoples *(dasa, dasyu, pani)*, whom they apparently came to dominate while adopting certain aspects of their cultures. (The older "invasion" theory is nowadays thought to overstate the violence or suddenness of Aryan expansion in southern Asia.) Vedic life oscillated between times of movement (yoga, harnessing)—for waging war, staging cattle raids, and shifting to new pasturage—and times of settlement *(kshema)*. Thomas Oberlies, an eminent scholar of ancient India, has recently suggested that individual people were invested with the leadership of the tribe in times of peace and warfare, even though the two functions are ascribed to a single individual. Over time the Aryans began to rely more heavily on agricultural practices, which were most likely adopted from the indigenous population.

By 1000–800 BCE Aryan social and ritual customs were codified in a corpus of four oral texts known as the "Vedas." The period is thus named for the culture attested in these four texts and in the ancillary ritual literature related to them. Scholars usually refer to the religious tradition attested in this period as "Brahmanism," after the dominant class of priests, the Brahmans, as opposed to Hinduism, which flourished around the beginning of the common era. The oldest text, the Rig-Veda (c. 1500–1200 BCE), attests a martial society and volatile political environment. Waves of migration were marked by warfare and shifting alliances, and tribes constantly struggled with each other and the indigenous people. Warriors *(kshatriya, shura, vira)* were skilled in horse and chariot combat, which the Aryans introduced into the subcontinent. By 1000 BCE iron weapons and implements were indigenously produced. Bands of aggressive young males *(vratya)* created further tension, and individual tribes had to take responsibility for them. Conquest and martial prestige are dominant motifs in the ritual hymns of the Vedas, and seasonal skirmishes and open warfare were central to Aryan ideology and life.

The earliest historical layers of the Rig-Veda verify the existence of five major tribes *(panca jana)* formed into subordinate clans *(vish)*. Chieftains *(rajan, rajanya)* ruled over the people and controlled large political units, crafts, and commerce and collected taxes. Most of the attested battles were over territorial or succession disputes between factional clans within the same tribe *(jana)*. Vedic society was dominated by two lineages of "royal" families (Puru and Bharata) and the lesser lineages of *vish* (a term equally applied to Aryan and non-Aryan people). Romila Thapar, the foremost historian of ancient India, argues that Vedic society became more focused on agricultural endeavors, but cattle rearing and cattle raiding remained significant, and over time the cattle-raiding warlords transformed into the territory-controlling Kshatriyas—indicating a new focus in power.

The post–Rig-Vedic evidence suggests that an alliance of two tribes, Kuru-Pancala, rose to dominance after conquering its enemies in a battle of ten kings. Michael Witzel, a prominent scholar of Vedic culture, demonstrates that the Kuru-Pancala alliance constituted the first large polity or state, which was divided into sixteen kingdoms. The kingdoms expanded their dominance eastward and established a new homeland *(kurukshetra)* in the fertile Ganges River plain. The realm of the Kuru-Pancalas became the center of Brahmanical (relating to the highest class traditionally assigned to the priesthood) orthopraxy (a term encompassing not only doctrine, but also the practice of elaborate rituals). Non-Aryan rulers from eastern territories legitimized themselves within Aryan hegemony (influence) by inviting priests to perform solemn rites *(shrauta)* and by adopting Aryan socio-religious practices and the Indo-Aryan language. The term *Aryan* came to designate an elite social status, and new solemn ritual traditions provided a means of upward social mobility for patrons *(yajamana)* and priests *(brahman, brahmana)*. Under Kuru dominance society was increasingly stratified, as seen in the unification of fifty or more smaller tribes, the systematization of priestly roles through specialized ritual functions, and the establishment of the traditional class system *(varna)* with elite Brahmans and Kshatriyas at the top.

Ritual Hymns

The ritual hymns of the Rig-Veda proclaim the ideal Aryan life, which revolved around breeding livestock and maintaining tracts of land in which to graze livestock. Other goals included material wealth, especially the preservation of fire *(agni)*, physical and mental health, a long life, and the continuation of individual lineages through male progeny. These are all seen as ordered, natural, divine, and in harmony with daily and seasonal changes *(rita)*, as opposed to everything unnatural, aberrant, or evil, such as darkness, lack of freedom, constricted movement, drought, poverty, disease, impotence, and death. The hymns to various gods

Selection from the *Bhagavad Gita* on War and Warriors

Considering also your duty as a warrior you should not waver. Because there is nothing more auspicious for a warrior than a righteous war. (2.31)

Only the fortunate warriors, O Arjuna, get such an opportunity for an unsought war that is like an open door to heaven. (2.32)

If you will not fight this righteous war, then you will fail in your duty, lose your reputation, and incur sin. (2.33)

People will talk about your disgrace forever. To the honored, dishonor is worse than death. (2.34)

The great warriors will think that you have retreated from the battle out of fear. Those who have greatly esteemed you will lose respect for you. (2.35)

Your enemies will speak many unmentionable words and scorn your ability. What could be more painful than this? (2.36)

You will go to heaven if killed, or you will enjoy the earth if victorious. Therefore, get up with a determination to fight, O Arjuna. (2.37)

Treating pleasure and pain, gain and loss, victory and defeat alike, engage yourself in your duty. By doing your duty this way you will not incur sin. (2.38)

The wisdom of Saamkhya (or the knowledge of the Self) has been imparted to you, O Arjuna. Now listen to the wisdom of Karma-yoga endowed with which you will free yourself from the bondage of Karma. (2.39)

In Karma-yoga no effort is ever lost, and there is no harm. Even a little practice of this discipline protects one from great fear (of birth and death). (2.40)

***Source:* EAWC Anthology: *The Bhagavad Gita*. Ramanand Prasad, Trans. Retrieved April 8, 2003, from http://eawc.evansville.edu/anthology/gita.htm**

highlight these goals and anxieties and also illuminate an Aryan martial ideology.

Central to this ideology are the continued exploits of the Aryan war god Indra, who set the model for human actions. Indra is not only the creator and sustainer of the universe, but also he annually slays the mythic serpent Vritra in order to release the monsoon rains. With his band of martial storm gods, the Maruts, Indra defeats both Aryan and non-Aryan enemies for his sacrificial patron and also undertakes cattle raids or rescues stolen livestock. He is glorified as the destroyer of forts and armies and grants the spoils of war to his worshipers. His primary weapon is a multipronged mace *(vajra)*, which can be wielded in melee combat or thrown. He further represents the ideal warrior in battle, embodying all the desirable characteristics of strength, power, speed, dexterity, virility, endurance, and mental resolve. A sacred juice (soma) pressed from a plant (probably a variety of ephedra) is said to have strengthened Indra's mettle before battle, and in turn Indra jealously monopolized the divine juice. The stimulant properties of soma may have been important for priests in order to sustain long ritual sessions as well as providing the extra physical and mental charge needed by warriors. Ritualized offerings of soma to Indra are the highest rites of the Brahmanical religion in the Vedic period. Within this ritual setting, Indra was intimately connected with the human patron of the sacrifice *(yajamana)*, who most often was a wealthy warlord or king.

Three other major gods—Mitra, Varuna, and Aryaman (collectively called the "Adityas")—upheld the principles of justice and punishment. Joel Brereton, a well-known historian of the Vedic period, says their respective cosmic functions represented Aryan social ideals of adherence to alliances, to commandments and authority, and to tradition. The gods not only governed these spheres of influence but also punished any transgressions. They were thus intimately involved in Aryan social interactions such as the family, community, trade, contracts, and castigation. Beyond this, they also embodied the ideals of Aryan kings and warriors. Like the human king, the Adityas and Indra protected Aryan society and maintained the natural order *(rita)*. As their human counterpart, the king imitated and enforced the gods' cosmic functions in human society, and various royal rituals consecrated the king with this duty. The ritual hymns to kings and warriors glorify, herald, and envisage victory and supremacy in battle and in the acquisition and maintenance of royal status *(rashtra)* and dominion *(kshatra)*. The legitimization of an elite status is possible only through participation in rituals, such as the "Drink of Strength" *(vajapeya)*, "Instigation of the King" *(rajasuya)*, and "Horse Sacrifice" *(ashvamedha)*, all of which are laden with martial metaphors and allusions. In a similar vein, the parallel ritual tradition of the Atharva-Veda includes rites for healing battle wounds and fever and for making protective amulets and talismanic armor.

Warrior Sacrifice

Jan Heesterman, a renowned interpreter of Vedic culture, has proposed a controversial theory that states that a controlled and safe ritual replaced an original (and hypothetical) warrior sacrifice that was the arena of conflict and alliance where honor and status were contended and where a consecrated warrior patron *(dikshita)* bestowed gifts on guests and took stock of his raids. The central problem was the resolution of killing and violence. Thus, the sacrifice was at once the place of generosity and munificence and death and destruction. It may have originally been a battleground where fire, food, and cattle were fought over. It was only through the intervention of specialized priests, who ordered and controlled the ritual, that the tension between patron and guests was pacified. Priestly involvement further allowed for any reciprocal exchange to be peacefully mediated. The priests thus created a harmless ritual from a once-ambivalent and violent warrior sacrifice (although the two roles of warrior and priest were originally not mutually exclusive).

By 600–400 BCE large kingdoms existed in northern India, and warfare played a substantial role in the political economy and in the nature of religious institutions and thought. Newly developed cities were administrative, commercial, and military centers of power. Within the competitive urban setting Brahmans and Kshatriyas cooperated with each other while also competing for power and prestige. By this period the Ashvamedha (Horse Sacrifice) was a dominant symbol and manifestation of royal power and also ritually stated the royal intention for warfare and conquest. Patrick Olivelle, the foremost cultural historian of ancient India, has demonstrated that within this cultural setting the notion of dharma as social duty and sacred law took its initial shape, especially as seen in the Upanishads and Dharmasutras, and was further codified in the notion of *kshatriya-dharma* or a specific code of conduct for warriors. By 100–200 CE the religious teachings of Manu (*Manava-Dharmashastra*) proclaim honorable warfare the eternal duty of warriors *(sanatana yodhadharma)*.

By the third century BCE a network of trade routes connected all of northern India, which acted as a connection point between eastern Mediterranean cultures under Roman rule and northwestern Chinese culture. A dominant political power, known as the Mauryan empire (c. 300–185 BCE), unified northern India under a centralized rule and spread urbanism and technology (e.g., iron, pottery) to remote areas. The Mauryans patronized Brahmans as well as new religious groups, such as adherents of Buddhism, which was founded about 400 BCE by a member of the warrior class, Prince Siddhartha Gautama, who rejected traditional Brahmanical values, such as sacrifice and strict social hierarchy, and promulgated a new ethical code based on nonviolence (ahimsa) and inward reflection. This period also brought a steady increase in foreign invasions from Bactrian-Greeks, Huns, and Persians, who brought with them new religious ideas and technologies. At the same time throughout India people increasingly worshiped individual deities (Vishnu, Shiva, Krishna, and the Goddess), and these new theologies were subsequently incorporated into or rejected by the Vedic religion and more specifically martial ideologies and warrior identities.

Jarrod L. Whitaker

Further Reading

Allchin, F. R. (1995). *The archaeology of early historic South Asia: The emergence of cities and states*. New York: Cambridge University Press.

Brereton. J. P. (1981). *The Rgvedic Adityas* (Vol. 63). New Haven, CT: American Oriental Society.

Erdosy, G. (Ed.). (1995). *The Indo-Aryans of ancient South Asia: Language, material culture and ethnicity*. Berlin, Germany: Walter de Gruyter.

Heesterman, J. C. (1985). *The inner conflict of tradition*. Chicago: University of Chicago Press.

Heesterman, J. C. (1993). *Broken world of sacrifice*. Chicago: University of Chicago Press.

Jamison, S. W. (1996). *Sacrificed wife/sacrificer's wife: Women, ritual, and hospitality in ancient India*. New York: Oxford University Press.

Liu, X. (1988). *Ancient India and ancient China: Trade and religious exchanges AD 1–600*. Delhi, India: Oxford University Press.

Olivelle, P. (1996). *The Upanisads*. Oxford, UK: Oxford University Press.

Olivelle, P. (1999). *Dharmasutras: The law codes of ancient India*. New York: Oxford University Press.

Olivelle, P. (in press). *The law code of Manu*. Oxford, UK: Oxford University Press.

Olivelle, P. (in press). Power of words: The ascetic appropriation and the semantic evolution of *dharma*. In P. Fluegel & G. Houtman (Eds.), *Asceticism and power in the Asian context*. London: Curzon.

Thapar, R. (1984). *From lineage to state: Social formations in the mid-first millennium BC in the Ganga Valley*. Bombay, India: Oxford University Press.

Witzel, M. (1997). The development of the Vedic canon and its schools: The social and political milieu. In M. Witzel (Ed.), *Inside the texts, beyond the texts: New approaches to the study of the Vedas* (Harvard Oriental Series Vol. 2) (pp. 257–345). Cambridge, MA: Harvard University:

Witzel, M. (1997). Early Sanskritization: Origins and development of the Kuru state. In B. Kolver (Ed.), *The state, the law, and administration in classical India* (pp. 27–52). Munich, Germany: R. Oldenbourg Verlag.

Hindu-Muslim Violence in India

Violence between Hindus and Muslims in India, often called "communal riots," has occurred sporadically for over a century. Hindus are the majority religious group in India at 81.3 percent of the population, and Muslims make up the largest minority at 12 percent of over a billion people. Most urban neighborhoods and rural villages include members of both groups, and there are Muslim majority communities in various parts of the country. As India is so heterogeneous, generalizations about the violence over the course of a century can be misleading. However, a study by the political scientist Ashutosh Varshney has recently demonstrated that Hindu-Muslim violence that occurred between 1950 and 1995 was concentrated in a limited number of areas. Whether this was true of earlier decades has not been studied, but it is known that Hindus and Muslims had lived together on the subcontinent for centuries before riots between the communities were recorded. While religious persecution and territorial warfare between adherents of the two faiths had occurred in precolonial India, the hostilities had been expressed more formally through political or military means, rather than social violence.

While many see the periodic outbursts of violence between the two groups as expressions of intrinsic hostilities between the communities or the incompatibilities of their religions, recent scholarship has emphasized the political and social causes for violent confrontations between the two, including both lack of integration in civic institutions and deliberate incitement by extremist groups on both sides to further political ends. They also cite the widespread poverty and lack of education as factors in social unrest in general. Although actual figures are highly contested, the death and destruction that results from the outbursts of violence is massive, and often one event will lead to reprisals in a bloody cycle.

Under the British Raj

Hindu-Muslim violence became a problem in the late nineteenth century, when India was part of the British Empire. Many date the Government of India Act of 1909 (also known as the Morley-Minto Reforms) as a watershed, as it made religious identity a political as well as social marker. The Reforms set up legislative councils that would include elected representatives, giving Indians their first opportunity to represent themselves, but they also introduced the principle of "communal representation," meaning that Hindus and Muslims voted in separate elections for parties representing them. The goal was to allay Muslim concerns about being overwhelmed by a Hindu majority in elections by providing them with separate electorates and weighting the proportion of representatives on the councils. For example, a province which had a population that was 20 percent Muslim and 80 percent Hindu and 100 seats in the Provincial Assembly would have separate elections for each confessional community and then distribute the seats in the assembly according

Call for a Separate Homeland for Muslims in South Asia

At the March 1940 meeting of the Muslim League in Lahore, League leader Mohammad Ali Jinnah called for a separate homeland for Muslims. Such a homeland was established in Pakistan but it did not end conflict among Hindus and Muslims in India nor in South Asia in general.

As far as our internal position is concerned we have also been examining it and, you know, there are several schemes which have been sent by various well-informed constitutionalists and others who take interest in the problem of India's future constitution, and we have also appointed a sub-committee to examine the details of the schemes that have come in so far. But one thing is quite clear. It has always been taken for granted mistakenly that the Mussulmans are a Minority and of course we have got used to it for such a long time that these settled notions sometimes are very difficult to remove. The Mussulmans are not a Minority. The Mussulmans are a nation by any definition. The British and particularly the Congress proceed on the basis, "Well, you are a Minority after all, what do you want?" "What else do the Minorities want?" Just as Baba Rajendra Prasad said. But surely the Mussulmans are not a Minority. We find that even according to the British map of India we occupy large parts of this country, where the Mussulmans are in a majority—such as Benga, the Punjab, North-West Frontier Province, Sind and Baluchistan.

Source: Jagdish Saran Sharma. (1965) *India's Struggle for Freedom: Select Documents and Sources.* Vol. 2. Delhi, India: S. Chand & Co., pp. 521–522.

to a 20–80 proportion; 20 seats in the assembly would be distributed among the winners of the Muslim elections and 80 seats would be distributed among the winners of the Hindu elections. Therefore, a party such as the Congress would run two separate campaigns in two distinct electorates. Were they to carry 50 percent of the votes in the Hindu elections and 25 percent of the Muslim electorate vote, they would get 45 seats in the assembly, i.e. 5 seats from those reserved for Muslims (25 percent of 20 seats) and 40 from the Hindu electorate, or half of the 80 seats. Because of the introduction of elections, the Indian National Congress (INC), originally founded in 1885, became a political party. Although it always claimed to be secular and national in the broadest sense, it included few Muslims at the top and was seen by many as being primarily Hindu in interests and orientation. Thus, the Muslim League was established in 1906 to protect and advance Muslims' political rights. Hindu nationalist groups such as the Arya Samaj (founded 1875) also gained popularity at this time; they felt that Hindu culture and religion (Hindutva) were central to Indian identity while the INC did not. Many nationalists accuse the British of codifying religious identity in order to maintain their control of India using a divide-and-conquer policy. Whether by design or not, communal identity was the defining marker of social and political identity in India in the twentieth century.

The Interwar Era

The decades between the two world wars eventually divided Hindus from many Muslims in their attitudes towards independence from Britain. There was a period of cooperation towards the end of World War I, when the INC and the Muslim League joined forces in 1916 (the Lucknow Pact) to demand self-government from Britain. A few years later, Mohandas Karamchand Gandhi (1869–1948) led a coalition of resistance movements under the slogans of Khilafat and Non-Cooperation. Khilafat referred to an Indian Muslim movement to preserve the strength of the defeated Ottoman Sultan in light of his simultaneous role as Caliph, or spiritual head, of Sunni Muslims. While the support of Gandhi for this admittedly Muslim concern helped create the coalition, it also alienated many Hindus that felt that the Ottoman Empire's recent defeat by the Allies Powers was not really India's concern. Furthermore, tensions regarding the issues of separate electorates and the definition of a "true" Indian identity led to increasingly fiery rhetoric and violent confrontations. More Hindu nationalist groups were founded, such as the Hindu Mahasabha (1915) and the Rashtriya Swayamsevak Sangh (RSS; 1925). Meanwhile, Muslims became increasingly alienated from the Hindu religious imagery used in nationalist discourse and feared loss of their social and political position, if not of their religion itself, in an overwhelmingly Hindu India. By 1930, a significant number of Muslims supported the "two nations" theory that claimed that India contained two separate nations, Muslim and Hindu, with different religions, histories, and cultures. In 1940, led by Mohammad Ali Jinnah (1876–1947), the Muslim League demanded the creation of an independent state in Muslim majority areas of British India (present-day Pakistan and Bangladesh, the latter being part of Pakistan until independence in 1971).

Partition

By the end of World War II, it had become clear that Britain would be granting India independence; and the issue of Pakistan was the paramount trigger for mass violence throughout India. The Muslim League won enough votes in national elections for an interim government to defend its claim of being the representative of Indian Muslims, even though there were Muslims such as Abul Kalam Azad (1888–1958) who were active in the INC as well. When the INC and the Muslim League refused to compromise on the issues of defining the character of the future State of India, both sides agreed to divide the country under the aegis of the new British viceroy, Lord Mountbatten (1900–1979). The British House of Commons passed the India Independence Act on 14 July 1947, partitioning the subcontinent into two states, with the contiguous Muslim majority areas (on either side of the subcontinent, with India between them) going to Pakistan. The five hundred "princely states," which technically did not belong to Britain, were free to choose to join either state, setting the stage for the Kashmir conflict when the Hindu prince of that Muslim majority province chose to join India. Independence was formally declared for Pakistan on 14 August 1947 and India on 15 August 1947.

But the scale of the violence that accompanied Partition was unforeseen. Hundreds of thousands of Hindus left the area allotted to Pakistan in fear for their lives and livelihoods, while a similar number of Muslims fled to Pakistan in similar panic. Families, communities, and even neighborhoods found themselves on opposite sides of an international border. Partition resulted in the largest transfer of population in recorded history, with an estimated 14 million people leaving their homes. Along with the mass migration, however, came the killings; mobs would attack members of the other community. It is estimated that 1.5 million people were killed in the chaos. The worst violence occurred in the provinces of Punjab and Bengal, which were divided between the new states. The leaders who had negotiated the partition had not expected the migrations or killings.

Independent India

India's constitution declared the nation to be a secular democratic republic and acknowledged and pledged to protect cultural, linguistic, and ethnic minorities. For many Indian citizens, this did not resolve issues such as the distribution of political power and resources, not to mention the ongoing debate over what comprised Indian identity. Hindu nationalists also continued to repudiate Partition as, in Gandhi's words, "a vivisection" of the Motherland; they blamed the new prime minister, Jawaharlal Nehru (1889–1964) for agreeing to Partition and felt the state's commitment to secularism was a betrayal of Indian heritage and identity. Gandhi himself was killed by a Hindu nationalist who believed that Gandhi had gone too far to appease the Muslims. The country still had millions of Muslim citizens. (Very few non-Muslims remained in Pakistan; most that did were in East Pakistan, the future Bangladesh.) Furthermore, each community blamed the other for the atrocities of Partition, and violence between the two groups has continued to flare up since 1947.

Violence tends to occur around elections and around symbols of identity, such as places of worship, or around incidents such as the killing of cows, which are sacred to Hindus. Those representing Hindu nationalist groups resent what they see as a special status accorded Muslims and other minorities. These groups also feel aggrieved over religious repression under the Muslims that ruled various parts of India for three centuries before the British. In addition, they believe present-day Muslims hold allegiances outside the subcontinent and most potently with Pakistan. Since there have been three wars between Pakistan and India, two over Kashmir, the argument that Muslims represent a fifth column (a group of people who act subversively out of a secret sympathy with the enemy of their country) in the country is a frightening one to them. Muslims, on the other hand, claim to be victims of discrimination and resent the implication that they are not true Indians. Some also fear that they will be forced to give up their religious beliefs.

An example of the issues that spark Hindu-Muslim tensions is the Shah Bano case of 1985, which pitted religious rights against civil law. Shah Bano had appealed to the Indian Supreme Court for alimony, which was her right according to secular Indian law, after the Islamic court that had granted her divorce ruled that she was not entitled to alimony under *shariʿa* (Islamic law). In response to pressure by Muslim groups that felt Islamic courts had been slighted, Parliament passed a law that allowed Muslim divorce cases to be removed from the jurisdiction of civil courts in favor of independent Islamic ones. This, however, created resentment on the part of many Hindus, whose civil affairs were subject only to the secular court system, which also does not allow for Hindu customs.

The Babri Masjid Incident

The most important flashpoint for Hindu-Muslim violence in the present, however, is the issue of the Babri Masjid (a mosque) in the city of Ayodhya in northern India, which a Muslim conqueror had been built on the site of an earlier temple that many Hindus believed was the birthplace of the Hindu god Ram. In 1986 the Vishwa Hindu Parishad (VHP), a Hindutva nationalist group, won a court ruling allowing Hindu worshippers to enter the mosque to pray to Rama, which Muslims felt was a violation of their holy space. The VHP was joined by other groups in a campaign to destroy the mosque, to them a symbol of oppression by Muslims, and rebuild the Ram temple. After years of increasingly violent protests by both communities, the mosque was destroyed by a Hindu mob on 6 December 1992.

The riots that followed spread throughout India, killing an estimated 2,200 people, 500 in Bombay (Mumbai) alone. The following March (1993), the Bombay Stock Exchange and other city landmarks were bombed, killing 200. An investigative tribunal found that the destruction of the mosque was deliberate and planned by a coalition of groups including the VHP, the Bajrang Dal, and the RSS. Muslim anger was also directed towards the government for not having stopped the mob action: The minister of the province was a member of the Bharatiya Janata Party (BJP), which had close alliances with Hindutva groups and had previously expressed support for the campaign to rebuilt the Ram temple.

Tensions increased over the following years as the BJP gained popularity on a platform that included a hard-line approach to dealing with Pakistan and abolishment of quotas and other legal instruments designed for Muslims. The party has won many provincial and national elections since 1992 and for a time ran the government. Human Rights Watch and other international nongovernmental organizations blame the BJP's use of Hindutva rhetoric for the rise in violence in the past two decades, while Hindutva groups blame Muslim intransigence and the enmity of "secularists" to the Hindu religion and identity.

In the New Millennium

Lowering Hindu-Muslim tensions remains one of India's main internal challenges in the twenty-first century. These efforts are complicated by the ongoing rivalry with Pakistan, the unresolved issue of Kashmir, and the polarization of politics that has accompanied the successes of the BJP and the groups that support it. The state has been ineffective in preventing violence, thus weakening it in the eyes of citizens of both communities. For example, an attack by Muslims on a train carrying Hindu worshippers in February 2002 sparked two months of rioting in the Indian state of Gujarat and claimed over a thousand lives. In September, gunmen attacked a Hindu temple in an admitted reprisal killing. Violence in Kashmir between separatists supported by Pakistan, the Indian Army, and a number of local groups continues. Numerous associations have been organized in India to promote intercommunal understanding, but their success is still quite limited.

Noor-Aiman I. Khan

See also Kashmir

Further Reading

Brass, P. (1997). *Text and context in the representation of collective violence*. Princeton, NJ: Princeton University Press.

Das, S. (1991). *Communal riots in Bengal, 1905–1947*. Delhi, India: Oxford University Press.

Das, V. (1992). *Mirrors of violence: Communities, riots and survivors in South Asia*. Delhi, India: Oxford University Press.

Engineer, A. A. (Ed.). (1984). *Communal riots in post-independence India*. New Delhi, India: Sangam Books.

Frietag, S. B. (1989). *Collective action and community: Public arenas and the emergence of communalism in north India*. Berkeley and Los Angeles: University of California Press.

Gopal, S. (Ed.). (1993). *Anatomy of a confrontation: The rise of communal politics in India*. London: Zed Books.

Hansen, T. B. (1999). *The Saffron Wave*. Princeton, NJ: Princeton University Press.

Hasan, M. (Ed.). (2000). *Inventing boundaries: Gender, politics and the partition of India*. Delhi, India: Oxford University Press.

Human Rights Watch. (1995). *Playing the communal card*. New York: Author.

Pandey, G. (Ed.). (1993). *Hindus and others: The question of identity in India today*. New Delhi, India: Viking Penguin Ltd.

Tambiah, S. (1996). *Leveling crowds: Ethnonationalist conflicts and collective violence in South Asia*. Berkeley and Los Angeles: University of California Press.

Van der Veer, P. (1994). *Religious nationalism: Hindus and Muslims in India*. Berkeley and Los Angeles: University of California Press.

Varshney, A. (2002). *Ethnic conflict and civic life: Hindus and Muslims in India*. New Haven, CT: Yale University Press.

Hizbullah

Literally, the "Party of God," Hizbullah is a party of radical Shiʿite Muslim militants that opposes Western hegemony and neocolonialism, seeks to create in Lebanon an Islamic fundamentalist state modeled on Iran, and to destroy the state of Israel. This group has been linked to numerous terrorist plots and attacks against Israeli and U.S. interests, including the suicide truck bombing of the U.S. embassy in Lebanon's capital, Beirut (1982), which killed more than two hundred U.S. Marines; the hijacking of TWA flight 847 (1985); and two major attacks on Jewish targets in Argentina—the 1992 bombing of the Israeli embassy (killing twenty-nine) and the 1994 bombing of a Jewish community center (killing ninety-five). Western intelligence sources indicate that Iran and Syria fund Hizbullah extensively; its bases of operation are the Shiʿite population centers in southern Lebanon, Lebanon's Bekaa Valley, and parts of Beirut. Hizbullah has established cells in North America, South America, Europe, Africa, and parts of Asia.

Historical Background

Hizb Allah is mentioned twice in the Qur'an (suras 5 and 58), referring to the body of Muslim believers who will triumph over the forces of Satan. The term was revived in 1979, when the Iranian supporters of Ayatollah Ruhollah Khomeini (1901–1989) described themselves as the "party of God." In that context Hizbullah referred to the unorganized Iranian masses that were recruited to support the overthrow of Mohammad Reza Shah Pahlavi (1919–1980) and the concomitant revolution that installed a cleric-based Shiʿite fundamentalist government (1979). Along with other paramilitary intelligence groups, the Hizbullah employed violence to disband opposition parties and to discourage political dissent.

In response to the 1982 Israeli invasion of Lebanon, Iranian Hizbullah organized, trained, and financed the development of disenfranchised Lebanese Shiʿites into one of Lebanon's most militant political associations. Both Iran's Hizbullah and Lebanon's Hizbullah shared a theological-political worldview that included a radical interpretation of Shiʿa Muslim doctrines, was anti-Zionist and anti-Israel, distrustful of Western governments, and had a propensity to use violence to achieve political goals. Today, Iranian Hizbullah operates in Iran as bands of vigilantes, while in Lebanon the group has transformed itself into one of Lebanon's most effective political parties with 12 seats in Lebanon's 128-member parliament.

Hizbullah's Successes: Southern Lebanon and Charity Work

Hizbullah's supporters number in the tens of thousands, with a small core of militants involved in terrorist or military actions. Scholars cite two reasons for the extensive support Hizbullah enjoys in Lebanon: the fact that it is credited with bringing about the withdrawal of Israeli troops from southern Lebanon in 2000, and its extensive social welfare network.

Military Success

Hizbullah's military triumph over Israeli forces in southern Lebanon and the subsequent Israeli withdrawal represents the only time an Arab government or group has been able to force the Israelis to relinquish occupied territory. For much of 1981, Israel contended that the Palestinian Liberation Organization (PLO) had launched attacks against northern Israel from Lebanon. When Abu Nidal's Fatah Revolutionary Council (an extremely radical offshoot of the PLO), attempted to assassinate the Israeli ambassador to Great Britain, Israel invaded Lebanon and established a "security zone" (June 1982). "Operation Peace for Galilee," led by Ariel Sharon (b. 1928), who at that time was Israel's defense minister, drove Israeli troops all the way to

United Nations Security Council Resolution 425 (19 March 1978)

The Security Council, Taking note of the letters of the Permanent Representative of Lebanon (S/12600 and S/12606) and the Permanent Representative of Israel (S/12607),

Having heard the statements of the Permanent Representatives of Lebanon and Israel, Gravely concerned at the deterioration of the situation in the Middle East, and its consequences to the maintenance of international peace,

Convinced that the present situation impedes the achievement of a just peace in the Middle East, Calls for strict respect for the territorial integrity, sovereignty and political independence of Lebanon within its internationally recognized boundaries;

Calls upon Israel immediately to cease its military action against Lebanese territorial integrity and withdraw forthwith its forces from all Lebanese territory;

Decides, in the light of the request of the Government of Lebanon, to establish immediately under its authority a United Nations interim force for southern Lebanon for the purpose of confirming the withdrawal of Israeli forces, restoring international peace and security and assisting the Government of Lebanon in ensuring the return of its effective authority in the area, the force to be composed of personnel drawn from States Members of the United Nations.

Requests the Secretary-General to report to the Council within twenty-four hours on the implementation of this resolution.

Source: **The Avalon Project. Retrieved April 7, 2003, from http://www.yale.edu/lawweb/avalon/avalon.htm**

Beirut, establishing Israeli military posts throughout southern Lebanon. In 1978, the United Nations Security Council issued Resolution 425, requiring that Israel immediately cease its military action against Lebanese territorial integrity and withdraw its forces. However, it was only after eighteen years of violent resistance by Hizbullah and other smaller groups that Israeli prime minister Ehud Barak (b. 1942) withdrew all troops in 2000. This David versus Goliath scenario captured the imagination of Palestinians, who see the current intifada (uprising) as an opportunity to duplicate Hizbullah's success in Lebanon. Globally, Hizbullah's successes have inspired radical Muslims in Chechnya and Dagestan, the Philippines, and Iraq.

Social-Welfare Work

The second powerful reason for Hizbullah's popularity in Lebanon lies in its extensive network of hospitals, schools, and charities in poor neighborhoods. Al-Rassol al-Aazam Hospital in southern Beirut was founded by Hizbullah. According to Hajj Mohammad Hijazi, the hospital's administrator, the hospital provides out-patient care for five thousand people per month and emergency room care for another three thousand patients per month. Patients—Sunni Muslims, Shiʿite Muslims, and Christians—use the hospital because of its low cost: An average visit costs approximately $10.00. Hizbullah also runs schools for the poor and supports the families of "martyrs" who die in an official operation. In a country where Shiʿa-majority areas are often underdeveloped, Hizbullah is seen as a legitimate political force.

Hizbullah and the United States

After the attacks of 11 September 2001, President Bush requested that Lebanon freeze all Hizbullah's assets in its country; Lebanon's prime minister, Rafiq Hariri, refused. In November 2001, the U.S. State Department listed Hizbullah as a foreign terrorist organization whose assets could be seized. Like Osama bin Laden (b. 1957), Imad Fayez Mughniyah (b. 1962), the head of Hizbullah's military operations, has a $25 million bounty on his head and is on the FBI's list of most-wanted terrorists.

American and European intelligence sources believe that Hizbullah and al-Qaeda are increasingly working together on logistics, explosives and tactical training, money laundering, weapons smuggling, and acquiring forged documents. The new alliance involves mid- and low-level operatives and stands in stark contrast to years of rivalry between the Shiʿa-dominated Hizbullah and the mostly Sunni al-Qaeda. Apparent cooperation notwithstanding, the worldviews of the two groups differ radically: Sheikh Muhammad Hussein Fadhlallah (b. 1935), Hizbullah's spiritual leader, condemned the 11 September attacks as "un-Islamic" and a perversion of the true meaning of jihad. He called the hijackers "merely suicides"—not martyrs—because they killed innocent civilians According to the Council on Foreign Relations' Terrorism Project, Sheikh Fadhallah accused bin Laden of "heeding personal psychological needs" rather than conducting Islamic jihad (www.terrorismanswers.-com/groups/hezbollah_print.html).

Hizbullah in the Twenty-First Century

It is entirely likely that, as more evidence surfaces connecting al-Qaeda and Hizbullah, and specifically connecting Mughniyah and Abu Zubaydah, (b. 1972) one of bin Laden's top lieutenants, Hizbullah will become a major target of George W. Bush's foreign policy and U.S. military power involving both Lebanon and Iran. Iranian links to bin Laden and al-Qaeda have been tentatively drawn by Israel's defense minister, Benjamin Ben-Eliezer (b. 1936), as well as by German terrorism expert Rolf Tophoven and Magnus Ranstorp, an expert on Hizbullah and deputy director of the Centre for the Study of Terrorism and Political Violence at the University of St. Andrews in Scotland. It seems likely that Hizbullah, Lebanon, and Iran will move to the forefront of U.S. foreign policy and demand more military and intelligence resources than they are currently allotted.

Kathryn M. Coughlin

See also Hamas; Palestine and Israel; Palestine Liberation Organization

Further Reading

As there are several systems of Arabic-English transliteration, electronic searches for information on Hizbullah should include its alternate spellings: Hezbollah, Hezbullah, Hizballah, Hizbollah, and Hizbullah. The group is also known as Ansar Allah, Islamic Jihad, Islamic Jihad for the Liberation of Palestine, Revolutionary Justice Organization, and Organization of the Oppressed on Earth.

Abi-Samra, M. (2000). *The women of Hizbollah* [Video recording]. New York: Icarus/First Run Films.

Haas, R. N., & Kennedy, D. M. (1994). *The Reagan administration and Lebanon*. Washington, DC: Institute for the Study of Diplomacy, School of Foreign Service, Georgetown University.

Humphrey, M. (1989). *Islam, sect and state: The Lebanese case*. Oxford, UK: Center for Lebanese Studies.

Israeli invasion of Lebanon (1982). [Video recording]. New York: WPIX-TV.

Jaber, H. (1997). *Born with a vengeance*. New York: Columbia University Press.

Kramer, M. (1987). *The moral logic of Hizballah*. Tel Aviv, Israel: Dayan Center for Middle Eastern and African Studies, Shiloah Institute.

Mounayer, M. (2001). *Hizbollah unveiled* [Video recording]. Princeton, NJ: Films for the Humanities and Sciences.

Norton, R. A. (1990). Lebanon: The internal conflict and the Iranian Connection. In J. L. Esposito (Ed.), *The Iranian Revolution*. Miami: Florida International University Press.

Norton, R. A. (1999). *Hizbullah of Lebanon: Extremist ideals vs. mundane politics*. New York: Council on Foreign Relations.

Ranstorp, M. (1997). *Hizb'Allah in Lebanon: The politics of the Western hostage crisis*. New York: St. Martin's Press.

Saad-Ghorayeb, A. (2002). *Hizbullah: Politics and religion*. London: Pluto Press.

Holy War Idea in the Biblical Tradition

"Holy War" is a Western concept referring to war that is fought for religion, against adherents of other religions, often in order to promote religion through conversion, and with no specific geographic limitation. This concept does not occur in the Hebrew Bible, whose wars are not fought for religion or in order to promote it but, rather, in order to preserve religion and a religiously unique people in relation to a specific and limited geography. The Western concept also presumes from the outset that there is such a thing as "holy war" in opposition to "profane war," but such a dichotomy is not always possible since wars that may be fought for material (economic) reasons may be couched in sacred terms. In some traditional societies where every dimension of life is experienced within the sphere of the sacred, wars to gain territory or appropriate material wealth may be considered "holy." This is certainly the case in many depictions of war in the Hebrew Bible, while in others, wars are depicted as occurring outside the broadest definition of "holy war" (Numbers 14:39–45; Deuteronomy 1:41–44). All wars depicted in the Hebrew Bible as national wars, whether by Israelites, Moabites, Phoenicians, or Egyptians, might be considered "holy wars" because they are fought by, for, and with the national gods of these nations. For the purposes of this article, biblical holy war is defined as war fought on behalf of the people of Israel either by or on the authority of the God of Israel. An example of wars fought by the deity itself is the destruction of the Egyptian armies at the Red Sea (Exodus 14). Most wars depicted for the conquest and settlement of the land of Israel and for its defense are fought on the command or authority of the Israelite God.

The Ancient Near Eastern Context

Nations and peoples in the ancient Near East had their own national deities whom they worshiped and who, in return, sustained them and protected them. It is likely that when independent communities or city-states came into political relationship or unification, they brought their gods into a corresponding relationship that resulted in a pantheon. Within that pantheon, the gods took on a differentiation that we recognize in the well-known Greek and Egyptian systems, but differentiation also occurred in Mesopotamia, the Levant, and most other areas of the ancient Near East.

In ancient Canaan, the land out of which emerged the Land of Israel and the People of Israel, there were warrior gods with characteristics that parallel some of the martial characteristics of the biblical God of Israel. It must be noted, however, that the God of Israel is not merely a warrior deity, but in fact combines all traits and associations of the major deities, including sustenance, fertility, and compassion. We concentrate on the martial aspects of the Israelite deity for the purposes of this article only. The god Yamm of Ugarit (broadly, in Canaan) had messengers who appeared as flaming warriors with flaming swords, parallel to the cherubs and flaming, turning sword put in place by the God of the Hebrew Bible in Genesis 3:24 (see also Numbers 22:31; Joshua 5:13; 2 Samuel 24:16–17; 1 Chronicles 21: 27–40), and the image of the God of Israel as warrior (Exodus 15:3), storm god (Genesis 7; Exodus14:21), and king (1 Samuel 8) parallels that of the martial god of Canaan known as Baʿal. In most cases in the ancient Near East, the gods fought one another in the heavens just as their human followers fought one another below. In only one case known from the literature of Ugarit does a deity fight human warriors as does the God of Israel, and this is the goddess Anat. It is theorized that Israel's rejection of the existence of gods aside from the God of Israel mitigated against the old presumption of gods fighting one another as their subject peoples fought one another, and necessitated the deity engaging directly in battles with the human enemies of Israel.

In Ancient Israel

Scholars of biblical holy war often refer to the phenomenon as "Yahweh war," meaning the war of the God of Israel, because the deity appears so prominently. In the Hebrew Bible, God may be referred to as the "man of war" (*ish milhamah*, Exodus 15:3). The common term "the Lord of Hosts" (*adonay zeva'ot*) may refer to heavenly warriors, though in some contexts the "hosts" may refer to a heavenly court for the divine king. God is consulted before engaging in war (Judges 1:1; 20: 18, 23), and certain burnt offerings are made before engaging in battle to entreat the assistance of God (Jeremiah 6:4; Micah 3:5; Joel 2:9). God himself fights for Israel (Exodus14:14). The Bible even records a battle cry: "For God and for Gideon!" (who was a tribal leader and warrior; Judges 7:18).

The ark of the covenant is the symbol and banner of God's presence in battle (1 Samuel 4:4; 2 Samuel 11:11), and this connection between the ark and the presence of God in war is made already in the desert in Numbers 10:35: "When the Ark was to set out, Moses would say: Advance, O Lord! May Your enemies be scattered and may Your foes flee before You!" (New Jewish Publication Society). The ark is like a battle station from which God fights for Israel and, although not mentioned in every battle, probably went forth often and is referred to in passing as a regular part of the battle array (Judges 4:14). The Philistine enemy was terrified of the ark itself and related to the ark as if it were the very appearance of God (1 Samuel 4:5–8).

The Hebrew Bible is a collection of literature spanning many centuries and reflecting a period considerably longer. The meanings of the ideas and institutions contained within it are therefore complex, sometimes even contradictory, and clearly reflect historical and conceptual development. This is certainly the case with the role of God in war. There is still no scholarly consensus regarding the process and details of the evolu-

The Biblical Rules of Engagement, Deuteronomy 20 (KJV)

1. When thou goest out to battle against thine enemies, and seest orses, and chariots, and a people more than thou, be not afraid of them: for the LORD thy God is with thee, which brought thee up out of the land of Egypt.
2. And it shall be, when ye are come nigh unto the battle, that the priest shall approach and speak unto the people,
3. And shall say unto them, Hear, O Israel, ye approach this day unto battle against your enemies: let not your hearts faint, fear not, and do not tremble, neither be ye terrified because of them;
4. For the LORD your God is he that goeth with you, to fight for you against your enemies, to save you.
5. And the officers shall speak unto the people, saying, What man is there that hath built a new house, and hath not dedicated it? let him go and return to his house, lest he die in the battle, and another man dedicate it.
6. And what man is he that hath planted a vineyard, and hath not yet eaten of it? let him also go and return unto his house, lest he die in the battle, and another man eat of it.
7. And what man is there that hath betrothed a wife, and hath not taken her? let him go and return unto his house, lest he die in the battle, and another man take her.
8. And the officers shall speak further unto the people, and they shall say, What man is there that is fearful and fainthearted? let him go and return unto his house, lest his brethren's heart faint as well as his heart.
9. And it shall be, when the officers have made an end of speaking unto the people, that they shall make captains of the armies to lead the people.
10. When thou comest nigh unto a city to fight against it, then proclaim peace unto it.
11. And it shall be, if it make thee answer of peace, and open unto thee, then it shall be, that all the people that is found therein shall be tributaries unto thee, and they shall serve thee.
12. And if it will make no peace with thee, but will make war against thee, then thou shalt besiege it:
13. And when the LORD thy God hath delivered it into thine hands, thou shalt smite every male thereof with the edge of the sword:
14. But the women, and the little ones, and the cattle, and all that is in the city, even all the spoil thereof, shalt thou take unto thyself; and thou shalt eat the spoil of thine enemies, which the LORD thy God hath given thee.
15. Thus shalt thou do unto all the cities which are very far off from thee, which are not of the cities of these nations.
16. But of the cities of these people, which the LORD thy God doth give thee for an inheritance, thou shalt save alive nothing that breatheth:
17. But thou shalt utterly destroy them; namely, the Hittites, and the Amorites, the Canaanites, and the Perizzites, the Hivites, and the Jebusites; as the LORD thy God hath commanded thee:
18. That they teach you not to do after all their abominations, which they have done unto their gods; so should ye sin against the LORD your God.
19. When thou shalt besiege a city a long time, in making war against it to take it, thou shalt not destroy the trees thereof by forcing an axe against them: for thou mayest eat of them, and thou shalt not cut them down (for the tree of the field is man's life) to employ them in the siege:
20. Only the trees which thou knowest that they be not trees for meat, thou shalt destroy and cut them down; and thou shalt build bulwarks against the city that maketh war with thee, until it be subdued.

tion of the ideas of holy war in ancient Israel, and part of the disagreement rests on the dating of early texts. All scholars, however, maintain that the biblical war narratives do not depict the actual history of the events they portray, but rather a literary interpretation. There is also general scholarly consensus that God's role in Israelite warfare evolved from one in which God assists alongside Israel in the actual fighting to one in which God is credited entirely and without human assistance with the protection of Israel.

The classic work of Gerhard von Rad is cited here as an example of scholarly thinking about this evolution. According to von Rad, Israel originally believed that they fought alongside God in their wars, but as they became influenced by the wisdom literatures of neighboring peoples, the human role was downgraded and God was seen as the sole warrior. Eventually, the idea of holy war became associated with the absolute miracle of God's deliverance, such as with the miracle at the Red Sea (Exodus 14), with Joshua at Jericho (Joshua 6), and with David and Goliath (1 Samuel 17). The prophets then spiritualized the idea and considered prophecy itself as the legal successor to holy war on behalf of Israel. Holy war was later reclaimed and institutionalized in the seventh century BCE under Josiah, when the nation needed a powerful incentive to fight wars of defense, but was again and finally spiritualized with the Deuteronomic rewriting of history and the book of Chronicles.

Another study, by E. W. Conrad, observes the different roles of God in war as two paradigms that are exemplified in two types of warriors. In the "Joshua paradigm," God engages actively in fighting battles that eventuate in winning the land of Israel for the people (Numbers 21:34; Deuteronomy 3:2; Joshua 8:1–2; 10:8; 2 Samuel 13:28; 2 Kings 25:24), while the "Abraham paradigm" represents Israel for whom God wages peace among the nations and promises great posterity (Genesis 15:1; 21:17–18; 46:3–4; Exodus 14:13–14; Nehemiah 4:8; Isaiah 7:4–9; 41:8–16; Jeremiah 30:10; Haggai 2:4–9). The Joshua warrior paradigm reflects memories of a heroic past when God delivered his people and granted victory in the struggle over the land, while the Abraham paradigm in the exilic and postexilic periods reflects Israel's imagining about the future restoration of offspring and a return to the land.

War Poetry

A great deal of poetry is embedded in Hebrew scripture and much of it consists of hymns of praise and thanks for God's protection of Israel and victory over Israel's enemies. Perhaps the most famous is the "Song of the Sea" of Exodus 15, which recounts God's deliverance of his people as he marches them out from Egyptian bondage to take the land for Israel. God throws Pharaoh and his chariots into the sea, drowning the enemy and blasting the waters with the breath of his nostrils. He foils the attempt of the enemy to despoil Israel and strikes fear in the hearts of the Canaanites who will melt away at the coming of Israel into the land.

The "Song of Deborah" in Judges 5 is a victory poem recounting the destruction of "the kings of Canaan" in a battle fought by the tribal chieftain Barak and the prophetess Deborah. It extols the acts of human heroes, excoriates the tribes who failed to fight, and attributes the victory to God for his people: "So may all Your enemies perish, O Lord! But may His friends be as the sun rising in might!" (5:31).

Various other poems in the Psalms and embedded within narrative contain victory songs and hymns of praise for divine acts in saving Israel. The images include the God of Israel and his heavenly host fighting with human armies to take the land or to conquer enemies after the original settlement, God establishing his kingship through his might and victory, requests for God to rise up against Israel's enemies, and even the celestial bodies responding to God's fighting for Israel (Deuteronomy 33; Joshua 10:12–13; 2 Samuel 18/Psalm 18; Psalms 7:7; 59:5–6; Isaiah 10:26; Habakkuk 3:3–15).

Psalm 68 contains fragments of a series of war songs or pieces of war poetry. "God will arise, His enemies shall be scattered, His foes shall flee before him. . . . O God, when You went at the head of Your army, when You marched through the desert, the earth trembled, the sky rained because of God. . . . The kings and their armies are in headlong flight; housewives are sharing in the spoils. . . . When Shaddai scattered the kings, it seemed like a snowstorm in Zalmon. . . . God's chariots are myriads upon myriads, thousands upon thousands. . . . You are awesome, O God, in Your holy places; it is the God of Israel who gives might and power to the people. Blessed is God."

Law

The Bible includes only a few formal laws associated with war; these laws are developed considerably later in rabbinic interpretation. Because God was understood to have some kind of presence within the war camp to protect the people and deliver the enemy, the camp must remain "holy" *(qadosh)*, meaning in this context that it must not be sullied by anyone in a state of ritual impurity. Those, therefore, who experience a nocturnal emission must leave the war camp until they can be rendered ritually pure, and an area must be designated outside of the camp for people to relieve themselves and bury their excrement (Deuteronomy 23:10–15). It is forbidden to rape captive women. If a captive woman is desired, she must be brought into the home of her captor, her captive clothing replaced, her hair and nails trimmed, and she must be allowed to mourn her parents for one full month before she may be taken to wife legally and sexually. If, once the heat of war has cooled during those thirty days, she is no longer desired, she must be released; she may not be enslaved (Deuteronomy 21:10–14).

Deuteronomy 20 provides encouragement for battle by ensuring that God will be with the troops to bring them victory (verses 1–4). At the same time, it provides for a series of military deferments. These apply to those who have built a new house but have not yet dedicated it, have planted a vineyard but have never harvested it, and have become engaged but have not consummated the marriage. All may return home lest they not enjoy the fruit of their love and labors. Likewise, those who are too fearful to engage in battle are relieved of duty lest their fear infect their comrades and hinder their fighting ability (verses 5–9).

Deuteronomy 20:10–18 provides rudimentary rules of engagement in war, presumably one of conquest, and these differ depending on whether the enemy lives in "towns that lie very far" or "the towns . . . belonging to the nearby nations." With regard to the former category, they are offered terms of surrender. If they agree they are subjected to forced labor; but as they retain ownership of their material possessions, this is not slavery as known in Western history. If they choose to fight and are defeated, the males are put to the sword and the women, children, livestock, and all material goods may be taken as spoil. With regard to the latter category, which is specified as certain Canaanite groups living within what is designated as the land of Israel, they must be proscribed through the *herem* (see below). Verses 19–20 then forbid the destruction of trees that are depended upon for sustenance. Only trees that are known do not yield fruit may be cut down for constructing siege works.

The *Herem*

The *herem* refers to something separated from the normal because of being either dedicated to God or proscribed as an abomination to him. In the first case, whatever one privately devotes to God as *herem* is sacred in the highest degree and is irrevocable, never to be redeemed by the devoter (Leviticus 27:28). It belongs, rather, to the priests who maintain the sacrificial system (Numbers 18:14; Ezekiel 44:29).

The second sense of the term refers to the absolute destruction of that which is abominable to the God of Israel. This may include Israelites themselves who worship other gods, whether individuals or an entire community (Exodus 22:19; Deuteronomy 13). In the case of *herem*, no benefit may be derived from such destruction. All livestock must also be destroyed and material goods burned, and in the case of a community, its buildings must be destroyed, never to be reoccupied.

The *herem* also applies to certain of the enemies of Israel, most often the Canaanite peoples who of course worshiped multiple gods and who represented the most persistent enemies that threatened the settlement of the People of Israel on the Land of Israel (Deuteronomy 2:32–35; Joshua 11:10–20). These peoples were also to be proscribed entirely, but in a number of cases such as some of those cited here, the spoil was not all destroyed but was taken by Israel. It is theorized that the institution of *herem* may have developed as a desperate means of ensuring the deity's support in war by promising the dedication to God of all spoils. In fact, however, there is noteworthy disparity within the Hebrew Bible itself regarding the *herem*, suggesting significant ideational development. Exodus 23:27–33, for example, commands the exile of the Canaanites to rid the land of idolatry, but not their destruction. The *herem* is not a purely Israelite phenomenon, as the Mesha Inscription demonstrates. According to this Moabite text, Mesha king of Moab reports that when he won back territory from Israel, he massacred the Israelite inhabitants as he made towns *herem* to the Moabite god, Ashtar-Chemosh.

The Seven Canaanite Nations and Amalek

The "Seven Canaanite Nations" is a literary construct, since the actual groups listed in the various references to them in the Hebrew Bible total at least ten. These are the local communities living in the land before and during the settlement, and the *herem* refers most frequently to them. In the rules of engagement listed in Deuteronomy 20, these are the peoples living in "the towns . . . belonging to the nearby nations." In fact, however, they serve as a literary trope in Deuteronomic material to represent the threat of idolatry and assimilation: "For they will turn your children away from Me to worship other gods, and the Lord's anger will blaze forth against you and He will promptly wipe you out" (Deuteronomy 7:4). The "Amalekites" hold a similar symbolic role, evident perhaps even in their designation, not as a people, but as an individual, "Amalek." Amalek was the first to attack Israel after the exodus from Egypt (Exodus 17:8–13), and Deuteronomy tells "how, undeterred by fear of God, he surprised you on the march, when you were famished and weary, and cut down all the stragglers in your rear" (25:18). God therefore commands that Amalek and his name be absolutely wiped out (17:14). Amalek thus becomes a symbol of absolute evil in Israel's enemies in biblical and postbiblical Jewish tradition, for "The Lord will be at war with Amalek throughout the ages" (17:16). In an enigmatic command, God command Israel to "blot out the memory of Amalek from under heaven. Do not forget!" (Deuteronomy 25:19b).

As in the case of the "Seven Canaanite Nations" and Amalek, the very notion of holy war in the Hebrew Bible takes on symbolic rather than practical meaning in its later layers. While clearly a functional category for various periods and occasions within the history of biblical Israel, "holy war" became a sacred category in the later periods that was rarely understood as applying in real time. That is, the wars of Israel in the exilic and postexilic periods were fought just as other nations fought their wars for material gain or national survival, though Israel retained the memory of the great battles in which God fought along Israel. In the latest biblical layers such as the book of Daniel, however, one begins to observe the phenomenon of apocalyptic, in which God's wars take on a symbolic meaning that transcends real time. Holy war ideology nevertheless remained an important part of biblical literature and helped to inform Israel's self-concept. Although doubtfully associated with Israel's actual wars in the late biblical period, its prominent position in sacred writings allowed for it to be revived in postbiblical periods such as under the Maccabees (second century BCE) and during the period of the Jewish revolt against Rome (66–70 CE) and the Bar Kokhba Rebellion (132–135 CE).

Reuven Firestone

Further Reading

Carmichael, C. M. (1974). *The laws of Deuteronomy*. Ithaca, NY: Cornell University Press.

Conrad, E. W. (1985). *Fear not warrior: A study of "al tira" pericopes in the Hebrew Scriptures*. Chico, CA: Scholars Press.

Lind, M. C. (1980). *Yahweh is a warrior*. Scottdale, PA: Herald Press.

Miller, P. D., Jr. (1973). *The divine warrior in early Israel* (Harvard Semitic Monographs 5). Cambridge, MA: Harvard University Press.

Niditch, S. (1993). *War in the Hebrew Bible*. New York: Oxford University Press.

Pedersen, J. (1940, 1953). *Israel: Its life and culture* (Vols. 3–4). London: Oxford University Press.

Rad, G. von. (1991). *Holy war in ancient Israel* (Marva J. Dawn, Trans.). Grand Rapids, MI: Eerdmans.

Saggs, H. W. F. (1978). *The encounter with the divine in Mesopotamia and Israel*. London: Athlone Press.

Schwally, F. (1901). *Der Heilige Krieg in alten Israel*. Leipzig, Germany: Dieterich'sche Verlagsbuchhandlung, Theodor Weicher.

Stern, P. (1991). *Biblical* herem: *A window on Israel's religious experience*. Atlanta, GA: Scholars Press.

Stolz, F. (1972). *Jahwes und Israels Kriege* [Yahweh's and Israel's Wars]. Zurich, Switzerland: Theologischer Verlag.

Inca

The Inca empire, which extended along the Pacific coast and Andean highlands from northern Ecuador to central Chile in South America, had a ritual-based, complex religion before it was conquered by the Spaniard Francisco Pizarro in 1532. After the conquest, the cross would follow (and often accompany) the sword as the Spaniards sought to convert the Inca to Catholicism and root out what the early missionaries viewed as the idolatrous practices of the Inca. The missionaries were, to a large degree, successful; although Andean religion survives partially among contemporary Andeans, much of it has been rooted out, destroyed, and lost from the historical record.

One reason for this loss was the lack of a sophisticated writing system among the pre-Hispanic Andeans. Whereas the ancient Mesoamericans developed a complex writing system and recorded much of their belief structure, particularly with hieroglyphic writings, the Inca did not. Thankfully, though, many of the early Christian missionaries (and chroniclers) saw the importance of recording the religion of the Inca, if only in order to better understand how to combat it. From these writings comes an understanding, although incomplete, of the official state religion as imposed by the Inca empire. The religious beliefs of this religion consisted of the Andean pantheon and the divinity comprising it and the place of humankind in the universe.

Growth of the Inca Empire

War spread the religion of the Inca. The Inca settled into a small village they called "Cuzco" in Peru in 1250. When an adjoining state attacked this village, the Inca rallied their allies, defeated the aggressor, and went on the offensive themselves to such a degree that by 1500 the Inca empire comprised nearly 5 million subjects and was made up of nearly 4,400 kilometers of territory. As the empire grew it incorporated the gods of the conquered into its pantheon. However, much as the ancient Greek city-states had a pan-Hellenic belief structure, so did the Andeans. The early Spanish chroniclers recorded this pantheon.

Once conquered, states were allowed to continue their worship of their local deities. However, one requirement of their new Inca overlords was that states support the cult of the Inca sun god as the religion of the empire. Likewise, the Inca would incorporate the deities of their newly conquered subjects into their pantheon of gods, transporting images of the gods of their conquered subjects to the sun temple in Cuzco. This act of absorbing the religions of the conquered would in turn ease the adoption of Christianity by the Inca during and after the Spanish conquest.

Religious observances—of the official state religion—united the different ethnic and language groups. The priests of the sun, the main deity in the Andean pantheon, were largely responsible for spreading the understanding of the language of the Inca—Quechua—among the newly conquered peoples. In Andean society the basic unit was the *ayllu*, the community or group of households related by blood or ritual ties. Each *ayllu* worshiped its own founding deities—spirits thought to inhabit plants, animals, or stones—as well as the new religion of the Inca. The Catholic priests sought ardently to destroy these deities.

Statue of Inca warrior and sun god, San Gabriel, Ecuador. March 2000. Courtesy Steve Donaldson.

For the Inca and their newly conquered allies, religion was a central feature of life, manifestations of which can be seen through ancestor worship, *huacas* (shrines or sacred places), and the official state religion.

Ancestors and *Huacas*

Each *ayllu* contained its own deities and shrines. If there were important matters to be discussed within each *ayllu*, the prominent ancestors would be consulted by the *ayllu* members. These prominent ancestors were deceased rulers, founders of the *ayllu*s, or *kuraka*s (leaders of the *ayllu*). After death, the bodies of these important members of society would be carefully preserved and brought out for ritual celebrations or consultations.

After the expansion of the Inca empire, royal ancestor worship was established and increased dramatically. When one Inca ruler died, the new ruler would not inherit the wealth of that office but rather merely the office itself. The male descendents of the emperor (with the exception of the chosen heir to the throne), or *panaca*, would receive the ruler's wealth and with it be charged with the responsibility of maintaining the mummy and the cult, treating the mummified ruler as though he were alive. These royal mummy cults were important because the new ruler would have to obtain his own wealth, fame, and honor through expanding the borders of the empire. With this aspect of the Inca religion, the Inca empire was sure to continue its expansion as long as military and political capabilities withstood defeat (as would come in the sixteenth century by the Spaniards).

Although many hills, houses, and other objects were considered sacred, the majority of *huaca*s were stones and springs. Also, places associated with the emperor were sacred, as was the entire city of Cuzco, as well as snow-capped mountains. If a person was born "unusual," such as born a twin, the person could be considered a *huaca* (or would often become a member of the priesthood). Priests and other specialists such as diviners, sacrificers, caretakers, and virgin women attended the most important of the *huaca*s.

*Huaca*s and mummified ancestors became especially important after the Spanish conquest as the friars sought to root out idolatry, beginning in 1551 when the Catholic Church launched a full-scale attack on all remaining Inca religious activities. Friars and government officials would root out and destroy all *huaca*s and burn all mummies they could find.

One immediate result of this suppression began in the 1560s and has been recorded by scholars as the first Latin American messianic movement, known as Taqui Onqoy (dance sickness). This movement's leaders preached that the Spaniards had conquered them because the Christian God had been stronger than the Peruvian deities. However, according to the leaders of this movement, the Peruvian deities were getting stronger and stronger. In order to help the Peruvian deities increase in strength, the Indians were to cease practicing Christianity and return to the worship of the *huaca*s. Severely repressed by the Spanish friars, this movement ended around 1570.

Official State Religion

The official state religion consisted not only of the royal mummy cults, but also of Inti, the sun god. Inti was the most important of three manifestations (comparable to the Trinity in traditional Christianity) of the sky god, who stood in the upper pantheon of Inca religion. The first manifestation of the sky god was that of Viracocha, the creator. Viracocha was thought to have a human form, as can be seen as his icons in a number of temples. Viracocha lived in the sky and, like Zeus for the Greeks, commanded a host of lesser supernatural beings who looked after the welfare of human beings. Jesuit Friar Manual M. Marzal quotes the following prayer to Viracocha as recorded in 1633 by the chronicler Bernabé Cobo:

> O Creator without equal, you are at the ends of the world, you gave life and valor to mankind, saying "Let me be man," and for the woman, "Let there be woman"; you made them, formed them and gave them life so that they will live safe and sound in peace and without danger! Where are you? By chance do you live high up in the sky or down below on earth or in the clouds and storms? Hear me, respond to me, and consent to my plea, giving us perpetual life and taking us with your hands, and receive this offering wherever you are, O Creator! (Marzal 1993, 89)

Note the similarities with the Christian Creation tradition. Some scholars question whether this was truly a prayer of the Inca or merely the chronicler's attempts to overly Christianize this Andean religion. Either way, it serves as a good explanation of the supreme being or deity of veneration by the Andeans. A prayer to Viracocha must precede any sacrifices to *huacas*.

The second manifestation of the sky god was Illapa, the god of thunder and weather. This god was extremely important for agriculture because he regulated rainfall. His clothes would give off flashes of lightning when he whirled his sling, and the crack of his sling would make the thunder and rain.

The third manifestation of the sky god was Inti, who, besides being the sun god, was the founder of the Inca royal lineage. He was the guardian of crops, and thus the agricultural ritual, with him at the center, was of great importance. As the Inca expanded their empire, temples were constructed to the sun throughout the empire.

An additional deity was Quilla, the goddess of the moon. Quilla was the wife of Inti, the sun god, and was linked to women's menstrual cycles as well as agricultural cycles. When eclipses of the moon occurred, this was seen as a puma or snake attacking Quilla to tear her apart. Thus, it was necessary for dogs to bark and howl. Women formed the membership of the cult of the moon.

Rituals

If religion was important in the life of the Inca, then ritual performances were the aspect that held the highest importance in religious veneration, much more so than mysticism and spirituality. These ritual performances centered around the supernatural increase of crops and animals and the health and well-being of the people. There were four basic types of Andean rituals.

The first type was curative. In Andean society there were evil spirits as well as good spirits. Most spirits were good—or at least those that are known to researchers were good. People prayed to these good spirits for help in life and after death. Thus, these spirits were helpful. Tied in with spirits were sorcery and countersorcery. Sorcery, which was quite prevalent, could cause illness as well as other misfortune. People could combat this misfortune through ritual: either public ceremonies led by priests or private ceremonies led by shamans or, in short, countersorcery.

The second basic type of Andean rituals was divinatory. Members of the priesthood (which consisted of a hierarchy, the apex of which was usually a close relative of the emperor) were expected to make divinations and interpret oracles, often through an examination of sacrificial entrails.

The third basic type of Andean rituals was penitential. Penitential rituals were required of a number of sins, such as failing to offer the correct sacrifices, not observing the obligatory fasts, resuming marital relations with women who have been unfaithful, committing murder (one of the worst of sins), and committing adultery. There were two types of sacrifices, although these were not confined to penitential rituals. The first was that of animal sacrifice, which was by far the most common. This type usually involved slitting the animal's throat and burning the corpse at a shrine. The second type was that of human sacrifice. This type was infrequent, especially when compared to practices of the other great empire of pre-Columbian times, the Aztec empire. Nonetheless, human sacrifice did occur. Victims would be strangled, after which their throats were slit or their hearts cut out.

The fourth basic type of Andean rituals was festive. These rituals were by far the most important. Public and solemn, they were celebrated at the advent of public crises, such as earthquakes, epidemics, droughts, or wars. They were also celebrated at times of the coronation of an Inca ruler. Major religious festivals of the Inca were annual and corresponded with the agricultural year or the calendar. The three most important ceremonies were Cápac-Raymi, Inti-Raymi, and Coya-Raymi.

Cápac-Raymi, celebrated in December, the first month of the year, was the festival in which Inca boys were initiated and knighted. This was the puberty ritual for adolescents of twelve to fifteen years of age where they received their final names.

The second of the three most important annual festivals was that of Inti-Raymi. Celebrated in June, this was the principal festival of Inti, the sun god. In this festival one hundred llamas would be sacrificed with the aid of the ruling Inca, himself a descendant of the Inti.

Finally, there was the festival of Coya-Raymi, also known as "Citua," which was celebrated in September. Because September was the beginning of the rainy season, which would bring with it hardship and disease, in this festival a supplication was made to Viracocha in order to prevent sickness and disease throughout the empire.

Inca Religion: Alive or Dead?

The Inca priests served as an arm of the state. The Inca, as they expanded their empire, adopted the gods of the vanquished into their own pantheon. The royal mummy cult served as an impetus for expansion. The official religion of the state included the worship of the sky god, manifested through Viracocha, the creator god; Illapa, the god of thunder and weather; and Inti, the sun god and founder of the Inca royal lineage. In addition, local people would support their own cults, along with shrines and a priesthood. This entire system was suppressed by the early Christian missionaries. Although many aspects of this religion still exist, it is, for the most part, a dead religion.

Kim Richardson

See also Aztecs

Further Reading

Classen, C. (1993). *Inca cosmology and the human body*. Salt Lake City: University of Utah Press.

Davies, N. (1995). *The Incas*. Boulder: University of Colorado Press.

Josephy, A. M., Jr. (1993). *The Americas in 1492: The world of the Indian peoples before the arrival of Columbus*. New York: Vintage Books.

Malpass, M. A. (1996). *Daily life in the Inca empire*. Westport, CT: Greenwood Press.

Marzal, M. M. (1993). Andean religion at the time of the conquest. In G. H. Gossen & M. León-Portilla (Eds.), *South and Meso-American native spirituality: From the cult of the feathered serpent to the theology of liberation* (pp. 86–115). New York: Crossroads Publishing.

Urton, G. (1981). *At the crossroads of the Earth and sky: An Andean cosmology*. Austin: University of Texas Press.

Zuidema, R. T. (1990). *Inca civilization in Cuzco* (J. Decoster, Trans.). Austin: University of Texas Press.

India *See* Buddhism: India; Hinduism, Classical; Hinduism: Early Medieval Period; Hinduism, Modern; Hinduism: Vedic Period; Hindu-Muslim Violence in India; Indo-European Mythology; Jainism; Kashmir; Sikhism; Thugs

Indo-European Mythology

The basic attitudes toward war and warriors are reflected in the several ancient Indo-European mythologies. It should be emphasized at the outset that warfare and the gods and heroes associated with it played an extremely important part in most if not all of the early Indo-European-speaking societies, from Ireland to India.

The Indo-European *Männerbund*

Like most pastoral nomads, contemporary as well as ancient, the Proto-Indo-Europeans, the ancestors of the Greeks, Hittites, Aryans, Iranians, Celts, Germans, and the rest of the ancient (and modern) Indo-European speakers, seem to have regarded warfare as a fundamental fact of life. Indeed, as Stig Wikander long ago pointed out, the *Männerbund* or war band was clearly the most important single ancient Indo-European social institution. Examples of it are legion, from the Kshatriya caste (or class, at least in the earliest period) of traditional Indian society to the ancient Germanic *comitatus*. Moreover, the presence of such a social stratum—that is, a class of military specialists—played a major role in the Indo-European expansion from the Kazakh steppes, beginning around 4500 BCE. Armed with battle axes and driving spoked-wheel battle chariots, the Indo-European war bands established themselves as ruling elites in the territories associated with this widespread language family in historic times. It was from these bands of fearless fighters and especially their leaders that the Indo-European warrior mythos developed.

The Ideology of the Second Function

According to the late Georges Dumézil (1898–1986), arguably the most important contributor to comparative Indo-European mythology since Friedrich Max Müller (1823–1900) established the discipline in the mid-nineteenth century, the ancient Indo-European speakers conceived of the world and their relationship to it in terms of three fundamental, hierarchically ranked ideological principles, or functions. In descending order, what Dumézil called the "first function" includes the social and supernatural manifestations of ultimate sovereignty and is typically reflected in a pair of deities, one of whom reflects juridical sovereignty, the other cosmic order (e.g., the Vedic Indian deities Mitra and Varuna and the Norse gods Tyr and Odin), as well as in a priestly social stratum (e.g., the Indic Brahmans, the ancient Irish Druids, and the Roman Flamines maiores); at the other end of this spectrum was the "third function," which reflected the sum total of activities and beliefs relating to the mass of society, the maintenance and promotion of physical well-being, fertility, and prosperity (e.g., the Vedic Nastaya, or Ashvins, the twin horsemen who were incarnations of fertility, etc.; the Roman deities Quirinus and Ops; and the Norse figures Njoror, his son Freyr, and his daughter Freyja). However, it is the intermediate or "second function" that is most relevant here, for it was to this function that the great war gods, such as the Vedic Indian deity Indra, the Roman god Mars, the Greek Ares, and the Norse warrior deity Thor belonged, as well as warlike demigods and heroes, such as the Indian epic figure Arjuna, Herakles, the Irish warrior hero Chuchulainn, the legendary Norse figure Starkaor, Siegfried (= the Norse Sigurd), King Arthur, Lancelot, Prince Igor, and a host of other similar figures throughout the ancient Indo-European-speaking domain. It is here also that the aforementioned military-oriented social institutions, such as the Kshatriya caste and other manifestations of the *Männerbund*, were located. The essence of the "second function" was the exercise of physical prowess, both in defense of the society and to conquer neighboring, non-Indo-European societies—although the ancient Indo-Europeans were far from a monolithic political entity, and the war bands were as apt to fight one another as they were outsiders.

The "War of Foundation"

One of the most important manifestations of the "second function" in a number of Indo-European mythologies is the so-called "War of Foundation." It involves a war between representatives of the first two functions and those of the third, wherein the latter are conquered and subsequently integrated into the social and divine systems. The best examples of this primordial conflict can be found in ancient Scandinavia and Rome. In Scandinavia, the tale is unabashedly mythological. The prime representatives of the first two functions, Odin, Tyr, and Thor, known collectively as the Aesir, attack and defeat the Vanir deities Njoror, Freyr, and Freyja, who according to Dumézil's scheme reflect the third function. The Aesir handily defeated their Vanir rivals and thus complete the functional integration of the divine realm.

Although some scholars have suggested that that this myth, found in the *Prose Edda* of Snorri Sturluson (1179–1241 CE) and other medieval Scandinavian texts, reflects the conflicts that must have occurred between the earlier Germanic-speakers and the indigenous, non-Indo-European inhabitants of northern Europe (e.g., the ancestors of the modern Finns, Lapps, and Estonians), the fact that the same story can be found in the ancient Roman pseudohistorical account of the Sabine War suggests that it is a common Indo-European cosmological tale and not specifically a reflection of the Germanic intrusion into northern Europe. In the Roman variant, shortly after founding the city, Romulus, the primeval sovereign, and his warlike male companions stole wives from their prosperous neighbors, the Sabines. After an inconclusive war, the whole Sabine community was incorporated into the Roman body politic. Thus, as in the Scandinavian case, the third function was defeated by a collation of representatives of the first two functions, thus rendering the community complete.

A somewhat less clear-cut reflex of this common Indo-European battle myth can be found in the Greek accounts of the Trojan War, in which the victorious figures Agamemnon, Menelaus, and the warrior figure par excellence, Achilles, are representatives of the first two functions, while the defeated Trojans, who fought in defense of their wealthy city, reflect the third function. Moreover, although the Trojans were not incorporated into the Greek polity at the end of the conflict, the fate of the Trojan women, including Helen, closely resembles that of the Sabine women.

The point here is that this account, which is so basic to the societies in question, focuses on war and the achievements of warrior figures like Thor and Achilles.

Sword Cults

Another important feature of the Indo-European warrior ethos, which appears in several ancient Indo-European-speaking traditions, is the presence of cult surrounding named, magical swords. Found among the Celts, Germans, and particularly among the Iranian-speaking nomads of the south Russian steppes (Scythians, Sarmatians, Alans, etc.), who appear to have diffused the cult westward in the early centuries CE, the best-known example is contained in the medieval legends surrounding King Arthur's magical sword, Excalibur. Another well-known medieval example is Roland's famous sword, Durandel. However, as early as the mid-fifth century BCE Herodotus (c. 484–between 430 and 420 BCE) described the Scythian practice of worshiping swords as the god "Ares," and in the fourth century CE Ammianus Marcellinus (c. 330–395) described the Alanic custom of thrusting a sword into the earth and worshiping it as "Mars." Moreover, the modern Ossetians, a people who live in the northern Caucasus, and who descend from the ancient Alans, preserve an epic tradition in which magical swords play an extremely important role.

Killing the Three-Headed Monster

Yet another important warlike theme that looms large in several ancient Indo-European traditions concerns the slaying of a three-headed monster or tricephalus that is threatening the community. The clearest example is found in the Indic *Mahabarata*, in which the war god Indra kills a voracious, three-headed monster called Vishvarupa. Additional reflexes of this theme can be found in the well-known Roman account of Horatius's defeat of the three Curiatii and the Irish tale of how the great hero Cuchulainn slew the three sons of Nechta Scene. To be sure, in these accounts, the monster has been euhemerized, respectively, into a set of Alban triplets and the three offspring of an enemy. But the basic theme is the same: an intrepid warrior slays a three-headed enemy and thus saves the day.

Ambivalent Attitudes toward the Warrior

Nevertheless, despite the centrality of warfare and warriors in the several Indo-European-speaking narrative traditions, there seems to have been, paradoxically, perhaps, a deep-seated ambivalence as far as the warrior was concerned. Indeed, all of the figures just discussed who slay three-headed (or triplicate) figures are seen as morally flawed. Indra was later punished because, despite his depravity, Vishvarupa was the son of Tvastr, chaplain to the gods and therefore a divine Brahman. Thus the god was guilty of Brahmanicide, a heinous crime indeed in the Indian tradition, modern as well as ancient. Both Horatius and Cuchulainn returned from their respective encounters engulfed by a battle frenzy that had to be exorcized. The Irish hero was immersed in three successive tubs of water to "cool" him off, while Horatius slew his own sister, who was betrothed to one of the Curiatii, and was forced to pass under a beam, which absorbed his furor (this appears to have been the origin of the Roman custom of building triumphal arches, the fundamental purpose of which was to divest a victorious army of its battle frenzy). Another manifestation of this socially disruptive frenzy can be seen in the Norse concept of the berserker, or the warrior who becomes like a raging bear and kills indiscriminately. Thus, the Indo-European warrior ethos had both a "dark" and a "light" (or chivalrous) aspect. Some warrior figures, such as Ares, Starkaor, and the Vedic figure Vayu, were inherently "dark" figures and prone to be unpredictable and treacherous. Others, like Mars, Thor, Indra, and Arjuna, belonged to the "light side" and were, for the most part, chivalrous and loyal to their respective sovereigns. However, as we have just seen, even the most chivalrous an d honorable warrior was, like Horatius, capable of causing harm, and this underscores an important Indo-European warfare-related theme, which Dumézil labeled "the three sins of the warrior."

The Three Sins of the Indo-European Warrior

The prime example here is Indra, who committed "sins" against each of the three ideological functions. His offense against the first or sovereign function was, of course, his aforementioned killing of Vishvarupa, a divine Brahman despite his monstrous nature. His offense against his own function (i.e., the second function) was an act of treachery. After swearing not to kill the demon Namuci with anything either wet or dry, he forged a weapon made of foam, and, when the demon's attention was diverted, he decapitated him. His sin against the third function was to assume the guise of a mortal and have intercourse with the man's wife.

He thus committed an illicit act of procreation. As a result of these three transgressions, the great Vedic war god lost his majesty, his physical prowess, and his physical beauty.

Another Indo-European warrior who commits a triad of sins is the Greek demigod Herakles, who (1) refused to obey his sovereign, King Eurystheus; (2) slew a fellow warrior, Iphitos, in violation of what amounted to a truce; and (3) abducted and then raped Astydamia after killing her father—again, an illicit act of procreation. Other sinning warriors include the Norse antihero Strakadr, who killed his sovereign, abandoned his comrades in battle, and murdered the Danish king Olo for money while he relaxed in a bath. Although illicit sex doesn't figure here, an illicit act for money does, which is also a violation of the ideology of the third function. Still other examples have been noted in the careers of Ares, Agamemnon, Siegfried, Sir Gawain, and Achilles.

The Indo-European Warrior-Deity as a Fertility Figure

Finally, it should be noted that despite their primary "mission," some of the best-known Indo-European warrior figures had close association with the promotion of agriculture and licit as well as illicit procreation. Mars, for example, in certain of his aspects, such as *Mars qui praest paci*, was regularly worshiped as a fertility figure. The Norse god Thor was also invoked as an agricultural deity, and his sexual prowess was almost as remarkable as his fighting ability.

In sum, despite their periodic bouts of antisocial behavior and occasional double duty as agricultural deities, the great Indo-European war gods and heroes, from Indra, Mars, and Thor to figures such as Herakles, Achilles, Arjuna, and Chuchulainn, occupied an extremely prominent niche in the ancient Indo-European belief systems, and a fair amount of the ideology that surrounded them survives to this day in the continuing importance, symbolic and otherwise, of military establishments in almost every modern Indo-European-speaking society.

C. Scott Littleton

Further Reading

Dumézil, G. (1956). *Aspects de la fonction guerrière chez les Indo-Européens* [Aspects of the warrior principles among Indo-Europeans]. Paris: Presses Universitaires de France.

Dumézil, G. (1983). *The stakes of the warrior* (D. Weeks, Trans.). Berkeley: University of California Press.

Littleton, C. S. (1970). Some possible Indo-European themes in the *Iliad*. In J. Puhvel (Ed.), *Myth and law among the Indo-Europeans* (pp. 229–246). Berkeley: University of California Press.

Littleton, C. S. (1982). *The new comparative mythology: An anthropological assessment of the theories of Georges Dumézil* (3rd ed.). Berkeley: University of California Press.

Littleton, C. S., & Malcor, L. A. (2000). *From Scythia to Camelot: A radical reassessment of the legends of King Arthur, the knights of the Round Table, and the Holy Grail* (2nd ed.). New York: Garland Publishing Inc.

Mallory, J. P. (1989). *In search of the Indo-Europeans: Language, archaeology, and myth*. London: Thames and Hudson.

Miller, D. A. (2000). *The epic hero*. Baltimore: Johns Hopkins University Press.

Puhvel, J. (1987). *Comparative mythology*. Baltimore: Johns Hopkins University Press.

Strutynski, U. (1980). Ares: A reflex on the Indo-European war god? *Arethusa, 13*(2), 217–231.

Strutynski, U. (1982). Honi soit qui mal y pense: The warrior sins of Sir Gawain. In E. Polomé (Ed.), *Homage to Georges Dumézil* (pp. 35–52). Washington, DC: The Journal of Indo-European Studies Monograph No. 3.

Wikander, S. (1938). *Der arishe Männerbund* [The Aryan war band]. Lund, Sweden: Ohlsson.

Indonesia

After centuries of peaceful coexistence, Muslims and Christians in Indonesia clashed violently in December 1998; violence declined only in 2002. The violence had many causes: social dissent, economic instability, political upheavals, and ethnic conflict that evolved into a religious war. The protracted political crises of intercommunal warfare resulted in atrocities by both sides: places of worship, homes, and businesses razed; people displaced; and nearly ten thousand people killed. Both Christians and Muslims perceived that they were being marginalized and fought to protect their territory.

Indonesia is the world's largest archipelago, the world's fourth-most-populous country at 230 million people, and the third-largest democracy. The archipelago straddles the equator and is a strategic location on major shipping routes from the Pacific Ocean to the Indian Ocean. It consists of seventeen thousand islands, of which six thousand are inhabited. Indonesia was part of the Netherlands' empire for three hundred years and was governed in an inhumane fashion. Indonesia achieved independence in 1949. The country has three hundred ethnic groups and 365 languages; the country's motto is "Unity in Diversity." In Indonesia 88 percent of the population are Muslim, 5 percent are Protestants, 3 percent are Roman Catholic, 2 percent are Hindu, 1 percent are Buddhist, and 1 percent are other religions. The head of government since 23 July 2001 is President Megawati Sukarnoputrim, daughter of Indonesia's founding father, President Sukarno, who founded the national ideology of Pancasila, promoting tolerance among the diverse religious and ideological groups. That ideology had worked until 1999.

Causes

One cause of the religious conflict was the weak government that succeeded President Mohaned Suharto (b. 1921), who was forced to resign in 1998 after thirty years of iron-fisted rule cloaked in democracy; this resignation led to a power vacuum. Suharto was succeeded by his vice president, Dr. Bacharuddin J. Habibie, who did not enjoy popular support. This situation was worsened by corruption, elite rivalries, confusing civil-military relations, an ineffective legal structure, opportunism, and violations of human rights. Habibie was forced to resign after losing a confidence vote in parliament. He was succeeded by Abdurrahman Wahid, who was forced to appoint Sukarnoputrim as vice president. This did not gratify the people, nor was the government effective in quelling the religious conflict.

The political cause of the conflict had religious underpinnings that led to serious altercations. Elections in Poso, Sulawesie, on 13 December 1998, for example, significantly altered the power-sharing structure. Traditionally a Muslim served as electoral head of district, as a *bupati*, whereas a Christian served as *sekwilda* (district secretary). The electoral shift in the fifty top district elected officials in Poso led to a drop in the Christian share of positions from 54 percent to 39 percent. The drop created antagonistic relations because Christians became economically vulnerable. The drop meant loss of aid, government contracts, and jobs, whereas gaining positions would have ensured strong economic prospects. Those people who were had lost their electoral offices, with the profit going to local government coffers. Looting of villages also contributed to economic loss for entire communities.

In addition, feelings ran high over the independence of East Timor. East Timor's lengthy struggle for independence was strongly supported by the U.N. The struggle caused problems for the national government. A strong nationalist backlash from politically powerful groups and the proud Indonesian peoples aggravated the problem.

President Suharto had destroyed political institutions while in power, leaving no avenue of release for the political grievances that had mounted up over the years. Christians, who had held prominent positions in Suharto's cabinet and military, were largely replaced by Muslims in the government of President Habibie. Although Suharto had tried to co-opt Islam to help him maintain power, Islam turned on him, and the extreme Islamic factions in Indonesia became radical. Muslims were happy because they had felt underrepresented in power positions under Suharto. However, Christians felt threatened.

Economics

Economic stagnation was another factor that led to religious conflict. A currency crisis caused banks to collapse, and savings were wiped out because the rupiah lost 85 percent of its value. Prices skyrocketed. High unemployment plunged Indonesia into chaos, with riots everywhere. People simply could not cope with the quickly changing socioeconomic structure; they had grown accustomed to better economic conditions under Suharto. An unexpected wave of immigrants from Asian countries upset the traditional communal balance and contributed to the volatile situation. The immigrants were not grounded in President Sukarno's Pancasila structure of religious tolerance and caused problems. Moreover, people's job losses were aggravated by government decentralization and lawlessness. Muslims deliberate destruction of destroyed businesses and property preyed on the Chinese business community in 1999. Although the ethnic Chinese owned 75 percent of Indonesia's wealth, they constituted only 3 percent of the population.

Religious War

The Moluccan Islands and central Sulawesie were the areas most seriously affected by religious conflict. The tinderbox ignited when conflict erupted in Poso, Sulawesie, in December 1998. Christian and Islamic youth

Grand Mosque, Medan, Sumatra, Indonesia. October 1996 Courtesy Steve Donaldson

fought in a street brawl, resulting in an Islamic man being stabbed. He roused believers in a nearby mosque to take revenge, and a four-year cycle of violence began. The result was hundreds dead and thousands homeless. Revenge resulted in Christian neighborhoods being besieged in Poso. Christians killed three hundred Muslims in the Kilo Nine massacre. Christians who were forced to give up defending their homes were decapitated when they were caught. Some witnesses claimed that people were killed with chainsaws. Thousands of Islamic men joined the conflict. The powerful 30 million-member religious education movement Nahdlatul Ulama circulated a menacing calendar stating that every month a local Christian was marked for execution. Security forces were largely ineffective; many people who had seen their family members killed or had their homes burned sided with their own religious faction.

The largely Christian capital city, Ambon, endured turmoil when fighting erupted there in January 1999. Over the course of the centuries Muslims, Catholics, and Calvinist Protestants had lived within a framework of religious tolerance. This tolerance was shattered when Muslims felt threatened. They were insulted by anti-Islamic graffiti on the streets. The violence of the Christians and Islamic gangs escalated.

Social Unrest

Social unrest based on religious rivalry was aggravated in May 1999 when the traditional torch ceremony honoring Pattimura (he never used a surname), a Christian who had fought the Dutch colonial policy, was changed. Instead of having a Muslim carry the torch, the honor went to a Christian, inflaming the Islamic community. This led to forty-five hundred Islamic jihad (holy war) warriors coming to the Moluccan Islands that month to defend the honor of their faith. The predominantly Islamic province of North Maluku separated from the old Maluku province in September 1999. By this time a pattern of violence sparked a civil war between Muslims and Christians and spread rapidly throughout the rest of the Moluccan Islands. Hundreds of people were targeted; during 26–29 November six hundred houses and six Christian churches were burned. From September to December 1999 seven thousand people were killed, and approximately 700,000 Moluccans became refugees.

Islamic provocateurs were intent on destroying Indonesia's political, economic, and civil integrity during this power vacuum. In January 2000 eighty thousand Muslims from Yemen, Saudi Arabia, and Afghanistan came from Java to join the Islamic cause. The Laskar Jihad (Holy War Warriors), a Java-based, disciplined, and unified fundamentalist Islamic militia, was founded in 2000 by an Indonesian cleric, Jafar Umar Thalib. Although he adheres to the Wahhabi creed of Islam embraced by suspected terrorist Osama bin Laden, Thalib postulates that bin Laden's ideology does not represent the true peaceful Islamic faith; a link between Thalib and al-Qaeda has not yet been proven. Thalib claimed that he wanted to focus on religious and social-welfare activities for Muslims, but he sent five thousand troops to the Moluccan Islands to squelch what he alleged was a Christian-based separatist movement. Moreover, Laskar Jihad classifies Christians in the Moluccans as *kafir harbi*, the most dangerous category of non-Muslims, providing the anti-U.S. Laskar Jihad with the religious basis to kill. Thalib had support from military hardliners who supported him in trying to destabilize the government of President Wahid, whom he considered anti-Islamic for oppressing Muslims and protecting Christians.

Thalib's troops had received training from sympathetic officers of the Indonesian National Military (TNI—Tentara Nasional Indonesia), were given modern weapons, supported by Islamic security forces, and financed with over $9 million from embezzled military funding. With Laskar Jihad's contingent of over ten thousand troops the tide of the conflict changed and put the Christian militias on the defensive. People were forced to convert, genital mutilation was enforced, and the *shariʿa* (Islamic law) as a form of government became the goal. The conflict raged out of control when humanitarian aid was obstructed, when troops failed to ensure neutrality by siding with Muslims, when the thinly stretched police force became incapable of providing support, and when the government under President Wahid failed to aid displaced people.

During the conflict the military established a centralized mobile reserve culled from the elite of the three armed services known as the "Joint Battalion" (Yon Gab). The reserve could be dispatched quickly to conflict areas. The Yon Gab was frequently confronted by Islamic militia and thus quickly gained a pro-Christian reputation. Although this reputation contributed significantly to the decline in fighting in 2001 the Yon Gab was alleged to have committed atrocities. It was withdrawn and replaced by the Indonesian army's special forces known as "Kopassus."

Aftermath

Both Muslims and Christians suffered during the four-year conflict, which left nearly ten thousand dead, countless more injured, and hundreds of thousands displaced. The destruction of property was unprecedented in Indonesia as homes, schools, businesses, and churches were razed.

By late 2001 Christians and Muslims had become polarized, with parts of Indonesia divided into Christian and Islamic sectors. The Baku Bae, a reconciliation movement, has sponsored informal meetings to facilitate reconciliation. Sukarnoputrim won the election in June 2001, and the national government finally intervened by imposing a civil emergency. The violence did not decline until 20 December 2001, when the Malino Declaration for Poso was signed by the belligerents. However, the declaration has repeatedly been violated. Ambon also signed the peace treaty in February 2002. Unfortunately, the fighting continues sporadically to support lucrative economic opportunities such as protection money payments from property owners. Christian youth gangs are still prepared to retaliate to any violent incidents. Thalib disbanded the Laskar Jihad after a bombing in Bali in October 2002. Although peace has eluded Indonesia, the latest developments are a step in the right direction.

Annette Richardson

Further Reading

Bandow, D. (2001). Letter from Indonesia. *Chronicles*. Rockford, IL.

McBeth, J., & Murphy, O. (2000). Bloodbath. *Far Eastern Economic Review*.

Ricklefs, M. C. (1993). *A history of modern Indonesia since c. 1300* (2nd ed.). Stanford, CA: Stanford University Press.

Silk, M. (2000, Spring). Religion in the news. *Wars of Religion, 3*(1).

Iranian Revolution of 1979

Following the violation of Iran's neutrality and the forced abdication of Reza Shah Pahlavi (1878–1944) in favor of his son Mohammad Reza Pahlavi (1919–1980) during World War II, Iran entered an lengthy period of turmoil as a result of foreign domination and instability, ultimately leading up to the Iranian Revolution. The consequences of the war were very damaging for the country and food and resources were extremely scarce. These realities eventually laid the foundation for Ayatollah Ruhollah Khomeini's (c. 1900–1989) rise to power, provoked by many economic, social, and religious factors.

Historical Background

Without the strict and efficient political control exercised by the previous shah before Mohammad Reza Pahlavi assumed the throne in 1941, many organizations and parties began to express their differing views actively, resulting in widespread political confusion and instability as exemplified by the Azerbaijan crisis and the emergence of the communist Tudeh Party. In December of 1945, the Azerbaijan Democratic Party declared the creation of an autonomous republic in the Azerbaijan region of Iran with Soviet suppot. Under Diplomatic pressure from the United States and Britain and after receiving oil concessions in the region from the Iranian government, the Soviet troops withdrew and the Iranian government regained control by the end of 1946. At the same time, the presence of an abundance of foreign troops and the foreign exploitation of oil resources created and added to nationalist and xenophobic sentiments.

By 1949, nationalization of Iran's oil industry became a major issue since foreign governments and companies were deriving more revenue from Iran's oil than Iran itself. Negotiations with the majority-controlling Anglo-Iranian Oil Company (AIOC) to remedy the exploitative situation failed. Soon after, Prime Minister Mohammad Mosaddeq (1880–1967), who was popularly elected but was accepted by the shah only after overwhelming protests, pursued the nationalization of the oil industry along with members of the legislative body, known as the Majlis. Nationalization was enacted finally in March of 1951.

Consequently, the production of oil was severely reduced as British oil experts left Iran and less trained workers took over. The British banned exports to Iran and challenged the legitimacy of the nationalization in the International Court of Justice. Britain's case failed, but the AIOC attempted to negotiate better terms with Iran under pressure from the United States. Mosaddeq and his supporters rejected AIOC's new offers, believing that the company would ultimately succumb to Iranian highest demands.

As a result of the strong xenophobic sentiments, the nationalization issue drove Mosaddeq to even higher levels of popularity and he moved to consolidate his power. Meanwhile, the United States was becoming increasingly skeptical of Mosaddeq, believing that the nationalization issue proved he was overwhelmingly against the Western powers and that he was increasing his ties with the communist Tudeh Party. The situation soon became volatile when the shah collaborated with the U.S. Central Intelligence Agency to overthrow Mosaddeq. A plan was enacted in August of 1953, but it seemed to fail at first and the shah fled Iran briefly. Following almost a week of rioting and demonstrations, the military acted in favor of the shah, who soon returned to the country, and Mosaddeq was sentenced to house arrest until his death more than a decade later.

In an attempt to support the shah's unstable government, the United States provided an aid package of $45 million. Relations were drastically improved with the West as a result of the shah's fear of increasing Soviet influence and new oil agreements were signed. Opposition to the shah was banned, enforced by a strong secret police force known as SAVAK (Sazeman-I Ettelate va Amniyat-I Keshvar, The National Organization for Intelligence and Security), and previously powerful political parties like the Tudeh and Mosaddeq's National Front were suppressed. A two-party system was created which was based upon loyalty to the shah and there was a strictly controlled election for the Majlis.

The new government struggled and it failed to address the concerns of the poorer classes. The shah's development plans were based upon utilizing increased oil revenues to industrialize and to modernize the Iranian military. The economy began to prosper, but the wealth gap between the rich and the poor continued to increase over the years.

In the ensuing years, banned political parties continued to exist secretly inside Iran and abroad. Also, political forces were unrelentingly suppressed within Iran, including Mehdi Bazargan (1907–1995) and the Iran Freedom Movement. In the late 1960s, Islam became more important politically. Ayatollah Khomeini, who was forced to leave Iran for exile in Iraq, attacked the government and the shah for their secular views, for the White Revolution program that empowered women, and for collaboration with the meddling Western powers who threatened Iran's traditional society.

The opposition had a growing support base from the poor who weren't benefiting from the shah's modernization policies and from younger Iranian students who embraced the revolutions enacted by guerrillas in Cuba, Vietnam, and China. By 1976–1977, the country faced severe economic trouble as a result of the Shah's overly ambitious plans to modernize. The shah was also facing criticism from U.S. President Jimmy Carter because of the poor state of human rights in Iran. As a result, certain rights were returned to the people and political parties used the new freedoms to reorganize and speak out.

Protests Presage the Revolution

From this point, the newly empowered political parties began to organize massive protests. The protest movement had two main stages. Intellectuals and secular politicians led the first protests primarily during 1977 with the goal of returning to constitutional rule. The protests early in 1978 were religiously motivated and led by the clerics. These protests focused on places that were representative of Western influence; symbols of moral corruption, economic exploitation, and political repression were targeted. From Iraq, Khomeini became even more vocal in advocating more demonstrations, refusal to compromise, and the forced removal of the shah.

The protests continued to gain strength and became more and more destructive and violent. The protest movement became explosive on 8 September 1978, the day after the shah declared martial law. At one particular protest, the military opened fire on the massive crowd at Jaleh Square in Tehran resulting in an official number of eighty-seven killed.

Soon after, the Iraqi government expelled Khomeini because they were unable to control his political activities. He settled in Paris, where he was able to maintain better contact with Tehran and to publicize his cause through the media. Iranian politicians and religious leaders were able to visit him often. Following one of their meetings in November of 1978, the opposition revolutionary group led by Khomeini issued a statement committing the group to ally with the National Front, to overthrow the shah, and to form a new "democratic and Islamic" government.

After failed attempts to address the protesters' concerns and correct the economic situation, the shah began to have discussions with the mainstream opposition, but they weren't successful because the leader of the National Front had by then allied with Khomeini. In December, the shah made an agreement with a rogue National Front leader, Shapour Bakhtiar (1915–1991). The agreement stipulated that Bakhtiar would become prime minister and the shah would leave the country. The Majlis confirmed the nomination of Bakhtiar on 3 January 1979, and the shah left the country on 16 January 1979, amid much jubilation by the populace.

Bakhtiar was dismissed from the National Front for collaborating with the monarchy and his attempts to appeal to the more radical opposition failed. Bakhtiar also failed to block the return on 1 February 1979 of Ayatollah Khomeini, who supported Mehdi Bazargan of the National Front as the rightful prime minister. Protests continued despite Bakhtiar's attempts at reconciliation, but by 12 February, Bakhtiar lost the support of the military and his government collapsed.

The Islamic Republic of Iran

Together, Bazargan and Khomeini moved to assert authority over all of Iran. The revolution had left the country fragmented and without a centralized government. Khomeini soon emerged as the supreme authority behind the new provisional government in Tehran and he established the Revolutionary Council as the supreme legislative body. Two new political parties were formed: Khomeini's Islamic Republican Party and the moderate Islamic People's Republican Party.

Khomeini moved quickly to end dissent from the previous regime and established revolutionary courts, which led to frequent and brutal executions. In late March of 1979, he authorized the provisional government to create a new constitution and he offered a yes or no referendum on the establishment of an Islamic republic. According to the government, 98 percent of the people voted in favor and Khomeini proclaimed the Islamic Republic of Iran on 1 April 1979. The new constitution ended up being virtually identical to the previous one with a strong president replacing the former monarch. However, after a clerical-backed Assembly of Experts reviewed the document, it was edited to reflect Shiʿa religious domination by the Revolutionary Council.

The government's first actions included the creation of a paramilitary force loyal to Khomeini and the clerics known as the Pasdaran in May of 1979 and the suppression of an uprising in the Kurdish areas in August of the same year. They also nationalized a variety of important industries, and attempted to maintain amiable relations with other Gulf states.

Meanwhile, the United States admitted the shah for medical treatment and outraged the Iranian people and government, who demanded his extradition. The people feared another U.S.-led coup to replace the shah and anti-American sentiment rose drastically. On 1 November 1979, massive protests were held to demand extradition and to denounce Prime Minister Bazargan for his current meetings with U.S. officials. On 4 November, militant students stormed the U.S. Embassy and took the remaining diplomats hostage. This event led to Bazargan's resignation and the final destruction of relations between Iran and the United States.

Utilizing anti-American sentiment as a unifying issue, the Revolutionary Council took complete control of the country until elections were held in January of 1980. Abolhassan Bani Sadr (b. 1931), an independent writer on the relationship between Islam and politics, surprisingly won the presidential election. Khomeini approved of his selection for the presidency, appointed him to be the chair of the Revolutionary Council, and relinquished the powers of commander in chief of the military to him.

Sadr hoped to use his position to promote presidential authority, to end revolutionary courts and the Pasdaran, to attempt to control the radical clerics, and to enact economic reform. His aspirations were overshadowed however; Sadr struggled to control the clerics' interference in political issues. Ultimately, his leadership signaled the end of the revolution with the opening of hostilities in the Iran-Iraq War on 22 September 1980, and the negotiated release on 21 January 1981 of the U.S. diplomats held hostage.

Arthur Holst

Further Reading

Esposito, J. L. (Ed.). (1990). *The Iranian revolution: Its global impact*. Miami: Florida International University Press.

History of Iran. (2001). Retrieved April 4, 2003 from www.iranchamber.com/history/history.php.

Hoveyda, F. (2003). *The shah and the ayatollah: Iranian mythology and Islamic revolution*. Westport, CT: Praeger.

Metz, H. C. (Ed.). (1987). *Iran: A country study*. Washington, DC: Library of Congress. Retrieved April 4, 2003 from http://lcweb2.loc.gov/frd/cs/irtoc.html

Spurgeon, B. (1999, February 9). 20 years later, images from the revolution. *International Herald Tribune*, p. 21.

Zahedi, D. (2001). *The Iranian revolution then and now: Indicators of regime instability*. Boulder, CO: Westview Press.

Zayar. (2000). The Iranian revolution—past, present, and future. Retrieved April 4, 2003 from www.marxist.-com/iran/index.html

Iroquois

From their first contact with Europeans in the seventeenth century until their settlement on reserves and reservations after the American Revolution, the Iroquois as a fighting force were held in high repute in eastern North America. Historians and anthropologists have focused on economic causes of their warfare, but the historian José António Brandão has argued that the Iroquois people's prime motive in war was to obtain war captives to maintain their population, which was stressed by losses to European diseases. Important in early Iroquois warfare was the view that the sun and Agreskwe, the god of war (the two deities may have been one and the same, as discussed below), demanded periodic sacrifice of war captives. Also important, though, was an emphasis on peace found in Iroquois traditions of the founding of the Iroquois confederacy, probably in the fifteenth or sixteenth century, and in the teachings of the prophet Handsome Lake (c. 1735–1815) in his revitalization of Iroquois religion over the period 1799 to 1815.

The Iroquois confederacy was originally made up of five nations whose aboriginal homeland stretched through what is now upstate New York from the valley of the Mohawk River to that of the Genesee. From east to west these nations were the Mohawk, the Oneida, the Onondaga, the Cayuga, and the Seneca. When encountered by Europeans in the first decade of the seventeenth century, the nations of the confederacy were at war with their neighbors to the north, and for much of the two centuries between this initial contact and the sale of their lands and their settlement on reservations they were at war with one or more of their neighbors. The Iroquois nations spoke closely related languages of the Iroquoian language family, as did those they fought to the north, west, and south: the Huron confederacy, the Wenro, the Neutral, the Erie, and the Susquehannock. To the east were the Algonquian-speaking Mahican and Delaware and the various Algonquian tribes of New England.

The Iroquois enjoyed considerable success in war. In the so-called Beaver Wars of the mid-seventeenth century they destroyed or dispersed the Wenro, the

Huron, the Petun, the Neutral, and the Erie nations, greatly expanding the area open to them for harvesting beaver pelts for the fur trade. They also established hegemony over several New England groups, ensuring a stream of tribute in the form of sacred wampum shell beads made from whelk and quahog gathered on the Atlantic shore, which was significant, as they were a landlocked people. At the peak of their power, Iroquois war parties struck far to the north, well into the Hudson Bay drainage, and as far west as the Mississippi. A key to their success was access to firearms from Dutch and English traders at Fort Orange (present-day Albany, New York). As their enemies, supplied by the French, became better armed, the Iroquois were less successful and in fact lost some of the territories they had conquered previously. After agreeing to a policy of neutrality with both the English and the French in separate treaties in 1701, they for the remainder of the century attempted to maximize their power through a combination of diplomacy and military strikes against selected enemies.

Iroquois Society

The Iroquois women planted and cultivated the Iroquois' principal food crop, corn (maize), as well as beans and squash to provide balance to the diet. Men did the heavy work of clearing the forest for the fields and contributed to the economy through hunting and fishing. After Dutch merchants became established on the edge of Iroquois territory at Fort Orange, the men also engaged in trapping for the fur trade. The fields surrounded relatively large villages of as many as three thousand people living in multifamily dwellings known as longhouses.

Each nation was divided into a number of clans. The Mohawks and Oneidas each had three clans, while the more western nations had eight or nine clans. The Wolf, Bear, and Turtle clans were found in all five Iroquois nations. One belonged to one's mother's clan and the clans were exogamous (that is, one had to marry someone from outside one's clan), thus one's father was from a different clan. The clans were divided into a number of localized lineages, each headed by an elder woman referred to as the clan or lineage matron. The longhouses were occupied by the women of a single lineage with their husbands and unmarried sons. One treated members of one's own generation of the same lineage or clan as siblings, but one had special obligations to one's father's lineage and clan.

Restoring Troubled Minds

It is difficult to segregate Iroquois religious beliefs from their general worldview and ideas of physical and spiritual well-being. A theme running through Iroquois behavior and social interaction and reflected in their mythology is the contrast between a clear mind and a troubled mind. According to Iroquois tradition, this world was created as a result of the actions of the leader of the sky world when his mind was troubled. Originally, this world was an endless sea, inhabited by waterfowl and marine animals. Above the celestial dome lived a population dependent upon a marvelous tree that grew at the center of their land. However, the chief of the sky world was troubled by fears of his wife's infidelity, and in this state he uprooted the celestial tree, then pushed his wife through the hole in the sky left by the tree's uprooting. The falling woman was caught by waterfowl and placed on the back of a turtle. An earth diver (most commonly a muskrat) came up with earth from the bottom of the sea, and the earth was placed on the turtle's back. This grew to continental size, creating solid land. There the woman—who had been pregnant when she fell—bore a daughter. That daughter later bore twin sons who created humans and the good and evil in the world (the elder twin, the Creator, providing for the good of humans, the younger twin spoiling the elder's creations and creating those things that plague humans).

The Iroquois believed that excessive grieving over the loss of a kinsman could cause a mind to become troubled, but that the mind could be restored to a normal state through war, and specifically through receiving two forms of trophy. These were either a war captive or the scalp of a slain enemy. Not all deaths would inspire such significant excessive grief, and normal funeral ritual would clear the mind in such cases. The historian Daniel Richter has appropriated "mourning wars," a name championed by anthropologist Marian Smith for similar wars of blood revenge on the North American Plains, as the designation for Iroquois war practices. The lineage matron played a leading role in urging action to secure one of these trophies to replace the deceased member of the lineage. The war party was recruited not from members of the deceased's lineage but rather from among men whose fathers belonged to the lineage of the deceased. Thus women (the clan matrons) played a leading role in initiating war activity, but they sent their brother's sons to war, not their own.

The taking of captives was such a significant part of the war complex that there was a specialized and often highly ornamented artifact that each warrior carried in addition to his weapons, food supply (dried maize), and spare moccasins. This was the prisoner tie, a collar ornamented with moose-hair false embroidery and beads with long cordage extending from each end. The collar was bound about the prisoner's neck and the two cords bound the prisoner's arms at the elbows behind his back and at the wrists in front. Part of a person's relationship with the spiritual world was a personal song that he or she would sing in certain ceremonies to communicate with supernatural powers. The prisoner was expected to sing this song from the point of his or her capture throughout the journey to the home village of his or her captors.

Both scalp and captive were received with ceremonial treatment. The women of the community would sing and dance for the scalp; captives, for their part, would be forced to run the gauntlet. This meant running between two rows of villagers armed with clubs and knives. Most survived this, and the majority of those captured were adopted into the village and incorporated into Iroquois society.

Ritual Torture and Sacrifice

Some captives, however, were destined to be sacrificed to Agreskwe or the sun. Agreskwe was a deity whom the seventeenth-century Iroquoians identified as the god of war and to whom they sacrificed first fruits, including war captives. It is unclear from the historical evidence whether the sun was the same deity as Agreskwe or a separate deity who also had an influence on war, but the sun or Agreskwe were addressed by both the victim and his tormentors during the torture ritual. An eyewitness to one of these torture rituals stated it was accompanied by an old man addressing Agreskwe in a loud voice: "we sacrifice to thee this victim, that thou mayst satisfy thyself with her flesh, and give us victory over our enemies" (quoted in Goddard 1984, 230). Ideally the torture victim was tormented through the night, but lived to be sacrificed upon the sight of the rising sun. At that time the dying victim was scalped and hot coals or ashes were thrown into the wound. He was killed, and his chest opened so that his heart could be removed. Sometimes the body was dismembered to be consumed by the torturers, although body parts were sometimes sent to allied communities so they might share in the sacrificial feast.

The anthropologist Peggy Reeves Sanday ties the torture and cannibalism ritual to the conflict between the Good Twin and the Evil Twin in the creation myth, to Iroquoian emphasis on desires of the soul expressed in dreams, to excessive grief on the death of a relative, and to a Freudian Oedipal conflict between senior males and junior males in Iroquoian society. She sees the stress introduced into seventeenth-century Iroquoian society by deaths from famine, disease, and warfare as creating conditions amenable the public display of torture and execution of war captives.

Voices for Peace

While the aid of Agreskwe was important to the Iroquois in gaining victory in war, other aspects of their belief system emphasized peace. The account of the founding of the Iroquois confederacy rivals the creation myth both in complexity and popularity. A central figure in this story is the Onondaga chief Thadodaho, a powerful and evil sorcerer with seven crooks in his body and snakes in his hair. He was tamed and brought into the League of Peace by the Peacemaker (a Huron man, born of a virgin mother) and his companion, the Mohawk chief Hiawatha. The Peacemaker cast the weapons of war into a pit, and planted over them the Tree of Peace. It is in the shade of that tree that the five nations of the Iroquois confederacy reside. The Iroquois were anxious throughout the colonial era to attract other to join them sitting in the shade of the Great Tree.

Another figure who had an important influence on Iroquois religion and issues of war and peace was the Seneca prophet Handsome Lake. Half-brother to the Seneca war chief Cornplanter (c. 1732–1836), Handsome Lake had fought through the American Revolution as an ally to the British and Loyalists. The defeat of the forces of the Crown in that conflict left the Iroquois and many other Native Americans facing an expansionist and land-hungry U.S. government. In this traumatic arena and era, Handsome Lake was one of several Native Americans who experienced visions that led them to attempt to revitalize indigenous traditions and provide a path for future policy. Unlike most of his fellow prophets, though, Handsome Lake preached a message of accommodation to the new United States. As the "peace prophet" he received the endorsement of the U.S. government, including Thomas Jefferson. The Iroquois did not participate in the bloody wars in the Ohio country and upper Great Lakes that followed the American Revolution, and Handsome Lake's teachings continue to have a strong influence on conservative elements in many Iroquois communities today in both Canada and the United States.

Thomas S. Abler

Further Reading

Abler, T. S. (1992). Beavers and muskets: Iroquois military fortunes in the face of European colonization. In R. B. Ferguson & N. L. Whitehead (Eds.), *War in the tribal zone: Expanding states and indigenous warfare* (pp. 151–174). Santa Fe, NM: School of American Research Press.

Abler, T. S. (1992). Scalping, torture, cannibalism and rape: An ethnohistorical analysis of conflicting cultural values in war. *Anthropologica, 34*(1), 3–20.

Abler, T. S., & Logan, M. H. (1988). The florescence and demise of Iroquoian cannibalism: Human sacrifice and Malinowski's hypothesis. *Man in the Northeast, 35*, 1–26.

Brandão, J. A. (1997). *Your fyre shall burn no more: Iroquois policy toward New France and its native allies to 1701.* Lincoln: University of Nebraska Press.

Deardorff, M. H. (1951). The religion of Handsome Lake: Its origin and development. *Bureau of American Ethnology Bulletin, 149*, 77–107.

Fenton, W. N. (1962). This island, the world on the turtle's back. *Journal of American Folklore, 75*(298), 283–300.

Fenton, W. N. (1978). Northern Iroquoian culture patterns. In B. Trigger (Ed.), *Handbook of North American Indians: Vol. 15. Northeast* (pp. 296–321). Washington, DC: Smithsonian.

Fenton, W. N. (1998). *The great law and the longhouse: A political history of the Iroquois.* Norman: University of Oklahoma Press.

Goddard, I. (1984). Agreskwe, a northern Iroquoian deity. In M. K. Foster, J. Campisi, & M. Mithun (Eds.). *Extending the rafters: Interdisciplinary approaches to Iroquoian studies* (pp. 229–235). Albany: State University of New York Press.

Hunt, G. (1940). *The wars of the Iroquois: A study of intertribal trade relations.* Madison: University of Wisconsin Press.

Richter, D. K. (1983). War and culture: The Iroquois experience. *William and Mary Quarterly (3rd ser.), 40*(4), 528–559.

Richter, D. K. (1992). *The ordeal of the longhouse: The peoples of the Iroquois League in the era of European colonization.* Chapel Hill: University of North Carolina Press.

Sanday, P. R. (1986). *Divine hunger: cannibalism as a cultural system.* Cambridge, UK: Cambridge University Press.

Smith, M. (1951). American Indian warfare. *New York Academy of Sciences Transactions (2nd ser.), 13*(8), 348–365.

Trelease, A. (1960). *Indian affairs in colonial New York: The seventeenth century.* Ithaca, NY: Cornell University Press.

Trelease, A. (1962). The Iroquois and the western fur trade: A problem in interpretation. *Mississippi Valley Historical Review, 49*(1), 32–51.

Wallace, A. F. C. (1958). Dreams and the wishes of the soul: A type of psychoanalytic theory among the seventeenth-century Iroquois. *American Anthropologist, 60*(2), 234–248.

Wallace, A. F. C. (1970). *Death and rebirth of the Seneca.* New York: Knopf.

Wallace, P. A. W. (1946). *The white roots of peace.* Philadelphia: University of Pennsylvania Press.

Woodbury, H. (Ed. and Trans.). (1992). *Concerning the League: the Iroquois League tradition as dictated in Onondaga by John Arthur Gibson.* Algonquian and Iroquoian Linguistics Memoir 8. Winnipeg: University of Manitoba.

Islam

See Afghanistan; Africa, West; Assassins; Babi and Baha'i Religions; Byzantine-Muslim War of 645; Crusades; Deobandism; Fundamentalism in Egypt and Sudan; Fundamentalism in Iran; Genocide in Bosnia; Hamas; Hindu-Muslim Violence in India; Hizbullah; Indonesia; Iranian Revolution of 1979; Islam: Age of Conquest; Islam, Qurʾanic; Islam, Shiʿa; Islam: Sufism; Islam, Sunni; Islamic Law of War; Islamic Movement of Uzbekistan; Jihad; Kashmir; Martyrdom; Palestine and Israel; Palestine: 1948 War; Palestine Liberation Organization; Shiite Rebellion of 815–819; Sudan; Sudanese War of 1881–1898; Tajik Civil War; Taliban; Wahhabism; Yoruba

Islam: Age of Conquest

The period of the early Muslim conquests, lasting approximately between 634 and 742 CE, was one of the most impressive bursts of military success in history. Although this age of conquest was comparatively short in duration (compared to the Roman, Spanish, British, or Russian conquests), its effects were long term (unlike those of the Mongols, Napoleon, or Hitler), changing the religious, cultural, and linguistic mosaic of late antiquity. These conquests were triggered by the decisions of the caliphs Abu Bakr (c. 573–634 CE) and ʿUmar ibn al-Khattab (c. 586–644 CE) to direct the energies of the population of the Arabian Peninsula outward against the two dominant empires of late antiquity, the Roman "Byzantine" Empire (centered at Constantinople) and the Persian Sasanian Empire (centered at Ctesiphon, present-day Iraq). The two empires had previously fought a lengthy war (602–628) that ended in the collapse of the Sasanian Empire, and the Pyrrhic victory of the Byzantines. The Muslims took advantage of this situation, conquered Syria and Egypt from the Byzantines, and swallowed the entire Sasanian Empire, which included the present-day countries of Iraq and Iran and parts of Afghanistan and central Asia.

After this initial phase of conquests, the Muslim empire fought a civil war (656–661) that resulted in the establishment of the Umayyad dynasty ruling from Syria with its capital in Damascus. A further civil war between 683 and 692 temporarily halted the conquests yet again, but another dynamic period between the late 680s and 717 saw the conquest of North Africa and Spain (Andalus) in the west, and that of Central Asia toward the borders of China in the east, and penetration of Sind and parts of the Indian subcontinent in the southeast. The Umayyad caliph Sulayman (674–717) mounted a major siege of the Byzantine capital of Constantinople, and control of the Mediterranean Sea in both its eastern and western parts (enabling raids on southern France and western Italy) passed to the Muslim navy. However, ultimately the Muslims failed to conquer Constantinople or any additional provinces of the Byzantine Empire other than those conquered during the first phase of the conquests (Syria, Egypt, North Africa). During the decades following 717 the Muslim empire suffered serious reverses on all fronts due to imperial overreach, and eventually collapsed into a third civil war (743–749) leading to the rise of the Abbasid dynasty (749–1258), according to K. Y. Blankinship. The western provinces of the empire (Spain, North Africa) split off during this period, and large-scale Muslim conquest came to an end (although the Abbasid army continued to dominate the region).

There is no consensus among scholars as to the reasons why the conquests happened or as to the reasons for their success. The various approaches as to the reasons can be summarized as follows:

1. Those following the Muslim sources who see the conquests as the result of a centralized decision on the part of the early Muslim caliphs and commanders to conquer territory (assumed above). There are a number of historical problems with this approach as the level of control presented by the Muslim sources on the part of the caliphs with regard to the armies stretches credulity, and regularly depends upon various miracles and foreknowledge of the future. However, despite these historical problems, this approach is the one assumed by most scholars.
2. Those following interpretations necessitating either environmental or economic compulsion (Marxist interpretations). These scholars have sought to find either a change in the climate of the Arabian Peninsula (marginal at the best of times) or economic factors that could have led to a large-scale invasion or migration of nomads into the surrounding regions. The evidence for these factors, unfortunately, is very partial and does not explain the success of the early Muslims nor how they managed to maintain themselves as a cohesive unity (despite their constant civil wars) in the newly occupied lands.
3. Those who see the conquests as either an illusion or an exaggeration on the part of the Muslim sources. These scholars have been frustrated by the near lack of corroborating historical or archeological evidence to back up the Muslim accounts of invasion. One scholar, P. Pentz, has even referred to it as "The Invisible Conquest" because of these problems. This approach to the conquests appears to envision a peaceful (or at least less violent) takeover of the core lands of the future Muslim empire (Syria, Iraq, Egypt) after the collapse of the two major empires, and then conquests of the additional territories that are better documented. Unfortunately, once again there is no compelling evidence for such an occurrence, and the theory does not appear to answer the basic questions of how this happened.
4. The conquests appear to have been justified as part of a program of religiously mandated expansion. An early tradition from ʿAbdallah b. al-Mubarak's (d. 797) *Kitab al-jihad* (the earliest book on the subject of *jihad*) states: "Behold! God sent me [Muhammad] with a sword, just before the Hour of Judgment, and placed my daily sustenance under the shadow of my spear" (*Kitab al-jihad*, pp. 89–90). This tradition and many others like it, coupled together with the later aggressive verses in the Qurʾan (especially those in *sura*) provide the basis for an ideology capable of the great conquests. The early Muslims were

not fighting for Muhammad so much as they were fighting for Islam. Thus the conquests are rightly seen as a vindication of the religion and an incontrovertible proof of its veracity. Many tribal groups such as the Berbers and the Turks, as well as the Persians, were attracted by this belief and converted to Islam.

Problems connected with the motivation of the early Muslim conquerors are equally difficult. For the most part the conquering armies were not dominated by Bedouin troops, but by those seminomadic inhabitants of Syria and Iraq that had previously been organized into "client kingdoms" by both the Byzantines and the Sasanians, usually with a member of the Muslim aristocracy for leadership. There is good evidence to suggest that many Muslims believed that their mission was to proclaim Islam by conquering the world, since the revelation of the Qur'an and other events suggested that the world was about to end. This is backed up by comparing the major thrusts of the campaigns described below with apocalyptic predictions (indicating the end of the world in the 660s, then in the 680s, and finally for the Muslim year 100/717–718).

However, discussion of motivation does not answer the question of why precisely the Muslims were able to defeat so many enemies during this period of one hundred plus years. It is clear, however, that the Byzantine and Sasanian empires they faced initially were very much weakened by their previous warring against each other. As the Muslims moved beyond the regions of these two empires, they found power vacuums in adjacent territories that had existed because of the weakness of the major empires and were able to quickly fill them. However, some of the Muslims' quick advance was achieved by ignoring the topographically difficult terrain of whatever region they conquered. Time after time during the centuries following the conquests, those mountainous regions were to serve as the base for a much smaller reconquest (in Spain, Armenia, Tabaristan, and Afghanistan).

Early Conquests (634–680 CE)

The early conquests were all led by close companions of the Prophet Muhammad (c. 570–632 CE) and involved lands either adjacent to the Arabian Peninsula or at least adjacent to a desert. Just before his death Muhammad had sent several columns toward the Byzantine province of Syria, where they were severely mauled. Abu Bakr, his immediate successor, continued to send troops that began raiding the undefended areas of Palestine and southern Syria in 634 to 637. This provoked the local Byzantine authorities to confront the different Muslim columns, during the course of which most of the latter were victorious. In the wake of these failures, the Byzantine emperor Heraclius (c. 575–641) assembled a large army in northern Syria to attack the Muslim raiders. Abu Bakr's successor ʿUmar ordered reinforcements from the Arabian Peninsula and Iraq to go to Syria, including the charismatic and successful commander Khalid ibn al-Walid (d. 642), who was not, however, placed in overall command. These two groups fought at Yarmuk (August 636), south of Damascus. The battle was a decisive victory for the Muslims, and the Byzantine army was for the most part annihilated.

During the following years cities and fortresses throughout Syria-Palestine were reduced one by one—Damascus (635), Jerusalem (638), Caesarea (640)—usually without a lengthy siege. The last areas to be conquered were the northern mountains of Syria, in which the Byzantines mounted guerrilla warfare into the first decades of the eighth century. After the taking of Caesarea, ʿAmr ibn al-ʿAs (d. 663), another Muslim commander, headed south for Egypt. With the exception of the major port city of Alexandria, Egypt fell to the Muslims with ease in 641, and they negotiated with the Byzantines for control of Alexandria. However, in 645 the Byzantines returned to Alexandria and retook the city, holding it until they were decisively defeated and expelled later that year. ʿAmr and other governors of Egypt then began to send out probing raids toward North Africa.

Iraq was easily conquered by the Muslims. As previously noted, the Sasanian Empire had virtually collapsed just before the Muslim invasions. During 634 the Bedouin chieftain al-Muthanna ibn Haritha (died c. 635–7) began raiding the border regions of Iraq. He was reinforced by Saʿd ibn Abi Waqqas (d. c. 661–80) with a large contingent of Muslim troops. On the Sasanian side, Emperor Yazdegerd III (d. 651) and his commander Rustam gathered a large army, and the two sides met, probably in 636 or 637, at al-Qadisiyah (Kadisiyah), to the southwest of Al-Kufa near the Euphrates River. This battle was a decisive victory for the Muslims, and virtually ended resistance in the area of Iraq. Muslim armies under ʿAbdallah ibn ʿAmir al-Qusim (d. c. 680) penetrated the Iranian heartlands in search of Yazdegerd, who was betrayed by his own supporters and killed. By the end of the early period of the

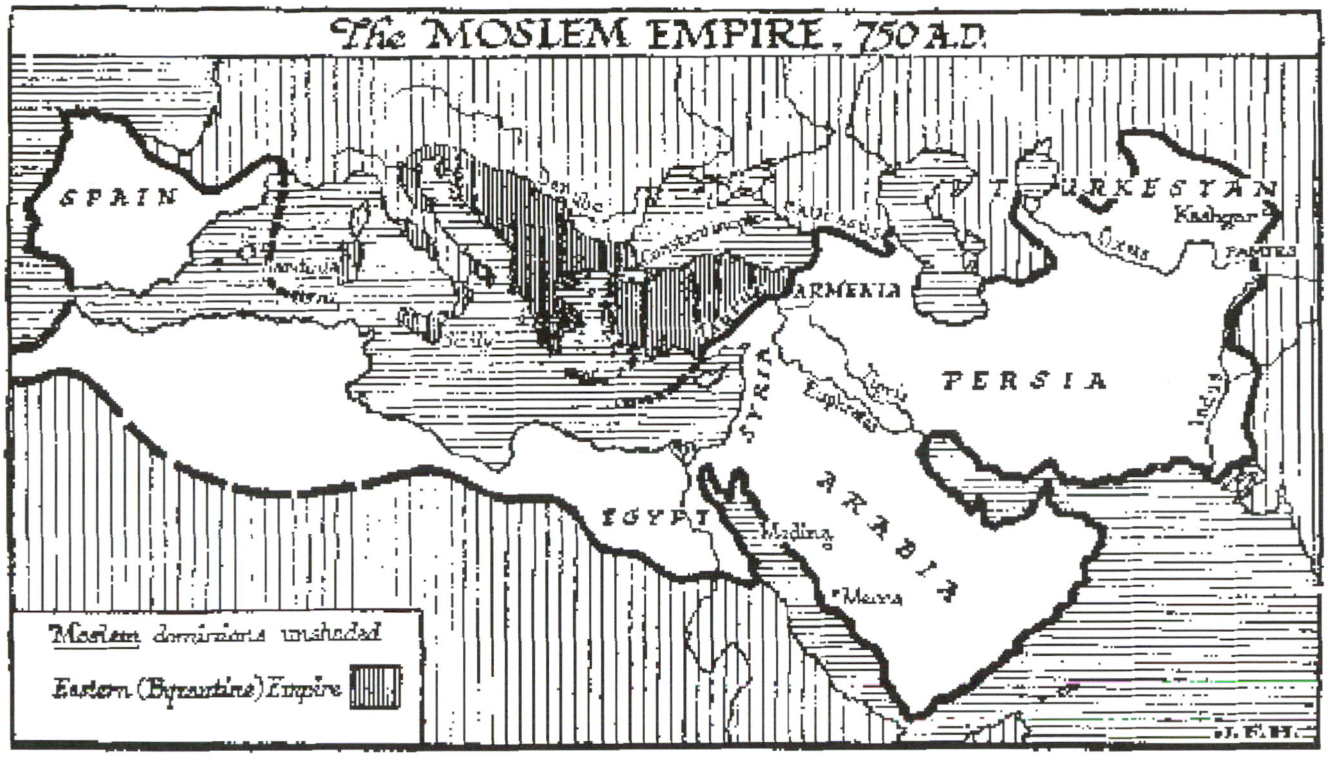

A map depicting the Muslim empire in 750 CE. Source: H.G. Wells, *A Short History of the World* (London: 1922).

Muslim conquests in 656, the area from Iran to the Great Salt Desert was subdued.

To the northwest, the area of Armenia and Azerbaijan was much more difficult for the Muslims to conquer, and was not fully subdued until the middle of the Umayyad period at the beginning of the eighth century. At that time, the Muslim armies went through the Derbent Pass (in Azerbaijan), but suffered numerous reverses going north toward the Khazar-controlled region of the north Caucasus Mountains. Effectively the Muslims did not advance in this direction for the following several centuries. We will now examine the later conquests in detail, first the eastern and then the western conquests.

Eastern Conquests (680–742 CE)

After the initial conquests, the eastern front in the region of present-day central Asia and Afghanistan was the toughest region for the Muslim conquerors. Topographically, this region is characterized by high mountains that are ideally suited for guerrilla warfare, in addition to being extremely distant from the Muslim primary bases in Al-Kufa and Basra (in southern Iraq). During the decade 705–715 CE the Muslim armies in central Asia were commanded by Qutaybah ibn Muslim (d. 715), who gradually managed to move through the Amu Darya (Oxus) and Jaxartes valleys to Fergana against the Turks. After Qutaybah's fall in 715 due to political schemes at the Umayyad court, the conquests toward the east stalled. His successor, Yazid ibn al-Muhallab (672–720), focused his attention on the previously ignored mountains of Tabaristan in northern Persia. Although al-Muhallab enjoyed some successes, Muslims did not conquer this difficult area for another 200 years.

Further to the east in Afghanistan, most of this time was spent in a largely fruitless effort to defeat the Turkish (or Iranian nomadic) tribesmen of the area. This war saw major reverses for the Muslims, although in the end they were able to defeat their foes and amalgamate them into their army. Yet further south in Sind the dynamic Muhammad ibn al-Qasim al-Thaqafi (d. c. 715–716) (governor 708–715) conquered the region and sent several raids into India itself, conquering Multan in 714. However, these successes were not followed up with large-scale settlement or conversion at this time. Muslim fleets during the following centuries came to dominate the Indian Ocean and repeatedly raided the Indian coast (especially in the region of Kerala), and eventually raided along the coast of eastern Africa as well.

For the most part the campaigns in the east were major operations supported by the Umayyad regime, which usually appointed its most successful general to this region. The Muslims achieved victory by outflanking their enemies on the plains (where their horsemen were dominant) and by relentlessly pursuing them in the hills and mountains (and by the occasional use of terror) until the latter were defeated. Muslim armies were supplemented and reinforced by a constant influx of converts from the Iranian population and from the defeated Turks.

Western Conquests (680–742 CE)

Like the conquests in the east, the western conquests were characterized by a high degree of mobility and long-range penetration of enemy territory coupled together with the successful integration of the Berber population into the Muslim army (to compensate for the lack of numbers). Muslim armies under ʿUqbah ibn Nafiʿal-Fihri (d. 683) penetrated (according to the sources) all the way to the Atlantic Ocean in 681 to 683. However, ʿUqbah was killed by Berbers while returning, and the region of North Africa was entirely lost. A secondary conquest attempt in 692 and 693 was partially successful, but was rolled back by a Berber revolt. Finally, in 698 to 710 the area of Ifriqiya (Tunisia) and then Morocco by Musa ibn Nusayr (c. 640–714), and the Berber tribesmen integrated into the Muslim armies.

During the year 711 Musa crossed over the Straits of Gibraltar to the Iberian Peninsula (supposedly at the invitation of a noble with a grudge against the Vandal king) and over the next three years together with Tariq ibn Ziyad (d. c. 720), his Berber subordinate, for whom Gibraltar is named, subdued most of the peninsula. As Arab and Berber tribesmen entered the region they continued northwards over the Pyrenees Mountains into the plains of southern France. Under the commander ʿAbd al-Rahman ibn ʿAbdallah al-Ghafiqi (d. c. 732) they encountered Charles Martel (c. 688–741; the grandfather of Charlemagne) in 732 at the Battle of Poitiers near Tours, several hundred miles south of Paris. This battle resulted in the Muslims' defeat. Most modern scholars have rejected the decisive importance of this battle, noting that Muslims continued to dominate the south of France for the next 150 years; however, it is a convenient point to note the high-water mark of Muslim conquest in the area. Muslims mounted raids against Sardinia and especially against Rome (846), but did not occupy these regions permanently. During the following century the Muslims of Ifriqiya (Tunisia) conquered Sicily and the southern region of the Italian Peninsula; other than these two latter conquests the Muslims never succeeded in following up their successes, probably because of logistical difficulties and lack of manpower.

Effects of the Islamic Age of Conquest

The age of Islamic conquest brought an end to the period of late antiquity and the unity of the Mediterranean basin. Although for the most part contemporary scholarship rejects the thesis of Henri Pirenne (1862–1935), who wrote that the division of the Mediterranean destroyed trade forever and led to the Dark Ages in western Europe, it is clear that the continual warfare of the seventh and eighth centuries led to completely different cultures developing on the opposite shores of the Mediterranean Sea. It is, however, incorrect to state that the Muslim and the medieval western Christian civilizations were not still closely linked by trade and other connections.

In the central region of the Muslim empire (Iraq, Syria, Egypt, Persia) the warfare with the Byzantine Empire (Anatolia and the southern Balkans) was inconclusive for the following 350 years until 1071, when the Battle of Manzikert (Malazgirt) permitted the Turkish tribesmen to enter and settle in Anatolia. Relations between these two empires were characterized by mutual respect and a high level of cultural and economic interdependence. On the eastern front, the Muslim conquests opened up communications between the world of the Mediterranean basin and China (the so-called Silk Road), and eventually led to the conversion of the Turkish peoples to Islam. To the southeast, the conquests in India at this time were abortive and not resumed until the time of Mahmud of Ghazni (971–1030). Further south and west, no serious attempt was made to conquer either one of the Christian kingdoms of Nubia or Ethiopia at this time.

The Islamic conquests formed the core lands still dominated by Muslims to this day, gave them a cultural and religious unity, and in many of them brought about a linguistic shift to the Arabic language (with the notable exception of Persia).

David B. Cook

Further Reading

Athamina, K. (1998). Non-Arab regiments and private militias during the Umayyad period. *Arabica, 45*, 347–378.

Blankinship, K. Y. (1994). *The end of the jihad state: The reign of Hisham b. ʿAbd al-Malik and the collapse of the Umayyads*. Albany: State University of New York Press.

Canard, M. (1926). Les expéditions des Arabes contre Constantinople dans l'histoirie et la légende [The Arab expiditions against Constantinople in history and legend]. *Journal Asiatique, 208*, 61–121.

Cook, D. (1996). Muslim apocalyptic and *jihad*. *Jerusalem Studies in Arabic and Islam, 20*, 66–104.

Donner, F. (1982) *The early Islamic conquests*. Princeton, NJ: Princeton University Press.

Donner, F. (1989). Centralized authority and military autonomy in the early Islamic conquests. In A. Cameron (Ed.), *The Byzantium and early Islamic Near East* (Vol. 3, pp. 337–360). Princeton. NJ: Darwin Press.

Hasan, S. A. (1970–1974). A survey of the expansion of Islam into central Asia during the Umayyad caliphate. *Islamic Culture, 44*, 165–176; *45*, 95–113; *47*, 1–13; *48*, 177–186.

Hasson, I. (1991). Les *mawali* dans l'armée musulmane sous les premiers umayyades [The *mawali* in the Muslim army under the first Umayyads]. *Jerusalem studies in Arabic and Islam, 14*, 176–213.

Huzayyin, S. (1995–56). Expansion of the Arabs: Its relation to climatic changes and other factors. *Bulletin d'Institute Egyptienne, 38*, 37–52.

Jandora, J. (1986). Developments in Islamic warfare: The early conquests. *Studia Islamica, 64*, 101–113.

Mazzaoui, M. (1993). The conquest of Alexandria. *Graeco-Arabica, 5*, 167–175.

McCormick, M. (2002). *The origins of the European economy*. Cambridge, UK: Cambridge University Press.

Noth, A. (1971). Der charakter der ersten grossen sammlungen von nachrichten zur frühen kalifenzeit. *Der Islam, 47*, 168–199.

Noth, A., & Conrad, L. (1994). *The early Arabic historical tradition* (M. Bonner, Trans.). Princeton, NJ: Darwin Press.

Pentz, P. (1992). *The invisible conquest: The ontogenesis of sixth and seventh century Syria*. Copenhagen, Denmark: The National Museum of Denmark.

Wenner, M. (1980). The Arab/Muslim presence in Medieval Central Europe. *International Journal of Middle Eastern Studies, 12*, 59–79.

Islam, Qur'anic

Although it accepts the reality of war in human life, allows the waging of war under certain circumstances, and provides instructions about conduct of war, the Qur'an regards war essentially as an exception to the rule of peace. Since the revelatory history of the Qur'anic text is inextricably tied to the history of the Prophet Muhammad's (c. 570–632 CE) efforts to establish Islam in Arabia, a study of the Qur'anic view of war will have to take into account both the Qur'anic text and Muhammad's conduct of war. But, first, a few words about the Qur'an's general perspective on war.

War in History

Qur'an 2:248–251 narrates the story of a war between the Israelites and the Philistines. The last verse in the passage reads: "So, they [Israelites] defeated them by God's will, and David killed Goliath, and God gave him kingship and wisdom and taught him whatever He wished. And were it not for God's repelling of one people by means of another, corruption would have overtaken the earth; God, however, is bountiful toward the people of the world" (Mustansir Mir, Trans.). This verse seems to speak of war as God's instrument to rid the world of evil and wickedness. But not every war qualifies as such an instrument, as the religious context of 2:251 itself suggests. The point is further clarified by 22:40, which justifies war with reference to religious and moral causes: "Were it not for God's repelling of one people by means of another, the result would have been demolition of monasteries, churches, synagogues, and mosques, in which God is frequently mentioned." In other words, it is only a just war that serves as God's instrument to purge the world of what the Qur'an calls corruption. This, of course, raises the question: What is a just war? While a detailed answer is not possible here, it can at least be said, in light of 22:40, that defense of houses of worship—and, by extension, (1) defense of the lands where such houses of worship are located and (2) defense of the general principle of religious freedom—would constitute a just war. A verse like the above-cited 2:251, which calls putting an end to *fasad*—which is here translated as "corruption," but which has a wider denotation—would seem to enlarge the scope of a just war even further.

Defensive War

Muhammad's prophetic career is divided into two phases, Meccan and Medinan. In the first phase, which lasted for about thirteen years (610–622 CE), the revelations received by Muhammad dealt largely with the fundamentals of the faith and the ethical principles deriving from those fundamentals. They contained no mention of war, or of the possibility of war, against the unbelievers; any such mention would have lacked relevance, since the Muslims, during the Meccan phase, were weak both in terms of numbers and in terms of resources and, hence, were incapable of militarily challenging the tribe of Quraysh, who ruled the city. The situation changed after the emigration of Muhammad and his followers to Medina in 622. Qur'an 22:39, revealed in the first year after the emigration, permits Muslims to take up arms against those who sought to fight them: "Permission is given to those who are being fought against, because they have been wronged." This verse would seem to establish several principles:

First, "permission is given" implies that Muslims can engage in a war only if it is religiously permissible for them to do so. In other words, war for its own sake or war for the sake of a religiously interdicted objective, such as plunder or hegemony, is proscribed.

Second, the passive voice of "those who are being fought against" signifies that the aforesaid permission is given not to initiate hostilities but to respond to hostilities initiated by an enemy.

Third, "because they have been wronged" states the circumstances justifying war: Muslims can fight to stop persecution or combat oppression. The immediately following verse explains the conditions under which the permission to go to war was given: because the Muslims "were ejected from their homes without any warrant." This is a reference to the fact that the Muslims were forced to emigrate from Mecca.

Qur'an 22:39–40 thus lays down the doctrine of defensive war. A number of other verses, for example, 2:191, support this doctrine. Historically, too, it is known that, after their emigration to Medina, the Muslims had to defend themselves in their new home against the repeated invasions of Mecca's Quraysh armies.

Offensive War and the Doctrine of Permanent War

But another set of data in the Qur'an seems to permit offensive war. For instance, 9:5 says: "When the Sacred Months have passed, kill the idolators wherever you find them; seize them, besiege them, and lie in wait for them in every place of ambush. If they repent and establish the prayer and pay the *zakah*, then leave them alone; God is Very Forgiving, Very Merciful." And 9:29 reads: "Fight those, from among those who were given the Book, who do not believe in God or in the Last Day, do not declare unlawful what God and His Prophet have declared unlawful, and do not follow the religion of truth." Verses like these—coupled, of course, with Prophetic *ahadith* (sayings; sing. hadith) of similar import—led classical Muslim jurists to posit what has been called the doctrine of permanent war or jihad. Historically, however, the doctrine passed through several stages, corresponding with the changing political and military fortunes of the so-called universal Islamic state. In its first formulation, the doctrine served to justify the spread of Islamic rule through the agency of an expanding state entity. With the arrest of the movement of conquest and expansion, the doctrine ceased to have an objective correlative and lost much of its substance and relevance, even though many jurists continued to subscribe to it nominally. In modern times, attempts have been made to state the Qur'anic concept of war as a defensive concept, but most of them are apologetic in character and do not succeed in offering a coherent view of the Qur'anic data on the subject. There is, however, one notable attempt made at reconciling the two apparently contradictory sets of Qur'anic data—one permitting resort to war only in self-defense and the other justifying offensive war. The main problem, of course, is how to explain offensive war. Amin Ahsan Islahi (1906–1997), a Pakistani Qur'anic exegete, offers the following interpretation of the Qur'anic verses that appear to sanction offensive war.

The essential mission of Muhammad was revival of the monotheistic faith of Abraham. Verses 129 and 151 of chapter 2 of the Qur'an, read together, explicitly state that God raised Muhammad as a prophet in response to Abraham's prayer to God that he may raise a prophet for the people of Arabia. Several verses in chapter 2 and elsewhere obligate Muslims to reclaim Arabia's principal sanctuary, the Kaaba in Mecca, in the name of Abrahamic monotheism. As such, the Qur'an put the idolatrous Quraysh on notice that control of the Kaaba will be wrested from them by Muslims. The Muslims' fundamental conflict, therefore, was with Arabia's idolators, and the offensive war sanctioned in the Qur'an is, essentially, the war that is to be waged against Arabian idolatry, which represented a vitiation of Abrahamic monotheism. It is in light of this rule—namely, that the only war that Muslims were religiously obligated to fight was the war fought under Muhammad to put an end to Arabian polytheism—that one should view the well-known but entirely misunderstood hadith of Muhammad: "I have been commanded to fight people until they should testify, 'There is no god but God and Muhammad is the Messenger of God,' and establish the prayer and pay the mandatory charity *(zakah)*." The word "people" in this hadith refers specifically to the idolators of Arabia and does not necessarily include all humankind, as both Muhammad's own conduct and Muslim historical practice would amply bear out.

But what about Qur'an 9:29, cited above, which enjoins Muslims to fight the people of the book—namely, the Jews and Christians? Islahi observes that the verse, read in its context, refers to the category of belligerent people of the book who have been subdued after a fight, as opposed to the category of nonbelligerent people of the book, with whom an Islamic state can reach any agreement that they would consider acceptable and honorable.

Islahi's interpretation of offensive war would seem to undermine in a powerful way the doctrine of permanent war as imputed to the Qur'an.

Jihad and the Peace Imperative

The foregoing does not mean that all wars other than those between Arabia's idolators and Muhammad's followers are unconditionally forbidden. Imposition of any kind of war must be resisted, given the ability and resources to resist. Accordingly, the Qur'an calls upon Muslims to fight in the way of God, promises reward to those who engage in such a fight (2:218; 4:74; 9:20, 88), and criticizes those who avoid combat (3:167–168; 48:16). Being a religion that has a program with both ethical and political dimensions, Islam seeks to create a polity whose defense, through military means if necessary, it naturally wants to ensure. The so-called jihad (literally, struggle, endeavor) thus becomes a logical and legitimate means for defending and perpetuating the Muslim polity, and is analogous to the means used by any other society to defend and perpetuate its existence.

The term jihad denotes much more than armed struggle, with which it is often confused. In principle, it represents any kind of struggle—not excluding ethical or spiritual—that a Muslim individual or a Muslim society makes in a religiously obligated or justified cause. The specific Qur'anic term for armed struggle is *qital*. Since *qital* can be undertaken only under certain specific conditions, it is incorrect to say that Islam divides the world only into a "House of Islam" and a "House of War" and, consequently, preaches a doctrine of universal and permanent war against non-Islam. It is sufficient to note that, even in classical Islamic law, a "House of Peace" is posited, and that nothing in Islam can be taken to militate against the concept of a Muslim state making peace or forging and maintaining peaceful relations with non-Muslim states. Today, with the development of international law, an Islamic state that becomes a member of an organization like the United Nations will be obligated to abide by the charter of such an organization. There is strong Qur'anic evidence to support the view that the "Other" is not necessarily to be cast in the role of hostile entity. Qur'an 8:61 explicitly states what may be called the peace imperative: "If they incline toward peace, then incline toward it." Qur'an 4:90, though it makes reference to a specific situation, lays down a general rule, supporting the principle enunciated in 8:61: "If they keep away from you and do not fight you and offer peace to you, then God does not allow you to make a move against them."

Rules of War and Peace

The Qur'an lays down several rules for the conduct of war. We have already noted the Qur'anic injunction concerning making peace (8:61). Another fundamental rule is stated in 2:190: "And fight in the way of God against those who fight you, but commit no transgression." In light of Qur'anic and hadith pronouncements, "transgression" in this context would mean violation of ethical rules by killing noncombatants without justification and wantonly destroying animal life and property. Islamic law specifically forbids the killing of monks and nuns, children, and old people; it also forbids mutilation of corpses. Qur'an 47:4, which says that prisoners may either be set free as a gesture of goodwill or held to ransom, clearly implies that prisoners cannot be treated in a brutal or inhumane manner. According to 9:6, under certain circumstances, the enemy's request for safe passage is to be granted, the verse implying that control over enemies is, by itself, no grounds for inflicting harm on them. A number of Qur'anic verses (for example, 8:72; 9:4, 7) command Muslims to abide by treaties made with non-Muslims, and this command is strongly reinforced by the moral exhortation to fulfill commitments. Islamic law stipulates that war can be declared and conducted only by competent authority. In view of the many restrictions it places on the conduct of war, Islam would seem to subscribe to the doctrine of minimum use of force in war.

A much misunderstood Qur'anic term is that of *jizyah*, usually translated as poll tax, which is levied on an Islamic state's non-Muslim citizens either (according to some) as a tax that is analogous to the *zakah* paid by the state's Muslim citizens or (according to others) as the price of protection and of exemption from military duty. Qurʾan 9:29 seems to suggest that payment of *jizyah* is a mark of the non-Muslim citizens' subordinate status. But the verse, as we have already noted, does not purport to lay down a rule for treating the entire category of the people of the book; it deals only with the belligerent people of the book, and not with the nonbelligerent people of the book, with whom the Islamic state may make any arrangement—including annulment of *jizyah* itself—that would be acceptable to both parties.

Civil War

While no armed strife took place among Muslims during the Prophet Muhammad's lifetime, a series of civil wars broke out in the decades following Muhammad's death. In juristic discussions about these wars, Qurʾan 49:9 served as the principal prooftext: "If two factions of Muslims should fight with each other, make peace between them. If one of them should commit transgression against the other, fight the one that has transgressed until it comes back to God's decree. If it comes back, make peace between the two in accordance with justice. And be just; indeed, God loves those who are just." The several possible scenarios of civil war admit of the application of different principles. For our purposes, it is sufficient to note that, according to 49:9, Muslim infighting, whether it involves two groups or two nations, must be a matter of grave concern to the larger body of Muslims, who should effect peace between the fighting parties, and, if it is necessary and within their means to do so, use force to bring the aggressor to justice. The aggressor in this case is technically known as a rebel, and Islamic law lays down rules for dealing with rebels, though it distinguishes between a war against Muslim rebels and that against unbelievers.

Classical Islamic law also has a concept of apostasy war, but underlying the concept is the assumption that apostates are not only religious renegades, but also traitors to the state. A different assumption would, of course, lead to a different conclusion.

Shiʿite Views

The account of the Qurʾanic view of war offered in this article is based on Sunni sources. Sunni and Shiʿite theories of war are similar in many respects, but one difference should be noted. According to Shiʿite theology (the reference here is to Twelver Shiʿism), the twelfth Imam is in a state of concealment, and, until his reappearance, only defensive war is allowed. For this reason, the Iranian people's struggle to remove the shah was called defense by those who led the struggle, and Iran's war with Iraq in the 1990s was similarly described by Iranian scholars.

Modern Times

The classical Islamic doctrines of war and peace were formulated during periods of Muslim political and military ascendancy, and political realities shaped those doctrines no less than Islamic religious norms and dictates. As a weakened and disintegrated Muslim world came under European colonial rule in the last two centuries, questions arose about the continued relevance of the classical theories. Scholars and writers who sought to reinterpret Islamic law in modern times found it both necessary and convenient to draw mainly (and sometimes exclusively) on the Qurʾan for guidance and inspiration—necessary in view of the Qurʾan's acknowledged primacy as a source of Islamic legislation, and convenient in view of the ease with which a direct appeal to the Qurʾan would render irrelevant, or at least undermine, the ponderous and complicated treatments of war in the classical works. Thus, referring principally to the Qurʾan, several modern Muslim scholars have held that Islam allows only defensive war. On the other hand, invoking the Qurʾan, radical Muslim groups have called for jihad not only against Western powers—which, after the cessation of their colonial rule in the Muslim world, are now called neocolonial powers because of their economic control of the Muslim world—but also against Westernized Muslim ruling elites, who are perceived as stooges in the hands of their anti-Islamic Western masters. Another redefinition—or, perhaps, metaphorical application—of jihad consists in the declaration of "war" against political oppression, economic exploitation, and social ills. Needless to say, a serious critical review of the classical theories of war and peace and a responsible reinterpretation of the Qurʾanic and other data on the subject in light of present-day realities remain a desideratum.

Mustansir Mir

Further Reading

Cornell, V. J. (1995). Jizyah. In J. L. Esposito, *The Oxford encyclopedia of the modern Muslim world* (pp. 377–378). New York: Oxford University Press.

Dajani-Shakeel, H., & Messier, R. A. (1991). *Jihad in Islam*. Ann Arbor: Center for Near Eastern and North African Studies, University of Michigan.

Islahi, A. A. (1968–1980). *Tadabbur-i Qurʾan* [Reflection on the Qurʾan]. Lahore, Pakistan: Anjuman-i Markazi Anjuman-i Khuddamuʿl-Qurʾan and Faran Foundation.

Kelsay, J. (1993). *Islam and war*. Louisville, KY: Westminster/John Knox Press.

Khadduri, M. (1955). *War and peace in Islam*. Baltimore and London: The Johns Hopkins Press.

Lewis, B. (1988). *The political language of Islam*. Chicago and London: University of Chicago Press.

Peters, R. (1979). *Islam and colonialism: The doctrine of jihad in modern history*. The Hague, Netherlands: Mouton Publishers.

Islam, Shiʿa

The article will examine the origins of the Shiʿas and discuss their distinctive perspective on war. The term Shiʿa refers to the party of ʿAli (c. 600–661 CE), the cousin and son-in-law of Muhammad (c. 570–632 CE). The Shiʿas claimed that ʿAli was the only legitimate successor (imam) to the Prophet Muhammad, having been explicitly designated by him at Ghadir Khum and other occasions. The Shiʿas further restricted leadership of the community to the family *(ahl al-bayt)* of the Prophet. Such leadership was designated by the term "imam" and is passed on from father to blood successor through a mode of conferring termed *nass*.

With the coming of ʿAli to power in 656 CE, Shiʿism emerged as an effective religious movement. The massacre of Husayn ibn ʿAli (c. 629–680 CE), the son of ʿAli, and his forces at Karbala during his uprising against Caliph Yazid I (c. 645–683 CE) in 680 CE was an important milestone in Shiʿite history as it affirmed notions of injustices endured by the progeny of the Prophet and exacerbated a passion for martyrdom. Husayn's activist movement was followed by other militant movements like those of Mukhtar ibn ʿUbayd al-Thaqafi (d. 687 CE) and Zayd ibn ʿAli (d. 740 CE), the grandson of Husayn.

Shiʿite Theology and Jurisprudence

Shiʿite theology and jurisprudence took definitive shape in the times of the fifth and sixth imams, Muhammad al-Baqir (d. 733/737 CE) and Jaʿfar ibn Muhammad (Jaʿfar as-Sadiq; 699/700 or 703/703–765 CE). The latter, in particular, was largely responsible for the construction of a Shiʿite legal edifice and the formulation of the Shiʿite doctrine of the imamate. The true imam, as-Sadiq stated, had to be divinely appointed. The imam was also believed to be infallible, hence empowered to provide authoritative interpretation of Islamic revelation. Designation and infallibility were complemented by the imam's possession of special knowledge that was either transmitted from the Prophet or derived from inherited scrolls.

Since they realized the futility of armed revolts against the political authority, the imams, starting with as-Sadiq, taught the doctrine of dissimulation *(taqiyya)* rather than jihad. Henceforth, Shiʿas were to conceive of jihad in terms of keeping their faith intact and paying allegiance to the imam rather than staging armed revolts against political authorities. Jihad was declared to be in abeyance until the time of the Mahdi, the promised messiah. He was expected to establish the kingdom of justice and equality and to eliminate injustice and tyranny. This belief was predicated on numerous apocalyptic traditions about the events that will unfold when he reappears. Henceforth, Shiʿite political theory taught coexistence with rather than opposition to tyrannical rulers. Dissimulation itself was construed as a form of defensive jihad since it protected the Shiʿas from tyrannical Muslim powers.

A turning point in Shiʿi history came in the year 874 CE when the eleventh imam, al-Hasan al-ʿAskari, died. Amidst competing claims for succession, his infant son Muhammad al-Mahdi al-Hujjah (d. c. 878 CE) was proclaimed to be the twelfth imam and promised messiah. This group formed the backbone of the Twelver Shiʿas, the largest of the Shiʿite factions. It is with this group that the rest of the article will be concerned.

The twelfth imam was believed to have entered a "minor" occultation from 874 to 940 CE. During this time, he reportedly communicated with agents, four of whom attained prominence. When the fourth agent died in 940, the imam was reported to have entered a "major" occultation. It was believed that he would reappear at the end of time to establish the kingdom of justice and equality.

When the Buyids (945–1055) came to power in Baghdad, Shiʿite jurists filled the leadership vacuum that was created by the major occultation. Prominent scholars like Ibn Babawayh (c. 923–991 CE), al-Mufid (d. 1022 CE), Sharif al-Murtada (d. 1044 CE), and Muhammad Jaʿfar at-Tusi (d. 1067 CE) composed important theological and juridical tracts. It was in this era that Shiʿite jurists examined and refined the Shiʿite doctrine of jihad during the occultation of the imam.

Shiʿism and Jihad

The Qurʾanic rationale on jihad was to bring the world under the sway of God's guidance so as to establish a righteous order based on justice and equality. Thus jihad was envisioned as an important tool in the community's attempt to build a world order in which peace, justice, and equality prevail according to Gods' providence. Since the Qurʾan stated that there was no compulsion in religion (2:256), Muslims were not to use jihad as a means to impose their beliefs on others.

Shiʿite theory of jihad resonates strongly with the views enunciated by Sunni jurists. Shiʿite scholars also see jihad as one of the pillars of Islam and a religious duty that is incumbent upon every Muslim who is male, free, and able-bodied. Many traditions in Shiʿite literature speak on the virtues of jihad. It is reported to be one of the gates to paradise; rich heavenly rewards are guaranteed for those who devote themselves to it. Due to the martyr's eminent status, his body does not have to be washed or shrouded. It can be buried in the same clothes in which he was killed.

Like the Sunni jurists of the classical period (570–1258 CE), Shiʿite jurists divided the world into the abode of Islam *(dar al-Islam)* and the abode of infidels. The former was seen as a political entity that upholds Islamic values and the *shariʿa* (Islamic law). It was also supposedly the territory of peace and justice. *Dar al-harb*, on the other hand, was the land of infidels, the epitome of heedlessness and ignorance that posed a threat to the Islamic moral order.

Both Shiʿite and Sunni jurists linked the universal ideals of Islam with jihad so as to justify the extension of the boundaries of *dar al-Islam*. This was contrary to the Qurʾanic view, which sanctioned jihad only in defense or to fight oppression. The jurists' vision of the world also allowed for the existence of the the "people of the book" (Christians, Jews, and Zoroastrians) within the Islamic community. If they agreed to submit to the political authority of Islam and to pay the poll tax *(jizya)*, jihad against them was not required. Jihad could also be directed against polytheists, apostates, and rebels or dissenters.

The Shiʿas also considered jihad as a collective duty of the community. It only became obligatory for each individual when his presence was necessary for the realization of the purpose envisaged by the law. Thus, when there was a group of Muslims whose number was sufficient to fulfill the needs of a particular conflict, the obligation of jihad no longer rested on others.

Offensive and Defensive Jihad

In contrast to the Sunnis, the Shiʿas restricted the expansionist dimension of war. Whereas for the Sunnis the caliph was empowered to declare and lead the jihad, the Shiʿas declared that the functions of calling people to respond to God's guidance and fighting those who undermine the creation of a just order were restricted to the figure of an infallible imam or his deputy. In the absence of the imam, offensive jihad was suspended until he reappeared. This juridical ruling was based on the premise that infallibility protects the imam from destroying or commanding to destroy any life without proper justification.

Thus the Shiʿas did not see it as incumbent to participate in a jihad that was declared by a caliph to extend the boundaries of Islam. Shiʿite jurists even declared that to fight for an illegitimate ruler was a sin. The Zaydis, a sect among the Shiʿas, did not recognize this dogma and followed the same teaching as that of the Sunni doctrine.

Although jihad has principally an offensive character, it assumes a defensive posture when Muslims have to defend their territory against aggression. Under the Buyids, the Shiʿite doctrine of jihad was revised by scholars like at-Tusi to state that during the occultation of the twelfth imam, defensive jihad was permitted. This form of jihad was understood as a response to an attack by infidels on *dar al-Islam*. Due to this Shiʿas were allowed join a tyrannical ruler to defend the interests of the Muslim community and their territory. However, this was not to be construed as joining hands with an unjust caliph. Rather, Shiʿite jurists ruled that the permission of the imam was not essential under such circumstances since defense of the self was a moral requirement.

Before the establishment of the Safavids in Iran in 1501, Shiʿite jurists were not in a position to advocate a military struggle against the numerically superior forces of the Sunni caliphs. Even after the Safavids came to power and declared a Shiʿite state, the jurists did not sanction any expansionist jihad. Using various types of hermeneutics that were based on rational grounds or traditions reported from the imams, scholars (ulama) like ʿAli ibn al-Husayn al-Karaki (d. 1533) and Zayn al-Din al-ʿAmili (d. 1558) argued that, in the absence of the imam, greater religious authority was to be assumed by the *faqih* or jurist. The jurists could now occupy judicial and political offices. They could, for example, serve as judges, collect religious taxes, and enforce legal penalties on behalf of the imam. Gradually, the Shiʿite ulama exercised greater control over the populace as they were incorporated into the state apparatus.

Subsequent jurists like Jaʿfar Kashif al-Ghitaʾ (d. 1813) played prominent roles in influencing the state's military decisions. He led a defensive war during the siege of An Najaf by the Wahhabis in 1805 CE. Kashif al-Ghitaʾ also maintained that a jurist could permit the monarch to engage in a jihad against the enemies of Islam or even lead one himself. The ulama declared jihad during the Perso-Russian wars of 1808–1813 and 1826–1828 and authorized Fath ʿAli Shah (1771–1834) to fight the Russians. Due to the dangers confronting the community, some juridical tracts written at this time even proclaimed that jihad was a personal rather a collective responsibility. Ayatollah Ruhollah Khomeini (c. 1900–1989) also declared jihad against the invading Iraqi forces in 1980 even though Iran was fighting against fellow Muslims, many of whom were Shiʿas.

Jihad against Rebels

Shiʿite jurists maintained that jihad was to be waged against both unbelievers and believers. In the latter category were rebels *(baghi)* and those who reject the authority of the imam *(muharibin)*. The Shiʿite view of war against rebels is distinguished by the view that the rebels are defined as those who wage war against the just imams, not against the caliphs. Thus the wars of ʿAli against ʿAʾishah (614–678 CE), Caliph Muʿawiyah I (c. 602–680 CE), and the Kharijites are all regarded as jihad against those opposing the imam of the time. In fact, in Shiʿite legal tracts, those who fight against the imams are regarded as unbelievers even if they formally accept Islam.

The struggle against the *bughat*, those Muslims who rebeled against the imam, is applicable only when there was opposition to an imam exercising political authority. Thus jihad against rebels was seen as void during the protracted occultation of the imam.

As in Sunnism, Shiʿite rules of engagement in a war with rebels are different from jihad against idolaters. Even though they are a threat to the territory of Islam, rebels are not to be killed as they remain Muslims. No war can be fought until the rebels initiate hostilities. Jihad against them can only be waged when they break allegiance with the imam and attack or pose a danger to Muslims. Their property cannot be confiscated and those rebels who are taken as prisoners of war must not be killed. They can only be exterminated in self-defense. The rules of war against rebels are different since it is hoped that they will return to the fold of the community. The goal of fighting rebels is to bring them back to the fold of submission, not to kill them.

Shiʿite jurists did not encourage their followers to rebel against Sunni governments. Rather, they were to obey the rulers and acquiesce in the face of an unjust government during the occultation of the imam. Rebellion by other groups against an unjust ruler was not to be fought or joined in.

Believers were allowed to fight against robbers and brigands in self-defense. Brigands and highway robbers are treated like rebels with some exceptions to the rules of combat. The punishment against a thief is contingent on whether he stole property or killed people. Highway robbers and brigands are also to be fought and punished either by execution or amputation of hands or feet.

The Shiʿite view on jihad is distinguished by its insistence on the need for the imam to declare and lead the jihad. Later on, it was accepted that a jurist could authorize a defensive jihad in the absence of an infallible imam.

Liyakat Takim

Further Reading

Esposito, J. L. (2002). *Unholy war*. Oxford, UK: Oxford University Press.

Firestone, R. (1999). *Jihad: The origin of holy war in Islam.* Oxford, UK: Oxford University Press.

Kelsay, J. (1993). *Islam and war: A study in comparative ethics*. Louisville, KY: Westminster/John Knox Press.

Khomeini, I. (1981). *Islam and revolution* (H. Algar, Trans.). Berkeley, CA: Mizan Press.

Kohlberg, E. (1970). The development of the imami Shiʿi doctrine of jihad. *Zeitschrift der deutschen Morgenlandischen Gesellschaft, 126*(1976), 64–86.

Lambton, A. (1981). *State and government in medieval Islam.* Oxford, UK: Oxford University Press.

Sachedina, A. (1988). *The just ruler in Shiʿite Islam: The comprehensive authority of the jurist in imamite jurisprudence*. New York: Oxford University Press.

Tyan, E. (1965). Djihad. *Encyclopedia of Islam* (Vol. 2, pp. 538–9). Leiden, Netherlands: E. J. Brill.

Williams, A. (1971). *Themes of Islamic civilization*. Berkeley: University of California Press.

Islam: Sufism

Sufism is Islamic mysticism. Just as there are many ways to be a Muslim, there are many ways to be a Sufi Muslim. Sufism is deeply rooted in the Qurʾan (the book of sacred writings accepted by Muslims as revelations made to the prophet Muhammad by Allah) and the example of Muhammad. There is in the revelations of the Qurʾan an intense direct experience of the divine.

Additionally, Muslims believe that Muhammad had a mystical experience, described in the first verse of the seventeenth chapter of the Qurʾan: "Glory to the one who took his servant on a night journey from the sacred place of prayer to the furthest place of prayer upon which we have sent down our blessing, that we might show him some of our signs. He is the All-Hearing, the All-Seeing" (Sells 1996, 47). This verse has traditionally been interpreted to describe Muhammad's night journey (*miʾraj* in Arabic) from the Kaaba in Mecca (the sacred place of prayer) to a place in Jerusalem (the farthest place of prayer). From Jerusalem (at a spot later marked with the building of the Dome of the Rock), Muhammad ascended through the seven heavens until he was brought into the presence of God. Muslims believe that they will be reunited with God on the Day of Judgment. In some respect, one can think of Sufis as those Muslims who yearn for that reunion in this lifetime, who long for the same experiences of the divine that Muhammad had when he received the Qurʾan and took the night journey.

Asceticism and a Name

Asceticism (strict self-denial as a measure of spiritual discipline) was not encouraged early in Islam. The world, being created by God, is considered to be a good thing by Muslims. However, in the second century of Islam, asceticism grew as a response to the worldliness that came with the increased political and economic power of the Umayyad dynasty. A famous early ascetic was Hasan al-Basri (d. 728). According to one authority, "He used to admonish his listeners to live strictly according to the rules laid down by the Qurʾan so that they would not be ashamed at Doomsday: 'O son of Adam, you will die alone and enter the tomb alone and be resurrected alone, and it is with you alone that the reckoning will be made!' " (Schimmel 1975, 30). The Sufi tradition received its name from this asceticism. In Arabic, the word *suf* means "wool," and those who deliberately wore ordinary garments of wool (as opposed to expensive garments of silk or other luxurious fabrics) came to be known as "Sufis."

Another famous early ascetic was Ibrahim ibn Adham (d. 777). He is usually credited with first classifying the stages of asceticism: "(a) renunciation of the world, (b) renunciation of the happy feeling of having achieved renunciation, and (c) the stage in which the ascetic regards the world as so unimportant that he no longer looks at it" (Schimmel 1975, 37). For ibn Adham asceticism extended to abstinence from sexual relations. In this respect he was clearly outside of the mainstream of the Islamic tradition that rejoices in the sexual relationship of a married couple.

Mysticism of Union

Although the term *Sufism* comes from a word that has a connection with asceticism, Sufism is not just or exclusively an ascetic movement. One trajectory that Sufism takes is different than that of asceticism. For many Sufis there was intense yearning for union with God. Sufis often used the vocabulary of analogies to describe their relationship with the divine. One of the most famous of these Sufis was Husayn ibn Mansur al-Hallaj (858–922). He expressed his union with the divine in the phrase "I am the Truth." To the pious and the conservatives around him, this statement smacked of blasphemy, implying that al-Hallaj was ascribing himself as a partner to God (in the Islamic tradition, "the Truth" is one of the most beautiful names of God). Instead, al-Hallaj was expressing a devout and devoted monotheism, claiming that nothing but God exists. For his assertion, al-Hallaj was put to death by the ruler of his time.

The most famous of these Sufis who used the vocabulary of analogies was Jalal al-Din Rumi, given the title of "Maulana" (our master) (1207–1273). Rumi was born in the province of Balkh in what is now Afghanistan and died in Konya, Turkey. At an early age Rumi studied jurisprudence as well as the sciences of the Qurʾan and Hadith (a narrative record of the sayings or customs of Muhammad and his companions). Rumi wrote two major books of poetry, the *Diwan* (collected works) and the *Mathnawi* (couplets), as well as other works of poetry and prose. Writing mostly in Persian, Rumi is one of the most beloved of Persian poets.

Through a number of English translations (most notably those of Coleman Barks), Rumi has become one of the best-selling poets in the United States. According to one scholar, "Most of the individual poems of the *Diwan* may be said to represent particular spiritual states or experiences, such as union with God or separation after union, described in appropriate images and symbols. . . . In contrast to the *Diwan*, the *Mathnawi* is relatively sober. It represents a reasoned and measured attempt to explain the various dimensions of spiritual life and practice to disciples intent upon following the Way" (Chittick 1983, 6). The *Mathnawi* begins with one of Rumi's most famous analogies—that of the reed. The reed is plucked from the reed bed and is made into a flute by its creator, who places nine holes in the reed. The flute then plays a song of its lament at being separated from the reed bed whence it came. The analogy is clear: People are the reed that has been plucked from the garden by their creator (God), who also puts nine holes in their bodies and breathes into them their existence. There is a further analogy in that the best pens for calligraphy, including the calligraphy of Qur'anic verses, are fashioned from the same cane reeds used for flutes. So the flute playing a song of lament becomes the pen writing the words of the Qur'an becomes the human longing for a return to the garden and union with the divine.

"Philosophical" Sufism

Sufism as a movement that emphasizes direct experience of the objects of faith is not anti-intellectual. The title of "Shaykh al-Akbar" (the greatest master) was given to one of the most creative philosophical thinkers of any era, Muhyi al-Din ibn al-ʿArabi (1165–1240). Ibn Arabi was born in Islamic Spain and died in Damascus. According to William Chittick, the greatest modern interpreter of his thought, ibn Arabi "wrote voluminously in Arabic prose and addressed every theoretical issue that arises in the context of Islamic thought and practice. His works are enormously erudite and exceedingly difficult, and only the most learned of Muslims, those already trained in jurisprudence, Kalam, and other Islamic sciences, could have hoped to read and understand them" (Chittick 2000, 28). Ibn Arabi gave tremendous importance to what the scholar Henry Corbin referred to as the "imaginal" world, or the world of the imagination. According to Chittick, "All religious traditions accord a central role to imagination, though not necessarily by this name. The *mundus imaginalis* is the realm where invisible realities become visible and corporeal things are spiritualized" (Chittick 1989, ix). Another concept that is associated with ibn Arabi is sometimes translated as the oneness or unity (although he never used the corresponding Arabic phrase *wahdat al-wujud*).

Sufism and Orthodoxy

There has been at times a tension between Sufis and conservative or orthodox Muslims. Sufism sometimes leads to antinomianism, the idea that Sufis were some sort of "elite" and so were not bound by the law incumbent on "ordinary" Muslims. However, for many Sufis, their practices were rooted in a deep understanding of the Qur'an and obedience to Islamic law. One cannot, for example, properly understand Rumi's poetry without a thorough understanding of the Qur'an and the Hadith. Nonetheless, some of the "orthodox" saw Sufism as incompatible with being a "true" Muslim. This notion was challenged by the great medieval Islamic theologian, Abu Hamid al-Ghazali (d. 1111). Al-Ghazali was responsible for the reconciliation of Sufism with Islamic orthodoxy. In his writings he articulated how one could simultaneously be a good Muslim and a Sufi. However, a number of Muslims still found certain Sufi practices to be incompatible with their understanding of what it means to be a Muslim. One of these practices was the worship at the shrines of the founders of Sufi orders or other "friends of god," as important Sufi figures came to be known. One of the actions of the Wahhabi movement, which began in Saudi Arabia in the eighteenth century, was the destruction of a number of Sufi shrines.

Islam was often spread through Sufi orders. Sufis through their faithful witness would inform those around them about Islam. In this respect one cannot deny the importance of Sufis to the propagation of the message of Islam.

Women and Sufism

It is important to note the role of women in the Sufi tradition. One of the most famous of the early Sufis was Rabi'a al-Adawiyya (713–801). She is usually credited with introducing the metaphor of love into the Sufi tradition. For Rabi'a, one should act only and always out of a love for God, not out of fear of punishment or hope of a reward. Rabi'a provided a good example for women and men to follow. The Sufi tradition often was the only one open to women. If one believed, as the Sufis did, that one can achieve union with the divine, then one's own gender is accidental. Being a woman or a man did not matter because gender fell away in the union with God, who is without gender. After Rabi'a women could be Sufi leaders where they might have been prevented from being trained in the more traditional Islamic sciences. Also, the shrines of Sufi saints, whether male or female, were often the preserve of women, a place where women had some measure of control. As such, one must consider the gender aspect when describing the tensions that often existed between Sufis and "orthodox" Muslims. The question must be asked: How much of the "orthodox" objection to Sufi practices was to the practices themselves, and how much of the objection was to a practice that allowed women no small amount of power?

Attitudes to War, Violence, and Peace

Not surprisingly, given the nature of the Sufi tradition, there is a strong pacifist strain and a rejection of violence. For many of the ascetics, there was a rejection of the world, particularly the political, economic, and temporal power that was sought by many Islamic rulers. For other Sufis, particularly those who expressed their thought in the vocabulary of analogies, the union with the divine left no room for war and hatred. These Sufis (and others) were fond of quoting the hadith where God says, "my Mercy takes precedence over my Wrath." An understanding of God in the aspects of love or beauty was stressed, not the aspects of power or majesty. Unfortunately, Islamic rulers often used Sufis as scapegoats. In the modern world as well as the ancient world, the persecution of "heretics" is often a convenient deflection of public opinion and support from the important issues of the day. Clearly, the execution of al-Hallaj must be seen in this light. Was he really killed for being a "heretic," or was his murder simply the exploitation of religious symbols and language to further political power?

In some cases Sufi orders and practices were threatened by political movements. Sufi groups were allied with political authority. This alliance often came from an emphasis on social activism practiced by some Sufis. For example, "social activism is integral to the traditions of Moroccan Sufism . . . many Moroccan saints saw themselves not only as teachers of disciples, but also as major players in local and regional politics" (Cornell 1998, 233). Reform movements during the eighteenth and nineteenth centuries included the Mahdi in Sudan and the Sanusi in Libya.

With regard to the spread of Islam, Sufis often practiced what Christians would understand as "faithful witness." Through their example, and not through forced conversion, Sufis would attract people to the Islamic tradition. In this way many of the conversions to Islam were nonviolent. In the modern world one sees a Sufi emphasis in a group such as the Muslim Peace Fellowship, which works for issues of peace and justice from within an Islamic framework. A famous contemporary Sufi was M. R. Bawa Muhaiyaddeen, who was born in Sri Lanka but immigrated to the United States and lived in Philadelphia until his death in 1986. His book, *Islam and World Peace: Explanations of a Sufi*, situates issues of peace and justice within his own Sufi framework.

Amir Hussain

Further Reading

Andrae, T. (1987). *In the garden of myrtles: Studies in early Islamic mysticism*. Albany: State University of New York.

Barks, C. (2002). *The soul of Rumi: A new collection of ecstatic poems*. San Francisco: Harper.

Chittick, W. C. (1983). *The Sufi path of love: The spiritual teachings of Rumi*. Albany: State University of New York.

Chittick, W. C. (1989). *The Sufi path of knowledge: Ibn al-ʿArabi's metaphysics of imagination*. Albany: State University of New York.

Chittick, W. C. (2000). *Sufism: A short introduction*. Oxford, UK: Oneworld.

Corbin, H. (1969). *Creative imagination in the Sufism of Ibn ʿArabi*. Princeton, NJ: Princeton University Press.

Cornell, V. J. (1998). *The realm of the saint: Power and authority in Moroccan Sufism*. Austin: University of Texas Press.

Ernst, C. W. (1997). *The Shambhala guide to Sufism*. Boston: Shambhala.

Hermansen, M. (2000). Hybrid identity formations in Muslim America: The case of American Sufi movements. *The Muslim World, 90*(1–2), 158–197.

Knysh, A. (2000). *Islamic mysticism: A short history*. Leiden, Netherlands: Brill.

Muhaiyaddeen, M. R. B. (1987). *Islam and world peace: Explanations of a Sufi*. Philadelphia: Fellowship Press.

Renard, J. (1996). *Seven doors to Islam: Spirituality and the religious life of Muslims*. Berkeley and Los Angeles: University of California Press.

Schimmel, A. (1975). *Mystical dimensions of Islam*. Chapel Hill: University of North Carolina Press.

Sells, M. A. (Ed. and Trans.). (1996). *Early Islamic mysticism: Sufi, Qur'an, Mi'raj, poetic and theological writings.* Mahwah, NJ: Paulist Press.

Trimingham, J. S. (1998). *The Sufi orders in Islam.* New York: Oxford University Press.

Islam, Sunni

Sunni Islam, by far the most widely followed school of thought among Muslims, has historically been a culturally and intellectually diverse tradition of Islamic interpretation. Sunni Muslims have accordingly produced a rich and broad-ranging literature on war and peace. This literature dates back to the revelation of the Qur'an itself and the earliest efforts to record the Prophet Muhammad's (c. 570–632 CE) teachings and actions (sunna). Moral and practical concerns relating to violence in general and warfare in particular were part of the formative experience of the early Muslim community led by the Prophet, and as the *ahl al-sunna wa'l-jama'a* (people of the Prophetic tradition and community), Sunnis claim to be upholding the interpretation and normative practice established by Muhammad and all of his companions on this, as on all other, issues.

The Qur'an and Sunna

The Qur'anic revelation is traditionally divided into two periods: the Meccan, lasting from 610 to 622 CE, and the Medinan, lasting from 622 to 632 CE. During the Meccan period, the Qur'an has very little to say on the subject of war. Indeed, there is no record whatsoever that the Prophet sanctioned or practiced the use of force at this time. His policy can only be described as nonviolent direct action. Because the Muslims at this time were a relatively small and powerless community, entirely reliant for their physical safety upon the system of tribal protection, this policy may have been determined by pragmatic considerations. Muslim biographers of Muhammad record escalating verbal and physical attacks directed against him by his polytheist opponents, but his status as a member of Mecca's ruling tribe, the Quraysh, assured him relative safety. A plot to kill the Prophet was hatched by the Meccans only when he was set to make the *hijra* (migration) from Mecca to Medina in 622 CE. The anti-Muslim persecution fell most harshly upon those converts who were not protected by tribal affiliations, namely, outsiders and former slaves. Muhammad instructed these Muslims to migrate to Abyssinia, a Christian kingdom, in 615 CE.

The Prophet's nonviolent policy in Mecca also accorded with the principles of the unfolding Qur'anic revelation. The few Meccan verses that deal with the use of force do not enjoin a completely pacifist policy. For example, Qur'an 42:39–43 describe Muslims as those who defend themselves when wronged. The verses do not mention the use of violence in such self-defense, but neither do they prohibit it. The Qur'anic message here and in other verses seems to be that war should only be seen as a last resort when other measures fail.

The Prophet's policy on the use of force changed on the eve of his migration to Medina. According to the pledge between him and his newly converted Medinan hosts, Muhammad agreed to "war against them that war against you and be at peace with those at peace with you" if the Medinans guaranteed his security (Ibn Ishaq 1990, 204). Within a year of coming to Medina, Muhammad launched a series of small-scale reconnoitering missions intended to impress upon his Qurayshi foes the newfound military strength of the Muslims. These raids resulted in the first major battle between the two parties at Badr two years after the migration. Over the next eight years, until the death of the Prophet in 632 CE, the Muslims fought a number of military engagements, primarily against the Quraysh and their bedouin and Jewish allies, but against Byzantine forces as well.

Qur'anic verses of the Medinan period reflect the changing conditions of the Muslim community. The majority of Qur'anic commentators believe the first verses explicitly permitting Muslims to use force in self-defense are 22:39–40. Subsequently, 2:190–191 convert the permission to fight into an obligation, with the argument that "oppression is worse than killing." Toward the end of the Prophet's life, two verses were revealed that many classical exegetes interpreted as marking a shift from purely defensive war to a war of conversion of the remaining polytheist Arabs (9:5) or a war of subjugation directed against other unbelievers, especially Christians and Jews (9:29).

The Classical Literature

Following Muhammad's death, subsequent Muslim generations expended much effort trying to understand the moral and legal significance of the Qur'an's

The Quʾran: Suras 9:5 and 9:29

9.5 So when the sacred months have passed away, then slay the idolaters wherever you find them, and take them captives and besiege them and lie in wait for them in every ambush, then if they repent and keep up prayer and pay the poor-rate, leave their way free to them; surely Allah is Forgiving, Merciful.

9.29 Fight those who do not believe in Allah, nor in the latter day, nor do they prohibit what Allah and His Apostle have prohibited, nor follow the religion of truth, out of those who have been given the Book, until they pay the tax in acknowledgment of superiority and they are in a state of subjection.

verses and the Prophet's actions and teachings on war. But Sunnis also thought and wrote about war using frames of reference outside the Qurʾan and sunna. We may therefore analyze the classical Sunni literature, produced roughly between the seventh and fifteenth centuries CE, according to different, broad genres: legal, ethical, philosophical, and historical.

The legal tradition has historically dominated Islamic intellectual life. For a number of reasons, not the least of which is that the Qurʾan contains a number of verses that may be understood to have a legal character, Muslim scholars produced a large body of legal rulings known as *fiqh*, purporting to offer the true believer a righteous path *(shariʿa)* through this earthly life. This legal literature drew upon the Qurʾan and authoritative accounts (hadith) of the Prophet's sayings and deeds. These sources were supplemented by the practice of the first four "rightly guided" caliphs and often by the personal preferences of the jurists themselves. Although numerous schools of law emerged at different times, only four Sunni schools *(madhhabs)* survived from the classical period: Hanafi, Maliki, Shafiʿi, and Hanbali. Each school produced a number of jurists who expounded the legal theory of war and peace, in works dealing with such topics as *siyar* (relations with non-Muslims), jihad (struggle to propagate Islam), or *kharaj* (tax on conquered land). In its broad outline, the Sunni legal theory of war and peace was rather consistent across the four schools. But the scholars did differ, sometimes with their colleagues in the same school, on some specific and significant points of interpretation.

The classical theory rested on the division of the world into two opposing realms, *dar al-Islam*, the area where Islamic law was enforced by the unitary Islamic state ruled by the caliph, and *dar al-harb*, where non-Islamic laws or anarchy prevailed. According to all four schools, the caliph's duty was to reduce *dar al-harb* by incorporating it into *dar al-Islam*, through peaceful means if possible, through forceful means if necessary. This "expansionist jihad" was a collective obligation of the Muslim community *(fard kifaya)*, which if performed by some exonerated others who were not financially or physically capable of participating in it. The goal of this jihad was to bring non-Muslims under Islamic law, not to convert them by force. So long as they accepted Muslim sovereignty, non-Muslim communities enjoyed *dhimmi* status whereby they retained a great deal of their communal autonomy. The expansionist jihad could be suspended through a truce with a non-Muslim power, creating what the Shafiʿi school labeled *dar al-sulh*. The general view was that such a truce could not exceed ten years, although nothing prohibited the caliph from renewing the truce indefinitely if the interests of the Muslims required it.

Jurists devoted comparatively little attention to a purely defensive jihad. It was commonly understood that Muslims had the right to defend themselves against aggression committed by non-Muslims. Such a jihad was *fardʿayn*, an obligation of every able-bodied Muslim, male or female, and did not require authorization by a governing authority.

Sunni writers were ambivalent on whether to treat wars among Muslims as jihad. For them, the defining intra-Muslim conflicts were the series of challenges to the caliphate of ʿAli (c. 600–661 CE). Sunnism arose in contradistinction to the Shiʿite claim that ʿAli was the Prophet's only legitimate successor, but Sunnis accepted ʿAli as the fourth caliph, following Abu Bakr (c. 573–634 CE), ʿUmar (c. 586–644 CE), and ʿUthman ibn ʿAffan (d. 656 CE). Therefore, Sunnis preferred not to pass judgment on the merits of either ʿAli's position or those of most of his opponents, preferring to consider the conflict as *fitna*, or "civil strife." Sunni writers

Temple Mount, Dome of the Rock, Jerusalem, Israel. November 1996. Courtesy Steve Donaldson.

did, however, treat one group of challengers, the Kharijites, as rebels. Some considered the state's suppression of such groups to be a form of jihad, while others considered fighting Muslim rebels to be a separate category of legitimate warfare.

In terms of the conduct of war, the jurists dealt with three broad questions: Who may be targeted for attack in war? What types of damage may be inflicted on different types of people? What types of damage may be inflicted on their property? Most scholars held women and children to be immune from intentional attack because they generally do not engage in fighting. Others included old and infirm men, merchants, peasants, hermits, and all those who ordinarily do not fight in the list of immune persons. Noncombatancy did not guarantee absolute protection from harm, however. All of the groups of people listed above, with the exception, perhaps, of hermits, could be enslaved at the discretion of the Muslim commanders. The jurists generally permitted Muslim armies wide latitude in the weapons and tactics they used to overcome the enemy. But the majority prohibited such acts as burning people alive, treacherously breaking oaths or violating amnesty, killing envoys, and mutilating the dead. As for the enemy's property, the majority prohibited the unnecessary destruction of orchards and the slaughter of livestock.

Based on the policies ʿAli had adopted to suppress the Kharijites, the rules for fighting rebels differed in some important ways from those relating to non-Muslims. Muslim rebels could not be pursued if in rout; if captured, the men could not be executed, nor could their women and children be enslaved; property seized from them was to be returned if they gave up their rebellion. The aim of all such rules was to preserve the Muslim identity of the rebels so as to facilitate their speedy rehabilitation into the Islamic body politic.

The ethical literature on war consists of practical manuals or "mirrors for princes" that counsel rulers on how to acquire and maintain power. This genre originated in pre-Islamic Iran and developed under Muslim writers into an eclectic blend of numerous oral and literary traditions. References to Qurʾanic verses and Prophetic hadith relating to war are mixed liberally with anecdotes and aphorisms drawn from pre-

Islamic Arabia and Iran, as well as from the lives of pious Muslim rulers after the Prophet. Because these works were intended to provide practical advice to rulers, the mirrors genre focuses little if any attention on jihad as a religious obligation, something with which Muslim rulers were only theoretically concerned by the second Islam century. Instead, war is treated as a mundane reality within the Islamic realm as much as against unbelievers, a problem that demanded clear understanding and adroit handling by the wise prince. Far from extolling war, the ethical literature treats it as a social calamity, a departure from a well-ordered society and polity, as in the *Siraj al-muluk* of the twelfth-century Andalusian writer al-Turtushi. Like illness in the human body, wars may be averted or lessened through effective preventive action.

The philosophical literature is traditionally identified with such thinkers as al-Farabi (c. 878–c. 950), Ibn Sina (980–1037), and Ibn Rushd (1126–1198), all of whom were strongly influenced by classical Greek philosophy. Of the three, only al-Farabi (who had Shiʿite leanings) discussed war in his philosophical works in any length, primarily in the context of the types of just war that a virtuous polity may fight. Yet, the most important work on war in the philosophical genre may be Ibn Khaldun's (1332–1406) *Muqaddima*. In it, Ibn Khaldun argues that war is a natural, universal feature of human society. It is the product of human beings' innate aggressiveness magnified by their desire to advance their own particular group's interests *(ʿasabiyya)*. Religion can only temporarily transcend such group loyalties, Ibn Khaldun writes, as Islam had under the leadership of Muhammad. But within twenty-five years of the Prophet's death, the uniting power of Islam had dissolved into civil war. Ibn Khaldun gives the standard Sunni view of the dispute between ʿAli and Caliph Muʿawiyah I (c. 602–680): "Each was right in so far as his intentions were concerned" (Ibn Khaldun 1967, 1:421).

Finally, Sunni writers produced a large historical literature in which wars fought by Muslims were chronicled in great detail. This literature begins with the biography of the Prophet written by Ibn Ishaq (c. 704–767) as preserved in the recension of Ibn Hisham (d. 828 or 833). This work, along with al-Waqidi's (747–823) history of the Prophet's military campaigns *(maghazi)*, may be seen as continuations of the pre-Islamic oral tradition of recording the martial valor of heroes, in this case Muhammad and his companions. The historical genre reached its apex with the monumental history of al-Tabari (c. 839–923), which begins with the Creation and proceeds to the ʿAbbasid caliphate in the early tenth century CE.

The Modern Literature

The classical juristic notion of an expansionist jihad against unbelievers was briefly revived under Ottoman rule in the fifteenth through seventeenth centuries. But in the period since, the Sunni Muslim literature on war has focused overwhelmingly on defending Muslim territories against European imperialism and on the legitimacy of violent means to reinstall Islamic law in increasingly secular Muslim states and societies.

Three strands may be identified in modern Sunni writings on war. The first is the apologetic literature, produced primarily by nineteenth-century Indian Muslim authors straining to answer the charge of Christian missionaries and orientalists that Islam was spread by the sword. According to the apologists, the wars of early Islam were purely defensive in nature, and jihad in modern times should be largely divested of its military connotations and reduced mainly to its spiritual aspects.

Such writings inevitably created a backlash among other Muslim interpreters. The modernists' goal is not so much to respond to criticisms of early Islamic history and dogma, but to reinterpret jihad in ways that make it compatible with the principles of modern international law. Thus, they reject much of the classical legal theory of jihad, pointing out that the idea of *dar al-Islam* in opposition to *dar al-harb* is not found in either the Qurʾan or hadith. Moreover, the modernists criticize the early writers for focusing on the Medinan period, while entirely neglecting the Meccan period of the Prophet's life. If the Qurʾan and the Prophet's teachings are taken as a whole, they argue, jihad cannot be properly understood as a war to spread Islam or subjugate unbelievers. It is waged only in self-defense, in conformity with international law, when the lives, property, and honor of Muslims are at stake.

The fundamentalists also appeal to the Qurʾan and hadith to challenge what they consider various false understandings of jihad. First, they refute the apologetic and modernist view that jihad means only a war in defense of Muslim territory. Jihad, according to them, meant by the end of the Qurʾanic revelation a struggle, through fighting if necessary, to establish the Islamic order over all unbelievers. But the category of unbelievers in fundamentalist writings includes nominal Muslims as well as non-Muslims. In arguments that hearken back to eighteenth- and nineteenth-century

Wahhabi justifications for the use of force to cleanse the faith of false doctrines and practices, contemporary fundamentalists justify violent means to overthrow entrenched secular or nominally Muslim rulers who do not apply *shariʿa*. The focus of fundamentalist arguments on war is thus inward, aimed at transforming allegedly hypocritical Muslim societies into true Islamic communities, led by true Muslim leaders.

As for the proper conduct of war today, the vast majority of Muslim scholars agree that principles of international humanitarian law are compatible with Islamic teachings. These include the notion of noncombatant immunity and the prohibition against inhumane forms of killing. A number of Muslim terrorist groups have sought to justify the killing of civilians on Islamic grounds, but their arguments and tactics have been condemned by mainstream scholars.

Sohail H. Hashmi

Further Reading

Abou El Fadl, K. (2001). *Rebellion and violence in Islamic law*. Cambridge, UK: Cambridge University Press.

Charnay, J. P. (1986). *L'Islam et la guerre: De la guerre juste à la révolution sainte* [Islam and war: From just war to sacred revolution]. Paris: Fayard.

Chiragh ʿAli. (n.d.). *A critical exposition of the popular jihad*. Karachi, Pakistan: Karimsons.

Hamidullah, M. (1961). *Muslim conduct of state* (7th ed.). Lahore, Pakistan: Shaykh Muhammad Ashraf.

Ibn Ishaq, M. (1990). *The life of Muhammad* (A. Guillaume, Trans.). Karachi, Pakistan: Oxford University Press.

Ibn Khaldun. (1967). *The Muqaddimah: An introduction to history* (F. Rosenthal, Trans.). Princeton, NJ: Princeton University Press.

Jansen, J. J. G. (1986). *The neglected duty: The creed of Sadat's assassins and Islamic resurgence in the Middle East*. New York: Macmillan.

Johnson, J. T., & Kelsay, J. (Eds.). (1990). *Cross, crescent, and sword: The justification and limitation of war in Western and Islamic tradition*. New York: Greenwood.

Kelsay, J. (1993). *Islam and war: A study in comparative ethics*. Louisville, KY: Westminster/John Knox Press.

Kelsay, J., & Johnson, J. T. (Eds.). (1991). *Just war and jihad: Historical and theoretical perspectives on war and peace in Western and Islamic tradition*. New York: Greenwood.

Khadduri, M. (1955). *War and peace in the law of Islam*. Baltimore: Johns Hopkins University Press.

Mawardi, A. M. (1996). *The ordinances of government: A translation of al-Ahkam al-sultaniyya wa al-Wilayat al-Diniyya* (W. H. Wahba, Trans.). Reading, UK: Garnet.

Morabia, A. (1993). *Le Gihad dans l'Islam médiéval: Le "Combat sacré" des origines au XIIe siècle* [The jihad in medieval Islam: The "holy war" from its origins to the twelfth century]. Paris: Albin Michel.

Nizam al-Mulk. (1978). *The book of government or rules for kings: The Siyar al-Muluk or Siyasat-nama of Nizam al-Mulk* (H. Darke, Trans.). London: Routledge & Kegan Paul.

Peters, R. (1979). *Islam and colonialism: The doctrine of jihad in modern history*. The Hague, Netherlands: Mouton.

Peters, R. (1996). *Jihad in classical and modern Islam*. Princeton, NJ: Markus Wiener.

Shaybani, M. (1966). *The Islamic law of nations: Shaybani's Siyar* (M. Khadduri, Trans.). Baltimore: Johns Hopkins University Press.

Tabari, M. (1989–1999). *Tarikh al-rusul wa al-muluk* [The History of al-Tabari] (Vols. 1–39; Trans.). Albany: State University of New York Press.

Turtushi, M. (1990). *Siraj al-muluk* [The light of kings] (J. al-Bayati, Ed.). London: Riad el-Rayyes Books.

Waqidi, M. (1966). *Kitab al-maghazi* [Book of military campaigns] (M. Jones, Ed.). London: Oxford University Press.

Zuhayli, W. (1981). *Athar al-harb fi al-fiqh al-islami: Dirasa muqarana* [The effects of war on Islamic law: A comparative study]. Beirut, Lebanon: Dar al-Fikr.

Islamic Law of War

The Islamic law of war is one aspect of inquiry into the *shariʿa*. The attempt to live according to the *shariʿa*, the ideal way, is a mark of *al-islam*, the "submission" to the will of God.

One comprehends the *shariʿa* by interpreting the "signs" of God, especially the Qurʾan and the example of the Prophet Muhammad. These become the foundation of a theory of practical reason known as *usul al-fiqh*, the "roots of comprehension." Attending to the Qurʾan and the testimony of sound reports concerning the prophetic example, and guided by precedents set by recognized scholars, Muslims through the ages attempt to comprehend the guidance of God.

The Islamic law of war is thus best understood as a kind of transgenerational conversation about the justification and conduct of war. In this conversation, one may identify (1) important contributors; (2) themes; and (3) modern developments.

Selection from the Constitution of Iran

Article 4 [Islamic Principle]

All civil, penal financial, economic, administrative, cultural, military, political, and other laws and regulations must be based on Islamic criteria. This principle applies absolutely and generally to all articles of the Constitution as well as to all other laws and regulations, and the wise persons

Source: **Iran Constitution. Retrieved April 17, 2003, from http://www.oefre.unibe.ch/law/icl/ir00000_.html**

Important Contributors

From the Islamic point of view, *shariʿa* reasoning is a duty. In one sense, the duty to comprehend God's guidance belongs to each and every Muslim. Yet the formal task of ascertaining the *shariʿa* regarding various questions is usually construed as a "collective" duty in which people whose talents and training set them apart carry the burden of *shariʿa* reasoning for others.

Historically, responsibility for Shariʿa reasoning fell to the *ulama* or "learned" class. These scholars issued opinions or *fatawa* in response to diverse questions about the justification and conduct of war, as well as many other topics. Their judgments are preserved in texts that collect their opinions, as well as in treatises on statecraft or on "public" law. Only a few of these are available in Western languages. Of these, one should note the ones described in the following paragraphs.

The Islamic Law of Nations: Shaybani's Siyar is a compendium of judgments by the early scholars of the Hanafi school (one of four recognized by the Sunni or majority of Muslims.) Al-Shaybani (d. 804 CE) practiced the art of *shariʿa* reasoning during the high period of the Abbasid caliphate. He and other scholars served as officials in the court of the great Harun al-Rashid (763 or 766–809), where they rendered judgments on questions of policy.

Al-Shaybani and his colleagues saw teaching as their primary task. Subsequent generations looked back to their judgments for guidance in the task of practical judgment. The *Siyar* deals with the "movements" of various classes of people between and within the geopolitical units the scholars termed the "territory of Islam" and the "territory of war."

The high period of the Abbasid caliphate is usually identified as around 750–935 CE. During this period, a number of the "fathers" of *shariʿa* reasoning did their work. Al-Tabari (c. 839–923) collected various opinions of these scholars in his *Book on the Disagreements among the Scholars Concerning Armed Struggle and Conquered Territory*. By the time of al-Tabari's death, however, the political context in which scholars practiced the art of *shariʿa* reasoning was changing. The power of the caliph to administer the territory of Islam waned, while the power of provincial governors increased. From the standpoint of Islamic law, the appointment of such governors and the designation of their territories was the responsibility of the aliph. Increasingly, however, strong governors refused the limits set by the caliph, and expanded their power accordingly.

Abu al-Hasan ʿAli al-Mawardi (d. 1058) recognized this reality, particularly as it related to the conduct of war, in his book on *The Ordinances of Government*. As with most members of the learned class of his day, al-Mawardi considered the establishment of legitimate government an obligation of justice. His vision of such government involved a unitary caliphate. The conduct of war in the interests of the Muslim community is the responsibility of the caliph and without this office, the possibility of just war is undermined. In al-Mawardi's day, the advance of provincial governors seemed to undermine the caliph's authority, and with it the possibilities for justice. Al-Mawardi judged that the caliph should recognize a strong governor, even one who takes power by "usurpation," and delegate responsibility for war to him. In return, the governor in question must recognize the caliph's role as the guardian of Islamic values. In this way, the caliph preserves important *shariʿa* values (for example, the unity of Islam). The governor, as designated commander of the armed forces, acts as a special agent of the caliph and is bound by the law of war.

Even as al-Mawardi wrote regarding the authority necessary for the just conduct of war, Shiʿite scholars developed their own set of judgments about the matter. The term "Shiʿite" describes the "partisans" of ʿAli ibn Abi Talib (c. 600–661). The various Shiʿite groups agree that God appoints one imam or leader in every generation. Only the imam possesses the authority to initiate fighting, because God protects him from injustice. Of the various scholars developing this line of thought, the work of al-Muhaqqiq al-Awwal, also known as al-Hilli, (d. 1277) is particularly illustrative.

Finally, no list of contributors to the law of war would be complete with the mention of Taqi Ibn Taymiyah (1263–1328). The various works of this scholar, many written from prisons in Damascus and Cairo, provide an important source for many contemporary Muslim groups. *Ibn Taymiyya on Public and Private Law in Islam* provides a translation of an oft-cited treatise dealing with the political implications of the *shariʿa*. With respect to the law of war, Ibn Taymiyah's work continues the discussion of right authority. His context, in which even the vestiges of the Abbasid caliphate so valued by al-Mawardi had vanished, raise multiple questions about the justice of fighting. What is the duty of Muslims in a time when authority is in question? To whom does the responsibility for commanding good and forbidding evil fall?

Themes

The notion that war can only be just when fought at the behest of a legitimate authority is persistent in the Islamic law of war. At the same time, war is supposed to serve the cause of justice, and must be fought with this intention. *Shariʿa* reasoning sees war as a means for promoting and defending justice, in connection with the policy of an established government.

The use of the term jihad provides one way to understand this. Literally, the term means "struggle." Jihad is intimately connected to the duty the Qurʾan describes as "commanding good and forbidding evil." One is supposed to struggle to fulfill this duty with means that accord with prudence or practical wisdom.

Many interpreters of the *shariʿa* spoke of participation in just wars as an aspect of jihad. They insisted, however, that any war deserving of this name be fought in the service of a legitimate authority. For majority Sunni interpreters like al-Mawardi, this meant the caliph or his designated representative. The caliph could authorize "offensive" fighting to increase the range of territory governed by Islamic values, or "defensive" fighting to protect the boundaries of the Islamic state.

For minority Shiʿite interpreters, the requirement of right authority led to different conclusions. Jamal al-Hilli, representing the *ithna ʿashari* or "Twelver" community, stressed that fighting deserved the name jihad only when ordered by the designated leader of the age. For the Twelvers, historical existence is characterized by an eschatological break, as God took the twelfth leader into hiding in 873/874 CE as a means of protecting him against the evil of the present age. The Twelfth Imam, also called *al-mahdi* or "the rightly guided one," will appear at a time of God's choosing. He will then summon the faithful to jihad. In the meantime, ordinary rulers lack the protection from error required to command jihad. Such "relatively just" rulers may, however, conduct "imposed" wars in which fighting is necessary to defend their people. For Shiʿite and Sunni authorities, a grave threat, for example from an invading enemy, indicates that the duty to fight for justice becomes an individual duty, whereby each Muslim is to join the fighting as he or she is able. In the extreme case, the duty to fight for justice actually becomes an "individual duty," whereby each Muslim is to join in the fighting as he or she is able.

Another persistent theme of *shariʿa* discussion of war has to do with the necessity of an invitation to Islam. Widely cited reports depict the Prophet ordering commanders to issue a summons inviting their enemies to adopt Islam as their way of life or, failing that, to place themselves under the protection of an Islamic state. Fighting that deserves the label "just" can only occur when these options are refused.

Following the spread of Islam in the seventh and eight centuries CE, some interpreters argued that such a formal invitation was no longer necessary, as familiarity with Islam could be presumed. An interesting question remains, however: Should the Muslim commander renew the invitation during the course of fighting, and thus allow the enemy to come to terms? Here, authorities were divided. Perhaps the best way to summarize is through the judgment of al-Shaybani: the renewal of the invitation is not required, but it is praiseworthy. The point, after all, is to promote Islamic values. Fighting is not an end in itself, but a means to this goal.

How should considerations of prudence enter into a decision to fight? Al-Mawardi, Ibn Taymiyah, and others often express concern that Muslims will avoid fighting for selfish or cowardly reasons. Hence there is much in their texts about the duty to fight, the rewards promised to those who struggle in God's way, and the promise of God to deliver the Muslims, even in contexts where they are outnumbered. At the same time, such writers counsel that the survival of the Muslims and of their ability to bear witness to Islamic values is critical. The ruler's duty in this regard may well lead to a judgment that fighting, even in a just cause, is not the best way to serve God in particular circumstances. Again, the critical role of legitimate authority in the Islamic law of war should be noted.

As regards the means of war, *shariʿa* authorities are very clear in maintaining that certain classes of enemy persons are presumed to be noncombatants. Women, children, the very old, and those physically or mentally disabled are not to be the direct and intentional target of military action. Of course, *shariʿa* interpreters know that the use of certain tactics and weapons is likely to lead to noncombatant deaths, even when the aim is to strike at military targets. In such cases, there is a way in which unintentional killing may be excused. Opinions differ regarding the question of whether soldiers responsible for such collateral damage must engage in acts of expiation.

Much of the discussion thus far presupposes conditions in which Muslims are fighting non-Muslims, or between the territories scholars called the "house of Islam" and the "house of war." There are cases where Muslims fight Muslims, however. Every authority writing on the law of war spoke about the rules for fighting rebels or dissenting groups, as well as for fighting apostates (those who "turn" from Islam) and brigands (those who break the law). These cases are perhaps better understood as punishment or policing than as war. They too proceed according to certain rules, and have the same purpose as fighting against non-Muslims: to promote or defend Islamic values, the values of justice.

Modern Developments

The judgments of Ibn Taymiyah and others stand as a kind of historical deposit to which modern Muslims recur in thinking about war and other matters. Many of the most important trends in modern Islamic thought should be seen in relation to the historic emphasis on right authority as a primary criterion for just war. This criterion was already under stress in the time of al-Mawardi. By the time of Ibn Taymiyah, it was even more unclear who could fill the role and exercise power legitimately.

During the middle period of Islamic history (c. 1400–1750), a de facto consensus placed the right of war in the hands of the heads of the Ottoman, the Safavid, and the Moghul empires. During the late eighteenth through the early twentieth centuries, these weakened and came more or less under the sway of European powers. When the Europeans loosened their grip, Muslim elites forging new states expressed ambivalence about historic institutions. At one extreme, the leadership of modern Turkey abolished the Ottoman caliphate in favor of republican governance. At the other, the movement for Indian independence saw Hindus as well as Muslims requesting a reinstitution of the caliphate as a symbol of "Eastern" unity.

In the absence of the unitary caliphate presupposed by al-Mawardi and others, the de facto right of war passed to individual states. These may be described as "Islamic" in the sense that the majority of their populations are Muslim; where constitutions exist, there is often also a legal establishment of Islam and a mechanism whereby *shariʿa* authorities may be consulted on matters of policy. Modern Islamic states participate in the international community, where states have the right of war in cases of self-defense, and a number of interpreters suggest that this is consistent with the *shariʿa*.

Not all interpreters consider this arrangement satisfactory. For example, the recognition of Israel by the international community proves a stumbling block for some, particularly so long as there is no parallel state for Palestinians. Some view the Israeli state as illegitimate as a matter of principle, and argue that Muslims are obligated to fight and regain land that God entrusted to the Muslim community. More judge that current political conditions deny basic rights to Palestinians, and that Muslims as well as others should support Palestinian resistance. In either case, discussions of resistance recall the historic *shariʿa* tradition, as scholars debate the legitimacy of "martyrdom operations" and other tactics.

From the *shariʿa* perspective, the problem of right authority in the modern world is not only a governmental problem. It also has to do with the right to interpret the *shariʿa*. Historically, interpretation of the *shariʿa* was the task of the learned class. One of the most striking features of modern Islam is the extent to which those who do not belong to that class put forward claims about the duties of Muslims to engage in armed resistance. For example, on 23 February 1998, the World Islamic Front issued a formal opinion stipulating that the duty of every Muslim was to fight Americans and their allies, without distinguishing between civilians and soldiers. None of the signatories (including Osama bin Laden) was a member of the learned class. More typical authorities published criticisms of the WIF declaration. It seems clear that the issue of legitimate authority in religion and politics is one that will occupy Muslims in the years to come.

John Kelsay

See also Jihad

Further Reading

Abou El Fadl, K. (2001). *Rebellion and violence in Islamic law*. Cambridge, UK: Cambridge University Press.

Al-Hilli, M. (1871–1872). *Droit Musulman* (A. Query, Trans.). Paris: Imprimerie Nationale.

Al-Mawardi, A. (1996). *The ordinances of government* (W. H. Wahba, Trans.). Reading, UK: Garnet Publishing Ltd.

Al-Tabari. (1998). *Book of the disagreement among Muslim jurists: The book of jihad* (Y. S. Ibrahim, Trans.). Tallahassee: M.A. thesis, Florida State University.

Cook, M. (2000). *Commanding right and forbidding wrong in Islamic thought*. Cambridge, UK: Cambridge University Press.

Firestone, R. (1999). *Jihad: The origins of holy war in Islam*. Oxford, UK: Oxford University Press.

Ibn Taymiyya, T. (1966). *Ibn Taymiyya on public and private law in Islam* (O. A. Farrukh, Trans.). Beirut: Khayats.

Johnson, J. T. (1997). *The holy war idea in Western and Islamic traditions*. University Park: Pennsylvania State University Press.

Johnson, J. T., & Kelsay, J. (Eds.). (1990). *Cross, crescent, and sword: The justification and limitation of war in Western and Islamic tradition*. Westport, CT: Greenwood Press.

Kelsay, J. (1993). *Islam and war: A study in comparative ethics*. Louisville, KY: Westminster/John Knox Press.

Kelsay, J., & Johnson, J. T. (Eds.). (1991). *Just war and jihad: Historical and theoretical perspectives on war and peace in Western and Islamic traditions*. Westport, CT: Greenwood Press.

Sachedina, A. A. (1988). *The just ruler in Shiʿite Islam*. Oxford, UK: Oxford University Press.

Islamic Movement of Uzbekistan

The Islamic Movement of Uzbekistan is a pan-Islamic militant organization established in 1996 by Islamic extremist leaders in Uzbekistan to overthrow the regime of President Islam Karimov (b. 1938) and replace it with an Islamic government. The IMU emerged as part of Islamic revivalism that engulfed Muslim Central Asia as soon as it became independent after the Soviet collapse in 1991. IMU followers in Uzbekistan included political dissidents, disaffected youth, and religious activists, some of whom had earlier played an active role in Islamic Renaissance Party's militant-political struggle against the government of Tajikistan. The Uzbek government repression contributed significantly to the rise of IMU. In June 2001 the IMU renamed itself the Islamic Party of Turkestan (however, the movement is still commonly identified with the old name) and expanded its goal to the creation of an Islamic state in the five Muslim Central Asian states (Kazakhstan, Kyrgyzstan, Tajikistan, Turkmenistan, Uzbekistan) and China's Muslim majority province of Xinjiang. The movement initially operated largely in the Fergana Valley, which straddles the Uzbek-Kyrgyz border, or from sanctuaries in northern Afghanistan under the Taliban rule.

Although IMU grew as an opposition movement in Uzbekistan, widespread repression under President Karimov's government led to violent confrontations between IMU and Uzbek authorities in the late 1990s. IMU was blamed for bombing attacks in February 1999, part of an alleged assassination attempt against President Karimov, which led to a bloody crackdown by the government. Two prominent IMU leaders, the military commander Juma Namangani (d. 2001), who had earlier fought in the Tajik civil war, and the political leader Tohir Yuldashev, who had led political Islam in Uzbekistan since independence, were sentenced to death in absentia.

The Afghan Connection

As a consequence of the crackdown, IMU leaders and followers moved to northern Afghanistan, where the Taliban allowed them to establish training camps. The IMU started to reflect the growing jihad culture, and allegedly received funding from al-Qaeda and Saudi-based Wahhabi charity organizations, as well as through drug trafficking. By the year 2000, the movement was believed to comprise some two thousand fighters from across Central Asia and Xinjiang. From its sanctuaries in Afghanistan, IMU launched a number of highly visible attacks in Kyrghzstan and Uzbekistan, including kidnapping Japanese and Americans in the Fergana Valley in 1999. The same year, Namangani led a group of more than eight hundred militants into southern Kyrgyzstan, where they captured villages and hostages, and threatened to attack Uzbekistan. In August 2000, IMU militants led by Namangani made incursions into southern Uzbekistan, mountainous areas just outside of Tashkent, and several areas in southern Kyrgyzstan.

A Crushing Blow

The demise of the Taliban regime in December 2001 was a major blow to IMU leadership and followers. In November 2001, Namangani was reported killed in heavy fighting near the northern Afghan city of Kunduz. As for Yuldashev, he, along with a number of IMU militants, were reported in early 2002 to be hiding in Pakistan's tribal Pashtun areas bordering Afghanistan.

The journalist Ahmed Rashid, an expert on Central and Southwest Asian Islamic extremism, comments, "Although IMU's Islamic ideology is not pure Wahhabi, its ideas of a universal jihad is strongly rooted in the Deobandi-Wahhabi teachings imported from Pakistan and Saudi Arabia—teachings that have little roots in traditional Central Asian Islam. IMU's inability to include the history and tradition of the people it purports to represent within its extremist Islamic ideology should limit its public support beyond the Fergana Valley" (Rashid 2002, 175). IMU's leadership may be in total disarray following the Taliban's fall in Afghanistan, but as long as the Uzbek government continues its repression of political and religious dissent, IMU may still be capable of attracting disgruntled youth in Uzbekistan.

Ishtiaq Ahmad

See also Tajik Civil War; Taliban

Further Reading

Ahmad, I. (2000–2001). Containing the Taliban: The path of peace in Afghanistan. *Perceptions*, *5*(4), 67–87.

Esposito, J. (2002). *Unholy war: Terror in the name of God.* New York: Oxford University Press.

Rashid, A (1999). The Taliban: Exporting extremism. *Foreign Affairs*, *78*(6), 22–35.

Rashid, A. (2000). *Taliban: Islam, oil and the new great game in Central Asia*. London: I. B. Tauris.

Rashid, A. (2002). *Jihad: The rise of militant Islam in Central Asia*. New Haven, CT: Yale University Press.

J

Jainism

The Jaina faith originated in India more than twenty-five hundred years ago. It emphasizes a philosophy of nonviolence (ahimsa) and has developed an array of techniques to cultivate a personal ethic grounded in the avoidance of harm to life, whether human, animal, microbial, or even elemental. Although the Jaina philosophers acknowledge that some violence cannot be avoided (accidents do happen, and eating requires the taking of even vegetable life), they advocate a lifestyle based in careful observance of precepts such as vegetarianism, fasting, and restricted travel that they deem effective in expelling the negative effects of residual violent tendencies (karma).

Jainism has a peculiar relationship with militarism and war. Though the precept "some violence is unavoidable" might be construed by some as a call for self-defense in times of attack, most Jainas would already have absented themselves socially from the possibility of violence. In the Indian social structure, certain castes specialize in the art of war and defense; Kshatriyas serve traditionally as soldiers and kings. The Jainas, on the other hand, tend not to initiate militarism but, as a group composed largely of merchants, have benefited from a division of labor that leaves security issues in the hands of others.

In the traditional social structures of India, the overarching principle of dharma mandated that certain individuals were born to complete some tasks and other individuals were scripted for other work. The person who established classical Jainism, Lord Mahavira (Vardhamana; c. 599–527 BCE), was born into the Kshatriya caste. According to one story accepted and promulgated by the Svetambara sect of Jainism, Mahavira originally entered the womb of a Brahmin woman called Devananda. The god Sakra (also known as Indra) deemed this unacceptable, stating that an Arhant or Tirthankara or Cakravartin or Baladeva or Vasudeva (all names for Jinas, Buddhas, or Avataras) cannot be born into a "low, mean, degraded, poor, miserly, or beggar's family, or a Brahmin family" (Bauer 1998, 60). Consequently, Sakra moves the fetus into the womb of a Kshatriya woman known by the name Trisala, who eventually gives birth to the baby Mahavira.

The entry of the future Jina into a Kshatriya household follows a pattern in stories of great Indian religious leaders. Siddhartha Gautama (c. 563–c. 483 BCE), who later became the Buddha, was born into a Kshatriya family. Lord Krishna was a Kshatriya, as were many other important figures in Indian history, both mythological and historical. All twenty-four Tirthankaras, of whom Mahavira is the most recent, hailed from the Kshatriya caste. Ironically, although the Jaina religion seems to have had a royal birth with the person of Mahavira, it eventually became a religion primarily followed by members of the Vaisya or merchant caste. In fact, one might observe that religious ritual and Vedic literature belong to the Brahmin caste, the great stories of the epic tradition, including the Bhagavad Gita, belong to the Kshatriya caste, and the Jaina largely finds its home in the Vaisya caste, though many other faiths are also represented among the merchants.

The name bestowed upon the liberated Mahavira, the Jina, also reflects his martial origins. The Jaina quest entails spiritual conquest, a war against the accretions

The *Uttaraadhyayan Sutra*, Chapter 20, verse 60

A person who is free from delusion (who understands things as they are), who has good qualities, who has good thoughts, speech and deeds, and who avoids violence of body, speech and mind, enjoys freedom like a bird, while living on this earth.

Source: **Kothari, Saroj. "Concept Of Nonviolence In Jainism: A System For Inner Peace And Happiness." Retrieved April 3, 2003, from http://www.jainstudy.org**

of karma that bind a person to repeated birth within samsara. The *Acaranga Sutra* includes many stories of the heroic acts of Mahavira as he struggled to free himself of all karma, including being assailed by sticks and stones by his detractors, and withstanding the extreme physical discomforts of heat and insects. In order for him to succeed in his spiritual quest, he needed the heroic strength of a warrior.

As Jainism developed and prospered, it came into relationship with various kings and kingdoms. Some scholars surmise that Chandragupta (Candragupta) Maurya (d. c. 297 BCE), the grandfather of Asoka (d. 238 or 232 BCE), in fact became a Jaina after ruling an empire that reached from Afghanistan to Bengal. He renounced the kingdom in later life and traveled to the south as part of his renunciation of the world. A clear linkage can be seen here between first accomplishing worldly conquest and then turning to spiritual conquest in later life.

Jainas had affiliation with and protection and patronage from a number of kings, both in the south in the north. Beginning with the early stories of the Mauryan ruling family's association with Jainism, we see that this religion permeated daily life in northern India. Many of the early converts to Buddhism hailed from the Jaina faith. Perhaps in response to a drought, many Jainas seem to have migrated to south India and to western India around the time of Chandragupta Maurya. In both locations, they experienced strong relations with a series of kings, some of whom clearly considered themselves to be Jains. In the south, a terrible repression of Jainism occurred in Madurai, resulting in the murder of many Jaina monks. According to Paul Dundas, many Hindu temples in the south include "lurid mural representations of the massacre by impaling of eight thousand Jains in Madurai for having taken Shiva's name in vain" (Dundas 1992, 109). In the northwest, invading Turks destroyed many Jaina temples. This relationship with the Muslims worsened at times and improved at others. While the emperor Akbar (1542–1605) looked favorably on individual Jainas and was sufficiently moved by the teachings of the Jaina monk Hiravijaya to proclaim in 1587 the banning of animal slaughter during the highest Jaina holy week (Paruysan), his grandson Aurangzeb (ʿAlamgir; 1618–1707), while governor of Gujarat in 1645, "desecrated, and turned into a mosque an ornate temple to Parsva, dedicated at colossal expense by Santidas Jhaveri, the richest and most influential merchant and financier of Ahmedabad" (Dundas 2002, 147). The Jainas were never in a position to fight their adversaries, and such events served "as a stark reminder to the Jains of their powerlessness in the face of a dominant Islam" (Dundas 2002, 147).

The Jaina community today retains its countercultural stance even within India. Only the rare Jaina will serve in the military, though I did have the pleasure in 1989 of meeting the chief of police in Madras (now Chennai) who is a Jaina. On occasion, a Jaina might adopt a promilitary stance against Pakistan, but would most likely not consider training to actually participate in any form of military action.

Unlike the Quakers, the Jainas have not issued a general antiwar proclamation. The Jaina lifestyle encourages members of the faith to engage in professions that entail little direct violence. Most Jainas are merchants and would have little or no occasion to support militarism or warfare. Undoubtedly, the extensive Jaina investments throughout India would include holding a stake in India's growing military-industrial complex. For the most part, however, Jainas remain a beacon of nonviolent behavior in an all-too-violent world.

Christopher Key Chapple

Further Reading

Bauer, J. H. (1998). *Karma and control: The prodigious and the auspicious in Svetambara Jaina canonical mythology.*

Unpublished doctoral dissertation, University of Pennsylvania.

Dundas, P. (1992). *The Jains*. London: Routledge.

Dundas, P. (2002). *The Jains* (2d ed.). London: Routledge.

Horner, I. B. (1990). *Women under primitive Buddhism: Laywomen and almswomen*. Delhi, India: Motilal Banarsidass. (Original work published 1930)

Murcott, S. (1991). *The first Buddhist women: Translations and commentary on the Therigatha*. Berkeley, CA: Parallax Press.

Sharma, J. P. (1999). The *Jinasattvas*: Class and gender in the social origins of Jaina heroes. In N. K. Wagle & O. Qvarnstrom (Eds.), *Approaches to Jaina Studies: Philosophy, Logic, Rituals, and Symbols*. Toronto, Ontario, Canada: University of Toronto Centre for South Asian Studies.

Smith, V. A. (1958). *The Oxford history of India* (3d ed.; P. Spear, Ed.). Oxford, UK: Clarendon Press.

Japan *See* Shinto, Ancient; Shinto, Modern; Zen and Japanese Nationalism; Zen, Modern; Zen, Premodern; Zen: Samurai Tradition

Japan: Tokugawa Period

The Tokugawa era in Japan (1603–1868) takes its name from the Tokugawa family, who united Japan under its military control and reestablished a national government. It initially allied itself closely with the emperor of Japan, who served as the chief Shinto priest as well as a nominal political leader of the country. Its weaknesses exposed after the arrival of American naval forces in 1853, the Tokugawa shogunate fell when rival feudal armies employed Western military technology to defeat the shogun's forces and persuaded the shogun to restore political power to the emperor.

Establishing the Tokugawa Shogunate

Though a centralized government did not exist in Japan between the mid-1400s and the late 1500s, the idea of it survived. In the late sixteenth century three powerful warlords brought Japan back together. The first, Oda Nobunaga (1534–1582), began the unification campaign in 1560. He had to overcome powerful Buddhist sects in central Japan, which wielded enough secular power that they rivaled many leading *daimyo*, or feudal lords. Between 1571 and 1580, Nobunaga waged a savage war against the Buddhists and broke their hold. His eventual successor, Tokugawa Ieyasu (1543–1616), completed the job of subjugation with a mix of military coercion and authoritarian legislation to control the Buddhist establishment.

When Nobunaga was killed in 1582, Toyotomi Hideyoshi (1537–1598) moved to avenge his master's death. He militarily reunified Japan by 1590. Hideyoshi's death in 1598 led to a brief power struggle among his five major daimyo. Tokugawa Ieyasu emerged victorious at the climactic Battle of Sekigahara, fought in late 1600. After Ieyasu consolidated power, in early 1603 the Heavenly Sovereign (*tenno*, or "emperor") elevated him to the office of shogun. Because the Japanese believed the Heavenly Sovereign was semidivine, the move gave legitimacy to Ieyasu's rule.

Ieyasu and his heirs allied themselves closely with the Heavenly Sovereigns, rebuilding palaces and mansions for them. But they also sought to control the royal family and its couriers. The Regulations concerning the Royal Court and Nobility issued by Ieyasu and his son Hidetada (1579–1632) in 1615 dictated the behavior of the Heavenly Sovereign and his court and isolated them from other nobility. The regulations forced the royal family to devote their lives to ceremonial pursuits and once again became the custodians of traditional culture. As a reminder of who held the real power, Ieyasu garrisoned samurai in the middle of Kyoto, the royal capital.

The shogun had to be careful not to abuse his power or he could face opposition from united daimyo. Ieyasu and his immediate successors, Hidetada and Iemitsu (1604–1651), carried out their obligation to supervise the warrior class and preserve the peace, just as their predecessors had done. But they also strengthened their government and national control with a strong standing army and absolute control of the office of shogun. To ensure that his family would retain control of the office, Ieyasu officially retired in 1605 and had the Heavenly Sovereign confirm his son Hidetada as the new shogun. Ten years later, Ieyasu and Hidetada led their armies against Hideyoshi's son, Hideyori (1593–1615), and nearly 100,000 of his followers at Osaka Castle. The army decimated Hideyori's fortress and its surroundings, slaughtered his followers, and drove Hideyori to suicide. When Ieyasu died a year later, he knew that his family firmly controlled the shogunate and, with it, the country.

Religion in the Tokugawa Period

Until the national government officially separated Shintoism and Buddhism in 1868, the two religions had always peacefully coexisted and shared practices and deities in Japan. Ieyasu understood the importance of these religions to his fellow countrymen. The first three shoguns of the Tokugawa Period personally journeyed to see the Heavenly Sovereign to receive investiture as shogun. Subsequent shoguns failed to do so, and by the mid–1800s, ignoring the Heavenly Sovereign had created a backlash against the shogun.

In addition to paying deference to the emperor, Ieyasu and his successors enveloped themselves in religious myth. Ieyasu converted to Tendai Buddhism. Following Ieyasu's wishes, one year after his death his remains were moved to a specially prepared mausoleum in Nikko, allegedly the home of numerous benevolent deities. Then the Heavenly Sovereign issued a proclamation deifying Ieyasu, giving him the posthumous title Tosho Dai Gongen, or "Illuminator of the East, August Avatar of Buddha." Japanese Buddhists believed that Buddha could assume many different forms, including Yakushi, the Buddha of Healing. Ranking below the Buddhas were bodhisattvas, who did not enter paradise but remained to help others find salvation. As Tosho Dai Gongen, Ieyasu, the avatar of Yakushi, would illuminate the pathway to enlightenment for the Japanese. The emperor's proclamation also meant that Ieyasu held a high place among the Shinto deities. He was celebrated as a *shinkun*, or "divine ruler," among those who practiced Shintoism. Thus, he was transformed from a fighting mortal into a powerful deity who protected his own descendents, the monarch and court, the samurai, and the people of the Japanese islands.

The Tokugawa shoguns also embraced Confucianism. They did so because Confucianism emphasized order, obedience, duty, and service to the family, community, and government. It provided a moral code that ran both directions. It required all subjects to be loyal to their leaders, and, in turn, required the leaders to be virtuous and moral. As the samurai transitioned from warriors to ruling bureaucrats, Confucianism helped ensure benevolent rule.

Hayashi Razan (1583–1657), an early Japanese Confucian scholar, served as an advisor to the Tokugawa shogunate for over thirty years. He drafted official documents and wrote the 1635 revision of the Regulations Concerning Warrior Households. After Ieyasu had consolidated power, the shogunate originally issued the regulations in 1615 to outline the samurai's mission under the new political system. The original regulations declared, "The study of letters and the practice of military arts, including archery and horsemanship, must be cultivated diligently" (McClain 2002, 78). But in a time of peace, there seemed to be little reason to work at such skills. A new sense of purpose for the samurai sprang from the concept of Bushido, the Way of the Warrior.

Early on, the Tokugawa shogunate adopted Confucian China's four-class system, with the samurai on top, followed by the peasants, artisans, and merchants. Bushido evolved as the code of conduct for the samurai. It was derived mostly from the contemporary philosophical texts of Miyamoto Musashi (1584–1645) and Yamaga Soko (1622–1685). Both men were samurai in the early Tokugawa period struggling to redefine their roles in peacetime. Miyamoto denounced the practice of ritual suicide, or *junshi*, and declared that warriors must always strive for success through preparation for whatever life may bring. One must not embrace death, he argued, but rather must try to achieve goals and victory in life. Committing suicide upon the death of one's master was a selfish act, not a selfless one.

Yamaga drew on Chinese Confucianism and the Chinese tradition. He argued that the *bushi*, or samurai, should emulate the Confucian intellectuals of the past and devote themselves to political and moral leadership. They should do so through diligent study of music, poetry, and other arts along with their military arts. They should strive to cultivate *makoto*, or "sincerity," the greatest virtue in Chinese Confucianism. As civil servants, they must allow *makoto* to guide their actions so that they could administer benevolently and for the good of all. He, too, denounced ritual suicide because loyalty to a master instead of the house of the master could wipe out much of a local government when the master died. But the practice remained such a problem that the shogunate prohibited *junshi* after 1664. Ultimately, though, Bushido included the traditional reverence for death held over from earlier times and added the new ideals of success as a virtue; the paramount importance of sincerity; and the obligations of the samurai to serve his government and contribute to society through honorable service.

The Persecution of Christians

In 1549, the Jesuit Francis Xavier (1505–1552) arrived as the first Christian missionary. By 1600 there were approximately 300,000 Japanese converts, though some claimed to be Christian because some Portuguese ship captains would only trade with fellow Christians. Christian beliefs ran contrary to the centuries-old practice of swearing allegiance and devotion to one's master. Prior to 1600, some Japanese had become suspicious of a religion that demanded exclusive loyalty to a god. Physical attacks on missionaries and their followers soon began. Undaunted by repeated assaults, Christian missionaries continued their work. Then in 1614, Ieyasu issued the most severe in a series of orders denouncing Christianity as seditious and demanded the departure of all missionaries. When several refused to obey the order and covertly continued their work, the shogun launched a campaign of extinction. Priests and their followers were hunted down throughout the country and executed. The campaign continued until the late 1630s. As many as four thousand believers were killed. The handful of remaining Christians retreated to isolated villages on the southern island of Kyosho, far from the vengeful shogun.

The third Tokugawa shogun, Iemitsu, equated Christianity with all Westerners, and broadened the ban on Christianity to a ban on Europeans in Japan. One Dutch ship a year was allowed in, but no others from Europe. The Chinese, however, were allowed to continue trading with the Japanese. They remained a source of information on the West for the Japanese, providing Chinese translations of Western books and news of the outside world. In contrast, due to the lack of western trade and contact with Japan, the country largely ceased to exist in the mind of most Westerners for the next two centuries.

Opening Japan and the Meiji Restoration

Though there was some intermittent contact with Europeans and Americans over the next two hundred years, Japan's isolation ended abruptly in 1853. The arrival of Matthew C. Perry (1794–1958) and four U.S. naval vessels to negotiate trade and diplomatic treaties in Edo Bay on 8 July 1853 left the shogunate in a difficult predicament. It knew that it could not repel the foreigners and their superior weaponry. If it opened the country, it might bring about the downfall of the shogunate. Japan's national integrity briefly remained intact after signing the Treaty of Peace and Amity on 31 March 1854, which opened to American ships two port towns where they could take on provisions. It did not, however, establish trade relations.

Two years later, Russia, France, and Britain demanded and received similar treaties. The arrival of an American consul who demanded the establishment of normal trade relations soon thereafter touched off a crisis for the shogunate that led to open warfare between those favoring capitulation to Western demands and those opposed to opening up the country. Opponents who embraced *sonno joi*, or the movement "to revere the Heavenly Sovereign and expel the barbarians," soon emerged. It quickly gained popularity among some of the younger samurai, known as *shishi*, from the *han*, or province, of Chosho at the southern tip of the main island and surrounding provinces.

The *shishi* claimed Japan's cultural and territorial integrity had been violated, and were angered by the inability of the weak and corrupt shogunate to cope with the severe economic problems faced by the majority of Japanese. They used the emperor as a rallying point and a justification for their actions, and sought to restore the Heavenly Sovereign to his rightful place as the leader of the nation. They gained control of Chosho and began arming themselves with Western military equipment to protect their domain. Satsuma, the second largest *han*, quickly followed suit. In early 1866, the two provinces agreed to an alliance. When the shogunate moved to put down the rebellion in Chosho, Satsuma refused to participate, and the shogunate's poorly armed forces were easily defeated. The days of the Tokugawa shogunate were numbered.

Sakamoto Ryoma (1835–1867), who had brought Satsuma and Chosho together, prevailed upon Shogun Keiki (1837–1913) to restore the powers of government voluntarily to the young Emperor Meiji (Mutsuhito; 1867–1912), who had just ascended to the throne in 1867. By doing so, Keiki hoped to avoid an all-out civil war and also hoped to head up the proposed new government. He believed turning power over to the emperor would bring the various factions into the government in time to prevent outside intervention by foreign powers, like had just occurred in China. The plan called for a parliamentary system. Keiki, the head of the Tokugawa clan, expected to lead the new government. However, anti-Tokugawa factions had no intention of allowing this, and defeated the Tokugawa forces at Toba-Fushimi, thus bringing the Tokugawa era to an end. It would be several years before Japan modernized and "westernized" and a new parliamentary government could exercise full power. But the Heavenly Sovereign had been restored to a central position in the national government, and a new era, known as the Meiji Restoration, was declared in 1868.

James G. Lewis

See also Confucianism: Han Dynasty; Confucianism, Classical; Confucianism, Modern; Confucianism: Neo-Confucianism; Zen: Samurai Tradition

Further Reading

Bellah, R. N. (1957). *Tokugawa religion: The values of pre-industrial Japan*. Boston: Beacon Press.
Hane, M. (1986). *Modern Japan: A historical survey*. Boulder, CO: Westview Press.
Korniki, P. F, & McMullen, I. J. (Eds.). (1996). *Religion in Japan: Arrows to heaven and earth*. Cambridge, UK: Cambridge University Press.
McClain, J. L. (2002). *Japan: A modern history*. New York: W. W. Norton.

The Jewish Revolt of 66–70 CE

The Roman Empire had controlled the land of Judaea (present-day Israel) since 63 BCE, when the Roman general Pompey the Great (106–48 BCE) invaded it; Judaea had been a Roman province since 6 CE. Decades of poor Roman administration in Judaea combined with social, economic, and religious tensions to spark a large Jewish rebellion in 66 CE. Roman armies, led first by the emperor Vespasian (9–79) and then his son Titus (39–81), systematically besieged and captured the rebel cities, in the end capturing Jerusalem and destroying the Second Temple. This ended a millennium of temple-centered Judaism; rabbinical Judaism soon became the dominant form of the religion.

Judaea under Roman Rule

Herod the Great (73–4 BCE) ruled a large Judaean kingdom as a Roman client-king until his death in 4 BCE. Emperor Claudius made Judaea a Roman province and ruled it through appointed procurators, with the brief exception of the three-year reign of Herod's grandson Agrippa (c. 10 BCE–44 CE), from 41 to 44. The procurators that followed Agrippa proved particularly poor administrators. Excessive taxation, harsh rule, cultural ignorance, religious intolerance, and routine massacres whose victims often numbered in the thousands led more and more Judaeans to oppose Roman rule. Minor rebellions and banditry became the norm in Judaea.

Poor Roman administration exacerbated tensions in Judaean society. Judaean landowners generally supported Roman rule, and tenant farmers came to see removing Rome as a necessary step in toppling the aristocracy and reforming society. Increasing numbers of Greeks immigrated to Judaea in these years, and religious clashes between Jews and Greeks became increasingly common and increasingly violent.

The Jews of Judaea were themselves split between the conservative Sadducees, the Pharisees, who worked to liberalize Jewish law and practice, and many smaller sects. Among the latter were the Sicarii who expected divine support for revolution. After their guerrilla struggle failed, they turned to assassinating Romans and Roman collaborators with daggers (*sica* in Latin). The Second Temple in Jerusalem remained the center of Jewish religious life, and Roman interference in Temple ritual, control of the priesthood, and repeated seizures of Temple funds sparked a series of increasingly violent clashes with religiously observant Jews.

Revolt Breaks Out

The Rebellion broke out in the spring of 66 after Procurator Gessius Florus (term 64–66 CE) seized Temple funds and ordered his troops to massacre protesters in Jerusalem. Angry mobs then drove the outnumbered troops from the city, and rebel groups began mobilizing for war. Agrippa's son, Agrippa II (c. 27–c. 93), who ruled a small kingdom that included some cities in Galilee, failed to persuade the rebels of the futility of fighting Rome and fled Jerusalem with much of the Jewish aristocracy, who had also pleaded for a peaceful solution.

Cestius Gallus (d. 67 CE), the governor of Syria, marched into Judaea with thirty thousand soldiers. Arriving outside Jerusalem in October, his army failed to capture it and retreated toward the coast. Jewish guerrillas harried the retreating Romans, killing more than five thousand soldiers. Afterward, various Jewish factions cobbled together a weak provisional government that included many moderates who still hoped for peace with Rome. The government divided the nation into six districts and appointed a military commander to each to prepare its defense. Galilee went to Josephus (c. 37–c. 100), the historian and general, and his later writings are the only substantial remaining contemporary account of the war.

View of Roman garrison below Masada, West Bank, Israel. November 1996. Courtesy Steve Donaldson.

Revolution in Judaea and Galilee

In Galilee, Josephus quarreled with rivals for leadership, and like other local commanders faced difficulties consolidating his leadership and convincing the local Jewish communities to support the revolution. The Roman general (and future emperor) Vespasian replaced Cestius in 67 and marched into Galilee with three legions, totaling about sixty thousand Roman soldiers and auxiliaries. Jewish resistance collapsed rapidly in the face of this large army. Many cities opened their gates to the Romans, and Vespasian captured the others quickly. Josephus gathered his surviving troops for a stand at the heavily fortified city of Jotapata, which fell after a forty-seven-day siege. Josephus surrendered to the Romans, changed sides, and became Vespasian's military adviser. Vespasian then conquered the remaining towns and cities of Galilee, only two of which put up sustained resistance.

Efforts by rebels to seize Roman-held cities in Judaea failed, and as Vespasian's army continued to advance south, refugees, defeated rebels, and new volunteers for the revolution poured into Jerusalem. Among the latter was a group Josephus termed Zealots. They were strongly committed to the revolution and to the creation of an egalitarian society. The death of Emperor Nero in 68 slowed the Roman juggernaut, but by July 69 Vespasian had captured all of Judaea except Jerusalem and a handful of fortresses. Vespasian then put his son Titus in command and left Judaea to seize control of Rome.

The Siege of Jerusalem

Titus began the siege of Jerusalem in the spring of 70. The Jewish provisional government had collapsed the previous year following a campaign of assassination by the Sicarii, who targeted some of its members, apparently doubting their sincerity in supporting the revolution. In particular, they assassinated Ananus, the son of Ananus, who was High Priest from 66 to 68 and the leader of the provisional government. They killed him both because they suspected he favored a negotiated settlement with the Romans and because they questioned his credentials as High Priest. There was a long-running dispute in the Jewish community in the

Second Temple Period as to who (based on bloodline) could be High Priest.

The Sicarii were in turn driven out of the city by other armed factions. The Zealots and other Jewish factions in the city then battled one another for control of the city, and particularly the Temple. Only the arrival of Titus and his legions stopped the fighting. Weakened by this bitter infighting, the rebels still put up fierce resistance. Jewish forays repeatedly destroyed Roman siege engines and inflicted considerable casualties. The Romans undermined the city's walls and captured the city neighborhood by neighborhood, razing the buildings and slaughtering the inhabitants. They captured and burned the Temple in August and the rest of the city shortly thereafter. Over the next few years, Roman soldiers captured the last rebel strongholds, including the fortress of Masada, whose garrison of Zealots and Sicarii committed suicide rather than surrender. All told, several hundred thousand Jews died in the fighting, and the Romans sold tens of thousands more into slavery.

The Aftermath

The destruction of the Temple brought an end to the Sadducees and temple-centered Judaism. In their place Rabbinic Judaism, whose foundation the Pharisees had laid, flourished in Judaea and the Diaspora. However, Jews remained restive under Roman rule. Jews in the eastern half of the Roman Empire launched a massive rebellion in 116, when Emperor Trajan (53–117) invaded Parthia, threatening the Jewish communities there. Led by Bar Kokhba (d. 135), Jews in Judaea rebelled again in 132.

Stephen K. Stein

See also Hellenistic Religions

Further Reading

Dio, C. (1924). *Roman history* (Vol. 7) (E. Carey, Trans.). Cambridge, MA: Loeb Classical Library.

Goodman, M. (1987). *The ruling class of Judaea: The origins of the Jewish revolt against Rome A.D. 66–70*. Cambridge, UK: Cambridge University Press.

Josephus, F. (1926). *Life*. (H. St. John Thackeray, Trans.). Cambridge, MA: Loeb Classical Library.

Josephus, F. (1999). *The Jewish war* (H. St. John Thackeray, Trans.). Cambridge, MA: Loeb Classical Library.

Josephus, F. (2000). *Jewish antiquities* (R. Marcus, Trans.). Cambridge, MA: Loeb Classical Library.

Rajak, T. (1984). *Josephus: The historian and his society*. Philadelphia: Fortress Press.

Smallwood, E. M. (1980). *The Jews under Roman rule from Pompey to Diocletian: A study in political relations*. Leiden, Netherlands: E. J. Brill.

Tacitus, P. C. (931–37). *Histories* (C. H. Moore, Trans.). Cambridge, MA: Loeb Classical Library.

Zeitlin, S. (1967). *The rise and fall of the Judean state: A political, social and religious history of the second commonwealth* (Vol. 2). Philadelphia: Jewish Publication Society of America.

Zeitlin, S. (1978). *The rise and fall of the Judean state: A political, social and religious history of the second commonwealth, 66 CE to 120 CE* (Vol. 3). Philadelphia: Jewish Publication Society of America.

Jihad

Jihad is the term most commonly used in Islam to denote fighting for a religious cause. As approximately 90 percent of the world's Muslims belong to the Sunni branch of Islam, this article will concentrate on Sunni views of jihad. The full idiom is *jihad fi sabil Allah*, meaning "striving in the path [or cause] of God." In fact, then, jihad does not necessarily mean fighting or warring at all. All words in Arabic derive from basic three-letter roots, and the root meaning of *j.h.d.* is "to strive, exert oneself, or take extraordinary pains." The Arabic lexicographers define the third form of this root, from which the noun jihad derives, as "exerting one's utmost power, efforts, endeavors, or ability in contending with an object of disapprobation" (Lane 1980, part 2, 473).

Jihad of the Tongue, Jihad of the Heart, Jihad of the Sword

The object of disapprobation against which one struggles may be a visible enemy, the devil, or aspects of one's own self. There are a number of kinds of jihad, therefore, and most having nothing to do with fighting or war. "Jihad of the tongue," for example, means exerting one's utmost efforts to speak on behalf of the good and against evil, and "jihad of the heart" denotes struggle against one's own sinful inclinations. According to Islamic tradition (the hadith), Muhammad outlined the types of jihad that a Muslim may engage in to defend Islam from corruption:

> Every prophet sent by God to a nation before me has had disciples and followers who followed in his ways and obeyed his commands. But after them came successors who preached what they did not pratice and practiced what they were not commanded. Whoever strives against them with one's hand is a believer, whoever strives against them with one's tongue is a believer, whoever strives against them with one's heart is a believer. There is nothing greater than [the size of] a mustard seed beyond that in the way of faith. (Muslim n.d., 1: 69–70)

In addition to jihad of the tongue, the hand, and the heart, however, is "jihad of the sword," and this is the term that most commonly denotes religiously authorized warring. When the term *jihad* is used without qualifiers such as "of the heart" or "of the tongue," it is understood universally as war on behalf of Islam.

Jihad is often divided into two types, greater jihad and lesser jihad. According to a famous but late legend concerning Muhammad (it cannot be found in any of the canonical collections of hadith) and narrated in a number of versions, either Muhammad or some of his warriors return from battle. Muhammad immediately remarks, "We [or you] have returned from the lesser jihad to the greater jihad." When asked what he meant by that, he is said to have replied, "The greater jihad is the struggle against the self" (ʿAli 1973, 12–13).

Jihad, then, may be done simply by striving to behave ethically and by speaking without causing harm to others, but it is generally understood as engaging actively in the defense or propagation of Islam. Within the broad range of meanings associated with defending Islam, it can also denote war against Muslims who are defined as apostates *(murtaddin)* rebelling against proper Islamic authority, dissenting Muslim groups *(bagh$_e$)* denouncing legitimate Muslim leadership, highway robbers and other violent people, and deviant or un-Islamic leadership.

Jihad tends to be directed outward, however, against non-Muslim polities that are perceived as threatening to the well-being of the Islamic community or nation, known as the *umma*. This form of jihad, which is authorized by the deity and directed against non-Muslims, corresponds most closely to the Western concept of holy war, and it is to this jihad that we now turn.

Jihad in the Qurʾan

The root *j.h.d.* occurs in the Qurʾan forty-one times in eighteen *suras* (chapters), but the word *qital* is more specific than jihad in its narrower meaning of fighting or making war. As with jihad, one may engage in *qital* in the path of God, and this is always religiously grounded war (the idiom occurs in 2:190, 2:244, 2:246; 3:13, 3:167; 4:74–76, 4:84; 9:111; 21:4; 73:20). *Harb* is a generic word meaning "war" in Arabic; it too is found commonly in the Qurʾan. *Harb* usually refers to wars that are not legitimized by religious authority and is not found as part of the idiom "in the path of God," so *harb* cannot be construed as religious war. Terms for war and battle in the Qurʾan, therefore, are not limited to jihad.

The Qurʾan is not consistent in its position on war. It includes a number of verses that would seem to call for a quietist or at least a nonmilitant approach to resolving conflict with non-Muslims. Q 6:106 says "Follow what has been revealed to you from your Lord; there is no God but He, and turn away from the idolaters" (all translations are the author's; see also Q 15: 94). Even in the face of strong opposition or treachery, some verses teach forgiveness and reconciliation. Q 5: 13 has in relation to the "Peoples of the Book" (Jews and Christians), "Because of their breaking their covenant, We cursed them and hardened their hearts. . . . You will continue to uncover treachery from all but a few of them, but be forgiving and pardon, for God loves the kindly." And when there is a serious quarrel, Q 29:46 teaches, "Only argue nicely with the People of the Book, except with the oppressors among them. Say: We believe in what has been revealed to us and revealed to you. Our God and your God is one, and it is Him to whom we surrender."

Other verses, however, express a militant approach to non-Muslims and to conflict. Some, such as Q 2: 190, call for fighting only in defense and with extreme caution not to exceed moral limits: "Fight in the path of God against those who fight against you, but do not transgress limits, for God does not love transgressors." But the following verses (191–193) give a far more agressive message: "Kill them wherever you find them, and drive them out of the places from which they drove you out, for temptation [most exegetes gloss: to engage in idolatry] is worse than killing. . . . And fight them until there is no more temptation and religion is entirely God's. But if they cease, let there be no hostility except to the oppressors."

Scriptural Abrogation and a Theory of War

Islamic tradition has treated the problem of apparent contradiction in the Qurʾan on this and other issues through a methodological approach called *naskh* (abrogation). Islam accepts as a given that the revelations of the Qurʾan are serial, meaning that they were given to Muhammad over the entire prophetic period of his life. According to the theory of abrogation, early revelations were given to Muhammad as advice in response to his very difficult early public life as prophet. These revelations prescribed certain behaviors in order to resolve specific difficulties he faced, but are not necessarily everlasting commands. Later revelations, however, when Muhammad was successful in leading his community of believers, are considered eternally valid. It was possible, therefore, to resolve conflicts between Qurʾanic pronouncements by determining a basic chronology of revelation.

According to virtually all traditional Muslim religious scholars and based on the science of determining the chronology of revelation, the militant verses were revealed later than those advocating more quietistic means of resolving conflict with idolaters and Peoples of the Book. Militant verses therefore abrogate the unwarlike verses and have thus become the primary sources upon which has developed Islamic law and expectations regarding war.

Two of the latest and therefore most eternally binding verses are Q 9:5 and 9:29. The first, which is commonly called the "sword verse" and is said to have abrogated as many as 140 other verses treating war, is understood by Muslim exegetes and jurists to refer only to those who worship idols: "When the sacred months [a limited period, according to most Muslim exegetes, during which believers were required to sever their relationships with nonbelievers] are past, kill the idolaters wherever you find them, and seize them, besiege them, and lie in wait for them in every place of ambush; but if they repent, pray regularly, and give the alms tax, then let them go their way, for God is forgiving, merciful." This verse serves as scriptural authority for the requirement to fight against true idolaters until they either accept Islam or die by the sword.

The second verse is understood to refer to Peoples of the Book: "Fight those who do not believe in God or the Last Day, and who do not forbid what has been forbidden by God and His messenger, nor acknowledge the religion of truth from among the People of the Book, until they pay the poll tax out of hand, having been brought low. This verse serves as scriptural authority for the requirement to fight Peoples of the Book until they are willing to accept Islamic religiopolitical hegemony and suffer the position of second-class social and religious status in Islamic society.

According to the classical Islamic position, then, as the early community of Muslims grew in numbers and strength, continuing divine revelations widened the conditions and narrowed the restrictions under which war could be waged, until it was concluded that war against non-Muslims could be waged virtually at any time, without pretext, and in any place. While this has been the classical position, its major weakness is that the classical Muslim scholars of the Qurʾan from the earliest period could not agree upon the chronology of revelations. It is therefore necessary to consider a different reading of the disparate verses. Conflicting verses of revelation may in fact articulate the views of different factions existing simultaneously within the early muslim commmunity of Muhammad's day and continuing for a period after his death, some militant and other quietiest or perhaps even pacifist as in early Christianity. Each faction would refer to different scriptural sources available from the oral and as yet unedited and uncanonized compendium of revelation for support of its views. When the militant factions won the day, they could not eliminate the scriptural support for nonmilitant behaviors because of the sacred nature of the references, but they could invalidate them through the theory of abrogation.

Jihad in Islamic Law

Muslim jurists developed a highly sophisticated legal doctrine of warring in the path of God. One of the greatest jurists, well-known even in the West, was Averroës (Muhammad ibn Rushd, 1126–1198 CE), who held the post of judge in Seville and his native Córdoba, Spain. In his legal handbook, Averroës makes the following points, though it should be noted that the juridical literature is both sophisticated and complex, with much legal and theoretical discussion and some disagreement over details: It is a collective legal obligation for healthy adult free men who have the means at their disposal to go to war. All polytheists should be fought (Jews and Christians are included in this group). The aim of warfare against Peoples of the Book is either conversion to Islam or payment of the *jizya* tax, signaling subjugation to Islam. Generally, collection of the *jizya* is only accepted from Jews, Christians, and Zoroastrians, though some scholars allow it for any polytheists (including, for example, Hindus) who are not Arabs. Damage inflicted on the enemy may consist of damage to property, injury to the person, or violation of personal liberty (slavery). This may be done to all polytheists, including men, women, and children, but Averroës notes that some scholars omit monks from such damages. Captives may be pardoned, enslaved, killed, or released either on ransom or as *dhimmi* (protected Peoples of the Book) who must then pay the *jizya* poll tax to the Muslim head of state. Some scholars forbid the killing of captives. Certain individuals among the enemy may be granted safe conduct in order to conduct political or economic activities that benefit the state. In time of war all adult able-bodied unbelieving males may be slain, but noncombatant women and children may not.

Further, there is much discussion in the juridical literature on rules of engagement, the use of weapons of mass destruction such as fire, how much damage may be inflicted on the property of the enemy, and so forth. Truce is permitted, but there is much discussion about who has the authority to call for it and under what conditions it may be called for. Some consider truce permitted at any time, provided that the ruler deems it in the interest of the Muslims, while other maintain that it is only allowed when the Muslims are pressed by sheer necessity.

Jihad and Realpolitik

Islamic doctrines of jihad were formulated during the classical period of Islam when Islam was the dominant religiopolitical civilization of southern and eastern Europe, the Mediterranean, and the Middle East, ascendant as far east as the Indian subcontinent. Its outstanding success could be measured in the arts and sciences as well as in politics and the military, and it seemed clear to Muslim believers that God was ensuring its unstoppable expansion. Perpetual war against the non-Muslim world seemed natural until victory, but the juggernaut did not continue forever. It slowed, continued in fits and starts, halted, and then reversed in some areas, such as Spain and southern and eastern Europe. However, there was little reevaluation of previous expectations. Reversals were considered temporary, so until the modern period Muslim scholars gave little new thought to Islamic military doctrines, whether legal or moral.

New thinking began with the impact of European colonization. Some responded to the shock of colonialism by calling for reform of Islamic doctrines and ideas, while others called for a return to military jihad and the pristine ways of early Islam in order to regain divine favor. Only in the last years of the twentieth century and the beginning of the twenty-first has there emerged much interest in other forms of conflict resolution, and this has taken place entirely in the West. The attack that destroyed New York City's World Trade Center and damaged the Pentagon, and the response of the United States in attempting to destroy what is often called "Islamic" terrorism has shocked the Muslim world and has encouraged some reevaluation of the doctrines of jihad. What will emerge from this will only become evident as the twenty-first century progresses.

Reuven Firestone

See also Islam, Sunni

Further Reading

ʿAli, M. (1973). *Al-jihad fil-sharʿiyya al-islamiyya* [Jihad in Islamic jurisprudence]. Cairo, Egypt.

Aziz Said, A., Funk, N., & Kadayifci, A. (Eds.). (2001). *Peace and conflict resolution in Islam*. Lanham, MD: University Press of America.

Blankinship, K. (1994). *The end of the jihad state*. Albany: State University of New York Press.

Dajani-Shakeel, H., & Messier, R. A. (Eds.). (1991). *The Jihad and its times*. Ann Arbor: University of Michigan.

Dekmejian, R. H. (1995). *Islam in revolution*. Syracuse, NY: Syracuse University Press.

Firestone, R. (1999). *Jihad: The origin of holy war in Islam*. New York: Oxford University Press.

Halim, H., et al. (1998). *The Crescent and the Cross: Muslim and Christian approaches to war and peace*. New York: St. Martin's Press.

Haykal, M. (1993). *Al-jihad wal-qital fil-siyasa al-sharʿiyya* [Jihad and fighting in politics and Islamic law] (Vols 1–3). Beirut, Lebanon: Dar al-Bayariq.Ibn Mansur. *Lisan al-ʿArab* (Vol. 13). Beirut, Lebanon: Dar Sadir.

Jamal al-Din Ibn Al-Jawzi. (n.d.). *Nawasikh al-Qurʾan* [Abrogation in the Qurʾan]. Beirut, Lebanon: Dar al-Kutub al-ʿIlmiyya.

Johnson, J. T., & Kelsay, J. (Eds.). (1990). *Cross, crescent, and sword: The justification and limitation of war in Western and Islamic tradition*. New York: Greenwood.

Kelsay, J. (1993). *Islam and war: The Gulf War and beyond: A study in comparative ethics*. Louisville, KY: Westminster/John Knox.

Kelsay, J., & Johnson, J. T. (1991). *Just war and jihad: Historical and theoretical perspectives on war and peace in Western and Islamic traditions*. New York: Greenwood.

Khadduri, M. (1955). *War and peace in the law of Islam*. Baltimore: Johns Hopkins University Press.

Lane, E. (1980). *An Arabic-English Lexicon*. Beirut, Lebanon: Librairie du Liban.

Muslim b. al-Hajaj. (n.d.). *Sahih Muslim*. Cairo, Egypt: Dar al-Kitab al-Misri.

Peters, R. (1996). *Jihad in classical and modern Islam*. Princeton, NJ: Markus Wiener.

Salmi, R., Adib Majul, C., & Tanham, G. K. (Eds.). (1998). *Islam and conflict resolution*. Lanham, MD: University Press of America.

Zayd, M. (1963). *All-naskh fil qu ʿan al-karim* [Abrogation in the glorious Qurʾan]. Cairo Egypt: Dar al-Fikr al-Arabi.

Judaism *See* Genocide in Europe; Jewish Revolt of 66–73; Judaism: Biblical Period; Judaism, Conservative; Judaism: Medieval Period; Judaism, Orthodox; Judaism, Pacifism in; Judaism, Reconstructionist; Judaism, Reform; Nazism and Holocaust; Palestine and Israel; Palestine: 1948 War

Judaism: Biblical Period

The lore preserved by ancient Israelites is rich in images and tales of war. As in the wider ancient Near East, creation is often perceived in terms of a battle against chaos, while the deity, Yahweh, is frequently depicted as a man of war, powerful and victorious in battle. Israelites' accounts of their own history describe both military successes and failures and include sophisticated intellectual engagement with issues pertaining to the causes and conduct of war. Exploring attitudes to war in ancient Israel, however, involves a number of methodological challenges. Questions arise about date, Israelite identity, and the relationship between the literature preserved in the Hebrew Bible and actual Israelites set in place and time. When one writes of attitudes to war in "biblical times," in the earliest period of Jewish history, precisely whose attitudes is one uncovering?

Biblical Textual History

The first eight books of the Bible trace a chronology from a period before the rule of kings in Israel (pre-tenth century BCE) through the time of the monarchies (tenth century BCE–586 BCE) to a period after the monarchies, when foreign superpowers take control (586 BCE on). It would be wonderfully convenient for the study of ancient Israelite history and culture if sources describing the various periods were historically accurate and if views of war expressed in biblical sources paralleled actual political developments. As is the case with the great epic literature of any culture, however, the relationship between the Bible and actual historical events is often difficult to ascertain, while trajectories of intellectual and social history and threads of ideology are difficult to unravel.

Biblical narratives, often expressed in the formulaic language and conventionalized patterns of traditional discourse, have a long history, written and oral. Layers of voices and contributors are reflected in any one account along with the point of view of the composer who got the last word. Variations persist in the rich array of manuscript traditions that lie behind the edited Bible that one now reads. In addition, extrabiblical literary sources and archaeological evidence must also enter any analysis of aspects of ancient Israelite history and culture. We begin, in fact, with a brief overview of the history of ancient Israel as revealed by archaeological evidence that richly, if sometimes enigmatically, informs our knowledge of the course of Israel's social and political history, both of these being intimately interwoven with attitudes to war, its causes, and conduct.

Israelite History and the Material Culture of War

The earliest known extrabiblical source in which Israel is mentioned is the Egyptian Merneptah Stele of the thirteenth century BCE, and it is with this date that most contemporary scholars feel confident in beginning the history of Israel. Archaeological evidence reveals settlement activity in the central frontier highlands of Israel at sites such as Ai, Bethel, and Shiloh. Hilltop villages were small in size, arranged in clusters of small, pillared, multiroom houses, probably reflecting kinship ties, as shown by the archaeologist Lawrence Stager. Water was stored in bell-shaped cisterns carved into the bedrock, and the villagers engaged in subsistence agriculture, growing grapes, figs, cereals, legumes, and other foodstuffs on terraced plots, with some variation depending upon the climate in each locale as Carol Meyers has noted. They were also engaged in pastoral activities, raising sheep, cows, and goats. Archaeologists picture an essentially prestate, nonurban culture having much in common with the cultures of other northwest Semitic peoples of the area.

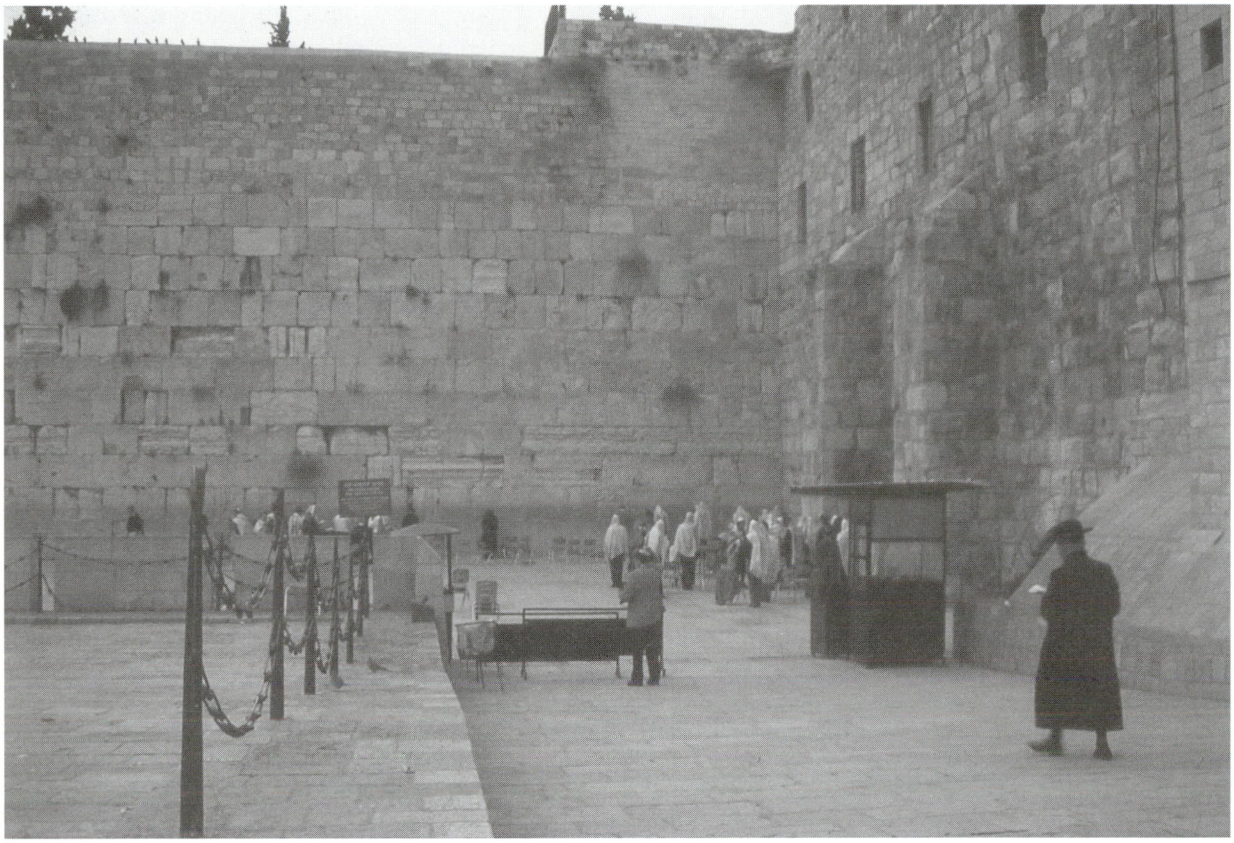

The Western Wall (Wailing Wall) in Jerusalem. November 1996. Courtesy Steve Donaldson.

We can assume the existence of a lively oral culture, the political role of certain local chieftains, and the presence of traders. Additional intriguing but difficult-to-interpret archaeological finds include religious artifacts such as an eighteen centimeter bronze bull and a perhaps-sacred circle of stones. We can also imagine the likelihood of the need for defense and the possible disputes that may have arisen between groups vying for control of land or water rights.

Certain features of war in ancient Israel pertain to this early period and all subsequent times. In Israel as in any traditional, premodern culture, wars, as the biblical scholar T. R. Hobbs notes, were "close order affairs" in which warriors "smelled their opponents as they fought." The fighting took place largely on foot, while "weapons were simple, thrown or pulled by the human arm" (Hobbes 1989, 18). Such physical realities inevitably affect not only images of war but also attitudes to fighting, one's views of the enemy.

Another ongoing feature of war throughout the ancient Near East involved the role of the deity. Not only was the deity himself a warrior who fought with or without human supporters, but he decided the outcome of battles and could use defeat in war as a means of punishing an unfaithful people. The deity was usually consulted before battle via oracle or another method to help leaders decide whether or how to engage in battle.

The Monarchical Period

While essential aspects of premonarchic culture thus continued throughout biblical times, the late tenth century BCE evidenced the existence a new urban culture as well, characterized by monumental architecture with fortifications, casement wall systems, six-chambered gateways, streets, drainage canals, and water projects. Archaeological evidence includes the remains of buildings used to support the military and bureaucratic infrastructure and increased use of the technology of writing. Finds also include hints of popular religious practice that differ in some respects from "proper" modes of religious behavior enjoined in the Bible. Actual references to wars in which Israelite kingdoms engaged is found in such artifacts as the ninth-century Mesha Stele and Tel Dan Stele inscriptions. While weapons such as "clubs, maces, spears, lances, daggers, and swords" (King and Stager 2001, 224) would have been common in the ancient Near East throughout biblical times, this period saw the transition from bronze to iron, which would have been imported to Israel and processed into steel via a carbonizing technology. As Israel made the transition to a more centralized state that controlled the lowlands as well as the hill towns, state-supported armies found use for chariots with iron axles. As T. R. Hobbs suggests, the existence monarchies led to more fully equipped armies and somewhat better weaponry.

After the Monarchical Period

The northern kingdom was conquered by Assyria in 721 BCE, the southern kingdom by Babylonia in 587/586 BCE, and the elites sent into exile by these superpowers in order to lessen the possibility of organized revolt. Major populations centers were disrupted, and a new frontier, in a sense, opened with the Persian conquest of the area in the late sixth century BCE, for Persia allowed Jews from the exiled aristocracy to return to Judea to live and lead under Persian rule. The temple in Jerusalem, which had been destroyed by the Babylonians, was rebuilt with Persian assistance. Some would suggest that these literate returnees, from the upper and priestly classes, are those who collected many of the Biblical traditions and wrote them down, putting their own ideologies and stamp on the material. They had an important role in preserving images of war in ancient Israel although the activity of actual, independent armies was over for the time being.

Certain threads in the archaeological record thus provide information about the evolution of weaponry and modes of warfare in ancient Israel, and these aspects of Israel's material culture do have a bearing on the way Israelites may have viewed participation in battle or their relationship to the enemy. On the other hand, artifacts lead only so far, and so we must turn to the Hebrew scriptures to explore attitudes expressed by Israelites themselves about war, keeping in mind the methodological challenges and complexities discussed above.

Ideologies of War

The integrated anthology of ancient Israelite writings, the Hebrew Bible, preserves a number of views of war, some of which overlap, some of which seems at odds with one another. Again, assigning these various ideologies of war to specific periods in Israelite history or to specific groups in Israelite society is no easy task, but one can, at least, provide an overview of some of the major threads in Israelite thinking about war and speculate about whose views they reflect and how such views may have operated in the complex process of asserting and understanding cultural identity.

The Ban

Perhaps the most troubling war ideology in the Hebrew Bible is that of the ban, or *herem*, a term rooted in the sacrificial meaning "devote to destruction" and sometimes associated with nonwarring contexts (see, for example, Leviticus 27:21, 28). The ban in war is imagined to be commanded by God and requires that all human enemy and sometimes also their animals be slaughtered and often burned in entirety, "a whole burnt offering to God" as Deuteronomy 13:16 states overtly. Spoil is often destroyed or set aside for God's use, unless exception is granted.

There are, in fact, two banning ideologies, the ban that treats the enemy as a sacrifice vowed to God, explicitly or implicitly (See Numbers 21:2–3; Deuteronomy 2:34–35; Joshua 6:17–21, 8:2, 24–28, 11:11, 14; and I Kings 20:35–38), and the ban that regards the killing as an execution of God's justice. In the latter version, the enemy is described as unclean, contaminating, and sinful. He must be rooted out (See Deuteronomy 7:2–5 and 23–26 concerning foreign enemies and 13:12–18, which concerns the idolatrous enemy within Israel.) Both versions of the ban may reflect an attempt to rationalize killing in war. God exacts the dead from the Israelites.

The ban as sacrifice is described in the Moabite Inscription of the ninth century BCE and appears to have been a concept shared by Israel's neighbors, but we have no way of knowing for certain when or if the ban was ever carried out in actual war settings. The ban, treated as God's justice, may well have been a response by Deuteronomic writers of the seventh century BCE to ancient traditions about devoting enemies for destruction, for such writers regarded Israel as a pristine entity that had become soiled by foreign influences and sin. The ban was thus treated not as a means of providing human offerings to a demanding deity, a notion which in unadorned form would have been anathema to these writers, but as a way of cleansing Israel from a contamination that separated them from God. Again, we have no way of knowing if the ban was ever enacted or publicly proclaimed as a call to specific battles. The biblical descriptions of the seventh-century-BCE reforms of Josiah, influenced by Deuteronomic thought, make no overt reference to the ban. This ideology is perhaps implicit in the coup of Jehu described in 2 Kings 9–10 as a violent change of power in the northern kingdom of the ninth century BCE. Because the ban was regarded as imposed by or expected by God, it appears to have come under the heading of just cause and just conduct in Israelite thought, which distances those traditions from modern concepts of just war. It can be argued, however, that these troubling traditions do reveal Israelites' discomfort with the violence of war in that the writers attempted to place responsibility for the killing outside Israel's own hands. God demands the enemy's death, or the enemy deserves to die in a grand plan of divine justice.

The Bardic Tradition

The bardic tradition, which is preserved traditional narrative style, glorifies the courage, daring, and skill of warriors. Enemies sometimes engage in stylized duels and taunting behavior, while war is described as men's sport (as, for example, in 2 Samuel 2:14) in which operates a code of fair play. Men should fight their equals in skill, for example (see 1 Samuel 17:43; 2 Samuel 2:22, 27). Thus elements of just conduct emerge. Spoil is desired and acquired, but sometimes leads to conflict among allies. This view of war, so similar to war as described in the epic traditions of other cultures, may well have originated in the royal courts of Judah or Israel during the period of the monarchies from the tenth century BCE on, but could also have roots in premonarchic oral literature extolling the heroes of old.

Tricksterism

Akin to guerrilla warfare, tricksterism is a war ethic of the oppressed, who must use deception to improve their lot. No guilt is attached to the enemy's death and no code governs fighting, although the cause is always just from the perspective of those out of power. This ideology may be as old as Israel itself and was no doubt available as a justification and explanation for war throughout their difficult history of subjugation. Tales of Samson (Judges 14–15), Ehud (Judges 3:12–30), and Jael (Judges 4–5) exemplify this ideology.

Expediency

This ideology suggests that any degree of cruelty is acceptable in order to achieve victory in battle. War is business as usual; naked aggression and brutal conquest are the activities of kings, including the great hero David (as, for example, in 2 Samuel 5:7–8; 8:2). Victory results in spoil, enslavement of enemies, and the paying of tribute by the losing state. This pragmatic ideology of war was common in the ancient Near East and possibly best relates to the ways in which actual wars were fought throughout Israel's history.

Nonparticipation

Rooted in biblical traditions that describe God's capacity to save Israel through miracles, the ideology of nonparticipation suggests that the Israelites need not fight wars themselves, for God who redeemed the helpless Israelite slaves in Egypt will rescue his people again. This ideology, reflected, for example, in 2 Chronicles 20, is the closest concept to pacifism found in the Israelite tradition. Human beings need not fight, but of course Yahweh himself is often expected or pictured to kill the enemy with the utmost violence and bloodshed. Nonparticipation does offer the powerless an alternative to the ethics of war that involve overt human aggression and seems to have been popular with the postmonarchic, fifth-century BCE writers of 1 and 2 Chronicles.

Complexities

The war ideologies of ancient Israelite tradition are neither self-contained nor related to one another in simple chronological or evolutionary sequences. Attitudes to war in ancient Israel were complex, various, and sometimes contradictory. There was more than one ideology of the ban, while the violent pragmatism of expediency is also reflected in the ideology of tricksterism. Those who produced the ennobling bardic tradition may well have practiced the brutal ideology of expediency. Those who imagined God himself fighting external enemies without the involvement of Israelite soldiers nevertheless express the desire to utterly destroy those they regard as sinners in their own group.

The war ideologies expressed in the Hebrew Bible do reveal Israelites' intense engagement with questions concerning the reasons for participation in war, the treatment of enemies, the conduct of battles, and the use of violence. Some texts, such as the battle directions in Deuteronomy 20 and the interesting declarations of Jephthah in Judges 11:4–28, prefigure just-war doctrine as articulated in later Western tradition, showing concern with proportionality in the fighting or matters of just cause. Even in such texts, however, those concerns intertwine with notions about the power of the divine warrior, the ritualization of battle, and the divine promises concerning the land and Israel's special status as God's people that provide the framework for much of Israelite thought.

Susan Niditch

Further Reading

Craigie, P. C. (1981). *The problem of war in the Old Testament*. Grand Rapids, MI: Eerdmans.

Good, R. M. (1985). The just war in ancient Israel. *Journal of Biblical Literature, 104*(3), 385–400.

Hanson, P. D. (1987). War, peace, and justice in early Israel. *Bible Review, 3*, 32–34

Hobbs, T. R. (1989). *A time for war. A study of warfare in the Old Testament*. Wilmington, DE: Michael Glazier, Inc.

Kang, S. (1989). *Divine war in the Old Testament and in the ancient Near East*. Berlin and New York: de Gruyter.

King, P. J., & Stager, L. E. (2001). *Life in biblical Israel*. Louisville, KY: Westminster/John Knox.

Lind, M. C. (1980). *Yahweh is a warrior: The theology of warfare in ancient Israel*. Scottdale, PA: Herald Press.

Mazar, A. (1992). *Archaeology of the land of Israel*. New York: Doubleday.

Meyers, C. (1997). The family in early Israel. In L. G. Perdue, J. Blenkinsopp, J. J. Collins, & C. Meyers (Eds.), *Families in ancient Israel* (pp. 1–47). Louisville, KY: Westminster/John Knox,.

Meyers, C. (1998). Kinship and kingship: The early monarchy. In M. D. Coogan (Ed.), *The Oxford history of the biblical world* (pp. 221–271). New York and Oxford, UK: Oxford University Press.

Niditch, S. (1993). *War in the Hebrew Bible. A study in the ethics of violence*. New York and Oxford, UK: Oxford University Press.

Niditch, S. (1997). *Ancient Israelite religion*. New York and Oxford, UK: Oxford University Press.

Rofé, A. (1985). The laws of warfare in the Book of Deuteronomy: Their origins, intent, and positivity. *Journal of the Study of the Old Testament, 22*, 23–44.

Rowlett, L. L. (1996). *Joshua and the rhetoric of violence: A new historicist analysis* (*Journal of the Study of the Old Testament* Supp. No. 226). Sheffield, UK: Sheffield Academic Press.

Smend, R. (1970). *Yahweh war and tribal confederation: Reflections upon Israel's earliest history* (Rogers, M. G. Trans.). Nashville, TN: Abingdon.

Stager, L. E. (1985). The archaeology of the family in ancient Israel. *Bulletin of the American Schools of Oriental Research, 260*, 1–35.

Stern, P. D. (1991). *The biblical herem: A window on Israel's religious experience* (Brown Judaic Studies No. 211). Atlanta, GA: Scholars Press.

Yadin, Y. (1963). *The art of warfare in biblical lands*. New York: McGraw-Hill.

Judaism, Conservative

Conservative Judaism is the middle movement in Judaism between the Orthodox on the right and the Reform on the left. Like Orthodox Jews, Conservative Jews believe that Jewish law is binding. Conservative Jews, however, study the texts and traditions of Judaism using modern techniques of scholarship as well as traditional ones, and those techniques reveal that Judaism changed over time. Those changes, though, were made as a community by the rabbis authorized to make them and through communal custom. Therefore, unlike Reform Jews, Conservative Jews believe that the decision to make changes in Jewish law rests not with each individual, but with the contemporary Jewish community, which seeks to obey Jewish law through its rabbinic interpretations of it in each generation and through Jewish customs. Conservative Jews believe that a historically authentic Judaism in our time requires that we study the tradition in its own terms and through new methods of archaeology, cross-cultural studies, and the like, and that we then use judgment in applying it to modern circumstances, making appropriate changes but, by and large, conserving the tradition as it has come down to us (hence the name *Conservative* Judaism).

That means that when it comes to any topic, Conservative Jews first study the tradition and then decide how best to apply it—if at all—to modern circumstances. First, then, here is a summary of Judaism's stance on war. While Judaism abhors war and yearns for a Messianic world in which it will cease, it recognizes that our world is unfortunately not Messianic. It provides guidelines for determining when war is necessary and when not, and it establishes rules for the just conduct of wars—all the time seeking to avoid war and to work for peace. Perhaps most telling is the fact that with the possible exception of the Maccabees, Jewish heroes are not military leaders; instead, Jewish heroes are rabbis, other scholars, physicians, and all who contribute to the betterment of the world.

Jews have only rarely had the responsibility of deciding when and how to wage war. Jews enjoyed judicial autonomy in many periods and places, and consequently Jewish sources on the whole gamut of civil and criminal legal concerns abound. It is only in three relatively short periods of Jewish history, though, that Jews also held political and military autonomy—namely, from the time of Moses to the destruction of the First Temple (c. 1300 BCE–586 BCE), during the Maccabean period (168 BCE–40 BCE), and since the establishment of the modern state of Israel in 1948. Thus while Jews have served in the armies of many nations, it is only in those three periods that Jews directly confronted the realities of power and the agonizing decisions of determining when to use it.

On Genocide

Conservative Jews living in the United States have taken official stands on three primary issues regarding war: genocide, Vietnam, and terrorism. Beginning with a 1950 resolution of the Rabbinical Assembly (the organization of Conservative rabbis) and continuing with resolutions in later years by the United Synagogue of Conservative Judaism (the organization of the movement's synagogues) and by the Women's League for Conservative Judaism, Conservative Jews have repeatedly urged the United States Senate to ratify the United Nations' Convention on Genocide, adopted in 1948 with the endorsement of the U.S. representative. Resolutions in 1954, 1963, 1965, 1966, 1971, and 1976 by one or another of the arms of Conservative Judaism demonstrate continuing frustration and embarrassment that the United States, which was instrumental in the U.N. effort to formulate and pass the Convention, failed to ratify it for so long. The Jewish experience in the Holocaust figures in several of the resolutions urging the Convention's adoption.

On Vietnam

During the Vietnam conflict, various organizations of Conservative Judaism opposed the war and urged steps toward peace, including unilateral withdrawal, while also condemning the North Vietnamese for their wartime atrocities. In 1966 the Rabbinical Assembly passed a resolution calling for a nonmilitary solution to the conflict and the halting of bombings, while simultaneously condemning North Vietnamese bombings and refusal to accept cease-fire proposals. The resolution concluded with a statement that affirmed that victory was to be gained through social and economic aid to Vietnam rather than by military means. A 1968 resolution of the Rabbinical Assembly stated these points more fully and vigorously, noting also that the U.S. government was failing to address domestic problems such as poverty and racial inequality adequately because of the burden of having to prosecute a war overseas. Another rabbinic resolution that year called on the U.S. government to recognize selective conscientious objection (that is, opposition to a particular war, but not to all wars) as a valid reason for people to serve their country in nonmilitary roles.

On Terrorism

On terrorism, Women's League resolutions in 1976 deplored rising occurrences of hijacking and terrorism, targeting both Israel and other countries, and urged international cooperation in bringing hijacking and terrorism to an end. A 1984 Women's League resolution most thoroughly articulated the stance of Conservative Judaism on terrorism. Before recommending steps to respond to it, the resolution spelled out in detail exactly what is objectionable about terrorism, which it describes as a declared war opposing civilized society. It points out that terrorism amounts to the moral justification of murder, that terrorism suppresses people's moral instincts, that terrorists reject political solutions, and that terrorism assists the spread of totalitarianism, as well as being dependent on it. Finally, it condemns terrorism for exploiting the trust and rights given to civilians of free societies. It supports establishing an international code for the punishment of terrorists and those agents (whether individuals or states) that support them, and rejects Jewish terrorist acts while applauding the government of Israel for moving decisively against acts that undermine that nation's sovereignty.

Finally, the Israeli branch of Conservative Judaism, called Masorti, has issued statements deploring the government's policy of granting military exemptions to seminary students, in widespread use by ultra-religious (haredi) Orthodox Jews there. The Conservative rabbinate there has ruled that as long as Israel is faced with the need to defend itself against armies and terrorists, Jewish law requires all Jews to serve in the army or in some other national form of service.

Elliot N. Dorff

Further Reading

Artson, B. S. (1988). *"Love peace and pursue peace": A Jewish response to war and nuclear annihilation*. New York:

United Synagogue of America, Commission on Jewish Education.
Baron, S., & Wise, G. S. (Eds.). (1977). *Violence and defense in the Jewish experience*. Philadelphia: Jewish Publication Society.
Bleich, J. D. (1989). Preemptive war in Jewish law. In *Contemporary Halakhic problems* (Vol. 3). New York: Ktav and Yeshiva University Press.
Commission on the Philosophy of Conservative Judaism. (c. 1988). *Emet Ve-Emunah: Statement of principles of Conservative Judaism*. New York: Jewish Theological Seminary of America.
Dorff, E. N., & Newman, L. E. (Eds.). (1995). *Contemporary Jewish ethics and morality: A reader*. New York: Oxford University Press.
Dorff, E. N. (1996). *Conservative Judaism: From our ancestors to our descendants*. New York: United Synagogue of Conservative Judaism.
Dorff, E. N. (2002). *To do the right and the good: A Jewish approach to modern social ethics*. Philadelphia: Jewish Publication Society.
Dresner, S. H. (1966). *God, man, and atomic war*. New York: Living Books.
Saperstein, D. (1983). *Preventing the nuclear holocaust: A Jewish response*. New York: Union of American Hebrew Congregations.
Walzer, M. (1985). *Exodus and revolution*. New York: Basic Books.

Judaism: Medieval Period

The Hebrew Bible has no specific term for holy war; most wars of ancient Israel were considered holy because they were authorized by God. The Talmud, however, differentiated between "commanded war" *(milhemet mitzvah)* or "required war" *(milhemet hovah)*, and "discretionary war" *(milhemet reshut)*. The former category corresponds roughly with the Western idea of holy war. This terminology became the norm in all formal Jewish discussion of war from the period of the Talmud (second to sixth centuries) into the twentieth century.

With very few exceptions, Jewish life in the Middle Ages was lived under the political and religious hegemony of non-Jews. Jews did evolve highly developed corporate organization under Christian and Muslim rule, but despite semi-independent courts of law and even occasional periods when Jewish communities could carry out capital punishment against their own members, Jews did not govern themselves in independent polities and had no standing armies. As a result of this unusual situation, ideologies of war had little relevance. With very few exceptions, therefore, medieval Jewish thinkers were not interested in war ideologies and did not extend the discussion much beyond that of the Talmud.

Rabbi Shlomo Yitzhaqi (d. 1105), for example, known universally as Rashi and the most widely read commentator on the Bible and Talmud, actually narrows the meaning and, therefore, theoretical application of holy war from what it is in the Talmud. In his commentary to the Talmud, he limits holy war to the ancient wars of conquest of the Land of Israel listed in the Book of Joshua. The only two medieval thinkers who reexamined the idea of holy war in a significant way were Moses ben Maimon, or Maimonides (1135–1204), and Moses ben Nahman, or Nahmanides (c. 1195–1270).

Maimonides

Maimonides was the first Jewish thinker to develop a systematic ideology of war, and this interest in systemization was clearly influenced by his Islamic environment (he emigrated from Córdoba, Spain, then a Muslim city, to Egypt around 1159). He was extreme in his position against all forms of idolatry and considered it a universal obligation to destroy idolatry, even if that meant invoking violence. In Maimonides' view, the Torah was given only to Israel and to those who wish to convert to Judaism. Those who choose not to convert are not forced to, but all humans are required to accept "the seven Noahide laws" that the rabbis of the Talmud considered the minimal moral duties enjoined upon all humanity. These include a prohibition against idolatry. "Those who will not accept [the Noahide laws] are to be killed" (*Mishneh Torah* "The Laws of Kings and their Wars" [henceforth, Kings] 8:10).

Maimonides' systemization includes universalization, which for the first time allowed for expanding the application of holy war beyond the borders of the Land of Israel. An Israelite king may conquer any and all lands he wishes because "his acts are for the sake of heaven since his goal and design is to strengthen the true religion, fill the world with righteousness, destroy the seed of the wicked, and fight God's wars" (Kings 4:10). The *Mishneh Torah* contains aggressive rhetoric with regard to this issue, but this is toned down in Maimonides' great philosophic opus, *The*

Old gravestones in the Jewish cemetery in Worms, Germany, in 1990. The cemetery was established in 1076 and the last person was buried there in 1911. The Jewish community in Worms was almost wiped out during the Crusades and again during the Holocaust. Courtesy David Levinson.

Guide for the Perplexed (henceforth, *Guide*). The Maimonidean scholar Gerald Blidstein has pointed out how Maimonides fluctuates between universal aggressiveness and restrained patience. While the king *may* conquer beyond the borders of the Land of Israel, he is never commanded (by God) to do so; but wherever the king conquers he is required to eradicate idolatry. The purpose of conquest and enforcing the Noahide laws is not to bring converts to Judaism, but rather to prevent the endangering of humankind through anarchy and violence. Maimonides does not articulate who would kill idolaters, and both that issue and the larger issue of war in general always remained theoretical.

The only war that the king is commanded to carry out is war against the seven Canaanite nations, against Amalek, and a war to save Israel from an attacking enemy (Kings 5:1). Destruction of the seven Canaanite nations and Amalek symbolizes for Maimonides the destruction of idolatry and associated immorality. This Maimonidean trope equating Canaanism with idolatry forces Maimonides to adopt a universal view regarding repentant idolaters that also finds a parallel in Islam, namely, that the way to repentance of idolatry and immoral behavior must always be left open, even for Canaanites and Amalekites. In Islam such renunciation requires conversion to Islam; to Maimonides, it is sufficient that the repentent accept the seven Noahide laws. Such a position would appear to fly in the face of the explicit biblical command to annihilate the Canaanites and Amalekites, but Maimonides quite clearly states in Kings 6:1 that acceptance of repentant idolaters is required both in discretionary and commanded wars.

Despite his position that a king may conquer beyond the borders of the Land of Israel, Maimonides nowhere suggests the option of going to war against any peoples who are already following the Noahide laws. He finds biblical proofs to justify his universal position on idolatry, and in so doing, universalizes the extinct Canaanites and Amalekites by making them into eternal symbols of idolatry and its associated evils. By emphasizing the universal nature of the issue, he shifts the discussion away from the particularity of the Land of Israel. Maimonides thus portrays the biblical wars against the Canaanites and Amalekites more as part of the divine will to bring humanity to right religion or universal morality than as the divine will for Israel to take possession of the Land. His universalizing, with the resulting negation of the centrality of the Land of Israel in his war ideology, is repeated in his *Book of Commandments*, a detailed enumeration of the 613 commandments that the rabbis of the Talmud believed the Torah contains. Because the divine command to destroy the Canaanites and Amalekites persists even though they no longer exist as distinct peoples, the command actually applies to the destruction of idolatry. A result of this universalizing is a reduction in the relative importance of the Land of Israel in Maimonides' system.

Nahmanides

Nahmanides took issue with Maimonides over his enumeration of the 613 commandments and wrote a critique of Maimonides' *Book of Commandments*. This critique is Nahmanides' *Hassagot* ("Criticisms"), which is found among the major commentaries in traditional printed editions of Maimonides' *Book of Commandments*. Nahmanides criticizes Maimonides for the latter's universalizing tendency because that tendency so clearly ignored what would appear to be undeniable divine commands to conquer and settle the Land of Israel In a famous comment that is often cited by activists and thinkers among Orthodox ultranationalist Jews today, Nahmanides notes that the importance for every individual Jew of conquering and settling the Land of Israel in every generation cannot be overstated. To Nahmanides, it is clear that the Land is never to be left in the hands of any other nation, that God's injunction to settle it is a command and not a promise or a statement of destiny.

The difference between Maimonides and Nahmanides on this issue became a classic controversy *(machaloqet)* in traditional Jewish scholarship and is cited, discussed and argued within traditional Jewry to this day. While both men agreed on the eternal validity of holy war (that is, "commanded war"), Maimonides minimized its importance in relation to the Land of Israel by universalizing the concept and understanding it largely as a command to end idolatry and the immorality that was understood to be intimately associated with idolatry. Nahmanides, on the other hand, understood the command to relate directly to the settling of the Land of Israel, and he believed Jews of every generation were obligated to fulfill the command. Individual fulfillment of the divine command, to Nahmanides, included settling and living in the Land of Israel with the goal of bringing back Jewish hegemony. It did not necessarily require violence and war.

Reuven Firestone

See also: Holy War Idea in the Biblical Tradition; Islamic Law of War; Judaism: Biblical Period; Roman Catholicism: Just-War Doctrine

Further Reading

Ariel, J. (1988). Conquest of the land according to the Ramban. *Crossroads, 2,* 189–195. (Original work published 1984 as Daʿat haramban bekibush ha'aretz [The view of Nahmanides on conquest of the Land]. *Techumin, 5*(3), 174–179)

Arzi, A. (1970). Takkanot mishum yishuv eretz yisra'el [Rabbinic enactments based on settling the Land of Israel]. *Shanah Beshanah*, 232–241.

Bleich, J. D. (1988, Fall). Of land, peace, and divine command. *Journal of Halachah and Contemporary Society, 16,* 56–69.

Blidstein, G. (1983). *Ekronot mediniyim bemishnat harambam* [Political concepts in Maimonidean Halakha]. Tel Aviv, Israel: Bar-Ilan University.

Brumberg, A. Y. (1964). *Galut ve'eretz yisra'el beferushey rabbi avraham ibn-ezra*. [Exile and the Land of Israel in the commentary of Abraham Ibn Ezra]. *Shanah Beshanah*, 236–241.

Epstein, Y. (1989). *Mored bemalkhut* [Rebelling against the government]. *Techumin, 10,* 90–107.

Goren, S. (1963). *Mitzvat yishuv eretz yisraʿel* [The commandment of settling the Land of Israel]. *Mahanayim, 67,* 6–7.

Horowitz, A. M. H. (1972). *Bi'ur divrey haramban shesover shelo hutru bemilchemet hareshut, raq achar kibush kol eretz yisrae'l, sheholekh leshitato sheyesh gam bizman hazeh mitzvat aseh likhbosh eretz yisraeʿel, velashevet bah*. [Clarification of the words of Nahmanides, who holds that discretionary war is allowed only after the conquest of the entire Land of Israel, this being according to his view that it is a positive commandment even today to conquer the Land of Israel and to settle it]. *Noam, 15,* 225.

Maimonides, M. (1956). *The guide for the perplexed* (M. Friedlander, Trans.). New York: Dover.

Maimonides, M. (1967). *The commandments* (C. Chavel, Trans.). London: Soncino.

Maimonides, M. (1972). *Mishneh Torah* (Uncensored Constantinople edition). Jerusalem: Makor.

Nachmanides, M. (1978). Rosh Hashanah sermon. In C. Chavel (Ed.), *Kitvey haramban* [The writings of Nachmanides] (pp. 249–250). Jerusalem: Mossad Harav Kook.

Rabinowitz, N. E. (1984). *Shitat haramban veharambam bemitzvat yerushat haʿaretz* [The method of Nahmanides and Maimonides on the commandment of inheriting the Land]. *Tehumin*, *5*, 180–186.

Rabinowitz, N. E. (1988). Conquest of the Land of Israel according to the Rambam. *Crossroads, 2*, 181–187.

Ravitzky, A. (1996). *Charut al haluchot* [Engraved on the Tablets: The Land of Israel in modern Jewish thought]. Jerusalem: Magnes.

Rivlin, Y. (1968). Torat eretz yisra'el bemishnat haramban [The law of the Land of Israel according to Nahmanides]. *Shanah Beshanah* 203–212.

Schacter, H. (1989). The Mitzvah of Yishuv Eretz Yisrael. In S. Spero &Y. Pessin (Eds.), *Religious Zionism after 40 years of statehood* (pp. 190–212). Jerusalem: World Zionist Organization. (Reprinted from *Journal of Halakhah and Contemporary Society, 8*, 14–33)

Yisraeli, S. (1984). Shitat harambam bekibush rabim vekhibush yachid [Maimonides' methodology regarding conquest of the many and individual conquest]. *Torah SheBeʿal Peh*, 15–17.

Judaism, Orthodox

Orthodox Judaism is the most observant of the three mainstreams of Judaism (Orthodox, Conservative, and Reform). Jewish law, as it applies to Jews, begins with the premise that man has no right to make war against his fellow. Standard translations of the Bible (such as the King James Version) render Exodus 15:3 as "The Lord is a man of war; the Lord is His name." The medieval Talmudic scholar Rashi (1040–1105), citing similar usages having the same connotation, renders the Hebrew term *ish* as "master" rather than "man." Thus the translation should read, "The Lord is the master of war; the Lord is His name." God is described as the master of war because only He may grant dispensation to engage in warfare. The very name of the Lord signifies that He alone exercises dominion over the universe. Only God as the creator of mankind and proprietor of all life may grant permission for the taking of the lives of His creatures.

Expectations of Jews

War is sanctioned only when commanded or permitted by God, that is, when divine wisdom dictates that such a course of action is necessary for fulfillment of human destiny. Wars explicitly commanded include the original conquest of the Promised Land and the war against Amalek, the enemy of the Israelites. Defensive warfare is also sanctioned. Other forms of warfare are translated as "permitted" or "discretionary war" but such warfare is discretionary only in the sense that it is initiated by man and does not serve to fulfill a divine commandment. However, even a discretionary war can be undertaken only upon the initiative of the monarch of the Jewish commonwealth pursuant to the approval of the Sanhedrin (the supreme council) and the acquiescene of the *urim ve-tumim*—the message conveyed via the breastplate of the High Priest—a form of prophecy granting divine authority for an act of aggression. Thus, Judaism sanctions violence only at the specific behest of the deity. Human reason is far too prone to error to be entrusted with a determination that war is justified in the service of a higher cause. Such a determination can be made solely by God. Thus, in historical epochs in which prophecy has lapsed, only defensive war can be sanctioned.

Expectations of Non-Jews

The teachings of Judaism with regard to non-Jews are somewhat complex. Non-Jews are not held to the same standards of behavior as Jews. Although the Noahide Code, which embodies divine law as it is binding upon non-Jews, prohibits murder, it does not necessarily prohibit the taking of human life under any and all circumstances. When confronted by a situation in which an individual's life is threatened, all persons, non-Jews as well as Jews, have an absolute right to eliminate the aggressor in self-defense. "If [a person] comes to slay you, arise and slay him first" (Sanhedrin 72a) is a universal principle. Accordingly, a defensive war would appear to require no further justification.

Acceptance of the premise that the principle of self-defense applies to non-Jews as well as to Jews does not serve to justify any and all military action, even in the context of a war of defense. War almost inevitably results in civilian casualties. Yet the taking of innocent lives certainly cannot be justified on the basis of what

War and Resettlement

The following extract of ethnographic text about the Hasidic (ultra-orthodox) Jews of Boro Park, Brooklyn, describes how the destruction of the Jewish communities of Europe in World War II led them to settle in the United States and establish their own communities based on their European cultural model.

Before the Second World War, most Hasidim viewed America as a *treyf* land (nonreligious country), inhospitable to their religious needs. No wonder that few made concerted efforts to come to the New World. Those who arrived in the 1920s had not, for the most part, planned to stay for good, hoping instead to earn some money and return home to Europe. Not that home was a promised land: Poached upon by secularists and ravished by the First World War, the Hasidim nonetheless preferred to live in the communities of their forefathers. All of this changed after the Holocaust, for the Hasidim, like other Jews, had simply no community or family to which they could return. . . . The Hasidim's worst fears for this treyf land were readily confirmed. Although America appeared to be a land of relative economic opportunity and religious tolerance, it had nurtured a permissive Jewish community, unable to sustain a robust Yiddishkeit.

"What happened to your young people?" they queried. "Where are the youth of your synagogue, where is the second generation?" The Hasidim quickly set about to reverse this trend. In the 1950s their progress was most evident in Williamsburg, home to many of the newcomers. The sociologist George Kranzler (1961) writes that as early as 1949, the Hasidim, mainly Hungarians, assumed leadership in this community. Thanks to the unifying power of their rebbes, they were able to seize the initiative in many areas of communal and religious life that had been neglected by others.

Source: Belcove-Shalin, Janet S. (1995). "Home in Exile: Hasidim in the New World."

New World Hasidim: Ethnographic Studies of Hasidic Jews in America (Janet S. Belcove-Shalin, Ed.). Albany: State University of New York Press, pp. 210–211.

is known as the law of pursuit, which provides that the life of the pursuer is forfeit in order that the life of the intended victim be preserved. The law of pursuit is not applicable in warfare because in warfare an innocent bystander may die when one is trying to eliminate the pursuer. However, should it be impossible to eliminate the pursuer other than by also causing the death of an innocent bystander, the law of pursuit cannot be invoked by the intended victim, much less so by a third party who is himself not personally threatened.

More fundamental is the question of whether or not there exists a general exclusion to the prohibition against homicide that can justify the taking of human life under conditions of war. One nineteenth-century authority does find grounds upon which to rule that non-Jews who engage in war are not guilty of murder. Rabbi Naphtali Zevi Judah Berlin (1817–1893), in his commentary on the Pentateuch, *Ha'amek Davar*, finds dispensation for warfare in the very verse which prohibits homicide to the Sons of Noah: "And surely your blood of your lives will I require . . . and at the hand of man, at the hand of every man's brother, will I require the life of man" (Genesis 9:5). The phrase "at the hand of every man's brother" appears to be entirely redundant since it adds nothing to the preceding phrase "at the hand of man." *Ha'amek Davar* understands the words "at the hand of every man's brother" as a limiting clause: "When is man punished? [If he commits homicide] when it is proper to behave in a brotherly manner." However, in time of war, when animosity reigns among nations, the taking of life in the course of military activity is not punishable.

Earlier, Rabbi Judah Loew of Prague (d. 1609), speaking of the action taken by the sons of Jacob against the inhabitants of Shechem, states that, in effect, the family of Jacob constituted a sovereign people that were permitted to do battle against another nation since war is not forbidden under the Noahide Code.

This permissive view is, however, contradicted by a number of other authorities. Moses Sofer (1763–1839) declares wars of aggression to be forbidden to Noahides under all circumstances. In support of his position, he cites a statement of the Talmud, Sanhedrin 59a, to the effect that non-Jews do not enjoy the legal prerogative of conquest. Since the Talmud affirms in Gittin 38a that non-Jews may acquire title to lands captured in war by virture of conquest, the notion that non-Jews do not enjoy the legal pererogative of conquest must be understood, he argues in *Hatam Sofer* (1855), as meaning that non-Jews have no right to engage in war for the purpose of conquest even though they may acquire title in this manner after the fact. That view was accepted by all subsequent rabbinic authorities who have addressed this topic.

Nuclear Holocaust

It must be noted that, even according to the authorities who maintain that non-Jews may engage in wars of aggression, there are strong grounds for concluding that the devastation inevitably associated with nuclear warfare renders such warfare illicit. The Talmud, Shevu'ot 35b, declares, "A sovereign power which slays one-sixth of the population of the universe is not culpable." It is to be inferred that the death of more than one-sixth of the world's population does engender culpability. The medieval authors of *Tosafot*, understanding the dictum as referring to the monarch of a Jewish state, indicate that the Talmud herein imposes a constraint upon discretionary war. The sovereign may not initiate a discretionary war if it is to be anticipated that an inordinate number of people will perish as a result of hostilities. Limitations upon warfare undertaken as a discretionary war would assuredly also apply to war undertaken by non-Jews. Hence, according to *Tosafot*, non-Jews may not engage in war that is likely to result in the annihilation of more than one-sixth of the population of the world. This restriction applies even to wars of defense in which not only the aggressors are destroyed but the lives of a large number of innocent victims are claimed as well. The nature of nuclear war is such that, in all likelihood, more than one-sixth of the world's population would be destroyed in a nuclear holocaust.

J. David Bleich

Further Reading

Bleich, J. D. (1983). War and non-Jews. In *Contemporary Halakhic Problems* (Vol. 2, pp. 159–166). New York: Ktav Publishing House.

Bleich, J. D. (1989). Nuclear warfare. In *Contemporary Halakhic Problems* (Vol. 3, pp. 4–10). New York: Ktav Publishing House.

Bleich, J. D. (1989). Preemptive war in Jewish law. *Contemporary Halakhic Problems* (Vol. 3, pp. 251–292). New York: Ktav Publishing House.

Landes, D. (Ed.). (1991). *Confronting omnicide: Jewish reflections on weapons of mass destruction*. Northvale, NJ: Jason Aaronson.

Judaism, Pacifism in

Judaism shows a radical commitment to the ideal of *shalom* (peace), teaching not only "to seek peace" but also to "pursue it" (Psalms 34:14, RSV; Numbers Rabbah, Hukkat 19:27). No Jewish tradition, however, precludes violence as a suitable option in situations of conflict, and Judaism is by no means a pacifist religion. It permits violence, but only that violence that can be permitted given that one aim in life is to pursue peace and work for the well-being of humanity. It calls for pacifism, but allows violence to ensure peace in a less than perfect world.

The Biblical Tradition and Pacifism

The Jewish position toward peace is based on the biblical tradition, which does not provide a dogmatic answer to the question of violence. On the one hand, the Bible contains glorified accounts of war and military victories (see, for example, Exodus 14–15 or Joshua 1–19), and includes a mandate for holy war that prescribes total annihilation of the enemy (Joshua 6:17). On other hand, it requires God's people to seek humane terms of peace with enemies of war (Deuteronomy 20:10–15, 19–20). Although the Israelites, like other peoples, recognized the responsibility of defending their people and nation, a newly married man's conjugal obligation to seek his spouse's happiness overrides the responsibility of military duties (Deuteronomy 24:5). The requirements of holy war can be set aside altogether for the sake of covenantal fidelity, even if the covenant was instituted through a ruse (see Joshua 9).

The covenant God made with Noah—a covenant Jewish traditions hold binding for all humanity—includes a stipulation that those who shed blood will be punished by having their blood shed (Genesis 9:6).

Sources of Jewish Pacificism

". . . they shall beat their swords into plowshares, and their spears into pruning hooks; nation shall not lift up sword against nation, neither shall they learn war any more" (Micah 4:3 NRSV).

"A war should never be waged against human beings until you call out to them '*Shalom*' " (Moses Maimonides, Hilchot Melachim, 86, 6:1; translation by author).

Rabbinic traditions, however, permit or even demand that violence may be used as the last resort to save one's own life or the lives of others. Categorical nonviolence could result in virtual suicide, which the Torah prohibits.

Throughout the Hebrew Bible, a mode of containment is pursued with regard to violence. For redress in violent injuries, the legal tradition stipulates the infamous *lex talionis* of eye for eye (Exodus 21:24; Leviticus 24:20; Deuteronomy 19:21), which actually was intended to prevent the escalation of violence that private justice may cause by seeking head for eye. In another context, vengeance is declared a divine prerogative (Deuteronomy 32:35), leaving private justice little room in the biblical teachings.

Pacifism as a Measure of Expedience

Over the centuries, as Judaism has worked on putting into practice the ideal of peace in an imperfect world, circumstances have served as the touchstone. One is to avoid and prevent violence if those actions promote peace and ensures the preservation of tradition and community.

In the first century CE, when the Roman army under Vespasian laid siege to Jerusalem, Johanan ben Zakkai took the pacifistic posture and opposed a war against the Romans. He negotiated with the Roman general (who became emperor later) and secured a concession to build a rabbinic academy at Jamnia (also called Yavneh). In 70 CE the Jewish military opposition gave in. The temple of Jerusalem was destroyed, but Judaism continued to live on with the study of the Torah at Jamnia. Toward the end of the first century CE the final shape of the Hebrew canon was fixed in a session at this academy. In the aftermath of the rebellion of Bar Kokchba in 135 CE, the Roman emperor Hadrian recognized the subversive side of the tactical pacifism of Judaism. He outlawed the Torah observances, and declared Jerusalem off limits to the Jewish people.

When military defeat is certain, the Talmud teaches pacifism as a means of survival. In the second century CE, the Jewish people are found taking an oath to adopt pacifism in order to ensure the survival of the Jewish people.

God and Pacifism

The adaptable pacifism of Judaism finds its overarching guide in the Jewish understanding of God. One should not shed blood, on the ground that human beings are made in God's image (Genesis 9:6). There should be no shedder of blood among the people of Israel, for God showed mercy by delivering the people of Israel out of bondage in Egypt (Torah temimah on Deuteronomy 21:8).

The Hebrew Bible often portrays God as a divine warrior, which is not necessarily in conflict with the notion of pacifism. Under the ideology of the divine warrior, the people do not wage a war, but take their place as observers in the work of God (see, for example, Exodus 14:13). At the same time, the rabbinic tradition displays discomfort for the violence that took place in the drowning of the Egyptian army, and alludes to the heart of God breaking at the drowning of the Egyptians, the work of God's hands (Babylonian Talmud, Sanhedrin 39b; Megillah 10b).

The Prophetic Vision of the Peaceable Kingdom

The prophets of the Hebrew Bible longed for the days when the nations would beat their swords into ploughshares, and their spears into pruning hooks (Isaiah 2:4; Micah 4:3), although they were keenly aware that military crisis might call for ploughshares and pruning hooks to be turned into swords and spears. In Isaiah's surrealistic vision of the peaceable kingdom, "The wolf shall dwell with the lamb, and the leopard shall lie down with the kid, and the calf and the lion and the fatling together, and a little child shall lead them" (Isaiah 11:6, RSV). The prophet calls for a radical rearrangement of interaction, let alone the diet of predatory members of nature. The prophetic vision leans toward a world beyond the historical realm.

Challenges of the New Millennium

Jewish tradition allows for a great deal of latitude when thinking of the relationship of war and peace, as it recognizes the difficult challenge of remaining committed to peace and at the same time being committed to ensuring one's own (or others') survival. The Holocaust of the twentieth century raises the question of the cost of pacifism for those who have been portrayed as sheep to the slaughter. Conflicts that have persisted in the Middle East from the founding of the state of Israel to the present times are constant reminders that the pacifism in Judaism has to continue its struggle to find faithful expressions in its pursuit of *shalom*.

Jin Hee Han

See also Anabaptist Pacifism; Eastern Orthodoxy, Pacifism in; Holy War Idea in the Biblical Tradition; Judaism: Biblical Period; Mennonites; Quakers; Roman Catholicism, Pacifism in

Further Reading

Burns, J. P. (Ed.). (1996). *War and its discontents: Pacifism and quietism in the Abrahamic traditions*. Washington, DC: Georgetown University.

Ferguson, J. (1977). *War and peace in the world's religions*. London: Sheldon Press.

Lackey, D. P. (1989). *The ethics of war and peace*. Englewood Cliffs, NJ: Prentice Hall.

Maier, J. (2000). *Kriegsrecht und Friedensordnung in jüdischer Tradition* [Law of War and Order of Peace in Jewish Tradition]. (Theologie und Frieden 14). Stuttgart, Germany: Verlag W. Kohlhammer.

Kellner, M. M. (Ed.). (1978). *Contemporary Jewish ethics* (Sanhedrin Jewish Studies). New York: Sanhedrin Press.

Kimelman, R. (1968). Non-violence in the Talmud. *Judaism, 17*(Summer), 316–334.

Nardin, T. (Ed.). (1996) *The ethics of war and peace: Religious and secular perspectives*. Princeton, NJ: Princeton University Press.

Polner, M., & Goodman, N. (Eds.). (1994). *The challenge of Shalom: The Jewish tradition of peace and justice*. Philadelphia: New Society Publishers.

Shapiro, D. S. (1975). *Studies in Judaica: Vol. 1. Studies in Jewish thought*. New York: Yeshiva University.

Smock, D. (1992). *Religious perspectives on war: Christian, Muslim, and Jewish attitudes to force after the Gulf War*. Washington, DC: Institute of Peace.

Wilcock, E. (1994). *Pacifism and the Jews*. Landsdown (Gloucestershire), UK: Hawthorn Press.

Judaism, Reconstructionist

Reconstructionist Judaism began as the philosophy of a U.S. rabbi, Mordecai Kaplan (1881–1985). Kaplan developed Reconstructionism as a means to help the United States' vast numbers of Eastern European Jewish immigrants at the beginning of the twentieth century maintain their connection to Jewish traditions while simultaneously participating fully in U.S. society. Kaplan produced many books and liturgical works. He served as the rabbi of the Society for the Advancement of Judaism in New York City, a synagogue that became the laboratory for his ideas. He also taught homiletics (the art of preaching) at the Jewish Theological Seminary of the Conservative movement, where he influenced a generation of rabbis. Among them was his future son-in-law, Ira Eisenstein (1906–2001), who institutionalized Kaplan's ideas by founding the Reconstructionist movement. Eisenstein edited a magazine, *The Reconstructionist*, which was the leading intellectual journal of post–World War II U.S. Jewry, and founded such institutions as the Reconstructionist Rabbinical College in Philadelphia (1968). While the movement remains small, accounting for less than 2 percent of Jews in the world today, its intellectual influence far exceeds the numbers of its adherents. Kaplan's ideas form the basis for understanding Reconstructionist Judaism's approach to the subject of war and peace.

Judaism as an Evolving Religious Civilization

Kaplan's greatest contribution to Jewish life was to define Judaism as an evolving religious civilization. According to Kaplan, Judaism is a civilization, not a religion or race. Like other civilizations, it has made important contributions to history and society. The main Jewish contribution has been in the area of religion. How that religion has been understood and practiced has evolved over time and in different cultural

Statement from Leaders of the Reconstructionist Movement: On the War In Iraq (21 March 2003)

Rabbi Yose HaGalili says, "How meritorious is peace? Even in time of war Jewish law requires that one initiate discussions of peace." ***(Leviticus Rabbah, Tzav 9)***

It was the hope of all people of good will committed to freedom that the threat posed to the international community by Saddam Hussein—and the repression, terror and tragedy visited by Hussein on the Iraqi people—might have been eliminated through international pressures short of war.

We are deeply saddened by the onset of war and the additional pain and destruction that it will bring. We now pray for the safety of those who serve; we pray for the minimizing of suffering and loss of life; we hope for a speedy conclusion of hostilities; and we give voice to the prayer that out of the tragedy of war might arise new conditions that might lead more firmly towards democracy and peace in the world.

Our communities reflect a range of opinion and emotion at this moment. We call on our communities to gather in order to share and hold the anxiety and uncertainty of these days, so that people may find comfort in solidarity, focus on prayers and hopes held in common, and keep faith with each other as we journey through this sad and challenging moment.

Source: **Reconstructionist Response to War in Iraq. Retrieved May 1, 2003, from www.jrf.org/news/joint-iraq-statement.html**

settings. A Reconstructionist approach to war begins with the understanding that there is no unified Jewish perspective. Not only have views changed over time, they are also based on texts that are subject to interpretation. For example, the ancient kingdom of Israel in its earliest stages (c. 1000 BCE) was actively involved in waging territorial war, but the prophets spoke out boldly against war and maintained a messianic vision of peace. Later, around the beginning of the first millenium of the common era, the Maccabees fought a civil war—the basis of the holiday of Hanukkah—but the rabbis who wrote about this event transformed the holiday into a celebration of the triumph of the spirit and downplayed the military dimension.

Tradition and Change

According to Kaplan, for Judaism to survive and grow, each generation of Jews must consciously reconstruct the tradition in accordance with the highest values and standards of the times in which they live. The process of reconstruction begins with a thorough understanding of Jewish traditions and ideas of the past in their complexity and multiplicity. Jewish teachings and traditions are accorded great respect, and discarded or changed only if there is some strong ethical or social motivation for doing so. Reconstructionist thinking about war is guided by Jewish texts that acknowledge some wars as obligatory. The texts do not support absolute pacifism, but individual conscientious objection is possible. The texts also demand that wars be fought without destruction of land, or, as far as possible, life. Finally, one of Judaism's central values is societal pursuit of peace. Reconstructionist Jews turn to these sources to decide their views on any given war.

Living in Two Civilizations

Reconstructionism teaches that U.S. Jews live in two civilizations—Jewish civilization and U.S. civilization—and that U.S. Jews have an obligation to be involved in and bring their Jewish values to bear on U.S. society. In their writings, Kaplan and Eisenstein expressed strong feelings about the wars the United States has fought. While they were unequivocal supporters of World War I and World War II, the leadership of the movement spoke out against the war in Vietnam (although not officially until January 1967) and against the threat of nuclear war in the 1980s. Although they opposed conscientious objection in both World Wars, the magazine wrote many editorials in support of dissenters during the war in Vietnam, and the Reconstructionist Rabbinical Association issued a strongly worded policy statement in favor of selective conscientious objection in 1981.

Reconstructionism and Zionism

Kaplan was an early supporter of the Zionist movement and strongly supported the establishment of the state of Israel and its early wars for survival in 1948 and 1956. While the Reconstructionist movement also supported subsequent Israeli war efforts, they maintained a critical stance towards those who celebrated Jewish militarism. An editorial in *The Reconstructionist* following the June 1967 war cautioned Jews not to become overly enthusiastic about the zealots at Masada, who died fighting against the Romans in the second century CE and whose exploits had become a popular example of Jewish bravery in war. The editorial suggested that the rabbis who at that time formed schools for learning and wrote eloquently about the pursuit of peace kept the Jewish people alive.

Reconstructionist Innovations

The Reconstructionist movement has been known for its liturgical innovation, and several of these efforts have focused on the pursuit of peace. In 1941 the movement published *The New Haggadah* (a radical version of the liturgy of the Passover seder). The early editions of the Haggadah omitted the ten plagues, because the act of celebrating the death and destruction of the Egyptians was deemed abhorrent. In subsequent years the plagues were reintroduced along with the midrash (interpretation) that pouring out wine from the cup at the mention of the plagues symbolized Jewish grief at the suffering of the Egyptians. The Reconstructionist Rabbinical College was the first home of the Shalom Center, the primary voice of the Jewish antinuclear movement in the 1980s. The Shalom Center originated Sukkat Shalom (tabernacles of peace), making the holiday of Sukkot (the fall harvest festival) into a time to focus on ending the threat of nuclear war. And Kaplan also suggested that Yom Kippur (the Day of Atonement when Jews fast, pray, and focus on self-renewal) become a day of protest against the waging of war.

Rebecca T. Alpert

See also Judaism: Biblical Period; Judaism, Pacifism in

Further Reading

Alpert, R., & Staub, J. (2001). *Exploring Judaism: A Reconstructionist approach* (2nd ed.). Wyncote, PA: The Reconstructionist Press.

Bokser, B. (1940, November). The Jews and war. *The Reconstructionist, 6*(14), 7–11, 16.

Kaplan, M. (1970). *The religion of ethical nationhood: Judaism's contribution to world peace.* New York: Macmillan.

Judaism, Reform

As a movement at the liberal, progressive end of the Jewish religious spectrum, Reform Judaism has been at the forefront of Jewish involvement with forces for social change and civic betterment ever since the movement's inception in Germany in the early 1800s. Originally founded as a response by Jewish laity to the perceived authoritarian rigidity of traditional or Orthodox Judaism and its rabbis, Reform Judaism emphasized liturgical reform, sermons in the vernacular, and the use of musical instrumentation. It received further impetus from the involvement of university-educated and trained rabbis such as Abraham Geiger (1810–1874), Samuel Holdheim (1806–1860), and David Einhorm (1810–1879). Under the Bavarian rabbi Isaac Mayer Wise (1819–1900), who came to the United States in 1846, the movement now known as Reform Judaism truly took hold. Under his leadership, its congregational parent body, the Union of American Hebrew Congregations (UAHC), was founded in Cincinnati, Ohio, in 1873; its rabbinical seminary, the Hebrew Union College, or HUC (which merged with the Jewish Institute of Religion, or JIR, in New York in 1947), was established in 1875, also in Cincinnati. Its professional organization, the Central Conference of American Rabbis (CCAR), was founded in 1889. While other organizations founded much later are today part of this worldwide Jewish religious movement (examples include the World Union for Progressive Judaism and the Association of Reform Zionists of America), the original three—the UAHC, the HUC-JIR, and the CCAR—continue to direct the present emphases and future course of Reform Judaism.

To understand Reform Judaism's outlook on religion and war, one can consider official statements—resolutions and responsa (written decisions given by rabbinic authorities in response to a question or problem)—of both the Union of American Hebrew Congregations and the Central Conference of American Rabbis, Reform Judaism's two decision-making bodies. (The Hebrew Union College-Jewish Institute of Religion, being an academic institution, does not make official statements on theological issues, but, rather, directs its energies to such matters as instructional curricula, faculty publications, educational outreach, and the like.)

Resolutions of the Union of American Hebrew Congregations

In accord with Jewish religious tradition, the Union of American Hebrew Congregations (UAHC)'s general position on war is that of support for both *defensive* wars and *obligatory* wars (terms used in rabbinic literature) where the safety, security and survival of innocents, not only Jewish innocents, are at stake, but, also, where aggressor-nations wantonly set their agendas as either land capture and/or subjugation or worse of those populations. Starting in 1941, in the midst of World War II, Reform Judaism's congregational parent body addressed the gamut of war-related concerns, promulgating resolutions on victims of war (1941), disarmament and world peace (1957, 1959, 1961, 1965, 1969), germ warfare (1969), genocide (1979), the many aspects of nuclear war and arms control (1979, 1981, 1983, 1989), and the apprehension and prosecution of war criminals (1997), among other topics. These resolutions reflect Reform Judaism's concerns with universal social issues. Reform Judaism has historically emphasized communal responsibility for social well-being both in the Jewish and larger communities as an inheritance and legacy of the biblical prophets of ancient Israel. Reform Jews, both laity and leadership, also believe that it is their moral and ethical responsibility to participate fully in the experience of U.S. democracy.

Throughout these resolutions runs a single unifying theme: translating the religious principles of Reform and indeed all Judaism into concrete actions. Thus, while espousing general religious ideals such as universal peace or humanity's capacity, working with God, to fashion a better world, the resolutions also recommend concrete and specific courses of action. Consistently, these resolutions urge those congregations affiliated with the UAHC to undertake serious programs of study at the adult level on such issues, enter into alliances with other like-minded religious and secular groups, and support both national (United States) and international (United Nations) legislation with which it agrees.

There are other resolutions that deal specifically with the ongoing crisis of Israel and her neighbors in the Middle East. More than fifteen Israel-related resolutions have been passed in convention, largely focusing on the questions and issues of *shalom* (peace); the survival, safety, and security of Israel and its primarily, but not exclusively, Jewish inhabitants; terrorist attacks on its civilian populations, particularly its children; and the overriding necessity of face-to-face dialogue between representatives on all sides in the dispute. For example, with regard to the so-called "Yom Kippur War" of 1973, the UAHC expressed strong support for the cease-fire urged by the United States government and the diplomatic efforts undertaken by the administration, commended then-Secretary of State Henry Kissenger for bringing together Israel and Egypt, and further urged face-to-face negotiations between all warring parties rather than the resumption of war itself.

Resolutions of the Central Conference of American Rabbis

Specific resolutions adopted in the last three decades of the twentieth century by the rabbinical arm of Reform Judaism have addressed the development of the neutron bomb (1978), statutes of limitations for Nazi war crimes (1979), the military draft (1980, 1982), terrorism (1981, 1985, 1995), nuclear arms control and nuclear war (1982, 1983, 1984, 1987), and genocide in Bosnia-Herzegovina (1993), among other topics.

Between the years 1889 and 1974, the CCAR also adopted numerous resolutions on such topics as conscientious objectors (twelve resolutions), international peace (sixteen resolutions), and war (nineteen resolutions). Since 1917, the first resolution on conscientious objection, for example, the CCAR has consistently supported the right of those who refuse to bear arms and voiced it strong object to punishment of such persons, arguing that freedom of conscience is an ideal of the Jewish religious tradition. In 1946, in the aftermath of the Second World War, the CCAR called on the president of the United States to "free all conscientious objectors still confined in federal prisons and to restore full civil rights to them and to the objectors who have already completed their sentences" (Central Conference of American Rabbis, 1946) has equally encouraged military service as a responsibility of citizenship. As with the UAHC, these resolutions are separate from

The Union of American Hebrew Congregations' Resolution on Gun Violence

ADOPTED RESOLUTION ON ENDING GUN VIOLENCE

Adopted by the General Assembly

Union of American Hebrew Congregations

December 15–19, 1999, Orlando

BACKGROUND

Too many Americans, especially children, die as a result of gun violence every day. The American people have been aroused by this ongoing, senseless slaughter. Statistics strongly affirm that gun control laws prevent gun violence. Canada's experience with decreasing gun violence after the enactment of strict gun control laws has demonstrated, clearly and unequivocally, that gun control works.

In prior resolutions, the Union has taken a strong stand in favor of gun control. However, merely enacting resolutions has been ineffective in advancing the cause of gun control in the United States. The power of the National Rifle Association (NRA) in controlling the debate on gun control by raising money and mobilizing a determined minority has yet to be met with an equal fervor on the part of those favoring effective gun control. Our reticence allows the NRA to score victory after victory. The time has come for us to do the same. We must counter the NRA with our own resources, our own organization and our own passion.

Our task as Reform Jews is to challenge America's conscience and to heed the biblical injunction that we must not stand idly by the blood of our neighbor. We must embark on a moral offensive and send the message to our elected officials that we care deeply about this issue and will hold them accountable.

The next nine months are critical in the battle over gun control. When the United States Congress reconvenes in January 2000, several gun control bills will be on the legislative schedule. If the horror generated by recent shootings across the United States is not enough to open the eyes of our elected officials, it is likely that gun control will be consigned to the dust heap for a generation, exposing our society to ever more violence caused by guns.

THEREFORE, the Union of American Hebrew Congregations resolves to:

1. **Call upon every congregation to organize a gun control advocacy effort and urge every congregant to write to his or her representative and senator demanding that effective gun control be enacted during the next congressional session;**
2. **Provide every congregation with a copy of the Religious Action Center's legislative action guide to implement their strategy for addressing gun control advocacy;**
3. **Urge our congregations to extend personal invitations to elected officials to appear in the congregation to explain their position on gun control; and**
4. **Urge congregants to become involved in broader anti-violence coalitions in their local communities that press for effective gun control at all levels.**

Source: UAHC. Retrieved March 19, 2003, from http://www.uahc.org/orlando/areso/guncontrol.shtml

the more than seventy-five resolutions that specifically address Israel and the Middle East.

Several resolutions that the Central Conference of American Rabbis passed in the 1980s and 1900s address the question of terrorism in the modern world. Significantly, the language of those resolutions appears to have gained new currency in the early years of the twenty-first century, when the United States is especially concerned with terrorism. The 1981 resolution "condemns all governments who train, support, or harbor terrorist organizations" and urges "the government of the United States to opposed all terrorist groups and governments, both right and left, who would threaten individual liberties and desecrate human life" (Central Conference of American Rabbis, 1981). The 1985 resolution expresses the "moral outrage and unequivocal opposition to international terrorism" (CCAR, 1985), most especially with regard to those who kidnap and murder. The 1995 resolution notes that "terrorist attacks, while made in the name of Islam, are, in reality, not expressions of religion, but instead are the products of antidemocratic, authoritarian political forces which disguise their activities with a religious mode of expression," and "condemns all acts of terrorism, and calls upon government leaders, particularly Arab leaders, to disavow terrorism and to condemn acts of terror, to close down the offices of terrorist organizations, and to imprison terrorists" (CCAR, 1995). It too calls for vigorous investigation of terrorist activity, the creation of an international treaty, federal antiterrorist statutes, and diplomatic, military, and economic sanctions—all of which are coming to be realized in the twenty-first century.

Both historically and contemporarily, the Reform rabbis have been at the vanguard of Reform Judaism's emphases on social change and civic betterment. Under their leadership, Reform Judaism has involved itself in the U.S. civil-rights movement and in opposition to the United States' military involvement in Vietnam, for example. As with resolutions passed by their lay counterparts, the resolutions passed by the Reform rabbis echo the ideals of religious Judaism, the particular emphases of this liberal Jewish denomination, and they move from the general and universal into the specific and tangible. Thus, with regard to "Bilateral Nuclear Arms Freeze and Reduction" (CCAR, 1982), for example, we find the following: "Our tradition speaks to us of *Sakanat Nefashot*, the danger of exposing ourselves to health hazards, *Bal Tashchit*, the abhorrence of willful destruction of the environment, and *Yishuv Haarets*, the betterment and guardianship of the earth." The CCAR then called upon advocates of nuclear disarmament to speak out publicly, and regional CCAR bodies and other organizations to endorse such freezes. It also advocated a special Washington convocation of all religious bodies, not only Jewish, on this issue "at the earliest feasible time."

Responsa of the Central Conference of American Rabbis

Almost from the inception of the rabbinate as a professional class in the aftermath of the Roman destruction of the Second Temple in ancient Palestine (70 CE), distinguished and learned rabbis found themselves sought after for advice by communities, congregations, and individuals. A tradition arose of written responses to such queries, and that tradition continues today among all Jewish religious denominations. An individual response is called a responsum; the plural is responsa. Reform Judaism's responsa are composed by a committee of rabbinic scholars of the CCAR who examine the collected rabbinic literature of the past as well as the present in addition to examining nonrabbinic literature (political, legal, psychological, and so forth) before arriving at their decisions.

Two relevant recent examples are responsa to the questions "How can we deal with nuclear war from within the Jewish tradition?" (asked of the CCAR Responsa Committee by Rabbi Douglas E. Krantz of Armonk, New York, 1989) and "Does our tradition countenance preemptive military action when there is suspicion, but no prima facie evidence exists, that a perceived enemy will attack?" (asked of the CCAR Responsa Committee by Rabbi Benno M. Wallach of Houston, Texas, 2002). The former responsum examined the distinction between the permissibility of war in general and nuclear war in particular, while the latter examined the distinction between commanded, discretionary, and preventive wars. The Responsa Committee concluded that such a discussion is part of a larger conversation on the permissibility of war governed by such constraints as the afore-mentioned principles of both defensive wars and obligatory wars , as well as a strong emphasis on the moral behavior and responsibility of all those who engage in war (CCAR, 1989). With regard to the second query, the Responsa Committee responded "An attack may be morally justifiable, but the government bears the responsibility to do all that it can to make the case that it is in the right" (CCAR, 2002).

Outlook for the Twenty-First Century and Beyond

The seemingly irresolvable Middle East crisis between Israel and her neighbors, the United States' post-11 September war on terrorism, as well as present and future global hot spots will continue to call forth both lay and rabbinic resolutions and rabbinic responsa on the part of Reform Judaism. Reform Judaism will continue to address issues of war and peace, nuclear disarmament, the tragic fate of victims of war, and genocide both in their human universality as well as their Jewish particularity. The ages-old Jewish dream of *shalom* (peace) continues to demand of its adherents nothing less.

Steven Leonard Jacobs

Further Reading

Central Conference of American Rabbis (CCAR). (1946, 1981, 1982, 1985, 1989, 1995). Resolutions. Retrieved May 9, 2003, from http://www.ccarnet.org/reso/

Central Conference of American Rabbis (CCAR). (1989, 2002). Responsa. Retrieved May 9, 2003, from http://www.ccarnet.org/resp/

Freehof, S. B. (1963). *Recent reform responsa*. Cincinnati, OH: Hebrew Union College Press.

Freehof, S. B. (1969). *Current reform responsa*. Cincinnati, OH: Hebrew Union College Press.

Freehof, S.B. (1970). *Modern reform responsa*. Cincinnati, OH: Hebrew Union College Press.

Freehof, S. B. (1974). *Contemporary reform responsa*. Cincinnati, OH: Hebrew Union College Press.

Freehof, S. B. (1977). *Reform responsa for our Time*. Cincinnati, OH: Hebrew Union College Press.

Freehof, S. B. (1980). *New reform responsa*. Cincinnati, OH: Hebrew Union College Press.

Freehof, S. B. (1990). *Today's reform responsa*. Cincinnati, OH: Hebrew Union College Press.

Jacob, W. (1987). *Contemporary American reform responsa*. New York: Central Conference of American Rabbis.

Jacob, W. (1991). *Questions and reform Jewish answers: New American reform responsa*. New York: Central Conference of American Rabbis.

Jacob, W. (Ed.). (1983). *American reform responsa: Jewish questions, rabbinic answers*. New York: Central Conference of American Rabbis.

Plaut, W. G, & Waschofsky, M. (Eds.). (1997). *Teshuvot for the nineties: Reform Judaism's answers for today's dilemmas*. New York: Central Conference of American Rabbis.

Union of American Hebrew Congregations (UAHC). (1973). Resolutions. Retrieved May 9, 2003, from http://uahc.org/docs/reso.shtml

K

Kashmir

Since their emergence as independent states, India and Pakistan have gone to war on four different occasions. The roots of the conflict between the two countries can be traced back to the time of independence and partition in 1947, a period when the conception of state building in both countries was fundamentally different. Throughout its struggle for independence against the British, the Indian nationalist movement under the leadership of the Indian National Congress had upheld the need for a secular and democratic post-independence India. Contrary to the ideological standpoint of the Indian National Congress, the Muslim League under the leadership of Mohammed Ali Jinnah sought to create a separate homeland for the Muslims of South Asia (1876–1948). It is against such a backdrop that one can undertake a study of the four wars between India and Pakistan to understand why both countries have continued to fight each other.

The First Kashmir War (1947–1948)

By the late 1940s, the Indian National Congress and the Muslim League reached a deadlock in their endeavors to arrive at a viable settlement for a unified India. The end of the British rule compounded the problem further because the princely states in India were faced with the critical choice of acceding either to India or to Pakistan.

The princely state most affected by the situation was Kashmir. It soon became clear that a controversy was brewing over signing the Instrument of Accession. Lord Mountbatten, the last viceroy of British India, gave assurances to Hari Singh, the Maharaja of Kashmir, that the Indian leaders would not consider it an "unfriendly act" if he acceded to Pakistan. On the other hand, Jawaharlal Nehru wanted the state of Jammu and Kashmir to be part of India as it symbolized India's secular ideology. Moreover Kashmir's accession to India would undermine Mohammed Ali Jinnah's two-nation theory.

In the months after partition, the prince of Kashmir, Maharaja Hari Singh (d. 1961), faced tremendous pressure from both India and Pakistan to accede, but he refused to accede to either country. Hari Singh wanted to maintain his own independence because the princely states had been nominally independent. Hari Singh was scared of joining a predominantly Muslim state, Pakistan. He also dreaded joining India because he knew he would lose all his power in Nehru's socialist-leaning and democratic India.

The Proximate Cause and the Onset of War

During the first week of October 1947, a tribal rebellion broke out in Poonch, a region in southwestern Kashmir. Sections of the Pakistani army chose to support the rebels and supplied them with personnel, weaponry, and transport. Within two weeks, these tribesmen supported by Pakistani troops captured Muzzaffarabad and moved on towards Srinagar, the capital of Jammu and Kashmir. The maharaja, who still had not acceded to either country, appealed to India for military assistance to prevent further encroachment by the intruders.

Selections from the Shimla Agreement between India and Pakistan (1972)

Shimla Agreement on Bilateral Relations between India and Pakistan signed by Prime Minister Indira Gandhi, and President of Pakistan, Z. A. Bhutto, in Shimla on July 3, 1972.

The Government of India and the Government of Pakistan are resolved that the two countries put an end to the conflict and confrontation that have hitherto marred their relations and work for the promotion of a friendly and harmonious relationship and the establishment of durable peace in the subcontinent so that both countries may henceforth devote their resources and energies to the pressing task of advancing the welfare of their people.

In order to achieve this objective, the Government of India and the Government of Pakistan have agreed as follows:

a. That the principles and purposes of the Charter of the United Nations shall govern the relations between the two countries.

b. That the two countries are resolved to settle their differences by peaceful means through bilateral negotiations or by any other peaceful means mutually agreed upon between them. Pending the final settlement of any of the problems between the two countries, neither side shall unilaterally alter the situation and both shall prevent the organisation, assistance or encouragement of anacts detrimental to the maintenance of peace and harmonious relations.

c. That the prerequisite for reconciliation, good neighbourliness and durable peace between them is a commitment by both the countries to peaceful coexistence respect for each other's territorial integrity and sovereignty and noninterference in each other's internal affairs, on the basis of equality and mutual benefit.

d. That the basic issues and causes of conflict which have bedeviled the relations between the two countries for the last 25 years shall be resolved by peaceful means.

e. That they shall always respect each other's national unity, territorial integrity, political independence and sovereign equality.

f. That in accordance with the Charter of the United Nations, they will refrain from the threat or use of force against the territorial integrity or political independence of each other.

[. . .]

In order to initiate the process of the establishment of durable peace, both the governments agree that:

a. Indian and Pakistani forces shall be withdrawn to their side of the international border.

b. In Jammu and Kashmir, the line of control resulting from the ceasefire of December 17, 1971, shall be respected by both sides without prejudice to the recognised position of either side. Neither side shall seek to alter it unilaterally, irrespective of mutual differences and legal interpretations. Both sides further undertake to refrain from the threat or the use of force in violation of this line.

c. The withdrawals shall commence upon entry into force of this agreement and shall be completed within a period of 30 days thereof.

Source: Embassy of India, Cairo. Retrieved May 14, 2003, from http://www.india-emb.org.eg/Section5/ShimlaAgreement_EnglV.html

India's prime minister, Jawaharlal Nehru (1889–1964), agreed to provide assistance to Hari Singh if two conditions were met: first, the maharaja would have to accede to India and second, the accession would have to be endorsed by Sheikh Abdullah(1905–1982), the political leader of Srinagar who commanded the sympathy of most Muslims and some Hindus. On 26 October, once the maharaja signed the Instrument of Accession and once Abdullah granted his approval, 300 troops from the First Sikh Battalion of the Indian army were airlifted into Kashmir. The Indian troops captured a third of the territory of the former princely state.

The Course of the War

The fall and winter of 1947 witnessed pitched battles in Kashmir between the Indian and Pakistani armies in which both sides suffered significant losses. The 161st Infantry Brigade led by Brigadier L.P. Sen on the Indian side successfully halted the advance of the Pakistani-backed forces. By 3 November, the raiders had pushed back one company belonging to the First Kumaon Regiment. The Pakistani invaders launched a series of attacks on a communications center located in Uri sector of Kashmir from Muzzafarabad, Domel, and Poonch. Around 7 November 1947, the Indian army launched a decisive counterattack, which caught the Pakistanis by surprise and enabled the Indians to secure the Srinagar airfield. By the afternoon of 8 November, the Indian forces entered Baramullah, forcing the raiders to retreat. On 13 November the Indians succeeded in entering Mahura.

By the winter of 1947, the Indian military began to slow the level of its operations. Not only were the Indian soldiers affected by the severe winter but they also lacked adequate supplies and high-altitude warfare equipment. Taking advantage of the weaknesses on the Indian side, the Azad Kashmir (literally "free Kashmir") forces (as the Pakistani-backed forces were called) compelled the Indians to retreat. In the spring of 1948, the Indians launched a counteroffensive that led to more direct Pakistani involvement in the war. To stop further Pakistani incursions, the Indians increased their force to two divisions, directing each at the Poonch and Uri sectors. However the Indian military had neither the resources nor the political will to pursue such a continued and effective strategy of targeting the Pakistani forces and as a consequence, the Indian interest in reclaiming the remainder of the former princely state began to wane.

Negotiations at the United Nations

On 31 December 1947, India referred the Kashmir dispute to the UN Security Council. Articles 34 and 35 of the UN Charter were invoked, which specifically addressed situations that pose a threat to international peace and security. The Government of India urged the UN Security Council to condemn Pakistan's aggression.

On 20 January 1948, the Security Council passed a resolution that created a three-member commission to investigate the situation and enable a speedy resolution to the dispute. However, the resolution achieved little due to grave differences in the Indian and Pakistani positions as discussed earlier. A second resolution was passed on 21 April 1948 that called on both the governments of Indian and Pakistan to withdraw the tribesmen and Pakistani nationals from Kashmir.

The resolution of 21 April 1948 was important because it endorsed the Security Council's stand on the Kashmir conflict. Under this resolution, India and Pakistan were urged to bring about a cessation of all hostilities and move towards the early restoration of peace and order in the region. Consistent with the maintenance of law and order, both countries were further encouraged to reduce the troops in Indian-controlled Kashmir. In addition, on the question of accession to India or Pakistan, the resolution urged both countries to conduct a free and fair plebiscite to determine the wishes of the Kashmiri people. Hence the resolution was hailed as the principal term of reference for future negotiations aimed at advancing a final solution to the Kashmir problem. On 20 January 1949, an agreement was reached in Karachi to delineate the Cease Fire Line (CFL) along the positions held by the two armies once hostilities ended.

The Second Kashmir War (1965)

There were a number of factors that precipitated the second India-Pakistan war. First, after India's referral of the Kashmir issue to the UN, the issue became deeply politicized. The government of India was skeptical about some of the conditions specified in the UN resolutions, more specifically on the plebiscite issue and the vague endorsement of the idea of Kashmiri self-determination. As a consequence, India displayed little interest in the implementation of the Security Council resolutions.

Second, India had suffered a humiliating defeat at the hands of the Chinese in the 1962 Sino-Indian war and was in the process of attempting to revamp its military infrastructure. Those actions were viewed with suspicion by the Pakistanis. Moreover Bhutto made Muhammad Ayub Khan (1907–1974) believe that in the event of a war with India, Pakistan would receive Chinese military assistance. This factor greatly increased Pakistan's belief that it could wage a successful war against India. Also, in early 1965, Pakistan had conducted a limited probe along a disputed area called the Rann of Kachchh in the western Indian state of Gujarat. India's apathetic response to the Pakistani attack further emboldened Pakistan's perceptions of winning a war against India.

Third, the Pakistani leaders remained unhappy with the disputed status of Kashmir. A majority of the population of Kashmir was Muslim, which provided Pakistan with the justification that Kashmir should be part of Pakistan. Moreover, the Pakistani elite believed that there was widespread popular support for Pakistan within the Kashmir valley because of anti-Indian sentiments that had erupted in the wake of the theft of a sacred relic of the Kashmiri Muslims from the Hazratbal shrine in 1963. Those feelings persisted despite the fact that the relic was later located and returned.

Military Maneuvers

On 26 May 1965, the Pakistani forces embarked on Operation Gibraltar. The infiltration began across the cease-fire line (CFL) in Kashmir around 5 August 1965. The Indian authorities were alerted to the incursion by native Kashmiris and dispatched forces to seal the borders. However on 14 August 1965 the Pakistanis infiltrated near the Azad Kashmir town of Bhimbar. In a series of actions on 15, 24, and 26 August, the Indian troops occupied three Pakistani posts in Kargil, two in the Tithwal sector, and one in the Haji Pir Pass sector. The Pakistanis launched a second counterattack which compelled the Indians to push further into Azad Kashmir. As the Indians made significant gains, the Pakistanis embarked on Operation Grand Slam (31 August to 1 September) in southern Kashmir.

As a result of the Pakistani incursions, the Indians suffered severe casualties. On 5 September 1965, after capturing the village of Jaurian, the Pakistanis moved towards the town of Akhnur with the aim of capturing it and sealing off the state of Jammu and Kashmir from the rest of India. On 6 September, the Indians attacked Lahore and Sialkot. However, they suffered heavy casualties in the Khem Karan and Fazilka sections. Finally on 9 September, Pakistan launched a counteroffensive on the Lahore front and occupied the town of Burki the following day.

UN Responses

The war continued for nearly seventeen days and provoked significant international attention. The UN Secretary General U Thant visited Islamabad from 9–12 September and New Delhi from 13–15 September, urging both sides to end hostilities. On his return, the UN Security Council passed a resolution on 20 September 1965 calling for the effective implementation of a ceasefire followed by the withdrawal of all armed personnel to the positions held by them before 5 August 1965. On 21 September 1965 the Indian government accepted the cease-fire resolution, and the Pakistani government accepted it the next day.

The end of this war led to growing foreign pressure on both India and Pakistan to arrive at a settlement to the Kashmir dispute. Pakistan's Ayub Khan and India's prime minister, Lal Bahadur Shastri (1904–1966), were invited by the Soviet Union to forge a postwar settlement. On 4 January 1966 negotiations began at Tashkent (the capital of present-day Uzbekistan) and a final agreement was reached on 10 January 1966. The Tashkent Declaration asserted that "all armed personnel of the two countries shall be withdrawn no later than 25 February 1966 to the positions they held prior to 5 August 1965 and both sides shall observe the terms of the CFL" (Brines 1968).

The Third India-Pakistan Conflict (1971)

The causes of the third India-Pakistan conflict were rooted in Pakistan's domestic politics. In October 1970, soon after Pakistan's first democratic election, East Pakistan (present-day Bangladesh) began to agitate for regional autonomy. The West Pakistani leaders, most notably Zulfikar Ali Bhutto, were averse to any meaningful power-sharing arrangements. The resulting deadlock in power-sharing negotiations pushed Pakistan's president, General Agha Muhammad Yahya Khan (1917–1980), to use extensive force against the population of East Pakistan. This led to a full-scale civil war by April 1971. The military launched Operation Searchlight on 25 March 1971. The main goal of this operation was to extinguish all sources of political opposition to the military regime in West Pakistan.

Over the next several months, the civil war led to the fleeing of an estimated 10 million refugees from East Pakistan into Indian territory. The Indian leadership found it more practical to resort to war than absorb this stream of people into its already dense population. Though India intervened on humanitarian grounds, one of the underlying reasons for its decision to join the war was to attack Pakistan's ideological foundation. India sought to demonstrate Pakistan's failure to stand united on the basis of Islam alone. In doing so it challenged the logic of Pakistan's irredentist claim on Kashmir.

By late October of 1971, India began to exert steady military pressure on Pakistan. The war started with a preemptive air attack by India on Pakistan's northern air bases on 3 December 1971. The Indian air force struck a number of West Pakistani air bases, including those at Islamabad, Sargodha, and Karachi. The forces on the East Pakistani side that aided the Indian efforts were called the Mukti Bahini (liberation force). While the Indians made significant victories in Sindh, the Pakistanis captured Chamb in Jmmu and Kashmir. By 6 December 1971, the Indian forces and the Mukti Bahini created two possible channels to mount an attack on the city of Dhaka (now the capital of Bangladesh). By 13 December, the Indian troops geared themselves for the final assault on Dhaka. By 16 December, the Pakistani forces were completely routed and the Indian army entered the city. On 17 December 1971 India's prime minister, Indira Gandhi (1917–1984), ordered a unilateral cease-fire and the Pakistan forces responded in a similar fashion, bringing the war to a close.

The Simla Agreement

Soon after the war, Indira Gandhi and the Zulfikar Ali Bhutto (1928–1979), the president of Pakisan, met in Simla, the former British colonial summer capital, in northwestern India, to reach a postwar settlement. The final negotiations took place between 28 June 1972 and 2 July 1972. Initially, there was no agreement as both sides voiced various concerns. Pakistan was not in favor of India's demand that the postconflict CFL in Kashmir be made the Line of Control. India wanted the UN observers on the cease-fire to leave. The agreement was finally signed on 3 July 1972.

As per the agreement, most Pakistani prisoners of war were repatriated. India and Pakistan reiterated their commitment to settling the Kashmir dispute through diplomatic channels. More significantly, they changed the nomenclature for the 1948 cease-fire line in Kashmir; henceforth it was to be called the Line of Control (LOC).

The end of the war established India as the dominant power in the subcontinent. It also removed the sense of humiliation that had haunted the Indians after their defeat at the hands of the Chinese in the 1962 war. The secessionist movement in Bangladesh also dealt a severe blow to Pakistan's ideological foundations by demonstrating that religion alone could not be the basis for state building in South Asia.

The Kargil War (1999)

In the summer of 1999, Indian forces failed to anticipate a Pakistani military incursion. Earlier in May 1998, both countries had conducted nuclear tests and became overt nuclear powers. Although the prime ministers of both nations signed an agreement in Lahore, the capital of Pakistani Punjab. In February 1999 to promote diplomatic relations with each other, the Pakistani military had been covertly planning a military operation against India with the intention of reviving the Kashmir issue on the international agenda.

The two nations' acquisition of nuclear weapons changed the security calculus in the subcontinent. Pakistan's intentions of precipitating the conflict can be understood in terms of the stability-instability paradox. The paradox states that nuclear weapons contribute to stability at high levels of conflict because of the fear of nuclear escalation. Yet they simultaneously create incentives for conventional conflicts in marginal areas as long as either side does not breach certain thresholds. Hence the Pakistanis saw no harm in infiltrating into unimportant areas like the upper reaches of the Kashmir valley.

By the last week of May, Indian soldiers realized that regular Pakistani forces and Kashmiri insurgents had occupied nearly seventy positions along the LOC. The Indian army then launched Operation Vijay to push back the intruders. The Indian air force was called into action and carried out a round of air strikes. Soon after, the regular infantry troops were called in and by early June, the Indian army had managed to recover twenty-one positions.

During the war both countries faced tremendous pressure from the United States to put an end to hostilities. In the last week of June, General Anthony Zinni, the commander in chief of the U.S. central command, visited Pakistan to persuade Nawaz Sharif, Pakistan's prime minister, to withdraw Pakistani troops from the LOC. Gibson Lanpher, the U.S. deputy assistant secretary of state for South Asia, visited New Delhi, urging India to exercise restraint.

The conflict continued till early July. By the first two weeks of July, the Pakistani forces were faced with artillery barrages and air attacks from the Indian military. The Indian capture of the strategic peak of Tiger Hills marked the beginning of the Pakistani defeat. On

12 July Nawaz Sharif visited Washington, and soon after he called for the withdrawal of Pakistani insurgents from the Indian positions. By 14 July the first set of infiltrators had withdrawn from the Indian side of the LOC.

Looking into the Future

The Kargil war revealed many gaps in Indian intelligence and also raised Indian concerns about the issue of cross-border terrorism. More importantly, it internationalized the Kashmir dispute, as foreign countries urging both India and Pakistan to exercise restraint, given the presence of nuclear weapons in the subcontinent. In the aftermath of a terrorist attack on the Indian Parliament in December 2001, the situation between both countries once again became tense. In the summer of 2002, the Indian army mobilized thousands of troops along its borders and made a clear attempt to manipulate the fear of nuclear war.

It remains to be seen whether the countries will continue to fight over Kashmir, whose future remains unresolved. All three attempts by Pakistan to wrest Kashmir from India have proved futile, but it is unlikely that Pakistan will abandon its efforts to fuel cross-border terrorism in India. India too seems unwilling to cede much ground on the Kashmir issue. Some Asian security specialists believe that changing the Line of Control into the de facto border between India and Pakistan could resolve the problem. However with both sides unwilling to make concessions on the Kashmir issue, it seems difficult to predict what shape the Kashmir conundrum will take in the near future.

Ayesha Ray

See also Hindu-Muslim Violence in India

Further Reading

Akbar, M. J. (1991). *Kashmir behind the Vale*, New Delhi, India: Viking Publishers.

Bajpai, K., Karim, A., & Mattoo, A. (Eds.). (2001). *Kargil and after: Challenges for Indian policy*. New Delhi, India: Har Anand Publications.

Brines, R. (1968). *The Indo-Pakistani conflict*. New York: Pall Mall.

Chari, P. R., & Major General Krishna, A. (2001). *Kargil: The tables turned*. New Delhi, India: Manohar Publishers.

Chopra, P. (1973). *India's second liberation*. New Delhi, India: Vikas Publishers.

Cohen, M. (1955). *Thunder over Kashmir*. Hyderabad, British India: Orient Longman.

Dawson, P. (1994). *The peacekeepers of Kashmir: The UN military observers group in India and Pakistan*. London: Hurst and Company.

Ganguly, S. (2002). *Conflict unending: India-Pakistan tensions since 1947*. Oxford: Oxford University Press.

Ganguly, S. (1999). *The crisis in Kashmir: Portents of war, hopes of peace*. Cambridge, UK: Cambridge University Press.

Hoffman, S. (1972). Anticipation, disaster and victory. *Asian Survey, 12*(11), 960–979

India, Government of (1999). *From surprise to reckoning* The Kargil Review Committee Report.

Johnson, A. C. (1953). *Mission with Mountbatten*. New York: Dutton.

Korbel, J. (1954). *Danger in Kashmir*. Princeton, NJ: Princeton University Press.

Lamb, A. (1992). Kashmir: A disputed legacy, 1846–1990. Karachi, Pakistan: Oxford University Press.

Mascarhenas, A. (1971). *The rape of Bangladesh*. New Delhi, India: Vikas Publishers.

Musa, M. (1965). Some aspects of the war. *Pakistan horizon, 18*(4), 328.

Musa, M. (1983). *My version: India-Pakistan war 1965*. Lahore, Pakistan: Wajidalis.

Noorani, A. G. (1964). *The Kashmir question*. Bombay: Manaktalas.

Quereshi, I. H. (1965). *The struggle for Pakistan*. Karachi, Pakistan: University Press.

Rahman, M.(1996). *Divided Kashmir*. Boulder, CO: Lynne Rienner Publishers

Singh, A. I. (1987). *The origins of the partition of India, 1936–47*. New Delhi, India: Oxford University Press.

Sawant, G. (2000). *Dateline Kargil*. New Delhi, India: Macmillan Publishers.

Sinha, Lieutenant General S. K. (1987). *Operation rescue*. New Delhi, India: Vision Books.

Swami, P. (2000). *The Kargil war*. New Delhi, India: Leftword Publishers.

Snyder, G. (1965). The balance of power and balance of terror. In P. Seabury (Ed.), *The balance of power* (pp. 185–201). San Francisco: Chandler.

Wirsing, R. G.(1994). India, Pakistan and the Kashmir dispute. New York: St Martin's Press.

Ku Klux Klan

A white supremacist organization founded in the United States after the Civil War, the Ku Klux Klan has a long history of vigilantism, guerilla warfare, terrorism, and political assassination targeting black people. It has also attacked Jews, Catholics, and others perceived as subverting an idealized White Protestant America. The Klan has mobilized in five different historic periods, and has repeatedly split into a number of contentious factions. Sometimes the Klan has maintained close ties to local law enforcement, while at other times it is the focus of law enforcement investigations. The Klan sees itself as a patriotic defense force preserving white rights, law and order, states' rights, and Protestant Christian values.

The Klan Is Born

The first-era Klan was founded in late 1865 or early 1866 in Pulaski, Tennessee as a social club for a handful of former Confederate soldiers. The words *Ku Klux* are wordplay derived from *kuklos*, corrupting the Greek word for circle or band; while the alliterative *Klan* came from the Scotch and Irish immigrant clan roots of the founders. What started as pranks against neighbors quickly spread to harassment of local black residents.

As Klan chapters spread across Tennessee they became more formalized, mixing the ceremonies and rituals of the burgeoning men's fraternal organizations of the period with a militarized style familiar to former soldiers. Thus their first leader was dubbed a *Grand Wizard* and was a former Confederate general, Nathan Bedford Forrest, who was recruited after a Spring 1867 reorganizing assembly attended by representatives of local KKK chapters. Within a few years, the Klan had spread from Tennessee to Alabama, North Carolina, South Carolina, Mississippi, Georgia, Florida, Arkansas, and Texas.

In the South, the period after the Civil War was called *Reconstruction*; this meant not only rebuilding the shattered economic infrastructure, but also reallocating power to former slaves, who ran for and were elected to public office. In addition to manipulating elections, whites seeking to marginalize blacks would refuse to sell them basic farm implements and other supplies, opening the market to peddlers from the North. That some peddlers were Jews lent an anti-Semitic component to the Klan's list of enemies, which also included the federal government (especially the Freedman's Bureau), northern Christian missionaries, local educators teaching blacks to read, and state officials enforcing tax payments and civil rights laws. All transplanted pro-Union Northerners were derogatorily referred to as *carpetbaggers* (based on the popularity of serviceable fabric-sided luggage), while local Southern supporters of the Union were called *scalawags*.

The Klan and its allies, who saw themselves as defending the Constitution and local laws against this malicious meddling as well as general post-war chaos and lawlessness, framed their work as the "redemption" of the South. In practice, the Klan became the primary vehicle for organized attempts to re-establish white male dominance and force freed slaves back into social, political, and economic subservience.

The Klan wore hoods and sheets as a disguise, and often rode in groups at night, so they became known as *night-riders*. Klansmen "threatened, exiled, flogged, mutilated, shot, stabbed, and hanged" blacks and their allies (Chalmers 1965, 10). York County, South Carolina saw one of the most intense terror campaigns. Starting in November 1870 and running for ten months, the Klan perpetrated "11 murders, more than 600 cases of whipping, beating, and other kinds of aggravated assault," plus other acts of intimidation, including the burning or destruction of several black churches and schools (Trelease 1995, 365).

The federal government was finally forced to restore order by passing anti-Klan statutes in 1870 and 1871, and by dispatching federal troops. Klan units had started to disband as early as 1869, and with federal intervention the process continued. By the mid-1870s the last of the active Klan chapters had collapsed.

Rebirth

White racism in a variety of forms was not uncommon in the United States at the beginning of the twentieth century, even among Protestant ministers such as Thomas Dixon Jr., who expanded from his New York City pulpit at the Twenty-third Street Baptist Church to write fiction as a way to spread his gospel warning of "creeping negroidism," and promoting Christian white supremacy (Wade 1987, 122–123).

Dixon's most popular book was *The Clansman*, a melodrama portraying the Reconstruction Klan as heroic soldiers in a war to protect the South against sinister Northern carpetbaggers, and to defend white southern women from rapacious black men. Filmmaker D. W. Griffith took *The Clansman* and transformed it into the first major cinema blockbuster. Retitled *The Birth of a Nation*, the film premiered in early 1915 and became a nationwide sensation.

In Atlanta, Georgia, the film's popularity coincided with an infamous criminal incident in which the rape and murder of fourteen-year-old Mary Phagan was

Ku Klux Klan parade in Washington D.C., September 13, 1926. Courtesy Library of Congress.

falsely blamed on her employer, Leo M. Frank, a Jew who had moved to the South from New York. After his conviction on clearly dubious evidence, Frank was jailed, then abducted and lynched by a mob—an act so popular in some circles, it prompted William J. Simmons to reorganize the Klan, adopting the flaming cross as a symbol from images in Dixon's book and the subsequent film. Within a few years, Klan vigilante attacks had been reported in Georgia, Alabama, Florida, Texas, and Oklahoma.

In the 1920s the Klan spread nationwide with soaring membership (often drawn from mainstream Protestant denominations), usually estimated at between 2 million and 4 million. Catholics and immigrants were added as major targets during this era, when membership in the Klan was often considered a political advantage for Protestant office-seekers. "The Klan was strongest in the Midwest; it briefly dominated Indiana politics and had important influence in such far-flung states as Texas, Oregon, Colorado, Georgia, and Maine" (Berlet & Lyons 2000, 97). The Klan's claim that it was defending hearth and home from alien ideas and forces attracted many women supporters. Violence still occurred, but many Klan leaders argued for other tactics. From its peak in the early 1920s, the KKK slowly declined until a demand for unpaid taxes forced it to disband in 1944.

Confronting Civil Rights

The Klan re-emerged in 1946 for a third era to confront post-World War II calls for racial tolerance. Throughout the 1950s the KKK was a marginal dissident movement engaged in sporadic "threats, cross burnings, floggings, and bombings" (Chalmers 1965, 349). As the civil rights movement grew in the 1960s, the Klan split into a variety of competing factions.

The Klan and other groups, such as the all-white Citizens Councils, defended segregation as being God's will. Biblical citations were used to defend keeping the races separate. The attack on God's plan for racial separation was fomented, according to popular conspiracy theories, by godless Communists who controlled the federal government in league with Jewish international banking families such as the Rothschilds and Schiffs. White supremacists believed these forces promoted racial unrest through outside agitators such as the Reverend Martin Luther King Jr. The logical end point of this conspiracy theory was that support for civil rights by the National Council of Churches and its membership of liberal Protestant denominations was evidence of Communist infiltration.

In the 1960s the most violent KKK factions and other racial hate groups murdered civil rights workers and bombed churches and synagogues, forcing the federal government to take belated action against the Klan, and exposing the friendly relationships between organized racists and some local law enforcement agencies in the South. The Klan was discredited for many Americans, and it fell apart.

In the mid-1970s the silver-tongued and photogenic David Duke of Louisiana tried to reframe the KKK as a white civil rights organization. Duke succeeded in briefly revitalizing the Klan, but it remained marginal. There was occasional violence from various Klan factions, peaking in 1979 with shootings at civil rights organizers in Alabama and an ambush in Greensboro, North Carolina, involving Klansmen and neo-Nazis that left five members of the Communist Workers Party dead and nine injured.

The fifth-era Klan began in the early 1980s with a call by Louis Beam to form an underground vigilante movement. Beam's 1983 essay on "Leaderless Resistance," published in his *Inter-Klan Newsletter & Survival Alert*, has helped spread the use of guerrilla tactics such as bombings and assassinations among members of organized hate groups.

Uncertain Future

The Ku Klux Klan has been eclipsed by a number of competing white supremacist organizations, and while scattered units still remain active, they are denounced by every Protestant denomination and monitored for criminal activity by local police and federal agencies. It is unlikely that in the near future they will be a vehicle for a mass social or political movement such as was seen in the 1920s; but the possibility of individual acts of violence from members of an organization rooted in terrorism and race hate should never be dismissed.

Chip Berlet

See also Christian Identity

Further Reading

Berlet, C., & Lyons, M. N. (2000). *Right-wing populism in America: Too close for comfort*. New York: Guilford Publications.

Blee, K. M. (1991). *Women of the Klan: Racism and gender in the 1920s*. Berkeley: University of California Press.

Chalmers, D. M. (1965). *Hooded Americanism: The first century of the Ku Klux Klan, 1865–1965*. Garden City, NY: Doubleday & Company.

Dixon, T., Jr. (1905). *The Clansman: An historical romance of the Ku Klux Klan*. New York: Doubleday, Page & Company.

Dobratz, B. A., & Shanks-Meile, S. L. (1997). *"White power, white pride!" The white separatist movement in the United States*. New York: Twayne Publishers.

Lay, S. (Ed.). (1992). *The invisible empire in the west: Toward a new historical appraisal of the Ku Klux Klan of the 1920s*. Urbana: University of Illinois Press.

Nelson, J. (1993). *Terror in the night: The Klan's campaign against the Jews*. New York: Simon and Schuster.

Ridgeway, J. (1995). *Blood in the face: The Ku Klux Klan, Aryan Nations, Nazi skinheads, and the rise of a new white culture*. (2nd ed.). New York: Thunder's Mouth Press.

Trelease, A. W. (1995). *White terror: The Ku Klux Klan conspiracy and southern reconstruction*. Baton Rouge: Louisiana State University Press.

Wade, W. C. (1987). *The fiery cross: The Ku Klux Klan in America*. New York: Simon and Schuster.

L

Latin America: Historical Overview

Religion has traditionally played an important role in Latin America. The majority of Latin Americans are still, even after the waves of Protestant incursions into Latin America, nominally Catholic. Yet this Catholicism is different from that in Europe or other regions. There are two reasons for this: the Iberian roots of Latin American Catholicism and the religious context provided by differing indigenous Native American nations and empires. This latter element in large part explains the increasingly violent reactions of Iberian Catholicism towards the inhabitants of the Americas, a reaction that culminated in papal pronouncements by the mid-sixteenth century regarding the humanity and proper treatment of the indigenous Native American populations.

Religion at the Time of Conquest

The Catholicism brought to the Americas in the sixteenth century was the historic product of Iberian conditions, and thus was Iberian rather than universal in nature. The Church was still in its formative stage when, in the beginning of the fifth century CE, the Visigothic tribes descended upon the Iberian peninsula. These tribes adopted Christianity. However, in 711, the Muslims burst into Spain, pushing the Christian-controlled land to the far north and northeastern areas of Iberia. The process of reconquering the lands from the Muslims took eight centuries and created a crusading, warring Christian mentality among the Spanish and Portuguese. It was this crusading mentality that characterized the worldview of the waves of Iberian conquistadores and settlers in the Americas. The Jesuit friar Manuel M. Marzal, writing today, describes the features of this Iberian Catholicism well, but as early as 1583 the friar Bartolome de las Casas (1484–1572), made the first bishop of the (now Mexican) diocese of Chiapas in 1543, was exposing its negative effects in his writings. Indeed the translation of his report on Spanish injustices against the indigenous peoples fueled the widely held "black legend" of Spanish injustice and cruelty in the Americas.

While the indigenous Native American inhabitants' reception of the Iberians had initially been friendly, relations rapidly deteriorated, especially when the Spaniards compelled the inhabitants of the Caribbean islands into forced labor to extract gold. This practice, especially on the island of Hispaniola (now the nations of Haiti and the Dominican Republic), was assumed by right of conquest. Spanish attempts to extirpate cannibalism and idolatry contributed to assumptions that the Native American inhabitants were not rational and thus less than human, and so could be justly enslaved.

Bartolomé de Las Casas, a settler who had converted to a religious life, objected to the enslavement and ill treatment of the local population. It was not that Las Casas thought that the Spanish Crown was not justified in its possession of the Americas. This right had been granted when Pope Alexander VI declared in 1492 that the Catholic monarchs of Spain held the right to the newly discovered lands to the West, provided those lands were not already held by a Christian monarch (as was the case with Brazil, which was deemed to be held by Portugal). But Las Casas did object to cruelty, and his objections led to the famed debate in Vallodolid, Spain, between De las Casas and Juan Ginés de Sepúlveda (1490–1573), who argued on Aristotelian grounds that the Native American inhabitants were natural slaves. Las Casas's arguments carried the debate, and the basic humanity of the Native American inhabitants was recognized, though in actuality the feudal practice enshrined in the practice of land grants or *encomienda* tended to obscure this. Thus conquest continued by force, with Nicholas de Ovando (1451–1511), conquistador of Hispaniola, being succeeded by Hernán Cortés (1485–1547) in Mexico and Francisco Pizarro (c. 1475–1541) in Peru, not to mention Diego Velásquez (1465–1524) in Cuba and many others.

The Church in Colonial Latin America

Throughout the colonial period (early sixteenth to early nineteenth centuries), the Roman Catholic Church was one of the most important political and cultural institutions in the New World. Reasons for this are threefold: First, the Church served as an agent of conquest, legitimizing, and participating in the process, ostensibly for the evangelization of the indigenous population. Second, the Church provided the colonies with economic backing in the form of loans and capital. And third, the colonial Church was an agent of social control; its clergy served as representatives of the Iberian crowns, maintaining social control by disciplining and providing a role for the masses to play in society. The Church also was responsible for social welfare, bringing hospitals and education to the colonies. Every facet of life (and death) during Latin America's colonial period, then, involved the Church and the clergy.

Agents of Conquest

The first role of the Church had been to legitimize conquest by giving it the evangelical mission of preaching the Gospels to the indigenous population. On the heels of every conquest of territory in the Americas followed efforts to convert the indigenous populations. When the Portuguese monarch King João III (1502–1557) sent Tomé de Souza (d. c. 1573), the first governor-general of Brazil, to the Americas in 1549, he stated "The main reason which leads me to colonize Brazil is to convert the people therein to our holy Catholic faith" (Bethell 1984, 541). The case was similar with the rest of Latin America. Upon entering Latin America, the religious orders immediately set out to convert the Indians. As an agent of conquest, the cross always accompanied the sword.

Agents of Economic Development

The Church also served in the economic development of Latin America. It was the principal source of loans in the colonies, and the Church also held property, businesses, and slaves, and accumulated a great deal of wealth. Many regular religious orders (such as the Benedictines, Jesuits, and Franciscans) attempted to become more independent of the Spanish and Portuguese Crowns by creating their own sources of income in the shape of farms, plantations, cattle ranches, sugar mills, and slaves. These often were obtained through donation, inheritance, or the promises of the faithful. Thus to a large degree, the clergy devoted themselves to money matters, buying and selling, and using the interest on loans to good avail. Indeed, this became the main concern of many priests, as only a minority was actually engaged in missionary activities.

Agents of Social Control

In addition to legitimizing the conquest of the New World and stimulating economic development through loans, the Church also served as an agent of social control. There were a number of key ways—all interrelated—in which the Church actively participated in the development of Latin America. It did so through a system of royal patronage: The Kings of Spain and Portugal authorized the collection of taxes in the New World for the Church, a 10 percent levy on whatever the lands produced—sugar, manioc, and so forth. This money was then theoretically to be put to use to support the Church in the New World, and the Church, in turn, would organize the colonies.

In addition to collecting the tithe, with which the Crown paid clergy's salaries and for the upkeep the Church, the Crown also appointed priests and bishops (although the latter in theory had to be approved by Rome). All priests desiring to work in the colonies first had to receive authority from the King through a personal interview; they also had to swear an oath of allegiance. Between Rome and the Church in the colonies there was no direct communication; all communication first passed through Iberia where, if the Crown granted permission, it would then be forwarded on to the colonies. In addition, only Catholics were legally allowed to enter the colonies.

The Church preached loyalty and obedience to the monarchy. Religious instruction prepared the indige-

Independence Mural at Instituto Geografico Militar, Quito, Ecuador. March 2000. Courtesy Steve Donaldson.

nous population to accept their permanently subordinate role in colonial society. In Hispanic cities, the clergy, whose role was to minister to the Hispanicized population, was to administer the sacraments and to handle problems of discipline.

Postcolonial, Independent Latin America

Prior to the nineteenth century, the Church in Latin America had been closely tied to the state through the system of royal patronage described above. When the independence movements began in the early 1800s, Simón Bolívar (1783–1830), who was known as "the liberator," took his task to be the liberation of the Spanish colonies. He drew inspiration from Las Casas, whom he described as a friend of humanity. Many clergy, whose ordination vows held them to obedience to the Spanish Crown, rejected the notion of national independence as symbolic of apostasy and modern, liberal error. From the 1830s onward a sharp division emerged in many Latin American nations between traditional, conservative clergy and a liberal, educated, and anticlerical ruling class.

These liberal governments tended to be anticlerical: After centuries of domination by an extremely powerful Church, they sought to diminish the role of the institutional Church and the clergy who administered it in society. They did not, however, seek to change fundamental Catholic beliefs.

Governments in Latin America during the nineteenth century and much of the twentieth century generally either were conservative or liberal. Liberal governments opted for religious toleration, an end to the *fueros* (the special privileges given to members of the priesthood, such as the right to trial in a church court rather than a secular one), and saw the Church's extensive landholdings as detrimental to progress. Liberals vocally advocated the confiscation of Church lands, as indeed eventually happened in Mexico.

An extreme version of the conflicts in which the Church became embroiled occurred in Mexico. In 1855 the liberal government of Mexico abolished ecclesiastical *fueros;* the following year it prohibited the corporate ownership of rural and urban estates. Following these laws, a number of additional ones were passed limiting clerical powers. This legislation led to the Mexican

Civil War of 1858–1861, in which the Church sided with the conservatives against the liberals, who used the war to radicalize their reforms. The pattern was repeated throughout Latin America, but in a less extreme fashion.

Conservatives, on the other hand, saw the Church as the religious foundation of Latin America. Thus they advocated a retention of the status quo. The Church, they argued, not only served as a lending institution, but financed hospitals, schools, and orphanages. Conservatives expected the clergy to play both secular as well as religious roles in the independent new nations. Liberalism, which advocated the secularization of institutions such as hospitals and schools, seemed heretical to the conservatives.

Until around 1930, Latin American governments were divided fairly equally between the liberal and conservative positions. Slowly, however, liberalism began to gain ground, and in response the Church became much more militant in its defense of its traditional rights. The scholar Jeffery Klaiber has outlined the historical course of the Latin American Church in his book *The Catholic Church in Peru, 1821–1985: A Social History*. Although his focus is Peru, his observations apply to Latin America in general. After the struggles between liberals and conservatives (as anti- and pro-clerical, respectively), the militant Church (1855–1930) gave way to a militant laity (1930–1955). In this period of twenty-five years or so, amidst the great internal and external tension accompanying worldwide depression, a world war, and the beginnings of the Cold War, the laity increasingly took it upon themselves to be the defenders of the Church in European-inspired movements such as Catholic Action.

Although there was limited religious toleration in the new Latin American states, the Roman Catholic Church remained in most cases the established Church, and it provided support for the national state's efforts at maintaining independence, settling boundary disputes, and seeking to modernize the state apparatus and services. The old issues surrounding the initial and subsequent conquest of the indigenous populations had long faded, although the unjust land distribution that earlier colonial practices had created remained, with the land merely changing hands after independence, from the Crown to the local ruling elite. This gross maldistribution of land was to rankle and provide fertile grounds for popular unrest through to the present century. Desire for land sparked numerous revolts during the twentieth century, often inspired by socialist organizations.

Such social unrest, coming from the landless peasantry, new radical political ideas, and the liberal agnosticism of much of the ruling elite, led in some cases to the Church taking a sharply conservative tone, advocating the maintenance of law and order against the impending threats of modernization. This process is well exemplified in the work of Dom Cardinal Sebastião Leme de Silveira Cintra (1882–1942), the first archbishop of Rio de Janeiro and the first Latin American cardinal. He thoroughly modernized the Brazilian Church, reorganized seminary training, and directed the national Church as a supporter of Vatican ideological and moral stances, as well as strategically offering the Church as a supporter of the state in exchange for state privilege.

The decade of the 1960s was marked in Roman Catholicism by the dramatic reforms enacted by the Second Vatican Council (1963–1965). Its declarations on human dignity and rights deeply influenced the Latin American bishops' conferences held at Medéllin (1968), and then in Puebla (1979). The decisions taken at those conferences provided support in the ensuing decades for a Church struggling against institutional violence within the countries of Latin America.

Reacting to the perceived threat of Communism and radical socialist land reform proposals suggested in the 1960s, the military in many Latin American nations led coups that replaced civilian democracies with military and authoritarian regimes. Thus, apart from such regimes already existing in the Caribbean and Central America, this period saw the governments of Brazil, Chile, Argentina, and numerous other nations become military dictatorships that lasted into the 1980s and in some cases longer. The imposition of such regimes led to a sharp increase in human-rights violations. The Church, one of the few—if not the only—institutions still able to function freely in such a context, responded by speaking out against abuses and calling for a return to democratic freedoms, actions that alienated the national governments.

The Church, a strong supporter of human rights since Vatican II, rejected Communism but opposed the indiscriminate use of force against citizens. Individual clerics such as Dom Helder Camara of Recife, Dom Evaristo Arns (archbishop of Sao Paulo, Brazil), Archbishop Oscar Romero of El Salvador, and numerous others gained world recognition for their opposition to military rule.

A critical role in this Church opposition to state policies was played by liberation theology, which emerged around 1971 from both the ideas of the Second Vatican Council and the Latin American context. Its first and most well-known proponents were the Peruvian priest Gustavo Gutierrez (b. 1928) and the Brazilian Franciscan Leonardo Boff (b. 1938). This theology, taking literally the example of Jesus, who preached freedom to the captives, rejected the traditional dualism between the spiritual and secular realms, and declared God's concern for all spheres of human life, political as well as spiritual. Liberation theology saw conflict and class division as the means by which God enabled the poor, acting responsibly, to effect their own liberation from oppression. Such a theological stance not only antagonized the state, in many cases it sharply polarized the Church itself, as it called into question the traditional Roman Catholic understanding of the Church as the channel of forgiveness and as a reconciler of peoples. These struggles within and without the Church played out differently in different nations, but the Church did help mobilize the previously disorganized lower classes, primarily the urbanizing poor.

While such opposition was rarely the stated position of the Church as a whole, it is nevertheless incorrect to charge the Roman Catholic Church with a failure to oppose oppressive regimes during the latter half of the twentieth century. Individual bishops did take a stand, and indeed the muted ecclesiastical reaction in some cases meant that the Church ended up being the mediator or the only trusted negotiator as transitions to civilian democratic rule took place. This was the case in Brazil, Argentina, and Chile. In other cases, the Church acted as an institutional base for numerous truth and fact-finding organizations, providing the materials for national truth and reconciliation commissions. This was the case with nations such as Argentina, Chile, El Salvador, Guatemala, and Honduras, though with varying degrees of success.

Thus the last half-century in Latin America witnessed internal civil conflict rather than conflict between nations, and the state, riven by deep social and racial cleavages, has often resorted to violence to maintain the privileges of the elite. Such action has been opposed by the institutional Church, which has also provided a space for peaceful negotiations to take place. Given that much of the inherited social order and patterns of land ownership remain unchanged, the peacemaking role of the Catholic Church—and also, now, the growing Protestant churches (especially in Brazil, Mexico, and Guatemala)—will no doubt increase.

Protestantism

From the 1960s onward membership in Protestant churches has been growing in Latin America. In the nineteenth century, as the Latin American countries one by one made freedom of worship legal, Protestant denominations increasingly entered Latin America. Today all Latin American countries have laws guaranteeing freedom of worship (although a few still declare official support for the Catholic Church).

The most important Protestant movement has been Pentecostalism. Many Latin Americans joined Pentecostal churches, converting from Catholicism because they were unhappy with the Catholic Church's role in social-reform movements. While Catholic Action workers and proponents of liberation theology were decrying corrupt governments and criticizing them for failing to provide adequate services for the poor, converts to Pentecostalism (the majority of whom were poor themselves) sought to turn to God and concentrate on their own, individual salvation. The belief was that if sin were to be eradicated, social and governmental evils would disappear.

Today, the two fastest-growing religious groups in Latin America are the Pentecostal churches and the Church of Jesus Christ of Latter-Day Saints (the Mormons). In Brazil and Guatemala, there are more Protestants than church-going Catholics (although Catholics continue to have overall numerical superiority). In addition, Buddhists, Hindus, Jews, worshipers of indigenous and African religions, and a whole array of other Protestant and non-Catholic religions (such as Jehovah's Witnesses and Seventh-Day Adventists, in particular) are common in Latin America.

Kim Richardson

See also Aztecs; Inca; Maya

Further Reading

Bethell, L. (Ed.). (1984). *The Cambridge history of Latin America: Vol. 1. Colonial Latin America*. Cambridge, UK: Cambridge University Press.

Burdick, M. (1995). *For God and the fatherland: Religion and politics in Argentina*. Albany: State University of New York.

Bushnell, D., & Macaulay, N. (1994). *The emergence of Latin America in the nineteenth century* (2nd ed.). Oxford, UK: Oxford University Press.

Costeloe, M. (1978). *Church and state in independent Mexico: A study of the patronage debate, 1821–1857*. London: Royal Historical Society.

De Las Casas, B. (1992). *A short account of the destruction of the Indies* (N. Griffin, Ed. & Trans.). London: Penguin Books.

Dussel, E. (Ed.). (1992). *Historia liberationis: 500 anos de história da Igreja na América Latina*. São Paulo, Brazil: Edições Paulinas.

Hankes, L. (1959). *Aristotle and the American Indian*. Bloomington: Indiana University Press.

Hayner, P. B. (2002). *Unspeakable truths: Facing the challenge of truth commissions*. New York: Routledge.

Klaiber, J. (1992). *The Catholic Church in Peru, 1821–1985: A social history*. Washington, DC: The Catholic University of America Press.

Knowlton, R. (1976). *Church property and the Mexican reform, 1856–1910*. DeKalb: North Illinois Press.

Levine, D. (1981). *Religion and politics in Latin America: The Catholic Church in Venezuela and Colombia*. Princeton, NJ: Princeton University Press.

Mainwaring, S., & Wilde, A. (Ed.). (1989). *The Progressive Church in Latin America*. Notre Dame, IN: Notre Dame University Press.

Martin, D. (1990). *Tongues of fire: The explosion of Protestantism in Latin America*. Oxford, UK: Basil Blackwell.

Mecham, J. L. (1966). *Church and state in Latin America: A history of politico-ecclesiastical relations* (Rev. ed.). Chapel Hill: The University of North Carolina Press.

Quirk, R. (1973). *The Mexican revolution and the Catholic Church, 1910–1929*. Bloomington: Indiana University Press.

Sigmund, P. E. (1990). *Liberation theology at the crossroads: Democracy or revolution?* Oxford, UK: Oxford University Press.

Smith, B. (1982). *The church and politics in Chile: Challenges to modern Catholicism*. Princeton, NJ: Princeton University Press.

Stoll, D. (1990). *Is Latin America turning Protestant? The politics of Evangelical growth*. Berkeley and Los Angeles: University of California Press.

Tangleman, M. (1995). *Mexico at the crossroads: Politics, the church and the poor*. Maryknoll, NY: Orbis.

Latin America: Modern Period

Since the colonial period, religion and war have been inextricably linked in Latin America. Churches, particularly the Catholic Church, have been organically connected to political and economic power structures and have played a variety of roles in times of conflict. They have allied with oppressive regimes, supported and even participated in liberation movements, and mediated violent conflicts between government armed forces and opposition groups. This article examines the influences that conditioned Catholic involvement in violent conflict as well as the diverse forms that involvement took in distinct countries from the 1960s to the present, focusing in particular on Central and South America. It also addresses the role that Protestants, whose numbers grew exponentially during this period, came to play in situations of conflict.

The Modern Catholic Church: Vatican II, Medellín, and Liberation Theology

A number of events in the 1960s forced the Latin American Catholic Church to break its alliance with the military and landed oligarchy, with which it had formed a triumvirate of power controlling society. The meetings of Vatican II, Medellín, and Puebla dramatically influenced the role the church would play in armed conflict in Latin America. The Second Vatican Council (1962–1965) was convened by Pope John XXIII to discuss theological and pastoral issues internal to the Church, such as faith and style of public worship, but issues formerly considered external to the Church were also addressed, most notably, social justice. One of the most important themes of Vatican II was the opening of the Church to the world, that is, the recognition that the Church must be involved in the realities and problems faced by the people, particularly by the poor. The Pastoral Constitution on the Church in the Modern World, titled *Gaudium et Spes* ("Joys and Hopes"), one of the documents produced as a result of Vatican II, denounces poverty, affirms that the Church must take action to support the poor, and proclaims the right of all people to have what is necessary to live.

Following these meetings, the Second General Conference of Latin American Bishops (CELAM) was held in Medellín, Colombia, in 1968 to reflect on the Church's new role. The bishops strongly denounced the structural injustice of Latin America, affirmed the Church's responsibility to work in solidarity with the poor, and called for *concientización*, or the promotion of political awareness and empowerment of popular sectors. The documents of Medellín condemn the ubiquitous violence in Latin America, including so-called institutionalized violence, that is, all forms of oppression and social injustice. The Conference supported the formation of ecclesial base communities (CEBs) to provide people with the opportunity to meet in small groups to discuss faith and scriptures and to interpret the conditions of their lives through the lens of Catholic doctrine. Although CEBs were not created for political motives, participants came to recognize that they shared common problems and began to learn leadership skills. As a result, they began to mobilize to change their situation.

The conclusions of Vatican II and Medellín were affirmed and deepened at a third CELAM meeting in Puebla, Mexico, in 1979. The concept of the preferential option for the poor, which emerged from the Medellin and Puebla meetings, demanded that the church commit itself to work with and for the poor.

Liberation theology, one of several pastoral lines that emerged from the meetings of Vatican II and Medellín, describes a God who takes the side of the poor and oppressed against the rich and powerful. Liberation theology asserts that oppression and domination are wrong, and that the Church should be working to protect human rights, especially in the defense of a dignified life for all human beings. In the liberation view, sins such as poverty and domination are collective or structural acts. Hence, the poor are not to be blamed for their poverty, because their suffering is due to "structural sin" or institutionalized violence.

This transformation ensured that some Catholics would become part of the violent conflicts in Central and South America in the 1960s and 1970s. Sectors of the Catholic Church came to advocate change, to ally with, and in some cases, to live among the poor. Not all members of the Catholic hierarchy followed the line of Vatican II. Indeed, as conservative members of the hierarchy denounced the conclusions of Medellín and other meetings, there was much conflict within the church about its proper role in addressing social issues.

Revolution in Central America

During the second half of the twentieth century, Central America was fraught with war and violence. The roots of Guatemala's civil war (1960–1996) can be found in the U.S.-sponsored coup that ousted elected president Jacobo Arbenz (1913–1971) in 1954. Some 75,000 people died in El Salvador's civil war (1980–1992) fought between the revolutionary opposition force the Farabundo Martí National Liberation Front (FMLN) and the government's army. In Nicaragua, the Sandinista Liberation Front (FSLN) ousted the dictator Anastasio Somoza Debayle (1925–1980) in 1979 and then fought U.S.-supported Contras (counterrevolutionaries) until 1990, when the Sandinistas were defeated in presidential elections. Opening the Church to the world meant giving up pretensions of political neutrality and becoming involved in these conflicts.

CEBs played a decisive role in Central American popular movements in the 1960s and 1970s, a time when military governments repressed labor unions and popular political organizations. Through participation in CEBs, people gained a vocabulary of protest founded in Catholic doctrine and an organizational structure to facilitate their struggle for social justice. Although the Church sought to maintain a separation between faith and politics, it recognized that faith could engender popular political organizing, and a number of political groups grew out of CEBs.

Catholic pastoral workers, from bishops to priests and nuns, played an important role in criticizing the abuses of repressive regimes. For example, Nicaraguan clergy influenced by Vatican II and Medellín denounced the Somoza dictatorship and supported the national movement that ousted him. Following the Sandinista victory, Catholic clergy served as representatives in the Sandinista government. Although these priests believed their political roles to be in keeping with the conclusions of Medellín, the Nicaraguan Church hierarchy with the support of the Pope asked them to either resign or to withdraw from the priesthood. Indeed, while a significant minority of Catholic clergy advocated social change, much of the hierarchy remained staunch advocates of the status quo.

The military responded to Catholic-based activism by violently suppressing representatives of these movements. When the Salvadoran priest Rutilio Grande, a supporter of CEBs who encouraged peasant farmers to organize, was machine-gunned to death in 1977, Archbishop Oscar Romero (1917–1980) responded by closing El Salvador's Catholic schools and canceling masses for three days. In a Lenten sermon in 1980, Romero called on military personnel to defy orders to kill innocent people, and days later the military responded by having Archbishop Romero shot while saying mass. Salvadorans engaged in the struggle for social justice identified Romero as a martyr who died for his religious beliefs and as a model for their faith-based activism. In the year of Romero's death, military personnel in El Salvador also raped and murdered four churchwomen from the United States, drawing international attention to human-rights violations. In 1989 the military again targeted clergy, murdering six Jesuits, their cook, and her daughter.

The situation in Guatemala closely paralleled that of El Salvador, but the violence was more intense and as a result the potential for political engagement less actualized. By 1981 some one hundred religious personnel had fled Guatemala because of assassinations, and CEBs were virtually clandestine. By adopting the "option for the poor," Catholic clergy became identified with opposition to the status quo and thus appeared a threat to the military and the landed oligarchy.

In Mexico's southern state of Chiapas, Bishop Samuel Ruiz Garcia (b. 1924) led his diocese to denounce poverty and oppression of the region and worked to empower indigenous peoples to become leaders within the Church. In January 1994, the Zapatista Army of National Liberation (EZLN), composed primarily of indigenous peoples and peasant farmers, occupied a number of towns and demanded democracy, land, indigenous rights, health care, and education, and other rights. Bishop Ruiz's diocese did not condone armed violence, but several Zapatista leaders had participated in the pastoral process of his diocese before joining the EZLN.

Military Rule in South America and the Catholic Church

In South America in the last four decades of the twentieth century, the Catholic Church did not have a unified response toward the military regimes; some laity and members of the hierarchy supported these regimes while others opposed them. Immediately following the 1964 coup in Brazil, sectors of the Church affiliated with the military. However, by the end of the 1960s, the National Conference of Brazilian Bishops formally denounced the violence, repression, poverty, and human-rights abuses associated with the military government. In addition, the Catholic Church played a prominent role in supporting democratization, creating social development programs, and strengthening civil society. CEBs were particularly important in Brazil where they provided space for group discussion at a time when unions, popular organizations, and student groups were under attack.

In Chile members of the Catholic hierarchy actively opposed the dictatorship of Augusto Pinochet (b. 1915; in power from 1973 to 1990) by denouncing human-rights abuses, protecting opposition organizations, defending the thousands of people arrested after the 1973 coup, and sponsoring social programs through its Vicariate of Solidarity. When the government shut down or attacked political parties, unions, university associations, human-rights organizations, and other groups, Catholic churches provided a crucial protected space in which people could meet.

In contrast to the cases of Brazil and Chile, the bishops of Argentina played an important role in legitimizing military rule during the "Dirty War" (1976–1983), a time of massive human-rights abuses, including the disappearance of an estimated 8,000 to 30,000 people. The military junta under the leadership of General Jorge Rafael Videla (b. 1925 in power from 1976 to 1983) appealed to the values of Western civilization and Christian democracy as he insisted on the necessity of eliminating subversives to protect national security. Key leaders in the Catholic Church remained silent in the face of repression, and some bishops echoed the junta's assertion that the disappeared were Communists or subversives. In September 2000, Argentina's bishops asked forgiveness for the Church's participation and complicity in the Dirty War.

Peace Negotiations, Truth, and Nonviolent Resistance

Throughout Latin America, because representatives of both the government and opposition forces recognized the Catholic Church as a legitimate authority, Church leaders played a significant role in peace negotiations. For example, the Salvadoran bishop Rivera y Damas (1923–1994) acted as mediator between the FMLN and the government from 1982 to 1990; the Guatemalan bishop Rodolfo Quesada Toruño(b. 1932) served as principal mediator between the government and the Guatemalan National Revolutionary Union guerillas from 1987 to 1994; and in Chiapas, Mexico, Bishop Samuel Ruiz Garcia served as the official mediator between the EZLN and the federal government from 1994 to 1998.

Central to negotiations was the recognition that there could be no peace without truth. In Chile, Argentina, Guatemala, and El Salvador, the Catholic Church established truth commissions, giving victims and, in some cases, perpetrators the opportunity to speak about human-rights violations. These commissions made people's voices of suffering and hope an integral part of historical memory of the periods of violence; they also demonstrated that the military was responsible for the overwhelming majority of human-rights violations in these countries. In 1985 the Archdiocese of São Paulo, Brazil, published a report titled *Brazil: Never Again* after secretly copying official documentation of the massive human-rights abuses of the military government. In Guatemala, just two days after presenting the conclusions of the 1998 Recovery of Historical Memory project (REMHI), Bishop Juan Gerardi (1923–1998) was killed by men acting under military orders.

Catholics and Protestants throughout Latin America have actively worked toward peace and justice by engaging in religiously based actions—fasts, pilgrimages, prayer—to protest injustice and work toward social change. One of the most well-known figures of nonviolent resistance is Argentina's Adolfo Pérez Esquivel (b. 1931), a Catholic, the founder of the Christian Service for Peace and Justice (SERPAZ). Pérez Esquivel won the 1980 Nobel Prize for Peace in recognition of his work for justice and human rights in Argentina and throughout Latin America. A very small number of priests took part in violent resistance, the most well-known being Columbian priest Camilo Torres (b. 1929) who joined the Columbian guerillas in 1965 and fought with them until 1966, when he was killed in combat. Overall the Catholic Church has promoted nonviolent means of resistance.

Protestants

The period of crisis and violence in Latin America corresponded with a dramatic increase in participation in Protestant mainline and evangelical denominations. The number of Protestants in Latin America grew from 5 million in the 1950s to over 20 million by 1980. Currently, around 10 to 15 percent of Latin Americans (well over 40 million people) are Protestant, while in some areas, such as Guatemala and Mexico's state of Chiapas, Protestants compose 20 to 30 percent of the population.

Although they were less prominent than Catholics, Protestants both resisted and collaborated with military regimes. In Chile, within weeks of the 1973 coup, Catholic, Methodist, Lutheran, and other churches formed the Committee for Cooperation for Peace in Chile (COPACHI). The Catholic bishop Fernando Ariztía Ruuiz (b. 1925) and the Lutheran bishop Helmut Frenz (b. 1933) acted as copresidents of COPACHI, which sought to protect people from abuse by the military government. But some Protestants aided the regime by sending a large delegation of laity and pastors to visit Pinochet and publishing a declaration of support in 1974.

Catholics formed the largest contingent of Christians supporting the opposition in Nicaragua and El Salvador, yet Protestants also participated. During El Salvador's Civil War, Lutherans, Episcopalians, and the Baptist Assembly took a progressive stance in supporting the opposition movements as well as the peace negotiations in the 1980s. In 1981, Salvadoran Catholic and Protestant organizations jointly issued a statement of support for the opposition movement. In Nicaragua, some Protestants supported or joined the Sandinistas in opposition to the Somoza dictatorship. Beginning in the final years of Nicaragua's Civil War, the Council of Evangelical Churches of Nicaragua (CEPAD) promoted dialogue and mediation at the local level in conflict-ridden zones.

Some scholars have suggested that in Guatemala people converted to Protestantism to protect themselves from the military. Throughout most of the civil war, the Guatemalan military targeted indigenous Catholic catechists and Catholic clergy, making conversion appear a pragmatic choice. The perception that conversion might protect people from military reprisals increased when Efraín Ríos Montt (b. 1926), a retired general and an elder in the Pentecostal church, gained power in a military coup in 1982. Montt ruled during the worst military abuses of the civil war, and justified the repression as a Christian holy war against evil. In Guatemala indigenous converts to Protestantism became a key force in the civil patrols organized by the military to fight the insurgents.

From 1980 to 1992 a Maoist guerilla group, Sendero Luminoso (Shining Path), waged a devastating war against the Peruvian national government. In this conflict, Protestants were killed both by government military forces, which mistook them for Senderistas, and by the guerillas, who viewed Protestants as a threat to their movement. Despite this targeting, the number of converts to Protestantism increased dramatically during the height of the violence in the 1980s. As was true in Guatemala, Protestants became a crucial force in civil patrols considered to be largely responsible for defeating Sendero Luminoso.

As the end of the twentieth century brought a transition to democracy in much of Latin America, military conflict lessened in many areas, but social conflict and institutional violence continued. A significant number of religious leaders and laity in diverse churches continue to promote the right to a dignified life and to draw attention to human-rights violations.

Christine Kovic
Susan Fitzpatrick Behrens

See also Liberation Theology; Millenarian Violence: Latin America; Roman Catholicism: Theology and Colonization

Further Reading

Archdiocese of Guatemala. (1999). *Guatemala: Never again!* Maryknoll, NY: Orbis Books, Catholic Institute for International Relations, Latin American Bureau.

Archdiocese of São Paulo. (1998). *Torture in Brazil: A shocking report on the pervasive use of torture by Brazilian military governments, 1964–1979*. Austin: University of Texas Press.

Berryman, P. (1984). *Religious roots of rebellion: Christians in Central America's revolutions*. Maryknoll, NY: Orbis Books.

Berryman, P. (1987). *Liberation theology: The essential facts about the revolutionary movement in Latin America and beyond*. New York: Pantheon Books.

Cleary, E. (1985). *Crisis and change: The church in Latin America today*. Maryknoll, NY: Orbis Books.

Cleary, E. (1997). *The struggle for human rights in Latin America*. Westport, CT: Praeger Press.

Cleary, E., & Stewart-Gambino, H., (Eds.). (1997). *Power, politics and Pentecostals in Latin America*. Boulder, CO: Westview Press.

Dorr, D. (1983). *Option for the poor: A hundred years of Vatican social teaching*. Maryknoll, NY: Orbis Books.

Garrard-Burnett, V., & Stoll, D., (Eds.). (1993). *Rethinking Protestantism in Latin America*. Philadelphia: Temple University Press.

Klaiber, J., S. J. (1998). *The church, dictatorships, and democracy in Latin America*. Maryknoll, NY: Orbis Books.

Lancaster, R. (1988). *Thanks to God and the revolution: Popular religion and class consciousness in the new Nicaragua*. New York: Columbia University Press.

Levine, D. (Ed.). (1986). *Religion and political conflict in Latin America*. Chapel Hill and London: University of North Carolina Press.

Levine, D. (1992). *Popular voices in Latin American Catholicism*. Princeton, NJ: Princeton University Press.

Mainwaring, S., & Wilde, A., (Eds.). (1989). *The progressive church in Latin America*. Notre Dame, IN: University of Notre Dame Press.

Martin, D. (1990). *Tongues of fire: The explosion of Protestantism in Latin America*. Oxford, UK: Blackwell.

Peterson, A. (1997). *Martyrdom and the politics of religion: Progressive Catholicism in El Salvador's civil war*. Albany: State University of New York Press.

Serbin, K. (2000). *Secret dialogues: Church-state relations, torture, and social justice in authoritarian Brazil*. Pittsburgh, PA: University of Pittsburgh Press.

Smith, B. (1982). *The church and politics in Chile: Challenges to modern Catholicism*. Princeton, NJ: Princeton University Press.

Smith, C. (1996). *Resisting Reagan: The U.S. Central America peace movement*. Chicago: University of Chicago Press.

Stoll, D. (1990). *Is Latin America turning Protestant?* Berkeley and Los Angeles: University of California Press

Weschler, L. (1998). *A miracle, a universe: Settling accounts with torturers*. Chicago: University of Chicago Press.

Williams, P. (1989). *The Catholic church and politics in Nicaragua and Costa Rica*. Pittsburgh, PA: University of Pittsburgh Press.

Liberation Theology

Liberation theology is a generic term for a range of theologies concerned with interpreting and mobilizing the Christian faith and mission in connection with contemporary social movements struggling against different forms of oppression. Among them: Latin American liberation theology; feminist, womanist, and *mujerista* (Latina feminist) theologies; African-American, Asian, and Latino theologies in the United States; ecotheologies; gay, lesbian, transsexual, and transgender theologies; some versions of African and Asian theologies.

In spite of the differences between and among them, these theological movements share several common features. First, they express the religious, spiritual, and ethical reflection of Christian groups engaged in social movements seeking radical social change. Second, these theologies promote ideological and institutional change in defense of the claims and rights of victims of oppression and pursue alternative arrangements and worldviews that may achieve liberation in church and society.

Finally, their theological method follows three distinct strategies with many variations. First, these theologies engage in ideological and ethical critique of practices, structures, and ideologies that promote and sustain particular forms of oppression (e.g., class, gender, race) in society and religious communities. Second, there is a deconstruction and critique of religious practices, sources, ideas, policies, institutions, and historical accounts that consent and promote, or ignore and dismiss, distinctive forms of oppression. Third, there is a retrieval and reconstruction of all these sources, policies, institutions, and historical accounts in making the case for Christian participation in liberation struggles. This last step is done in critical dialogue with contemporary secular theories and discourses of liberation, the popular religious practices and insights of poor and oppressed Christians resisting oppression; and the political and religious practices and ideas of militant Christians already involved in struggles against oppression. The efforts in constructing a theology of liberation seek to formulate a theological, ethical and pastoral vision that may mobilize and sustain Christians in the struggle for liberation in church and society.

Latin American Liberation Theology

Latin American liberation theology has dealt from its origin in the mid-1960s with practical and theoretical issues related to the use of violence by Christians. This is due to at least three factors: (a) the continuous presence and challenge of revolutionary movements in Latin American countries, (b) the option of many Christians to support or participate in such liberation efforts, and (c) the theoretical impact of Marxism inacademic and political circles. A minority of Catholic and Protestant Christians in many countries has joined the ranks of both militant pacifist and revolutionary movements to protest and change conditions of economic, political, social, and cultural oppression of majorities (the poor, peasants, urban workers) and minorities (indigenous people, women, blacks). From the early call of Camilo Torres Restrepo (1965), the Colombian revolutionary priest, to the manifesto of Christians for Socialism in Chile (1971), to the triumph of the Sandinista Revolution in Nicaragua (1979), to the death of martyr Archbishop Oscar Romero (1917–1980) in El Salvador, to the struggle of indigenous people in Chiapas (1994), Mexico, there has been a steady stream of liberationist Christians opting for radical social change. Christian participation in liberation struggles has resulted in tens of thousands of known and unknown martyrs, persecuted and tortured survivors, and disappeared, displaced, and exiled people. It is from these militant sectors in churches that theology of liberation emerged.

Arguments for Social Change

Contrary to popular belief, not all liberation theologians in Latin America have endorsed armed revolution as a mean for liberation; others have defended the option of nonviolent resistance. The majority and leading representatives of the movement have supported the idea of "just revolution or insurrection" as last resort (Camilo Torres, Gustavo Gutiérrez, José Míguez Bonino). This position differentiates itself from and criticizes four other positions on resistance: revolution as the only mean for change; the idea of a holy war; nonresistance (conscientious objection); and nonviolent resistance. However, a significant number of liberationist Christians and theologians have argued for nonviolent resistance (Hélder Cámara, Oscar Romero).

Although differing in the use of violence as a mean for sociopolitical change, most Latin American liberation theologians share similar analysis and critique of the system in place, the goals to pursue, and the religious-ethical reasons for radical change. In general, liberationist Christians in Latin America have justified their commitment to social change by integrating components of two major sources: the Christian tradition and some sort of radical social theory or ideology, like Marxism. In supporting their commitment to social change, they develop a political, ethical, and religious reasoning that involves a number of specific claims.

Political and Economic Arguments

The first claim is that the capitalist system generates a disparity favoring rich and powerful minorities. This divide between the haves and have-nots is expressed in massive poverty and its deadly consequences; economic exploitation of workers and peasants; high unemployment or underemployment; denationalization of the economy and excessive dependency on foreign capital; increasing national and international debt; limited resources to attend to general social needs and massive funding for projects and defense benefiting the few; government corruption; unequal distribution of and access to wealth, services, and goods.

Second, this economic situation generates the conditions for class and social conflict that, along with other unmet basic social needs and the violation of human rights by the state, has resulted in the escalation of institutional violence and popular counterviolence. In many countries the economic and political control of the elites has contributed to the collapse or corruption of democratic processes and institutions, leaving very few or no effective means for opposition and social change. In other cases, the instauration of authoritarian governments or military juntas has led to the debunking of democratic institutions; the proscription and elimination of organized opposition; violent repression by police, military, and paramilitary groups.

Finally, this situation of oppression has received the direct or indirect support of the church's hierarchy, who since colonial times have legitimized the interests of the elites. Oppressors and their allies deny religion or use it to their advantage by promoting spiritualist interpretations of Christianity that call for detachment from social reality and struggles. Other church and political leaders propose reformist theologies that support capitalism and condemn the demonic character of socialism and communism. This whole situation is diagnosed by liberation theologians as one of internal colonialism, external neocolonial dependency, and structural violence, and is considered morally and theologically as inhumane, unjust, and a situation of social sin.

Arguments Posed by Theologians

The main theological arguments developed for participation in social change towards liberation include traditional and new Christian concepts in Catholic and Protestant thought found in church's documents and the work of theologians. The vision of God in these theological works put emphasis on the God of the exodus, who wishes and brings liberation in history; and in Christ the liberator who preached and lived among the poor; resisted and died at the hand of the powerful; and who was resurrected to sustain the hope for a new liberated world. The understanding of the human person constructed by liberation theologians argues for the dignity of free human beings, created in the image of God; the ethical preferential option for the poor, weak, and innocent; and the priority of full human development over development that is simply economic. Further, this understanding of humanity calls for personal and structural conversion in a true revolution; awareness of the social and political nature of human life; the interdependence of the private and the public realms; the unity of theory and practice in ethics and epistemology; and social conflict as part of social reality and change.

Social Arguments

Liberation social ethics insists on the duty to love and do justice to the neighbor; the need for efficacious love mediated by historical actions and social means; the common good as a social goal for churches and governments; the social ends of property; poverty, injustice, and oppression as social evils and expressions of social sin; the state's responsibility for justice, fairness, freedom, and human rights; and peace as a consequence of social justice. There are several other important religious themes informing liberation theologies. Salvation is not only transcendental but also historical and political. The church is called to be: servant of God and the world; sign and sacrament of the Kingdom of God (a kingdom of peace, justice, and freedom); and a church of and for the poor.

The main concern of liberation theologians is the promotion of radical social change as part of Christian mission, and not the use of violence per se. The issue of the people's right to insurrection, as a last resort, is a secondary but realistic concern in light of conflictive and violent social situations they experience.

Arguments for Armed Revolution

The main arguments for justifying the use of violence as a legitimate means for social change are based on concepts and criteria found already in the Christian tradition of just-war theory and the right of people to insurrection under certain conditions. This reasoning includes some of the following claims. Violence is not Christian, but Christians must struggle for social justice and solidarity, without which there is no peace. The first option should be a nonviolent resistance strategy that Denounces and publicly opposes oppression, and promotes structural and personal change. If militant pacifism becomes ineffective because of the opposition or violence of the powerful, then revolution can be a legitimate option as last resort and as an act of legitimate defense. It can be legitimate in the case of an evident and prolonged personal or structural tyranny that violates basic human rights and damages dangerously the common good of the country. It is legitimate if inspired by love for the oppressor and oppressed; for the sake of the liberation of all with a preferential (not exclusive) option for the poor; after a careful and conscientious analysis that predicts a reasonable chance of success with the least amount of violence and damage, and a proportionate chance for the establishment of an alternative and viable social arrangement. Participation in revolution will always be a tragic option in a world marked by sin. It is thought to be an option for Christians only after all other peaceful means have been explored, and there is no other way out to promote social change toward legitimate goals, for the right reasons, with the correct attitudes, the maximum restraint in the use of violent means, and the willingness to avoid and if necessary correct new oppressive conditions in a postrevolutionary situation.

Arguments for Nonviolent Resistance

Those who favor nonviolent resistance are interested in promoting radical change through organized non-collaboration, disobedience, and dialogue, but without the use of violence as a means for change and/or self-defense. They differentiate between and oppose several forms of violence: (a) institutionalized violence, that is, the adverse results on majorities generated by an unjust socioeconomic and political systems that benefit a minority in power; (b) repressive violence of the state or the use of violence by state security forces to contain the aspirations and change efforts of the majority; (c) terrorist violence of right or left extremist groups; (d) spontaneous or not calculated or organized violence used for self-defense in response to illegitimate acts of aggression but marked by desperation and improvisation. Even when they recognize the argument for the legitimate use of violence in the Christian tradition, they favor the power of nonviolent resistance.

Violence is never an end in itself, and cannot be the first choice to promote good or advance human rights. Violence tends to generate more violence, usually with grave unintended results of new injustices, imbalances, and disasters.

Just-war criteria are difficult to apply in today's world and to many forms of contemporary warfare. Changes in structures without changes in consciousness and relationships are ineffectual and not conforming to human dignity. Nonviolent means to promote social justice conform better to the gospel and God of peace, justice, and love, and to Jesus' nonviolent way. Nonviolent resistance calls for a greater balance of beneficence over malficence is more effective in unveiling the violence of the oppressor; helps to deescalate the spiral of violence; resists the temptation of the cult of violence; can contribute to a deeper persuasion and a lasting conviction for the way of peace, even at the price of martyrdom.

Luis Rivera-Rodriguez

See also Latin America: Modern Period; Millenarian Violence: Latin America; Roman Catholicism: Theology and Colonization

Further Reading

Abbott, W. M. (Ed). (1966). *The documents of Vatican II.* New York: Herder & Herder.

Cámara, H. (1971). *Spiral of violence* (D. Couling, Trans.). Denville, NJ: Dimension Books.

Cámara, H. (1984). *Hoping against all hope* (M. J. O'Connell, Trans.). Maryknoll, NY: Orbis Books.

Cámara, H. (1987). *Questions for living* (R. R. Barr, Trans.). Maryknoll, NY: Orbis Books.

Cámara, H. (1993). *Utopias peregrines* [Pilgrim utopias]. Recife, Brazil: Editora Universitária da Universidade Federal de Pernambuco.

Castro, D. (Ed.). (1999). *Revolution and Revolutionaries: Guerrilla Movements in Latin America.* Wilmington, DE: Scholarly Resources Inc.

Centro de Estudios y Publicaciones. (1973). *Signos de liberación: Testimonios de la iglesia en América Latina, 1969–1973* [Signs of liberation: Testimonies of the Church in Latin America]. Lima, Perú: Centro de Estudios y Publicaciones.

Centro de Estudios y Publicaciones. (1983). *Signos de vida y fidelidad: Testimonios de la iglesia en América Latina, 1978–1982* [Signs of life and faithfulness: Testimonies of the Church in Latin America]. Lima, Perú: Centro de Estudios y Publicaciones.

Concha, M. J. I. (1977). *Cristianos por la revolución en América Latina* [Christians for revolution in Latin America]. Chapultepec Morales, Mexico: Editorial Grijalbo.

Eagleson, J. & Scharper, P. J. (Eds.) (1979). *Puebla and beyond: Documentation and commentary* (J. Drury, Trans.). Maryknoll, NY: Orbis Books.

García, I. (1987). *Justice in Latin American theology of liberation.* Atlanta, GA: John Knox Press.

Gutierrez, G. (1998). *A theology of liberation: History, Politics, and Salvation* (Sister C. Inda and J. Eagleson, Eds. & Trans.; Rev. ed.). Maryknoll, New York: Orbis Books.

Lora, Carmen, et. al. (1978). *Signos de lucha y esperanza: Testimonios de la iglesia en América Latina, 1973–1978* [Signs of struggle and hope: Testimonies of the Church in Latin America]. Lima, Perú:

Medellín, conclusiones: La iglesia en la actual transformación de América Latina a la luz del Concilio.

Míguez Bonino, J. (1976). *Christians and Marxists.* Grand Rapids, MI: Wm. B. Eerdmans.

Míguez Bonino, J. (1983). *Toward a Christian political ethics.* Philadelphia: Fortress Press.

Romero, Oscar. (1981). *A martyr's message of hope: Six homilies by Archbishop Oscar Romero.* Kansas City, MO: Celebration Books.

Romero, Oscar. (1985). *Voice of the voiceless: The four pastoral letters and other statements* (M. J. Walsh, Trans.). Maryknoll, NY: Orbis Books.

Romero, Oscar. (1988). *The violence of love: The pastoral wisdom of Archbishop Oscar Romero* (J. R. Brockman, Compiler and Trans.). San Francisco: Harper & Row.

Silva Gotay, S. (1980). *El pensamiento Cristiano revolucionario en América Latina y el Caribe* [Christian revolution thought in Latin America and the Caribbean]. Salamanca, Spain: Ediciones Sígueme.

Smith, C. (1991). *The emergence of liberation theology: Radical religion and social movement theory*. Chicago: The University of Chicago Press.

Torres, Camilo. (1970). *Cristianismo y revolución* (O. Maldonado, G. Oliviéri, & G. Zabala, prologue, selection, and notes). N.p.: Ediciones Era.

Lutheran Germany

The German religious reformer Martin Luther (1483–1546) was the foremost leader of the Protestant Reformation (a sixteenth-century religious movement marked ultimately by rejection or modification of some Roman Catholic doctrine and practice and establishment of the Protestant churches). Luther is notable as the first outspoken opponent of medieval Christian crusade ideology. From his day to the present he has been criticized from some quarters for his stance on political matters, mainly with an accusation that he demanded unquestioned subservience of subjects and lower magistrates to their higher authorities; for example, the U.S. author William Shirer in his best-selling book, *The Rise and Fall of the Third Reich* (1959), charged him with responsibility for obedience to German leader Adolf Hitler and the Nazi regime.

To the European mind after the Middle Ages, God established the Holy Roman Empire, centered on Germany, and the papacy as his highest authorities in the temporal and spiritual spheres of life. Yet, power in sixteenth-century Germany was shared contentiously between the empire on the one side and many principalities and some self-ruling cities on the other. Government everywhere was in the hands of aristocratic and patrician elites; common people were simply subjects without recognized political voice. Lutheran political thinking reflected this situation. In considering the issue of war, Luther, his colleague Philipp Melanchthon (1497–1560), and other Lutherans focused on whether violence can ever be in accord with Christian teaching and, if so, how Christians may participate in it. For them warfare also demanded consideration of the question of whether disobedience or even resistance to higher authorities is ever acceptable. Luther and his followers explored these issues within the context of his teachings on two kingdoms and two governments *(zwei Reiche, zwei Regimente)*. The Peasants' War of 1524–1525, Turkish incursion on the southeastern border of the Holy Roman Empire in the same decade, and hostility and threat of war from Catholic princes in Germany and Emperor Charles V (1500–1558) during that and following decades shaped their views.

Luther's Doctrine of Two Kingdoms and Two Governments

Contrasting with medieval papal assertions of predominance, Luther insisted upon the independence of the secular realm and secular government from the Church and its authorities. One sees this from early in his Reformation years, principally in his *Temporal Authority: To What Extent It Should Be Obeyed* (1523). In Luther's view, in the earthly paradise God established two realms of existence: a spiritual kingdom of salvation and a temporal kingdom to order natural life *(zwei Reiche)*. The entrance of sin introduced an earthly battleground between legions of God and Satan; somewhat confusingly to his readers Luther spoke of these two entities also as kingdoms—a kingdom of God and a kingdom of Satan. Whereas Satan's kingdom dominates earthly existence, throughout history God has gathered a small crowd of believers to himself. A spiritual government of the Word and a temporal government of the sword *(zwei Regimente)* are God's instruments to prevent Satan's destruction of his two kingdoms; the measure of law, order, and peace achieved by temporal government not only preserves this world, but also allows his small Church to continue.

Each government has its own place and purpose in God's plan for his creation. The spiritual is an inward government, without external force; here ministers are entrusted with preaching the Word of salvation, but all Christians stand equal to each other before God. Reason, natural law, and, because sin prevails in this life, coercion are the tools of temporal government; here inequality of persons exists. Because reason and wisdom are the marks of good rulers, non-Christian rulers and heathen governments can perform their tasks admirably, although Luther preferred true Christian rulers and magistrates because they would serve in Christian love, concerned solely about the welfare of those under their charge.

Satan seeks to undermine the two governments. He gets spiritual and temporal authorities to interfere in each other's government. Luther pointed to the pope's claims of supremacy over temporal government and to rulers who legislate in religious matters, forcing their beliefs on their subjects. (He came to believe that Christian rulers can assist church reform as long as they do not introduce the sword into the Church.) In the spiritual sphere the papacy imposes its own laws as binding upon believers. Satan tempts temporal rulers and magistrates to turn their office to their own gain, neglecting their duties to those in their charge, and tempts subjects to rebel, which in Luther's view can result only in destruction of government and chaos.

Jesus's injunction in the Sermon on the Mount to turn the other cheek (Matthew 5:39, RSV) led a few people of the time—the Anabaptist forefathers of the Mennonites and Amish—to conclude that the sword is forbidden to Christians and therefore participation in an office of temporal government. Drawing on his two kingdoms doctrine, Luther responded that in their own cause Christians can indeed have no recourse to violence, accepting suffering instead, but they also have callings in the temporal world as magistrates or subjects, and here they serve for the care and protection of their fellow humans—when necessary with coercion.

Luther's Views of War and Rebellion

Luther addressed the specific issues relating to war and rebellion briefly in *Temporal Authority*, more fully in *Whether Soldiers, Too, Can Be Saved* (1526), and in treatises and sermons at the time of the Peasants' War and at the height of the Turkish threat in 1529. Armed conflict for him is caused by Satan's objective of destruction. Nevertheless, armed conflict sometimes is a necessary evil and—depending upon the circumstances and manner of conduct—must be pursued. Here he drew upon the just war theory from the Christian tradition, specifically insisting that states may wage only defensive war and may wage it only after exhausting all efforts at negotiation, that civilians must be spared, and that in victory Christians must act mercifully toward the defeated. The Turkish advance had been seen in Central Europe for more than a century as a threat, and already in that there had been calls at the papal and imprial courts for revival of the crusades against Islam. Luther condemned warfare for religion as a monstrous confusion of the two governments. His ire about clergy who involve themselves in any warfare was striking; their vocation is to preach and pray, not to bear arms; God's anger at the notion of papal or bishop's armies leads to their certain defeat. Nor may the emperor lead Christendom in a crusade attacking the Turks; however, he must as the supreme temporal authority defend the empire against any invasion, including that of the Turks.

Throughout the 1520s Luther's intense fear of chaos as well as the disciple Paul's injunction, "Let every person be subject to the governing authorities" (Romans 13:1, RSV), dictated his consideration of violence of subjects toward all authority or even of lower magistrates toward higher authorities. They may have just grievances against their lords, as he recognized in many of the peasants' demands in his treatise, *Admonition to Peace*, in 1525, but he recognized therein no just cause of rebellion. Good never comes of revolt: He wrote, "There is as great a difference between changing a government and improving it as the distance from heaven to earth" (Luther 1955–1980, 46, 111–112). Whereas in the *Admonition* he criticized the nobility for their utter lack of equity toward their peasants, when the latter would not desist from riot, he issued his infamous *Against the Robbing and Murdering Hordes of Peasants*, in which he called on lords to strike down rebelling peasants without mercy. Nor would he accept an alliance of Lutheran princes against Charles V, despite his threats. He brushed aside the princes' legal arguments to justify the alliance, such as that the emperor would not be in compliance with his own coronation oath if he attacked. Luther accepted only their wars against equals (other princes) and only when fought in self-defense and for the sole purpose of protecting their subjects.

Warfare and the Issue of Resistance to Higher Authority

Luther's *Temporal Authority* was prompted by orders of Catholic princes that subjects turn in any copies of his translation of the New Testament in their possession. Because for him secular government rules only over the external person, and the Bible is God's word, necessary for salvation, Luther advised their subjects to refuse to comply. They were to engage solely in passive disobedience, however, accepting any punishment that ensues. He gave similar advice three years later in *Whether Soldiers:* When a Christian soldier ascertains that his prince is pursuing an unjust war, he must refuse to participate on pain of his eternal soul. To cause death in unjust violence is to commit murder; that soldier must instead accept punishment by his prince, even if it is capital punishment. (He also advised soldiers to flee the battlefield when they saw flags of the pope or bishops flying at the front of their own army!)

Luther's advice of passive disobedience in the 1520s appeared in widely read treatises; a fruit of twentieth-century scholarship was the uncovering of Luther's espousal of active resistance in the 1530s. Heightened fear of imperial intervention in Germany led Protestant princes to pressure Luther and his fellow theologians at the University of Wittenberg to accept armed resistance to the emperor and thereby permit a Protestant political alliance. Their jurists presented a constitutional argument that the princes and city councils were the emperor's partners—not agents—in governing the empire and consequently had the duty to protect their own subjects from him, if necessary. Also, they argued that there was a natural right of self-defense (seen as a duty to protect family and neighbors) and that in Roman and Germanic law a superior forfeited his authority when he acted beyond his jurisdiction or with undue force. The theologians conceded at this point, and in 1532 the princes and cities formed the Schmalkaldic League. As the decade progressed Luther came more and more to regard Charles V's threat in the context of an apocalyptic struggle between the papal Antichrist and God's people, with the emperor now seen simply as the pope's agent. Those walls that Luther had erected between spiritual and secular governments began to show cracks when he now spoke of a role for princes to protect God's people.

Months after Luther's death Charles V brought on the Schmalkaldic War, and by April 1547 he had defeated the Lutheran forces. In the meantime, Melanchthon and his fellow Wittenberg theologians flooded the book market with tracts to justify Protestant resistance to the emperor. They printed materials from the previous decade that showed the change in thinking about resistance, and they added treatises of their own. Another resistance argument appeared. From the late 1520s onward Luther augmented his two kingdoms discourse with the notion of three hierarchies (he often called these the "orders of creation"): the family with its head, the father, alongside the spiritual and temporal governments. Fathers and clergy have the duty, so the argument went, of opposing erring rulers. After the war one Lutheran city, Magdeburg, managed to hold out against the imperial forces. In 1550 its pastors issued the *Magdeburg Confession (Confession, Instruction, and Admonishment of the Pastors and Preachers of the Christian Churches of Magdeburg)*, which brought together under one cover all of the previous thinking on political resistance. The book was soon known in Calvinist Geneva and from there inspired and help shape the literature of revolution among Calvinists in France (the Huguenots), the Netherlands, Scotland, and England.

Although Luther's early advice of passive disobedience was clearly aimed at the common person, most scholars have insisted that the Lutherans limited leadership in armed resistance to lower magistrates and noblemen. The resistance argument based upon the constitutional structure of the empire could work only for lower authorities, and because the Calvinists took only that argument from the Lutherans, their literature clearly restricts the duty of resistance to lower authorities. Doubtlessly Luther and Melanchthon and the others in the 1530s had solely that intent. This author, however, has found a change in the literature produced in the crisis of the Schmalkaldic War. In employing self-defense, apocalyptic imagery of forces of the Antichrist, and especially orders of creation in their call to Lutheran Germany to resist the emperor, the Wittenberg theologians blurred the distinction between political authorities and subjects—for example, praising subjects such as William Tell for acts of tyrannicide (the act of killing a tyrant). The American scholar Oliver Olson (1972) has observed in the *Magdeburg Confession* a similar call to subjects to resist.

Lutherans, the State, and War

Luther claimed that in comparison to the medieval situation he had established a new dignity as well as a greater responsibility for the state. He could call princes "scoundrels" and yet insist that their offices were divinely established and that they must be obeyed (almost always). Some scholars argue that in church affairs he handed over too much authority to rulers, observing, for example, that when he perceived in the late 1520s that local parishes needed reform, he accepted their direction as "bishops in necessity" *(Notbishof)*. His revival of just war theory is important, although because his age had almost constant warfare, his demand that princes fight only defensive wars seems to have had little effect. Yet, his rejection of the crusade undercut clerical pretensions to use political means to advance God's kingdom. A recent study of Luther's rejection of any Turkish crusade states that "he charted new territory" and that contained in his opposition are "the seeds of an admission that the Turks are a God-permitted authority that deserves the obedience of its subjects (even its Christian ones)" (Miller 2002, 41, 52).

In considering German Lutherans and war, the most controversial issue is the question of Luther and obedience to higher authority. Claims that he demanded unquestioning obedience from subjects, such as William Shirer's assertion, seem substantiated by *Against the Robbing and Murdering Hordes of Peasants*. In fact, however, circumstances might dictate that subjects and lower magistrates must disobey or even resist higher authority. Anyone seeking an answer to the question of obedience to Hitler might better examine the political messages of eighteenth- and nineteenth-century Lutheran and Catholic clergy, both of whom were by then essentially state servants. What most distinguishes the Lutherans of the Reformation on the issue of war is their resistance theory; through its influence upon Calvinist thought it became a source of the liberal revolutionary tradition that led through the English philosopher John Locke (1632–1704) to the American Revolution.

Luther D. Peterson

Further Reading

Althaus, P. (1972). *The ethics of Martin Luther* (R. C. Schutz, Trans.). Philadelphia: Fortress Press.

Cargill Thompson, W. D. J. (1984). *The political thought of Martin Luther*. Totowa, NJ: Barnes and Noble Books.

von Friedeburg, R. (2002). *Self-defence and religious strife in early modern Europe: England and Germany, 1530–1680*. Aldershot, UK: Ashgate Publishing.

Kirchner, H. (1972). *Luther and the Peasants' War* (D. Jodock, Trans.). Philadelphia: Fortress Press.

Luther, M. (1955–1980). *Luther's works* (Vols. 45–47). St. Louis, MO: Concordia Publishing.

Miller, G. J. (2002). Fighting like a Christian: The Ottoman advance and the development of Luther's Doctrine of Just War. In D. M. Whitford (Ed.), *Caritas et Reformatio: Essays on church and society in honor of Carter Lindberg* (pp. 41–57). St. Louis, MO: Concordia Publishing.

Olson, O. K. (1972). Theology of revolution: Magdeburg, 1550–1551. *Sixteenth Century Journal, 3*(1), 66–79.

Peterson, L. D. (1987). Melanchthon on resisting the emperor: The *Von der Notwehr Unterricht* of 1547. In J. Friedman (Ed.), *Regnum, Religio, et Ratio: Essays presented to Robert M. Kingdon* (pp. 133–144). Kirksville, MO: Sixteenth Century Journal Publishers.

Scheible, H. (Ed.). (1982). *Das Widerstandsrecht als Problem der deutschen Protestanten 1523–1546* (The right of resistance as a problem of the German Protestants 1523–1546). Gütersloh, Germany: Gerd Mohn Verlag.

Skinner, Q. (1980). The origins of the Calvinist theory of revolution. In B. C. Malament (Ed.), *After the reformation: Essays in honor of J. H. Hexter* (pp. 309–330). Philadelphia: University of Pennsylvania Press.

Stelmachowicz, M. J. (Ed.). (1986). *Peace and the just war tradition: Lutheran perspectives in the nuclear age*. St. Louis, MO: Concordia Publishing.

Whitford, D. M. (2001). *Tyranny and resistance: The Magdeburg Confession and the Lutheran tradition*. St. Louis, MO: Concordia Publishing.

M

Manichaeism

Manichaeism was a religion founded in Mesopotamia during the first half of the third century CE that incorporated aspects of Zoroastrianism, Judaism, Christianity, and Buddhism. It was the only sect emerging from the Near Eastern Gnostic traditions to survive beyond the first three centuries CE and to attain global status. At various points in medieval times its influence extended from France to China and its popularity rivaled Catholic Christianity and Buddhism. The teachings of Manichaeism came to influence conceptions of war, violence, pacifism, and the priesthood, especially in the West.

History of the Movement

Manichaeism was founded by Manes, or Mani (216–276 or 277 CE), a Persian physician who proclaimed himself "the messenger of God come to Babel" and the paraclete (Holy Sprit). He held that God had revealed himself at various times and places in human history: as the Buddha in India, Zoroaster in Persia, and Jesus in Palestine. Mani believed that each of these figures taught that the path to salvation came through gnosis (spiritual knowledge) rather than through faith or acts. In 242 Mani set out to disseminate his message publicly, traveling extensively in central Asia and apparently visiting India and China. While only fragments of his written works survive today, they reveal that Mani certainly had familiarity with the Christian synoptic Gospels and the epistles of Paul, Jewish orthodox and noncanonical texts, Zoroastrianism, and Mahayana Buddhism. Mani's challenges to the Zoroastrian priesthood, the Magi, led to his execution in 276 or 277.

Mani's teachings, however, spread rapidly. By 370 Manichaean churches could be found throughout much of the Roman Empire, from southern France to North Africa. While violently suppressed in the old Roman provinces in the sixth century, Manichaeism continued to flourish in Persia and Chinese Turkisten for centuries, even becoming the state religion of the (Chinese) Uighur empire in 762. A final, significant revival of Manichaeism occurred in Western Europe, especially France, in the eleventh to thirteen centuries. Labeled the Albigensian heresy, its challenge to the Catholic Church was perceived as so great that Pope Innocent III (reigned 1190–1216) ordered a crusade against the "scourge of God," bringing a violent end to the movement.

Cosmology of War

Warfare is at the very heart of the Manichaean mythological worldview. Like the Zoroastrian and Gnostic belief systems that influenced it, Manichaeism portrays the universe in radically dualistc terms. The universe is constituted by two oppositional forces: light and darkness. Light corresponds to the spiritual realm, the realm of goodness. Darkness corresponds to the material and bodily realm, which is evil. History is to be played out in three stages: a golden age when the realms of darkness and light are distinct and separate; a middle age in which light and darkness battle for control of the universe; and a final age in which the realms again will be separated, with the spiritual returning to the realm of light and the material being relegated to the realm of darkness. We presently are in the middle age, the time of the great cosmic battle between the forces of good and evil.

The realm of light is ruled by and equated with God, who is known as the King of Light or the Father of Light. The material realm is ruled by an independent and equally powerful Archon of Darkness or Hyle (matter), who uses the process of creation to trap light in fleshly cell. The two gods are in cosmic battle, with the universe as their battlefield. Christ, the Buddha, and other prophets came to earth to impart to humans knowledge of how to release the light imprisoned within the material realm by the God of Darkness. In some Manichaean depictions, the creator God of Genesis *is* the Archon of Darkness, and Christ is the serpent in the garden, imparting good knowledge to Adam and Eve as a path to liberating the light. In China, Mani himself became known as the Buddha of Light.

Manichaean dualism and its resulting cosmic war are used to account for the existence of evil in the world: Evil emerges in this realm when the Archon of Darkness wins a battle over the good, but not omnipotent, King of Light. The Manichaean cosmology has another important implication: All material creation is evil in its very conception. Humans, being spirit incarnate, are in a tragic and flawed state, subject to evil and ignorance through the imprisonment of their spiritual essences in fleshly bodies.

Manichean Prescriptions about War

Because during this life humans live in the corrupt, material realm, Manichaeanism attempted to separate them from the actions of the Archon of Darkness as much as possible. Manichaean clergy were held to the highest standards of purity: sexual abstinence (since each new birth constituted another spirit imprisoned in the flesh and hence a victory for the forces of Darkness), vegetarianism (since meat was judged to be more highly impure than vegetables), refusal to participate in food preparation (since even the chopping of vegetables harmed the light trapped within them), and abstinence from all forms of violence against human or animal (for the spiritual light could be liberated properly from living entities only by knowledge, not by slaughter).

Significantly, of these priestly prohibitions (likely a reflection of the influence of Buddhism), only the dictate against all forms of killing was required equally of the Manichaean laity, making Manichaeism a completely pacifistic religion in theory. Not surprisingly, the practice was somewhat different, with Manichees who fell short of the pacifistic ideal often attributing their failing to a determinism resulting from their role as pawns in the cosmic battle between the King of Light and the Archon of Darkness.

Augustine, the Manichee

While the influences upon Manichaeism were multiple and varied, the lasting importance of Manichaeism to Western attitudes towards war and violence may be traceable largely to a single man, the profoundly influential Christian bishop and theologian Augustine of Hippo (354–430). Born in North Africa under Roman rule, Augustine served for nine years as a Manichaean novice before his conversion to orthodox Christianity in 386. While the mature Augustine produced strong letters condemning the Manichaeanism of his youth and rejecting its tenets, some scholars observe that he continued to understand the world in Manichaean terms. Augustine established one of the earliest Christian monastic orders on the premise that the spiritual person must separate himself from the temptations of the fleshly realm and embrace abstinence and pacifism. When justifying the laity's participation in war in *City of God*, Augustine offers a rationale that seems to owe much to Manichaean anthropology: In this life, humans are torn between two opposite domains, the fleshly City of Man and the spiritual City of God; their dualistic nature as spiritual beings trapped in fleshly bodies makes the attainment of true and lasting peace impossible in this realm. War, while regrettable, must be used to minimize the victories of the flesh over those of the spirit. Hence, despite the fact that Augustine labeled Manichaeism heretical, scholars believe that Manichaean tenets found their way into the Christian discourse of war by means of Augustine's writings.

Manichaeism and War Today

In contemporary intellectual discussions, Manichaeism is most often used as a perjorative term, describing a radical dichotomy between good and evil that allegedly misconstrues the nature of reality. The U.S. Conference of Catholic Bishops, for example, writes that it is "a Manichean heresy to assert that war is intrinsically evil and contrary to Christian charity" (National Conference of Catholic Bishops 1983, 162). The historian Bernard Lewis claims that the tendency of some forms of modern-day Islam to demonize Christians and Jews as "enemies of God" is attributable to Manichaeism's influenence on Islam. Whether such accusations are fair or not, the Manichaean depiction of the world as a place of cosmic conflict between the forces of the spirit and those of the flesh doubtlessly has had a profound influence on Jewish, Christian, and Muslim discussions of and attitudes toward warfare.

Timothy M. Renick

See also Greek Religions; Indo-European Mythology; Roman Religions; Zoroastrianism

Further Reading

Asmussen, J. (1975). *Manichaean literature: Representative texts*. Delmar, NY: Scholars Facsimiles and Reprints.

Augustine. (1984). *City of God*. New York: Penguin Books.

Barnstone, W. (1984). *The other Bible*. San Francisco: Harper San Francisco.

Brown, P. (1967). *Augustine of Hippo: A biography*. Berkeley and Los Angeles: University of California Press.

Burkitt, F. (1925). *The religion of the Manichess*. Cambridge, UK: Cambridge University Press.

Coyle, J. K. (1997). The idea of the "good" in Manichaeism. In W. Sunderman (Ed.), *Proceedings of the fourth international conference on Manichaeism* (pp. 124–137). Berlin: Claudius Naumann.

Lewis, B. (1990, September). The roots of Muslim rage. *Atlantic Monthly, 266*(3), 47–60.

Lieu, S. (1994). *Manichaeism in Mesopotamia and the Roman east*. New York: E. J. Brill.

National Conference of Catholic Bishops. (1983). The challenge of peace: God's promise and our response (the pastoral letter on war and peace). In J. Elshtain (Ed.), *Just war theory* (pp. 77–168). New York: New York University Press.

Robinson, J. (1977). *The Nag Hammadi libray*. San Francisco: Harper Collins.

Rossbach, S. (1999). *Gnostic wars: The cold war in the context of a history of western spirituality*. Edinburgh, UK: University of Edinburgh Press.

Martyrdom

The most basic meaning of martyrdom is the suffering of a violent death for the sake of adherence to religious law, faith, or any cause despite threats and pressure to do otherwise. The martyr is recognized posthumously for his or her courage and, within the framework of organized religion, is expected to receive transcendent reward. The word derives from the Greek word for witness, *martys*, the meaning of which finds a semantic parallel in the Arabic term for martyr, *shahid*.

Martyrdom beyond Religion

Martyrdom is a political as well as religious act, and like organized violence, social or economic pressure, intimidation, negotiation, and war, martyrdom can be a tool for promoting change. While most of the aforementioned tactics may be employed by any group negotiating power, martyrdom is a tool of the unempowered. Although destroyed by the dominant power, the martyr's very willingness to die is a powerful symbol of the resistance and solidarity of the undergroup. In cultures influenced by the Abrahamic religions (that is, Judaism, Christianity, and Islam), martyrdom is a kind of self-sacrifice symbolic of a sacrificial animal, typically unblemished (Leviticus 1:1–4, 1 Corinthians 5:7, Qur'an 3:140), that is served up to a higher power. As a human sacrifice, it attains an absolute sanctity that serves to delegitimize the authority of the establishment. It imbues sanctity to resisting authority and inspires the undergroup to continue with its resistance.

To be effective, martyrdom must be a public act, and if it is not, it must be publicized after the fact to inspire members of the subgroup while challenging the legitimacy of the empowered. After the act, stories or legends of the martyrdom may become a canonical tradition used for solidarity and educational inspiration even after achieving political dominance. Martyrdom transcends the boundaries of religion and may be committed for deeply held political or ideological as well as religious reasons.

Martyrdom is a statement that survival of the group and its norms takes precedence over survival of the individual, that ideals take precedence over biological self-interest. Nevertheless, even zealots would not normally consider committing this ultimate deed. The most zealous within the wider community of devotees, therefore, sometimes form cells that condition individuals and support them throughout the ordeal leading to the final act.

Before the emergence of Greece and the influence of Hellenic systematic thinking, religion in most of the world tended to be localized and associated with ethnic or tribal groups. The deity or deities were therefore associated only with particular communities. When battles occurred between groups, people often invoked their particular gods, who were understood as fighting

A martyr-saint, depicted in a Fourteenth Century mosaic in the outer narthex of the mosque of Kahrieh Djami, Istanbul.

one another in their own realms while their human worshippers fought on earth. Wars tended to be driven unself-consciously by material needs and were not, at this time, couched in ideological terms. Noncombatants were killed in this kind of conflict, of course, but they were not considered martyrs, as martyrdom requires that death come about because of determined adherence to one's ideals, not as a mere accident or consequence of battles that are not considered ideological.

Martyrdom in Eastern Religions

Martyrdom became possible only when religion was understood as an ideological as well as supernatural system. Religious references to very ancient acts of martyrdom may, in fact, be nothing more than a reading of contemporary ideals back into ancient contexts. This seems to be the case in Zoroastrianism, where (late) tradition fairly unanimously understands the death of Zarathushtra (Zoroaster; c. 628–c. 551 BCE) as a martyrdom within the context of holy wars between the Iranian king Vishtaspa, Zarathushtra's convert, and the great enemy of the faith, the Turanian Arejataspa (or Arjasp). According to the tradition, Zarathushtra was killed with eighty of his priests within the fire temple, and the fire was quenched with their blood.

Such may also be the case with legends of the Buddha collected in later *Jataka* tales, which record the sufferings and deaths of bodhisattvas (those who refrain from the final attainment of enlightenment in order to help others come closer to achieving it) and their disciples, especially while exhibiting the virtues of patience and self-sacrifice. The bodhisattva suffers for the sake of the dharma (Buddhist law), which is often identified with the Buddha himself, though in most cases the persecution is not due to the bodhisattva's being a Buddhist per se. Later teachings in Mahayana Buddhism (the school of Buddhism practiced in China, Korea, Vietnam, and Japan) describe in great detail the gruesome suffering, often self-inflicted, borne for the sake of the dharma. These demonstrate the educational aspect of legendary martyrdom. Whether or not the ancient religious leaders or prophets actually died a martyr's death or were considered to have done so by their contemporaries is irrelevant from the standpoint of the religious system. The tradition establishes the merit of martyrdom and it becomes, by virtue of emulation, an ideal. Such a view was renewed in World War II when Japanese kamikaze pilots were taught to deny the individual self in order to achieve complete enlightenment through Zen teachings.

Martyrdom in the Hebrew Bible

Although some post biblical works and commentaries refer to episodes such as the death of Saul as acts of biblical martyrdom, the Hebrew Bible itself does not exhibit a consciousness of martyrdom aside from the Book of Daniel, the final layer of biblical literature, datable to the Hellenistic period. The Hebrew term used in the later Rabbinic Judaism for martyrdom, *kiddush ha-Shem* (sanctifying God's name), does occur in biblical texts in relation to its antithetical term, *hillul ha-Shem* (Leviticus 22:31–32, Numbers 20:12, Deuteronomy 32:51, Ezekiel chapters 20, 36, 39), but this does not refer in the biblical layers to martyrdom. Even the Book of Daniel does not depict martyrdom as actually having been carried out, but Chapter 3 describes the attempted execution of three Jews, Shadrakh, Meshakh, and Abed-Nego, for refusing, despite coercive force, to worship Nebuchadnezzar's golden statue. The very existence of this narrative in a canonical biblical text demonstrates that late biblical Judaism had begun to absorb the idea of martyrdom in the Hellenistic period.

Martyrdom in Hellenistic Jewish Texts

The works known as the Books of Maccabees depict famous acts of Jewish martyrdom. These works depict Jewish individuals as an underclass being forced by the Hellenistic powers to forsake their religion by violating religious law. The Jews refuse and usually suffer a gruesome death as a result, but not before brave soliloquys extolling the merits of God's true religion and the preference of death to public apostasy, breaking Jewish ritual law, or even the semblance of either of the two (2 Maccabees 6:18–31, 7, 4 Maccabees). The context for these stories is the long war between traditional Judeans and Hellenists, and these acts of martyrdom served as inspiration for the subdominant group of Judeans. The books not only commemorated the subgroup's eventual victory and testified to the authority of its rule, but also encouraged group solidarity and resistance in the face of the temptation to become assimilated. While the term *martyr* does not appear in these texts, the acts portrayed in them demonstrate a clear understanding and adoption of the concept.

Martyrdom in Rabbinic Judaism and Christianity

The fluid expressions of Rabbinic Judaism and Christianity emerge simultaneously as new religious systems, both evolving out of the multicultural and polyglot Semitic-Greco-Roman world. They eventually formed distinct systems, but during the first through fourth centuries CE, they shared ideas so intimately that they were in many ways impossible to distinguish, as their own texts witness (and about which they often complain). One shared aspect was their developing ideas about martyrdom.

In both systems, the words for martyr evolved out of terms that did not originally denote suffering and violent death, and both the terms and the concepts appear to have developed in historical parallel and under a significantly shared worldview. In the pre-Christian, pre-Rabbinic Jewish Hasmonean period represented by 2 Maccabees, the martyr's execution occurred as a result of refusing to violate one's religious integrity. By the fourth century martyrdom is portrayed in both Jewish and Christian texts as being actively sought as a spiritual goal or even a spiritual requirement that was impossible to fulfill in any other manner. The Jewish martyr Akiba ben Joseph (c. 40–c. 135) and the Christian martyr Polycarp (second century) portrayed martyrdom as the ultimate statement of religion. To Akiba, it is the declaration of the oneness of God via the recitation of *Shema Yisra'el*, "Hear O Israel: the Lord God is one!" To Polycarp, it is the declaration of the essence of self: *Christianus sum*, "I am a Christian!" In rabbinic and medieval Jewish texts, martyrdom is depicted as the ultimate and final statement of love for God, and among the Christian moral theologians of the same period it is treated as the chief act of the virtue of fortitude and the ultimate and final confession of love for Christ. While both Polycarp and Akiba lived in the second century, the depictions of their martyrdoms are found in later texts that are of questionable historical value for their historicity but of great importance for the development of the concept of martyrdom.

One significant distinction must be stressed between the Christian and Jewish types of martyrdom during the first centuries of the common era. While both Christians and Jews were martyred for public association with their religion through teaching, preaching, and witnessing, Jews were martyred within a context of open military and political rebellion while Christians were not. In the wake of the nearly absolute destruction of the Jewish communities of Palestine that ensued as a result of the aborted Jewish rebellions of the first and second centuries, later Jewish texts downplayed the militancy of the movements. They stressed the civil rather than military disobedience of the early martyrs, sometimes rewriting stories entirely.

Within the Christian Church there soon developed a cult of the martyrs that included annual commemoration rituals and *Acta Martyrum*, or martyrology books. Martyrdom was seen as an act of conquest whereby the unempowered triumphed over the earthly depravities of the dominant enemy. During the centuries of persecution by the pagan Roman empire, the idea of martyrdom served as a source of encouragement and solidarity and as inspiration to observers outside of the group. Justin Martyr (c. 100–c. 165) and other Church thinkers and leaders claimed that the heroic example of Christians suffering and dying for their religious convictions brought them to conversion. After the Roman empire became a Christian polity, martyrology became a means of community formation and retention against constant centrifugal social and religious forces. Especially in the West, the martyrdom of Jesus in the Crucifixion became the ultimate symbol of the Church.

Judaism also has its martyrologies, but no cult, and this may be attributed to the greater Jewish emphasis on a this-worldly existence. Nevertheless, a particularly powerful martyrology, the Midrash of the Ten Martyrs, entered into Jewish liturgy during the Gaonic period of Jewish literature (sixth–eleventh centuries) and is recited on the Day of Atonement (Yom Kippur). It details the suffering and executions of ten great rabbis for having founded schools for the study of Torah in defiance of an imperial Roman edict. Other famous stories and liturgical poems in the Ashkenazic (European Jewish) world also extol the willingness of martyrs to suffer torture and death, or even jubilantly to take their own lives rather than submit to forced conversion by the dominant Christian power. As in Christianity, then, Jewish martyrdom became an act of belligerence by a powerless group. It was violent and aggressive and often did not help the individuals or even communities involved find a means of survival, but nevertheless it was successful as a means of resistance and in helping the survival of the faith as a whole. This trend in Jewish martyrdom reached its highest point in Europe in the wake of the Crusades (twelfth and thirteenth centuries).

Martyrdom in Islam

Martyrdom in Islam began similarly to the way it began in early Christianity and rabbinic Judaism. Unempowered followers of Muhammad were persecuted by their fellow Meccan tribesmen, and some were killed for civil and religious resistance to the dominant authority. After the *Hijra* (the emigration to Medina) in 632, however, the early Muslim community under the leadership of the Prophet was no longer powerless. While not yet dominant, it could muster a military force. The early Muslim community was confronted with a unique economic problem, however, since it had no economic base after the move to Medina. It therefore mustered forces to conduct raids for economic reasons against enemy tribes and tribal confederations. Such raiding invited reprisals, and the community was then confronted with the problem of raising the requisite forces for survival.

Many early Muslims did not agree to go out to battle, and the Qur'an repeatedly complains of resistance to fighting among the earliest believers (2:216, 3:156, 167–168, 4:72–77, 9:38–39). As a result of this resistance, numerous Qur'an verses stress the rewards for engaging in military campaigns. Qur'an 4:74 states, "Let those fight in the path of God who sell the life of this world for the other. Whoever fights in the path of God, whether he be slain or victorious, on him We shall bestow a vast reward." (See also 3:157, 169, 9:111, 47:4–6.)

The ideal of military martyrdom continued in Islam even after the community became politically and militarily dominant. A large corpus of post-qur'anic traditions extol the rewards of martyrdom, especially in combat. All the martyr's sins will be forgiven, he will be protected from the torments of the grave, he will be married to seventy-two houris (heavenly maidens), and his intercession will be accepted for up to seventy of his relatives.

Not all martyrdom in Islam is military martyrdom. People may also be considered martyrs and granted divine rewards for dying for their beliefs, being murdered while in the service of God (as was the case with some of the early caliphs), dying a natural death while on pilgrimage, or even, according to some authorities, dying from disease or accident while leading a virtuous life. But battlefield martyrs achieve the highest level of martyrdom. According to the scholar Etan Kohlberg, "A martyr's death in combat is the apogee of the believer's aspirations; it is the noblest way to depart this life (hence the motif of the old man who rushes forth to battle) and is a guarantee of God's approval and reward" (Kohlberg 1999, 205).

Praise of battlefield martyrdom may have been a historic necessity in the early stages of Islam's emergence in Arabia, as it was confronted with violent and aggressive resistance, but it remained an ultimate statement of religious aspiration long after Islam had become a dominant, hegemonic religious civilization. Unlike in Judaism, there was no need in Islam to reinterpret martyrdom through war as civil disobedience, because Islam remained a powerful political authority long after its rise to ascendancy. During periods of stress, such as during the Crusades, stories of martyrdom were reinvoked and intensified.

In addition to the basic Islamic veiw of martyrdom in domination, one may also find the paradigmatic martyrdom of the unempowered. The classic expression of this form, observed so prominantly in Christian and Jewish systems, occurs in Shiʿa Islam, the largest minority stream of Islam. For Shiʿites, the martyrdom of Husayn ibn ʿAli (626–680) represents the ultimate act of resistance to illegitimate authority—for Shiʿites, the ruling dynasties of Sunni Islam (the majority stream of Islam). From ʿAli (Muhammad's son-in-law and cousin; c. 600–661), the first Imam (authoritative leader) of Shiʿa Islam, onward, Imams suffered and many were killed, until the last Imam (the seventh or twelfth, depending on the branch of Shiʿa Islam) finally disappeared and remains hidden, to return at some future point to redeem the suffering of the followers of true (that is, Shiʿite) Islamic authority. Sufi expressions of Islam also carry a tradition of martyrdom of the unempowered, epitomized by the death of the ninth-century al-Hallaj.

Martyrdom and the Discourse of Ultimate Meaning

Oppression and war have always caused human suffering and death. Because meaning evolves in relation to prevailing political and intellectual temperaments, the meaning of suffering and death changes as it is interpreted and reinterpreted through what may be called a discourse of martyrdom. The discourse of martyrdom has always related closely to the discourse of war in general. Beginning in the early modern period and continuing into the postmodern, the discourse of war has been increasingly one in which belligerence is considered legitimate only if employed for the pursuit of justice. Because war for material gain is considered illegitimate by virtually all ethicists and social philosophers, even materially driven wars must be couched today in terms of noble ideals. All victims of war, therefore, whether noncombatants or warriors, and whether aggressors or defenders, are increasingly seen as martyrs. Life requires meaning, and death without meaning is no life. Meaningless death in the current age, therefore, has often become death with applied meaning.

Reuven Firestone

See also Hamas; Hellenistic Religions; Hizbullah; Jewish Revolt of 66–73

Further Reading

Abu Daud, Sulayman b. al-Ashʿath al-Sijistani. (1988). *Sunan Abi Daud* (Vols. 1–4). Cairo, Egypt: Dar al-Misriyya wal-Lubnaniyya.

Ben Sasson, H. H. (1971). Kiddush Hashem: Historical aspects. In C. Roth and G. Wigoder (Eds.), *Encyclopaedia Judaica* (Vol. 10, pp. 981–986). Jerusalem: Encyclopaedia Judaica.

Bowersock, G. W. (1995). *Martyrdom and Rome: The Wiles Lectures given at the Queen's University of Belfast*. Cambridge, UK: Cambridge University Press.

Boyarin, D. (1999). *Dying for God: Martyrdom and the making of Christianity and Judaism*. Stanford, CA: Stanford University Press.

Bukhari, M. b. Ismaʿil al-, & Muhsin, M. (Ed.). (1979). *Sahih* (Vols. 1–9). Lahore, Pakistan: Kazi.

Firestone, R. (1999). *Jihad: The origin of Holy War in Islam*. New York: Oxford University Press.

Frend, W. H. C. (1965). *Martyrdom and persecution in the early Church*. Oxford, UK: Blackwell.

Jacobs, I. (1982). Eleazar ben Yair's sanction for martyrdom. *Journal for the Study of Judaism in the Persian, Hellenistic and Roman Period, 13*(2), 183–186.

Kohlberg, E. (1999) *Shahid*. In H. A. R. Gibbs, B. Lewis, C. Pellat, C. Bosworth, et al. (Eds.). *Encyclopaedia of Islam* (2nd ed, Vol 9, pp. 203–207). Leiden, Netherlands: Brill.

Lamm, N. (1971). Kiddush Ha-shem and Hillul Ha-shem. In C. Roth and G. Wigoder (Eds.), *Encyclopaedia Judaica* (Vol 10, pp. 977–986). Jerusalem: Encyclopaedia Judaica.

Maimonides, M. (1979). *Iggeret Hashemad*. In M.D. Rabinowitz (Ed.), *Iggrot HaRambam* [Letters of Maimonides] (pp. 13–68). Jerusalem: Mossad Haravd Kook.

Massignon, L. (1982). *Passion of al-Hallaj: Mystic and martyr of Islam* (Vols. 1–4). Princeton, NJ: Princeton University Press.

Peters, R. (1996). *Jihad in classical and modern Islam*. Princeton, NJ: Marcus Wiener.

Rajak, T. (1997). Dying for the law: The Martyr's portrait in Jewish-Greek Literature. In M. J. Edwards & S. Swain (Eds.). *Portraits: Biographical representation in the Greek and Latin literature of the Roman Empire* (pp. 39–67). Oxford, UK: Oxford University Press.

Sachedina, A. (1981). *Islamic Messianism: The idea of the Mahdi in Twelver Shiʿism*. Albany: State University of New York Press.

Spiegel, S. (1967). *The last trial*. Philadelphia: Jewish Publication Society.

Tirmidhi, A. I. M. b. Isa al- (n.d.). *Sunan al-Tirmidhi* (Vols. 1–5). Beirut, Lebanon: Dar al-Kutub al-ʿIlmiyya.
Victoria, B. (1997). *Zen at War*. New York: Weatherhill.

Maya

The Maya were a number of Maya-speaking peoples living in present-day Guatemala, Belize, Honduras, El Salvador, and southern Mexico, including the Yucatan Peninsula. For the Maya, religion was all-important, defining their world and manipulating their environment. The religion of the Maya, however, came to be a synthesis of indigenous religion and values from millennia of development. By the sixteenth century their religion had been influenced by traditions from Mexico as well as from farther north.

For the Maya two central themes were interrelated: religion and war. Therefore, looking at the classic Maya, postclassic Maya, and the influence of religion on warfare is vital to understanding the Maya. In 1517 the Maya first encountered the Spaniards, an encounter that would change their lives and religion forever. Already composed of a synthesis of religions, their new, synthesized belief structure took on a new life, a "Maya Catholicism" (Maurer Avalos 1993, 228). Today, then, Mayan religion is both Christian and Mayan. Much of the knowledge of the Mayan religion comes from oral traditions (such as those recorded by Friar Diego de Landa, early missionary and chronicler) as well as from the *Popol Vuh*, a document written in Latin in 1555 by a Quiché (Mayan) scribe.

The time from about 250 to 900 CE is the "classic period." Even before this period, ruler and elite members of Mayan society both served as members of the priesthood and held political powers. Through bloodletting rituals (drawing blood from tongues, lips, and genitals), Mayan kings were able to communicate with the gods as well as to facilitate communication with deified royal ancestors. Every stage in life and every important event, such as the erection of buildings, the sowing of fields, birth, marriage, or death, required sanctification through bloodletting.

After 900 CE a priestly class began to emerge separate from royalty, although this separation was not complete. Like the positions of the political royalty, the positions of the priestly class were inherited. The priests kept track of lineages and produced divinations and prophecy, generally through the use of hallucinations. They also directed human sacrifices when the gods required it.

As with the Aztecs and other pre-Columbian civilizations, warfare with the Maya served a central role. Particularly during the classic period, wars were waged for territorial expansion. Wars for expansion, however, were the exception. In general, wars had religious meanings and featured religious rituals. Fought during the hot and dry spring when less labor was required for agricultural cultivation, these wars were preceded by days of fasting in order to ensure support of the gods. Additionally, kings and members of the upper nobility performed ritual purification.

The winning side in a war ritually sacrificed the elite—such as kings and members of the upper nobility—who were captured in battle. Generally, wars failed to be decisive and ended with such sacrifices instead of territorial gains or losses or the overturning of lineages. Thus, war for the Maya held religion and religious symbolism in high regard.

Mayan Deities

The Mayan religious structure at the time of European encounter (1517) was the result of contact between Mayan groups with non-Mayan religious ideals. The Aztecs, for example, entered Mayan cities to confer on scientific matters, no doubt bringing many aspects of their religion with them. However, the principal purpose of Mayan religion seems to have remained constant: to maintain and ensure life, health, and sustenance.

Religion, then, permeated every facet of life. All of the most important Mayan deities were connected with the growth of corn, the four main deities being the creator god, the sun god, the moon goddess, and the rain gods.

The creator god was Hunab Ku. The Maya, perhaps surprisingly, paid little attention to the creator god because he was too far away to be interested in human beings. However, extremely important were the cyclical stages of history. These cycles, or cosmic stages, began in 26,502 BCE with the First Creation, leading to the Fourth Creation, the making of humankind (from the sacred food of corn) in 3,114 BCE (which, incidentally, is scheduled to end in 2015 CE). The first three attempts at creation failed because of the ingratitude of the beings created; they did not worship God and were destroyed.

The sun god and moon goddess were important in the pantheon because they were the ancestors of the

The Importance of Saints (Santo) in Yucatec Maya Culture

Considered as worship, the name-day festival is an annual homage offered to the santo by the people to whom the santo gives special protection. The people make the expected offerings, and the santo gives them health and good fortune. A sort of perpetual vow, which must be annually renewed, exists between santo and community. Failure to perform the festival in the traditional manner is regarded as a breach of the obligation. If for such a special reason as a year of relative poverty the people find themselves unable to perform the festival as usual, it is felt that the obligation is added to the commitment to perform the festival at the next anniversary. In such a case some prayers will be offered, perhaps a mass will be paid for (a sort of token payment), and the individuals in that year responsible for the festival will "explain" the situation to the santo.

Source: **Redfield, Robert. (1941).** ***The Folk Culture of Yucatan.*** **Chicago: University of Chicago Press, p. 271.**

human race (perhaps much like Adam and Eve for Western Christianity)—they were the first inhabitants of the world. The sun was the god of hunting, and the moon was the goddess of weaving crops, medicine, and women.

Fourth in the pantheon were the four rain gods (although sometimes they were regarded as one god). Each of the rain gods was assigned a geographic location and a color: Red Chac was assigned to the East, White Chac to the North, Black Chac to the West, and Yellow Chac to the South. These Chacs, whether one representing the four directions or four separate deities, were thought to have evolved from snakes. As rain gods, they had great jars in which they stored rain. However, if annoyed, these gods could send hail or other devastating precipitation. Whenever the Earth needed rain, the gods could sprinkle water from these jars onto the Earth. Accompanying rain is thunder—thunder was caused when these gods hurled stone axes to the Earth.

The gods were involved in all the myths regarding creation, the movements of the heavenly bodies, and the coming of the seasons.

Because religion permeated Mayan life, separating the religious from the secular is difficult because nearly all aspects of Mayan life were controlled by the gods, and the gods played large roles in the agricultural cycles. Moreover, life and death themselves were caught in the middle of an eternal struggle between good and evil over the destiny of humans. Religion demanded a great deal of worship. Worship of deities was important, and great monuments—many of which are still standing—were built to honor them. Monuments were the locus of prayers, incense burning, self-mutilation, and, occasionally, human sacrifice.

Priesthood

The priesthood, an integral part of Mayan religion, was hierarchical. The upper or high priests were, of course, concerned with religion. However, they were also concerned with astronomy, mathematics, administration, and other forms of scholarship. The Mayan religion excelled in mathematics and astronomy and created a calendar. This calendar came from the movements of the planets and stars and gave meaning as well as names to the cyclical periods of time.

There also were lesser priests, including sun priests, who were the lowest and most general order of the priesthood and performed divination, curing, and witchcraft, all three of which continue to be performed today. Divination was linked to the knowledge of the 260-day religious or sacred calendar. After all, for the Maya, the calendar and religion were inseparable—days and months were represented by individual deities. Divination would occur through the casting of dice, the interpretation of omens or entrails, the flight of birds or arrows, or dreams, trances, or other such methods, often with the aid of hallucinogens. Prophecy, then, was important for the Maya.

Curing rituals also were performed by the sun priests. These rituals normally were performed at the patient's bedside, in temples, or at shrines. However, when a priest was called upon to cure someone afflicted with an illness, the priest would, if the case was serious, have to find out who sent the illness and then turn it back to the sender. Thus, sorcery and countersorcery were vital functions of the priesthood.

The Maya believed in immortality; the afterlife consisted of a heaven and a hell. In Mayan cosmology (a branch of metaphysics that deals with the nature of the universe), the sky consisted of thirteen layers, the lowest layer being the Earth. Beneath the Earth were nine underworlds, with the death god residing in the lowest of the underworlds in skeleton form.

Mayan Catholicism

The Spanish conquest of the Maya was begun by Francisco de Montejo a decade after the Maya first encountered the Spaniards in 1517, although not until 1545 were the Spaniards able to establish effective political control. Spanish priests immediately entered the region, endeavoring to convert the Maya to Catholicism. Today there is a Mayan and Christian synthesis. Anthropologist Eugenio Maurer Avalos argues that the Mayan religion is neither pagan nor Western Christian in primary orientation. Its beliefs, as outlined by Maurer Avalos, consist of a four-fold belief structure: a belief in God, Jesus Christ, the Cross, and the saints, especially the Virgin Mary. The roots of these beliefs were in preconquest times but have been adapted to Christianity, the religion of the conquerors. Many of the writings of the Maya prior to the sixteenth century—scrolls and books, in particular—were burned by the early Christian missionaries in their process of rooting out idolatry. The Spaniards destroyed many of the sacred images found in temples along with documents and pictographs. Temples and religious dwellings were torn down and replaced by Christian churches. The new Mayan Christian religion, however, would retain elements of preconquest belief.

Today the Maya retain a belief in God. He is often referred to as the "Unified God," "the Mother," and "the Father." Like the Christian Trinity, these represent one god. Perhaps this is the incarnation of the creator god. God, however, as a supreme being does not govern directly but rather through his agents, or saints, who are his representatives in each village.

Also important is Christ. Christ is believed to be a real man, son of the Virgin Mary. Just as the sun god held importance before the advent of Christianity, Christ holds importance in his stead. In Mayan Catholicism, then, Christ is associated with the sun. Although God does not govern directly, Christ is believed to always be present in the community; his images, for example, adorn many churches.

Crosses command particular adoration and reverence. They, together with the Virgin Mary, angels, and thunderbolts, are believed to live in caves in sacred mountains. The axis of the Earth had been depicted for over a thousand years in the form of a cross. Thus, not only was it a powerful symbol, but also it would assist in the conversion of the Maya to Christianity.

Saints are deities who serve as intermediaries between humans and God, and each Mayan community has its own patron saint, or representative of God. The principal role of saints is to protect people from harm. The most powerful of the saints is the Virgin Mary, and the leader of them all is Christ himself. Incidentally, as Christ is associated with the sun, the Virgin Mary is associated with the moon.

Harmony is important for the Maya. To achieve true happiness, people must be in harmony with themselves, the community, and the gods. To achieve happiness, one must offer ritual offerings to the patron saint. Then the patron saint will bestow divine protection on the person and community—unless witchcraft is involved, in which case a curer must be summoned. Now known as *principale*s, curers receive their power from the patron saint. This power, however, can be used for good (such as to cure illness or ward off evil) or for bad (such as sending an illness or other type of affliction).

In sum, the religion of the Maya formed millennia before the common era. By the time of the Spanish conquest, many aspects, such as the main gods, had crystallized. Although after the conquest the Maya as a whole adopted Christianity, they retained many aspects of their traditional religion, forming a Mayan Catholicism.

Kim Richardson

See also Aztecs

Further Reading

Avalos, E. M. (1993). The Tzeltal Maya-Christian synthesis. In G. H. Gosse & M. León-Portilla (Eds.), *South and Meso-American native spirituality: From the cult of the feathered serpent to the theology of liberation* (pp. 228–250). New York: Crossroads Publishing.

Bricker, V. R. (1981). *The Indian Christ, the Indian king: The historical substrata of Maya myth and ritual*. Austin: University of Texas Press.

Clendinnen, I. (1987). *Ambivalent conquests: Maya and Spaniards in the Yucatan, 1517–1570*. New York: Cambridge University Press.

Dumond, D. E. (1985). Talking crosses of Yucatan: A new look at their history. *Ethnohistory, 32*(4), 291–308.
Edmunson, M. S. (1993). The Mayan faith. In G. H. Gosse & M. León-Portilla (Eds.), *South and Meso-American native spirituality: From the cult of the feathered serpent to the theology of liberation* (pp. 165–185). New York: Crossroads Publishing.
Estévez, M. G. (1993). The Christian era of the Yucatec Maya. In G. H. Gosse & M. León-Portilla (Eds.), *South and Meso-American native spirituality: From the cult of the feathered serpent to the theology of liberation* (pp. 251–278). New York: Crossroads Publishing.
Gruzinski, S. (1989). *Man-gods in the Mexican highlands: Indian power and colonial society, 1520–1800.* Stanford, CA: Stanford University Press.
Schele, L., & Friedel, D. (1990). *A forest of kings: The untold story of the ancient Maya.* New York: William Morrow.
Tedlock, B. (1992). *Time and the highland Maya.* Albuquerque: University of New Mexico Press.

Mennonites

Throughout most of their five centuries of history, Mennonites have been opposed to warfare and have expressly discouraged or forbidden their members from participating in warfare and other forms of violence. Since the early twentieth century, Mennonites have been known—along with the Society of Friends and the Church of the Brethren—as one of the historic peace churches. Today Mennonites' opposition to violence often is expressed around the globe in positive forms of peacemaking and service in the name of Christ.

Traditionally, Mennonites' peace position has been rooted in the biblical portrayal of Jesus' way of love and his willingness to suffer on the cross. Mennonites believe Jesus' demonstration of love in all relationships should be normative for his followers. Often in Mennonite history the faithful response to violence has been characterized as nonresistance, a term derived from Jesus' injunction during the Sermon on the Mount to "not resist an evildoer" (Matthew 5:39, NRSV), but to turn the other cheek. For Mennonites, nonresistance has been a way of being a faithful disciple of Jesus Christ, not a strategy for achieving peace. Such a posture, espoused most articulately by the Mennonite historian Guy F. Hershberger (1896–1989) in his mid-twentieth-century book *War, Peace, and Nonresistance,* was broader than simple conscientious objection or refusal to participate in warfare; nonresistance had implications for all dimensions of Christian life. While many Mennonites still speak in terms of nonresistance, in the last half of the twentieth century—influenced in part by the successful activist movements of Mohandas (Mahatma) Gandhi and Martin Luther King, Jr.—Mennonites have debated the appropriateness of nonviolent resistance, sociopolitical activism, and justice making. Such debates have pushed at Mennonites' traditional theological and ethical boundaries.

Anabaptist Peacemaking Origins

Contemporary Mennonites and related groups, who number about 1.2 million around the world, with about 60 percent of those living in the southern hemisphere, trace their faith origins to the sixteenth-century Anabaptists (rebaptizers), who were part of what became known as the "left wing" of the Protestant Reformation. The Anabaptists agreed with much of what the Reformers were seeking to do, but believed the Reformers were not going far enough on some issues. Of central importance to early Anabaptist leaders to whom contemporary Mennonites trace their ancestry was the autonomy of the church from the state in matters of worship and religious practice; the separation of Christians from the "worldly" realm of politics; the necessity for baptism into the church to be voluntary, based on an adult commitment to follow in the way of Christ; and, most importantly in this context, rejection of "the sword."

Not all early Anabaptists were pacifists, but the surviving groups of Mennonites' ancestors were. Both because a small number of sixteen-century Anabaptists were violent, and because the pacifist Anabaptists refused to obey civil authorities on matters such as infant baptism, they were perceived as a threat to social order. Within months after their beginnings in 1525, their first martyrs were killed, initially at the hands of Catholic authorities and later by Protestants. Over the course of the next century, thousands of Anabaptists were killed, and those in the movement fled to other lands and rural areas safe from the avenging arm of religious and civil authorities. Hundreds of these martyr stories are told in a collection titled *Martyrs Mirror of the Defenseless Christians* (J. F. Sohm, trans.), a huge volume in continuous publication since 1660 and a staple in many Mennonite homes. Although the movement began in Switzerland and South Germany, soon many Anabaptists came to be called Menists and then Mennonites,

Selection from *Martyrs Mirror Of The Defenseless Christians*

Anna of Rotterdam, Put to Death in That Place, A. D. 1539 (abridged)

The following is the Testament which Anna of Rotterdam left and presented to her son, Isaiah, on the 24th of January, A.D. 1539, at nine o'clock in the morning, as she was preparing herself to die for the name and testimony of Jesus, and took leave of her son, at Rotterdam:

Isaiah, receive your testament:

My son, hear the instruction of your mother; open your ears to hear the words of my mouth. Behold, today I go the way of the prophets, apostles and martyrs, and drink of the cup which they all have drunk. . .

See, my son, this way has no retreats; there are no roundabout or crooked little paths; whoever leaves to go to the left or the right inherits death. Behold, this is a way found by so few, and walked by still fewer, for there are some who know well this is the way to life, but it is too hard for them, it pains their flesh. . .

Therefore my child, do not regard the great number, nor walk in their ways. Take your feet far from their paths. . . But where you hear of a poor, simple, cast-off little flock, which is despised and rejected by the world, join them. For where you hear of the cross, there is Christ; from there do not depart. Flee the shadow of this world; become one with God; fear Him alone; keep His commandments; observe all His words, to do them. . . Observe that which the Lor commands you, and sanctify your body to His service, that His name may be sanctified, praised, and made glorious and great in you. Don't be ashamed to confess Him before men; do not fear men. Better to give up your life than to depart from the truth. . .

Therefore my child, strive for righteousness unto death and arm yourself with the armor of God. . . May the Lord cause you to grow up in His fear, and fill your understanding with His Spirit. Sanctify yourself to the Lord, my son; sanctify your whole conduct in the fear of your God. . . Whatever the Lord gives you by the sweat of your brow, more than what you need yourself, share it with those whom you know love the Lord. Don't keep it until tomorrow, and the Lord will bless the works of your hands, and give you His blessing for your inheritance . . .

O holy Father, sanctify the son of Thy handmaiden in Thy truth, and keep him from the evil, for Thy name's sake, O Lord.

Thereupon she sealed this with her blood, and thus, as pious heroine and follower of Jesus Christ, she was received among the number of witnesses of God who were offered up.

***Source: Martyrs Mirror Of The Defenseless Christians.* Retrieved March 13, 2003, from http://www.homecomers.org/mirror/intro.htm**

after the Dutch Anabaptist leader Menno Simons (1496–1561), who managed to avoid early martyrdom.

"All Christians," wrote Simons in 1552, "are commanded to love their enemies; to do good unto those who abuse and persecute them; to give the mantle when the cloak is taken, the other cheek when one is struck." Citing Isaiah 2:4 and Micah 4:3, he said such Christians "have beaten their swords into plowshares and their spears into pruning hooks. . . . Neither shall they learn war any more" (Simons 1956, 555).

Most sixteenth-century Anabaptists agreed with the Reformation leader Martin Luther that the state was ordained to preserve order in a fallen world, adopting some version of a dualistic, two-kingdom understanding of the world, building on the writings of St. Augustine and of their contemporaries. The surviving strains of Anabaptism, however, parted ways with Luther on the issue of the Christian's role in the two kingdoms. For Luther, Christians stood squarely in the midst of both kingdoms: In their private, personal

Anonymous engraving, circa 1800, influenced by Van Sichem, depicting Menno Simons. Courtesy Mennonite Church, USA.

lives, they were in the kingdom of God, and in their public lives they were in the earthly kingdom. Persons were essentially split down the middle in their loyalties: Christian love called them to act in both kingdoms, abiding by the ethic of each when working in that realm and not expecting to effect much change in the earthly kingdom.

For most of the Anabaptists, it was the *world*, not individuals, who were split: Faithful Christians lived in the kingdom of God and abided by its ethic, and others were in the earthly kingdom. God had instituted civil government, the Anabaptists said, and therefore it should be obeyed—up to the point where the state's demands clearly contradicted God's authority. Because of their understandings of the commandments of Christ, however, they believed the Christian could not kill—even when the state had legitimated killing in the cases of war and capital punishment. Therefore, although they believed the state was divinely instituted, most Anabaptists said the true Christian could not participate in the government's work, because the civil realm required the use of violence for maintaining order and was therefore "outside the perfection of Christ," as the Schleitheim Confession of 1527 says. Even the Anabaptist leader Pilgram Marpeck (c. 1495–1556), who himself served as a civil engineer, said, in effect, that one can be a Christian magistrate, but not for long.

Influenced by the Mennonite theologian John H. Yoder (1927–1997) and other Mennonite leaders, many twentieth-century Mennonites began to question the traditional church-world dualism of their faith heritage. Beginning in the 1960s, many Mennonites began to speak of the "lordship of Christ" over not just the church but all the world. That theological shift justified and perhaps mandated a Mennonite witness to the state—asking the state to embody more fully the norms Christ revealed, norms which were relevant for both individuals and institutions, including nations. In the case of nations, what might be expected are modified norms, sometimes referred to as "middle axioms," theological-ethical mediating grounds that ask political leaders to work toward a more just society. In Yoder's classic *Politics of Jesus* (1972), he also argued that Jesus' ethic is a relevant social strategy for the contemporary world: Believers should create a distinct community through which the gospel works to change other sociopolitical structures.

In this spirit, twentieth-century Mennonites were not content only to maintain a negative attitude toward war. Especially in North America, many felt a need to do some corresponding positive act whereby they could assist their countries and the world. The Mennonite historian James C. Juhnke has contended that in the United States, the Mennonite tragedy was not that they became Americans so slowly, but that "they so desperately wanted to be good American citizens and could not fulfill the requirements without violating their consciences or abandoning the tradition of their forebears" (Juhnke 1975, 156). Juhnke attributes to this tension "whatever was creative in the Mennonite experience"—relief programs, development of positive alternatives to military service, and scattered criticism of U.S. nationalism from a pacifist perspective (Juhnke 1975, 156–157).

Mennonite Practice of Conscientious Objection

In countries where they originated or to which they have migrated, Mennonites have usually sought legal status as conscientious objectors (COs) to warfare, both for their own young men and women and for others with religious or humanitarian objections to military service. Prior to World War II, Mennonites and other historic peace churches in the U.S. created the National Service Board for Religious Objectors, later known as the National Interreligious Service Board for Conscientious Objectors and now called the Center on Conscience and War.

In some countries where Mennonites have lived, obtaining CO status has been difficult or impossible, at times prompting Mennonites to accommodate and at other times forcing emigration to CO-friendly lands. Because of a variety of social and legal pressures, Mennonites in central and western Europe had nearly abandoned their nonresistant position by the beginning of the twentieth century. Many young Mennonites from Germany, Switzerland, and the Netherlands served militarily in World Wars I and II.

About eighteen thousand Mennonites emigrated to North America from Russia in the 1870s and 1880s, when their status as conscientious objectors there was jeopardized. Mennonites who remained in Russia suffered immensely in the following decades—through the turbulent Communist Revolution of 1917, a severe famine, banditry by various anarchists in the 1920s, and extraordinary state-sponsored persecution during the 1930s and 1940s. About 50 percent of Mennonite families lost their providers during those years, and all Russian Mennonite churches were closed by 1934–1935. In total, in the twentieth century far more Russian Mennonites died both directly and indirectly at the hands of the Soviets than the four thousand or so Mennonites who were martyred in the sixteenth century. In the midst of the volatile years following World War I—and in response to anarchist and Bolshevik attacks—some Russian Mennonites organized a short-lived military self-defense (*Selbstchutz*) force to protect their local villages. During World War II, after most Russian Mennonite spiritual leaders had been executed, large numbers of Mennonite young men were drafted into the Soviet Union army with little resistance. In Latin America, Mennonites occasionally have been granted noncombatant options, though official recognition of CO status is rare. In recent decades Mennonites in nearly all of these countries in Europe and Latin America have witnessed a resurgence of the Mennonite peacemaking commitment.

In the American colonies prior to the American Revolution, Mennonites perceived that their pacifism was compatible with good citizenship. They voted, helped select candidates, and held certain local offices. By the early stages of the revolution, however, the test of membership in the newly forming state was willingness to participate in local "associations" and to pledge to bear arms to protect American liberties. Nonresistant Mennonites failed the test. Eventually, the revolution contributed to U.S. Mennonites' withdrawal from public life and political marginalization.

During the U.S. Civil War, Mennonites responded in various ways. Some young Mennonites served militarily for the northern or southern forces, some hired substitutes to serve in their stead, others made "voluntary" contributions, and others paid commutation fees. Both during and after the war, the practices of military service, hiring substitutes, and voluntarily contributing to the war effort were condemned by many Mennonite leaders. In the late nineteenth century and afterward, renewed teaching and writing on the way of the cross, coupled with waves of immigration from lands where Mennonites were not receiving CO status, strengthened the North American Mennonite commitment to the principle of nonresistance.

Mennonites in the United States and Canada made up a plurality of conscientious objectors during their countries' twentieth-century wars; nonetheless, many Mennonite young men served militarily in World Wars I and II, the Korean War, and Vietnam. U.S. Mennonites were unprepared for the patriotic fervor engendered by World War I. Many individual Mennonites suffered persecution in their communities for not buying war bonds or otherwise refusing to support the war. In Oklahoma and Michigan, local vigilantes burned Mennonite church buildings. In other areas Mennonite young men were conscripted into U.S. military training camps with the promise that they would not be coerced against their conscience into combatant service. However, once there, some abandoned their nonresistant heritage under verbal and physical abuse by military officials and their peers. About 150 conscripted Mennonite men were court-martialed and imprisoned for refusing military orders. The Hutterites, Mennonites' sibling denominational group, were particularly victimized, and about a thousand Hutterites emigrated to Canada to escape continued persecution.

To avoid reliving the tragic experiences of World War I, leaders from the historic peace churches met several times prior to World War II to establish a Civilian Public Service (CPS) program for their young men and other conscientious objectors. CPS, administered by the church rather than the U.S. military, allowed twelve thousand Mennonite, Friends, Brethren, and other COs to serve in constructive ways in work "of national importance," without militarily defending their country. Much to Mennonite leaders' chagrin, even with the option of CPS, nearly 54 percent of Mennonite young men chose military service. In 1951 another alternative service program (1-W) was inaugurated by U.S. Mennonites, and that program continued until conscription ended in 1973. With increased efforts at teaching the peacemaking heritage during and after World War II, the percentage of Mennonites participating militarily in the Korean, Vietnam, and Persian Gulf wars declined dramatically. By the early twenty-first century, Mennonite peacemaking convictions were perhaps as strong as they ever had been in the church's history.

Peacemaking in the Twenty-First Century

During and since the Vietnam War, North American and European Mennonites frequently have issued public statements opposing various war-making initiatives. In addition, they have taught their young men and women the "way of peace," supported their young people who have refused draft registration in the United States and conscription elsewhere, engaged in ecumenical dialogues with those from nonpacifist religious traditions, peacefully participated in demonstrations opposing war and other forms of violence, argued for significant reductions in or elimination of military budgets, and increased their service efforts in suffering nations around the globe. Mennonites also are aware that with volunteer armies, technological developments, and the corresponding need for fewer conscripted soldiers to fight modern wars, the impact of individual conscientious objection may lessen. Instead, peacemaking Christians' financial and social entanglement in their nations' war making may become a more pressing issue. Some U.S. Mennonites have refused to pay voluntarily the percentage of their income taxes which goes to support present and past wars, and Mennonites have been at the forefront of the War Peace Tax Fund efforts in the United States.

In the contemporary context, Mennonite concerns about warfare and violence have stimulated extensive development of peace studies and conflict transformation programs in Mennonite colleges and universities, and they have birthed creative peacemaking efforts in Mennonite denominational and interdenominational agencies, such as the Mennonite Central Committee (MCC). An active peacemaking group, Christian Peacemaker Teams (CPT) emerged in the 1980s with the support of the three historic peace churches. In hot spots such as Haiti, Hebron, Afghanistan, and Iraq, CPT sends small teams of workers to stand between hostile groups, document and report atrocities and human-rights violations, and actively intervene in violent situations.

How these various efforts at active peacemaking will reshape Mennonite commitments and theology remains to be seen. Many within the tradition call for greater attention to a heritage of nonresistance, others emphasize nonviolent direct action as the most faithful response, and a few ask whether justice may be best served, on some occasions, by violent revolution. Some notion of church-world separation likely will be maintained as Mennonites sort through a number of possible models for embodying the peaceful way of Christ in the twenty-first century. In any event, it seems clear that the practice of warfare as well as support for warfare will continue to be seen by most Mennonites as contrary to the teaching and spirit of Christ and the Gospel.

Keith Graber Miller

See also Anabaptist Pacifism; Judaism, Pacifism in; Lutheran Germany; Quakers; Roman Catholicism, Pacifism in

Further Reading

Bender, H. S., et al. (Eds.). (1955–1959). *Mennonite encyclopedia* (Vols. 1–4). Scottdale, PA: Mennonite Publishing House.

Bender, R. T., & Sell, A. P. F. (1991). *Baptism, peace and the state in the Reformed and Mennonite traditions*. Waterloo, Canada: Wilfrid Laurier University Press.

Burkholder, J. L. (1989). *The problem of social responsibility from the perspective of the Mennonite Church*. Elkhart, IN: Institute of Mennonite Studies. (Original work published 1958)

Burkholder, J. R. (1977). *Continuity and change: A search for a Mennonite social ethic*. Akron, PA: Mennonite Central Committee Peace Section.

Burkholder, J. R., & Gingerich, B. N. (1991). *Mennonite peace theology: A panorama of types*. Akron, PA: Mennonite Central Committee Peace Office.

Bush, P. (1998). *Two kingdoms, two loyalties: Mennonite pacifism in modern America*. Baltimore: Johns Hopkins University Press.

Driedger, L., & Kraybill, D. E. (1994). *Mennonite peacemaking: From quietism to activism*. Scottdale, PA: Herald Press.

Dyck, C. J., & Martin, D. D. (1990). *Mennonite encyclopedia* (Vol. V). Scottdale, PA: Herald Press.
Friesen, D. K. (1986). *Christian peacemaking and international conflict: A realist pacifist perspective*. Scottdale, PA: Herald Press.
Gingerich, M. (1949). *Service for peace: A history of Mennonite civilian public service*. Akron, PA: Mennonite Central Committee.
Graber Miller, K. (1996). *Wise as serpents, innocent as doves: American Mennonites engage Washington*. Knoxville: University of Tennessee Press.
Hershberger, G. F. (1944). *War, peace, and nonresistance*. Scottdale, PA: Herald Press.
Hershberger, G. F. (1958). *The way of the cross in human relations*. Scottdale, PA: Herald Press.
Hershberger, G. F. (1991). *The Mennonite Church in the Second World War*. Scottdale, PA: Mennonite Publishing House.
Juhnke, J. C. (1975). *A people of two kingdoms: The political acculturation of the Kansas Mennonites*. Newton, KS: Faith and Life Press.
Juhnke, J. C. (1989). *Vision, doctrine, war: Mennonite identity and organization in America, 1890–1930*. Scottdale, PA: Herald Press.
Kauffman, J. H., & Driedger, L. (1991). *The Mennonite mosaic: Identity and modernization*. Scottdale, PA: Herald Press.
Klaassen, W. (Ed.). (1981). *Anabaptism in outline: Selected primary sources*. Kitchener, ON: Herald Press.
Loewen, H. (2003). A Mennonite-Christian view of suffering: The case of Russian Mennonites in the 1930s and 1940s. *Mennonite Quarterly Review, 77*(1), 47–68.
MacMaster, R. K. (1985). *Land, piety, peoplehood: The establishment of Mennonite communities in America, 1683–1790*. Scottdale, PA: Herald Press.
Peachey, U. (Ed.). (1980). *Mennonite statements on peace and social concerns*. Akron, PA: MCC U.S. Peace Section.
Roth, J. D. (2002). *Choosing against war: A Christian view*. Intercourse, PA: Good Books.
Sawatsky, W. (2002). Historical roots of a post-gulag theology for Russian Mennonites. *Mennonite Quarterly Review, 76*(2), 149–180.
Schlabach, T. F. (1988). *Peace, faith, nation: Mennonites and Amish in nineteenth-century America*. Scottdale, PA: Herald Press.
Simons, M. (1956). *The complete writings of Menno Simons*. (J. C. Wenger, Ed.). Scottdale, PA: Mennonite Publishing House.
Snyder, C. A. (1995). *Anabaptist history and theology: An introduction*. Kitchener, Canada: Pandora Press.
Snyder, C. A. (Ed.). Peace theology in a pluralistic world. *Conrad Grebel Review, 14*(1), 1–123.
Swartley, W. (Ed.). (1988). *Essays on peace theology and witness*. Elkhart, IN: Institute of Mennonite Studies.
Swartley, W., & Dyck, C. J. (Eds.). (1987). *Annotated bibliography of Mennonite writings on war and peace*. Scottdale, PA: Herald Press.
Toews, P. (1996). *Mennonites in American society, 1930–1970: Modernity and the persistence of religious community*. Scottdale, PA: Herald Press.
Van Braght, T. J. (1950). *The bloody theater or martyrs mirror of the defenseless Christians*. Scottdale, PA: Herald Press.
Yoder, E. G. (1992). *Peace theology and violence against women*. Elkhart, IN: Institute of Mennonite Studies.
Yoder, J. H. (1964). *The Christian witness to the state*. Newton, KS: Faith and Life Press.
Yoder, J. H. (1992). *What would you do?* Scottdale, PA: Herald Press.
Yoder, J. H. (1994). *The politics of Jesus: Behold the man! our victorious lamb*. Grand Rapids, MI: William B. Eerdmans Publishing Company.
Yoder, J. H. (1997). *For the nations: Essays public and evangelical*. Grand Rapids, MI: William B. Eerdmans Publishing Company.

Methodism

Methodism began as an evangelical revival movement in England in the early eighteenth century under the leadership of John Wesley (1703–1791), a priest in the Church of England. The Methodist Episcopal Church was among the largest Protestant denominations in the United States in the early nineteenth century, becoming "the most extensive national institution in antebellum America other than the federal government" (Goen 1985, 57). Today its successor, the United Methodist Church, claims almost 8.4 million members and clergy in the United States and 9.7 worldwide. The World Methodist Council claims 70 million Methodist or related churches in 130 countries. This article focuses on developments in the United States relating to issues of war and peace.

Wesley and his followers emphasized both justifying grace, whereby sinners were forgiven for their sins and restored to fellowship with God, and sanctifying grace, an experience of personal moral renewal that enabled believers to achieve "Christian perfection" or "holiness." The Methodist minister and theologian

Selections from the United Methodist Social Principles

Military Service

We deplore war and urge the peaceful settlement of all disputes among nations. From the beginning, the Christian conscience has struggled with the harsh realities of violence and war, for these evils clearly frustrate God's loving purposes for humankind. We yearn for the day when there will be no more war and people will live together in peace and justice. Some of us believe that war, and other acts of violence, are never acceptable to Christians. We also acknowledge that most Christians regretfully realize that, when peaceful alternatives have failed, the force of arms may be preferable to unchecked aggression, tyranny and genocide. We honor the witness of pacifists who will not allow us to become complacent about war and violence. We also respect those who support the use of force, but only in extreme situations and only when the need is clear beyond reasonable doubt, and through appropriate international organizations. We urge the establishment of the rule of law in international affairs as a means of elimination of war, violence, and coercion in these affairs

We reject national policies of enforced military service as incompatible with the gospel. We acknowledge the agonizing tension created by the demand for military service by national governments. We urge all young adults to seek the counsel of the Church as they reach a conscientious decision concerning the nature of their responsibility as citizens. Pastors are called upon to be available for counseling with all young adults who face conscription, including those who conscientiously refuse to cooperate with a system of conscription.

We support and extend the ministry of the Church to those persons who conscientiously oppose all war, or any particular war, and who therefore refuse to serve in the armed forces or to cooperate with systems of military conscription. We also support and extend the Church's ministry to those persons who conscientiously choose to serve in the armed forces or to accept alternative service.

War and Peace

We believe war is incompatible with the teachings and example of Christ. We therefore reject war as a usual instrument of national foreign policy and insist that the first moral duty of all nations is to resolve by peaceful means every dispute that arises between or among them; that human values must outweigh military claims as governments determine their priorities; that the militarization of society must be challenged and stopped; that the manufacture, sale, and deployment of armaments must be reduced and controlled; and that the production, possession, or use of nuclear weapons be condemned. Consequently, we endorse general and complete disarmament under strict and effective international control.

Source: **General Board of the Church and Society the United Methodist Church. *The United Methodist Social Principles.* Retrieved November 11, 2002, from: http://www.umc-gbcs.org/sp.htm**

Thomas Langford called the idea of Christian perfection "the most distinctive aspect of Wesley's theology" (Langford 1983, 40), although the theologian S. Paul Schilling pointed out that neither Wesley nor his followers "developed the social implications of his doctrine" (Schilling 1960, 230).

From its inception Methodism has had an ambivalent attitude toward war. It has consistently condemned war as "incompatible with the teachings and example of Christ" (UMC 1972a, para. 75), but it has never regarded a commitment to nonviolence as an essential aspect of Christian life. It has tended to regard military service as an appropriate form of obedience to governments, which are thought to have their authority from God. It has left the choice of participation to individuals, but Methodists have generally tended to respond uncritically to their governments' calls to arms; only a relatively small number have committed to pacifism.

John Wesley on War

Wesley abhorred war and wrote eloquently and passionately of the moral tragedy it represented. Wesley regarded war and its often trivial justification as evidence supportive of the doctrine of original sin. He believed that God used war to punish humans beings for their sin and thereby to call them to repentance.

Wesley did not regard participation in war as inconsistent with Christian perfection. He regarded defensive wars as justified and believed that the Bible enjoined people to obey governing authorities in the matter of going to war as in other matters. Wesley's analysis amounted to a theory of a just war, but he did not reflect on the possible conflict between Christian love of one's neighbor and killing that neighbor in war. Furthermore, he did not promote just-war criteria among Methodist people as a resource for discerning when they should obey the government's call to war and when they should not. There is also evidence of Wesley's tolerance of a pacifist position among Methodists.

John Wesley, founder of the Methodist Church. Courtesy General Board of Global Ministries, The United Methodist Church.

The Eighteenth and Nineteenth Centuries

In the eighteenth and nineteenth centuries, the vast majority of Wesley's followers in the United States shared his views that duty to one's government required participation in war. Not only did the northern and southern wings of Methodism (which had split over slavery in 1844) vigorously support their respective governments in the Civil War, the Methodist historian C. C. Goen has argued that Methodists, Baptists, and Presbyterians actually led the country into war.

Methodists also offered enthusiastic support for the Spanish-American War (1898), advocating wholeheartedly both the war and the subsequent annexation of Spanish territory. These positions were not seen as being in any way at odds with loyalty to Christ.

There were, however, exceptions to this general pattern of support for and participation in the nation's wars. Many preachers were conscientious objectors during the American Revolution, and Francis Asbury (1745–1816), the founder of Methodism in North America, opposed ministers serving in the armed forces. There was also some Methodist involvement in the American Peace Society, founded in 1828, whose purpose was the abolition of war.

Methodism and the Wars of the Twentieth Century

In the decades prior to World War I, efforts to reduce and eliminate war through international arbitration intensified, and Methodists participated in such efforts, often using the Wesleyan theme of social holiness. The 1908 and 1912 Episcopal Addresses to the General Conference of the Methodist Episcopal Church, for example, celebrated the establishment at the Hague of an international tribunal for resolving international disputes.

Immediately after World War I broke out in Europe in 1914, Methodists tended to support a policy of neutrality. After Germany sank the Lusitania, public opinion shifted toward U.S. involvement, and Methodists' sentiments followed the general trend. Once the United States entered the war in 1917, the Methodist population for the most part supported the war effort enthusiastically. They shared in the optimistic belief that civilization was progressing toward a democratic utopia in which war would be obsolete—a belief particularly significant among liberal or modernist Protestants committed to social reform. Methodists accepted Woodrow Wilson's notion of saving the world for democracy as a Christian duty and equated faith with patriotism.

In the 1920s and early 1930s, reacting to the horrors of World War I, U.S. churches, the Methodist Church among them, worked intensely for the promotion of world peace. An example of the Methodist commitment to international peace was the Methodist Episcopal Church's establishment in 1924 of the Commission on World Peace. The bishops of the Methodist Episcopal Church South told their 1934 General Conference: "War is another enemy to the human race which should no longer be tolerated by an intelligent, conscientious, honorable people. It is archaic, belongs to the jungle period of human development, and should be branded as an iniquitous and inhuman procedure" (Long 1992, 52–53, quoting MECS 1934, 367). The same General Conference affirmed the right to conscientious objection. In 1939, the newly reunited Methodist church stood opposed "to the spirit of war now raging in the world" and called for "a system of Christian education which shall seek to eradicate the causes of war and train our children for Christian participation in the arts of peace" (Long 1992, 55, quoting MEC 1939, 698). Even as war raged in Europe, the 1940 General Conference declared that the Methodist Church would not endorse war.

Affected by the pacifism that swept the United States following World War I, five thousand Methodists had registered their status as conscientious objectors with the Methodist Commission on World Peace by 1940. Except for members of the historic peace churches, Methodists were the largest group provided alternative service in the Civilian Public Service during World War II.

Official statements changed after the bombing of Pearl Harbor on 7 December 1941. After declaring the war inevitable, the bishops' "Wartime Message" said: "We condemn the processes of war even while accepting the awful alternative, not of our own making, forced upon us by the selfishness and perversity of men" (Will 1984, 64–65, quoting MB 1942, 7–8). After bitter debate, the 1944 General Conference said, "We are sending over a million young men from Methodist homes to participate in the conflict. God himself has a stake in the struggle, and we will uphold them as they fight forces destructive of the moral life of men." It continued to offer respect for conscientious objectors but said, "We cannot accept their position as the defining position of the Christian church" (Will 1984, 71–72, quoting MC 1944, 178–179). Yet as the historian Fredrick Norwood observed, despite this shift to unambiguous support for the war, "Relatively little of the emotional patriotism so noticeable in World War I found expression this second time around" (Norwood 1974, 411).

The Methodist Church was divided over the Vietnam War. Steadily, however, significant opposition to it emerged. In 1968 the General Conference of the now United Methodist Church called for the withdrawal of all outside military forces from Vietnam, and in 1970 the Episcopal address to the General Conference condemned the war strongly. The General Conference of 1972 declared that participation in the war had been a sin and referred to the actions of the United States in the region as a crime against humanity.

The Social Principles of the United Methodist Church approved by the 1972 General Conference rejected war as an instrument of foreign policy but stated that when peaceful alternatives have failed, warfare was preferable to "unchecked aggression, tyranny and genocide" (UMC 1972a, para. 74).

Nuclear Disarmament and *In Defense of Creation*

In 1928, the Methodist Episcopal Church called for international disarmament. Attention to disarmament increased after the dropping of the atomic bombs in Japan at the end of World War II—an act that the Methodist Commission on World Peace condemned. In 1986 the United Methodist Council of Bishops published *In Defense of Creation: The Nuclear Crisis and a Just Peace.*

The bishops said they addressed issues related to nuclear weapons because such weapons threatened the whole of creation. Drawing upon the just-war criteria that war requires a reasonable hope of success, discrimination, and proportionality, the bishops clearly opposed nuclear war and any use of nuclear weapons. The bishops intentionally went beyond their Roman Catholic counterparts, who three years previously had come out against nuclear weapons as a form of deterrence but had not called for immediate unilateral nuclear disarmament.

The bishops argued that the issues involved in the nuclear crisis went beyond those that pacifism and the just-war tradition addressed. They pointed to the fact that the nuclear arms race threatened social justice by swallowing up economic resources while the world's poor continued to suffer and die. The bishops' guiding principles for "a new theology for a just peace" (UMB 1986, 13), however, drew heavily on the just-war tradition as they continued to rely on just-war criteria for justification for resorting to force and to reaffirm their condemnation of the use of nuclear weapons.

The Contributions of Paul Ramsey and Stanley Hauerwas

Two United Methodist theologians have made significant contributions to contemporary theological discussions of issues related to war and peace in the United States. Paul Ramsey (1924–1988) explored the just-war tradition and criticized Methodist statements related to war, including *In Defense of Creation*, for their failure to more heartily affirm a just-war approach. As a member of the committee that prepared the Social Principles in 1972, Ramsey proposed an amendment that said "war is *ultimately* incompatible with the teachings and example of Christ," meaning to signal that "until Christ finally consummates the Kingdom, war is not completely outside faithful Christian living" (Long 1992, 65). Ramsey's amendment was defeated. The 2000 General Conference did amend the Social Principles, rejecting "war as a *usual* instrument of national foreign policy" (UMC 2000a, para. 74).

Stanley Hauerwas (b. 1940) vigorously defends Christian pacifism. However, his understanding of the theological basis for such a commitment is very different from that which seems to have driven official Methodist opposition to war in the twentieth century. He has no confidence that modern states can be convinced to abandon war or that war can be eliminated from human history. Moreover, he was critical of *In Defense of Creation* for seeming to base its rejection of nuclear weapons on a fear for human survival. Hauerwas calls the Christian community to a nonviolent way of life on the grounds that through Jesus Christ we see that God is nonviolent. Jesus, he says, "reveals the effective power of God to create a transformed people capable of living peaceably in a violent world" (Hauerwas 1983, 83). Though war cannot be eliminated from human history, Hauerwas asserts that it has already been eliminated for the Christian community. Hauerwas's approach points to a possible modern development of the social implications of Wesley's doctrine of holiness.

Terrorism

The 2000 General Conference condemned all acts of terrorism, without exception. It also opposed "the use of indiscriminate military force to combat terrorism, especially where the use of such force results in casualties among noncombatant citizens who are not themselves perpetrators of terrorist acts" (UMC 2000, 787).

In the immediate aftermath of the September 11 terrorist attacks in the United States, both the General Board of Church and Society and the Council of Bishops responded. The Board of Church and Society said that the teaching of Jesus was to pray for one's enemies and not to respond to violence with violence; further, the Board said it believed military actions would not end terrorism. The bishops called upon the church to work toward addressing the social conditions, such as poverty, that are exploited by terrorists. Both statements were criticized, particular by those seeking an affirmation of the U.S. military response to the attacks. *Good News Magazine*, a publication of an unofficial, evangelical renewal movement within the United Methodist Church, called for an explicit affirmation of the U.S. military response on just-war grounds.

Future Directions

It seems reasonable to expect that Methodism will continue to be torn between the two poles of its ambiguous legacy. Church leaders and official pronouncements will continue to express abhorrence for war and seek methods for its elimination without clearly embracing pacifism or the just-war tradition. Left to their individual consciences a majority of Methodists will continue to respond to their nations' calls to war.

Barry Penn-Hollar

Further Reading

Goen, C. C. (1985). *Broken churches, broken nation*. Macon, GA: Mercer University Press.

Hauerwas, S. (1983). *The peaceable kingdom: A primer in Christian ethics*. Notre Dame, IN, and London: University of Notre Dame Press.

Hauerwas, S. (1985). *Against the nations: War and survival in a liberal society*. Minneapolis, MN, Chicago, and New York: Winston Press.

Langford, T. A. (1983) *Practical divinity: Theology in the Wesleyan tradition*. Nashville, TN: Abingdon Press, 1983.

Long, D. S. (1992). *Living the discipline: United Methodist theological reflections on war, civilization, and holiness*. Grand Rapids, MI: William B. Eerdmans Publishing Company.

Marquardt, M. (1992). *John Wesley's social ethics: Praxis and principles*. Nashville, TN: Abingdon Press.

Methodist Bishops (MB). (1942). *Wartime Message of the Council of Bishops*. Chicago: The Methodist Publishing House.

Methodist Church (MC). (1939). *The discipline of the Methodist church*. Nashville, TN: The Methodist Publishing House.

Methodist Church (MC). (1940). *The discipline of the Methodist church*. Nashville, TN: The Methodist Publishing House.

Methodist Church (MC). (1944). *The journal of the Methodist church*. Nashville, TN: The Methodist Publishing House.

Methodist Episcopal Church (MEC). (1928). *The discipline of the Methodist Episcopal Church*. New York: The Methodist Book Concern.

Methodist Episcopal Church South (MECS). (1934). *Journal of the twenty-second general conference*. Nashville, TN: The Methodist Publishing House.

Methodist Episcopal Church South (MECS). (1934a). *The discipline of the Methodist Episcopal church south*. Nashville: The Methodist Publishing House.

Miller, R. M. (1964). *The history of American Methodism: Vol. 4. Methodism and American society*. New York and Nashville, TN: Abingdon.

Norwood, F. A. (1974). *The story of American Methodism*. Nashville, TN: Abingdon.

Ramsey, P. (1968). *The just war: Force and political responsibility*. New York: Charles Scribner's Sons.

Ramsey, P. (1988). *Speak up for just war or pacifism: A critique of the United Methodist Bishops' pastoral letter in defense of creation*. University Park, PA, and London: Pennsylvania University Press.

Salango, B. (1970). *The Methodist foreign policy response, 1939–1964*. Unpublished doctoral dissertation, Johns Hopkins University, Baltimore, MD.

Schilling, S. P. (1960). *Methodism and society in theological perspective*. New York and Nashville, TN: Abingdon Books.

United Methodist Bishops (UMB). (1986). *In defense of creation: The nuclear crisis and a just peace*. Nashville, TN: Graded Press.

United Methodist Church (UMC). (1972). *The book of resolutions of the United Methodist Church*. Nashville, TN: The Methodist Publishing House.

United Methodist Church (UMC). (1972a). *The discipline of the United Methodist Church*. Nashville, TN: The Methodist Publishing House.

United Methodist Church (UMC). (2000). *The book of resolutions of the United Methodist Church 2000*. Nashville, TN: The Methodist Publishing House.

United Methodist Church (UMC). (2000a). *The discipline of the United Methodist Church*. Nashville, TN: The Methodist Publishing House.

Weber, T. R. (2001). *Politics in the order of salvation: Transforming Wesleyan political ethics*. Nashville, TN: Abingdon Press.

Will, H. (1984). *A will for peace: Peace action in the United Methodist Church: A history*. Washington, DC: The General Board of Church and Society.

Middle East

See Assassins; Babi and Baha'i Religions; Byzantine-Muslim War of 645; Crusades; Deobandism; Fundamentalism in Egypt and Sudan; Fundamentalism in Iran; Hamas; Hizbullah; Iranian Revolution of 1979; Islam: Age of Conquest; Islam, Qur'anic; Islam, Shiʿa; Islam, Sufism; Islam, Sunni; Islamic Law of War; Judaism: Biblical Period; Manichaeism; Palestine and Israel; Palestine: 1948 War; Palestine Liberation Organization; Shiʿite Rebellion of 815–19; Wahhabism

Millenarian Violence: Latin America

A millenarian is, in its simplest definition, someone who believes that the millennium will occur. The millennium is the thousand-year period in which Christ will rule the earth with his followers preceding the last or final judgment, as described in the New Testament in chapter twenty of the book of Revelation.

Christianity itself began in this tradition as the early Christians were looking in anticipation for the return of the Messiah. When the second coming of Christ failed to materialize immediately, the idea began to form among the early Christians that it would come to pass only after the gospel had been preached to all corners of the earth. In the fifteenth century, Christopher Columbus himself viewed the discovery, exploration, and colonization of all the ends of the earth to be the fulfillment of the prophecies of the apocalypse. In fact, Columbus estimated that only fifty-five years remained until the end of the world. In that same century, Nicholas of Cusa (1401–1464) reinvigorated millennial speculation by his trinitarian speculations that the world was now in the third and final age of the Spirit. The Franciscan order in particular was deeply influenced by such speculation and understood their missionary work as bringing this final age to fruition.

Immediately following the Spanish conquest of Mexico in 1521, twelve Franciscan missionaries arrived in Mexico, referring to their mission as the final preaching of the gospel before the advent of the end of the world. Holding the image of the apocalypse in high regard, these Franciscans viewed the very discovery of the New World as part of God's plan to spread the gospel to the four corners of the world.

Millenarian Violence

A millenialist and apocalyptic tradition was thus brought by the Europeans to the New World. Closely related is millenarianism, of which various movements occurred throughout the history of Latin America. Millenarianism is the quest for complete collective salvation in *this* world. Such millenarian movements understand human activity as actively participating in the creation of a holy society here and now. These social movements seek radical change in accordance with a predetermined divine plan. They are, in short, a form of popular revolution.

The difference between a political revolution and a millenarian movement is that political revolutionaries have a predetermined plan about what their new society is going to look like and how they are going to obtain this society. Millenarianists, on the other hand, are simply rejecting the established order. The new society as well as the process of bringing it about will be according to God's will and plan, divine intervention being the key ingredient. The process of rejecting the established society and preparing oneself for Christ's reappearance as a warrior-messiah to establish his kingdom on earth and reign a thousand years often sparks violence.

Although millenarianism has European roots, it is not merely Christian in content. The first violent millenarian movement occurred not in favor of a Christian New World, but in opposition to one. In 1564, the Peruvian Indians had recently been conquered by the Spaniards. A rebellion among the Indians arose known as Taki Onkoy (also spelled Taqui Onqoy), in which the leaders preached that they had been conquered by the Spaniards simply because the Christian God had been stronger than the Peruvian deities. In order that the Peruvian deities increase in strength, then, they would have to cease the practice of Christianity and embrace the traditional indigenous customs. Along the way they must destroy the Spanish colonial economy and murder all Spaniards. Their reward would be a new millenarian paradise. By 1570, however, the Spanish priests had succeeded in crushing this uprising. Throughout the colonial period, millenarian movements would continue to intensify as a form of political protest and cultural revitalization—the results of a longing for a return to an idealized past golden age. These movements were challenging civil authority and therefore generally became violent.

In Mexico, a millenarian movement also occurred, particularly from 1889 to 1892. In 1889 a woman named Teresa Urrea in Cabora, Sonora, located in northwestern Mexico, lapsed into unconsciousness. Thought to be dead, her body was prepared for burial. However, she regained life and reported having spoken to the Virgin Mary, who had bestowed upon her the powers to cure.

Once these powers were known, people began flooding to Cabora in order to seek her help. One Indian village of Tomochic adopted Teresita (as they called her) as their saint, placing a statue of her in their church. This village rebelled against the government of Mexico in 1892 and asked Teresita to interpret God's will. As was the case with other millenarian movements, the Mexican army crushed this rebellion brutally, destroying the Indian village and killing all males over the age of thirteen. Teresita was a leader opposed to violence, but when 200 Mayo Indians attacked the town of Navojoa shouting, "Viva la Santa de Cabora!" she was exiled to the United States.

The most famous Latin American episode of millenarian violence, however, occurred in Brazil. By 1893 a religious mystic and penitent known as Antônio Conselheiro had wandered the Brazilian Northeast for twenty years preaching against ungodly behavior and of the necessity of rebuilding the rural churches and cemeteries. Conselheiro led a group of followers to Canudos, an inaccessible mountain valley in the interior of Bahia. Soon thousands of followers flocked to this area in order to live according to God's commandments and await the coming of the millennium, when the weak would inherit the earth and fertility would return to this drought-ridden region. Landless and peasants largely made up this group, for which this promise of inheriting the earth proved a strong pull, although landowners themselves cringed at the thought of a possible social revolution of the underclass.

The followers, who fled to Canudos, soon to be the second-largest city in Bahia, had previously made up the labor force in the countryside. Now, seeing their labor flee to Canudos, landowners began to demand government intervention. Simultaneously, Conselheiro advised his followers not to pay taxes, thus alienating the government. The church authorities denounced him, resenting his influence over the masses. Twice landowners led excursions against the settlement, both resulting in defeat for the attackers. A third wave, lasting for two years, involved the Brazilian army itself. In October of 1897 the army overran the redoubt of Canudos and its inhabitants were defeated.

The Millenarian Tradition

A key ingredient of Christianity was the return of the Messiah to establish his kingdom on Earth. Yet he has not yet returned, so there will continue to be millenarian movements accompanied with violence to prepare the way. And though not solely Christian by nature, all such movements have been influenced and molded by the coming of a golden age: a millennium.

Kim Richardson

Further Reading

Burns, E. B. (1994). *Latin America: A concise interpretive history* (6th ed.). Englewood Cliffs, NJ: Prentice-Hall.

da Cunha, E. (1944). *Rebellion in the backlands* (H. Putnam, Trans.). Chicago: University of Chicago Press (Original work published 1902)

Della Cava, R. (1970). *Miracle at Joaseiro*. New York and London: Columbia University Press.

Diacon, T. (1991). *Millenarian vision, capitalist reality: Brazil's contestado rebellion, 1912–1916*. Durham, NC, and London: Duke University Press.

Gossen, G. H., & León-Portillo, M. (Eds.). (1993). *South and Meso-American Native spirituality: From the cult of the feathered serpent to the theology of liberation*. New York: The Crossroad Publishing Company.

Graziano, F. (1999). *The millennial new world*. New York and Oxford: Oxford University Press.

Phelan, J. L. (1970). *The millennial kingdom of the Franciscans*. Berkeley, CA: University of California Press.

Millenarian Violence: Thai Buddhism

The existence of Buddhist millenarian movements presents at least two problems in the context of the conventional view of Buddhism. First, how can a religion that is in essence otherworldly be the basis for movements that are primarily concerned with this world? Second, how can violence be embraced, when it is clearly contrary to the teachings of the Buddha?

Millennialism and Buddhist Millennialism

The concept of millennialism originates in Christianity's belief that in the future Christ will establish a new order in a supernatural way. This belief differs from similar beliefs found in other religions in that the arrival of this future is believed to be imminent and the new order to be located on Earth rather than some celestial plane of existence. For the new order to come into being, the existing order must be destroyed, as must those who are not chosen to enjoy the new order. The anthropologist Stanley Jeyaraja Tambiah defines millennial Buddhism as:

> "the totality of beliefs, expectations, practices, and actions that have as their object the reconstitution of an existing social order in terms of an ideal order, a future utopia, which at the same time is a return to an ideal and positive beginning . . . [M]illennial Buddhism is the antinomy of the established Buddhist polity wherever it is seen to be corrupt and debased, or to require restoration and resurrection in the face of social decline or alien intrusion . . . it is a counter-statement, dedicated to the substitution and a future replacement, and capable of becoming rebellious." (Tambiah 1984, 319)

The anthropologist Charles F. Keyes's explanation for the existence of such movements focuses on two specific aspects of Theravada Buddhism—the dominant form of Buddhism in Thailand. He argues that the central concept for most Thai Buddhists is not nirvana (the attainment of enlightenment) but karma (the principle of cause and effect). While karma affects one's existence, not only is one unable to know the effects that past karma will have on this present existence, one does not know when those effects will emerge. Thus, one is permitted to struggle to improve one's life without violating karmic theory. Keyes continues by postulating that the "crucial belief is that 'merit' generated through positive *karma* (i.e., through good actions) can be shared with or transferred to others" (Keyes 1977, 287). Theravadin Buddhism holds that there are individuals who have accumulated vast reservoirs of merit in past lives, who can in turn use that merit to improve the lives of those associated with them. This belief appears closer to Mahayana Buddhism's belief in bodhisattvas, those who, although destined for enlightenment, choose to postpone its attainment in order to help as many others as possible. While Mahayana Buddhism allows for many bodhisattvas, the Theravada school holds to only two: the historical Buddha and Maitreya, the Buddha to come. It is said that Maitreya will come at the end of a period of decline and will renew the teachings (dharma) of the Buddha. Such a renewal would include the overthrow of existing orders, including political authority. The combination of the belief in the sharing of merit and the coming of Maitreya opens the door to millennial expectations.

Individuals of Charisma

Thai Buddhism recognizes two types of individuals who are critical to millennial movements: the *phu wiset* (literally, "men with extraordinary powers"), who are able to perform miracles, and the *phu mi bun*, people who have merit. The *phu mi bun* is the more significant of the two as a basis for millennial expectations. While the *phu wiset* are more plentiful, only a few achieve any prominence. The transformation of a miracle worker into a person who has merit is not a mystical affair but a change in social relationships. The transformation occurs when the followers of a *phu wiset* face a common threat. His followers often act against the existing political order with the goal of establishing a more just order.Justification for rebellion is found in the anticipated coming of Maitreya and the restoration of the teachings set down by the Buddha.

Uprisings in Northeast Thailand (1899–1902)

While Myanmar (Burma) may provide the best illustrations of millennial cults and uprisings (for example, consider the Saya San rebellion in the 1930s), the revolts at the beginning of the twentieth century in northeast Thailand are among the most recent and possess the best documentation.

Toward the end of the nineteenth century, the political order in northeast Thailand and in neighboring areas in Laos and Cambodia was radically changed. Thailand was threatened by French expansion to the east and British expansion to the west. Having surrendered its authority over Cambodia in 1867, the Thai court began to develop and institute a new political system in northeast Thailand. As friction increased between the French and Thai governments, the political situation in northeast Thailand became very confused. Economic conditions deteriorated as the Thai authorities raised taxes, hurting those who were struggling to survive.

In 1899 Thai officials began to receive reports about men who claimed to be *phu wiset*. "At the same time, troubadour singers—apparently from French Laos—were traveling about the region singing, in a popular form know as *kham phaya*, about the coming of *phu mi bun*" (Keyes, 295). There were also handwritten manuscripts of the *phu mi bun* message circulating, with at least four such versions known to exist from different parts of the region. Their content was similar, beginning with a prediction of imminent catastrophe, during which "many normal things were to be radically transformed" (Keyes, 296). The message went on to predict the coming of a savior, who was given various designations, such as Lord Righteous Ruler, the lord who has merit, or the man who has merit. Those who followed the savior and did what was ordained by him would not only escape the coming holocaust but also prosper, while those who failed to do as commanded would be eaten by giant demons (*yaksa*s).

For a time, Thai officials dismissed these reports as mere superstition. By 1902, however, they could no longer ignore the fact that disturbing events were taking place in the region. In some places, rice in the fields remained unharvested, as people were obsessed with the *phu mi bun*. The first direct government action was to reprimand three ranking monks for having performed the cleansing ceremony (when a person who has committed evil deeds is sprinkled with sacralized water to make him/her pure). The movement continued to grow around four men claiming to be *phu mi bun*. Their goal (according to a minor leader interviewed after the rebellion was put down) was to establish a kingdom which was not under either the Thai or French, and to achieve this objective the movement was to destroy by force Thai and French power in the area. Once this was accomplished, each of the *phu mi bun* would rule a part of the region. Military force, that is, violence, was their intended means of achieving their goal.

The decisive battle took place on 2 April 1902, when government troops attacked the rebel force of as many as two thousand. The government force was armed with repeating rifles and cannon while the rebels had knives, swords, spears, and old flintlock rifles. According to one account, after a four-hour battle, more than 200 rebels had been killed, more than 500 wounded, and another 120 captured. According to Keyes, "Not a single government soldier was even injured" (298). The leaders were captured and, with the exception of one monk, executed.

Millennial movements are but symptoms of significant social crises. In the case of the 1902 uprising, we can identify at least three underlying causes. Those from northeast Thailand cite the poverty of the region as the primary cause for the uprising; poverty continues to plague the region. Political changes instituted by Thai authorities at the time were also a significant factor, as the rapid changes displaced certain individuals and made them potential rebel leaders. There was an ideological cause as well. While the Thai government saw all legitimate authority as flowing from the monarchy, the people of the region believed that powerful individuals could emerge from among the local population and be identified by their religious charisma.

Solutions

Theravadin societies have a variety of means for dealing with Buddhist millenarian movements. Many scholars believe that it would be unwise to view such movements primarily as political uprisings that must be suppressed. The scholar Yoneo Ishii, for example, contends that "Millenarism is "essentially a prepolitical phenomenon' " (Ishii 1975, 26). Instead, they should be considered symptoms of potential crises and instability. Governments should act to alleviate or mitigate the circumstances responsible for the upheaval. The key to any millenarian movement is its leadership. As the government of Thailand has discovered, channeling "the charismatic appeal of *phu mi bun* into established institutions . . . [helps reduce] the incidence of millennial uprisings within the kingdom" (Keyes, 291).

Damon L. Woods

See also Buddhism, Mahayana; Millennialism

Further Reading

Harris, I. (1999). Buddhism and politics in Asia: The textual and historical roots. In I. Harris (Ed.), *Buddhism and politics in twentieth-century Asia* (pp. 1–25). New York: Pinter.

Ishii, Y. (1975). A note on Buddhistic millenarian revolts in Northeastern Siam. *Journal of Southeast Asian Studies*, 6(2), 121–126.

Keyes, C. F. (1977). Millennialism, Theravada Buddhism, and Thai Society. *Journal of Asian Studies, 36*(2), 283–302.

Tambiah, S. J. (1984). *The Buddhist saints of the forest and the cult of amulets: A study in charisma, hagiography, sectarianism, and millennial Buddhism*. New York: Cambridge University Press.

Millenarian Violence: United States

Millenarian violence—violence that is catalyzed by belief in an imminent eschatological event in which the course of history is about to be brought to a violent close, opening a posthistorical epoch of peace, justice, and terrestrial power for the believers—has been a regular occurrence in the history of the West. The phenomenon was first named and brought into academic study of violence by British historian Norman Cohn in his 1957 classic *Pursuit of the Millennium: Revolutionary Millenarians and Mystical Anarchists of the Middle Ages*. The book examined a number of cases of medieval millenarian violence. The original edition included a controversial chapter applying the theory to Nazi Germany. By the early 1960s it stimulated other scholars—anthropologists in particular—to apply the model of millenarian violence to their own studies of non-Western indigenous groups. The theory then disappeared for a time before being resurrected in the 1970s by American scholars and applied both to American religious history (Michael Barkun) and to Nazi Germany (James Rhodes). This new burst of interest stimulated a new round of examination by anthropologists and others (most notably, Michael Adas), resulting in significant new contributions to the literature of millenarian violence.

According to Cohn's model, millenarian violence comes about as a response by marginalized groups or individuals to bewildering conditions of rapid social change. Once violence occurs, millenarian violence is characterized by its totality. Nothing and no one is spared, and believers fight with suicidal audacity for a dream of a radically purified terrestrial paradise. In Christian terms, the dream is of a final judgment in which a returned Jesus rewards his righteous remnant, punishes the wicked majority, and institutes a thousand-year reign of peace and prosperity on this earth. It is important to note, however, that millenarian movements are not tied to the calendar. What is at issue is not the particular date—even so portentous a date as the turning of the millennium in the years 1000 and 2000 of the Gregorian calendar. Rather, millenarian leaders are ever vigilant for the "signs of the times"—current events—as interpreted through the lens of inerrant text. The Bible and CNN in contemporary America (albeit with a growing contribution from the Internet, which relays signs of the times, real and imagined, with remarkable speed) provide the primary texts for this interpretive endeavor.

The Taborites in Bohemia (early sixteenth century) and the brief spasm of revolutionary millenarian violence at Münster (1530s) under the leadership of such radical Anabaptist figures as Thomas Münzer and Jan Beuckelzoon (who styled himself as King John of Leiden) were two of the most successful movements. This entry, however, will concentrate entirely on millenarian violence in the United States, examining cases of actual violence (the nineteenth-century Ghost Dance religion and the twentieth-century cases of Christian Identity and the pro-life rescue movement) and violence that was anticipated by many but never came to pass (the year 2000).

The Ghost Dance

The Ghost Dance represents a phenomenon that was not uncommon in the nineteenth century: a nativist reaction to the imminent destruction of their traditional way of life combined with a newly acquired Christian end times narrative in which Jesus would return to punish a colonial power and return the world to its precontact balance. From the Sudan to southern Africa, and from New Zealand to the Americas, this pattern tended to vary remarkably little. In each case, the impact of the colonial power had reached a stage where the culture of the colonized people was seen as imperiled. When events reached this stage and the passing of an ancient way of life could be perceived as imminent, a prophet would arise who was fired by a vision composed of an amalgamation of traditional beliefs and Christian apocalypticism. This native prophet would then preach his message of redemption to his people, many of whom would rally to his cause. On occasion, the message would be quite violent. More often, it would be a redemptive message in which the world would be rectified by supernatural intervention, without the need for the faithful themselves to take up arms. In either case, the colonial power invariably interpreted the prophet and his movement as threatening, and would often react violently to suppress the movement. Such was the case of the Ghost Dance.

There were two distinct waves of Ghost Dancing. The first in 1870 ran its course peacefully, but the second in 1890 ended in the tragedy of the Wounded Knee massacre. In 1870, a Paiute prophet in Nevada named Wodziwob (d. 1872) had an apocalyptic vision of the destruction of the earth, followed by a general resurrection of the dead, the regeneration of game animals, and a reconstituted traditional life-cycle for his people. To bring about this felicitous denouement, however, the people were urged to renew their age-old traditions by performing dances—dancing being a form of spiritual practice analogous to prayer. The Ghost Dance quickly spread throughout the western United States, with a number of tribes taking part. This first phase of the Ghost Dance phenomenon ran its course and ended without bloodshed.

In 1890, Wavoka (d. 1932), another Paiute prophet, had a vision similar to that of Wodziwob. In the intervening two decades, however, the situation of the Native American had become more precarious, and Wavoka's vision was consequently darker than that of Wodziwob. The Lakota Sioux, who were at the heart of the 1890 events for example, were faced with the virtual extinction of the buffalo herd, disastrous crop failures on reservation land (which was ill-equipped for agriculture in the first place), epidemic diseases, and the threat of deportation to even less habitable lands. Thus, to the vision of resurrection and the restoration of the world to its pristine condition was added the promised destruction of the white race.

The 1890 phase of the Ghost Dance arose in Nebraska and spread throughout the Midwest, with a particular epicenter in the Dakotas. This time, however, the Indian Agency and the military reacted. Through a catastrophic series of misunderstandings and miscalculations on both sides, violent clashes flared between the American military determined to end the Ghost Dance and Lakotas equally determined to seize what they viewed as their last, best chance for cultural survival. From the Lakota side, the flavor of this vision may be heard in the words of Short Bull (1845–1915), a medicine man from the Rosebud reservation. James Mooney's 1896 account recounts Short Bull's promise to his people:

> We must continue this dance. If the soldiers surround you four deep, three of you, on whom I have put holy shirts, will sing a song, which I have taught you, around them, when some of them will drop dead.

> Then the rest will start to run, but their horses will sink into the earth. The riders will jump from their horses, but they will sink into the earth also. Then you can do as you desire with them. Now, you must know this, that all the soldiers and that race will be dead. (Peasuntabee 2000, 70)

This promise, and others like it from Short Bull and the Minniconju medicine man Kicking Bear (c. 1850–1890), which assured their people that ghost shirts would render the wearer immune to bullets, all played their part in the tragedy that followed. But in the end, it was the overreaction of the government and the brutality of soldiers, whose claims to have engaged only armed Indians were belied by the murder of twenty-six children under the age of thirteen and the killing of women and children over a two-mile pursuit. This tragedy at the Rosebud Sioux Reservation at Wounded Knee, South Dakota, in December 1890 brought the Ghost Dance to a violent end.

Contemporary Cases: Christian Identity and the Rescue Movement

Christian Identity evolved from nineteenth-century British-Israelism, an eccentric form of biblical interpretation that posited the British people as the descendants of the biblical Israelites. Transplanted to the United States, British-Israelism combined with anti-Semitic currents drawn from the *Protocols of the Elders of Zion* and the "International Jew" series run in Henry Ford's company newspaper, the *Dearborn Independent*, to create by the 1940s the virulently anti-Semitic and racist doctrines of Christian Identity. Identity's most distinctive theological motif is the "two seeds doctrine," which posits the Jewish people as the demonic offspring of Eve and the serpent in the Garden of Eden (Genesis 3:1–4). The nonwhite races in this interpretation are seen as the "beasts of the field" (Genesis 2:19–20), over whom Adam as the first white man was given dominion (Genesis 1:28–30). Identity Christians see the book of Revelation's dread tribulation period as imminent, but these believers have no hope of supernatural rescue via the rapture, or the rising into the air of the faithful to await the culmination of the apocalypse at the side of Jesus (1 Thessalonians 4:17). Added to this biblical world view is the acceptance of the Zionist Occupation Government discourse, which holds that the Jews have succeeded in establishing control not only over the American government, but over the world system itself (John 8:44; Revelation 2:9; 3:9).

Despite the often violent rhetoric emanating from Christian Identity quarters, the movement has rarely initiated violence. This may be attributed to the faithful's awareness of their own tiny numbers (between ten thousand and fifty thousand worldwide) and to disagreements over the interpretation of world events within the apocalyptic scenario of the Bible. Yet throughout the 1980s, there were confrontations between state authorities and Identity communities that took place at several isolated compounds, most notably at the Covenant, Sword, and Arm of the Lord in rural Missouri in 1985. These confrontations were invariably resolved with the peaceful surrender of the besieged Identity believers.

There were a handful of individuals, however, who attempted to take action against the state or against those whom they identified with the state (i.e., the Jews). The most important of these were the Brüderschweigen (the Silent Brotherhood more popularly known as the Order), a revolutionary group centered in the Northwest, which was composed of a mix of Identity Christians and neopagan Odinists under the charismatic leadership of Robert Mathews. In the mid–1980s, the Order undertook a brief course of revolutionary violence that included at least two murders, the robbery of several armored cars, counterfeiting, and sundry crimes and misdemeanors. The group was smashed and Mathews killed in a shoot-out with federal agents on 8 December 1984.

The pro-life rescue movement, defined as pro-lifers who practice "interposition" (in rescue parlance "those who interpose their bodies between the killer and his victim" [Trewhella & Sedlak], i.e., the abortionist and the unborn child), emerged slowly from the religious opposition to the 1973 Roe v. Wade Supreme Court decision legalizing abortion. The first halting attempts at interposition, primarily in the form of minor vandalism, were undertaken in the early 1980s by individuals such as Joan Andrews. The punishments meted out to Andrews and others for these early forays were sufficiently draconian to inspire her and others to attempt to do more serious damage, correctly assuming that the sentences would be no worse for the greater level of destruction.

Operation Rescue was formed under the leadership of Randall Terry in 1986. Operation Rescue marked both the emergence of a large, organized rescue movement and the shift in the movement from a primarily Roman Catholic to a primarily evangelical and fundamentalist Protestant constituency. Operation Rescue's tactical approach involved large-scale demonstrations aimed at shutting down abortion clinics in selected cities for limited periods of time. Thus, in such cities and towns as Buffalo, Fargo, North Dakota, Los Angeles, Pittsburgh, and culminating in Atlanta during the 1988 Democratic Convention, Operation Rescue mobilized supporters throughout the country. Operation Rescue however, consciously modeled its actions on the nonviolent civil disobedience of the 1960s-era civil rights movement and insisted that anyone seeking to take part in their actions sign a pledge to eschew violence in any form.

The experience of the Atlanta jails split the movement, and after 1988 new rescue groups appeared, some of whom were less committed to nonviolence than Operation Rescue. The Lambs of Christ, for example, a primarily Catholic rescue group, is led by a priest named Norman Weslin, who, like his second-in-command Ron Maxson, is from a military background. The Lambs added an element of increased militancy to the rescue movement. The Milwaukee-based Missionaries to the Pre-Born, led by two former Operation Rescue stalwarts, Joseph Foreman and Matt Trewella, added direct confrontations with abortionists, destruction of property, and a form of spiritual warfare they called imprecatory prayer (i.e., calling upon God through the use of certain Old Testament Psalms to either show the abortionist the error of his ways or to strike him dead).

Meanwhile, in the mid-1980s and early 1990s, individuals such as John Brockhoeft, Marjorie Reed, Michael Bray, and Shelley Shannon began to take more resolute action by firebombing clinics. They were scrupulous in their determination that the destruction of buildings would be accomplished with absolutely no loss of life. Moreover, all of them explained their actions by reference to biblical texts and their passionate belief that abortion was symptomatic of the fact that these were indeed the last days and that God's judgment on a fallen nation was nigh. Thus, when Michael Griffin, a peripheral figure in the tightly knit rescue community, shot and killed Dr. David Gunn in Pensacola, Florida, in 1993, the final barrier to lethal violence was broken. In short order, Shelley Shannon attempted to kill Dr. George Tiller in Milwaukee and Paul Hill shot and killed another Pensacola doctor, John Britton, and his volunteer bodyguard.

The core group of rescuers who opted for force—Shannon, Brockhoeft, Bray, Reed, and a few others around the country—created an organizational symbol in the early 1990s called the Army of God (AOG). The AOG produced a manual that contained the experiences of the group as they tried to learn from scratch the methods of domestic terrorism. The AOG manual offered both the optimum recipes for bombs and fervent expressions of religious faith. Today, the primary outlet for the views of the proforce wing of the rescue movement is via the Nuremberg Files website, which offers an apocalyptic analysis of American society; the names, addresses, and whereabouts of abortion providers throughout the nation; and explicit endorsements of the use of lethal force.

The Year 2000

The increased scholarly attention given to millennial violence in recent years—from the disastrous siege at Waco, Texas, in 1993 to the Oklahoma City bombing in 1995 and the Aum Shinrikyo cult's release of sarin gas in the Tokyo subway, also in 1995—did not go unnoticed by government security agencies in the run-up to the new millennium in the year 2000. Complicating security concerns was the fear that the so-called Y2K bug would cause computers to malfunction, grinding industrial civilization to a halt and inducing widespread panic and chaos. Government authorities began to make contact with concerned scholars, and from this interaction emerged a series of government reports warning of the dangers of millenarian violence to accompany the turn of the calendar year.

In 1999, these reports began to go public in several countries. The highly publicized American contribution, the *Megiddo Report* issued by the FBI, was the most alarmist. The Canadian *Doomsday Religious Movements* report followed, seeking to present the level of threat as much less than the *Megiddo Report* suggested. Even the Israelis issued a report with the ungainly title *Events at the End of the Millennium: Possible Implications for the Public Order in Jerusalem* (reprinted in Kaplan 2002). In the event, the year 2000 passed quietly enough. Ominously in light of what was to come on 11 September 2001, the only serious plot to commit terrorist violence was reportedly undertaken by operatives of al-Qaeda, when a group led by Ahmad Rassam and including Mokhtar Haouari, Abdelmajid Dahoumane, and Abdel Ghani Meskini (who later exchanged his testimony against his comrades for leniency) were arrested when trying to enter the United States or were extradited to the United States subsequent to the initial arrests. Their putative target appears to have been Los Angeles International Airport, which would have been crowded with holiday travelers.

With the advantage of hindsight, it is significant that the threat of real terrorist violence came not from Western millenarians, but from an Islamist movement that emerges from a culture whose lunar calendar did not reflect the turn of the chronological millennium and whose attraction to taking action on the New Year seems to have been occasioned by the opportunity of expected crowds at airports and public events and, apparently, the widespread press speculation that millennial violence was imminent. The full import of these arrests was unknown at the time, and before 11 September 2001 set new paradigms for our understanding of terrorism, the threat of violence by Western millenarians was considered to be both real and serious by many governments, and by more than a few scholars.

As this entry suggests however, the dangers posed by violent Western millenarians, while real enough, pale in comparison to the level of terrorist violence demonstrated on 11 September. This should serve to remind those who follow these movements—press, governmental authorities, and scholars alike—that what millenarians do best is wait. They wait for the signs of the times to accord with a reliable interpretation of inerrant text by charismatic leaders entrusted with the task. These leaders in turn, as contemporary history teaches, are canny judges of the prevailing balance of forces. Given the minute numbers of the faithful, the vast array of forces that could be mobilized against them, and the dearth of indisputable signs of the times, the small fraction of the millenarian community who might be attracted to violence remains content to wait, and to watch, and to dream.

Jeffrey Kaplan

See also Christian Identity; Millennialism

Further Reading

Adas, M. (1979). *Prophets of rebellion: Millenarian protest movements against the European colonial order*. Chapel Hill: University of North Carolina Press.

Ahlstrom, S. E (1972). *A religious history of the American people*. New Haven, CT: Yale University Press.

Barkun, M. (1974). *Disaster and the millennium*. New Haven, CT: Yale University Press.

Barkun, M. (1994). *Religion and the racist right*. Chapel Hill: University of North Carolina Press.

Billington, J. H. (1980). *Fire in the minds of men: Origins of the revolutionary faith*. New York: Basic Books.

Coates, J. (1987). *Armed and dangerous: The rise of the survivalist right*. New York: Hill and Wang.

Cohn, N. (1970). *Pursuit of the millennium: Revolutionary millenarians and mystical anarchists of the Middle Ages*. New York: Oxford University Press.

Flynn, K., & Gerhardt, G. (1990). *The silent brotherhood*. New York: Signet.

Gill, S. (1987). *Native American religious action: A performance approach to religion*. Columbia: University of South Carolina Press.

Girard, R. (1979). *Violence and the sacred*. Baltimore: Johns Hopkins University Press.

Kaplan, J. (1996). Absolute rescue: Absolutism, defensive action, and the resort to force. In M. Barkun (Ed.), *Millennialism and violence* (pp. 128–163). London and Portland, OR: Frank Cass.

Kaplan, J. (1997). *Radical religion in America*. Syracuse, NY: Syracuse University Press.

Kaplan, J. (2000). *Encyclopedia of white power: A sourcebook on the radical racist right*. Walnut Creek, CA: AltaMira Press.

Kaplan, J. (2002). *Millennial violence: Past, present, and future*. London: Frank Cass & Co.

Marty, M. E. (1986). *The irony of it all 1893–1919*. Chicago: University of Chicago Press.

Marty, M. E. (1991). *The noise and the conflict 1919–1941*. Chicago: University of Chicago Press.

Marty, M. E. (1996). *Under God indivisible 1941–1960*. Chicago: University of Chicago Press.

Melton, J. G. (1987). *Encyclopedia of American religion* (2nd ed.). Detroit, MI: Gale Publications.

Pesantubbee, M. E. (2000). From vision to violence: The Wounded Knee massacre. In C. Wessinger (Ed.), *Millennialism, persecution, and violence* (pp 62–81). Syracuse, NY: Syracuse University Press.

Rhodes, J. M. (1980). *The Hitler movement: A modern millenarian revolution*. Stanford, CA: Hoover Institution Press.

Saint Clair, M. J. (1992). *Millenarian movements in historical context*. New York: Garland.

Tabor, J. D., & Gallaghe, E. V. (1995). *Why Waco? Cults and the battle for religious freedom in America*. Berkeley: University of California Press.

Trewhella, M., & Sedlak, W. (n.d.). *The historic Christian doctrine of interposition*. Milwaukee, WI: Missionaries to the Preborn.

Walls, R. (Ed.). (1982). *Millenarianism and charisma*. Belfast, Northern Ireland: Queens University.

Wilson, B. R. (1973). *Magic and the millennium*. New York: Harper & Row.

Court Cases

Roe v. Wade, 410 U.S. 113 (1973)

Millennialism

Millennialism is a term used by scholars of religion to denote a pattern of religiosity that has its peaceful as well as violent aspects. The term has its origins in the prediction in the Christian New Testament book of Revelation that God's kingdom on Earth would last 1000 years, but scholars have identified the millennial religious pattern in diverse religious and purportedly secular traditions. A range of behaviors is associated with millennialism, and in extreme manifestations millennial worldviews are used to justify warfare. Many conflicts are characterized by millennial motivations.

Building on the definition of millennialism first offered by Norman Cohn (1957), millennialism is defined here as involving belief in an imminent transition to a collective salvation. The expected collective salvation may be heavenly or earthly. When it is earthly, people may engage in social work to create the millennial kingdom; they may engage in nation-building, which can involve revolution against perceived tyranny, or violent actions to defend the elect community; they may fight wars to extend their rule over other nations; and they may engage in genocide to cleanse the elect of perceived polluting and disruptive elements.

Citizens or law enforcement agents may attack a millennial group because they perceive the group as being threatening, but millennialism should not be considered inherently dangerous and violent. Numerous people with millennial worldviews never engage in violence or become caught up in violent episodes.

There is, however, a noteworthy connection between millennialism and war. Millennialism has two major expressions that are not mutually exclusive: catastrophic millennialism and progressive millennialism. The views of believers may shift between whether they expect the transition to the collective salvation to occur catastrophically or progressively. A sense of being persecuted often enhances catastrophic expectations.

Catastrophic millennialists believe that the old order is so evil and corrupt that it must be destroyed to make way for the new millennial kingdom. Many catastrophic millennialists believe that the old order will be destroyed by divine intervention and that their role is to wait in faith. Other catastrophic millennialists believe they are called by God or some other superhuman agent to take up arms to destroy the old order so the new one can be created.

Progressive millennialists have a more optimistic view of society and a strong faith in "progress," a conception of history that became prominent in the Enlightenment. They believe humans acting according to a divine or superhuman plan can create the millennial kingdom. It is not a matter of human effort alone; rather, it will take human effort cooperating with the will of a higher power to create the collective salvation. Peaceful progressive millennialists engage in reform, peace, and reconciliation work, as in the example of the Protestant Social Gospel movement and the Roman Catholic "special option for the poor" emphasis of Vatican II. However, some believers in progress are, according to Robert Ellwood, impatient to speed progress up, sometimes to an apocalyptic degree. They will do anything—including wage war or kill people—to hasten the transition to the millennial kingdom.

On the violent end of the millennial scale, revolutionary progressive millennialists and revolutionary catastrophic millennialists are very similar to each other in outlook and behavior. Both types of believers desire social transformation and are willing to utilize violence to achieve it. They see the world in rigid dualistic terms, dividing people into "us and them" or "good and evil." Ellwood has identified Nazism, with its goal of the Third Reich for the benefit of the German *Völk*, as an expression of progressive millennialism. Richard C. Salter has shown that the Khmer Rouge in Cambodia were progressive millennialists desiring to start Cambodian history and society over again in the "Year One." Scott Lowe has written of the Maoist Communist movement in China as an expression of progressive millennialism. Jacqueline Stone has highlighted catastrophic millennial ideas deriving from Nichiren *Lotus Sutra* Buddhism as being a factor in militant Japanese nationalism culminating in World War II. Statements by Osama bin Laden before and after 11 September 2001 indicate that he was motivated by a desire to defeat evil as embodied in the United States and "hypocritical" Muslim regimes. Bin Laden encouraged Muslims to take up arms to fight a revolution that would produce a true Islamic state, obedient to Allah and his commands as expressed in Islamic law. In other words, bin Laden's goal was a collective salvation for an elect that is characteristic of millennialism.

When revolutionary millennialists succeed in attracting a significant segment of society willing to fight a revolution for the sake of establishing their vision of the millennial kingdom, they produce wars involving extensive suffering and death. For instance, the Taiping Revolution in China, which from 1853 to 1864 had its Heavenly Capital of the Taiping Heavenly Kingdom in Nanjing, resulted in the deaths of millions.

The Axis of Evil

In his State if the Union address on 29 January 2002, President George W. Bush characterized North Korean, Iran and Iraq as the "Axis of Evil." His use of the word "evil" to describe nations which he sees as threat to world peace and security is in accord with the actions of many leaders of millennial movements through history who have defined the enemy as evil so as to justify their destruction.

Our second goal is to prevent regimes that sponsor terror from threatening America or our friends and allies with weapons of mass destruction. Some of these regimes have been pretty quiet since September the 11th. But we know their true nature. North Korea is a regime arming with missiles and weapons of mass destruction, while starving its citizens.

Iran aggressively pursues these weapons and exports terror, while an unelected few repress the Iranian people's hope for freedom.

Iraq continues to flaunt its hostility toward America and to support terror. The Iraqi regime has plotted to develop anthrax, and nerve gas, and nuclear weapons for over a decade. This is a regime that has already used poison gas to murder thousands of its own citizens—leaving the bodies of mothers huddled over their dead children. This is a regime that agreed to international inspections—then kicked out the inspectors. This is a regime that has something to hide from the civilized world.

States like these, and their terrorist allies, constitute an axis of evil, arming to threaten the peace of the world. By seeking weapons of mass destruction, these regimes pose a grave and growing danger. They could provide these arms to terrorists, giving them the means to match their hatred. They could attack our allies or attempt to blackmail the United States. In any of these cases, the price of indifference would be catastrophic.

Source: President Delivers State of Union Address. (2002, January 29). Retrieved April 5, 2003, from http://www.whitehouse.gov/news/releases/2002/01/20020129–11.html

When revolutionary millennialists do not have a critical mass in society, they engage in acts of terrorism that they hope will spark the revolution that they desire. For example, Timothy McVeigh, the perpetrator of the 19 April 1995 bombing of a federal office building in Oklahoma City, Oklahoma, participated in a broad, diffuse, and not socially dominant Euro-American (white supremacist) revolutionary millennial movement in the United States, which included disaffected military men and police officers, Identity Christians, Neo-Nazis, Odinists, and others.

A revolutionary millennial movement that is avowedly secular in its ideology will still refer to a superhuman agent, such as Adolf Hitler's Nature or Marxism's dialectical materialism, as tending toward the collective salvation of the elect. Secular revolutionary millennialists and overtly religious revolutionary millennialists share a common ultimate concern to destroy the old order and create the new, and they believe a superhuman agent is on their side in the battle.

Messianism is a common, but not a necessary, component of millennial movements. The word *messiah* is used here to denote an individual who is believed to be empowered by a divine or superhuman agent to create the collective salvation. There have been numerous messiahs of revolutionary millennial movements, including Hitler, Mao, and Hong Xiuquan of the Taiping Revolution, to mention just a few. Political leaders in times of warfare may be invested with messianic charisma by devoted followers. But not all millennial movements, including revolutionary millennial movements, have messiahs. The contemporary Euro-American nativist movement thus far lacks a unifying messianic figure.

Fanaticism, like millennialism, is varied in intensity and expression. Fanaticism involves a rigid, dualistic worldview—a strong sense of good and evil, us and them—a conviction that the true believers have access to an infallible source of authority, and an unwillingness to grant legitimacy to other points of view and ways of life. A violent fanatic has taken the position that the end justifies the means; any means, even violent ones, can be used legitimately to bring about the desired goal, which for millennialists is the collective salvation of the elect, the millennial kingdom.

Revolutionary millennialism, like other religious expressions, can change; people can lose their revolutionary and fanatic fervor. The conviction that the transition to the collective salvation is imminent can wane. Stone has pointed out that if a revolutionary millennial movement suffers a devastating defeat, pacifist movements can arise out of the ashes. She identified this shift from militarism to pacifism in the Nichiren Buddhist groups and thinkers that emerged in Japan after World War II. Ian Reader (2000) has coined the phrase "pragmatics of failure" to refer to the way a millennial movement changes its methods if those previously used fail to achieve the collective salvation. If violent methods are shown to be futile in achieving the goal of a millennial kingdom, believers may resort to peaceful means. Conversely, if a peaceful movement or nation feels threatened and attacked, believers may resort to violence.

Millennial expectations were important in motivating American colonists to fight the American Revolution against England. Probably most wars are associated with millennial dualism. If people on the opposing side are dehumanized as evil and "other," then it becomes easier and even virtuous to kill them. The vision of the millennial kingdom, the earthly well-being of the sacred elect community, provides strong motivation for the extreme actions of killing and dying to achieve salvation for others, if not oneself. Ultimately the winners write the history and determine which parties to war are glorified as righteous patriots and which ones are vilified as evil.

Catherine Wessinger

See also Christian Identity; Millenarian Violence: Latin America; Millenarian Violence: Thai Buddhism; Millenarian Violence: United States

Further Reading

Cohn, N. (1957). *The pursuit of the millennium.* London: Secker & Warburg.

Cook, D. (2002). Suicide attacks or "martyrdom operations" in contemporary jihad literature. *Nova Religio: The Journal of Alternative and Emergent Religions 6*(1), (pp. 7–44).

Ellwood, R. (2000). Nazism as a millennialist movement. In C. Wessinger (Ed.), *Millennialism, persecution, and violence: Historical cases* (pp. 241–260). Syracuse, NY: Syracuse University Press.

Lowe, S. (2000). Western millennial ideology goes east: The Taiping Revolution and Mao's Great Leap Forward. In C. Wessinger (Ed.), *Millennialism, persecution, and violence: Historical cases* (pp. 220–240). Syracuse, NY: Syracuse University Press.

Reader, I. (2000). Imagined persecution: Aum Shinrikyo, millennialism, and the legitimation of violence. In C. Wessinger (Ed.), *Millennialism, persecution, and violence: Historical cases* (pp. 158–182). Syracuse, NY: Syracuse University Press.

Salter, R. C. (2000). Time, authority, and ethics in the Khmer Rouge: Elements of the millennial vision in the year zero. In C. Wessinger (Ed.), *Millennialism, persecution, and violence: Historical cases* (pp. 281–298). Syracuse, NY: Syracuse University Press.

Stone, J. (2000). Japanese *Lotus* millennialism: From militant nationalism to contemporary peace movements. In C. Wessinger (Ed.), *Millennialism, persecution, and violence: Historical cases* (pp. 261–280). Syracuse, NY: Syracuse University Press.

Wessinger, C. (2000). *How the millennium comes violently: From Jonestown to Heaven's Gate.* New York: Seven Bridges Press.

Wessinger, C. (Ed.). (2000). *Millennialism, persecution, and violence: Historical cases.* Syracuse, NY: Syracuse University Press.

Wojcik, D. (1997). *The end of the world as we know it: Faith, fatalism, and apocalypse in America.* New York: New York University Press.

Mormons

War and religious conflict have played an important part in the history and theology of the Mormons. From their early days, Mormons encountered violence in the surrounding community. Those encounters are instructive in understanding the United States' struggle with an emerging pluralism in the nineteenth century and in understanding how Mormons' attitudes toward war and other forms of conflict developed.

Mormonism is the religious movement associated with the beliefs and practices of the Church of Jesus Christ of Latter-Day Saints. Mormons distinguish themselves from Protestant Christianity in referring to their movement as restorationist rather than reformationist. This restoration is said to have begun with the revelations given to Joseph Smith (1805–1844), which communicated the need for a restoration of the true church and the authority to perform necessary rites and ordinances. Arguably the most important revelation given to Joseph Smith was the Book of Mormon (published in 1830), which is part of the Latter-Day Saint canon along with the Bible, the Doctrine and Covenants, and the Pearl of Great Price (the latter two being primarily collections of other revelations to Joseph Smith. In addition to accepting this expanded canon, the Church of Latter-Day Saints differs from traditional Christian religions in its acceptance of continuing revelation from God through the leaders of the Church, the need for additional sacred ordinances performed in temples dedicated for this purpose, and in conceiving of God and Jesus Christ as embodied beings.

Pronouncements on War and Violence in the Book of Mormon

Scripture plays an important role in shaping Mormon attitudes toward war and the use of violence. The Book of Mormon is particularly valuable because one of the central themes of the book is the justification and use of war for righteous and unrighteous ends. Published in 1830, the Book of Mormon is believed by Mormons to be an ancient book of scripture that records the sacred history of Jewish colonizers on the American continent between approximately 600 BCE and 400 CE. The book records the spiritual and military struggles of two warring factions known as the Nephites and Lamanites. The centerpiece of the book is the account of the appearance of Jesus Christ on the American continent shortly after his death and resurrection, during which he commands the people to "offer up unto me no more the shedding of blood" (3 Nephi 9:19). The Book of Mormon contains more than a hundred accounts of armed conflict, and it addresses such issues as pacifism, conditions for a just war, divine deliverance, and religious freedom.

The ideal of pacifism is familiar in the development of Christianity and Judaism. However, "The Book of Mormon presents the only instance in scripture of a society committed by covenant to pacifism, the rejection of war in all forms through passive nonresistance to violence" (Firmage 1985, 46). This account involves a group of Lamanites who were converted to righteousness by Nephite missionaries. As part of their conversion and repentance for the murders they had committed in past wars, they covenanted never to take up arms again under any circumstances.

> Oh how merciful is our God! And now behold, since it has been as much as we could do to get our stains taken away from us, and our swords are made bright, let us hide them away that they may be kept bright, as a testimony to our God at the last day, or at the day that we shall be brought to stand before him to be judged, that we have not stained our swords with the blood of our brethren since he imparted his word unto us and has made us clean thereby. . . . [A]nd this they did, vouching and covenanting with God, that rather than shed the blood of their brethren they would give up their own lives; and rather than take away from a brother they would give unto him; and rather than spend their days in idleness they would labor abundantly with their hands. (Alma 24:15, 18)

As a result of their conversion, this group of Lamanites changed their name to symbolize their commitment to peace. Shortly thereafter, the Lamanites who had not converted attacked the new converts, who responded by prostrating themselves on the ground in front of their attackers. When the Lamanites discovered that their former allies would not retaliate, they threw down their weapons, and many were converted by this extraordinary act of courage.

There are also repeated accounts specifying the conditions for engaging in warfare, which are limited to the defense of freedom, self, family, or property and only as a last resort. In many respects, the Book of Mormon's strictures parallel traditional Christian just-war doctrine. Both specify what are known as "just causes," the reasons for engaging in conflict, and "just conduct" which specifies the appropriate range of actions while engaged in conflict.

> Now the Nephites were taught to defend themselves against their enemies, even to the shedding of blood if it were necessary; yea, and they were also taught never to give an offense, yea, and never to raise the sword except it were against an enemy, except it were to preserve their lives. And this was their faith, that by so doing God would prosper them in the land. . . Now, they were sorry to take up arms against the Lamanites, because they did not delight in the shedding of blood; yea, and this was not all—they were sorry to be the means of sending so many of their brethren out of this world into an eternal world, unprepared to meet their God. Nevertheless, they could not suffer to lay down their lives, that their wives and their children should be massacred by the barbarous

The Nauvoo Legion

The first Saturdays of May and September and the 4th of July were set aside for parades when the Nauvoo legion was organized. They were day long affairs and were held on the official parade grounds near Joseph Smith's farm east of Nauvoo. They featured a speech and inspection of the troops by the commander in-chief. There were also sham battles and field exercises. Many people attended these affairs but because of the publicity and the purpose of the Legion neighboring settlers were alarmed and called for the disarming of them. The Prophet Joseph always attended these gatherings as commander-in-chief. In September 1843 the Neighbor announced the parade for the 16th at the usual site. This time, however, there were no dignitaries present. Sensing the climate and aware of the troubled days ahead, the Prophet Joseph reviewed the troops and then told the officers to increase their size and numbers. This was their last parade . . .

Governor Ford sent troops to disarm the Legion of their state held arms. A short time later Governor Ford dispatched troops under a Captain Singleton where he was ordered to assemble the Legion and see if they were disbanded and unarmed. In a matter of two hours, two thousand men assembled with their personal arms and weapons. We don't know of the Captain's response to this. We only know that the Legion against the state's warnings quietly went about gathering more arms. . . .

In August 1844 Brigadier Charles Rich received orders to parade the armed and equipped Legion. Brigham Young turned the Legion over to Rich who quietly and efficiently set about turning the legion into a no-nonsense fighting force . . .

Hyrum Smith had prophesied before his death that the governor would yet call upon the legion to maintain the supremacy of the law, and sure enough the governor wrote a letter to Brigham Young ordering him to "hold in readiness a sufficient force under your command of the Nauvoo Legion to guard the court and protect it or its officers from the violence of the mob."

The legion would eventually follow the saints on their exodus to the West and years later would remember their time in Nauvoo when they were reorganized and moved into defensive positions in Echo Canyon in Utah awaiting the arrival of Johnston's army.

Source: **Givens, George W. (n.d.).** ***In Old Nauvoo: Everyday Life in the City of Joseph. Consisting of Becky Porter's selected excerpts from the book.*** **Retrieved January 13, 2003 from http://rnsmith.com/wpsmith/oldnauv.html**

> cruelty of those who were once their brethren, yea, and had dissented from their church, and had left them and had gone to destroy them by joining the Lamanites. (Alma 48:14–15; 23–4)

A further component of this defensive approach to war is the repeated practice of seeking a peaceful resolution in the midst of battle and the refusal to annihilate the enemy. During one campaign, the armies of general Moroni surrounded the Lamanites. Upon seeing the Lamanites' terror, Moroni ordered his army to withdraw and said to Zerahemnah, the Lamanite general, "Behold, Zerahemnah, that we do not desire to be men of blood. Ye know that ye are in our hands, yet we do not desire to slay you. Behold we have not come out to battle against you that we might shed your blood for power; neither do we desire to bring any one to the yoke of bondage" (Alma 44:1–2).

The Book of Mormon makes clear that the use of violence may be necessary, but only as a last resort when peaceful alternatives are exhausted. Wars conducted in the interest of expansionism or revenge are expressly prohibited, as illustrated in the account of subsequent wars in which the Nephites disregarded the just-war criteria of earlier generations and engaged in war against the Lamanites as an act of revenge for the slaughter of their people. As a result, Mormon (the

Joseph Smith, in a copy of a daguerreotype taken just before his death in 1844. Courtesy The Church of Jesus Christ of Latter-Day Saints.

general of the Nephite armies) refused to participate and watched as his people engaged in atrocities such as torture and cannibilism.

The Book of Mormon ends with the destruction of the Nephites due in part to their unjustified use of violence and with a prophetic plea to modern readers to apply the lessons of the book to their own experience. Because Mormons believe the Book of Mormon was preserved in order to come forth in the "latter days," their approach to issues in contemporary society is deeply affected by the central themes of the book. Spencer W. Kimball (1895–1985), President of the Church of Jesus Christ of Latter-Day Saint from 1973 to 1985, stated that the Book of Mormon "should convince all living souls of the futility of war and the hazards of unrighteousness. A few prophets, swimming in a sea of barbarism, find it difficult to prevent the crumbling and final collapse of a corrupt people" (Kimball, 1982, 414). The Book of Mormon shares with the Hebrew Bible and the New Testament the repeated theme of reliance on God as the deliverer instead of on one's own strength, which will inevitably lead to self-destruction. Without faith in God, the prophet Mormon records that "the strength of the Lord was not with us; yea, we were left to ourselves, that the Spirit of the Lord did not abide in us; therefore we had become weak like unto our brethren" (Mormon 2:26).

The Mormon Experience

For Mormons, questions of the appropriate use of and response to violence have been more than hypothetical, as they faced violence and persecution from the founding of the Church of Latter-Day Saints in 1830. Conflict with their non-Mormon neighbors in New York, Ohio, Missouri, and Illinois led Mormons to leave the United States and settle in the Utah Territory in 1847, but there they soon faced confrontation with the U.S. federal government (described below).

Although the Church of Jesus Christ of Latter-Day Saints has always "renounced war and proclaimed peace" (Doctrine and Covenants 98:16), its response to persecution has varied with the circumstances. As the Mormons moved from Ohio to western Missouri beginning in 1831, their initial response was one of pacifism. However, as the persecution intensified, the Church wrestled with the conditions under which it could respond to violence with violence.

One of the most important contributions in understanding this struggle is the revelation Joseph Smith received in 1833 during a period of intense persecution in Missouri when dozens of Mormons were driven from their homes and their bishop was stripped of his clothing and covered with tar and feathers in the public square.

> And again, this is the law that I gave unto mine ancients, that they should not go out unto battle against any nation, kindred, tongue, or people, save I, the Lord, command them. And if any nation, tongue, or people should proclaim war against them, they should first lift a standard of peace unto that people, nation, or tongue; And if that people did not accept the offering of peace, neither the second nor the third time, they should bring these testimonies before the Lord; Then I, the Lord, would give unto them a commandment, and justify them in going out to battle against that nation, tongue, or people. And I, the Lord, would fight their battles, and their children's battles and their children's children's, until they had avenged themselves on all their enemies, to the third and fourth generation. (Doctrine and Covenants 98: 33–36)

The revelation also commands that as long as their enemies seek forgiveness for their wrongdoings, Mormons are commanded to forgive them "until seventy times seven."

By 1838, however, relations between Mormons and many of their neighbors had grown so acrimonious that Sidney Rigdon, Joseph Smith's assistant and spokesman, declared that the time had finally come for Mormons to aggressively defend themselves against continued attacks. In his infamous Fourth of July speech at Far West, Missouri, Rigdon declared:

> We have not only when smitten on cheek turned the other, but we have done it, again and again, until we are wearied of being smitten, and tired of being trampled upon. . . . We take God and all the holy angels to witness this day, that we warn all men in the name of Jesus Christ, to come on us no more forever; for from this hour, we will bear it no more, our rights shall no more be trampled upon with impunity. The man or set of men who come on us to disturb us, it shall be between us and them a war of extermination, for we will follow them, till the last drop of their blood is spilled, or else they will have to exterminate us: for we will carry the seat of war to their own homes, and their own families, and one party or the other shall be utterly destroyed. Remember it all men. We will never be the aggressors, we will infringe upon the rights of no people; but shall stand for our own until death. We claim our own rights, and are willing that all others shall enjoy theirs. (Rigdon 1839, 12)

As a result of Rigdon's speech, a new wave of violence ensued that led Missouri's governor at that time, Lilburn Boggs, to declare that "Mormons must be treated as enemies, and must be exterminated or driven from the state if necessary, for the public peace" (Arrington and Bitton 1979, 44). In the winter of 1838–39, five thousand Mormons left Missouri and eventually found refuge in Nauvoo, Illinois, on the upper Mississippi River.

The experience in Missouri led the Mormon to have a more resolute attitude toward war and peace. Once in Illinois, Joseph Smith established the Nauvoo Legion, an army of several thousand soldiers, and was named its lieutenant general. By 1845, the Nauvoo Legion was one-quarter the size of the entire U.S. Army. The U.S. government feared that the Mormons represented an organized threat to the stability of the region and violent skirmishes ensued along with legal and political maneuvering. In June 1843, upon being released from custody for changes stemming from the Missouri period, Joseph Smith declared:

> If our enemies are determined to oppress us & deprive us of our rights and privileges as they have done & if the Authorities that be on the earth will not assist us in our rights nor give us that protection which the Laws &Constitution of the United States & the State guarantees unto us: then we will claim them from higher power from heaven & from God Almighty. . .I will lead you to battle & if you are not afraid to die & feel disposed to spill your Blood in your own defence you will not offend me. Be not the aggressor. Bear untill they strike on the one cheeck. Offer the other & they will be sure to strike that. Then defend yourselves & God shall bear you off. Will any part of Illinois way we shall not have our rights? Treat them as strangers & not friends & let them go to Hell. (Ehat and Cook, 217–18)

The Mormons under Brigham Young

In the summer of 1844, after continued skirmishes with the law and anti-Mormon mobs, Smith was arrested and taken to Carthage, Illinois, where he was murdered by a group of rogue militia men while waiting to stand trial. The Mormon reaction to the death of their prophet showed remarkable restraint. One editorial stated that "we will suffer wrong rather than do wrong. . . . The gospel whispers peace" (Walker 1982, 45). In early February 1846, the Latter-Day Saints, now under the leadership of Brigham Young (1801–1877), fled from Nauvoo and, in one of the great migrations in U.S. history, emigrated to the Great Salt Lake Valley in the Utah Territory. Although there continued to be mixed attitudes toward the United States government during this time, Brigham Young was interested in participating in national affairs by supporting the Mexican-American War (1846–48), to which he sent five hundred troops.

The Mormons found that even in Utah Territory the U.S. federal government was not content to let them establish an independent religious community in peace. In 1857 President James Buchanan, influenced by reports that the Mormons were acting in defiance to federal authority, sent a military force to Utah. Fearful for their lives and wary of the government's intentions, Brigham Young reactivated the Nauvoo Legion and sent troops to do all it could to obstruct the advance of the army short of bloodshed. As outright war approached in 1858, Young weighed his options and was determined to lead the Mormons out of Utah to avoid further violence. However, the situation ended without bloodshed when it was agreed that the U.S. Army would not attack if the Mormon military forces would disband. After the U.S. Civil War (1861–65), Young declared that "God never institutes war; God is not the author of confusion or of war; they are the results of the acts of the children of men. Confusion and war necessarily come as the results of foolish acts and policy of men; but they do not come because God desires they should come" (Hildreth 1982, 217).

Religious Commitment and Duties toward One's Country

Utah was granted statehood in 1896, after which Mormons became increasingly involved in the issues of larger society, including the question of U.S. involvement in World Wars I and II. These conflicts compelled the Church to deal with issues such the duties of church members as citizens of a nation at war. The Twelfth Article of Faith of the Church of Jesus Christ of Latter-Day Saints reads: "We believe in being subject to kings, presidents, rulers, and magistrates, in obeying, honoring, and sustaining the law." The conflicting duties of proclaiming peace and submitting to civic authority led the church to clarify its position. In the 1942 General Conference of the Church, president David O. McKay (1873–1970) stated that

> The Church is and must be against war. . . It cannot regard war as a righteous means of settling international disputes . . .
>
> But the Church membership are citizens or subjects of sovereignties over which the Church has no control. . . . When, therefore, constitutional law, obedient to these principles, calls the manhood of the Church into the armed service of any country to which they owe allegiance, their highest civic duty requires that they meet that call. . . . It would be a cruel God that would punish His children as moral sinner for acts done by them as the innocent instrumentalities of a sovereign whom He had told them to obey and whose will they were powerless to resist. (McKay 1942, 94–95)

Thus it was determined that military service to one's country overcame ecclesiastical objection to war. McKay further stated that soldiers were not morally responsible for their actions as soldiers, and that justification for the actions of the state in warfare is left to the wisdom of God. However, one criterion for assessing international relations that church leaders have repeated for the past several decades is that the golden rule is "equally binding on nations, associations, and individuals. With compassion and forbearance, it replaces the retaliatory reactions of 'an eye for eye, and a tooth for a tooth' " (Nelson 2002, 39).

The Church of Jesus Christ of Latter-Day Saints Today

The Church of Jesus Christ of Latter-Day Saints has grown from a small sect with violent encounters with its frontier neighbors to a global church with members who are subjects of a variety of political regimes. Its history shows a pattern of trying to negotiate a balance between early pacifist ideals and the justified use of violence. The Church strongly opposed the MX missile project, a project proposed in 1979 and carried out in the 1980s to develop third-generation intercontinental ballistic missiles. The Church has acknowledged the rights of conscientious objectors, but it has also placed significant emphasis on civil obedience, personal righteousness over social activism, and deference to God in judging state warfare. Although Church leadership has repeatedly called upon states to find peaceful resolutions for their differences, "Nationalism and the growing internationalization of the Church required not only international military compliance during WWII, but demanded that such compliance be automatic and dispassionately neutral" (Walker 1982, 53–4).

These competing principles of pacifism vs. justified violence, allegiance to church vs. state, and individual purity vs. social activism have long divided Western religious traditions. Contemporary Mormon responses to war and violence mirror in many respects those of other mainline Christian denominations. The millennial enthusiasm of Mormon responses to war and violence early in their history has developed into a more tempered approach characteristic of a global religion.

Brian D. Birch

Further Reading

Arrington, L. J., & Bitton, D. (1979). *The Mormon experience: A history of the Latter-Day Saints*. New York: Alfred A. Knopf.

Blais, P. (1984). The enduring paradox: Mormon attitudes toward war and peace. *Dialogue: A Journal of Mormon Thought 17*(4), 61–73.

Ehat, A. F. & Cook, L. W. (1980). *The words of Joseph Smith*. Provo, UT: Religious Studies Center, Brigham Young University.

England, E. (1982). Can nations love their enemies? An LDS theology of peace. *Sunstone, 7*(6), 49–56.

Firmage, E. B. (1983). Allegiance and stewardship: Holy war, just war, and the Mormon tradition in the nuclear age. *Dialogue: A Journal of Mormon Thought, 16*(1), 47–61.

Firmage, E. B. (1985) Violence and the gospel: The teachings of the Old Testament, the New Testament, and the Book of Mormon. *Brigham Young University Studies, 25*(1), 31–53.

Hildreth, S. A. (1982). The first presidency statement on MX in perspective. *Brigham Young University Studies, 2*(2), 215–225.

Hill, M. S. (1989). *Quest for refuge: The Mormon flight from American pluralism*. Salt Lake City, UT: Signature Books.

Kimball, S. W. (1976). The false gods we worship. *Ensign, 6*(7), 3–7.

Kimball, E. L. (Ed.). (1982). *The teachings of Spencer W. Kimball*. Salt Lake City, UT: Bookcraft.

McKay, D. O. (1942). *One hundred and twelfth annual conference of the Church of Jesus Christ of Latter-Day Saints.* Salt Lake City, 72.

Nelson, R. M. (2002). Blessed are the peacemakers. *Ensign, 32*(11), 39–41

Ricks, S. D., & Hamblin, W. J. (Eds.). (1990). *Warfare in the Book of Mormon*. Salt Lake City, UT: Deseret Book Company.

Rigdon, S. (1839). Oration *Delivered by Mr. S. Rigdon on the 4th of July, 1838*. Far West, MO: The Journal Office.

Shipps, J. (1985). *Mormonism: The story of a new religious tradition*. Chicago: University of Illinois Press.

Walker, R. W. (1982). Sheaves, bucklers, and the state: Mormon leaders respond to the dilemmas of war. *Sunstone, 7*(4), 43–56.

Wood, R. S. (1992). War and peace. In D. H. Ludlow, (Ed.). *Encyclopedia of Mormonism* Vol. 4, New York: Macmillan Publishing Company, 1547–50.

Muslim Brotherhood *See* Fundamentalism in Egypt and Sudan

N

Native America *See* Aztecs; Inca; Iroquois; Maya; Pueblo Revolt of 1680

Nazism and Holocaust

That the Holocaust and much of the *Ostkrieg* (the eastern war against the Soviet Union) were conceived by the Nazis as part of a larger religious conflict is a little-understood but essential element of the Nazi phenomenon. This lack of understanding is due to three misconceptions. First, the long-held belief that the Nazis were solely a secular political movement is incorrect and fails to consider how the Nazis viewed themselves. The leadership of the movement, and many of its followers, always considered Nazism to be a spiritual movement that arose to meet the spiritual needs of Germany and, in fact, the world. The Nazis were fond of saying that those who see their "movement" (a term they favored over "party") as merely a political organization failed to grasp what Nazism was truly about.

Second, many contemporaries and many historians still today mistakenly equate Nazi anti-Christian views with an overall antispiritual perspective. However, rejecting certain aspects of traditional Christianity, especially any connection to Judaism, did not make Nazism an antispiritual movement. On the contrary, the Nazis saw their movement as a spiritual force inspired by divine powers to counter a demonic force bent on world annihilation.

Third, the Nazi emphasis on biological matters, especially involving the supposedly superior Aryan race, has led some to conclude that such a biological emphasis somehow makes the movement antispiritual. This proposition fails to grasp that the Nazis considered race to be both a biological and a spiritual principle, two aspects of the same thing. Thus the German word *Volk* meant for the Nazis "people," "race," and "race soul." It encompassed the totality of a people's racial characteristics, both physical and spiritual. The two could not be separated, and for this reason the Nazis set out to purify both body and soul. The Nazi eugenics program, which involved sterilization, euthanasia, and, on a grand scale, wholesale extermination, was the biological component of a larger salvational mission.

Despite these misunderstandings, a number of scholars, such as Gamm, Heer, Pois, Viereck, and Voegelin, have noted religious aspects of Nazi rhetoric, symbolism, and propaganda. More recently, scholars such as Redles, Rhodes, and Wistrich have noted that what underscored this religiosity was a profound millenarian and apocalyptic worldview. A new generation of German scholars, including Bärsch, Ley, and Vondung, have returned to the original writings of Nazi elites and concluded that Nazism was essentially a religious movement. This newer research has found that Nazism arose as a millenarian movement, responding to the apocalyptic chaos of Weimar Germany with a professed desire to save the world. Hitler saw himself as combining the roles of prophet and messiah, a John the Baptist and a Jesus Christ, sent from above to warn of impending apocalypse and to save the world. The writings of Hitler's inner circle, and of his disciples in the lower echelons of the movement, demonstrate that they accepted Hitler as this heaven-sent prophet and

From Darkness to Light

There is only one German Reich, one German Volk under one Führer Adolf Hitler, who leads us out of darkness to the light, from misery to happiness. All of Germany strongly supports him and all know that this Third Reich, that our Führer created, will stand for a millennium, and that after us the Hitler Youth will take this great earth in their loyal hands and build strongly upon it. Thus with a sense of the National Socialist Weltanschauung as an eternal value and as God-sent we will be able to hand over to the loyal hands of the coming Hitler Generation. And still I know one day that through Hitler and his *Weltanschauung* not only Germany, but the entire world will recover. Truth lights the road ahead and so one day the rest of the world will view us as the most harmonious Volk on earth. . .

Source: **Hubert Schummel, an Old Guard Nazi describing the Third Reich. From the Theodor Abel Collection, number 60, p. 26. Stanford, CA: Hoover Institute on War, Revolution, and Peace.**

savior. This acceptance legitimated Hitler's messianic self-perception and emboldened his desire to realize his apocalyptic and salvational worldview. That many individuals who became Nazis reported to have had conversion experiences to what they termed Hitler's "holy idea" only strengthened the religious nature of the movement.

The Spiritual Origins of Nazism

The Nazi movement had its origins in the German Worker's Party, an organ of the Thule Society, a political action group founded by the occultist anti-Semitic lodge the Germanenorden (Order of Teutons). The Thule Society created the German Worker's Party to attract workers away from the Communists, whom they conceived as Jewish Bolsheviks, a demonic force that was attempting to takeover the world. The unexpected loss of World War I and the chaos that characterized the early years of the Weimar Republic, combined with the wide release of the notorious hoax *The Protocols of the Elders of Zion* (which was interpreted as an apocalyptic tract), seemed to indicate to many anti-Semites that the Jews were making a final push at world domination. When Hitler and his inner circle took over the German Worker's Party, now renamed the National Socialist German Worker's Party, it is clear that they believed that Germany's salvation, and ultimately world salvation, could only come about through the annihilation of the Jews. Hitler's earliest known political statements from this time repeatedly associate salvation with the extermination of Germany's Jews.

The linkage of Bolshevism, the Jews, and the threat of world annihilation, combined with a counterthreat for the extermination of the Jewish race, would remain with the Nazis throughout their existence. In 1924 Hitler's mentor Dietrich Eckart, in *Der Bolschewismus von Moses bis Lenin* (Bolshevism from Moses to Lenin), argued that the signs of the times indicated that the Jews were on the threshold of taking over the world, and that if this occurred the inhabitants of the world would be exterminated. Hitler argued the same thing in *Mein Kampf*, saying, "If, with the help of this Marxist creed, the Jew is victorious over the other peoples of the world, his crown will be the funeral wreath of humanity and this planet will, as it did millions of years ago, move through the ether devoid of men" (Hitler 1943, 452). From this point on the Nazis argued that the salvation of the so-called Aryan race (seen to be the Creator's true chosen race) was tied inextricably to the extermination of Jewish Bolshevism. It is essential to understand that the Nazis believed that Bolshevism was not simply a political system or theory, but a demonic spiritual force. Hitler and his inner circle believed that after World War I the Jewish attempt at world domination was imminent and would ultimately lead to the annihilation of the world. The world therefore had reached a historical turning point of eschatological significance. A racial struggle that was considered to be both biological and spiritual, one that had been waged for thousands of years, was now coming to an imminent apocalyptic end. The Nazis conceived themselves as chosen not only to witness this final battle, but also to take an active part in its realization. Hitler was the God-sent savior who would create a movement that that would win this "final showdown," as he termed it, and usher in the *tausendjährige Reich* (millennial kingdom).

The death camp at Auschwitz, 1985. Courtesy Karen Christensen.

The Eastern War and the Holocaust as Aspects of an Apocalyptic Religious War

On 30 January 1939, with Europe on the brink of world war, Hitler gave his yearly speech to the Reichstag commemorating his assumption of power and with it, the dawn of the millennial Third Reich, also referred to as the Final Reich. He assumed his role as End Times prophet, stating, "I will today again be a prophet: if international finance Jewry within and without Europe should succeed in plunging the peoples yet once again in a world war, then it will result not in the bolshevization of the earth and thereby the victory of Jewry, but rather the annihilation of the Jewish race in Europe" (Domarus 1962–1963, vol. 2, 1058). The linking of the war with a threat to exterminate the Jews follows the beliefs of Hitler and his inner circle, held for nearly two decades. Hitler would return to his prophecy a number of times during the course of the war, and after the Final Solution was underway. Not unimportantly, Hitler and various Nazi publications misdated the prophecy to September 1, 1939, when the Nazis invaded Poland and began the Second World War. The final struggle against the Jews was inextricably tied to the war itself, for it was the same religious conflict. When war in the east was about to be launched some two years later, Hitler made it clear that this was the real war, the final war he prophesied so many years earlier. The war in the east was conceived as both an "ideological war" (*Weltanschauungskrieg*) and a war of extermination (*Vernichtungskrieg*). The two concepts were intricately and inextricably related. It is important to understand that the notion of a war between opposing *Weltanschauungen*, which literally means something like "ways of seeing the world," but is usually translated somewhat misleadingly as "ideologies," meant for the Nazis more than simply a struggle between political ideas (in this case Nazism versus Communism). It was always conceived as a final battle of diametrically opposed world views, conceived as cultural and spiritual forces rooted in and stemming from two conflicting races, one divinely inspired and constructive, and the other demonic and destructive. These two spiritual forces were mutually exclusive and now, with invasion of the Soviet Union (the supposed homeland of Jewish Bolshevism), locked in the very same final war (*Endkrieg*) that Hitler had always prophesied was imminent.

It is not surprising then that Hitler's orders to his generals for the conduct of the war in the east linked the extermination of Bolshevism to the extermination of the Jews.

Subsequently, Hitler's generals, including Hoepner, von Reichenau, von Manstein, and Hoth, gave orders to their troops characterizing the war in the east as one that would result in the complete and final extermination of the so-called "Jewish Bolshevik system." A phrase from one such order, and one that was used as a model for subsequent orders, stated: "The soldier must be brought to the understanding for the necessity of the harsh atonement for Jewry, the spiritual bearer of Bolshevik Terror" (Streit 1978, 116).

A Most Deadly Religious War

Therefore, with the eastern war Hitler's long-prophesied final showdown between Nazism and Jewish Bolshevism had truly begun. The apocalyptic extermination orders concerning the treatment of Soviet commissars, which included all Jews by definition, were quickly and ruthlessly carried out as the war in the east progressed. Beginning precisely with the invasion of June 1941, mass killings by the *Einsatzgruppen* (Special Forces) began, escalated in late July and early August, and then again in September and October. When Japan declared war on the United States on 7 December 1941, and Hitler subsequently declared war on the United States on 11 December 1941, the war finally became the true "world war" Hitler had prophesied in 1939. It was perhaps at this time that he made some general order to begin a more systematic plan for the extermination of all the Jews of Europe, a plan that began to come to its horrible fruition with the Wannsee Conference in January 1942. The apocalyptic religious war between Nazism and Jewish Bolshevism had reached its eschaton; some six million Jews, twenty-five million Soviet soldiers and citizens, and seven million Germans would lose their lives. Millions of other nationalities would die as well. By the end of the war in Europe a total of forty million people would be dead. If seen from the perspective of being conceived as a religious war between Aryans and Jewish-Bolsheviks, however imaginary the construct was, it was unquestionably the most deadly religious war in human history.

David Redles

See also Genocide in Europe

Further Reading

Bärsch, C. E. (1998). *Die politische Religion des Nationalsozialismus: Die religiöse Dimension der NS-Ideologie in den Schriften von Dietrich Eckart, Joseph Goebbels, Alfred Rosenberg und Adolf Hitler* [The Political Religion of National Socialism: The religious dimensions of NS ideology in the writings of Dietrich Eckart, Joseph Goebbels, Alfred Roesenberg and Adolf Hilter]. Munich, Germany: Wilhelm Fink Verlag.

Bartov, O. (1991). *Hitlers army: Soldiers, Nazis, and war in the Third Reich*. New York: Oxford University Press.

Boepple, E. (Ed.). (1925.) *Adolf Hitler Reden* [Adolf Hitler's Speeches]. Munich, Germany: Deutscher Volksverlag.

Domarus, M. (Ed.). (1962–1963). *Hitler: Reden und Proklamationen, 1932–1945* [Hitler: Speeches and Proclamations, 1932–1945] (Vols. 1–2). Neustadt, Germany: Aisch Schmidt.

Eckart, D. (1924). *Der Bolschewismus von Moses bis Lenin: Zwiegespräch zwischen Adolf Hitler and mir* [Bolshevism from Moses to Lenin: Dialogue between Adolf Hitler and me]. Munich, Germany: Hoheneichen-Verlag.

Gamm, H. J. (1962). *Der Braune Kult: Das Dritte Reich und seine Ersatzreligion. Ein Beitrag zur politischen Bildung* [The brown cult: The Third Reich and its pseudo religion. A contribution on political formation]. Hamburg, Germany: Rütten & Loening.

Goodrick-Clarke, N. (1992). *The occult roots of Nazism: Secret Aryan cults and their influence on Nazi ideology: The Ariosophists of Austria and Germany, 1890–1935*. New York: New York University Press.

Heer, F. (1968). *Der Glaube des Adolf Hitler: Anatomie einen politischen Religiosität* [The faith of Adolf Hitler: Anatomy of a political religiosity]. Munich, Germany: Mechtle.

Hitler, A. (1943). *Mein Kampf* [My struggle] (R. Mannheim, Trans.). Boston: Houghton Mifflin.

Ley, M. (1993). *Genozoid und Heilswartung: zum Nationalsozialistischen Mord am Europäischen Judentum* [Genocide and salvation: On the national socialist murder of European Jews]. Vienna: Picus.

Ley, M., & Schoeps, J. (Eds.). (1997). *Der Nationalsozialismus als politische Religion* [National socialism and political religion]. Bodenheim b. Mainz, Germany: Philo Verlagsgesellschaft.

Pois, R. (1986). *National Socialism and the religion of nature*. New York: Palgrave Macmillan.

Redles, D. (forthcoming) *Hitler and the apocalypse complex: Salvation and the spiritual power of Nazism*. New York: New York University Press.

Rhodes, J. M. (1980). *The Hitler movement: A modern millenarian revolution*. Stanford, CA: Hoover Institute Press.

Schramm, P. E. (1961). *Kriegstagebuch des Oberkommando der Wehrmacht (Wehrmachtführungstab) 1940–1945* [War diary of the supreme command of the armed forces]. Frankfurt, Germany: Bernard & Graefe.

Spielvogel, J., & Redles, D. (1986). Hitler's racial ideology: Content and occult sources. *Simon Wiesenthal Center Annual, 3*, 227–246.

Streit, C. (1978). *Keine Kameraden: Die Wehrmacht und die sowjetischen Kriegsgefangenen, 1941–1945* [None are comrades: The armed forces and the Soviet prisoners of war]. Stuttgart, Germany: Verlags-Anstalt.

Tal, U. (1980). Nazism as a political faith. *The Jerusalem Quarterly, 15*, 71–90.

Viereck, P. (1965). *Metapolitics: The roots of the Nazi mind*. New York: Capricorn Books.

Voegelin, E. (1999). *Hitler and the Germans* (The collected works of Eric Voegelin, 31; D. Clemens & B. Purcell, Eds., & Trans.). Columbia: University of Missouri Press.

Vondung, K. (1971). *Magie und Manipulation: Ideologischer Kult und politische Religion des Nationalsozialismus* [Magic and manipulation: Ideological cult and the political religion of national socialism]. Göttingen, Germany: Vandenhoeck & Ruprecht.

Vondung, K. (1988). *Die Apokalypse in Deutschland* [The apocalypse in Germany]. Munich, Germany: Deutscher Taschenbuch Verlag.

Wistrich, R. (1985). *Hitler's apocalypse: Jews and the Nazi legacy*. New York: St. Martin's Press.

Nigeria

Nigeria is the most populous country in sub-Saharan Africa with an estimated population of over 120 million. Its ethnic-cultural landscape is highly complex and diverse with about 374 ethnic stocks. Nigeria is characterized by a multiplicity of religious traditions including the indigenous religion, the various strands of Christianity and Islam, as well as spiritual science movements. The major religions are Christianity and Islam, both deeply influenced by the indigenous religions. Census figures measuring the numbers of Christians and Muslims are controversial in the context of the enduring debate on Nigeria's status as a "secular" state. As there is no concise official figures, the unauthenticated percentages of Christians and Muslims are projected between 40–50 percent for either of the traditions depending on the information source. The indigenous tradition and other minority religions are believed to share between 10–20 percent of the population. Religion has become a matter of political significance and tension in Nigeria. This religious tension has a clear connection with the growth of uncompromising Muslim and Christian activism. The relationship between Islam and Christianity has led to a growing culture of religious violence particularly in northern Nigeria. Religious and political issues and conflicts have revolved largely around the activities of, and the interrelationships between, Islam and Christianity. Their involvement in regional and national politics is aptly illustrated by their activities in postindependent Nigerian politics.

Religion and the Nigerian Civil War (1967–1970)

The fragile politics of Nigeria's First Republic (1960–1966) is partly attributed to religious factors in which the ruling northern elite were accused of indirectly perpetuating a "jihad" to enlarge the borders of the Sokoto caliphate. The jihad movement of Uthman dan Fodio (1804–1908) launched to purify Islam, succeeded in establishing a theocracy, the Sokoto caliphate, and in influencing the course of events since the birth of Nigeria. The British colonial administration inherited a religious-political system, which it retained as part of the indirect rule system in Northern Nigeria. The Sokoto caliphate helped to facilitate the consolidation of Hausa-Fulani hegemony in the political developments of the First Republic. The belief that northerners were bent on unleashing a pogrom on the Christian Igbo and other southerners drew Christianity into center stage as a rallying point for the Biafra-Nigeria civil war (1967–1970). The Christian and anti-Muslim self-identification of Biafra was colored by the pre–1966 situation of the Sardauna's tours and the uninhibited proclamations of militant Islam that they reflected. No sooner had political independence been achieved than the premier of Northern Nigeria, Sir Ahmadu Bello (then Sardauna of Sokoto) embarked on a religious crusade or politics that became the foundation stone for religious politics in the nascent nation. Following the assassination and overthrow of Aguiyi Ironsi's military government in 1966, the Biafrans under the leadership of Emeka Ojukwu fought in 1967 to secede from the Federal Republic of Nigeria on grounds that include political marginalization and the inequitable sharing of the national cake. The civil war was for Biafrans a religious war. Religion became a cohesive force for the Biafrans and a self-conscious Christian profession became an integral part of their self-identity. On 16 January 1968, S. M. Ojukwu said: "Biafra is a Christian country, we believe in the ability of the Almighty God to come to the aid of the oppressed and give us victory as he gave victory to young David over Goliath" (Walls 1978, 207). As Christianity gave self-identity to Biafra, so was a Muslim identity bestowed upon the Federal Republic of Nigeria. Although the Biafrans lost the war in 1970, yet it had sent red signals that religion and ethnicity would remain the canister upon which the nation may explode, if not consciously handled in Nigeria's political theatre. The role of Christian churches during the war was ambivalent. Many became accused of complicity in and praise of the federal government's actions against the Biafrans, a development that provoked harsh criticisms from the Biafran side. "The war conditions nurtured humanist ideologies and their attacks on Christianity. As the so-called 'Christian Britain' supported genocide in Biafra, the mission churches were the butt of socialist attacks as agents of imperialism and bastions of neo-colonialism" (Kalu 1996, 272). The Biafrans also emphasized religious sentiments in order to garner external support and assistance. Most of the sources of aid were Christian; church bodies were so prominent among the expressions of support as to reinforce the self-consciousness of a Christian state facing a jihad supported by a Muslim household of faith. As a further mark of the international links forged under the canopy of religion, the World Council of Churches and the Vatican joined those clamoring for a ceasefire. Such links were significant for the Biafrans as it drew worldwide attention and sympathy to their cause rather than seeing themselves as fighting a lone battle. The response from the world Christian bodies reinforces the Biafran consciousness that they were engaged in a religious battle. In an attempt at religious legitimation,

Biafra's self-identification with biblical Israel became a commonplace. The theme of Biafra as the "Elect People of God" was popular when they fared well during the war, but as the situation worsened, the significance of suffering and identification with the biblical nation elected to suffer and triumph became the religious catchwords. Prophecies assumed a crucial role especially in Biafra, as diviners played out their roles in influencing ground fighting. The aftermath of the civil war witnessed a revitalization of indigenous aspects of Christianity and traditional African religion, as a survival technique to cushion the untold hardship and displacement. Other Christian groups such as the Pentecostals, the charismatics, and the evangelicals became active and enlarged their clienteles and modes of operation.

Religion in the Post-Civil War Era

Religion has continued to assume a volatile presence in the Nigerian body politic such that ethnic politics is almost being supplanted by religious politics. The consequences of the incessant violent interaction between Muslims and Christians, particularly in northern Nigeria, have left the political entity in a very fragile state where the "religious gunpowder" is waiting to explode at the slightest provocation. The mutual suspicion and distrust engendered by religious functionaries, coupled with the evolution of religious and ethnic bigotry, intrudes into the overall security and well-being of Nigeria. Thus, religion became a crucial factor in contemporary Nigerian politic against the backdrop of religious unrest, inter- and intrareligious conflicts, and the accompanying wanton destruction of lives and property. Religious cleavages took a more conspicuous role than ethnicity and class in the political intrigues that have characterized the military dictatorship in Nigeria.

The interplay of religion and politics in Nigeria is intricately linked with the virulent competition for the "national cake." Religion is becoming more and more a factor in both politics and policy-making, such that the consuming power of religion in Nigerian politics and society looms large. One characteristic of this kind of religious politics is that every government move or utterances as well as the actions of religious groups are watched, highlighted, and analyzed. It is within this context that the Christian Association of Nigeria (CAN) emerged as the political watchdog to checkmate the activities of Jamaʿatu Nasril Islamiyya (Society for the Victory of Islam), one of the most active Islamic organizations. The radicalization of CAN has been partially due to a new politic ethic among Pentecostals. The subversion of religion for political ends, such as supporting and sustaining the hegemony of the status quo, has often resulted in religious violence and riots, reaching frightening proportions and leading to an intermittent but steady displacement of people. Religious affiliations are seen or often suspected of dictating political and public actions of public officials. Suspicion that one religious group is accorded preferential treatment by the government in power often ignites agitation and countercollaboration by unfavored religious groups as a measure to safeguard their interests and credibility in the Nigerian polity. The somewhat crude, extralegal actions such as the "fire-brigade approach" of the government, reprisals by victims from an opposing religious groups, often undertaken to resolve such anomalies heighten insecurity and precipitate unwarranted displacement and mass emigration. Religious buildings (churches), private homes, and businesses have become frequent targets of the forms of religious violence that erupt in northern Nigeria, sometimes met with reprisals in other parts of the country. As religiously inspired violence has become a recurring feature of the Nigerian religious landscape, its focus has shifted from intrareligious strife to interreligious disturbances. Public violence has often occurred in total defiance of section 10 of the Nigerian 1979 constitution, which states: "the Federal Government or the State shall not adopt any religion as a State religion."

Military rule of the Federal Republic of Nigeria began on 15 January 1966 under Aguiyi Ironsi, an Ibo Christian. Although he denied the claim, some believed that Ironsi undertook the coup to protect the rights of Christians. Religious bias became more pronounced under Yakubu Gowon between 1966 and 1975, as many Northern Muslims were suspicious of and uncomfortable with having a Christian at the helm of national affairs. The current wave of religious violence and unrest in Nigeria took root in the late 1970s. The Maitsatsine movement under Muhammad Marwa struck with riots during the era of Muhammadu Buhari and Tunde Idiagbon, both Muslims. One significant feature of this period is the politics surrounding the Constituent Assembly of 1978 and the implantation of the *shariʿa*. The 1980s witnessed the resurgence of old and the upsurge of new Islamic fundamentalist groups typified by the Muslim Students' Society (MSS) and the Yan Izala movement, with their campaign to restore pristine Islam and the *shariʿa* as a panacea to the socie-

Is Biafra Still an Option?

Thirty-one years after the end of the civil war, leader of the defunct Biafra, Chief Emeka Odumegwu-Ojukwu says Biafra remains a worthy alternative if Nigeria is not better.

I have carried a lot of blame for Biafra. And before you ask me, I will tell you plainly that if Nigeria is not better, then Biafra is a worthy alternative, Chief Ojukwu declared in a marathon interview to mark the Armed Forces Remembrance Anniversary.

He said: These are the things we have to look into. Certainly, when you compare death and Biafra, I will choose Biafra. When you compare strangulation to death and Biafra, I will choose Biafra. When you compare lack of reconciliation and marginalisation and Biafra, I will choose Biafra. When you compare the lack of economic enterprises in one part of the country, and discrimination to Biafra, I prefer Biafra.

Expressing disappointment over the socio-political situation in the country, Chief Ojukwu said: We've gone through the year 2000. Like everybody in the world, we all had great expectations of that year. Ours was even more because it was the first year of true democratic practice. When I say true, I mean true in the sense that we all looked forward to better democratic practice; a truer form of democracy. But if you have to judge the year just gone by, I believe we have to look at it in a normal form, which is economic well being; social well being and political well being.

Nigeria entered the year 2000 it was as though the country was pregnant and at a point of giving birth. I regret that at the end of the year, we would seem still, expecting the birth of something. The year 2000, in actual fact, was eaten up by internal squabbles. Year 2000 was eaten up by posturing on the part of our various leaders, without actually giving birth to policies that we can grapple with. In year 2000, probably more people had been killed on the streets of Nigeria than we have ever had under any form of government.

He reiterated his call for a national conference to discuss Nigeria's problems, saying he would personally be prepared in the next conference to lay on the table an Igbo charter where I would say to Nigeria, these are the sine qua non of our membership of the Nigerian federation. Take it or leave it.

***Source:* "Biafra Remains Worthy Choice If. . ." (2001, January 15). *Vanguard.* Retieved March 12, 2003, from World History Archives, http://www.hartford-hwp.com/archives**

tal ills of Nigeria. These groups targeted non-Muslims, but also other Islamic groups for their complacency of faith.

Between 1980 and 1985, a renewed wave of religious riots spread beyond the confines of university campuses into the wider society. The Maitatsine resurfaced and took center stage in these riots. Mayhem was again unleashed on thousands of innocent, unsuspecting Nigerians. One of the most severe riots during this period occurred in Kano in 1982, owing to disagreements about the intended location of a cathedral within the vicinity of a mosque. The Kafanchan riot was a result of rejection by the MSS of the perceived provocative evangelistic strategy of the Federation of Christian Students (FCS) at the College of Education. The fracas that broke out spread like wildfire to other northern cities including Kaduna, Zaria, and Katsina and it took the intervention of the Nigerian army to quell the inferno. The Kafanchan riots gave impetus to other incidents, which occurred at the slightest provocation in educational institutions, marketplaces, towns, villages, and even within sacred spaces.

Religious politics reached its zenith between 1985 and 1993 during the military dictatorship of Ibrahim Babangida. His discreet registration of Nigeria as a permanent member of the Organization of Islamic Countries in January 1986 met with uproar and rejection, thus reinforcing the battle lines along the religious divide. The Advisory Council for Religious Affairs, set up in 1987 to mitigate this crisis, was itself stultified with controversy on its composition and modus operandi. The botched Gideon Orkar coup of 22 April 1990 was an attempt to contain the "Muslim threat," a reason for which the coup was perceived as Christian-motivated. The execution of a legion of military personnel, the incarceration and harassment of activists, and the restriction on religious activities further heightened the already delicate religious mood in the country. The campaign of the German evangelist Reinhard Bonnke on 14 October 1991 in Kano city resulted in unprecedented bestiality as Muslims took to the streets, questioning his right to hold an open-air crusade in the heartland of Nigerian Islam. In Zango-Kataf, a long dispute between the Christian Kataf and the Muslim Hausa culminated in violence, in a battle that spread to Kaduna and its environs and left in its wake hundreds of corpses and the destruction of private and public buildings.

Babangida's annulment of the 1993 presidential elections, the freest and fairest election in Nigeria's political history, ostensibly won by a southern Muslim, Moshood Abiola; the seizure of power by Sanni Abacha on 18 November 1993 from a political stooge, Ernest Shonekan, through a "palace coup"; the subsequent gruesome murders of Moshood Abiola, Ken Saro-Wiwa, and many others; and the unrelenting hunt for several prodemocracy activists by the military junta all helped to aggravate the tense religious climate.

Intrareligious violence has not yet abated even in the face of the third democratic period in Nigeria's history. The election of President Olusegun Obasanjo, a Southerner, Christian, and former military leader, has raised new fears of reprisals and marginalization, especially in the north. It is against this backdrop that the resurgence of the Sharia Law and the "shariazation" of many northern states is seen to have political more than religious undertones. Provisions of the Sharia legal system were not new in the Nigerian constitution. What was however new was the recent tendency of some state governors to extend the scope of Sharia to embrace criminal processes and invoked the punishments from the Maliki legal structure. The *shariʿa* controversy and the planned stoning of Safiyya Hussaini on grounds of infidelity is a case in point. Another recent incident that led to a debacle was the planned Nigerian hosting of the "Miss World Pageant 2002" and a newspaper article that made allusions that not only inflamed religious sentiments but was used as another excuse to unleash terror on innocent citizens in Kaduna during the sacred time of the Muslim month of Ramadan. Thus, the sporadic, spontaneous dimension of these religiously, economically, and politically motivated "wars" has left Nigeria in a quagmire of uncertainty and insecurity, a situation that may only change for the better when a genuine and enduring strand of democracy takes shape in which all Nigerian peoples, irrespective of religion or ethnicity, can have a sense of belonging.

Afe Adogame

Further Reading

Chukwuma, M. (1985). *Nigerian politics and the role of religion: An analysis of the role of religion in Nigerian politics at the early stages of national integration*. Bonn, Germany: Friedrich-Wilhelms-Universität.

Falola, T. (1998). *Violence in Nigeria: The crisis of religious politics and secular ideologies*. Rochester, NY: University of Rochester Press.

Kalu, O. U. (1996). *The embattled gods: Christianization of Igboland, 1841–1991*. Lagos, Nigeria: Minaj Publishers.

Madiebo, A. (1980). *The Nigerian revolution and Biafran war*. Enugu, Nigeria: Fourth Dimension.

Nwankwo, A., & Ifejika, S. U. (1969). *The making of a nation: Biafra*. London: C. Hurst and Co.

Olupona, J. K. (Ed.). (1991). *Religion and society in Nigeria*. Ibadan, Nigeria: Spectrum Books.

Olupona, J. K. (Ed.). (1992). *Religion and peace in multi-faith Nigeria*. Ile-Ife: Obafemi Awolowo University Press.

Walls, A. F. (1978). Religion and the press in "the Enclave" in the Nigerian civil war. In E. Fashole-Luke, et al. (Eds.), *Christianity in independent Africa* (pp. 207–215). Bloomington: Indiana University Press.

Williams, P. (1997). Religion, violence, and displacement in Nigeria. In P. E. Lovejoy & P. A. T. Williams (Eds.), *Displacement and the politics of violence in Nigeria* (pp. 33–49). Leiden, Netherlands: Brill.

Williams, P., & Falola, T. (Ed.). (1995). *Religious impact on the nation state*. Aldershot, UK: Avebury.

Northern Ireland

Northern Ireland (also known as Ulster), and particularly its capital of Belfast, illustrates clearly the interplay of religion, politics, and communal turmoil. Catholics (also called Republicans or Nationalists) often object to the phrase "Northern Ireland" and instead refer derisively to the area as "the six counties." This linguistic nicety has for Catholics two references: it points to the twenty-six counties in the rest of Ireland (i.e., Eire with its capital in Dublin) and it notes that the north of Ireland was historically composed of nine counties. Northern Ireland today comprises the six counties of Antrim, Down, Armagh, Fermanagh, Tyrone, and Londonderry. The Catholic population of Ulster has risen from one-third in 1922 to more than 40 percent by the 1990s. Among young people, as of 2002 there was at least near parity between Catholics and Protestants.

Catholics want the area to be (again) part of the rest of Ireland, while Protestants (also known as Loyalists or Unionists) single-mindedly want to remain part of Great Britain. Surprisingly for the twenty-first century, Unionists verbalize their position in the explicit antipopery polemics of the sixteenth century, while Republicans formulate their political position in the quasi-religious nation-forming terminology of the nineteenth century.

The Role of Religion

Religion has more than a superficial or epiphenomenal role in this ongoing dispute, and most religious leaders (while suffering from the violence along with their flocks) show little inclination to deemphasize church positions and interests for the sake of peace and unity. For at least the past two centuries, this religious conflict has been partially subsumed into the overtly political nationalistic question. The intense worldwide twentieth-century debate on class plays almost no realistic part in this Northern Ireland dispute, except among Marxist-inclined commentators.

Catholics divide between "Constitutional" Nationalists who prefer a peaceful political solution and "Republican" Nationalists who feel that only violence can resolve the Northern Ireland imbroglio. Protestants naturally divide by denominations, the largest number (21 percent of Northern Ireland in 1991) being of a Presbyterianism heavily influenced by evangelical revivals, and becoming increasingly exclusivist in the last decades of the twentieth century. The slightly smaller (18 percent in 1991) Church of Ireland is usually low church in orientation. Many of the 10 percent (in 1991) who refuse to state a religion are young males from the Protestant community, forming an uncertain element in the usual Protestant-Catholic divide. Many of the over forty smaller denominations (8 percent in 1991) share an evangelical ethos. Antipope sermons started the 1850s Belfast riots, and an American fundamentalist (W. P. Nicholson) in the 1920s helped guarantee working-class Protestant loyalty to the new Northern Ireland state by his revivalist rhetoric. Rev. Ian Paisley today personifies this fundamental populism in his Free Presbyterian Church, his Democratic Unionist Party, and his strong electoral support.

The 1641 and 1689 Roots

Northern Ireland adversaries rely for credibility on a similar victim version of history. For both sides, relevant history begins in the first decade of the seventeenth century, when the most Gaelic/Irish part of the island finally succumbed to English military force at the end of the Nine Years' War. Originally this conquest had little religious significance, but shortly after the 1607 "Flight of the Earls," the English began the "Plantation" of Ulster. That is, the land left behind in northern Ireland by the fleeing and recently defeated old Gaelic elite was assigned to new—mostly Protestant—owners from Scotland and northern England. Perhaps because Ulster was seriously underpopulated at that time, any ethnic or religious antagonism was at first masked. In 1641, however, a series of political moves sparked a ferocious Catholic jacquerie featuring a slaughter of perhaps a fourth of the 40,000 recently arrived Protestant Scots and English settlers of the Ulster. The resultant Protestant fear led to what historians call the "siege mentality" of Northern Ireland Protestantism. These dreadful murders were repaid with interest by Cromwell's army in 1649–1652.

In the iconic 1689 siege of Londonderry, Protestant defenders successfully held off the forces of James II. While this clash of kings was not a Catholic-Protestant event, the Northern Ireland Protestants perceived it as a providential release from another 1641-type communal slaughter. Protestants then passed the Penal Codes, which simultaneously put down the Catholics and guaranteed Protestant ascendancy. These effective codes, which set the Catholic church back a century in Ulster, came to personify for Catholics their crushed position in their own homeland.

The Ulster Scots/Scotch-Irish

Williams's victory in the Glorious Revolution of 1688 led also to a large new immigration of Scots into Ulster, the largest movement of people in Europe during the time. Counties Antrim and Down are both the closest

Selection from the Penal Code, 7 Will III c.5 (1695): An Act for Better Securing the Government, By Disarming Papists

Sec. 1. All papists within this kingdom of Ireland shall before the 1st day of March, 1696, deliver up to some justice of the peace or corporation officer where such papist shall dwell, all their arms and ammunition, notwithstanding any licence for keeping the same heretofore granted. Justices of the peace, mayors, sheriffs, and chief officers of cities and towns and persons under their warrants, may search and seize all arms and ammunition of papists, or in the hands of any persons in trust for them, wherever they shall suspect they may be concealed. And such arms shall be preserved for the use of his Majesty.

Sec. 2. Searches of dwellings shall be made only between sunrise and sunset, except in cities and their suburbs, and market towns. If no arms are seized, chief magistrates may cause suspected persons to be examined on their oath concerning concealed arms.

Sec. 3. Every papist who shall have or keep any arms or ammunition, or who shall refuse to declare what arms or ammunition they or any other to their knowledge shall have, or shall hinder the delivery thereof to the said justices, or being summoned, shall refuse to appear or make discovery under their oath, shall forfeit, if a peer or peeress, for the first offence, one hundred pounds sterling, and for a second offence, suffer praemunire*. If such offenders are under the degree of peer, they shall for a first offence forfeit thirty pounds and suffer imprisonment for one year, and until they pay the penalty, and for a second offense, incur the penalties of a person attainted in a praemunire. The penalties and sums forfeited shall go one half to his Majesty, one half to the informer who shall sue for the same.

[. . .]

Sec. 10. No papist shall be capable of having or keeping for his use, any horse, gelding or mare of five pounds value. Any protestant who shall make discovery under oath of such horse, shall be authorized with the assistance of a constable, to search for and secure such horse and in case of resistance to break down any door. And any protestant making such discovery and offering five pounds five shillings to the owner of such horse, in the presence of a justice of the peace or chief magistrate, shall receive ownership of such horse as though such horse were bought in the market overt.

Source: **Laws in Ireland for the Suppression of Popery. Retrieved March 13, 2003, from http://www.law.umn.edu/irishlaw/weapons.html**

to Scotland and the most Protestant (and Presbyterian) in Ireland. Many of these Scots were of a militant Calvinistic branch of Presbyterianism—the Seceders and Covenanters. Many of the new Ulster Scot immigrants were (as the historian D. H. Fischer has shown) also of a tougher, more violent sort who found it healthier to leave Scotland as the English authorities vigorously stamped out the civic anarchy that had marked Scotland's society for centuries.

No matter what their background, these recent arrivals in Ireland began to acquire the most fertile parts of Northern Ireland. While this acquisition of land was mostly by economic means, the dramatic increase of population in the late eighteenth century caused such an intense competition for land that the ever-poorer Catholic lower class gradually accepted the views of the dispossessed old Catholic gentry that Catholics had been forcibly evicted by Protestants from old family lands. At the very least, Catholics of all ranks realized that their religion by this date kept them firmly from any political power. At the same time, Presbyterians felt threatened by the tendency of Catholics to accept the substantially increased cost for leasing land. When combined with certain other economic (and at times, religious) restrictions, this practice of Catholics accepting a lower standard of living in order to regain ten-

Selection from the Belfast or Good Friday Agreement of 1998

DECLARATION OF SUPPORT

1. **We, the participants in the multi-party negotiations, believe that the agreement we have negotiated offers a truly historic opportunity for a new beginning.**
2. **The tragedies of the past have left a deep and profoundly regrettable legacy of suffering. We must never forget those who have died or been injured, and their families. But we can best honour them through a fresh start, in which we firmly dedicate ourselves to the achievement of reconciliation, tolerance, and mutual trust, and to the protection and vindication of the human rights of all.**
3. **We are committed to partnership, equality and mutual respect as the basis of relationships within Northern Ireland, between North and South, and between these islands.**
4. **We reaffirm our total and absolute commitment to exclusively democratic and peaceful means of resolving differences on political issues, and our opposition to any use or threat of force by others for any political purpose, whether in regard to this agreement or otherwise.**
5. **We acknowledge the substantial differences between our continuing, and equally legitimate, political aspirations. However, we will endeavour to strive in every practical way towards reconciliation and rapprochement within the framework of democratic and agreed arrangements. We pledge that we will, in good faith, work to ensure the success of each and every one of the arrangements to be established under this agreement. It is accepted that all of the institutional and constitutional arrangements—an Assembly in Northern Ireland, a North/South Ministerial Council, implementation bodies, a British-Irish Council and a British-Irish Intergovernmental Conference and any amendments to British Acts of Parliament and the Constitution of Ireland – are interlocking and interdependent and that in particular the functioning of the Assembly and the North/South Council are so closely inter-related that the success of each depends on that of the other.**
6. **Accordingly, in a spirit of concord, we strongly commend this agreement to the people, North and South, for their approval.**

Source: Government of Ireland, Department of Foreign Affairs. Retrieved January 9, 2003, from http://www.gov.ie/iveagh/angloirish/goodfriday/default.htm

ancy caused a large number of the recently arrived Scots (and English) to begin the great Atlantic migration that placed around 200,000 of these so-called Scotch-Irish in 1776 as enthusiastic supporters of revolutionary America.

The 1801 Act of Union

French revolutionary ideas appeared in 1790s Ireland, encouraging the 1798 series of unsuccessful anti-English revolts. Nationalist Republicans today preach that 1798 showed how both Protestants (especially dissatisfied Presbyterians) and Catholics could unite politically in a nonsectarian sway. Protestant Unionists, however, portray 1798 as one more attempt by disaffected Catholics to eliminate Protestants. The Orange Order as the defender of Protestantism appeared at this time and its lodges mark the areas of the most intense Protestant-Catholic clashes. In any case, the idea of common Catholic and Protestant revolutionary endeavor against English rule was stillborn.

A small French army, however, landed in 1798 just south of Ulster to stiffen the Irish anti-English revolt, but the English under General Cornwallis easily crushed the Franco-Irish army. At the same time, other British army units rather easily scattered popular uprisings of Catholics and Presbyterians in Northern Ireland and in the rest of the country. Nevertheless, England found 1798 so potentially dangerous to its national interest that on 1 January 1801 it incorporated Ireland into Great Britain. Catholics at first welcomed the Union, but in a short time came to regard the political union as an outrage. Conversely, Protestant Ulster complained about the Union at first, but then Protestants came to rely on this England/Ireland linkage as the bedrock of Ulster security. Thus Daniel O'Connell's 1840s emphasis on eliminating the 1801 Union sent shock waves through the Ulster Protestant community. In a similar fashion, C. S. Parnell (although a Protestant) in the 1880s frightened Northern Ireland Protestants by advocating "Home Rule" for all of Ireland.

Northern Ireland: 1921–1972

After two unsuccessful attempts—both accompanied by major Protestant riots in Belfast—the third Home Rule Bill passed the English Parliament in 1912. Under the slogan "Home Rule is Rome Rule," Protestants formed an army to resist the implementation of the Home Rule Bill. World War I put the question on the back burner for all but the most rabid of Republicans, who unsuccessfully tried to revolt in Dublin in 1916. England attempted to satisfy both parties by granting in the 1921 Anglo-Irish treaty the quasi-freedom of dominion status (which went beyond home rule) to the twenty-six southern counties that were overwhelmingly Catholic, while allowing the six most Protestant of the nine Ulster counties to remain a protected Protestant enclave under their own form of home rule. Unfortunately, rabidly nationalist areas such as southern Armagh and southern Down were not assigned over to the Dublin government. The newly formed Irish Free State divided over the British compromise solution and a bloody civil war broke out whose heritage was a paralyzing, bitter divide in its own political landscape. Northern Ireland Protestants were thus left free to form their own government. After a year of great Catholic violence toward the new government of Northern Ireland, the Protestant authorities gained complete control and quickly Northern Ireland became in the word of its prime minister, James Craig, a "Protestant parliament and a Protestant state." For example, a complete Unionist control of the heavily nationalist city of Londonderry/Derry was achieved by gerrymandering.

The Depression and World War II and its aftermath did nothing to alter the Northern Ireland picture of dominant Protestantism and a quiescent and submerged Catholic people. The Unionist selection in 1963 of the reformer Terence O'Neill as prime minister encouraged middle-class Catholics to demand their civil rights. For the increasing number of middle-class Catholics, the old nationalist vision of one Ireland seemed irrelevant. Civil rights demonstrations started marching only to be subjected in January 1969 to hostile Protestant crowds and an obviously biased Northern Ireland police establishment. Thus began a thirty-year civil war that is known in Ireland as "the troubles." In 1972, England prorogued the Northern Ireland Parliament and took over direct rule of Northern Ireland. Besides the British army and the regular police force (which was predominantly Protestant) to keep order, Unionist paramilitary groups reappeared. Their criminal activities and their horrendous sectarian killings quickly tarnished their reputations even in Unionist circles.

Ambiguous Military Position: 1972 to Present

England realized quickly the quagmire it had gotten into and tried a variety of political and military ways to extricate itself. The slow changes in the political landscape required the presence of the British military to negate both Republican and Loyalist objectors. For centuries, the British army had maintained a large presence in Ireland in support of the local police establishments. Ireland almost always found itself under some form of martial law that gave the forces of law and order extraordinary discretionary powers. Mere military presence, sometimes with a judicious use of force, had helped keep Ulster most years free of widescale disturbances by Catholics.

Therefore, when Northern Ireland was formed in 1921, the military helped in the difficult first year, and then thereafter maintained a small force indicating London support for the Northern Ireland government. With the appearance in the 1960s of the disturbances following the civil rights demonstrations, the British army acquired a prominent policing role. So severe was the Unionist reaction that England in 1969 intervened to protect the Catholic community. For a short period of time, the British army was looked upon as the protectors of the Catholic people. This ended spectacularly when on the 30th of January, 1972 (now known as "Bloody Sunday") paratroopers fired into a Catholic crowd, killing thirteen. With the slow emergence of the Provisional Irish Republican Army (PIRA, also known as the Provos), the army was forced to fulfill two jobs simulate simultaneously: to continue keeping the Catholics and Protestants from killing each other, and to fight a guerrilla war in both urban and rural areas. Thus, the army in a complex way contributed mightily to the Northern Ireland problem and yet protected the area from a savage sectarian war.

Draconian "special legislation" and legally dubious interrogation techniques supported military intelligence. While Catholics realized that they were generally safer under the professional British army personnel than under the Northern Ireland police establishment, Catholics nevertheless perceived the army as merely a coercive wing of the British government. The army gradually took command of the large urban centers, and the Royal Ulster Constabulary (police) could there appear to be functioning normally. In the cities the PIRA began to realize that the English army could not lose as long as there was a political resolve in London. Rural areas of largely nationalist Catholics, however, certainly presented the Protestant RUC with an impossible task and even gave the army huge problems.

Political Initiatives: 1973 to Present

England began a series of political initiatives that the Unionists rightly saw as undermining their basic position. In 1973, England, Eire, and Northern Ireland government officials signed the Sunningdale Agreement that called for a Council of Ireland to help express the Irish Catholic dimension. A general, provincewide Ulster strike by Protestant labor killed this power-sharing scheme. Significantly, though, the general-strike tactic failed in 1977 when orchestrated by Rev. Paisley. In 1985, the Anglo-Irish Agreement allowed Eire to advise officially on legal, social, and economic matters of Northern Ireland. The agreement called for an Inter-Governmental Conference. This so disturbed Unionists that they staged widespread confrontations, including attacks on the (Protestant) police. Unionists again succeeded in negating the agreement. In 1991, talks restarted, again centering on the "three strands" of the Northern Ireland problem: Ireland-England relations; Northern Ireland–Eire relations; and Republican-Unionist relations. Finally, in 1998 all parties, representing both sides of the religious divide, signed the Good Friday or Belfast Agreement, a new version of the Sunningdale plan.

What had made the talks increasingly successful was the remarkable series of changes taking place in Eire. Ireland saw in the 1970s the departure of Eamon de Valera, the Republican symbol of all that the Unionists detested; Eire's enthusiastic joining of the European community; and the breaking of the hegemony of Fianna Fail, the Irish party most supportive of violent Republicanism. The 1985 founding of the Progressive Democrats showed how even some Fianna Fail leaders were accepting European political views and repudiating the old political—ultimately sectarian—divisions of the Irish past. The changes in the Catholic church started by Pope John XXIII slowly began to transform Eire's confessional underpinnings. For example, in 1990, Eire elected as president Mary Robinson, well known for her support of laws permitting divorce and the sale of contraception devices.

The growing political rapprochement between London and Dublin (and America) helped the argument of PIRA's political wing, Sinn Fein, of the need for something besides a military solution. All sides of the war realized, for example, that Bobby Sands—incarcerated by the British for fire bombing a furniture store—scored a public relations coup by going on a hunger strike. He died, of course, but not before he was elected by the Catholics of Northern Ireland to the British Parliament. Many Provos, in addition, began to believe that while they might never lose, they could not win a military struggle with the British army. Realizing this, leaders like Gerry Adams slowly inched a majority of the Provo gun-bearers toward a political solution as part of their program. However, few who know Irish history expect that the resultant Good Friday Agreement will, in the short run, permanently dispel all Irish communal strife.

Leroy V. Eid

Further Reading

Aughey, A., & Morrow, D. (1996). *Northern Ireland politics*. London: Longman.

Bardon, J. (2001). *A history of Ulster*. Belfast, Northern Ireland: Blackstaff Press.

Brooke, P. (1994). *Ulster Presbyterianism: The historical perspective, 1610–1970*. Belfast, Northern Ireland: Athol Books.

Cassidy, E., McKeown, D., & Morrow, J. (2001). *Belfast: Faith in the city*. Dublin, Ireland: Veritas.

Donohue, L. K. (2001). *Counter-terrorist law and emergency powers in the United Kingdom, 1922–2000*. Dublin, Ireland: Irish Academic Press.

Duffy, S. (1997). *Atlas of Irish history*. Dublin, Ireland: Gill & Macmillan.

Elliott, M. (2001). *The Catholics of Ulster*. New York: Basic Books.

Fitzspatrick, D. (1998). *The Two Irelands 1912–1939*. Oxford, UK: Oxford University Press.

Fischer, D. H. (1989). *Albion's Seed*. New York: Oxford University Press.

Gray, T. (1972). *The orange order*. London: The Bodley Head.

Harris, M. (1993). *The Catholic church and the foundation of the Northern Irish state*. Cork, Ireland: Cork University Press.

Holmes, J. (2001). *Religious revivals in Britain and Ireland*. Dublin, Ireland: Irish Academic Press.

Kennedy-Pipe, C. (1997). *Present troubles in Northern Ireland*. New York: Addison Wesley Longman.

Livingstone, D., & Wells, R. (1999). *Ulster-American religion*. Notre Dame, IN: University of Notre Dame Press.

McGarry, J., & O'Leary, B. (1999). *Policing Northern Ireland: Proposals for a new start*. Belfast, Northern Ireland: Blackstaff Press.

Moloney, E. (2002). *A secret history of the IRA*. New York: W. W. Norton.

Moody, T. W. (1974). *The Ulster question 1603–1973*. Dublin, Ireland: Mercier Press.

Mulholland, M. (2002). *The longest war: Northern Ireland's troubled history*. Oxford, UK: Oxford University Press.

Rafferty, O. P. (1994). *Catholicism in Ulster, 1603–1983*. Columbia: University of South Carolina Press.

Sloan, B. (2000). *Writers and Protestantism in the north of Ireland*. Dublin, Ireland: Irish Academic Press.

P

Pacifism *See* Eastern Orthodoxy, Pacifism in; Judaism, Pacifism in; Mennonites; Quakers; Martyrdom; Roman Catholicism, Pacifism in

Palestine: 1948 War

The 1948 Arab-Israeli war is the subject of fierce historiographical debate. This debate began in earnest in the late 1980s when a number of Israeli historians—known as the "new historians"—challenged what they regarded as the official Israeli narrative on the war. This official narrative tended to center around a cluster of myths—as the new historians labeled them—about the birth of Israel. These myths included the following: that the British were more supportive of Palestinian claims to statehood than of Jewish claims; that the military balance was weighed heavily in favor of the Palestinians and the Arab states; that the Palestinians became refugees because they were instructed to leave Palestine by the Arab states; that the declared Arab war aim "to push the Jews into the sea" reflected the reality of a united Arab army fighting on behalf of Palestinian nationhood; and that the blame for the failure to make peace after the war lay entirely with the Arab states. The new historians challenged all of these assumptions and their revised accounts of the war are now accepted by most professional historians of this period of Middle Eastern history. Readers should be aware, however, that a definitive account of the 1948 War—to the extent that such a thing is possible—remains to be written. Apart from the debates that still flare over particular issues of interpretation, there are important topics that even now are largely unexplored. Most prominent of these is the history of the political and military dynamics within each of the Arab states during the war, a task that is hindered by the difficulty of obtaining documentary evidence from the Arab state archives.

Origins

The 1948 War, called Milhemet ha-Atzmaʿut ("The War of Independence") in Israel and al-Nakba ("The Catastrophe") by Palestinians, was the culmination of nearly thirty years of conflict between European Jewish immigrants and indigenous Palestinian Arabs in Palestine. This conflict had begun in earnest under the rule of the British, who in World War 1 had seized control of Palestine from the Turks by military conquest, and who—in the famous Balfour Declaration of 1917—had promised the land to the Jews as a national home. Although the Balfour Declaration required that the "civil and religious [note, not political] rights of existing non-Jewish communities in Palestine" be respected, the British made this promise without consultation with the Palestinians, that is to say, the inhabitants of Palestine. British rule was characterized by increasingly unsuccessful attempts to manage and placate conflicting Jewish and Palestinian claims to the land. In 1947, as part of their broader postwar policy to shed their imperial responsibilities, the British announced their intention to leave Palestine and handed over the Palestine problem to the United Nations. On 29 November 1947 the United Nations General Assembly voted to divide the country into a Jewish state and an

The Balfour Declaration

Foreign Office

November 2nd, 1917

Dear Lord Rothschild:

I have much pleasure in conveying to you. on behalf of His Majesty's Government, the following declaration of sympathy with Jewish Zionist aspirations which has been submitted to, and approved by, the Cabinet:

His Majesty's Government view with favor the establishment in Palestine of a national home for the Jewish people, and will use their best endeavors to facilitate the achievement of this object, it being clearly understood that nothing shall be done which may prejudice the civil and religious rights of existing non-Jewish communities in Palestine, or the rights and political status enjoyed by Jews in any other country.

I should be grateful if you would bring this declaration to the knowledge of the Zionist Federation.

Yours,

Arthur James Balfour

Arab state, with an international enclave encompassing Jerusalem and its environs. The Jews accepted the partition resolution and the Palestinians rejected it. In 1947 the vast majority of Jews in Palestine were those who had come from Europe in the first half of the twentieth century in order to participate in the Zionist project of establishing a Jewish nation there. This immigration had increased during the 1930s as the persecution of Jews in Europe had intensified. The UN's 1947 offer of statehood in half of the territory was considered a triumph, by and for Jews, particularly in the wake of the horrors of the Holocaust; now, it seemed, there would at last be a place for Jews to live where they would not be a minority. By contrast, the indigenous Palestinians had witnessed their neighbors—Transjordan (called Jordan from 1949), Lebanon, and Syria—gaining independence from British and French rule in the mid–1940s. They were unwilling to give up half of the land to Jewish settlers from Europe whom they regarded as colonizers. This UN vote in favor of partition sparked the beginning of the battle between Jews and Palestinians for the land that the British would be leaving in less than six months.

The Civil War

The first phase of the 1948 war is usually called the civil war. This is the period between the announcement of the UN vote in favor of partition on 29 November 1947 and the departure of the British on 14 May 1948. This period saw fighting between Palestinians and Jews and a volunteer force of about three thousand Arabs from neighboring states that the Arab League had sent into the theater of war. The regular armies of the Arab states were not involved in the fighting during this period. Casualties mounted on both sides, but the Jewish forces were better organized and better led than the Palestinians and they quickly gained the upper hand. Major Palestinian towns and villages, including Safad, Tiberius, Haifa, Acre, and Jaffa, fell to Jewish troops. By the time of the departure of the British and the declaration of the State of Israel on 14 May, Jewish forces had taken most of the land allocated to the Jewish state by the UN as well as some of the land allocated to the Palestinians.

The Interstate War and Its Aftermath

On 14 May 1948 the last British High Commissioner, General Alan Cunningham (1887–1983), left Palestine and David Ben-Gurion (1886–1973), the leader of the *Yishuv* (the Jewish community in Palestine), declared the establishment of the State of Israel. The next day, units from the regular armies of Egypt, Transjordan, Syria, and Iraq attacked the new Jewish state, and the struggle for the land became an international conflict.

The Arab Legion, which was the British-trained army of King Abdullah (1882–1951) of Transjordan, posed the greatest threat to Israel, and the Arab Legion and the Israeli army engaged in some fierce fighting, particularly in and around Jerusalem. The armies of other Arab states made some gains at the beginning of the war, but they were preoccupied with the threat posed to them by King Abdullah's own territorial ambitions in Palestine. In addition they failed to coordinate effectively, and they were poorly equipped and trained.

The fighting can be divided into three phases: 14 May until the beginning of the first truce on 10 June, 8–18 July (sometimes called the ten days' war), and October 1948–January 1949. All three phases saw Israeli gains, but it was during the ten days' war and the final period of fighting between October 1948 and January 1949 that Israeli forces seized large portions of land that had originally been allocated to the Arab state under the terms of the partition resolution, in the Galilee, the Tel Aviv-Jerusalem corridor, and the Negev.

By January 1949 Israeli forces had beaten the Arab armies. The Arab Legion had possession of the West Bank (allocated to the Arab state under the terms of the partition resolution), and the eastern part of Jerusalem, including the old city of Jerusalem. Israel had conquered the western part of Jerusalem. The Arab Legion did not fight to seize control of territory that the partition resolution had allocated to the Jewish state. Most professional historians of the modern Middle East now accept the argument (for example, as given in Avi Shlaim's *Collusion Across the Jordan: King Abdullah, the Zionist Movement, and the Partition of Palestine*) that this was due to a secret agreement, secured between Israel and King Abdullah, in which Israel agreed not to contest Transjordanian claims to the West Bank as long as Transjordan did not attempt to conquer land allocated to the Jewish state. By the end of hostilities Israel had secured all the territory allocated to it by the UN in addition to a significant portion of the land allocated to the Arab state. In fact, following the armistice negotiations that were conducted on the island of Rhodes after the war, the Jewish community in Palestine emerged with a state of Israel that was bigger by a third than the area originally allocated to it under the terms of the partition resolution. Egypt occupied a small strip of land on the southern coast of Palestine (allocated to the Arab state under the terms of the partition resolution) that became known as the Gaza Strip. After the conclusion of the armistice agreements at Rhodes, attempts were made to conclude a lasting peace treaty. These attempts, which failed due to intransigence on both sides, became known as the Lausanne Peace Talks.

Outcome

Jewish casualties in the war were high (6,500 people, over 1 percent of the population), but the new state of Israel had won an impressive military victory. In addition it had received diplomatic recognition from most foreign powers, including the United States and the Soviet Union. Only three years after the liberation of the concentration camps in Europe, the establishment of the state of Israel seemed like an astounding achievement for the Jewish people. The exact number of Palestinian and other Arab deaths is difficult to establish, but some estimates put the total at around 10,000. For the Palestinian people the 1948 War was a catastrophe. Not only did they end up stateless, but roughly 750,000 (well over half of the Arab population of Palestine) had become refugees, consigned to living in camps in the West Bank, the Gaza Strip, and the neighboring Arab states. Some of these Palestinians left as a result of direct expulsions by Jewish forces, others fled in fear when the news of Jewish massacres of Palestinians spread through the villages and towns. The most infamous of these massacres took place in the village of Dayr Yasin in April 1948. Most of the Palestinians who left did so in the belief that they would be able to return to their homes after the Arab armies had fulfilled their widely broadcast promise to "push the Jews into the sea." The Palestinian refugee problem remains unsolved to this day. Its resolution is one of the key hurdles that needs to be overcome in order for there to be any lasting peace between Palestinians and Israelis.

In the Arab world the defeat of 1948 is treated as a cataclysmic moment in the history of the twentieth century. The defeat discredited the leaders of the newly independent Arab states, who were just then struggling to establish their legitimacy. In many Arab countries they were quickly replaced by military regimes, which led to a general radicalization in Arab politics. The struggle for Israel/Palestine, one of the many legacies of British imperialism in the Middle East, continues to dominate the political landscape in the Arab world.

Laila Parsons

See also Palestine and Israel; Palestine Liberation Organization

Further Reading

Karsh, E. (1997). *Fabricating Israeli history: The "new historians."* London: Frank Cass.

Kurzman, D. (1970). *Genesis 1948*. New York: The World Publishing Company.

Louis, W. R., & Stookey, R. W. (Eds). (1986). *The end of the Palestine Mandate*. Austin: University of Texas Press.

Masalha, N. (1992). *Expulsion of the Palestinians: The concept of "transfer" in Zionist political thought, 1882–1948*. Washington, DC: Institute for Palestine Studies.

Morris, B. (1988). *The birth of the Palestinian refugee problem, 1947–1949*. Cambridge, UK: Cambridge University Press.

Morris, B. (1990). *1948 and after: Israel and the Palestinians*. Oxford, UK: Oxford University Press.

Pappe, I. (1991). *The making of the Arab-Israeli conflict, 1947–1951*. London: I. B. Taurus.

Rogan, E., & Shlaim, A. (Eds). (2001). *The war for Palestine: Rewriting the history of 1948*. Cambridge, UK: Cambridge University Press.

Shlaim, A. (1988). *Collusion across the Jordan: King Abdullah, the Zionist movement, and the partition of Palestine*. Oxford, UK: Oxford University Press.

Palestine and Israel

The continuing violent conflict between Israelis and Palestinians results from a complex network of factors ranging from competing nationalisms to economics, the legacy of Western colonialism and imperialism, anti-Semitism and religion. All of these factors impact each other in ways that blur clear lines of distinction, so that the issue of competing nationalisms, for example, incorporates aspects of all the other issues within it. Although holy war ideologies clearly inform attitudes and behaviors of both Muslims and Jews with regard to the conflict, it is not a religious conflict per se. On the Palestinian side, for example, not all activists are Muslims. Influential and active Arab Christians are counted among Palestinians striving to establish an independent state. Other Palestinians, although nominally Muslim, function in their personal lives and in relation to the conflict largely in secular terms. And on the Israeli side, a large non-Jewish minority of Arabs, both Muslim and Christian, is divided and ambivalent with regard to its position in the conflict. Among Jewish Israelis, the majority define themselves as secular or nominally religious. Only a small but politically powerful minority in what is often referred to as the "national religious" camp relates to the conflict in strongly religious terms. Ideas of religious war are limited mostly to the radically religious Muslim nationalist minority among Palestinians and the radically religious Jewish nationalist minority among Israelis, both of whose nationalist principles include aspects of holy war ideologies.

Zionism as a Secular Nationalist Movement

Zionism is the term for the various expressions and ideologies of modern Jewish nationalism that consider "Zion," a term referring to the biblical land of Israel, as the Jewish national home. Zionism emerged in late–nineteenth-century Europe as a secular movement that saw its future in parallel with the national movements that emerged as a result of the weakening and eventual collapse of the Russian, Hapsburg, and Ottoman empires. Within the groups making up the broad range of Zionism's political and social spectrum, its leaders, avant-garde, and rank and file were virtually all secular Jews who identified as members of the Jewish *nation* rather than *religion*. Only a small minority of Zionists observed Jewish ritual life as prescribed by the tradition, and this minority was opposed by the overwhelming majority of "religious" Jews.

"Religious" Jews, which for the purposes of this article will henceforth be distinguished from secular Jews by the designation "religiously Orthodox," relied on a famous passage from the Babylonian Talmud (*Ketubot* 111a) that had been interpreted by most Jews in the Middle Ages to mean that God forbade emigrating on mass to the land of Israel until the coming of the Messiah (Ravitzky 1996, 211–234). While the overwhelming secular majority of Zionists completely disregarded the talmudic prohibition in their zeal to establish a secular Jewish state along the lines of other modern secular states emerging in Europe, a few Orthodox Jews were energized by the tremendous excitement of Jewish nation-building. Religiously Orthodox Zionists were confronted with a very difficult problem: how to justify engaging in what appeared to be not only a secular and therefore godless movement, but also one that appeared to disregard in a most egregious manner a divine prohibition. This small group of Orthodox Jews remained committed to Zionism but had difficulty justifying its commitment. Some announced that their goal was to bring wayward secular Jews back to religious Orthodoxy by working with them in their

Selection from the Oslo Accords of 1993

Declaration of Principles on Interim Self-Government Arrangements:

The Government of the State of Israel and the PLO team (in the Jordanian-Palestinian delegation to the Middle East Peace Conference) (the "Palestinian Delegation"), representing the Palestinian people, agree that it is time to put an end to decades of confrontation and conflict, recognise their mutual legitimate and political rights, and strive to live in peaceful coexistence and mutual dignity and security and achieve a just, lasting and comprehensive peace settlement and historic reconciliation through the agreed political process. Accordingly, the two sides agree to the following principles:

Article I: Aim of negotiations:

The aim of the Israeli-Palestinian negotiations within the current Middle East peace process is, among other things, to establish a Palestinian Interim Self-Government Authority, the elected Council (the "Council"), for the Palestinian people in the West Bank and the Gaza Strip, for a transitional period not exceeding five years, leading to a permanent settlement based on Security Council resolutions 242 (1967) and 338 (1973). It is understood that the interim arrangements are an integral part of the whole peace process and that the negotiations on the permanent status will lead to the implementation of Security Council resolutions 242 (1967) and 338 (1973).

***Source:* Islamic Association for Palestine. Retrieved April 10, 2003, from http://www.iap.org**

project. Others justified their involvement as working toward finding a shelter for Jews who were being persecuted and even massacred in the pogroms occurring at the time in Eastern Europe. Most believed that perhaps the coming of the messiah and God's final redemption of the Jewish people was nigh. This was extremely controversial and was not articulated outright; it endangered the acceptance of religiously Orthodox Zionists among the overwhelming majority of coreligionist non-Zionists because the same talmudic passage (*Ketubot* 111a) forbids attempting to "force the hand of God" by moving to the land of Israel en masse before God decides it is time to bring the messiah. Religiously Orthodox Zionists were thus largely marginalized, both within the Zionist movement by its secular leadership and rank and file, and by Orthodox Jewry that considered them wayward and transgressing a divine command. Secular Zionism would prevail and succeed in creating a secular state, a Jewish state to be sure, but one in which non-Jews would also be voting citizens and the democratic rule of law would prevail.

The position of Orthodox Zionism would hardly change, even after the surprisingly successful victory of the War of Independence in 1948, until the famous "Six Day War" of 1967. The tremendous success of the Israeli army was recognized by Jews throughout the world, whether secular, liberally religious, or Orthodox, as a divine miracle or something suggestive of such. Facing the combined threat of five larger armies and the Egyptian president's promise to destroy the Jewish state and throw its citizens into the sea, Israeli forces managed not only to survive a terrifying situation (particularly in light of the Holocaust that had occurred only twenty-five years previously), but even succeeded in expanding its territory, winning for the Jewish state almost all of the biblically defined "land of Israel." Most of the Orthodox Jewish world would come to interpret this success as a divine miracle, a sure harbinger of the coming messiah. Coupled with a generally increasing ethnic consciousness in the West, most Jews throughout the world, whether religious or secular, became staunch Zionists. Religiously Orthodox Zionists were energized by the experience and began to take on (and were granted) more leadership roles in the Zionist movement and in the national government as secular Zionist ideologies weakened and corruption in government stained the secular leadership. Although still a relatively small minority, religiously Orthodox expressions of Zionism have become much more prominent and their ideas far more influential. A general ideology of religious nationalism that had been quietly emerging was now thrust into the public arena to justify religious Orthodoxy's involvement in Zionism, in war, and in retaining what is considered to be the divine gift of Jewish hegemony over the biblical lands of Judea and Samaria, the two areas of the region that, ironically, are most densely populated by Palestinian Arabs. This aggressive emerging religious nationalist ideology would clash violently with emerging Palestinian nationalist ideologies, including those of Islamic revivalist movements.

A Modern Jewish Holy War Ideology

The most activist and radical segment of religiously Orthodox Zionists are members of the "Settler Movement" who make up most of the Jewish inhabitants of the territories on the West Bank (or Judea and Samaria) conquered in the 1967 war. There is no single holy war ideology among religious Orthodox Zionists, but there is basic conformity along fundamental beliefs, expectations, and requirements. At the core is the belief that the coming of the messiah is imminent. God demonstrated this through the divine "signs and wonders" of the successes of the War of Independence in 1948 and the Six Day War of 1967. These signs have neutralized the talmudic prohibition against mass emigration, settlement, and premature political hegemony over the biblical land of Israel, and have simultaneously reactivated the old rabbinic category of "commanded war" *(milhemet mitzvah)*. Only "commanded war" is divinely authorized, and this Jewish equivalent to "holy war" applies to the conquest of the land of Israel. Its purpose is to secure the land of Israel for the people of Israel or to defend the people and its land. It does not apply to expanding Jewish hegemony beyond the borders established by the Bible except in the case of defending Jews from attack. Before the messianic coming, it applied only to the biblical conquest, but with the messiah's imminence it may apply also to contemporary Israeli wars to conquer and retain the sacred land. Wholesale slaughter of the enemy, including noncombatants, was traditionally allowed only in "commanded war" directed against the seven Canaanite nations and the Amalekites. Some radicals today would allow such rules of engagement in relation to Palestinians, whom they consider present-day Canaanites.

Some military reverses such as the Yom Kippur War in October of 1973 are understood to reflect divine displeasure in response to government willingness to hand over biblical lands to non-Jews (Palestinians) in a peace process, or government unwillingness to conform more fully to the religious laws of Orthodox Judaism. Settler activists consider themselves the avant-garde of the messiah. When the majority Israeli population wavers in its desire to retain the God-given lands, this vanguard must work all the harder to make sure they do not fall away from Jewish control. Such an imperative transcends all interest in democracy, since the divine command transcends all human authority. What is at stake for these activists is the very future of Israel, not only the state but the people, for the people of Israel has been given only one opportunity in the last two thousand years to bring the messiah and, therefore, the redemption of the entire world. If they fail, the very universe will be shaken asunder.

Palestine Nationalist and Islamist Movements

The Palestinian Liberation Organization (PLO) is the umbrella organization of Palestinian national movements and has been the primary Palestinian institution to confront the state of Israel from the 1948 *Nakba* (or "Disaster," as the establishment of the state of Israel is referred to in the Palestinian national narrative) until the period of the first *Intifada* or "uprising" (literally, "quaking") in 1987. The PLO is a secular nationalist movement that has generally worked through political and military means to establish a Palestinian state. Even before the establishment of the PLO, however, Palestinian Arabs had formed clubs, societies, and political organizations under the British mandatory government whose purpose was to promote a sense of modern Arab identity in Palestine and, eventually, national independence.

Parallel to Arab interest in Westernizing and secular nationalism can be found a negative reaction to Western influence that has stimulated the emergence of Islamic revivalist (Islamist) movements, the most famous and influential of which is the Muslim Brotherhood, founded in Egypt in 1928 by Hasan al-Banna. While Islamist movements differ over tactics and ideology, they agree on a basic analysis and core goals. The Islamic world has weakened, according to this analysis, as a result of Western corruption identified as modernism and secularism and various political and social ideas such as socialism, nationalism, democracy, and liberalism. Love of the West has weakened the religious and moral integrity of Muslims as they seek modernity and an easy materialistic life. The Islamic world, though nominally Muslim, is actually turning toward apostasy. It is reverting to a modern *jahiliyya* or state of barbaric ignorance that parallels the horrible state of *jahiliyya* in Arabia that precipitated the divine

Memorial Park and statue commemorating The Six Day War, Golan Heights, Israel. November 1996. Courtesy Steve Donaldson.

intervention of God revealing the Qur'an and Islam. Governments in the Islamic World are hopelessly secular dictatorships that disregard the rights of the people by disregarding the laws of Islam. The only way to rectify this heresy, defiance of God, and cruelty to the Arab people is to return the Islamic world to the pristine period when believers truly lived according to God's will as articulated through the Qur'an and the leadership of the Prophet Muhammad.

While the goal of eliminating the state of Israel is shared by radical secular nationalists and Islamists alike and while both groups consider violent confrontation to be a legitimate form of resistance against Israel, they disagree entirely over how the Jewish state should be replaced. The nationalists want a modern Palestinian state, while the Islamists want Palestine to be a region run according to Islamic law as part of a larger Islamized Middle East. Nationalists, whose ranks include Christians as well as Muslims, tend to identify more as Arabs than Muslims and are more likely to agree to a two-state solution, while Islamists are adamant in their call to eliminate any non-Islamic entity in the Middle East.

Violence against the state of Israel and, in some cases, against Israelis and Jews living or traveling outside the state, had been a part of nationalist Palestinian resistance long before the rise of Islamist activism in the latter two decades of the twentieth century. Until the early 1980s, this militancy tended to be justified through secular revolutionary ideology, and until the first Intifada of the late 1980s and early 1990s, Islamism was not a significant political force, though Palestinians were increasingly attracted to religious revivalism since the early 1970s. By the 1980s, the failure of the PLO to achieve its nationalist goals and the increasingly obvious corruption among its leaders had begun to decrease the support of rank-and-file Palestinians. At the same time, Islamic revivalism had grown substantially and had succeeded in attracting followers through its expanding social-service network. As a result, Islamic revivalist groups and leaders achieved a tremendous increase in support by the second Intifada (the "Al-Aksa Intifada") in the first decade of the twenty-first century.

Both nationalists and Islamists use the term jihad (holy war) in their political rhetoric, because of its primary importance in Arab and Islamic history. Various modern interpretations of the term and its applicability to contemporary events have been proffered in the Islamic world, from accommodation with colonialism to violence against all forms of non-Western ideas and influence. The more radical and activist Islamists among Palestinians and throughout the Middle East, however, understand the term as a religiously authorized effort to rid first the region and then the world of negative non-Islamic influence. It should be noted that such jihad is not directed only against Jews, Christians, and adherents of other religions, but also against secularist or liberal Muslims themselves who may be decried as non-Muslims or apostates.

Virtually all Palestinians are Sunni Muslims, as opposed to Shiʿite, and they draw their Islamist ideologies from traditional Sunni thinkers such as Ibn Taymiyah (1263–1328) and twentieth-century leaders such as Hassan al-Banna and Sayyid Qutb as developed and interpreted through the Muslim Brotherhood. They have found significant inspiration also, however, from the activism and militancy of Shiʾite groups such as those that succeeded in the Iranian revolution and the Hezbollah in southern Lebanon.

A Modern Islamist Ideology of Jihad

God has demanded monotheism of all humankind, according to Islamists, and has given revelations to all human groups, some of which we know as the Hebrew Bible and the New Testament. Unfortunately, however, all extant expressions of monotheism have become corrupted, and only Islam expresses the whole truth of the divine will. In addition to this problem, most contemporary Muslims have become corrupted by the temptations of unbelief, so it is incumbent upon all good Muslims to encourage their coreligionists to return to the proper path. The world is divided into two spheres, one of Islam (the "Abode of Islam") and the other of idolatry and apostasy (the "Abode of War"). True Muslims in the Abode of Islam must strive (which is the meaning of jihad) until the entire world counts itself in the Abode of Islam. This striving may occur on a number of levels, from education to war.

Palestine is a region of the Islamic Middle East that has been within the Abode of Islam from its initial conquest by Muslims in the 630s until the present, with only two short interruptions. The first was under the Crusaders and the second under modern British and Western colonialism since the collapse of the Ottoman Empire. Just as the Crusaders were repelled by jihad in the Middle Ages, so too must the Jews and their Western supporters be repelled by a modern jihad. Some Palestinian Islamists believe that success will come only after all Palestinian Muslims return to proper belief and practice, after which a war with Israel will be successful because the fighters will be religiously pure and will thereby gain victory through divine aid. Others believe that the profaning influence of the West through the state of Israel will prevent Muslims from returning to proper belief and practice, so that the dismantling of the Jewish state must first occur before the region can return to true Islam.

After the destruction of Israel, Palestine will revert to its status as an Islamic region ruled according to Islamic rather than secular (Western) law. According to most public statements, most Jewish survivors will be free to live within Islamic Palestine as *dhimmi* (protected) peoples with full religious and economic rights on the condition that they accept the religious and political hegemony of Islam and pay a special tax levied on non-Muslim monotheists, the so-called "People of the Book." Most classical writings on jihad, however, note that People of the Book who fight against Muslims may be taken as slaves or, upon the discretion of the ruler, the males or men of fighting age may be killed.

Conflicting Religious Visions

Both radically religious Jews and radically religious Muslims believe that they are waging a war authorized and commanded by God. In such religious war ideologies, there can be no compromise with the divine will. The Jewish vision is geographically limited to Jewish religious and political rule of the biblical land of Israel, while the Islamic vision is one in which the entire world must eventually come under Islamic religious and political rule. Even in the geographically limited Jewish vision, however, the future of the world is at stake because the messianic advent will bring redemption not only to world Jewry, but to all humankind.

While both religiously militant Jews and Muslims remain minorities within their respective national communities, they wield an inordinate influence (based on sociological, historical, and political factors that extend beyond the limits of this entry). Their impact on the conflict waxes and wanes, and at the time of this writing early in the first decade of the twenty-first century, both wield considerable influence on the rank-and-file and leadership of their respective communities. National conflicts that center around material issues such as territory, natural resources, and economics are essentially quantitative and may be negotiated to arrive at some kind of compromise. Religious conflicts, on the other hand, are ideological and qualitative, deriving from creed and belief, and are much more difficult to negotiate. The conflict between Israelis and Palestinians began largely as a national conflict, but frustration at continuing violence and lack of resolution has helped to propel it into an increasingly religious conflict. A reversal of this trend is necessary for any solution to be achieved.

Reuven Firestone

Further Reading

Abu-Amr, Z. (1994). *Islamic fundamentalism in the West Bank and Gaza*. Bloomington: Indiana University Press.

Bleich, Rabbi J. (1988). Of land, peace, and divine command. *Journal of Halachah and Contemporary Society 16*, 56–69.

Firestone, R. (1996). Conceptions of holy war in biblical and Qur'anic tradition. *The Journal of Religious Ethics 24*, 801–824.

Firestone, R. (1999). *Jihad: The origin of holy war in Islam*. New York: Oxford University Press.

Friedman, R. I. (1992). *Zealots for Zion: Inside Israel's West Bank settlement movement*. New Brunswick, NJ: Rutgers University Press.

Hertzberg, A. (1971). *The Zionist idea*. New York: Atheneum.

Peters, R. (1996). *Jihad in classical and modern Islam*. Princeton, NJ: Markus Wiener.

Ravitzky, A. (1996). *Engraved on the tablets: The land of Israel in modern Jewish thought*. Jerusalem: Magnes.

Ravitzky, A. (1996). *Messianism, Zionism, and Jewish religious radicalism*. Chicago: University of Chicago Press.

Schacter, H. (1989). The mitzvah of Yishuv Eretz Yisrael. In S. Spero & Y. Pessin (Eds.), *Religious Zionism after 40 years of statehood* (pp. 190–212). Jerusalem: World Zionist Organization. (Reprinted from *Journal of Halakhah and Contemporary Society 8* (1984), 14–33)

Silberstein, L. (Ed.). (1993). *Jewish fundamentalism in comparative perspective*. New York: New York University Press.

Sivan, E., & Friedman, M. (Eds.). (1990). *Religious radicalism and politics in the Middle East*. Albany, NY: State University of New York Press.

Palestine Liberation Organization

The Palestine Liberation Organization (PLO; in Arabic, *Munazzamat al-Tahrir al-Filas Tiniyah*) is the umbrella organization of the movement for an independent Palestinian nation, and serves as the main international political entity of the Palestinian people. Since the Madrid Peace Conference in 1991, the PLO has served as the negotiating party with the State of Israel to resolve the Palestinian-Israeli conflict.

Early History

As a result of the establishment of the state of Israel and the war surrounding its independence in 1948, millions of Arab inhabitants of the former British Mandate of Palestine fled to the surrounding Arab countries. Throughout the subsequent decade, many Palestinian resistance cells and guerilla movements formed to organize opposition to Israel and pressure the Arab states to act on their behalf. In 1959, a number of leading Palestinian activists assembled in Kuwait and within three years organized *Harakat At-Tahrir Al-Filistiniya* (Palestinian Liberation Movement); the reverse acronym, *fateh*, by which the organization came to be known, is Arabic for *conquest*. Among the founders of Fateh was Yasser Arafat, an engineering graduate of Cairo University and founder of the General Union of Palestinian Students. Arafat has served as Fateh's spokesperson since 1968.

Among Fateh's founding principles was the common goal of liberating Palestine, a call for an armed struggle to achieve this goal, and an emphasis on Palestinian self-organization. Fateh's philosophy contrasted sharply with the dominant Arab political discussions of the time, which held that Arab unity was essential for the liberation of Palestine. The leaders of Fateh insisted that the liberation of Palestine was a goal unto itself, and that the unity of the Arab states could come about only after Palestinians engaged in a grassroots effort to liberate their homeland.

In January 1964, the president of Egypt, Gamal Abdel Nasser, convened the first Arab Summit. Attended by the leaders of thirteen Arab states, the meeting was initially conceived to discuss Israel's diversion of water from the Sea of Galilee to the Negev Desert. While unable to prevent that action, a collective decision was made—one that marks the summit's contribution to history—to create a Palestinian political entity. The leaders hoped that the creation of this entity, the Palestinian Liberation Organization, would contain

Selection from The Palestinian National Charter: Resolutions of the Palestine National Council, July 1–17, 1968

Article 1: Palestine is the homeland of the Arab Palestinian people; it is an indivisible part of the Arab homeland, and the Palestinian people are an integral part of the Arab nation.

Article 2: Palestine, with the boundaries it had during the British Mandate, is an indivisible territorial unit.

Article 3: The Palestinian Arab people possess the legal right to their homeland and have the right to determine their destiny after achieving the liberation of their country in accordance with their wishes and entirely of their own accord and will.

Article 4: The Palestinian identity is a genuine, essential, and inherent characteristic; it is transmitted from parents to children. The Zionist occupation and the dispersal of the Palestinian Arab people, through the disasters which befell them, do not make them lose their Palestinian identity and their membership in the Palestinian community, nor do they negate them.

Article 5: The Palestinians are those Arab nationals who, until 1947, normally resided in Palestine regardless of whether they were evicted from it or have stayed there. Anyone born, after that date, of a Palestinian father—whether inside Palestine or outside it—is also a Palestinian.

Article 6: The Jews who had normally resided in Palestine until the beginning of the Zionist invasion will be considered Palestinians.

Article 7: That there is a Palestinian community and that it has material, spiritual, and historical connection with Palestine are indisputable facts. It is a national duty to bring up individual Palestinians in an Arab revolutionary manner. All means of information and education must be adopted in order to acquaint the Palestinian with his country in the most profound manner, both spiritual and material, that is possible. He must be prepared for the armed struggle and ready to sacrifice his wealth and his life in order to win back his homeland and bring about its liberation.

Article 8: The phase in their history, through which the Palestinian people are now living, is that of national *(watani)* struggle for the liberation of Palestine. Thus the conflicts among the Palestinian national forces are secondary, and should be ended for the sake of the basic conflict that exists between the forces of Zionism and of imperialism on the one hand, and the Palestinian Arab people on the other. On this basis the Palestinian masses, regardless of whether they are residing in the national homeland or in diaspora *(mahajir)* constitute – both their organizations and the individuals – one national front working for the retrieval of Palestine and its liberation through armed struggle.

Article 9: Armed struggle is the only way to liberate Palestine. Thus it is the overall strategy, not merely a tactical phase. The Palestinian Arab people assert their absolute determination and firm resolution to continue their armed struggle and to work for an armed popular revolution for the liberation of their country and their return to it. They also assert their right to normal life in Palestine and to exercise their right to self-determination and sovereignty over it.

Article 10: Commando action constitutes the nucleus of the Palestinian popular liberation war. This requires its escalation, comprehensiveness, and the mobilization of all the Palestinian popular and educational efforts and their organization and involvement in the armed Palestinian revolution. It also requires the achieving of unity for the national *(watani)* struggle among the different groupings of the Palestinian people, and between the Palestinian people and the Arab masses, so as to secure the continuation of the revolution, its escalation, and victory.

Article 11: The Palestinians will have three mottoes: national *(wataniyya)* unity, national *(qawmiyya)* mobilization, and liberation.

Source: **Kadi, Leila S. (Ed.). (1969).** ***Basic Political Documents of the Armed Palestinian Resistance Movement.*** **Beirut, Lebanon: Palestine Research Centre, pp. 137–138.**

and organize Palestinian activism. Furthermore, they hoped that by imposing an institutional framework on the various guerilla groups, they could prevent them from unilaterally taking action on Israel that could provoke a potentially destabilizing military response.

Within months, the new PLO formed a parliament, the Palestine National Council (PNC), a body consisting of 422 members. The PNC's charter called for the elimination of Israel and the establishment of an independent Palestinian state in its stead. The National Council also elected an executive committee of fifteen members, which chose as its chairman Ahmed Shuqairy. Shuqairy had previously served as a Palestinian delegate to the Arab League and Ambassador to the United Nations for Saudi Arabia.

The Aftermath of the 1967 War

The 1967 Six Day War proved a turning point in the development of the Palestinian Liberation Organization. After soundly defeating the combined armies of Egypt, Syria, and Jordan, Israel was able to occupy both the West Bank and the Gaza Strip, previously under the control of Egypt and Jordan, respectively, and home to many large Palestinian communities. More Palestinian refugees were created, and the leaders of the Arab states and the PLO were widely discredited for their seeming lack of military prowess and their inability to improve the Palestinian's situation. Fateh, chief among other factions, seized the opportunity to begin acting against Israel independently of the PLO umbrella.

A series of small Palestinian guerilla raids and attacks against Israel led to a violent retaliatory strike against the Jordanian town of Karama in March 1968. Karama, just east of the Jordan River, was the command center of Fateh's operations in the West Bank. The guerillas strongly resisted the incursion and inflicted heavy casualties on the Israeli forces, though Palestinian deaths still far outnumbered those of Israelis. The small victory was subsequently inflated in Fateh's rhetoric, and the movement found itself rehabilitated with new recruits and financial support from the Arab Gulf states. As a result, Fateh quickly became the dominant faction in the PLO.

In July 1968, an amendment to the Palestine National Charter reflected Fateh's underlying principles: it called on Arab states to avoid direct involvement in Palestinian affairs and for the liberation of Palestine by the Palestinians themselves. In February 1969, Yasser Arafat was elected Chairman of the Executive Committee of the Palestine National Council. Under Arafat, the PLO solidified its role as a loose confederation of a number of different Palestinian factions. While maintaining the larger goal of an independent Palestine, these factions in fact often worked at cross purposes. Included under the PLO umbrella was the Marxist group the Popular Front for the Liberation of Palestine (PFLP), its non-Marxist splinter group, the Democratic Front for the Liberation of Palestine (DFLP), and the PFLP–GC, the Popular Front for the Liberation of Palestine–General Command.

Throughout their history, these rival groups have offered varying degrees of resistance to and competition with Yasser Arafat and the Fateh faction within the PLO. Arafat has frequently been criticized for not articulating a guiding ideology for the Palestinian movement, but instead reacting to each individual crisis. Arafat and his Fateh colleagues have also been accused of subverting the democratic ideals of the PLO through cronyism, corruption, and the Chairman's own autocratic style. Serious infighting has occurred when the Fateh faction, which came to be seen as relatively centrist and moderate, has openly disagreed with the more radical and leftist facets of the PLO. Such internecine fighting occurred as a result of Fateh's condemnation of plane hijackings by the PFLP and PFLP-GC in 1969 and 1970. At times, certain groups have completely or temporarily withdrawn from the PLO in protest of its leadership. In other instances, the leftist groups have ensnared the PLO as a whole in extremely difficult entanglements. These include involvement in the civil wars in Jordan (1970) and Lebanon (1976).

The PLO in Lebanon

Despite infighting and competition among the various Palestinian groups, the Palestine National Council under Arafat was successful in serving as a government-in-exile for the hundreds of thousands of Palestinians living in Lebanon in the 1970s. Through this effort, the PLO found itself with increased status and stature on the world stage. An Arab League meeting in October, 1974 appointed the PLO as the official representative body of the Palestinian people. In November 1974, Yasser Arafat was invited to address the United Nations upon the granting of observer status to the PLO. By 1982, the Palestinian Liberation Organization was recognized by over one hundred nations.

In setting up both political and economic institutions in Lebanon, the PLO seriously undermined the sovereignty and authority of the Lebanese government, exacerbating the existing instability between Lebanon's Christian and Muslim communities. The PLO ensnared itself in the Lebanese civil war while at the same time incurring Israel's wrath for using the southern part of the country as a base against Israel's northern border. The Israeli government invaded Lebanon in June 1982, seeking to fully neutralize the PLO. This effort was unsuccessful; the PLO leadership quickly relocated to Tunisia, leaving thousands of Palestinian refugees in southern Lebanon unprotected. In September, the Phalange, a Christian militia with Israeli backing, invaded the Sabra and Shatilla refugee camps, killing between 800 and 1,500 Palestinians.

Israel's extended occupation of southern Lebanon (which did not end until June 2000) did not prevent Arafat from attempting to reassert PLO control there within a year of the expulsion. These efforts were thwarted both by the Israelis' military presence and the opposition of rival Palestinian factions loyal to Syria. The PLO leadership returned to Tunis, where Israel once again tried to undermine their authority with a failed bombing attack on PLO headquarters.

Peace Plans and Peace Agreements

In March 1979 Egyptian President Anwar Sadat signed a peace agreement with Israeli Prime Minister Menachem Begin at Camp David, under the direction of U.S. President Jimmy Carter. In so doing, Sadat broke ranks with the other Arab states who had long opposed the concept of a "separate peace." The agreement also isolated the PLO by excluding their participation, while calling for limited Palestinian autonomy within Israel instead of an independent Palestinian state. In ending the threat of Egyptian military action against Israel, the Camp David Accords gave Israel greater freedom of action, which it exercised in the invasion of Lebanon three years later. President Ronald Reagan's peace plan, also put forth in 1982, was based on the Camp David Accords and similarly prevented participation by the PLO.

In the early 1970s, the position of the PLO had evolved to reflect the recognition of Israel's permanence on the Middle Eastern landscape. At two subsequent assemblies of the Palestine National Council, in 1974 and 1977, a two-state solution was proposed and supported by the body. These proposals, as well as a later plan put forth by King Fahd of Saudi Arabia, called for the establishment of a Palestinian state in the West Bank and Gaza. Such proposals were rejected by the Israeli government, and the limited Palestinian autonomy called for in the Camp David Accords failed to materialize throughout the 1980s.

An uprising by Palestinians living in the occupied territories in December 1987 refocused world attention on the intractable situation in the West Bank and Gaza. This *intifada* ("shaking off") reflected the Palestinians' frustration not only with the ongoing Israeli military occupation, but with the inability of the PLO to change their lot for the better. In response, the PLO, at the direction of Yasser Arafat, undertook a number of political and diplomatic steps in late 1988: It was at this time that the organization established a Palestinian "government-in-exile" with Arafat at its head, and endorsed U.N. resolutions 181 (the 1947 partition plan), and 242 (the 1967 "land for peace" proposal). In response to these changes, and a formal renunciation of terrorism, the government of the United States commenced talks with the PLO, despite Israel's refusal to join them.

In August 1990, the Iraqi army invaded neighboring Kuwait, drawing condemnation from the international community that would eventually precipitate a U.S.-led military operation, Desert Storm, in 1991. In the negotiations preceding the invasion, Hussein attempted to link his withdrawal from Kuwait to an Israeli withdrawal from Palestine. This gambit, as well as Israel's refusal to participate in talks, prompted Arafat to support Iraq during the crisis. This proved to be a divisive issue with many of the Gulf states, as they were also threatened by the Iraqi regime. The funding they had previously provided to the PLO was soon drastically reduced or eliminated. With the collapse of the Soviet Union, another major source of funding evaporated. The combination of the two weakened the organization such that it had little choice but to accept the United States' peace initiative that culminated in the Madrid Peace Conference of 1991.

The Madrid Conference was followed by two years and ten rounds of negotiations between the PLO and Israel that produced few tangible results. Among other obstacles, the PLO considered the United States to be anything but an "honest broker," the role assigned to it at the conference. However, at the behest of Norway, a back channel for negotiations was opened in Oslo through which Israel and the PLO eventually accepted mutual recognition. A Declaration of Principles was signed at the White House in September, 1993. The agreement called for a five-year period of limited Palestinian autonomy in the West Bank and Gaza, then elections for a Palestinian Council and further Israeli withdrawal from other parts of the West Bank. A key aspect of the agreement was the postponing of negotiations on "final status issues" until 1999. Such issues included the status of Jerusalem (claimed as a capital by both parties), Jewish settlements, and the status of Palestinian refugees of the 1948 War.

The Israeli Defense Force (IDF) withdrew from Jericho and parts of the Gaza Strip in 1994, ceding control to a Palestinian civil administration and Palestinian police. In the face of ongoing civilian violence on both sides and protracted negotiations, a handful of interim agreements were successfully reached. The second Oslo accord was one such an agreement, signed 25 September 1995. Under this agreement, known as Oslo II, Israel agreed to withdraw fully from 30 percent of the West Bank and accepted the establishment of the Palestine National Authority (PNA) to govern the area. Since 1995, the PNA has been the representative body of Palestinians living in the West Bank and Gaza, while the PLO remains the representative of those living outside the area, and the negotiating partner with Israel when there are talks.

However, attempts at resolving the final status issues identified in the Oslo Agreement have thus far failed. In July 2000, President Bill Clinton convened a peace conference at Camp David, Maryland, with Arafat and Israeli Prime Minister Ehud Barak. These talks proved unproductive and further convinced many within the Palestinian and Israeli populations that nearly a decade of peace talks had done little to improve the conditions of their everyday lives. In September 2000, a visit by Israeli Prime Minister Ariel Sharon and Israeli soldiers to Muslim holy sites in Jerusalem triggered what is now called the al Aqsa intifada—another, more violent, demonstration of Palestinian frustration with both Israel and their own leadership. Subsequent plans to quell the violence of both parties, including those put forth by former U.S. Senator George Mitchell and Saudi Crown Prince Abdullah, have failed. In the event of future negotiations that lead to the establishment of an independent Palestinian state, the PLO will have thus negotiated itself out of existence, its ultimate objective achieved.

Irving Birkner

See also Hamas; Hizbullah; Palestine and Israel

Further Reading

Cobban, H. (1984). *The Palestinian Liberation Organization.* Cambridge, U.K.: Cambridge University Press.

Gresh, A. (1988). *The PLO: The struggle within.* London: Zed Books Limited.

Usher, G. (1997). *Palestine in crisis: The struggle for peace and political independence after Oslo.* London: Pluto Press.

Papal Imperial Conflict

The wars between the papacy and the medieval German Holy Roman Empire were part of a long-term pattern of church-state interaction. The violence that intermittently troubled papal-imperial relations in the high Middle Ages strengthened the papacy, weakened the German monarchy, and secured the independence of the Italian city-states. By 1250 the Roman church had outlasted its most bitter rival, Frederick II Hohenstaufen, but this victory did not prevent future church-state conflicts. The ruthlessness with which the papacy disposed of the Hohenstaufen dynasty introduced a wariness into relations between popes and secular governments that persisted into modern times.

The Investiture Conflict (1076–1122)

In the mid-eleventh century reforming churchmen grew more and more opposed toward lay appointment (that is, appointment by secular, not religious, authorities) of bishops and abbots. This hostility was the initial source of papal-imperial conflict. In 1046, Henry III of Germany went to Rome to be crowned emperor. There he found three men who claimed to be pope. Henry deposed all three and then installed a series of German bishops as pope. The third of these, Leo IX (reigned 1049–1054), initiated a reform movement that altered the distribution of power in western Europe.

By deposing and installing popes, Henry was acting in a way that was essentially theocratic. From the time of Charlemagne, kings had claimed that God had conferred on them a right and a duty to provide for the safety and welfare of God's people. This doctrine of royal theocracy gained strength during the troubles of the ninth and tenth centuries. Churchmen themselves asserted royal primacy as an alternative to anarchy. To help maintain order, kings were accorded the right to install and remove bishops and abbots in their territories.

Kings also conferred political office on the higher clergy to strengthen royal power. During the tenth and eleventh centuries, the German monarchy depended heavily on its ecclesiastical vassals in its ongoing struggles with the nobility. A prelate frequently held *regalia*—royal lands, incomes, and rights—along with the *spiritualia* (things such as: the emblems of ecclesiastical office (the ring and staff); tithes; church properties; jurisdiction over clerics, monks, and nuns; jurisdiction over the laity in spiritual matters) that pertained to ecclesiastical office. Many bishops and abbots in Germany and Italy ruled as counts or dukes.

The kings openly participated in ecclesiastical elections. They conferred the emblems of ecclesiastical office—the ring and staff—upon the bishop or abbot at his consecration. This act, known as investiture, transferred the *regalia* and *spiritualia* to the candidate, who thus became both prelate and vassal by royal action. This practice was commonplace in every kingdom in western Europe.

Under Leo IX, however, lay investiture of bishops and abbots was opened to criticism. A leading reformer, Cardinal Humbert, questioned the lawfulness of lay investiture in 1055. The issue did not become the centerpiece of the reforming program until later, but Humbert's remarks initiated a concerted campaign to restructure Christendom.

The reformers sought first to free the papacy from lay control. Pope Nicolas II (reigned 1059–1061) promulgated a papal election decree in 1059. It conferred on the Roman cardinals the sole right to elect a pope and thus effectively prevented direct royal intervention in papal elections. Nicholas II also prohibited lay investiture of any priest. During the pontificate of Pope Alexander II (reigned 1061–1073) the reformers consolidated their program. A contemporary alliance with the Norman princes of southern Italy provided the papacy with protection from royal reprisals.

Henry III died in 1056. His six-year-old son, Henry IV (1050–1106; reigned 1056–1106), succeeded him. During his turbulent minority, Henry IV suffered humiliating losses at the hands of German princes. After he reached his majority in 1065 he depended on his ecclesiastical vassals to rebuild royal power. Henry did not intend to relinquish his control over the appointment of high churchmen.

Henry clashed with reformers over the appointment of the archbishop of Milan in 1072. The archbishop ruled the city as an imperial governor, but the see of Milan was also the most important in Italy after Rome. Ecclesiastical liberty, the term by which reformers denoted the independence of the church from lay control, was clearly at stake. The appointment of the archbishop was closely intertwined with the struggle between the aristocratic elite and the rising middle class for control of Milan. Henry's appointment favored the older noble establishment. Townsmen and knights elected a reformer. The violence that ensued previewed papal exploitation of Italian city-states as proxies in its twelfth- and thirteenth-century struggles with the German emperors.

The fierce reformer Hildebrand succeeded Alexander II as pope. As Gregory VII (reigned 1073–1085), he was determined to end lay control of ecclesiastical appointments. Gregory immediately warned Henry to desist in Milan and to correct abuses in Germany. The king, who was facing a serious uprising in Saxony, agreed to do so. In 1075, Gregory presided over a synod in Rome that prohibited lay investiture. He then composed the *Dictatus papae*, a list of propositions that laid out a program of papal theocracy. Henry, meanwhile, had defeated the Saxons and was now ready to take on the pope. At a synod of German bishops, Henry declared Gregory unfit for papal office. The pope responded by excommunicating and deposing Henry in February 1076, an unprecedented act that functioned as a claim of jurisdiction over secular rulers.

Rebellious German princes collaborated with Gregory to summon the king to a Diet at Augsburg in 1077 at which the pope would preside. In December 1076, Henry intercepted the northbound pope at Canossa in Tuscany. The penitent king begged Gregory for absolution, which the pope reluctantly granted. Henry was restored to his royal title. Angry German princes elected their own king, Rudolf, and civil war raged in Germany for three years. Henry defeated and killed his rival and then turned to Italy. He laid siege to Rome and took the city in 1084. An antipope—a pope whom someone, like an emperor or king, arranged to have elected to create an alternative to the canonically elected pope—crowned Henry emperor in Rome, but Gregory's Norman allies drove Henry and the antipope from the city. The Normans sacked Rome and then withdrew south and took Gregory with them. He died in Salerno in 1085.

Henry profited little from the death of Gregory VII. The election of Urban II (reigned 1088–1099) brought to the papacy a reformer who was smart, determined, and methodical. He codified and assiduously applied the entire papal reforming program, including the use of excommunication and deposition to protect ecclesiastical liberty. Urban condemned the kings of England and France for lay investiture and supported the opposition to Henry in Germany. When Henry IV died in 1106, even his heir, the future Henry V, was in rebellion against him.

Henry V (1081–1125; reigned 1106–1125) took up the battle with the church in 1111. He captured the city of Rome, where he extracted from Pope Pascal II (reigned 1099–1118) a total renunciation of the holding of *regalia* by churchmen. This proposal met with stiff opposition among both the Roman cardinals and the German bishops. In the twelfth century, churchmen universally agreed that ecclesiastical liberty required power that could come only from land, income, and jurisdiction. In 1122 Henry negotiated the Concordat of Worms with Pope Calixtus II (reigned 1119–1124). It allowed the king to attend the election of bishops and to invest them with *regalia*, but only after the bishops had been canonically installed in their spiritual office. The Concordat effectively thwarted royal theocracy, but papal theocracy did not take its place.

Frederick Barbarossa's Conflicts with the Papacy

The death of Henry V in 1125 accelerated the loss of imperial power to the German princes and the city-states of northern Italy. Endemic civil war plagued the reigns of two weak emperors, Lothar II (reigned 1125–1137) and Conrad III (reigned 1137–1152). When Conrad died, the princes sought to end the anarchy by electing a strong king, Frederick I Hohenstaufen (1152–1190), known as Barbarossa. Frederick was determined to strengthen the German monarchy.

Frederick pursued two strategies. First, he attempted to convert the German princes into royal vassals on the French model. This approach enjoyed only limited success. The princes did not allow him to accumulate royal demesne; that is, Frederick did not gain control over the lands of the German princes. This approach enjoyed only limited success. Unlike the contemporary kings of France, who were able to add the fiefs that they confiscated from rebellious vassals to their personal domains, the German princes forced Frederick to grant out the lands that he confiscated. It was as much as he could do to balance the power of the princes against one another. Frederick was left with his second strategy, to assert his imperial rights in the prosperous cities of northern Italy. He decided to invade Italy, which brought him into conflict with the papacy.

By the middle of the twelfth century, the townsmen and knights of northern Italy had taken control of the cities away from the bishops who had once ruled them as imperial vassals. These independent city-states, known as communes, warred with each other relentlessly. The cities were loosely joined into two rival factions under the leadership of Milan and Cremona.

Frederick claimed the right to participate in the selection of communal officials; he also claimed direct imperial jurisdiction over the *contado*, or rural hinterland, of the communes. Frederick marched south in 1154 with a small army to claim his rights. He made common cause with Cremona and its allies against Milan, but with little effect. Pope Adrian IV (reigned 1154–1159) crowned him emperor in Rome in 1155, but only after tense negotiations. The Germans abruptly departed after the coronation, which left Adrian without the help that Frederick had promised him against the pope's erstwhile allies, the Normans. Adrian reluctantly renewed the papal alliance with the king of Sicily.

Papal-imperial strains intensified in 1057 when a papal legate, Rolandus Bandinelli, asserted at an imperial Diet that, by virtue of papal coronation, Frederick held the imperial crown from the papacy as a *beneficium*, an ambiguous legal term that could mean either a benefit or a fief. The emperor was outraged. In 1159, Rolandus was elected Pope Alexander III. Frederick reacted by immediately appointing an antipope.

In 1162 Milan rose up against Frederick's persistent efforts to exercise imperial jurisdiction in the city and its *contado*. Frederick and his Italian allies defeated the Milanese and razed the city. However, the subsequent heavy-handed rule of imperial vicars induced the fractious communes to form the first Lombard League in 1167. Pope Alexander III (reigned 1159–1181) was instrumental in organizing and financing the League. In 1176 Frederick's army engaged Lombard forces at Legnano, where he was crushingly defeated. Frederick negotiated a truce with the communes and recognized Alexander as pope. He returned to Germany and spent several years settling scores with the princes who had refused to assist him in his Italian campaigns, most notably his cousin, Henry the Lion of Welf.

Frederick returned to Italy in 1183 and negotiated the Peace of Venice, which confirmed the independence of the communes. The communes agreed to pay the emperor for the right to exercise imperial jurisdiction. Frederick installed imperial vicars in Tuscany, Ancona, and Spoleto. He married his son, Henry, to Constance, the aunt of King William II of Sicily. This flurry of activity brought the empire into conflict with the papacy, which claimed the lands that Frederick had seized in central Italy. Of even greater concern to the papacy was the possibility of being crushed between Hohenstaufen holdings to the north and south of Rome.

These fears were well founded. Frederick Barbarossa died on crusade in 1190 and was succeeded by his son, who became Henry VI (1165–1197; reigned as emperor 1190–1197). William II of Sicily had died in 1189, and in 1194 Henry invaded Sicily to press the claim of his wife against William's successor, Tancred of Lecce. Henry's army handily defeated Tancred, and Henry became king of the rich, well-governed Norman state. The emperor had little interest in Germany, but did manage to convince the princes to elect his young son, Frederick (1194–1250), as king. Henry attempted to negotiate an understanding with the pope, but Hohenstaufen control of the entire Italian peninsula was a nightmare scenario that no pope could entertain. Henry died in 1197 as he was planning an expedition against the Byzantine empire. Constance died the next year. In her will, she commended her son to the care of the pope. Frederick grew up in Sicily at the mercy of German warlords, despite the efforts of his papal guardian.

Frederick II's Conflicts with the Papacy

The medieval papacy reached its zenith under Pope Innocent III (reigned 1198–1216). Innocent contended that the pope was Vicar of Christ, the supreme agent of God's power on earth. Under Innocent, the authority of the papacy briefly approached that of the theocratic emperors of an earlier age. Innocent claimed that he exercised "fullness of power" *(plenitudo potestatis)* within the church and that papal jurisdiction over sinners allowed him to intervene in political matters. A struggle for the imperial title followed the death of Henry VI. Innocent energetically exploited the turmoil in Germany. In the decretal (papal decree) *Venerabilem* (1200) he claimed the right to arbitrate the disputed imperial election. He quickly passed over Frederick on the grounds of youth. He rejected Philip of Hohenstaufen as a chronic offender of ecclesiastical liberty. He chose the Welf candidate, Otto of Brunswick (c. 1174–1218), who swore to defend the Roman church and return papal holdings in central Italy.

Innocent crowned Otto as emperor in 1208, but Otto IV (reigned 1209–1218) reneged on his promises to the pope and prepared to invade the kingdom of Sicily. Innocent dispatched Frederick to Germany to win Germany away from Otto, but first he made Frederick swear that he would not unite the crowns of Sicily and the Holy Roman Empire in his person. The pope declared Otto deposed at the Fourth Lateran Council (1215) and confirmed Frederick's earlier election in Aachen as king of Germany.

Frederick II spent the following years consolidating his position in Germany. He was crowned emperor in 1220, but he convinced Pope Honorius III (reigned 1216–1227) to allow him to keep both his imperial and royal titles. Honorius's main interest was the recovery of the Holy Land. Frederick's preoccupation with Germany prevented him from participating in the ill-fated Fifth Crusade (1217–1221), even though he had taken the cross at the Fourth Lateran Council in 1215. Honorius pressed Frederick to launch a new expedition and even arranged in 1225 for Frederick to marry Yolande, heiress of the kingdom of Jerusalem, as an inducement.

Rebellion in Sicily and Lombard resistance to imperial claims delayed Frederick's crusade until September 1227. He fell ill soon after embarking for the Holy Land and returned to Italy along with many other stricken crusaders. A new pope, Gregory IX (reigned 1227–1241), was an unbending proponent of papal supremacy. He considered Frederick the most serious threat to the primacy and independence of the Roman church. When Frederick failed to fulfill his crusading vow, Gregory promptly excommunicated him, and when Frederick departed unabsolved on crusade in 1228, Gregory launched an invasion of the kingdom of Sicily.

This war was one of the very few in which forces under the papal standard of the Keys of St. Peter waged offensive war against Frederick. Later popes would proclaim crusades against Frederick and his immediate successors, but those were largely proxy wars. Frederick negotiated with the Muslim sultan of Egypt, al-Kamil, for the return of Jerusalem and several other holy sites in Palestine to Christian control. The emperor's bloodless victory in 1229 enraged the Latin patriarch of Jerusalem, a fiery papalist whose animosity toward the excommunicated Frederick exceeded his hatred of the Muslims. When word of the papal invasion reached the emperor, he hastened back to Italy and made short work of the invaders. In 1230 Frederick made peace with the pope, who lifted the excommunication.

Both Frederick and Gregory had reason to patch up their differences. The emperor wanted papal support against the resurgent Lombard League. The pope wanted imperial forces to suppress his opponents in Rome, who had driven him from the city in 1228. This uneasy coalition lasted until the pope made peace with his Roman adversaries in 1235, after which papal-imperial relations deteriorated again. Gregory excommunicated Frederick on 20 March 1239 and preached a crusade against the emperor in 1239–1240, but most of the fighting was between Frederick and the Lombard cities. During this war papal legates actively organized and financed the League. Few if any papal forces were involved. In 1241 Gregory called a general council in Rome to depose the emperor, but an imperial fleet captured most of the council fathers. Gregory died in August 1241 as Frederick's army closed in on Rome. Hostilities ceased with the pope's death.

Gregory's successor, Celestine IV, died less than a month after his election. A two-year interregnum ended with the election of Innocent IV (reigned 1243–1245), who fled to Lyons in 1244 to escape imperial pressure to lift the excommunication. At the First Council of Lyons (1245) Innocent deposed the emperor. The papal sentence weakened Frederick, but not decisively. He renewed the war against the Lombard cities, and it dragged on inconclusively for the remainder of his life. He was on the offensive in Italy when he died at Castel Fiorentino on 13 December 1250. Innocent IV declared his death an act of divine deliverance.

Papal animosity toward the Hohenstaufen continued unabated after Frederick's death. His son, Conrad IV (1228–1254; reigned 1250–1254), established himself in the kingdom of Sicily but died shortly thereafter. Conrad's half-brother, the illegitimate Manfred (c. 1232–1266), seized power and ruled as regent for Conrad's son, Conradin (1252–1268). Manfred successfully defended the kingdom against attacks from crusading armies financed by King Henry III of England, who sought to win the southern kingdom for his son, Edmund. Manfred soundly defeated these forces in 1258. The papacy then offered the Sicilian throne to Charles of Anjou, the brother of King Louis IX of France. Charles defeated and killed Manfred at Benevento in 1266 and established himself as king of Sicily. Conradin led a German army into Italy in 1268, but Charles defeated, captured, and executed him.

By the thirteenth century, the conflict over lay investiture had broadened into a bitter struggle over right order in Christendom. From the eleventh century on, papal reformers led an assault on royal theocracy that eventually freed most ecclesiastical operations from secular interference. The papacy successfully established a monarchy over the church. However, the popes could not make good on their more radical claims of papal theocracy. Political and religious leaders continued to test one another's power with mixed results well into the modern era.

John Phillip Lomax

Further Reading

Abulafia, D. (1988). *Frederick II, a medieval emperor*. London: Allen Lane/The Penguin Press.

Alighieri, D. (1998). *Dante's Monarchia* (R. Kay, Trans.). Toronto, Canada: Pontifical Institute of Mediaeval Studies.

Carson, T. (Ed. and Trans.). (1994). *Barbarossa in Italy*. New York: Italica Press.

Berman, H. J. (1983). *Law and revolution: The formation of the western legal tradition*. Cambridge, MA: Harvard University Press.

Bernard of Clairvaux. (1976). *Five books on consideration: Advice to a pope* (J. D. Anderson & E. T. Kennen, Trans.) (Cistercian Fathers Series No. 37). Kalamazoo, MI: Cistercian Publications.

Blumenthal, U. (1988). *The investiture controversy: Church and monarchy from the ninth to the twelfth century*. Philadelphia: University of Pennsylvania Press.

Brentano, R. (1974). *Rome before Avignon: A social history of thirteenth-century Rome*. New York: Basic Books.

Chodorow, S. (1972). *Christian political theory and church politics in the mid-twelfth century: The ecclesiology of Gratian's Decretum*. Berkeley and Los Angeles: University of California Press.

Fuhrmann, H. (1986). *Germany in the High Middle Ages, c. 1050–1200*. Cambridge, UK: Cambridge University Press.

John of Paris. (1971). *On royal and papal power* (J. A. Watt, Trans.). Toronto, Canada: The Pontifical Institute of Mediaeval Studies.

Ladner, G. (1954). The concepts of "ecclesia" and "christianitas" and their relation to the idea of papal "plenitudo potestatis" from Gregory VII to Boniface VII. *Sacerdozio e regno da Gregorio VII a Bonifacio VIII: Miscellanea Historiae Pontificiae, 18*, 49–77.

Matthew, D. (1992). *The Norman kingdom of Sicily*. Cambridge, UK: Cambridge University Press.

Morris, C. (1989). *The papal monarchy: The Western Church from 1050–1250*. Oxford, UK: The Clarendon Press.

Munz, P. (1969). *Frederick Barbarossa: A study in medieval politics*. Ithaca, NY: Cornell University Press.

Oakley, F. (1973). Celestial hierarchies revisited: Walter Ullmann's vision of medieval politics. *Past and Present, 60*, 3–48.

Pacaut, M. (1970). *Frederick Barbarossa* (A. J. Pomerans, Trans.). New York: Scribners.

Partner, P. (1972). *The lands of St. Peter: The Papal State in the Middle Ages and the early Renaissance*. London: Eyre Methuen.

Robinson, I. S. (1990). *The Papacy, 1073–1198: Continuity and innovation*. Cambridge, UK: Cambridge University Press.

Tellenbach, G. (1948). *Church, state, and Christian society at the time of the investiture contest* (R. F. Bennett, Trans.). Oxford, UK: Basil Blackwell.

Tierney, B. (1964). *The crisis of church and state*. Englewood Cliffs, NJ: Prentice-Hall.

Ullmann, W. (1962). *The growth of papal government in the Middle Ages* (2nd ed.). London: Methuen & Co.

Waley, D. P. (1978). *The Italian city-republics* (2nd ed.). New York: Longman.

Watt, J. A. (1964). The theory of papal monarchy in the thirteenth century: The contribution of the canonists. *Traditio, 20*, 179–317.

Protestantism *See* Anabaptist Pacifism; Bishop's Wars (England 1639, 1640); Christianity and Revolution; English Civil Wars; European Wars of Religion; Mennonites; Methodism; Northern Ireland; Quakers; Reformed Christianity; Thirty Years' War; World Council of Churches

Pueblo Revolt of 1680

The Pueblo Revolt of 1680 was a successful effort by various Native American Pueblo Indians in New Mexico to oust the Spaniards, who did not retake the colony until 1692–1693. When the Spaniards did return, they treated the Pueblo Indians less harshly.

In 1598 Juan de Oñate (c. 1552–1626) traveled to New Mexico with settlers to found a colony for Spain. They settled in towns (called pueblos) already inhabited by Pueblo Indians. Franciscan missionaries worked to convert the Pueblos to Christianity and to eliminate native religion, while Spanish settlers and officials forced the Indians to labor and to pay tribute. Though some small-scale revolts and individual acts of rebellion occurred, the Pueblos lived with the Spanish settlers for almost a century. The Spaniards were not a united group during the seventeenth century, as religious and government officials quarreled for power.

In the late 1600s, the Pueblos faced many problems in addition to the demands that the Spaniards placed upon them. Years of drought in the 1660s and 1670s caused crop failure, loss of livestock, and famine. Apache and Navajo Indians, also hurt by the drought, increased their raiding of Pueblo settlements to procure food and resources. By 1680, many of the Pueblo Indians had returned to their native religion and were ready to revolt. Several decades of suffering made the Indians believe that the Christian God was not helping them as their own gods could.

A San Juan Pueblo Indian named Popé (c. 1630–c. 1690) coordinated most of the people in each village or the Pueblo Indians in each pueblo, who had their own leaders, in the attack. Runners delivered knotted strings to the Pueblos. Each day one knot was to be untied until the final knot was undone on 11 August 1680, the planned day of the offensive. The revolt actually began one day earlier, 10 August 1680, because several Indians divulged the plan to the Spaniards.

The Indians attacked both settlers and missionaries, but the Pueblos largely directed their anger towards the religious people and objects. The Indians destroyed churches and religious items and killed twenty-one of the thirty-three missionaries in New Mexico. Around 400 of 2,500 settlers perished as well. Spanish survivors fled to Isleta pueblo, which did not join the revolt, and Santa Fe. On 14 September 1680, the Spaniards and many Indians continued to flee to El Paso, while those in Santa Fe stayed to fight. After an unsuccessful effort, the Spaniards abandoned Santa Fe for El Paso on 21 September 1680.

The Pueblos maintained control of northern New Mexico for about a decade before Diego de Vargas (1643–1704) led the reconquest from El Paso in 1692–1693. Though there were some small revolts in the following years, the Spaniards remained in New Mexico. They did, however, improve their treatment of the Pueblos. They did not demand as much labor, and the missionaries allowed the Indians more religious freedom and lessened harsh punishments for what the missionaries perceived as sacrilegious or disrespectful behavior, including running away from the missions and praying to other gods. The Pueblo Revolt was just one of several revolts among Native Americans in northern New Spain, but it was the largest and most successful, changing the ways that the inhabitants lived together in the colony.

Amy Meschke

A barrier blocks the entrance to a kiva (underground ceremonial chamber) in Taos Pueblo in 1990. The effort by the Spanish to destroy the kiva-based pueblo religions was one cause of the Pueblo Revolt. Pueblo Peoples have been protective of their religions ever since. Courtesy David Levinson.

See also Roman Catholicism: Theology and Colonization

Further Reading

Gutiérrez, R. (1991). *When Jesus came, the corn mothers went away: Marriage, sexuality, and power in New Mexico, 1500–1846*. Stanford, CA: Stanford University Press.

Knaut, A. (1995). *The Pueblo Revolt of 1680: Conquest and resistance in seventeenth-century New Mexico*. Norman: University of Oklahoma Press.

Riley, C. (1995). *Rio del Norte: People of the upper Rio Grande from earliest times to the Pueblo Revolt*. Salt Lake City: University of Utah Press.

Silverberg, R. (1970). *The Pueblo Revolt*. New York: Weybright and Talley.

Weber, D. (Ed.). (1999). *What caused the Pueblo Revolt of 1680?* Boston: Bedford/St. Martin's.

Q

Quakers

Quakers, members of a denomination formally known as the "Religious Society of Friends," have opposed violence since their 1652 inception in England. Much of the justification for the pacifistic stand of Quakers is drawn from the "peace testimony," which serves as a fundamental part of the Quaker body of principles. As first articulated by founder George Fox in 1660, the peace testimony forbids Quakers from participating in war by serving as soldiers or by offering any other form of military aid. The very vagueness of this prohibition has allowed subsequent generations of Quakers to develop different interpretations of appropriate conduct for a soldier of Christ in times of war.

Founding

The Quaker movement began in the turmoil surrounding the English Revolution of 1650 to 1660. Although the aristocracy generally followed the form of Protestantism that had developed during King Henry VIII's Reformation, much of the landed gentry and the merchant class adopted the strict Calvinist Protestantism that had developed on the European continent in the mid-sixteenth century. This continental Protestantism brought a form of religious worship more suited to the independent and entrepreneurial spirit of the English commoners.

In the British Isles a variety of Calvinism known as "Puritanism" sprang up in the early part of the seventeenth century. George Fox (1624–1691), one of the Puritans who had severed ties with the Church of England, capitalized on the resentment against ecclesiastical authority to expound upon his idea that Christ is the only authority and that he can be known directly through the human heart without going through a clerical intermediary. Fox founded the Society of Friends in the process of advocating a return to a simpler form of religion than the austere, unemotional, and complicated Church of England doctrine. Quakerism involved four core beliefs: the internal locus of religious authority, the internal source for teaching, the profound sense of human unworthiness, and the absolute certainty of the availability of temporal salvation. All of these beliefs would play a role in the development of Quaker thought about war.

Fox traveled throughout England spreading his message and, although welcomed by some, met with considerable opposition for his blasphemy. In May 1652 Fox climbed to the top of a hill near Clitheroe, Lancashire, and had a vision of "a great people to be gathered." Swarthmore Hall, a large house near Ulverston that was occupied by the liberal Judge Fell and his Quaker convert wife Margaret, subsequently became the headquarters of the Society of Friends. From this site, small groups of missionaries went forth to spread Fox's message throughout the country. The Quaker movement had begun, and converts quickly flocked to the cause.

Quaker Beliefs

The Quakers were never quiet about their beliefs. The doctrine of predestination put forth by the French theologian John Calvin had struck a chord within the Quakers and other Puritans that would resonate politically

Movies on Peace and War Issues Recommended by Quakers

The following is a list of some movies posted to the Quaker-L e-mail list which individual Quakers recommend as helping teach about the Quaker perspective on war and peace.

All Quiet on the Western Front
Angel and the Badman
Born on the 4th of July
The Burmese Harp
The Diary of Anne Frank
Europa Europa
For the Boys
For Whom the Bell Tolls
Friendly Persuasion
Gallipoli
Gandhi
Glory
The Hiding Place
Johnny Got His Gun
Johnny Shiloh
The Killing Fields
Lest Innocent Blood Be Shed
Little Big Man
MASH
A Midnight Clear
Paths of Glory
Red Badge of Courage
The Russians Are Coming, the Russians Are Coming
Sergeant York
The Search
The Summer of My German Soldier
The War

Source: Movies on Peace and War Issues. Retrieved April 8, 2003 from http://www.spont.com/moviesintro.htm

for ages. Predestination holds that only inward belief and outward righteousness reveal one's fate, which God alone knows and has already decided. With this doctrine, Calvinists rejected those human laws that did not agree with their inner sense of righteousness. In short, Calvinists became revolutionaries willing to defy any temporal authorities perceived to be in violation of God's laws. Predestination would imbue Quakers with the strength to oppose high government officials on a variety of matters, including war.

Notably confrontational and confident, Quakers believed that they expressed the viewpoints of Christ because an "Inner Light" exists within all beings. This fundamental doctrine of Inner Light maintains that, because the relationship between Christ and each individual is an organic one, all human beings have a common tie to God and to one another. The Inner Light produced a strong sense of social responsibility within the faithful that prompted them to speak out, typically loudly and without fear of reprisal.

Unlike some groups, notably the Fifth Monarchists, that sprang from the Puritan trunk, Quakers never sanctioned violence. They renounced it as being incompatible with the Kingdom of God. Unfortunately, they

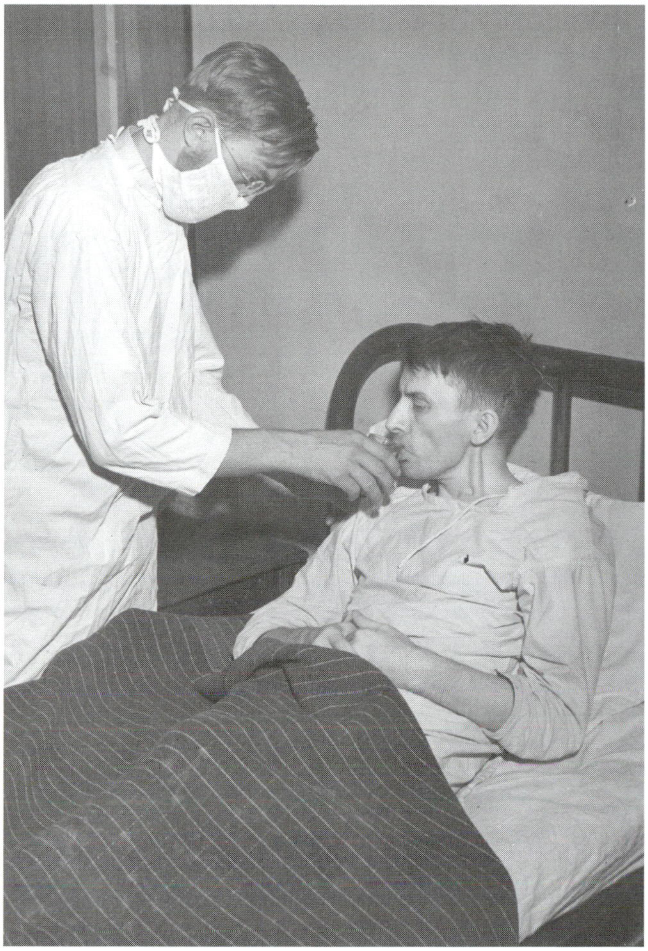

A Civilian Public Service (CPS) orderly assists a patient at the Cleveland State Mental Hospital in Cleveland, Ohio. The Historic Peace Churches (which include the Quakers) established CPS during World War II to allow their conscientious objectors, and those from other traditions, to serve in work "of national importance" without militarily defending their country. Courtesy Mennonite Central Committee, Mennonite Church USA Archives.

were often perceived to be a societal danger because of a similar background and some shared beliefs with the violent branch of Puritanism. Violent attacks upon Quakers became common. The Quakers and the disorder that they represented led to officially sanctioned violence against these dissenters as well as such repressive measures as the Quaker Act of 1662. Thousands of Quakers were imprisoned, and hundreds died in jail. Mindful of Jesus's new covenant and his admonition to love one's enemies, Quakers tolerated this abuse and did not fight back. Until King James II's Declaration of Indulgence of 1687 and rulers William and Mary's Toleration Act of 1689 bought respite, Quakers suffered considerably.

Fell's Peace Statement

In an effort to ward off this persecution, Margaret Fell wrote the first peace declaration of the Society of Friends in 1660. Signed by thirteen Quakers who witnessed for its truth, *A Declaration and an Information from Us the People of God Called Quakers to the King and Both Houses of Parliament* had the aim of convincing King Charles II and his government that Quakers were not a danger to English society. It appears to have been chiefly a preemptive strike designed to prevent Charles, newly restored to the throne of England, from launching further attacks on the Quakers. The declaration stressed the sufferings that Quakers had already endured, argued that these sufferings had been unjustly inflicted, and cataloged Quaker habits that had been misunderstood in the past, such as the refusal to take oaths. Fell explained that a righteous people, such as the Quakers, would be free of the passions leading to strife and would have no need of government regulation embodied by oath taking. To elaborate upon the Quaker peace position, she employed four biblical references: to Christ's kingdom being not of this world, to Christ having come not to destroy people's lives but rather to save them, to Christ's weapons being not carnal but rather spiritual, and to offering up one's body to suffering. She ended the declaration by stressing that Quakers opposed all manner of treachery and plotting.

Peace Testimony

Eight months after Fell presented her declaration to the king, the Fifth Monarchists rose up against the government, and George Fox rushed to protect the Quakers from probable antidissenter reprisals. *A Declaration from the Harmless and Innocent People of God*, written in late 1660, was directed exclusively to issues of nonviolence. Witnessed by several of the same Quakers who had signed Fell's document, Fox's declaration attempted to remove all suspicions of sedition by pointing to the Quaker history of refraining from violence even when personally attacked. It built upon a collection of ideas that Fox had been developing for about ten years.

Of the many ideas that ended up in the peace testimony, perhaps the most significant is the notion that national interests are of little importance to a person of God. In 1550 Fox had first articulated this notion when he stated that he had the divine right to refuse military service. Given a choice to be placed in prison for committing blasphemy and disturbing the peace or to join English soldier and statesman Oliver Cromwell's Puritan army, Fox picked prison. In the peace testimony, he explained the reasoning behind this decision. Pride, vanity, and greed cause wars and will be eliminated in a divine society. The Inner Light flowed through Fox and made it impossible for him to associate with the ungodly spirit from which war developed. He could not be both a soldier of Christ and a soldier of Cromwell.

As a result of Fox's teachings, Quakers refused to offer assistance to the military. However, the lack of specifics within the peace testimony meant that no consensus developed as to a definition of military aid. Quakers always refused to pay war taxes and resisted conscription into the military services, but agreement among them on other issues related to war did not develop for years. Some Quakers believed that offering medical aid to wounded soldiers and sailors does not promote war, whereas others argued that such help does indeed serve to associate a Quaker with an ungodly purpose.

The Discipline

Although the dictates of the peace testimony were so vague as to leave considerable freedom of action to each Quaker, this situation changed over the next few decades. Besides the Inner Light, Quakers came to be governed by a strict code of behavior called the "Discipline." This code evolved over the years to encompass appropriate standards of conduct, basic Quaker beliefs, and rules of everyday living. Any Quaker who failed to obey all of the standards in the Discipline faced penalties that could include loss of membership in the Society of Friends. By 1776 the Discipline included requirements for conduct during wartime.

Quakers in Times of War

Religious persecution in England had prompted a substantial number of Quakers to leave Europe for the fairer shores of North America. Most of the Quakers settled in Rhode Island and Pennsylvania, but their goal of balancing an allegiance to the government with the religious principles of their society became increasingly difficult as relations with the mother country soured. In 1756 Pennsylvania Quakers withdrew from the colonial assembly because revolutionaries had begun promoting violence. By 1776 the political climate in the colonies had worsened to the point that Quakers were placed under considerable pressure to declare themselves in support of a revolution or against it. In an attempt to clarify the relationship between pacifism and civil government, the Quakers periodically circulated tracts and statements outlining their position relative to specific situations. The 1776 peace statement, written by a committee appointed by a grand council of Quakers from all the colonies, is the first comprehensive statement on the position and conduct of Quakers during war.

The statement discouraged all Quakers from participating in civil government in any way because the authorities in power were funded and supported in the spirit of war. Quakers were forbidden to bear arms and to pay any fine, penalty, or tax in lieu of personal military service. They could not engage in any business that would promote the war effort. Any infraction of these rules could result in disownment by the society.

Free Quakers

Although the majority of Quakers remained neutral during the American Revolution, some actively supported the colonial efforts. As promised, patriots paid a price as 1,276 members were disowned from the Religious Society of Friends for such offenses as committing military deviations, paying taxes and fines, subscribing to loyalty tests, assisting the war effort, accepting public service, and such miscellaneous misdoings as watching military drills and celebrating independence. Quakers from Pennsylvania and New England formed the Free Quakers to reconcile their patriotism with their religious convictions.

The Free Quakers believed that God justifies a defense of a democratic system based on a popularly elected government and the exercise of free trade. Samuel Wetherill Jr., a Philadelphia weaver who founded Free Quakerism, strongly opposed the 1765 Stamp Act by backing the nonimportation resolutions of the Pennsylvania assembly. During the war his textile factory furnished the Continental Army with cloth for uniforms. In 1779 Wetherill took an oath of loyalty to Pennsylvania. Other prominent Free Quakers included Owen Biddle, the deputy commissioner of forage for the Continental Army; Timothy Matlack, clerk of the Continental Congress; and Timothy Davis, author of *A Letter from One Friend to Some of His Intimate Friends on the Subject of Paying Taxes* (1775). As this dispute among Quakers indicates, the very complexities of war have made rigid opposition to it difficult to sustain.

Quakers and War

The idea that the Inner Light could lead an individual to peace or to violence means that Quakers have struggled to develop a consensus about war. Generally, Quakers provide relief services such as food aid and ambulance help but do not pick up arms. Quaker men have claimed conscientious objector status in wartime, and some have refused entirely to comply with a military draft. Both sexes have aided those who refuse to serve in uniform. Although Quakerism is a pacifist movement, the Quakers have taken an individualistic approach to participation in war by relying upon the Inner Light for guidance.

Caryn E. Neumann

Further Reading

Goosen, R. W. (1997). *Women against the good war: Conscientious objectors and gender on the American home front, 1941–1947*. Chapel Hill: University of North Carolina Press.

Kashatus, W. C., III. (1990). *Conflict of conviction: A reappraisal of Quaker involvement in the American Revolution*. Lanham, MD: University Press of America.

Nelson, J. S. (1991). *Indiana Quakers confront the Civil War*. Indianapolis: Indiana Historical Society.

Newman, D. (1972). *A procession of friends: Quakers in America*. Garden City, NJ: Doubleday.

Weddle, M. B. (2001). *Walking in the way of peace: Quaker pacifism in the seventeenth century*. Oxford, UK: Oxford University Press.

R

Reformed Christianity

Reformed churches are those Protestant Christian churches that trace their historical origins to the theology and church reforms of John Calvin (1509–1564), who, though French, led the reform of the Catholic Church in Geneva, Switzerland. The European Reformation and post-Reformation periods saw Reformed ecclesiastical institutions dominate in the northern cantons of Switzerland, the Netherlands, Scotland, northern Germany, and episodically in Eastern Europe, France, England, and the New England colonies. They are represented today by state churches in Germany, Switzerland, and Scotland, and worldwide by Christian denominations encompassing the Reformed, the Evangelical and Reformed (both Hervormde and Gereformeerde mean Reformed, though they are differing denominations), the Christian Reformed, the Presbyterians, the Congregationalists (or the United Churches of Christ), the United Reformed, and some Baptist Churches. The Reformed tradition has supported the traditional just-war theory in the conviction that an imperfect world requires the use of force to restore order, justice, and peace. Thus the Christian struggles to maintain order, not as an end in itself, but so that there may be a just peace. This is in contradistinction to dictatorships that have stressed order and even peace, but without justice.

Calvin's Mediaeval Predecessors

Augustine (354–430) taught that due to Adam's original sin, human love is disordered and expresses itself not in love of God and neighbor, but in selfish ways, with radical consequences for all human social ordering. Consequently, individuals—and this tendency is magnified in nations—seek their own ends rather than the common good, and conflict becomes inevitable. Given that reality, Augustine argued that although wars were the result of human pride and selfishness, Christians could nevertheless engage in them (provided they were determined to be just), but always with regret and with the awareness that in the given circumstance war was the lesser of two evils. Thus war, in seeking to deliver humanity from evil, must always be undertaken with peace as the eventual goal.

Thomas Aquinas (1225–1274), drawing upon the same exegetical tradition as Augustine, specified three conditions that had to be met to make a war just: Declaration by a competent authority; the existence of a just cause; and right intention of engaging in war to achieve peace. Later these criteria were expanded to include the proportionate prosecution of the war—the idea that the evil caused by war must not exceed the evil caused by not going to war.

Calvin and the Reformed Tradition

Calvin, following Augustine's understanding of a good world now disordered by sin, saw the state and the exercise of force as necessary to establish, maintain, and extend order and God's purposes. Consequently, in the last book of his primary theological work, *The Institutes of the Christian Religion*, Calvin followed his predecessors in teaching nonresistance to the state authorities. However, Calvin's stress on the absoluteness of God's commands did permit him to allow excep-

Selection from John Calvin's *Institutes of the Christian Religion* IV: 20, 11 on War

11. *On the right of the government to wage war*

As it is sometimes necessary for kings and states to take up arms in order to execute public vengeance, the reason assigned furnishes us with the means of estimating how far the wars which are thus undertaken are lawful. For if power has been given them to maintain the tranquillity of their subjects, repress the seditious movements of the turbulent, assist those who are violently oppressed, and animadvert on crimes, can they rise it more opportunely than in repressing the fury of him who disturbs both the ease of individuals and the common tranquillity of all; who excites seditious tumult, and perpetrates acts of violent oppression and gross wrongs? If it becomes them to be the guardians and maintainers of the laws, they must repress the attempts of all alike by whose criminal conduct the discipline of the laws is impaired. Nay, if they justly punish those robbers whose injuries have been inflicted only on a few, will they allow the whole country to be robbed and devastated with impunity? Since it makes no difference whether it is by a king or by the lowest of the people that a hostile and devastating inroad is made into a district over which they have no authority, all alike are to be regarded and punished as robbers. Natural equity and duty, therefore, demand that princes be armed not only to repress private crimes by judicial inflictions, but to defend the subjects committed to their guardianship whenever they are hostilely assailed. Such even the Holy Spirit, in many passages of Scripture, declares to be lawful.

***Source:* Calvin, John. (1599). *Institutes of the Christian Religion.* Henry Beveridge, Trans. London: Arnold Hatfield.**

tions in cases where the commands of the state came in conflict with the commands of God. This exception was to widen from the 1530s onwards as the reformers and their congregations came under greater military threat. Probably following the example of Philipp Melanchthon (1497–1560) and other Lutherans, the Reformed tradition adopted the interpretation of scripture that required resistance in order to uphold the true religion. However, as Calvin stated in the last edition of the *Institutes of the Christian Religion*, only properly instituted lower authorities or magistrates could initiate such resistance. The Reformed tradition recognized the sphere of the state and its authority as granted by God, but declared that authority to be legitimate only insofar as it upholds justice. In fact, according to Reformed thought, the legitimacy of the state and the obedience owed to it, which is enjoined by Romans 13, applies only so far as the state legitimately uses its God-given powers. Otherwise it becomes the beast depicted in Revelation 13, to whom no Christian obedience is necessary.

Calvin on the Right of Resistance

In perhaps one of the most influential sections of his *Institutes*, Book IV "On the Duty of Magistrates," Calvin states that this duty includes removing any tyrannical ruler. Calvin makes clear that this power does not rest in individuals or in the common citizenry, but only in those who occupy a position or rank to counter any abuse of power, here of course referring to the authority of the magistrates. Resistance is not anarchy. Calvin was well aware of the excesses of the radical reformers, the horrors subsequent to the Peasants Revolt of 1525, and sought to address the Roman Catholic criticism that Protestant reform was promoting anarchy. Following from the belief in God's absolute sovereignty, no government is regarded as absolute, and in fact church resistance to unjust or illegitimate aspects of a government's rule is in fact its highest act of service, serving in effect as God's loyal opposition, preventing the state from perverting justice: The state must always resist the temptation to give up justice as its foundation in favor of order or peace or even force. Thus the Scots Confession of 1560, declares at Article 14 that Christians are called to "save the lives of innocents, to repress tyranny, and to defend the oppressed" (*Constitution of the Presbyterian Church* 1996, 17). Thus opposition to tyrannical power is not merely permitted, it is positively commanded. Though Calvin had stressed obedience to the state authorities, with perhaps some exceptions, this did not prevent later Reformed thinkers from pursuing diverging directions, as is evident from the political and military struggles that ensued in countries such as France, the Netherlands, Scotland, and England.

A Brief History of Reformed Christianity

The Reformed tradition has always displayed an interest in the political order. While over the last five hundred years Reformed thinkers have exhibited a range of views, it would be accurate to say that the tendency has been to favor representative forms of civil ordering. While recognizing the state's role in preventing chaos, the Reformed tradition has always focused on maintaining right order, fostering the common good, and establishing peace. Thus Reformed theologians spoke up in Europe for justice, popular sovereignty (the principle that government requires the consent of the people to be legitimate), and the right of resistance against tyranny. For example, François Hotman (1524–1590), a contemporary and friend of Calvin, advocated French popular sovereignty and Johannes Althusius (c. 1563–1628), a Swiss-trained official in Emden, northern Netherlands, wrote the influential *Politics Methodically Set Forth* (1603), which set forth a fundamental view of political principles based on social contract and organic thought. Hugo Grotius (1583–1645) was the most prominent developer of the emerging science of international law. He wrote the treatise *The Rights of War and Peace* (1625), and this work and that of Althusius received renewed attention in the twentieth century. Grotius argued that war is only justified as an act of self-defense, and that the ultimate goal must be peace. In Scotland, figures such as George Buchanan (1506–1582), John Knox (1513–1572), and Samuel Rutherford (1600–1661) all supported a people's right, when led by lower-ranking authorities, to revolt, as did the English Puritans. Thus Calvin's limited comments on the powers of the magistrates have had a powerful influence, and they continue to today.

The impact of the first modern wars that were "total" in their scope, beginning with the U.S. Civil War (1862–1865), the Anglo-Boer War (1899–1902) and peaking at World War I (1914–1918), was critical in forming the modern pacifist reaction against war. The destruction of the World War I led to the foundation of the Fellowship of Reconciliation (FOR) in 1914, an interdenominational German-British, then American, voluntary organization that sought to resolve conflicts between nations without resorting to war. The FOR gained much support not only from traditionally pacifist churches, but also from the clergy of Reformed churches. However, this support ended during the 1930s as the threat of totalitarianism increased. The theologian Reinhold Niebuhr (1892–1971) made his sharp and highly publicized break with FOR summed up in his pamphlet, *Why the Christian Church is not Pacifist*. Niebuhr reiterated the Augustinian point that the pacifist potion failed to take account of the depths of human sin. Tragically for humanity, he argued, the fact of humanity's sin leads to war and defensive responses to prevent even greater sin.

Similarly, the Swiss Reformed theologian Karl Barth (1886–1968), in declaring his opposition to the German Nazi State in 1938, directly quoted Calvin's description of the role of subordinate magistrates or lower-ranking authorities. Barth is quite clear that in the modern state, every Christian who adheres to Romans 13:1–7 by being a loyal subject of his or her state has a part, directly or indirectly, in state violence. Thus even a pacifist is involved in state violence. Accepting the state means accepting and being coresponsible for all its actions, including the exercise of force. In a situation where the state is acting unjustly—as, for instance, in Nazi Germany—resistance is demanded and the question becomes what form this divine obedience must take. Is violent resistance required or not? Karl Barth again provides a useful criterion, that of boundary situations, supremely despair-inducing situations that force one to rely utterly on God, as one no longer has any spiritual, physical, or other resources of one's own. Thus only when all attempts at peace have failed, and the situation is marked by drastic contraventions of justice, can violence be justified. This situation occurred for Barth by 1938, and in his correspondence with friends in Great Britain and the United States he actively encouraged them to advocate war against Germany, in order to restore proper government there. War then becomes part of God's grace towards Germany. Indeed war is a judgment, but as such it has a restorative purpose in God's providence. War is the last resort, brought into play to reestablish a just peace.

After World War II and the formation in 1948 of the World Council of Churches, the Protestant ecumenical organization, Reformed member churches continued to stress the necessity of states providing conditions for peace, particularly in the civic and economic spheres. The reality of total war and the sense of urgency conveyed by the threat of nuclear holocaust from the 1950s onwards led to a radical questioning of the whole just-war theory. The theologian Paul L. Lehman (1906–1994) and the Presbyterian ethicist J. C.

Bennett (1902–1995), among others, questioned the viability of traditional just-war criteria. In question here was the seeming impossibility of placing limits on collateral damage, that is, of applying the proportionality criterion in contexts where total destruction of everything is assured. The Reformed tradition, along with most Christian traditions, spent the ensuing thirty years up to the end of the Cold War in 1989 in vigorous questioning of even the possibility of a just war. While no Reformed church completely endorsed pacifism, greater stress was laid on peacemaking in order to avoid the possibility of war.

Roughly contemporaneous with the Western European and North American Reformed churches' discomfort with the applicability of the traditional just-war criteria in the nuclear age was the increased interest on the part of Reformed churches in the largely postcolonial Third World in revolutionary movements' attempts to justify violence. However, apart from some Reformed bodies, mainly in southern Africa, most Reformed traditions, though perhaps sympathetic, rejected legitimizing such movements since they did not seem to uphold law, order, and justice. The national churches were then faced with evaluating what level of injustice justified the use of force. Did apartheid in South Africa justify it? Oppression of the poor? Religious oppression?

Looking Ahead

Since the end of the Cold War, the possibility of nuclear strife has abated, but unfortunately the waging of war by means has increased. Iraq's invasion of Kuwait in 1990 and the U.S.-led coalition that started the first Persian Gulf War prompted a revival of just-war theory. Rapidly changing global contexts encourage critical reflection on the criteria and their applicability.

Nonetheless, the Cold War and its rather troubling aftermath has left the just-war criteria intact, but again, as criteria of last resort. The twentieth century has witnessed the dramatic democratization of most of the world's peoples and the increased pluralization of populations along ethnic, cultural, and religious lines. Thus with some major exceptions, conflict over the past century has increasingly been intranational instead of international. Given the wide acceptance of human-rights criteria and religious adherence to the divine image in humanity, peacemaking efforts in the political and economic spheres in particular are taking a prominent place in any just-war disputation. While positions such as pacifism and conscientious objection are recognized within the Reformed tradition, they are understood as decisions reached by individuals and have not been advocated as social norms.

Iain Maclean

See also Lutheran Germany

Further Reading

Allen, A. W. (1928). *Political thought in the sixteenth century*. London: Methuen & Co.

Barth, K. (1961). *Church dogmatics* (Vol. III, part 4). Edinburgh, UK: T & T Clark.

Calvin, J. (1960). *Institutes of the Christian religion* (Vols 1–2) (F. L. Battles, Trans.; J. T. McNeill, Ed.). Philadelphia: Westminster Press.

Chenevière, M. E. (1937). *La Pensée politique de Calvin*. Geneva, Switzerland: Labor.

Constitution of the Presbyterian Church (USA). (1996). Scots confession (Part 1: Book of Confessions, Article 14, pp. 17). Louisville, KY: The Office of the General Assembly.

Decosse, D. E. (Ed.). (1992). *But was it just? Reflections on the morality of the Persian Gulf War*. New York: Doubleday.

Miller, R. B. (Ed.). (1992). *War in the twentieth century: Sources in theological ethics*. Louisville, KY: Westminster/John Knox Press.

McNeil, J. T. (1954). *The history and character of Calvinism*. New York: Oxford University Press.

Niesel, W. (1956). *The theology of Calvin* (H. Knight, Trans.). Philadelphia: Westminster Press.

Skinner, Q. (1978). *The foundations of modern political thought: Volume 2. The age of Reformation*. New York: Cambridge University Press.

Stone, R. H. (Ed). (1983). *Reformed faith and politics*. Lanham, MD: University Press of America

Villa-Vicencio, C. (1988). *On reading Karl Barth in South Africa*. Grand Rapids, MI: William B. Eerdmans.

Religion, Violence, and Genocide

With the twentieth century, the violence of warfare took a grim new turn. Suddenly, the systematic mass murder of civilian populations became an instrument of official or quasi-official governmental policy, with entire ethnic or cultural groups sometimes being slated for brutal elimination. Prime examples include the murder of up to 1.5 million Armenians by Turks during the first World War, as well as the extermination of close to six million Jews under Adolf Hilter. In 1944, with the Nazi destruction of the European Jews in mind, Raphael Lemkin coined the word *genocide*, meaning the deliberate attempt to destroy an entire people. In addition, the American deployment of two atomic bombs at Hiroshima and Nagasaki in 1945 effectively ushered the world into a stark new age of manmade mass death. Not only did this change the face of modern warfare; it created a crisis for religion as well, a crisis that has been felt with special theological force among Jews and Christians in the West.

The Destruction of the Jews

The paradigmatic case of modern genocide was the attempt by Adolf Hitler, leader of the neopagan National Socialist movement in Germany, to destroy the whole of European Jewry during the Second World War. Often this destruction is referred to as the "Holocaust," a word that comes from the Greek *ʿolokaustos*, which means "whole burnt," or more literally, "that which goes up in smoke." Because the Nazi-inspired violence was reprehensible and thus far from the pure offering to God contemplated in the biblical sacrifice, many have rejected the term "Holocaust" in favor of the Hebrew word *Shoʾah*, meaning simply "destruction."

Inspired as it was by a neopagan ideology focused on racial purity, the Nazi persecution of the Jews began almost immediately upon Adolf Hitler's assumption of power in 1933. The initial point of this persecution apparently was to force Jews to emigrate from Germany, a strategy that soon gave way to forced labor, the creation of ghettos, and death by hit squads. Eventually, these strategies too were superseded by the so-called "Final Solution," in which all European Jews were to be transported to one of six extermination camps operated on Polish soil (Auschwitz, Belzec, Chelmo, Majdanek, Sobibór, and Treblinka) and annihilated. This grisly business was performed through gas chambers with the bodies then incinerated in crematoria. Through deliberate extermination, starvation, exhaustion, or otherwise, it is estimated that between 5 and 6 million Jews died at the hands of the Nazis.

Without in any way minimizing the extent of Jewish suffering, it needs to be added that the Nazis targeted Gypsies and certain persons who were mentally and physically handicapped for elimination as well. Some scholars would include these two groups as well in the definition of the Holocaust. Indeed, beginning in 1939 the physically and mentally handicapped seem to have been targeted for death even before the Jews through a systematic program of euthanasia. Male homosexuals and certain enemies of the Reich were subject to similar persecution.

Genocide, Violence, and the Crisis of Western Religion

Too often religion has played a supporting role in acts of genocide. One thinks, for example, of Puritan preachers writing justifications for the mass slaughter of Native Americans. In the case of the *Shoʾah*, the Christian doctrine of supersessionism (the teaching that the church superseded historic Israel) together with centuries of religious, cultural, and racial anti-Semitic sentiment cannot be ignored. Sometimes the Christian churches deliberately preached against the Jews, which prompted harassment and outbreaks of violence against them. As Franklin Littell has noted, most of the people who carried out the day-to-day devastation of the *Shoʾah* were baptized Christians, none of whom was ever disciplined by any church court for their actions. Moreover, the policy of neutrality toward Hitler adopted by the Vatican under Pope Pius XII has stirred particular consternation.

On the other hand, religion also helped motivate acts of resistance, which were more pervasive than previously believed and sometimes included sporadic armed uprisings. Yet it is still a debated point whether a pervasive belief in divine sovereignty contributed to attitudes of passivity among Jewish victims. The religious motivation of rescuers is hard to determine, but there are some 16,000 documented cases of people who risked their lives to save Jews.

Suffice it to say the event of the *Shoʾah* shook subsequent Jewish and Christian belief to their foundations. The writings of Auschwitz survivor Elie Wiesel speak to the profound difficulty some face in continuing to believe in God. In the 1960s the Jewish theologian Richard Rubenstein argued in *After Auschwitz* that traditional Jewish belief in the God of the covenant has been made meaningless. In a more positive vein, the Jewish philosopher Emil Fackenheim maintained that though the saving presence of God has been rendered problematic, God's commanding presence can still be felt. And that command was simply to survive. For to allow Judaism to die would be to grant Hitler a posthumous victory. Rather than give in to death, Jews are to seek *Tikkun olam*, the reconstitution of the world.

The Feed Thine Enemy Campaign

The following excerpt describes a unique, scripture-based approach to preventing war. The same tactic was used by some opposed to the U.S./Britain-Iraq War of 2003.

In the mid–1950s, the pacifist Fellowship of Reconciliation, learning of famine in China launched a "Feed Thine Enemy" campaign. Members and supporters mailed thousands of little bags of rice to the White House with a tag quoting the Bible, "If thine enemy hunger, feed him." As far as anyone knew for more than ten years, the campaign was an abject failure. The President did not acknowledge receipt of the bags publicly; certainly, no rice was ever sent to China.

What nonviolent activists only learned a decade later was that the campaign played a significant, perhaps even determining role in preventing nuclear war. Twice while the campaign was on, President Eisenhower met with the Joint Chiefs of Staff to consider U.S. options in the conflict with China over two islands, Quemoy and Matsu. The generals twice recommended the use of nuclear weapons. President Eisenhower each time turned to his aide and asked how many little bags of rice had come in. When told they numbered in the tens of thousands, Eisenhower told the generals that as long as so many Americans were expressing active interest in having the U.S. feed the Chinese, he certainly wasn't going to consider using nuclear weapons against them.

***Source:* Albert, David H. (1985). *People Power: Applying Nonviolence Theory.* Philadelphia: New Society Publishers, p. 43.**

The religious crisis was by no means limited to Judaism. Christians, too, found it necessary to question their traditional beliefs. Roman Catholic and Protestant churches issued repudiations of supersessionism and anti-Semitism and voiced their unique relationship to and solidarity with Judaism among the religions of the world. At a deeper level, however, the age of manmade mass death has raised profound questions concerning the very cogency of the traditional theological belief systems. What is one to make of the fact that such heinous events could occur in the heart of supposedly Christian Europe? And what is one to make of a God who was apparently powerless to stop such events? These questions still present a challenge to contemporary religious thought.

This has led many to wonder about the relationship in general between religious belief and violence. In the Hebrew Bible holy war is not only to be pursued on behalf of the deity but the God of Israel is a prime actor in war. In the medieval Crusades, in which Muslims, Jews, and Eastern Christians were massacred in the name of religious orthodoxy, this holy war tradition lived on in Christianity. Similarly, the Islamic counterpart to holy war—jihad—signifies a struggle for righteousness in which all Muslims are required to support a legitimate Islamic ruler in battle against the infidel. Hinduism, too, contains certain admonitions to support violence. And although there is a long tradition of pacifism in Buddhism, even Buddhists in the modern era have engaged in religiously sanctioned mass death (see below).

Other Cases of Religious Violence and Genocide

In the aftermath of the *Sho'ah*, numerous war trials were held, including twelve trials conducted by the American military in Nuremberg from 1946 to 1949. In 1948 the United Nations rendered genocide a crime in international law, defining it to include not only acts of killing members of an identified group but other violent and coercive acts, including maiming members of an identified group; causing them mental distress; creating conditions designed to bring about a group's whole or partial demise; preventing childbirth; and forcibly transporting children for the purpose of what today is known as "ethnic cleansing."

Despite the unique features of the *Sho'ah*, it was not the first, the only, nor even the most numerically destructive act of religious or ideologically driven mass violence in the modern era. The first such outbreak of official mass murder was the killing by Muslim Turks during the First World War of between 1 and 1.5 million Armenians, most of them Christians, through direct acts of violence or mass starvation. Another precursor was the pillaging of the Chinese city of Nanking (Nanjing) by the Japanese in 1937–1938, part of a resurgence of Shinto nationalism. Numerically speaking, the quasi-religious ideology of Communism has inspired close to 100 million deaths, with some 20 million killed in purges under Josef Stalin in the former Soviet Union; between 44.5 and 72 million destroyed under Mao Zedong in China; and between one and 1.7 million wiped out more recently under the Khmer Rouge in Cambodia.

All the major religions have been implicated in mass violence. In 1971, for example, an outbreak of rape, assault, and death was unleashed by Pakistani Muslim soldiers in occupied Bangladesh, much of it aimed at the minority Hindu population, with some 3 million killed and 9.5 to 10 million made refugees. Or again, Eastern Orthodox Serbs, Roman Catholic Croats, and Muslim Slavs were pitted against each other in a series of bloody conflicts from 1990 to 1999 following the breakup of the former multiethnic, multireligious state of Yugoslavia. Even in Buddhism, despite its long tradition of pacifism, religion and violence have sometimes gone hand in hand, as when religion bolstered the claims of Buddhist Sinhala nationalism in Sri Lanka in the persecution and slaughter of the Tamil minority; or again, in 1995 when the Buddhist sect Aum Shinrikyo released sarin nerve gas in the Tokyo subway.

The disconcerting inability of religion to temper violence is evidenced in the protracted struggle between Protestants and Catholics in Northern Ireland; the ongoing conflict between Jews and Palestinians in Israel; and the 1994 outbreak of violence in Rwanda, in which the plane crash of Rwandan President Juvénal Habyarimana prompted a dramatic 10-day period of killing by Hutu rebels of approximately 750,000 of the racial Tutsi minority and between 10,000 and 30,000 Hutu of more moderate persuasion. In the Rwandan situation, the racist teachings of the Roman Catholic Church under colonialism had accentuated the rift, with some church members actually participating in luring Tutsi victims to their deaths in Christian sanctuaries.

With the 11 September 2001 attacks by Islamic fundamentalist terrorists against the United States, religious violence entered a new phase. The al-Qaeda organization had earlier instigated the 1992 bombing of a hotel in Yemen housing U.S. troops (2 killed); a prior bombing of the World Trade Center in 1993 (6 killed); the 1993 attack on U.S. soldiers in Somalia (18 killed); an attack in 1995 of U.S. military headquarters in Riyadh, Saudi Arabia (6 killed); the 1996 bombing of U.S. military barracks in Dhahran, Saudi Arabia (19 killed); the bombings of American embassies in Kenya and Tanzania in 1998 (224 killed); and the attack in 2000 on the *U.S.S. Cole* in Yemen (17 killed). With the September 11 attack on the Pentagon and destruction of the World Trade Center in New York, it was clear that manmade mass death had now become the weapon of choice for certain religious terrorist groups too.

Plumbing the "Meaning" of Religious Violence

Robert J. Lifton has argued that a "genocidal mentality" grips the modern world, a mentality with striking religious overtones. Whether we are speaking of Hitler's storm troopers, of those trained to drop modern nuclear weapons, or of today's new breed of suicide bombers, what they have in common is a special elite trained in the delivery of death and the art of killing upon demand, an elite driven by the allegedly higher purpose of "killing in order to heal."

Sociologist Mark Juergensmeyer has argued that the very belief structure of religion becomes a breeding ground for violence. Spurred by a zeal that will admit of no compromise and taking on the aura of a symbolic performance, this peculiar sort of violence pits the religious adherent as protagonist against the forces of evil.

René Girard has uncovered how religious violence marks the very founding of culture. Human beings are fundamentally mimetic, imitating the desires and actions of others, making them imitate acts of violence that tend to escalate. In order to relieve the resulting cycle of violence and counterviolence, blame is projected onto a scapegoat, whose death provides expiation for the bloodshed. Girard, a Roman Catholic, claims that in the biblical religions of Judaism and Christianity this scapegoating mechanism is exposed as evil and is rejected. In the story of Jesus of Nazareth in the Gospels, God stands with the innocent victim and not with perpetrators of scapegoating.

Perhaps the most provocative understanding of violence is that of the Jewish philosopher Emmanuel Levinas, who argues in *Totality and Infinity* that the Western fascination with thinking in terms of the totality has led it repeatedly into the violent subjugation of the "Other." Outbursts of violence derive not from the breakdown of reason but from employing the wrong sort of reason, the sort that leaves no place for the Other. With the *Sho'ah* in mind, Levinas argues that true religion is found in being bound to the Other, even to the extent of giving the Other the bread from my own table. Encountering the face of the Other calls me into question, arrests my attention, and summons me to a hospitality that impinges upon me prior to any action. Being for the Other is, indeed, what makes moral action possible in the first place. One of Levinas's most provocative claims is that this stance in the Other's behalf is somehow obligatory even when the Other is my persecutor. It is as though Levinas were placing all moral agents in the shoes of the survivor, with the attendant sense of guilt and responsibility to live for the Other that this entails. From a Levinasian point of view, there is no inherent meaning to be found in the violence of our age other than that which is to be found in the righteousness of our response. It is only through our response that a new cycle of violence can be avoided.

Although cruelty and mistreatment of others have been enduring features of war, the *Sho'ah* and events like it served to raise questions about the violent nature of modernity itself. Never before had a modern state made it a matter of official and deliberate public policy to carry out the complete and total annihilation of a people. Did the *Sho'ah,* or other similar events, represent the utter breakdown of modernity or did they, instead, constitute one of modernity's own logical results? From a cultural point of view, the social and intellectual condition we now call "postmodernity" is to a certain extent a by-product of living in a post-Holocaust age, for the indelible character of this event has helped engender the widespread skepticism and malaise that make postmodernity what it is. Yet, at the same time, the sheer magnitude of so much genocidal carnage has served to call this very same skepticism and malaise into question. In the face of such overwhelming evil, the postmodern world is challenged not to wallow in its hesitancy and doubt but to formulate a response that will never again let such nightmares be unleashed on human beings.

William Stacy Johnson

See also Genocide in Africa; Genocide in Bosnia; Genocide in Europe; Nazism and Holocaust

Further Reading

Bauer, Y. (2001). *Rethinking the Holocaust*. New Haven, CT, and London: Yale University Press.

Chang, I. (1998). *The rape of Nanking: The forgotten holocaust of World War II*. New York: Viking Penguin.

Dadrian, V. N. (1995). *The history of the Aremenian genocide: Ethnic conflict from the Balkans to Anatolia to the Caucasus*. Providence, RI: Berghahn Books.

Fackenheim, E. (1970). *God's presence in history: Jewish affirmations and philosophical reflections*. New York: New York University Press.

Fackenheim, E. (1994). *To mend the world: Foundations of post-Holocaust Jewish thought*. Bloomington, IN: Indiana University Press.

Hilberg, R. (1985). *The destruction of the European Jews* (Vols. 1–3). New York: Holmes & Meier.

Girard, R. (1986). *The scapegoat*. Baltimore: Johns Hopkins University Press.

Gutman, I. (Ed.). (1990). *Encyclopedia of the Holocaust* (Vols. 1–4). New York: Macmillan.

Johnson, W. S. (2002). Probing the "meaning" of September 11, 2001. *The Princeton Seminary Bulletin, 23*(1), new series, 36–53.

Judah, T. (1997). *The Serbs: History, myth, and the destruction of Yugoslavia*. New Haven, CT: Yale University Press.

Juergensmeyer, M. (2000). *Terror in the mind of God: The global rise of religious violence*. Berkeley: University of California Press.

Katz, S. T. (1994). *The Holocaust in historical context: Vol. 1. The Holocaust and mass death before the modern age*. New York: Oxford University Press.

Kiernan, B. (1998). *The Pol Pot regime: Race, power, and genocide under the Khmer Rouge, 1975–79*. New Haven, CT: Yale University Press.

Lepore, J. (1999). *The name of war: King Philip's war and the origins of American identity*. New York: Random House.

Lemkin, R. (1994). *Axis rule in occupied Europe*. Washington, DC: Carnegie Endowment.

Levinas, E. (1969). *Totality and infinity: An essay on exteriority* (A. Lingis, Trans.). Pittsburgh, PA: Duquesne University Press.

Lifton, R. J., & Marcusen, E. (1990). *The genocidal mentality: Nazi Holocaust and nuclear threat*. New York: Basic Books.

Littell, F. (1987). *The crucifixion of the Jews*. Macon, GA: Mercer University Press.

Mamdani, M. (2001). *Why victims become killers: Colonialism, nativism, and the genocide in Rwanda*. Princeton, NJ: Princeton University Press.

Prunier, G. (1997). *The Rwanda crisis: History of a genocide*. New York: Columbia University Press.

Rubenstein, R. (1966). *After Auschwitz: Radical theology and contemporary Judaism*. Indianapolis, IN: Bobbs Merrill.

Rubenstein, R. (1992). *After Auschwitz: History, theology, and contemporary Judaism* (Rev. ed.). Baltimore: Johns Hopkins University Press.

Tambiah, S. J. (1992). *Buddhism betrayed? Religion, politics, and violence in Sri Lanka*. Chicago and London: The University of Chicago Press.

Religious Feminism and War

Connections between women and war can be found in a host of ancient religious traditions, ranging from Greek and biblical to Hindu. As early as 2000 BCE, ancient Babylonians were telling a creation account in which the fierce primordial goddess Tiamat battled the male warrior god Marduk for control of the cosmos. Around the fourth century CE, stories about Hindu warrior goddesses such as Durga and Kali began to emerge among the indigenous, non-Aryan peoples of India. Indeed, if Merlin Stone is correct that "at the very dawn of religion, God was a woman," we should not be surprised that, in the earliest religious accounts, goddesses regularly were involved in the task of subduing the violent and unpredictable cosmos (Stone 1978, 1).

The phenomenon of religious feminists writing specifically on issues of war and peace, however, is a relatively recent phenomenon, having its origins in the twentieth century. To date, the field has been dominated by authors working from within the religious traditions of the West, where feminism initially took root. Like any relatively new intellectual discourse, religious feminist commentary on war seeks to work through a series of foundational questions. By means of the answers offered by individual feminists to these questions, one can map out the broad range of positions that define the field.

Is There a Feminist Perspective on War?

One question posed by religious feminists is whether there even exists something that rightfully can be labeled a feminist perspective on warfare.

For Jean Bethke Elshtain, a leading just-war theorist who focuses on issues of religion, the answer is clear: "There is no separate feminist tradition on war and peace" (Elshtain 1996, 214). Elshtain bases her position not merely on the obvious point that women, even feminists, often disagree on issues of warfare, but also on the observation that "each articulated feminist position represents an evolution within or a break-out from a previous historic discourse" (Elshtain 1996, 214). In other words, there are feminists who write from the perspective of Christian pacifism, realism, and just-war thought; there are Jewish, Muslim, and Buddhist feminists. But there is no position on war that is identifiably "feminist" as such.

Sarah Tobias challenges Elshtain's conclusion. Tobias argues that feminists are linked by their desire to end the subordination of women and to challenge gender distinctions. As a result, "feminists have developed new understandings of domination and subordination, authority and resistance, violence and peace. Feminists' ontological and epistemological claims are drawn from women's experience, and they neither replicate nor simply refurbish familiar philosophical concepts" (Tobias 1996, 229). According to Tobias, the experiences, goals, and methodologies that feminists share have allowed them to develop perspectives on warfare that, while far from uniform, collectively present an important alternative to prevailing patriarchal attitudes.

How Is War Defined?

Another important question for feminists concerns the very definition of the word *war*. Some religious feminists subscribe to the "conventional" definition of war as state-centered military action. Elshtain, for instance, writes of war as "collective violence in defense of the state" (Elshtain 1987, 257).

For Mary Daly, a former Catholic nun who came to advocate a radical feminist spirituality, the prevailing definition of war perpetuates sexism through privileging a certain type of violence as significant and legitimate—that in defense of one's community or state—while ignoring the wide range of violence inflicted on women, often by these very same social and political entities. Daly writes of the mass burnings of women as witches by American and European communities in the fifteenth to eighteenth centuries, the "genital mutilation" historically performed on young girls within certain African traditions, and the use of lobotomies on American women as "treatment" by the psychological profession during the first half of the twentieth century as three examples of organized and horrific violence against women that is not counted as "war" by the conventional definition. As a result, Daly argues, these acts of violence are neither acknowledged by society nor held up to moral scrutiny. For Daly, violence against women and warfare are inextricably linked as common expressions of "phallocentric power" and constitute what she calls the "Most Unholy Trinity of Rape, Genocide, and War." She writes:

> These are structures of alienation that are self-perpetuating, eternally breeding further estrangement. The circle of destruction generated by the Most Unholy Trinity and reflected in the Unwhole Trinitarian symbol of Christianity will be broken when women, who are by patriarchal definition objects of rape, externalize and internalize a new self-definition whose compelling power is rooted in the power of being. The casting out of the demonic Trinities *is* female becoming. (Daly 1973, 122)

For Daly, women must stop fighting to defend institutions such as the state and Christianity—institutions that wage "war" on women but that fail to call it such—and must "vaporize the constricting walls imposed upon the Self" by the patriarchal culture of violence (Daly 1978, 380). When the roots of war, rape, and genocide are exposed to be one and the same, the rejection of all three—and of violence in general—becomes possible.

Religious Feminism and Pacifism

In 1911, Olive Schreiner was among the first feminists to draw the connection between feminism and pacifism. For Schreiner, the experiences of women as bodily entities are distinct from those of men: women are (or at least can be) mothers. This fact grounds and informs women's attitudes toward killing and war:

> No woman who is woman says of a human body, "it is nothing." . . . On this one point, and on this one point alone, the knowledge of woman, simply as woman, is superior to that of man; she knows the history of human flesh; she knows its cost; he does not. (Ruddick 1990, 231)

According to Schreiner, the fact that women experience bodily life differently than do men leads to women's rejection of violence: "It is not because of woman's cowardice, incapacity, nor, above all, because of her general superior virtue that she will end war when her voice is finally and fully heard" (Ruddick 1990, 231). It is because, as woman and mother, she knows each human life to be unique and valuable.

A host of religious women have followed Schreiner in a feminist rejection of all violence and war, offering an array of religious rationales for their pacifism. The Jewish author Halina Birenbaum, a survivor of Auschwitz, founds her stance on "the hopes which are shattered time and time again" by violence and on the dignity of the human being grounded in the tenets of Judaism (Berndt 2000, 7). Dorothy Day, a Roman Catholic and former editor of *The Catholic Worker*, traces a connection between Christ's love for the poor and the downtrodden, on the one hand, and his pacifism, on the other. The Irish Catholic Mairead Maguire, corecipient of the Noble Peace Prize in 1976 for her efforts in addressing violence between Protestants and Catholics in Northern Ireland, holds that "people kill in order to defend their identity, their Britishness or Irishness" and asserts that peace and reconciliation are possible "only when humanity is recognized as the binding foundation" (Berndt 2000, 43). The Moroccan Muslim feminist, Fatima Mernissi, sees the core values of Islam "to be shaped by *rahma*, by mercy, sensibility and tenderness. . ." and argues that by confronting violence in general Muslim society can address the problem of violence against women (Berndt 2000, 71–72). Stella Tamang, a Nepalese Buddhist and a leader of the International Network of Engaged Buddhists, writes, "For me, non-violence is both active and passive"; Tamang holds that the Buddhist commitment to "the dignity of all life" grounds her pacifist fight against violence and injustice (Berndt 2000, 104).

Christian theologians Sallie McFague and Rosemary Radford Ruether are among the religious feminists, so-called "eco-feminists," who argue against militarism on the grounds that war poses a threat to the very survival of the species and planet. For McFague and Ruether, warfare is part of a complex web of social challenges—including poverty, environmental issues, and sexism—that emerge from the Western tendency to create hierarchies and divisions of various sorts: male/female, rich/poor, humans/nature, us/them. Ruether explains:

> The "four horsemen" of destruction—human population explosion at the expense of the plants and the animals of the earth; environmental damage to air, water, and soil; the misery of growing masses of the poor; and a global militarization aimed at retaining unjust advantage over the earth's resources for a wealthy elite—create a combined set of catastrophic scenarios. (Ruether 1992, 111)

For Ruether, war is a violent manifestation of the desire of the powerful to maintain the status quo. As such, the "struggle to reconcile justice in human relations," including efforts on behalf of sexual and gender equality, and the fight to promote a "sustainable life community on earth" are one and the same (Reuther 1992, 111).

Feminism and Just War

A number of contemporary feminists locate their arguments within the diverse just war tradition—as advocates, critics, or, in some cases, both.

Mary C. Segers suggests that Roman Catholic thinking on just war has been shaped by the tendency of the Catholic Church to turn important ethical discourse into "private realm issues" (Segers 1990, 79). Using the 1983 pastoral letter of the (U.S.) National Conference of Catholic Bishops as an example, she argues that the voices of women are summarily and uniformly excluded from the formulation of a "Catholic" position on war and peace, evidencing an "apparent distrust of women as moral decision-makers" (Segers 1990, 79). The result is an inconsistent "life ethic" that asserts the sanctity of human life in the case of abortion but justifies widespread slaughter in the name of so-called "just" war. Segers writes: "women with the medical option of abortion . . . continue to appear, in the bishops' eyes, to be a greater danger to life than men armed with tanks, missiles and bombs" (Segers 1990, 79).

Lucinda Peach, while sympathetic to just-war thought, cautions against its tendencies to engage in depersonalizing abstractions and dichotomies. Building upon the work of Carol Gilligan, Peach fears that the just-war tradition's "capacity for abstraction . . . enables the denial of suffering because it replaces actual lives with hypothetical people" (Peach 1996, 198). Amid just-war language, the individual becomes a "combatant," "casualty," or "collateral damage" and the enemy becomes the one-dimensionally evil "Other." Peach argues not for the scrapping of just-war thought, though, but for its "revitalization." Existing *jus ad bellum* (right or justice at the time of war) criteria should be preserved, but their application must be rethought in light of the insights offered by feminists. With regard to the concept of "last resort," she suggests, "The emphasis on collaboration in much feminist theory could . . . be creatively applied to the development of new international or multinational frameworks for assessing if and when resort to armed force is morally necessary" (Peach 1996, 204). In a parallel way, by replacing abstract thinking with greater attention to context and particularity, feminists can alter the way just-war theory applies *jus ad bellum* criteria like "proportionality" and "reasonable hope of success" (Peach 1996, 204). For Peach, just-war theory and feminism are thus largely compatible, with the latter serving as corrective to the former.

Religious Feminism and Realism

Jean Bethke Elshtain holds that the problem with contemporary discussions of the morality of war rests not primarily with just-war theory but with "realism." Using Hobbes and Machiavelli as historical examples of realists, Elshtain defines realism as the perspective that the world is constituted by hostile, autonomous individuals ("monads") guided by fear, force, and instrumental calculation. Each individual seeks his or her self-interest, and nation states behave in a like manner. From the realist perspective, then, war is inevitable because self- (and state) interests inevitably conflict, and only power and force, or the threat thereof, are effective in deterring the aggression of one's opponent. The realist rejects and brands "idealistic" notions that concepts like love, forgiveness, and reconciliation play any effective role in the political arena. Strength is what counts.

Elshtain laments the fact that some feminists have adopted this realist perspective: "Hardline feminist realists . . . endorse a Hobbesian social ontology and construe politics as a battleground, the continuation of war by war-like means" (Elshtain 1992, 398). For such feminists, the way for women to combat a violent, coercive, patriarchal culture is for them to learn to be violent and coercive; they must learn to "fight dirty." Such feminists claim that for women to be equal to men socially, they must be equal partners in the extant power structures of violence: the National Guard, sheriff departments, the military, and so forth. According to Elshtain, this was the stance taken by the National Organization of Women (NOW) in the 1980s when it challenged all-male military registration in the American courts. If women are to be equal—if they are to possess "first-class citizenship," as the NOW legal brief put it—they must have the equal right to fight and to kill.

Elshtain argues, "such feminist realists share with their Hobbesian forefather a self-reproducing discourse of fear, suspicion, anticipated violence, and force to check-mate force" (Elshtain 1992, 399). She asks, is such realism *realistic*? Does it produce the promised results? Elshtain thinks not. First, in many circumstances, no amount of force can right the wrongs that have been committed in the past (e.g., the Nazi Holocaust, South African apartheid). In such cases, Elshtain holds, there is greater value to come through forgiveness and a peaceful and public disclosure of past wrongs than through retaliation and force (Elshtain 2001, 43). In direct contrast to the assumptions of realism, she cites Charles Villa-Vicencio: "It is important that we treat one another in the best possible manner" (Elshtain 2001, 51). The effect can be transformative—recasting age-old relationships of animosity and violence into new associations of tolerance, if not acceptance.

Second, building upon Hannah Arendt's notion of "natality," Elshtain questions one of the central tenets of realism, the belief that human agents necessarily will pursue self-interested and violent acts. Natality holds that, in the birth of each new human being, there is a new beginning and a new opportunity to change the ways of the past. For Elshtain, human proclivities toward self-interest and violence are far from inevitable. As conduits of natality, women have unique insights into the potential of humanity for change, innovation, and rebirth; and, as chief caregivers to each new generation, women possess unique opportunities to promote such change.

The Contribution of a Religious Feminism of War

The debate among religious feminists on the nature of war revisits issues at the heart of two existing intellectual discourses. On the one hand, individual feminists come to represent each of the major positions in the philosophical discourse on the moral nature of war: pacifism, just-war theory, and realism. On the other hand, their writings reflect and replay the sharp divisions among feminists with regard to questions at the core of feminism in general: Do there exist essential differences between male and female? Should women seek to integrate themselves into existing structures of power or should they reject these institutions and start anew? The promise of a religious feminism of war rests in the hope that in bringing these two divergent dialogues together—feminist discourse and the discourse of war—feminists can shed new light on both.

Timothy M. Renick

Further Reading

Alonso, H. (1993). *Peace as a women's issue: A history of the United States movement for world peace and women's rights*. Syracuse, NY: Syracuse University Press.

Berndt, H. (2000). Non-violence and the world religions. London: SCM Press.

Birenbaum, H. (1994). *Hope is the last to die: a personal documentation of nazi terror*. Oswiecim: Publishing House of the State Museum.

Daly, L. (1994). *Feminist theological ethics: A reader*. Louisville, KY: Westminster/John Knox Press.

Daly, M. (1973). *Beyond God the father*. Boston: Beacon Press.

Daly, M. (1978). *Gyn/ecology*. Boston: Beacon Press.

Day, D. (1972). *The long loneliness*. New York: Harper and Row.

Elshtain, J. (1987). *Women and war*. New York: Basic Books.

Elshtain, J. (1992). Reflection on war and political discourse: Realism, just war, and feminism in a nuclear age. In R. Miller (Ed.), *War in the twentieth century* (pp. 395–416). Louisville, KY: Westminster/John Knox Press.

Elshtain, J. (1996). Is there a feminist tradition of war and peace? In T. Nardin (Ed.), *The ethics of war and peace* (pp. 214–227). Princeton, NJ: Princeton University Press.

Elshtain, J. (2001). Politics and forgiveness. In N. Biggar (Ed.), *Burying the past* (pp. 40–56). Washington, DC: Georgetown University Press.

Gilligan, C. (1982). *In a different voice: Psychological theory and women's development*. Cambridge, MA: Harvard University Press.

McFague, S. (1989). *Models of God: Theology for an ecological, nuclear age*. Philadelphia: Fortress.

Mernissi, F. (1995). *The harem within*. New York: Batam Books.

National Conference of Catholic Bishops. (1983). *The challenge of peace: God's promise and our response (a pastoral letter on war and peace)*. New York: Crossroad Publishers.

Peach, L. (1996). An alternative to pacifism: Feminism and just-war theory. In K. Warren & D. Cady (Eds.), *Bringing peace home: Feminism, violence, and nature* (pp. 192–210). Indianapolis: University of Indiana Press.

Ruddick, S. (1990). The rationality of care. In J. Elshtain, & S. Tobias (Eds.), *Women, militarism, and war* (pp. 229–254). Savage, MD: Rowman and Littlefield Publishers, Inc.

Ruether, R. (1992). *Gaia and God: An ecofeminist theology of earth healing*. San Francisco: HarperSanFrancisco.

Segers, M. (1990). A consistent life ethic: A feminist perspective on the pro-peace and pro-life activities of the American Catholic Bishops. In J. Elshtain & S. Tobias (Eds.), *Women, militarism, and war* (pp. 61–84). Savage, MD: Rowman and Littlefield Publishers, Inc.

Stone, M. (1978). *When god was a woman*. Philadelphia: Harcourt.

Tobias, S. (1996). Toward a feminist ethic of war and peace. In T. Nardin (Ed.), *The ethics of war and peace* (pp. 228–241). Princeton, NJ: Princeton University Press.
Young, S. (1994). *An anthology of sacred texts by and about women*. New York: Crossroad.

Roman Catholicism

See Bishop's Wars (England 1639, 1640); Central and South America; English Civil Wars; European Wars of Religion; Liberation Theology; Roman Catholicism: Just War Doctrine; Roman Catholicism: Theology and Colonization; Roman Catholicism, Pacifism in; Spanish Christian-Muslim Wars

Roman Catholicism: Just-War Doctrine

In Catholic teaching war is not inevitable and thus we can hope for the abolition of war. Tempering this hope is the understanding that in a sinful world conflict is unavoidable. Without deliberate and serious commitment to manage it, conflict can evolve into the armed violence of war. Yet, even in war the moral dimension of human existence must not be ignored. There ought to be restraints upon both the judgment to go to war and the means whereby war is waged. Just-war doctrine developed to articulate those restraints.

Historical Background

Moral reflection on war, in particular, and violence, in general, dates back to the beginnings of the church in the apostolic period of the first century CE. During the first three centuries of Christianity there was a widespread sensibility that violence could not be reconciled with belief in the teaching and practice of Jesus. Still, there were pastoral problems to be addressed as converts to the new faith spread beyond the boundaries of Judaism and the region of Palestine. On occasion a new convert to Christianity was a member of the Roman military, or held a position of civic administration and governance involving the employment or approval of violent force. Could such persons remain in their preconversion roles or must converts now abandon earlier responsibilities? As time passed that question was answered differently by various leaders of the church community.

In the fourth century CE, as the emperor himself accepted Christian baptism and ever larger numbers followed his example, practical guidance for following the gospel led to new theories of what was, and was not, permissible for disciples of Jesus. As the growing Christian population moved from a socially marginal to a leading role in the empire, the topic of war was viewed in a new way. Within this changing context the doctrine of just-war gradually evolved. Teachers such as Ambrose (339–397 CE) and then Augustine (354–430 CE) began to defend military action if undertaken with the proper attitude and in the right circumstances. In the construction of their theories they relied upon Old Testament texts in which God was seen as supporting Israel's military conquest of Palestine, as well as the wisdom of non-Christian writers like Cicero (106–43 BCE) and Marcus Aurelius (121–180 CE). Because of the prestige of Augustine later Christian thinkers tended to adopt his view of war as analogous to a police action, punishing evildoers and protecting innocent people.

In subsequent centuries scholars such as Thomas Aquinas (1225–1274 CE), Francisco Vitoria (c. 1481–1546 CE), and Francisco Suárez (1548–1617 CE) further systematized Catholic thought on war. They developed theories that reflected the particular historical circumstances of their respective times, i.e., feudal rivalries, the presence of militant Islam, the rise of sovereign nation-states, and European expansion in the new world. The doctrine of just-war, never far removed from the actual circumstances of the time, was formulated, questioned, reconsidered, and reformulated throughout the centuries.

The emergence of a new context for just-war thinking is forcing the tradition to once more undergo development. Among the elements of the new context are the diminishing threat of nuclear war imperiling humankind's survival, the increasing incidence of conflict inspired by ethnic and religious differences, greater sensitivity to human rights abuses, the ever stronger ties of interdependence, and the pressures both within and without territorial borders that recast traditional notions of state sovereignty.

The Substance of the Doctrine

At the center of the doctrine or teaching on just-war stand several convictions: (1) violence, though always regrettable, is not inherently or necessarily a moral wrong; (2) the harm caused by war's violence may be justified, at least in some cases, by an appeal to the goods protected or obtained by war; and (3) the use of armed force within war is a rule-governed activity, for even war is subject to ethical assessment and governance.

Over the course of history the just-war doctrine served a variety of purposes: the legitimization of armed force authorized by political leaders; a restraint upon force used by warriors and states; a set of norms to govern combat in a divided world; a form of criticism of various military strategies and weapons; the basis for an argument supporting selective conscientious objection; and finally, a means of ethical evaluation of government policies and military doctrines.

Of course, within Roman Catholicism there are supporters of nonviolence who question the soundness of the just-war doctrine. Can Christian disciples countenance resorting to violence to achieve values such as justice and peace? Is it possible to use violence as a means to express love of neighbor? These issues are best discussed not in the abstract but by people amidst the situation of the world as it is, a world in which human beings engage in a variety of unwarranted behaviors: treating others unjustly, undermining the common good, seizing what is not theirs. What may the followers of Christ do in response to such behavior and on behalf of the victims of aggression? Just-war doctrine is an attempt to fashion a reply to the question.

Elements of Just-War

One significant statement of just-war doctrine is found in a pastoral letter written by the National Conference of Catholic Bishops of the United States in 1983. Entitled *The Challenge of Peace: God's Promise and Our Response*, the document was the most extensive treatment of the moral problem of war ever undertaken by the American bishops. It received wide attention among Catholics and others, both in the United States and abroad. In their letter the bishops listed a set of criteria for a just-war under the traditional headings of *jus ad bellum* (justice in going to war) and *jus in bello* (justice in waging war). Under the former category they stipulate seven criteria.

1. Just Cause: war is permissible only for a sound moral reason such as the protection of innocent life or the defense of basic human rights. With the devastating force of modern weaponry the harm of war has been increased to such an extent that a cause which may have justified war in an earlier age, when the harm was less, may not now be sufficient.

2. Competent Authority: war is not a private vendetta but a public act and must be declared by those who can legitimately speak and act on behalf of the state. In a democracy like the United States it is important that the nation's leaders follow the legally established processes for declaring and undertaking war.

3. Comparative Justice: the use of the modifier "comparative" is meant to signify that neither side in a conflict may be simply "just" in an unqualified way. Nor may the opposing side be characterized as purely evil or unjust. Yet, this criterion requires that on balance, the case plausibly be made that one side has a clear "edge" in its claim that the values it defends outweigh the claim made by the opponent.

4. Right Intention: this criterion is closely linked to just cause. The actual intent of those waging war cannot be different than the cause that is publicly espoused, e.g., war cannot be declared to defend against an unjust aggressor while the real intent of the war is to seize territory or destroy the culture of the enemy.

5. Last Resort: since war is always regrettable, all realistic alternatives must be studied before going to war. This requires a willingness to take prudent risks and to explore options short of armed force to avoid the tragedy of war.

6. Probability of Success: this is not an expectation that we can predict the future but a reminder that if war is to be seen as a morally rational activity there must be a plausible expectation that the goods for which a war is fought are, in fact, obtainable. A reckless and foolhardy call to arms, even for the sake of a just cause, is ruled out by this criterion.

7. Proportionality: when viewed under the *jus ad bellum* rubric this requires a judgment that the overall harm caused by war is proportionate to the good gained by armed conflict. Obviously as the devastation of modern war increases it becomes more difficult to satisfy this criterion. Indeed the bishops expressed great doubt as to whether a nuclear war could ever be proportionate.

As criteria for the *jus in bello* the bishops note two items.

8. Proportionality: seen under the heading of justice in war, this criterion means that the particular strategies, tactics, and individual actions employed in the conduct of war must be proportionate in terms of the evil brought about in pursuit of the good. Even within a war that has satisfied the first seven criteria, the means of fighting the war can be unjust, e.g., torturing

prisoners of war as a way to gather military intelligence or using weapons that will cause long-term devastation of the environment.

9. Discrimination: this final criterion proposes that some persons and places are not legitimate targets for attack. Deliberately attacking hospitals or shooting at civilians extends the range of war's damage beyond proper bounds. Even in war there are crimes and denying to noncombatants immunity from direct attack is one of the clearest crimes.

Just-War and Peace

In Catholic moral theology peace has never been accorded an absolute value. This is especially true when peace has been understood in the minimalist sense of peace as the absence of violence. Catholic teaching has traditionally maintained that such a minimal peace is not even a true peace, for peace requires more than "merely the absence of war" (Vatican II 1965, par. 78).

A better understanding recognizes peace as constituting more than the minimal definition often used in secular politics. For peace "is rightly and appropriately called 'an enterprise of justice' " (Vatican II 1965, par. 78, quoting Isaiah 32:7). For this reason, it is correct to say that war is not the opposite of peace. Rather, the outbreak of armed violence can be understood as an effort to establish a true peace in a situation of injustice. It is not a contradiction, therefore, in Catholic moral theory to state that a just-war can be fought in the name of peace.

Just-War as a Middle Path

Just-war teaching has sought to occupy a middle position on the question of war and morality. The polar opposites in the debate share a common premise that war cannot be subject to moral norms. This is the premise the just-war doctrine rejects. Much space exists between those who in the name of "national security" dismiss all talk of moral restraints in war as sentimental and those who in the name of nonviolence deny the possibility of any moral legitimacy to war. Occupying the middle territory are proponents of just-war who continue to develop theories in response to the ever-changing situations of history. Seen in this way, the just-war doctrine and its elements should be understood as a structure for moral reasoning about warfare, not a definitive list of precise rules to be mechanically applied.

Kenneth R. Himes

Further Reading

Bainton, R. (1960). *Christian attitudes toward war and peace.* Nashville, TN: Abingdon.

Cahill. L. S. (1994). *Love your enemies.* Minneapolis, MN: Fortress Press.

Himes, K. (1991). Pacifism and the Just-war tradition in Roman Catholic social teaching. In J. Coleman (Ed.), *One hundred years of Catholic social thought.* Maryknoll, NY: Orbis Books.

Hollenbach, D. (1983). *Nuclear ethics.* New York: Paulist Press.

Miller, R. (1991). *Interpretations of conflict.* Chicago: University of Chicago Press.

Murnion, P. (1983). *Catholics and nuclear war.* New York: Crossroad Publishing.

National Conference of Catholic Bishops. (1983). *The challenge of peace: God's promise and our response.* Washington, DC: United States Catholic Conference.

Powers, G. D., & Hennemeyer, C. R. (Eds.). (1994). *Peacemaking: Moral and policy challenges for a new world.* Washington, DC: United States Catholic Conference.

Shannon, T. (Ed.). (1980). *War or peace?* Maryknoll, NY: Orbis Books.

Vatican II. (1965). *Pastoral constitution on the church in the modern world.* Vatican City: Vatican Polyglot Press.

Walzer, M. (1977). *Just and unJust-wars.* New York: Basic Books.

Roman Catholicism, Pacifism in

"All citizens and all governments are obliged to work for the avoidance of war" (*Catechism of the Catholic Church* 1994, § 2308). While all members of the largest branch of Christianity especially share in this call to be peacemakers (Matthew 5:9), most Roman Catholics are not pacifists. In general, pacifism involves the belief that, morally, all killing is intrinsically wrong, including killing in war, revolution, policing, capital punishment, and self-defense. In addition, pacifists often reject other uses of force, including nonlethal force, which cause physical or psychological harm. This absolute form of pacifism is known typically as sectarian, doctrinal, or witnessing pacifism. In reality, however, there is "no such thing as a single position called 'pacifism,' to which one clear definition can be given and which is held by all 'pacifists' " (Yoder 1971, 10). Indeed, some pacifists do not rule out absolutely all uses of force; rather, they may prohibit participation in war while accepting, possibly, nonlethal though forceful forms of defending others from attack, or perhaps police use of force and international police actions. This form of pacifism often is called utopian, internationalist, or world-order pacifism. Still other pacifists advocate nonviolent resistance as a way to defend and promote a just peace. This activist form of pacifism characteristically is referred to as prophetic, pragmatic, or prudential pacifism. Each of these broad forms of pacifism may be found historically and today within Roman Catholicism.

The Early Church Period

There is no straightforward evidence of Christians serving in the Roman military until approximately 170–180 CE, though there probably were a few soldiers who converted to Christianity prior to that time as mentioned, for example, in the New Testament (Luke 7:9; Acts 10:47). Also, given the Roman custom that soldiers' sons usually became soldiers themselves—a compulsory practice for one son (or his substitute) of an officer—it may be inferred that when substantial evidence is found of Christians in the military in the late second century, there must have been some Christians in the same legion in the previous generation and perhaps a few in the generation prior to that. Although Christian participation in the Roman military gradually grew during the first three centuries of the early church's existence, a number of sociological and theological reasons may have contributed to why most Christians did not serve as soldiers.

First, as a minority sect or group, Christians periodically experienced persecution at the hands of the Romans, which naturally would give rise to reluctance on the part of Christians to serve in the army of their persecutors. Second, up to this time only citizens could become Roman soldiers. Because most Christians belonged to social groups, including slaves and freedmen, that were not eligible for such service, not many were able to join the army. Third, the Roman Empire tended to recruit for the military from rural areas. Since most of the early Christians lived in urban areas, few of them volunteered to be in the military. Fourth, rituals were required of Roman officers, which soldiers had to attend and thereby give their indirect support of, including sacrifices to, and worship of, the Roman emperor, Caesar. Related to this, many military units often had their own cult, wherein a particular god was worshiped in return for that god's favor and assistance. Because for Christians "Jesus is Lord," they refused to join the Roman military with its idolatrous practices. Along similar lines, early Christians rejected swearing oaths, which were required in the military and which usually involved an invocation of some deity and thereby was binding. Fifth, sexual immorality was associated with being in the military, and Christians were appalled by, and forbidden from, such behavior. Sixth, there was an intense eschatological anticipation among the early Christians of Jesus' return, the coming of the kingdom of God, and the end of the present age. Given this fervent expectation, most Christians did not bother to join the ranks of the Roman military. Finally, aside from some police functions such as the guarding of prisoners, the protection of the roads, and firefighting, being a Roman soldier commonly entailed killing in war. Because the early Christians abhorred bloodshed, they refused to kill as part of the Roman military.

Early Christian pacifism, therefore, was not solely due to the absolute prohibition against killing, although this appears to be an important reason, especially given the incompatibility of killing with Jesus' teachings and example. In his Sermon on the Mount, Jesus commanded his disciples to love their enemies (Matthew 5:44) and, moreover, not to resist evil (Matthew 5:39). Indeed, Jesus himself adhered to his own teaching, especially during his crucifixion. For early Christians, Jesus' nonviolent sacrifice on the cross out of love for others, including his enemies, witnessed to the way in which God resists and overcomes evil, thereby reconciling people with God and one another. They believed that all Christians were called to follow the way that Jesus taught and exemplified. Their pacifism was an important component of their way of life faithful to their Lord Jesus Christ.

It is noteworthy that no patristic writers offered any theological justification for participation in the military by Christians. Indeed, during this period prior to 325 CE all church theologians and bishops who addressed the subject opposed Christian involvement in the military, including Justin Martyr (c. 100–c. 165 CE), Tertullian (c. 155 or 160–after 220), Origen (c. 185–c. 254), Clement of Alexandria (c. 150–between 211 and 215), Cyprian of Carthage (c. 200–258), and Lactantius (c. 240–320). The primary theological reasons given for Christian antipathy toward military service—including repugnance toward idolatry, oaths, or killing—varied from one to another of these writers perhaps depending on their geographical region.

For instance, in his *On Idolatry*, Tertullian addressed the question "whether a believer may turn

Dominicans in West Africa

The following text discusses the goals of Dominican missionaries in northwest Nigeria in the early 1970s.

The Dominicans, of course, feel that any changes they bring in Dukawa life that forward the acceptance of Catholicism are good changes, even though they admit such changes may temporarily be disturbing. They have studied the works of Father Luzbetak (1971) and are attempting to lessen the chance for traumatic changes by studying the "personality of culture" and adapting their methods to lessen the shock of change.

The Dominicans expect the following changes in the lives of their converts. They expect them to have a monogamous marriage, to stop attending indigenous religious ceremonies, to stop using "native magic" to attend Catholic religious services and to use Catholic sacraments whenever possible. They expect them to refrain from non-marital sexual relations and to "live a good Christian life." Some minimum knowledge of the catechism is also expected.

Source: **Salamone, Frank A. (1974).** ***Gods and Goods in Africa: Persistence and Change in Ethnic and Religious Identity in Yauri Emirate, North-Western State, Nigeria.*** **New Haven, CT: Human Relations Area Files, Inc., pp. 162–63.**

himself unto military service, and whether the military may be admitted unto the faith," replying that Jesus at the time of his arrest in the Garden of Gethsemane, "in disarming Peter, unbelted every soldier" (Holmes 1975, 43–44). Also, in his *Against Celsus*, a work aimed at Celsus, who had criticized Christians for refusing to protect the empire by fighting in the Roman military, Origen answered that while Jesus "nowhere teaches that it is right for His own disciples to offer violence to any one, however wicked," Christians nevertheless accept the role of government in a fallen world and "fight" on behalf of the Roman emperor by "forming a special army—an army of piety—by offering our prayers to God" (Holmes 1975, 48–49). In addition, there were soldier-martyrs who refused to join or continue to serve in the Roman military, including Maximilianus, who was martyred in Carthage in 295, and Marcellus, who was martyred in Tangiers in 298. At the same time, many of these patristic writers and martyrs critically presupposed or alluded to the gradually growing "acceptance by *other* Christians of participation in war and military service" (Johnson 1987, 19).

Echoes of Pacifism in Roman Catholic Tradition

The slow shift during these first few centuries toward Christian acceptance of military service in order to protect the empire from injustice and attacks by criminals within its borders or by barbarians on the frontier gained momentum in 313 CE with Emperor Constantine's Edict of Milan, making Christianity the official religion of the Roman Empire. Subsequently, more Christians were found among the ranks of the Roman military, and some of the key principles of the just-war tradition were set forth by theologians, such as Ambrose (339–397) and Augustine (354–430), in order to justify Christian participation in war and limit their use of force. From that time to the present, the just-war tradition has been the primary ethical framework within Roman Catholicism concerning the morality of war and the use of force.

Nevertheless, the just-war tradition did not completely supplant pacifism. Indeed, although they held that the use of force in defense of others was justified, Ambrose and Augustine did not permit personal self-defense against attack. Thus a residual trace of the earlier pacifist stance remained in early just-war theory, though restricted to cases of personal self-defense. Pacifism moreover remained as a possible way of life for Christians called to be clergy and monks. The earlier prohibition against killing in war no longer was regarded as a mandated precept for all Christians but instead came to be seen as a counsel of perfection for monks and clergy. During the Middle Ages, monastic and religious movements within Catholicism preserved pacifism as "one strand of Catholic tradition from the time of Jesus down to the present day" (Hollenbach 1983, 8). One of the medieval examples of such Roman Catholic pacifism was Francis of Assisi (1181

Activist pacifists, including Des Moines Diocesan Roman Catholic priest Father Frank Cordaro (far right side), protesting the U.S. war against Iraq moments before trespassing onto Camp Dodge, Iowa, property and being arrested on March 22, 2003. Courtesy Jeffrey Hage, Press Citizen Newspapers.

or 1182–1226) and his Franciscan Order. Francis also reopened the door to pacifism for laypeople in the Franciscan Third Order, which required for membership their refusal to bear arms against anyone. During the twelfth century, the Waldensians and Cathars also attempted to mandate nonviolence for all Christians; however, the Catholic Church regarded these groups as heretics and employed violence against them in an attempt to force their return to orthodox Roman Catholic beliefs at the time. In addition, beginning in the sixteenth century, this thread of absolute pacifism was maintained by a few non-Catholic Christian sects after the Protestant Reformation, including Mennonites, Brethren, Hutterites, and Quakers. Most of these groups appealed to Jesus' teachings in the Gospels and the example of the early Christians for support of their pacifism.

World-order pacifism surfaced during the Middle Ages in the thought of Dante Alighieri (1265–1321) and Marsilius of Padua (c. 1280–c. 1343). While not considering themselves pacifists, they began to consider how a just and ordered society might be extended at the level of Christendom. As a society internally is peaceful, so too might a more international society internally be peaceful. There would be no more war, though room would be allowed for police type of force, for the sword would remain, but only in the hands of a just sovereign. During the Renaissance, such world-order pacifism was articulated by the Catholic humanist Desiderius Erasmus (c. 1466–1536), especially in *The Complaint of Peace*, and by Thomas More (1478–1535), who wrote about such an ideal community in his *Utopia*.

Twentieth-Century Catholicism

Through the first half of the twentieth century, the just-war tradition was the dominant approach, though not having doctrinal status, within Roman Catholicism. Social ethicist John Ryan (1869–1945), for example, wrote that pacifism "finds no support in either the law of revelation or the law of nature," adding that the teachings of Christ "have always been interpreted by the Catholic Church as counsels of perfection" rather than "precepts" mandated for everyone, and that as such "they were addressed to individuals, not to states," because citizens and nations are authorized by natural law to defend themselves and others "by force against unjust aggression" (Ryan 1928, 25). Similarly, Pope Pius XII (1876–1958), in his Christmas message of 1956, rejected absolute pacifism, or the conscientious objection to all war, as an option for Catholics.

Nevertheless, in the face of the rise of modern, total warfare, the world-order peace vision has been advocated officially by Catholicism beginning especially with Pope John XXIII (1881–1963) and his *Pacem in terris*, which called for an international order that would replace war with arbitration, judicial structures, and, if necessary, international police actions. In addition, activist or pragmatic pacifism emerged among Catholics at this time and gained official church support especially at the Second Vatican Council (1962–1965) and its document *Gaudium et spes*, which praised individuals who choose not to vindicate their rights by armed force and instead employ nonviolent methods to defend and promote the common good. The council moreover called upon governments to recognize legally the right of conscientious objection, allowing for pacifists to work for the common good through other forms of service. This activist form of pacifism, involving nonviolent resistance, has been exemplified and articulated by Dorothy Day (1897–1980) and the Catholic Worker movement, Philip (1923–2002) and Daniel (b. 1921) Berrigan, and others. These pacifists believe that nonviolence as a method is more effective than war, is less costly in human lives than war, and can even lead to reconciliation. At the same time, however, they often understand and defend their pacifism not merely with pragmatic reasons but as anchored theologically in Jesus' teachings and example.

In 1983, the United States Catholic bishops issued a pastoral letter, *The Challenge of Peace*, affirming the teaching of Vatican II and observing that Catholics "choose different paths to move toward the realization of the kingdom in history" (National Conference of Catholic Bishops 1983, 62). While all Catholics are obligated to defend peace against aggression, some may do so by using force in accordance with the just-war tradition while others may do so by active nonviolence. Although the bishops "believe work to develop nonviolent means of fending off aggression and resolving conflict best reflects the call of Jesus both to love and to justice," they continue to recognize "that force, even deadly force, is sometimes justified and that nations must provide for their defense" (National Conference of Catholic Bishops 1983, 78). At the time, the bishops noted that pacifism therefore is an option available only to individuals and not to nations.

The Future

In their 1994 statement appearing in the wake of successful nonviolent revolutions in the Philippines and in Eastern Europe, the American bishops observe, "Although nonviolence has often been regarded as simply a personal option or vocation, recent history suggests that in some circumstances it can be an effective public undertaking as well" (National Conference of Catholic Bishops 1994, 5). Indeed, this leads them to entertain the possibility that nonviolence should now be placed on an equal footing with the just-war tradition in the public order rather than relegated to the personal, individual level. They furthermore call for governments to promote research, education, and training in nonviolent methods of resisting injustice and aggression, even though they continue to note that this does not deny a nation's right and duty to defend its citizens with force in accordance with the just-war tradition. In view of this, at this time all three of the broad forms of pacifism—witnessing, world-order, and pragmatic—currently are represented within Roman Catholicism. Perhaps in the future they will be reconciled and integrated more with one another and, perhaps, with the just-war tradition.

Tobias Winright

See also Eastern Orthodoxy, Pacifism in; Judaism, Pacifism in; Mennonites; Quakers; Martyrdom

Further Reading

Allen, J. L. (2001). *War: A primer for Christians*. Dallas, TX: Maguire Center and Southern Methodist University Press.

Bainton, R. H. (1960). *Christian attitudes toward war and peace*. New York: Abingdon Press.

Cahill, L. S. (1994). *Love your enemies: Discipleship, pacifism, and just war theory*. Minneapolis, MN: Fortress Press.

Catechism of the Catholic Church. (1994). New York: Image/Doubleday.

Douglass, J. W. (1968). *The non-violent cross: A theology of revolution and peace*. New York: Macmillan.
Egan, E. (1999). *Peace be with you: Justified warfare or the way of nonviolence*. Maryknoll, NY: Orbis Books.
Hollenbach, D. (1983). *Nuclear ethics: A Christian moral argument*. Ramsey, NJ: Paulist Press.
Holmes, A. F. (Ed.). (1975). *War and Christian ethics: Classic readings on the morality of war*. Grand Rapids, MI: Baker Book House.
Johnson, J. T. (1987). *The quest for peace: Three moral traditions in Western cultural history*. Princeton, NJ: Princeton University Press.
Marrin, A. (Ed.). (1971). *War and the Christian conscience: From Augustine to Martin Luther King, Jr.* Chicago: Henry Regnery Company.
Murray, J. C. (1960). *We hold these truths: Catholic reflections on the American proposition*. Kansas City, MO: Sheed and Ward.
National Conference of Catholic Bishops. (1983). *The challenge of peace: God's promise and our response*. Washington, DC: United States Catholic Conference.
National Conference of Catholic Bishops. (1994). *The harvest of justice is sown in peace*. Washington, DC: United States Catholic Conference.
Ryan, J. A. (1928). *International ethics*. Washington, DC: Catholic Association for International Peace.
Winright, T. (1999). From police officers to peace officers. In S. Hauerwas et al. (Eds.). *The wisdom of the cross: Essays in honor of John Howard Yoder*. Grand Rapids, MI: Eerdmans Publishing Company.
Yoder, J. H. (1971). *Nevertheless: The varieties and shortcomings of religious pacifism*. Scottdale, PA: Herald Press.
Zahn, G. (1967). *War, conscience, and dissent*. New York: Hawkthorn.

Roman Catholicism: Theology and Colonization

The word "colony" and its cognates derive from the Latin term *colonia*, which can mean "land," "estate," or "settlement." Colonies in the Roman sense were official settlements created by law, which specified location, size, leadership, and those citizens enrolled. "If sufficient volunteers were not forthcoming," as one scholar notes, "compulsion could be used, for the foundation of a colony was, in a sense, a military expedition"(Jolowicz 1952, 61 n. 4). Among the Romans, such colonies were typically established to secure and govern conquests.

The Catholic tradition in the Latin West grew up on the foundations laid by Rome. It accepted as fact the urban establishments that had started as colonial settlements and the need for such settlements to safeguard the imperial order. Thus in Catholic religious thought colonization and colonialism have no independent status; they are matters for legal and political reflection. Nonetheless, Catholic moral theology, particularly as it dealt with mission and conquest, had much to say about the activities that made colonization possible.

Mission

The Christian tradition has always been a missionary religion. The church has a responsibility to spread the message of salvation as a matter of charity, the love each person owes to God and neighbor. When, in the fourth century CE, the church was embraced by the rulers of the Roman Empire, it was generally assumed that the state could suppress pagan religion and heresy as threats to the spiritual and social well-being of the community. Belief itself, however, could never be coerced and faith proper was a gift of God, positions articulated most fully, in the early Latin tradition, by Augustine of Hippo (354–430 CE). To say that belief could not be coerced, however, should not be confused with modern notions of toleration. Both restraint and correction were the duty of the authorities.

Crusade

Canon law and the crusading movement each, beginning in the eleventh century, helped to clarify the legal status of mission, particularly as it related to the peoples of foreign lands. Gregory VII (c. 1020–1085 CE), in the reforming conflicts of his papacy, gave impetus to the development of a general justification for the use of force to secure the goods of the church. He attempted to enlist the European nobility into the *militia Christi* and set the stage for the ecclesiastical authorization of war. In 1095, Pope Urban II (c. 1035–1099 CE), earlier a chief advisor and executor of Gregory's reforms, preached war for the recovery of the holy land and the rescue of the Eastern Church.

In legal theory this was a just war for the recovery of Christian patrimony, unjustly occupied by a hostile people. It was, in principle, no different from the war for the recovery of Christian Spain that the papacy also backed. In the language of the time, the First Crusade was a pilgrimage with arms. It was not a war of conversion, though the crusaders' success, their wonder at the relics of the holy land, and the visionary experiences of several among them contributed, as Jonathan Riley-Smith puts it, "to the conviction that the crusade was God's own war"(Riley-Smith 1986, 107). Religious motives were not the only impetus to crusade, however. The crusaders famously, and brutally, sacked Constantinople in 1204 and were more than willing to turn on each other for practical and political gain.

Among Muslims and Christians both, by the end of the crusading era, the most noble figure to emerge from these conflicts was the Muslim leader Saladin (1137 or 1138–1193 CE). Dante places him, with Hector, Aeneas, Caesar, and the elder Brutus, among the noble souls in Limbo. In the next generation, Boccaccio's Filomena recounts a tale of Saladin and Melchizedek, whose wealth Saladin hopes to expropriate. But the wise Jew tells a story of the equality of Judaism, Christianity, and Islam, at which point Saladin admits his unworthy intention, Melchizedek volunteers to help him, and they both live on in great honor. That this story captured something of the popular feeling of subsequent centuries, despite the efforts of Counter-Reformation authorities, emerges in the work of the Italian historian Carlo Ginzburg.

European Expansion and Canon Law

In the mid-thirteenth century Pope Innocent IV (d. 1254 CE) elaborated a theory of divine government that justified papal intervention well beyond anything allowed by the just war theory. On Innocent's account, when the Psalmist proclaims that "the earth is the Lord's," he is making a statement of legal fact. Government devolved from God to his various agents, culminating in the Christian emperor. The pope, as the heir of Peter, is ultimately responsible for both the spiritual direction of the empire and, by extension, the spiritual well-being of those rebellious subjects who fail or refuse to acknowledge imperial rule. This authority is obviously de jure, as opposed to de facto, but it is legitimate nonetheless for the pope to empower the emperor to act in the best interests of both the universal church and its wayward subjects.

This does not mean that non-Christian rulers hold power illegitimately. God bestows power on nonbelieving rulers to pursue the common good of their people. But if the proper authorities do not abide by the dictates of the natural law, which is in principle known to all, then concern for the spiritual welfare of even alien peoples falls to the pope as Vicar of Christ. He can authorize a Christian army to invade a non-Christian land to suppress injustice, idolatry, or sexual perversion. But in general the point of Innocent's theory was to establish a basis for protecting Christians from persecution and abuse. For Innocent and his successors this was particularly important with regard to Christian communities in North Africa.

The need for papal protection could also apply to Christians faced with colonial incursions by other Christians. With the expansion of the German peoples during the agricultural take-off of the eleventh and twelfth centuries, colonization and conversion generated problems. Expansion across the Elbe brought Christians into conflict with a variety of pagan peoples along the Baltic coast. Secular authorities were happy to justify dispossessing these people, when possible, on the grounds of their paganism, but as the indigenous population responded to the preaching of Christianity, religious and secular authorities began to clash. As dynastic families accepted Christianity, the native peoples came, nominally, under the protection of the church, but as Joseph Muldoon notes, the Germans and the Poles continued to devastate and displace the Lithuanians even after the conversion of their king in the mid-thirteenth century. "The territorial aims of the Christian neighbors of the Lithuanians," he writes, "overrode the Church's goals" (Muldoon 1979, 33).

One of the most remarkable acts of Innocent IV, at least to modern readers, must be his embassy to the Mongols in 1245. The grandson of Genghis Khan (c. 1162–1227 CE), Guyuk (d. 1248), was rebuked by Innocent's ambassador for his attacks on Christians and warned of the eternal peril of his soul. His only chance, wrote Innocent, was to seek salvation in Christ and place himself under the authority of the pope. The khan reflected that his own great conquests could hardly be contrary to divine will and directed Innocent's ambassador, Friar John, to inform the pope that he should come himself to submit to the ruler of the world. The stalemate was never resolved.

Innocent's was not, however, the last world on secular authority and nonbelief. Henry of Segusio (d. 1271), a contemporary of Innocent at the law school in Bologna, known to posterity simply as Hostiensis, argued that the advent of Christ rendered the authority of all nonbelievers null and void. While, in principle, this would justify dispossessing all nonbelieving rulers, such actions would be precipitous and unwise. Though nonbelievers ought, in both fact and law, to

Dorothy Day on Pacifism

In this letter published in *The Catholic Worker* one month after Pearl Harbor, Dorothy Day, founder of the Catholic Worker Movement, emphasizes the movement's commitment to Gospel-based pacifism.

DEAR FELLOW WORKERS IN CHRIST:

Lord God, merciful God, our Father, shall we keep silent, or shall we speak? And if we speak, what shall we say?

I am sitting here in the church on Mott Street writing this in your presence. Out on the streets it is quiet, but you are there too, in the Chinese, in the Italians, these neighbors we love. We love them because they are our brothers, as Christ is our Brother and God our Father.

But we have forgotten so much. We have all forgotten. And how can we know unless you tell us. "For whoever calls upon the name of the Lord shall be saved." How then are they to call upon Him in whom they have not believed? But how are they to believe Him whom they have not heard? And how are they to hear, if no one preaches? And how are men to preach unless they be sent? As it is written, "How beautiful are the feet of those who preach the gospel of peace." (Romans X)

Seventy-five thousand Catholic Workers go out every month. What shall we print? We can print still what the Holy Father is saying, when he speaks of total war, of mitigating the horrors of war, when he speaks of cities of refuge, of feeding Europe . . .

We will print the words of Christ who is with us always, even to the end of the world. "Love your enemies, do good to those who hate you, and pray for those who persecute and calumniate you, so that you may be children of your Father in heaven, who makes His sun to rise on the good and the evil, and sends rain on the just and unjust."

We are at war, a declared war, with Japan, Germany and Italy. But still we can repeat Christ's words, each day, holding them close in our hearts, each month printing them in the paper. In times past, Europe has been a battlefield. But let us remember St. Francis, who spoke of peace and we will remind our readers of him, too, so they will not forget.

In *The Catholic Worker* we will quote our Pope, our saints, our priests. We will go on printing the articles which remind us today that we are all "called to be saints," that we are other Christs, reminding us of the priesthood of the laity.

We are still pacifists. Our manifesto is the Sermon on the Mount, which means that we will try to be peacemakers. Speaking for many of our conscientious objectors, we will not participate in armed warfare or in making munitions, or by buying government bonds to prosecute the war, or in urging others to these efforts.

But neither will we be carping in our criticism. We love our country and we love our President. We have been the only country in the world where men of all nations have taken refuge from oppression. We recognize that while in the order of intention we have tried to stand for peace, for love of our brother, in the order of execution we have failed as Americans in living up to our principles.

We will try daily, hourly, to pray for an end to the war, such an end, to quote Father Orchard, "as would manifest to all the world, that it was brought about by divine action, rather than by military might or diplomatic negotiation, which men and nations would then only attribute to their power or sagacity."

Continues

Continued

"Despite all calls to prayer," Father Orchard concludes, "there is at present all too little indication anywhere that the tragedy of humanity and the desperate need of the world have moved the faithful, still less stirred the thoughtless masses, to turn to prayer as the only hope for mankind this dreadful hour.

"We shall never pray until we feel more deeply, and we shall never feel deeply enough until we envisage what is actually happening in the world, and understand what is possible in the will of God; and that means until sufficient numbers realize that we have brought things to a pass which is beyond human power to help or save.

"Those who do feel and see, however inadequately, should not hesi-tate to begin to pray, or fail to persevere, however dark the prospects remain." Let them urge others to do likewise; and then, first small groups, and then the Church as a whole, and at last the world, may turn and cry for forgiveness, mercy and deliverance for all.

"Then we may be sure God will answer, and effectually; for the Lord's hand is not shortened that it cannot save, nor His ear heavy that it cannot hear." Let us add, that unless we combine this prayer with almsgiving, in giving to the least of God's children, and fasting in order that we may help feed the hungry, and penance in recognition of our share in the guilt, our prayer may become empty words.

Our works of mercy may take us into the midst of war. As editor of *The Catholic Worker*, I would urge our friends and associates to care for the sick and the wounded, to the growing of food for the hungry, to the continuance of all our works of mercy in our houses and on our farms. We understand, of course, that there is and that there will be great differences of opinion even among our own groups as to how much collaboration we can have with the government in times like these. There are differences more profound and there will be many continuing to work with us from necessity, or from choice, who do not agree with us as to our position on war, conscientious objection, etc. But we beg that there will be mutual charity and forbearance among us all.

This letter, sent to all our Houses of Hospitality and to all our farms, and being printed in the January issue of the paper, is to state our position in this most difficult time.

Because of our refusal to assist in the prosecution of war and our insistence that our collaboration be one for peace, we may find ourselves in difficulties. But we trust in the generosity and understanding of our government and our friends, to permit us to continue, to use our paper to "preach Christ crucified."

May the Blessed Mary, Mother of love, of faith, of knowledge and of hope, pray for us.

***Source:* Day, Dorothy. (1942, January). "Our Country Passes from Undeclared War to Declared War; We Continue Our Christian Pacifist Stand." *The Catholic Worker, 1*(1). Retrieved April 6, 2003, from http://www.catholicworker.org/dorothyday/**

be subject to Christians, Hostiensis agreed with Innocent that the best approach was through the preaching of the gospel. In theory, however, nonbelievers could not legitimately hold dominion of their own.

The Spanish Critique of Papal and Imperial Authority

In the centuries that followed, the claims of Innocent and Hostiensis did not go unchallenged. Nor did the more extravagant claims of the advocates of empire. Beginning in 1493, Pope Alexander VI (1431–1503 CE) issued a series of pronouncements dividing the arena of exploration and exploitation between Spain and Portugal. In the previous century Portugal had taken the lead in developing trade with Africa. Spain, of course, had just laid claim to the lands discovered by Columbus. To forestall the sorts of conflict that had erupted over the Canaries and other islands off the west African coast, the pope proposed dividing the spheres of interest along an imaginary line that eventually gave Brazil to the Portuguese and the rest of the Western Hemisphere to Spain.

In the explorations and conquests of the sixteenth century one of the professed purposes was to spread the gospel. Soon after Columbus's first voyages Queen Isabella was exhorting the colonists to do their duty by the New World natives. Particularly in the Americas, missionary priests found themselves at odds with the explorers and conquistadors when they spoke out against the abuse of native populations. Shortly before Christmas of 1511, the Dominican friar Antonio de Montesinos (d. 1545), preaching in Santo Domingo, in what is now the Dominican Republic, "launched 'with pugnacious and terrible words' into an attack on the conscience of the Spaniards, which he likened to a 'sterile desert' "(Pagden 2001, 66). Montesinos's denunciation was not, in general, favorably received. But among those who did responded was Bartolomé de Las Casas (1474–1566 CE), who took up the cause of the natives and pushed it with vigor until his death in 1566.

Las Casas, however, was only the most visible, and vocal, of the Spanish critics of imperial conquest. Francisco de Vitoria (c. 1492–1546 CE) and Domingo de Soto (1494–1560), the leading moral theologians at Salamanca in the first half of the sixteenth century, rejected the claims of emperor and pope. The Spaniards viewed themselves as following their Dominican precursor, Thomas Aquinas (1225–1274 CE), who himself recognized that the missionary impulse, when backed by the power of the state, could overstep the bounds of "natural justice"(Aquinas 1989, 341–42). Vitoria wrote that neither natural nor human law could confer universal dominion on the emperor, since human beings are free under natural law and there is no human law that can claim legitimacy throughout creation. In theory, God could give dominion to a single authority, as he gave stewardship to Adam in Eden, but in fact, Vitoria argued, it is not the case that any such authority was ever issue or claimed by God.

Not only, for this tradition, did the pope and emperor overstep their authority in claiming dominion, but the conquests carried out on their behalf were manifestly unjust. The background to this judgment rested in the Thomist account of the just war. The indigenous peoples, while more primitive in their technology than the Spanish, had standing institutions of government, marriage, and the like that attested to their human maturity. They could not maintain those institutions if they were not, as Soto would point out, as sound of mind as the average Spaniard. And given the bellicose appearance of the Spaniards, it was not unreasonable for the natives to repel the newcomers. In the end their fears were well founded. Vitoria and Soto concluded not only that the conquest and occupation were unjust, but that in all honesty the king of Spain was liable for the return of goods.

The natural law argument of the Spanish Dominicans set the standard for the analysis of conquest and thus when colonization could be just. At least as important as Las Casas for establishing Thomas's teaching in the New World was Vitoria's student, the Augustinian friar Alonzo de la Vera Cruz (c. 1507–1584), who left Salamanca for Mexico in 1536 and spent the next forty-eight years writing and lobbying for the rights of the indigenous peoples. Franciscans and Jesuits as well maintained, at least in principle, the basic Thomist position. The Royal Orders for New Discoveries, issued in 1573, themselves reflected the Spanish position that "missions contend for the souls of Indians through friendly persuasion rather than . . . minister to alienated peoples conquered by force" (Weber 1992, 95). This spirit continued to animate the mission to Upper California at the end of the eighteenth century.

It was, however, a standard that the European powers studiously managed to avoid. The Dutch lawyer Hugo Grotius (1583–1645 CE) led the way in subverting the Aristotelian and Thomist argument against conquest. Grotius was followed, in English-speaking lands, by John Locke (1632–1704 CE), whose justification for the British usurpation of North America lay in the absence of widespread native agriculture. Locke's indifference to the claims of indigenous peoples was expanded by John Stuart Mill (1806–1873 CE), for whom it was axiomatic that "despotism is a legitimate mode of government in dealing with barbarians, provided the end be their improvement, and the means justified by actually effecting that end" (Mill 1989, 14). It is unclear whether Mill knew that the argument for paternalism had been critically dissected by Vitoria and Soto four hundred years earlier.

Toward Independence

Between the end of the eighteenth century and the independence movements that culminated in the 1960s, colonialism followed in the wake of trade. Missions during this period were perhaps even more conflicted than earlier, often seeing themselves as advocates for native peoples while at the same time dependent on the colonial government. On the one hand, as Roger Aubert puts it, "the work of colonisation and the work of mission, although not totally unrelated, was kept clearly distinct." On the other, missions "allowed themselves to become actively or passively linked with the colonial system, often in compromising fashion" (Aubert 1978, 410).

By the last great period of European conquest, the "scramble for Africa" of the final quarter of the nineteenth century, Catholic and Protestant missions had been at work in the interior of Africa for fifty years. It was only after the middle of the nineteenth century that bringing the gospel to the Africans began to energize the popular imagination. Central to this new interest were the reports, notably by David Livingstone (1813–1873 CE), of the brutality of the slave trade. Livingstone's call for "commerce, Christianity, and civilization" as an antidote to the trade in east and central Africa did much to spur missionary zeal in the English-speaking world. By the end of the nineteenth century the churches were often identified with colonial power, while at the same time they served as advocates for indigenous rights, a complex dynamic captured, in "the tranquil twilight of the colonial period," on the edge of independence, by Roland Oliver (Oliver 1965, viii). Mission remains central to the identity of the church; conquest, and the colonialism it made possible, have generally received the condemnation Vitoria and Soto thought they richly deserved.

G. Scott Davis

See also Latin America: Historical Overview; Latin America: Modern

Further Reading

Aquinas, T. (1989). *Summa theologiae: A concise translation* (T. McDermott, Ed.). Allen, TX: Christian Classics.

Aubert, R. (1978). *The church in a secularized society* (J. Sondheimer, Trans.). London: Darton, Longman & Todd.

Augustine of Hippo. (2001). *Political writings* (R. M. Atkins & R. J. Dodaro, Ed. & Trans.). Cambridge, UK: Cambridge University Press.

Baum, G. (1966). *The teachings of the second Vatican Council*. Westminster, MD: Newman Press.

Bolton, H. E. (1964). *Bolton and the Spanish borderlands* (J. F. Bannon, Ed.). Norman: University of Oklahoma Press.

Boxer, C. R. (1978). *Church militant and Iberian expansion, 1440–1770*. Baltimore: Johns Hopkins University Press.

Canny, N. (Ed.). (1998). *The origins of empire: Oxford history of the British empire* (Vol. 1). Oxford, UK: Oxford University Press.

Dante. (1980). *Inferno* (A. Mandelbaum, Trans.). Berkeley: University of California Press.

Friede, J. & Keen, B. (Eds.). (1971). *Bartolome de Las Casas in history: Toward an understanding of the man and his work*. Carbondale: Southern Illinois University Press.

Ginzburg, C. (1980). *The cheese and the worms: The cosmos of a sixteenth century miller* (J. & A. Tedeschi, Trans.). Baltimore: Johns Hopkins University Press.

Hanke, L. (1949). *The Spanish struggle for justice in the conquest of America*. Philadelphia: University of Pennsylvania Press.

Jolowicz, H. J. (1952). *Historical introduction to the study of Roman law* (2nd ed.). Cambridge, UK: Cambridge University Press.

Kamen, H. (1997). *The Spanish Inquisition: A historical revision*. New Haven, CT: Yale University Press.

Markus, R. A. (1988). *Saeculum: History and society in the theology of St. Augustine* (rev. ed.). Cambridge, UK: Cambridge University Press.

Mill, J. S. (1989). *On liberty and other writings* (S. Collini, Ed.). Cambridge, UK: Cambridge University Press.

Muldoon, J. (1979). *Popes, lawyers, and infidels: The church and the non-Christian world, 1250–1550*. Philadelphia: University of Pennsylvania Press

Murphy, T. P. (Ed.). (1975). *The holy war*. Columbus: Ohio State University Press.

Oliver, R. (1965). *The missionary factor in East Africa* (2nd ed.). London: Longman.

Oliver, R., & Atmore, A. (1967). *Africa since 1800*. Cambridge, UK: Cambridge University Press.

Pagden, A. (1995). *Lords of all the world: Ideologies of empire in Spain, Britain and France, c. 1500–1800* New Haven, CT: Yale University Press

Padgen, A. (2001). *Peoples and empires*. New York: Modern Library.

Pakenham, T. (1991). *The scramble for Africa: The white man's conquest of the dark continent, 1876–1912*. New York: Random House.

Parry, J. H. (1966). *The Spanish seaborne empire*. New York: Alfred A. Knopf.

Riley-Smith, J. (1986). *The first crusade and the idea of crusading*. Philadelphia: University of Pennsylvania Press.

Spence, J. (1984) *The memory palace of Matteo Ricci*. Harmondsworth, UK: Penguin Books.

Tuck, R. (1999). *The rights of war and peace: Political thought and the international order from Grotius to Kant*. Oxford: Oxford University Press.

Vera Cruz, A. de la. (1968). *In defense of the Indians: Their rights* (E. J. Burrus, Ed. & Trans.). Rome: Jesuit Historical Institute.

Vitoria, F. de. (1991). *Political writings* (A. Pagden & J. Lawrance, Eds. & Trans.). Cambridge, UK: Cambridge University Press.
Weber, D. (1992). *The Spanish frontier in North America*. New Haven, CT: Yale University Press.
Williams, R. A. (1990). *The American Indian in Western legal thought: The discourses of conquest*. Oxford, UK: Oxford University Press.

Roman Religions

Roman religions typically are analyzed from two perspectives: (1) Roman religion as religion *in* Rome—that is, the study of generically "religious" beliefs and practices, whether imported from outside the Roman world or born from within it, and their sociological and political effects throughout Rome's history and (2) the evolution of a distinctively "Roman religion" from its earliest origins early in the first millennium BCE through its evolution into the official pagan state religion and manifold distinct civil cults both "official" and "unofficial"; of these only a few would survive, with one of them—Christianity—ultimately dominating.

Given the quality and quantity of historical evidence that fuel such analyses, neither perspective by itself seems adequate; but when they are taken together, one can distill two significant themes upon which to contextualize further inquiry: the role of religion as validative and protective of the state—especially in times of war and civil unrest—and the role of the state as validative and protective of religion. The operation of these two complementary themes is central throughout the history of Rome, through its growth from city to kingdom to republic to empire and finally to Christian capital.

The Early Years

The oldest surviving writings dealing with Roman religion date to the third century BCE. From these and later works, it is known that Romans believed their city to have been founded by Romulus, their first king, in 753 BCE—an endeavor that involved two key activities, both grounded in conflict. The first was his establishment of the city's *pomerium* (sacred boundary), designed and demarcated in accord with the wishes of gods. The desecration of the *pomerium* by Remus, Romulus's twin brother, resulted in Remus's swift death by his brother. The second activity was Romulus's construction of Rome's first temple, dedicated to Jupiter in thanksgiving for Romulus's military victories. The official state religion in coming years would also include the other great gods—Juno, Mars, Minerva, and so forth—most of whom derived from the Greek pantheon and its associated mythological tradition. Manifold subordinate gods would be added over the years, each associated with a specific function, and in general the primary interface between Romans and all their gods was the proper performance of public ritual.

The establishment of Rome's collegiate priestly religious authority by Romulus's successor, Numa (according to tradition), was equally significant to the formation of the complementary relationship between religion as validative and protective of the state and the state as validative and protective of religion. Throughout Rome's transition from kingdom to republic to empire, the very business of government itself—the convening of the senate, city architecture and construction, the planning of wars—depended upon the rituals, analysis, opinion, and advice of priests for validation. At the same time, however, the power to effect decision and action of any kind, including matters of religious policy and often even the performance of the religious rituals themselves, lay with the officers of government—the senators and magistrates. By the third century BCE the colleges would draw their priestly membership from the leading senators of the republic.

The Republic

One reason for this development might have been the appearance of organized cult religions in the early republic, from the fifth through the third centuries BCE. The gods of these cults were either drawn from the traditional Roman pagan tradition and elevated (the Bacchus cult, for example), or they were imported from other civilizations. The cults of the Egyptian goddess Isis and the Jewish god Yahweh are examples, as would be the cults of the Persian god Mithras and Christianity by the time of imperial Rome. Initially, religious pluralism was tolerated (apart from practices deemed "magic" and "witchcraft" by Rome's priestly authority). However, this influx of foreign or otherwise unorthodox religious traditions which continued with Rome's expansion, fueled greatly by the wars of the third and second centuries, eventually began to place a strain on the traditional state religion. For if Rome's growth, fueled largely by war, depended on the pleasure and protection of the gods secured through the advice and rituals of the priestly colleges, then the government had a reciprocal responsibility to protect Rome's state religion. Drawing upon the senate for priestly membership seems a natural product of this attitude, clearly embodied in these words of Cicero:

> Many things, O priests, have been devised and established with divine wisdom by our ancestors; but no action of theirs was ever more wise than their determination that the same men should superintend both what relates to the religious worship due to the immortal gods, and also what concerns the highest interests of the state, so that they might preserve the republic as the most honourable and eminent of the citizens, by governing it well, and as priests by wisely interpreting the requirements of religion. (Yonge 1891, 1)

The Empire

By the time of imperial Rome in the first century BCE, this relationship would become even more acute. During the transition from republic to empire the statesman Julius Caesar was deified after his death (and even while alive, he claimed genealogical lineage to the goddess Venus). His successor and adopted son Octavian, Rome's first emperor, referred to himself as "*divi filius*" (son of god) and took the name "Augustus," meaning "sacred" or "revered." From this point forward emperors would serve as *pontifex maximus*, the head of Roman state religion. For Augustus, previous political crises were the direct result of neglected state religion, and in coming years more attention was paid to the proper regulation of cults and the distinction between valid religion and mere superstition. The complementary themes of religion as protective and validative of the state and the state as protective and validative of religion were closely fused under Augustus through the revitalization of traditional state religion and the regulation and selective proscription of the manifold cults operative in Roman society.

Christianity was one such cult, variously tolerated and proscribed throughout the following centuries. After periods of severe Christian persecution under the emperors Nero in the first century CE and Diocletian at the beginning of the fourth century CE, Roman religion would undergo a marked transformation in 312 CE when the emperor Constantine defeated his rival Maxentius in the Battle of Milvian Bridge. Like Romulus a millennium earlier, Constantine was said to have attributed his military victory to divine providence—only instead of Jupiter, it was the Christian God to whom Constantine owed his debt. It is said that on the eve of battle, Constantine had a dream that inspired him to renounce the gods of Rome and pledge his allegiance, and that of his army, to the Christian god. Victory was granted in return.

The protection and validation of Rome's power were now entrusted to the Christian god, and likewise, the protection and validation of the Christian religion were now entrusted to the Roman government under Constantine as the new *pontifex maximus*. Thus, the operation of the double theme of the Roman state owing its preservation and validity to Roman religion and Roman religion owing its preservation and validity to the Roman state would continue.

Michael Epperson

Further Reading

Beard, M., North, J., & Price, S. (1998). *Religions of Rome*. Cambridge, UK: Cambridge University Press.

Brown, P. (1995). *Authority and the sacred: Aspects of the Christianization of the Roman world*. Cambridge, UK: Cambridge University Press.

Feeney, D. (1988). *Literature and religion at Rome: Cultures, contexts, and beliefs*. Cambridge, UK: Cambridge University Press.

Ferguson, J. (1970). *The religions of the Roman Empire*. Ithaca, NY: Cornell University Press.

Fowler, W. (1971). *The religious experience of the Roman people, from the earliest times to the age of Augustus*. New York: Cooper Square Press.

Grant, R. (1986). *Gods and the one God*. Philadelphia: Westminster Press.

MacMullen, R. (1983). *Paganism in the Roman Empire*. New Haven, CT: Yale University Press.

North, J. A. (1986). Religion and politics, from republic to principate. *Journal of Roman studies, 7*(6), 251–258.

Taylor, L. (1988). *The divinity of the Roman emperor*. Philadelphia: American Philological Association.

Wardman, A. (1985). *Religion and statecraft among the Romans*. Amherst, MA: Prometheus Books.

Yonge, C. D., & London, B. A. (Trans.). (1891). *The orations of Marcus Tullius Cicero*. London: George Bell & Sons.

S

Shiʿite Rebellion of 815–819

Disagreements regarding the leadership of the *umma* (community of Muslim believers) began almost immediately after the Prophet Muhammad's (c. 570–632 CE) death in 632 CE and have divided the Islamic world throughout its subsequent history. While the majority of the early Muslims held that the leader, or caliph, should be chosen by a representative sampling of the community based on merit, some believed that only descendants of the Prophet—through his son-in-law ʿAli ibn Abi Talib (c. 600–661)—were divinely sanctioned to lead the *umma*. This minority group became known as Shiʿites (those of the party of ʿAli). In the tumultuous years following the Fourth Civil War (809–813) of the Islamic Empire, simmering Shiʿite frustrations erupted in a rebellion that spread to the most influential cities in the empire—Basra, Al-Kufa, Mecca, and Medina. These rebellions, occurring between the years 815 and 819, demonstrated the dissatisfaction of Shiʿites with the leadership of the Abbasids (750–1258), the second dynasty of the Islamic Empire, and were emblematic of the continual struggle to determine who was most qualified to lead the Muslim people.

The Abbasids

Named for al-ʿAbbas ibn ʿAbd al-Muttalib (566–c. 653), an uncle of the Prophet from whom they descended, the ʿAbbasids came to power after the Third Civil War (744–750), ostensibly as champions of Islamic justice against the perceived sensuality and corruption of the previous rulers, the Umayyads (661–750). Because the ʿAbbasids descended from someone closely related to the Prophet, the Shiʿites viewed their cause as a return to rightful leadership and supported them in the civil war. Once in power, however, the ʿAbbasids abandoned the interests of the Shiʿites, appointing only ʿAbbasids to positions of power. To avoid a scramble for power between his sons, the fifth ʿAbbasid caliph, Harun ar-Rashid (763 or 766–809), divided the empire between them: Muhammad al-Amin (787–813) would be caliph, while ʿAbd Allah al-Maʿmun (786–833) would rule Khurasan and the eastern provinces with full autonomy until becoming caliph upon al-Amin's death. When al-Amin appointed his son, rather than al-Maʿmun, as his successor in 810, however, the Fourth Civil War (811–813) resulted. Baghdad fell in 813, and al-Amin was beheaded. Al-Maʿmun was declared caliph but chose to stay in Khurasan and to allow one of his ministers, al-Hasan ibn Sahl, to govern in Baghdad in his stead. At its height, under the fifth Abbasid caliph, Harun ar-Rashid (763 or 766–809), the ʿAbbasid empire stretched from the Mediterranean coast of North Africa, beginning in what is now Algeria, encompassed the entire Arabian Peninsula, and ended in Khurasan. To avoid a scramble for power between his sons, ar-Rashid divided the impressive empire between them: Muhammad al-Amin (787–813) would be caliph, while ʿAbd Allah al-Maʾmun (786–833) would rule Khurasan and the eastern provinces with full autonomy until becoming caliph upon al-Amin's death. "after the sentence," Once in power, however, the ʿAbbasids abandoned the interests of the Shiʿites, appointing only ʿAbbasids to positions of power.

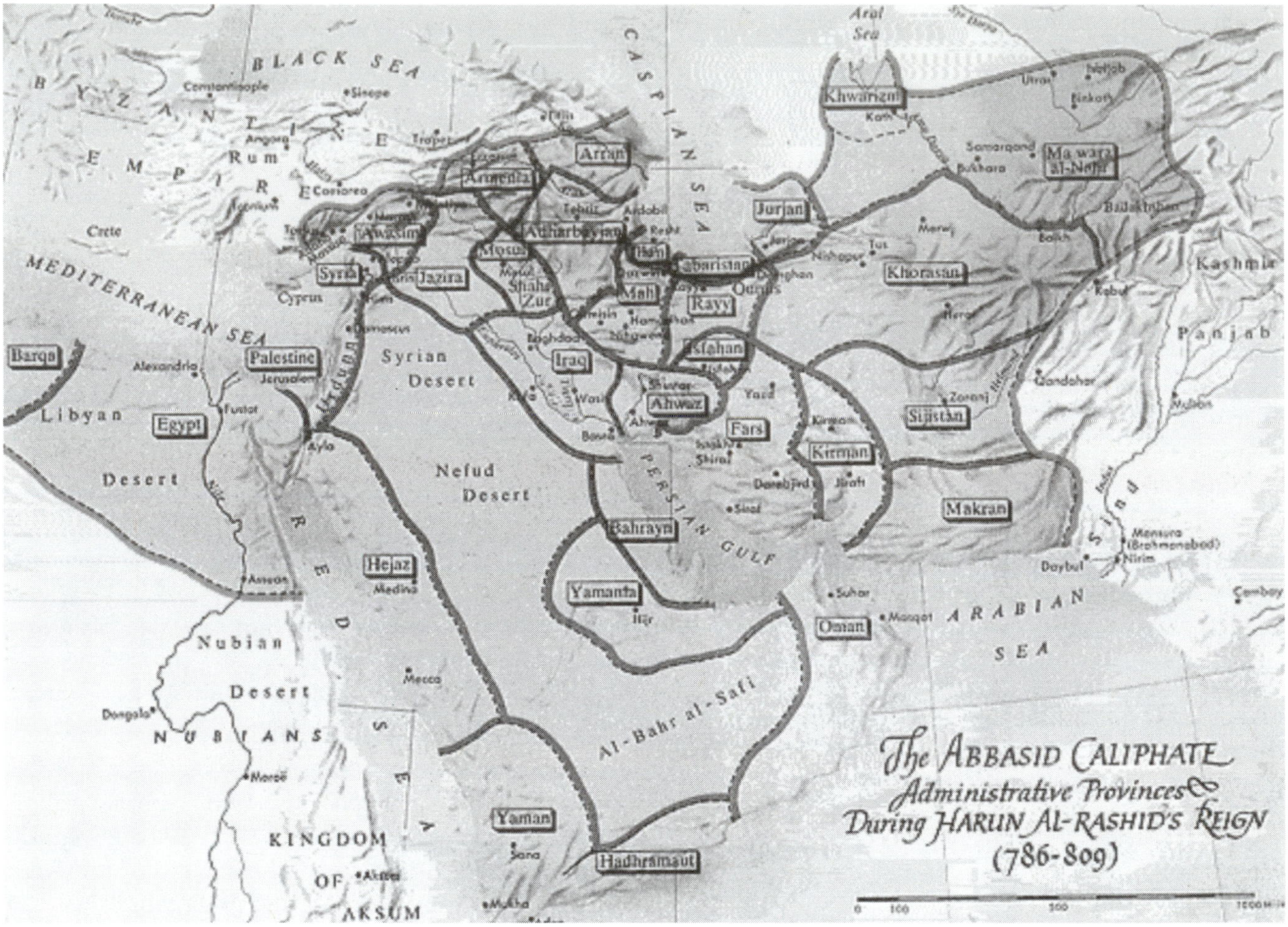

The Abbasid Caliphate Administrative Provinces. From the "Historical Atlas of the Muslim Peoples" compiled by Roelog Roolvnik, Amsterdam, Djambatan 1957.

The Kufan Revolt

The lack of centralized authority engendered by the civil war presented itself to opposition groups as an opportunity to seize power. Abu ʿl-Saraya (d. October 815), a former army commander, sent out a call to arms to Shiʿites in Al-Kufa, a city about eighty miles south of Baghdad, in January of 815, with the support of a religious figure known as Muhammed ibn Tabataba (d. 15 February 815). Al-Hasan ibn Sahl dispatched a veteran general to quell the fledgling uprising. Although few in number and poorly armed, the rebel forces defeated Sahl's troops on 14 February 815. In the midst of the celebrations the following day, however, Ibn Tabataba died. Abu ʿl-Saraya replaced him with a young, inexperienced man, and thus retained the real power. Hoping to spread the rebellion to other parts of the empire, he sent envoys to Basra, Mecca, and Medina who met with surprising success. Unable to suppress the rebellion, Sahl turned to his rival, the Khurasanian general Harthama ibn Aʿyan, in March 815. Harthama defeated Abu ʿl-Saraya and had him beheaded on 18 October 815. The rebel leader's head was sent to al-Maʾmun in Marv (Merv), but his corpse was sent to Baghdad to be cloven in half and hung at each end of a bridge over the Tigris River as a warning.

The Rebellion Spreads

Despite the defeat of Abu ʿl-Saraya, Shiʿite control spread to other cities and regions under the leadership of his commanders. In Basra in February 815, Zayd ibn Musa—later known as Zayd al-Nar (the Firebrand)—zealously attacked the ʿAbbasids, burning many of them alive in their homes. Shortly after Harthama defeated Abu ʿl-Saraya in October of 815, however, he recaptured Basra and sent Zayd al-Nar to Merv. Several months later, in June 816, Zayd al-Nar escaped and led another rebellion, with Abu ʿl-Saraya's brother Abu Abdallah, just west of Baghdad. They were soon captured.

Meanwhile, Abu ʿl-Saraya's forces in western Arabia easily took the cities of Mina, a city on the Arabian Peninsula about 3 miles southeast of Mecca, and ʿArafat, a city about 9 miles southeast of Mecca. As the rebels neared Mecca and Medina, the governor of the cities fled, and Ibrahim ibn Musa entered Medina without resistance while Husayn al-Aftas took control of Mecca. Al-Aftas declared Muhammad ibn Jaʿfar, a well-respected ʿAlid (descendant of ʿAli) who was popular with the Meccans, caliph on 13 November 815. In February 816, the ʿAbbasid general Hamdawayh recaptured Mecca and Medina. Muhammad ibn Jaʿfar escaped but later surrendered on 19 July 816, when he returned to Mecca to formally divest himself of power.

Ibrahim ibn Musa, a brother of Zayd al-Nar, extended Shiʿite control into Yemen in October 815, earning the nickname al-Jazzar, "the Butcher," after killing large numbers of ʿAbbasids and taking power with bloodthirsty enthusiasm. Hamdawayh suppressed this revolt after recapturing Mecca.

Al-Maʾmun's Pro-Shiʿite Policy and Its Repercussions

In an attempt to conciliate his Shiʿite subjects, al-Maʾmun briefly embarked upon a pro-Shiʿite policy. He appointed ʿAli ibn Musa (765–818), the brother of two of the ʿAlid rebel leaders, as his successor in March 817, calling him ʿAli ar-Rida (the Chosen One; c. 768–818). He installed another of the brothers, al-ʿAbbas ibn Musa, as governor in Al-Kufa in October 817.

The ʿAbbasid aristocracy in Baghdad reacted violently to these concessions to the Shiʿites. They deposed al-Maʾmun and proclaimed one of his uncles, Ibrahim ibn al-Mahdi, caliph on 20 July 817. Al-Mahdi sent forces who ousted al-'Abbas in November 817. Early in 818, Abu ʿl-Saraya's brother rebelled in Al-Kufa, but he was killed in battle by al-Mahdi's army.

When al-Maʾmun learned of the ʿAbbasid revolt in Baghdad, he decided to return and to restore the city as the administrative capital of the empire. On the journey to Baghdad, ʿAli ar-Rida died in September 818. Shiʿite tradition maintains that he was poisoned by al-Maʾmun. Al-Maʾmun entered Baghdad in August 819, consolidated his power, and abandoned his efforts to appease the Shiʿites.

Although the rebellion ultimately failed, its impressive initial successes, wresting much of southern Iraq and western Arabia from the ʿAbbasid caliphate at the height of its power, demonstrated the depth of Shiʿite convictions, which lie at the historical root of the Shiʿite movement that continues to thrive today.

Elisabeth Markese

Further Reading

Amoretti, B. S. (1960). Ibn Tabataba. In H. A. R. Gibb, J. H. Kramers, E. Levi-Provencal, J. Schacht, B. Lewis, & C. Pellat, C. (Eds.), *The encyclopedia of Islam* (Vol. 1, pp 950–951). London: Luzac and Company.

Arjomand, S. A. (1984). *The shadow of God and the hidden imam: Religion, political order, and societal change in Shiʿite Iran from the beginning to 1890*. Chicago: University of Chicago Press.

Black, A. (2001). *The history of Islamic political thought: From the prophet to the present*. Edinburgh, UK: Edinburgh University Press.

Bosworth, C. E. (Trans. and Ed.). (1987). *The history of al-Tabari: Vol. 32. The reunification of the ʿAbbasid Caliphate*. Albany, NY: State University of New York Press.

Donaldson, D. (1984). *The Shiʿite religion: A history of Islam in Persia and Irak*. New York: Luzac and Company.

Donner, F. M. (1981). *The early Islamic conquests*. Princeton, NJ: Princeton University Press.

Frye, R. N. (1975). The Abbasid caliphate in Iran. In R. N. Frye (Ed.), *The Cambridge history of Iran: Vol. 4. The Period from the Arab invasion to the Saljuqs* (pp. 57–89). New York: Cambridge University Press.

Hodgson, G. S. (1974). *The venture of Islam: Conscience and history in a world civilization: Vol. 1. The classical age of Islam*. Chicago: University of Chicago Press.

Jafri, S. (2000). *The origins and early development of Shiʿa Islam*. New York: Oxford University Press.

Kennedy, H. (1981). *The early ʿAbbasid caliphate: A political history*. Totowa, NJ: Barnes and Noble Books.

Kennedy, H. (1986). *The prophet and the age of the caliphates: The Islamic Near East from the sixth to the eleventh century*. New York: Longman.

King, D. A. (1991). Makka. In C. E. Bosworth, E. Van Donzel, B. Lewis, & C. Pellat (Eds.), *The encyclopedia of Islam* (Vol. 6, pp. 144–187). Leiden: E. J. Brill.

Lewis, B. (1960). Abbasids. In H. A. B. Gibb, J. H. Kramers, E. Levi-Provencal, J. Schacht, B. Lewis, & C. Pellat (Eds.), *The encyclopedia of Islam* (Vol. 1, pp. 15–23). London: Luzac and Company.

Lewis, B. (1960). Ali al-Rida. In H. A. B. Gibb, J. H. Kramers, E. Levi-Provencal, J. Schacht, B. Lewis, & C. Pellat (Eds.), *The encyclopedia of Islam* (Vol. 1). London: Luzac and Company.

Lewis, B. (1960). Alids. In H. A. B. Gibb, J. H. Kramers, E. Levi-Provencal, J. Schacht, B. Lewis, & C. Pellat (Eds.), *The encyclopedia of Islam* (Vol. 1). London: Luzac and Company.

Sourdel, D. (1970). The ʿAbbasid Caliphate. In P. M. Holt, A. K. S. Lambton, & B. Lewis (Eds.), *The Cambridge history of Islam: Vol. 1. The central Islamic lands.* New York: Cambridge University Press.

Shinto, Ancient

Shinto (lit. "Way of the Gods") comprises in its broadest sense a variety of beliefs in Japanese indigenous deities *(kami)*. *Kami* range from powerful nature and ancestor deities to spirits of insignificant objects, and are virtually infinite in number. Beliefs and forms of worship are equally heterogeneous, but are often directed at objects of nature such as trees, rocks, or rivers. To many foreign observers, Shinto has therefore appeared as a particularly gentle, peaceful religion. Nevertheless, Shinto has played a crucial role in building up a Japanese nationalistic ideology, the so-called State Shinto, in the nineteenth and twentieth centuries. State Shinto prepared the ground for Japan's aggressive imperialist policies on the Asian continent and in the neighboring Pacific regions, culminating in the Pacific War (1941–1945). This article discusses some recurrent motives or possible forerunners of belligerent Shinto nationalism that can be found in what we know about Shinto in the premodern history of Japan.

Mythology

According to the earliest Japanese chronicles, *Kojiki* ("Records of Ancient Matters," written in 712 CE) and *Nihon shoki* ("Chronicles of Japan," 720 CE), heaven and earth were originally inhabited by distinct deities until the deities from heaven sent down a representative to become a new ruler on earth. This was Ninigi, the grandson of the (female) sun deity Amaterasu and who became at the same time the ancestor of the imperial clan of the Japanese Tenno ("heavenly ruler"). Together with Ninigi, several other ancestor deities of aristocratic court clans descended from heaven. Today there is a general consensus that these mythical accounts reflect the early subjugation of indigenous inhabitants (the "earthly deities") by a particular ethnic group ("heavenly deities"), which certainly did not occur without violent conflicts. The chronicles, however, tend to avoid images of warlike battles in this context. Also in later ritual texts *(norito)*, read at important ceremonies at the imperial court, Ninigi's enterprise is euphemistically portrayed as turning a land of "unruly deities" into "a land of peace" *(yasukuni)*. Drastic violence is clearly taboo in the depiction of the first Japanese "imperialist" conquest.

There are many further reports of warfare in *Kojiki* and *Nihon shiki*, which tend to become more realistic the closer they approach the times of their authors. However, in most cases, such as the famous "conquest of the East" (alleged date 667–661 BCE) led by Jimmu Tenno, or the campaign against the Korean kingdom of Silla (alleged date 200 CE) by Empress Jingu, military success is attributed to divine aid rather than to military supremacy. This indicates that there are no moral objections against warfare as such by the *kami*. Moreover, in later times these mythical or semimythical battles served as models for legitimate warfare.

Kamikaze

The word "kamikaze" has earned a sad reputation in the West because the Japanese used it for their suicide bomber planes in the Pacific War. Translated as "divine wind," the expression clearly bears religious connotations that are rooted in a famous historical precedent. In 1274 and 1281 CE the Mongols who had successfully conquered China and Korea set out to attack Japan as well, but failed in both cases. Each time typhoons are said to have destroyed their huge fleets. In Japan, military defense was at that time accompanied by substantial religious activities all over the country. Consequently the eventual defeat of the Mongols was seen as the result of divine protection. While Buddhist temples and Shinto shrines both engaged in ritual activities, the favorable typhoons were attributed to the native *kami*, rather than to the foreign Buddhas, and were called *kamikaze*—winds of the *kami*. This notion is to be seen in close connection to the idea that Japan is a "land of the gods," i.e., a land blessed by the native *kami*. Naturally, this idea prospered significantly after the Mongols had been defeated by the *kami* winds.

Is There a God of War in Shinto?

It would be a mistake, however, to construct a dichotomy between pacifist Japanese Buddhism and militarist Japanese Shinto from this example. The complexity of the religious situation at the time of the Mongol attacks is evidenced, for instance, by the fact that one of the most prominent religious activists at that time was the eminent Buddhist monk Eison (1201–1290 CE), who performed rituals for Buddhist and native deities alike. Among the *kami*, he addressed in particular Hachiman, still one of the most popular deities in Japan. Hachiman epitomizes the merger of Buddhist and native beliefs common at that time. He was depicted as a *kami* who had taken Buddhist vows and was thus called a Bodhisattva, indicating that he had attained Buddhist enlightenment. At the same time he was regarded as the son of the belligerent Empress Jingu, mentioned above, and thus figured as a kind of ancestor deity for many samurai clans of the country. To early Western observers, Hachiman therefore appeared comparable to the war god of ancient Rome and they called him the "Japanese Mars," an image still reflected in Western secondary sources on Japan. In fact, however, Hachiman is rather a god of the warriors than a god of war, and does not carry particularly violent connotations. The Japanese samurai, on the other hand, found models of warrior virtues in Buddhist ethics rather than in Shinto.

Shinto and National Cult

In contrast to universalistic religions such as Buddhism or Christianity, Shinto did not produce a body of doctrines or an ethical code, let alone a pacifist commandment. Rightful behavior according to Shinto is rather guided by ritual avoidance (taboo regulations) than by the quest for the morally good. This implies that one cannot find explicit statements in favor of or against war. There is, however, a long historical relationship between the belief in the *kami* and the Japanese Tenno, which ranges from ancient mythology to the various religious duties of the Tenno, some of which are still performed according to ancient precedents. It is almost impossible to imagine a nationalist ideology in Japan that would not make use of this rich legacy of politicoreligious traditions. On the other hand, if we take a careful look at these traditions, we actually find a great deal of ambiguity concerning war or violence, as shown in the examples above. Clearly, the *kami* were always considered a crucial factor in warfare, but there were never religious wars in the name of Shinto in premodern times. Also, premodern Japanese never conceived of themselves as the means of destructive *kami* power as the suicide bombers did (at least if we take the modern kamikaze literally). Moreover, there always were and still exist beliefs in the *kami* that are independent from Tennoism and a national cult. Thus, ancient Shinto traditions certainly contributed to modern nationalist propaganda, but do not provide a sufficient explanation for the emergence of modern Japanese State Shinto.

Bernhard Scheid

Further Reading

Breen, J., & Teeuwen, M. (Eds.). (2000). *Shinto in history: Ways of the kami*. London: Curzon Press.

Guth, C. (1985). *Shinzo: Hachiman imagery and its development*. Cambridge, MA: Harvard University Press.

Kojiki (D. L. Philippi, Trans.). (1968). Tokyo: University of Tokyo Press.

Kuroda T. (1981). Shinto in the history of Japanese religion (J. Dobbins & S. Gay, Trans.). *Journal of Japanese Studies 7*(1), 1–21.

Kuroda T. (1996). The discourse on the land of the kami *(Shinkoku)* in medieval Japan: National consciousness and international awareness (F. Rambelli, Trans.). *Japanese Journal of Religious Studies 23*(3–4), 353–386. (Original work published 1994)

Naumann, N. (1996). *Die mythen des alten Japan* (Myths of ancient Japan). Munich, Germany: C. H. Beck Verlag.

Nihongi. (1998). *Chronicles of Japan from the earliest times to A.D. 697* (W. G. Aston, Trans.). Tokyo: Tuttle. (Original work published 1896)

Norito. (1969). *A new translation of ancient Japanese ritual prayers* (D. L. Philippi, Trans.). Tokyo: University of Tokyo Press.

Rambelli, F. (1996). Religion, ideology of domination, and nationalism: Kuroda Toshio on the discourse of *Shinkoku*. *Japanese Journal of Religious Studies 23*(3–4), 387–426.

Teeuwen, M., & Scheid, B. (Eds.). (2002). Tracing Shinto in the history of kami worship (special issue on Shinto studies). *Japanese Journal of Religious Studies 29*(3–4).

Shinto, Modern

Of all the world's religious traditions, only a very few evoke a direct connection with and responsibility for the disaster of war. Shinto, Japan's oldest religion, is one of those traditions. Attributing Japanese aggression in World War II to a kind of religiously inspired nationalism is commonly taught around the world. How else are we to explain what appears to be a fanatical devotion to an emperor, a military campaign based on racial superiority and divine destiny, and a willingness to end one's life in battlefield charges or kamikaze attacks? As in any stereotype, a certain element of truth can be found in the claim of Shinto's responsibility for the war, but it will be the task of this short discussion to provide a clearer understanding of Shinto's role and influences upon Japan's recent militaristic past.

Beginnings in the Meiji Era

What we today call "Shinto" is largely an invented tradition, born out of political expediency during the first years of the Meiji era (1868–1912 CE). Of course, the idea of supernatural deities *(kami)* interacting with human societies and endeavors is a very ancient one in Japan, with similar beliefs holding sway in Korea and China as well. This tradition of venerating deities in order to ensure a bountiful harvest, many children, good health, or a peaceful kingdom has been central to all forms of political authority throughout Japanese social history—from emperors to warlords to local village chiefs to the heads of households. While there were certain continuities—in ritual practices and in the powers of popular deities—*kami* veneration can be characterized more accurately by its regional, economic, occupational, and political diversity.

After the Meiji revolution in 1868 ended Japan's feudal period, the government began crafting these diverse practices into an ideology of service to the developing state. Precedents for this kind of move came from the powerful industrialized nations and their use of Christianity as the spiritual engine propelling colonization throughout the world. In Japan, shrines venerating deities such as Hachiman, known for his powers in archery and war, were drawn into a system of symbols, new interpretations, and reconfigured meanings that now extolled the revitalized institution of the emperor and the cultural and civic identity of people as specifically "Japanese." To this day, most Japanese have little understanding of the abstract term "Shinto." Instead, their interaction with this tradition comes through rituals and festivals at shrines large and small, with a focus on educational or occupational success, family stability, land and economic productivity, and prosperity of all kinds.

In 1871, shrines were designated as sites for the performance of state ritual, with the catchphrase "reverence for the deities and respect for ancestors" *(keishin sûso)* intended to form a bond between the citizenry and the state. This led to long-lasting tensions between shrines stressing religious themes and those aligning themselves with the state emphasizing nonreligious or civic themes of patriotism, duty, and national destiny. The cult of the emperor was steadily gaining greater awareness and prominence among ordinary Japanese, but after the failure of the short-lived Department of Divinity (Jingikan, 1868–1871) there was no governmental bureau in charge of coordinating and systematizing the nation's more than 193,000 shrines until the establishment of the Bureau of Shrines (Jinjyakyoku) in 1900.

The Russo-Japanese War of 1904–1905 added new impetus to better coordinating the role shrines and Shinto would play in the nation's colonizing agendas. Already established (1869) and functioning was Tokyo's Yasukuni shrine, devoted to commemorating the nation's war dead. After the 13,619 spirits of the military dead of the Russo-Japanese War were enshrined, a new funding scheme passed in the diet that, for the first time, created from prefectural budgets a stable source of income for many government-affiliated shrines. The government also eliminated 83,000 civic shrines during its disruptive merger campaign (1905–1929) to have only one shrine per village. The death of the Meiji emperor and subsequent enthronement of his son, both occurring in 1912, provided an additional opportunity to establish "the most profound linkage between shrines and the imperial court and the state . . . (a linkage that) must be impressed upon people far and wide," according to Home Minister Oura Kanetake (Sakamoto 2000, 277).

Developments Related to the Two World Wars

Japan's entry into World War I in 1914, primarily to seize German territories in Asia, was announced to deities at major shrines all over the nation by emissaries from the imperial palace. Local shrines as well held notification rituals, and priests were called on to help raise "martial spirit." Although Japan's expansionistic agendas were checked by other colonial powers in the region, Japan had already invaded and colonized Korea in 1910, followed after the war by Manchuria in 1931. In both cases, shrines were established and local populations forced to pay homage at these outposts of state and imperial authority.

Domestically, Japan's new colonies and continuing military successes had stoked patriotic fever among the population, which could always be expressed at a local shrine. Elementary children made periodic visits to shrines, and after the Manchurian invasion it became common to pray for victory at these same institutions. It's important to note here that support for Japan's military expansion and state authority extended to all mainstream Buddhist and even Christian institutions, with many clergy from the former ministering to troops overseas. Thus, it is less than accurate to use the term "State Shinto" as a blanket category for the ups and downs of government policy as well as the variety of other religious institutions serving as intermediaries in the government's war propaganda effort.

By 1937, the state's use of Shinto was reaching its apex. Nearly forty years of persistent efforts to link the state, the emperor, and the nation's shrines and deities provided an ideological map for Japan's aggressive military expansion and led to such horrors as Nanking, Bataan, Unit 731's biological experimentation on prisoners of war, kamikaze and other suicide attacks, and a refusal to surrender, which resulted in the 1945 firebombing of Tokyo (110,000 killed) and the atomic bombs on Hiroshima and Nagasaki (140,000 and 75,000 killed, respectively).

Despite this association with war, the allied occupation forces recognized in a policy statement in 1945 that "the spiritual strength of the Shinto faith properly directed need not be dangerous" (Dower 1999, 283). After Japan's crushing defeat and unconditional surrender, shrines were neither disbanded nor their priests arrested; instead, the government was chastised for having appropriated and perverted for its own ends this venerable tradition. The word "Shinto" may never be able to evoke the pre-Meiji origins and religious diversity of this tradition. But for the majority of Japanese people, as long as there are shrines, *kami*, and festivals honoring those deities, the practices of acknowledging and petitioning the *kami* will continue to have relevance to their cultural identity as Japanese.

John K. Nelson

Further Reading

Antoni, K. (1988). Yasukuni-Jinja and folk religion: The problem of vengeful spirits. *Asian Folklore Studies 47*, 123–136.

Bix, H. (2000). *Hirohito and the making of modern Japan*. New York: HarperCollins.

Breen, J., & Teeuwen, M. (2001). *Shinto in history: Ways of the kami*. Honolulu: University of Hawaii Press.

Buruma, I. (1994). *The wages of guilt: Memories of war in Germany and Japan*. New York: Farrar, Straus & Giroux.

Creemers, W. (1968). *Shrine Shinto after World War II*. Leiden, Netherlands: E. J. Brill.

Dower, J. (1999). *Embracing defeat: Japan in the wake of World War II*. New York: W. W. Norton & Co.

Field, N. (1991). *In the realm of a dying emperor: Japan at century's end*. New York: Pantheon Books

Hammond, E. (1995). Politics of the war and public history: Japan's own museum controversy. *Bulletin of Concerned Asian Scholars 27*(2), 56–60.

Hardacre, H. (1989). *Shinto and the state: 1868–1988*. Princeton, NJ: Princeton University Press.

Iwai, T. (Ed.). (1988). *Kindai Nihon shakai to tennosei* (Modern Japanese society and the emperor system). Tokyo: Kashiwa Shobo.

Nelson, J. (2000). *Enduring identities: The guise of Shinto in contemporary Japan*. Honolulu: University of Hawaii Press.

O'Brien, D. (1996). *To dream of dreams: Religious freedom and constitutional politics in postwar Japan*. Honolulu: University of Hawaii Press.

Sakamoto, K. (2000). The structure of state Shinto. In J. Breen & M. Teeuwen (Eds.), *Shinto in history: Ways of the kami* (pp. 272–294). Honolulu: University of Hawaii Press.

Tsubouchi, Y. (1999). *Yasukuni*. Tokyo: Shinchosha.

Sikhism

Recognizing only the one God, Sikhism preaches equality of sex, religion, and race. It firmly rejects the rituals of worship used in other faiths, prohibits the use of intoxicants (tobacco, alcohol), and sets strong moral and family values as a goal toward spiritual salvation. Sikhs believe in the Ten Gurus (spiritual leaders) and the Guru Granth Sahib (scriptures), and respect the Khalsa (pure) ideal.

Guru Nanak

Sikhism developed in the Punjab region of India when Guru Nanak (1469–c. 1539) first began teaching a faith quite different from the prevailing religions of Hinduism and Islam. Preaching the worship of one God and criticizing the blind rituals of Hindus and Muslims, Guru Nanak was the first of ten living gurus who developed Sikhism over the next 239 years (1469–1708). Born into an orthodox Hindu family on 15 April 1469, Guru Nanak received his initial education in Sanskrit

Changing Sikh Views on War

No one is my enemy
No one is a foreigner
With all I am at peace
God within us renders us
Incapable of hate and prejudice.
—Guru Nanak (1469–1534), the first Sikh Guru

When all efforts to restore peace prove
useless and no words avail,
Lawful is the flash of steel,
It is right to draw the sword.
—Guru Gobind Singh (1666–1708), the tenth and last Guru

from the local pandit (teacher of traditional learning) before going on to be educated in Persian and Arabic at the Talwandi Muslim School. Between the ages of thirty and fifty Guru Nanak undertook a series of reflective journeys both inside and outside his native India. Traveling as far as Tibet and Sri Lanka, he visited the important religious centers of both Hindus and Muslims. He spent this period (1500–1521) as a wandering teacher, debating with followers of the many religious sects and cults in India at that time. Debating not only religion but politics and society in general, he was a reformer who spoke out and acted against the caste system. In his fifties Guru Nanak finally settled at Kartarpur on the banks of the river Ravi, devoting the remainder of his life to teaching his beliefs to all those who visited Kartarpur. The followers of Guru Nanak became known as Sikhs from the Sanskrit *shishya*, or disciple.

The Ten Gurus

Guru Nanak, born in Talwandi in 1469, was the founder of the Sikh religion and first Guru until his death in 1539. Guru Angad (1504–1552) developed the idea of a free kitchen as a means of breaking the caste barriers and freeing Sikhism from social taboos. He was followed by Guru Amar Das (1479–1574), who trained traveling missionaries to extend the message of Sikhism throughout India. Guru Ram Das (1534–1581) established a new township called Ramdaspur (later Amritsar) on land purchased from local landowners. Guru Arjan (1563–1606) continued to develop Amritsar as an industrial center and was responsible for the laying of the foundations of the Golden Temple (a Sikh religious site). Guru Arjan, who was tortured and killed for his faith by the emperor Jahangir (1569–1627), became the first Sikh martyr. It was not until the sixth Guru, Guru Hargobind (1595–1644), that steps were taken to militarize the Sikh community as a means of preserving their faith in the face of opposition. Guru Har Rai (1630–1661) promoted self-discipline and meditation. He was followed by Guru Hari Krishen (1656–1664), who became Guru at the age of five. Known as the Child Guru, he died from cholera while giving comfort to other sick children. After fighting a number of battles (Amritsar 1634, Lehra 1637, Kartarpur 1638) in defense of their faith, the Sikhs coexisted in relative peace until 1675, when the ninth Guru, Guru Tegh Bahadur (c. 1621–1675), was executed by the Mughal Emperor Aurangzeb ('Alamgir; 1618–1707), after Guru Tegh Bahadur's refusal to accept the Islamic faith. In 1699 the Khalsa was created by the tenth and last personal Guru, Guru Gobind Singh (1666–1708), as a military group of men and women with the intention that the Sikhs should forever be able to defend their faith. Also established under Gobind Singh, the rite of initiation *(Khandey di Pahul)* and the five K's (symbols worn by members of the Khalsa) give Sikhs their unique appearance and culture.

Banda Singh Bahadur (1670–1716) was the first military leader of the Sikhs to follow the Gurus. He led a successful campaign against the Mughals until his capture and execution in 1716. The eighteenth century continued as a period of continual conflict with the

Mughal emperors as the Sikhs gained more territory at the expense of the Indian Mughals. In 1801 Ranjit Singh (1780–1839) established the Punjab as an independent state with a Sikh minority population. It was after Ranjit Singh's death in 1839, when internal leadership battles weakened the Sikh forces, that the British defeated the Sikh armies in 1845–1846 and the rule of the British Empire was established over the Sikh territories. The Sikhs coexisted amiably with their British rulers until the Amritsar massacre in 1919. In April of that year British troops commanded by General Reginald E. H. Dyer (1864–1927) opened fire without warning on 10,000 people who were holding a protest meeting. The troops killed 379 and wounded 1,000. The British retired General Dyer but appeared to countenance his actions by first promoting him. The Amritsar massacre gave enormous moral strength to the growing movement for Indian independence and is recognized as the single event that began the decline of the British Empire in India.

Partition

In 1947 British India was partitioned along religious lines as an integral part of independence, in the process creating the secular but largely Hindu state of India and the Islamic state of Pakistan. The frontier between India and Pakistan ran through the Sikh homeland of the Punjab. Unable to press their claim for a separate Punjab in the face of Pakistan aggression, the Sikhs chose to join India, establishing themselves in the Indian section of the Punjab. However, this came only after an extended period of religious conflict and communal massacres as millions of Sikhs, Hindus, and Muslims tried to cross the border to the country of their choice, resulting in the Sikhs losing much of their land and privileges. The Sikh determination to create a separate state was always close to the surface, creating friction with an Indian government that was not prepared to concede any territorial rights. The government held firm to the ideal that India was created as a secular state and it would be inappropriate to set a precedent by allowing the Sikhs to create a separate state based primarily on religious grounds. It was felt that to give in to their demands would open the floodgates to the numerous religious groups and cults in India. Undaunted, the Sikhs continued to press their demand and in 1966 India divided the Punjab into three, in the process creating a subnational state with a Sikh majority. Unfortunately, Sikh anger at the boundaries of their new state continued to create friction with the central government.

Golden Temple, Amritsar, India. August 1996. Courtesy Steve Donaldson.

The Golden Temple

As Sikh discontent grew in the 1970s and 1980s the focus of conflict changed from political to religious confrontation between Hindus and Sikhs, often breaking out into large-scale violence with large numbers of dead on both sides. The matter came to a head in 1984 with the invasion of the Golden Temple at Amritsar. The Golden Temple (also known as Harmandir Sahib or "God's Temple") was completed in 1604 and is the most significant religious center for Sikhs. Although it is the inspirational and historical center for Sikhism and the most revered site in the Sikh world, in keeping with the teachings of Guru Nanak it is not a mandatory place of pilgrimage or worship. In 1983 militant Sikhs took refuge in the Golden Temple complex at Amritsar. Under the belief that the temple was being used as a militant command post, an armory, and a sanctuary for criminals, the Indian government issued instructions for the Indian army to attack the temple. The resulting battle (Operation Bluestar), in June 1984, in which the Indian army used tanks and helicopters to attack the Golden Temple, killed many of those inside and seriously damaged the buildings. The attack had far-reaching repercussions for India and for the Sikhs. The desecration of their holiest site infuriated even the most conservative Sikhs and their anger was directed at Indian Prime Minister Indira Gandhi (1917–1984). In October 1984 Indira Gandhi was assassinated by two of her Sikh bodyguards while Sikh soldiers in the Indian army mutinied. Several days of anti-Sikh rioting followed the assassination with the official figures of Sikh dead put at 2,700. However, death tolls as high as 17,000 were put forward by newspapers and human-rights groups and those who carried out the atrocities went unpunished. Ever since, militant Sikhs have responded to this massacre by killing members of the Hindu community and political leaders who oppose the rights of Sikhs to religious freedom and political self-determination.

Guru Granth Sahib

Before he died in 1708, the tenth Guru, Guru Gobind Singh, ordained that the teachings compiled by him and earlier Gurus, called the Guru Granth Sahib, should be adhered to and should be recognized as the Guru. He felt that all the wisdom needed by Sikhs for spiritual guidance in their daily lives could now be found in the Guru Granth Sahib. Although the Guru Granth Sahib is accorded the status of being the spiritual head of the Sikh religion, it also contains the writings of saints of other faiths whose ideals were considered compatible with those of the Sikh Gurus. The Guru Granth Sahib is written mainly in Panjabi. It is in the form of poetry and the scriptures are intended to be sung. The Guru Granth Sahib is not worshiped for itself but is revered for the spiritual content contained within—the Granth Sahib is merely the physical manifestation of the scriptures.

The Gurdwara

The Gurdwara is the place where Sikhs come together for congregational worship. Translated from Punjabi, Gurdwara means "the residence of the Guru." Any place that contains a copy of the Guru Granth Sahib is considered equally holy for Sikhs. The first Gurdwara was built at Kartarpur in 1521–1522 by Guru Nanak. Sikhs worship the one God, who is regarded as without physical form; therefore the Gurdwara contains no statues, idols, religious pictures, candles, bells, or other ritualistic trappings. Priests were abolished by Guru Gobind Singh, as he felt that they had become corrupt and full of false pride. Any Sikh is free to read the Guru Granth Sahib in the Gurdwara or in their home. The only appointed position is that of the custodian of the Guru Granth Sahib (known as the Granthi), who organizes daily services. The Gurdwara serves many purposes in the Sikh faith. It is a place to learn spiritual wisdom, a place where Sikh customs and traditions are taught, and a place for religious ceremonies. It is also a center for the local Sikh community and every Gurdwara contains a free community kitchen (Langar), which serves meals to people of all faiths, regardless of caste or belief.

Beliefs

There is only one God, according to Sikh belief. Because there is only one God Sikhs believe that all religions have the same God, a God who has no physical form and is therefore neither male nor female, and a God who is the creator of everything and before whom everyone is equal. God is sometimes described as Parmeshur (ultimate being), Sat Guru (the divine teacher), or Karta Purukh (the creator). Sikhs focus their lives around their relationship with God, and being a part of the Sikh community. Sikhs believe that God is inside everyone, and that everyone can change his or her life for the better by accepting God. Sikhs have three duties: (1) *Nam Japna*, keeping God in mind at all times; (2) *Kirt Karna*, earning an honest living within the bounds of their beliefs including the avoidance of gambling, alcohol, or tobacco; and (3) *Vand Chhakna*, giving to charity and caring for others, which for many Sikhs takes the form of unpaid work in the community. As well as adhering to the three duties, Sikhs are also at pains to avoid the five vices that they believe make people self-centered and ungodly: lust, envy and greed, materialism, anger, and pride. Spiritual liberation can be achieved by overcoming these vices.

Customs

The majority of Sikh customs relate to the Khalsa, the body of initiated Sikhs to which most adult Sikhs belong. The Amrit ceremony is an initiation ceremony that Sikhs can undertake as soon as they are old enough to understand the full commitment that they are making. The ceremony takes place in a Gurdwara, before the Guru Granth Sahib, and in the presence of five initiated Sikhs who represent the first five Sikhs to be initiated. After the ceremony Sikh men take the name "Singh" (lion) and women take the name "Kaur" (princess).

The Five K's

The five K's are the physical symbols worn by Sikhs who are members of the Khalsa. Each individual K has its own particular significance. Uncut hair *(Kesh)* is regarded as a sign of holiness, strength, modesty, and the adoption of a simple life. Another reason put forward is that keeping one's hair uncut indicates a willingness to accept God's gift as God intended it. However, others give a simpler explanation: that it merely follows the appearance of Guru Gobind Singh, founder of the Khalsa. A steel bracelet *(Kara)* is worn as a symbol of restraint and gentility, and acts as a reminder that the Sikh is linked to the Guru. It also symbolizes God having no beginning or end and is made out of steel rather than precious metals because it is not regarded as an ornament. A wooden comb *(Kanga)* is worn to symbolize a clean mind and body, and the importance of looking after the body that God created. Cotton underwear *(Kaccha)* in the form of breeches that must not come below the knee are worn to symbolize chastity. The sword *(Kirpan)* represents the struggle against injustice or the defense of the weak, although many see it simply as a metaphor for God. The sword is ceremonial and plays an important part in the initiation ceremony when it is used to stir a mixture of sugar and water, which the initiate must drink. When creating the Khalsa, Guru Gobind Singh introduced the five K's for specific reasons. The Sikh who wears them shows personal dedication to a life of devotion and submission to the Guru, who felt that adopting these symbols would identify members of the Khalsa, thereby encouraging members of the community to feel more strongly bound together.

Festivals

Gurpurbs are festivals that relate to the lives of the Gurus. They are celebrated with a complete and continuous reading of the Guru Granth Sahib over a period of forty-eight hours, finishing on the day of the festival. The most important Gurpurbs are the birthday of Guru Nanak (November), the birthday of Guru Gobind Singh (January), the martyrdom of Guru Arjan (June), and the martyrdom of Guru Tegh Bahadur (November/December). Vaisakhi is the Sikh New Year festival, which is held on 13 or 14 April (depending on the lunar calendar) and is celebrated in the same fashion as Gurpurbs. This festival also coincides with celebrations to commemorate the founding of the Khalsa in 1699 by Guru Gobind Singh.

In the aftermath of partition many Sikh professionals settled in the United States, Canada, and Great Britain and, while becoming valuable assets in their adopted communities, Sikhs worldwide continue to look toward the Punjab as their spiritual and cultural home. Controversy continues with the adoption of a new Sikh calendar (the Nanakshahi Calendar), which celebrates the anniversary of the death of the two Sikh assassins who killed former Indian Prime Minister Indira Gandhi as martyrdom days.

Derek Rutherford Young

See also Hinduism, Modern

Further Reading

Coakley, S. (Ed). (2002). *Religion and the body*. Cambridge, UK: Cambridge University Press.

Cole, W. O. (1995). *Sikhism*. Berkshire, UK: McGraw Hill.

Cole, W. O., & Sambhi, P. S. (1978). *The Sikhs: Their religious beliefs and practices*. London: Routledge and Kegan Paul.

Cole, W. O., & Sambhi, P. S. (1993). *Sikhism and Christianity: A comparative study*. London: The Macmillan Press.

Dhanjal, B. (2002). *Sikhism*. Berkshire, UK: McGraw Hill.

Grewal, J. S. (1990). *The Sikhs of the Punjab*. Cambridge, UK: Cambridge University Press.

Kapur, R. A. (1986). *Sikh separatism*. New Delhi, India: Vikas.

Mann, G. S. (2003). *Sikhism*. London: Routledge.

Mann, G. S., Numrich, P. D., & Williams, R. B. (2002). *Buddhists, Hindus, and Sikhs in America*. Oxford, UK: Oxford University Press.

McLeod, H. (1998). *Sikhism*. London: Penguin Books.

McLeod, W. H. (1989). *The Sikhs: History, religion, and society*. New York: Columbia University Press.

McLeod, W. H. (2000). *Aspects of Sikh identity, culture, and thought*. Oxford, UK: Oxford University Press.

Singh, D. (1991). *Western perspective on the Sikh religion*. New Delhi, India: Sehgal.

Singh, P. (2002). *The Sikhs*. New York: Doubleday.

Uberoi, J. P. S. (1999). *Religion, civil society, and the state: A study of Sikhism*. Oxford, UK: Oxford University Press.

Spanish Christian-Muslim Wars

In 711 CE, Muslims crossed over the Strait of Gibraltar from Africa into Iberia, quickly occupying nearly the whole of the Iberian Peninsula and in doing so destroying the Visigothic kingdom that had been established there since the fifth century. That turn of events set the stage for the Spanish Christian-Muslim wars, more commonly known as the *Reconquista*, or Reconquest—

The Reconquest of León

The following historical reconstruction describes León as it appeared to the Christians who reoccupied and restored it following Muslim rule.

With its old Roman walls still standing, but its hot public baths and similar monuments more or less in ruins, León was a ghost town for almost a century. It seems to me that when he was finally able to resume the Reconquest, Ramiro I would have found it deserted. At the very least, the effort required to recapture it must have been so small that not even his grandson the chronicler nor the chronicle attributed to a monk from Albelde, mention his occupation of the town. However, it is beyond doubt that a Christian population established itself there during his reign, because various Muslim historians tell us how this population fled in 846 in the face of a Moorish attack. These same sources reveal the strength (and therefore the origin) of the town walls when they tell us that, after having set fire to the town, the Moors tried to destroy its fortified area but had to retreat without success as a result of the depth and strength of the walls. The fire and the failed attempt to raze the walls are good proof that the troops from Córdoba did not even consider garrisoning the conquered town, which must have continued to be deserted. This is how King Ordoño found it in 856, when he left behind the mountain barrier that surrounded the kingdom of Asturias to settle the plain below, restored Astorga and Amaya at the foot of the hills, and occupied León. As he generally did with all new lands, he repopulated it with Christians from the north, who had come to seek their fortune on the frontier, and with Mozarabs who were fleeing from civil strife in Muslim Spain.

Source: Albornoz, Claudio Sánchez. (1999). *Daily Life In The Spanish Reconquest: Scenes from Tenth-Century León.* Simon Doubleday, Trans. The American Academy of Research Historians of Medieval Spain, the AARHMS Library. Retrieved May 14, 2003, from http://www.uca.edu/aarhms/LEON2.htm

the attempts of the northern Christian kingdoms to control the entire peninsula. More importantly, however, it was during this time of Reconquest that the inhabitants of Iberia created distinctively Hispanic societies.

The territory that the Muslims conquered in Iberia (broadly speaking, the southern and eastern parts of the peninsula) became known as al-Andalus, or "Vandal Land." Whereas the Visigothic capital had been Toledo, the Muslims established their capital at Córdoba.

In the first couple of centuries after conquest, the Muslim invaders were demographically a small percentage of the population. However, by the end of the tenth century, Islam was the religion of the majority of the population in Iberia. The cultural mixing that occurred between Muslims and Christians came about for two main reasons: Intermarriage of Muslim men with Christian women and as a result of Muslim soldiers being compensated for their services with land, thus the reverse—Muslim women with Christian men —tended to be the exception rather than the rule.

The Muslim stronghold of Granada was not defeated until 1492, the year of the voyage of Christopher Columbus. Although all Jews were expelled from Spain in this year, it was another decade before the remaining Muslims were expelled from Spain. The Reconquest, then, spanned nearly eight centuries and left the Spanish and Portuguese with a warring and crusading mentality that they took with them to the New World.

Islamic Invasion

In the year 711 the Muslim invader Tariq ibn Ziyad (d. c. 720) led an army of Arab soldiers and North African Berber recruits over the Strait of Gibraltar. Religious devotion to the spreading of the Island combined with political and economic motives (much like the Christian Crusades) spurred these soldiers. From 711 to 718, the Muslims advanced, establishing control over much of the territory of Iberia. The sections they did not conquer, the extreme north and northwest, remained in the hands of the Christians. It was among those Christians that resistance to the Muslims began. In the year 718, a band of Christians, led by Pelayo (d. 737), a Visigoth who had been elected king, clashed with the Muslims in a battle near the caves of Calvadanga in the

Cantabrian Mountains in the northwestern area of the peninsula. The Christians triumphed, and although the battle itself was quite small, it marked the beginning of the Reconquest.

Despite this first sign of Christian resistance, the Muslims continued farther into Iberia through sheer momentum. Continuing on into France, however, their advance was finally halted at the famous Battle of Tours (732), in which the Muslims were thrown back by the Franks, led by Charles Martel (c. 688–741). As a result of the Battle of Tours, the Muslims advanced no further north than the Iberian Peninsula.

The Berber recruits from North Africa who participated in the invasion of Iberia, themselves new converts to Islam, were known as Moors by Western Europeans. The newly established emirate (a type of governorship) of al-Andalus made up part of the Islamic Umayyad dynasty (661–750) centered in Damascus (Syria). The Umayyad dynasty was defeated by the Abbasid dynasty (750–1258), which moved its capital to Baghdad and turned its attention east. Abd al-Rahman I (reigned 756–788), the last of the Umayyads, established an independent Spanish Umayyad dynasty in al-Andalus in 756. Many Spaniards, particularly in the ninth century, converted to Islam, and the century was one of religious tolerance in the region, with communities of Muslims, Christians, and Jews (whom many historians believe came to Spain after the destruction of the Second Temple of Jerusalem in 70 CE, though Jewish lore suggests they had been living there for centuries earlier) living relatively harmoniously under Muslim rule. The Reconquest, then, was not a continuous struggle between Christianity and Islam; the situation was much more complex.

Reconquest

Although we can date the Reconquest to Pelayo's defeat of the Muslims in battle, the process of Reconquest actually began with the subsequent repopulation of the wastelands, an ill-defined area, more or less uninhabited, between the two peoples.This repopulation followed on the heels of this first Reconquest battle. Each time that the Muslims were pushed back, this area would also be pushed back. As a general rule, once Reconquest began, the Christians were the aggressors and the Muslims the defenders. Then came resettlement. The resettling of these areas involved the formation of communities, the establishment of a government system, and attention to the people's spiritual and material welfare. These things could only occur when demographics—not military might—favored the Spanish Christians, that is, when there was a sufficient resident population.

During the Reconquest, military operations most commonly had as their goal the acquisition of land or booty—generally in the form of slaves. These frontier raids, called *algaras* by the Muslims and *cabalgadas* by the Christians, were quite common. Religious zeal, while playing a large part, was usually a secondary factor. In fact, in various instances Christian lords would side with Muslim rulers against their fellow Christians, and vice versa.

Once the Muslims had been pushed back and new territory was opened up to the Christians, there were four types of people that took possession of the newly conquered lands: kings, nobles, members of religious orders, and commoners. When kings took possession of the new lands in person (which was not always the case), they created large rural estates. When nobles acquired the lands in the name of kings, though they kept four fifth of everything they won, sending one fifth back to the king, they would create rural manors. When monks acquired land which had been left vacant, they would undertake its agricultural and pastoral (grazing of the animals) colonization. As for commoners, they founded the lands once they had become vacant, founding villages in which they held fields and pastures in common.

This state of affairs continued into the eleventh century, with an uneasy balance existing between Muslims and Christians until both sides began to feel the rumbles of an impending holy war. In 1031 the Umayyad dynasty was overthrown by rival Mislim emirates and the citizens of Córdoba established an oligarchic republic. The rest of al-Andalus broke up into a number of small, petty kingdoms. Seizing the opportunity, the Christians took the offensive, pushing to the center of the peninsula to Toledo, the old Visigothic capital, which they captured in 1085. The Christian victory fired up religious enthusiasm among the Muslims, who appealed to the Muslims in North Africa for aid in driving back or at least halting the Christian advance.

Holy War

Although the pope had preached a holy war against the Moors in Spain as early as 1064, military and demographic factors stalled the Reconquest until the period from 1146 to 1147, when another wave of Muslims arrived from North Africa. At this point religion came to the forefront, and the fighting became increasingly fierce. The Christian kings began to depend heavily on religious orders such as the Knights Templar and the Knights Hospitaler, which had a military focus. Although those two orders came to the peninsula from the Holy Land (the area around Jerusalem), domestically the orders of Calantrana (1158), Alcántara (c. 1165), and Santiago (c. 1170) all came to play a large military-religious role. From 1157 to 1230 it was the military orders that did the bulk of the fighting (both offensive and defensive) against Muslim Spain. The religious orders were given large estates in return for their services, and on these estates they put the subjugated Muslims to work. The estates were defended by large monastery-castles.

Enlisting the aid of the Crusaders on their way to the Holy Land in 1147, the king of Portugal promised land, plunder, and protection to all who would help him attack Lisbon. His recruitment efforts succeeded, and nearly all of Lisbon's Muslim inhabitants fled or were slain.

As in previous centuries, the Christians would push the Muslims back and then repopulate the newly conquered lands. However, while the nobility had been the most powerful force in the first four centuries of Reconquest, kings came to the forefront in the twelfth century. As the Christian kings grew more powerful through consolidating their control over the nobility, the process of repopulation changed. Jealous of their rights, the kings insisted on maintaining closer control over resettlement (at the expense of the power of the traditional nobility). Thus while the north had previously been resettled and repopulated somewhat informally, in the center and south the kings would delegate the authority to hand-selected individuals or groups. The main instruments of repopulation were towns. Individuals would receive the authority from the king in the form of charters (called *cartas pueblos* or *fueros*) which authorized them to found municipalities and additionally granted them privileges and immunities as incentives.

The process of Reconquest was one of the most culturally shaping forces of the twelfth and thirteenth centuries. During the height of the Reconquest two emblems of Christian spirit and strength were hailed by Christian forces: the city of Santiago de Compostela and the hero El Cid. The importance of Santiago began in the ninth century, when the tomb of St. James was discovered in Galicia in what is now northwestern Spain. The town of Santiago de Compostela grew up around the tomb, which became an important pilgrimage site and the religious center of Christian Spain. El Cid, born Rodrigo Días de Vivar (1043–1099), was a Castilian hero. Eventually he became the ruler of the Muslim kingdom of Valencia, where he established a new Christian see on the site of the city's main mosque. El Cid became one of Spain's national heroes, someone whom the Iberian Christians could emulate.

Climax and Expulsion

The territory held by the Christians increased dramatically in the thirteenth century. In the years 1150 to 1212, the Iberian Peninsula consisted of León in the northwest, Castile in the north, Navarre in the far northeast, Aragón in the east, Portugal in the west, and al-Andalus, including Granada, in the south. In 1212 the North African Almohads, a Muslim dynasty, attempted a large-scale invasion of central Spain. However, because the archbishopric of Toledo had been preparing to launch a Crusade against Islam, the Castilian forces had been dramatically reinforced. In the battle of Las Navas de Tolosa, Alfonso VIII of Castile defeated the Almohad leader, which was forced to retreat to North Africa. In 1229, Ferdinand of Castile (c. 1201–1252) took the Muslim city of Mérida, and the following year the lands of Léon and Castile united under Ferdinand. This increased the power of Castile and made possible the virtual completion of Christian conquest.

After the conquest of Mérida, Ferdinand went on to receive the surrender of Córdoba, the historic capital of Muslim Spain, in 1236. He continued on to conquer Murcia in 1243 and Seville in 1248. This meant that by the time of Ferdinand's death all that remained of Muslim-controlled Spain was a thin wedge of territory around Granada (southeastern Spain) as well as a small foothold on the shore of the Strait of Gibraltar. In all other areas, Muslims were forced to either convert to Christianity or emigrate. In Christian Spain, the kingdoms of Castile and Aragón dominated the weaker kingdoms (with the exception of Portugal, which became an independent country in 1385).

In 1478, Tomás de Torquemada (1420–1498), a Dominican prior, established the Spanish Inquisition in order to ensure the sincerity of the Jews and Muslims who had accepted Christianity. Four years later, all unconverted Jews were ordered to leave Spain. In 1481, Isabella I (1451–1504) launched a new attack against Granada, and on 6 January 1492, she and her husband, Ferdinand V (1452–1516), made their victorious entry into Granada. The remaining Muslims were forced to convert to Christianity or leave Spain in 1502.

Reconquest Heritage

In the year that Granada fell, Christopher Columbus discovered a new frontier where the Reconquest—now simply a Conquest—could continue. As the historian Jonathan Brown notes in his social history of colonial Latin America, the experience of the Reconquest nurtured the crusading fervor and economic opportunism that the Spaniards brought to the New World. It was during the Reconquest that the Spaniards began dividing up the spoils of victory and setting aside portions for their king. They came to expect the Church to grant moral sanction for their conquest and developed an impatience for those who refused to convert.

Kim Richardson

See also Crusades; Holy War Idea in the Biblical Tradition; Roman Catholicism: Theology and Colonization

Further Reading

Brown, J. C. (2000). *Latin America: A social history of the colonial period*. Fort Worth, TX: Harcourt College Publishers.

Glick, T. F. (1979). *Islamic and Christian Spain in the early Middle Ages: Comparative perspectives on social and cultural formation*. Princeton, NJ: Princeton University Press.

Lomax, D. W. (1978). *The reconquest of Spain*. New York: Longman.

Mackay, A. (1977). *Spain in the Middle Ages: From frontier to empire, 1000–1500*. London: Macmillan.

McAlister, L. (1984). *Spain and Portugal in the New World, 1492–1700*. Minneapolis: University of Minnesota Press.

O'Callaghan, J. F. (1975). *A history of medieval Spain*. Ithica, NY: Cornell University Press.

Ramsey, J. (1973). *Spain: The rise of the first world power*. Tuscaloosa, AL: University of Alabama Press.

Sri Lanka

Few twentieth-century postcolonial wars have betrayed as complicated a relationship between religion and nationalism as the interethnic struggle that has torn Sri Lanka since 1983. It would be too simplistic to characterize that war as one between Buddhism and Hinduism, the religions, respectively, of the majority of Sinhalese and Tamil people who make up the bulk of the population of Sri Lanka. Self-consciously Buddhist, linguistic, chauvinistic, and mytho-historical in the Sinhalese case; reactive, largely secular, linguistic, and heritage-invoking in the Tamil case, both nationalisms got their start during the last phase of Sri Lanka's long (1505–1948) colonial history as Hindu and Buddhist revivalist movements reacting against the missionary Christianity that accompanied colonization. By 1948, when Ceylon—as Sri Lanka was then known—gained its independence from Britain, the last of its three European colonizers, the stage was set for a struggle between nationalisms that eventually coalesced in 1983 into a protracted and bloody civil war. Hence, while it cannot be said that Sri Lanka's war was a contest between Buddhism and Hinduism, or even between Hindus and Buddhists, it is clear that this conflict cannot be understood without grasping the historical role played by those two religions in the events that led up to the war. For that, some background knowledge of Sri Lanka and its history is required.

Background

Sri Lanka is a teardrop-shaped island nation located just south of the Indian subcontinent. It is roughly 432 kilometers north to south and about 240 kilometers wide east to west, except where it tapers at its northern end into the hook-shaped Jaffna peninsula, which points toward India's southernmost state, Tamil Nadu. The bulk of Sri Lanka's Tamil populace live in the island's northern and eastern districts, and most regard the town of Jaffna, which is located there, as their unofficial capital. For many Sinhalese people the geographic proximity of Sri Lanka's Tamil minority to 54 million Tamil speakers in Tamil Nadu is a fact of grave alarm, and the cause of what some scholars have characterized as the Sinhalese majority's "minority complex." A central mountain range divides the island into two climatic zones: a relatively dry northern and eastern one-third that includes the Jaffna peninsula and much of Sri Lanka's east coast, and a relatively wet and verdant southern and western two-thirds that includes the mountains, and, south of Mannar, almost the entire west and south coast, including the area surrounding Sri Lanka's capital, Colombo. This part of Sri Lanka is where the majority of Sinhalese people live.

In 1991 there were 19.6 million people living in Sri Lanka, of whom 74 percent were Sinhalese, 18.2 percent were Tamil, and 7.4 percent were Muslim—Mus-

Buddhist Monks and Political Violence

One development of the long war between Buddhist Sinhalese and Hindu Tamils in Sri Lanka was recognition of the fact that Buddhist monks were involved in the conflict and in other conflicts in South and Southeast Asia as well. The following written by the leading anthropological scholar of Sri Lanka points to the difficulty this causes for Buddhists.

Nevertheless, it is necessary to realize that many Buddhists among the ranks of the laity as well as the sectarian communities of monks must necessarily experience a profound misgiving, even consternation, when monks become caught up in political violence. There are central normative rules linked in doctrinal terms to the monks' vocation, which advocate nonviolence and the necessity to repudiate and to be distanced from all forms of taking life and inflicting injury. There is an inescapable dilemma here which surely must tug at the conscience and moral sensibilities of all Buddhists. It cannot be ignored; it has to be confronted, even if it cannot be satisfactorily resolved.

***Source:* Tambiah, Stanley Jeyaraja. *(1992) Buddhism Betrayed?: Religion, Politics and Violence in Sri Lanka.* Chicago: University of Chicago Press, p. 101.**

lim being used in this context as both an ethnic and a religious designation. But there are some complexities in the relationship between ethnicity, religion, and nationalism that require explanation. First, there are a substantial number (about 8 percent) of Sinhalese and Tamil people who are Christian. Most of these Christians are Catholic, and whether Sinhalese or Tamil, many tend to be members of maritime castes—the Sinhalese Karava and the Tamil Karaiyar—a fact that perhaps reflects the emphasis placed on conversion by the Portuguese when they dominated Sri Lanka's spice-producing coasts from 1505 until the Dutch took over in 1640. It is interesting and important to note that some of the most radical nationalists on both sides have been Christians. Second, although most of the island's Muslims speak Tamil at home, they do not regard themselves as Tamil. Yet such Muslims, one must note, make up close to 50 percent of the population of Sri Lanka's eastern Batticaloa District, which figures to be an important part of the Tamil independent state that Tamil nationalists hope to create. Third, about one-third of the Tamil population are "Hill Country Tamils," Tamil people whose (often low-caste) ancestors were brought to Sri Lanka from India by British planters in the nineteenth century to work as laborers in colonial Ceylon's important coffee and, later, tea plantations. These people were stripped of their citizenship by an act of Parliament in 1949, and although some of their rights were later restored they remain a vulnerable population anxiously poised between the Sinhalese they live among (who have frequently rioted against them) and the Sri Lankan Tamils (that is, those claiming Sri Lanka rather than India as their ancestral home), who have tended to look down upon them. Sri Lankan Tamils also tend to be divided amongst themselves between the more urban, better educated, Vallalar-caste-dominated Tamils of Jaffna and the more rural, often less wealthy and thus less well-educated Tamils of the east coast. Finally, the Sinhalese population, like the Tamil population, is also internally divided by caste and region, especially between low-country Sinhalese, descendants of the coastal populations first exposed to European colonial domination, and up-country Sinhalese, who are descendants of inhabitants of the Sinhalese mountain kingdom of Kandy, which remained independent until 1815. Complicating all this further is the fact that prior to the twentieth century there was substantial mixing going on among all these groups. Hence, though Sri Lanka's nationalisms have striven hard, with some success, to create internally homogenous, precisely bounded, and, in the Sinhalese and Muslim case, religiously defined, ethnic groups, and to present such groups as primordial, in truth the situation is more complex and the conflicts of more recent origin.

Before and during Colonialism

When Europeans first came to Ceylon in the sixteenth century, the ancient empires chronicled in the sixth-century *Mahavamsa* (a quasi-historical account of the Sinhala dynasty of the Anuradhapura Kingdom from roughly 500 BCE to 300 CE) had long ago disintegrated. What the Europeans found instead was a number of small, independent kingdoms Specifically, there was the largely Hindu, Tamil Jaffna kingdom in the north, and two largely Sinhalese and Buddhist kingdoms: Kotte, along the cinnamon-producing, lowland southwest coast, and Kandy, located high in the island's mountainous center. By the 1590s, all the coastal kingdoms had been conquered by the Portuguese, who were replaced by the Dutch in 1758. Kandy alone remained an independent state until the British, after taking over lowland Ceylon from the Dutch in 1796, captured it in 1815.

These kingdoms were all "galactic"; that is, they participated in a pan-Indian ideology of universal sovereignty. This is the kind of sovereignty in which a monarch is envisioned as standing in the center of a cosmic, ceremonially maintained, moral and physical order, with the rest of the social system, a complex system of ranked castes and communities, comprising a widening series of encircling emanations around it. It is important to note that within such galactic polities it was always possible to contain people of various languages and religions because the key to membership in them was participation in the ritual practices rather than expressed belief in the doctrines of the religion (Hindu or Buddhist) associated with the state's cosmically centered monarch. Hence, Hindus could be found in the primarily Buddhist kingdom of Kotte, Buddhists in the primarily Hindu kingdom of Jaffna, and the ostensibly Buddhist Kandyan kingdom could, and did, set up (some) politically beholden Hindu communities on the Tamil-speaking eastern coast of Sri Lanka. This galactic form of governance also explains why one of the dynasties that ruled Hindu Jaffna was Sinhalese, while the last dynasty to rule Buddhist Kandy was of South Indian, Hindu origin.

This fuzziness of boundaries between polities was replicated, in some ways, in Hinduism and Buddhism themselves as these religions were practiced in precolonial times. The form of Hinduism associated with the Jaffna Kingdom was Saivism (or Saiva Siddhanta). The form of Buddhism associated with the Buddhist kingdoms was Theravada Buddhism. These two religions often touched, however, at the village level and in their pilgrimage systems. Theravada Buddhism as practiced in Sri Lanka displayed both an otherworldly concern with cosmic morality and personal salvation, as articulated in the Buddhist *Dhamma* (or Pali canon; Sanskrit: Dharma), symbolized by important relics, and preached by Ceylon's important orders of monks (the *Sangha*), and an equally impassioned this-wordly devotion to a large number of gods, Hindu in origin, who, though morally and ontologically inferior to the Buddha's doctrine and example, were nevertheless powers who could be manipulated into intervening in the everyday world.

British rule tended to neaten and harden both communal and religious distinctions, though perhaps accidentally. The 1815 Kandyan Convention, signed to mark British control of the Kandyan kingdom, seemed to proclaim the colonial government's responsibility to protect the "Religion of the Boodhas"; beyond this, British colonial law tried to rationalize local customary law by drawing upon, and therefore legally fixing in place, local customary practices pertaining to caste, community, and religious identity and practice. At the same time, the colonial government struggled with the demands of evangelically minded British and U.S. missionaries to be given access to the local population. Eventually, Christian missionary societies became responsible for running most of the English-medium schools (at the primary level, mostly) on the island—schools the colonial government needed to supply its administration with personnel. Such schools became particularly pervasive in Jaffna, where U.S. missionaries were allowed to open a large number of English-medium schools. Jaffna's Vellalar caste majority, therefore, began to specialize in English, and become a disproportionate source of clerical and professional labor throughout Ceylon, and an inspiration of envy for many Sinhalese people. British colonialism also produced a tiny, rich, English-speaking, largely Anglophilic and Anglican, Tamil, and Sinhalese elite. Generally centered in Colombo in one residential district, these so-called "cinnamon gardens" people constituted the "educated Ceylonese" upon whom a series of British administrative reform commissions (in 1832, 1920, and 1931) drew for an advisory legislative council for the governor.

In the nineteenth century Hindus and Buddhists began to react against what many saw as concerted attacks on their religions, and this led to both Hindu and Buddhist revival movements. The Hindus were first. Arumuka Navalar (1822–1879), a missionary-educated Jaffna Tamil, started protesting the dominance of missionaries over education, and began to fashion a muscular, modern, Tamil prose style fit for vernacular education and anti-Christian polemics. He also began to set up Tamil-medium schools. Although presented as a Hindu movement, it is interesting that for Navalar the emphasis was firmly on redressing the alienation of Jaffna Tamils from their cultural, rather than religious, past. In contrast, the Buddhist revival began a bit later, in the 1860s and 1870s, and was more religiously oriented right from the beginning. Monks, stung by Victorian Christian criticisms of Buddhism, staged a series of debates with missionaries, culminating in the famous 1873 Panadura debate, in which the Buddhist monk Migettuwatte Gunananda (1823–1890) roundly trounced his Christian attackers. It was this debate that inspired the U.S. Theosophist H. S. Olcott (1832–1907) not only to visit Ceylon in 1880, but to announce shortly thereafter his public conversion to Buddhism. Olcott then founded the Buddhist Theosophical society and helped organize a specifically Buddhist political movement with a flag and a stated purpose: to purify Buddhism of its "non-Buddhist" (that is, Hindu-like) admixtures, and to modernize it into a religion proper for forward-thinking elites. One of Olcott's students, who was born Don David Hevaviritarnana and later changed it to Anagarika Dharmapala (1864–1933), went on to become the spokesmen for this movement, but later broke away from it and its solely religious ambitions to become the fashioner, eventually, of the new, nationalist, Buddhist, and racist, Sinhalese discourse that became the foundation for the Sinhalese-Buddhist chauvinist nationalism of the twentieth century.

Dharmapala's Sinhala-Buddhist nationalism answered to a felt need among Ceylon's "native" colonial elites. With the introduction of universal suffrage for the election of members of the Legislative Council in 1931, Sinhalese and Tamil elites needed to be able to rally support among populaces with whom they often shared very little real cultural commonality. For this purpose the rhetorical condemnations of other communities that Dharmapala's ideology allowed came in handy—although the 1915 anti-Muslim riots also made it obvious that such talk could go too far. Nevertheless, it quickly became as apparent to both Sinhalese leaders such as D. S. Senanayake (1881–1952) and Tamil leaders such as G. G. Ponnambulam (1901–1977) that under majority rule the fruits of democracy were going to be distributed by and for the Sinhalese majority. Between 1931 and 1948, therefore, Ponnambulam pushed for a fifty-fifty constitutional rule that would split legislative representation evenly between the Sinhalese majority and the remaining minorities, and Sinhalese elites pushed just as hard against this idea. The communal representation scheme was ultimately turned down by the 1947 Soulbury Commission in favor of a first-past-the-post, Westminster-style parliamentary government, with a clause in the constitution protecting minorities against discrimination. Thus was Ceylon left positioned by its colonial past for future ethnic conflict.

Independence and Civil War

After independence, conflict between the communities took on a more desperate, violent tone. Acts of the Sinhalese-dominated Parliament eliminated a third of the country's Tamil voters by stripping the Hill Country Tamils of citizenship. Thereafter, the two largest Sinhalese political parties, the United National Party (UNP) and the Sri Lankan Freedom Party (SLFP), tried to outdo each other in decrying each other's lack of toughness against Tamils. Tamils, for their part, formed a Federal Party (FP) under S. J. V. Chelvanayakam (1898–1977) whose stated purpose was to push for a federal system of government in which Tamils would have some form of regional autonomy. Things took a more violent turn in 1956 when S. W. R. D. Bandaranaike, campaigning to lead his SLFP-led coalition to victory, promised to institute an act making Sinhalese (Sinhala) the only official language of Ceylon. This "Sinhala Only" act both won the election and sparked off anti-Tamil rioting, the first of an escalating series of more serious anti-Tamil riots occurring between 1956 and 1983. Bandaranaike, appalled by the violence, eventually tried to back off his pledge to institute this rule by signing a pact with Chelvanayakam, a move protested and decried by the UNP and which set off the 1958 anti-Tamil riots. Bandaranaike was assassinated by a Buddhist monk in 1959, and, in defiance of the pact with Chelvanayakam, the Official Language Act was eventually instituted by his widow, Sirimavo Bandaranaike, in 1960. Various Sinhalese majority governments then instituted a series of laws that further alienated and hampered the Tamil minority. These included irrigation and colonization schemes that relocated poor Sinhalese communities to traditionally Tamil parts of the country; laws making it difficult for Tamils to participate in the police force, army, or civil service; and laws that effectively limited the admission of high-scoring Jaffna Tamils to Sri Lanka's universities. In 1970 a constitutional assembly voted to drop the section of the constitution that protected minorities. It also renamed Ceylon "Sri Lanka"—a designation both more Sinhalese and Buddhist—and officially recognized Buddhism as the religion of the Sri Lankan state.

Attempts by the Federal Party to protest these developments through acts of peaceful civil disobedience were violently suppressed. Between 1972 and 1975, therefore, the Federal Party, pushed hard by younger Tamils angered by the new university laws, transformed itself—first into the Tamil United Front, which still demanded a secular, federal state; and then, in a meeting at Vaddukoddai, into the Tamil United Liberation Front (TULF), which, for the first time, called for an independent Tamil state or Eelam. Paralleling this development were more radical moves by younger Tamils, who were growing more and more suspicious of the abilities and parliamentary tactics of the old Colombo and Jaffna elites. Their Tamil Students Movement, formed in 1970, became the Tamil New Tigers and then the Liberation Tigers of Tamil Eelam (LTTE) in 1975. Led by Velupillai Prabhakaran (b. 1954), a ruthless but brilliant military leader, the LTTE, though a tiny organization, began to pursue its goal through small guerrilla attacks on banks and police stations—perhaps inspired by the example, if not by the spectacular lack of success, of the brutally suppressed 1972 insurrection by the neo-Marxist, Sinhalese, People's Liberation Front (the Janatha Vimukthi Peramuna, or JVP). Although the 1977 elections returned an all-TULF slate to Parliament, making them, indeed, the balancing block of votes in a nearly evenly divided Parliament, the inability of the TULF leaders to translate this into gains for the Tamil populace, plus additional outrages by the Sri Lankan government such as the burning of the Jaffna Library and the passage of a draconian Prevention of Terrorism Act (which allows detention without trial by the military), encouraged the LTTE and spurred the creation of many more such groups, thirty-six eventually, also dedicated to fighting for an independent state. Most of these groups, however, were later destroyed by the LTTE.

In 1983 an ambush laid by the LTTE killed thirteen Sinhalese soldiers and sparked the most violent anti-Tamil riots Sri Lanka had ever seen, in which, according to some estimates, rioters burned over 100,000 Tamil homes and some 178,000 Tamils fled abroad. It was widely believed that this rioting was government sanctioned and even government led. In the aftermath, large numbers of Tamil youths rushed to join the various Tamil militant groups. The Sixth Amendment to the constitution, passed immediately after the riots, demanded an oath of allegiance to a unitary state, thereby effectively ending the role of the TULF in parliament. This left Tamil people without any representation—and the field clear for the militants. And so the war began.

The war itself lasted for nineteen years, went through many phases, and is not yet completely settled. There were breaks in the fighting in 1987, 1990, and 1994 during which ceasefires were declared and peace talks were held, only to have war break out again. There were also periods of intense fighting and some moments of odd alliance. At one point, from 1987 to 1990, an Indian army (the Indian Peace Keeping Force, or IPKF) occupied the northern and eastern parts of Sri Lanka, ostensibly to ensure peace and disarm Tamil militants, and was fought to a standstill by an LTTE that was itself, perhaps, being secretly aided by a Sri Lankan government simultaneously fighting its own guerilla war against a renewed JVP in the south. Similarly, after 1987, the rump remains of many of the Tamil militant groups destroyed by intense internecine fighting with the LTTE allied themselves first with the IPKF and later with the Sri Lankan government against the LTTE. For the most part, however, this war, which ground to a military standstill by 1997, was between the Sri Lankan government and a ruthless and militarily efficient LTTE. This war was also fought by both sides with incredible brutality, with large numbers of civilians being killed, tortured, imprisoned and made refugees, and with ultimate casualty estimates (especially if you count the JVP insurrection as part of it) ranging from 60,000 to 100,000. The current, Norwegian-facilitated, ceasefire, signed on February 22, 2002, may have finally spelled the end of this war, but people remain wary.

Religion, War, and Sri Lanka's Future

Sri Lanka's war clearly shows the role religions can play in the violent identity politics of interethnic civil war. But it also demonstrates that the relationship between religion, ethnicity, and nationalism is not a simple one and must be seen against a complex backdrop history. Buddhism and Hinduism per se were not in conflict in Sri Lanka; rather, these religions became one polity-solidifying tool among many used in a competition for state resources between two groups primed for this role by prior colonial politics. It can only be hoped that the current peace talks will result in a future free from further war.

Mark P. Whitaker

Further Reading

De Silva, K. M. (1981). *A history of Sri Lanka*. Delhi, India: Oxford University Press.

Gamage, S., & Watson, I. B. (Eds.). (1999). *Conflict and community in contemporary Sri Lanka: "Pearl of the East" or "Island of Tears"?* New Delhi, India: Sage Publications.

Gombrich, R., & Obeyesekere, G. (1988). *Buddhism transformed: Religious change in Sri Lanka*. Princeton, NJ: Princeton University Press.

Gunasingam, M. (1999). *Sri Lankan Tamil nationalism: A study of its origins*. Sydney, Australia: MV Publications.

Manogaran, C., & Pfaffenberger, B. (Eds.). (1994). *The Sri Lankan Tamils: Ethnicity and identity*. Boulder, CO: Westview Press.

Seneviratne, H. L. (1978). *Rituals of the Kandyan state*. Cambridge, UK: Cambridge University Press.

Spencer, J. (Ed.). (1990). *Sri Lanka: History and the roots of conflict*. New York: Routledge.

Tambiah, S. J. (1986). *Sri Lanka: Ethnic fratricide and the dismantling of democracy*. Chicago: University of Chicago Press.

Whitaker, M. (1999). *Amiable incoherence: Manipulating histories and modernities in a Batticaloa Hindu Temple* (Sri Lanka Studies in the Humanities and the Social Sciences No. 8). Amsterdam: VU University Press.

Wickremeratne, A. (1995). *The roots of nationalism: Sri Lanka*. Colombo, Sri Lanka: Karunaratne & Sons.

Wilson, A. J. (2000) *Sri Lankan Tamil nationalism: Its origins and development in the nineteenth and twentieth centuries*. Vancouver, Canada: UBC Press.

Sudan

In September 1983, the Sudanese dictator Ja'far Nimeiri (b. 1930) broke sharply from his record as a secular socialist by declaring the countrywide application of Islamic *shariʿa* law. Based in theory upon injunctions from the Qur'an, his "September laws" forbade gambling and alcohol consumption and applied corporal punishments such as amputation for petty theft. For many southern Sudanese intellectuals, most of whom were Christian, Nimeiri's Islamization program added to deep-seated and long-mounting grievances against the central government based in the capital Khartoum. When civil war broke out in 1983, after a twelve-year lull that had followed an earlier bout of fighting (1955–1972), religion—or more precisely, the role that the religion of the Muslim majority should play in shaping national identity and political life—emerged as an important point of contention.

Outside observers often describe the Sudanese civil war as a conflict between Arab Muslim peoples of the North and African Christians of the South, with the northerners backing the Khartoum government and the southerners supporting rebel organizations—notably, since 1983, the Sudan People's Liberation Movement and Army (SPLM/SPLA). The truth is more complex, for two reasons. First, there is substantial diversity of religious belief and practice, ethnicity, and political opinion within the northern and southern regions, so that lines of opposition have not always been clear-cut. Second, while the war has been in part a battle to define Sudanese national identity in terms of religion and ethnicity, it has equally been a struggle waged by disempowered groups to gain access to economic and political resources, including revenues from oil exports and fair representation in government offices.

Historical Background

The territory that makes up present-day Sudan has a long and rich history. Three thousand years ago, it enjoyed strong trading connections to Pharaonic Egypt and boasted a distinctive civilization in Nubia, the northernmost region of the country. In the sixth century, Christianity arrived in Nubia and became the religion of political elites before dwindling and disappearing entirely several centuries later. Meanwhile, beginning in the mid-seventh century, Islam began to spread slowly and for the most part peacefully, as Arab nomads and traders arrived, intermarried with local peoples, and spread their religion. In 1820 armies of the Muhammad Ali dynasty of Egypt invaded the country and established a regime led by military men from the wider Ottoman Empire, thereby initiating a period of Turco-Egyptian imperialism in Sudan. Decades later, in 1881, a local Arab scholar named Muhammad Ahmad declared himself *al-Mahdi*—the Rightly Guided One—whose arrival, according to Muslim millenarian beliefs then prevailing, would herald the end of time and Judgment Day. Attracting many followers, the Mahdi initiated a jihad movement and in 1885 founded a Sudanese Islamic state based in Omdurman, near Khartoum. The Mahdist state survived until 1898, when British and Egyptian forces invaded Sudan and initiated a new period of colonial domination.

British Colonialism: Precursor to Conflict?

The Sudanese civil war first broke out in 1955, just months before the country gained independence fol-

British Repression of Indigenous Religion in Southern Sudan

The repression of indigenous religions in Sudan by the British as described below is one factor underlying the continuing ethnic/religious/political violence in the modern Sudan.

Secret societies have spread from the south and west and prospered all over Zandeland since European administration. They are nevertheless not indigenous institutions and are still "subterranean and subversive." In the past they were suppressed by the chiefs, and Lagae suggests that the Congo chiefs would have eliminated them completely but for the diminution of their powers by the Administration. In the Sudan few secret societies were known under Gbudwe (d. 1905) and they were so persecuted that they had only a small clandestine following. By 1919 their influence had increased so much that the Sudan Government felt impelled to make "The Unlawful Societies Ordinance" for the suppression of dangerous and obscene rites. The Congo authorities had taken action some time before 1915. Official opposition, however, served to direct the purpose of the societies "against the vagaries of European rule" so that they flourished as centres of opposition to European occupation.

The magic and rites of each society have always been secret and acquired by its members only after initiation and payment, but formerly the actual existence of the societies was not kept secret, nor did the members conceal their purpose or meeting places. As a sign of membership Mani members used to wear a blue bead. Later, government persecution forced the societies to keep not only their rites but also their membership and very existence secret.

Source: Baxter, P. T. W, & Butt, Andre. (1953). "The Azande, and Related Peoples of the Anglo-Egyptian Sudan and Belgian Congo." In Daryll Forde (Ed.), *Ethnographic Survey of Africa, East Central Africa*, Part IX. London: International African Institute, p. 91.

lowing a half-century of British control. To understand the reasons for the war's outbreak and persistence, one must consider the role of historical legacies and attitudes in seeding internal resentments.

In 1898, at a time when European imperial powers were competing to secure colonial territories in Africa, Britain worked in nominal partnership with Egypt to conquer the region that became known as the Anglo-Egyptian Sudan. Within its new and to some extent arbitrarily drawn borders, the Sudan became the largest territory in Africa, covering a region of enormous social diversity.

In this Anglo-Egyptian period (1898–1956), Britain administered the Sudan along an internal North-South divide. In overwhelmingly Muslim northern areas, and particularly in Arabic-speaking towns in the central riverine region along the Nile, British authorities concentrated meager resources—for example, by establishing modern schools and hospitals and extending transportational networks. By contrast, they did little to develop social services and infrastructures either in southern regions, which were inhabited mainly by practitioners of local religions, or in remote parts of the North, namely, western and eastern regions (bordering Chad and the Red Sea, respectively) that were inhabited by Muslim but non-Arabic-speaking peoples. In the long run, these colonial practices perpetuated and accentuated patterns of uneven development and economic inequality within the Sudan territory.

In the South especially, British policies reflected a kind of apathetic paternalism. That is, while British authorities expressed a desire to protect the South from northern Muslims, who had exploited southern peoples in a vigorous nineteenth-century slave trade, they were reluctant to spend scarce resources on the development of nonliterate societies that they regarded as primitive. Thus they imposed de facto internal border controls to keep northerners and southerners apart, a move that isolated and further marginalized the South vis-à-vis the affairs of the Khartoum government. They made Arabic the official language of administration and education in the North, with English (supplemented to some extent by local vernaculars) filling that role in the South. They also invited foreign Christian missionary societies into the South—notably the Church Missionary Society (British Anglicans), the Verona Fathers (Italian Catholics), and the American Presbyterians—and relinquished the region's educational development to them. By the early 1950s, this educational policy was giving rise to a small southern educated class of young men from various ethnic backgrounds (such as Dinka, Nuer, and Bari) who had attended English-medium Protestant or Catholic mission schools and in the process converted from traditional religions to Christianity. Relative to their educated Arabic-speaking counterparts in the North, this new southern intelligentsia was smaller, more atomized, and more removed—culturally and geographically speaking—from the center of power at Khartoum.

After World War II, as decolonization began to seem imminent, British authorities decided that the Sudan would proceed to independence as a single entity, not divided in half as North and South. Members of the northern Sudanese elite were delighted, for as primary beneficiaries of British educational and employment policies and as the country's earliest nationalist organizers, they stood to inherit the reins of political power. Educated northern Sudanese stepped into jobs that Britons vacated. Eager to fulfill their dream of the Sudan as an Arab-Islamic nation, if necessary by promoting policies of cultural assimilation, northern politicians moved to make Arabic the sole official language in a country where scores of languages were spoken and welcomed Muslim proselytizers into regions where Christian groups had enjoyed exclusive privileges during the colonial period.

Meanwhile, many southerners watched decolonization with dismay, not least because British authorities and northern nationalists failed to include them in major discussions. Late in 1952, a group of educated southerners issued a memorandum arguing that the South was not ready for rapid independence (in light of its underdeveloped condition) and that it needed more time before it could hope to participate as a fair partner in union with the North. These concerns went unheeded, plans for independence proceeded, and tensions mounted in the South as northerners arrived to assume leadership roles. In August 1955, with independence from Britain less than five months away, mutiny erupted among soldiers based at Torit in East Equatoria, the Sudan's southernmost province, leading to massacres of northern officials and civilians followed by government reprisals. Most historians believe that these events marked the start of the Sudanese civil war.

War and Peace in Independent Sudan

In the decade following independence the northern-dominated government tried to consolidate Sudanese national identity while maintaining a very fragile political order. Although the government enlisted Sudan in the Arab League immediately after independence in 1956, it later joined the Organization of African Unity (OAU) as a founding member along with Egypt and the other North African Arabic-speaking countries. In 1958, with factionalism rife among northern Muslim politicians, the military staged a coup that ended parliamentary rule. Continued instability in the South dislocated populations and produced refugees, among them southern intellectuals who moved to neighboring Uganda, where they collectively organized. In 1963, some of these exiles formed the guerrilla army known as the Anya-Nya, which battled government forces in the South in an escalation of the war.

In the late 1950s and early 1960s the government responded to the continuing mutiny, as it called the war in this period, by more aggressively pursuing its Arabization and Islamization policies. These efforts went hand-in-hand with attempts to suppress Christian missionary activity. Thus, in 1957, northern politicians took over Christian missionary schools in the South, arguing that education should be government-run and should promote common national values. In 1960 the government changed the day of rest in the South to Friday (the day of Muslim congregational prayer), making Sunday part of the work week; two years later, it passed an act restricting missionaries from operating beyond the bounds of church premises. Finally, in 1964, the government expelled foreign Christian missionaries from the country altogether. It justified the expulsion on the grounds that missionaries had been compromising national sovereignty and impeding national integration by promoting southern cultural distinction based on Christianity and an English lingua franca, and by stirring up fear and antipathy towards northerners while fomenting wartime hostilities.

In spite or perhaps because of these government measures, Christianity flourished and expanded among southerners, gaining wide ground among people who had previously practiced traditional religions. An indigenous Catholic and Protestant church leadership developed and publicized southern issues and perspectives through connections with Africa-wide and international Christian organizations. Ultimately, Christianity did for the South what northern politicians had feared it would do: it helped to rally displaced and ethnically heterogeneous southern populations under the banner of common religion.

In late-twentieth-century Sudan Islam also expanded among practitioners of traditional religions, who encountered the Muslim faith through Islamic schools and charitable foundations. Among southern peoples, however, religious identity did not (and to this day has not) automatically determined one's role in the midst of civil war. Just as some southern Christians chose to work with the central government, remaining optimistic about prospects for national coexistence, some southern Muslims opted to join the resistance against successive Khartoum regimes.

In 1969, following five years of parliamentary rule during which northern politicians considered an Islamic constitution and held abortive discussions on ending the war, Sudan experienced another coup, which propelled Ja'far Nimeiri to power. Nimeiri was from the start an authoritarian ruler who crushed his political rivals, Islamists and communists alike. In some sense it was his stranglehold on political dialogue that enabled him to stop the war in 1972 by sponsoring the Addis Ababa Accord. This agreement granted the southern provinces a degree of regional autonomy, arranged for fairer southern representation in the national assembly and armed forces, and permitted the use of English and local languages for southern administrative and educational purposes. In 1973 a new constitution also affirmed the country's dual Arab and African heritage as well as respect not only for Islam but also for Christianity and traditional beliefs.

Some scholars suggest that the Addis Ababa Accord was a rare victory for ethnic pluralism and political inclusion in postcolonial Sudan. Yet it proved to be far better in theory than practice, failing to fulfill its promises. Among southerners, one growing cause for disillusionment was the central government's growing interest in exploiting and siphoning off southern resources, water and oil especially. As the government explored plans for digging the Jonglei Canal, which would drain White Nile water to increase the main Nile flow, southern thinkers began to question why their local environment should be disrupted for a hydrological scheme that would ultimately benefit Egypt and northern Sudan. Similar concerns arose following the discovery of oil deposits in Bentiu in 1979, future revenues of which (by the terms of the Addis Ababa Accord) should have been earmarked for southern development. Not only did the central government try to redraw provincial boundaries in 1980 to situate these oil deposits in the North, it also began to transfer northern troops into the oil field areas in an assertion of its authority. By the time Nimeiri overturned the Addis Ababa Accords in 1983 and declared Islamic *shari'a* law, southern leaders were already planning their resistance and the SPLM/SPLA was taking shape.

War resumed in 1983. Within a few years fighting spread beyond the South to the Nuba Mountains of Kordofan in central Sudan, where the SPLM/SPLA found support among Nuba peoples, Muslims and Christians alike, who resented the region's political marginalization and the central government's longstanding attempts at cultural assimilation through Arabization. Nimeiri fell from power in 1986, yet his successors in government—parliamentarians first and dictators later—retained his commitment to Islamic laws in various forms, and in the process affirmed the idea of the Sudan as a monocultural Arabic-speaking Muslim state.

The Cost of War and the Issues at Stake

In 1989 the civil war gained a new ideological charge when a military coup brought the regime of General Omar Bashir (b. 1945) to power. Working in collaboration with the National Islamic Front (NIF) and its chief spokesman, Hasan al-Turabi (b. 1932), the Bashir regime zealously pursued an Islamization agenda and tried to impose its strictures on all Sudanese. Many Arabic-speaking Muslim intellectuals sought exile abroad to escape the atmosphere of political repression. In 1992 the regime began increasingly to characterize the civil war as a jihad, or Islamic holy war, attributing moral dimensions to the struggle. At the same time it reached out to international Islamic militant groups, for example, by welcoming the Saudi radical Osama bin Laden (b. 1957) into northern Sudan and allowing him to set up mujahideen (Islamic guerrilla) training camps.

Criticized for its human-rights abuses, for its conduct in the war against southern and Nuba peoples, and for its purported connections to terrorist organizations, Sudan in the 1990s became what many observers called a pariah state. The Bashir regime's support of Iraqi president Saddam Hussein during and after the Persian Gulf War of 1990–1991 increased its isolation on the international stage. Meanwhile, drought, famines, and epidemics buffeted the country, while southern and Nuba peoples—women and children especially—fell victim to local government-backed Arab militias that carried out abductions that amounted to slave raiding. Some observers debate whether this situation reflects the revival or continuation of local slavery traditions. Still others debate whether foreign humanitarian groups helped to perpetuate the recent slave trade by offering Arab militia members sums of money to redeem their captives, thereby giving them a financial incentive to continue their raiding.

In the 1990s the SPLM/SPLA fragmented, leading to internecine fighting as its leaders competed for power and argued about long-term goals. SLPM/SPLA mainstream leaders contended that the Sudan could theoretically emerge from the war as a unitary nation-state, provided that a peace agreement backed by the central government acted on two principles: first, the decentralization of power (so as to deliver, once and for all, a fair allocation of political authority and economic resources), and second, the affirmation of ethnic and religious diversity, by officially identifying Sudan as a multicultural, not exclusively Arab-Islamic, state. The SPLM/SPLA splinter groups took a more pessimistic view. Despairing of the possibility for genuine reform within the central government, these groups declared long-term coexistence to be impossible in the absence of mutual tolerance, and therefore they called for secession and for the creation of a new independent country in southern Sudan. In either case, the point was moot. Eager to retain claims to the whole territory and to the South's lucrative reserves of water and oil, the Bashir regime refused to entertain the possibility of secession. At the same time, it insisted that the Arab-Islamic heritage provided the Sudanese nation-state with its necessary social and ethical glue.

International observers estimate that 2 million Sudanese, mostly southerners, have died since 1983 from war-related causes, and that as many as 4 million (out of a total population of 36 million) have been displaced as refugees, internally or abroad in neighboring countries. Casualties continue to mount, and still the war goes on.

How Will It End?

Many observers argue that in Sudan, as in other post-colonial countries, the political and cultural exclusivism of the bastions of power has propelled the civil war. The Arab-Islamic ideal of nationhood propagated by a narrow political elite appears inadequate to encompass the country's heterogeneity. For the war to end, only two humane solutions seem possible: Either the country must split into distinct national fragments, or the idea of the nation must embrace cultural pluralism.

Heather J. Sharkey

See also Fundamentalism in Egypt and Sudan; Sudanese War of 1881–1898

Further Reading

Barsella, G., & Guixot, M. A. A. (1998). *Struggling to be heard: The Christian voice in independent Sudan, 1956–1999*. Nairobi, Kenya: Paulines Publications Africa.

Beshir, M. O. (1968). *The southern Sudan: Background to conflict*. London: C. Hurst and Co.

Central Intelligence Agency (CIA). (2001). Sudan. In *World Factbook 2002*. Retrieved April 2, 2003, from http://www.odci.gov/cia/publications/factbook/geos/su.html

Hamdi, M. E. (1998). *The making of an Islamic political leader: Conversations with Hasan al-Turabi* (A. A. Shamis, Trans.). Boulder, CO: Westview Press.

Holt, P. M. & Daly, M. W. (2000). *A history of the Sudan* (5th ed.). London: Longman.

Jok, J. M. (2001). *War and slavery in Sudan*. Philadelphia: University of Pennsylvania Press.

Lesch, A. M. (1998). *The Sudan: Contested national identities*. Bloomington: Indiana University Press.

O'Ballance, E. (2000). *Sudan, civil war and terrorism, 1956–99*. Houndmills, UK: Macmillan Press.

Rahhal, S. M. (Ed.). (2001). *The right to be Nuba: The story of a Sudanese people's struggle for survival*. Lawrenceville, NJ: The Red Sea Press.

Ruay, D. D. A. (1994). *The politics of two Sudans: The south and the north, 1821–1969*. Uppsala, Sweden: The Scandinavian Institute of African Studies.

Sharkey, H. J. (2003). *Living with colonialism: Nationalism and culture in the Anglo-Egyptian Sudan*. Berkeley and Los Angeles: University of California Press.

Sidahmed, A. S. (1996). *Politics and Islam in contemporary Sudan*. New York: St. Martin's Press.

Sudan Government, Ministry of the Interior. (1964). *Expulsion of foreign missionaries and priests from the southern provinces*. Khartoum, Sudan: The Republic of the Sudan.

U.S. Committee for Refugees. (2002). *Country report: Sudan*. Retrieved April 2, 2003, from http://www.refugees.org/world/countryrpt/africa/sudan.htm

Wai, D. M. (Ed.). (1973). *The southern Sudan: The problem of national integration*. London: Frank Cass.

Warburg, G. R. (1992). *Historical discord in the Nile Valley*. Evanston, IL: Northwestern University Press.

Wheeler, A. C. (Ed.). (1997). *Land of promise: Church growth in a Sudan at war*. Nairobi, Kenya: Paulines Publications Africa.

Wöndu, S., & Lesch, A. (2000). *Battle for peace in Sudan: An analysis of the Abuja conferences, 1992–1993*. Lanham, MD: University Press of America.
Woodward, P. (1990). *Sudan: The unstable state, 1898–1989*. Boulder, CO: Lynne Rienner.

Sudanese War of 1881–1898

This war consisted of a series of battles in and around the Nile valley region by followers of the Mahdi (in Arabic, literally, "the one who is rightly guided") and various groups, Muslims and non-Muslims, who opposed the movement or stood in its path of expansion. The last of the battles was fought against a massive British force, with large Egyptian participation, under Sir Herbert Kitchener. The Battle of Karari of September 1898, popularly known as the Battle of Omdurman, was the end for the independent Mahdist state and movement.

The Sudanese Mahdi became known in eastern Sudanic Africa in June 1881 when he began to dispatch letters to local leaders proclaiming himself the expected Mahdi. Diverse charismatic leaders in the Islamic world have claimed the title of Mahdi at various intervals. In the Sudanese instance, he was Muhammad Ahmad ibn as-Sayyid ʾAbd Allah (c. 1844–1885) and less than forty years old. He had been a member of the Sammaniyya sufi order in the north of the country but due to dissatisfaction with one of his teachers he left it and moved to the Nile River island of Aba, south of Khartoum. There he established himself with a small band of followers, among which was his future successor ʾAbd Allah ibn Muhammad at-Taʾiʾshi (1846–1899).

The Sudan was then an Ottoman-Egyptian colony and the regime was known locally as the Turkiyyah. By the 1870s the colonial state was thoroughly neglected by the rulers based in Egypt, creating opportunities for revolt. The administration and significant sectors of the colonial economy had substantial European participation right up to the level of governor. A few Sudanese were part of the government but most of the indigenous people resented their foreign rulers. The exclusion of Muslim Sudanese from leading roles in the colony and the inclusion of non-Muslim Europeans disturbed pious Muslims such as the Mahdi. Slavery was under attack by the British and abolition threatened many northern slave traders who were benefiting from the trade. These slave-traders would throw their weight behind the Mahdist movement.

The Mahdi came to address what he and his followers thought was an oppressive authority, which was contravening Islamic precepts. They challenged this situation and believed that a movement would emerge throughout the land to overthrow the regime. The Mahdi's calculation, however, that a countrywide revolt would follow his calls was never realized. But his movement was only partly political. Much support for the Mahdi was based on the belief that he was a divinely inspired figure. The religious dimension of his mission was perhaps more significant than its political impact.

The Mahdiyyah

The Mahdiyyah (meaning Mahdist Movement) was an indigenous northern Sudanese phenomenon but the Mahdi modeled himself and his movement on the early Islamic community of the Prophet of Islam in the Arabian Peninsula. His followers were called Ansar (helpers), just as the Prophet's supporters in Medina were named; he preached jihad against the infidels, collected *zakat* (tax on wealth) instead of the range of colonial taxes, and strove to impose *shariʿa* prohibitions and punishments. His successor, who was appointed on his deathbed, was given the title *khalifa* (caliph), as was the Prophet's successor. Indeed, Khalifa ʾAbd Allah was named *khalifa as-Siddiq*, the latter term usually associated with the first caliph of Islam, Abu Bakr (c. 573–634).

For the first two years the Mahdi was confined to the province of Kordofan, and then his forces spread slowly to the north along the Nile River. Thereafter his supporters increased and brought large parts of the west and east of the country under their control. Important towns such as El-Obeid, the main city of Kordofan, fell in January 1883, and the defeat of the expedition of Colonel William Hicks (1830–1883) in September of the same year at Shaikan bolstered the movement tremendously.

The already weak government in Cairo was unable to do much to stem the tide of the Mahdi's success, and the British, who had recently occupied Egypt (in 1882), were hesitant to act. When General Charles Gordon (1833–1885) was dispatched to the Sudan he was sent with contradictory instructions: to restore "good government" and to evacuate the colony. When he reached Khartoum he wrote to the Mahdi offering him the sultanship of Kordofan, which he rejected. The

Mahdi had much bigger ambitions that transcended mere political authority, especially that in an isolated province.

In October 1884 the Mahdi arrived on the banks of the Nile River opposite Khartoum and laid siege to the capital. In January of the following year Khartoum fell to the Mahdists. But instead of installing himself there he established a new capital called Omdurman, opposite the old one. There he died in June 1885, was buried, and a tomb was built for him. But the Mahdi's tomb was destroyed, and his body disinterred, in the reconquest of the Sudan by Sir Herbert Kitchener (1850–1916) in 1898.

Khalifa ʾAbd Allah's reign opened with the new state's armies engaged on multiple fronts: in the west to pacify the state of Darfur, on the Ethiopian borderland marches against the Christian state, and on the Egyptian border. Against the Ethiopian fighters the Mahdists were successful but not elsewhere. The khalifa also had to deal with a number of pretenders, "false mahdis." Furthermore, internal schisms surfaced between various layers of supporters who were dissatisfied with the khalifa's policies. The Ashraf, from the Mahdi's own kinsmen, were dissatisfied with the hegemony of the Taʿiʿsha, the khalifa's clan. There were also a series of ecological challenges including bad harvests and epidemics that led to famine between 1889 and 1890. As a result, by the early 1890s the khalifa's armies were easily beaten in numerous engagements. Their final defeat came at the hands of a determined British command with superior weaponry. It began in August 1897 and ended with the last battle at Karari, outside Omdurman, in September 1898. Thousands of Sudanese fighters were killed and wounded while the Anglo-Egyptian losses numbered fewer than fifty, with fewer than four hundred wounded. This was the beginning of British rule in the Sudan.

Accomplishments of the Mahdiyyah

In its short history the Mahdist state was actually able to put in place the foundations of a coherent and workable administration. There was a judiciary and judgments were based on the classical Islamic methods of juristic thought, although the Mahdi also sometimes relied on his own intuition as the Mahdi, a man with divinely inspired authority. There was a *Bayt al-Mal* (roughly, a Department of Finance or Treasury), which kept detailed records, taxed the subjects, and distributed wealth. The state minted its own coins for the local economy. Then there was the military. Under the khalifa the administration put in place by the Mahdi lost its reputation and tended to become corrupt. The khalifa, for instance, acquired a private army for himself and a separate share of the *Bayt al-Mal*. But the state under the khalifa was not wholly corrupt as it has sometimes been judged, although it did divert from the strict and puritanical path of its founder.

Shamil Jeppie

Further Reading

Holt, P. M. (1958). *The Mahdist state in the Sudan 1881–1898: A study of its origins, development, and overthrow.* Oxford, UK: Clarendon Press.

Holt, P. M., & Daly, M. W. (2000). *A history of the Sudan: From the coming of Islam to the present day* (5th ed.). Essex, UK: Longman.

Trimingham, J. S. (1949). *Islam in the Sudan*. London: Oxford University Press.

T

Tajik Civil War

The civil war in Tajikistan, a republic in Central Asia, was rooted in longstanding ethnic, religious, regional, and clan animosities as rival factions—with competing ideologies—fought to fill the power vacuum left by the collapse of the Soviet Union in 1991. The new Khujandi-based neo-Soviet elites that emerged victorious were secular-oriented and opposed Islamic fundamentalism, the dominant ideology emerging in southern post-Soviet Tajikistan. In the search for a post-Communist identity, local and regional clan elders in southern Tajikistan adopted an increasing religious orientation when Islamic fundamentalism began making significant inroads—as when former Afghan mujahideen (Islamic guerrilla fighters) established contact with Islamic activists in Tajikistan. Tajikistan's porous borders with Afghanistan willingly allowed the export of Islamic fundamentalism, which had gained credibility following the Soviets failure to win a quick, decisive victory in Afghanistan.

From Tribal Politics to Sovietization

Historically, the basic governing unit of Tajiks was the village. The village was the organizing unit of economic life, residence, local authority, law, and administration. The khanates (states or jurisdictions of a khan, or chieftain) that governed Tajikistan prior to Russian rule adopted the Persian pattern of government in which government was imposed on local communities. Tribal kin groups often settled in the same locality, so that in some villages and sometimes in cities extended kin groups retain clan identity. Settlement patterns secluded Tajiks into four regions marginally connected with each other, which would later become the basis of the republic's constituent regions. When the Bolsheviks came to power, they began superimposing Communism on the traditional Tajik social structures.

Sovietization in Tajikistan began with the establishment of Communist control. Traditional political elites were either assimilated or eliminated. Clan chiefs disappeared but often reappeared in the guise of district administrators. Administrators often gave preference to members of their own clan or region when making appointments and other decisions. The patronage system that developed under the native nomenclature had a dual purpose: First, party and state officials were Communist party functionaries; second, they were traditional local chiefs, often favoring their clan over another, fueling regional and clan animosities. Over time the clan from the northern region of Khujand (now Sogd) gained a monopoly on power within the Communist Party as well as in state organs at the expense of the other provinces of the republic—Kurgan-Tyube, Kulyab (now Khatlon), Garm, and Gorno-Badakhshan—so that by the end of World War II, Khujandis dominated political and economic life in Tajikistan. Not until the 1970s did the clan from the southern region of Kulyab manage to break the domination of the Khujandi elite.

The Combatants

The collapse of Soviet control and the introduction of perestroika (reform) in Tajikistan initiated the fragmentation of politics. The geographic isolation of the population centers and the development of regionalism during the Soviet era led to the emergence of clan-based regionally oriented political parties drawing support from their native region while receiving marginal support from neighboring regions. The combatants of the civil war were comprised of five major groups: the Communist Party against a four-part coalition called the "United Tajik Opposition" (UTO) of secular and democratic parties: the Democratic Party of Tajikistan, the Rastokhez (Resurgence) Movement, the Islamic Renaissance Party (IRP), and a regional party, La'li Badakhshan (Rubies of Badakhshan).

The Khujandi elite who dominated Soviet-era politics coalesced into a neo-Communist political party following independence, even retaining the Communist Party name. The Democratic Party of Tajikistan advocated the introduction of democracy, a market economy, and the end to Soviet rule and garnering limited support from the intelligentsia in the capital, Dushanbe. The Rastokhez Movement was the first officially recognized opposition movement registered in 1988. Led by Tahir Abdul Jabbar, Rastokhez had a nationalistic orientation favoring the sovereignty of Tajikistan, the recognition of Tajik culture, and the adoption of the Tajik language as the state language. The Islamic Renaissance Party (IRP) offered a competing ideology—Islamism—to that of failed communism and democracy and found support in the more rural, conservative South, where former Afghan mujahideen had established contact with Tajik Islamic activists—via organizations sponsored by Pakistan's Inter-Service Intelligence (ISI) based in the refugees across the border in Afghanistan— in hopes of establishing a friendly Islamic state. These connections introduced a fundamentalist version of Islam that was overtly anti-Soviet, and thereby, anti-Russian, with ties to the Jamaʾat-e-Islami, a powerful religio-political organization based in Pakistan.

Precursor to War

The attempted right-wing coup against the government of Soviet leader Mikhail Gorbachev in August 1991 created political turmoil in Tajikistan because the government supported the thwarted coup. When the coup failed, the Tajik Communists were forced from power by a coalition of antigovernment forces. Following three months of political instability, the Communist Party, led by Rakhmon Nabiev, won contested multiparty elections over the candidate of the Islamic-democratic coalition, Davlat Khudonazarov, and began consolidating power. Nabiev assumed dictatorial power, eliminating rivals from other clans. His sacking of a popular interior minister brought mass protests in Dushanbe. After a month of peaceful protests, the government announced the formation of a national guard, ostensibly comprised of neo-Soviets and former criminals from Kulyab. The opposition responded in kind by forming its own militia. Soon fighting erupted in the streets of Dushanbe. After gun battles between the two rival militias, the opposition seized the presidential palace, television station, and airport on 5 May 1992. Hostilities ceased on 11 May when a truce was reached between President Nabiev and the Islamic-democratic coalition. The truce—which was short-lived—included the opposition retaining the portfolios of eight key ministries as well as half of the seats in the newly formed parliament.

From Civil War to Chaos

In violation of a later truce proclaimed during the November 1992 session of the Tajik Republican Parliament, a coalition of Soviet-era political elites from Khujand and criminal elements from Kulyab known as the "Popular Front of Tajikistan" (PFT) attempted to eliminate the coalition of Islamic and secular pro-democracy militias. Supported by Russian and Uzbek forces, the PFT launched offensives into the IRP strongholds of Kulyab, Kurgan-Tyube, and Khazand, destroying homes and forcing as many as 100,000 refugees to flee across the border into Afghanistan. Soon the PFT routed opposition forces in Komsomolabad, Navabad, and Garm, consolidating control over much of the countryside, forcing the IRP leadership to flee to the relative safety of Afghanistan while the Islamic and democratic militias continued fighting from mountain bases and camps in Garm and Gorno-Badakhshan as well as from camps across the border in Afghanistan. After the defeat of the opposition forces, Tajikistan's civil war degenerated into bloodshed and chaos as criminal elements from within the PFT roamed the countryside committing atrocities against long-time ethnic, religious, regional, and clan rivals.

Geopolitical Implications

After intermittent ceasefires, peace negotiations began in 1994, and a ceasefire was eventually agreed to in June 1987 when the regime of Imomali Rakmonhov and the opposition agreed to an amnesty for opposition combatants, legalization of opposition political parties, exchange of prisoners, repatriation of refugees living in Afghanistan, and establishment of the National Reconciliation Commission to oversee the transition to multiparty elections.

The Tajik Civil War destabilized much of central Asia, and Russia used the war as justification to station its 201st Motorized Rifle Division along the 1,448-kilometer-long Afghan-Tajik border, claiming that Russia needed to secure its southern flank as a shield against the spread of regional and clan violence as well as against the perceived threat of Islamic fundamentalism, which could spread to other central Asian republics.

Keith A. Leitich

See also Afghanistan; Islamic Movement of Uzbekistan; Jihad

Further Reading

Atkin, M. (1997). Tajikistan's civil war. *Current History, 96*(612), 336–340.

Emadi, H. (1994). State, ideology and Islamic resurgence in Tajikistan. *Central Asian Survey, 13*(4), 565–573.

Gretsky, S. (1995). Civil war in Tajikistan: Causes, developments, and prospects for peace. In E. Sagdeev & S. Eisenhower (Eds.), *Central Asia: Conflict, resolution, and change* (pp. 217–248). Chevy Chase, MD: CPSS Press.

Hetmanek, A. (1993). Islamic revolution and jihad come to the former Soviet central Asia: The case of Tajikistan. *Central Asian Survey, 12*(3), 365–378.

Hyman, A. (1994). *Power and politics in central Asia's new republics*. London: Research Institute for the Study of Conflict and Terrorism.

Jawad, N., & Tadjbakhsh, S. (1995). *Tajikistan: A forgotten civil war*. London: Minority Rights Group.

Khudonazar, D. (1995). The conflict in Tajikistan: Questions of regionalism. In E. Sagdeev & S. Eisenhower (Eds.), *Central Asia: Conflict, resolution, and change* (pp. 249–264). Chevy Chase, MD: CPSS Press.

Niyazi, A. (1998). Tajikistan I: The regional dimension of conflict. In M. Waller, B. Coppieters, & A. Malashenko (Eds.), *Conflicting loyalties and the state in post-Soviet Russia and Eurasia* (pp. 145–170). Portland, OR: Frank Cass Publishers.

Olimova, S. (1998). Political Islam and conflict in Tajikistan. In L. Jonson & M. Esenov (Eds.), *Political Islam and conflicts in Russia and central Asia* (Conference Paper No. 24) Stockholm: Swedish Institute of International Affairs.

Roy, O. (1993). *The civil war in Tajikistan: Causes and implications*. Washington, DC: United States Institute for Peace.

Taliban

The Taliban are an extremist Islamic movement that formed in October 1994 in Kandahar province in southeastern Afghanistan. The Taliban captured Kabul, Afghanistan's capital, in September 1996 and governed most of the country until they were overthrown by U.S. forces by the end of 2001. The Taliban ruled Afghanistan according to a strict version of *shariʿa* (Islamic law) that had no parallel in earlier Islamic history.

The Taliban's Beginnings and Rise to Power

The Arabic word *taliban* means "religious students" and indeed, the Taliban were mostly young students of Qurʾanic learning at Islamic seminaries called *madrasahs* in Kandahar and neighboring areas in Pakistan. Ethically, most were Pashtuns, the most populous ethnic group in Afghanistan. Their leadership consisted mainly of former Pashtun mujahideen (Islamist guerrillas) who had fought the invading (and later, occupying) Soviet troops in Afghanistan in the 1980s.

Following the withdrawal of Soviet troops in 1989, most of these mujahideen, including Mullah Mohammed Omar (b. 1962), the Taliban's spiritual leader, started Qurʾanic teaching at the *madrasahs* in Afghanistan. However, factional warfare, especially the oppressive acts of certain Afghan commanders against the citizenry of Kandahar, led Mullah Omar and other former mujahideen to transform the Taliban into a movement with a political, as well as a religious, component.

Militarily assisted by Pakistani authorities for regional strategic reasons, financed by Saudi Arabia as part of its mission to spread Wahhabism, a conservative sect of Islam, in South and Central Asian Muslim regions, and overlooked by the United States, the Taliban movement initially aimed to ensure peace and enforce *shariʾa*. Taliban leaders abhorred the quest for power, blaming it as the chief reason for intra-Afghan warfare. They pledged to work for the common good of the Afghan people. However, as the Taliban made successive territorial gains across Afghanistan, hunger for power overwhelmed the desire to establish peace.

The Taliban Impose More Bans on Nationals; *The Daily MUSLIM*, May 24,1997

Peshawar: Besides imposing other restrictions on individual freedom, the Taliban in Afghanistan, have banned the keeping of pigeons and playing with the birds, describing it as un-Islamic.

The violators of the ban, according to a report from Kabul will be imprisoned and the birds shall be killed. The kite flying has also been stopped.

Another interesting rule on the subject related to what it described the promotion of Islamic hairstyle. They have advised the Afghans not to go for the American and British hair styles which could land them in jail. The concerned department has also authorized to shave the hair of such people and charge expenses.

The male tailors have been banned from sewing ladies dresses and taking their body measurements, adding that if any woman or magazines were found at the tailors shop, the owner will be arrested.

***Source:* Recent Reports form Afghanistan. Retrieved April 28, 2000, from http://www.rawa.org/recent.htm**

In September 1995 the Taliban captured the province of Herat in the west; in September 1996 they took Kabul, and in August 1998, they were in control of Mazar-e Sharif, a city in northern Afghanistan. At their strongest they controlled 95 percent of the territory of Afghanistan, leaving only a couple of northeastern provinces in the hands of the Northern Alliance, an alliance composed primarily of Tajiks, Uzbeks, and Hazaras, minority peoples in Afghanistan.

Taliban Extremism

Traditionally, 90 percent of Afghans belonged to the Sunni Hanafi sect, the most liberal branch of Sunni Islam (Sunni Muslims comprise 90 percent of the world's Muslims). Sufism, a branch of Islam that emphasizes mysticism, was also enormously popular in Afghanistan.

Before the Taliban, none of Islam's extreme orthodox sects had made any inroads in Afghanistan's traditional social structure, where tribe and ethnicity were more important than religion. The Taliban were able to succeed only because the collapse of civil society brought on by years of warlordism created a political vacuum: There was no other strong ideological or political movement around. The Taliban began as reformers, following an established tradition in Islamic history based on the notion of jihad, or struggle. Jihad generally has been used to imply a holy war against infidels, but the Taliban took it to extremes, using it to justify attacks on rival ethnic and sectarian groups

The Taliban's conception of *shari'a* was based on their understanding of Deobandism, an Islamic reformist movement that developed in British India in the mid-nineteenth century, but Saudi funding of the *madrasah*s where future Taliban studied meant that the curriculum leaned toward Wahhabism. One example of the overbearing influence of Wahhabism on the Taliban's Deobandi origins could be seen in Mullah Umar's insistence on destroying the Bamiyan Buddhas. For, unlike Wahhabism, Deobandism did not consider sacred Islamic sites, such as tombstones and shrines, as "idolatrous"—and, therefore, worthy of destruction.

The Taliban practice of *shari'a* required women to cover up from head to foot in public and forbade men to shave their beards: People not complying could be beaten. Women were forbidden to be educated. Music was forbidden completely, and the Ministry for Fostering Virtue and Preventing Vice even disrupted sport activities, invoking Mullah Omar's fat was (religious edicts) about their un-Islamic character. The Taliban also became host to Osama bin Ladin (b. 1957), the leader of the terrorist organization al-Qaeda. It was while a guest of the Taliban government that bin Laden issued his February 1998 fatwa urging Muslims to "kill the Americans and their allies" (Griffin 2001, 196) and realized it in the August 1998 bombing of two U.S. embassies in East Africa and the September 11 attacks on New York City's World Trade Center and the Pentagon in Washington, D.C.

It is true that the rise of the Taliban took place as a consequence of anarchic circumstances, involving internecine warfare by rival mujahideen warlords and the accompanying social unrest. The Taliban can be given the credit for disarming the rival factions, and restoring civic order. However, in their bid to reunite Afghanistan on the basis of shariʾa, the Taliban crushed the very delicate ethno-religious balance that had held the Afghan society together for ages. The evil surely outweighed the good during the Taliban period in Afghanistan. The domestic extremist posture on the part of Taliban's bigoted leaders eventually assumed a regional/global dimension as they forged closer ties with the Laden-led al Qaeda.

The Aftereffects

The Taliban may have fallen in Afghanistan, but the domestic and regional fallout from their extremist legacy is far from over. The rise of Taliban in Afghanistan had a spillover impact on all the Muslim nations bordering Afghanistan, particularly Pakistan, Tajikistan, and Uzbekistan. It fuelled Islamic extremism in Tajikistan and Uzbekistan, and led to what is called the "Talibanization of Pakistan" (Ahmad 2000–2001, 69). Owing to their pan-Islamic outlook, the Taliban did not recognize international borders. Consequently, from Chechnya in Russia to Kashmir in India, the Taliban made their militant—and terrorist—presence felt for the respective state authorities.

The Taliban's practice of Islamic *shariʾa* was so cruel in humanitarian terms and so out of keeping with the spirit of the modern age that their demise has led to a renewed debate in the Muslim world on how Islam can coexist productively with modernity. For many in the Western world as well, the Taliban's success in Afghanistan led to renewed questions about Islam's compatibility with democracy and modernity. While the remnants of the Taliban continue to endanger peace and security in Afghanistan, the Afghani people may now look forward to a future free from the horrors of the Taliban era.

Ishtiaq Ahmad

See also Afghanistan; Deobandism; Wahhabism

Further Reading

Ahmad, I. (2000–2001). Containing the Taliban: The path of peace in Afghanistan. *Perceptions, 5*(4), 67–87.

Ahmad, I. (2002). Post-war Afghanistan: Rebuilding a ravaged nation. *Perceptions, 7*(2), 25–39.

Cooley, J. K. (2002). *Unholy wars: Afghanistan, America and international terrorism.* London: Pluto Press.

Griffin, M. (2001). *Reaping the whirlwind: The Taliban movement in Afghanistan.* London: Pluto Press.

Gohari, M. J. (2000). *The Taliban: Ascent to power.* New York: Oxford University Press.

Marsden, P. (1999). *The Taliban: War, religion and the new order in Afghanistan.* London: Zed Books.

Maley, W. (1998). *Fundamentalism reborn? Afghanistan and the Taliban.* London: C. Hurst.

Rashid, A. (2002). *Jihad: The rise of militant Islam in Central Asia.* New Haven, CT: Yale University Press.

Rashid, A. (2000). *Taliban: Islam, oil and the new Great Game in Central Asia.* London: I B Tauris.

Rashid, A (1999). The Taliban: Exporting extremism. *Foreign Affairs, 78*(6), 22–35.

Terrorism, Religious

Religious terrorism can be literally defined as the deliberate use of violence against civilians for religious ends. As compared to ethnonationalist or ideologically inspired terrorism, religious terrorism is the oldest, most consistent, and deadliest in terms of its current global reach and impact. Religious terrorists could hail from both main religious faiths and small religious cults, and target not only the followers of other religious faiths but also fellow believers refusing to follow their diktats.

For centuries, religion has been a source of violence, terrorism, and war. However, never before did it emerge as the principal source of terrorism at the global scale as it has since the start of the 1990s. The 11 September 2001 terrorist attacks against the United States carried out by Osama bin Laden's al-Qaeda network thus far represent the optimal stage of transnational Islamic terrorism. These and a number of other successive attacks against Western targets claimed by al-Qaeda and other radical Islamic organizations reflect the likely enormity of Islamic terrorism in the twenty-first century.

Historical Background

The history of religious terrorism is as old as the history of religion itself. The just-war doctrine is a religious precept, and as old as war itself. Parts of the Bible hint at it, and St. Thomas Aquinas synthesized it in *Summa Theologicae*. Some of the English words used to describe terrorists and their acts today are derived from the names of Jewish, Muslim, and Hindu religious groups active centuries ago. For example, the word *zealot* comes from a Jewish sect, which fought in the first century against the Roman occupation of what is now Israel. The word *assassin* is derived from a radical offshoot of Shi'ite Islam, which fought between the eleventh and thirteenth centuries with Christian crusaders attempting to conquer present-day Syria and Iran. The assassin would eat hashish before committing murder. The origin of the word *thug* is from a Hindu association of professional robbers and murderers who, between the seventh and nineteenth centuries, ritually strangled travelers as sacrificial offerings to Kali, the Hindu goddess of terror and destruction.

In fact, until the end of the nineteenth century, religion provided the only justification for terrorism. From the start of the twentieth century up to the 1980s, however, religious terrorism was overshadowed by ethnonationalist, separatist, and ideologically motivated political terrorism. These included anticolonial and postcolonial movements for national liberation in the shape of ethnonationalist terrorism, as well as right-wing and left-wing terrorism. Even terrorist movements with a strong religious component—such as the Palestine Liberation Organization (PLO)—had a political, rather than religious, motivation. It was only after the 1979 revolution in Iran that religious terrorism revolving around the Shi'ite Islamic principle of martyrdom started to surface in the Middle East.

Religion became a far more popular motivation for terrorism in the post–Cold War era as old ideologies were discredited by the collapse of the Soviet Union and communist ideology. Samuel P Huntington's 1993 clash of civilizations thesis in the book of the same title, even though quite controversial, placed religion at the heart of regional and global conflicts in the post–Cold War period. According to it, at least eight primary cultural paradigms or civilizations with religion as the key determinant are dominating the modern world, including Western, Confucian, Japanese, Islamic, Hindu, Slavic-Orthodox, Latin American, and African. Each civilization has religious zealots who seek to impose their views on others.

Unsurprisingly, the proportion of religious terrorist groups among all active international terrorist organizations grew radically during the 1990s. The decade, in particular, saw the rise of militant Islamic extremism, while terrorism by religions other than Islam as well as obscure sects and cults also increased. By the mid–1990s, nearly half of the fifty-six known active international terrorist groups were religiously motivated. Today well over half of the world's terrorist organizations are religiously motivated; a number of Islamic terrorist groups have been added to the list of terrorist organizations by the U.S. government since September 11.

Relative Lethality

Religion is a major force behind terrorism's rising lethality. The 11 September 2001 attacks were by far the most lethal in the recent history of religious terrorism. In the 1990s and beyond, the biggest transformation in religious terrorism is that its operational scope is no more limited to a particular country or a specific region; rather, it has become global, transcending international boundaries, penetrating even the most powerful of nations such as the United States.

The emergence of religion as a driving force behind the increasing lethality of international terrorism shatters some of the main assumptions about terrorists. In the past, most analysts tended to discount the possibility of mass killing involving chemical, biological, radiological, or nuclear terrorism. Few terrorists, it was argued, knew anything about the technical intricacies of either developing or dispersing such weapons. Political, moral, and practical considerations also were perceived as important restraints. The compelling new motives of the religious terrorist, coupled with increased access to critical information and to key components of weapons of mass destruction, render conventional wisdom dangerously anachronistic. The motives of current religious terrorist groups go far beyond the creation of a theocracy based on a particular deity. They may include mystical, transcendental, or divinely inspired imperatives as well as a staunchly antigovernment/state populism reflecting conspiracy theories based on a volatile mixture of seditious, racial, and religious maxim.

The reasons why religious terrorism results in so many more deaths than political terrorism may be found in the radically different value systems, mechanisms of legitimization and justification, concepts of morality, and worldviews embraced by the religious terrorist.

According to terrorism expert Bruce Hoffman, "holy terror" contains a value system that stands in opposition to "secular terror." Secular terrorists operate within the realm of a dominant political and cultural framework. They want to win, to beat the political system oppressing them. Their goal may be to destroy social structure, but they want to put something in its place. Secular terrorists would rather make allies than discriminately kill their enemies. Holy terrorists, however, are under no such constraints. They see the world as a battlefield between the forces of light and darkness. Winning is not described in political terms. The enemy must be totally destroyed.

For political terrorists, killing is the outcome of an operation. Again, religious terrorists differ. According to Hoffman, for holy terrorists, "violence (is) first and foremost a sacramental act or divine duty executed in direct response to some theological demand or imperative" (White 2002, 51). For example, the Islamic radicals who adhere to the aggressive and militaristic interpretation of jihad divide the world into *dar al-Islam* (House of Islam) and *dar al-harb* (House of War). For them, the purpose of terrorism is to either kill the enemies of God in *dar al-harb* or convert them to Islam so as to bring them to the fold of *dar al-Islam*.

Contemporary Examples

Religious terrorism afflicts every region of the world, developed and developing, Muslim and Western. However, it is most prevalent in the Middle East—the birthplace of Judaism, Christianity, and Islam. While Jewish fundamentalist groups like Kach and Kahane Chai want to establish the greater Israel of biblical times, the secular Muslim organizations such as the PLO and the Popular Front for the Liberation of Palestine (PFLP) want to liberate Palestine from Israeli occupation. For their part, radical Islamic movements such as the Shi'ite extremist Hizbullah in Lebanon, Islamic Jihad and Hamas in Palestine, and Gam'a al-Islamiyya in Egypt not only want to end the state of Israel but also wish to overthrow their pro-Western Arab regimes, which they view as oppressive. The Palestinian freedom struggle took a more violent Islamic turn with the start of the second Intifada in 2000, involving suicide bombings against Israeli civilians primarily by members of Hamas and Islamic Jihad. Since 11 September 2001, the Israeli government has intensified its campaign to crush the Palestinians in the guise of fighting terrorism, which has only further strengthened the hands of religious extremists among the Palestinians vis-à-vis the traditionally secular Palestinian organizations like the PLO and the PLFP.

Africa is not far behind in the contemporary wave of religious terrorism. The Islamic regime of Sudan, a country inhabited in the north by Muslims of Arab descent and in the south by Christians of African descent, has resorted to various means of terror to suppress the Christian population. In Algeria, the extremist Armed Islamic Group does not spare the regime as well as the general public in its terrorist operations. Nigeria and Kenya are two other African states depicting a growing trend of indigenous religious terrorism (Muslim-Christian violence in Nigeria's Muslim majority provinces under *shari'a* rule) and transnational Islamic terrorism (the November 2002 attacks against Israeli targets in Mombasa, Kenya, claimed by al-Qaeda).

In the Balkan wars of the 1990s, the Catholic Croats fought with the Orthodox Serbs, and the Orthodox Serbs fought against the Muslims of Bosnia and Kosovo. Each side accused the other of practicing terrorism. In Kosovo, for instance, while terrorism committed by Serbian forces of the Yugoslav Federation was quite obvious, the Serbian leadership accused the Kosovo Liberation Army of committing terrorism. And when NATO started to bomb Yugoslavia, the Slavic-Orthodox Serbian leadership even perceived a Western Christian conspiracy in it. However, apart from religion, ethno-racial identity—Slavic Serbs versus Albanian Kosovars in Kosovo—could be identified as a major factor in the Balkan wars. Huntington's clash of civilizations thesis had predicted greater conflict in "torn countries"—regions inhabited by more than one civilization, such as the Balkans. The Balkan wars were mainly a result of believers of conflicting faiths literalizing symbols and myths, and subjugating them to ethnic and nationalistic aims.

In the eastern Mediterranean island of Cyprus, the Muslim Turks have been on the receiving end of Greek Orthodox Christianity's Hellenic ambition of enosis, the island's unification with Greece. In Eurasia, the two conflict situations—the dispute over Nagorno-Karabakh between Azerbaijan and Armenia, and the Chechen independence movement in the Russian Federation—involve much of the same ethno-religious tendency, except that the issue of Chechnya is believed to be closely associated with a worldwide jihad movement led by al-Qaeda. In central Asia, radical Islamic groups like the Islamic Movement of Uzbekistan have committed a number of terrorist attacks against foreigners and government authorities in Uzbekistan and Kyrgyzstan.

In southeast Asia, radical Islamic organizations such as Abu Sayyaf in the Philippines and Malaysia and Jama al-Islamiyya in Indonesia have been involved in a number of terrorist acts targeting Western tourists, the most recent and lethal being the bombing in Bali in November 2002, allegedly by militants of Jama al-Islamiyya. In west Asia, the Taliban and al-Qaeda in Afghanistan terrorized not just the Muslim people of Afghanistan, and nations and regions surrounding Afghanistan, but also U.S. interests at home and abroad, including the 1993 terrorist attack against the World Trade Center, the August 1998 bombings of the U.S. embassies in east Africa, and the 11 September 2001 terrorist attacks.

In south Asia, religion has been a major source of terrorism. Examples include the conflict between the separatist Tamil-speaking Hindus and the ruling Sinhalese-speaking Buddhists in Sri Lanka and the Hindu extremist violence against minority Muslim, Christian, and Sikh people in India. The Kashmir dispute between India and Pakistan has fueled Islamic extremist passions in Pakistan and Hindu nationalist feelings in India, and set in force a spiral of competing religious extremisms in the Indian subcontinent that could have catastrophic consequences, given that both India and Pakistan are nuclear powers. The Hindu-Muslim conflict, which led to the bloody partition of the Indian subcontinent in 1947, is at the root of India-Pakistan hostility and threatens to destroy the secular fabric of India's polity. Moreover, Islamic radicalism has become synonymous with the Kashmir dispute since 1989, when mujahideen from the anti-Soviet Afghan war shifted their attention to liberating Kashmiri Muslims from Indian rule. Since September 11, the U.S. government has placed a number of radical Kashmiri groups, including Lashkar-e-Toyaba, Jaish-e-Mohammad, Harkat-ul- Mujahideen, and Hizb-ul-Mujahideen, on the list of international terrorist organizations.

Religious terrorism also exists in the Western or developed world, even though at a far lesser scale than the developing or Muslim parts of the world. In Northern Ireland, for instance, religion is definitely the fuel that inflames the passions of the rival Protestant and Catholic extremists. Catholic extremists use the Catholic label to describe nationalistic revolutionaries who want no part of Britain. Protestant extremists use the Protestant label to define who will use terrorism to keep Northern Ireland associated with the United Kingdom. That explains why the Catholic Sinn Fein and Protestant Ulster Unionists disagree over power sharing in Northern Ireland and demilitarization of the Irish Republican Army (IRA). This also explains the continuity of terrorist acts by spin-off groups like the Real IRA, which has been placed on the U.S. government list of international terrorist organizations.

Terrorism by doomsday or apocalyptic religious cults has affected in particular Japan and the United States. Apocalyptic cults believe that the world is coming to an end and that members of the cult will play some role in the eschatological event. Doomsday cults believe they must take offensive action to bring about the end of the world. In March 1995, the Aum Shinrikya (Supreme Truth) sarin gas attack on Tokyo's subways killed twelve and injured more than 5,000. It was the world's first mass-scale chemical terrorist attack. The 1993 debacle in Waco, Texas, where seventy-four persons were killed, including twenty-one children, and the eighty-one-day standoff between the Freemen, a Montana militia organization, and the FBI in April 1996, which concluded peacefully, are two recent examples of the growth of religious cults and their terrorist streaks in the United States.

Religious extremist movements in the United States, in addition to such apocalyptic cults, include black supremacy groups such as the Nation of Islam, white supremacists like the Ku Klux Klan, and other Christian identity movements like the Aryan Nation. All of them are racist and anti-Semitic. The Christian identity movements are of special concern, given their emphasis upon a future racial and religious Armageddon, a holy war between Yahweh's Aryan race on the one side and the Jews and other "subhuman races" on the other. These movements represent a powerful religious ideology whose teachings or teachers may have influenced Timothy McVeigh, convicted and executed for the 1995 Oklahoma City bombing.

Future Prospects

While religious terrorism, especially with an ethnonationalist cover, is most widespread in developing and Muslim regions of the world, Islamic terrorism has emerged as a global phenomenon targeting American-Western-Christian and Israeli-Jewish interests worldwide. The September 11 terrorist attacks, according to Strobe Talbott and Nayan Chanda, prove that religious terrorism in the twenty-first century will involve an enemy who is invisible and unpredictable, who acts without a stated military objective, who does not spare even a power with the most awesome military capability, and who aims at mass killings, even involving the use of weapons of mass destruction.

Fighting such an enemy requires more than traditional strategies and conventional means. Reversing the global expansion of religious terrorism and eventually limiting its social impact require the adoption of new, multipronged approaches, employing military, political, and economic means. While the international community cannot ignore the violent ramifications of religious terrorism, it cannot as well overlook the larger political and economic causes, which provide a breeding ground for religious hatred and radicalism, and the consequent religious terrorism. It may be easier to reintegrate American or Japanese religious, doomsday cults into mainstream society by addressing the particular socioeconomic grievances of their followers. For it is these grievances which could encourage them to develop alienated worldviews and apocalyptic thinking. However, de-radicalizing religious terrorist networks like al-Qaeda and groups like Hamas is an uphill task, which may not be accomplished until the larger political, social, and economic context in which religious radicalism occurs regionally or internationally is properly understood.

Given that, it may be a mistake to single out Islam as a religion of terror. Terrorism has been practiced by the radical elements belonging to all religious faiths. Islam has yet to experience the sort of reformation that Western Christianity underwent centuries ago, after which it started its march to modernity. It is due to the deep modernity crisis facing Islam that radical Islamic forces traditional on the fringes have come to the forefront of religious expression in a terrorist way, hijacking even genuine causes of Muslim liberation in the world. Obviously, the U.S.-Western conduct vis-à-vis the Muslim world—based upon political duplicity (unduly backing Israel on Palestine or supporting authoritarian Arab regimes) and economic exploitation (getting cheap oil from the Persian Gulf even to the extent of overlooking the Saudi bid to spread Wahhabism)—may also have contributed to the radicalization of a section of Islamic believers. While the international community cannot ignore the use of military and nonmilitary means to tackle the violent ramifications of Islamic terrorism, it cannot overlook "the larger political and economic causes, which provide a breeding ground for religious hatred and radicalism, the rise of extremist movements, and recruits for the Bin Ladens of the world" (Esposito 2002, 160). It is only by duly addressing these causes that the current global wave of Islamic terrorism can be reversed credibly, and its potentially cataclysmic consequences avoided.

Ishtiaq Ahmad

See also Assassins; Crusades; Fundamentalism in Egypt and Sudan; Fundamentalism in Iran; Genocide in Africa; Genocide in Bosnia; Genocide in Europe; Hamas; Hizbullah; Indonesia; Jihad; Kashmir; Ku Klux Klan; Martyrdom; Mormons; Nazism and Holocaust; Nigeria; Palestine–1948 War; Palestine-Israel; Pueblo Revolt of 1680; Religion, Violence and Genocide; Sri Lanka; Sudan; Thugs; Zealots

Further Readings

Akbar, M. (2002). *The shade of swords: Jihad and the conflict between Islam and Christianity*. London: Routledge.

Ali, T. (2002). *The clash of fundamentalisms: Crusades, jihads, and modernity*. London: Verso.

Combs, C. (2003). *Terrorism in the twenty-first century*. Upper Saddle River, NJ: Prentice-Hall.

Ellis, M. (1997). *Unholy alliance: Religion and atrocities in our time*. Minneapolis, MN: Fortress Press.

Esposito, J. (1999). *The Islamic threat: Myth or reality?* New York: Oxford University Press.

Esposito, J. (2002). *Unholy war: Terror in the name of Islam*. New York: Oxford University Press.

Gallagher, E. (1997). God and country: Revolution as a religious imperative on the radicalright. *Terrorism and Political Violence, 9*(3), (pp. 63–79).

Hoffman, B. (1999). *Inside terrorism*. New York: Columbia University Press.

Huntington, S. (1996). *The clash of civilizations and the remaking of world order*. New York: Simon & Schuster.

Jaffrelot, C. (1996). *The Hindu nationalist movement in India*. New York: Columbia University Press.

Juergensmeyer, M. (2001). *Terror in the mind of God: The global rise of religious violence*. Berkeley: University of California Press.

Kaplan D., & Marshall, A. (1996). *The cult at the end of the world*. New York: Crown Publishers.

Laqueur, W. (1999). *The new terrorism*. New York: Oxford University Press.

Reich, W. (1998). *Origins of terrorism: Psychologies, ideologies, theologies, states of mind*. Washington, DC: Woodrow Wilson Center Press.

Schofield, V. (2000). *Kashmir in conflict: India and Pakistan and the unfinished war*. New York: I. B. Tauris.

Stern, J. (2001). *The ultimate terrorists*. Cambridge, MA: Harvard University Press.

Talbott, S., & Chanda, N. (2001). *The age of terror: America and the world after September 11*. New York: Basic Books.

White, J. (2002). *Terrorism: An introduction*. Belmont, CA: Wadsworth.

Thirty Years' War

The Thirty Years' War, 1618–1648, was a conflict in which Germany (the Holy Roman Empire) was the primary battleground. While the war began as a conflict among princes of the empire, by the end, all of Europe from England to Russia had taken part, and battles waged in Hungary, Poland, Denmark, Italy, the Netherlands, as well as Germany. Ultimately, the conflict in Germany was brought to an end by the Peace of Westphalia in 1648, but the combatants continued to wage war outside the empire until 1659 (when France and Spain finally made peace).

The Background

The roots of the war lay in two major factors. First of all, the Protestant Reformation had broken the religious unity of the Holy Roman Empire. Martin Luther (1483–1586) had been declared an outlaw at the Imperial Diet of Worms in 1521 but survived because of the protection given him by his ruler, Frederick the Wise (1463–1525) of Saxony. In the course of the 1520s a number of princes and many imperial cities had adopted Protestantism. After walking out of the Imperial Diet of Augsburg in 1530 (the "protest" that gave Protestantism its name) the Protestant rulers and cities took up arms to defend their decisions on religious matters. These religious wars came to a temporary end with the Peace of Augsburg in 1555. There the right of princes to choose the religion of their territories was recognized (though not given legal standing). This right, *cuius regio, eius religio* (whose the region, his the religion), was limited to Lutherans and Catholics. Calvinism remained illegal and the question of whether bishops and other churchmen who were also rulers of secular states had the right to convert to Protestantism (and in the process alter the confession of their territories) remained unresolved. In addition, the status of Catholic institutions and property (monasteries and bishoprics) within Protestant territories remained unclear. Could Protestant rulers seize such property and force the closure of monasteries? Most Catholics, including the emperor and the pope, viewed the Peace of Augsburg as a temporary concession.

The other major cause of the Thirty Years' War was the Habsburg family's territorial ambitions. Over the years, in part by luck, in part by military success, but above all by marriage policy, the Habsburgs had risen to be the most powerful family in Europe. Its members ruled Spain, Portugal, and their foreign possessions; Burgundy and the Netherlands; Austria, Hungary, Bohemia, and southern Italy. A Habsburg had been elected emperor repeatedly. This concentration of power, even if different people wielded it after the abdication of the Holy Roman emperor Charles V (1500–1558), was viewed with alarm by many in the empire and of course by France, England, and the papacy.

The Immediate Cause: The Revolt in Bohemia

Though relations between the papacy and the Habsburgs were often stormy, for the most part the Habsburgs were devout Catholics. In Spain and the New World, they championed Catholicism. In the Netherlands, they fought a long and bloody struggle against the Dutch Estates, which were dominated by Calvinists. In Central Europe, though, they had adopted a policy of accommodation toward the Protestants. In Bohemia and Austria, the Protestant Reformation had made significant inroads, particularly among the Estates. Habsburgs ruled both of these kingdoms, but their hereditary rights to the crowns were disputed by the estates who argued that both crowns were electoral.

The situation in Bohemia was complicated by the presence since the fifteenth century of an indigenous alternative to the papal church. The Czech Brethren, descended from the views of Jan Hus (1372– or 1373–1415), had dominated Bohemian religious life and had succeeded in gaining significant local control over religious life and practice (including the right to receive both bread and wine in communion). In both Bohemia and Austria, there was widespread support for Protestantism among the nobility, the merchant classes, and even among peasants and miners. In Austria, perhaps 80 to 90 percent of the nobility were Protestant by 1580.

The Estates were able to force religious concessions, especially in Bohemia, including freedom of worship for Protestants and clerical marriage. Indeed, the Estates were so powerful that they were able to force the resignation of Rudolf II (1552–1612) as king of Bohemia. He was succeeded in 1611 by Matthias (1557–1619). Matthias had been King of Hungary since 1608 and would be elected Holy Roman emperor in 1612. Matthias was childless and both Habsburgs and the Estates were concerned about the succession to the throne of Bohemia. The Habsburg favorite was Ferdinand (1578–1637) and indeed the Estates had elected him king-designate in 1617. Matthias's efforts to reestablish Habsburg power in Bohemia meant that he attacked both the political privileges of the Estates as well as their Protestantism. The Estates resisted. In 1618, Matthias declared their assembly illegal. In response, members of the Bohemian Estates tossed three Habsburg officials out of the window of the Hradschin palace on 23 May 1618 (the "defenestration of Prague"). This was the immediate cause of the Thirty Years' War.

The Bohemian Revolt

This course of events roused anti-Habsburg feelings throughout Europe. The Bohemians were joined in the revolt by Lusatia, Silesia, and Upper Austria in the summer of 1618, and by Moravia and Lower Austria in 1619. The Bohemians hinted that they might offer the crown to Frederick, Elector of the Palatinate (1596–1632), who had also sent some troops. In May 1619 Bohemian forces led by Count Thurn (1567–1632) (who had participated in the defenestration), besieged Vienna. In response, Ferdinand raised an army and invaded Bohemia.

The siege of Vienna was lifted in 1619, but the Estates solemnly deposed Ferdinand and on 26th of August 1619 elected in his stead Frederick, Elector of the Palatinate. He was not the best choice. A contemporary described him as "a man who had never seen either a battle or a corpse, . . . a prince who knew more about gardening than fighting" (Parker 1987, 52). But he was well connected, related to most of the major Protestant houses of Europe, including Sweden, and married to the daughter of King James I (1566–1625) of England. In the weeks that followed, the Protestant forces again seemed to have the upper hand. With the support of Gabor Bethlen (1580–1629), Prince of Transylvania, who with help from the Ottoman Turks invaded Hungary, the Protestants again laid siege to Vienna. It was in this context that Ferdinand was unanimously elected Holy Roman emperor on 28 August 1619.

Diplomatic moves now isolated the rebels. The Habsburgs convinced the Turks to withhold support for Gabor Bethlen. James I of England sharply criticized his son-in-law's actions in Bohemia and urged the Protestants to compromise. Hopes that Louis XIII (1601–1643) might bring France in on their side came to nothing. On 17 July 1620, a Catholic army of 30,000 (including René Descartes) led by Count Tilly (Johann Tserclaes; 1559–1632) marched against Bohemia. On 8 November 1620, the rebels made their stand on the White Mountain, just outside Prague. The battle resulted in a total victory for the Catholic forces, ending the Bohemian revolt, and dashing Frederick's aspirations to be king of Bohemia. He would die in exile in the Netherlands in 1632, deposed by the emperor and his territory stripped of its electoral status.

The War

The war itself is an enormously complex phenomenon. The Protestant cause was weakened by internal dissension. Some doubted the validity of Frederick's election as king of Bohemia. The leading Protestant prince of the empire, Elector of Saxony Johann Georg (1585–1656), viewed anyone who took up arms against the emperor as an unjustified revolutionary. Moreover, he and many other Lutherans perceived Calvinism as a greater threat than Catholicism. Frederick's efforts to broaden the Protestant cause by gaining support outside the empire foundered. Frederick received some financial support from the Dutch, whose own conflict with the Spanish flared up again in 1621 after a truce of some ten years. Even Frederick's father-in-law, James I of England, sought to end the conflict. The Catholics were led by the imperial forces under the command of two famous generals, Tilly and Albrecht von Wallenstein (1583–1634). In addition they could call on support from the Habsburg forces of Spain. The leading Catholic power in Germany was the Duchy of Bavaria, whose ruler Maximilian I (1573–1651) was a champion of Catholic reform and eager to enhance his status within the empire.

By the late 1620s, the outlook for the Protestants was bleak indeed. Denmark's entry into the war in the mid–1620s succeeded only in broadening the devastation into northern Germany. King Christian IV (1577–1648) was also an imperial vassal as Duke of Holstein. He wanted to broaden his influence in northern Germany to counterbalance Sweden's growing power in the eastern Baltic. His campaign in northern Germany was a failure but the cost to the empire and its supporters of maintaining Wallenstein's army in the north became too high to bear. In 1629, Ferdinand made peace with Christian. It seemed that Habsburg forces were triumphant.

But the emperor overplayed his hand and issued the Edict of Restitution in the same year. Catholics demanded that ecclesiastical states and properties be returned to the status quo in 1552. This would have meant that many of the ecclesiastical institutions, including the important prince-bishoprics of northern Germany, secularized in the second half of the sixteenth century, would have returned to Catholic hands. Even though militarily weak, the Protestants could not accept such a demand. More importantly, the edict made clear that to both sides that the war was about much more than Frederick's desire to be king of Bohemia.

Gustavus Adolphus and the Protestant Resurgence

Protestant fortunes changed with the entry of Sweden in 1632. Gustavus Adolphus (1594–1632), the king of Sweden, had been fighting in Poland and Lithuania. After Wallenstein intervened in Poland against him, Gustavus Adolphus decided to challenge the Habsburgs head-on. In addition to his grievance over Habsburg activity in Poland, he feared the Habsburgs' intentions in the Baltic Sea, which had become a sphere of Swedish dominance. So Gustavus Adolphus landed in the north German port of Peenemünde in 1630.

Although much of northern Europe, including the Danish province of Jutland, was occupied by imperial forces, Gustavus's intervention received little initial support from Protestant territories. It was only when his single declared ally, the city of Magdeburg, was seized, plundered, and burned by imperial forces that Gustavus became the champion of the Protestant cause. Now with the support of Brandenburg, Gustavus defeated the imperial forces under Tilly's command at Breitenfeld in 1632. This victory brought more Protestants into the Swedish camp and Gustavus pursued the campaign, entering Munich, the capital of Bavaria, on 17 May 1632. Imperial forces regrouped under Wallenstein and eventually pushed the Swedes back into Saxony. In November 1632, the two armies fought again at Lützen, near Leipzig. The Swedish victory was overshadowed by the death of Gustavus Adolphus.

The French Intervention

For the next two years, the imperial forces regained the upper hand. In 1635, the Peace of Prague altered the situation considerably. The emperor suspended the Edict of Restitution, granted Saxony new territories, and gained Saxony and the Protestant territory of Hesse-Darmstadt for the conflict with Sweden. The Peace of Prague altered the religious aspect of the war as well. The formal alliance of Protestants with the Catholic emperor meant that no longer would the two sides in the conflict be religiously monolithic, and no longer would imperial policy be driven by the ultra-Catholic party.

In the same month as the Peace of Prague was declared, King Louis XIII of France declared war on the emperor. So began the third and final phase of the war. France was primarily interested in limiting Habsburg power, and most importantly in preventing the formation of a compact, absolutist state in the Holy Roman Empire. Even though the king's chief ministers, first Cardinal Richelieu (Armand-Jean du Plessis; 1585–1642), then Cardinal Mazarin (Giulio Mazarini; 1602–1661), were churchmen, they pursued a consistent policy of challenging imperial forces. From this point on, if not before, the war had become truly international in scope and the reasons for continued conflict were no longer primarily or even partially religious. Now the reasons for fighting had to do overwhelmingly with the long-term struggle between the French monarchy on the one side and the Habsburgs, especially the Spanish Habsburgs, on the other.

The Peace of Westphalia

With the entrance of the French, the balance of power tilted dramatically away from the imperial (Habsburg) side. In order to raise funds to combat the combined Swedish and French forces, the new emperor Ferdinand III (1608–1657) was forced to convene the Imperial Diet at Regensburg, its first meeting since 1613. In a meeting that lasted over a year (September 1640–October 1641), the Imperial Estates gained important concessions, including ultimately the right to participate in any peace conference.

With all participants exhausted by war, peace negotiations began. The first diplomats arrived in Münster and Osnabrück in 1643, but the Swedes and the French opened negotiations for a conference with the emperor only in 1645. The conference began seriously in late 1645, and the Peace of Westphalia was finally signed on 24 October 1648. It brought an end to the conflict in the empire, although war between Spain and France continued for another eleven years.

The peace was significant in several respects. First, it established firmly in law the principle of *cuius regio, eius religio*. Rulers could no longer intervene in the religious affairs of other territories. Calvinism was given the same legal standing as the other two confessions. In addition, the status of Catholic institutions and properties in Protestant territories was established. Those that had been in existence in 1624 were permitted to continue, but there would be no rollback of earlier seizures or reforms. Thus Europe began its slow move toward religious tolerance. Lutheran communities in Catholic territories were also promised some measure of religious freedom. Most significantly, religion would no longer function as a primary foreign policy interest. France's insistence in the 1630s that *raison d'état* (reason of state) supersedes religious concerns won the day.

The Impact of the War

The Thirty Years' War had other significant legacies for the religious life of Europe and especially Germany. While rulers may have become less inclined to view religion as an appropriate goal of foreign policy, the battles of the war and the widespread propaganda, especially pamphlet literature, helped to harden confessional boundaries. Catholics celebrated the Battle of White Mountain as a sure sign of God's favor. Gustavus Adolphus became for Protestants the savior of the faith, praised in his life and revered after his death, memorialized in countless broadsides and commemorative objects.

But at the same time there is evidence of another development. The devastation of the war, reducing Germany's population anywhere from 25 to 50 percent (depending on the scholarly estimate, and on the locale), meant that the effects of the war—the plague, starvation, economic ruin—had an enormous effect on religious life. Pastors saw their congregations shrink and occasionally vanish entirely. Contemporaries described the general decline in religious activity in both Protestant and Catholic territories. Efforts to enforce religious behavior and to expand religious institutions foundered on the lack of available financial resources.

For some, the violent religious conflict was directly related to the theological polemics that had dominated relations both among and within the confessions. The Protestant mystic Jacob Böhme (1575–1624), a resident of Bohemia, was an eyewitness of the devastation caused by the war. He was sharply critical of the religious and political disputes that led up to the war, and hoped that the war's destruction would pave the way for a "new reformation." He criticized clergy of both confessions and warmongering princes and saw the conflict as the struggle of "a persecuting church of Cain against a persecuted church of Abel," the latter encompassing religious dissidents of all stripes (Weeks 1991, 218).

Another response was a move away from the arid theological debate that had characterized Lutheranism since the death of Luther in 1546. Pastors like Paul Gerhardt (1607–1676) who survived the war sought to recover Luther's own interest in personal piety and depth of devotional feeling. Their efforts led them not only to the spiritual writings of their own tradition, but to those of late medieval mysticism and even of Catholic authors like St. Teresa of Avila (1515–1582). Here lie two of the sources of what would become the German Pietist movement of the late seventeenth century.

The economic and social upheaval of the war had another effect on religious life in the decades after the war. For some rulers, just as religion no longer played a role in foreign policy, so too its rule in domestic policy became less important than other issues. Thus, the rulers of the Palatinate, faced with a countryside that had lost much of its population during the war, responded to this by inviting religious minorities, specifically Anabaptists (Mennonites), to settle and promised them freedom of religion as well.

D. Jonathan Grieser

Further Reading

Asch, R. G. (1997). *The Thirty Years War: The Holy Roman Empire and Europe, 1618–1648*. New York: St. Martin's Press.

Burkhardt, J. (1992). *Der Dreissigjährige Krieg*. Frankfurt, Germany: Suhrkamp.

Gutmann, M. P. (1988). The origins of the Thirty Years' War. *Journal of Interdisciplinary History, 18*, 749–770.

Haude, S. (2000). Life, death, and religion during the Thirty Years' War. In R. J. Bast & A. C. Gow (Eds.), *Continuity and change: The harvest of late Medieval and Reformation history: Essays presented to Heiko A. Oberman on his seventieth birthday* (pp. 417–430). Leiden, Netherlands: E. J. Brill.

Heckel, M. (1983). *Deutschland im konfessionellen zeitalter*. Göttingen, Germany: Vandenhoek/Ruprecht.

Langer, H. (1980). *The Thirty Years' War*. Poole, UK: Blandford.

Mortimer. G. (2001). Did contemporaries recognize a Thirty Years' War? *English Historical Review, 116*, 124–136.
Parker, G. (Ed.). (1987). *The Thirty Years' War*. London: Routledge.
Polisensky, J. V. (1971). *The Thirty Years War*. Berkeley: University of California Press.
Polisensky, J. V., & Snider, F. (1978). *War and society in Europe 1618–1648*. Cambridge, UK: Cambridge University Press.
Schmidt, G. (1996). *Der Dreissigjährige Krieg*. Munich, Germany: Beck.
Sutherland, N. M. (1992). The origins of the Thirty Years' War and the structure of European politics. *English Historical Review, 107*, 581–625.
Thiebault, J. C. (1995). *German villages in crisis. Rural life in Hesse-Kassel and the Thirty Years' War, 1580–1720*. Atlantic Highlands, NJ: Humanities Press International.
Thiebault, J. C. (1994). Jeremiah in the village: Prophecy, preaching, pamphlets, and penance in the Thirty Years' War. *Central European History, 27*, 441–460.
Wedgewood, C. V. (1939). *The Thirty Years' War*. New Haven, CT: Yale University Press.
Weeks, C. A. (1991). Jacob Boehme and the Thirty Years' War. *Central European History, 24*, 213–221.

Thugs

People may be acquainted with the inaccurate depiction of the Thuggee cult from the 1984 movie *Indiana Jones and the Temple of Doom*. The actual Phansigars, or stranglers, as they were once called, roamed the countryside of India until their suppression in the nineteenth century by the British colonial powers. Their name came from the Hindustani word *phansi*, which means noose. In northern India they were called Thuggees, derived from the Hindustani *thag-lana*, meaning "the deceivers," hence the English derivative thug. Thousands of Thuggees traveled as bandit groups whose goal was robbery and ritual sacrifice.

Because Thuggees functioned as a fiercely guarded secret society without written records, mystery veils the history of the cult and any detailed account of its membership. Thuggees were supposedly depicted in a rock carving at the Ellora Caves in central India (c. 760–800 CE), which indicates indigenous activity. But according to Francis Tuker, their practices originated with the Sagartii of Persia, a people described by Herodotus in 440 BCE. They possessed few weapons except for leather cords that they used to trip horses and to strangle men. During the Islamic invasions that began in during the tenth century AC, descendents migrated to India making their homes near Delhi. Some traditions say that a fourteenth-century Moslem holyman, Nizam-ud-din Auliya, founded the Thuggee.The first written account of the cult came from historian Zia-ud-Barni in 1356 when he wrote about Firoz Shah, who freed one thousand captured Thuggees sending them to Bengal in about 1290. Under the reign of Akbar the Great (1556–1605), five hundred Thuggees were arrested for their nefarious activities. Ironically, Muslims and Hindus, who ordinarily were ideological opposites, joined the secret society without any religious conflict. In some cases, men joined because of various times of economic displacement, although primarily Thuggee families maintained hereditary involvement. As a subcultural adaptation and possibly by absorbing preexisting groups of native gangs, the Thuggees adopted occult Hindu ritual. While the historical record remains sketchy on the origins of the Thuggees, their mythological underpinnings and devotion to the Hindu Mother Goddess, Kali, are very clear. The mythological origins of the Thuggees are retold in the legends of Kali and her specific personification as Bhavani.

Thuggees worshipped the Hindu goddess of destruction, Kali. Kali once tackled a demon called Raktabija ("Blood-seed"). When this demon was wounded, new demons would sprout from drops of its blood. In order to defeat the demon, Kali swallowed it and its progeny so that no blood would be spilled. To honor the goddess, Thuggees kill their victims without shedding blood. According to legend, the first Thuggees devised a bloodless death through strangulation. According to another legend, the first two Thuggees sprang from the sweat under Kali's arms. She gave them handkerchiefs, instructing them to kill demons using the handkerchiefs. Since yellow was Kali's favorite color, many Thuggees conducted their ritual killings using a yellow scarf, which they kept knotted around their waists. After dispatching their victim, they performed a ritual called Tuponee, which involved eating yellow sugar *(goor)*. The band of devotees sprinkled sugar on the ground or on a cloth upon which they placed a pickaxe (ordinarily used to dig graves). On the cloth, they placed a piece of silver or silver string, which was often part of the noose used to kill their victims. Following prayers and a gesture imitating strangulation, those who took part in the deed ate the sugar offering. Every group employed a ritual butcher, who would cut up and mangle corpses so they could not be recognized.

The Thuggees' creed dictated that no victim would survive an encounter, with the exception of young boys, whom they brought up to be the next generation of Thuggees. Young men were required to strangle an unsuspecting person in order to become formal members of the secret society. Most sects only attacked men, because female sacrifice displeased Kali and remained taboo.

The Thuggees regularly divided their plunder with local authorities in exchange for protection. Some booty ended up as temple offerings, enriching priests of the goddess. During colonial times, Thuggees stalked non-Europeans because they feared reprisals if they attacked Europeans. Being apolitical, Thuggees did not oppose colonial rule. In 1822, William Sleeman, a British officer, began to investigate the cult's activity; his investigations led to the eventual arrests of more than three thousand. By 1848, after many trials and hangings, the group's activities came to an end. Subsequent generations learned new trades, and the cult of Thuggee passed into history.

Diana Tumminia

Further Reading

Bruce, G. (1968). *The stranglers: The cult of Thuggee and its overthrow in British India*. New York: Harcourt, Brace & World.

Davies, N. (1981). *Human sacrifice: In history and today*. New York: William Morrow.

Lung, H. (1999). *Ancient art of strangulation: An ancient cult of silent assassins*. Boulder, CO: Paladin Press.

MacKenzie, N. (Ed.). (1967). *Secret societies*. New York: Collier Books.

Sleeman, W. H. (1973). *Rambles and recollections of an Indian official* (Rev. ed.; V. A. Smith, Ed.). Karachi, Pakistan: Oxford University Press. (Original work published 1844)

Tuker, F. I. S. (1961). *The yellow scarf; the story of the life of Thuggee Sleeman, or Major-General Sir William Henry Sleeman, K. C. B., 1788–1856, of the Bengal Army and the Indian Political Service*. London: Dent.

Tyrannicide, Medieval Catholic Doctrine of

The term tyrannicide, derived from the Greek *turannos* ("absolute ruler"), applies to the act of killing a despotic ruler. Today we would more generally refer to it as political assassination, and it is regarded by some as belonging to a set of political phenomena that can include terrorism and revolution. Whereas other kinds of killing, such as killing in self-defense or in war, may be considered legal, tyrannicide has seldom, if ever, been considered a legal act; rather, it is generally regarded as an instance of murder. However, theologians and philosophers who have written on the topic of tyrannicide have evaluated it not in terms of the laws of a particular state, but from the viewpoint of morality, either secular or religious.

History of the Doctrine

Although *tyrant* was a morally neutral term in ancient Greece, meaning simply one who exercises absolute power, ancient Greek philosophers opposed tyranny as a morally corrupt form of governance, one which, in the words of Aristotle (384–322 BCE), "no free man willingly endures" (Aristotle 1977, 4:9), and consequently they considered the killer of a tyrant to be worthy of public honors. The historian Xenophon (c. 430–350 BCE), in his dialogue on tyranny, wrote: "Instead of avenging them, the cities heap honors on the slayer of the despot . . . [and] put up statues to them in holy places" (Xenophon 1925, 4:5). Among the earliest monuments erected in Athens are those commemorating Harmodius and Aristogeiton for attempting to assassinate the tyrants Hipparchus and Hippias in 514 BCE.

Roman writers elaborated on the Greek doctrine of tyrannicide. The statesman Cicero (106–43 BCE), for example, developed the doctrine in the context of a natural-law morality. He wrote: "For we have no fellowship with tyrants, but rather are separated from them by the widest gulf; nor is it contrary to nature to despoil, if we can, him whom it is honorable to kill" (Cicero 1975, 3:6). Later, the philosopher Seneca (4 BCE–65 CE) presented the doctrine in a theological context more suitable to medieval Catholicism. "For natures like this," he wrote, "exit from life is the only remedy. . . . No offering is more acceptable to God than the blood of a tyrant" (1974, 8:20).

Christian theologians of the early Church developed the doctrine along two distinct lines of thought, both with biblical warrants. Following the epistles of Paul, some emphasized the biblical imperative of submission to political powers. "Let every person be subject to the governing authorities," Paul wrote, "for there is no authority except from God, and those that exist have been instituted by God" (Romans 13:1, RSV).

Similarly Peter wrote: "Be subject for the Lord's sake to every human institution. . . . Honor the emperor" (I Peter 2:13, 17, RSV). Later, after the conversion of the Roman emperor Constantine (d. 337) in the fourth century, the duty of submission to political powers was strengthened by the close alliance between the Church and Roman empire. Even the unjust, wicked, or tyrannical ruler was to be regarded as God's agent. Augustine (354–430) argued that at times God would permit the coming to power of ruthless tyrants as a punishment for the sins of the people (1972, 5:21). Killing the tyrant would, therefore, be an act against God. As Pope Gregory the Great (540–604) put it, "Those who murmur against the rulers set over them speak not against a human being but against him who disposes of all things by divine order" (quoted in Carlyle 1930, 153, n. 1).

But other theologians of the early Church held an entirely different view. Chrysostom (c. 347–407), writing in the fourth century, interpreted Paul's words in Romans 13 as meaning that God had ordained the office of ruler, but not the ruler himself. Hence the tyrant, by the misuse of power, failed to act as God's minister, and killing him would, therefore, not be an act against God. This view of the doctrine finds biblical warrants in the Hebrew scriptures recounting how the people of Ehud, Jehu, and Judith were freed by the killing of tyrannical rulers. Later, the scholar Isidore of Seville (c. 560–636) revived the ancient Greek distinction between king and tyrant. His work significantly influenced the thought of medieval writers. "Kings," he wrote, citing an old proverb, "are so called by their ruling. . . . Therefore by doing rightly the title of king is kept, by wrongdoing it is lost" (Carlyle 1930, 221).

The Medieval Period

The doctrine of tyrannicide was first introduced into medieval Catholicism in the twelfth century by the theologian John of Salisbury (1115–1180) in the latter chapters of his book *Policratus*. The doctrine was not standard medieval political fare, and John's motive for introducing it has therefore been a subject of scholarly debate among contemporary writers. Opinions range from John's possible yet undocumented indignation at the tyrannical conduct of some of the nobles and rulers of his time (for example, Roger II of Sicily) to the more plausible suggestion that John merely developed the doctrine he found in the republican literature of classical writers such as Cicero and Seneca. Regardless of John's motive, his defense of tyrannicide exerted significant influence upon political thought, religious and secular alike, from the Middle Ages to the early modern period.

John's defense of tyrannicide is not in all ways consistent, but his main points may be summarized thus. A prince, that is, a legitimate ruler, is one who "rules in accordance with the laws" (John of Salisbury 1963, 335); the laws themselves are from God. Law is "the gift of God, the model of equity, a standard of justice, a likeness of the divine will, the guarding of well-being" (335). The prince, by obeying the law, shows reverence and obedience to God. He is "a kind of likeness of divinity" (335). But a tyrant is a ruler who does not obey the law, one "who oppresses the people by rulership based upon force" (335); in his disobedience the tyrant is the "likeness of wickedness" (336) and assails God, who "in a sense is challenged to battle" (335). For that reason the tyrant "is generally to be even killed" (336). John declares that "it has always been an honorable thing to slay [tyrants] if they can be curbed in no other way" (356) and "even priests of God repute the killing of tyrants as a pious act" (370). It may even be a mandatory act, as when John says that the wickedness of the tyrant is "always punished by the Lord," who sometimes uses a "human hand . . . [as] a weapon wherewith to administer punishment to the unrighteous" (375).

In the *Policratus*, John appeals not only to classical writers, but also to Hebrew texts. For example, he quotes the Book of Judith 9:12–15: "Bring to pass, Lord, that by his own sword his pride may be cut off. . . . Grant to me the constancy of soul that I may despise him, and fortitude that I may destroy him . . . [as] a glorious monument of Thy name" (1963, 371). Similarly, he cites the Book of Judges 4:17–21 and 5:24–26 recounting the story of Jael, who killed the tyrant Sisera with a tent peg and a hammer, crushing his head and piercing his temple. In these and other instances John stresses that God can and does have wicked rulers killed at the hands of the virtuous.

The most systematic presentation of the doctrine was given by Thomas Aquinas (1225–1274). Making use of the ancient distinction between two types of tyrants, those who become tyrants by illegitimate acquisition of power (a *tyrannos in tituto*) and those who become tyrants by abuse of power (a *tyrannos in regimine*), the former, Aquinas says, may be killed "by any one [to] resist such dominion. . . . For in that case he who kills the tyrant for the liberation of his country is praised and receives a reward" (Gabriel Palmer-Fernandez, Trans.). While here Aquinas seems to affirm teachings of earlier writers, notably John of Salisbury, in later writings he was considerably more hesitant than they in upholding the right of tyrannicide against a king who degenerates into a tyrant, that is, a *tyrannos in regimine*. In this case Aquinas restricts if not removes from "any one," that is, any person or private citizen, the right to kill the tyrant, for unless the tyranny is "excessive it would be more expedient to endure [it], rather than bring about many dangers graver than the tyranny itself" (1982, 1:6). The right to remove this kind of tyrant lies then not in the hands of a private individual, but in the community. He writes: "If a given community has the right to appoint a ruler it is not unjust for the community to depose the king or restrict his power if he abuses it by becoming a tyrant" (1982, 1:6).

Most other medieval writers emphasized the right of the individual to kill the tyrant, agreeing with John of Salisbury rather than adopting the more cautious view that some kind of public deliberation and community decision was required, as Aquinas suggested. Either way, the discussions were primarily academic and seldom, if ever, a dominant theme of medieval political thought. They were essentially logical developments of the deeply held belief that the king had an objective purpose instituted by God. Its neglect could well forfeit the king's authority. But in the later Middle Ages the doctrine became a very practical issue.

On November 1407 the Duke of Orléans, brother of the King of France, was killed. His cousin John the Fearless, the Duke of Burgundy, was suspected of complicity in the act. Jean Petit (d. 1411), a French cleric at the University of Paris, justified the killing. He wrote: "It is lawful for any subject, without any order or command, according to moral, divine, and natural law, to kill or cause to be killed a traitor and disloyal tyrant. It is not only lawful, but honorable and meritorious, especially when he is in such great power that justice cannot well be done by the sovereign" (quoted in Jászi and Lewis 1957, 29; Ford 1985, 132). Several years later, Jean Gerson (1363–1429), chancellor of the University of Paris, denounced Petit's teaching and instructed his contemporaries on the correct interpretation of those authorities, especially Aquinas, whom Petit had employed in his justification. Gerson had earlier supported the doctrine in a sermon preached before Charles VI of France, but like Aquinas held that it required a public authority: "Wise philosophers, expert jurists, legists, theologians, men of good life, of good natural prudence, and of great experience should be consulted and confidence should be placed on them" (quoted in Jászi and Lewis 1957, 29–30).

At two subsequent Church councils, the Council of the Faith held in Paris in 1414 and the General Council of the Church convened in Constance in 1415, Gerson's condemnation of Petit's teaching on tyrannicide was approved. Although Petit's name was never mentioned at either council, the proposition that it was lawful and meritorious for any subject to kill any tyrant, even resorting to trickery if necessary to do so, was declared heretical. A sufficiently wicked tyrant could still be killed—provided the proper authorities gave their approval— but the act must be accomplished without ambush or ruse. Aquinas seems to have won the debate. For the remainder of the Middle Ages, almost all theologians affirmed the condemnation of Petit's justification. But the condemnation did not extend to the killing of a tyrant who had gained power by force (that is, a *tyrannus in titulo*). The killing of such a tyrant could be justified by an individual's natural right of self-defense as a means to liberate the community.

Postmedieval Developments

In 1599, Juan de Mariana (1536–1623), a Spanish Jesuit theologian, published his major work *The King and the Education of the King*, which specified in great detail the nature of a king's duties, the meaning of a good man, and especially of a good Christian. Chapter Six addresses the question of whether it is right to destroy a tyrant, offering one of the last justifications for tyrannicide by a Catholic author. By the middle of the seventeenth century, the doctrine practically disappears and we see the gradual emergence of the doctrine of popular revolution, the main lines of which continue relatively unchanged to the present day.

Mariana begins his defense of tyrannicide by recounting the story of a young Dominican monk, Jacques Clement, who in 1589 assassinated Henry III, King of France, as Henry laid siege to the city of Paris. Clement had received instruction on the great medieval Catholic authors from the theologians at the Dominican college. "He was told by the theologians whom he had consulted, that a tyrant may be killed legally" (Mariana 1948, 143). Because a tyrant is a public enemy, "he may be removed by any means and gotten rid of by as much violence as he used in seizing power. . . . [Tyrants] can be killed not only justly but with praise and glory" (1948, 147). Although the assassin himself might die for his deed, as Clement did, whoever takes the initiative to kill a tyrant is held in great honor. So Clement, Mariana concludes, is to be considered an "eternal honor to France [in whom] a greater power strengthened his normal power and spirit" (144). From the pulpits in Paris Clement was "proclaimed as 'the holy martyr of Jesus Christ,' who had delivered France from 'that dog of a Henry de Valois.' Even the pope, Sixtus V (1521–90), regarded the event as a sign that God still watched over the kingdom of France" (Jászi and Lewis 1957, 65–66).

A few years later, the Jesuit theologian Francisco Suárez (1548–1617) argued that the condemnation of tyrannicide issued at the Council of Constance did not say that no tyrant may be slain but merely that not every tyrant may be slain before sentence has been pronounced against him. He argued that when a private individual slew a tyrant, he was acting by the authority of the state and God, since God had given all men the right to defend themselves and their state from the violence a tyrant inflicts. Suárez adds a novel feature to the long tradition that began with the Greek philosophers: A heretical king (that is, a Protestant), he argues, may be deposed by the pope, by virtue of the pope's temporal authority. Once dethroned and after sentence has been pronounced, he may be killed as a *tyrannos in titulo* by any private individual, whether subject to that king or not. Such a king, by reason of his heresy, is "deprived of his dominion [which] is to pass to his lawful Catholic successor" (Suárez 1964, 717).

Suárez's *Defence of the Catholic and Apostolic Faith* brought great indignation among Protestant rulers, particularly James I (1566–1625) of England, who had this work publicly burnt in London in 1613, as it was also in Catholic France. Even the Jesuit General Aquaviva (1543–1615) prohibited any discussion of Suárez's defense of slaying the heretical ruler. Nonetheless, Suárez's ideas were "exploited in the Protestant world without acknowledgment of the source" (Wilenius 1963, 85–86), and may well have been a pioneering source in the popular right of revolution.

Gabriel Palmer-Fernandez

See also Roman Catholicism: Just-War Doctrine

Further Reading

Aquinas, T. (1929–1947). *Scriptum in IV Libros Sententiarum* [Commentary on the sentences of Peter Lombard] (P. Mandonnet & M. F. Moos, Eds.). Paris: A Cattier.

Aquinas, T. (1982). *On kingship* (G. B. Phelam, Trans.). Toronto, Canada: Pontifical Institute of Medieval Studies.

Aristotle. (1977). *Politics* (H. Rackham, Trans.). Cambridge, MA: Harvard University Press.

Augustine. (1972). *City of God* (H. Bettenson, Trans.). London: Penguin.

Carlyle, A. J. (1930). *A history of medieval political theory in the west* (Vols. 1–6). Edinburgh, UK: William Blackwood & Sons.

Cicero. (1975). *De Officiis* (W. Miller, Trans). Cambridge, MA: Loeb Classical Library.

Ford, F. L. (1985). *Political murder: From tyrannicide to terrorism*. Cambridge, MA: Harvard University Press.

Jászi, O., & Lewis, J. D. (1957). *Against the tyrant: The tradition and theory of tyrannicide*. Glencoe, IL: The Free Press.

John of Salisbury (1963). *Policratus, The statesman's book of John of Salisbury* (J. Dickinson, Trans.). New York: Russell & Russell.

Lewy, G. (1957). A secret papal brief on tyrannicide during the Counterreformation. *Church history, 26*(4), 319–324.

Mariana, J. de (1948). *The king and the education of the king* (G. A. Moore, Trans.). Washington, DC: Country Dollar Press.

Palmer-Fernandez, G. (2000). Justifying political assassination: Michael Collins and the Cairo gang. *Journal of Social Philosophy, 31*(2), 160–176.

Seneca. (1974). *De Beneficiis* (A. Golding, Trans.). Norwood, NJ: W. J. Johnson.

Suárez, F. (1964). A defence of the Catholic and apostolic faith. In Williams, G., Brown, A. & Waldron, J. (Trans. & Eds.), *Selections from three works* (Book VI, Ch. IV, pp 705–725). New York: Oceana.

Strauss, L. (1948). *On tyranny: An interpretation of Xenophon's Hiero*. Glencoe, IL: The Free Press.

Wilenius, R. (1963). *The social and political theory of Francisco Suárez*. Helsinki, Finland: Societas Philosophica Fennica.

Xenophon. (1968). Hiero IV, 5. In Marchant, E.C. (Ed.), *Scriptura Minor* (pp. 17). Cambridge, MA: Loeb Classical Library.

Zellner, H. M. (Ed.). (1974). *Assassination*. Cambridge, MA: Schenkman.

U

United States *See* Christian Identity; Christianity: African-American Traditions; Iroquois; Judaism, Conservative; Judaism, Orthodox; Judaism, Reform; Judaism, Reconstructionist; Ku Klux Klan; Mormons; Pueblo Revolt of 1680; Quakers; U.S. Civil War and Christian Churches; U.S. Revolutionary War

U.S. Civil War and Christian Churches

Christian churches provided various forms of support during America's civil strife. This support was for good and ill as they encouraged congregants to stand by their convictions, to support their government and way of life, and to provide aid for the suffering.

The U.S. Civil War wasn't the result of one cause or event, but it was the culmination of multiple issues in various segments of American culture. Ever since the arrival of immigrants and explorers upon the shores of North America there has been turmoil and tension as opposing groups and ideas competed. Contention would mark the political and religious life of the emerging nation. Also, the search for autonomy instilled an attitude of self-reliance and independence that became a major issue in the sectionalism that plagued the nation.

Religious and Social Context

Although the colonies gathered and formed a union, the differences between the geographic regions caused difficulties. The harsh struggle, rapid growth, technological inequality, and inaccessibility fostered sectionalism and misunderstanding. As colonies and young states the Southern economy had relied upon the use of cheap labor from slaves. Being less urban and industrial than their Northern counterparts, the South relied on economic methods that would soon become obsolete and the object of national debate.

Alongside political turmoil, religious turmoil also surfaced as theological debate separated churches and traditional ideas were challenged. Rationalism had begun to change the notions that people held as theologians questioned the basic tenets of the dominant Christian faith. The certainty of the Bible, the nature of true religion, and the reality of Jesus and his nature were doubted.

However, revivals also arose during these times of doubt. The Great Awakening (1740s) and the Second Great Awakening (1790s–1810s) were times of spiritual renewal that reshaped the nation. The first awakening so captured the attention of the colonies that one of this awakening's greatest orators, George Whitefield (1714–1770), garnered nearly one-third of the total colonial publishing market with his books and sermons.

The second awakening had the greatest impact upon the form and function of religion in America, especially on that which the Union and Confederate soldiers practiced. The evangelical character that came to the fore influenced its theological tendencies and social contributions. It was in the years following this awakening that most of the institutions emerged that became known as the "Benevolent Empire." This "empire" consisted of institutions like the American Bible Society, the American Tract Society, and others that

Proclamation Appointing a National Fast Day, March 30, 1863

By the President of the United States of America.

A Proclamation.

Whereas, the Senate of the United States, devoutly recognizing the Supreme Authority and just Government of Almighty God, in all the affairs of men and of nations, has, by a resolution, requested the President to designate and set apart a day for National prayer and humiliation.

And whereas it is the duty of nations as well as of men, to own their dependence upon the overruling power of God, to confess their sins and transgressions, in humble sorrow, yet with assured hope that genuine repentance will lead to mercy and pardon; and to recognize the sublime truth, announced in the Holy Scriptures and proven by all history, that those nations only are blessed whose God is the Lord.

And, insomuch as we know that, by His divine law, nations like individuals are subjected to punishments and chastisements in this world, may we not justly fear that the awful calamity of civil war, which now desolates the land, may be but a punishment, inflicted upon us, for our presumptuous sins, to the needful end of our national reformation as a whole People? We have been the recipients of the choicest bounties of Heaven. We have been preserved, these many years, in peace and prosperity. We have grown in numbers, wealth and power, as no other nation has ever grown. But we have forgotten God. We have forgotten the gracious hand which preserved us in peace, and multiplied and enriched and strengthened us; and we have vainly imagined, in the deceitfulness of our hearts, that all these blessings were produced by some superior wisdom and virtue of our own. Intoxicated with unbroken success, we have become too self-sufficient to feel the necessity of redeeming and preserving grace, too proud to pray to the God that made us!

It behooves us then, to humble ourselves before the offended Power, to confess our national sins, and to pray for clemency and forgiveness.

Now, therefore, in compliance with the request, and fully concurring in the views of the Senate, I do, by this my proclamation, designate and set apart Thursday, the 30th. day of April, 1863, as a day of national humiliation, fasting and prayer. And I do hereby request all the People to abstain, on that day, from their ordinary secular pursuits, and to unite, at their several places of public worship and their respective homes, in keeping the day holy to the Lord, and devoted to the humble discharge of the religious duties proper to that solemn occasion.

All this being done, in sincerity and truth, let us then rest humbly in the hope authorized by the Divine teachings, that the united cry of the Nation will be heard on high, and answered with blessings, no less than the pardon of our national sins, and the restoration of our now divided and suffering Country, to its former happy condition of unity and peace.

In witness whereof, I have hereunto set my hand and caused the seal of the United States to be affixed.

Done at the City of Washington, this thirtieth day of March, in the year of our Lord one thousand eight hundred and sixty-three, and of the Independence of the United States the eighty seventh.

By the President: Abraham Lincoln William H. Seward, Secretary of State.

Source: Basler, Roy P. (Ed.) *The Collected Works of Abraham Lincoln.* Retrieved April 2, 2003, from Abraham Lincoln Online, http://www.netins.net/showcase/creative/lincoln/speeches

were established with a national (though mainly Northern) character and ecumenical scope and emerged to help shape the path and nature of a young nation. The American Tract Society stated that it wished to "lengthen the cords and strengthen the stakes that bind together the body politic" (Gaustad 1972, 11). Like the American Tract Society, some of these societies were purposefully national in nature and tried to advance a moderate position on some issues; others like the American Anti-Slavery Society were not so inclined. The American Tract Society, whose major tenet was to not condone or condemn any practice that did not receive full agreement among all Christians, eventually split over slavery.

The fracture of the American Tract Society was mirrored throughout the country as individuals in the same city and of the same denomination failed to agree on this topic. In October 1845 at the request of the General Assembly of the Presbyterian Church (Old School), Jonathan Blanchard (1811–1892), former lecturer for the American Anti-Slavery Society and pastor of the Sixth Street Presbyterian Church, and Nathan Lewis Rice (1807–1877), pastor of the Central Presbyterian Church, debated for several days before the citizens of Cincinnati—and the nation after the publication of their debates—on the evils and benefits of slavery. Both men argued with logic and the Bible, a tool in the hands of both men as each interpreted it as supporting his position.

The general character of the American culture is reflected in its reformist/voluntarist nature. Many were not afraid to take on the task of reform and this was especially true for the abolitionist movement. Many of the benevolent societies successfully utilized this feature of reform and recruitment as they couched their goals in language that spoke of national interest and security.

Denominational Strife

As a group, the Methodist Episcopal Church exhibits the traits of this reformist nature. Begun by John Wesley (1703–1791), Methodism—an offshoot of the Anglican Church—grew from a backward, unappealing, and reviled "sect" to a mature denomination. This did not, however, occur without growing pains as American Methodism split over the issue of slavery. The editorials of Charles Elliott (1792–1869), longtime editor of the *Western Christian Advocate* and author of *Sinfulness of Slavery Proved from its Evil Source*, did nothing to help mend the rift that was growing within the denomination. The *Western Christian Advocate* was the official Methodist newspaper that was printed in Cincinnati, Ohio, and was a hotbed of abolitionist thought and activity.

American Christianity held some responsibility for the Civil War that ensued, because the eventual denominational separations were a prelude to an eventual geographical/political separation, which is seen in the withdrawal of West Virginia from Virginia proper in 1865 and had been mirrored in the denominational division in the Methodist Episcopal Church South that occurred years earlier. Additionally, politicians, preachers, and military men on either side used the name of God to "christen" their cause as the nation moved toward civil war.

If the church was the cement of society as John C. Calhoun (1782–1850) stated, a church divided over such an issue as slavery would result in a nation divided. As early as 1846 in the preface to the published debates between Jonathan Blanchard and Nathan L. Rice, the publisher states, "there is no subject at this moment receiving a greater share of the attention of Christendom than this—none involving more important consequences to our civil and ecclesiastical institutions" (Blanchard et al. 1846, iii). Unfortunately, this prophetic statement was eventually fulfilled.

Few events in American history have experienced such overwhelming encouragement from religious bodies as did the principles from which the American Civil War arose. In both the North and South the churches fully supported their respective governments and offered their spiritual resources for the war.

Denominational figures led the way in the search to support the rightness of their cause. At the request of Abraham Lincoln (1809–1865), Catholic Archbishop John Hughes (1797–1864) of New York sided with the Union and took a goodwill tour of the nation. Matthew Simpson (1811–1884), cousin of Ulysses Simpson Grant (1822–1885) and a Methodist Episcopal bishop, traveled extensively and lectured on behalf of the Union. His lecture, "Our Country," was a great propaganda weapon. Simpson was also an editor of the *Western Christian Advocate* and helped define its character as an abolitionist paper. Congregationalists were quite vocal on the sinfulness of slavery, but their message was heard only in the North due to their low representation in the South. Additionally, the Society of Friends strove to separate the activities of church and state. Despite persecution as pacifists, the Quakers served in hospitals and among liberated slaves.

The example of the squabbling Methodist Church was echoed in many of the major American denominations, even in those that intentionally sought unity. The issue of slavery grew to the fore. Eventually, the major denominations split along geographic lines, echoing the political sectionalism that had existed for decades. Even in the year of Methodism's fracture in 1844, Bishop Leonidas Hamline (1797–1865) deemphasized the social evils of the day, instead focusing on evangelism and missions.

American Presbyterianism experienced division just as Methodism had over the issue of slavery and on how the church and civil government should interact. Many in the Southern Presbyterian Church saw that the two spheres should never interact or be confused. Stuart Robinson (1814–1881) exhorted the Presbyterian Church in the South to remember that "the civil power derives it authority from God as Author of nature, whilst the power of ecclesiastical comes alone from Jesus as mediator" (Robinson 1995, 85). The strict division between church and state allowed slavery to go unchallenged from the Southern pulpits.

As slavery grew so too did the abolitionist movement. One of its greatest leaders was Theodore Dwight Weld (1803–1895). Adding his voice to the one-hundred-year-old American antislavery cause, Weld, a Presbyterian, helped unite thousands of clergy and laypeople in the struggle to eradicate slavery. With the assistance of Lewis Tappan (1788–1873) and others, Weld formed the American Anti-Slavery Society in late 1833. This organization, though not the beginning of the antislavery movement, was a significant catalyst in bringing the issue before the people.

Military Chaplains

One way in which the organized church participated more directly in the Civil War was through the provision of chaplains to the military. The military chaplaincy has a rich history of clerics accompanying soldiers throughout history's crusades and campaigns, all the while hoisting the banner of the cross and leading soldiers to battle and possible death. These clerics attended to the spiritual needs of the soldiers, as well as the political maneuvering of the leaders. Chaplains often helped sway the public and the warrior with impassioned calls to service and sacrifice.

Both armies enlisted the aid of chaplains, who were viewed as half officer and half civilian, and became in many ways a necessary part of the organizational and methodological structure of the armed forces. Chaplains were frequently in a tough situation as they were often forbidden to fight, and repeatedly unable to preach. Though many soldiers may have not been religious, they appreciated the services and commitment of the chaplains. These hard-working ministers boosted the morale of the men and in the middle of confusion and turmoil chaplains spoke words of encouragement to frightened men and boys.

However, some soldiers did not give their complete respect to chaplains because they saw them as "long-jawed, loud-mouthed ranters" (Jacobson 1972, 33), who talked of heaven and its glories, while at times seeking refuge in rear areas. Though the Confederate States of America did not officially appoint chaplains until 1863, Catholic chaplain Father John B. Bannon (1829–1913), of Saint Louis, Missouri, began serving in 1861. Bannon was constantly in the midst of the battle and he was noted for his bravery and was ordered by his superiors on numerous occasions to withdraw to safety, but Bannon was driven to minister as he gave hasty baptisms and last rites to dying soldiers. Bannon, and a few others, was willing to serve as a chaplain in the front lines, even disobeying commands to care for his own safety, rather than in the rear areas where chaplains usually stayed.

As chaplains served spiritual purposes, they often filled the roles needed as battle demanded. One of the roles in which the chaplains served was through encouraging the soldier concerning the worthiness of the cause for which they fought. Bannon believed that the Confederate cause was divinely justified and his sermons emphasized that God was blessing the South. These emotionally and psychologically empowering sermons were echoed throughout the camps of the North and the South and fell from the lips of chaplains of all denominations. As situations dictated, spiritual needs and assistance were neglected as sermons, prayers, and Mass were set aside as battles raged and men fought. Days would pass before time was available to gather a crowd, or stand upon a stump, or erect a chapel tent.

United States Christian Commission

Another major service of Christian churches during the Civil War was the United States Christian Commission (USCC). The object of the commission was to promote the spiritual and temporal welfare of the brave men in arms. They proposed to do this by aiding chaplains and others in their work by furnishing to them religious tracts, periodicals, and books and by facilitating communication between soldiers and their friends and families.

Many factors helped bring about the establishment of the USCC and its parent organization, the Young Men's Christian Association (YMCA). One strong influence was the above-mentioned religious awakenings that emerged as the nation grew. Lemuel Moss (1829–1904), chronicler of the history of the USCC, stated, "The years 1857–'8 witnessed a religious awakening of unparalleled extent and power throughout the United States. In the light of subsequent events that period becomes invested with new significance. It was the preparation of the nation and the church for the hour of trial" (Moss 1868, 64).

Though individual Young Men's Christian Associations were actively working with the young men who entered the war, efforts were not centralized. This changed with the establishment of the commission and its efforts "to take active measures to promote the spiritual and temporal welfare of the soldiers in the army and the sailors [and marines] in the navy, in co-operation with the chaplains [and others]" (Moss 1868, 105). As stated in its first resolution, the commission sought to work in union with other agencies. The sixth resolution deemed that "all organizations, designed to promote the spiritual and temporal welfare of the army, be cordially invited freely to make use of the facilities afforded by the Commission" (Moss 1868, 105).

Despite the seeming scarcity of women in relation to the church and the civil war, women were at work in various capacities. Women were indispensable in denominational benevolence associations, antislavery societies, and efforts of medical mercy. Some of the faithful women who showed themselves worthy of praise and honor were the Sisters of Charity, who volunteered their services by erecting and coordinating hospitals during the war. These volunteers at times found themselves quite close to the battle lines as they worked in infirmaries and Father Bannon found some of these kindly sisters working in a hospital in Memphis. Though not filling the role of official chaplains, these ministers served the spiritual needs of many, as well as the physical.

America had a long history of slavery and opposition to it and it was inevitable that the two could not forever coexist without resulting in conflict. Though the eventual civil strife that consumed the resources and lives of the nation was not fought solely for the abolition of slavery, but also for the preservation of the Union and the character of American government, the role of the slave trade and the churches' denunciation of it must be considered as consequential. Calhoun alluded to the relationship of the church and state and their near-symbiotic association, and this can be seen as the church through its activities of reform and education enlightened and alienated the nation. Its activities, though beneficial, also revealed a deficiency. Though some commentators have applied some of the blame for the Civil War upon the church, that same church responded greatly to the needs that emerged. The church became grace in a time of need and an ever-present agent of mercy. Through the efforts of various denominations and thousands of individuals the church was able to alleviate suffering, comfort the weary, and assist the country through a difficult time.

David B. Malone

Further Reading

Bennett, W. W. (1877). *A narrative of the great revival which prevailed in the Southern armies*. Philadelphia: Claxton, Remsen, and Haffelfinger.

Blanchard, J., & Rice, N. L. (1846). *A debate on slavery*. Cincinnati, OH: Wm. H. Moore.

Brockett, L. P. (1866). *The camp, the battle field, and the hospital*. Philadelphia: National Publishing.

Durkin, J. T. (Ed.). (1960). *Confederate chaplain: A war journal of Rev. James B. Sheeran, C.S.S.R.* Milwaukee, WI: Bruce.

Gaustad, E. (Ed.). (1972). *Documents of the American Tract Society, 1825–1925*. New York: Arno Press.

Headley, J. T. (1864). *The chaplains and clergy of the Revolution*. New York: Charles Scribner.

Jacobsen, L. A. (1972). Religion in the Confederacy, 1861–1865. Unpublished master's thesis, Wheaton College, Wheaton, Illinois.

Jones, J. W. (1887). *Christ in the camp, or, religion in Lee's army*. Richmond, VA: B. F. Johnson.

McPherson, J. M. (1997). *For crusade and comrades: Why men fought in the Civil War*. New York: Oxford University Press.

Miller, R. M., Stout, H. S., & Wilson, C. R. (Eds.). (1998). *Religion and the American Civil War*. New York: Oxford University Press.

Moss, L. (1868). *Annals of the United States Christian Commission*. Philadelphia: Lippincott.

Norton, H. (1961). *Rebel religion*. St. Louis, MO: Bethany Press.

Robinson, S. (1995). *The church of God as an essential element of the gospel*. Greenville, SC: GPTS Press.

Romero, S. (1983). *Religion in the rebel ranks*. New York: University Press.

Shattuck, G. (1987). *A shield and hiding place: The religious life of the Civil War armies*. Macon, GA: Mercer University Press.

Smith, T. L. (1980). *Revivalism and social reform: American Protestantism on the eve of the Civil War*. Baltimore: Johns Hopkins University Press.

Tucker, P. T. (1992). *The Confederacy's fighting chaplain: Father John B. Bannon*. Tuscaloosa: University of Alabama Press.

Woodworth, S. E. (2001). *While God is marching on: The religious world of Civil War soldiers*. Lawrence: University Press of Kansas.

U.S. Revolutionary War

The relationship between religion and the American Revolution can be discussed under the following questions. First, what circumstances of a specifically religious nature influenced the course and development of the revolution? Second, how did religious ideas influence the development of the war for American independence? Third, what role did religious institutions actually play in the war? Fourth, how did the war affect the thought and behavior of the American churches?

Revolutionary Antecedents

Most students of American history are familiar with the outline of events that led to the American War of Independence: having incurred war debts during the French and Indian War (known in England as the Seven Years' War), the British Parliament began in 1764 to take specific steps to raise revenues in the American colonies. The Sugar Act became the first law enacted by Parliament for the express purpose of raising revenues for the crown. This was followed by the Stamp Act of 1765 and the Townshend Acts of 1767, which reaffirmed the Parliament's view that it had a right to raise revenues in the colonies for the purposes of civil administration. Finally, the Tea Act of 1773 granted the East India Company a virtual monopoly over the tea trade in the colonies, which led to the Boston Tea Party.

Two other circumstances that galvanized colonial opposition to the crown were the possible appointments of Anglican bishops in the colonies and the Quebec Act of 1774. By 1770 the Church of England had achieved a wider presence throughout the thirteen colonies than any other denomination. Hence, many Anglicans believed the time had come to establish one or more bishops on American soil. They reasoned that this would improve the administration of the church throughout the colonies and make it possible for clergy to be trained and ordained in America without having to make the difficult journey back to England. Although this idea sounds innocuous to modern ears, for the majority of non-Anglican Protestants in British America the possibility of an Anglican episcopate raised considerable fear and worry. The widespread belief that bishops of the Church of England were beholden to royalist policies had deep roots in English political history. What would prevent an eventual tax-supported establishment of the Church of England throughout the colonies and the imposition of religious discrimination toward non-Anglicans? Such fears grew dramatically during the 1760s as colonists realized that if Parliament could tax Americans for general revenues without the consent of the colonial legislatures, it could also tax them for the support of bishops. In John Adams's (1735–1826) opinion, this concern was as important as any other in leading common people to reflect on the authority of Parliament over the colonies.

In addition to the perceived threat of episcopacy, Americans also disliked the Quebec Act of 1774, which confirmed the privileged position of Roman Catholicism in Quebec and granted French-speaking Canadian Catholics religious toleration and full civil rights. By extending the boundaries of Quebec to the Ohio River, some colonists believed that the English government was infringing on their rightful territories and making an unholy alliance with French Catholics against the interests of English-speaking Protestants. Many clergy and members of the Continental Congress spoke out vehemently against this act and used it to gain support for the patriot cause.

Intellectual Influences

Religious ideas, whether self-consciously articulated or not, influenced many Americans to take up arms against Britain. What were these ideas, and how did they affect the way colonial Americans viewed a war for independence? In general, historians have focused on three areas of thought that contributed to the revolutionary spirit: the Puritan religious tradition, the Whig political tradition, and the Enlightenment political philosophy of John Locke (1632–1704). Although the latter two are usually treated as political philoso-

Selection from a Sermon by Samuel West "On the Right to Rebel Against Governors," Colony of the Massachusetts Bay, May 29, 1776

***Put them in mind to be subject to principalities and powers, to obey magistrates, to be ready to every good work,* -Titus 3:1**

From hence it follows that tyranny and arbitrary power are utterly inconsistent with and subversive of the very end and design of civil government, and directly contrary to natural law, which is the true foundation of civil government and all politic law. Consequently, the authority of a tyrant is of itself null and void; for as no man can have a right to act contrary to the law of nature, it is impossible that any individual, or even the greatest number of men, can confer a right upon another of which they themselves are not possessed; i.e., no body of men can justly and lawfully authorise any person to tyrannise over and enslave his fellow-creatures, or do anything contrary to equity and goodness. As magistrates have no authority but what they derive from the people, whenever they act contrary to the public good, and pursue measures destructive of the peace and safety of the community, they forfeit their right to govern the people. Civil rulers and magistrates are properly of human creation; they are set up by the people to be the guardians of their rights, and to secure their persons from being injured or oppressed,—the safety of the public being the supreme law of the state, by which the magistrates are to be governed, and which they are to consult upon all occasions. The modes of administration may be very different, and the forms of government may vary from each other in different ages and nations; but, under every form, the end of civil government is the same, and cannot vary; it is like the laws of the Medes and Persians—it altereth not.

***Source:* Great American Sermons. Retrieved April 3, 2003, from http://www.frii.com/~gosplow/sermons1.html**

phy in modern textbooks, to the eighteenth-century person, political thought and religious ideas were usually so closely intertwined as to be virtually indistinguishable. Thomas Paine (1737–1809), for example, argued in his Revolutionary War pamphlet *Common Sense* that monarchy was the result of sin according to the Bible.

Puritanism

Although the term Puritan was old-fashioned by the time of the Revolution, the spirit and culture of Puritanism continued to live on in the thought and attitudes of most American Protestants, particularly those that had ancestral ties to the "dissenting" sects of English Puritanism: Congregationalists, Presbyterians, and Baptists. Puritans were part of the Reformed tradition of Protestantism that was inspired by sixteenth-century religious reformers such as John Calvin (1509–1564). Across Europe, Reformed Protestantism was often associated with antimonarchical feelings among the middle classes of merchants and professionals. Nowhere was this more apparent than among radical English Puritans, who believed that obedience to Scripture was a higher duty than an unquestioning obedience to the king or to traditions of the church. If Scripture did not sanction bishops, then the king ought to purify the church of bishops, they reasoned, thus striking a blow at one source of royal power and influence. For the Puritans the king was not above the law, and if the king violated the laws of God, then many English Puritans believed that it was their religious duty to overthrow the king, which they did in the 1640s. Therein were the seeds of revolution planted.

Whig Political Thought

Closely allied with the Puritan vision of a moral society based on the laws of God was the Whig political ideology that grew out of the seventeenth-century power struggles between king and Parliament. In this political theory, unchecked power in a monarchy was inherently corrupting and led inevitably to tyranny. This view merged comfortably and often imperceptibly with the Puritan view of the inherently sinful nature of human beings. Concerned with the question of how best to preserve liberty within society, which Puritans conceived as a blessing of the gospel, eighteenth-century theorists argued that power should be divided between different branches of government, and that civic virtue was necessary to maintain the health of society. These "republican" ideals often merged with Christian themes in subtle ways. If the apostle Paul, for example, had said that the gospel sets us free, then perhaps he also meant freedom from political tyranny. Or again, if tyranny results from the evils of aristocratic excess, then the struggle against the king is also a struggle of virtue against the vices of political corruption, luxury, and sloth. Armed with such arguments, it was not unusual for colonial ministers to translate the patriot cause into a struggle of Christian virtue against the evils of unfettered monarchy, and some even identified the king with the Antichrist or the beast of Revelation 13.

Enlightenment Thought

Finally, the natural rights philosophy of John Locke and other political theorists of the Enlightenment became increasingly important in the years prior to the revolution, as Americans sought to justify their revolt against Britain. These ideals, summarized and enshrined in American political discourse in the Declaration of Independence, include the propositions that all people are created equal and that the creator has endowed human beings with unalienable rights of life, liberty, and the pursuit of happiness. These natural rights are "self evident," asserted Thomas Jefferson (1743–1826), because they are rational truths known by the human mind without the assistance of divine revelation. Jefferson grounded his idea of natural rights in the God above nature, as did almost all thinkers of his day, but in keeping with his rationalist views, he wrote of "nature's God," "the Creator," "the Supreme Judge," and "divine Providence." More orthodox Christians than Jefferson could accept these terms on the assumption that they applied to the God of the Bible, even though for many religious rationalists they implied a rejection of traditional Christian views of God.

In a more religious context, many Christians were troubled by the injunctions of the apostle Paul to obey governmental authority, because government is ordained by God, and whoever resists government "shall receive to themselves damnation" (Romans 13:1–8, KJV). A sermon by Congregational pastor Jonathan Mayhew (1720–1766), preached in 1750, used a blend of Puritan and Enlightenment ideas to reinterpret Paul's counsel on obedience. Christians believe in obedience to government, argued Mayhew, but not an unqualified obedience: God has so ordered "the nature and end" of government to be the welfare of society. Therefore, if a ruler becomes a tyrant and oppresses his people, then the apostle does not require passive obedience, but to the contrary, "implicitly authorizes and even requires" resistance, whenever necessary " to the public safety and happiness" (Mayhew 1969, 28–29).

The Role of Religious Institutions

Religious leaders played an important role in preparing people to enter the war with Britain. The influence of preaching was significant. In colonial times, sermons were often published in newspapers and could therefore reach a wider audience than today. Prior to the war, thousands of sermons were preached that laid out the reasons for the patriot cause of freedom. Usually these sermons portrayed the conflict in biblical imagery: for example, they often identified the American colonists with Israel, and Britain with Egypt or Babylon, thus transforming the language of war into a righteous battle against the enemies of God. Many religious leaders served as military chaplains in the Continental Army, and some even took part in military engagements. One example was John Peter Gabriel Muhlenberg (1746–1807), a Lutheran minister who commanded American troops at Yorktown.

Support for independence came slowly for most ministers. As late as the outbreak of fighting in 1775, most ministers probably still hoped for reconciliation with Britain. However, as events unfolded and it became clear that war was inevitable, the leaders of the colonial churches took sides in the conflict. Historians have made the following general observations about how the churches responded to the war.

Congregational Churches, direct heirs of the Puritans, strongly supported the war, with few exceptions. So widespread was their support that their clergy were derisively called "the black regiment," referring to the color of their robes. Congregationalists were predominantly centered in New England, and included such patriots as Samuel Adams (1722–1803), John Adams, and John Hancock (1737–1793). Likewise, Presbyterians in the middle colonies also supported the war. Joseph Galloway (c. 1731–1803), a loyalist member of the Pennsylvania Assembly, blamed the revolution in part on Presbyterian and Congregational principles of religion. Foremost among Presbyterian patriots was John Witherspoon (1723–1794), a Scot Presbyterian and president of Princeton College. Witherspoon was accused of turning Princeton into a "seminary of sedition"; he was also the only clergyman to sign the Declaration of Independence.

There were many Dutch Reformed, German Reformed, and Lutheran communities in the middle colonies. These groups were less uniform in their response to the war, preferring neutrality in many instances, but by 1776 the majority supported independence. Members of pacifist churches, Quakers, Mennonites, Moravians, and German Brethren, declared themselves neutral or opposed to the war. Quakers were generally regarded as loyalist in their sentiments, although officially they declared themselves neutral. Many were persecuted for their stance. A few Quakers who decided the war was just were disowned: among these was Nathanael Greene (1742–1786), who became a general in the Continental Army.

Baptists in New England and Roman Catholics in Maryland usually supported the patriot cause because they believed that their prospects for religious freedom would be better under a new American government. There were about 2,000 Jews in America at the time of the revolution, most of them in Rhode Island, New York, and Charleston, South Carolina. Just as in every denomination, colonial Jews were divided by the war, but the majority supported independence.

The largest bloc of loyalist opposition to the war came from the Anglican clergy. For most Anglicans, the revolution went against the divinely ordained monarchical rule of society. Moreover, Anglican priests at their ordination had sworn allegiance to the king. Hence, more than half of the Anglican clergy in America left their pulpits during the war, and some served as chaplains in the British army. One exception to Anglican loyalism lay in the South, where a class of wealthy Anglican gentry provided the center of intellectual leadership for independence: Thomas Jefferson, Patrick Henry (1736–1799), George Mason (1725–1792), George Washington (1732–1799), and James Madison (1751–1836) were nominal Anglicans influenced by Enlightenment rationalism. Two-thirds of the signers of the Declaration of Independence were Anglicans.

The Effects of the War on Religion

On the one hand, the disruption of normal life caused by the War of Independence led to what Sydney Ahlstrom has called a "religious depression" (Ahlstrom, 1972, 365): pulpits were left vacant and church organizations were disrupted. On the other hand, the war also stimulated other religious expressions not easily measured by church statistics. Many soldiers experienced religion for the first time in field revivals held by military chaplains. Moreover, the stress of war led naturally to a heightened sense of religious sensitivity. The Continental Congress, for example, ordered regular days of public fasting and prayer throughout the war. Apocalyptic modes of thinking were accentuated, as the war stimulated religious speculation about the end of the world and the final judgment.

The revolution brought the issue of religious liberty into bolder relief. As already noted, some groups supported the war because they were given assurances that their religious rights would be secured under a new American government. This hope induced many frontier Baptists and Presbyterians in the southern colonies to make common cause with Anglican rationalists like Thomas Jefferson. Conversely, the war weakened religious establishments of colonial governments, because popular support was needed to carry out the war effort. Anglican establishments were repealed quickly in five colonies, and even in New England and Virginia where disestablishment was delayed, efforts were made to relax religious discrimination.

The war also weakened the control of religious institutions by elites. After the war most churches reorganized themselves into voluntary denominations. The result of this process led to a "democratizing effect," as lay people came to have more influence in the leadership of their religious institutions.

Finally, historians have discussed extensively the emergence of a national civil religion during the revolution. By "civil religion," historians mean the ways that public ceremonies and symbols reinforce commonly held beliefs of a nation about its history, meaning, and destiny. For example, the celebration of July 4 as a holiday gave public and symbolic expression to the unity of the colonies and their destiny to form one people out of many. The Declaration of Independence became one of many documents that function as a sacred canon for the self-understanding of the nation. The motto "Novus ordo seclorum" gave expression to the special role of the new nation as a beacon of light to the world. These and other ideas, symbols, and ceremonies led to the development of a national civil religion during and after the American Revolution.

Daniel W. Draney

Further Reading

Ahlstrom, S. E. (1972). *A religious history of the American people*. New Haven, CT: Yale University Press.

Albanese, C. L. (1976). *Sons of the fathers: The civil religion of the American Revolution*. Philadelphia: Temple University Press.

Bailyn, B. (1967). *The ideological origins of the American Revolution*. Cambridge, MA: Harvard University Press.

Bonomi, P. U. (1986). *Under the cope of heaven: Religion, society, and politics in colonial America*. New York: Oxford University Press.

Corbett, M., & Corbett, J. M. (1999). *Politics and religion in the United States*. New York: Garland Publishing, Inc.

Hudson, W. S. (1981). *Religion in America*. New York: Charles Scribner's Sons.

May, H. F. (1976). *The Enlightenment in America*. New York: Oxford University Press.

Noll, M. (1977). *Christians in the American Revolution*. Washington, DC: Christian University Press.

Smith, P. (Ed.). (1976). *Religious origins of the American Revolution*. Missoula, MT: Scholars Press.

W

Wahhabism

Wahhabism is the name given by outsiders (adherents call themselves *muwahhidun*, meaning "unitarians") to a radical Islamic reform movement in Sunni Islam (the branch of Islam followed by 90 percent of the world's Muslims) that began in mid-eighteenth-century Arabia. Today it forms the ideological basis of the Islamic Kingdom of Saudi Arabia. Wahhabism denotes an ultraconservative brand of Islam that is literalist, rigid, and exclusivist. Since the 1970s, Wahhabism has not been confined to Saudi Arabia alone, as the Kingdom has exported it to the rest of the world, particularly the conflict-ridden Muslim regions of South and Southeast Asia, Central Asia, and the Caucasus. A number of extremist Islamic movements and organizations, including al-Qaeda, the Taliban, and the Islamic Movement of Uzbekistan, adhere to the puritanical Wahhabi doctrine.

History

Wahhabism was founded by Muhammad ibn Abd al-Wahhab (1703–1791), who studied law and theology in Mecca and Medina and advanced the radical Islamic doctrine of Ibn Taymiyah (1263–1328), a medieval Muslim theologian. Al-Wahhab was disillusioned by the spiritual and moral decline he perceived in Arab society in the eighteenth century. To him, any idea added to Islam after the third century of the Muslim era (mid-tenth century CE) was false and had to be expunged. This was the time when the Ummiyyad dynasty was replaced by Abbasids, and the fundamentals of Islam, as upheld by Prophet Muhammad's companions and their Ummiyyad sucessors, started to be influenced by other religious/spiritual factors such as Sufism. The Wahhabi view regarded the veneration of saints, ostentation in worship, and luxurious living as being typical of *jahiliyyah*, or pre-Islamic ignorance and barbarism.

Besides denouncing the prevailing popular Islamic beliefs and practices as idolatry, al-Wahhab rejected much of the medieval law of the ulema (Muslim clergy) as *bid'a* (condemnable innovations, and called for a fresh interpretation of Islam that returned to its revealed sources. Central to al-Wahhab's theology and movement was the doctrine of God's unity *(tawhid)*, an absolute monotheism reflected in the Wahhabis' self-designation as unitarians—those who uphold the unity of God. Al-Wahhab identified himself with Prophet Muhammad, and tried to equate contemporary Arab society with the sort of heathen culture the Prophet had striven to overthrow.

Citing the tradition that Prophet Muhammad had destroyed the pantheon of gods in his Meccan shrine, Wahhabi forces set out to destroy "idolatrous" shrines, tombstones, and sacred objects, including the tombs of the Prophet and his Companions in Mecca and Medina, as well as the Shi'ite pilgrimage site at Karbala (in Iraq) that houses the tomb of Husayn ibn 'Ali, one of Shi'a Islam's greatest martyrs (Shi'a Islam is followed by approximately 10 percent of the world's Muslims). The destruction of this venerated site has contributed to the historic enmity between Wahhabi Saudi Arabia and Shi'ite Iran. Wahhabi iconoclasm remains strong: It inspired the Taliban, the radical Is-

Selection from the Constitution of Saudi Arabia, adopted March 1992

The following articles of the Constitution of Saudi Arabia make clear the centrality of the Wahhabism in Saudi Arabia.

Chapter 1 General Principles

Article 1

The Kingdom of Saudi Arabia is a sovereign Arab Islamic state with Islam as its religion; God's Book and the Sunnah of His Prophet, God's prayers and peace be upon him, are its constitution, Arabic is its language and Riyadh is its capital.

Article 2

The state's public holidays are Id al-Fitr and Id al-Adha. Its calendar is the Hegira calendar.

Article 3

The state's flag shall be as follows:

(a) It shall be green.

(b) Its width shall be equal to two-thirds of it's length.

(c) The words *"There is but one God and Mohammed is His Prophet"* shall be inscribed in the center with a drawn sword under it. The statute shall define the rules pertaining to it.

Article 4

The state's emblem shall consist of two crossed swords with a palm tree in the upper space between them. The statute shall define the state's anthem and its medals.

Chapter 2 [Monarchy]

Article 5

(a) The system of government in the Kingdom of Saudi Arabia is that of a monarchy.

(b) Rule passes to the sons of the founding King, Abd al-Aziz Bin Abd al-Rahman al-Faysal Al Saʾud, and to their children's children. The most upright among them is to receive allegiance in accordance with the principles of the Holy Koran and the Tradition of the Venerable Prophet.

(c) The King chooses the Heir Apparent and relieves him of his duties by Royal order.

(d) The Heir Apparent is to devote his time to his duties as an Heir Apparent and to whatever missions the King entrusts him with.

(e) The Heir Apparent takes over the powers of the King on the latter's death until the act of allegiance has been carried out.

Article 6

Citizens are to pay allegiance to the King in accordance with the holy Koran and the tradition of the Prophet, in submission and obedience, in times of ease and difficulty, fortune and adversity.

Article 7

Government in Saudi Arabia derives power from the Holy Koran and the Prophet's tradition.

Article 8 [Government Principles]

Government in the Kingdom of Saudi Arabia is based on the premise of justice, consultation, and equality in accordance with the Islamic Shariʿah.

Source: International Court Network. Retrieved May 14, 2003, from http://www.oefre.unibe.ch/law/icl/sa00000_.html

lamic group that ruled Afghanistan from 1996 to 2002, to destroy the ancient Bamiyan Buddha statutes in Afghanistan in March 2001.

In the eighteenth century, ibn Saud (c. 1880–1953), a tribal leader in Arabia, adopted Wahhabism and channeled the religious zeal it generated toward the unification of Arabia. Like the Kharijites of the seventh century CE, the Wahhabis viewed fellow Muslims who did not accept their uncompromising viewpoints as unbelievers who must be fought and killed; Wahhabism permitted warfare against Muslims who disputed Wahhabi teachings.

Since ibn Saud's official founding of the kingdom of Saudi Arabia in 1932, the kingdom has combined politics with religion. Successive Saudi kings have enjoyed strong support from the Wahhabi establishment, though occasionally since the 1990 Gulf War and the stationing of U.S. troops in Saudi Arabia in its aftermath Saudi dissidents have criticized the House of Saud for compromising Wahhabi principles.

Global Spread

Since the 1970s, the Saudis, both through government-sponsored organizations and wealthy individuals, have exported a puritanical and at times militant version of Wahhabi Islam to other countries and communities in the Muslim world and the West. Wahhabi ulema have consistently exported Wahhabism throughout the Muslim world. The Saudi royal family remains extremely sensitive to the opinion of these ulema, who were also instrumental in securing, despite the latter's growing ties with Osama bin Laden. Wahhabism has deeply impacted a number of militant Islamic movements in the late twentieth century and early twenty-first century. These include the global al-Qaeda terrorist network, as well as Jamiyat-e-Ulema Islam in Pakistan, the Islamic Movement of Uzbekistan, and Gamʿaal-Islamiyya in Egypt. Its critics call Wahhabism regressive because it refuses to reinterpret traditional Islamic law in accordance with the norms of modernity, and because it depicts everyone, Muslim or non-Muslim, who does not adhere to Wahhabism as *jahiliyyah*—meaning Western or pro-Western.

Wahhabism and the War on Terrorism

The House of Saud cannot end its support of Wahhabism without risking its political survival and its position of leadership in the Islamic world. But as long as Wahhabism thrives in Saudi Arabia, and as long as Saudi backers support Wahhabism in the rest of the world, especially among extremist Islamic forces, the United States may find the prosecution of its war terrorism an uphill battle.

Ishtiaq Ahmad

See also Islamic Movement of Uzbekistan; Taliban; Deobandhism

Further Reading

Ahmad, I. (2000–2001). Containing the Taliban: The path of peace in Afghanistan. *Perceptions*, 5(4), 67–87.

Akbar, M. J. (2002). *The shade of swords: Jihad and the conflict between Islam and Christianity*. New York: Routledge.

Algar, H. (2002).*Wahhabism: A critical essay*. London: Islamic Publications International.

Ali, T. (2002). *The clash of fundamentalisms: Crusades, jihads and modernity*. New York: Verso.

Esposito, J. (1999). *The Islamic threat: Myth or reality?* New York: Oxford University Press.

Esposito, J (2002). *Unholy war: Terror in the name of God*. New York: Oxford University Press.

Hiro, D. (2002). *War without end: The rise of Islamic terrorism and global response*. New York: Routledge.

Juergensmeyer, M. (2001). *Terror in the mind of God: The global rise of religious violence*. Berkeley and Los Angeles: The University of California Press.

Rashid, A. (2000). *Taliban: Islam, oil and the new Great Game in Central Asia*. London: I. B. Tauris.

Schwartz, S. (2002). *The two faces of Islam: The House of Saud: from tradition to terror*. New York: Doubleday.

World Council of Churches

The World Council of Churches (WCC) unites 340 Protestant and Orthodox churches, denominations, and fellowships in 120 countries to pursue Christian aims and advance ecumenism. To achieve its aim of protecting all people made in God's image, the WCC has offered assistance to war victims and opposed weapons of mass destruction while controversially providing funds to violent liberation movements through the Program to Combat Racism.

Formation

On 12 May 1938, 80 Christian leaders representing 130 branches assembled at Utrecht, Netherlands, to adopt a provisional constitution for an organization dedicated to improving international relations through the cooperation of all Christian churches. A few months later in July 1939, with war clouds massing, the embryonic WCC gathered thirty-five leading Christians to propose ways in which to check the drift toward war. The statement issued by this conference summarizes WCC opinion of war: "We believe that no decision secured by force of arms will be just and that out of the evil forces, thereby set in motion, more evil is bound to come" (Macy 1960, 66). The WCC, not yet officially formed, called for negotiations conducted free from the threat of force. Once World War II began, the budding ecumenical movement entered a holding pattern but the WCC did manage to provide some chaplaincy service and give limited assistance to prisoners of war, Jews, and other refugees. With the end of war, the WCC boxed Bibles for delivery to war-torn areas, offered medical, clothing, and food aid, and rebuilt churches. Orthodox leaders, who had joined the Roman Catholic Church in reacting suspiciously to ecumenism and had refused to join the WCC, were the main beneficiaries of construction aid and this assistance prompted them to participate in the official formation of the WCC at Amsterdam on 23 August 1948. The Catholic Church never joined, though it later cooperated with the WCC. With its formation, the WCC became the most visible ecumenical movement of the twentieth century.

After World War II

The 147 churches from 44 countries participating at the 1948 WCC Assembly charged that the horrors through which the world had just lived testified in part to the failures of the churches to promote peace and justice. These representatives condemned war as being contrary to the will of God and incompatible with the teachings of Jesus Christ, adding, "the part which war plays in our present international life is a sin against God and a degradation of man" (Macy 1960, 115). To help prevent future wars and heal the wounds of World War II, the WCC joined the new United Nations and it is now one of the largest Non-Governmental Organizations within this body.

Cold War

While the WCC opposes war, it is not a pacifist organization. Members have always argued that some violence may be justified, and this view prompted the WCC to voice support for the U.N. police action in response to hostilities in Korea in 1950. This is the only occasion where the WCC has approved the use of military force. The WCC statement, issued shortly after the war broke out, approved by a majority of member churches, praised the United Nations as an instrument of world order.

As the Cold War intensified, the WCC responded both to the increased threat of world destruction and to the continued menace of nationalism. At its second assembly in 1954 in Evanston, Illinois, the WCC rejected the notion that war is inevitable by arguing that God's will is peace. The organization called on all Christians to rise above nationalism and celebrate Christ by bringing all ethnicities, races, and classes together. Responding directly to the increased threat from nuclear bombs, the Evanston delegates called for the prohibition of all weapons of mass destruction and the sharp reduction of all other armaments. The WCC called for international inspection and control of weapons with the inspectors presumably drawn from the United Nations. The group also sought assurances from nations that no country would engage in or support aggressive or subversive acts in other countries.

While the WCC did not issue a statement directly addressing Vietnam, the organization consistently focused on areas of concern that touched on aspects of that war, such as conflict resolution, human rights, and racism. It has typically sought to provide a channel of communication between opposing parties but has occasionally attempted mediation.

Its best known and most successful mediation effort, the Addis Ababa agreement, ended the Sudanese civil war in 1972. But peace collapsed by 1982.

Controversy and Decline

As the WCC grew, members from Third World countries initiated a debate on the theological justification of armed revolution. The Program to Combat Racism, created in 1969, supported disciplined revolutionary violence as a last resort in the belief that such violence did not undermine the democratic process. This branch of the WCC gave a grant in 1978 to the Patriotic Front of Zimbabwe, which was then engaged in an armed struggle to overthrow the white minority government of Rhodesia. In protest, both the Salvation Army and the Presbyterian Church of Ireland withdrew from the WCC while European and American churches began to debate their commitment to the group. The WCC pointed out that the funds were to be used for humani-

The World Council of Churches on the 2003 Iraq War

The World Council of Churches (WCC) remains extremely concerned with the continued calls for military action against Iraq both by the US and UK governments despite Iraq's compliance with United Nations Resolution for UN weapons inspection, agreeing for the "immediate, unconditional and unrestricted access to sites in Iraq".

We were greatly alarmed and saddened by the US Congressional Joint Resolution to authorize use of force against Iraq passed by the US House of Representatives and Senate on 10th October, 2002, authorizing, inter alia, the President of the USA to use its armed forces in order to enforce all relevant UN Security Council resolutions regarding Iraq.

As you prepare for further deliberations of the United Nations Security Council this week, I would like to draw your attention to the numerous voices of Christians around the world, who, committed to the teachings of Jesus Christ and the prophetic vision of peace, strongly believe that pre-emptive war against Iraq is illegal, immoral and unwise.

The World Council of Churches' governing body meeting in September this year, urged the international community to uphold the international rule of law, to resist pressures to join in pre-emptive military strikes against a sovereign state under the pretext of the "war on terrorism", and to strengthen their commitment to obtain respect for United Nations Security Council resolutions on Iraq by non-military means.

They deplored the fact that the most powerful nations of this world continue to regard war as an acceptable instrument of foreign policy, in violation of both the United Nations Charter and Christian teachings.

The WCC has always advocated for every member state to comply with binding UN resolutions and to resolve conflicts by peaceful means. Iraq can be no exception. Since the end of the Gulf War we have repeatedly called the Government of Iraq to destroy its weapons of mass destruction and related research and production facilities, to cooperate fully with UN inspectors deployed to oversee compliance, and to guarantee full respect of the civil and political, economic, social and cultural human rights for all its citizens.

We are deeply concerned by the potential human costs of a new war and the prospects of large-scale deplacement of people. The people of Iraq have suffered enough under a sanctions regime since 1991. Inflicting further punishment on innocent civilians is not morally acceptable to anyone. Churches around the world also caution against the potential social, cultural, and religious as well as diplomatic long-term consequences of such a war, especially a unilateral one. Further fueling the fires of violence that are already consuming the region will only sow more seeds of intense hatred strengthening extremist ideologies and breeding further global instability and insecurity.

The WCC joins its voices with church leaders and Christian communities around the world, especially from the USA and UK, praying that you focus your attention on addressing the root causes of this conflict and to put an end to the dire humanitarian crisis in Iraq and the Middle East region as a whole. I call upon you as members of the United Nations Security Council to act wisely, responsibly and courageously.

We pray that God will guide you to take decisions based on moral principles and legal standards.

"No nation shall lift up sword against nation, neither shall they learn war any more' Isaiah 2:4"

Source: World Council of Churches Press Update. (2002, September 20). Retrieved April 6, 2003, from http://www2.wcc-coe.org

tarian aid, not arms, but critics charged the group had become pro-leftist and anti-Western. WCC membership and influence began to drop in the West as part of the resulting conservative backlash.

Subsequent WCC meetings did little to appease critics. At the 1975 Nairobi Assembly, Third World participants attacked industrialized nations for using science and technology to serve their own military and economic interests in ways that brought about great suffering. The 1983 Vancouver Assembly drew further controversy by condemning the "blatant misuse of the concept of national security to justify repression and foreign intervention" (Koshy 1994, 53). The delegates alleged that no nation is secure as long as the right to self-determination as well as social and economic justice are denied to individuals. The WCC further took the position that churches should declare the use, production, and deployment of nuclear weapons to be a crime against humanity. It declared that Christians should state their refusal to participate in any conflict involving weapons of mass destruction or weapons with indiscriminate effects, such as chemicals.

Throughout the years, the WCC has struggled to reach a consensus on how to best serve God. Striving to obey the teachings of Jesus Christ, it has balanced opposition to war with a desire for worldwide social and political justice. While its success is difficult to measure, it has made a considerable contribution to peace by bringing the churches together and by coordinating worldwide humanitarian relief and development projects.

Caryn E. Neumann

Further Reading

Koshy, N. (1994). *Churches in the world of nations: International politics and the mission and ministry of the church*. Geneva, Switzerland: World Council of Churches.

Macy, P.G. (1960). *If it be of God: The story of the World Council of Churches*. St. Louis, MO: Bethany Press.

VanElderen, M., & Conway, M. (2001). *Introducing the World Council of Churches*. Geneva, Switzerland: World Council of Churches.

Webb, P. (Ed.). (1994). *A long struggle: The involvement of the World Council of Churches in South Africa*. Geneva, Switzerland: World Council of Churches.

World Council of Churches. (1988). *And so set up signs: The World Council of Churches' first forty years*. Geneva, Switzerland: World Council of Churches Publications.

Y

Yoruba

The Yoruba are an ethnic group concentrated in the West African country of Nigeria (there is a smaller population in neighboring Benin) whose population numbers more than 20 million. Even though they are usually considered a homogenous cultural group, there are many subgroups within their ranks; these include the Ife, Ketu, Awori, Egbado, Egba, Ibadan, Ijebu, Ijesha, Oyo, Ondo, Owo, Ekiti, and Igbomina. These subgroups have frequently engaged in intraethnic strife reflected in competing political views, economic interests, and religious conflict.

The Yoruba in the Nineteenth Century

Established in the fourteenth century, the Yoruba kingdom of Oyo enjoyed peaceful stability under the reign of Alafin Abiodun at the beginning of the nineteenth century. Fulani Muslims, poised just north, sought to expand their influence by converting the Yoruba to Islam. Abiodun's successor, Awole Arogangan, destabilized the Oyo kingdom by ordering his nephew, Afonja, the commander of the northern territory of Ilorin, into war against the Muslims further north over a personal grudge. Sensing the futility of such a battle, Afonja mutinied instead and forced Awole to abdicate his throne and commit suicide. Afonja was eventually killed by his Muslim allies in 1831. Oyo attempted to recapture Ilorin, but because of intraethnic struggling among the Ife, Egba, Ibadan, and Ijebu, there was little unity. Ultimately, the Ilorin-based Fulani leader Usman dan Fodio conquered Oyo. Refugees from the defeated northern Yoruba towns were captured and sold to European slave traders.

The dissolution of the Oyo empire created a vacuum in Yorubaland (the territory occupied by Yoruba peoples) and led to wars among various groups. During the 1830s there were many temporary political alliances and rivalries among the Ibadan, Ijebu, and Egba, but wars broke out in 1835 and 1836. Later in the decade, the Egba fought the Egbado over the port city of Abeokuta for direct trade links with the British, who were active in the region long before the beginning of the nineteenth century. There was a twenty-year general armistice before Yoruba intraethnic fighting over territorial lines broke out once more in the Ijaye War of 1860–1865.

By the 1870s, intra-Yoruba disputes were as economic as they were religious and political. The Ijebu were the ultimate beneficiaries of the internal struggling because they fought mostly outside their own territory but still maintained a trading relationship with Britain, with whom they had once trafficked in human cargo, and other equipment. Seeking western education became a goal of many Ijebu, which meant members of other subgroups came to rely on Ijebu skills. (Among those who sought them out were traditional chiefs, who relied on Ijebu letter writers to complain to the British government.) Nineteenth-century intraethnic clashes nurtured resentment and mistrust among Yoruba subgroups that lasted well into the twentieth century, and politicians were quick to exploit these collective hurts for personal and political gain.

Religion, Ethnicity, Class and Marriage in Nigeria

Nigeria is one of the more socially complex nations in the world. That complexity is indicated by the various factors that must be considered in selecting a marriage partner. The following example is from northern Nigeria.

Since it was anticipated that few, if any, individuals would indicate willingness to marry a white woman, or a non-Moslem, the choices which were offered were limited to tribes who are all present in the area and who are known to the people of the community of Geidam. The Fulani are all Moslem and the Hausa almost all Moslem; in the case of the Babur and the Yoruba who are partly Moslem, the question was specifically phrased: would you marry a Moslem Yoruba, or a Moslem Babur woman? . . .

The most popular tribe was the Hausa, and 43 per cent said they would marry a Hausa woman. The next in order of popularity was the Babur tribe, a part-Moslem, part-pagan people living in Bornu Province and strongly acculturated to the Kanuri; 38 per cent indicated willingness to marry a Babur woman. Fewer people are willing to marry a Fulani woman; though the Fulani are Moslems like the Kanuri, they are pastoralists who live in the bush and differ greatly from the urban Geidamites; 30 per cent would marry a Fulani woman. The least popular choice was the Yoruba woman, selected by only 27 per cent of the sample. Though the Yoruba who live in Northern Nigeria are all urban people, and the question referred specifically to Moslem Yoruba who are numerous, the Yoruba are generally identified as a southern tribe of very different background.

Considering each group in turn, the Aristocracy are noteworthy in their willingness to marry Yoruba women, whom they seem to prefer above the other three choices. This might be attributed to their wider orientation as a group. The Koranic Malams show no difference in their preferences among the four tribes. The Canteen Operators are almost unanimous in rejecting three of the four tribes, yet a majority of them (67 per cent) would marry a Hausa woman. This curious and striking result can be explained quite simply by looking at the role of the Canteen Operators. Their normal activities in trade bring them into contact with Hausas and they all speak Hausa. Because of the frequency of their interaction with members of that culture they show a willingness to marry Hausa women. This does not extend to women of other tribes in the form of a general willingness to marry out, as can readily be seen by their responses in columns 3, 4, and 5. The NA Malams are willing to marry with women of three of the tribes, including the unpopular Fulani, but unlike the Aristocracy they are not willing to marry a Yoruba woman.

Source: Rosman, Abraham. (1966). *Social Structure and Acculturation among the Kanuri of Northern Nigeria.* Ann Arbor, MI: University Microfilms Publications, pp. 320–322.

The Growth of Separatist Christian Churches among the Yoruba

In the late 1880s, there was a Yoruba urban elite in Lagos that was joined by Yoruba returnees of Spanish and Portuguese influence (that is, Africans who had been enslaved in Brazil or Latin America who were repatriated or voluntarily returned). This added a religious component to the internal strife. The urban Christian Yoruba began seeking autonomy from their U.S. and European mission churches.

Between 1890 and 1920 a separatist church movement spread among the Yoruba and gained momentum in other parts of the African continent. Among the churches that emerged as a result of a break from their mission churches were the Native Baptist Church, the United Native Africa Church, the Bethel African Church, and Jehovah Shalom Church. By 1917 fourteen African churches had sprung up in southern Nigeria. Cosmetic efforts were made to incorporate indigenous cultural expressions in their services, but doctrinally they remained similar to the parent church. Although there is no reliable data, by the beginning of the twentieth century, Yoruba north of Oyo tended to be Muslims and those south of it were more likely to be Christian.

By World War I outside colonial, social, and economic pressures nearly closed the separatist churches. Economic hardships brought rural Yoruba into major cities like Lagos seeking employment, and with them came self-styled itinerant evangelists who preached from street corners, in marketplaces, and in other informal settings. Their hellfire-and-damnation style was punctuated with dramatic apocalyptic prophecies and promises to cure the influenza outbreak that ravaged the region at the time. Several of these evangelists held prayer meetings or formed praying bands that gained popularity within some of the separatist churches. One of the praying bands, the Cherubim and Seraphim Society (1925), became very popular among the Yoruba after its unusual beginnings.

One founder of the society was Christianah Abiodun Akinsowon (later known as Captain Mrs. Abiodun Emanuel), a teenage girl living in Lagos, who began having frequent angelic visitations in her sleep in June 1925. The story goes that although she became friendly with her angelic visitor, on one occasion she was taken by a different angel before an angelic council and told that unless she answered several biblical questions, she would be unable to return to her normal consciousness. Unbeknownst to the council, Abiodun's friendly angel stood behind her and supplied her with the correct answers.

To the outside world, however, Abiodun appeared to be comatose for several days. Her relatives sent for one of the itinerant preachers in the area, Moses Orimolade Tunolashe. It was Tunolashe (in the form of the Abiodun's friendly angel) who gave her the answers to the complex biblical queries posed by the angelic council. When this story was reported, it was seen as a miracle because Moses Orimolade Tunolashe could neither read nor write. When Abiodun came out of her trance and was told about Tunolashe, she located him and with him formed the Cherubim and Seraphim Society. This developed into the first denomination of the Aladura ("owners of prayer") church. Within ten years of the Cherubim Society's emergence, there were several Aladura churches in and around Lagos.

In their effort to Africanize Christianity, the Aladura churches allowed plural marriages, acknowledged the presence of negative magical forces (and prophylactic measures to counteract those forces). They held fast to a belief in visions such as Abiodun and other prophets had experienced. The primacy of prayer and its healing power, however, was the paramount tenet. Aladura worship includes the use of drums, bells, and, in more recent times, instruments like trumpets and electric guitars. In the 1940s the Aladura movement spread outside Yoruba-speaking Nigeria to other parts of the continent and eventually to Europe and the United States.

Independent Nigeria

In 1960 Nigeria attained its independence, but in the mid–1960s, intraethnic violence reemerged with a vengeance among the Yoruba. Politicians exploited old rivalries and jealousies among the Yoruba even to the point of drawing artists and dramatists into the fray. To incite matters further, politicians fanned smoldering interethnic angers, rivalries, and biases, such as Igbo dislike for Yoruba or Yuruba dislike for Hausa and Fulani, and played on those prejudices when it came to appointments and passing out political favors. Ethnic tensions were heightened by obviously rigged national elections in 1964 and regional elections in 1965 in Yoruba-dominated parts of the country. In January 1966 all of the intra- and interethnic violence throughout the country came to a halt when midlevel military officers carried out the country's first coup d'état by assassinating the majority of senior politicians and military leaders.

The fact that those political and senior military leaders killed were from the north (that is, they were Hausa and Fulani) and the west (and therefore Yoruba) and that eastern leaders (primarily Igbo) were largely spared fueled suspicions that the coup was an Igbo plot to rule the country. (Many of the officers who led the coup were Igbo.) When an Igbo officer, Major General J. Aguiyi Ironsi, emerged as the new military head of state, those suspicions were confirmed in the minds of many. A subsequent coup later that year took place in which Ironsi and other eastern officers were killed, and there were attacks on easterners resident in northern parts of the country. Nigeria plunged into a full-scale civil war between 1967 and 1970.

Although religion was not the primary dynamic in the fighting, the dual identities of northern Nigerians (religiously Muslim and ethnically Hausa-Fulani) and eastern Nigerians (religiously Christian and ethnically Igbo) were used in the propagandistic literature circulated throughout the respective regions. After the surrender of the Biafran forces (Biafra was the name of the Igbo secessionist state) in 1970, the restored Nigerian federal government made efforts to ameliorate the ethnic and religious divide among its young people by requiring them to perform a mandatory one-year term of service in a section of the country other than that which they were from (or to which they had ancestral ties).

Among the Yoruba, religious conflict continues to manifest itself because unlike any other major ethnic group in Nigeria, there are significant numbers of both Christians and Muslims within that population. There are estimates that fifty percent of Yorubas are Muslims and forty percent are Christians, with the remainder being practitioners of tradition beliefs systems. In the early 1980s, the Saudi Arabian government provided the funds to build a mosque on the campus of the primarily Yoruba University of Ibadan. After its completion, worshippers complained that as they prayed to the east, they could see the cross of the Catholic cathedral that had been on the campus for close to seventy-five years. They demanded that the cross be removed. Christians were vehemently opposed to even discussing the matter and the issue simply died off.

Throughout the 1990s and into the twenty-first century, there continue to be debates among the Yoruba (and the rest of the country) over the Muslim-Christian divide. There are those who believe the country is on the brink of a religious war. The adoption of Islamic *shari'a* law in the northern states has been another contentious issue early in the new century. Keeping such tensions under control appears to be the ongoing challenge of the Nigerian government.

Christopher Brooks

See also Nigeria

Further Reading

Ajayi, J. F. (1965). *Christian missions in Nigeria: 1841–1891*. London: Longman.

Ajayi, J. F., & Smith, R. (1964). *Yoruba warefare in the ninteenth century*. Cambridge, UK: Cambridge University Press.

Akintola, V. L. (1982). *Akintola: The man and the legend*. Lagos, Nigeria: Delta.

Anifowose, R. (1982). *Violence and politics in Nigeria*. New York: NOK.

Azikiwe, N. (1970). *My odyssey: An autobiography*. London: C. Hurst.

Bascom, W. (1969). *The Yoruba of southwestern Nigeria*. New York: Holt, Rhinehart and Winston.

Brooks, C. (1989). *Duro Ladipo and the Moremi legend: The socio-historical development of the Yoruba music drama and its political ramifications*. Unpublished doctoral dissertation, University of Texas, Austin.

Clarke, J. H. (Ed.). (1974). *Marcus Garvey and the vision of Africa*. New York: Vintage Books.

Crowder, M. (1966). *A short history of Nigeria*. New York: Frederick A. Praeger.

Johnson, S. (1921). *The history of Yorubas*. London: Routledge and Kegan Paul.

Omoyajowo, J. A. (1971). *The Cherubim and Seraphim in Nigeria*. Unpublished doctoral dissertation, University of Ibadan, Nigeria.

Osuntokun, A. (1984). *Chief S. Ladoke Akintola: His life and times*. London: Frank Cass.

Peel, J. D. Y. (1968). *Aladura: A religious movement among the Yoruba*. London: Oxford University Press.

Z

Zealots

The Zealot movement was a nationalistic and violent reaction to the Roman occupation of Judea and Hellenized monarchies of Herod Antipas (21 BCE–39 CE) and Herod the Great (73–4 BCE). The movement, active from approximately 45 BCE to 72 CE, centered around a dynasty of religious leaders beginning with Hezekiah, a Pharisee whose protests against the semidivine monarchy of Herod Antipas provoked Roman suppression so severe the Sanhedrin in Jerusalem protested. Hezekiah was executed in 47 BCE, but one of his descendants, probably a son, Judas of Galilee, surfaced in 6 CE in response to the Roman occupation of the region and the call for an imperial census.

Concepts and Practices

Judas of Galilee, aided perhaps by a priest, Zadok (whose historical existence is unproven), formulated the Zealot philosophy based on two simple concepts: that there should be no ruler of Judea except God, and that God would only intervene on behalf of a people who showed themselves willing to seize their liberty by any means. This struck at the heart of Roman rule, since Zealots could not pay taxes, participate in the census, offer obligatory sacrifices to the emperor, or tolerate Roman contamination of the temple or synagogues by placing pagan statuary in them and by adding the Antonia Tower to the temple as a defensive fortification. Zealots wished to purify the faith and took as key scriptural references passages in Exodus identifying God as "a man of war" and Numbers, in which Aaron's son Phineas used violent means to defend the Jewish people (Exodus 15:3; Numbers 25:11–13). Other role models were King David, Israel's warrior king, and Elijah, who called on the power of God to remove the priest of Baal from Israel (2 Samuel 8: 1–14; 1 Kings 18:1–40).

Between the census and the Jewish Revolt of 66 CE, the Zealots frequently ran afoul of Roman authorities, who classified them as robbers or brigands. Judas of Galilee and two of his sons were executed, and perhaps hundreds of Zealots were martyred after being captured for conducting guerrilla attacks on Roman officials and Jewish collaborators, as well as being punished for refusing to participate in the Hellenized life of the Roman province, which forbade circumcision and demanded sacrifices for the emperors. The Zealots embraced martyrdom, on the grounds that their deaths represented to God the commitment, not just of their group, but of the entire Jewish people. More practically, Zealots favored death to the imprisonment that would force them to break Jewish law and preferred the suicide of their women and children rather than have them raped or sold as slaves. This was a particular fear regarding Zealot children, who might be taken from their parents and raised as pagans.

Until the outbreak of the revolt in 66 CE, the Zealots operated out of Galilee, waging a guerrilla war in hopes of attracting the support of the entire Jewish people, whose taking up of arms, they believed, would trigger God's intervention and lead to the restoration of the kingdom of God. During this period, Zealots were in deep conflict with more accommodating factions, particularly the followers of Jesus, who may have had former Zealots (Simon) amongst the apostles (Mark 3:18). The separation of church and state as well as the pacifisms inherent in the teaching of Jesus were antithetical to the Zealots, who regarded them as a betrayal of the Jewish faith and the Mosaic law.

Success and Decline

The Jewish Revolt of 66 CE, triggered by a particularly sensitive Zealot issue, sacrilege, seemed to be the start of a unification of the Jews in order to remove the Romans from Judea. Zealots quickly seized key positions, including the Temple Mount in Jerusalem and the fortress of Masada, while another group of Zealots ambushed and killed the Roman governor of Syria, Gallusin 67 CE, and his soldiers in the pass at Beth Horon as he arrived to quell the rebellion. Jewish unity, however, splintered as the Romans, now led by Vespasian (9–79 CE), sacked Galilee in 67 CE and moved to lay siege to Jerusalem.

The Zealots holding the temple, who had already purged the area they held of Romans, sacrilegious Jews, and the foreign spouses of Jews, attempted to rule the city as "deliverers." Unfortunately, the kingdom of God as interpreted by the Zealots did not include practical governing concepts, only a belief that God would assume control of their military efforts through divine inspiration, and the situation degenerated quickly into a massacre of Sadducees and triggered fighting between the Jewish factions holding the city, even while Vespasian attacked the city itself. When Jerusalem fell, numerous Zealots sought martyrdom defending the temple against the Romans, and deliberately died in the fire that destroyed it.

Surviving Zealots, angered at the interference of more moderate factions, who sought peace with the Romans or agreed, like Josephus, to change sides, gathered for a last stand at Masada, which they had taken in the early days of the revolt. Led by Eleazer, another descendent of Hezekiah, the Zealots held out against a besieging Roman legion for seven months before deciding to commit mass suicide rather than fall into Roman hands in 72 CE. The movement died out quickly with the deaths of most of its leaders, and the Romans seemed to have made a deliberate effort to seize any living descendents of Hezekiah or of King David in order to prevent further Zealot leaders emerging. Interestingly, although a dangerous force against the Romans, the Zealots were always officially categorized under Roman law as robbers or *sicarii* (assassins) rather than an army or military force, mandating their treatment as criminals rather than recognized combatants.

Margaret Sankey

Further Reading

Brandon, S. G. F. (1967). *Jesus and the Zealots: A study of the political factor in primitive Christianity*. Manchester, UK: Manchester University Press.

Farmer, W. (1956). *Maccabees, Zealots, and Josephus*. New York: Columbia University Press.

Hengel, M. (1989). *The Zealots* (D. Smith, Trans.). Edinburgh, UK: T. & T. Clark.

Pearlman, M. (1969). *The Zealots of Masada*. London: Hamilton.

Roth, C. (1959). *The historical background of the Dead Sea scrolls*. New York: Philosophical Library.

Zen and Japanese Nationalism

Until recently, the relationship between Zen and modern Japanese nationalism has been one of the least understood aspects of the Zen tradition. This is because Zen apologists such as Daisetz T. Suzuki (1870–1966) have consistently presented this school of Buddhism to the West as transcending not only good and evil, life and death, but history itself including such related "isms" as capitalism, communism, and, of course, nationalism.

Zen before World War II

The truth, however, is the very opposite, for the Zen tradition has been among the most loyal and faithful servants of the modern Japanese state since the Meiji Restoration of 1868. Given that Zen was wedded to the ruling samurai (warrior) class since its introduction to Japan in the early 1200s, it could hardly have been otherwise. In fact, it was D. T. Suzuki himself who first described the role not only Zen but also Japanese Buddhism as a whole was destined to play in the modern Japanese state.

Specifically, in November 1896, the twenty-six-year-old Suzuki published a book entitled *A Treatise on the New [Meaning of] Religion (Shinshukyo-ron)*. Chapter 15 was entitled "The Relationship of Religion and the State" and began with the claim that "religion should, first of all, seek to preserve the existence of the state, abiding by its history and the feelings of its people." In this, religion shared a common responsibility with Japan's military, the latter having the added burden of "preventing [the state] from being encroached upon by unruly heathens" (Victoria 1997, 23–24).

While Suzuki did not identify the "unruly heathens" he had in mind, Japan had just emerged victorious from its first modern conflict, i.e., a war with China in 1894–1895 in which Japan acquired its first overseas colony—Taiwan. The pretext for the war had been China's attempt to block Japan's expansion onto the Korean peninsula. Given this, it not surprising that Suzuki went on to claim:

> "If a lawless country comes and obstructs our commerce, or tramples on our rights, this is something that would truly interrupt the progress of all of humanity. In the name of religion our country could not submit to this. . . . Instead, we would simply punish the people of the country representing injustice in order that justice might prevail." (Victoria 1997, 24–25)

By the end of the chapter Suzuki laid out the fundamental position Buddhist leaders would collectively adhere to until Japan's defeat in 1945. Namely: (1) Japan had the right to pursue its commercial and trade ambitions as it saw fit; (2) should unruly heathens *(jama gedo)* of any country interfere with that right, they deserved to be punished for interfering with the progress of all humanity; (3) such punishment would be carried out with the full and unconditional support of Japan's religions; (4) soldiers must, without hesitation, offer up their lives to the state in carrying out such religion-sanctioned punishment; and (5) discharging out one's duty to the state on the battlefield is a religious act.

Suzuki, it should be noted, was not necessarily the originator of the preceding ideas, for they can also be found in the writings of Shaku Soen (1859–1919), Suzuki's Rinzai Zen master. It was Soen who demonstrated just how easy it was to put Suzuki's theory into practice. He did this by going to the battlefield as a Buddhist chaplain attached to the First Army Division shortly after the outbreak of the Russo-Japanese War in February 1904. As to why he went, Shaku stated: "I wished to have my faith tested by going through the greatest horrors of life, but I also wished to inspire, if I could, our valiant soldiers with the ennobling thoughts of the Buddha, so as to enable them to die on the battlefield with the confidence that the task in which they are engaged is great and noble" (Victoria 1997, 26).

A photo of "god of war" Lt. Col. Sugimoto Gorô (1900–1937) as the embodiment of the Zen ideal of the "unity of Zen and the sword" within the context of Japanese militarism. He did this through his writings on Zen and the imperial military entitled *Taigi* (*Great Duty*). More than 100,000 copies would be published in 1938 after his battlefield death in north China.

Courtesy Brian Victoria.

In fairness to Suzuki, Shaku, and others like them, it should be pointed out that Japan's traditional Buddhist sects, Zen included, had come under severe verbal and even physical attack by Shinto adherents even prior to the advent of the Meiji Restoration. Shintoists claimed that because Buddhism was a foreign religion, it had no place in a uniquely divine country ruled over by an emperor who was a direct descendant of the Shinto sun goddess Amaterasu. Thus, Japan's Buddhist leaders had to demonstrate to their detractors, including government officials, that they were patriots who could contribute to Japan's modernization, not least of all by rallying popular support for Japan's expansionist policies.

Because of its long involvement in the spiritual training of Japan's warrior class, Zen was particularly well placed to support Japan's increasing emphasis on the military. In 1938 D. T. Suzuki explained the importance of Zen training for the military, past and present, in *Zen and Japanese Culture:* "A good fighter is generally an ascetic, or stoic, which means he has an iron will. This, when needed, Zen can supply" (Suzuki 1959, 62).

The practical impact Zen had on the Japanese military is best demonstrated by "god of war" *(gunshin)* Lieutenant Colonel Sugimoto Goro (1900–1937). Sugimoto was a lay disciple of Rinzai Zen Master Yamazaki Ekiju (1882–1961), who praised his military disciple for having achieved full enlightenment. Sugimoto described why he practiced Zen:

> The reason that Zen is important for soldiers is that all Japanese, especially soldiers, must live in the spirit of the unity of sovereign and subjects, eliminating their ego and getting rid of their self. It is exactly the awakening to the nothingness *[mu]* of Zen that is the fundamental spirit of the unity of sovereign and subjects. Through my practice of Zen I am able to get rid of my ego. In facilitating the accomplishment of this, Zen becomes, as it is, the true spirit of the imperial military. (Victoria 1997, 125)

Zen and World War II

Zen influence on the imperial military went far beyond individual soldiers like Sugimoto. Key elements of Zen doctrine were purposely incorporated into the very foundation of the military's program of "spiritual education" *(seishin kyoiku)* used to instill a fanatical willingness to die in soldiers. This is revealed in a booklet published in January 1941 by the Department of Military Education Department entitled "Shisei Ichinyo" ("Death and Life Are One"), itself an expression of traditional Zen doctrine.

After pointing out just how critical a proper understanding of life and death is to the maintenance of military discipline, the booklet continued:

> It was the Zen sect that furnished the warrior spirit with its ideological and spiritual foundation. The Zen sect overthrew the earlier belief in rebirth in Amitabha Buddha's Western Paradise [as taught by the Pure Land school of Buddhism] and replaced it with the teaching that one's very mind is the Buddha, coupled with a call to rely on one's own efforts [to achieve salvation]. It caused people who were vainly yearning for rebirth in the innumerable lands of Amitabha's Western Paradise to immediately focus on the here and now, to reflect on the original nature of the self. That is to say, the Zen sect emphasized the dignity and power of the self and concluded that belief in gods, Buddhas, paradises, or hells outside of the self was total delusion.
>
> On the one hand it can be said that it was only natural for warriors to be able to fearlessly and calmly enter the realm of life and death based on their prior experience on the actual battlefield. Nevertheless, it is also true that the teachings of the Zen sect exerted a strong influence on the warrior spirit . . .
>
> It can therefore be said that the time-honored, traditional spirit of our country [as embodied in Shinto mythology] was tempered by the belief in the oneness of life and death that had been incorporated into the Zen training of the warriors of the Kamakura period [1185–1333]. . .thus becoming the deeply and broadly held view of life and death of the Japanese people . . .
>
> It is this view of life and death that is one of the primary factors in the maintenance of strict military discipline in the midst of a rain of bullets. Coupled with this, of course, is the sublime greatness of the imperial military's mission, making it possible to sacrifice one's life without regret in the accomplishment of that mission. (Victoria 2002, 118–9)

The claim that the oneness of life and death had also become the "deeply and broadly held view of life and death of the Japanese people" is significant in that it suggests Zen influence was not limited to the military alone. D. T. Suzuki also advocated this position as revealed in an article he wrote in 1942 entitled "The Japanese People's View of Life and Death." After noting that the "Zen view of life and death is now that of the Japanese people as a whole," Suzuki went on to claim that the warrior class had been "the most Japanese-like" of all classes, its superior character allowing warriors to play the leading role in Japan's development:

> It is the warrior spirit that can be rightly said to represent the Japanese people. I believe that if the warrior spirit, in its purity, were to be imbibed by all classes in Japan—whether government officials, military men, industrialists, or intellectuals—then most of the problems presently troubling us would be swept away as if at the stroke of a sword. (Victoria 2002, 120)

This absolute faith in the Zen-inspired warrior spirit was destined to have ever more tragic consequences for the Japanese people, especially as it became clear from late 1943 onwards that an Allied invasion of the Japanese mainland was only a matter of time. It was then that Zen leaders, virtually to a man, called on the civilian population to be prepared to repel the Allied invasion even at the cost of national suicide. One such leader was Harada Sogaku, who in postwar years would be introduced to the West as the very model of a fully enlightened Zen master. In a July 1944 article entitled "Be Prepared, One Hundred Million [Subjects], for Death with Honor!" Harada wrote:

> It is necessary for all one hundred million subjects [of the emperor] to be prepared to die with honor. . . . If you see the enemy you must kill him; you must destroy the false and establish the true—these are the cardinal points of Zen. It is said that if you kill someone it is fitting that you see his blood. It is further said that if you are riding a powerful horse nothing is beyond your reach. Isn't the purpose of the [Zen] meditation we have done in the past to be of assistance in an emergency like this? (Victoria 1997, 140)

In addition to exhortations like these, as the territories colonized and occupied by Japan increased, the Zen school, including both the Rinzai and Soto sects, established branch headquarters and missions throughout Asia and willingly cooperated with the colonization policy. The two Zen sects also offered prayers and gave sermons in support of military victory, dispatched military chaplains to encourage war sentiment, and supported the arming of ordained clergy to serve on the battlefield. Both sects also carried out military drills, conducted fund-raising drives to purchase military aircraft, and otherwise supported the war effort both spiritually and materially, under the rallying cry of "Preach the Dharma and Serve the Nation."

In short, up through Japan's surrender on 15 August 1945, the relationship between Zen and Japanese nationalism can best be characterized by the famous Zen dictum: "Not two" *(funi).*

Brian Daizen Victoria

Further Reading

Cleary, T. (1991). *The Japanese art of war.* Boston: Shambhala.

Leggett, T. (1978). *Zen and the ways.* Rutland, VT: Charles Tuttle.

Suzuki, D. T. (1959). *Zen and Japanese culture.* Princeton, NJ: Princeton University Press.

Varley, P. H. (with I. & N. Morris). (1970). *The samurai.* London: Weidenfield and Nicholson.

Victoria, B. (1997). *Zen at war.* New York: Weatherhill.

Victoria, B. (2003). *Zen war stories.* London: Routledge Curzon.

Zen, Modern

Given the Zen school's deep complicity in Japanese militarism during and prior to the Asia-Pacific War, one might imagine that the Zen school, like other Buddhist sects, would have been subjected to severe criticism in the immediate postwar period. However, for a variety of reasons, this did not occur.

Yanagida Seizan (b. 1922), one of Japan's greatest postwar Zen scholars, provided one explanation for Zen and institutional Buddhism's lack of accountability:

> All of Japan's Buddhist sects—which had not only contributed to the war effort but had been one heart and soul in propagating the war in their teachings—flipped around as smoothly as one turns one's hand and proceeded to ring the bells of peace. These sectarian leaders had been among the leaders of the country who had egged us on by uttering big words about the righteousness [of the war]. They acted in a totally shameless manner. (Victoria 1997, 162)

A second factor was the allied occupation forces' determination that the spiritual foundation of Japanese militarism had been State Shinto, not Buddhism. Thus they initially focused on ending state support for the Shinto faith and then applied pressure on Emperor Hirohito to issue a proclamation 1 January 1946 denying, at least indirectly, his status as a Shinto deity. Once this had been done, occupation authorities left Japan's religions to fend for themselves.

Buddhist War Responsibility in Japan

Not everyone, however, was ready to ignore the past. D. T. Suzuki (1870–1966) first broached the topic of Buddhist war responsibility in October 1945 when he wrote a new preface for his *Nihonteki Reisei* (Japanese Spirituality). While, like the occupation authorities, Suzuki blamed Shinto for providing the "conceptual background" to Japanese militarism, he went on to discuss the Buddhist role as follows:

> It is strange how Buddhists neither penetrated the fundamental meaning of Buddhism nor included a

global vision in their mission. Instead, they diligently practiced the art of self-preservation through their narrow-minded focus on "pacifying and preserving the state." Receiving the protection of the politically powerful figures of the day, Buddhism combined with the state, thinking that its ultimate goal was to subsist within this island nation of Japan.

As militarism became fashionable in recent years, Buddhism put itself in step with it, constantly endeavoring not to offend the powerful figures of the day. Out of this was born such things as totalitarianism, references to [Shinto] mythology, "Imperial Way-Buddhism," etc. As a result, Buddhists forgot to include either a global vision or concern for the masses within the duties they performed. In addition, they neglected to awake within the Japanese religious consciousness the philosophical and religious elements, and the spiritual awakening, that are an intrinsic part of Buddhism. (Victoria 1997, 150–1)

As insightful as Suzuki's words were, he failed to address his own Zen-based support for Japan's war effort. Further, when he later explained the war years to his English-speaking readers, he left out all reference to Buddhism's war responsibility. Specifically, in an autobiographical account of his life entitled *A Zen Life: D. T. Suzuki Remembered*, Suzuki claimed:

The Pacific War was a ridiculous war for the Japanese to have initiated; it was probably completely without justification. Even so, seen in terms of the phases of history, it may have been inevitable. It is undeniable that while British interest in the East has existed for a long time, interest in the Orient on the part of Americans heightened as a consequence of their coming to Japan after the war, meeting the Japanese people, and coming into contact with various Japanese things. (Victoria 1997, 154)

There were, nevertheless, a few critics in the West who expressed concerned about Zen (and Suzuki's) apparent lack of moral awareness. Arthur Koestler was one of the first to raise these concerns in a book published in 1960 entitled *The Lotus and the Robot*. He began his discussion of Zen as follows:

Zen was introduced into Japan in the late 12th century—more than five centuries after Confucianism and earlier forms of Buddhism. It took immediate roots; but it became radically transformed in the process, and the flower was characteristically Japanese. By a feat of mental acrobatics, of which perhaps no other nation would be capable, the gentle, non-violent doctrine of the Buddha became the adopted creed of the murderous samurai. . . . How was this possible?

The secret is not in the Buddha's smile, but in a simple formula applicable to all these diverse activities, the panacea of Zen: trust your intuition, short-circuit reflection, discard caution, act spontaneously. It is amazing what wonders this prescription can achieve. (Koestler 1960, 242–3)

Koestler later went on to discuss both Suzuki and some of those Western intellectuals, such as Alan Watts and Christmas Humphreys, who considered themselves to be his disciples. Koestler first noted that both Watts and Humphreys found *Alice in Wonderland* to be imbued with the spirit of Zen. Koestler then wrote:

This brings me back, for almost the last time, to Professor Suzuki and the question whether he and his disciples are trying to fool the reader or themselves. Since *Alice* is now being used as a Zen manual, I may as well confess that I have always been puzzled by Dr. Suzuki's striking spiritual resemblance either to Tweedledum or Tweedledee, whose twin suchnesses are no doubt meant to symbolize the identity of tea and no-tea, arrow and target, author and reader, the deluding and deluded mind. (Koestler 1960, 259–60)

Although Koestler was a journalist and not a scholar, Suzuki's writings were also of concern to two noted scholars, Paul Demiéville and R. J. Zwi Werblowsky. Demiéville, a French specialist in East Asian Buddhism, noted his concerns in a 1966 review of Suzuki's *Zen and Japanese Culture* while Werblowsky wrote an article in 1967 entitled "Some Observations on Recent Studies of Zen." Writing from a Jewish standpoint, Werblowsky was particularly troubled by Suzuki's statement in *Zen and Japanese Culture*, first published in 1938, that "[Zen] may be found wedded to anarchism or fascism, communism or democracy" (Suzuki 1959, 63). After quoting this passage, Werblowsky went on to add, "Dr. Suzuki forgot to add to the list of possibilities also Nazism with its gas chambers (as the annoying Mr. Koestler has rudely pointed out)" (Werblowsky 1967, 321). What both of these men found unacceptable was the way in which Suzuki placed Zen above all moral considerations.

Zen Leaders Grapple with War Responsibility

While these critiques were taking place in the West, in Japan itself the leaders of the Rinzai and Soto Zen sects saw no need to reflect on their wartime activities. On the contrary, some Zen leaders continued to insist that Japan had truly been engaged in a holy war. Rinzai Zen master Yamada Mumon (1900–1988), for example, had edited a strongly prowar book published in 1942 entitled *Bushidô no Kôyô* (The Promotion of the Way of the Warrior). Following the war, Yamada became both president of Rinzai-affiliated Hanazono University and chief abbot of Myoshin-ji, the largest branch of the Rinzai Zen sect. More importantly, he was one of the founders of the Association to Repay the Heroic Spirits [of Dead Soldiers] (Eirei ni Kotaeru-kai). The association's purpose was to lobby the Japanese government for reinstatement of state funding for Shinto-affiliated Yasukuni Shrine, where the "heroic spirits" of Japan's war dead were venerated.

At the association's inaugural meeting held on 22 June 1976, Yamada released a statement entitled "Thoughts on State Maintenance of Yasukuni Shrine" containing the following passage:

> Japan destroyed itself in order to grandly give the countries of Asia their independence. I think this is truly an accomplishment worthy of the name "holy war." All of this is the result of the meritorious deeds of two million five hundred thousand heroic spirits in our country who were loyal, brave, and without rival. I think the various peoples of Asia who achieved their independence will ceaselessly praise their accomplishments for all eternity. (Victoria 1997, 165)

At least in the Zen school, a belief in holy war had not disappeared and neither had the right-wing politics that sustained that belief. This latter feature is illustrated in the comments made by Zen Master Yasutani Haku'un (1885–1973) in January 1972 about Japanese labor unions, etc.:

> It goes without saying the leaders of the Japan Teachers' Union are at the forefront of the feebleminded [in this country]. . . . They, together with the four Opposition political parties, the General Council of Trade Unions, the Government and Public Workers Union, the Association of Young Jurists, the Citizen's League for Peace in Vietnam, etc. have taken it upon themselves to become traitors to the nation. . . .
>
> The universities we presently have must be smashed one and all. If that can't be done under the present Constitution, then it should be declared null and void just as soon as possible, for it is an un-Japanese constitution ruining the nation, a sham constitution born as the bastard child of the Allied Occupation Forces. (Victoria 1997, 171–2)

It is noteworthy that Yasutani was one of the most influential transmitters of Zen to the West in the 1960s. However, right-wing comments like the above were noticeably absent from his talks about Zen during his seven trips to the United States.

Nonetheless, by January 1993 Soto Zen leaders felt compelled to issue a statement admitting their war responsibility. It must be stressed, however, that this statement emerged not from any sudden moral awakening on the sect's part but from a well-publicized series of human rights abuses that the sect could no longer ignore. The statement read in part:

> Although the Soto sect cannot escape the feeling of being too late, we wish to apologize for our negligence and, at the same time, apologize for our cooperation with the war. . . . We recognize that Buddhism teaches that all human beings are equal as children of the Buddha. And further, that they are living beings with a dignity that must not, for any reason whatsoever, be impaired by others. Nevertheless, our sect, which is grounded in the belief of the transference of Shakyamuni's Dharma from master to disciple, both supported and eagerly sought to cooperate with a war of aggression against other peoples of Asia, calling it a holy war. (Victoria 1997, 158–9)

Despite the Soto sect's admission, the Rinzai Zen sect refused to admit its war responsibility until September 2001, fifty-six years after war's end. In fact, it was not until after the terrorist attack of 11 September 2001 on the United States that the large Myoshin-ji branch of the Rinzai Zen sect acknowledged for the first time that they, too, had once engaged in holy war. Their statement, issued on 27 September 2001, began:

> As we reflect on the recent events [of 11 September 2001 in the United States], we recognize that in the past our own country engaged in hostilities, calling it a "holy war," and inflicting great pain and damage to various countries. Even though it was national policy at the time, it is truly regrettable that our sect, in the midst of wartime passions, was unable to maintain a resolute anti-war stance and ended up cooperating with the war effort. In light of this, we wish to confess our past transgressions and critically reflect on our conduct. (Victoria 2002, 232)

The following year, in September 2002 the Myoshin-ji branch issued a much longer statement providing concrete examples of the numerous ways in which the sect had supported Japan's war effort. Significantly, the secretary general of this branch, Hosokawa Kei'itsu, called on his fellow priests to investigate "the root causes of these [war-related] errors and implement the reforms necessary to insure that they never happen again" (Me o sorasazu 2002).

It is too early to judge whether the Rinzai and Soto sects have the will to honestly examine the causes of their war collaboration and initiate the reforms necessary to insure that the Zen school never again finds itself a war enthusiast. Among other things, questions must be raised about the doctrinal and historical relationship between Zen and the state, let alone between Zen and the emperor. Is, for example, Zen's traditional role as a "protector of the nation" an intrinsic part of Zen or merely a historical accretion? What was the spiritual cost to Zen of the patronage it long enjoyed from Japan's warrior (and later military) class? Similarly, is the vaunted unity between Zen and the sword an orthodox or heretical doctrine?

It is no exaggeration to say that Zen's future, at least as an authentic part of the Buddhist tradition, depends on the answers to these and related questions.

Brian Daizen Victoria

Further Reading

Heisig, J. W., & Maraldo, J. C. (Eds.). (1995). *Rude awakenings*. Honolulu: University of Hawaii Press.

Ives, C. (1992). *Zen awakening and society*. Honolulu: University of Hawaii Press.

Koestler, A. (1960). *The lotus and the robot*. London: Hutchinson & Co.

Me o sorasazu hansho shi zange [Repenting and reflecting without pretense]. (2002, October 1). *Chugai Nippo* (newspaper).

Sharf, R. H. (1993). The Zen of Japanese nationalism. *History of Religions, 33*(1), 1–43.

Suzuki, D. T. (1959). *Zen and Japanese culture*. Princeton, NJ: Princeton University Press.

Victoria, B. (1997). *Zen at war*. New York: Weatherhill.

Victoria, B. (2003). *Zen war stories*. London: RoutledgeCurzon.

Werblowsky, R. J. Z., et al. (Ed.). (1967). *Studies in mysticism and religion presented to Gershom G. Scholem*. Jerusalem: Magnes Press, Hebrew University.

Zen, Premodern

The East Asian Buddhist tradition known variously by its Japanese *(Zen)*, Chinese *(Chan)*, Korean *(Son)*, and Vietnamese *(Thien)* names—all of which mean "meditation"—has adopted a variety of stances toward war and other forms of violence, especially in its premodern history. Any account of Zen Buddhist attitudes toward war must take into account both the commitment to nonviolence shared by Zen with all Buddhist traditions and the ways in which Zen Buddhists have cooperated with nationalistic and militaristic efforts in various East Asian cultures.

Buddhism as a Tradition of Nonviolence

"Enmities never cease by enmity in this world; only by non-enmity do they cease. This is an ancient law" (*Dhammapada* 5, in Harvey 2000, 239).

At the heart of the Zen Buddhist tradition is the basic Buddhist commitment to nonviolence. All Buddhists, whether laypersons or monastics, pledge to abide by five simple moral principles known as the Five Precepts. Foremost among these is the obligation to avoid causing harm to beings (human or otherwise). Early Buddhist scriptures such as the *Dhammapada* and the *Anguttara-nikaya* (probably recorded in written form during the second century BCE) underscore the importance of nonviolence by linking violent actions to negative karma (in Sanskrit, "action," referring to moral retribution in future rebirths) and understanding violence as an outgrowth of attachment to the false idea of a permanent self, which in turn is seen as the cause of all suffering.

The basic Buddhist teaching, or dharma (Sanskrit, "law"), about suffering is that it results from attachment to a changing, impermanent, and dissatisisfying reality. One can avoid suffering, however, by learning to accept reality for what it truly is (i.e., dynamic, temporary, and incapable of providing lasting happiness). Once one has learned to do this, one may live in blissful calm (nirvana—Sanskrit, "blowing out," i.e., extinguishing suffering), understanding the interdependence of all beings and exercising compassion for all beings. The role of nonviolence in spiritual practice leading to enlightenment and nirvana is obvious to all early Buddhist commentators.

From this, it would seem to follow that no Buddhist would voluntarily involve himself or herself in acts of violence, including war. Yet Buddhists in every age have become embroiled in violent conflicts, and because of Zen's unique understanding of the dharma, Zen Buddhists in particular have been drawn into militarism and other facets of war.

The Mahayana Background of Zen

In order to understand how a tradition that explicitly forbids violence came to be associated, at least in some instances, with state-sponsored killing, it is necessary to know something about the distinctive teaching of the Mahayana (Sanskrit, "Greater Vehicle") movement to which the Zen sect belongs.

Mahayana Buddhism arose in India during the first century CE, in part as a response to debates about the accessibility of practice and enlightenment and the sources of teaching authority for Buddhist communities. It emphasizes the "emptiness" (Sanskrit, *shunyata*) or impermanence of all concepts and entities, the utility of "skillful means" (Sanskrit, *upaya*) or expedient methods of communicating Buddhist teachings (regardless of how unorthodox or even immoral these may appear to the unenlightened), and the cultivation of "compassion" (Sanskrit, *karuna*) as the primary value of Buddhist doctrine and practice.

With the emergence of the Mahayana, Buddhists began to see how it might be possible to perform ordinarily prohibited actions (such as killing) as an expression of skillful means and/or compassion. For example, the *Upaya-kaushalya Sutra*, an early Mahayana scripture, tells how a bodhisattva (a Sanskrit term for a heroic, self-sacrificing figure who vows to help all beings attain enlightenment) saves the lives of hundreds of people when he kills a thief who otherwise would have robbed and murdered them all. This violation of the First Precept is described as a combination of compassion and skillful means. Other early Mahayana scriptures suggest that those who kill in order to protect the Buddhist state actually acquire positive karma, rather than negative karma, because their violent actions help to preserve and propagate the dharma.

Critics of such Mahayana apologies for violence were rebuked, if not silenced, by the Mahayana claims that the unattached mind of the Buddha does not recognize dualistic concepts such as "good" and "evil," that all sentient beings possess this Buddha-mind, or "Buddha-nature," inherently, and that enlightenment consists of coming to view reality through the nondualistic lens of "Buddha-mind," rather than "ordinary mind."

Zen, Militarism, and the State in Premodern East Asia

"If people within a country uphold the Buddhist rules governing moral behavior, the various heavenly beings will protect that country. . . . The Zen school maintains the principle of "protecting the country" (Eisai [1141–1215 CE], in Welter 1999, 69–70).

One way to explain the development of the Zen Buddhist tradition is to see it as the product of the encounter between Indian Mahayana Buddhism, imported into China by merchants and missionaries around the beginning of the common era, and indigenous Chinese social and spiritual values, defined primarily by the Confucian tradition of state authoritarianism and "sage kings" and the Taoist tradition of individualistic mysticism and esoteric meditation techniques. This marriage of moralistic ideologies and idiosyncratic insights gave birth to the peculiarly East Asian Buddhist tradition best known today by its Japanese name, Zen, and which flowed from China to Korea, Japan, and Vietnam over the course of the early medieval period (c. fourth through sixth centuries CE).

The Mahayana concepts of skillful means and "Buddha-nature," in particular, became important in the growth of the Zen tradition. Rather than meditating on the Tao (Chinese, "way" or the cosmos as an organic whole), early Chinese Zen practitioners meditated on their own "original nature" or "Buddha-nature"—studying the self to forget the self, as the Japanese Zen master Dogen (1200—1253 CE) famously put it. Rather than cultivating Confucian wisdom in order to advise or become a "sage king," later Japanese Zen thinkers such as Eisai taught that the embrace of Zen by the medieval East Asian state was the best way in which to protect the state, both materially (e.g., from natural disasters and enemy invasions) and spiritually (e.g., from the damning karmic consequences of attachment, desire, etc.).

Perhaps because of arguments such as Eisai's, or perhaps because of the increasing efforts of East Asian states to control Buddhist institutions during the medieval period, or perhaps because of both factors, "there emerged a doctrine of the identity of the Buddhist law and the imperial law, and, related to this, the doctrine that truth is identical with *upaya*" (Hirata 1995, 6). This, in turn, made possible the startling spectacle of armies of Buddhist monks, fighting to protect the imperial thrones of China and Japan.

The Legacy of Premodern Zen Ethics

"The Buddha-seed grows in accordance with not taking life" (Dogen, in Aitken 1984, 24).

At the end of the premodern period in East Asia, Zen had become associated with an emphasis on spontaneous action as an expression of one's Buddha-nature within, rather than on principled ethical life in accordance with scriptural canons of discipline and morality, as in the early Indian Buddhist tradition. Its unique flavor can be summarized in the well-known Zen saying that samsara (Sanskrit, "revolving," meaning the cycle of rebirth) and nirvana (i.e., freedom from rebirth) are one and the same. For premodern Zen Buddhists, it was possible to interpret this saying in two rather different ways: as an exhortation to moral responsibility (including nonviolence) as a sign of one's enlightenment, or as a license to transgress moral norms (such as nonviolence) in the name of skillful means and even compassion.

Jeffrey L. Richey

Further Reading

Aitken, R. (1984). *The mind of clover: Essays in Zen Buddhist ethics*. San Francisco: North Point Press.

Dumoulin, H. (1988). *Zen Buddhism: A history: Vol. 1. India and China* (J. W. Heisig & P. Knitter, Trans.). New York: Macmillan.

Dumoulin, H. (1990). *Zen Buddhism: A history: Vol. 2. Japan* (J. W. Heisig & P. Knitter, Trans.). New York: Macmillan.

Harvey, P. (2000). *An introduction to Buddhist ethics*. Cambridge, UK: Cambridge University Press.

Hirata, S. (1995). Zen Buddhist attitudes to war. In J. W. Heisig & J. C. Maraldo (Eds.), *Rude awakenings: Zen, the Kyoto school, and the question of nationalism* (pp. 3–15). Honolulu: University of Hawaii Press.

Mitchell, D. W. (2002). *Buddhism: Introducing the Buddhist experience*. New York and Oxford, UK: Oxford University Press.

Welter, A. (1999). Eisai's promotion of Zen for the protection of the country. In G. J. Tanabe Jr. (Ed.). *Religions of Japan in practice* (pp. 63–70). Princeton, NJ: Princeton University Press.

Zen: Samurai Tradition

The close relationship that developed in Japan between Zen and the samurai (warrior) class is one of the most controversial episodes in Buddhist history. How was it possible for Buddhism, which takes "Do not kill" as its first and cardinal precept, to become so intimately involved with a class of men whose duty it was to kill on command?

The great Zen scholar D. T. Suzuki saw no conflict in this regard, for he claimed that, from both moral and philosophical points of view, Zen was the ideal religion for the samurai class. "Morally," he explained, "because Zen is a religion which teaches us not to look backward once the course is decided upon; philosophically, because it treats life and death indifferently" (Suzuki 1959, 61).

Historically, it is difficult to argue with Suzuki because the first great warrior patron of Zen, Regent Hojo Tokimune (1251–1284), underwent Zen training in order to prepare himself mentally for a feared Mongol invasion of Japan in 1279. Shortly before the invasion, Tokimune sought guidance from Zen Master Bukko (1226–1286):

> "The greatest event of my life is here at last."
> Bukko asked, "How will you face it?"
> Tokimune shouted, "Katsu!" as if he were frightening away all his enemies actually before him.
> Bukko was pleased and said, "Truly, a lion's child roars like a lion!" (Dumoulin 1990, 35)

This exchange became a model for subsequent generations of samurai who sought to acquire fearlessness in battle through Zen training. In a deeply Confucian-oriented, hierarchical society, Zen's early success at the very pinnacle of Japanese society was also a significant factor in its rapid spread among the warrior class, the de facto rulers of the country from the Kamakura period (1185–1333) onwards. It is noteworthy that Tokimune's Zen master, Bukko, was Chinese, not Japanese, demonstrating that Chinese Zen masters were no less willing than their Japanese counterparts to place Zen training in the service of martial prowess.

As important as fearlessness in the face of death was to the samurai, it was only one of many features in Zen they found attractive. Zen doctrine was straightforward, teaching that through the single-minded practice of Zen meditation it was possible to see deeply into one's nature, become a Buddha, and "transcend life and death." While a Zen master might provide guidance, it was nevertheless a spiritual journey based on self-reliance, a key warrior virtue. Furthermore, Zen's emphasis on plain and frugal living appealed to the rough and unsophisticated temperament of the samurai.

Over the following centuries, the Zen spirit would go on to permeate the value system of the warrior class, eventually becoming codified in the late Middle Ages as Bushido (Way of the Samurai). In Bushido, Zen's emphasis on intuitive action, coupled with its teaching of the oneness of life and death based on the nonexistence of the self, became the basis for the unquestioning, loyal, and self-sacrificial spirit expected of the warrior. In the *Hagakure* (Hidden under the Leaves), an early-eighteenth-century formulation of Bushido, the essence of this spirit was expressed in its opening lines: "The Way of the Samurai is found in death" (Yamamoto 1979, 17).

Brian Daizen Victoria

Further Reading

Cleary, T. (1991). *The Japanese art of war*. Boston: Shambhala.

Dumoulin, H. (1990). *Zen Buddhism: A history (Japan)*. New York: Macmillan.

Leggett, T. (1978). *Zen and the ways*. Rutland, VT: Charles Tuttle.

Suzuki, D. T. (1959). *Zen and Japanese culture*. Princeton, NJ: Princeton University Press.

Varley, P. H. (with I. & N. Morris). (1970). *The samurai*. London: Weidenfield and Nicholson.

Victoria, B. (1998). *Zen at war*. New York: Weatherhill.

Yamamoto T. (1979). *Hagakure: The book of the samurai* (W. S. Wilson, Trans.). Tokyo: Kodansha International.

Zimbabwe

The nation which is now Zimbabwe possesses an unusual degree of geographical and historical coherence. It lies between three natural boundaries, the Zambezi river to the north, the Limpopo river to the south, and the Kalahari desert to the west. For hundreds of years this large area was inhabited by peoples speaking dialects of a single language, Shona. They were not conscious of a single identity and there was intense competition among their chieftancies and states. But there were similar cultural, including religious, institutions and ideas right across the zone.

In this context wars arose in three main ways. There were wars among different houses fighting to control a chieftancy. There were wars between chieftancies. Some chieftancies developed into large kingdoms, owning large herds of cattle, exacting tribute, and controlling trade. Such kingdoms could raise large numbers of fighting men, though they did not possess standing armies. Finally, there were wars waged by and against invaders from outside the region defined by the rivers and desert.

Some of these enemies were African, such as the armies that crossed the Zambezi from the north in the sixteenth and seventeenth centuries or the cattle-raiding Ndebele warriors who entered the Zimbabwean southwest in the 1830s and established their own state there. Some were European, such as the gold-seeking Portuguese who sought to dominate the Mutapa kingdom of the northeast in the sixteenth and seventeenth centuries. The Portuguese fought "just wars," supposedly to punish the murder of Catholic missionaries; they also imposed puppet kings and tried to repress rebellions. Eventually the Portuguese withdrew from the Zimbabwean plateau and did not seek to invade it again until the nineteenth century.

Up until the late nineteenth century all these wars were fought on roughly equal terms. Neither the Portuguese firearms nor the Ndebele assegais (a type of spear) gave an overwhelming advantage. In any case by the middle of the nineteenth century firearms had spread to all groups on the Zimbabwean plateau, and there was a military balance between the Shona-speaking chieftancies, the Ndebele, and the Portuguese. This changed decisively in the 1890s. The white adventurers recruited by Cecil Rhodes's British South Africa Company and the British soldiers who supported them in the wars of 1893 and 1896 possessed not only repeating rifles but machine guns and artillery. After their victories in these wars, the whites disarmed Africans throughout what became Southern Rhodesia. It was not until the guerrilla wars of the 1960s and 1970s that modern weapons came into African hands.

Foreign incursions into Zimbabwe always had religious connotations. In the fifteenth and sixteenth century Swahili traders from the East African coast, who came up the rivers to seek for gold and to trade with African kings and chiefs, brought Islamic ideas and technologies with them. They encouraged the Mutapa kings to kill Christian missionaries, and they were themselves expelled by Portuguese soldiers fighting a "holy" war. Three hundred years later, settlers with the British South African Company were accompanied by Protestant clergy when they entered the country in 1890. The white victory over the Ndebele in 1893 was seen by most missionaries as opening up the area for the work of God. African wars and resistances, meanwhile, were always suffused with religion.

Traditional Religion in Zimbabwe

African religion in Zimbabwe drew upon two main spiritual principles. One was the concept of the High God, creator of the world, maker of rain and guarantor of fertility. The High God, Mwali, embodied both male and female creative power—the male power of lightening from the sky and the female power of water in the earth. The worship of Mwali transcended the operation of kinship networks and of political patriarchy. Both priests and priestesses operated at the Mwali shrines, and pilgrims came to them from many different kin, chieftancies, and even language groups. At the shrines, which were generally in caves and rock overhangs and beside sacred pools, divinely possessed priestesses spoke in the voice of God. Attendant priests translated Mwali's commands to the congregation. In earlier times such shrines operated in many parts of the region, but by the nineteenth century they were concentrated in the Matopos mountains in the southwest, in the area where the Ndebele established their state.

Mwali was preeminently the god of social harmony and of natural abundance. But Mwali could be forcefully angry too: Evildoers and witches were punished, and rulers who disobeyed Mwali's laws were given up to the power of their enemies. There were shrines for rain and for healing, but there were also shrines for war. These war shrines empowered rulers in their wars against their enemies; they also offered cleansing to soldiers returning from the war. To make a just war meant getting the blessing of the shrines. To make a lasting peace meant getting cleansing from them.

The patriarchal system, which allocated dominance over women, kinship groups, and chieftancies to male elders, was sustained by another spiritual principle—the concept of the founding ancestors of the clan or the polity. It was believed that the spirits of these dead ancestors could return as lions and could possess living mediums Like the Mwali cult, the cult of the great ancestral spirits both afforded a fruitful relationship with the environment and legitimized the use of disciplinary violence and war. The great spirits were owners of the land and its resources; further, many of the founders had been conquerors, and they were able to empower soldiers and to offer guidance in war. Belief in the power of spirits also provided a means for controlling illegitimate violence. If a man killed an innocent person, then he or his descendants could be haunted by the vengeful *ngozi* spirit of the killed person until reparation and atonement were made. While the Mwali High God shrines were concentrated in the southwest by the nineteenth century, the system of ancestral spirit mediums was concentrated in the northeast.

Zimbabwean Religion and the Europeans

Most of our evidence for the history of Zimbabwean religion before the twentieth century comes from European commentators. These writers said little about African religion's focus on fertility and peace. They were mostly concerned to show that the resistance of African chiefs and kings was brought about by "witch doctors" who ordered the kings and chiefs to oppose Christianity. A sixteenth-century Portuguese commentator described how the Mutapa kings consulted the mediums of the royal ancestors: "The devil enters into one of the kaffirs . . . saying that he is the soul of the dead king"; climbing the mountain to meet one of these "demoniacs," the king talks with him "as amicably as if with his dead father, asking him if there will be war" (Mudenge 1988, 121–125). Two hundred years later, after many wars between the Portuguese and African chiefs, another Portuguese claimed that the ancestral mediums could "order the Emperor that he may or may not declare war . . . whom he may or may not slay" (Mudenge 1988, 121–125). These reports were blatant distortions, since patriarchal religion had nothing to do with the devil and resistance was certainly not the product of irrational superstition. But they do show that African religion was very much involved in war.

It was the same story with the British invasions of the 1890s. The British too believed that they were bringing commerce, civilization, and Christianity to the Ndebele and the Shona. African resistance to the obvious benefits of white rule was once again seen as the result of superstition. The African uprising of 1896 was blamed on "witch doctors" and "witches." Priests of the Mwali shrines were arrested and shackled; one priest was shot dead in his cave. Senior spirit mediums were captured, tried, and hanged. Some historians have dismissed all this as white ignorance and have emphasized that priests and mediums were concerned with rain and crops and social relations and not with violence. What seems likely, though, is that the Mwali war shrine in the Matopos both gave power for war and later authorized negotiations for peace. Moreover, the very concern of priests and mediums with rain and fertility led them to blame the whites for the droughts, the cattle diseases, and the locusts which were ravaging the land. After the suppression of the uprisings, optimistic missionaries thought that African religion had been "exploded" and that there was now no obstacle to their triumph.

In fact, organized African religion was merely driven underground. During the twentieth century it coexisted with Christianity. The Ndebele kingdom no longer existed, but the Mwali shrines in the Matopos mountains continued to function. The royal states of the northeast had gone but the senior ancestral spirits still possessed mediums. White administrators, anthropologists, and historians increasingly studied Zimbabwean religion and came to depict it much more positively, stressing its role in maintaining harmony in African societies. Operating among a disarmed people, the priests and mediums seemed to have nothing to do with violence and war.

But this view was as one-sided as the earlier one had been. The religious authorities still had political and even military potential. In the 1950s African nationalist movements emerged. Nationalist leaders visited Mwali shrines and senior mediums to ask for spiritual power to overthrow white rule; mass nationalist rallies sang hymns to the spirit mediums executed in 1897. African religion connected modern Zimbabweans to past kings and generals; it laid a profound African claim to the soil and the landscape. The atmosphere of the shrines had a powerful influence on the imagination of cultural nationalists. Joshua Nkomo (1917–1999), widely known as "Father Zimbabwe," who first visited the war shrine in the Matopos in 1953 as a young urban politician, continued to visit the shrines until his death more than forty years later.

The earliest region of Zimbabwe to produce large numbers of Christians—Anglicans, Methodists, Catholics—was Manicaland in the east. In the early 1930s there arose in Manicaland several African prophets, inspired by the Voice of God, who established Apostolic churches. The two most influential prophets both called themselves John (Yohana) after John the Baptist. These were Yohana Masowe (John of the Wilderness) and Yohana Maranke (Maranke being the name of his birthplace). Astonishingly both the Masowe and the Maranke Apostolic churches were to become multinational movements, each with millions of adherents throughout southern Africa. The Apostolic churches were a specifically Zimbabwean type of African Christianity, with a strong emphasis on prophetic vision, on exorcism and healing. In southern Zimbabwe very large numbers of people joined the so-called Zionist churches, which focused around holy Zion Cities established by their leaders. Missionaries regarded these Apostolic and Zionist churches as anti-European and nationalist historians have seen them as expressions of African resistance. They were persecuted and repressed. But it has become clear that their real intention was to do the job that the missionaries had failed to do—namely, to transform and fully Christianize African society. Missionaries often accused them of being "disguised paganism" but in fact their relationship to African religion was quite different. Apostolics and Zionists regarded African religion as diabolical; forbade the veneration of ancestors; and claimed that the Voice of God was truly expressed by their prophets but corrupted and distorted by the Mwali shrines. They were thus much more opposed to and by Zimbabwean African religion than was mission Christianity.

These churches were also not nationalist. They refused the authority of the colonial state but they repudiated the authority of any state, withdrawing into cities of God. However, when the guerrilla war became intense in the 1970s these churches were drawn in to the resistance to settler rule. Guerrillas made great use of Zionist and Apostolic prophets because of their powers to predict, to heal, and to render witches harmless. Since guerrillas also made great use of spirit mediums and Mwali shrines these two forms of African religion were brought together during the war.

Zimbabwean Religion and the Fight for Independence

As nationalism turned into guerrilla war in the later 1960s and 1970s, the old combatant role of African religion was rediscovered. Because the first formidable guerrilla incursions took place over the northeastern border between Zimbabwe and Mozambique, it was the ancestral mediums of the Mutapa state system that were first mobilized. It was only in the late 1970s that guerrillas reached the Matopos and interacted with the Mwali shrines.

In 1985 the anthropologist David Lan published *Guns and Rain: Guerrillas and Spirit Mediums in Zimbabwe*, a study of the role of the mediums in the northeastern war. Lan did his research in the Dande, the core area of the old Mutapa state. He showed how the great mediums used their power over both history and nature to assist the guerrillas. They portrayed the young fighting men as ancestral warriors, the true sons of the soil. They put the forces of nature at the guerrillas' disposal—eagles hovered to warn them of ambush, it was believed; rivers rose to block Rhodesian troops. In return, the mediums imposed taboos on the young fighters, prohibiting offenses against the environment and society. By the mid-1970s the Rhodesian administration was only too well aware of how much the mediums could offer to the guerrillas. An extraordinary "Shamanism Book" was compiled to instruct administrators about the history, cosmology, and politics of the Mwali shrines and the five great networks of spirit mediums. A "spirit index" was drawn up that aimed to include every priest and medium in Zimbabwe and to note which ones were supporting the "terrorists." Many mediums were arrested. Some were killed, either by Rhodesian soldiers or by guerrillas who believed them to be collaborating with the regime.

Today many spokesmen and women for African religion in Zimbabwe offer an explanation for the problems faced by the country since independence in 1980—problems such as the violence in Matabeleland in the 1980s, drought, hunger, AIDS, and political instability. These arise, they say, because the new rulers of Zimbabwe used the Mwali shrines and the spirit mediums to help them make war, but have not used them to make peace. After 1980, they say, the politicians relied on socialist or capitalist ideologies and turned their backs on African religion. Spirit mediums have been redefined as healers; Mwali shrines have been classified as national monuments. This sidelines or mummifies the religion. There has been no great national ceremony of cleansing from violence and of making peace.

Terence O. Ranger

Further Reading

Bucher, H. (1980). *Spirits and power. An analysis of Shona cosmology*. Cape Town: Oxford University Press.

Daneel, M. E. (1970). *The God of the Mtopo Hills: An essay on the Mwari Cult in Rhodesia*. Mouton: The Hague.

Fry, P. (1976). *Spirits of protest. Spirit mediums and the articulation of consensus among the Zezuru of Southern Rhodesia*. Cambridge, UK: Cambridge University Press.

Lan, D. (1985). *Guns and rain. Guerrillas and spirit mediums in Zimbabwe*. London: James Currey.

Maxwell, D. (1999). *Christians and chiefs in Zimbabwe*. Edinburgh, UK: Edinburgh University Press.

Mudenge, S. I. G. (1988). *A political history of Munhumutapa, c.1400–1902*. Harare, Zimbabwe: Zimbabwe Publishing House.

Presler, T. (1999). *Transfigured night. Mission and culture in Zimbabwe's vigil movement*. Unisa: Pretoria.

Ranger, T. O. (1967). *Revolt in Southern Rhodesia, 1896–7*. London: Heinemann.

Ranger, T. O. (1999). *Voices from the rocks: Nature, culture and history in the Matopos Mountains*. Bloomington: University of Indiana Press.

Zionism *See* Palestine and Israel

Zoroastrianism

Zoroastrianism postulates a universal battle at both the spiritual and corporeal levels between order (*asha*), which is equated to righteousness and good, and confusion (*drug*), which is equated to chaos and evil. War is considered an appropriate means of combat or struggle *(koxshishn)* against all forms of evil during the period, known as the time of the long dominion *(zaman i dagrand-xwaday)*, when order and confusion are in a state of interminglement *(gumezishn)* within corporeal creations. Zoroastrians believe that all evil must be battled so that it can be defeated and rendered separate *(wizarishn)* from good, resulting in an eschatological renovation (*frashagird*) when absolute order will be reestablished.

History

Each devotee customarily refers to himself or herself as *Mazda-yasna* ("Mazda worshiper") because the religion's creator deity or God is Ahura Mazda, or the Wise Lord. Designations such as *Zarathushtri* or Zoroastrian and *Majus* or Magian are based on the faith's founder Zarathushtra and the male clergy or magi. Zoroastrianism's basic doctrines are traced back to a devotional poet named Zarathushtra, who much later was called Zoroaster by the classical Greeks. Zarathushtra's time and place of ministry are uncertain. Most likely, he lived between the eighteenth and sixteenth centuries BCE, during the late Bronze Age. Most probably, he preached somewhere in central Asia. His words gradually drew followers and, around 1500 BCE, after the Proto-Iranians had migrated to the land that gained its name—Iran—from them, Zarathushtra's hagiography was modified to depict him as the prophet of ancient Iran and the first major religious founder. From among the newly resettled Iranian tribes, first the Medes (673–550 BCE) and then the Achaemenian clan of the Persians (550–331 BCE) founded empires that at a zenith extended from Egypt to the Indus river valley. After the reign of Darayavahush or Darius I (550–486 BCE), Zoroastrianism was clearly the official faith of Iran although other religions were freely practiced as well. Conflict between Iranians and Greeks eventually resulted in the Greco-Macedonian conquest led by Alexander the Great (356–323 BCE) in 334–331 BCE and the Seleucid kingdom (312–238 BCE). Iranian rule and Zoroastrianism as the official religion were reestablished in the region from the Euphrates River to western central Asia under the Parthian (247 BCE–224 CE) and then the Sassanian (224–651 CE) kingdoms. Arab Muslims conquered Iran in the seventh century CE, and Zoroastrianism gradually became a minority faith through conversion to Islam between that time and the thirteenth century CE. In the tenth century CE, a few Zoroastrians migrated from Iran to the Indian subcontinent to freely practice their own religion. Their descendants are called Parsis or Persians by other Indians. Even though a very small minority in demographic terms, Zoroastrians spread throughout India in the centuries thereafter, contributing to culture, politics, and economy. They also survived in Iran, again in small numbers. From the eighteenth century CE onwards, Zoroastrians have migrated to other countries as well and now form a worldwide community of approximately 154,000 individuals.

Doctrines

According to the Avesta or Zoroastrian scripture, Zarathushtra spoke of ethical and moral dualism between *asha* and *drug*, personifying the former in Ahura Mazda and the latter in Angra Mainyu, or the Destructive Spirit. Followers of Zarathushtra were required to "differentiate between the just and the unjust" (Ushtauuaiti Gatha, Kamnamaeza Haiti, Yasna 46:15). The devotional poet is said to have commented: "O Ahura Mazda, you know about the many disruptive deeds through which (each) evil person seeks fame, . . . ravages the pastures and wields a weapon against the follower of order" (Ahunauuaiti Gatha, Xvaetumaiti Haiti, Yasna 32:6, 10). Such persons were said to have "missed the veracity of the straight (path), . . . strayed from the path of order" (Vohuxshathra Gatha, Vohuxshathra Haiti, Yasna 51:13). Zarathushtra wished to know, for his followers and himself, "When the disparate hordes confront each other . . . to whom will you grant victory?" (Ushtauuaiti Gatha 44:15, Tat-thwa-peresa Haiti, Yasna 44:15). "I seek strong power for myself, through good thought, with the increase of which we may defeat confusion" (Ahunauuaiti Gatha, Ta-ve-uruuata Haiti, Yasna 31:4), he is supposed to have stated. Confident in the correctness of his views, Zarathushtra predicted: "Destruction will come to confusion" (Ahunauuaiti Gatha, At-ta-vaxshiia Haiti, Yasna 30:10), because "the (evil) mob fears us, for (we) the strong one(s) smite (those) weaker one(s) according to the strictness of your law, O Mazda" (Ahunauuaiti Gatha, Ya-shiiaothana Haiti, Yasna 34:8). He urged his deity to "place a mighty sword upon the evil ones to bring tribulation and harm to them, O Mazda" (Ushtauuaiti Gatha, Tat-thwa-peresa Haiti, Yasna 44:14) and enjoined his congregation to "strike sharply at cruelty" (Spentamainiiu Gatha, Yezidha Haiti, Yasna 48:7). According to Zarathushtra's message, persons who fight, morally and tangibly, for order will reach their "promised prize" in the paradisiacal "house of song" (Vohuxshathra Gatha, Vohuxshathra Haiti, Yasna 51:15). On the other hand, those who spread confusion and harm would, upon death, be condemned by their own actions to be "guests indeed in the (spiritual) house of deceit" according to Zarathushtra's sarcastic words (Spentamainiiu Gatha, At-maiiauua Haiti, Yasna 49:11). So the stage was set for a universal battle between the forces of order and confusion within the religion's worldview.

By medieval times, the magi began to write that humans had been created by Ahura Mazda to function as the deity's troops in the struggle against Angra Mainyu's confusion. According to one important passage: "Ahura Mazda deliberated with the perceptions and immortal souls of humanity . . . (saying) 'incarnate you can battle with evil and vanquish it.' . . . (Humans) agreed to enter the material world to become perfect and immortal in the final body at eternity" (Bundahishn 3:23–24). Owing to belief in this contract between God and humans, the life-purpose of every Zoroastrian is thought to involve combating *drug* in all its manifestations—religious, social, and political—using all appropriate means including warfare if necessary. The central notion is that good actions by people in the corporeal state can ensure the eventual triumph of order over confusion, of righteousness over evil, on the spiritual level.

Zarathushtra is credited, accurately, with having laid the framework for belief in universal eschatology (Ahunauuaiti Gatha, At-ta-vaxshiia Haiti, Yasna 30:8; Ahunauuaiti Gatha, Ta-ve-uruuata Haiti, Yasna 31:14, 20; and Ushtauuaiti Gatha, Kamnamaeza Haiti, Yasna 46:10), a notion that spread, eventually, to other faiths

Rock relief at Taq-e Bostan, Iran, depicting the Sasanian king of kings Ardashir II (ruled 379–383 CE) standing (center) over the body of a slain foe. As the victor in battle, Ardashir receives a diadem of sovereignty from the Zoroastrian god Ahura Mazda (right) while the divinity Mithra (left) with sword in hand protects the king. Courtesy R.N. Frye.

like postexilic Judaism, Christianity, and Islam. The magi built upon his basic ideas, producing complete, written apocalyptical and eschatological schemes by the Middle Ages. In Zoroastrian belief, signs that the end of the world is approaching include a steady increase in evil and suffering—including wars—on pious persons. Saviors will "wield the triumphant mace" (Zamyad Yasht, Yasht 19:92), it was said in the hymn whose ideas predate Achaemenian times but whose canonization probably dates to the third century BCE. The final confrontation between order and confusion, represented in medieval texts as an apocalyptic battle between good and evil, supposedly will involve deity and devotees—including resurrected mythic heroes who will "smite the triumphant mace on the head(s)" of legendary villains—fighting victoriously side by side it is still believed (Ayadgar i Jamaspig 6:6; Bundahishn 33:29–34:32; Wizidagiha i Zadspram 35:34–47; Zand i Wahman Yasht 4:3–68; 9:1–23).

Myths and Legends

The theme of combat between good and evil was also incorporated into Yashts or hymns to lesser divinities said to have been created by Ahura Mazda (in fact, these beings had been assimilated into Zoroastrian belief from early Iranian religiosity and had been made subordinate to Ahura Mazda). So, a female *yazata* or praiseworthy spirit called Aredwi Sura Anahita (later Ardwisur Anahid) was portrayed in the Avesta as "driving her chariot," "overcoming the opposition of all enemies—demonic and mortal," and granting mythic heroes such as Haoshyangha (later Hoshang) and Yima Xshaeta (later Jamshed), who had allied themselves with *asha*, the power to "smite two-thirds of the demons and villains" and "wrest goods, revenue, flocks, and herds from evil ones" (Ardwisur Yasht, Yasht 5:11, 13, 22, 26). In keeping with the notion that the armies of persons allied with *drug*, such as the legendary archenemy Azi Dahaka (later Azdahag), should not be assisted in battle, when beseeched by foes of Zoroastrians, this female divinity "did not grant this boon" (Ardwisur Yasht, Yasht 5:31). Rather, it was said that she assisted the Zoroastrians of Iran in "smiting the Turanians with one hundred blows for every fifty (the enemies deliver), with one thousand blows for every hundred blows (the enemies deliver)" (Ardwisur Yasht, Yasht 5:54). Eventually, Anahita would come to be regarded as the divinity of kingship, depicted on Sassanian silver coinage or *drahm* bestowing diadems upon monarchs. A male *yazata* called Mithra (later Mihr), who oversaw covenants, contracts, and social order, was depicted in an Avestan hymn from late Achaemenian times as bearing "spears with sharp tips and long shafts, the far-shooting archer, . . . who protects Ahura Mazda's creatures" (Mihr Yasht, Yasht 10:102–103). Mithra served as the patron of Ahura Mazda's mortal rulers and armies "as they descend upon the battlefield against the bloodthirsty enemy troops," armies who sought from that divinity "the ability to rout hostile enemies" believing that Mithra "takes his stand in battle" by their side (Mihr Yasht, Yasht 10:8, 11, 36). This divinity was thought to serve as the foremost, ever watchful scout "who has ten thousand spies" working on the behalf of Zoroastrians who uphold order (Mihr Yasht, Yasht 10:60, 82). Associated with Mithra was said to be the divinity of victory, named Verethraghna (later Wahram), who flies in front of the former's chariot "mixing together the bones, hair, brains, and blood (of enemies) on the ground," "killing with a single blow" (Mihr Yasht, Yasht 10:72; Wahram Yasht, Yasht 14:15).

The theme of battling opponents of Zoroastrianism became a central part of the Iranian national epic as well. That text is a mixture of myth and history, heroism and romance. It represents epic on a grand scale, was read under the Middle Persian title *Xwaday namag* in the Sassanian era, and was finalized in New Persian verse during the eleventh century CE. Tracing the history of Iran from the first mythological rulers up to the defeat of the last Sassanian king of kings by the Arabs in the middle of the seventh century CE, it proved an ideal bridge between the religious and the secular. Among its literary subcycles were ones on the prophet Zarathushtra and his royal patron king Vishtaspa (later Goshtasp), Alexander (Iranian renderings as Iskandar/Sikandar), and the east Iranian Saka or Scythian tribal hero Rostam. Rostam in particular epitomized the epic—he was depicted battling villains, male and female ghouls, and monsters, brought kings to power, defended the kingdom repeatedly, and in one tragic episode (supposedly predetermined by destiny playing upon the hero's hubris) failed to recognize his own son and slew that youth after a mighty one-on-one combat. The unifying theme of this epic is the concept of kingship bestowed by God—sacral kingship, which upholds social and moral order and stresses honor, freedom, and patriotism while opposing all forms of disorder, even by war if necessary. Rostam, like Vishtaspa, was cast as a model of the protector of state, faith, and sacral kingship battling for the welfare of Zoroastrians (Levy 1973, 60–1, 108–9, 176–7).

Customs and Praxes

The notion of sacral kingship would become clearly enshrined as socioreligious ideology and practice during the Sassanian period as reflected by statements by magi including "religion and state were born from one womb, joined together never to be separated" (Minovi 1932, 33–4) and "essentially, royalty is religion and religion is royalty" (Madan 1911, 47). Yet its practice by Zoroastrian rulers dates back at least to Darius I. That Achaemenian king of kings justified his ascension to power and military suppression of rivals with words in Old Persian such as "by the will of Ahura Mazda, I am king; Ahura Mazda granted me the kingdom" and "by the will of Ahura Mazda, my army defeated that rebellious army completely . . . (when) we fought the battle" (Kent 1982, 1:11–12, 94–96; cf. 2:34–37, 40–42). So he would command his troops: "Go forth! Vanquish that army that does not ally itself to me" (Kent 1982, 3:14–15, cf. 2:20–21, 83–84). His successor, Xshayarsha or Xerxes I (c. 519–465 BCE), continued the use of war to enforce socioreligious authority: "When I became king there was among the lands inscribed above one which was in rebellion. Then Ahura Mazda bore me aid. By the will of Ahura Mazda, I smote that land and put it down in its place" (Kent 1982, H 28–35). Likewise, the founder of the Sassanian dynasty, Ardashir I (ruled 224–240 CE) is reported to have equated rebellion to heresy against crown and religion, "commanding that the fortress be demolished . . . he dispatched his army against (rebels) in Kerman" (Anita 1900, 13:18–19).

Military instruction was emphasized for princes and courtiers so that they could uphold the laws of state and faith. Darius I claimed: "I am trained to use both hands and feet. As a rider, I am a good rider. As an archer, I am a good archer both on foot and on horseback. As a lancer, I am a good lancer both on foot and on horseback" (Kent 1982, B 40–45). A Middle

Persian text captures the essence of Sassanian education—combining secular and sectarian education with military instruction—in the words of a pageboy: "I was placed in school and was steadfastly zealous in studies. I memorized completely the Yasht, Hadhoxt, Yasna, and Videvdad like a theologian and studied their interpretation passage by passage. My scribal skill is such that I am well versed in fine literature and calligraphy, seek knowledge, and am capable of rhetoric. My prowess in riding and archery is such that the opponent is fortunate if he can escape my arrow while riding. My prowess in throwing the spear is such that unfortunate is the rider who seeks combat with me on horseback using spear and sword" (Monchi-Zadeh 1982, ll. 8–12).

Specific Conflicts

Religious tenets carried over to historical campaigns because the idea of order versus confusion, good against evil, could be applied to secular warfare arising from political situations—even if only as casus belli. According to the Greek historian Herodotus (c. 484–between 430 and 420 BCE), the Achaemenian monarch Xerxes I had a divinely inspired dream that supposedly foretold success in battles against the Greeks (Herodotus, *History* 7:12–15). Later when a storm washed away bridges, he commanded that the Hellespont be "scourged with three hundred lashes, and a pair of fetters be thrown into the sea" while admonishing the water as "bitter"—presumably because he believed that the water had not cooperated with his plans and thus had been allied with the forces of evil (Herodotus, *History* 7:35). In another case, the Sassanian king of kings Shapur I (ruled 241–272 CE) inscribed at Naqsh-e Rostam his reasons of war against the Romans, including the idea that untruths had been spoken—thereby implying that the Romans were allied with *drug* and Angra Mainyu: "Caesar lied again and attacked Armenia, so we attacked the Roman empire" (Back 1978, l. 4). War as a means of establishing Zoroastrianism was also mentioned by Shapur I in the same inscription: "We have sought and seized many lands with the aid of the divinities so that in every land we would establish many (holy) Wahram fires, confer benefits upon many magi, and expand the cult of the divinities" (Back 1978, l. 17). As Shapur I had defeated the Roman leaders Gordianus III (225–244 CE), Philip the Arabian (d. 249 CE), and Valerian (d. 260 CE), those victories were depicted on monumental rock reliefs imbued with religious symbolism. Ardashir II's (ruled 379–383 CE) advent to kingship after he had defeated opponents in battle was also depicted on a rock relief (see photograph).

Attempts at protecting of Zoroastrianism were another factor that resulted in particular battles. When Armenian rulers, who had been Zoroastrians allied religiously and politically with Iran against Byzantium, adopted Christianity in the early fourth century CE, the Sassanian king of kings Shapur II (309–379 CE) conducted many military campaigns in a futile effort to have them reconvert to Zoroastrianism and re-ally with Iran. According to later accounts, when Arab Muslim troops invaded Iranian territory in the seventh century CE and laid siege to the Sassanian capital city of Ctesiphon: "Iranians who saw Muslims crossing the [Tigris] river cried out, 'The devils have come.' They then said to each other, 'By god, we are not waging war against mortals. Rather, we are fighting none other than [evil] spirits.' So they fled" (De Goeje 1866, 263; and Abu Jaʿfar Muhammad b. Jarir al-Tabari 1879–1901, 1:2440–1). By the ninth century CE, the defeat of the Sassanians and the conversion of most Zoroastrians to Islam had been rationalized by incorporating those events into eschatology and attributing a premonition back to Zarathushtra: "Ahura Mazda said, 'The seventh age, of alloyed iron, entails evil rule by disheveled demons (descended) from the clan of Xeshm' " (Cereti 1995, 1:6, cf. 3:29). The term Xeshm, usually the name for the Zoroastrian demon of wrath, was employed in this passage as a pun on Hashim, founder of the prophet Muhammad's clan. Likewise, in 1465 CE, Parsis fought unsuccessfully alongside Hindus against the Muslim troops of the Muzaffarid sultan Mahmud I Begath (ruled 1458–1511 CE) to defend the city of Sanjan—resistance that bought time to facilitate their transferring a holy fire to the safety of a cave in a hill at the nearby locale of Bahrot for the next twelve years (Eduljee 1991, 54–7). Parsi Zoroastrians, as citizens of colonial British India, volunteered for service in the armed forces of the British empire during World War II. They served duty against the Japanese forces in Burma and Southeast Asia, fighting for the Allied cause that they believed to be both good and just. Others served as physicians in the British forces. The concept of assisting communities and nations that provide safety for followers of the faith continues to the present day as evidenced by Parsis in modern India both serving in that country's armed forces at all levels including as generals and assisting in development of that country's aviation and nuclear programs as engineers and physicists.

Implications

Essentially in Zoroastrianism war became a socioreligious notion, theoretically although not always successfully directed at protecting Zoroastrianism and its adherents against political and sectarian domination. Less often in the history of Zoroastrian societies has war been utilized ideologically and practically as a means of spreading faith. Zoroastrians usually have viewed themselves not as holy warriors combating infidels but as allies of God spreading righteous order while doing as little harm as possible and working with, rather than against, established regimes. This situation is especially so at present, when as religious minorities in Iran, India, and other countries adherents of Zoroastrianism attempt to maintain a low religious profile so as not to attract proselytization or persecution from members of other sects.

Jamsheed K. Choksy

Further Reading

Abu Jaʿfar Muhammad b. Jarir al-Tabari. (1879–1901). *Taʿrikh al-rusul waʿl-muluk* (Vols. 1–15; M. J. De Goeje, et al. [Eds.]). Leiden, Netherlands: E. J. Brill.

Anklesaria, T. D. (Ed.). (1908). *The Bundahishn*. Bombay, India: British India Press.

Antia, E. K. (Ed. & Trans.). (1900). *Karnamak-i Artakhshir Papakan*. Bombay, India: Fort Printing Press.

Back, M. (Ed.). (1978). *Die sassanidischen Staatsinschriften* (Acta Iranica 18). Leiden, Netherlands: E. J. Brill.

Bivar, A. D. H. (1972). Cavalry equipment and tactics on the Euphrates Frontier. *Dumbarton Oaks Papers 26*, 273–291.

Boyce, M. (1979). *Zoroastrians: The religious beliefs and practices*. London: Routledge and Kegan Paul

Boyce, M. (1982). *A history of Zoroastrianism* (Vol. 2). Leiden, Netherlands: E. J. Brill.

Boyce, M. (1989). *A history of Zoroastrianism* (Vol. 1, 2d ed.). Leiden, Netherlands: E. J. Brill.

Boyce, M., & Grenet, F. (1991). *A history of Zoroastrianism* (Vol. 3). Leiden, Netherlands: E. J. Brill.

Cereti, C. G. (Ed. & Trans.). (1995). *The Zand i Wahman Yasn: A Zoroastrian apocalypse* (Serie Orientale Roma 75). Rome: Istituto per il Medio ed Estremo Oriente.

Choksy, J. K. (1988). Sacral kingship in Sasanian Iran. *Bulletin of the Asia Institute*, new series 2, 35–52.

Choksy, J. K. (1997). *Conflict and cooperation: Zoroastrian subalterns and Muslim elites in medieval Iranian society*. New York: Columbia University Press.

Dandamayev, M. A., & Lukonin, V. G. (1989). *The culture and social institutions of ancient Iran*. Cambridge, UK: Cambridge University Press.

De Goeje, M. J. (Ed.). (1866). *Futuh al-buldan*, by Ahmad b. Yahya al-Baladhuri. Leiden, Netherlands: E. J. Brill.

Dodgeon, M. H., & Lieu, S. N. C. (Eds.). (1991). *The Roman eastern frontier and the Persian Wars AD 226–363: A documentary history*. London: Routledge.

Eduljee, H. E. (Trans.). (1991). *Kisseh-i Sanjan*. Bombay, India: K. R. Cama Oriental Institute.

Frye, R. N. (1984). *The history of ancient Iran*. Munich, Germany: C. H. Beck.

Frye, R. N. (1998). Women in pre-Islamic central Asia: The Khatun of Bukhara. In G. R. G. Hambly (Ed.), *Women in the medieval Islamic world: Power, patronage, and piety* (pp. 55–68). New York: St. Martin's Press.

Geldner, K. F. (Ed.). (1982). *Avesta: The sacred books of the Parsis* (Vols. 1–3). Delhi, India: Parimal Publications. (Original work published 1886–1895)

Gignoux, M. P. (1985–1988). L'apocalyptique iranienne est-elle vraiment la source d'autres apocalypses? *Acta Antiqua Academiae Scientiarum Hungaricae 31*, 67–78.

Gignoux, M. P. (1986). Nouveaux regards sur l'apocalyptique iranienne. *Comptes Rendus de l'Académie des Inscriptions et Belles-Lettres*, 334–346.

Gignoux, M. P., & Tafazzoli, A. (Ed. & Trans.). (1993). *Anthologie de Zadspram* (Studia Iranica cahier 13). Louvain, Belgium: Peeters.

Godley, A. D. (Ed. & Trans.). (1981). *Herodotus* (Loeb Classical Library Vols. 117–120). Cambridge, MA: Harvard University Press. (Original work published 1920–1925)

Hinnells, J. R. (2000). War and medicine in Zoroastrianism. In J. R. Hinnells (Ed.), *Zoroastrianism and Parsi studies* (pp. 277–300). Aldershot, UK: Ashgate Publishing.

Kent, R. G. (Ed.). (1982). *Old Persian: Grammar, texts, lexicon* (2d ed.). New Haven, CT: American Oriental Society. (Original work published 1953)

Levy, R. (Ed. & Trans.). (1973). *The epic of kings: Shah-Nama, the national epic of Persia, by Ferdowsi*. London: Routledge and Kegan Paul.

Madan, D. M. (Ed.). (1911). *The complete text of the Pahlavi Dinkard* (Vols. 1–2). Bombay, India: Society for the Promotion of Researches into the Zoroastrian Religion.

Messina, G. (Ed.). (1939). *Libro apocalittico persiano: Ayatkar i Zamaspik*. Rome: Pontifico Istituto Biblico.

Minovi, M. (Ed.) (1932). *Tansar nama*. Tehran, Iran: Majles Printing House.

Monchi-Zadeh, D. (Ed. & Trans.). (1982). Xusrov i Kavatan ut Retak. In idem, *Monumentum Georg Morgen-*

stierne II (Acta Iranica 22; pp. 47–91). Leiden, Netherlands: E. J. Brill.

Nicolle, D. (1996). *Sassanian Armies: The Iranian Empire Early 3rd to Mid–7th Centuries AD*. Stockport, UK: Montvert Publications.

Nikonorov, V. P. (1997). *The armies of Bactria: 700 BC–450 AD* (Vols. 1–2). Stockport, UK: Montvert Publications.

Russell, J. R. (1987). *Zoroastrianism in Armenia* (Harvard Iranian Series 5). Cambridge, MA: Harvard University Department of Near Eastern Languages and Civilizations.

Tafazzoli, A. (2000). *Sassanian Society: I. Warriors, II. Scribes, III. Dehqans*. New York: Bibliotheca Persica Press.

Zulu

With nine million members, the Zulu form the largest black ethnic group in South Africa. Although they are the largest, they have a relatively brief history as an independent group. The term "Zulu" refers to the Nguni-speaking people in KwaZulu-Natal in South Africa. The Zulu are a branch of the southern Bantu, who have close ethnic, linguistic, and cultural ties with other groups in the area such as the Xhosa and the Swazi.

The Zulu are the least Christianized group in South Africa. That does not keep the Zulu from using millenarian Christian rhetoric to advance their cause. Chief Mangosuthu Buthelezi's (b. 1928) Inkatha Freedom Party's campaign slogan during the 1994 democratic election was "The last shall be first." Buthelezi thus claimed a sacred origin for Zulu nationalism, freely using Christian terms promising a divine destiny.

Buthelezi's slogan is in the Zulu tradition of using religion to strengthen Zulu nationalistic objectives. The rise of the Zulu and their consolidation of power and resistance to British power and later to other ethnic groups in the new South Africa follow a common pattern of the union of religious ideas with nationalistic ones, and this pattern forms the outline of this article.

Early Period

In the early nineteenth century the Nguni, under Shaka (c. 1787–1828), united the Zulu clan of the Nguni with other Nguni people in Natal, forming the Zulu nation. Shaka used his clan name, Zulu, for the united peoples. Through expansive conquest and using new principles of warfare, Shaka formed the powerful Zulu Empire.

There is no question that Shaka was a military mastermind who was unable to rule in peacetime. Shaka was born about 1787 to the Zulu clan of the Nguni. His father was a Zulu chieftain. Shaka had a turbulent childhood. His parents split up when he was about six years old. When he was around fifteen his mother's people, the Langeni clan, drove him and his mother out. They found refuge with the Dietsheni clan. This clan belonged to the Mtetwa people, a very powerful group. Shaka stayed with the Mtetwa as a warrior until he became the Zulu chief when his father died in 1816.

It was at this time that he showed his military skill in reorganizing the military. This reorganization changed warfare from a series of skirmishes into a bloody ordeal. Sword replaced spears, leading to close-quarter fighting. Shaka also divided the army into four parts. Shaka used Zulu age-grades as a basis for military organization. Age-grades consist of all males born within certain periods. Members of each grade go through all culturally defined states of life together. These units then learned how to surround the enemy. In a brief time, he had built up his empire.

Historically, the Zulu were farmers who kept large herds of cattle. They kept up the size of these herds through cattle raids. During the nineteenth century European settlers fought the Zulu, taking grazing land and water resources from them. The Zulu had little option but to hire themselves out for labor on European farms or in urban areas. Shaka's heirs had little time to enjoy the fruits of their conquest. They found themselves battling with Boer settlers migrating north into Natal. These Boers, Dutch descendants who were farmers, were moving away from British settlers and their government, a movement entitled The Great Trek. Dingane (d. 1840), the Zulu chief, ambushed Boers moving through his territory, killing around 500 people. This massacre occurred in 1838. Andries Pretorius (1793–1853), a Boer general, retaliated at the Battle of Blood River, killing about 3,000 Zulus. In 1840, the Boer intruded into Zulu domestic politics, resulting in the toppling of Dingane and the rise to power of Mpande (1798–1849), who became a vassal of the Boer republic of Natal.

Religious Ideas

There is a close relationship between Zulu religious ideas and their prowess in war. The Zulu have a belief in a Supreme Being; called Unkulunkulu. Some scholars argue that the term originally referred to the first man. In any case, Zulu use the term to refer to the Ancient One who has created all things and who is also the ancestor of humans. This Ancient One organized human societies. Additionally, the Zulu use the terms Lord of Heaven and Chief in the Sky, the latter referring to a storm god.

There are also other supernatural agents, including animal spirits and sacred snakes, which aid in rainmaking. They also have a female spirit, Inkosazana. Inkosazana aids in the growing of corn. There are rituals, performed by young women in the spring, to celebrate her power.

In common with other related peoples, the Zulu regard the chief as the symbol of tribal unity. The chief is a priest and sorcerer. He is the ruler and lawgiver of his people. He is also general and source of wealth. Under Shaka, the king became godlike. Simply put, he was a sacred being whose people prostrated themselves before him. He was a demigod and passed on this persona to his heirs.

Despite these views, people could and did abandon the king. Coups could take place, even civil wars. His enemies assassinated Shaka. Provocation for these actions had to be great and both the Boers and the British learned how to foment and abet such provocation.

The firstfruits festival was an important ceremonial time for the Zulu. It was a time of the gathering of a large number of people. Diviners, herbalists, and other ritual specialists gathered and the sense of unity around the power of the king was enhanced by these ritual ceremonies.

Christianity came into Zululand in 1835 with Christian missionaries of many denominations. In 2000 about 50 percent of the people were Christians. Most of these people belong to African Independent Churches. However, there are Zulu Catholics, Anglicans, and members of the Dutch Free Church and other Christian denominations. Most of these Christians also observe traditional religious practices along with Christian ones. Thus, the nationalistic notions of traditional religion get absorbed into Christianity in the Zulu area.

Anglo-Zulu Wars

When the British succeeded the Boers as rulers of Natal in 1843, they found Mpande's son Cetewayo (c. 1826–1884) to be opposed to their interests. In 1878, he refused to accept an ultimatum to submit to British rule. Great Britain reacted to this refusal by attacking Zululand in 1878. Although the Zulu inflicted serious defeats on them, the British conquered the Zulu in July 1879. In 1897, the British annexed Zululand because the Zulu continued to resist British rule and staged a number of raids against them.

The Anglo-Zulu War began on 11 January 1879. The British sent about 15,000 troops into Zululand. There were about 7,000 British regulars, 7,000 conscripted African troops, and roughly 1,000 colonial volunteers. The attack took place at the sacred time of the firstfruits festival. Cetewayo had his entire army of about 30,000 assembled at Isandhlwana for the festival. He counterattacked and defeated the British and then sued for peace. He had refrained from killing civilians and invading Natal.

The Zulu inflicted the greatest defeat that any European army had ever encountered at the hands of an African force. Almost every soldier on the British side died. The British refused to allow any peace to be negotiated and sought revenge and in July 1879 they burned Lundy, the royal homestead, and captured the king.

Bambatha's Rebellion

The last armed Zulu rebellion against the British was Bambatha's Rebellion (1869–1906). Bambatha was a chief of the Zondi people, a group related to the Zulu. He was born about 1865 in Natal. He became a ruler in Natal in 1904. His opposition to the fiscal policies of the British colonial administration led to his removal in 1905. Bambatha found refuge among the Zulu and organized opposition to an unfair poll tax.

Bambatha led a guerrilla resistance against the poll tax. The resistance continued even after the British killed him at the Battle of Mome Gorge on 10 June 1906. However, when the Natal colonial forces turned to modern weapons, including heavy artillery, machine guns, magazine dries, and dum-dum bullets, they routed the outmatched Zulu. About 24 Natal colonial forces and their allies were killed while over 2,000 Zulu died. After the rebellion ended, around 5,000 Zulu were imprisoned and the British punished these Zulu with floggings and other punishments.

Bambatha's rebellion was the flourish of Zulu military might against Europeans. Its consequences have lasted into the present. British troops destroyed kraals, burned Zulu crops, and stole Zulu cattle. As a result of the poverty consequent on the war, multitudes of Zulu men sought work in the Transvaal goldfields. The rebellion pushed whites to form a union of Cape Colony, Orange River Colony, Transvaal, and Natal.

The failure of armed resistance impressed on Africans the need to form another means for resistance. Black South Africans turned to more political means of organization. In 1912 Zulu were among the organizers of the South African Native National Congress. This Congress later became the African National Congress.

Implications

There was a close relationship between the power of the Zulu king, religion, and military organization. Shaka built on both Zulu religion and the sacred nature of the chief to supplement his military reorganizations. So powerful did he make the Zulu people and their military that the Zulu came close to driving the British from Natal and caused great discontent in Great Britain regarding the colonial endeavor in South Africa.

Zulu religion stresses the age-grade system, the importance of cattle, and the importance of matrilineal ties. These ties stretch back to ancestors from whom the elders descend and whose authority they wield. The belief system centers on ancestor worship and this strengthens ties in the group and the power of the king. The king is in charge of all magic, rainmaking, and other significant rites. These rites increase his power.

Shaka's heirs as priests and shamans as well as sacred people commanded a great deal of respect. They were able to harass the British and Boers until the end of the nineteenth century and proved to be a force to be reckoned with during the last years of white rule in South Africa. Much of their cohesion has come from their knowledge of their traditional customs and religion. Their reverence for the old and willingness to adapt to changing times, a part of their tradition, has enabled them to continue as an essential part of South Africa's future.

The Zulu nationalist movement has been comprised of intellectuals, traditionalists, and Christians of various beliefs. The Africanist churches have taken the lead in weaving the various strands together in support of a modernized Zulu monarchy. The best known of these African Christian religions is the amaNazarite movement. The "prophet" Isaiah Shembe founded the movement in 1912. The amaNazarite movement has about three quarters of a million followers, most of whom are Zulu. Shembe's religion keeps essential Zulu cultural beliefs and practices but merges them with modern ideas. Shembe included Europeans and Indians in his movement while encouraging education. He used biblical ideas to strengthen Zulu nationalism and modernization.

Frank A. Salamone

See also Apartheid

Further Reading

Beck, R. B. (2000). *The history of South Africa*. Westport, CT: Greenwood Press.

Callaway, H. (1868–1870). *The religious system of the Amazulu*. Springvale, Australia: A. J. Blair.

Chidester, D. et al. (1997). *African traditional religion in South Africa: An annotated bibliography*. Westport, CT: Greenwood Press.

Davenport, T. R. H. (1998). *The birth of a new South Africa*. Toronto, Canada: University of Toronto Press.

Elphick, R., & T. R. H. Davenport. (1997). *Christianity in South Africa: A political, social, and cultural history*. Berkeley: University of California Press.

Gluckman, M. (1963). *Order and rebellion in tribal Africa: Collected essays, with an autobiographical introduction*. New York: Free Press of Glencoe.

Gorman, G. E., & Homan, R. (Eds.). (1986). *The sociology of religion: A bibliographical survey*. New York: Greenwood Press.

Gump, J. O. (1994). *The dust rose like smoke: The subjugation of the Zulu and the Sioux*. Lincoln: University of Nebraska Press.

Keto, T. C. (1977). Race relations, land, and the changing missionary role in South Africa: A case study of the American Zulu Mission. *The International Journal of African Historical Studies 10*(4), 600–627.

Krige, E. J. (1936). *The social system of the Zulus*. London: Longman, Green.

Miller, R. B. (1992). (Ed.). *War in the twentieth century: Sources in theological ethics*. Louisville, KY: Westminster John Knox Press.

List of Contributors

Abler, Thomas S.
University of Waterloo
Iroquois

Adogame, Afe
Universitaet Bayreuth
Nigeria

Ahmad, Ishtiaq
Eastern Mediterranean University
Afghanistan
Deobandism
Islamic Movement of Uzbekistan
Taliban
Terrorism, Religious
Wahhabism

Akinade, Akintunde E.
High Point University
Fundamentalism in Egypt and Sudan

Alpert, Rebecca T.
Temple University
Judaism, Reconstructionist

Axtell, Rick
Centre College
Christianity, Early: Jesus Movement

Barkun, Michael
Syracuse University
Christian Identity

Berlet, Chip
Political Research Associates
Ku Klux Klan

Birch, Brian D.
Utah Valley State College
Mormons

Birkner, Irving
University of Chicago
Palestine Liberation Organization

Bleich, J. David
Yeshiva University
Judaism, Orthodox

Bresciani, Umberto
Taipei, Taiwan
Confucianism, Modern

Brooks, Christopher
Virginia Commonwealth University
Africa, West
Christianity: African-American Traditions
Yoruba

Campbell, Courtney S.
Oregon State University
Christianity and Revolution

Chapple, Christopher Key
Loyola Marymount University
Jainism

Chibi, Andrew A.
University of Leicester
European Wars of Religion

Choksy, Jamsheed K.
Indiana University–Bloomington
Zoroastrianism

Cook, David B.
Rice University
Islam: Age of Conquest

Coughlin, Kathryn M.
Georgetown University
Hamas
Hizbullah

Crumbley, Deidre
University of Florida
Africa, West

Davis, G. Scott
University of Richmond
Roman Catholicism: Theology and Colonization

Dorff, Elliot N.
University of Judaism
Judaism, Conservative

Draney, Daniel W.
Fuller Theological Seminary
U.S. Revolutionary War

Eid, Leroy V.
University of Dayton
Northern Ireland

Epperson, Michael
University of Chicago
Roman Religions

Evans, Connie
Baldwin-Wallace College
Bishop's Wars (England 1639, 1640)

Firestone, Reuven
Hebrew Union College
Holy War Idea in the Biblical Tradition
Jihad
Judaism: Medieval Period
Martyrdom
Palestine and Israel

Fitzhugh, Michael L.
Washington University in St. Louis
Confucianism: Han Dynasty
Daoism, Huang-Lao

Fitzpatrick Behrens, Susan
California State University, Northridge
Latin America: Modern Period

Forêt, Philippe
Swiss National Science Foundation
Buddhism: Tibet

Forrest, Francesca M.
Belchertown, Massachusetts
Daoism, Medieval

Friedman, Saul S.
Youngstown State University
Genocide in Europe

Graber Miller, Keith
Goshen College
Mennonites

Grieser, D. Jonathan
Furman University
Thirty Years' War

Han, Jin Hee
New York Theological Seminary
Judaism, Pacifism in

Harrington, Peter
Brown University
Art

Hashmi, Sohail H.
Mount Holyoke College
Islam, Sunni

Hassig, Ross
Norman, Oklahoma
Aztecs

Herman, Jonathan R.
Georgia State University
Confucianism, Classical
Daoism, Classical

Himes, Kenneth R.
Boston College
Roman Catholicism: Just-War Doctrine

Holst, Arthur
Widener University
Iranian Revolution of 1979

Hussain, Amir
Califonia State University, Northridge
Islam: Sufism

Jacobs, Steven Steven
University of Alabama
Judaism, Reform

Jeppie, Shamil
University of Cape Town
Sudanese War of 1881–1898

Johnson, William Stacy
Princeton Theological Seminary
Religion, Violence, and Genocide

Kaplan, Jeffrey
University of Wisconsin, Oshkosh
Millenarian Violence: United States

Kapparis, Konstantinos
University of Florida
Greek Religions

Kelsay, John
Florida State University
Islamic Law of War

Khan, Noor-Aiman I.
Urbana, Illinois
Hindu-Muslim Violence in India

Kovic, Christine
University of Houston, Clear Lake
Latin America: Modern Period

Lambden, Stephen N.
Athens, Ohio
Babi and Baha'i Religions

Lawson, Russell
Bacone College
Hellenistic Religions

Lazich, Michael C.
Buffalo State College
Buddhism, Mahayana

Leitich, Keith A.
Seattle, Washington
Buddhism: Taiwan
Tajik Civil War

Lepak, Keith John
Youngstown State University
Genocide in Bosnia

Levinson, David
Berkshire Publishing Group
Ghost Dance

Lewis, James G.
Falls Church, Virginia
Japan: Tokugawa Period

Lewis, Todd T.
College of the Holy Cross
Buddhism: India

Littleton, C. Scott
Pasadena, California
Indo-European Mythology

Lomax, John Philip
Ohio Northern University
Papal Imperial Conflict

Lorenzen, David N.
El Colegio de Mexico
Hinduism: Early Medieval Period

Lubin, Timothy
Washington and Lee University
Hinduism: Late Medieval Period

Maclean, Iain
James Madison University
Reformed Christianity

Malone, David B.
Wheaton College (IL)
U.S. Civil War and Christian Churches

Markese, Elisabeth
University of Chicago
Shiʿite Rebellion of 815–19

Masondo, Sibusiso
University of Cape Town
Apartheid

McBride II, Richard D.
University of Iowa
Buddhism: China

Meschke, Amy
Dallas, Texas
Pueblo Revolt of 1680

Minch, Michael L.
Utah Valley State College
Anabaptist Pacifism

Mir, Mustansir
Youngstown State University
Islam, Qurʾanic

Mukherjee, Anup
Jabalpur, India
Hinduism, Modern

Nelson, John K.
University of San Francisco
Shinto, Modern

Neumann, Caryn E.
Ohio State University
Quakers
World Council of Churches

Niditch, Susan
Amherst College
Judaism: Biblical Period

Palmer-Fernandez, Gabriel
Youngstown State University
Tyrannicide, Medieval Catholic Doctrine of

Parsons, Laila
Yale University
Palestine: 1948 War

Penn-Hollar, Barry
Shenandoah University
Methodism

Peterson, Luther D.
State University of New York, Oswego
Lutheran Germany

Ranger, Terence O.
Oxford University
Zimbabwe

Ray, Ayesha
University of Texas, Austin
Kashmir

Redles, David
Cuyahoga Community College
Nazism and Holocaust

Renick, Timothy M.
Georgia State University
Crusades
Manichaeism
Religious Feminism and War

Richardson, Annette
University of Alberta
English Civil Wars
Fundamentalism in Iran
Indonesia

Richardson, Kim
University of Texas, Austin
Inca
Latin America: Historical Overview
Maya
Millenarian Violence: Latin America
Spanish Christian-Muslim Wars

Richey, Jeffrey L.
Berea College
Daoism, Modern
Zen, Premodern

Rivera-Rodriguez, Luis
McCormick Theological Seminary
Liberation Theology

Rixon, Diane
Savannah, Georgia
Assassins
Byzantine-Muslim War of 645

Rutherford Young, Derek
University of Dundee
Sikhism

Salamone, Frank A.
Iona College
Zulu

Sankey, Margaret
Minnesota State University, Moorhead
Zealots

Scheid, Bernhard
Austrian Academy of Sciences
Shinto, Ancient

Sharkey, Heather J.
University of Pennsylvania
Sudan

Skedros, James
Holy Cross Greek Orthodox School of Theology
Christianity, Early: Constantinian Movement

Smith, Jr., Allyne L.
Mercy College of Health Sciences
Eastern Orthodoxy, Pacifism in

Stein, Stephen K.
University of Memphis
Jewish Revolt of 66–70

Takim, Liyakat
University of Denver
Islam, Shia

Thompson, Kirill Ole
National Taiwan University
Confucianism, Neo-Confucianism

Tumminia, Diana
California State University–Sacramento
Thugs

Victoria, Brian Daizen
University of Adelaide
Zen: Samurai Tradition
Zen and Japanese Nationalism
Zen, Modern

Wan-Tatah, Victor F.
Youngstown State University
African Religion: Warrior Cult
Genocide in Rwanda

Wessinger, Catherine
Loyola University
Millennialism

Whitaker, Jarrod L.
University of Texas, Austin
Hinduism: Vedic Period
Hinduism, Classical

Whitaker, Mark P.
University of South Carolina, Aiken
Sri Lanka

Whitsel, Brad
Pennsylvania State University
Aum Shinrikyo

Winright, Tobias
Walsh University
Roman Catholicism, Pacifism in

Woods, Damon L.
California State University, Long Beach
Buddhism: Myanmar (Burma) and Thailand
Millenarian Violence: Thai Buddhism

INDEX

Note: Main encyclopedia entries are indicated by **bold** type.